铁路技术标准中英文大词典

A CHINESE-ENGLISH & ENGLISH-CHINESE DICTIONARY
FOR RAILWAY TECHNICAL STANDARD

主编单位　中国铁路经济规划研究院有限公司
副主编单位　中铁第一勘察设计院集团有限公司
　　　　　　中铁一局集团有限公司
　　　　　　中铁十五局集团有限公司
　　　　　　中国铁建电气化局集团有限公司
　　　　　　中国土木工程集团有限公司
　　　　　　北京时代大语国际翻译有限公司

人民交通出版社股份有限公司
北京

图书在版编目(CIP)数据

铁路技术标准中英文大词典 / 中国铁路经济规划研究院有限公司主编. — 北京：人民交通出版社股份有限公司，2021.6
ISBN 978-7-114-16969-4

Ⅰ. ①铁⋯ Ⅱ. ①中⋯ Ⅲ. ①铁路运输管理—词典—汉、英 Ⅳ. ①U29-61

中国版本图书馆 CIP 数据核字(2020)第 244390 号

Tielu Jishu Biaozhun Zhongyingwen Da Cidian
书　　名：铁路技术标准中英文大词典
著　作　者：中国铁路经济规划研究院有限公司
责任编辑：王　霞　张　晓
责任校对：孙国靖　扈　婕　宋佳时
责任印制：张　凯
出版发行：人民交通出版社股份有限公司
地　　址：(100011)北京市朝阳区安定门外外馆斜街 3 号
网　　址：http://www.ccpcl.com.cn
销售电话：(010)59757973
总　经　销：人民交通出版社股份有限公司发行部
经　　销：各地新华书店
印　　刷：北京印匠彩色印刷有限公司
开　　本：787×980　1/16
印　　张：41.75
字　　数：1856 千
版　　次：2021 年 6 月　第 1 版
印　　次：2021 年 6 月　第 1 次印刷
书　　号：ISBN 978-7-114-16969-4
定　　价：408.00 元

(有印刷、装订质量问题的图书由本公司负责调换)

编辑委员会

主　　　任：吴克非
副 主 任：倪光斌　孔　遒　雷升祥　王争鸣　董　勇
　　　　　　黄　超　张学伏　安国勇　黄昌富　程庆海
　　　　　　寇宗乾　胡社忠　李昌宁　张立新
编　　委：王　磊　薛吉岗　吕生禄　桑翠江　孙　炜
　　　　　　黄双林　徐　宏　王春晓　阚绍忠　黄国胜
　　　　　　王振文　柯迪民　潘建华　高　策　董学武
参 编 人 员：代永翔　戴　宇　董晓光　方文珊　伏松平
　　　　　　黄建勇　黄一昕　霍建勋　蒋函珂　李　峰
　　　　　　李光华　李海珍　李毓娟　梁　超　林传年
　　　　　　刘传朋　刘　华　刘　珣　刘　喆　马莉亚
　　　　　　王凯林　王　生　王雪原　吴歆彦　夏　炎
　　　　　　许开达　闫宏伟　杨常所　杨全亮　杨思博
　　　　　　张洪涛　张　凌　张晓东　许洲峰　赵生亮
　　　　　　赵永红　赵泽宇　周勇政　朱飞雄　梁　进
　　　　　　张启龙　张　辉　卢明坤　倪天聪
主要审稿人：霍保世　卢有杰　汪吉健　吴命利　刘彦明
　　　　　　刘化宇　杜永昌　张立成　赵　龙　秦学珍
　　　　　　王玲玲　马琳君　张德祥　王雅珺　赵国斌
　　　　　　戴若愚　郄春生　胡建伟　王　可

序

  国家主席习近平在致第 39 届国际标准化组织大会的贺信中指出：标准是人类文明进步的成果。伴随着经济全球化深入发展，标准化在便利经贸往来、支撑产业发展、促进科技进步、规范社会治理中的作用日益凸显。标准已成为世界"通用语言"。世界需要标准协同发展，标准促进世界互联互通。

  党的十八大以来，我国铁路尤其是高速铁路建设取得了举世瞩目的成就，在复杂地基处理、千米级超大跨度桥梁、大断面隧道、轨道工程、牵引供电、通信信号、现代客站等方面不断取得技术突破，成功研制"复兴号"动车组、CTCS 列控系统和智能综合调度等系统，建立了结构合理、衔接配套、覆盖全面、具有世界先进水平的铁路技术标准体系，为铁路工程建造、装备制造、运输服务的安全高效提供重要技术支撑。

  世界铁路的高质量发展需要国际铁路市场的推动，鉴于标准在其中的基础性和战略性作用，铁路标准国际化是今后一定时期内技术标准工作的重中之重。当前，世界铁路发展有市场有需求，中国铁路发展有优势有能力，以此为契机，《铁路技术标准中英文大词典》顺应时势编制而成。本词典具有统一铁路工程技术、经济、涉外法律法规等方面专业词汇和促进铁路技术国际对接互认的积极作用，可有效推动国际铁路技术交流，更好地展示中国铁路技术优势，提升中国铁路的国际影响力，助力于中国铁路的工程建造、技术装备、综合运输国际合作。

本词典既秉持国际视野，又呈现中国理念；既凝练技术特征，又覆盖发展规律；既反映专业引领，又力求表意精准。内容扎实、精益求精，撮要纳新、释义简明，是铁路行业较为理想的中英双语词典，可供广大铁路科研、设计、施工、管理人员以及高校师生、翻译人员参考使用。

目前我国铁路仍处于快速发展的黄金机遇期，广大铁路科技工作者生逢其时，发展舞台广阔。希望广大铁路科技工作者，立足国内、胸怀世界，不断提升专业和外语水平，持续关注国际铁路发展前沿，掌握更多铁路核心关键技术，为中国铁路创新发展努力奋斗，为"一带一路"建设和铁路国际合作做出新的更大的贡献。

中国科协副主席
中国工程院副院长

2020 年 7 月

编写说明

《铁路技术标准中英文大词典》由中国铁路经济规划研究院有限公司（以下简称：经规院）主持编写，副主编单位包括中铁第一勘察设计院集团有限公司、中铁一局集团有限公司、中铁十五局集团有限公司、中国铁建电气化局集团有限公司、中国土木工程集团有限公司、北京时代大语国际翻译有限公司，于2021年6月由人民交通出版社股份有限公司出版发行。为保证词典编写质量，编写组从词典内容、参编人员、编写过程等三个方面严格把控，以期为广大读者奉献一本专业、全面、实用的铁路行业工具书。

《铁路技术标准中英文大词典》主要服务于广大铁路科研管理及专业技术人员，尤其是铁路技术标准翻译和审查人员。词典取词遵循了专业性、全面性和实用性的原则。词条主要来源于现行铁路工程建设标准，涵盖了地质、测量、路基、桥梁、隧道、线路与轨道、站场、通信、信号、电力、电牵、防灾、灾害监测、信息、机务车辆设备、房屋建筑、给排水、环保、混凝土、试验检测和工程经济、智能铁路、BIM等专业领域，同时也收录了国际工程管理领域的相关专业词汇。词典收录词条两万七千余条，涵盖了铁路工程建设的各个方面，力求全面反映当前铁路技术发展的最新进展，满足国际交流的需要。

参与中文词条选取工作的单位包括中铁第一勘察设计院集团有限公司、

中铁一局集团有限公司、中铁十五局集团有限公司、中国铁建电气化局集团有限公司、中国土木工程集团有限公司，参与人员均为具有丰富理论和实践经验的工程技术人员，涵盖站前、站后所有专业，确保了取词的专业性和全面性。参与词条翻译的北京时代大语国际翻译有限公司长期致力于铁路交通领域的翻译工作，具有系统全面的语料库储备、过硬的翻译业务能力和丰富的翻译实践经验。参与词条审查的50多位专家分别来自各设计院、工程局、科研院所以及相关高校，长期参与工程技术标准翻译审查工作，具有较高的英语水平和专业技术能力，确保了词典的准确性和权威性。

  词典编写历时两年多，从项目策划、中文词条选取、词条翻译，再到专家函审、会审、定稿，每个环节都由经规院组织专业人员严格把关，程序规范、严谨，确保了词典编写的顺利实施和编纂质量。

  由于水平所限，词典难免存在疏漏之处，恳请广大读者多提宝贵意见，以便下次修订予以改进。

编辑委员会

2020 年 7 月

目 录

PART Ⅰ 汉英部分

- A 3
- B 5
- C 19
- D 37
- E 62
- F 64
- G 77
- H 101
- I 118
- J 119
- K 148
- L 157
- M 170
- N 175
- O 179
- P 180
- Q 187
- R 197
- S 202
- T 230
- U 244
- V 245
- W 246
- X 256
- Y 271
- Z 291

PART Ⅱ 英汉部分

A	323
B	346
C	361
D	401
E	421
F	438
G	452
H	460
I	468
J	483
K	485
L	486
M	501
N	516
O	523
P	533
Q	559
R	561
S	580
T	616
U	636
V	642
W	648
X	656
Y	657
Z	658

PART I

汉英部分

A

AT 段　AT section
AT 供电方式　auto-transformer feeding system, AT feeding system
AU 指针调整　AU pointer adjustment
A 组填料　fill material of group A
埃洛石　halloysite
矮型信号机　dwarf signal, low signal
艾滋病预防　HIV-AIDS prevention
隘谷　gulley
安拆费及场外运费　charges for installation and removal and off-site delivery
安定性　soundness
安检仪　X-ray inspection machine
安全　safety, security
安全门　emergency door
安全报告　safety report
安全标准　safety standard
安全程序　safety procedure
安全出口　emergency exit
安全措施　safety measure, protective measure, accident prevention, security measure, measure of security
安全代表　safety representative
安全岛　safety island, pedestrian island
安全等级　safety level
安全地线　safety earth wire
安全第一，防范为主　safety and prevention first
安全电路　vital circuit
安全度　degree of safety
安全阀　safety valve
安全法规　safety regulation
安全防护　safety protection
安全防护距离　safety protective distance
安全防护装置　safety protection device
安全附件　safety accessory
安全工作条件　safe working conditions
安全钩　safety hook
安全护栏　safety fence

安全计划　safety program
安全计划费用　cost of safety program
安全计算机　vital computer
安全技术　safety technology
安全监控　safety monitoring
安全监控系统　safety monitoring and controlling system
安全检查　safety inspection
安全接地　safety earthing
安全接点　safety contact
安全净距　safety clearance
安全距离　safety distance
安全苛求　safety critical
安全连挂　safe coupling
安全帽　safety helmet, hardhat
安全门　metal detector door
安全培训　safety training
安全审计　security audit
安全生产　safety production
安全生产费　safety production costs
安全生产责任制　accountability system for construction safety
安全疏散功能　safety evacuation function
安全套接层　Secure Sokets Layer(SSL)
安全系数　safety factor
安全系数法　safety factor method
安全线　catch siding, safety siding
安全性　safety
安全宣贯　safety promotion
安全预防措施　safety precaution
安全制动距离　safe brake distance
安全制动器　safety brake
安全装卸　safe handling
安全装置　safety controls, safety installation
安山岩　andesite
安置补助费　settlement subsidies
安装　erection
安装测试　installation test

A

安装拆卸费　installation and removal expenses
安装调试　installation and commissioning
安装费　installation fee, erection cost
安装高度　mounting height
安装工程　installation works
安装工程费　installation cost
安装工程进度表　schedule of erection works
安装工程一切险　erection all risks (EAR)
安装工具　installation tools
安装工作量曲线　installation quantity curve
安装架　mounting rack
安装曲线　installation curve
安装容量　installed capacity
安装图　assembly drawing, installation diagram
安装资料　erection information
岸边式取水构筑物　riverside intake structure
岸坡　bank slope
岸溶盆地　shore dissolving basin
岸上合同　onshore contract
按比例　pro rata
按比例分摊　pro rata distribution
按成本计价　valuation at cost
按成果付酬工资制　payment-by-results
按份额　by share
按固定价格付款　payment on fixed price basis, pay at fixed price
按揭　mortgage
按揭人　mortgagor
按里程碑付款　milestone payment
按面值　at par
按年分期付款　yearly installments
按年计　per annum
按年计算　annualization
按钮　button
按钮表示　button indication
按钮表示器　button indicator
按人计算　capitation
按日计　per diem
按日计息贷款　day loan
按容积配合　volume batching
按条件付款　payment on terms
按通知交货　delivery on call
按物价水平调整的报表　price-level-adjusted statement
按现价　in current price
按现时成本　at current cost
按现值　current basis
按预定计划　on schedule
按月计　on a monthly basis, monthly
按月支付　monthly payment
按照　comply with, in compliance with, according to, based on
按照合同　in accordance with contract
按重量配合　proportioning by weight
案件处理费　handling fee
案件受理费　registration fee
案例　case
暗沟　blind ditch
暗管　buried pipe
暗河　underground river
暗设　concealed installation
暗示　imply, implication
暗线　buried wiring
凹坡　concave slope
凹陷　sag
凹形垫块　concave washer
凹形站台　concave platform
奥长环斑花岗岩　rapakivi granite
奥氏体不锈钢　austenitic stainless steel
奥陶纪　Ordovician period
奥陶系　Ordovician system

B

BIM 建模软件　BIM modeling software
BIM 设计交付物　BIM design deliverables
BIM 视图成果　BIM views deliverables
BIM 应用模型　BIM application model deliverables
BIM 执行计划书　BIM execution plan
B 组填料　fill material of group B
扒砟机　ballast raker
拔起高度　lifting height
拔桩机　pile extractor
坝　dam, barrage
坝顶　crest
罢工　strike, stoppage, walk off the job, down tools
罢工险　strikes riots and civil commotions（SRCC）
白班　day shift
白点　flake failure
白垩纪　Cretaceous period
白垩系　Cretaceous system
白光带　white light strip
白光图像处理　white-light image processing
白榴石　leucite
白榴石响岩　leucite phonolite
白天　day-time
白铁矿　marcasite
白铁皮　galvanized iron, tinned plate
白云母　muscovite
白云石　dolomite
白云石质灰岩　dolomitic limestone
白云岩　dolomite
百分比　percent
百分表　dial indicator
百分率　percentage
百米标　100-meter post
百米桩（百米标）　100-meter stake
百年洪水位　flood level in return period of 100 years
百叶窗　louver
百叶形风口　shutter type air outlet
柏油路　tar coated road
摆式发码器　pendulum type coder

败诉　losing a suit, defeated suit
败诉方　losing party, defeated party
拜访位置寄存器　visitor location register（VLR）
扳道电话　switchman's telephone
班　shift
班机　flight
班轮　liner
班轮公会运价　conference rate
班轮条件租赁　berth charter
班轮运输　liner transport
班组费用　gang cost
颁布　publish, issue, issuance
颁发　issue
颁发招标文件　issue bidding documents
斑点板岩　spotted slate
斑点状构造　spotted structure
斑杂构造　taxitic structure
斑状构造　porphyritic structure
搬迁　relocate, relocation
搬迁安置费用　relocation settlement costs
搬迁费　relocation cost
搬运　transportation
搬运费　handling charges, handling expenses, removal expenses
搬运工　loader, porter
板　plate, plank
板拱桥　slab arch bridge
板块　plate
板肋　open rib
板梁　plate girder, slab beam
板桥　slab-type bridge
板式岔区　slab-type turnout area
板式轨道　slab track
板式换热器　plate heat exchanger
板式楼梯　slab-type stairway
板式排烟口　plate-type smoke outlet
板式橡胶支座　laminated rubber bearing
板系结构　plated structure

板岩　slate
板柱—剪力墙结构　slab-column shear wall structure
板桩　sheet pile
板桩结构　pile-plank structure
板桩式挡土墙　sheet-pile retaining wall
板状　slaty
板状构造　tabular structure, slaty structure
版权　copyright
办公费　expenses for administration, office expenses
办公建筑　office building
办公时间　office hours
办公室管理费　office overhead costs
办公网　office network
办公信息系统　office automation system
办公用房　office premises
办理保险　insure, take out insurance, arrange insurance
办事员　clerk, officer
半补偿接触网　semi-compensated overhead contact line system
半成品　semi-finished product
半堤半堑　part-cut and part-fill, cut-and-fill
半地下室　partly-exposed basement
半分开式扣件　mixed direct and indirect fastening
半封闭声屏障　semi-enclosed sound barrier / semi-enclosed noise barrier
半干旱地区　semi-arid region
半公里标　half kilometer post
半功率带宽法　half-power bandwidth method
半功率点带宽　half-power point bandwidth
半固定沙丘　semi-fixed dune
半挂车　semi-trailer
半官方的　quasi-official
半环形枢纽　semicircular terminal
半金属光泽　semi-metallic luster
半晶质结构　hypocrystalline texture
半开放式办公室　semi-open office
半坡角度　bevel angle
半球形摄像机　semi-dome camera
半熟练工　semi-skilled labour
半填半挖　part-cut and part-fill, cut-and-fill
半通行地沟　semi-accessible trench
半无限弹性体　semi-infinite elastic body
半循环运转制　half circular routing system of locomotive
半压力式涵洞　culvert in the case of only one of the inlet/outlet submerged
半主动控制　semi-active control
半自动闭塞　semi-automatic block
拌和比　mix ratio, mix proportion
拌和机　mixer
拌和区　mixing area
拌和水　mixing water
拌和站　mixing plant
拌合物温度　fresh concrete temperature
拌合物性能　mixture properties
帮宽路基　subgrade widening
帮宽值　widening value
浜沟　creek ditch
绑架赎金险　kidnap ransom insurance
绑扎钢筋　assembling reinforcement
绑扎骨架　tied framework
棒状温度计　bar thermometer
傍山隧道　mountainside tunnel
包乘制　residency system
包干酬金　lump sum remuneration
包干项　lump sum items
包工包料合同　contract for labour and materials, contract for work and materials
包工合同　contract for labour
包裹　package, parcel
包裹单　bill of parcel
包含　include, contain
包括　comprise, cover
包括的　inclusive
包络线　envelope curve
包气带　aeration zone
包气带水　suspended water
包容　containment
包退包换　caveat venditor
包修制　contracted repair
包装　pack, packaging, package
包装不良　bad packing
包装成本　packing cost
包装单　packing slip (sheet)
包装费　packing expense
包装容积　bale capacity
包装须知　packing instructions
包装与标记　packing and marking
饱冰冻土　ice-saturated permafrost
饱和　saturated
饱和冻土　saturated frozen soil
饱和度　saturation degree
饱和含水率　saturated water content
饱和密度　saturation density
饱和器　saturator
饱和曲线　saturation curve
饱和土　saturated soil
饱和吸水率　saturated absorption rate
饱和蒸汽　saturated steam

饱和蒸汽压力　saturation vapor pressure
饱和重度　saturated unit weight
饱水带　saturation zone
饱水系数　water-saturation coefficient
保安器　protector
保安人员　security guard
保安系统　security system
保本点　break-even point
保本分析　break-even analysis
保本图　break-even chart
保持
　　keep, maintain, maintenance, preserve, retain
保持价值　maintenance of value
保持入　hold-in
保持有效　remain in force
保单　insurance policy, insurance certificate
保单持有人　policy holder
保兑　confirmation
保兑信用证　confirmed letter of credit
保兑银行　confirming bank
保付支票　certified check（cheque）
保管　custody, storage
保管费　storage charge
保管费率　storage rate
保管期　retention period
保管人　keeper
保管证书　back bond
保函　guarantee, letter of guarantee（L/G）
保函退还　release of security
保函样本　form of letter of guarantee
保护　protect, protection
保护半径　protective radius
保护层　protective layer
保护措施　protective measure
保护导体　protective conductor
保护范围　protective range
保护接地　protective earthing
保护面积　protection area
保护模式　protective mode
保护屏　protection panel
保护器　protective device
保护区　protection zone
保护区段　protection section
保护条款　safeguard clause
保护误动作　protection malfunction
保护线　protective wire（PW）
保护线（PW线）回流
　　current return via protective wire
保护性关税　customs duties
保护余量　margin

保护整定值　protection setting value
保护主义　protectionism
保价信　insured letter
保留　reserve, reservation, retain, retention
保留的　reserved
保留金　retention money
保留金保函　retention money guarantee
保留金比例　retention percentage
保留金的退还　release of retention money
保留金起扣额　retention free amount
保留金限额　limitation of retention money
保留期　retention period
保留权　retention option
保留条件　proviso
保留条款　saving clause, proviso clause
保密　confidentiality, secrecy, non-disclosure
保密的　confidential, secret
保密事项　confidential details
保密条款　confidential clause
保密性　confidentiality
保赔保险条款　protection and indemnity clause
保释　bail, bailment
保释金　bail
保释金保函　bail bond
保释人　bailer, bailor
保水性　water-retaining property, water retention
保水增稠材料
　　water-retention consistence-increasing material
保税仓库　bonded warehouse, bonded stores
保税港　bonded port
保税货物　bonded goods
保税区　bonded area, free trade zone
保卫　defend, safeguard, guard
保温　thermal insulation
保温保湿养护
　　curing at moisture-retention and heat-insulation
保温材料　thermal insulation material
保温层　thermal insulation layer
保温窗　thermal insulation window
保温工程　thermal insulation works
保险　insurance
保险标的　object of insurance, object matter of insurance, insurance subject
保险储备存量　buffer inventory
保险代理人　insurance agent
保险担保书　guarantee of insurance
保险单　insurance policy, policy, certificate of insurance
保险单的解释　construction of policy
保险单据　insurance documents

保险单正本　original policy
保险单转让　assignment of policy
保险的　insured
保险的完备性　adequacy of insurance
保险对象　insured object
保险额　insurance amount, sum insured
保险法　law of insurance, insurance law
保险范围　scope of cover, insurance cover (coverage)
保险费　insurance premium, premium
保险费率　insurance rate, rate of premium, premium rate
保险费总额　gross premium
保险风险　insurance risk
保险公估人　insurance assessor
保险公司　insurer, insurance company
保险估价　insurance assessment
保险惯例　insurance practice
保险合同　contract of insurance, insurance contract
保险基金　insurance fund
保险集团　insurance group
保险价值　value of insurance, insured value
保险鉴定人　insurance surveyor
保险金　insurance premium
保险金额　amount of insurance, amount insured
保险经纪人　insurance broker
保险客户　insured, policy holder
保险利益　benefit of insurance, insurance interest
保险赔偿　indemnity of insurance, insurance compensation, insurance indemnity
保险凭证　certificate of insurance, insurance certificate
保险期限　insurance period, period of insurance
保险人　insurer, assurer, underwriter
保险商　underwriter
保险申请人　insurance applicant
保险事件　insurance incident
保险受益人　insured, assured
保险索赔　insurance claim
保险条件　terms of insurance
保险条款　insurance clauses
保险箱　strong box, safe box
保险要素　essence of insurance
保险责任　insurance liability, insured liability
保险闸　safety brake
保险证书　certificate of insurance, insurance certificate
保险总额　insured amount, insurance cover
保修　warranty
保修费用　warranty expenses
保修阶段　warranty phase
保修期　term of service, period of warranty
保养　maintenance, service
保养费　maintenance charge
保障　indemnify, indemnification, insurance
保障方　indemnifying party
保障区　support district
保障条款　safeguard clause, indemnity clause
保障协议　indemnity agreement
保证　guarantee, ensure, assure, pledge, warranty
保证保险　guarantee insurance
保证表　schedule of guarantees
保证金　earnest money, deposit, warrant money, guarantee deposit
保证率　guarantee rate
保证期　guaranty period, guarantee period, warranty period
保证契约　deed of undertaking
保证人　guarantor, surety
保证人佣金　surety commission
保证书　guarantee, letter of guarantee, surety bond, letter of assurance
保证条款　engagement clause
保证最大价格　guaranteed maximum price
报表　statement
报表和支撑文件　statement and supporting documents
报酬　remuneration, fee, pay
报废　retirement
报废资产　dead asset
报告　report
报告式资产负债表　report form of balance sheet
报告书格式　form of report
报关　declare at the customs, apply to the customs, customs declaration
报关程序　procedure of customs
报关代理人　clearing (clearance) agent, customs agent
报关代理行　customs agency
报关单　customs entry, bill of entry
报关费　customs clearing charges (fee)
报关经纪人　customs broker
报关行　customs broker
报关人　declarant
报价　bid, offer, quote
报价单　quotation
报价函　letter of offer
报价人　offerer, offeror
报价有效期　offer period, validity of offer
报价摘要　abstract quotation
报价最高的投标人　highest bidder

报警　alarm
报警阀　alarm valve
报警复位　alarm resetting
报警设施　alarm facilities
报警速度曲线　warning speed profile
报警终端　alarm terminal
报警主机　alarm host
报销　apply for reimbursement
抱杆　derrick
抱箍（支柱上）　hoop
抱箍（坠陀限制架）　guide strap
暴跌　slump, break, crash
暴动　insurrection
暴风　storm
暴利　windfall profit
暴露　exposure
暴露声级　sound exposure level
暴乱　riot
暴雨　cloudburst
暴雨历时　rainstorm duration
暴雨强度　rainstorm intensity
暴雨特征值　rainstorm characteristic value
爆破　blast, explode, detonate
爆破材料　explosive
爆破地震效应　blasting seismic effect
爆破工　shot-firer, hole man
爆破循环进尺　cycle advance of blasting
爆破噪声　blasting noise
爆破振动　blasting vibration
爆炸极限　lower explosion limit
爆炸挤密法　blasting compaction method
爆炸物测探仪器　explosive detector
爆炸作用　explosion action
杯形基础　cup-type foundation
北向接口　northbound interface
北亚热带　northern subtropics
贝得石　beidellite
贝氏体钢轨　bainite rail
贝状断口　conchoidal fracture
备案　file, file a record
备查资料　backup data
备抵　allowance, provision
备抵坏账　allowance for bad debts, reserve for bad debts, provision for bad debts
备抵销贷折扣　allowance for sales discount
备抵折旧　reserve for depreciation, provision for depreciation, allowance for depreciation
备购时间　lead time
备件　spare parts
备品备件　spare parts

备忘录　memorandum, aide-memoire, memo
备选报价　alternative offer
备选的　alternative
备选方案　alternative plan
备选方案分析　options analysis
备选投标书　alternative bid
备选项目　alternative item
备用泵　emergency pump
备用材料　spare material, spare unit
备用车停留线　stabling siding for spare vehicles
备用成本　standby cost
备用的　standby
备用电源　standby power source
备用轨　spare rail (emergency rail stored along the way)
备用机车　spare locomotive
备用机车停留线　hold track for reserved locomotive
备用井　emergency shaft
备用客车存放线　stabling siding for spare passenger cars
备用品　stores, standby
备用冗余 UPS　standby UPS
备用设备　standby equipment, optional equipment, spare unit
备用现金　till money, petty cash
备用箱　spare box
备用信用证　standby letter of credit
备用资金　expendable fund
背对背　back to back
背对背信用证　countervailing credit, back-to-back (letter of) credit
背风坡　leeward slope
背光效果　backlight effect
背景　background
背景材料　background material
背景无线电噪声场强
　radio-noise field strength of background
背景噪声　ambient noise, background noise
背景噪声对照点　reference point of background noise
背面　back
背书　endorse, indorse, endorsement, indorsement, back
背书人　endorser, indorser
背书支票　back a check
背斜　anticline
背斜谷　anticlinal valley
背压回流　back-pressure back flow
倍频带声压级　octave-band sound-pressure level
被保风险　insured perils
被保释人　bailee
被保损失　insured loss

被保险财产　insured property
被保险人　insured, assured, insurant
被保证人　warrantee
被背书人　endorsee, indorsee
被查封账户　attached account
被担保者　vouchee
被抵押资产　hypothecated assets
被动红外探测器　passive infrared detector
被动控制　passive control
被动土压力　passive earth pressure
被告　accused person, defendant, respondent
被告承认书　cognovit
被空间包含　contained in spatial structure
被控站(子站)　controlled station (slave station)
被扣货物　detained goods
被任命人　nominee
被申请人　respondent
被授权方　authorized party, accredited party, authorized person
被索赔人　claimee
被提名人　nominee
被委任的　accredited
被委任者　appointee
本币　local currency
本地电话网　local telephone network
本地控制　local control
本地控制器　field controller
本地人　native, local
本地维护终端　Local Craft Terminal (LCT)
本构关系　constitutive relation
本国　home country
本国的　domestic, native
本国人　native
本国制成品　domestic manufacture
本金　principal, corpus, principal sum
本金偿还日　principal payment date
本金支付　principal payment
本利　principal and interest, capital and interest
本量利分析　cost-volume-profit analysis
本年度拨款　current appropriation
本票　promissory note, cashier's cheque
本期　current period
本期费用　current expense
本期利润　profit for the term
本期收益　current income
本钱　principal sum
本土承包商　indigenous contractor, local contractor
本务端设备　leading unit
本务机车　leading locomotive
本息　principal and interest
本质　essence
崩积的　colluvial
崩积黄土　colluvial loess
崩解　disintegration
崩解量　disintegration quantity
崩塌　toppling collapse
崩塌堆积　collapse accumulation
崩塌及岩堆路基　subgrade in collapse and talus zone
崩塌节理　collapse joint
泵送混凝土　pumped concrete
泵站　pumping station
逼近度　degree of approximation
鼻状凸丘　nose-like hump
比奥固结理论　Biot's consolidation theory
比表面积　specific surface area
比长仪　comparator
比贯入阻力　specific penetration resistance (Ps)
比焓　specific enthalpy
比价　relative price
比较财务报表　comparative financial statement
比较资产负债表　comparative balance sheet
比例　proportion
比例尺　scale
比例估算法　ratio estimation method
比例扩张　scale expansion
比例税率　flat rate
比例责任制　pro rata liability system
比率　ratio, proportion, rate
比色管　color comparison tube
比色皿　cuvette
比特误码率　bit error rate
比重　specific gravity
比重瓶　pycnometer, specific gravity bottle
比重瓶法　pycnometer method
笔误　clerical error, typographical error, typo
币值　monetary value
币值调整因数　currency adjustment factor
币值稳定　monetary stability
必备文件　requisite document
必测项目　required monitoring item
必要的　prerequisite, requisite
必要条件　prerequisite
毕托管　pitot tube
毕肖普简化条分法　Bishop's simplified method of slice
闭合测量导线　closure survey traverse
闭合差　misclosure
闭合导线误差　closure error of traverse
闭合环边数　number of closed loops
闭合水准路线　closed leveling line (route)

闭合中误差　closed mean square error
闭环电码化　closed-loop coding
闭口控制曲线　closed entry control curve
闭路式轨道电路　normally energized track circuit
闭塞　blocking
闭塞分区　block section
闭塞分区逻辑状态　logic state of block section
闭塞分区设备状态　state of block section device
闭塞机　block instrument
闭塞类型　block type
闭塞线　block line
闭式回水　closed return
闭式满管回水　closed full flow return
闭式水箱　closed water tank
闭锁　interlock
闭锁装置　interlocking device
壁柜　closet
壁后注浆　grouting for the backside void of segment lining
壁厚　wall thickness
壁龛　niche
壁式框架　wall-frame structure
避车洞　refuge niche, refuge recess
避车台　refuge platform
避开干扰　avoidance of interference
避雷带　lightning strip
避雷器　surge arrester
避雷网　lightning net
避雷针　lightning rod
避免/裁决争议协议的一般条件　general conditions of dispute avoidance/adjudication agreement
避免　avoidance
避免干扰　avoidance of interference
避免双重征税　avoidance of double taxation
避免争议　avoidance of disputes
避难层　refuge storey
避难所　refuge
避难屋　refuge room
避难走道　fire-protection evacuation walk
避税　tax avoidance, avoidance of tax, tax shelter
臂板电锁器联锁　interlocking by electric locks with semaphore, interlocking system of semaphore signal
臂板接触器　semaphore contact, contacts operated by semaphore
臂板信号机　semaphore signal
臂式起重机　boom hoist
边长较差限差　side difference tolerance
边长相对中误差　relative mean square error of side length

边长中误差　mean square error of side length
边沟　side ditch, gutter
边滚刀　gauge disc cutter
边际　margin
边际成本　marginal cost, marginal costing
边际利润　marginal profit
边际收入　marginal revenue
边际收益　marginal income
边角测量　triangulateration
边角交会　linear-angular intersection
边角交会法　linear-angular intersection
边角联合交会　linear-angular combined intersection
边角网　triangulateration network
边界　boundary
边界保护　perimeter security
边界网关　border gateway (BG)
边界网关协议　BGP Border Gateway Protocol
边境交货　delivered at frontier
边坡　slope
边坡剥落　slope spalling
边坡防护　slope protection
边坡防护正面图　front view of slope protection
边坡挂网锚喷防护　anchoring shotcrete with wire mesh on slope
边坡开挖　slope cutting
边坡溜坍　sliding of slope surface layer
边坡绿色防护　slope protection with vegetation
边坡平台　slope bench
边坡坡率　slope gradient
边坡清筛机　shoulder ballast cleaning machine
边坡渗沟　infiltration ditch of side slope
边坡坍塌　slope collapse
边坡稳定系数　slope stability factor
边坡稳定性　slope stability
边坡稳定性观测　observation of slope stability
边坡桩　slope stake
边坡桩测设　slope stake locating
边墙　side wall
边石堤　side stone bank
边修线　side repair track
边缘处理　edge processing
边缘热带　marginal tropics
编标　bid preparation
编发线　marshalling-departure track
编号　serial number
编号错误　numbering error
编绘原图　compiled original
编解码器　coder-decoder
编码　coding
编制　formulate, prepare

编制办法　budgetary estimate making regulation
编制层次　budgetary estimate making hierarchies
编制单元　budgetary estimate making unit
编制方法　cost making method
编制计划　planning
编制内容　compilation content
编制年度　cost making year
编制期　cost making period
编制期机械台班单价　machine shift price of cost making period
编制期价格　cost making period price
编制期价格水平　price level of cost making period
编制期综合工费单价　unit price of comprehensive expense of labors of cost making period
编制投标文件　bid preparation, preparation of bid
编制预算　compilation of budget, planning budget
编组屏　train coach position display
编组线　marshalling track, marshalling line
编组站　marshalling station, marshalling yard
鞭梢效应　whipping effect
贬值　devaluation, depreciation, decrement, depreciation of value
扁疤　tread flat
扁铲侧胀试验　flat dilatometer test
扁平颗粒　tabular grain
扁平率　flat ratio
扁千斤顶法　flat jack technique
变成构造　metamorphic structure
变电所　transformer substation
变电站　substation
变动　variation
变动成本　variable cost
变动成本计算　variable costing
变动水头注水　varying head water injecting
变动预算　flexible budget, variable budget
变风量空气调节系统　variable-volume air conditioning system
变刚度调平设计　variable stiffness leveling design
变更　vary, variation, change
变更程序　variation procedure
变更的单价　varied rate
变更的费率　varied rate
变更的工作　varied work
变更的估价　valuation of variation
变更和调整　variations and adjustments
变更建议书　change proposal, variation proposal
变更进路　alternative route
变更控制　change control, variation control
变更控制程序　variation control procedure
变更命令　change order, instruction for variation
变更命令记录簿　change order log
变更请求　change request
变更权　rights to vary
变更日志　change log
变更申请　request for change (RFC)
变更所有权　change of ownership
变更条款　change clause, variation clause
变更通知　notice of change
变更指令　change order, order for variation, change instruction (CI), variation order (VO)
变换光束测图　affine plotting
变焦摄像机　zoom lens camera
变截面梁　variable cross-section beam
变晶结构　crystalloblastic texture
变频调速恒压给水系统　variable frequency speed regulation constant pressure water supply system
变坡点　point of gradient change
变水头法　variable head method
变现　liquidation
变形　deformation
变形参数　deformation parameter
变形测量　deformation survey
变形二阶效应　deformation second-order effect
变形分析　deformation analysis
变形缝　deformation joint
变形观测控制网　deformation observation control network
变形监测　deformation monitoring
变形监控量测　deformation monitoring measurement
变形控制网　deformation control network
变形模量　deformation modulus
变形速率　rate of deformation
形变压力　deformation pressure
变形验算　deformation check
变形因子　deformation factor
变压器　transformer
变压器电抗　transformer reactance
变压器空载试验　no-load test for transformer
变压器在线监测　online monitoring of transformer
变异系数　coefficient of variation
变异应力　altered stress
变余构造　palimpsest structure
变余结构　palimpsest texture
变制冷剂流量多联分体式空气调节系统　variable refrigerant flow multi split air conditioning system
变质　deterioration

变质砾岩　metamorphic conglomerate
变质砂岩　metasandstone
变质岩　metamorphic rock
变质作用　metamorphism
便道　service road
便桥　temporary bridge
便条　note
便线　temporary line
(铁路)便线　detour line
便携电台　portable radio
便携终端　portable terminal
辨别　discriminate, discrimination
辩护　defence, defense, defend
辩护律师　defence counsel, counsel, counselor
辩护人　advocate
标本　specimen, sample
标称尺寸　nominal dimension
标称电流　nominal current
标称电压　nominal voltage
标称精度　nominal accuracy
标称频率　nominal frequency
标称容量　nominal capacity
标称声压级　nominal sound pressure level
标称阻抗　nominal impedance
标尺　rod, staff
标的(物)　object
标底　base price, tender price
标定　calibration
标段　bid lot
标杆　surveying stake, staff
标杆管理　benchmark, benchmarking
标高　elevation
标高金　mark-up
标记　mark, label
标价　bid price, pricing
标价单　bidding sheet
标价的工程量表　priced bill of quantities
标距　gauge length
标距长度　gauge length
标牌　brand name
标签　tag, label
标前会议　pre-bid meeting
标石　markstone
标识　label, marking, sign
标题　subject, title, caption
标线　guide line
标志　mark, sign
标志层　marker bed
标志牌　sign board
标桩　stake

标准　standard, criteria, norm
标准保险费率　manual rates
标准操作程序　standard operation procedures
标准差　standard error
标准长度钢轨　standard length rail
标准成本　standard cost
标准尺　gauge
标准稠度　normal consistency
标准稠度用水量
　　water requirement of normal consistency
标准的　normal, standard
标准冻结深度　standard frost depth
标准分流感度　standard shunting sensitivity
标准分路电阻　standard shunt resistance
标准分路灵敏度　standard shunting sensitivity
标准格式　standard form
标准工程招标文件　Standard Bidding Documents
　　for Works (SBDW)
标准工况　standard working condition
标准工时　normal hour
标准工资率　standard labour rate
标准固结试验　standard consolidation test
标准贯入器　standard penetrometer
标准贯入试验　standard penetration test (SPT)
标准轨距　standard gauge
标准轨距铁路　standard gauge railway
标准合同　standard contract, model contract
标准荷载计算参数
　　calculation parameter of standard load
标准横断面　standard cross section
标准化　standardization
标准化管理　standardization management
标准化图像格式
　　Common Intermediate Format (CIF)
标准活载　standard live load
标准机械工时　standard machine hour (time)
标准检定场　standard calibration site
标准黏度计　standard viscometer
标准配置点　standard collocation point
标准喷头　standard sprinkler
标准偏差　standard deviation
标准曲线　standard curve
标准人工工时　standard labour hour (time)
标准溶液　standard solution
标准融深　standard thawing depth
标准砂　standard sand
标准设防　standard fortification
标准设计　standard design
标准设计费　standard design fee
标准试件　standard specimen

标准条款　standard clause, standard terms
标准协议书　standard agreement
标准养护试件　standard curing specimen
标准养护温度　standard curing temperature
标准值　standard value
标准制冷量　standard cooling capacity
标准组合　characteristic combination
表层覆土　covering soil
表层土　top soil
表单　schedules
表干时间　tack-free time
表格　table, form, sheet
表观密度　apparent density
表观黏度　apparent viscosity
表决　vote
表决权　voting right
表流　tableflow
表面波法　surface wave technique
表面冲洗　surface washing
表面处理　surface treatment
表面的　prima facie
表面负荷　hydraulic loading rate
表面力　surface force
表面裂缝　surface crack
表面排水　surface drainage
表面气泡　surface bubble
表面扫洗　surface sweep washing
表面式换热器　surface heat exchanger
表面装修　surface finish
表明　indicate, indication, show
表示　indication
表示灯　indication lamp
表示灯电源　power source for indication lamp
表示电路　indication circuit
表示杆　indication rod
表示盘　indication panel
表示器　indicator
表示条件　indication requisition
表示周期　indication cycle
表土　topsoil
表现　show, performance, manifestation
滨海路基　coastal subgrade
滨海平原　coastal plain
滨海相　littoral facies
滨河路基　riverside subgrade
濒危野生动物　endangered wildlife
冰雹　hail
冰川　glacier
冰川槽谷　glacier trough
冰川沉积　glacial deposit
冰川地貌　glacial landform
冰川相　glacial facies
冰床　ice bed, glacier bed
冰冻线　frost line
冰斗　kar, cirque
冰盾　ice sheet
冰盖　ice cover
冰荷载　ice load
冰湖　ice lake
冰积平原　glacial deposition plain
冰夹层　ice interlayer
冰坎　cross-wall
冰砾阜　kame
冰瀑布　ice fall
冰碛　glacial drift
冰碛地形　morainal topography
冰碛阜　moraine kame
冰碛丘陵　moraine hill
冰碛黏土　morainic clay
冰前扇地　glacial marginal fan
冰丘　ice mound
冰舌　ice tongue
冰蚀崖　glacial erosion scarp
冰水沉积　outwash
冰水阶地　fluvioglacial terrace
冰水扇　glaciofluvial fans
冰楔　ice wedge
冰压力　ice pressure
冰缘的　periglacial
冰缘地貌　periglacial landform
冰缘区　periglacial region
冰缘作用　periglacial process
兵险　war risk
并联电容补偿装置　shunt capacitor bank
并联电容器　parallel capacitor, shunt capacitor
并联电容器补偿　parallel capacitor compensation
并联分支钢轨连接线　parallel branching railway connector
并联负载均分性能　parallel load equipartition performance
并联供水　parallel water supply
并联冗余UPS　parallel UPS
并联式轨道电路　parallel track circuit
并联条件　parallel condition
并列式枢纽　parallel arrangement type terminal
并列运行　parallel running
并行双线　parallel double-track
并置信号点　double signal location

病毒	virus

病毒　virus
病毒防范　anti-virus
病害类型　defect types
病假　sick leave
病假工资　sick leave pay
病原体污水　sewage with pathogens
拨(款)　allocate, appropriate
拨道　track lining
拨道机　track lining machine
拨付　payment by transfer
拨款　appropriation, allocation, allotment
拨款额　amount allocated
拨款通知　allotment advice
拨款要求　requisition for money (payment)
波传播速度　wave propagation velocity
波动　fluctuation, fluctuate
波动传播系数　wave propagation coefficient
波段色散特性　waveband dispersion characteristics
波分复用　wavelength division multiplexing(WDM)
波幅　amplitude
波痕构造　ripple structure
波浪爬高　wave runup
波浪侵袭高　swash height of wave
波浪压力　wave pressure
波谱　spectrum
波速　wave velocity
波速测井　wave velocity logging
波速测井法　wave velocity well logging method
波纹补偿器　corrugated compensator
波纹效应　ripple effect
波形　waveform
波形磨耗　rail corrugation
波状层理　current bedding
波状沙地　undulating sandy land
波状沙丘带　undulating dune zone
波状斜层理　undulate diagonal bedding
玻化岩　buchite
玻基橄榄岩　meimechite
玻基辉橄岩　rizzonite
玻基辉岩　limburgite
玻璃电极　glass electrode
玻璃钢腕臂　glassfiber reinforced plastic cantilever, GRP cantilever
玻璃工　glazier
玻璃光泽　glassy lustre
玻璃纤维薄毡　glass fiber felt base
玻璃纤维增强塑料　glassfiber reinforced plastic
玻璃纤维毡防水卷材　glass fiber mat waterproof sheet
玻璃质的　glassy, vitreous

玻纤网　glass fiber grid
玻纤增强聚酯毡　glass fiber reinforced polyester felt
玻纤毡　glass fiber felt
剥夺　deprive, divestiture
剥夺所有权　expropriation
剥离表层土　stripping
剥离强度　peel strength
剥露　uncover
剥落量　scale mass
剥蚀　denudation
剥蚀残山　denudated mountain
剥蚀平原　denudation plain
剥蚀坡　denudation slope
驳不倒的　irrefutable
驳斥　disproof, confute
驳船　barge
驳回　dismiss, ignore, reject, set aside
驳载　transshipment
泊松比　Poisson ratio
泊位　berth, berthage
泊位包租条款　berth clause
勃氏法　Blaine method
铂器皿　platinum dish
箔式应变片　foil strain gauge
薄壁取土器　thin-wall sampler
薄壁堰　plate weir
薄层　thin layer
薄壳　shell
薄利　narrow margin
薄膜　membrane
薄膜烘箱试验　thin film oven test
薄膜水　film water
薄细层　laminated layer
补偿　compensate, compensation, indemnify, indemnity, reimburse, reimbursement
补偿保险　compensation insurance
补偿电容　compensation capacitor
补偿合约　contract of compensation
补偿滑轮　tension pulley
补偿棘轮　toothed(ratchet) wheel tension assembly
补偿金　stipends consideration money, honorarium
补偿贸易　compensation trade
补偿器　compensator
补偿事件　compensation events
补偿收缩混凝土　shrinkage-compensating concrete
补偿条款　compensation terms
补偿原则　principle of compensation
补偿装置　tensioning device
补充　complement, supplement

补充材料单价表 unit price sheet of supplementary materials
补充财务报表 supplementary financial statement
补充测点 additional measure point
补充的 complementary, supplementary
补充定额 supplementary quota
补充定线测量 additional location survey
补充合同 supplemental contract
补充勘测 additional survey
补充清单 supplemental bill
补充条件 supplementary conditions
补充协议 supplementary agreement
补充资料 supplementary information
补充资料表 schedule of supplementary information
补发的工资 retroactive pay
补给半径 recharge radius
补给率 recharge rate, replenishment rate
补给区 recharge area
补给水泵 make-up pump
补机 helper locomotive, assistant locomotive, banking locomotive
补机地段 helper locomotive section
补机始终点站 helper locomotive station
补救 remedy, rectify, repair, redress
补救办法 method of redress
补救措施 remedial action, remedial measure
补救工作 remedial work
补码 complement
补票 pay excess fare
补票机 ticket machine for excess fare
补税 tax make-up
补贴 subsidy, allowance, grant
补遗 addendum, amend
补助费 allowance
补助金 subsidy, benefit
捕虏体 xenolith
不包括 exclude, except
不保兑信用证 unconfirmed letter of credit
不保事项 exclusion
不变成本 constant cost
不变承诺 firm commitment
不成文法 lex non scripta
不承兑期票 dishonour a bill
不承认 disclaimer
不充分的 inadequate
不出庭 default
不带息票据 no-interest-bearing note
不当的 inappropriate, unwarranted
不当损失 undue loss
不得超过的期限 cut-off period

不等向固结 anisotropic consolidation
不定期租赁 tenancy at will
不定值保险 unvalued insurance
不动产 fixed property, real estate, real property, immovables
不动产抵押贷款 loan on actual estate
不动产清册 cadastre
不动产增值 betterment
不动产债权 encumbrance
不对称脉冲轨道电路 asymmetrical impulse track circuit
不对称侵蚀淤积 asymmetrical erosion and siltation
不法行为 illegal act, delict, barratry, tort
不方便 inconvenience
不妨害 without prejudice to
不分开式扣件 direct fastening
不封锁 unblocked
不符合 discrepancy, noncompliance
不符合合同条件 noncompliance with contractual conditions
不符合技术规范 noncompliance with specifications
不符合要求的投标 non-responsive bid
不公开投标 private bidding (tendering)
不公平 unfair, injustice
不公平竞争 unfair competition
不固结不排水剪 unconsolidated and undrained shear
不固结不排水剪试验 unconsolidated and undrained shear test
不规则块体试验 irregular lump test
不规则三角网 irregular triangulateration network
不合格 disqualification
不合格产品 unqualified product, subquality product, non-conforming product
不合格的 non-eligible, improper, underproof
不合格的工作 condemned work
不合格货物 disqualified goods
不合格来源国 non-eligible country
不合格桩 defective pile
不合要求报告 non-conformance report
不极化电极 nonpolarizable electrode
不记名背书 blank endorsement, endorsement in blank
不记名提单 bearer bill of lading, open bill of lading
不记名债券 bearer bond
不记名支票 bearer cheque
不间断电源 uninterruptible power supply (UPS)

不间断供电　uninterruptible power supply
不接受　non-acceptance
不接受报价　decline an offer
不洁提单　dirty bill of lading, foul bill of lading, unclean bill of lading
不均匀沉降　uneven settlement
不均匀沉陷　unequal settlement
不均匀程度系数　non-uniformity coefficient
不均匀度　unevenness
不均匀系数　coefficient of non-uniformity
不可保风险　uninsurable risk
不可避免的　inevitable, unavoidable
不可编辑的记录　un-editable record
不可撤销的　irrevocable
不可撤销的保函　irrevocable letter of guarantee
不可撤销的跟单信用证　irrevocable documentary (letter of) credit
不可撤销的合同　firm contract
不可撤销的信用证　irrevocable letter of credit, irrevocable credit
不可调解的　irreconcilable
不可兑换　inconvertibility
不可分割的　indivisible, inalienable
不可分割协议书　non-separation agreement
不可分债务　indivisible obligation
不可抗力　force majeure
不可抗力条款　force majeure clause
不可控风险　uncontrollable risks
不可控制成本　uncontrollable cost
不可逆正常使用极限状态　irreversible serviceability limit state
不可预见　unforeseeable
不可预见的工作　unforeseen work
不可预见的事件　unforeseeable event
不可预见的外部障碍　unforeseeable physical obstructions
不可预见的物质条件　unforeseeable physical conditions
不可预见费　contingency cost, contingency sum, contingency
不可预见性评估　contingency evaluation
不可预见因素　unpredictable element
不可原谅的拖期　non-excusable delays, inexcusable delays
不可转让单据　non-negotiable document
不可转让的　non-assignable, non-negotiable
不可转让提单　non-negotiable bill of lading
不可转让信用证　non-transferable credit, nontransferable letter of credit
不利的天气条件　adverse weather conditions
不利地段　unfavorable section
不利条件　unfavourable conditions
不利自然条件　adverse physical conditions
不连续级配土　gap-graded soil
不良地质　unfavorable geology
不良地质隧道　tunnel in unfavorable geological conditions
不良地质现象　unfavorable geological phenomena
不良地质作用　unfavorable geological process
不良级配土　poorly-graded soil
不履行　failure, breach
不履行付款义务　default of payment
不履行合同　breach of contract
不履行义务　default
不履行债务　financial default
不落轮镟轮库　under-floor wheel lathe workshop
不满意通知　notice of dissatisfaction (NOD)
不满载　partial load
不明确的条文　imprecise terms
不能理解的　baffling, puzzling
不能履行　failure to perform, inability to perform
不能履行的合同　frustrated contract
不能自由兑换的货币　inconvertible currency, irredeemable currency
不凝性气体分离器　non-condensable gas separator
不排水剪切内摩擦角　internal friction angle under undrained shearing
不排水剪强度　undrained shear strength
不平等　inequality
不平等条款　unequal terms
不平衡(报价)　unbalanced, front loaded
不平衡报价　unbalanced bidding
不平衡报价法　unbalanced bidding method
不平衡电阻　unbalanced resistance
不平衡绝缘电阻　unbalanced insulation resistance
不平衡牵引电流　unbalanced traction current
不平衡投标　unbalanced bidding
不平稳系数　unstability coefficient
不歧视待遇　rum-discriminatory treatment
不弃权　non-waiver
不起诉　non-prosecution, waive
不燃烧体　non-combustible substance
不扰动土样　undisturbed soil sample
不实陈述　misrepresentation
不舒适眩光　discomfort glare
不熟练工人　unskilled labour
不通行地沟　unpassable trench
不同速度限制　different speed restriction
不透水层(隔水层)　impermeable layer (aquiclude)
不透水性　watertightness, water impermeability

不透水仪　watertightness tester, waterproof apparatus
不限时人工解锁　manual non-time release
不锈钢　stainless steel
不一致　discrepancy, repugnance
不摘车修理　in-train repair
不整合接触　discordant contact, unconformable contact
不正当竞争　unfair competition
不支付期票　dishonour a bill
不执行　non-execution
不主动信托　inactive trust
不追溯条款　grandfather clause
不准进入　no trespassing
不足　short, shortage, inadequate, deficient
不足额　deficiency
不遵守　noncompliance
不作废条款　non-forfeiture condition
不作为　fail, default, in default, breach of contract, non-performance
(法定义务的)不作为　act of omission
布告　notice, notification
布局　layout
布线　wiring, cabling
布线系统　wiring system
布辛涅斯克理论　Boussinesq theory
布置图　layout plan

步进　launching
步行板　foot plank
步增成本　step cost
部　ministry
部长　minister
部分　section, proportion, portion
部分保险　partial coverage
部分补偿　partial compensation
部分的　partial
部分废除　derogation
部分监控模式　partial supervision mode (PS)
部分交货　partial delivery
部分赔付　partial coverage
部分损失　partial loss
部分预应力混凝土梁　partially prestressed concrete beam
部分预应力混凝土桥　partially prestressed concrete bridge
部分占有　partial possession
部分支付　partial payment
部件　component, unit
部门　division, department, sector, section
部门经理　department manager, section manager
部门主会计师　division controller
簿记　bookkeeping
簿记员　bookkeeper

C

CBR 顶破强度　CBR burst strength
CD 法　central diaphragm method (CD method)
CRTSⅠ型板式　CRTS-Ⅰ slab
CRTSⅡ型板式　CRTS-Ⅱ slab
CRTSⅢ型板式　CRTS-Ⅲ slab
CRTS Ⅰ型板式无砟轨道
　　CRTS-Ⅰ slab ballastless track
CRTS Ⅱ型板式无砟轨道
　　CRTS-Ⅱ slab ballastless track
CRTS Ⅲ型板式无砟轨道
　　CRTS-Ⅲ slab ballastless track
CRTSⅠ型双块式　CRTS-Ⅰ bi-block
CRTSⅡ型双块式　CRTS-Ⅱ bi-block
C 组填料　fill material of group C
擦伤　scratch
材料　material
材料表　bill of materials (BOM)
材料采购　procurement of materials
材料采购及保管费
　　material purchase and storage expenses
材料厂　large scale material storehouse
材料成本　material cost
材料出库单　material delivery note
材料单价　unit price of materials
材料单重　unit-weight of material
材料弹性模量　elasticity modulus of materials
材料定额消耗量　quota consumption of materials
材料短缺　lack of materials
材料发放　release of material, issue of material
材料费　material cost
材料供应　material supply
材料供应方案/计划　material supply plan
材料购买　materials purchasing
材料合格证　material certification
材料和工艺　plant, material and workmanship
材料基价　base price of materials
材料计划　materials planning
材料价差　difference in price of materials
材料价差系数
　　coefficient of difference in price of materials
材料抗震强度
　　seismic resistance strength of materials
材料抗震强度设计值　design value of earthquake-resistant strength of materials
材料库　material store
材料力学性能　mechanical properties of materials
材料明细表　material specification
材料签收报告　material receiving report
材料强度标准值
　　standard value of material strength
材料强度设计值
　　design value of material strength
材料蠕变影响系数
　　influence coefficient of creep of material
材料设备存放场　lay-down yard
材料试验机　material testing machine
材料收据　material receipt
材料说明　description of materials
材料统计　material take-off (MTO)
材料退回　return of materials
材料消耗　consumption of material
材料消耗定额　material consumption norm
材料消耗量　material consumption amount
材料性能的标准值
　　characteristic value of material properties
材料性能分项系数
　　partial factor of material property
材料性能设计值
　　design value of material property
材料异常报告
　　material exception report (MER)
材料预算价格　budgetary price of materials
材料原价　original price of material
材料运输方案　material transport plan
材料证明　certificate of materials
材料种类　material types

材料转运	material handling
材料综合单价	all-in material rate
财产	property, assets, estate
财产保险	property insurance
财产保险费	property insurance premium
财产保险合约	contract of property insurance
财产抵押行为	hypothecation, incumbrance
财产扣押	arrestment
财产权	right of property, property
财产收回	recovery of property
财产受领人	abandonee
财产受托命令	vesting order
财产税	tax on property, property tax
财产损失	property damage
财产所有权	title to property
财产增益税	accession tax
财产转让	conveyance of estate
财产转让契约	deed of assignment
财产租赁权	right to leased property
财力	resources, financial ability
财团成员	member of consortium
财务报表	financial report, statement
财务报告	financial statement, financial report
财务备忘录	financial memorandum
财务比率	financial ratio
财务成本	financial cost
财务代理人	fiscal agent
财务担保	financial guarantee
财务费用	financial cost, financial expenses
财务分析	financial analysis
财务干系人	financial stakeholder
财务杠杆	financial leverage
财务顾问	financial counsellor (consultant)
财务管理	financial management
财务会计	financial accounting
财务会计标准	financial accounting standards
财务建议书	financial proposal
财务结算	financial settlement
财务能力	financial capacity
财务评估	financial appraisal
财务评价	financial evaluation
财务清账	financial closing
财务审计	financial audit
财务审计报表	audited financial statement
财务收入	financial means
财务收益率	financial rate of return
财务数据	financial data
财务文件	financial document
财务盈利能力分析	profitability analysis
财务预测	financial projection
财务预算	financial budget
财务援助	financial aid
财务账目	financial accounts
财务主管	treasurer
财务专员	financial commissioner
财务状况	financial status, financial position, financial condition
财务状况表	statement of financial position
财务咨询	financial counselling
财务资产	financial assets
财务租赁	financial lease
财政措施	fiscal measures
财政当局	monetary authorities
财政的	fiscal, financial, monetary
财政拮据	financial embarrassment
财政年度	fiscal year, financial year, budget year
财政收入	fiscal revenue
财政收支平衡	balance of revenue and expenditure
财政危机	fiscal crisis
财政委员会	treasury board
财政政策	fiscal policy
财政资源	financial resources
财政资助	financial aid
裁定	determination, rule, award, ruling
裁决	adjudication, arbitration, ruling, verdict
裁决的有效性	validity of an award
裁决规则	adjudication rule
裁决令	adjudication order
裁决人	arbitrator, adjudicator
裁决书	award, arbitral award
采购	purchase, procure, procurement
采购办法	procurement methods
采购包	procurement packages
采购费	charges for procurement, storage and maintenance
采购备忘录	purchase memorandum
采购部	purchasing department
采购策略	purchasing strategy
采购代理	purchasing agency
采购费	purchase expense
采购工作计划	procurement schedule
采购管理	procurement administration
采购及保管费	purchase and storage expenses
采购及保管费率	rate of purchase and storage expenses
采购计划	procurement program
采购计划编制	procurement planning
采购进度报告	procurement status report
采购控制	acquisition control

采购评估　acquisition evaluation
采购申请单　purchase requisition
采购审计　procurement audit
采购限制　procurement restraints
采购员　purchasing clerk, procurement clerk
采购指南　guidelines for procurement
采光　daylighting
采光系数　daylight factor
采光系数标准值　standard value of daylight factor
采集单元　acquisition unit
采掘场　quarry
采空区　mined-out area
采暖　heating
采暖度日数　heating degree days
采暖管道　heating pipe
采暖期室外平均温度
　　average temperature outside during heating period
采暖期天数　days of heating period
采暖室外计算温度
　　design outdoor temperature for heating
采取交钥匙的形式　on a turnkey basis
采取行动　take action
采石场　quarry
采石工程　quarrying
采样间隔　sampling interval
采样率　sampling rate
采样频率　sampling frequency
彩色合成　color composite
彩色红外片　color infrared film
彩色红外摄影　color infrared photography
彩色片　color film
菜地开发建设基金
　　vegetable field development and construction fund
参差状断口　uneven fracture
参考　reference, refer
参考地　reference earth
参考价格　reference price, price indication
参考模型　reference model
参考平面　reference plane
参考椭球（体）　reference ellipsoid
参数　parameter
参照点　reference point
参照建筑　reference building
残积　residual deposit
残积土　residual soil
残积相　eluvial facies
残疾抚恤金　disablement pension
残料　salvage
残留层　residual layer
残留风险　residual risk

残丘　monadnock
残压　residual voltage
残压峰值　residual voltage peak value
残余变形　residual deformation
残余强度　residual strength
残余上下视差　residual vertical parallax
残值　remaining value salvage value, residual value
仓储成本　warehouse cost
仓储费　storage fee
仓储损耗费　stock loss fee
仓储损耗费率　stock loss rate
仓单　manifest, warehouse receipt
仓库　storehouse, warehouse, depot
仓库端墙轴线　end wall axis of warehouse
仓库交货　ex store, delivery ex-warehouse
仓库交货价　ex-warehouse, ex store
仓库宽度　warehouse width
仓库凭证　warehouse certificate
仓库收据　warehouse receipt
仓库账簿　warehouse book
仓至仓条款　warehouse to warehouse clause
舱面货物险　on deck risk
舱面交货提单　on deck bill of lading
舱位包租　berth charter
舱位损失　broken space
操纵台　operating console
操作　operation
操作电源　power supply for operation
操作工　operator
操作规程　job specification, working rules
操作规范　operational specification
操作过电压　switching overvoltage
操作和维修费用　operation and maintenance cost
操作和维修手册
　　operation and maintenance manuals
操作及显示界面　operation and display interface
操作检查　operation inspection
操作系统　operating system
操作与维护中心
　　operation and maintenance center（OMC）
操作终端　operation terminal
糙率　roughness coefficient
槽道盖板　conduit cover slab
槽钢　trough iron, channel steel
槽碛　trough moraine
槽碛垄　trough moraine ridge
槽式列车　bunker train
槽探　trench exploration
槽铁　trough iron
槽形梁　Trough-type girder, Trough-type beam

C

草案	draft, protocol, outline, rough draft
草本植物	herbs
草地	meadow
草稿	draft, sketch
草块移植	turf transplanting
草拟	drawing, draft
草坪	lawn
草签	initial, initialling
草签合同	initial a contract
草图	draft, layout, sketch, rough draft, rough sketch
草原	grassland, steppe, prairie
草种	grass seed
侧方交会	lateral intersection, side intersection
侧沟	side ditch
侧沟平台	side ditch berm
侧接触式接触轨	side-contact conductor rail
侧面冲突	side-on collision
侧面磨耗	side wear
侧面式叉车	side forklift
侧模	side formwork
侧摩擦阻力	shaft friction
侧碛	lateral moraine
侧碛垅	lateral moraine ridge
侧式中间站台	side intermediate platform
侧视图	side view
侧吸罩	side-draught hood
侧限	lateral confinement
侧线	sidings
侧向承载基础	side bearing foundation
侧向挡块	lateral stop block
侧向接发列车	lateral train reception and departure
侧向进路	diverging route
侧向水平联结系	lateral bracing system
侧向弯曲	lateral bending
侧向位移	lateral displacement
侧向压力	lateral pressure
侧向有效应力	lateral effective stress
侧向约束膨胀率	swelling ratio under lateral restraint condition
侧压力系数	lateral pressure coefficient
侧胀板头	flat dilatometer
（轨道板）侧置立放	(track slab) vertically placed on the side
侧撞防护	lateral collision protection
测边交会法	linear intersection
测长	distance-to-coupling measurement
测点	measuring point
测点变位	deflection of measure point
测回	observation set
测绘标准	standard of surveying and mapping
测绘范围	scope of surveying and mapping
测绘仪器	instrument of surveying and mapping
测记法成图	mapping by picket-point method
测角中误差	mean square error of angle measurement
测井	well logging
测距仪	diastimeter, distance measuring instrument
测距中误差	mean square error of distance measurement
测孔	sampling hole
测力计	dynamometer
测力装置	dynamometric device
测量	admeasurement, survey, measuring, measure, measurement
测量安置	measuring installation
测量标距	measuring gauge length
测量标志	survey marker
测量标桩	survey peg
测量觇标	observation target
测量电极	measuring electrode
测量电极距	measuring electrode spacing
测量规范	specifications of surveying
测量机器人	geo-robot, robotic total station
测量基准	geodetic datum
测量检查	measurement and inspection
测量控制网	survey control network
测量平差	survey adjustment
测量曲线	curve calibration
测量日期	date of survey
测量时窗	measuring time-window
测量学	surveying
测量仪器	surveying instrument
测量与成本补偿合同	measurement and cost reimbursement contract
测量员	surveyor
测区代号	code of survey area
测区范围	coverage of survey area
测区名称	title of survey area
测区平均高程面	mean height surface of survey area
测深点	sounding point
测深点间距	interval between sounding points
测深定位	location of sounding point
测深线	sounding line
测时水位	timing water level
测试	test
测试案例	test case
测试环线	test loop
测试孔	test hole
测试序列	test sequence

测试支架　testing scaffold
测试值　test value
测速　speed measurement
测图放大系数　plotting magnification factor
测微器行差　run error of micrometer
测线　measuring line
测斜管　inclinometer tube
测压管水头　piezometric head
测验　examination
测站　survey station
测站归心　reduction to station centre
测振传感器　vibration measuring sensor
测振放大器　vibration-measuring amplifier
测振记录装置　vibration-measuring recording device
测值修正　measure value modification
测置队　survey party
测置师　surveyor
测钟　test clock
测重　weight sensing
测桩　measuring peg
测阻　rollability measurement
层高　floor height
层高利用系数　utilization factor of storey height
层间劈理　interlaminar cleavage
层间水　interbedded water
层理　stratification, bedding
层理构造　bedding structure
层流　laminar flow
层析成像　computerized tomography
层系　stratum series
层系组　coset
层状构造　stratified structure
层状裂纹　lamellar tearing
叉车　forklift
叉车日均作业时间　average daily operation time of forklift
叉管　branch pipe
叉簧　hookswitch
叉心　frog point rail, crossing nose
插入式混凝土振捣器　immersible concrete vibrator, internal concrete vibrator, penetrating vibrator
插入式继电器　plug-in relay
插入式振捣器　vibrator poker
插入损耗　insertion loss
插入损失　insertion loss (IL)
插图　figure
插腿式叉车　straddle forklift
查漏仪　leakage detector
查询　interrogation

查询响应时间　inquiry response time
查账　audit, inspection of accounts
查账人　auditor
查账条款　auditing clauses
查账追踪　audit trail
查照间隙　check gauge
岔后直线段长度　straight section length after the turnout
岔线　branch line
岔枕　turnout sleeper
岔枕组件　turnout sleeper components
岔中绝缘　insulated joints within a turnout
差动保护　differential protection
差额　difference, balance amount
差分GPS　difference of GPS
差分服务　Differentiated Services (DiffServ)
差分改正　differential correction
差价　price difference
差价税　variable levy
差减法　minusing
差流元件　differential current element
差旅费　travel expense
差旅交通费　travel and transportation expenses
差模试验　differential mode test
差热分析　differential thermal analysis
差压流量计　differential pressure flowmeter
差异沉降　differential settlement
差异性　differentiation
拆包　unpack
拆除　demolish, dismantle, dismantlement, pull down
拆除费　demolition cost
拆除工程　demolition works
拆模　stripping
拆铺　removal and laying
拆迁　demolition, disassembly, relocation
拆迁安置　demolition and resettlement
拆迁补偿　demolition compensation
拆迁成本　demolition and relocation cost, removal cost
拆迁范围　demolition range
拆迁费　demdition and relocation
拆迁人　demolitioner
拆迁许可　demolition permit
拆卸　disassembly
拆装式桁架　demountable truss
拆装箱场　stuffing and destuffing yard
拆装箱库　stuffing and destuffing shed
拆装箱作业　stuffing and destuffing operation
拆装箱作业站台　stuffing and destuffing platform
柴草沙障　straw barrier

柴油打桩机　diesel pile driver
柴油捣固机　diesel tamping machine
柴油发动机叉车　diesel engine forklift
柴油机　diesel engine
觇标　observation target
掺饵光纤 EDF　erbium-doped fiber (EDF)
掺合料　admixture
掺假　adulterate
缠丝过滤管　wire-wrapped filter tube
产出　yield
产地检验证书　inspection certificate of origin
产地交货单　loco invoice
产地交货价格　loco price
产地证书　certificate of origin
产量保证　production quantity guarantee
产量定额　output quota
产量折旧法　production method of depreciation
产品成本　production cost
产品回购　buy-back of product
产品鉴定证书　product appraisal certificate
产品生命周期　product life cycle
产品试板　production test
产品寿命　life of product
产品税　product tax
产品责任保险　product liability insurance
产品质量保证　product quality guarantee
产权　equity, property right
产权待定　abeyance
产权归属说明书　abstract of title
产权纠纷　property dispute
产权使用费　royalty
产权式合营　equity joint venture
产权所有权　equity ownership
产权所有人　owner of title
产权要求　property claim
产权转移　alienate, title transfer
产权资本　equity capital
产业税　industry tax
产业所有权　domain
产状　occurrence, attitude
铲斗　bucket
铲斗挖土机　scoop shovel
铲土机　shovel
铲运机　scooptram / scraper
颤振　chattering
长波不平顺　long wave irregularity
长大笨重货区　heavy and bulky goods area
长大坡道　long steep grade
长吊环　extended clamp for suspension
长定位单环　extended drop bracket
长定位环　extended steady ring
长定位双环　extended twin drop bracket
长杆贯入仪　penetration test apparatus
长钢轨存放区　long rail storage area
长钢轨运输作业列车　transport and working train of welded long rails
长钢轨纵向水平力　longitudinal horizontal force of long steel rails
长轨条　long rail string
长回路阻抗　long loop impedance
长交路　long route, locomotive long runs
长距离预报　long distance forecast
长链　lengthened chain
长名单　long list
长期保单　long-term policy
长期贷款　long-term loan
长期订单　standing order
长期负债　long-term liabilities
长期规划　long-term planning
长期模量　long-term modulus
长期投资　long-term investment
长期稳定性　long-term stability
长期效应组合　combination of long-term action effects
长期协议　long-run agreement
长期许可证　standing permit
长期预测　long-term forecast
长期债权　long-term claim
长期债务　long-term debt, funded debt
长期资产　long-lived assets
长期租赁　long-term lease
长期租用　long-term rental
长石　feldspar
长石砂岩　arkose
长时制　permanent
长丝机织土工布　filament woven geotextile
长丝针织土工布　filament knitted geotextile
长隧道　long tunnel
长途电话网　long-distance telephone network
长途电路　long-distance circuit
长途人工交换系统　long distance manual exchange system
长途通信系统　long-distance communication system
长途线路　long-distance line
长细比　slenderness ratio
长英岩　arkose quartzite
长枕埋入式轨道　long sleeper embedded track
长周期采购项目　long-lead items
常闭隔离开关　normally closed disconnector

常闭节点　normally closed contacts
常差　constant error
常规　convent ion，custom
常规试验　routine test
常开隔离开关　normally open disconnector
常开节点　normally open contacts
常任争议评判委员会　full-term DAB
常水头法　constant head method
常水位　normal water level
常务董事　standing director
常务董事会　executive board
常压泌水率　bleeding rate at normal pressure
常用贷款　evergreen credit
常用制动　service braking
常用制动模式曲线　service braking mode curve
常住　residency
常驻代表　resident representative
偿付　pay back，repay
偿付款　disbursement
偿付能力　ability to pay
偿付协议　agreement of reimbursement
偿还
　repay，repayment，pay back，reimburse，satisfy
偿还保函　repayment guarantee
偿还贷款　repayment of loan，loan repayment
偿还能力　repayment ability
偿还期　repayment period
偿还日　maturity date
偿还预付款　repayment of advance payment
偿还债务　refund，pay back debts，liquidation
偿清　pay off，extinguish
偿依能力比率　liquidity ratio
偿债能力　solvency
偿债能力分析　debt service analysis
厂发料　material delivered from temporary large size storage site
厂家　manufacturer
厂价　price at factory
厂界　boundary
厂界环境噪声　ambient noise at boundary
厂界噪声　noise at boundary
厂内生产能力　in-house capacity
厂商代理人　manufacturer's agent
厂商发票　manufacturer's invoice
厂商协调会议　vendor coordination meeting（VCM）
厂商证明书　manufacturer certificate
场地　field，ground，site，yard
场地分析　site analysis
场地环境类型　type of site environment
场地浸淋水　site leachate

场地类别　site category
场地烈度　site intensity
场地平面图　site plan
场地平整　site leveling，site grading
场地评价　site assessment
场地清理费　expense of site clearing
场地使用计划　site utilization planning
场地填筑　site reclamation
场地条件　site condition
场地土　site soil
场地土类型　site soil type
场地租约　ground lease
场间联系电路　liaison circuit between yards
场景重组　scene reorganization
场内道路　in-site road
场内经纪商　floor broker
场内停车场　in-site parking lot，stabling yard
场坪标高　elevation of ground leveling
场坪高程　yard elevation
场强覆盖　field strength coverage
场所　place，spot，location
场外停车场　off-site parking lot
唱标价　announced bid price，read-out bid price
抄件　copy，duplicate
抄平　levelling
超长附加费
　overlength charges，long length charges
超出额　excess
超出预算　exceed the budget
超大体积　oversize
超低能耗建筑　ultra low energy building
超额利润　super profit
超范围维修　repairs beyond the scope of repairing course
超高　superelevation，cant
超高时变率　superelevation time-varying rate
超高顺坡　superelevation runoff
超高顺坡率
　superelevation runoff rate，superelevation rate
超固结
　over consolidation ratio（OCR），overconsolidated
超固结土　overconsolidated soil
超过　exceed，overrun，outgo
超基性碱性岩　ultrabasic alkaline rock
超基性岩　ultrabasic rock
超静定结构　statically indeterminate structure
超静定桥梁结构
　statically indeterminate bridge structure
超静水压力　excess hydrostatic pressure
超孔压比　excess pore pressure ratio
超滤法　ultrafiltration

超滤膜　ultrafiltration membrane
超前导坑　advance heading
超前导坑预报法　advance heading forecast method
超前导坑预测法　prediction by advance heading
超前地质预报　geology forecast
超前管棚　pipe roof
超前锚杆　advance anchor bolt
超前探测　advance detection
超前相　leading phase, wild phase
超前小导管　forepoling, advance small duct
超前预注浆　advance grouting
超前支护　advance support
超前钻探　advance exploration drilling
超前钻探预报法　advance drilling forecast method
超声波法　ultrasonic method
超声波式风速风向传感器
　ultrasonic wind speed and direction sensor
超声成像测井　ultrasonic imaging well logging
超声阻滞法　ultrasonic blocking method
超速防护　overspeed protection
超速连挂　overspeeding in coupling
超填　overfill
超挖　overbreak, overexcavation
超压排风　overpressure ventilation
超载　overload
超支　outspend, overexpenditure
超重　overweight
超重费　charge for overweight
朝向修正率　correction factor for orientation
潮间带　intertidal zone
潮湿　humid, moist, moisture, damp
潮湿程度　humidity
潮湿基面黏结强度
　adhesive strength of moist surface
潮位重现期　recurrence interval of tide level
潮汐河流　tidal river
潮汐区　tidal zone
车(船)队保险单　fleet policy
车船使用税　vehicle and vessel use tax
车次　train number
车次表示　train number indication
车底　train-set
车底取送走行线　running track for train-set placing-in and taking-out
车底数　amount of passenger train sets
车底停留场　train-set parking yard
车钩缓冲装置　coupler buffer device
车号自动识别系统
　automatic train identification system
车间　workshop

车间测试　shop testing
车间副主任　assistant superintendent
车辆　vehicle
车辆安全防范预警系统
　vehicle safety early warning system
车辆的动态限界　kinematic load gauge
车辆的静态限界　static load gauge
车辆调度　vehicle scheduling
车辆动态包络线　kinematic envelope
车辆段　rolling stock depot, car depot
车辆段修　rolling stock depot repair
车辆辅修　rolling stock auxiliary repair
车辆购置附加费
　rolling stock purchase additional charge
车辆滚动轴承故障轨边声学诊断系统
　faulty trackside acoustic detection system of train rolling bearing
车辆计算长度
　calculated length of railway vehicles
车辆技术交接作业场
　freight car technical handing-over yard
车辆技术整备场　car technical servicing yard
车辆加速器　car accelerator
车辆检修设备　car inspection and repair facilities
车辆减速器　car retarder
车辆减速器动力室　powerhouse of car retarder
车辆交接　delivery-receiving of wagon
车辆溜放阻力　car rolling down resistance
车辆能高　car energy head
车辆平均长度　averaged length of car
车辆平均溜放速度　mean rolling speed of car
车辆蛇形摆幅　amplitude of snake-like movement
车辆设备　rolling stock facility
车辆税　vehicle tax
车辆脱轨系数　coefficient of train derailment
车辆洗刷线
　vehicle-washing track, vehicle cleaning siding
车辆运行安全监测站
　monitoring station for train operation safety
车辆运行品质轨边动态检测系统　track side dynamic detection system for train riding quality
车辆运用维修
　rolling stock operational maintenance
车辆振动周期　vehicle vibration period
车辆轴温智能探测系统
　train hotbox detection system (THDS)
车轮厂　car wheelset repair shop
车轮传感器的电气中心线
　electric center line of wheel sensor
车轮滑行　wheel sliding

车轮空转　wheel slipping
车门自动控制　automatic train door control
车桥耦合动力响应
　　vehicle-bridge coupling dynamic response
车载安全计算机　onboard vital computer
车载地面检测设备　trackside equipment for testing onboard equipment
车载钢轨涂油器　on-board rail lubricator
车载设备　onboard equipment
车载司法记录单元
　　on-board juridical recorder unit（JRU）
车载通信单元　onboard communication unit
车载卫星终端　on-board satellite terminal
车载信号　Train-borne signaling
车站　station, terminal
车站电台　station radio
车站调度交换机　station dispatching switch
车站分布　station distribution
车站股道电码化　coding for tracks in station
车站广播　station broadcasting
车站集成管理平台
　　station integrated management platform
车站技术作业过程
　　technical operation process at station
车站接发车进路电码化
　　coding for station receiving-departure route
车站客运广播设备　station passenger service broadcasting equipment
车站控制　station control
车站通信机房　station communication equipment room
车站信号　station signal
车站咽喉区　station throat area
车站自律机　station autonomous computer
车组　train set
撤场　demobilization
撤防　cancellation of protected area
撤回　withdraw, withdrawal
撤回索赔　waiver of claim
撤回投标书　bid withdrawal
撤销　cancel, rescind, revoke, abandon, set aside
撤销订货单　recall an order
撤销合同
　　cancellation of a contract, cancel a contract, recession of contract, annulment of contract
撤销权　right of revocation
撤销授标　annulment of award
撤销诉讼　abatement of action
撤销投标　withdrawal of bid（tender）
撤销银行保函　release of bank guarantee
撤销执照　revocation of licence

撤资　disinvestment
辰砂　cinnabar
沉淀　sedimentation
沉淀池　sedimentation tank
沉淀井　settling pond, decant pond
沉淀系统　sedimentation system
沉管　immersed tube
沉管法　immersed pipeline method
沉管隧道　immersed tube
沉积平原　depositional plain
沉积岩　sedimentary rock
沉降　settlement, subsidence
沉降板　settlement plate
沉降变形　subsidence deformation
沉降变形观测
　　observation of subsidence deformation
沉降变形监测
　　settlement deformation monitoring
沉降差　differential settlement
沉降带　subsidence zone
沉降缝　settlement joint
沉降观测　settlement observation
沉降观测断面　observed profile for settlement
沉降计算深度　settlement calculation depth
沉降量　settlement
沉降评估　evaluation of settlement
沉降剖面管　profile settlement tube
沉降曲线　settlement curve
沉降室　settling chamber
沉降速率　settlement rate
沉井　open caisson, well-sinking
沉井法施工测量
　　construction survey by caissons
沉井基础　open caisson foundation
沉井刃脚　cutting edge of open caisson
沉没　sunk
沉没系数　sinking coefficient
沉溺谷　drowned valley
沉砂池　desilting basin, grit chamber
沉陷　subsidence
沉箱　caisson
沉箱基础　caisson foundation
沉箱桩　caisson pile
沉渣　sediment, dregs
衬垫（物）　liner
衬砌　lining
衬砌变形　lining deformation
衬砌腐蚀　lining corrosion
衬砌厚度　lining thickness
衬砌裂损　lining crack

衬砌内轮廓　inner contour of lining
衬砌渗水情况　lining seepage
衬套　sleeve
称量　weigh
称量法　weighing method
称量盒　weighing box
称量瓶　weighing bottle
称重法　weighing method
撑杆　brace, strut
(TBM)撑靴　gripper
成本　cost
成本、数量、利润分析　cost-volume-profit analysis
成本、保险费、运费加班轮费用(价)　cost, insurance, freight, liner terms (CIF liner terms)
成本、保险费、运费加船舱底交货(价)　cost, insurance, freight, ex-ships hold (CIF ex-ships hold)
成本、保险费、运费加吊钩下交货价　cost, insurance, freight under ship's tackle
成本、保险费、运费加卸货费(价)　cost, insurance, freight, landed terms (CIF landed terms)
成本、保险费、运费加佣金(价)　cost, insurance, freight and commission (CIF and C.)
成本、保险费、运费加战争险价　cost, insurance, freight and war-risks (CIF and W.)
成本编码　cost code
成本编码系统　cost code system
成本变动调整　adjustments for changes in cost
成本补偿　cost reimbursable
成本补偿合同　cost reimbursement contract
成本差异　cost variance
成本差异分析　analysis of cost variance
成本超支　cost overrun
成本单　cost sheet
成本定率(折旧)法　fixed-percentage-of-cost method (of depreciation)
成本分解　cost breakdown
成本分解结构　cost breakdown structure
成本分类细则　cost breakdown detail
成本分摊　cost contribution, cost allocation
成本分析　cost analysis
成本工程师　cost engineer
成本估算　estimate of cost, cost estimate
成本固定百分比(折旧)法　method of fixed percentage on cost
成本管理　cost control
成本管理员　cost clerk
成本回收　cost recovery
成本核算　cost account
成本会计　cost accounting
成本计算　costing
成本加成　mark-up
成本加成合同　cost-plus contract
成本加成计价法　cost-plus pricing
成本加酬金合同　cost-plus-fee contract, cost-and-fee contract
成本加定比酬金合同　cost-plus-percentage-fee contract
成本加浮动酬金合同　cost-plus-fluctuating-fee contract
成本加固定酬金合同　cost-plus-fixed-fee contract
成本加固定最大酬金合同　cost-plus-upset-maximum contract
成本加激励酬金合同　cost-plus-incentive-fee contract
成本加奖金合同　cost-plus-incentive-fee contract, cost-plus-award-fee contract
成本加利润　cost plus profit
成本加运费(价)　cost and freight (CFR)
成本控制　cost control
成本明细表　cost schedule
成本目标合同　cost target contract
成本偏差　cost variance
成本曲线　cost curve
成本收益　cost benefit
成本投入　cost input
成本现值　present value of cost
成本项目　cost items
成本削减　cost cutting
成本效益比　cost-benefit ratio
成本效益分析　cost-benefit analysis (CBA), cost-effective analysis
成本效益评价　cost-benefit evaluation
成本因素　cost factor
成本影响分析　cost impact analysis
成本与承诺费　cost and commitment
成本预测　cost forecasting
成本预算　cost estimation
成本账户　cost account
成本直接分摊法　direct method of allocation of cost
成本咨询顾问　cost consultant
成件包装货区　packed goods area
成交　strike a bargain, conclude a transaction
成交价值　transaction value
成交量　turnover
成孔　borehole-forming
成品　finished product
成品厂　finished product factory

成束筒结构　bundled tube structure
成套备件　set of spare parts
成套技术　package technology
成套商业单据　commercial set
成套设备　complete set of equipment, complete plant, complete set of equipment
成套设备总价　total price of the package
成套图纸　complete set of drawings
成文法　formal law, written law, lex scripta, statute law
成文合同　literal contract
（试件）成型　molding
成型温度　molding temperature
成员资格　membership
成组装车　wagon loading by groups
成组装卸　wagon loading and unloading by groups
诚信　good faith, integrity
诚信原则　principle of good faith
承按人　mortgagee
承包　contracting, contract
承包单位　contractor
承包工程　project contracting, construction contracting
承包工程一切险　contractor's all risks insurance (C.A.R)
承包合同价　contract price
承包企业　contracting firm
承包商　contractor
承包商代表　contractor's representative
承包商带资承包合同　contractor-financed contract
承包商的保障　indemnities by contractor
承包商的酬金　contractor's fee
承包商的风险和成本　contractor's risk and cost
承包商的记录　contractor's records
承包商的监督　contractor's superintendence
承包商的交通运输　contractor's traffic
承包商的索赔　contractor's claim
承包商的现场作业　contractor's operations on site
承包商的一般义务　contractor's general obligations
承包商的职员　contractor's staff
承包商短名单　contractor short-list
承包商发票　contractor invoice
承包商放弃索赔　contractor's claims release
承包商付款请求　contractor payment request
承包商付款系统　contractor payment system
承包商供货范围　scope of supply by contractor
承包商供应设备　contractor furnished equipment
承包商过错终止　termination for contractor's default
承包商过错终止后的估价　valuation after termination for contractor's default
承包商过错终止后的支付　payment after termination for contractor's default
承包商机具　contractor's equipment
承包商建议书　contractor's proposals
承包商利润　contractor's profit
承包商联合体　consortium of contractors
承包商联营体　contractor's joint venture
承包商全险保险　contractor's all risks insurance (C.A.R)
承包商人员　contractor's personnel
承包商融资　contractor's financing
承包商设备　contractor's equipment
承包商设备保险单　contractor's equipment floater
承包商设备报表　returns of contractor's equipment
承包商设备运输险　contractor's equipment floater
承包商设施　contractor's facilities
承包商试验　testing by the contractor
承包商提供的保险　insurance to be provided by the contractor
承包商违约　contractor's default, default of contractor, breach of contractor, default by contractor
承包商文件　contractor's documents
承包商宣誓书　contractor's affidavit
承包商暂停　suspension by contractor
承包商暂停和终止　suspension and termination by contractor
承包商责任保险　contractor's liability insurance
承包商终止　termination by contractor
承包商终止后的支付　payment after termination by contractor
承包商主导的设计团队　contractor-led design teams
承保　accept insurance, acceptance, insure, underwriting
承保单　cover note, open cover
承保短量险　insurance against loss in weight
承保人　assurer, insurer
承保条　insurance slip
承保险别　coverage
承保协议　binder
承保证明　risk note
承插粘接　socket bonding
承担　bear, undertake
承担法律责任　bear legal liability
承担费用　bear expenses
承担风险　acceptance of risks
承担能力　affordability
承担赔偿责任　honour one's liability
承兑　acceptance, accept, honour

承兑合同　acceptance contract
承兑汇票　acceptance credit, acceptance bill, D/A draft
承兑汇票手续费　acceptance commission
承兑交单　documents against acceptance(D/A)
承兑交货　delivery against acceptance
承兑结算　settlement by acceptance
承兑金额　acceptance amount
承兑票据　acceptance bill, honour a bill
承兑票据登记簿　acceptance register
承兑人　acceptor
承兑商行　accepting house
承兑提示　presentment for acceptance
承兑信贷　acceptance credit
承兑信用证　acceptance credit, acceptance letter of credit
承兑银行　acceptance bank, accepting bank
承兑责任　liability for acceptance
承付人　acceptor
承购合同　offtake contract
承购协议　offtake agreement
承轨槽　rail seat
承轨台　rail seat
承轨台磨削加工　abrasive machining of rail support stand
承力索　messenger wire
承力索弛度　messenger wire sag
承力索电连接线夹　electrical connection clamp for messenger wire
承力索吊弦线夹　dropper clip for messenger wire
承力索滑动吊弦线夹　sliding dropper clip for messenger wire
承力索接头线夹　messenger wire splice
承力索双线支撑线夹　support clamp for double messenger wires
承力索线夹　messenger wire clamp
承力索中心锚结绳线夹　clamp for midpoint anchor rope of messenger wire
承力索中心锚结线夹　midpoint anchor clamp for messenger wire
承力索终端锚固线夹　terminal anchor clamp for messenger wire
承诺　accept, acceptance, commit, commitment
承诺费　commitment charge (fee)
承诺付款额　commitment
承诺价值　commitment value
承诺期限　time limit for acceptance
承诺权　commitment authority
承诺人　accepter, acceptor
承诺时限　commitment time
承诺授权书　commitment authorization
承诺文件　commitment document
承诺信　commitment letter
承诺与授予　commitment and award
承认　admission, acknowledgement
承认和执行外国仲裁裁决公约　convention on the recognition and enforcement of foreign arbitral awards
承台　pile cap
承台效应系数　pile cap effect coefficient
承托　haunch board
承托层　graded gravel layer
承压板　bearing plate
承压管　pressure pipe
承压含水层　confined aquifer
承压区　confined area
承压水　confined water
承压水头　confined water head
承压应力　bearing stress
承押人　mortgagee
承运　acceptance for carriage
承运人　carrier, haulier, transportation carrier
承运人留置权　carrier's lien
承运人责任保险　carrier's liability insurance
承运人责任豁免　immunities of the carrier
承运商　forwarding agency
承载比　bearing ratio
承载比试验　test of california bearing ratio
承载力　bearing capacity
承载力因数　load-bearing capacity factor
承载能力　bearing capacity
承载能力极限状态　ultimate limit states
承载平台　bearer platform
承载通路连接　bearer channel connection (BCC)
承载网　bearer network
承载系数检定　load factor rating
承重基础　gravity foundation
承重结构　bearing structure
承重墙　bearing wall
承重桩　bearing pile
承租人　lessee, tenant, leaseholder
城际铁路　intercity railway
城市(镇)排水管网　urban sewer network
城市测量　urban survey
城市轨道交通工程信息模型　information model of urban rail transit engineering
城市设施　urban facilities
城市维护建设税　urban maintenance and construction tax
城镇污水　urban wastewater

城镇污水系统　urban wastewater system
乘务方式　working mode of locomotive crew
乘务员连续工作时间
　　working duration of locomotive crew
程序　program, programme, procedure, proceeding
程序法　procedural law, adjective law
程序流程图　program flow chart
程序设计　programming
程序图　flow chart
惩罚条款　penalty clause
惩罚性赔偿费　punitive damages
澄清　clarification
澄清池　settling tank
澄清请求函　request for information
呈交要求　file a claim
池塘　pond
弛度　sag
驰振　gallop, galloping
迟到的付款　late payment
迟到的投标书　late bid
迟付　postpone payment
迟付款项利息　interest on late payments
迟误　laches
持荷时间　load holding duration
持久设计状况　persistent design state
持力层　bearing stratum
持水度　water retaining capacity
持水性　water retention capacity
持续　last, continue
持续的误期　prolonged delay
持续的暂时停工　prolonged suspension
持续时间　time of duration
尺长改正　correction for tape length
尺寸　dimension
尺寸偏差　dimensional deviation
尺度　criteria, scale
尺度效应　scale effect
齿缝破坏　saw-tooth joint failure
赤道热带　equatorial tropics
赤泥库　red mud pond
赤平极射投影　stereographic projection
赤平面　equatorial plane
赤平投影　stereographic projection
赤平投影法　stereographic projection method
赤铁矿　hematite
赤字　deficit, red balance
赤字财政　deficit financing
赤字开支　deficit spending
赤字预算　deficit budget
充电　charging

充电电源间　charging source chamber
充电法　mise-a-la-masse method
充电模块　charging module
充电式冲击扳手　charging impact wrench
充满度　depth ratio
充气机　inflator
充气压力　inflation pressure
充实水柱　full water columns
充水比　fill ratio
充填层　filling layer
充填式垫板　filling pad
充填体滑坡　fill-mass landslide
充填性　filling ability
充盈度　filling degree
充盈率　suffuse degree
充装压力　charging pressure
冲断层　thrust
冲沟　gully
冲洪积平原　alluvial-proluvial plain
冲击波　impact wave
冲击地震　impact earthquake
冲击电流　impulse current
冲击电压转移系数
　　transfer coefficient of impulse voltage
冲击法　impact method
冲击放电电压　impulse discharge voltage
冲击负载　impulse load, impact load
冲击荷载　impact load
冲击激振器　impact vibration exciter
冲击接地电阻　impulse grounding resistance
冲击力　impact force
冲击碾压　impact rolling
冲击韧性　impact ductility
冲击式钻机　percussion drill
冲击系数　impact factor
冲击系数测定　determination of impact coefficient
冲击仪　impact tester
冲击因数　impact factor
冲击振动　impact vibration
冲击钻进　percussive drilling
冲击钻孔机　jack-hammer
冲积　alluviation
冲积堆　alluvial deposit
冲积平原　alluvial plain
冲积扇　alluvial fan
冲积土　alluvial soil, alluvium
冲剪破坏　punching shear failure
冲孔器　puncher, piercer
冲孔洗井　punching well flushing
冲片机　sheet-punching machine

冲蚀　washout
冲刷系数　scouring factor
冲填土　dredger fill
冲突　conflict
冲突法规　conflict rules
冲洗　rinse
冲洗废水　washing wastewater
冲洗强度　wash rate
冲洗液　flushing fluid
冲洗周期　flushing cycle
冲销　elimination, abatement, charge off, offset
冲账　set-off, off set
重叠　superposition, overlap
重叠区段　overlap section
重订还债期限　debt rescheduling
重复保险　overlapping insurance
重复检查　repeated check
重复显示　repeating indication
重建　reconstruction, rehabilitation, restitution
重现期　recurrence interval
重新筹集资金　refinance
重新估价　revaluation
重新计量　remeasurement
重新计量合同　remeasurement contract
重新检验　retest
重新评估　re-evaluate
重新确认　reconfirm
重新试验　retesting
重新招标　retender, rebid
重置　replacement
重置成本　replacement cost, reproduction cost
重置价值　replacement value
重置价值保险　reinstatement value insurance
虫害　insect and pest nuisance
抽查　spot test, test check
抽气法　degassing method
抽水试验　pumping test
抽水洗井法　pumping flushing
抽头　tapping, tap
抽样　sampling
抽样方案　sampling plan
抽样方法　method of sampling
抽样检查　sample inspection, sampling inspection
抽样检验　sampling inspection
抽样试验　sample test
酬金　remuneration, reward, consideration money
酬劳费　charge for trouble
稠度　consistency
稠度界限　consistency limit
筹备费　preparation expenses
筹措资金　raise funds
筹资　financing, fund raising
筹资成本　financing cost
臭氧　ozone
臭氧消毒　ozone disinfection
臭氧氧化法　ozone oxidation method
出版原图　original printing
出差津贴　mission allowance
出厂单价　unit price EXW
出厂价　factory price, ex-factory price
出厂试验　delivery test
出厂税　factory tax
出厂说明书　shop instruction
出发　departure, depart
出发场　departure yard
出发港　port of departure, port of embarkation
出发线　departure track
出港　clear a port
出港结关　port clearance
出港手续费　outward port charges
出港许可证　clearance permit
出货区　dispatch area
出借人　lender
出境文件　exit documents
出具保函　providing a guarantee
出具收据　providing a receipt
出口　export, exit
出口报关
　declaration for exportation, declaration outward
出口报关单　export entry, entry outward
出口补贴　export subsidy
出口担保　export documents
出口单证　export documents
出口发票　export invoice
出口风速　outlet air velocity
出口港　port of exit
出口关税　export tariff
出口价　export price
出口检验证　certificate for export
出口结关证书　out ward clearance certificate
出口免税　free export
出口手续　process of export
出口税　export duty, export tax
出口限制　export restriction
出口信贷　export credit
出口信贷担保　export credit guarantee
出口信用保险　export credit insurance
出口信用证　export letter of credit
出口许可证
　export incense（permit）, certificate of shipment

出口许可证申请书　application for export licence
出口银行保函　export bank guarantee
出口装船须知　export shipping instructions
出库通知单　warehouse-keeper's order
出库许可证　permit for withdrawing
出门按钮　exit button
出纳员　cashier
出票人　drawer
出勤率　work attendance
出入段线　transfer track for depot, entrance and exit line for depot
出入境手续　entry and exit procedural
出入口　entrance/exit
出入口通道　access to entrance and exit
出入库检测　entrance/exit inspection
出入权　right to access
出示　present, production, produce
出示证据　presentation of evidence, tender evidence
出售　sell, sale, dispose, disposal, disposition
出售价格　offered price, disposal price
出水量　water yield
出庭　appear in court, presence
出土角　arriving angle
出席　attendance, presence, present
出险通知　loss advice
出线　outgoing feeder
出押人　mortgagor
出渣　mucking
出站　exit
出站大屏　information display at arrival lobby
出站通道屏　information display of exit corridor
出站信号机　departure signal
出证方　licenser, licensor
出资人　sponsor
出租　lease, rental, let
出租人　lessor, hirer
初步估算　preliminary estimate
初步计划　tentative plan, outline plan, rough plan
初步计算　preliminary computation
初步建议书　preliminary proposal
初步评价　preliminary evaluation
初步设计　preliminary design
初步设计阶段　preliminary design stage
初步设计批复　approval of preliminary design
初步设计图纸　preliminary drawings
初步验收证书　preliminary acceptance certificate
初步预算　preliminary budget
初步证据　prima facie evidence
初测　preliminary survey
初测导线　preliminary traverse

初沉污泥　primary sludge
初次沉淀池　primary settling tank
初次付款　down payment
初级会计师　junior accountant
初级律师　solicitor, attorney
初级市场　primary market
初勘　reconnaissance
初滤水　initial filtrated water
初凝　pre-setting, initial setting
初凝时间　initial setting time
初凝时期　presetting period
初喷　primary shotcreting
初期　initial stage
初期豁免　initial exemption
初期价格　initial price
初期控制估算　initial control estimate (ICE)
初期支护　primary support
初始报告　inception report
初始沉降　initial settlement
初始地应力　initial ground stress
初始地应力场　initial ground stress field
初始风险　initial risk
初始计划　initial programme
初始剪应力比　initial shear stress ratio
初始模量　initial modulus of elasticity
初始强度　initial strength
初始水位　initial water level
初始应力　initial stress
初始预算　initial budget
初速度试验　initial speed test
初位移试验　initial displacement test
初至　first arrival
除尘　dust removal
除尘器　dust remover
除尘效率　dust removal efficiency
除磷　phosphorus removal
除皮重量　tare gross
除湿　dehumidification
除水器　dehydrator
除外风险　excepted risk
除外条款　exclusion clause, exception clause
除外责任　excluded liability
除外责任条款　exclusion
除锈　rust removal
除氧装置　deaerator
除油设施　oil removal facilities
厨房　kitchen
杵环杆　ball with eye rod
杵座鞍子　ball socket end clamp
杵座双耳　ball socket with clevis

C

杵座楔形线夹　socket end wedge-type clamp
储备　reserve, reservation, stock, stockpile
储备库存量　reserve stock
储存　store, stockpile
储存量　storage volume
储存区　storage area
储存压力　storage pressure
储风罐　air reservoir
储户　depositor
储料仓　storage bin
储能剪切模量　storage shear strength modulus
储水层　aquifer
储水池　storage tank
储水系数　water storage coefficient
储酸室　acid storage room
储蓄存款　saving deposit, deposit accounts
储蓄账户　saving account, thrift account
储油区　oil storage area
储值卡票　stored value card, stored value ticket
处罚　punish, penalty, sanction
处理　handle, dispose, disposal, take up, treatment, handling
处理单元　processing unit
处理能力　processing capability
处理效率　processing efficiency
促进　promote, promotion
触变性　thixotropy
触摸屏调度台　touch screen dispatching console
(开关)触头　contact
穿墙套管　wall-through bushing
穿销防爬器　wedged rail anchor
穿越电流　through current/through fault current
传动检查　driving inspection
传动系统　driving system
传感器　sensor
传力杆　dowel steel
传热　heat transfer
传热系数　heat transfer coefficient
传声损失　transmission loss（TL）
传输　transmission
传输电平　transmission level
传输干扰时间　transmission interference period
传输控制协议　transmission control protocol(TCP)
传输网　transmission network
传输无差错时间　error-free period
传输系统　transmission system
传输线路　transmission line
传输协议　transmission protocol
传输质量　transmission quality
传送　convey, deliver
传送带　belt conveyor, conveyer belt
传送机　conveyer
传送设备　conveyor, conveyer
传送系统　conveying system
传真　facsimile（fax）
传真电报　facsimile telegraph
传真发送　facsimile transmission
传真机　fax machine
传真通知　notice by fax
船　ship, boat, craft
船边交货　outboard delivery
船边交货价　free alongside ship（F.A.S）
船边交货提单　alongside bill of lading
船舶保险　hull insurance
船舶费用保险　disbursement insurance
船舶费用条款　disbursement clause
船舶险　hull insurance
船舶运价　shipping freight
船货　cargo, lading, shipment
船货检查员　jerquer
船货清单　shipping bill, manifest
船级社　bureau of shipping
船龄　age of vessel
船期延误保险条款　overdue risk
船上交货　delivered ex ship（DES）
船体保险单　hull policy
船位　berth
船坞　dock
船坞费　dockage
船运　shipment
船运公司　shipping company
串联电容器补偿　series capacitor compensation
串联供水　series water supply
串联式轨道电路　series track circuit
串通　collusion, collude
串通投标　collusive bid（tender）
串通行为　collusive practice
串音防卫度　signal to crosstalk ratio
串音干扰　crosstalk interference
串音衰耗测试器　crosstalk attenuation tester
窗函数　window function
窗间墙宽度　breadth of wall between windows
窗口对讲器　counter intercom
窗口售票机　booking office machine
窗口双屏　dual monitors at ticket counter
窗墙面积比　area ratio of window to wall
窗式空气调节器　window-type air conditioner
创办费　initial expenses
吹风机　blower
吹蚀　deflation

垂线偏差　deviation of plumb line
垂向力　vertical force
垂直并联板　vertical parallel plate
垂直单管采暖系统
　　vertical single-pipe heating system
垂直度　verticality
垂直度测量　plumbing survey
垂直反力　vertical reaction
垂直缝　vertical joint
垂直刚度　vertical rigidity
垂直荷载　vertical load
垂直接地极　vertical earth electrode
垂直接地体　vertical earth electrode
垂直面　vertical section
垂直渗漏带　vertical percolation zone
垂直渗透系数
　　coefficient of permeability normal to the plane
垂直式存放　vertical storage
垂直天窗　vertical window time
垂直位移　vertical displacement
垂直位移测量　vertical displacement measuring
垂直位移监测网
　　vertical-displacement monitoring network
垂直旋转角度　vertical rotating angle
垂直压力　vertical pressure
垂直匀布压力
　　vertical uniformly-distributed pressure
锤垫　pallet
锤击法　hammering method
锤击检查　hammering check
锤式打桩机　monkey engine
纯保险费　pure premium
纯粹风险　pure risk
纯单价合同　straight unit rate contract
纯费率　net rate
纯灰浆　neat plaster
纯剪应力　pure shear stress
纯利　net profit
纯利息　pure interest
纯水　pure water
纯损失　dead loss
纯支出　net expenditure
纯资本　net capital（N/C）
唇音同步　lip synchronization
词句引申义　secondary meaning of words
瓷护套　ceramic sheath
瓷支持绝缘子　porcelain post insulator
瓷支柱绝缘子　porcelain post insulator
瓷砖　ceramic tile
辞职和终止　resignation and termination

磁场强度　magnetic field intensity
磁带库　tape library
磁法　magnetic method
磁法勘探　magnetic prospecting
磁方位角　magnetic azimuth
磁化率　magnetic susceptibility
磁环　ceramic ferrule
磁介质纸质热敏票
　　magnetic medium thermal paper ticket
磁力搅拌机　magnetic stirrer
磁路系统　magnetic circuit system
磁盘空间　disk space
磁盘阵列　redundant array of inexpensive disk（RAID）
磁偏角　magnetic declination
磁屏蔽　magnetic shielding
磁倾角　magnetic inclination
磁石电话　magneto telephone
磁铁矿　magnetite
磁异常　magnetic anomaly
磁子午线　magnetic meridian
此端向上　this side up
次边侧　low voltage side, secondary side
次干道　secondary trunk road
次高级路面　sub-high type pavement
次固结　secondary consolidation
次固结沉降　secondary consolidation settlement
次固结系数　coefficient of secondary consolidation
次火山岩　subvolcanic rock
次级品　subquality product
次坚石　secondary hard rock
次棱角状　subangular
次梁　secondary beam
次氯酸钠　sodium hypochlorite
次品　defective goods, offal, spoiled product（goods），
　　seconds
次深海相　bathyal facies
次生矿物　secondary mineral
次生盐渍化　secondary salinization
次生应力　secondary stress
次序　order
次要缺陷　minor defect
次要债务　subordinate debt
次要站线　auxiliary station track
次应力　secondary stress
次应力系数　coefficient of secondary stress
次重型轨道　secondary heavy track
次子类　sub-subtype
刺点　punching point
刺点相片　punching point photograph
刺破强度　piercing strength

从价关税率　ad valorem tariff
从价进口税　ad valorem import duty
从价税　ad valorem duties, ad valorem tax
从价税率　ad valorem rate of duty
从价提单　ad valorem bill of lading
从价运费　ad valorem freight
从权利　collateral rights
从文本到语言(也称语音合成)　text to speech(TtS)
从属抵押品　collateral
从属面积　tributary area
从属损失　consequential damage (loss)
从属信号机　dependent signal
从属债务人　accessory debtor
粗糙度　roughness
粗差　gross error
粗差检验　gross error checking
粗估　guesstimate
粗骨料　coarse aggregate
粗骨料分级比例　grading proportion of coarse aggregate
粗加工　rough making
粗角砾土　coarse angular gravel soil
粗颗粒　coarse particles
粗颗粒土　coarse grained soil
粗砾土　cobbly soil
粗粒土　coarse-grained soil
粗料石　coarse dressed stone
粗略定向　rough orientation
粗面岩　trachyte
粗砂　coarse sand
粗砂岩　gritstone
粗筛　coarse sieve
粗圆砾土　coarse round gravel soil
促凝剂　accelerator
促凝外加剂　accelerating admixture
促销　promotion
催促　prompt
催促交货　expedite deliveries
催单　reminder
催付　ask for payment
催交　expediting
催缴　call, ask for payment
催款单　prompt
催款信　call letter
催债　dun
脆断　brittle failure
脆性　brittleness
脆性断裂　brittle fracture
脆性破坏　brittle failure
脆性转变温度　brittle transition temperature
淬火处理　quenching treatment
淬火轨　quenched rail, head hardened rail
存车场　stabling yard
存储服务器　storage server
存储卡　memory card
存储模型　storage model
存储能力　storage capacity
存储区域网络　Storage Area Network(SAN)
存储设备　memory device
存放数量　storage quantity
存货　goods in stock, inventory, stock
存货不足　understock
存货短缺　stockout
存货分类账　stock ledger
存货估价　inventory valuation
存货管理　inventory control
存货盘点表　inventory sheet
存货数据　inventory data
存货允许限度　inventory allowance
存货周转　inventory turnover
存款　deposit
存款不足　not sufficient funds(N.S.F.)
存款单　deposit slip, certificate of deposit
存款利率　deposit rate
存款收据　deposit receipt
存款银行　bank of deposit
存梁区　girder storage area
存梁台座　girder storage pedestal
存梁周期　girder storage period
存轮棚　wheel pair assembly shed, wheelset storage shed
存水弯　trap
存续期　duration
存砟场　ballast storage yard
搓条法　thread twisting method
磋商　consult, consultation
措辞　wording, expression
措施　measure, step
措施项目　measurement items
错落　dislocation
错落体　dislation
错台　staggering
错误　error, mistake
错误办理　wrong handling
错牙接头　rail end step in gauge line or surface

D

D 组填料　fill material of group D
搭拆费　building and removing cost
搭接　splice
搭接长度　overlap length
搭接节点　overlap joint
搭卖合同　tying contract
搭卖条款　tie in clause
搭载测试　carrying test
达成　conclude
达成协议　reach an agreement, agree
达到　achieve, obtain
达到标准　up to par
达西定律　Darcy law
答辩　statement of defence
答辩人　respondent
打靶控制　target aiming control
打靶区　shot area
打包　pack
打道钉机　spike driver
打弓　collapse of pantograph
打夯机　ramming machine, tamper
打捞公司　salvage company
打磨装配区　grinding and assembling area
打印机　printer
打桩机　pile driver
打钻瓦斯动力现象
　　drilling gas dynamic phenomenon
大比例尺地形测图　large-scale topographic mapping
大比例尺地形图　large-scale topographical map
大比例尺航空摄影测量
　　large-scale aerial photogrammetry
大避车洞　big refuge niche
大变形围岩
　　surrounding rock with serious deformation risk
大便槽　stool groove
大便器　stool device
大地测量　geodetic surveying
大地测量系统　geodetic surveying system
大地导电率　earth conductivity
大地电磁测深　telluric electromagnetic sounding
大地电磁测深及剖面法
　　magnetotelluric sounding and profiling method
大地电阻率　earth resistivity
大地高　geodetic height
大地控制数据库　geodetic control data base
大地水准面　geoid
大地水准面差距　geodetic leveling difference
大地原点　geodetic origin
大地坐标　geodetic coordinate
大地坐标系　geodetic coordinate system
大风　fresh gale
大功率转辙机　heavy duty switch machine
大轨缝　excessive joint gap
大号码道岔　large-size turnout
大火灾　conflagration
大机检修库　large track maintenance machinery repair workshop
大揭盖清筛机　ballast cleaning machine with removed track panels
大口井　dug well, open well
大口井出水量　large-diameter well yield
大跨度结构　long-span structure
大里程端　large mileage end
大理岩(石)　marble
大梁　girder
大楼综合定时供给设备
　　Building Integrated Timing Supply(BITS)
大陆法　civil law, continental law
大陆法系　continental law system, civil law system
大陆架　continental shelf
大陆隆　continental rise
大陆坡　continental slope
大律师　barrister
大能力驼峰　large capacity hump
大偏心受压构件
　　compression member with large eccentricity

大屏幕显示设备　video wall
大气　atmosphere
大气密度　density of air
大气污染　air pollution / atmospheric pollution
大气压力　atmospheric pressure
大气影响急剧层深度
　　depth of sharp atmospheric effect
大气影响深度
　　depth of atmosphere/atmospheric effect
大气折光　atmospheric refraction
大桥　long bridge (with length from 101 m to 500 m)
大水滴喷头　deluge sprinkler
大体积混凝土　mass concrete
大写金额　sum in words, amount in words
大型编组站　large scale marshalling station
大型车站　large station
大型工程　heavy construction, mega project
大型滑坡　large scale landslip
大型矿车　large scale mine car
大型临时设施　large scale temporary facilities
大型临时设施和过渡工程费
　　expenses of large scale temporary facilities and transitional works
大型旅客车站　large passenger station
大型企业　large-scale enterprise
大型全断面清筛机
　　heavy duty full section ballast cleaning machine
大型养路机械段
　　large track maintenance machinery depot
大型养路机械停放线　parking track for large track maintenance machinery
大型站房　large station building
大修　heavy maintenance
大修费用　cost of overhaul
大修基金　capital repair fund
大修间隔台班
　　the amount of machine shift between major repair
大修修理费　major repair cost
大洋盆地　oceanic basin
大宗材料　bulk material
呆账　bad debt, bad account, dead account
呆滞存货　inactive stock, dead stock
呆滞贷款　dead loan
呆滞资本　dead capital
呆滞资产　slow assets
呆滞资金　inactive money
歹字形构造　zeta type structure
代办人　attorney
代表权的授予　grant of representation
代表团　delegation, mission
代表性断面　representative section
代表性工点　representative construction site
代偿责任　vicarious liability
代购佣金　purchasing commission
代理　act, agency, surrogate
代理存款　escrow deposit
代理费　agency fee
代理公司　agent firm
代理合同　agency contract
代理机构　agency
代理经理　acting manager
代理权　agency, proxy, power of representation
代理人　agent, alternate
代理人侵权行为　agent's tort
代理融通费　factoring charges
代理融通公司　factoring company
代理商　agent
代理商佣金　factorage
代理手续费　agency commission
代理协议　agency agreement
代理行　correspondent bank
代理业　factorage
代理银行　correspondent bank, agent bank
代理佣金　commission, override
代码　code
代签　sign for
代收人　collecting agent
代收银行　collecting bank
代售点　ticket agency
代位履行　vicarious performance
代位求偿权　subrogation right
代位授权书　letter of subrogation
代销行　sales agency
代用材料　replacement material
代运人　forwarder
带壁柱墙　wall with pilaster
带电概率　energized probability
带电间隔　energized bay, energized compartment
带电结构　energized structure
带电体　live part
带电作业　live working
带动道岔　switch with follow-up movement
带动道岔测试
　　test of switch with follow up movement
带短路指示器电动隔离开关　motorized disconnector with short-circuit indicator
带耳环的长棒式绝缘子
　　long rod insulator with eye end cap
带回流线的直接供电方式
　　direct feeding system with return conductor

带奖励的固定价格合同　fixed price contract with incentives
带孔油毡　perforated asphalt felt
带式输送机　belt conveyer
带式装料机　belt loader
带息票据　interest-bearing note
带薪休假　leave with pay
带薪休假期　paid holiday, holiday with pay
带有分项工程表的标价合同
　　priced contract with activity schedule
带有分项工程表的目标合同
　　target contract with activity schedule
带有工程表的目标合同
　　target contract with bill of quantities
带有工程量表的标价合同
　　priced contract with bill of quantities
带云台的摄像机　pan-tilt-zoom camera
带载分闸能力　load-breaking capacity
带载合闸能力　load-making capacity
带状地形图　strip topographic map
带状构造　banded structure
带状平面图　zone plan
带状黏土　banded clay
贷方　creditor, credit side
贷方栏　credit column
贷方余额　credit balance
贷记　credit
贷款　loan, credit
贷款本金　principal amount
贷款财团　loan consortium
贷款偿还期　loan repayment period
贷款担保　security of loan
贷款对象　prospective borrower
贷款额　size of the loan
贷款额度　credit line
贷款方　lender
贷款货币　loan currency
贷款利率　loan interest rate, lending rate, offered rate
贷款利息　loan interest
贷款期限　lending term, term of loan
贷款条件　lending terms
贷款委员会　loan committee
贷款文件　loan document
贷款限额　loan ceiling, lending limit
贷款协议　loan agreement
贷项　credit
贷项通知单　credit memorandum(memo), credit note
待班台位　temporary rest position
待定　hold
待定赔款准备金　outstanding loss reserve
待分配利润　retained profit
待机模式　standby mode
待检查物品单　bill of sufferance
待结付的补偿　executory consideration
待履行的合同　executory contract
待清理账户　clearing account, suspense account
待摊成本　unabsorbed cost
待修箱　to be repaired box
待验工　works to be measured
待用品　backup
待遇　treatment, terms of employment
待运提单　received for shipment bill of lading
怠工　slacking at work, idle
袋装砂井　sand wick
袋装水泥　bagged cement
丹霞地貌　Danxia landform
担保　bond, guarantee security, warrant
担保成本　cost of bond
担保承兑　collateral acceptance
担保代理人　bonding agent
担保额度　bonding capacity
担保费率　bonding rate
担保负债　secured liabilities
担保公司　bonding company, surety company
担保金额　amount secured
担保能力　bonding capacity
担保品抵押　collateral mortgage
担保契约　deed of guarantee
担保权益　security interest
担保人　surety, guarantor, underwriter
担保人身份　suretyship
担保书　warranty, surety bond
担保债券　collateral bond, surety bond
担架　hand barrow
单边供电　single-end feeding
单层百叶型风口
　　single-layer shutter-type air outlet
单层存梁　girder storage in single layer
单层矩形布置
　　single layer rectangular arrangement
单掺　single-doped
单承力索吊弦线夹
　　dropper clip of single messenger wire
单程票　single trip ticket
单纯背书　absolute endorsement
单纯承兑　absolute (clean) -acceptance
单纯计件工资制　straight piece work system
单代号网络
　　precedence diagram, activity-on-node (AON)
单代号网络图　precedence network

单点沉降　single point settlement
单点法　single-point method
单点激振　single point excitation
单动双管取芯钻进
　　single-swivel double-tube core drilling
单斗挖土机
　　single bucket excavator, monobucket excavator
单独海损　particular average
单独海损不赔偿
　　free from particular average (FPA)
单独海损赔偿　with particular average (WPA)
单独事项　particulars
单独折旧　individual depreciation
单独酌处权　sole discretion
单渡线　single crossover
单端接地　single-end earthing
单端张拉　tensioning at one end
单断　single break
单耳连接器　cross link (eye/eye)
单方废约　unilateral denunciation
单方合约　unilateral contract
单方面　ex parte
单方宣告无效　unilateral denunciation
单管顺序式采暖系统
　　one-pipe series-loop heating system
单轨条轨道电路　single rail track circuit
单轨小车　monorail trolley
单轨楔体焊接
　　single track wedge-shaped welding
单护盾掘进机　single shield TBM
单机测试　single machine test
单机牵引区段　single-locomotive traction section
单级架构　single-level architecture
单价　unit price
单价表　schedule of rates
单价分析　breakdown of price
单价合同
　　contract based on unit price, unit price contract
单间式办公　single-room office
单剪试验　simple shear test
单建掘开式工程　cut-and-cover works
单井抽水试验　single-well pumping test
单据　document, voucher
单开道岔　single turnout, simple turnout
单孔法　single hole method
单矿物　monomineral
单利　simple interest, single rate
单粒结构　single-grained structure
单梁式架桥机
　　single-armed girder-erecting machine

单列布置　single row layout
单溜放　single humping
单路画面　single-channel image
单面坡道　one-way slope
单面坡口　single groove
单面坡隧道　one-way slope tunnel
单面山　cuesta
单面索斜拉桥　single-plane cable-stayed bridge
单面斜道　single-sided ramp
单模光纤　single mode optical fiber
单母线分段　sectionalizing of single busbar
单盘检测　single drum test
单偏光镜　single polar
单频　single frequency
单频感应器　single frequency inductor
单曲线　single curve
单刃滚刀　single-edge disc cutter
单双管混合式采暖系统
　　mixed single and double pipe heating system
单体测试　standalone test
单体工程　unit project
单体试验　individual test, single test
单体蓄电池　battery cell
单推单溜　single humping and single rolling
单驼峰　single-hump
单位　unit
单位成本　unit cost
单位风阻力　unit windage resistance
单位工程　section of works, unit works
单位估计表　sheet of unit estimation
单位估价法　method of unit estimation
单位利润　unit profit
单位面积质量　mass per unit area
单位权　unit weight
单位权方差(又称"方差因子")　variance of unit
　　weight (also known as "variance factor")
单位权中误差　mean square error of unit weight
单位人工成本　unit labour cost
单位生产能力估算法
　　unit capacity estimate method
单位吸浆量　specific grout absorption capacity
单位吸水量　specific water absorption capacity
单位制动能高　unit energy head of braking
单务协议　unilateral agreement
单线　single-track
单线臂板信号机
　　single-wire operated semaphore signal
单线地段　single-track section
单线桥　single-track bridge
单线石质路堑　single-track rock cutting

单线隧道　single-track tunnel
单线铁路　single-track railway
单线土质路堑　single-track soil cutting
单线往复式　single line reciprocating type
单相负荷　single phase load
单相工频交流制　"industrial frequency single-phase AC traction system"
单相接地短路　single-phase ground short-circuit
单相结线　single-phase winding connection
单相牵引变压器　single phase traction transformer
单相三线制　single-phase three-wire system
单向板　one-way slab
单向编组站　unidirectional marshalling station
单向混合式编组站　unidirectional combined type marshalling station
单向拉伸　unidirectional stretching
单向铺轨　track laying using one set of track laying machinery
单向图形　unidirectional layout
单向土工格栅　uniaxial geogrid
单向推力墩　unidirectional thrust-force pier
单向纵列式编组站　unidirectional longitudinal type marshalling station
单项概(预)算　budgetary estimate (budget) of single construction
单项工程　single construction
单项工程量清单　activity bill of quantities
单项工作程序　individual job procedure
单项估算　individual estimate
单项估算表　individual estimate sheet
单项活动　activity
单项索赔　single case claim
单项预估算　individual pre-estimate
单项预估算表　individual pre-estimate sheet
单项招标　single tender
单项折旧　item depreciation
单斜　monocline
单斜谷　monoclinal valley
单斜晶系　monoclinic system
单信号选择性　single signal selectivity
单液浆　single-fluid grout
单一安全系数法　single safety coefficient method
单一负责制　single point responsibility
单一墙　simple wall
单一税制　single tax system
单一责任　single liability
单元　element, unit
单元板　panel
单元工程清单　elemental bill of quantities
单元轨节　unit rail link

单元式办公室　unit office
单枕长轨连续铺设法　long rail continuous method
单证　certificate, document
单值评价量　unit value assessment
单置信号点　single signal location
单重　unit weight
单轴抗压强度　uniaxial compressive strength
单桩承载力　single pile bearing capacity
单桩复合地基载荷试验　load test of composite ground with single pile
单桩竖向承载力特征值　characteristic value of the vertical bearing capacity of a single pile
单桩竖向极限承载力　ultimate vertical bearing capacity of a single pile
单桩竖向抗拔承载力　vertical uplift bearing capacity of single pile
单桩竖向抗压承载力　vertical compression bearing capacity of single pile
单桩水平承载力　horizontal bearing capacity of single pile
单子　slip, sheet, list
胆矾　calcantite, blue vitriol
但书　saving clause
淡季　dead season, off season
淡水　fresh water
淡水湖泊相　freshwater lake facies
蛋白石　opal
当班　on duty
当班工长　shift boss
当场　on the ground
当场检查　sight test, spot check
当场交货　spot delivery
当地材料　local material
当地承包商　local contractor, domestic contractor
当地代理人　local agent
当地法规　local statute
当地工人　local worker, local labour
当地供应商　local supplier
当地购买　local shopping
当地货币　local currency
当地价格　local price, price loco
当地居民　local resident
当地开支　local expenditures
当地利率　local interest rate
当地人员　local personnel
当地政府　local government
当局造成的延误　delays caused by authorities
当量长度　equivalent length
当量阻抗　equivalent impedance
当面谈判　face to face negotiation

当年投资　investment of the said year
当期利润　profit for the term
当期营业收入　current revenue
当前工资简报　current wage bulletin
当前实施计划　current programme
当事人　principal, client concerned, client
当事人的承诺和赔偿
　　the parties's undertaking and indemnity
当事双方的一般义务
　　general obligations of the parties
(补偿坠陀)挡板　obstacle board
挡车器　stop buffer
挡尘板　dust board
挡块　baffle block
挡水建筑物　barrage, water retaining works
挡土构件　earth-retaining component
挡土墙　retaining wall
挡土墙纵断面
　　longitudinal section of retaining wall
挡烟垂壁　ceiling screen
挡油墙　fire suppression and barrier wall
档案　file
档案资料　file data
刀间距　cutter spacing
刀盘　cutter head
刀盘功率　cutter head power
刀盘密封　cutter head sealing
刀盘扭矩　cutter head torque
刀盘推力　cutter head thrust
刀盘微动机构
　　cutter head micromotion mechanism
刀盘支承壳体　supporting shell of cutter head
刀盘轴承　cutter head bearing
刀盘转速　cutter head rotation speed
刀圈　cutter ring
刀圈寿命　cutter ring life
刀圈直径　cutter ring diameter
刀体　cutter hub
刀轴　cutter shaft
刀座　cutter housing
导爆索装药　charging along detonating fuse
导电率　conductivity
导洞　pilot tunnel
导高　contact wire height
导管　conduit
导管调整器　pipe compensator
导管灌注混凝土　tremie concrete
导管装置　pipe installation
导轨　closure rail, lead rail, curved stock rail
导轨架　guiding track bracket

导航卫星全球定位系统
　　navigation satellite global positioning system
导流　diversion
导流板　deflector
导流槽　diversion trench
导流洞　diversion tunnel
导流建筑物　diversion structures
导流渠　diversion channel
导轮　guide wheel
导曲线支距　offset of lead curve, offset of closure rail
导热系数　thermal conductivity coefficient
导入高程测量　induction height survey
导水系数　coefficient of transmissibility
导通电压　break-over voltage, turn-on voltage
导线边　traverse side
导线测量　traversing
导线导轮　wire carrier
导线点　traverse point
导线调整器　wire compensator
导线反正扣　wire-adjusting screw
导线方位角闭合差　azimuth closing error of traverse
导线横向误差　lateral error of traverse
导线节点　traverse node
导线控制网　traverse control network
导线立轮　vertical wheel
导线疲劳　fatigue of contact wire
导线平轮　horizontal wheel
导线平轮组　horizontal wheel assembly
导线曲折系数　meandering coefficient of traverse
导线全长闭合差
　　total length closing error of traverse
导线网　traverse network
导线相对闭合差　relative closing error of traverses
导线折角　traverse angle
导线装置　wire installation
导线纵向误差　longitudinal error of traverse
导向安全侧偏差　safe side-oriented deviation
导向标志　guidance sign
导向危险侧偏差　wrong side-oriented deviation
导油管　oil conduit
岛弧　island arc
岛架　island shelf, insular shelf
岛坡　island slope, insular slope
岛式站台　island platform
岛屿　island
岛状冻土区　island-like permafrost region
岛状多年冻土　patchy permafrost
岛状融区　island talik
捣固　tamping
捣固车　tamping car

捣固道床　ballast tamping
倒锤线观测（又称"倒锤法"）　inverse plummet observation（also known as "inverse plummeting"）
倒代措施　switchover measure
倒涵管　dive culvert
倒虹吸管　inverted siphon
倒虹吸涵　inverted siphon culvert
倒换时间　switchover time
倒镜　reversing telescope
倒流防止器　backflow preventer
倒排工期　back scheduling
倒填日期　antedate, foredate, backdate
倒填日期支票　antedated check
倒转背斜　overturned anticline, inversion anticline
倒转产状　inverted attitude
倒转岩层　inverted strata
到岸成本　landed cost
到岸价　cost, insurance and freight（CIF）
到岸价格加班轮条件　cost, insurance, freight, liner terms（CIF liner terms）
到岸价格加卸货费　cost, insurance, freight, landed terms（CIF landed terms）
到岸价格加佣金　cost, insurance, freight and commission（CIF and C.）
到岸轮船舱底交货　cost, insurance, freight, ex-ship's hold（CIF ex-ship's hold）
到岸品质　landed quality
到场时间　show-up time
到达　arrival, arrive
到达场　receiving yard
到达地完好货价　sound arriving value
到达日　date of arrival
到达线　receiving track
到发场　receiving-departure yard
到发线　receiving-departure track
到发线出岔测试　test for switching midway in receiving-departure track
到发线出岔电路　protection circuit for switching midway in receiving-departure track
到发线通过能力　carrying capacity of receiving-departure track
到发线有效长度　effective length of receiving-departure track
到货合同　arrival contract
到货条件　arrival terms
到货通知　arrival notice, advice of arrival, cargo delivery notice, notice of arrival
到货质量　arrival quality
到期　fall due, at maturity
到期付款　payment at maturity
到期付款净额　net account due
到期负债　matured liability
到期利息　interest due
到期票据　bill of maturity
到期清单　due date checklist
到期日　expiration date, date due
到期未付款　overdue payment
到期应付　due
到期债务　debt due
到期支付　payment in due course
到期值　maturity value
盗窃　larceny
盗窃保险　theft insurance
道岔　turnout, switch, switch and crossing, points and crossings
道岔安装装置　turnout installation device
道岔表示　switch indication
道岔表示器　switch indicator
道岔侧股　diverging track of turnout
道岔测量　turnout survey
道岔错误表示　false indication of a switch
道岔打磨车　turnout grinding car
道岔定位表示　switch normal indication
道岔动作电源　power source for switch operation
道岔对向布置　opposite arrangement of turnouts, face-passing arrangement of turnouts
道岔反位表示　switch reverse indication
道岔封锁　switch closed up
道岔附加阻力　additional resistance of turnouts
道岔号数　turnout number
道岔后长　rear length of turnout
道岔护轨　guard rail of turnout, check rail of turnout, restraining rail of turnout
道岔恢复　switch resetting
道岔基线　reference line of turnout
道岔几何状态检测　turnout geometry inspection
道岔结构　turnout structure
道岔控制电路　switch control circuit
道岔拉杆　switch rod
道岔类型　type of turnout
道岔理论长度　theoretical length of turnout
道岔理论导程　theoretical lead of turnout
道岔连接杆　connecting rod of turnout
道岔梁桥　railway-turnout girder bridge, railway-turnout beam bridge
道岔密贴　switch closure, switch close-up
道岔密贴检查装置　turnout closure detector
道岔铺换机组　turnout laying and replacement crew

道岔铺换设备　turnout laying and replacement device
道岔启动　switch starting
道岔前长　front length of turnout
道岔清筛机　turnout ballast cleaning machine
道岔区轨枕埋入式无砟轨道　sleeper-embedded ballastless track in turnout area
道岔区坡　gradient within the turnout area
道岔全长　total length of turnout
道岔缺口　switch machine indicating gap, switch gap
道岔人工解锁　switch manual release
道岔失去表示　loss of indication of a switch
道岔实际长度　actual length of turnout
道岔始端　front end of turnout
道岔顺向布置　back-passing arrangement of turnouts
道岔顺序启动　sequential starting of switches
道岔顺序转换　sequential transition of switches
道岔锁闭　switch locking, switch lock out
道岔锁闭表示　turnout locking indication
道岔跳线　switch jumper
道岔外锁闭装置　outside turnout locking device
道岔稳定车　turnout stabilizer
道岔握柄　switch lever
道岔辙叉跟　frog heel
道岔直股　straight track of turnout
道岔中途转换　switch thrown under moving train
道岔中心　turnout center, intersection point of turnout
道岔终端　rear end of turnout
道岔主线　main line of turnout
道岔柱　turnout mast
道岔转换　switch transition
道岔转换及锁闭测试　turnout setting and locking test
道床　track bed
道床边坡　ballast slope
道床边坡夯实机　ballast shoulder consolidating machine
道床沉陷　ballast bed depression
道床底砟夯实机　sub-ballast consolidating machine, sub-ballast compactor
道床电阻　ballast bed resistance
道床顶面宽度　top width of track bed
道床覆盖　ballast cover
道床夯拍机　ballast compactor
道床横向阻力　lateral resistance of track bed
道床厚度　thickness of track bed, depth of ballast bed
道床肩宽　width of ballast shoulder
道床密度　ballast density
道床配砟整形车　ballast distributing and profiling car
道床清扫机　ballast cleaning machine
道床系数　ballast coefficient
道床脏污　ballast contamination, ballast fouling
道床砟肩　ballast shoulder
道床整形　ballast trimming, ballast regulation
道床支承刚度　supporting stiffness of track bed
道床纵向阻力　longitudinal resistance of track bed
道床作业　ballast maintenance
道德标准　ethical standard
道德风险　moral risk
道德准则　ethics, moral standard
道钉　track spike
道钉锤　spike hammer
道间距　wave receiver interval
道口　level crossing, grade crossing
道口安全　level crossing safety
道口报警　alarm at level crossing
道口标志　sign at level crossing
道口电话　telephone at level crossing
道口防护　protection at level crossing
道口房　level crossing cabin
道口接近区段　approach section of highway level crossing
道口栏木　crossing barrier
道口轮缘槽　flangeway of level crossing
道口平台　level stretch of grade crossing
道口铺面　level crossing pavement
道口闪光信号　highway level crossing flashing signal
道口室外音响器　highway crossing outdoor audible device
道口通知设备　highway level crossing announcing device
道口信号　level crossing signal
道口信号机　highway crossing signal
道口遥信遥测设备　remote surveillance and telemetering for highway crossing
道口遮断信号　level crossing obstruction signal
道口折算交通量　converted traffic volume of level crossing
道口自动栏杆　automatic level crossing barrier
道口自动通知　automatic level crossing announcement
道口自动信号　automatic level crossing signal
道路　road, way
道路边缘　road edge
道路标准荷载　rated load of road, standard load of road
道路工程测量　road engineering survey
道路红线　boundary lines of roads
道路交叉口　intersection

道路路面　road pavement
道路通行权　right of way, wayleaves
道心　mid-track
道义索赔　ex gratia claim
道义支付　ex-gratia payment
道砟　ballast
道砟表面清洁度　cleanliness of ballast surface
道砟槽　ballast trough
道砟存放场　railway ballast storage yard
道砟电阻　ballast resistance
道砟电阻率　ballast resistivity
道砟更换　ballast replacement
道砟更换机　ballast replacement machine
道砟级配　ballast grading
道砟犁　ballast plough
道砟桥面　ballasted deck
道砟清筛　ballast cleaning
道砟清筛机　ballast cleaning machine
道砟陷槽　ballast depression trough
灯光水位计　light water level gauge
灯光转移　transfer of lighting indication
灯具效率　luminaire efficiency
灯具效能　luminaire efficacy
灯具遮光角　cutoff angle of a luminaire
灯笼(导线缺陷)　birdcaging
灯桥　bridge lighting
灯丝断丝　filament burn-out
灯丝断丝报警　filament burnout alarm
灯丝转换装置　filament transfer device
登记　register, enter
登记簿　register
等电平远端串音功率和　power sum ELFEXT attenuation(loss)(PS ELFEXT)
等电平远端串音衰减　equal level far end crosstalk attenuation(loss)(ELFEXT)
等电位　equipotential
等电位连接　equipotential connection
等高距　contour interval
等高线　contour line
等高线图　contour map
等积投影　equivalent projection
等级　classification, grade, scale
等级转换　grade shift
等价　par
等角投影/正形投影　conformal projection
等截面梁　uniform beam
等截面柱　constant cross-section column
等径圆杆　circular pole of equal diameter
等距投影　equidistant projection
等离子体　plasma
等量代替法　equivalent replacement method
等偏摄影　parallel-averted photography
等倾摄影　equally tilted photograph
等权代替法　method of equal-weight substitution
等深距　isobath interval
等深线　isobath
等势线　equipotential line
等温射流　isothermal jet
等向固结　isotropic consolidation
等效A声级　equivalent A-weighted sound level
等效n次谐波　equivalent n-th harmonic
等效剪切波速　equivalent shear wave velocity
等效均布荷载　equivalent uniform load
等效均布活荷载　equivalent uniform live load
等效客站能耗计算模型　energy performance equivalent building of railway station
等效孔径　effective pore size
等效连续A声级　equivalent continuous A-weighted sound pressure level
等效声级　equivalent sound level
等效弯矩系数　equivalent moment coefficient
等压水位线法　isobaric waterline method
等黏温度　equal viscosity temperature
等震线　isoseismal
等震线图　isoseismal map
等值货币　money equivalent
等值货币价值　money's worth
等值距　interval of isoline
等值线　isoline
等值线法　isoline method
等轴晶系　cubic system
等阻线　resistance isoline
低动力污水处理设施　low-power sewage treatment facilities
低发射率膜玻璃　low emissivity coated glass
低负荷生物滤池　low-rate trickling filters
低高度梁　shallow beam
低估　underestimate, undervalue, undervaluation
低路堤　low embankment
低热水泥　low-heat cement
低山　low mountain
低税地区　tax haven
低填浅挖　low fill and shallow cut
低洼地　low-lying land
低温冰柜　low temperature refrigerator
低温烘干法　low temperature drying method
低温基本稳定冻土区　basically stable low-temperature permafrost
低温基本稳定区　low-temperature and basically stable area

低温试验　low temperature test
低温送风空气调节系统
　　low temperature air supply air conditioning system
低温稳定冻土区　stable low-temperature permafrost
低温稳定区　low-temperature stable area
低温性能　low temperature properties
低息贷款
　　easy money, cheap money, cheap credit, soft loan
低效率　inefficiency
低压侧　low voltage side, secondary side
低压断路器　low-voltage circuit breaker
低压膜过滤装置
　　low pressure membrane filter device
低压配电　low-voltage power distribution
低压缩性　low compressibility
低压系统　low pressure system
低压消防给水系统
　　low pressure fire water supply system
低应变法　low-strain integrity testing
低应变反射波法　low strain reflected wave method
低周反复作用　low frequency alternate action
低桩承台　low pile cap
堤　embankment
堤坝施工测量　dam construction survey
滴定　titration
滴定法　titration
滴定管　burette
滴入(加)　dropwise add
迪凯石　dickite
敌对进路　conflicting route
敌对信号　conflicting signal
敌对行为　hostilities
抵岸价　landed price
抵埠通知　arrival notice
抵偿　compensate, cover
抵偿高程面　compensation level surface
抵税　tax credit
抵消　offset, set-off
抵消税　countervailing duty
抵消账户　contra account, offset account
抵押　mortgage, hypothecate, pledge
抵押贷款　mortgage loan, collateral loan, secured loan
抵押贷款人　mortgagee
抵押单　mortgage
抵押借款　pledge against a loan
抵押借款人　mortgagor
抵押款　mortgage
抵押凭证　pawn ticket
抵押契约　deed of mortgage
抵押权　lien, mortgage
抵押权益　security interest
抵押人　pledger, mortgagor
抵押条款　mortgage clause
抵押物　pledge, things mortgaged
抵押债券　mortgage bond
抵押证书　memorandum of deposit, letter of hypothecation, letter of deposit
抵押资产　hypothecated assets
抵制　boycott, resist, curb
底板　base slab, base plate
底辟　diapir
底部剪力法/拟静力法　bottom shearing force method/quasi-static method, equivalent base shear method
底价　bottom price, floor price, base price
底砾岩　basal conglomerate
底梁　ground beam
底流　underflow
底盘　base plate
底漆　prime coating
底碛　ground moraine
底线　base line
底砟(垫层)　sub-ballast
底座　base
地板辐射采暖　radiant floor heating
地表沉降或隆起
　　ground surface subsidence or upheaval
地表径流　surface runoff
地表碾压措施　surface rolling measure
地表水　surface water
地表水环境质量标准
　　environmental quality standard for surface water
地表下沉　ground surface settlement
地表下沉量测　ground depression measurement
地表形态　surface relief
地表旋喷桩
　　jet grouting pile constructed from ground surface
地表移动观测站
　　observation station of surface movement
地材　local material
地槽　geosyncline
地层　stratum
地层层序　stratigraphic sequence
地层单元　stratigraphic unit
地层分界线　stratum boundary
地层观测点　stratum observation point
地层结构　stratigraphic structure
地层时代　stratigraphic age
地层岩性　formation lithology, stratum lithology
地层柱状图　stratum column
地产　landed property, estate

地产信托证　land trust certificate
地磁场　geomagnetic field
地带　zone
地道　underpass tunnel
地道风　tunnel air
地底点　ground nadir point
地对车信息传输　ground-train information transmission
地盾　shield
地方长官　commissioner
地方当局　local authority
地方电源　local power source
地方法规　by-law
地方法院　local court
地方供电部门　local power supply authority
地方税　local tax
地方铁路　local railway
地方性编组站　local marshalling station
地方杂税　miscellaneous local taxes
地沟　trench
地鼓　ground heave
地核　earth's core
地回流　earth return current
地基　subsoil, foundation soil
地基沉降　subsoil settlement
地基承载力　subsoil bearing capacity
地基承载力抗震调整系数　seismic adjustment coefficient of subgrade bearing capacity
地基承载力特征值　characteristic value of subsoil bearing capacity
地基处理　ground treatment
地基加固　ground stabilization, ground treatment
地基缺陷　subgrade defect
地基土　subsoil
地基微动测定　ground microtremor testing
地基系数　coefficient of subgrade
地基系数 K30　coefficient of subsoil K30
地基下沉　setting of ground
地籍图　cadastral map
地籍信息系统　cadastral information system
地价　land price
地脚螺栓　anchor bolt
地界　boundary
地界测量　land boundary survey
地壳　crust
地壳应力　crustal stress
地垒　horst
地理位置　geographic(al) position
地理信息　geographic information
地理信息系统　geographic information system
地理坐标参考系　geographical coordinate reference system
地理坐标网　geographic coordinate graticule
地裂　ground fracture
地裂缝　ground fissure
地龙式协作货位　earthworm-like freight section
地漏　floor drain
地脉动　ground micro-tremor
地幔　mantle
地锚　ground anchor
地貌　geomorphy, landform
地貌单元　landform unit, geomorphic unit
地貌观测点　landform observation point
地貌图　geomorphological map
地面　ground surface, floor
地面沉降　land subsidence, ground settlement
地面粗糙度　ground roughness
地面电子单元　lineside electronic unit(LEU)
地面感应器　wayside inductor
地面钢轨涂油器　track-side rail lubricator
地面高程　ground elevation
地面横坡　lateral slope of ground
地面横坡倾角　dip angle for lateral slope of ground
地面集水时间　inlet time, time of concentration
地面控制部分　ground control segment
地面坡度　surface slope
地面摄影测量　terrestrial photogrammetry
地面摄影测量坐标系　terrestrial photogrammetric coordinate system
地面塌陷　surface collapse
地面线　ground track
地面信号　trackside signal
地面应用节点　ground application node
地面预注浆　pre-grouting performed from ground surface
地面转换自动过分相区段　changeover section
地名数据库　geographic-name data base
地契　land certificate, title deed
地堑　graben
地堑谷　graben valley
地球曲率　earth curvature
地球椭球　earth ellipsoid
地球物理勘探　geophysical prospecting
地球形状　figure of the earth
地球仪　tellurian
地区　area, locality, region
地区差价　regional price differential
地区电缆　regional cable
地区法庭　district court, district tribunal
地区规划　regional planning

地区检察官　district attorney
地区经验　local experience
地区审计员　district auditor
地区统一定额　regional uniform quota
地区限制　territorial limitation
地区线路　regional line
地区性优惠　regional preference
地热　geotherm
地台　platform
地图　map
地图编制　map compilation
地图规范　map specifications
地图集　atlas
地图数据库　map database
地图数据库管理系统　map database management system
地图投影　map projection
地图印刷　map printing
地图整饰　map decoration
地图制版　map plate-making
地图制图学　cartography
地图注记　map annotation
地网　earthing network
地位　standing position, status
地温分区　ground temperature zoning
地温年变化深度　ground temperature annual change in depth
地温梯度　geothermal gradient
地物　ground feature
地物波谱特性　spectrum characteristic of ground feature
地物点　ground feature point
地下测量　underground surveying
地下车站　underground station
地下电缆　underground cable, ground cable
地下洞室　underground cavity
地下工程　underground works
地下管线　underground pipeline
地下管线测量　underground pipeline survey
地下管线探测　underground pipelines detection
地下河　subterranean stream
地下混凝土　buried concrete
地下结构　substructure
地下径流　subsurface runoff, groundwater runoff
地下径流模数　underground runoff modulus
地下径流深度法　underground runoff depth method
地下连续墙　underground diaphragm wall
地下埋设物　underground installation
地下排水管　underdrain
地下室　basement

地下水　ground water
地下水 pH 值　pH value of groundwater
地下水补给量　groundwater recharge
地下水储存量　groundwater storage
地下水存储量　groundwater storage
地下水等水位线图　contour map of groundwater level
地下水动力学　groundwater dynamics
地下水动力学法　groundwater dynamics method
地下水动态　groundwater regime
地下水富集区　ground water abundant area
地下水监测　groundwater monitoring
地下水控制　groundwater control
地下水侵蚀性　corrosiveness of groundwater
地下水取水构筑物反滤层　inverted filter layer of groundwater intake structure
地下水水化学图　hydrogeochemical map of groundwater
地下水位　groundwater level
地下水污染　groundwater pollution
地下水源　underground water source
地下水总矿化度　total mineralization of groundwater
地下物探　underground geophysical prospecting
地下物探仪　underground geophysical prospecting instrument
地下线　underground track
地线　earth wire
地线连接检查　earthing connection inspection
地线弯卡　curved holder for earth wire
地线线夹　earth wire clamp
地心坐标系　geocentric coordinate system
地形　terrain, topography
地形采样　terrain sampling
地形测量　topographic survey
地形测图　topographic mapping
地形地貌调查　topography investigation
地形点　topographic point
地形点间距　interval of topographical point
地形数据库　topographic database
地形条件　terrain condition
地形图　topographic map
地形图比例尺　topographic map scale
地形图分幅　topographic map-subdivision
地形图数据库　topographic map database
地形图图式　topographic map symbols
地形图修测　topographic map revision
地形图要素　topographic map content elements
地形线　landform line
地形校正　topographical rectification
地形原图　topographic original map

地役权	easement
地应力场	ground stress field
地域范围	territory
地源热泵	geothermal heat pump
地震	earthquake
地震安全性评估	seismic safety evaluation
地震安全性评估费	assessment fee for seismic safety
地震波	seismic wave, earthquake wave
地震波反射法	seismic wave reflection method
地震次生灾害	secondary disaster of earthquake
地震带	earthquake zone, seismic belt
地震动参数	seismic ground motion parameter
地震动参数区划图	seismic ground motion parameter zoning map
地震动峰值加速度	seismic peak ground acceleration
地震动加速度反应谱特征周期	characteristic period of the acceleration response spectrum
地震动水压力法	earthquake dynamic water pressure method
地震动土压力法	seismic earth pressure calculation method
地震峰值加速度	earthquake peak acceleration
地震荷载	seismic load
地震活动	seismic action
地震基本烈度	seismic basic intensity
地震加速度	seismic acceleration
地震加速度计	earthquake acceleration meter, seismic accelerator
地震监测	earthquake monitoring, seismic monitoring
地震监测报警预警	earthquake monitoring alarm and early warning
地震监测传感器	earthquake monitoring sensor
地震监测台站	earthquake monitoring station
地震紧急处置	seismic emergency handling
地震勘探	seismic prospecting
地震勘探仪	seismic exploration instrument
地震坑	seismic pit
地震力	seismic force
地震烈度	seismic intensity
地震漏报	failure to predict an earthquake
地震强度	earthquake intensity
地震群集	earthquake grouping
地震设计状况	earthquake design state
地震危害分析	seismic hazard analysis
地震系数	seismic coefficient
地震影响系数	seismic influence coefficient
地震原生灾害	primary earthquake disaster
地震灾害	earthquake disaster
地震震级	earthquake magnitude
地震作用标准值	standard value of earthquake action
地震作用效应	seismic action effect
地址变更	address modification
地址更正	address correction
地址解析协议	address resolution protocol (ARP)
地址录	directory
地质不良地段	unfavourable geological section
地质不良路基	subgrade with unfavorable geological conditions
地质测量	geologic survey
地质测试	geological test
地质超前预报	geological prediction
地质调查法	geological survey method
地质调绘	geological investigation and mapping
地质分析法	geological analysis method
地质复杂程度分级	classification of geological complexity
地质构造	geological structure
地质横剖面图	geological cross section
地质环境	geological environment
地质环境要素	geological environmental factor
地质界线	geological boundary
地质勘探	geological investigation
地质雷达	geological radar, ground penetrating radar (GPR)
地质雷达法	ground penetrating radar method
地质力学模型试验	geomechanical model test
地质年代	geochron
地质判释	geological interpretation
地质平面图	geological plane map
地质剖面图	geological profile
地质素描	geological sketch, geological mapping
地质缩图	geological abbreviated drawing
地质填图	geological mapping
地质条件	geological condition
地质选点	geological location
地质灾害	geological hazard
地质灾害危险性评估	geological hazard assessment
地质灾害危险性评估费	assessment fee for geological hazard risk
地质纵断面图	geological longitudinal section drawing
地质纵剖面图	geological longitudinal profile
地质作图法	geological mapping method
地中电缆盒	underground cable terminal box
地中电流	earth current
递耗资产	diminishing assets, wasting assets
递减	decrease
递减税	regressive tax

递减折旧　degressive depreciation
递交　deliver, forward
递交投标书　tender submission
递延保险金　deferred premium
递延成本　deferred cost
递延贷项　deferred credits
递延费用　deferred charges (expenses)
递延负债　deferred liabilities
递延股权　deferred equity
递延借项　deferred debits
递延收入　deferred revenue (income)
递延资产　deferred assets
递增成本　increasing cost
第二接近区段　second approach section
第二离去区段　second departure section
第二循环管　secondary circulating system
第三方　third party
第三方保险　third party insurance
第三方合同　third party contract
第三方试验检测机构　third party test and inspection body
第三方收费　third party charges
第三方索赔　third party claim
第三方托管账户　escrow account
第三方责任　third party liability
第三方责任强制保险　compulsory third party insurance
第三国货币　third-country currency
第三纪　Tertiary period, Tertiary
第三类贷款业务　third window loan
第三离去区段　third departure section
第三系　Tertiary system
第三者责任险　third party insurance
第四纪　Quaternary, Quaternary period
第四系　Quaternary system
第一抵押权　first mortgage
第一接近区段　first approach section
第一离去区段　first departure section
第一手资料　first-hand information
第一损失保险　first loss insurance
第一循环管　primary circulating system
第一优先权　first priority
缔结　enter into, conclude, conclusion
缔结和约　conclude a contract
缔结协议　strike an agreement
缔约　conclude a treaty
缔约能力　capacity to contract, competency, contractual capacity
典型地段绿化图　greening design drawing of typical sections
典型工点　typical construction site
典型工点设计　design of typical construction site
典型开发建设项目　typical development and construction projects
典型列车　representative trains
典型弃土场水土保持防护图　soil and water conservation design drawing for typical spoil ground
典型取土场水土保持防护图　soil and water conservation design drawing for typical borrow pit
点对点普通语音通信业务　point-to-point speech service
点对点协议　point-to-point protocol
点荷载强度指数　point loading strength index
点荷载试验　point load test
点连式　intermittent-continuous mode
点连式调速　intermittent-continuous speed control
点连式调速系统　point-continued type speed control system
点式　intermittent mode
点式传输　intermittent transmission
点式调速　intermittent speed control
点式设备　intermittent device
点位稳定性检验　stability test of point location
点位误差　position error
点位中误差　mean square error of positions
点下对中　centering under point
点之记　description of station
点状符号　point symbol
碘化物　iodide
碘量法　iodometry
碘量分光光度法　Iodine spectrophotometric method
电伴热　electric heat tracing
电报　telegraph
电报交换机　telegraph exchange
电报通信　telegraph communication
电报终端　telegraph terminal
电表　kilowatt-hour meter
电测井　electric logging
电测剖面法　electric profiling
电测深法　electrical sounding method
电测式量测装置　electrical logging measuring device
电测水位计　electric water level gauge
电测仪器　electrical logging apparatus
电厂　power station, power plant
电场法　electric field treatment
电场强度　electric field strength

电池槽　battery jar
电池组　battery bank
电传　telex
电磁　electromagnetism
电磁波 CT　electromagnetic wave CT
电磁波测距
　　electromagnetic distance metering（EDM）
电磁波测距标称精度
　　nominal accuracy of EDM
电磁波测距三角高程测量
　　trigonometric leveling by electromagnetic ranging
电磁波测距仪　electromagnetic distance meter instrument（EDMI）
电磁波测距仪极坐标法
　　polar coordinate method with EDMI
电磁波测距最大测程
　　maximum range of EDM
电磁波测距最佳观测时间段
　　best observation period for EDM
电磁波法　electromagnetic wave method
电磁波反射法
　　electromagnetic reflection method
电磁波速　velocity of electromagnetic wave
电磁波透射法
　　electromagnetic wave transmission
电磁测井　electromagnetic logging
电磁阀　electromagnetic valve
电磁辐射　electromagnetic radiation
电磁干扰　electromagnetic interference（EMI）
电磁感应　electromagnetic induction
电磁感应法　electromagnetic induction method
电磁环境　electromagnetic environment
电磁继电器　electromagnetic relay
电磁兼容　electromagnetic compatibility（EMC）
电磁脉冲　electromagnetic pulse
电磁频谱仪　electromagnetic spectrum device
电磁屏蔽　electromagnetic shielding
电磁式测试系统　electromagnetic test system
电磁式电流互感器
　　electro-magnetic current transformer
电磁式轨道继电器　electromagnetic track relay
电磁污染　electromagnetic pollution
电磁污染防护
　　electromagnetic radiation protection
电导池常数　conductivity cell constant
电导法　conductivity method
电导率　conductivity
电笛　electric whistle, electric siren
电动臂板电锁器联锁　interlocking by electric locks with electric semaphore

电动臂板信号机　electric semaphore signal
电动操作机构　motorized operating mechanism
电动车组　Electric Multiple Units（EMU）
电动传送设备　electric conveyer
电动起重机（又称"电动葫芦"）
　　electric hoist（also known as "electric block"）
电动发电机　dynamotor
电动钢轨钻孔机　electric rail drilling machine
电动隔离开关　motorized disconnector
电动机　electric motor
电动机式发码器　motor-type code sender
电动卷扬机　electric winch, electric hoist
电动开关操作机构
　　operating mechanism for motorized disconnector
电动抗折机
　　electric bending resistance machine
电动压缩机　electric compressor
电动振捣器　electric vibrator
电动转辙机　electric switch machine
电度表　watt-hour meter
电镀　electroplating
电法　electrical method
电法勘探　electrical prospecting
电法勘探仪　electrical prospecting instrument
电分段　electrical sectioning
电分相　phase break
电复　tele-reply
电杆　pole
电感耦合等离子体原子发射光谱法　inductively coupled plasma atomic emission spectrometry
电镐　portable electric tamper, electric pick
电锅炉　electric boiler
电焊　electric welding
电焊设备　welding equipment
电荷放大器　charge-amplifier
电弧擦伤　arc strike
电弧焊　electric arc welding
电弧焊机　electric arc welder
电弧焊接头　arc welding joint
电化法　electrochemical process
电化股道　electrified track
电化线路　electrified track
电化学加固　electrochemical stabilization
电化学探头法　electrochemical probe method
电话闭塞　telephone blocking
电话订票系统　telephone booking system
电话衡重杂音电压　telephone weighted noise voltage
电话会议电路　telephone conference circuit
电话会议设备　telephone conference equipment
电话机　telephone set

电话交换　telephone switch
电汇　telegraphic transfer（T/T）, wire transfer, cable transfer
电汇费率　cable rate
电汇汇款单　telegraphic money order
电汇申请单　wire request
电机集中联锁　electro-mechanical interlocking
电极距　electrode spacing
电加热法　electrical heating method
电加热器　electric heater
电价　electricity price
电监控通路　electrical supervisory channel（ESC）
电解液　electrolyte
电抗补偿　reactance compensation
电抗器　reactor
电空传送设备　electro-pneumatic conveyer
电空阀　electro-pneumatic valve
电空转辙机　electro-pneumatic switch machine
电缆　cable
电缆标志　cable mark
电缆槽　cable trough
电缆充气　cable inflation
电缆分线夹　cable tee connector
电缆分支箱　cable branch box
电缆盖板　cable cover
电缆沟　cable trench, cable trough
电缆沟(线路两侧预留的)　cable duct
电缆沟(需要回填土的)　cable trench
电缆沟盖板　cable trench cover
电缆故障测试仪　cable fault testor
电缆故障探测仪　cable fault detector
电缆管道　culvert
电缆盒　cable box
电缆基本线对　fundamental wire pair of cable
电缆夹层　cable interlayer
电缆架　cable bracket
电缆检修孔　cable manhole
电缆接头　cable joint
电缆井　cable shaft
电缆控制长度　cable control length
电缆盘　cable drum, cable reel
电缆配线图　cable layout
电缆腔　cable chamber
电缆桥架　cable ladder（tray）
电缆竖井　cable shaft
电缆套管　cable sleeve
电缆线卡　cable clamp
电缆线路　cable route
电缆支架　cable support, cable rack, cable tray, cable ladder, cable riser
电缆终端杆　cable terminal pole
电缆终端头　cable terminal
电离层延迟　ionospheric delay
电力　power
电力叉车　electric forklift
电力电缆　power cable
电力调度电话　electric power dispatching telephone
电力调度中心　power dispatching center
电力复合脂　conductive grease
电力工程　power project, electric power, traction power supply, communications and signalling
电力贯通线路　run-through power line
电力机车　electric locomotive
电力开闭所　power switching station
电力牵引　electric traction
电力牵引干扰　electric traction interference
电力线材　power cable material
电力谐波分析仪　power harmonic analyzer
电力远动系统　power remote control system
电力资源　power resources
电连接线夹　electrical connection clamp
电流保护　current protection
电流波形　current waveform
电流电压保护　current-voltage protection
电流互感器　current transformer
电流速断保护　instantaneous trip current protection
电流元件　current element
电流增量保护　current increment protection
电路倒换　circuit switchover
电路故障　circuit failure
电路交换　circuit switching
电路台账　circuit table
电路图　circuit diagram
电码轨道电路　coded track circuit
电码化　coding
电码化轨道电路　coded track circuit
电码继电器　code relay
电码自动闭塞　automatic block with coded track circuit
电能计量装置　electric energy metering device
电能利用效率　power usage effectiveness（PUE）
电能损失　electrical energy loss, power energy loss
电能质量分析　electrical energy quality analysis
电能质量监测　electrical energy quality monitoring
电钮　push button
电平　electrical level
电平表　level meter
电平振荡器　level oscillator
电瓶车　battery locomotive, storage battery car
电剖面法　electric profiling method

电气安装　electrical installation

电气安装	electrical installation
电气防护	electrical protection
电气隔离	electric isolation
电气工程师	electrical engineer
电气化	electrification
电气化附加费	additional charge of electrification
电气化附加费费率	additional rate of electrification
电气化改造	electrification transformation
电气化干扰	electrification interference
电气化里程	electrification mileage
电气化区段	electrification section
电气化铁道	electrified railway
电气化铁路	electrified railway
电气集中	electric concentration
电气集中联锁	electric interlocking
电气绝缘节	electrical insulated joint
电气联锁	electrical interlocking
电气路牌闭塞	electric tablet block system
电气路牌机	electric tablet instrument
电气路签闭塞	electric staff block system
电气路签机	electric staff instrument
电气石	taltalite
电气试验	electrical test
电气试验车	electrical testing vehicle
电气锁闭	electric locking
电气照明	electrical lighting
电桥	electrical bridge
电热板	electric hot plate
电热干燥箱	electrically heated drying oven
电热鼓风烘箱	electric heat oven
电热水器	electric water heater
电容补偿	capacitance compensation
电容和介质损耗	capacitance and dielectric loss
电容器	capacitor
电容器充电	capacitor charge, condenser charge
电容器电抗	capacitor reactance
电容器放电	capacitor discharge
电容器室	capacitor room
电容器组	capacitor bank
电容式电压互感器	capacitor voltage transformer
电渗法	electro-osmotic drainage
电渗析法	electrodialysis process（ED）
电式机车信号	electric cab signaling
电视测井	television logging
电视电话会议	video conference
电视会议电路	video conference circuit
电视信号场强	television signal field strength
电寿命	electrical endurance
电锁器	electric lock
电锁器联锁	interlocking by electric locks
电梯	lift, elevator
电梯井	lift shaft
电梯责任保险	elevator liability insurance
电通量	electric flux
电通量测定仪	permeability tester
电网	power grid
电网传感器	power grid sensor
电位测量仪	potentiometric tester
电位滴定法	potentiometric titration
电位法	potentiometry
电务检测车	communication and signal inspection car
电修间	electrical repair shop
电压	voltage
电压保护	voltage protection
电压不平衡度	voltage unbalance factor
电压等级	voltage level
电压调整率	voltage regulation factor
电压放大器	voltage amplifier
电压互感器	voltage transformer
电压畸变率	voltage distortion（VD）
电压降	voltage drop
电压升	voltage rise
电压损失	loss of voltage
电压突变	rapid voltage change
电压下降	voltage dip
电压值	voltage value
电压自动调整器	automatic voltage regulator
电液转辙机	electro-hydraulic switch machine
电源	power supply
电源板测试台	power strip test board
电源电压	power supply voltage
电源端子	power supply terminal
电源防雷箱	power lightning protection box
电源容量	power capacity
电源室	power supply room
电源线	power line
电源转换屏	power switching over panel
电站	power plant
电子秤	electronic scale
电子方式开标程序	electronic bid opening procedures
电子方式投标程序	electronic bid submission procedures
电子票	E-ticket
电子汽车衡	electronic truck scale
电子倾斜仪	electronic inclinometer
电子速测仪	electronic tachometer
电子速测仪测量	electronic tachometer measurement

D

电子锁　electronic strike
电子天平　electronic balance
电子文档管理系统
　　electronic document management system
电子信息系统　electronic information system
电子支付　e-payment, digital payment
电子执行单元　electronic execution unit
电阻率　resistivity
电阻率法　resistivity method
电阻损失　resistance loss
电阻温度系数　temperature coefficient of resistance
电阻系数　coefficient of resistance
电阻应变传感器　resistance strain sensor
电阻应变片　resistance strain gauge
电阻应变片法　resistance strain gauge method
电阻应变式　resistance strain type
电阻应变仪　resistance strain gauge
垫板　pad
垫板焊　backing weld
垫层　cushion course, bedding course
垫付　make advance
垫片　gasket, washer, shim
垫圈　washer
奠基石　corner stone
吊锤投影　projection by suspended plumb
吊顶　suspended ceiling
吊斗　lift bucket
吊杆　suspender
吊沟　suspended ditch
吊罐　bucket
吊环　eye clamp
吊架　hanger
吊筋　hanging bar
吊孔　suspended span
吊跨　suspended span
吊篮　hanging basket
吊缆　suspension cable
吊笼　suspension coop
吊桥　suspension bridge
吊扇　ceiling fan
吊绳　lifting rope
吊索　bridle wire
吊索导向托座　bridle wire guiding bracket
吊索滑轮装置　bridle wire-and-pulley suspension
吊弦　dropper
吊弦间距　dropper spacing
吊弦线夹　dropper clip
吊线　messenger wire
吊销执照　cancellation of licence
吊柱　drop tube

吊装　hoisting
调查　investigation
调查价　price by investigation
调查结果　findings
调查人　inquirer, surveyor
调车表示器　shunting indicator
调车表示器电路　shunting indicator circuit
调车测试　shunting test
调车场　shunting yard
调车场尾部　tail of shunting yard
调车场中部　middle part of shunting yard
调车监控模式　shunting monitoring mode
调车进路　shunting route
调车模式　shunting mode (SH)
调车区电气集中联锁
　　all-relay interlocking for shunting area
调车设备　shunting equipment
调车手持台　operational purpose handset/handheld for shunting (OPS)
调车线　shunting track
调车线内减速器　retarder within shunting track
调车线始端减速器　tangent retarder
调车信号　shunting signal
调车信号机　shunting signal
调车员室　shunter's cabin
调车转线　shunting transfer track
调车作业模式通信
　　shunting mode communication
调车作业区　shunting area
调度　despatch, dispatch
调度电话分机　dispatching extension
调度集中系统　centralized traffic control system
调度监督　dispatching supervision
调度监督系统　dispatching supervision system
调度交换机　dispatching switch
调度控制　dispatching control
调度区段　train dispatching section
调度所　dispatching post
调度台　dispatching console
调度用户区域标识　dispatching user zone ID
调度总机　dispatching switchboard
调绘　annotation
调绘相片　annotated photograph, surveying picture
调遣　mobilize
调遣费　redeployment expense
掉块　spalling
掉码　code missing
跌价　beat down
跌落式熔断器　drop-out fuse
跌水槽　drop chute

叠层石　stromatolite
叠合构件　composite member
叠合墙　superposition wall
叠合式混凝土受弯构件
　　laminated reinforced concrete flexural member
叠加电码化　overlapped coding
叠加轨道电路　overlap track circuit
叠加荷载　superimposed load
叠接　splice
叠瓦式断层　imbricate fault
叠压供水　pressure-superposed water supply
碟式仪　disk-type apparatus
碟式仪法　dishing liquid limit method
蝶式液塑限仪　disk-type liquid-plastic limit apparatus
丁坝(又称"挑水坝")　spur dike
丁苯橡胶改性沥青　styrene butadiene rubber(SBR) modified asphalt
顶板　roof, top plate
顶管法　pipe jacking method
顶管过轨　pipe jacking through track
顶护盾　roof support
顶进法　jack-in construction method
顶进桥涵
　　bridge/culver by jack-in construction method
顶帽　top cap
顶面高程　elevation of top surface
顶棚　ceiling, ceiling board
顶棚吊顶　ceiling hanger
顶棚辐射采暖　ceiling radiant heating
顶棚速度监视区　ceiling speed surveillance area
顶升机构　jacking mechanism
顶铁　jacking block, stud
顶推法　incremental launching method
顶推式架设法
　　erection by incremental launching method
订单　booking order, purchase order
订单积压　backlog
订购　place an order
订合同　enter into a contract
订货　order, place an order, indent
订货单　order, order sheet, indent
订货单格式　order form
订货档案　order file
订货费用　ordering cost
订货付现　cash with order
订货合同　purchase contract, ordering contract, contract for goods
订货卷宗　order file
订货量　order quantity
订货人　orderer
订货周期　lead time
订立合同
　　conclude a contract, enter into a contract with
订约人　contractor, promisor, contracting party
定测导线　traverse of location survey
定程租船　voyage charter
定尺钢轨　length-fixed rail
定点报警　fixed spot alarm
定点检测　fixed point detection
定点取送
　　taking-out and placing-in at designated places
定点停车　stopping a train at a target point
定点误差　fixed point error
定额　quota
定额备用金　imprest fund
定额备用现金　imprest cash
定额备用制　imprest system
定额拨款　definite appropriation
定额测定　quota measurement
定额抽换　quota exchange
定额工期　construction period quota
定额工天　quota man-day
定额计价　quota valuation
定额价　quota price
定额年金　constant annuity
定额体系　quota system
定额投资基金　closed-end investment fund
定额增加幅度　quota increase range
定额直接工程费
　　quota direct engineering expense
定反位锁闭　normal and reverse locking
定风量空气调节系统
　　constant-volume air conditioning system
定价　pricing, price, value
定焦摄像机　fixed focus camera
定金
　　down payment, earnest money, purchase money
定金保函　down payment guarantee
定居　residency
定量分析法　quantitative analysis method
定硫仪　sulfur determinator
定率递减折旧法
　　fixed-percentage-on-declining-balance method
定期保函　limited duration guarantee
定期保险　regular insurance
定期报表　periodical statement
定期报告　periodic report
定期测量　periodic measurement
定期存款　time deposit, term deposit, periodical deposit, fixed deposit

定期贷款　time loan, term loan
定期贷款协议　term loan agreement
定期付款　scheduled payment, time payment, periodic payment, payment on terms
定期复测　regular re-measuring
定期合同　fixed-term contract
定期汇票　date draft, time draft, time bill, term bill, period bill, periodic bill
定期会议　periodic meeting
定期检查　routine inspection, periodic inspection
定期盘存　periodic inventory
定期票据　day bill
定期信贷　term credit
定期信用证　term credit
定期修　periodical repair
定期支付　regular payment
定期租船　time charter
定伸保持器　tensile retainer
定速　constant speed
定位标志　location mark
定位钢筋　spacer bar
定位钩　hook clip
定位管　registration tube
定位管卡子　registration tube clamp
定位管支撑　registration tube brace, registration tube strut
定位焊　tack welding
定位环　eye clamp
定位基准点　location reference
定位接点　normal contact
定位块　positioning block
定位器　steady arm
定位器销钉　pin for steady arm
定位索　cross-span wire
定位索线夹　cross-span wire clamp
定位锁闭　normal locking
定位显示　normal position indication
定位信息　localization information
定位修　location repair
定位(支)柱　registration mast
定位装置　registration assembly
定线　alignment
定线测量　layout survey, route locating survey
定向点　orientation point
定向连接测量(又称"连接测量")　orientation connection survey (also known as "connection survey")
定向天线　directional antenna
定向钻法　directional drilling method
定型模板　typified formwork
定性分析　qualitative analysis
定性分析法　qualitative analysis method
定义　definition
定义阶段　definition phase
定值设计法　deterministic design method
定制建造　build-to-suit
丢包率　packet loss rate
东道国　host country
东道国政府　host government
冬季空气调节室外计算温度　design outdoor temperature for air conditioning in winter
冬季空气调节室外计算相对湿度　design outdoor relative humidity for air conditioning in winter
冬季通风室外计算温度　design outdoor temperature for ventilation in winter
冬期施工　winter construction
董事　director
董事长　chairman, chairman of the board
董事会　board of directors, board
董事会会议　board meeting
董事及高级职员责任险　directors and officers liability insurance
董事主席　board chairman
动态变形　dynamic deformation
动产　movable property, chattel, personal property
动产抵押　chattel mortgage
动车段(所)　EMU depot (section)
动车所　EMU running shed
动车运用所　EMU operation shed
动车组　Electric Multiple Units (EMU)
动车组出入段(所)　EMU transfer track
动车组存车场　EMU stabling yard
动车组存放线　EMU stabling siding
动车组地面电源　ground electrical power source for EMUs
动车组管理信息系统　EMU management information system
动车组进出段(所)线　EMU depot access track
动车组设备　EMU facilities
动车组试验线　EMU running test track
动车组走行线　running track for EMU
动程　stroke
动单剪试验　dynamic single shear test
动荷载　dynamic load
动机　motive, intention
动剪切模量　dynamic shear strength modulus
动接点　heel contact
动力车间　power room
动力触探试验　dynamic penetration test

动力电缆　power cable
动力黏度　dynamic viscosity
动力切断　power cut
动力三轴试验　dynamic triaxial test
动力水位　dynamic water level
动力特性试验　test for dynamic parameter
动力头式钻机　power head drilling rig
动力稳定机　dynamic track stabilizer
动力系数　coefficient of dynamic force
动力相似　dynamic similarity
动力黏滞系数　coefficient of kinetic viscosity
动能坡度　momentum gradient
动扭剪试验　dynamic torsional shear test
动强度　dynamic strength
动强度试验　dynamic strength test
动三轴试验　dynamic triaxial test
动水压力　residual/running pressure
动态　dynamic state
动态变形模量　dynamic deformation modulus
动态标识　dynamic sign
动态不平顺　irregularity of track under train load
动态参数识别　dynamic parameter identification
动态测试　drive test
动态穿孔　dynamic perforation
动态电阻应变仪　
　　dynamic resistance strain gauge
动态放大倍数　dynamical magnification
动态风险　dynamic risk
动态风压　dynamic wind pressure
动态管理　dynamic management
动态荷载　dynamic load
动态几何形位　dynamic track geometry
动态立体摄影　dynamic stereo photography
动态密封指数　dynamic seal index
动态挠度　dynamic deflection
动态设计　dynamic design
动态试验　dynamic test
动态试验线　running test track
动态速度曲线　dynamic train speed profile
动态抬升　dynamic uplift
动态投资　dynamic investment
动态投资回收期　
　　dynamic investment pay-back period
动态无功补偿装置　
　　dynamic reactive power compensator
动态性能　dynamic characteristic, dynamic performance, dynamic behavior
动态验收测试　dynamic acceptance test
动态应力　dynamic stress
动态质量　dynamic mass
动态主机配置协议　
　　dynamic host configuration protocol (DHCP)
动态作用　dynamic action
动弹模量测定仪　dynamic elastic modulus tester
动弹性模量　dynamic elasticity modulus
动稳定电流　dynamic stability current, rated peak withstand current
动物胶凝聚重量法　gravimetric method of animal glue
动应力　dynamic stress
动应力衰减比　attenuation ratio of dynamic stress
动员　mobilize, mobilization
动员费　mobilization fee, mobilization charges
动员预付款　mobilization advance
动载试验　dynamic loading test
动载性能　dynamic load performance
动作负载试验　operation duty test
动作杆　throw rod
动作计数器　operation counter
动作连接杆　operating rod for driving a switch
动作时间　switching time
冻拔石　frozen pulling stone
冻结　freeze
冻结层　freezing layer
冻结存款　blocked deposit
冻结法　freezing method
冻结货币　blocked currency
冻结接头　frozen rail joint
冻结结构土　frozen structure soil
冻结泥炭化土　peatificated permafrost
冻结强度　frozen strength
冻结深度　depth of frost
冻结温度　freezing temperature
冻结账户　blocked account, frozen account
冻结指数　freezing index
冻结资产　frozen assets
冻结资金　blocked fund
冻裂点　freezing breaking point
冻融　freezing-thawing
冻融分选　freeze-thaw sorting
冻融破坏　freezing-thawing damage
冻融侵蚀　freeze-thaw erosion
冻融侵蚀区　freeze-thaw erosion area
冻融蠕流　freeze-thaw creeping flow
冻融损失率　freezing-thawing loss rate
冻融损失率 L 或 Q　
　　freezing-thawing loss ratio L or Q
冻融循环　freezing-thawing cycle
冻深　frost depth
冻土　frozen soil
冻土导热系数　frozen soil thermal conductivity

冻土地貌　permafrost landform
冻土路基　permafrost subgrade
冻土区路基　subgrade in permafrost region
冻土融化圈　permafrost thawing circle
冻土融化压缩试验　thawing and compression test of frozen soil
冻土上限　permafrost table
冻土天然上限　natural permafrost table
冻土下限　permafrost base
冻土沼泽　permafrost swamp
冻土总含水率　total water content of frozen soil
冻胀　frost heave
冻胀等级　frost heave grade
冻胀分级　classification of frost heaving
冻胀力　frost heaving force
冻胀量　frost-heave capacity
冻胀率　frost heaving ratio
冻胀敏感性　sensitivity of frost heaving
冻胀丘　frost heaving mound
峒室爆破　chamber blasting
洞口　portal
洞口边仰坡　side and front slopes at tunnel portal
洞口缓冲结构　portal buffer structure
洞口投点　setting horizontal point of portal
洞门　portal
洞门墙　portal wall
洞内控制测量　controlling survey inside tunnel
洞室围岩变形监测　monitoring of deformation of surrounding rock
洞探　adit excavation, adit exploration
洞体　cave body
洞外控制测量　controlling survey outside tunnel
洞穴　cavern
洞穴堆积　cave deposit
洞轴　cave axis
斗车　tipper
斗淋　doline
斗式联合卸煤机　bucket combined coal unloader
斗式升降机　bucket elevator
斗式提升机　bucket elevator, skip elevator
斗式挖土机　bucket excavator
斗式装载机　bucket loader
抖动　jitter
抖振　buffeting
陡壁　steep wall
陡坎　scarp
陡立岩层　steep strata
陡坡路基　steep slope subgrade
陡倾岩层　deeply inclined strata
陡崖　cliff
豆状结构　pisolitic texture
逗留检测　loitering detection
毒品　drug
独家承包合同　monopoly contract
独家代理　exclusive agency, sole agency
独家代理人　exclusive agent, sole agent
独家经销　exclusive distribution
独家经销商　exclusive dealer, sole distributor
独家销售代理商　exclusive selling agent
独家专利权　exclusive patent right
独立保险人　independent insurer
独立承包商　independent contractor, separate contractor
独立磁盘冗余阵列　redundant array of independent disks(RAID)
独立代理人　independent agent
独立电源　independent power source
独立订约人　independent contractor
独立法人　separate legal entity
独立符合性审计　independent compliance audit
独立工程师　independent engineer
独立供电线　independent feeder
独立管理　standalone management
独立合同　separate contracts
独立和公正　independence and impartiality
独立会计师　independent accountant
独立基础　independent foundation
独立交会高程点　elevation point by independent intersection
独立理赔人　independent claim settling clerk
独立模型法区域网平差　block adjustment using independent-model method
独立审计　independent audit
独立一方　independent party
独立坐标系　independent coordinate system
独任仲裁员　sole arbitrator
独特方法　unique method
独销市场　exclusive market
独资　individual proprietorship
独资企业　solely foreign-owned enterprise, enterprise owned by sole investor
读卡器　card reader
渎职　malfeasance, dereliction of duty
渎职罪　offence of dereliction of duty, misconduct offense
堵门　block door
度盘　dial
渡槽　aqueduct
渡槽流水压力　pressure of water flow in aqueduct
渡船费　ferriage

渡轮	ferryboat
渡线	crossover
镀锌	galvanizing, zinc coating
镀锌铁皮	galvanized iron
镀锌铁丝	galvanized iron wire
端承桩	point bearing pile
端刺	end spine

端到端呼叫(连接)建立时间　end to end call connection establishment delay
端到端时延　end-to-end delay
端横梁　end transverse floorbeam
端口速率　port rate
端口运用台账　port distribution table
端口运用图(表)　port distribution diagram (table)
端墙　end wall
端站　terminal station
端子　terminal
端子排　terminal board
端子箱　terminal box
短波不平顺　short wave irregularity
短号码　short dialing codes
短加劲肋　short stiffener
短距离预报　short distance forecast
短链　short chainage, shortened chain
短量险　risk of shortage
短路　short circuit
短路电动力　short-circuit electrodynamic force
短路电流　short-circuit current
短路电流(持续)时间　duration of short-circuit current
短路故障　short-circuit fault
短路基　short subgrade
短路容量　short-circuit capacity
短路损耗　short-circuit loss
短路特性　short-circuit characteristic
短路阻抗　short-circuit impedance
短名单　short list
短期保险　short-term insurance
短期贷款　short-term loan, temporary loan
短期垫款　temporary advance
短期放款　money at call
短期合同　short-term contract
短期计划　short-term planning
短期流动资金　hot money
短期期票　short bill
短期同行拆借　money at call, call loan
短期投资　short-term investment, temporary investment, current investment
短期效应组合　combination of short-term action effects
短期信贷　short-term credit
短期银行贷款　current loan
短期债务　current debt, current liabilities, floating debt, short-term debt
短期租赁　short lease
短时制　temporary
短隧道　short tunnel
短纤非织造土工布　Synthetic staple fiber nonwoven geotextile
短纤化学黏合非织造土工布　Synthetic staple fiber chemical bonding nonwoven geotextile
短纤热黏非织造土工布　Synthetic staple fiber thermal bonding nonwoven geotextile
短纤维针织土工布　Synthetic staple fiber knitted geotextile
短纤针刺非织造土工布　Synthetic staple fiber needle-punched nonwoven geotextiles
短消息服务中心　short message service center(SMSC)
短溢装条款　allowance clause, more or less clause (M/L clause)
短暂设计状况　transient design state
段管线　depot track
段修　depot repair
段修率　rate of locomotive shed repair
段修循环系数　circulating factor of depot repairing
段中阻抗　mid-section impedance
断层　fault
断层带　fault zone
断层谷　fault valley
断层角砾岩　fault breccia
断层面　fault plane, fault surface
断层泥　fault gouge
断层破裂带　fault fractured zone
断层泉　fault spring
断层线　fault line
断层崖　fault scarp
断电释放　release after power-off
断缝　broken rail gap
断高　broken height
断轨保障　broken rail protection
断轨检查　broken rail detection
断轨检查灵敏度　broken rail detection sensitivity
断轨力　rail breaking force in CWR on bridge
断轨盲区　broken rail dead zone
断距　fault displacement
断口　fracture
断块地貌　fault block landform
断链　broken chain
断裂　fracture
断裂负荷　fracture load

断裂构造破碎带　shattered fault zone
断裂荷载　breaking load
断裂力学　mechanics of fracture
断裂破碎带　fracture zone
断裂韧度　fracture toughness
断裂伸长率　elongation at break
断裂延伸率　fracture elongation
断流器　circuit breaker
断路开关　circuit breaker
断路器　circuit breaker（CB）
断面　cross section
断面测量　cross-section survey
断面尺寸　section size
断面方　cut-fill volume evaluated based on average cross section
断面基线　base line of section
断面间距　section spacing
断面净空　transverse section
断面扫描　profile scanning
断（截）面图　sectional view
断面形式　section form
断盘　fault wall
断线　breakage, wire fracture
断言　assertion
断桩　broken pile
锻造　forge
堆放　stock pile
堆放层数　stacking layers
堆货场　freight storage yard
堆积　accumulate
堆积层滑坡　accumulation landslide
堆积地貌　accumulation landform
堆积阶地　accumulation terrace
堆积密度　apparent density
堆积平原　accumulation plain
堆料场　stock pile area, stockpile
堆码层数　stacking tier
堆石坝　rock-fill dam
堆塌　heap collapse
堆载预压　preloading with surcharge fill, surcharge preloading
对比　contrast
对策　countermeasure
对称道岔　symmetrical turnout, equilateral turnout
对承包商违约的反索赔　counterclaim for contractor's defaults
对等贸易　countertrade
对工程的损害　damage to works
对国内承包商的优惠　preference for domestic contractors
对国内制造商的优惠　preference for domestic manufacturers
对价　consideration
对角线差　diagonal deviation
对接　butt joint
对接接头　abutting joint
对进口货课税　lay duty on imports
对开信用证　reciprocal letter of credit
对开账户　back-to-back account
对流层延迟　troposphere delay
对外借贷　foreign borrowing
对外贸易　foreign trade, external trade
对外事务　external affairs
对物税　objective tax
对向单开道岔　facing single turnout
对向连接　opposite connection
对向重叠进路　route with overlapped section in the opposite direction
对象　object
对账　verification of account
对账单　bank statement, check sheet
对植　opposite planting
兑付支票　honour a cheque
兑换　exchange, convert, conversion
兑换价格　conversion price
兑换率　conversion rate, exchange rate, rate of exchange
兑现　cash
吨次费　tonnage-time fees
吨位（费）　tonnage
吨位税　tonnage duty（tax）
敦促　urge
墩　pier, pillar
墩帽　pier cap
墩身　pier shaft
墩台防撞　collision prevention for pier and abutment
墩台基础挖验　excavation of foundations of piers and abutments for inspection purpose
墩台基础钻探测量　drilling exploration of foundations of piers and abutments for inspection purpose
墩台拓宽加固法　strengthening method by pier/abutment widening
墩周冲淤　scouring and depositing around pier
趸船　wharf boat, pontoon, landing stage
盾构法　tunnelling by shield machine
盾环进尺　cycle length
多边合同　multilateral contract
多边合作　multilateral cooperation
多边结算　multilateral settlement

多边贸易	multilateral trade
多边清算	multilateral clearing
多边税收协定	multilateral tariff treaty
多边协定	multilateral agreement

多边形立体护坡网　polygon three-dimensional slope protection network

多边形平差	polygon adjustment
多边形屋架	polygonal top-chord roof truss
多边援助	multilateral aid
多冰冻土	ice-moderate permafrost
多波段图像	multiband image
多层矩形布置	multilayer rectangular arrangement

多层立体式候车室　multi-storey stereoscopic waiting room

| 多处理器 | multiprocessor |
| 多次覆盖(叠加) | multiple coverage (overlay) |

多次支付(等额现金流)　multiple payments (equal cash flow)

多次重复作用	repeated action
多次重合闸	multiple-shot reclosing
多道抗震设防	multiaspect seismic fortification
多点激振	multipoint excitation
多点控制单元(设备)	multipoint control unit (MCU)
多点位移计	multipoint displacement meter
多斗挖沟机	continuous bucket ditcher
多斗挖土机	multi-bucket excavator
多段厌氧处理	multistage anaerobic treatment
多方案报价法	multi-plan bidding
多方仲裁	multi-party arbitration
多光谱图像	multispectral image
多合同发包	multiple contracting
多合同招标	multiple bidding
多级架构	multi-level architecture
多级用能计量措施	multistage measuring instrument of energy consumption
多计算机切换器	Keyboard Video Mouse (KVM)
多井抽水试验	multiple-well pumping test
多孔混凝土	cell concrete
多孔砖	porous brick
多路径效应	multipath effect
多媒体	multimedia
多模光纤	multimode optical fiber
多年冻土人为上限	artificial permafrost table
多频信号显示器	multi-frequency signal display
多时像图像	multitemporal image
多式联运	multimodal transport
多数裁定原则	majority rule
多驾驶员通信	multi-driver communication
多塔楼结构	multi-tower structure
多特征脉冲	multi-feature pulse
多推双溜	multiple pushing and double rolling
多险种保险	multiple line insurance
多线桥	multi-track bridge
多线隧道	multiple-track tunnel
多协议BGP	MP-BGP Multi-Protocol BGP
多协议标记交换	Multi-Protocol Label Switching (MPLS)
多协议标签交换	Multi-Protocol Label Switching (MPLS)
多业务传送平台	Multi-Service Transport Platform (MSTP)
多优先级功能	Enhanced Multi-level Precedence and Pre-emption service (eMLPP)
多余观测	redundant observation
多遇地震	frequently occurred earthquake
多圆锥投影	polyconic projection
多种方式联运	multimodal transport
多种风险保险	multiple perils insurance
多重关税制	multiple tariff system
多转接段电路	circuit with multiple transit sections
躲避	dodge, evade, avoid
惰行	coasting

E

EXPRESS 语言的图形子集　Express-G
E 组填料　fill material of group E
讹传　misrepresentation
鹅卵石　cobble
额定的　nominal
额定电流　rated current
额定电压　rated voltage
额定峰值耐受电流　rated peak withstand current
额定负荷　rated load
额定工作压力　rated operating pressure
额定功率　rated power
额定关合电流　rated making current
额定荷载　nominal load
额定荷载利用系数　utilization factor of rated load
额定开断电流　rated breaking current
额定利率　nominal interest rate
额定量程　rated measuring range
额定流量　rated flow
额定马力　rated horsepower
额定容量　rated capacity
额定值　rated value
额外成本　extra cost, additional cost
额外的　extra, additional
额外费用　extra cost
额外费用索赔　claim for extra cost
额外服务　exceptional service
额外付款　additional payment
额外工作　extra work, additional work
额外建设成本　additional cost of construction
额外津贴　extra allowance, bonus
额外开支　extra charges (expenses)
额外利润　extra profit, premium returns
额外时间　extra time
扼流变压器　choke transformer
扼流线圈　choking coil
恶化　deteriorate, deterioration, exacerbate
恶劣天气　inclement weather, adverse weather
恶性通货膨胀　galloping inflation
恶性循环　vicious circle
恶意　in bad faith
恶意破坏　malicious damage
恩式黏度　Engler viscosity
鲕状粒岩的　oolitic
鲕状构造　oolitic structure
耳环杆　eye end rod
耳环悬式绝缘子　suspension insulator with eye end cap
耳墙　wing wall
耳墙式桥台　abutment with cantilevered retaining wall
二长岩　monzonite
二沉污泥　secondary sludge
二次搬运　double handling
二次变形模量　secondary deformation modulus
二次参数　secondary parameter
二次侧　low voltage side, secondary side
二次沉淀池　secondary settling tank
二次衬砌　secondary lining
二次电流　secondary side current
二次负荷　secondary side load
二次核定估算　production check estimate (PCE)
二次回风　secondary return air
二次回路　control circuit
二次接线　secondary wiring
二次设备　secondary side equipment, equipment at secondary side
二次污染　secondary pollution
二次系统　secondary side system
二次仪表　secondary instrument
二次支护　secondary support
二次装卸　double handling
二叠纪　Permian period
二叠系　Permian system
二级处理　secondary treatment
二级检修　second-level inspection
二级评价　second class environmental impact assessment

二级强化处理　secondary strengthening treatment
二级水源保护区
　　second class water conservation district
二甲酚橙分光光度法
　　xylenol orange spectrophotometry
二阶弹性分析　second order elastic analysis
二阶非线性分析　second order nonlinear analysis
二流商品　seconds
二手设备　second-hand equipment
二维码扫描枪　2D barcode scanner
二维条码票　2D barcode ticket
二显示自动闭塞　two-aspect automatic blocking
二线接收电平　two-wire reception level
二氧化硅　silicon dioxide
二氧化氯消毒法　chlorine dioxide disinfection
二氧化钛含量　content of titanium dioxide
二氧化碳含量　content of carbon dioxide
二氧化碳灭火剂
　　carbon dioxide fire extinguishing agent
二氧化碳灭火系统
　　carbon dioxide fire-extinguishing system
二氧化物含量　content of dioxide
二乙基二硫代氨基甲酸银光度法　silver-diethyldi-thiocarbamin acid spectrophotometry
2×2取2冗余结构
　　double 2-vote-2 redundant structure
Ⅱ类接入节点　Class Ⅱ access node
Ⅱ型轨道板预制场　precast yard for Ⅱ type track slab

E

F

发包策略　contracting strategy
发布　issue, issuance
发车表示器　departure indicator
发车表示器电路　departure indicator circuit
发车进路　departure route
发车进路信号机　route signal for departure
发车进路与区间状态联锁关系测试
　　test of departure route and section state interlocking relation
发车信号　departure signal
发车信号机　departure signal
发电　power generation
发电厂　power house (plant)
发电轨道车　power generating rail car
发电机　electric generator, generator
发电机组　generator set
发电能力　generating capacity
发电站　power station, generating station
发电走行两用车
　　self-propelled power generating car
发光二极管　light emitting diode(LED)
发光强度　luminous intensity
发光效能　luminous efficacy
发光性　luminescence
发函日期　date of letter
发货　shipping, shipment
发货单　shipping document, bill of sale, dispatch list
发货港　port of discharge
发货国　country of dispatch
发货清单　shipping list, invoice
发货人　consignor, consigner, vendor, sender
发件人　addresser
发料点　material departure point
发码器　code transmitter
发盘　offer, make an offer
发盘人　offerer, offeror
发票　invoice
发票副本　duplicate invoice
发票价值　invoice value
发热电缆　heating cable
(声波)发射　excite
发射电极　current electrode
发生　occur, occurrence, happen
发生器　generator
发送　forward, dispatch
发送光功率　transmitting optical power
发文簿　table of distribution
发薪日　payday, pay date
发信电平　transmitting level
发信人　addresser
发行　issue, publish
发展　develop, development, expand, grow
发展基金　development fund
发展论坛　development forum
发展银行　development bank
罚金　fine, forfeit, penal sum, pecuniary penalty, forfeiture
罚金条款　penalty clause
罚款　financial penalty, penalty, levy a fine
阀控式密封铅酸蓄电池
　　valve-regulated sealed lead-acid battery
阀式避雷器　valve type arrester
阀式轨道电路　valve type track circuit
筏形基础　raft foundation
法案　act, bill
法典　code
法定　statute
法定保险　legal insurance
法定贬值　official devaluation
法定代表
　　statutory representative, legal representative
法定代表权　right of legal representation
法定代理人
　　legal representative, legal agent, statutory agent
法定单位　legal entity
法定的　lawful, legal

法定负债	legal liability
法定股本	authorized capital stock
法定汇率	official exchange rate, official rate
法定货币	lawful money, legal tender
法定价格	official price
法定假日	legal holiday, official holiday
法定利率	official rate
法定赔偿	legal compensation
法定清算	legal liquidation
法定权利	statutory right, legal right
法定权益按揭	legal mortgage
法定身份	legal capacity
法定声明	statutory declaration
法定税率	statutory tax rate
法定所有权	legal title
法定文件	statutory instruments
法定义务	statutory duty
法定重量	legal weight
法定资本	legal capital (value), capital authorized
法定资产	legal assets
法定资格	legal title
标准方程	normal equation
法官	judge
法官席	tribunal
法规	code, statute, legislation
法规要求	code requirement
法截弧曲率半径	curvature radius of normal section arc
法拉第笼	Faraday cage
法兰	flange
法兰连接	flange connection
法令	act, decree, statute, ordinance
法律	laws
法律冲突	conflict of laws
法律的	legal
法律的解释	interpretation of law
法律顾问	counsel, legal adviser
法律管辖区	jurisdiction
法律规定	legal provisions, legal rules
法律和当地惯例要求的其他保险	other insurance required by laws and local practice
法律界	law circle
法律上的推定	presumption of law
法律身份	legal standing
法律事实	legal fact
法律释义	legal construction
法律诉讼程序	legal proceedings
法律文件	legal document
法律效力	force of law
法律行为	legal act
法律依据	legal basis, merits
法律责任	legal liability
法律制裁	legal sanction
法律咨询	legal consultation
法人	artificial person, legal person, judicial person
法人单位	legal entity, impersonal entity
法人实体	legal entity
法人团体	body corporate
法人业主	corporate owner
法人资格	legal personality
法庭	court, tribunal
法庭费用	court fee, adjudication fee
法系	legal system
法向冻胀力	normal frost-heave force
法向拉力	normal tension
法向应力	normal stress
法院	court, law court
砝码	balance weight, weight
翻车机	tippler
翻斗车	dumper, skip car
翻斗式雨量传感器	tipping bucket rainfall sensor
翻浆冒泥	mud-pumping
翻译	translate, translation, translator, interpretation, interpreter
繁荣	boom
反S形构造	reversed S-shaped structure
反避税措施	anti-avoidance measures
反驳	refute, contradict, disproof, contravene
反补贴税	countervailing duty
反铲挖沟机	trench hoe
反铲挖土机	backhoe
反常贬值	abnormal depreciation, special discount
反常费用	abnormal cost
反常利润	abnormal profit
反担保	back bond
反担保函	counter guarantee
反到	reverse receiving
反定位	push-off
反发	reverse departure
反购	counterpurchase
反光镜	retroreflector
反击	back flashover
反控诉	countercharge
反馈	feedback
反力	reaction
反力墙	reaction wall
反力装置	counter-force device
反立体镜	pseudo-stereoscope
反滤层	inverted filter, reverse filter
反面证据	proof to the contrary

反倾销税　anti-dumping duty, countervailing duty
反射比　reflectance ratio
反射波　reflected wave
反射波法　reflection method
反射镜　reflector
反射体　reflector
反射眩光　glare by reflection, reflected glare
反渗透法　reverse osmosis process (RO)
反诉　counterclaim
反索赔　counterclaim
反逃税措施　anti-evasion measures
反托拉斯法　anti-trust law
反驼峰方向　reverse-hump direction
反位接点　reverse contact
反位锁闭　reverse locking
反向贸易　countertrade
反向曲线　reverse curve
反向容许信号
　　permissive signal for reverse direction
反向属性　inverse attribute
反向转极值　reverse pole-changing value
反循环旋转钻机　reverse circulation drilling rig
反压护道　loading berm
反压力　back pressure
反压平台　back-pressure platform
反演分析　inverse analysis
反义居先原则　contra proferentum
反应谱　response spectrum
反应谱特征周期
　　characteristic period of response spectrum
反之亦然　vice versa
反转片　reversal film
反装　left-handed machine
返工　reworking
返工成本　rework cost
返还保留金　release of retention money
返还系数　release factor
返回　return
返销　buy-back
返销协议　buy-back agreement
返修　repair
犯法　offence
犯罪　convict, crime, commit a crime
范例　example
范围　scope, limit, range, gauge
范围变更　scope change
范围定义　scope definition
范围核实　scope verification
范围说明　scope statement
方案　scheme, plan, program, proposal

方案设计　conceptual design, scheme design
方案设计阶段　schematic design phase
方案设计水平年　target year of design
方案图　scheme drawing
方差—协方差传播律
　　variance-covariance propagation law
方差—协方差矩阵(又称"积差阵")
　　variance covariance matrix (also known as "variance-covariance matrix")
方法　method, means, way, approach
方格法　square method
方格网点　square grid point
方解石　calcite
方里网　square grid
方铅矿　galena, gelenite
方位　locality, direction
方位角　azimuth
方位角闭合差　closure error of azimuth
方位角条件　azimuth condition
方位角中误差　mean square error of azimuth
方位线　orienting line
方位元素　orientation element
方向电源　directional traffic power source
方向附合导线　direction-annexed traverse
方向观测法　method of direction observation
方向角　direction angle
方向线交会法　method of traverse line intersecting
方向转接器　directional switch
方枕器　tie respacer
方正轨枕　tie respacing
芳香分　aromatics of asphalt
防爆　explosion proof
防爆波电缆井
　　anti-explosion wave electric cable well
防爆波化粪池
　　anti-explosion wave digestion tank
防爆地漏　anti-explosion floor drain
防爆电气设备
　　explosion-proof electric apparatus
防爆罐　anti-explosion tank
防爆墙　blastproof partition wall
防爆区　explosion-proof area
防爆毯　anti-explosion blanket
防波堤　breakwater
防潮　moisture proof
防潮层　damp-proof coating
防尘　dust-proof
防尘网检查清洗
　　dust screen inspection and cleaning
防窜中心锚结　anti-creeping device

防倒塌棚架	collapse-proof shed
防冻	anti-freezing
防毒通道	gas protection passage
防堵性	block resistance property
防断中心锚结	anti-breakage midpoint anchor
防范索赔	defense/prevention against claim
防风固沙	wind break and sand fixation
防风固沙工程	wind break and sand fixation works
防风固沙林	wind break and sand fixation forest
防风拉线	windstay
防风走廊路基	subgrade in anti-wind corridor
防腐	anticorrosive
防腐剂	preservative substance, corrosion preventive
防腐蚀措施	anticorrosion measures
防腐蚀的	corrosion-proof
防腐蚀强化措施	intensified anti-corrosion measures
防涸地漏	anti-dry floor drain
防洪功能	flood control function
防洪河段	flood control reach
防洪排导工程	flood control and draining project
防洪水位	flood control level
防护变压器	protective transformer
防护措施	protective measures
防护带	protective belt
防护单元	protective unit
防护道岔	protective switch
防护道岔测试	protective turnout test
防护等级	levels of protection
防护钢管	protective steel pipe
防护工程	protection works
防护涵洞	protection culvert
防护栏杆	guard railing, safety railing
防护门	protection door
防护墙	protection wall
防护区段	protected section
防护套管	protection tube
防护栅栏	protection fence
防护罩	protective cover
防滑地面	anti-slip floor
防滑扣件	skid resistant fastener
防化通信值班室	communication duty room of chemical defense
防回流装置	backflow preventer
防火	fireproof
防火阀	fireproof valve
防火费用	cost of fire protection
防火风管	fireproof air duct
防火封堵	fire stopping
防火隔墙	fireproof partition
防火间距	fireproof distance
防火净距	fire separation clearance
防火门	fireproof door
防火墙	firewall
防火水幕带	fire-fighting water curtain belt
防火套管	fireproof casing
防火性能	fire protecting performance/fire resistance
防静电地板	anti-static floor
防空洞	air-raid shelter
防雷	lightning protection
防雷保安器	lightning arrestor
防雷变压器	lightning-proof transformer
防雷地线	lightning protection earth wire
防雷分线柜	lightning protection cable cabinet
防雷设备	lightning protection equipment
防雷箱	lightning protection box
防雷元件	lightning protection components
防雷元件测试仪	lightning protection component tester
防爬器	anti-creeper, rail anchor
防爬支撑	anti-creep strut
防沙体系	sand control system
防渗	seepage-proof
防渗护面	membrane
防渗铺盖	impervious blanket
防渗墙	cut-off, diaphragm
防暑降温	workplace temperature control
防水	waterproof
防水板	waterproofing sheet
防水层	waterproof layer
防水隔离层	waterproofing insulation layer
防水工	waterproofing worker
防水混凝土	waterproof concrete
防水基层	waterproof base course layer
防水剂	water-repellent admixture
防水卷材	waterproof coiled material
防水林	forest against flood
防水密封材料	waterproof seal material
防水抹面	waterproofing plaster coat
防水透气材料	water-proof and vapor-permeable material
防水涂料	waterproof coating
防水性	waterproofness
防锈材料	rust-resisting material
防锈的	antirust
防锈剂	corrosion preventive
防锈漆	anticorrosive paint
防烟	smoke prevention
防烟分区	smoke bay

防烟楼梯间　smoke proof staircase
防雨　rain proof
防灾通风　disaster prevention ventilation
防灾系统　disaster prevention system
防振锤　damper, stockbridge damper
防震挡块　shockproof block
防震缝　seismic joint
防震架　shock absorber base
防撞破凌　breaking up ice run to avoid collision
防坠安全器　anti-falling safety device
妨碍　interfere, interference, obstruct, objection, impede
妨害　nuisance
妨害失效　obstructive failure
房产税　building tax
房地产　real estate, real property, property assets
房地产公司　property company
房间空气调节器　room air conditioner
房屋检测人员　building inspector
房屋建筑　construction of buildings
房屋建筑安全评估　housing construction safety assessment
房屋建筑工程　building construction engineering
房屋建筑结构安全　structural safety of building
房屋建筑使用安全　serviceability safety of building
房屋界线　building line
仿真模拟　simulation
访问控制　access control
放电　discharge
放电电流　discharge current
放电管　discharge tube
放电间隙　discharge gap
放电器　discharger
放电容量　discharge capacity
放电时间　discharge time, time of discharge
放电线圈　discharging coil
放款　disbursement
放慢速度　slow down
放气阀　bleed valve
放弃　disclaim, waive
放弃合同　abandonment of contract, repudiation of contract
放弃权利　abandonment of right, waive one's right
放弃权利者　releasor
放弃上诉　abandonment of appeal
放弃索赔　release claim
放弃索赔权　waive right of claim, abandonment of claim
放弃条款　waiver clause
放弃责任　disclaimer of responsibility
放弃者　disclaimer
放射强度　intensity of radioactivity
放射性测井　radioactivity logging
放射性勘探　radioactivity prospecting
放射性探测法　radioactive detection method
放射性污染　radioactive contamination
放射状　radiated
放渗　seepage
放线　paying out
放线装置　unreeling device, decoiling device, stringing device
放样　setting out
放样测量　setting-out survey
放置　lay
飞车　run away
飞模　flying form
非安全电路　non-vital circuit
非标准圆锥台体试件　non-standard circular cone specimen
非常站控　emergency station control
非承压锅炉　non-bearing boiler
非承重墙　nonbearing wall
非传统水源　non-traditional water source
非弹性变形　non-elastic deformation
非等温射流　non-isothermal jet
非地形摄影测量　non-topographic photogrammetry
非电化股道　non-electrified track
非电化线路　non-electrified line
非定期保证　unlimited duration guarantee
非法的　illegal, unlawful
非法合同　illegal contract
非法解雇　wrongful dismissal
非法利润　illegal profit
非法码字　invalid code
非法途径　back door
非法行为　illegality
非法支付　illegal payment, illicit payment
非工作支　outgoing contact line
非货币性负债　non-monetary liabilities
非货币性资产　non-monetary assets
非机械化驼峰　non-mechanized hump
非集中道岔　locally operated switch
非集中联锁　non-centralized interlocking
非几何信息　non-geometric information
非价格准则　non-price criteria
非碱活性骨料　non-alkali-active aggregate
非接触测量　non-contact measurement
非接触量测　non-contact measurement
非接触式 IC 卡　non-contact IC card

非接触式卡　contactless card
非结构构件抗震设计
　　seismic design of non-structural element
非结构节理　nonstructural joint
非结合水　unbound water
非金属材料风管　nonmetallic air duct
非金属性短路　non-metallic short circuit
非紧坡地段　section of insufficient grade
非进路调车　shunting operation without interlocking
非进路调车电路　non-route shunting circuit
非经常性项目　extraordinary item
非晶质结构　amorphous texture
非晶质体　amorphous body, non-crystalline
非竞争性报价　non-competitive bid
非绝缘锚段关节　non-insulated overlap
非绝缘转换(支)柱　non-insulated transition mast
非联锁道岔　non-interlocking switch
非联锁区　non-interlocked zone
非量测摄影机　non-metric camera
非流动资金　illiquid fund
非贸易收入　non-trade receipt
非平衡传输线　unbalanced transmission line
非屏蔽双绞线　unsheilded twisted paired(UTP)
非破损检验　non-destructive test
非设备集中站　non equipment centralized station
非渗水土　impervious soil
非渗水土路基　impermeable soil subgrade
非生产性建设项目
　　non-productive construction project
非贴现票据　non-discountable bill
非完整井　partially penetrating well
非稳定流　unsteady flow
非稳定流抽水试验　unsteady flow pumping test
非稳态传热　unsteady-state heat transfer
非稳态噪声　non-steady noise
非物质资本　immaterial capital
非线性失真　non-linear distortion
非线性误差　non-linear error
非泄流轮对　non-leakage flow wheel set
非营利性项目　nonprofit-oriented project
非营业费用　non-operating expenses
非营业利润　unearned profit
非营业收入
　　non-operating income, non-operating revenue
非营业性支出　non-operating outlay
非运用车系数　coefficient of cars not in service
非正常成本　abnormal cost
非正常利润　abnormal profit
非正常收益　abnormal gains
非正常损失　abnormal loss

非正式合同　informal contract
非正式记录　informal record, memorandum
非正式协定　informal agreement
非正式协议　unofficial agreement, agreement of understanding
非正式协助　informal assistance
非自复式按钮　stick button
非自重湿陷性黄土
　　non-self-weight collapsible loess
菲涅尔区　Fresnel zone
废标　rejection of all bids
废除　annul, rescind, withdraw
废除合同　rescission of contract
废除条款　defeasance clause
废除原合同　abrogate the original contract
废轨　scrap rail
废料处理　waste disposal
废气　waste gas
废弃财产　abandoned property
废弃地　waste land
废弃工程　abandoned works
废弃物　debris, rubbish, garbage
废弃资产　abandoned assets
废热　waste heat
废水　wastewater
废约　invalidate the contract
废渣　slag muck
沸溢性油品　boiling spill oil
沸煮法　boiling method
费率　rate
费用　cost, charge, expense, fee
费用变更　change in cost
费用补偿　cost reimbursement
费用超支　cost overrun
费用分摊　expense allocation
费用估算　cost estimate
费用和工期延长(EOT)的索赔
　　claims for payment and / or EOT
费用和开支　fees and expenses
费用计划　cost planning
费用监测　cost monitoring
费用率　expense ratio
费用清单　statement of expenses
费用指数　cost index
分包　subcontracting
分包工程费　cost of subcontracted works
分包供货商　sub-supplier
分包合同　subcontract
分包合同包　subcontract package
分包商　subcontractor

分包商的违约　default of subcontractor
分包商的误期　delays by subcontractor
分贝　decibel
分辨力　resolution, resolution capacity
分辨率　resolution
分标　bid division
分布电容　distributed capacitance
分布钢筋　distribution reinforcement, distribution bar
分布荷载　distributed load
分布式　distributed
分布式拒绝服务　distributed deny-of-service (DDoS)
分步成本计算法　process costing
分步收益表　multiple-step income statement
分部标定法　sectional calibration method
分部工程　part of works, divisional works
分部工程的接收　taking over parts
分层抽水试验　stratified pumping test
分层度　layering degree
分层空气调节　stratified air conditioning
分层碾压　layer-wise rolling and compaction
分层铺垫　layered bedding
分层填筑　layered filling
分层填筑高度　height of layered filling
分层总和法　layer-wise summation method
分插复用器　add-drop multiplexer (ADM)
分场分束供电　swtiching groups feeding
分场供电　switching groups feeding
分贷　relending
分担　share, contribution
分担差价　absorb the price difference, share the price difference
分担风险　share risks
分度值　division value
分段后退式注浆　segmented retrograde grouting
分段绝缘器　section insulator
分段前进式注浆　segmented advance grouting
分段压水试验　sectional water pump-in test
分段装置(电分段装置)　electrical sectioning device
分发　distribution
分割区段　cut section
分公司　branch, division, affiliate, subsidiary company, branch office
分光光度比浊法　spectrophotometric turbidimetry method
分光光度计　spectrophotometer
分合闸电流　making and breaking current
分户热计量　household heat metering
分户账　ledger

分级堆放　graded stockpiling
分级费率　class rate
分级计量　graded measuring
分级检验　classified inspection
分拣区　sorting area
分接抽头　tap changer
分接电压　tapping voltage
分解温度　decomposition temperature
分界　demarcation
分界线　boundary
(各类地质结构构造的)分界线　demarcation line
分开式扣件　indirect fastening
分类日记账　ledger journal
分类账　ledger
分类账表格　ledger form
分类账科目　account as recorded in a ledger
分类折旧　classified depreciation
分类折旧法　group method of depreciation
分离度　degree of separation
分离式钢柱　separated steel column
分料器法　distributor method
分流堤　water-dividing dyke
分流制　separate system
分录　journal entry
分录簿　journal
分录凭单　journal voucher
分路　shunting
分路不良　defective shunting
分路残压　shunting residual voltage
分路残压超标　excessive residual voltage for branching
分路道岔　branch switch
分路电阻　shunting resistance
分路电阻超标　excessive resistance for branching
分路灵敏度　shunting sensitivity
分路死区　shunting dead zone
分路效应　shunting effect
分路状态　shunting state
分年度投资表　annual investment schedule
分年度投资额　annual investment amount
分年度资金供应量　annual funding amount
分凝冰　segregated ice
分配额　amount allocated
分批成本单　job cost sheet
分批成本预算法　batch costing
分批法　job lot method
分批交货　delivery in instalment
分批预算　batch budgeting
分批装运　installment shipment, partial shipment
分坡平段　level grade between opposite gradients
分期偿付计划　amortization schedule

分期偿还	amortization
分期偿还贷款	amortization loan, amortizing loan
分期偿还抵押贷款	amortized mortgage loan
分期偿还率	amortization rate
分期偿还条件	terms of redemption
分期分批	installment
分期付款	installment, pay by installments
分期购买	installment buying / hire / purchase
分期合同	installment contract
分期汇票	bill payable by installments
分期销售	installment sale
分期支付	payment on account, installment
分汽缸	steam distribution header
分区	partition
分区插播	zoning broadcast
分区防水	partitioning waterproofing
分区兼开闭所	combination of TSP and SP
分区两管制水系统	zoning two-pipe water system
分区所	track sectioning post (TSP), track sectioning cabin (TSC)
分散发电	distributed power generation
分散构造	decentralized structure
分散式串联电容补偿装置	compensator with decentralised series capacitors
分散性黏土	dispersive clay
分散自律调度集中系统	decentralized and autonomous CTC system
分散自律控制	decentralized and autonomous control
分散自律约束条件	decentralized and autonomous constraints
分输	offtake
分束供电	switching groups feeding
分水岭	watershed, water divide
分水器	water separator
分摊保险	contributing insurance
分摊成本	allocate cost
分摊价值	contribution value
分摊数额	apportionment
分摊条款	share clause
分体式空气调节器	split air conditioner
分位值	fractile
分析纯	analytical reagent (AR)
分析价	analysis price
分析筛	analysis sieve
分析天平	analytical balance
分析指标	analysis index
分线盘	distributing terminal board
分线箱	distribution box
分相绝缘器	phase break device
分相区	neutral zone, dead zone
(列控系统)分相区	non-energized section
分向电缆盒	cable branching terminal box
分项发包合同	separate contract
分项工程	item of works, subdivisional works
分项价格	itemized price, breakdown price
分项说明	description of items
分项系数	partial factor
分项系数表达式	expression of partial factor
分项系数设计方法	partial factor design method
分销	distribution
分销网	distribution network
分行	affiliate bank
分选机	separator, sizer, grader
分押	submortgage
分样器	riffle sampler, sample splitter
分闸回路	opening circuit
分闸时间	opening time, breaking time
分闸线圈	opening coil, breaking coil
分支并联跳线	branching parallel jumper
分支机构	branch affiliate
分支接线	branch connection
分支结线	branch connection
分支手套	breakout boot
分中心	branch center
分转向角	auxiliary deflection angle
分子缔合	molecular association
分子吸水率	molecular water absorption ratio
分组传送网	Packet Transport Network (PTN)
分组观测	grouped observation
分组交换	packet switching
分组控制	packet control
分组域	packet switched domain
酚的质量浓度	mass concentration of phenol
酚类	phenols
酚醛胶泥	phenolic mastic
酚酞指示剂	phenolphthalein indicator
粉尘	dust
粉尘采样仪	dust sampler
粉尘含量	dust content
粉尘浓度	dust concentration
粉粒	silt grain
粉煤灰	fly ash
粉煤灰硅酸盐水泥	Portland-fly ash cement
粉末活性炭吸附	powdered activated carbon adsorption
粉喷桩	powder jet mixing pile
粉砂	silty sand
粉砂岩	siltstone
粉砂质黏土	silty clay

粉砂质土　silty soil
粉砂状　aleuritic
粉体喷射搅拌桩　powder injection mixing pile
粉毡　powder surfaced asphalt felt
粪便污水　fecal sewage
丰水期　high-water period
风　wind
风杯式风速风向传感器
　　cup-type wind speed and direction sensor
风成的　aeolian
风成黄土　aeolian loess
风城　wind-erosion castle
风道　air duct
风动凿岩机　pneumatic rock drill
风洞　wind tunnel
风干土　air-dried soil
风镐　air pick, pneumatic pick
风管吊架　air duct hanger
风管路调压设备　air pipeline pressure governor
风管系统　air duct system
风管支架　air duct support
风荷载　wind load
风荷载体形系数　drag coefficient of wind load, drag factor of wind load
风荷载阻力系数　drag coefficient of wind, drag factor of wind load
风化　weathering
风化程度　weathering degree
风化带　weathering zone
风化节理　weathering joint
风化颗粒　weathered particles
风化壳　weathering crust
风化破碎带　shattered weathered zone
风化系数　weathering coefficient
风化岩石　weathered rock
风化作用　weathering
风机过滤器单元　fan filter unit(FFU, FMU)
风机盘管机组　fan-coil unit
风积　aeolian deposit
风积地貌　aeolian landform
风积沙　aeolian sands
风积土　eolian soil
风级　wind scale
风季　wind season
风冷　air cooling
风冷机组　air-cooled unit
风冷式冷凝器　air-cooled condenser
风力　wind force
风力等级　wind force/ wind power
风力侵蚀　wind scale

风量　blowing rate
风流偏角　drift angle
风玫瑰图　wind rose diagram
风偏　wind deflection
风沙地区路基
　　subgrade in wind-blown sand regions
风沙流　sand flow
风沙区　dust bowl
风扇　fan
风蚀　wind erosion
风蚀残丘　deflation unaka
风蚀城堡　wind-erosion castle
风蚀地貌　wind-erosion landform
风蚀谷　wind valley
风蚀蘑菇　aeolian mushroom
风蚀盆地　blowout basin
风蚀强度　wind erosion intensity
风蚀洼地　deflation hollow
风俗习惯　custom, manners and customs
风速　wind velocity, wind speed
(通风)风速　air speed
风速风向传感器　wind speed and direction sensor
风速风向计　wind direction and speed meter, anemometrograph
风速监测报警　wind speed monitoring alarm
风险　risk
风险保费　risk premium
风险辨识　identification of risks
风险承担者　risk bearer
风险处理　risk treatment
风险的分离　isolation of risk
风险登记　risk registration
风险等级　risk grade
风险等级划分　risk rating
风险度　degree of risk
风险分担
　　allocation of risks, risk allocation, risk sharing
风险分级　risk ranking
风险分散　distribution of risks, risk reduction, diversification of risk, exposure diversification
风险分摊　risk apportionment
风险分析　risk analysis
风险概率分析　risk probability analysis
风险估计　risk estimation
风险管理　risk management
风险规避　risk avoidance
风险合同　risk contract
风险记录单　risk register
风险监测　risk monitoring
风险监控　risk monitoring and control

风险减轻　risk mitigation
风险减少　risk reduction
风险接受准则　risk acceptance criteria
风险控制　risk control
风险类别　risk category
风险累积　accumulation of risk
风险利用　risk speculation
风险赔偿　indemnity for risk
风险评估　risk assessment
风险评级　risk rating
风险评价　risk evaluation
风险识别　risk identification
风险事故　peril
风险事件　risk event
风险数据库　risk database
风险投资　venture investment
风险型工程管理模式　at-risk CM
风险意识　sense of risks
风险因素　risk factor
风险应对计划　risk response plan
风险责任的起期　attachment of risk
风险指标体系　risk index system
风险转移
　　passing of the risk, risk deflection, risk transfer
风险准备金　risk allowance
风险自留　risk retention
风向　wind direction
风向风频玫瑰图
　　rose diagram of wind direction and wind speed
风向频率　frequency of wind direction
风雪流　snow-bearing wind, snow-driving wind
风压　wind pressure
风压高度变化系数
　　height variation coefficient of wind pressure
风压钳夹式减速器　pneumatic clamp retarder
风压重力式减速器　pneumatic gravity-like reducer
风压钻进　air pressure drilling
风影区　wind shade
风振　wind vibration
风振系数　wind vibration coefficient
风钻　pneumatic drill
风嘴　wind fairing
封闭防水　sealing water proof
封闭施工　enclosed construction
封闭式声屏障
　　enclosed sound barrier / enclosed noise barrier
封闭式市场　closed market
封边模板　gap sealing formwork
封端混凝土　blocking concrete
封锚　anchorage sealing

封锁　close up
封装模型　package model
峰顶　hump crest
峰顶净平台　net platform at hump crest
峰顶跨道岔铺面
　　cross-turnout pavement at hump crest
峰顶联结员室　couper's cabin at hump crest
峰顶平台　hump crest platform
峰峰值　peak to peak value
峰高　hump crest height
峰林地形　peak forest terrain
峰前到达场　pre-hump crest receiving yard
峰丘　peak hill
峰值　crest value, peak value
峰值强度　peak strength
蜂鸣器　buzzer
蜂窝　honeycomb
蜂窝结构　honeycomb structure
否认合同有效　repudiate the contract
弗拉斯脆点
　　Fraass bursting point, Fraass breaking point
伏安特性　volt-ampere characteristics
扶壁式挡土墙　counterfort retaining wall
扶手　hand rail, rail
服务范围　scope of services
服务费　service charge
服务GPRS支持节点
　　serving GPRS support node (SGSN)
服务合同　contract for service, service contract
服务器　server
服务协议书　service agreement
服务质量　quality of service(QoS)
氟含量　content of fluorine
氟化物　fluoride
浮标水位计　buoy water level gauge
浮称法　floating weighing method
浮充　floating charge
浮充充电　floating charge
浮充电流　floating charge current
浮充电压　floating charge voltage
浮充供电　floating charge power supply
浮动工资　wage in sliding scale
浮动汇率　floating exchange rate
浮动价格　sliding price
浮动价格合同　fluctuating price contract
浮动利率　floating interest rate
浮动利率票据　floating rate note (FRN)
浮动密封　floating seal
浮动时间　slack time, float time
浮力　buoyancy

浮码头　landing stage
浮桥　float bridge, pontoon bridge, floating bridge
浮时　float time
浮式沉井基础　floating caisson foundation
浮式起重机　floating crane
浮岩　pumice
浮游测标　gliding mark
浮运架桥法　bridge erection by floating crane method
浮重度　buoyant unit weight
符合进度表　compliance with a schedule
符合性投标　responsive bid
符山石　idocrase, vesuvianite
幅频曲线　amplitude-frequency curve
幅频特性　amplitude vs frequency characteristic
幅值　amplitude
辐流沉淀池　radial flow settling tank
辐射变换　radiation transformation
辐射采暖　radiant heating
辐射井　radial well
辐射井出水量　radiant well yield
辐射强度　radiation intensity
辐射照度　irradiance
辐射状构造　radial structure
福费廷交易　Forfeiting
福利　welfare, tip, gratuity
福利费　welfare benefits, welfare expenses
福利基金　welfare funds
抚恤金　pension
辅修　auxiliary repair
辅助保护　auxiliary protection.
辅助表达方式　secondary presentation methods
辅助材料　auxiliary materials
辅助承力索　auxiliary messenger wire
辅助道路　service road
辅助调车场　auxiliary marshalling yard
辅助墩　auxiliary pier
辅助工资　supplementary wage
辅助轨　auxiliary rail
辅助回路　auxiliary circuit
辅助记录　subsidiary record
辅助开关　auxiliary switch
辅助坑道　construction adit, service gallery
辅助母线　auxiliary bus bar
辅助热源　assistant heat source
辅助人员　support personnel
辅助设备　auxiliary equipment
辅助设施　auxiliary facility
辅助生产设施　auxiliary operation facilities
辅助收益　ancillary benefits
辅助提示测试　auxiliary prompt test
辅助箱场　auxiliary container yard
辅助眼　driving hole
辅助账簿　auxiliary book
辅助账户　subsidiary account
辅助证据　secondary evidence
腐蚀　corrosion
腐蚀环境　corrosion environment
腐蚀性　corrosiveness
腐殖土　humus soil
付还　pay back
付款　payment
付款保函　payment guarantee
付款程序　disbursement procedure
付款代理人　paying agent
付款地点　place of payment
付款国　country of payment
付款后交货　cash before delivery (CBD)
付款计划表　schedule of payment
付款交单　document against payment (D/P)
付款交货　cash and delivery, delivery against payment, delivery on payment
付款结算　settlement by payment
付款期限　prompt
付款清单　bill of payment, paying list
付款人　drawee, payer
付款日　due date (pay day)
付款申请　application for payment, requisition for money (payment)
付款提示　presentment for payment
付款条件　terms of payment
付款通知　advice of payment, payment order, bill of credit
付款信用证　payment credit
付款延误　delayed payment
付款银行　paying bank
付款证据　evidence of payments
付款证明　evidence of payment, certificate for payment
付款证书　payment certificate
付讫　paid off
付讫支票　canceled check, paid check
付清　pay off, take up, pay in full, clear a bill
付清本息　pay off the principal and interest
付清的　paid-off
付息日　interest payment date
付现　pay cash
付现成本　out-of-pocket cost
付现费用　out-of-pocket expenses
负担损失　bear a loss
负地形　negative relief

负荷　load
负荷均分系统　load equipartition system
负荷开关　load switch
负荷率　load rate
负荷容量　load capacity
负荷试验线　load test track
负摩阻力　negative skin friction
负片　negative film
负视速度法　negative apparent velocity method
负水头　negative hydraulic head
负现金流量　negative cash flow
负序　negative sequence
负序补偿度　negative sequence compensation degree
负序电流　negative sequence current
负序分量　negative sequence component
负序增量　negative sequence current increment
负压区　negative pressure area
负压吸蚀作用　negative pressure suction erosion
负延时　negative delay
负硬度　negative hardness
负载均衡器　load balancer
负载损耗　on-load loss
负增长　negative growth
负债　liabilities
负债净额　net liabilities
负债人　debtor
负债账户　negative assets account, liabilities account
负债准备金　liability reserves
负债资产比　debt to equity ratio
负债总额　total liabilities
负资产账户　negative assets account
附参数条件平差
　　condition adjustment with parameters
附带担保　collateral warranty
附带费用　incidental expenses
附带服务　incidental service
附带事件　incidental
附带收入　incidental revenue
附带损害　collateral damages
附带条件　side conditions
附带条件贷款　tied loan
附费率表的总价
　　lump-sum price with schedule of rates
附工程量表的总价
　　lump-sum price with bill of quantities
附合导线　connecting traverse
附合水准路线　connecting leveling line
附加　add-on
附加安全系数　additional safety factor
附加保险费　additional premium, extra premium

附加成本　supplementary costs
附加导线(电力)　additional conductor
附加导线(航测)　annexed traverse
附加费　surcharge, fringe cost, additional cost
附加费率　additional rate
附加费用　additional charge
附加费用的补偿　compensation of additional cost
附加服务　additional service
附加福利　fringe benefits
附加工况　additional working condition
附加工资　extra wage
附加工作　additional work
附加轨道电路　additional track circuit
附加耗热量　additional heat loss
附加合同　accessory contract, contract of adhesion
附加荷载　additional load
附加价值　value added
附加抗拉强度　additional tensile strength
附加力　additional force
附加受保人　additional assured
附加水准路线　annexed leveling line
附加税　surtax, tax surcharge
附加条款　attached clause, additional clause, additional provision
附加物　addendum
附加险　additional risk
附加限制　ancillary restrictions
附加应力　additional stress
附加运费　additional freight
附件　annex, appendix
附建公共用房　attached public houses
附属　affiliation
附属贷款协议　subsidiary loan agreement
附属担保品　collateral
附属担保协议　collateral warranty agreement
附属工程　subsidiary works, external works
附属合同　collateral contract
附属机构　subsidiary
附属建筑物　easement, auxiliary structures
附属企业　auxiliary enterprise
附属设备　auxiliary equipment
附属装置　fixture
附条件背书　restrictive endorsement
附条件参数平差(又称"附条件的间接平差")
　　parameter adjustment with conditions (also known as "condition adjustment with indirection")
附条件承兑　qualified acceptance
附意合同　adhesion contract
附有单证的发票　invoice with document attached
附约　accessory contract

附则　additional contract clauses
附着度　adhesion
附着式混凝土振捣器　external concrete vibrator, attached concrete vibrator
附着装置　attachment device
复测　repeating survey
复耕　land rehabilitation
复工　resumption of work
复轨器　rerailing apparatus
复合保险　multiple line insurance
复合材料风管　composite material duct
复合掺合料　composite mineral admixture
复合衬砌　composite lining
复合带　composite belt
复合地基　composite ground
复合地基载荷试验　load test for composite ground
复合电极　composite electrode
复合箍筋　compound stirrup
复合关税　compound duties, compound tariff
复合管　composite tube
复合硅酸盐水泥　Portland-composite cement
复合滑动面　composite slip surface
复合货币单位　basket unit
复合基桩　composite pile foundation
复合剪切模量　composite shear strength modulus
复合接地网　compound earthing mesh
复合绝缘子　composite insulator
复合墙　composite wall
复合式衬砌　composite lining
复合土钉墙　composite soil nailing wall
复合土工布　composite geotextile
复合土工膜　composite geomembrane
复合土工膜隔断层　composite geomembrane insulating course
复合土工排水材料　drainage material of composite geomembrane
复合土工织物　composite geotextile
复合型沙丘　compound dunes
复合油毡　composite malthoid
复核　re-check
复活谷　resurgent valley
复检　re-inspection
复利　compound amount, compound interest, interest compound
复利计算　compounding
复利率　compound rate
复链形接触网　overhead contact line system with compound suspension
复链形接触悬挂　compound suspension catenary
复喷　secondary shotcreting

复曲线　compound curve
复审　review
复示信号　repeating signal
复示信号机　repeating signal
复示站　repeating station
复示终端　repeating terminal
复式税则　complex tariff, multiple tariff system
复式梯线　ladder track with multiple frog angles
复式账户制　double-account system
复税制　multiple taxation
复位进程　restoration process
复印件　copy, xerox copy
复用段　multiplexing section
复用器　multiplexer
复用设备　multiplex equipment
复原　restore, restoration, resurrent
复原费用　reinstatement cost
复照　rephotography
复制　duplicate
复制品　duplicate
副本　copy, duplicate
副变质岩　para-metamorphite
副担保书　collateral warranty
副灯丝　spare filament
副交点　auxiliary intersection point
副签　countersign
副通气立管　auxiliary ventilation riser
副院长　assistant superintendent
赋予权力　vesting, vest
傅里叶变换　Fourier transform
富冰冻土　ice-rich permafrost
富混凝土　rich concrete, fat concrete
富水程度　water abundance
富水地层　water-rich stratum
富水岩溶隧道　tunnel in water-rich karst region
富余系数　extra coefficient
腹板　web
腹板屈曲后强度　post-buckling strength of web plate
腹杆　web member
覆冰　ice coating
覆冰荷载　ice load
覆盖　cover
覆盖层　overburden
覆盖层厚度　overburden thickness
覆盖厚度　overburden thickness
覆盖率　percentage of coverage
覆盖型岩溶区　covered karst area
覆盖压力　overburden pressure
覆土　earth covering
覆土高度　soil covering height

G

G-M 法　G-M method
GPRS 归属服务器
　　GPRS home subscriber server (GROS)
GPRS 接口服务器　GPRS interface server (GRIS)
GPRS 业务交换点
　　GPRS service switching point (gprsSSP)
GSM 业务交换点
　　GSM service switching point (gsmSSP)
改编列车　remarshaling train
改编能力　remarshaling capacity
改编作业量　marshaling workload
改变结构体系加固法
　　strengthening method by changing structural system
改动　change, alter, alteration
改建　rebuilding, reconstruction
改建—运营—移交
　　rehabilitate-operate-transfer (ROT)
改建费用　improvement cost
改建工程　upgrading/renewal works
改建既有线　existing line reconstruction
改建既有线路基
　　subgrade renovation of existing line
改建铁路　reconstructed railway
改进成本　improvement cost
改良措施　ameliorative measures
改良土　improved soil
改良土拌和站　mixing station of improved soil
改签　reschedule ticket
改线　realignment
改性剂　modifying agent
改正后的投标价　corrected bid price
改正通知　notice to correct
钙离子含量　content of calcium ion
钙镁硅酸盐角岩
　　calcium magnesium silicate hornfels
钙镁离子浓度
　　concentration of calcium and magnesium ions
钙质胶结　calcareous cementation
钙质页岩　calcareous shale
盖板　cover plate
盖板涵　slab culvert
盖梁　bent cap
盖挖法　cover-excavation method
盖挖顺筑法　cover and cut-bottom up
盖章合同　contract under seal
概况　overview, profile
概率分布　probability distribution
概率分析　probability analysis
概率估算　probability estimate
概率极限状态设计法
　　probabilistic limit state design method
概率设计法　probabilistic design method
概略施工组织方案意见　outline construction scheme
概念设计　conceptual design
概算　budgetary estimate
概算定额　budgetary estimate quota
概算价值　budgetary estimate
概算造价　budgetary estimate
概算指标估算法
　　index method of budgetary estimate
概算指标计价法　index calculation method of budg-
　　etary estimate indexes
概算总额　total amount of budgetary estimate
概要计划　outline plan
干捣水泥砂浆　dry tamped cement mortar
干法成孔工艺　dry drilling technology
干粉灭火器　dry powder fire extinguisher
干粉灭火系统　powder extinguishing system
干工况　dry condition
干谷　dry valley
干管　main pipe
干过滤　dry filtering
干旱　drought
干旱地区　arid region
干空气　dry air
干料　drier, dry materials

干流　mainstream
干密度　dry density
干喷法　dry-mix shotcreting method
干喷混凝土机　dry shotcreting machine
干砌片石　dry rubble / dry masonry
干砌墙　mortarless wall
干砌石护坡　dry pitching
干砌石圬工　dry-stone masonry
干球温度　dry-bulb temperature
干扰　interference, disturbance
干扰保护比　carrier and interference ratio
干扰波　interfering wave
干扰电流阶梯曲线
　　step curve of interference current
干扰异常　interference anomaly
干筛法　dry sieving method
干筛分析法　dry sieving method
干湿交替环境
　　dry and wet alternating environment
干湿球温度表　psychrometer
干湿循环　drying and watering cycle
干式变压器　dry-type transformer
干式空芯电抗器　dry type air-core reactor
干式凝结水管　dry condensation pipe
干式喷水灭火系统　dry sprinkling system
干式消火栓　dry hydrant
干式蒸发器　dry evaporator
干缩　dry shrinkage
干缩裂缝　desiccation fissure
干土　dry soil
干土法　dry soil method
干系人　stakeholder
干线　trunk line
干线长途通信网
　　trunk long-distance communication network
干硬性混凝土　dry concrete
干硬性砂浆　stiff consistency mortar
（制动）干预曲线　(brake) intervention curve
干燥器　dryer
干燥箱　drying oven
干重度　dry density
甘特图　Gantt chart, bar chart
杆件　member
杆上电缆盒　cable terminal box on a post
杆体　body of rod
杆系结构　bar structure
坩埚　crucible
赶工　expedite
赶工报价　quotation for acceleration
赶工成本　crash costs

赶工费用　payment for acceleration
赶工工期　crash duration
赶工计划　recovery plan (schedule)
感官法　sensory testing method
感光材料　photosensitive material
感量　sensitivity
感温/感烟探测器　heat/smoke detector
感温火灾探测器
　　temperature sensing fire detector
感温性　temperature sensitivity
感烟火灾探测器　smoke sensing fire detector
感应　induction
感应电流　induced current
感应电压　induced voltage
感应雷　inductive thunder
橄长岩　troctolite
橄辉煌板岩　olive brilliant slate
橄榄石　olivine
橄榄玄武岩　olivine basalt
橄榄岩　peridotite
刚弹性方案　rigid-elastic analysis scheme
刚度　stiffness, rigidity
刚构　rigid frame
刚构桥　rigid frame bridge
刚果红试纸　Congo red test paper
刚架拱　rigid-framed arch
刚架结构　rigid-framed structure
刚架桥　rigid frame bridge
刚接　rigid connection
刚接板梁法　rigid-jointed plate method
刚性导体　rigid conductor
刚性方案　rigid analysis scheme
刚性横墙　rigid transverse wall
刚性基础　rigid foundation
刚性扣件　rigid fastening
刚性—塑性分析　rigidity-plasticity analysis
刚性系杆　rigid tie bar
刚性系杆柔性拱桥　flexible arch bridge with rigid tie
刚性支座连续梁
　　rigidly supported continuous girder
刚性桩　rigid pile
刚玉　corundum
刚域　rigid zone
岗上培训　on-the-job training
岗位津贴　pecuniary allowances for job
纲要设计　outline design
钢板　steel plate
钢板梁　steel plate girder
钢板橡胶止水带
　　water stop tie of steel sheet and rubber type

钢板止水带　water stop tie of steel sheet type
钢板桩　steel sheet pile
钢材　steel
钢材洛氏硬度计　Rockwell hardness tester for steel
钢材牌号　standard grade of steel
钢尺量距　steel tape odometer
钢格栅　steel lattice girder
钢拱架安装器　steel rib installing machine
钢构　steel structure
钢构件变形容许值
　　allowable value of deformation of steel member
钢构件容许长细比
　　allowable slenderness ratio of steel member
钢挂尺　steel tapeline
钢管混凝土拱桥
　　concrete-filled steel tube arch bridge
钢管混凝土构件　concrete-filled steel tube
钢管混凝土桥　concrete-filled steel tube bridge
钢管结构　steel tubular structure
钢管柱　tubular steel pole
钢管桩　steel pipe pile
钢轨　rail
钢轨—大地电位　rail-earth potential
钢轨擦伤　rail scratch
钢轨打标记　mark stamping of rails
钢轨打磨　rail grinding
钢轨打磨车　rail grinding car
钢轨低接头　dipped rail joint
钢轨电气断离　rail electrical disconnection
钢轨电位　rail potential
钢轨定尺　rail sizing
钢轨断裂　rail fracture, rail breakage
钢轨更换　rail replacement
钢轨更换机　rail replacement machine
钢轨工作边
　　running surface of rail, gauge side of rail
钢轨焊补　rail repair welding
钢轨焊接　rail welding
钢轨焊接车　rail welding car
钢轨回流　rail return current
钢轨基础模量　rail supporting modulus
钢轨极性　steel rail polarity
钢轨急救器　emergency joint bar
钢轨加热　rail heating
钢轨加热器　rail heater
钢轨矫直　rail straightening
钢轨接头　rail joint
钢轨接头配件　components of rail joint fastening
钢轨接续线　rail bond
钢轨绝缘　rail insulation

钢轨拉伸器　rail tensor, rail puller
钢轨裂纹　rail crack
钢轨螺栓孔　rail bolt hole
钢轨落锤试验　drop test of rail
钢轨磨耗　rail wear
钢轨磨损检查车　rail wear measuring car
钢轨磨损检查仪　rail wear measuring device
钢轨爬行　rail creeping
钢轨刨边机　rail-head edges planing machine
钢轨疲劳　rail fatigue
钢轨伤损　rail defect
钢轨伸缩调节器　rail expansion joint
钢轨锁定　rail fastening-down
钢轨踏面　rail tread
钢轨探伤　rail flaw detecting
钢轨探伤车　rail flaw detecting car
钢轨探伤仪　rail flaw detector
钢轨涂油　rail lubricating
钢轨涂油器　rail lubricator
钢轨推凸机　rail weld seam shearing machine, rail
　　weld trimmer
钢轨位移观测桩
　　rail creep indication post, rail creep observation pile
钢轨温度　rail temperature
钢轨泄漏电阻　rail leakage resistance
钢轨锈蚀　rail corrosion
钢轨引接线　track lead
钢轨应力　rail stress
钢轨折断　brittle fracture of rail
钢轨支点弹性模量　elastic modulus of rail support
钢轨直度测量尺　rail straightness measuring scale
钢轨纵向连接　rail longitudinal connection
钢轨阻抗　rail impedance
钢轨钻孔机　rail drilling machine
钢轨钻孔器　rail drilling tool
钢桁梁　steel truss girder
钢架　steel rib, steel arch
钢绞线　steel strand
钢结构　steel structure
钢结构安装　steel erection
钢结构工程　structural steelwork
钢结构塑性设计　plastic design of steel structure
钢筋　reinforcing bar, reinforcement bar, (steel
　　bar, rebar, bar)
钢筋安装工　re-bar fixer
钢筋保护层　concrete cover
钢筋保护层厚度　thickness of concrete cover
钢筋布置　arrangement of reinforcement
钢筋测力仪(计)　reinforcement meter
钢筋层距　rebar layer spacing

G

钢筋搭接　bar splicing
钢筋搭接长度　lapped length of steel bar
钢筋电弧焊　arc welding of rebar
钢筋调直机　steel bar straightener
钢筋工　re-bar worker
钢筋混凝土　reinforced concrete (RC)
钢筋混凝土保护层　concrete cover to reinforcement
钢筋混凝土保护层最小厚度　minimum thickness of concrete cover
钢筋混凝土结构　reinforced concrete structure
钢筋混凝土桥　reinforced concrete bridge
钢筋混凝土套箍或护套加固法　strengthening method by reinforced concrete hoop or sheath
钢筋混凝土压力水管　reinforced concrete pressure pipe
钢筋混凝土柱　reinforced concrete pole
钢筋混凝土桩　reinforced concrete pile
钢筋机械连接　rebar mechanical splicing
钢筋加工场　reinforcement yard
钢筋间距　spacing of reinforcement
钢筋接头　bar splice
钢筋截断机　bar cutter
钢筋抗拉强度标准值　standard value of tensile strength of steel bar
钢筋抗拉强度设计值　design value of tensile strength of steel bar
钢筋抗压强度设计值　design value of compressive strength of steel bar
钢筋可焊性　weldability of steel bar
钢筋容许拉伸应变　allowable tensile strain of reinforcement
钢筋冷拉机　steel bar cold-drawing machine
钢筋连接　connection of steel bars
钢筋锚固长度　anchorage length of steel bar
钢筋母材　base metal of steel-bar
钢筋切断机　steel bar cutter, bar shearing machine
钢筋闪光对焊　flash-butt welding of rebar
钢筋试验　steel bar test
钢筋弯曲机　steel bar bender, bar shearing machine
钢筋网　wiremesh, reinforcing fabric, mesh reinforcement
钢筋网片/骨架绑扎台座　reinforcement mesh/skeleton binding pedestal
钢筋位置　position of steel bars
钢筋性能检验　performance test of steel bar
钢筋锈蚀　corrosion of steel bar
钢筋阻锈剂　"steel anti-corrosion admixture, corrosion inhibitor for steel"
钢卷尺　steel tape
钢梁腐蚀裂纹　corrosion-induced crack of steel girder
钢梁加固　strengthening of steel girder
钢梁疲劳损伤　fatigue damage of steel girder
钢梁应力腐蚀裂纹　stress/corrosion-induced crack of steel girder
钢梁油漆　protective coating of steel bridge
钢梁整体稳定系数　overall stability coefficient of steel beam
钢铝复合接触轨　aluminium-steel composite conductor rail
钢桥　steel bridge
钢桥养护　steel bridge maintenance
钢丝　steel wire
钢丝反复弯曲机　steel wire reverse bend test machine
钢丝绳　wire rope
钢丝束　steel tendon
钢丝刷除锈　descaling by brush
钢筋网　fabric reinforcement
钢丝网套　cable stocking
钢套管　steel casing
钢纤维　steel fibre
钢纤维混凝土　steel fiber reinforced concrete
钢纤维喷射混凝土　steel fiber reinforced shotcrete
钢纤维水泥混凝土　steel fiber cement concrete
钢箱梁　steel box girder, steel box beam
钢斜拉桥　steel cable-stayed bridge
钢芯铝绞线　aluminum conductor steel reinforced (ACSR)
钢与混凝土组合梁　composite steel and concrete beam
钢枕　steel sleeper
钢支架　steel support
钢支柱(钢柱)　steel pole, steel mast
钢支座　steel bearing
钢制散热器　steel radiator
钢柱底座　base plate of steel pole, pedestal of steel pole
钢柱分肢　steel column component
钢柱脚　steel column base
钢桩　steel pile
港口　port
港口费用　port charge, port dues, groundage
港口附加费　port surcharge
港口工程　port works
港口惯例　custom of port
港口检验人员　surveyor of port
港口税　harbor duty, port dues

港口税率　rate of port dues
港口条例　harbor regulations
港口吞吐量　port handling capacity
港口拥挤附加费　port congestion surcharge
港湾防波堤　harbour breakwater
港湾工程　harbor works
港湾项目　harbor project
港湾站　harbour station
港务费　harbor dues
港务局　port authority
杠杆比率　leverage ratio
杠杆固结仪　lever arm oedometer
杠杆压力仪装置　lever-type pressure apparatus
杠杆原理法　lever rule method
杠杆作用　leverage
高边坡　high slope
高标价投标　high priced bid
高层建筑　high-rise building
高层谈判　high-level talks
高差　elevation difference
高差偶然中误差　random mean square error of elevation difference
高差全中误差
　　total mean square error of elevation difference
高差同步法　elevation synchronization method
高潮位　high tide level
高程　elevation, level
高程测量　vertical survey, elevation survey
高程导线　height traverse
高程点　elevation point
高程基准　vertical datum
高程控制测量　elevation control survey
高程控制点　elevation control point
高程控制网　elevation control network, vertical control network
高程投影面　altitude projection surface
高程系统　elevation system
高程异常　height anomaly
高程中误差　elevation mean square error
高程注记点　elevation annotation point
高处作业　working at height
高弹性人造橡胶薄膜
　　high elasticity synthetic rubber membrane
高低　longitudinal level, profile
高低差　height difference
高地　highland
高地温　high ground temperature
高额关税　prohibitive duty
高分子防水卷材　high polymer waterproof sheet
高风险工程　high risk works

高峰　peak time
高峰交通量　peak traffic flow
高峰小时发送量　peak hour volume
高峰小时功率需求
　　peak traffic hour power demand
高(低)负荷生物滤池　high(low) rate biofilter,
　　high(low)-rate biological filters
高估　overestimate, overstate
高管层　top management
高寒区　cold area
高级工程师　senior engineer
高级管理人员　executive
高级检修　advanced repair
高级路面　high type pavement
高级数据链路控制协议
　　high-level data link control (HDLC)
高级音频编码技术—低延迟规格
　　advanced audio coding-low delay (AAC-LD)
高价　high price, long price
高架公路　high-flying highway
高架候车室　elevated waiting room
高架桥　viaduct, overpassing
高架桥下公路　underpass
高架线　elevated line, viaduct
高阶地　high terrace
高阶振型　high mode
高径比　height-diameter ratio
高空作业　work at height
高跨比　depth to span ratio
高岭石　kaolinite
高岭土　kaolin
高路堤　high embankment
高氯酸脱水质量法　gravimetric method of perchloric acid dehydration
高漫滩阶地　high flood plain terraces
高密度电法　high-density electrical method
高密度剖面法　high density profiling method
高频开关　high frequency switch
高频开关电源　high frequency switching power supply
高强度等级水泥　high-quality cement
高强度钢筋　high-tensile steel bar
高强度螺栓　high strength bolt
高强度螺栓摩擦面抗滑移系数　slip resistance coefficient of friction surface for high strength bolt
高强混凝土　high-strength concrete
高强水泥　high-strength cement
高清摄像机　high-definition camera
高山　high mountain
高山冰川　mountain glacier
高式水沟　deep gutterway

高斯—克吕格投影　Gauss-Kruger projection
高斯平面直角坐标系　Gaussian planimetric rectangular coordinate system
高斯投影长度变形　length variation in Gaussian projection
高斯投影分带　zone-dividing of Gaussian projection
高斯投影面　Gaussian projection plane
高斯约化法　gauss method of reduction
高耸结构　high-rise structure
高速车场　high-speed yard
高速公路　expressway
高速轨检车　high-speed track inspection car
高速摄影　high-speed photography
高速铁路　high-speed railway（HSR）
高速铁路精密工程测量　precise engineering survey of high speed railway
高速铁路网　high-speed railway network
高填深挖　high fill and deep cut
高通滤波器　high-pass filter
高位水池　elevated tank
高位消防水池　gravity fire reservoir
高位消防水箱　elevated fire tank
高温不稳定冻土区　non-stable permafrost region at high temperature
高温不稳定区　high-temperature unstable area
高温极不稳定区　high-temperature and extremely unstable area
高温计　pyrometer
高温茂福炉　high temperature muffle furnace
高温消化　thermophilic digestion
高息贷款　dear money
高效减水剂　superplasticizer
高效节能　energy-efficient
高性能混凝土　high performance concrete
高压泵　high pressure pump
高压侧　high voltage side, primary side
高压断路器　high voltage circuit breaker
高压绝缘子　high-voltage insulator
高压配电室　high voltage power distribution room
高压喷射注浆法　jet grouting method
高压全封闭式组合电器　high voltage gas insulated switchgear
高压试验　high voltage test
高压室　high-voltage room
高压缩性　high compressibility
高压套管　high-voltage bushing
高压系统　high pressure system
高压消防系统　high-pressure fire system
高压旋喷桩　high pressure jet grouting pile
高应变法　high-strain dynamic testing
高应力反复拉压试验　high stress repeated tensile and compression test
高原　plateau
高原寒带　plateau frigid zone
高原铁路　railway in plateau region
高原温带　plateau temperate zone
高原亚寒带　plateau subfrigid zone
高原亚热带　plateau subtropics
高站台　high platform
高柱信号机　high signal
高桩承台　high pile cap
高阻保护　high impedance protection
高阻轮对　high resistance wheel set
告警　alarm
割线模量　secant stiffness
格构式钢柱　latticed steel column
格里菲斯准则　Griffith criterion
格网板　grid plate
格网间隔　grid interval
格栅　bar screen
格子线　graticule
蛤壳式抓斗　clamshell bucket
隔板絮凝池　spacer flocculating tank
隔爆电气设备　flameproof electrical equipment
隔断层　insulating course
隔绝通风　isolation ventilation
隔离变压器　isolating transformer
隔离层　isolation layer, separation layer
隔离剂　separant
隔离开关　disconnector
隔离开关杆　disconnecting switch pole
隔离模式　isolation mode（IS）
隔离区　Demilitarized Zone（DMZ）
隔离系数　segregation coefficient
隔离纸　interleaving paper, release paper
隔墙　partition wall
隔热　heat insulation
隔热材料　thermal insulation material, heat-insulating material
隔热屏　heat screen
隔声　sound insulation
隔声材料　sound insulator
隔声窗　sound insulation window
隔声观察窗　sound insulation watching door
隔声量　sound reduction factor（index）
隔声门　soundproof door
隔声罩　acoustic enclosure（shield）
隔水层　aquifuge
隔音板　acoustical board
隔油沉淀池　oil separation and sedimentation tank

隔油池　grease tank, oil separator
隔油井　grease tank
隔振　vibration isolating
隔振管桩　vibration isolation pipe pile
隔振减振基础　vibration isolation and damping base
隔振器　vibration isolator
隔振墙　vibration isolation wall
隔震技术　seismic isolation technique
镉含量　cadmium content
个别辨认法　specific identification method
个别留置权　particular lien
个别设计　individual design
个人财产　personal property, personal effects
个人的　individual, private, personal
个人劳保用品　personal protective equipment
个人侵权行为　personal tort
个人所得　individual income
个人所得税　individual income tax, personal income tax
个人责任　personal liability
个人咨询专家　individual consultant
个人资产　personal assets
个体　entity, individual
个体企业　individual enterprise
个体业主　individual owner
各向异性　anisotropy
各向异性指数　anisotropy index
各专业　disciplines
各自负有连带和单独责任　joint and several liability
各自责任　several liability
铬化物　chromium compounds
铬胶翻版　chromium gel reprint
给承包商的指示　instruction to contractor
给水　water supply
给水泵站　water supply pump station
给水厂　water supply plant
给水度　specific yield
给水干管路　trunk pipeline for water supply
给水管　water supply pipe
给水机械　water supply machine
给水能力　water supply capacity
给水排水工程　water supply and sewerage works
给水配件　water supply fittings
给水特点　water supply property
给水系统　water supply system
给水站　water supply station
给水装置　water works
给予　extend, vest
给予权利　entitle
给予特许　franchise
根本性变更　cardinal changes
根本性违约　fundamental breach
根本责任　ultimate liability
根据　pursuant to, in accordance with
根开　root span
根开(铁塔)　center to center distance between tower feet
根系发育状况　root development
根源　source
跟单汇票　documentary bill (draft)
跟单汇票托收委托书　advice for collection of documentary bill
跟单托收　collection on documents, documentary collection
跟单信用证　documentary letter of credit
更改　alter, alteration, modify, modification
更换　replace, replacement, substitute
更换支座　replacement of bearing seat
更替型合同　novation contract, contract of novation
更新　renew, renewal, updating, upgrade
更新—拥有—运营　rehabilitate-own-operate (ROO)
更新成本　replacement cost
更新的进度计划　updated schedule
更新世　Pleistocene epoch
更新统　Pleistocene series
更正　amend, amendment
耕地　cultivated land
耕地开垦费　reclamation cost of farmland
耕地占用税　farmland occupation tax
工人　navvy
工厂　plant, works, workshop
工厂化　industrialization, member fabrication in plant
工厂交货　ex works (EXW), ex-factory
工厂交货价　ex-works price, price of ex-factory
工厂漆　factory painting
工厂生产能力　plant capacity
工场　workshop, yard
工潮　labour disturbance
工程　works
工程部经理　engineering manager
工程保险　insurance of works, project insurance
工程保险费　project insurance expenses
工程保修　project warranty
工程报表　bill of works
工程报告　engineering report
工程变更　alteration of works, job changes, variation of work
工程变更单　bill of variations

工程财产保险　project property insurance
工程采购　procurement of works
工程彩色制图　color engineering drawing
工程测量　engineering survey
工程场地地震安全性评价
　　seismic safety assessment of construction site
工程成本　engineering cost
工程成本分类账　job cost ledger
工程成本记录　job cost record
工程成本日记账　job cost journal
工程成本预算　work cost budget
工程承包　project contracting, work contracting
工程承包费　engineering contract fee
工程船舶　engineering vessel
工程措施　engineering measure
工程的估价　valuation of works
工程地点　project location
工程地质　engineering geology
工程地质测绘
　　engineering geological investigation and mapping
工程地质调绘　engineering geological mapping
工程地质勘察报告
　　engineering geological investigation report
工程地质勘查大纲
　　outline of engineering geological investigation
工程地质勘探　engineering geological prospecting
工程地质评价　engineering geological evaluation
工程地质剖面图　engineering geological profile
工程地质手册　engineering geology manual
工程地质条件　engineering geological condition
工程地质图　engineering geological map
工程地质选线
　　engineering geological route selection
工程地质柱状图　engineering geological column
工程地质钻探
　　engineering geological drilling exploration
工程定额测定费　project quota measurement fee
工程定位复测　location survey
工程独立坐标系
　　independent engineering coordinate system
工程范围变更索赔　scope of work claim
工程范围数据库　engineering scope database
工程费　job overhead cost
工程分解结构　engineering breakdown struture(EBS)
工程分析　engineering analysis
工程风险　project risk
工程服务贷款　engineering service loan
工程概况　project profile
工程管理员　clerk of the works
工程合同　project contract

工程和单位工程的接收
　　taking over the works and sections
工程滑坡　engineering landslide
工程及费用名称　description of works and fees
工程计划　project program
工程计划概要　outline programme
工程价款结算　settlement of project cost
工程监测　engineering monitoring
工程监理费　engineering supervision fee
工程监理与咨询服务费
　　engineering supervision and consulting service fees
工程检查报告　project inspection reports
工程建设定额　engineering construction quota
工程接口　engineering interface
工程结(决)算期　engineering settlement (final accounting) period
工程结构　engineering structure
工程结构地震破坏等级
　　earthquake damage grade of engineering structure
工程结构设计　engineering structure design
工程进度　rate of progress
工程进度表
　　schedule of construction, schedule of works
工程竣工　completion of works, job completion
工程竣工结算　completion settlement of project
工程竣工图　as-built drawing of project
工程开工　commencement of works
工程勘察　engineering investigation
工程抗震　engineering earthquake resistance
工程控制网　engineering control network
工程扩建　extension of works
工程蓝图　blueprint of the project
工程类比法　engineering analogy method
工程量　quantity
工程量变更　variation of quantity
工程量标价　quantity pricing
工程量表　bill of quantities
工程量表合同　bill of quantities contract
工程量计算　quantity take-off
工程量检查证　inspection certificate of quantity
工程量清单　bill of quantities
工程量清单汇总表　summary of bill of quantities
工程量折扣　quantity discount
工程列车　engineering train
工程描述　description of works
工程排污费　project pollution discharge fees
工程期限　period of construction
工程签证人　certifier
工程缺陷　work defect
工程设计　project design

工程设计方案　project design plan
工程设计阶段　engineering design phase/stage
工程摄影测量　engineering photogrammetry
工程师　engineer
工程师代表　engineer's representative
工程师的初始响应　engineer's initial response
工程师的检查和调查
　　engineer's inspection and investigation
工程师的期中支付证书
　　engineer's interim certificate
工程师的确定　engineer's determination
工程师的替换　replacement of the engineer
工程师的同意　engineer's consent
工程师的委托　delegation by the engineer
工程师的职责和权限
　　engineer's duties and authority
工程施工一切险　contractor's all risks insurance
工程实施　execution of the works
工程实体质量　engineering entity quality
工程试验室　engineering laboratory
工程数量　engineering quantity
工程说明书　description of project
工程宿营车　dormitory van
工程统计　works statistics
工程投资　project investment
工程维修　maintenance of works
工程物理勘探　engineering physical exploration
工程详细报告　detailed project report
工程项目投标　bid for engineering project
工程项目招投标　bidding of engineering project
工程项目总承包
　　general contracting for engineering project
工程性质　nature of works
工程延期　deferment of a project
工程延误　delays in engineering
工程岩体分级
　　rock mass engineering classification
工程验收
　　acceptance of works, acceptance of a project
工程遥感　engineering remote sensing
工程用地红线图
　　boundary map for construction land
工程用电综合单价　comprehensive unit price for
　　power supply for construction
工程用水　engineering water
工程用水综合单价　comprehensive unit price for
　　water supply for construction
工程造价　construction cost
工程造价管理
　　management of construction cost
工程造价信息　construction cost information
工程造价增长率
　　growth rate of construction cost
工程造价增长预备费
　　budgetary reserve for rise of construction price
工程造价增长预留费
　　budgetary reserve for rise of construction price
工程造价指数　construction cost index
工程照管和免责　care of works and indemnities
工程直接费　hard costs
工程质量安全监督费
　　engineering quality and safety supervision fee
工程质量检测费
　　engineering quality inspection fee
工程专用　exclusive use for the works
工程状况　status of a project
工程准备阶段文件
　　document of project preparation stage
工程咨询公司　engineering consultancy firm
工程咨询合同　engineering consulting contract
工程总量　total quantities of works
工程组织机构　job organization
工地
　　site, construction site, job site, work site, field
工地保管费　on-site custody fee
工地备用品　stores on site
工地布置　site arrangement
工地范围　site coverage
工地记录本　field book
工地监工员　contractor supervisor
工地搅拌　mixed-in-place
工地勘察　job site survey
工地平整　site grading
工地漆　field painting
工地清理　job site cleanup
工地日志　site diary
工地设备　site equipment
工地设施　job site facilities
工地试验室
　　site laboratory, on job lab, field laboratory
工地视察　field inspection
工地照明　lighting of the site
工地装配　field connection
工点表　list of construction sites
工点地形图　topographic map of construction site
工点卡片　card of construction site
工点说明　introduction of construction site
工段长　section foreman
工法　construction method
工后沉降　post-construction settlement

G

工会　labour union, trade union
工会经费　trade union funds
工件　workpiece
工匠　craftsman, workman
工具　tool, instrument, facility
工具轨　tool rail
工具用具使用费
　　charge for using tools and appliances
工控机　industrial personal computer
工料测量　quantity survey
工料测量师　quantity surveyor (QS)
工料测量学　quantity surveying
工龄　working years
工棚　site hut
工频磁场　power frequency magnetic field
工频电场　power frequency electric field
工频接地电阻
　　industrial frequency grounding resistance
工频耐压　power frequency withstand voltage
工频耐压有效值
　　power frequency withstand voltage r. m. s
工频闪络电压　power frequency flashover voltage
工期　construction period
工期成本　cost concerning construction period
工期的延长　extension of time (EOT)
工期计算　duration calculation
工期落后　slippage
工期拖延　construction delay
工期压缩　duration compression
工期延长　extension of time
工区　work section
工人　labour, workman
工人抚恤金　workman's compensation
工日　man day
工伤　industrial injury, injury on job
工伤保险费　industrial injury insurance premium
工伤补偿　compensation for injury
工伤事故　accident work injury, work accident, working accident
工伤事故保险
　　insurance against accident to workmen
工商企业　business
工商所得税　industrial and commercial income tax
工时　working hours, man hour
工时报告单　time report
工时成本　time cost
工时分配　time distribution
工时记录　time keeping
工时记录卡　time card
工时率　labour hour rate

工天定额　man-day quota
工头　leading hand, task master
工项　work result
工项分解结构　work breakdown structure (WBS)
工薪税　payroll tax
工形梁　I-girder, I-beam
工序　work procedure
工序分析　process analysis
工序控制　process control
工业产权　industrial property right
工业废水　industrial wastewater
工业基础类　industry foundation classes (IFC)
工业建筑　industrial building
工业通风　industrial ventilation
工业站　industrial station
工艺　workmanship, technology, process
工艺包　process package
工艺发表　process release
工艺工程师　process engineer
工艺检验　technology inspection
工艺控制图　process control diagram (PCD)
工艺流程图　process chart, process flow chart, process diagram, process flow diagram (PFD)
工艺设备　process plant
工艺设计　process design
工艺性试验　operative test
工艺装置　process unit
工长　foreman
工种工程量表　trade bill of quantities
工资　pay, wage
工资标准　wage level, wage rate
工资标准和劳动条件
　　rates of wages and conditions of labour
工资表　payroll, wages sheet
工资表格　payroll form
工资记录　payroll records
工资率　wage rate
工资水平　wage level, wage rate
工资所得税　wages income tax
工资支票　pay cheque, payroll check
工资指数　index of wage, wage index
工资总额　total salary amount
工资总额单　wage bill
工资最高限额　wage ceiling
工字钢　I-shaped section steel
工字梁　I-girder, I-beam
工作包　work package
工作报告　work report
工作变动　work changes
工作场所　workplace

工作成果	work result
工作大纲	terms of reference (TOR)
工作单项	work item
工作底稿	work sheet
工作电流	working current
工作范围	scope of work
工作范围说明	work scope description
工作方案	work program, work plan
工作费用	working expenses
工作分解结构	work breakdown structure (WBS)
工作负荷	workload
工作管	operating pipe
工作规范	job specification
工作基点	operation base point
工作计划	work plan, work program
工作计划成本	scheduled cost of work
工作记录	job record
工作接地	functional earthing
工作进度表	work-schedule
工作井	launching shaft
工作量	quantity of work, work capacity, workload
工作流程	workflow
工作面	working face
工作内容	work content
工作能力	ability to work, work capacity
工作缺陷	faulty work
工作人员	staff
工作人员工资	staff salary
工作人员条例	staff regulations
工作日	working day, workday
工作溶液	working solution
工作时间	working hours
工作台	mounting rack
工作条件	working condition
工作条件系数	coefficient of working condition
工作通知单	work order
工作完成	job completion
工作文件	working papers
工作项目或费用名称	work item or expense description
工作效率	working efficiency, labour efficiency
工作协调	coordination of work
工作行程	working stroke, operating stroke
工作许可	working papers, employment permit, work permit
工作许可证	work permit
工作业绩	job performance
工作站	work station
工作张力	working tensile stress
工作支	in-running contact line
工作执行流程表	work execution flowsheet
工作值	working value
工作指令	working instruction
工作中断	work interruption
工作周期	job cycle
弓头	pantograph bow, pantograph head
弓网关系	interaction behavior between pantograph and OCS
弓形腕臂	curved cantilever
公安管理信息系统	police management information system
公布	announce, publish
公布账目	accounting released
公差	tolerance
公称长度	nominal length
公称力	nominal force
公称粒径	nominal particle size
公称直径	nominal diameter
公断人	arbitrator, arbiter, umpire
公断书	arbitration award
公法	public law
公告	announcement, proclamation
公共安全系统	public security system
公共参与调查	inquiry in public participation
公共电网	public grid
公共福利	public welfare
公共工程	public works
公共关系	public relation
公共基础设施	infrastructure
公共假日	public holiday
公共建筑	public building
公共交换电话网	public switched telephone network (PSTN)
公共绿地	public green area
公共设施	public facilities, common facilities, service
公共信道信令	common channel signaling
公共责任	public liability
公共政策	public policy
公共资产	public assets
公害	hazard
公函	official letter
公积金	reserve fund, accumulated funds
公开报价	public offer
公开竞争	open competition
公开投标	open bid (tender)
公开招标	public bidding, open bidding (tendering), competitive bidding
公款	public money
公里标	kilometer post

G

公里桩　kilometer stake
公路　highway
公路干线　primary highway
公路工程　road engineering, highway engineering
公路活载　live load of road
公路运距　haul distance of highway transportation
公路运输　carriage by road
公路运输用集装箱半挂车
　　container semitrailer for road transport
公路运输用集装箱牵引车
　　container tractor for road transport
公路支线　feeder road
公路综合运价率　comprehensive freight rate
公平价格　fair price, reasonable price
公平交易　fair dealing, arm's length transaction
公平交易法　fair trading act
公平竞争　fair competition
公平市价　fair market price
公平性　fairness
公认的国际惯例
　　established international practice
公认会计原则　generally accepted accounting principles (GAAP)
公式调价法　formula price adjustment
公司　company
公司本部　home office
公司本部费用　home office cost
公司财产　company property
公司创办人　incorporator
公司法　corporation act (law), company act, company law, law of company
公司合并　corporate merger
公司汇票　house bill
公司利润税　corporate profit tax
公司收购　corporate acquisition
公司税　corporation tax (CT), corporate tax
公司税法　corporation tax act (CTA)
公司所得税　corporate income tax
公司条例　company act, corporation regulation
公司印章　corporation seal
公司债券　corporate bond, debenture
公司章程　charter of company, corporation bylaws, memorandum of association
公司执照　corporate charter, charter
公司重组　corporate restructuring
公司注册地　place of incorporation
公司注册手续　incorporation procedure
公司注册证书　certificate of incorporation
公司资产　corporate assets
公私合营企业　joint state and private enterprise
公私伙伴关系　public private partnership (PPP)
公铁两用桥　rail-cum-road bridge
公务电话试验　service telephone test
公务护照　service passport
公务员　officer
公用工程　public works
公用设施　public utility
公用事业　utility, public utility, public services
公用箱　common box
公寓式办公楼　apartment-office building
公约　convention, pact
公债　government bond, bond
公章　official seal, common seal
公正性　impartiality
公证　notarize, notarization
公证人　public notary, notary, notary public
公证手续　notarial acts
公证文件　notarial document
公证证书　notarial certificate
公制　metric system
公制换算　metric conversion
公制计量　metric measure
公众的便利　convenience of the public
公众紧急呼叫　public emergency call
公众责任险　public liability insurance
功分器　power splitter
功率放大器　amplifier
功率密度　power density
功率损耗　power loss
功率因数　power factor
功率因数补偿　power factor compensation
功能函数　performance function
功能号　function number (FN)
功能检验　functional test
功能欠佳赔偿费　low performance damages
功能区　function area
功能试验　functional test
功能寻址　functional addressing (FA)
功能置换　functional replacement
供不应求　in short supply
供电臂　feeding section
供电臂平均电流　average current of feeding section
供电臂瞬时最大电流
　　transient maximum current of feeding section
供电臂有效电流
　　effective current of feeding section
供电臂有效电流系数
　　effective current coefficient of feeding section
供电臂最大电流
　　maximum current of feeding section

供电臂最大有效电流　maximum effective current of feeding section

供电臂最大有效电流
　　maximum effective current of feeding section
供电侧　sending end
供电电极　current electrode
供电电极距　current electrode spacing
供电电缆　feeder cable, feeder
供电段　power supply equipment maintenance management department
供电方案　power supply plan
供电方式　power supply mode
供电复示系统　indication system for traction power supply system
供电干线　main supply
供电计算　traction power supply calculation
供电可靠性分析　reliability analysis of traction power supply system
供电维修　power supply maintenance
供电线路　power supply line
供电线上网（点）　feeding point
供电线阻抗　impedance of feeder cable
（施工）供风　compressed air supply
供货厂商先期确认图　advanced certified final drawings（ACF）, advanced certified vendors' drawings, preliminary vendor drawings（PD）
供货厂商最终确认图　certified final drawings（CF）, certified vendor drawings（CD）
供货担保　supply bond
供货价格　supply price
供货商名单　vendor list
供冷年耗冷量　annual cooling demand
供料斗　feed hopper
供料线　charging line
供暖年耗热量　annual heating demand
供暖系统　heating system
供气压力　gas supply pressure
供求　demand and supply
供水　water supply, water service
供水方案　water supply plan
供水方式　water supply mode
供水管　feed pipe, charging line
供水量　output of supplying water
供水系统　water supply system
供应　supply, furnish, furnishings, provision
供应范围　scope of supply
供应方案　supply plan
供应品　supply
供应渠道　supply channel
供应商　supplier, materialman, vendor
汞含量　mercury content
汞蒸气测定仪　mercury vapor meter

拱　arch
拱坝　arch dam
拱板　arched slab
拱背线　extrados
拱波　transverse auxiliary arches
拱部　arch
拱顶　arch crown
拱顶下沉　crown settlement
拱度　camber
拱腹　arch soffit
拱腹线　intrados
拱高　rise of arch
拱涵　arch culvert
拱架　lagging jack
拱肩　spandrel
拱脚　arch springing
拱结构　arch structure
拱肋　arch rib
拱梁　arched girder
拱桥　arch bridge
拱圈　arch ring
拱上建筑　structure above arch
拱石　arch stone
拱矢　arch rise
拱式桥　arch bridge
拱推力　arch thrust
拱形屋架　arched roof truss
拱腰　haunch
拱座　arch impost, skewback
共保交叉责任条款　joint insured cross liability clause
共电电话　common battery telephone
共模试验　common mode test
共同保险　co-insurance
共同保障　shared indemnities
共同承保人　co-assurer
共同承兑人　co-acceptor
共同错误　common mistake
共同贷款　participating loan
共同担保人　co-guarantor
共同管理人　co-manager
共同过错　contributory negligence
共同海损　general average（G. A.）
共同海损保函　general average guarantee
共同海损保证金　general average deposit
共同海损保证书　average bond
共同海损补偿　make good on general average
共同海损担保　general average security
共同海损担保书　general average guarantee
共同海损费用保险
　　general average disbursement insurance

共同海损分摊　general average contribution
共同海损基金　general average fund
共同海损理算　general average adjustment, adjustment of general average
共同海损理算书　general average statement
共同海损赔偿理算　adjustment of claim for general average
共同海损损失　general average loss
共同海损条款　general average clause
共同海损行为　general average act
共同和各自的责任　joint and several liability
共同基金　mutual funds
共同借款人　co-borrower
共同市场　common market
共同受益人　co-beneficiary
共同诉讼　joinder
共同所有权　joint ownership
共同行为　joint act
共同延误　concurrent delay, overlapping delays
共同义务　joint liability
共同债权人　joint creditor
共同债务人　co-debtor
共同资助　cofinancing
共同租赁人　joint tenant
共线条件方程　colinearity condition equation
共享保护环　shared protection ring(SPRing)
共用接地　common earthing
共用作业场　shared operation yard
共振　resonance
共振法　resonance method
共振速度　resonance velocity
共振系数　resonance factor
共振柱试验　resonant column test
沟、槽、管和洞　trench, groove, pipe and hole
沟槽　drainage blind ditch, pipeline, trench
沟谷　gulley
钩车　cars per cut
钩螺栓　hooked bolt, claw bolt
钩损险　risk of hook damage
钩头鞍子　hook end clamp
构件　element
构件变形容许值　allowable value of deformation of structural members
构件长期刚度　long term rigidity of members
构件承载力抗震调整系数　seismic resistance adjustment coefficient of components bearing capacity
构件承载能力　load-bearing capacity of member
构件承载能力设计值　design value of bearing capacity of members
构件端面承压强度标准值　standard value of pressure bearing strength for member end
构件短期刚度　short term rigidity of members
构件抗剪刚度　shearing rigidity of members
构件抗拉刚度　tensile rigidity of members
构件抗扭刚度　torsional rigidity of members
构件抗弯刚度　flexural rigidity of members
构件抗压刚度　compressive rigidity of members
构件库　component library
构件模型几何表达等级　geometric expression level of component model
构件挠度容许值　allowable value of deflection of structural members
构件性能检验　performance test of structural member
构件纵向弯曲系数　longitudinal bending coefficient of components
构造　structure
构造带　tectonic zone
构造地震　tectonic earthquake
构造钢筋　structural reinforcement
构造观测点　structure observation point
构造轨缝　structural rail joint gap
构造角砾岩　tectonic breccia
构造配筋　constructional reinforcement
构造坡　structural slope
构造速度　design speed, structural speed
构造体系　tectonic system
构造要求　structural requirements
构造应力　tectonic stress
构造应力场　tectonic stress field
构造柱　constructional column
购电协议　power purchase agreement
购方企业　acquiring enterprise
购货成本　cost of goods purchased, purchasing cost
购货代理人　purchasing agent
购货单　buying order, purchase order
购货发盘　buying offer
购货发票　purchase invoice
购货合同　contract for purchase
购货确认书　purchase note
购货日记账　purchase journal
购货样品　purchase sample
购货约定　purchase commitment
购买—更新—运营　procure-upgrade-operate(PUO)
购买地价格　price loco
购买方　acquiring party
购买力　purchasing power, ability to pay
购买要约　buying offer
购置财产　acquisition of property
购置成本　acquisition cost

购置费	purchase expenses
估定价值	assessed value, constructed value
估计残值	estimated residual value, estimated salvage value
估计负债	estimated liabilities
估计工程量单价合同	bill of approximate quantity contract
估计价格	estimated price
估价	assess, assessment, estimate, value, valuation
估价财产人	assessor
估价单	bill of estimate, estimate sheet
估价人	appraiser, estimater
估价条款	valuation clause
估价文件	estimate documentation
估量	takeoff
估税人	tax assessor
估税员	tax assessor
估算	estimate, assess, approximate estimate
估算成本	estimated cost
估算工程量	estimated quantities
估算价	rough estimation
估算师	estimator
估算指标	index of estimate
估损人	claim assessor
孤植	specimen planting
箍筋	stirrup
箍筋间距	stirrup spacing
箍筋肢距	spacing of stirrup legs
古德曼经验式	Goodman empirical formula
古董	antiquities
古河道	ancient channel/riverway
古生代	Paleozoic era
古生界	Paleozoic erathem/ group
古树名木	ancient and rare trees
古太古代	Paleoarchean era
古太古界	Paleoarchean erathem
古土壤	paleosoil
古物	antique
古新世	Paleocene epoch
古新统	Paleocene series
古元古代	Paleoproterozoic
谷冰川	valley glacier
谷地相	valley facies
股本	capital stock
股本持有者	equity holder
股道间电连接	electrical connection between tracks
股道空闲长度	unoccupied track length
股东	shareholder, stockholder
股东大会	shareholder's meeting
股东分户账	stock ledger
股东权益	shareholder's equity, proprietary equity, stockholder's equity
股东协议	shareholder's agreement
股份	stock capital
股份公司	incorporated company
股份有限公司	company limited by shares, limited liability company, corporation
股利收入	dividend earned
股利支付率	dividend payout ratio
股票	stock, share, equity
股票股利	capital bonus
股票基金	equity fund
股票市场	equity market, stock market
股票溢价	stock premium
股权	equity, interest
股权式联营合同	equity joint-venture contract
股息	dividend
骨干层	backbone layer
骨干传输网	backbone transmission network
骨干同步网	backbone synchronization network
骨干网络	backbone network
骨架	framework, skeleton
骨架护坡	skeleton slope protection, skeleton revetment
骨架内植草	planting grass in skeleton
骨架曲线	skeleton curve
骨料	aggregate
骨料仓	aggregate bin
骨料冲击韧度	aggregate impact toughness
骨料的碱活性	alkali reactivity of aggregate
骨料分离	aggregate segregation
骨料级配	aggregate gradation
骨料加工厂	aggregate processing plant
骨料碱活性试验	alkali reactivity test of aggregate
骨料水泥比	aggregate-cement ratio
骨料压碎率	aggregate crushing rate
鼓包夹板	protruding joint bar, bulged fishplate
鼓风烘箱	air-circulating oven
鼓风机	fan blower, blower, air blower
鼓丘	drumlin
鼓式张裂缝	drum tension crack
鼓筒式混凝土搅拌机	reversing drum mixer, non-tilting mixer
固弹指数	solid elastic index
固定备用	permanent standby
固定闭塞	fixed blocking
固定臂起重机	fixed-boom crane
固定并联电容无功补偿装置	reactive compensator with fixed parallel capacitors
固定布水器	fixed distributor

G

固定成本　fixed cost, constant cost, unavoidable cost
固定酬金　fixed fee
固定酬金合同　fixed-fee contract
固定单价合同　fixed unit price contract
固定断面　fixed cross section
固定费率项目　fixed rate item
固定费用　fixed cost, fixed charges, fixed expenses
固定分保　obligatory reinsurance
固定工程量总价合同　lump sum on firm bill of quantities
固定工资　fixed wages
固定管理费　fixed overhead
固定价格　fixed price, definite price
固定价格合同　fixed price contract, firm fixed price contract（FFP）
固定价格加激励酬金合同　fixed price plus incentive fee contract
固定开支　fixed expenses
固定劳工工资等级　fixed labour rates
固定利率贷款　fixed rate loan
固定区　non-breathing zone
固定沙丘　fixed dune
固定设备　fixed equipment, capital equipment
固定式开关柜　fixed-type switchgear
固定式液压登车桥　stationary hydraulic yard ramp
固定式液压升降台　stationary hydraulic lifting platform
固定式真空卸污　fixed facility for sewage discharge by vacuum
固定式重力卸污　fixed type gravity sewage discharge
固定水头注水　fixed head water injection
固定水位　fixed water level
固定台位式　fixed position type
固定提成　fixed royalty
固定体积法　fixed volume method
固定投资总额　gross fixed investment
固定误差　fixed error
固定限速　fixed speed limit
固定信贷额　fixed credit line
固定信号　fixed signal
固定辙叉单开道岔　single turnout with fixed frog
固定支架　fixed support
固定支座　fixed bearing
固定装置　fixing device
固定资本　fixed capital
固定资产　fixed property, fixed assets, capital assets, permanent assets, non-trading asset, plant assets
固定资产报废　retirement of fixed assets
固定资产标准　standard of fixed assets
固定资产残值　fixed assets salvage value
固定资产的处置　disposal of fixed assets
固定资产净值　fixed assets net value, net value of fixed assets
固定资产使用费　expenses for using fixed assets
固定资产税　fixed assets tax
固定资产摊销　amortization of fixed asset
固定资产统计师　actuary
固定资产投资　fixed-asset investment
固定资产账户　capital account
固定资产折旧　depreciation of fixed assets
固定总价合同　firm lump sum contract
固化剂土　solidified agent soil
固结　consolidation
固结不排水剪　undrained consolidated shear
固结不排水剪切内摩擦角　internal friction angle under consolidated-undrained shear
固结不排水剪试验　consolidated undrained shear test
固结不排水三轴试验　consolidated-undrained triaxial test
固结沉降　consolidation settlement
固结度　degree of consolidation
固结灌浆　consolidation grouting
固结快剪　consolidated quick shear
固结快剪试验　consolidated quick shear test
固结排水剪　drainage consolidated shear
固结排水剪试验　consolidated drained shear test
固结排水三轴试验　consolidated-drained triaxial test
固结曲线　consolidation curve
固结试验　consolidation test
固结系数　consolidation coefficient
固结仪　consolidometer, consolidation apparatus
固结应力　consolidation stress
固结应力比　consolidation stress ratio
固沙防火带　sand stabilization and fire prevention belt
固态水　solid water
固体废弃物污染　solid waste pollution
固体废物　solid waste
固体废物处置　solid wastes disposal
固体负荷　solid load
固体含量　solid content
固体燃料　solid fuel
固体试剂法　solid reagent method
固体网垫　earth-securing mesh cushion

固相　solid phase
固有频率　natural frequency
故意破坏　vandalism
故意侵权行为　intentional tort
故意行为　intentional act
故障　fault
故障—安全　fail-safe
故障板件　fault board
故障办理　fault treatment, emergency treatment after failure
故障测距　fault locating
故障测试　fault test
故障定位　fault locating
故障复原　fault restoration
故障管理　fault management
故障积累　fault accumulation
故障判别装置　fault identification device
故障升级　escalation of fault
故障检修　corrective maintenance
故障再现　breakdown reappearance
故障诊断　fault diagnosis
顾客　client, customer
顾客信贷　customers' credits
顾问　adviser, advisor, consultant, counselor
顾问费加成功费合同　retainer and success fee contract
顾问委员会　advisory committee
雇工　hired labour
雇工惯例　labour practice
雇工合同　contract of hire of labour
雇工许可证　employment permit
雇佣　engagement, employment, hire
雇佣合同　employment contract, contract of employment
雇用条件　conditions for employment, conditions of engagement, terms of employment
雇员　employee
雇员履历表　employee experience profile
雇员伤害　injury to employees
雇主　employer, hirer
雇主的风险　employer's risks
雇主的接收　employer's taking over
雇主的义务　employer's obligation
雇主的责任　employer's liability
雇主的责任保险　employer's liability insurance
雇主供材料　employer-supplied materials, materials supplied by the employer
雇主决定终止　termination for employer's convenience
雇主决定终止后的付款　payment after Termination for Employer's Convenience
雇主决定终止后的估价　valuation after termination for employer's convenience
雇主提供的保障　indemnity by employer
雇主违约　employer's default
雇主暂停　employer's suspension
雇主暂停后果　consequences of employer's suspension
雇主责任的终止　cessation of employer's liability
雇主终止　termination by employer
刮板输送机　scraper conveyer
刮弓　collapse of pantograph
挂车　trailer
挂钩　hook
挂号信　registered letter
挂号邮件　registered mail
挂扣式脚手板　sticky hook scaffold
挂篮　formtraveler (used for cast-in-place cantilever construction)
拐肘　crank
关闭信号　closing signal
关键部件　key component
关键点　critical point
关键工序　critical process
关键活动　critical activity
关键绩效指标　key performance index
关键里程碑　key milestone
关键路径　critical path
关键路径方法　critical path method (CPM)
关键路径网络图　critical path network
关键路线进度表　critical path schedule
关键人员　key personel
关键日期计划表　critical date schedule
关键事件　critical event
关键事件进度表　key event schedule
关键条款　red flag clause
关键线路　critical path
关键项目清单　critical items list
关键组成部分　key component
关节电连接　electrical connection at overlap
关节式电分相　phase break with overlaps
关境　customs territory
关卡　pike
关联协议　bridging agreement
关税　customs duty, duty, tariff, customs dues
关税保护　tariff protection
关税壁垒　customs barrier, tariff barrier
关税减让　concession of tariff, concession of custom duty
关税率　tariff, tariff rate

关税率表　tariff schedule
关税配额　tariff quota
关税同盟　custom union
关税未付　duty unpaid
关税协议　tariff agreement
关税已付　duty paid
关税优惠　tariff preference
关税征收　collection of customs duty
关税最高限额　tariff ceiling
观察孔　observation hole
观测点　observation point
观测点位置图　plan of observation points
观测墩　observation monument
观测方程(又称"误差方程")　observation equation (also known as "error equation")
观测孔　observation well
观测时段　observation session
观测数据　observation data
观测误差　observation error
观测仪器　observation instrument
观测站　observation station
观测周期　observation period
观测桩　observation pillar
观察检查　visual inspection
观察孔　sightglass
观感质量　appearance quality
官方兑换率　official rate
官方公报　official gazette
官方汇率　official exchange rate
官方价格　official price
冠幅　crown diameter
冠梁　crown beam
管道　pipe, conduit, pipe run, drainage blind ditch, pipeline, trench
管道安装　piping erection
管道保温　pipeline thermal
管道壁厚　pipe wall thickness
管道测量　pipeline surveying
管道防腐　pipe anticorrosion
管道覆土厚度　overlying soil thickness on pipe
管道工　plumber
管道工程　pipe work, plumbing
管道井　pipe shaft
管道埋深　burial depth of the pipe
管道内底　inner bottom of pipe
管道配件　pipe fittings
管道平面布置图　piping layout drawing
管道平面设计图　piping planning
管道仪表流程图
　　piping and instrument diagram (PID/P & ID)
管道运输　pipage
管道综合图　synthesis chart of pipelines
管顶埋深　burial depth of pipe top
管沟　pipe trench
管箍　hoop
管涵　pipe culvert
管界标　section sign
管井　deep well, drilled well
管井出水量　tubewell yield
管卡　pipe clamp
管理策略　management strategy
管理成本　administration cost
管理承包　management contracting
管理承包商　management contractor
管理措施　management measure
管理费　management cost
管理费分配　overhead allocation
管理费账户　overhead account
管理费总价合同
　　management fee lump sum contract
管理顾问　management consultant
管理规定
　　administration rules, administration practice
管理合同　management contract
管理会计
　　managerial accounting, management accounting
管理会计师　managerial accountant
管理机构　government
管理计划　management plan
管理控制系统　management control system
管理协定　management agreement
管理信息　management information
管理信息系统　management information system (MIS)
管理职能　management function
管帽　tube cap
管棚注浆　pipe-roof grouting
管片　segment
管片模具　segment mould
管渠　ditch, channel
管网　network
管网漏失水量　water leakage from pipeline
管辖法律　governing law
管辖权　jurisdiction
管线　line, pipeline, pipe run
管线工程项目　pipeline project
管靴止水器　tube boot sealing device
管涌　piping
管涌潜蚀　subsurface erosion / piping
管制价格　controlled price
管柱基础　tube column foundation

管柱桩　caisson pile
管桩　pipe pile
管桩基础　pipe pile foundation
管子脚手架　tubular scaffold
贯穿性裂缝　penetrating crack
贯流式通风机　tangential ventilator
贯入度　penetration
贯入法检测　penetration inspection
贯入量　penetration rate
贯入仪　penetrometer
贯入阻力　penetration resistance
贯入阻力仪　penetration resistance apparatus
（隧道）贯通　breakthrough
贯通测量　break through survey
贯通地线　through earthing wire
贯通误差　passing error
惯例　convention, custom, practice, usage, general practice
惯例法　customary law
惯性测量系统　inertial surveying system
灌溉　irrigation
灌溉渠　irrigation channel
灌溉田　sewage farming
灌浆　grouting
灌浆泵　grout pump
灌浆机　grouting machine
灌浆试验　grouting test
灌浆压力　grouting pressure
灌木　shrub
灌渠　irrigation canal
灌砂法　sand cone method
灌水法　water replacement method
灌水试验　water filling test
灌注　pouring, casting
灌注孔　pouring hole
灌注砂浆饱满度　plumpness of mortar grouting
灌注桩　filling pile
灌注桩后注浆　post grouting for cast-in-situ pile
罐　silo
罐体安全装置　tank safety device
罐体连接装置　tank connecting device
罐体输送装置　tank delivery device
光传送段　optical transmission section (OTS)
光传送网　optical transport network (OTN)
光船租赁　bareboat charter
光带　light strip
光带式表示　light-strip indication
光点式表示　light-spot indication
光电参数　photoelectric parameter
光电测距　electro-optical distance measurement

光电测距导线　photoelectric distance measuring traverse
光电测距仪　electro-optical distance measurement instrument
光电隔离器　optoelectronic isolator
光电缆引入　optical eletrical cable lead-in
光电缆引入柜　optical eletrical cable lead-in cabinet
光电式挠度仪　photoelectric type flexural meter, photoelectric deflectometer
光电式液塑限联合测定仪　photoelectric type liquid-plastic limit combined tester
光电转换器　photoelectric converter
光分配网络　optical distribution network (ODN)
光复用段　optical multiplex section
光复用段保护　optical multiplex section protection (OMSP)
光功率　optical power
光功率计　optical power meter
光监控通路　optical supervisory channel (OSC)
光距条件　optical ranging condition
光可变衰耗器　variable optical attenuator
光缆　optical cable
光缆监测系统　optical cable monitoring system
光轮压路机　smooth wheel roller, smooth-wheeled roller
光面爆破　smooth blasting
光面管散热器　pipe radiator
光幕反射　veiling reflection
光缆配线架　optical distribution frame (ODF)
光票　clean bill, clean draft
光票托收　clean (bill for) collection, collection on clean bill
光票信用证　clean (letter of) credit
光谱纯　Spectrography
光谱分析仪　spectrum analyzer
光强分布　light distribution
光栅传感器　grating sensor
光时域反射仪　optical time-domain reflectometer (OTDR)
光衰耗器　optical attenuator
光通道　optical channel
光通道数据单元　Optical Channel Data Unit (ODU)
光通量　light flux
光通量维持率　luminous flux maintenance factor
光通路传送单元　optical channel transport unit
光通路净荷单元　optical channel payload unit
光网络单元　optical network unit (ONU)
光纤　optic fibre
光纤存储交换机　fabric switch

光纤到户　Fiber to the Home(FTTH)
光纤到楼宇/分线盒
　　Fiber to the Building/Curb(FTTB/C)
光纤端面　fiber end face
光纤监测系统　optical fiber monitoring system
光纤交换机　FC switch
光纤连接　optical connection
光纤配线架　optical distribution frame(ODF)
光纤熔接机　optical fiber fusion splicer
光纤收发器　fiber optical transceiver
光纤通道　optical channel, fiber channel (FC)
光纤线路自动切换保护装置　optical fiber line auto switch protection equipment(OLP)
光纤余长　residual length of optical fiber
光线路终端　optical line terminal(OLT)
光线束法区域网平差
　　block adjustment using bundle method
光信噪比　Optical Signal to Noise Ratio(OSNR)
光学对中器　optical centering device
光学机械纠正　optical-mechanical rectification
光学立体模型　optical stereoscopic model
光学图像处理　optical image processing
光学镶嵌　optical mosaic
光学准直　optical alignment
光源　light source
光泽　luster
光中继器　optical repeater
光转换器单元　optical transponder unit (OTU)
广播电缆　audio cable
广播分区　zoning of public address system
广播控制器　controller of public address system
广播通信　broadcast communication
广播星历　broadcast ephemeris
广域网　wide area network
归并　incorporation
归档　archiving
归还保函　restitution of the guarantee, release of the guarantee
归零差　misclosure of round
归属位置寄存器　home location register (HLR)
归心元素　centering element
归一化　uniformization
规避　dodge
规程　specification
规定日期　specified date
规定声压级　specified sound pressure level
规范　specification, code, standard
规范验证　code verification
规费　specified costs
规格　specification

规格响应表　specification compliance form
规划　planning
规划测量　planning survey
规划当局　planning authority
规划同意书　planning consent
规划许可　planning permission, zoning permit
规划选线　planning-based railway location
规模　scale
规则　rule
规章制度　rules and regulations
硅华　fiorite
硅灰　silica fume
硅灰石　wollastonite
硅镁石　stevensite
硅钼蓝分光光度法
　　silicon molybdenum blue spectrophotometry
硅酸盐　silicate
硅酸盐矿渣水泥　portland slag cement
硅酸盐水泥　Portland cement
硅线石　sillimanite
硅橡胶护套　silicone rubber sheath
硅元件　Silicon components
硅藻土　diatomaceous earth
硅质胶结　siliceous cementation
硅质岩　silicalite
硅质页岩　siliceous shale
轨撑　rail brace
轨道　track
轨道暗坑　voids under sleeper/tie
轨道板　track slab
轨道板编号　serial number of track slab
轨道板精调　fine adjustment of track slab
轨道板偏移　track slab deflection
轨道板铺设　track slab laying
轨道板上浮　track slab floating
轨道板预制场　precast yard for track slab
轨道板运输　track slab delivery
轨道板中线位置　centerline position of track slab
轨道板纵向连接
　　longitudinal connection of track slabs
轨道变形　track deformation
轨道变压器箱　track transformer box
轨道变阻器　track rheostat
轨道不平顺　track irregularity
轨道参数　track parameter
轨道残余变形　track residual deformation
轨道车　rail car
轨道车库　rail car shed
轨道承载力　track carrying capacity
轨道单元板　unit slab

轨道道床漏泄电阻　track bed leakage resistance
轨道电抗器　track reactor
轨道电路　track circuit
轨道电路长度　track circuit length
轨道电路电码化　coding overlapped on track circuit
轨道电路读取器　track circuit reader
轨道电路分割　separation of track circuit
轨道电路分路状态　shunting state of track circuit
轨道电路构成　constitution of track circuit
轨道电路区段　track circuit section
轨道电路死区段　dead section of track circuit
轨道电路蓄电现象　track storage effect
轨道电路一次调整　track circuit adjustment at once
轨道电位　rail potential
轨道动力稳定车　dynamic track stabilizer
轨道动力学　track dynamics
轨道附属设备　track auxiliary component
轨道工程　track works, track engineering
轨道衡　rail weighing bridge
轨道基准点　track datum mark
轨道几何尺寸容许公差　track geometry tolerances
轨道几何形位　track geometry
轨道检测　track inspection
轨道检测设备　track inspection device
轨道检查车　track inspection car
轨道检查小车　track inspection trolley
轨道接触器　track treadle
轨道结构　track structure
轨道绝缘　track insulation
轨道空闲　track unoccupied
轨道控制网　track control network（CPⅢ）
轨道框架刚度　rigidity of track panel
轨道类型　type of track
轨道力学　track mechanics
轨道滤波器　track filter
轨道明坑　visible pit of track
轨道平车　rail flat car
轨道谱　track geometry spectrum
轨道起重机　track-bound crane
轨道强度　track strength
轨道区段　track section
轨道区段设备状态　state of track section device
轨道设计　track design
轨道生电现象　track galvanic effect
轨道失效　track failure
轨道施工测量　construction survey of track works
轨道式集装箱门式起重机
　　rail mounted container gantry crane
轨道受电变压器
　　transformer at track circuit receiving end
轨道水平尺　track level
轨道条件测试　track condition test
轨道系统　track system
轨道信息接收单元
　　specific transmission module（STM）
轨道信息接收天线
　　track information receiving antenna
轨道养护标准　track maintenance standard
轨道养护维修　track maintenance and repair
轨道占用　track occupied
轨道占用检查　track occupation check
轨道质量指数　track quality index（TQI）
轨道状态　track condition
轨底　rail base
轨底崩裂　burst of rail base
轨底坡　rail base slope, rail bottom inclination, rail cant
轨顶　top of rail（TOR）
轨端崩裂　burst of rail end
轨缝　rail joint gap
轨缝调整器　rail gap adjuster
轨回流系统　track return system
轨检车　track inspection car
轨检车评分　evaluation by track inspection car
轨距　track gauge
轨距挡板　gauge apron, guide plate
轨距杆　gauge rod
轨距加宽　gauge widening
轨距加宽递减率　declining rate of gauge widening
轨距块　track gauge block
轨料存放区　track material storage area
轨面　rail plane
轨排　track panel, track framework
轨排存放区　storage area of track section
轨排调整　track panel adjustment
轨排基地　track panel base
轨排拼装　assembly of track section
轨排生产区　production area of track section
轨排生产作业线　production line of track section
轨排运送车　track panel transport car
轨排组装　track panel assembling
轨排组装机　track panel assembling machine
轨旁电子单元　trackside electronic unit
轨头　rail head
轨头剥离　rail head shelling
轨头发裂　rail head checks
轨头肥边　flow of rail head, lip of rail head
轨头核伤　transverse fatigue crack in rail head,
　　tache ovale, transverse fissure in rail head
轨头磨损　rail head wear
轨头劈裂　split of rail head

G

轨头微细波纹　detail fracture of rail head
轨头压溃　crushing of rail head
轨头整形　rail head reprofiling
轨温监测　rail temperature monitoring
轨隙片　rail gap slice
轨下垫板　rail pad
轨下基础　substructure, sub-rail structure
轨向　alignment of track
轨向水平逆向复合不平顺
　　reverse composite irregularity of the track cross level and the alignment
轨行式起重机　rail mounted crane
轨行式装运机械　rail-mounted handling and transportation machine
轨腰　rail web
轨腰劈裂　split of rail web
轨枕　sleeper
轨枕抽换机　tie replacing machine
轨枕更换　sleeper replacement
轨枕更换机　sleeper replacement machine
轨枕盒　sleeper crib
轨枕铺设　sleeper laying
轨枕伤损　sleeper defect
轨枕修补　sleeper repair
轨枕预制场　precast yard for rail sleeper
贵务—产权比率　debt-equity ratio
辊压复合土工膜　roll-in composite geo-membrane
滚刀　disc cutter
滚刀承载能力　load-bearing capacity of disc cutter
滚刀数　number of disc cutters
滚焊机　seam welder
滚筒式拌和机　drum mixer
滚轴支座　roller bearing
锅炉　boiler
锅炉房　boiler room
锅炉热效率　heat efficiency of boiler
锅穴　pot hole
国别风险　country risk
国别配额　country quota
国产的　domestic
国籍　nationality
国际避税　international tax avoidance
国际博览会　international fair
国际财团　consortium
国际电信联盟远程通信标准化组　international telecommunication union-telecommunication Sector (ITU-T)
国际法　international law, law of nations
国际工程　international project, international construction project
国际公司　international corporation
国际公约　international convention
国际惯例　international customs, international practice, international convention
国际货物运输保险　international cargo transportation insurance
国际价格　international price
国际监管箱　internationally supervised containers
国际借贷差额　balance of international indebtedness
国际金融　international finance
国际竞争性招标
　　international competitive bidding (ICB)
国际开发协会信贷　IDA credit
国际贸易　international trade
国际贸易法　international trade law
国际贸易货币　international trade currency
国际贸易逆差
　　adverse balance of international trade
国际贸易术语　international commercial terms
国际贸易术语解释通则　international rules for the interpretation of trade terms (INCOTERMS)
国际双重征税　international double taxation, international double tax imposition
国际税收协定　international taxation agreement
国际私法　private international law
国际通行货币　international currency
国际效力　international validity
国际询价采购　international shopping
国际移动用户识别码
　　international mobile subscriber identity (IMSI)
国际银团贷款　international syndicated loan
国际运费　international freight charge
国际制裁　international sanctions
国际仲裁裁决书　international arbitral award
国际仲裁法庭　international arbitral tribunal
国际咨询工程师联合会　FIDIC
国际字典框架
　　international framework for dictionaries (IFD)
国家　nation, country, state
国家保险　national insurance
国家标准　national standard
国家财政　national finance
国家法令　national statute
国家公债　national bond
国家海关辖区　national customs territory
国家税收　national revenue
国家铁路　national railway
国家重点文物保护单位
　　national key cultural relics protection units
国家主权　national sovereignty

国家坐标系　national coordinate system
国境　frontier
国库　treasury
国库券　treasury bill
国民　nationals
国民总收入　national product
国民待遇　national treatment
国民经济评价　national economic evaluation
国民生产净值　net national product (NNP)
国民生产总值　gross national product (GNP)
国民收入总值　gross national income (GNI)
国民所得　national dividend
国内财政　domestic finance
国内代理人　domestic agent
国内费用　domestic cost
国内工程项目　domestic project
国内合伙人　domestic partner
国内合同　domestic contract
国内汇兑　domestic remittance, domestic exchange
国内货运保险
　domestic cargo transportation insurance
国内竞争性招标　local competitive bidding (LCB),
　national competitive bidding
国内贸易　domestic trade
国内生产总值　gross domestic product (GDP)
国内市场　national market
国内市场价格　domestic market price
国内税　domestic tax, internal tax
国内提单　inland bill of lading
国内提单条款　inland bill of lading clause
国内通货膨胀率　domestic inflation rate
国内消费　home consumption
国内消费品进口报关单　entry for home use
国内销售额　domestic turnover
国内优惠　domestic preference
国内优先　domestic priority
国内运费　home-freight
国内制造　home made
国内仲裁裁决　domestic arbitral award
国内资源成本　domestic resources cost
国内总产值　gross domestic product (GDP)
国税　national tax
国土基础信息系统　basic information system of land
国外分部　overseas branch
国外分支机构　foreign branch
国外付款　payment abroad
国外工程　overseas works
国外汇票　foreign draft
国外培训　overseas training
国外市场　foreign market

国外投资　foreign investment
国外项目　overseas project
国外子公司　foreign subsidiary
国有企业　state-owned enterprise
国债　national debt
过岔速度
　turnout passing speed, turnout through speed
过超高
　cant excess, cant surplus, surplus superelevation
过程控制　process control
过程天窗　possessive interval for process
过道　aisle
过电流　overcurrent
过电流保护　overcurrent protection
过电压　overvoltage
过电压保护　overvoltage protection
过电压保护装置　overvoltage protection device
过度改正　overcorrection
过渡贷款　bridge loan
过渡段　transition section
过渡段工程　transition section works
过渡方案　transition scheme
过渡工程　transitional works
过渡工程费　cost of transitional works
过渡滚刀　transitional disc cutter
过渡孔　transition span
过渡区　transition area
过渡相　transition facies
过渡性融资　bridge financing
过放电　over-discharge
过负荷　overload
过负荷保护　overload protection
过负荷能力　overload capability
过负荷曲线　overload curve
过轨敷设　laying through track
过轨钢管　steel pipe passing through track
过户　transfer
过户结账日　pay day, account day
过境国　transit country
过境签证　transit visa
过境权　right of way
过境手续　transit formalities
过境税
　transit tax, transit duty (dues), passenger duty
过境运价　transborder rate
过梁　lintel
过硫酸铵分光光度法
　ammonium persulfate spectrophotometry
过滤　filtration
过滤层　filter course

过滤器　filter
过滤器初阻力　initial resistance of filter
过滤器终阻力　final resistance of filter
过滤吸收器　gas particulate filter
过滤效率　filtration efficiency
过期　past-due
过期保险单　stale policy
过期利息　over interest
过期票据　past-due bill (note)
过期提单　stale bill of lading
过期未付的　overdue
过期未付款　back money, overdue payment
过期支票　out-of-date check, stale check, overdue check
过热蒸汽　superheated steam

过筛　sieving
过失　negligence
过失侵权诉讼　action for negligence
过失行为　negligent act
过失性大超差　faulty excessive out-of-tolerance
过失责任　liability for fault
过失罪　error of omission, negligent crime
过时设备　out-of-date equipment
过水断面　discharge cross-section
过堰流量　weir flow
过氧化氢　hydrogen peroxide
过账　post, posting
过账依据　posting reference
过走防护区　overlap
过走防护区段　passing protected section

H

H 形钢柱　H-shape steel pole
H 形管　H pipe
H 形型钢　H-shaped section steel
海岸　coast
海拔　height above sealevel
海滨　seashore
海成　marine origin
海地地貌　submarine geomorphy
海峰　seapeak
海港　maritime port
海工建筑　maritime works
海沟　trench
海关　customs, customs house, maritime customs
海关保税保证书　customs bond
海关登记　customs entry
海关发票　customs invoice
海关法　customs law
海关放行证　customs clearance
海关估价　customs appraised value, customs valuation
海关关长　chief of customs
海关官员　customs house officer
海关检查　rummage
海关检查证　jerque note
海关检验　customs examination
海关检验人员　surveyor of customs
海关进口手续　customs entry
海关进口税则　customs import tariff
海关境域　customs territory
海关申报单　customs declaration form
海关收据　customs receipt
海关手续　customs procedures, customs formalities
海关署长　controller of customs
海关税率　rate of customs duty
海关税则　customs tariff, tariff
海关条例　customs regulations
海关通行证　customs pass
海关退税单　debenture
海关委托人　customs consignee
海关许可证　customs permit
海关验货单　customs examination list
海关佣金　customs brokerage
海积阶地　sea terrace
海积平原　marine deposition plain
海积土　marine soil
海里　nautical mile
海岭　ridge, ocean ridge
海陆交互沉积　interactive marine and terrestrial deposit
海陆联运　ocean and rail (O. & R.)
海绿石　glauconite
海难　perils of the sea
海难救援公司　salvage company
海泡石　sepiolite
海盆　sea basin
海侵层序　transgression sequence
海砂　sea sand
海山　seamount
海商法　marine law, maritime law
海上保险契约　contract of marine insurance
海上的　marine
海上风险　perils of the sea, maritime perils
海上火灾　fire on the sea
海上建筑物　marine structure
海上救助　salvage
海上综合保险　all risks marine insurance
海蚀壁龛　wave cut notch
海蚀窗　marine window
海蚀地貌　abrasion geomorphy
海蚀拱桥　marine arch
海蚀平台　marine platform
海蚀穴　sea cave
海蚀崖　marine erosion cliff
海蚀岩柱　marine stack
海事法庭　maritime court
海事索赔　maritime claim

海事仲裁委员会　maritime arbitration commission
海水　sea water
海损　average, sea damage, maritime loss
海损保险单　average policy
海损代理人　average agent
海损分摊　average contribution
海损精算书　adjustment letter
海损理算　adjustment of average
海损理算人　average taker, adjuster
海损条款　sea damage terms
海损协议　average agreement
海滩　beach
海图　chart, marine chart
海退层序　regressive sequence
海外　overseas, abroad
海外办事处　offshore office
海外代理商　overseas agents
海外工程　overseas project
海外津贴　overseas allowance
海外市场　overseas market
海外投资　overseas investment
海湾　gulf
海西期　Hercynian age/stage
海峡　strait
海相　marine facies, sea facies
海相沉积　marine deposit
海啸　tsunami
海洋地貌　marine geomorphy
海洋货运保险　cargo marine insurance
海洋污染　marine pollution
海洋运输保险　maritime transportation insurance
海洋运输货物保险　ocean marine cargo (transportation) insurance
海运　ocean carriage, shipping
海运保险　marine insurance, sea insurance
海运保险单　marine insurance policy
海运保险费　marine premium
海运承运人　ocean carrier
海运的　maritime
海运费　sea freight, ocean freight
海运公会　shipping conference
海运公会运价　conference rate
海运合同　contract of ocean carriage
海运提单　ocean waybill, ocean bill of lading, marine bill of lading
含尘浓度　dust concentration
含镉污水　cadmiferous sewage
含碱量　alkali content
含量　content
含泥量　silt content
含铅污水　leady sewage
含湿量　moisture content
含水比　water content ratio
含水冰层　water-bearing ice layer
含水层　water bearing stratum, aquifer
含水层露头地区　aquifer outcrop areas
含水带　water-bearing zone
含水量　water content
含水率　water content
含水沙层　water bearing sand
含土冰层　soil-containing ice layer
含油率　oil length
含油生产污水　oily production sewage
含油污水　oily sewage
含重金属污水　heavy metals contained sewage
焓湿图　enthalpy-humidity diagram
焓值　enthalpy
涵洞　culvert
涵洞测量　culvert survey
涵洞出水口　culvert water outlet
涵洞进水口　culvert water inlet
涵洞孔径　culvert span
寒冷地区　cold region
寒漠带　cold desert zone
寒温带　cold temperate zone
寒武纪　Cambrian period
寒武系　Cambrian system
罕遇地震　seldomly occured earthquake
夯　rammer
夯具　compactor
夯实　compaction
夯实道床　ballast consolidating, ballast compaction
夯实地基　rammed ground
夯实水泥土桩复合地基　composite foundation with rammed soil-cement piles
夯土机　earth-rammer
旱地　dry farm
旱桥　dry bridge
焊缝　weld seam
焊缝金属拉伸试验　all-weld tensile test
焊工　welder
焊轨机　rail welding machine
焊轨生产线　rail welding production line
焊后热处理　postweld heat treatment
焊脚尺寸　leg length
焊接　welding
焊接(用于电子设备的锡焊)　soldering
焊接材料　welding consumable
焊接长度　welding length
焊接长钢轨　welded long rail

焊接长钢轨运送车　transport car of welded long rails
焊接钢结构　welded steel structure
焊接钢梁　welded steel beam
焊接骨架　welded framework
焊接接头　welded rail joint
焊接式钢轨接续线　welded bond
焊头　welding head
焊修钢轨　rail repair welding
航次　voyage
航次租船　charter by voyage
航带设计　flight strip design
航道测量　channel survey
航道绘图水位　channel surveying reference level
航高差　flight level difference
航海日志　logbook
航迹线　flight trajectory
航空货运　air freight
航空货运单　air-way bill
航空日志　logbook
航空摄影　aerial photography
航空摄影比例尺　aerial photographic scale
航空摄影测量　aerial photogrammetry
航空摄影测量学　aerial photogrammetry
航空摄影分区　flight block
航空托运单　air consignment note（CAN）
航空遥感　aerial remote sensing
航空运费　air freight
航空运输货物保险
　　air transportation cargo insurance
航空照片　aerial photo
航偏角　drift angle
航空摄影绝对漏洞　aerial photographic absolute gap
航空摄影漏洞　aerial photographic gap
航空摄影相对漏洞　aerial photographic relative gap
航天遥感　space remote sensing
航天遥感技术　space remote sensing technology
航线　line, route, air line, air route, airway, shipping line, way, itinerary, azimuth, pathway, trajectory, course line
航线段　segment of flight strip
航线弯曲度　strip deformation
航线网　network of flight strip
航向倾角　longitudinal tilt
航向重叠　longitudinal overlap
航行　voyage, navigate, sail, fly
航运公会　shipping conference, freight conference
行规　professional etiquette, guild regulations, industrial rules
行话　jargon, cant, slang
行距　inter-line spacing
行情　conjuncture, tone, business condition, market quotations, market information, price
行业惯例　industry practice, industry routine, trade practice
行业惯例标准　standards of industry practice
行长　president
毫米锁闭　mm locking
好氧　aerobic, oxic
好氧处理　aerobic treatment
好氧泥龄　oxic sludge age
好氧区　oxic zone, aerobic zone
好氧稳定塘　aerobic pond
好氧消化　aerobic digestion
耗电　power consumption
耗电输热比
　　ratio of power consumption to heat output
耗减准备　depletion reserve, reserve for depletion
耗减资产　wasting assets.
耗尽　deplete, exhaust, expiration
耗煤　coal consumption
耗能剪切模量
　　energy consumption shear strength modulus
耗热量　heat loss
耗水　water consumption
合并　merge, amalgamation, combination
合并报价　combined quotation, merge offer
合并财务报表　consolidated financial statement, combined financial statement
合并发盘　combined offer, merge offer
合并资产负债表　consolidated balance sheet, amalgamated balance sheet
合成轨枕　composite sleeper
合成纤维　synthetic fibre
合点控制　vanishing-point control
合法　legality, legitimacy
合法持票人　bona-fide holder, lawful bearer
合法当局　constituted authority, legal authority
合法的　legal, lawful, legitimate, rightful, licit
合法抵押　legal mortgage
合法继承人　legitimate heir, lawful successor, heares legitimus, successor legitimus
合法码字　valid code
合法请求　legitimate claim, legal requests
合法权利　legitimate right, lawful right
合法收入　legitimate income, lawful earned income
合法授权　legal authorization
合法性　legality
合格材料　acceptable materials, qualified materials
合格产品　eligible product, acceptable product

合格承包商　eligible contractor, qualified contractor
合格的　eligible, acceptable, qualified
合格来源国　eligible source country
合格票据　eligible bill, eligible paper
合格投标者　eligible bidder, eligible tenderer
合格性　eligibility
合格性检验
　test for suitability, conformity test, approval test
合格性限制　restriction on eligibility, eligibility limit
合格证　certification
合格质量　acceptable quality
合格桩　qualified piles
合股人　partner
合规性验证体系　compliance verification system
合规性验证文件
　compliance verification documentation
合伙　partnership
合伙关系　partnership, copartnery
合伙企业　partnership, partnership enterprise, partnership business establishment
合伙契约
　deed of partnership, contract of copartnery, partnership contract, partnership agreement
合伙人　associate, partner
合伙受让人　coassignee, partnership assignee
合伙受托人　partnership trustee
合架供电线　along-track feeder
合金轨　alloy rail
合理驳回　fair dismissal
合理索赔　legitimate claim, resonable claim
合流污水泵站　combined sewage pumping station
合流制　combined system
合龙　closure
合拢　closure joint
合同　contract
合同安排　contractual arrangement
合同版本　contract version
合同包　contract package
合同变更　contract variation, contract change, modification of contract, alteration of contract
合同标的　contract object
合同补充条款　additional contract clauses, supplementary terms of the contract
合同不履行　non-implementation of contract, non-performance of contract
合同草稿　contract draft
合同超支额
　contract overrun, contract overexpenditure
合同承诺　contractual commitments
合同担保　contract bond, the contract guarantee
合同档案　contract file
合同到期　expiration of contract
合同缔结　conclusion of contract
合同额　contract amount
合同法　contract law, law of contract
合同范本　model contract, standard form of contract, model agreement
合同范围　contract package scope
合同范围变更　contract scope changes
合同分类账　contract ledger
合同风险　contract risk
合同附件　appendix to contract
合同格式　contract form, formality of contract
合同各方　parties to contract
合同工程师　contract engineer
合同公证费　contract notarial fees
合同构成　contract formation
合同关系　contractual relationship
合同关系不涉及第三者原则　privity of contract
合同管理
　contract administration, contract management
合同管辖法　proper law of the contract, law governing the contract, law of contract jurisdiction
合同惯例　contractual practice, contractual usage
合同规定
　contract provisions, provisions of contract, contract stipulations, contractual specification
合同规定的货币　currency of contract, contract currency, the currency specified in the contract
合同规模　contract size
合同货物验收证书
　acceptance certificate of the contract goods
合同记录　contract records
合同计量类型　admeasurement type of contract
合同价格
　contract price, contract amount, contract sum
合同价格调整公式指数　indices for contract price adjustment formula
合同价格和付款　contract price and payment
合同价值　contract value
合同接口　contract interface
合同节余额　contract underrun, contract balance
合同解除　contractual release, discharge of contract, rescission of contract, dissolution of contract, termination of contract
合同解释　interpretation of contract
合同金额的充分性
　sufficiency of the contract amount
合同经理　contract manager
合同卷宗　contract files

合同类型　contract type
合同履行　implementation of contract, performance of contract, fulfilment of contract
合同落空　frustration of contract
合同批准通知　approval notice of the contract
合同期　contract period, period of contract, duration of contract
合同期的延长　extension of contract period
合同期满　contract expiry, expiration of contract
合同签订程序　procedure for concluding a contract
合同签署　signing the contract
合同签署日期　contract signature date
合同前的程序　pre-contract procedures
合同权利　contractual right
合同权益转让　assignment of contract rights, transfer of contractual interest
合同审核　contract review, contract verification
合同生效　entry of contract into force, execution of contract, effectiveness of contract, validate contract
合同生效日期　starting date of contract, effective date of contract
合同实施　performance of contract, contract execution, contract implementation
合同收尾　contract close-out
合同授权　contract authorization
合同数据　contract data
合同数据表格资料　contract data
合同谈判　contract negotiation
合同条件/本条件　conditions of contract/these conditions
合同条款　contract clause, provisions of contract, contract terms
合同外索赔　ex-contractual claims
合同完成日期　contract completion date
合同完成证书　contract completion certificate
合同文件　contract documents, contract file
合同文件的编制　preparation of contract documents
合同文件的优先次序　priority of contract documents
合同文件分析　contract document analysis
合同文件审核　contract document review
合同项目　contract project
合同项下的投入　contractual input
合同协议书　contract agreement
合同序号　contract serial number
合同续订　contract renewal, renewal of contract
合同要点　point of contract
合同一般责任　general contractual liabilities
合同一方/当事人　party/parties

合同义务　contract duty, contract obligation, contractual obligation
合同意识　sense of contract, contract consciousness
合同有效期　contract period, term of contract, life of contract, duration of contract
合同有效性　validity of contract
合同语言　contract language, language of contract
合同预付款　advance payment for contract
合同约定价格　contract price
合同约束　contractual restrictions, contract constraint
合同暂停　contract suspension
合同责任　contractual liabilities
合同债务　contract debt
合同展期　renewal of contract
合同争议　contract dispute
合同支付担保　contract payment bond, contract payment guarantee
合同终止　contract termination
合同仲裁费　contract arbitration fees
合同转让　assignment of contract
合同准据法　proper law of the contract, applicable law of contract
合同最终评审　final contract review
合意裁决　consent award
合意解决　accord and satisfaction
合约正本　original of the contract
合闸回路　closing circuit
合闸母线　closing power source bus
合闸时间　closing time, making time
合闸线圈　closing coil, making coil
合重　total weight
合资公司　joint venture company, co-partnership company, consortium company
合资企业　joint venture, consortium
合资企业协议　joint venture agreement, consortium agreement
合资铁路　joint venture railway
合资银行　joint venture bank, share-holding bank, consortium bank
合作　co-operation
合作合同　collaboration contract, cooperation contract
合作生产　co-production, joint production
和解　conciliate, conciliation, compromise, reconciliation
和解协议　composition, agreement of dispute resolution, settlement agreement
和易性　workability
河岸　riverbank, riverside

河岸冲刷路堤　embankment with riverbank scouring
河槽　river channel
河槽糙率系数　channel roughness coefficient
河槽宽度　channel width
河槽天然冲刷　natural scour of river channel
河成相　fluvial facies
河床　river bed
河床比降　riverbed gradient
河床变迁　deformation of river bed
河床冲刷　riverbed scouring
河床宽度　river bed width
河床铺砌　river bed paving
河床式取水构筑物　riverbed intake structure
河道　river course
河道调查　river course survey
河道取砂(砾)料　sand material excavated from river course
河底　river bottom
河谷　river valley
河谷阶地　valley terrace
河间地块　interfluve
河间洼地　interfluve depression
河口三角洲　estuarine delta
河漫滩　flood plain, alluvial flat
河漫滩相　flood plain facies, alluvial flat facies
河渠疏浚　channel dredging
河砂　fluvial sand
河水　river water
河滩　floodplain
河滩路堤　embankment of the benchland
荷载　loading
荷载标准值　load standard value
荷载布置　load arrangement
荷载代表值　representative values of a load
荷载分项系数　partial factor for load
荷载工况　load case
荷载横向分布　transverse distribution of load
荷载换算系数　load conversion coefficient
荷载检验　load test
荷载率　load rate
荷载偶然组合　occasional combination of loads
荷载频遇值　frequent value of a load
荷载强度　load strength
荷载设计值　design value of a load
荷载试验　load test
荷载效率　load efficiency
荷载效应　load effect
荷载效应准永久组合　quasi-permanent combination of load effect
荷载效应组合　combination of load effect
荷载效应最不利组合　most unfavorable combination of load effect
荷载准永久值　quasi-permanent value of a load
荷载组合　load combination
荷载作用标准值　standard value of load
荷载作用代表值　representative value of load
荷载作用分项系数　partial factor of load
荷载作用设计值　design value of load
荷载作用准永久值　quasi-permanent value of load
荷重率　load rate
核查　review, examine, inspection
核磁共振探视法　nuclear magnetic resonance method
核单　vouching
核定股本　authorized capital stock
核对符号　check mark
核对清单　checklist, punchlist, verify a statement
核对账目　verification of account, check up account
核风险　nuclear risk
核实　verify, check, prove
核算　accounting, computation
核销　charge off, cancel after verification
核心节点　core node
核心竞争力　core competitiveness, core competence
核心网　core network
核装置　nuclear assembly, nuclear device
核准　authorize, authorization, examine and approve, check and approve
核准书　written authorization, project charter, remittance permit, project proposal for approval
核准资本　authorized capital, approved capital
核子密度湿度测试仪　nucleon density and humidity tester
核子射线法　nuclear ray method
褐煤　lignite
褐铁矿　limonite
鹤管　loading arm
黑球温度　black globe temperature
黑曜岩　obsidian, hyalopsite
黑云母　biotite
恒荷载　dead load
恒量　constant
恒温烘箱　constant temperature oven
恒温水槽　thermostatic water bath
恒温养护箱　constant temperature curing box
恒应力压力机　constant stress press machine
恒载　dead load
恒张力放线车　constant tension wire barrow
桁架　truss
桁架拱　truss arch

桁架拱桥	trussed arch bridge
桁架横梁	truss crossbeam
桁架桥	trussed bridge
横波	transverse wave
横财	windfall
横承力索	head-span wire
横承力索线夹	head-span wire clamp
横道图	Gantt chart, bar chart
横断层	cross fault
横断面	cross section
横断面测量	cross-section survey
横断面图	cross section drawing
横腹杆预应力钢筋混凝土支柱	transverse web prestressed reinforced concrete pole
横杆	cross-bar
横隔板	diaphragm
横谷	transverse valley
横管	horizontal pipe
横基尺视差法	subtense method with horizontal staff
横截面	cross section
横跨结构	cross-span structure
横联	sway bracing
横梁	transverse floorbeam, cross beam
横列配置	transverse arrangement, lateral arrangement
横列式编组站	transverse marshalling station
横列式区段站	transverse district station
横坡	transverse slope
横墙刚度	rigidity of transverse wall
横墙间距	spacing of transverse walls
横式	horizontal type
横通道	cross tunnel, cross passage, connection tunnel, connection passage
横卧板	lateral stiffener
横线支票	cross(crossed) check(cheque)
横向测井	lateral logging
横向电连接	transverse electrical connection, electrical connection between MW and CW
横向分布	transverse distribution
横向分布钢筋	transverse distribution bar
横向刚度	lateral stiffness, rigidity, inflexibility
横向钢筋	lateral reinforcement
横向环流	transverse circulation
横向加劲肋	lateral stiffener
横向结构物	lateral structure
横向连接	transverse link
横向排水设备	lateral drainage facility
横向排水设施	transverse drainage facility
横向偏差	lateral deviation
横向坡度	transverse gradient
横向沙丘	transverse dune
横向水平力系数	lateral force factor
横向水平支撑	transverse horizontal bracing
横向撕裂力	lateral tear force
横向协议	horizontal agreement
横向斜撑	transverse diagonal brace
横向增大系数	lateral enlargement factor
横向振动加速度	lateral vibration acceleration
横向振幅	lateral vibration amplitude
横移梁	lateral launching of girder, lateral launching of beam
横轴	abscissa axis, transverse shaft, transverse axis, lateral axle, horizontal axis
横轴投影	transversal projection
横坐标	abscissa
衡量	measurement
衡平法按揭	equitable mortgage
衡平租赁	leveraged lease
衡重式挡土墙	balance weight retaining wall
衡重噪声	weighted noise
烘干法	oven drying method
烘箱	oven
红层	red bed
红利	bonus. dividend
红利股	bonus share (stock)
红黏土	red clay
红黏土路基	red clay subgrade
红土	laterite
红外	infrared
红外测距	infrared distance measurement
红外对射探测器	infrared opposite emission detector
红外勘探	infrared detection
红外摄影	infrared photography
红外探测	infrared detection
红外线测温仪	infrared thermometer
红外线辐射器	infrared radiator
红外线轴温探测设备检测所(红外所)	maintenance center for hotbox detection system
红外线轴温探测系统	infrared journal temperature detection system, ultrared hotbox detection system, THDS
宏观结构	macrostructure
宏观预测	macro-forecast
虹吸	siphon, syphonage, syphon
虹吸管	siphon
虹吸管法	siphon tube method
虹吸涵洞	siphon culvert
虹吸回流	siphon backflow

虹吸滤池　siphon filter
虹吸筒法　siphon cylinder method
洪峰　flood peak
洪峰流量　peak flow, peak discharge
洪积的　pluvial
洪积扇　proluvial fan
洪积土　diluvial soil
洪积相　pluvial facies
洪水　flood
洪水标记　flood mark
洪水调查　flood survey
洪水流量　flood discharge
洪水频率　flood frequency
洪水位　flood level
洪水淹没　flood inundation of railway
洪水影响评价报告编制费　compilation fee of flood influence assessment report
后备保护　backup protection
后备计划　program backup, backup plan
后备人员　reserve personnel
后备式 UPS　offline UPS
后处理差分改正　post-processed differential correction
后端分析　back-end analysis
后方交会　resection
后继条件　condition subsequent
后浇带　post-poured strip
后接点　back contact
后配套　backup system
后配套设备　back-up equipment
后评价　post evaluation
后期支护　afterwards backup
后勤　logistics, rear services
后勤保障　logistics support
后圈　back coil
后审查　post review, post-grant review, after action report (AAR)
后退信号　humping back signal
后续安全评估的年限　age limit for subsequent safety assessment
后续活动　successor activity, subsequent activity
后续事件　subsequent event
后续投资　follow-up investment
后张法　post-tensioning
后张法有黏结预应力混凝土结构　post-tensioning bonded and prestressed concrete structure
后张法预加应力　post-tensioned prestressing
后张法预应力混凝土结构　post-tensioned prestressed concrete structure
后张法预应力梁　post-tensioned concrete girder

后张钢丝索　post tensioning cable
后照管工程师　aftercare engineer
后支承　rear support
厚壁敞口取土器　thick-wall open mouth soil sampler
厚层　thick layer
厚层滑坡　thick layer landslide
厚层松散堆积体　thick loose deposit
厚度计　thickness gauge
候车　waiting for the train
候车区　waiting area
候车引导屏　information display in waiting hall
候选公司名单　short listed firms
呼叫等待　call waiting
呼叫（连接）建立失败概率　connection establishment error ratio (CER)
呼叫（连接）建立时间　connection establishment delay (CED)
呼叫列队　call queuing
呼叫限制　call barring service
呼叫信号　call signal
呼损率　call loss probability
呼吸器　respirator
忽略　omit, omission, neglect, ignore, elide, lose sight of, overlook, neglection
弧垂　sag
弧弦长　arc-chord length
弧形闸门　radial gate, tainter gate
弧形支座　curved bearing
湖泊　lake
湖积　lacustrine deposit
湖积平原　lacustrine plain
湖水　lake water
互差　mutual deviation
互感器　instrument transformer
互购　counterpurchase
互换　exchange, swap, interchange, counterchange, mutual exchange, double replacement, interconversion, reciprocate, transposition, permutation
互换修　cannibal repair
互换许可证　cross license, swap license
互惠　mutual benefit
互惠待遇　reciprocal treatment
互惠的　reciprocal
互惠关税　reciprocal tariff, mutually preferential tariff
互惠合同　reciprocal contract
互惠基金　mutual funds
互惠贸易　reciprocal trade
互惠协定　reciprocal agreement
互惠信贷　swap credits

互利　mutual benefit
互联功能单元　inter working function（IWF）
互联互通　interoperability
互联网售票　online ticket sales
互联网数据中心　internet data center(IDC)
互联网协议　internet protocol(IP)
互联网协议第 4 版
　　internet protocol version 4(IPv4)
互联网协议第 6 版
　　internet protocol version 6(IPv6)
互谅　mutual understanding
互相谅解　mutual understanding
互意条款　reciprocity clause
互助保险公司　mutual insurance company
互阻抗　mutual impedance
护岸　revetment, shore protection
护岸工程　bank protection work, banking protection works, shore protection engineering
护岸护滩　revetment and beach protection
护道　berm
护堤　dike
护盾　shield
护盾式掘进机
　　shielded TBM, shield tunnel boring machine
护拱　stiffened end of arch
护管壁　casing pipe
护筋性　steel bar protection property
护栏　rail, railing
护轮轨　guard rail
护目镜　goggle
护坡　revetment, slope protection
护墙　parapet wall
护套偏心度　sheath eccentricity
护筒　pile casing
护罩　protection cover
护桩　guard stake
花岗斑岩　granite porphyry
花岗闪长斑岩　granodiorite-porphyry
花岗闪长岩　granodiorite
花岗伟晶岩　granite-pegmatite
花岗岩　granite
华力西期　Variscan age/ stage
滑触线　conductor bar
滑床板　slide plate
滑道　slideway
滑动层　sliding layer
滑动吊弦线夹　sliding dropper clamp
滑动接触电流法　sliding contact current method
滑动面　sliding surface
滑动模板　slip form

滑动双承力索吊弦线夹
　　sliding dropper clamp of double messenger wire
滑动土　sliding soil
滑动稳定系数　anti-sliding stability coefficient
滑动油缸　sliding oil cylinder
滑环　slip ring
滑轮　pulley
滑轮组补偿装置　pulley assembly tensioning device
滑码　slip code
滑模施工　slip-form construction
滑劈理　slip cleavage
滑坡　landslide
滑坡壁　slip cliff
滑坡仓　gravity loading storage
滑坡床　landslide bed
滑坡地段路基　subgrade in landslide section
滑坡堆积　landslide deposit
滑坡规模　landslide size
滑坡监测　landslide monitoring
滑坡节理　landslide joint
滑坡舌　slide tongue
滑坡塌方　landslide
滑坡台地　landslide platform
滑坡台坎　landslide terrace
滑坡体　landslide mass
滑坡洼地　landslide depression
滑石　talc
滑塌　slump
滑移　slippage
化粪池　septic tank
化石　fossil, reliquiae, petrification
化学沉淀法　chemical sedimentation
化学堆积　chemical accumulation
化学法　chemical methods
化学分析　chemical analysis
化学风化　chemical weathering
化学改良法　chemical amendments
化学改良土　chemical improved soil
化学灌浆　chemical grouting
化学剂破坏影响系数
　　influence coefficient of damage due to chemicals
化学结构　chemical constitution
化学侵蚀　chemical corrosion
化学侵蚀环境　chemical erosion environment
化学危险品　hazardous chemicals
化学稳定性　chemical stability
化学洗井　chemical flushing
化学需氧量　chemical oxygen demand（COD）
化学絮凝强化池
　　enhanced pool with chemical flocculation

化验　test, assay
化验间　laboratory
划分　demarcation, dividing, divide, partition, re-partition
划线支票　cross (crossed)-check (cheque)
话路强插　preemptive call
话筒　microphone
话务量　traffic volumn
坏账　bad debt, bad account, uncollectible account, bad loans
坏账准备　reserve for bad debts, bad-debt provision
还本付息　debt service, repay (the) capital and interest, repay capital with interest
还价　counter offer, abate a price, counter-bid
还款时间表　repayment schedule
还盘　counter offer
还息贷款额　loan amount with interest
还息年度　year of loan interest payment
还债　money returned, pay a debt, debt retirement
环保选线　Railway location based on environmental protection factors
环刀　cutting ring
环刀法　cutting-ring method
环到　ring receiving
环发　ring departure
环筋　hoop reinforcement
环境　environment
环境保护　environmental protection
环境保护费　environmental protection expenditure
环境保护选线　environmental friendly route selection
环境保护政策　environmental protection policy
环境保护专项监理费　special supervision fee for environmental protection
环境承载力　environmental carrying capacity
环境地质　environmental geology
环境地质条件　environmental geological conditions
环境调查　environmental survey
环境分析　environmental analysis
环境风险保险　environmental risk insurance
环境工程　environment engineering
环境管理体系　environmental management system
环境及电源监控系统　environment and power monitoring system
环境监测系统　environmental monitoring system
环境监控　environmental monitoring
环境监理　environmental supervision
环境敏感区　environmentally sensitive area
环境水文地质　environmental hydrogeology
环境特征　environmental characteristics
环境条件　environmental condition

环境微振动　environmental micro-vibration
环境温度　ambient temperature
环境污染　environmental pollution, environment contamination
环境效益　environmental benefit
环境应力开裂时间　environmental stress cracking time
环境影响　environmental impact
环境影响报告　environmental impact statement (EIS)
环境影响报告编制与评估费　compilation and assessment fees of environmental impact report
环境影响评价　environmental impact assessment (EIA)
环境灾害　environmental disaster
环境噪声　environmental noise
环境噪声测量方法　environmental noise measuring method
环境噪声监测点位　environmental noise monitoring points
环境噪声污染　environmental noise pollution
环境振动试验　environmental vibration test
环境资源　environment resource
环境作用等级　environmental action grade
环路电阻　loop resistance
环球法　ring and ball method
环线　loop
环向　circumferential
环向缝　circumferential joint
环向盲管　circumferential filter pipe
环形道路　ring road
环形接地体　ring earthing electrode
环形开挖预留核心土法　ring cut method
环形枢纽　circular junction terminal
环形通气管　annular vent pipe
环形网　ring network
环氧混凝土　epoxy concrete
环氧树脂涂层钢筋　epoxy resin coated steel bar
环氧涂层　epoxy coating
环状供电　looped power supply
环状构造　circular structure
环状管网　loop pipe network
缓变温度计　slowly varying thermometer
缓冲基金　buffer fund
缓冲结构　buffer structure
缓冲库存　buffer inventory, buffer stock
缓冲区　buffer zone, transition zone
缓冲装置　buffer bumper
缓放继电器　slow release relay
缓放时间　slow release time

缓和坡段	transitional grade section

缓和坡段 transitional grade section
缓和曲线 transition curve, spiral curve
缓和曲线测设 transition curve locating
缓解 release
缓解措施 mitigating action
缓解时间 releasing time
缓解制动模式曲线 braking release mode curve
缓凝剂 retarder
缓凝水泥 retarded cement, slow setting cement
缓凝型 set retarding-type
缓坡 gentle slope
缓倾岩层 low dipping stratum
缓释药剂消毒 controlled-release chemical disinfection
缓吸时间 slow pick-up time
缓圆点 SC, point of change from spiral to circular curve
缓直点 ST, point of change from spiral to tangent
换汇 exchange, swap
换汇成本 exchange cost
换能器 transducer
换铺法(铺轨) track laying with replacement method
换气次数 ventilation frequency
换热器 heat exchanger
换热效率 heat transfer efficiency
换算长度 converted length
换算长细比 equivalent slenderness ratio
换算截面惯性矩 inertia moment of conversion section
换算截面面积 area of conversion cross section
换算截面模量 section modulus of conversion section
换算均布活载 equivalent uniform live load
换算列车对数 converted train pairs
换算土柱 converted soil column
换算土柱高度 height of converted soil
换算系数 conversion coefficient
换算箱 twenty-foot equivalent unit (TEU)
换填 fill replacement
换填垫层 replacement layer of compacted fill
换向器 commutator
黄铁矿 pyrite
黄铜矿 chalcopyrite
黄土 loess
黄土碟 loess plate
黄土高原 loess plateau
黄土滑坡 loess landslide
黄土井 loess well
黄土梁 loess ridge
黄土路基 loess subgrade
黄土峁 loess hill, loess hillock
黄土平原 loess plain
黄土桥 loess bridge
黄土丘陵 loess hill
黄土湿陷性试验 loess collapsibility test
黄土陷穴 loess sink hole
黄土塬 loess tableland
黄土桩 loess pile
黄土状土 loess-like soil
黄玉 topaz
煌斑岩 lamprophyre
灰度级 greyscale
灰分 ash content
灰浆 plaster
灰阶 gray level
灰土 lime soil
灰土换填夯实法 replacement method by tamping lime-soil cushion
灰土(水泥土)挤密桩 lime-soil (cement-soil) compaction pile
灰土挤压桩 lime soil squeezing pile
灰土桩 lime-soil pile
挥发酚 volatile phenols
挥发性固体 volatile solid
挥发性固体去除率 removal percentage of volatile solids
挥发性固体容积负荷 cubage load of volatile solids
挥发性有机化合物 volatile organic compound
恢复 restore, restoration, recover, recovery, restitution, resume, renew, return to, regain, recuperate, revive, reinstate, rehabilitate, resurgent, resurrect, reinstate sb. in, regenerate
恢复力模型 restoring force model
恢复原状 reinstatement, repristination
辉长岩 gabbro
辉绿岩 diabase
辉石 pyroxene
辉岩 pyroxenite
回车道 turning lane for vehicles
回程阀 return valve
回程时间 return time
回程运费 back freight, home-freight
回弹变形 resilient deformation
回弹率 rebound ratio
回弹模量 modulus of resilience
回弹仪 resiliometer, rebound apparatus
回弹指数 resilience index
回访 return visit

回风百分比　percentage of return air
回风方式　air return mode
回风口吸风速度
　　suction velocity at return air inlet
回复　reply, response
回购　buy-back
回购产品　buy-back of product
回购交易　buy back deal
回归模型　regression model
回国探亲津贴　home leave allowance
回函　reply (to a letter), letter of acknowledgement, counter-notice, response letter
回扣　brokerage, kickback, rebate
回流比　reflux ratio
回流导体　return conductor
回流电缆　return cable
回流电路　return circuit
回流轨　return rail
回流回路（包括走行轨、回流轨、回流线、接地线、回流电缆、导通回流组件）
　　return circuit (including running rail, return current rail, return conductor, earthing wire, return cable, other components conducting return currents)
回流区　recirculation zone
回流污泥　returned sludge
回流污染　backflow pollution
回流系统　return circuit
回流线　return conductor
回流线回流　current return via return conductor
回收价值　recovery value, returned value, reclamation value
回收利用　reuse and recycling
回收期　payback period
回收期评估法　payback method
回水　return water
回水管　water return pipe
回填　backfill, reclamation, refilling
回填料　backfill, backfill material, backfilling
回填土　backfilling soil
回填土压力　pressure of backfilled soil
回填注浆　backfilling grouting
回头曲线测设　switch-back curve locating
回线环路　loop
回线台账　loop account
回执　acknowledgment of receipt
回转取土器　rotary sampler
回转线　turnaround track
回转钻进　rotary drilling
回租　leaseback

汇编　proceedings, collect and edit, compile, assemble, assembler, assembly, directory, pandect, compilation, collection, corpus
汇兑　remittance, transfer, exchange
汇兑风险　exchange risk
汇兑商　cambist
汇兑损益　foreign exchange gains and losses
汇兑银行　exchange bank
汇付　remittance, pay to
汇还本国　repatriation
汇集线　bus conductor
汇寄　remit
汇价　exchange rate, conversion rate
汇接　tandem
汇接架　tandem shelf
汇接设备　tandem device
汇接移动交换中心
　　tandem mobile switching center (TMSC)
汇聚层　convergence layer
汇聚节点　convergence node
汇款　remit, make remittance, remittance, transfer of funds
汇款单　money order, cash remittance note
汇款结算　remittance settlement
汇款人　remitter
汇款通知单　remittance slip, remittance advice
汇款银行　remitting bank
汇流量　confluence amount
汇流面积　catchment area
汇流排　overhead conductor rail
汇流排地线线夹
　　earth wire clamp for overhead conductor rail
汇流排电连接线夹　electrical connection clamp for overhead conductor rail
汇流排定位线夹　overhead conductor rail clamp
汇流条　bus bar
汇率　exchange rate, rate of exchange
汇率保值条款　exchange proviso clause, exchange rate hedging clause
汇率调整　exchange adjustment, exchange rate adjustment, currency exchange adjustment
汇率走势　tendency of exchange rate
汇票　bill of exchange (B/E.), bill for remittance, bill of draft, draft
汇票汇款　remittance by draft
汇票金额　amount of a draft
汇票贴现　discount of draft
汇票正本　original bill
汇票支付　payment by draft
汇票支付日期　maturity of a draft, date of draft

汇水面积　catchment area
汇水面积测量　catchment area survey
汇油管　oil converging pipe
汇总　aggregation, collection, gather, summarization
汇总估价表　estimate summary
会场　meeting place
会话启动协议交换
　　session initiation protocol truck (SIP Truck)
会签　countersign
会签栏　countersignature block
会让站　passing station, crossing station
会谈　conference, talk
会议　conference, meeting, convention
会议电视　video conference
会议电视终端　video conference terminal
会议调度车间　conference dispatching room
会议分机　conference extension
会议记录本　minute book
会议纪要
　　minutes of the meeting, meeting notes, minutes
会议签到单格式　meeting attendance form
会议室回损　return loss of conference room
会议系统　conference system
会议总机　conference switchboard
绘图　drawing
绘图聚酯薄膜　drawing polyester film
贿赂　corrupt, bribe
贿赂费　hush money, bribes
贿赂物　bribe
贿赂行为　corrupt practice, venal practices
贿赂罪　offence of bribery, bribery crime
毁坏　destroy, collapse, devastate, damage, break, decay, ruin, ravage, erode, deface
毁灭　destroy, destruction, exterminate, ruin
毁约　declare off, breach of contract, breach of promise, to break the contract
浑圆状　rounded
浑浊程度　turbidity
混合　amalgamation, mix, blend, mingle, admix, mixture, mix-up, interfusion, commixture, blending, creolization, mixing, compound, compounding, hybrid, intermix
混合比　mixture ratio, mix proportion, blending ratio
混合成本　mixed cost
混合抽水试验　mixed pumping test
混合关税　compound tariff, mixed duties, compound duties, mixed tariff
混合胶结　mixed cementation
混合结构　composite structure
混合控制　hybrid control
混合料　all-in, mix, mixture, compound
混合溶液　mixed solution
混合砂　mixed sand, blend sand
混合砂浆　composite mortar
混合税　mixed duties, compound duty
混合税率　mixed tariff, compound tariff
混合土　mixed soil
混合显色剂　mixed chromogenic reagent
混合液回流　mixed liquid recycle
混凝剂　coagulant
混凝土　concrete
混凝土板　concrete slab
混凝土拌和　mixing of concrete
混凝土拌和厂　batching plant, concrete mixing plant
混凝土拌和楼　concrete mixing plant, batching plant
混凝土拌合物　fresh concrete
混凝土保护层　concrete cover
混凝土保护层测定仪　concrete cover tester
混凝土保护层厚度　thickness of concrete cover
混凝土保护层最小厚度
　　minimum thickness of concrete cover
混凝土泵　concrete pump
混凝土泵车　concrete pump truck
混凝土衬砌　concrete lining
混凝土稠度　concrete consistency
混凝土打毛机　chipping machine
混凝土大板结构　large panel concrete structure
混凝土单向板　one-way concrete slab
混凝土道岔板　concrete turnout slab
混凝土道床板　concrete track slab
混凝土底座　concrete base
混凝土吊斗　concrete skip
混凝土冻融循环试验
　　concrete freezing and thawing cycle test
混凝土工　concrete worker
混凝土构造柱　concrete structural column
混凝土骨料　concrete aggregate
混凝土含气量　concrete air content
混凝土含气量测定仪
　　concrete air content measuring instrument
混凝土和易性　workability of concrete
混凝土缓凝剂　concrete retarder
混凝土基础　concrete foundation
混凝土极限压应变
　　ultimate compressive strain of concrete
混凝土集中拌和站
　　centralized concrete mixing plant
混凝土浇筑　concrete placement, concreting
混凝土浇筑设备　placing plant
混凝土搅拌车　concrete truck, motormixer

H

混凝土搅拌机　concrete mixer
混凝土搅拌楼　concrete mixing plant
混凝土搅拌运输车　ready-mix concrete truck
混凝土搅拌站　batching plant
混凝土结构　concrete structure
混凝土抗冻等级　frost resistance class of concrete
混凝土抗冻性　concrete freezing resistance
混凝土抗冻性能　frost resistance of concrete
混凝土抗腐蚀性　concrete corrosion resistance
混凝土抗渗仪　concrete anti permeability apparatus
混凝土抗压强度　concrete compressive strength
混凝土块　concrete block, concrete brick
混凝土块路面　pavement of concrete block, concrete pavement
混凝土快速养护　accelerated curing of concrete
混凝土宽枕　concrete broad sleeper
混凝土立方体抗压强度标准值　standard value of compressive strength for concrete cube
混凝土裂缝　concrete crack
混凝土裂纹　concrete crack
混凝土氯离子扩散系数　diffusion coefficient of chloride ion of concrete
混凝土模板　concrete formwork
混凝土耐久性　durability of concrete
混凝土内部充填物　internal filling of concrete
混凝土配合比　concrete mixing ratio
混凝土配筋　concrete reinforcement
混凝土气泡间距系数　air bubble spacing factor of concrete
混凝土砌块　concrete block
混凝土砌块专用砂浆　mortar for concrete small hollow block
混凝土强度　concrete strength
混凝土强度标准值　standard value of concrete strength
混凝土强度等级　strength grade of concrete
混凝土强度检验评定　inspection and evaluation of concrete strength
混凝土强度设计值　design value of concrete strength
混凝土桥　concrete bridge
混凝土蠕变　creep of concrete
混凝土入模温度　concrete casting temperature
混凝土设备　concrete equipment
混凝土实体质量　entitative quality of concrete
混凝土试件　concrete specimen
混凝土收缩　concrete shrinkage
混凝土受压弹性模量　compressive elastic modulus of concrete
混凝土输送泵　concrete delivery pump
混凝土双向板　two-way concrete slab
混凝土坍落度　concrete slump
混凝土摊铺机　concrete paver
混凝土弹性模量　elastic modulus of concrete
混凝土碳化　carbonation of concrete
混凝土透气系数　permeability coefficient of concrete
混凝土外加剂　concrete additive
混凝土弯曲抗压强度标准值　standard value of bending compressive strength of concrete
混凝土弯曲抗压强度设计值　design value of bending compressive strength of concrete
混凝土小型空心砌块　small-sized hollow concrete block
混凝土斜拉桥　concrete cable-stayed bridge
混凝土心墙　concrete core wall
混凝土芯部温度　core temperature of concrete
混凝土徐变　concrete creepage
混凝土养护　concrete curing
混凝土预制块　prefabricated concrete blocks
混凝土折板结构　folded-plate concrete structure
混凝土枕　concrete sleeper
混凝土枕道岔　concrete sleeper turnout
混凝土枕螺栓钻取机　concrete sleeper bolt drilling and pulling machine
混凝土真空保水机　vacuum water saturation instrument of concrete
混凝土振动台　concrete vibrating stand
混凝土支撑层　concrete supporting layer
混凝土支承层　concrete supporting layer
混凝土支柱　concrete pole, concrete mast
混凝土轴心抗拉强度标准值　standard value of axial tensile strength of concrete
混凝土轴心抗拉强度设计值　design value of axial tensile strength of concrete
混凝土柱　concrete column
混凝土柱帽　concrete column cap
活动层　active layer
活动层水　active layer water
活动断层　active fault
活动断裂带　active fault zone
活动滑坡　active landslide
活动脚手架　jenny scaffold, mobile staging
活动模板　traveling formwork, collapsible form
活动桥　movable bridge
活动区　active region
活动图像　moving image
活动性指数　activity index
活动支架　movable support

活动支座　movable bearing
活度　activity
活断层　active fault
活荷载折减系数　reduction coefficient of live load
活荷载准永久值　quasi-permanent value of live load
活荷载组合值　combination value of live load
活期存款　demand deposit, current deposit
活期贷款　demand loan, call loan, call money
活期账户　current account, checking account
活塞　piston
活塞式压缩机　piston compressor
活塞洗井法　piston flushing
活塞组合件　piston subassembly
活套闭水接头单管钻进　single-tube drilling with movable casing water-blocking connector
活性矿物　active mineral
活性炭　active carbon
活性炭吸附　active carbon adsorption
活性炭吸附池　activated carbon adsorption tank
活性污泥　activated sludge
活性污泥法　activated sludge process
活性氧化沟　oxidation ditch
活性指数　activity index
活跃账户　active account
活载　live load
活载系数　live load coefficient
火车、汽车装卸单价　unit prices of loading and unloading for train or truck
火车运价　train freight rate
火车运输　delivering by train
火成岩　igneous rock
火花间隙　spark gap
火炬信号　torch signal
火力发电厂　fuel-burning power plant, fuel electric plant, steam electric plant, thermal power plant
火山地貌　volcanic landform
火山地震　volcanic earthquake
火山堆　volcanic deposit
火山堆积　volcanic deposit
火山灰质硅酸盐水泥　portland-pozzolana cement
火山活动　volcanic activity, volcanism, volcanism
火山角砾构造　volcanic breccia structure
火山角砾岩　volcanic breccia
火山锥　volcanic cone
火焰除锈　descaling by flame
火焰光度法　flame photometry
火羽流　fire plume
火源辐射　fire radiation
火灾　fire, conflagration

火灾保险　fire insurance
火灾报警　fire alarm
火灾报警器　fire alarm
火灾报警系统　fire alarm system (FAS)
火灾风险　fire risk
火灾风险事故　fire perils, fire risk accident
火灾和拓展范围险　fire and extended cover insurance
火灾危险等级　fire risk level
伙伴关系　partnering, partnership
或取或付合同　take-or-pay contract
或有费用　contingent expenses
或有负债　contingent liabilities
或有利润　contingent profit
或有权益　contingent interest
货币　currency, money
货币比例　currency proportion
货币贬值　currency depreciation, currency devaluation, devaluation of the currency
货币贬值调整　devaluation adjustment
货币贬值损失　loss on devaluation
货币储备　currency reserve
货币单位　monetary unit
货币的　monetary, nummary
货币掉期　currency swap
货币兑换　conversion of currency, currency conversion, currency exchange
货币兑换性　convertibility
货币风险　currency risk
货币互换　currency swap
货币汇率　monetary exchange rate, monetary exchange rate
货币可兑换性　currency convertibility
货币期货合同　currency futures contract
货币期权　currency option
货币升值　currency appreciation, currency revaluation, appreciation of a currency
货币时间价值　time value of money
货币市场　money market, monetary market, currency market
货币损益　monetary gain or loss
货币套期保值　currency hedge
货币限制　currency restriction, monetary restraint
货币性资产　monetary assets
货币性资产或负债　money assets or liabilities
货币性资金　monetary capital
货币债务　monetary liabilities
货币政策　monetary policy
货币周转　money turnover
货币自由兑换性　currency convertibility

货场　freight yard
货车　truck, freight car
货车保有量　daily stock of freight cars, number of freight cars on hand
货车车辆段　freight car depot
货车车辆设备　freight car facilities
货车故障轨边图像检测系统　track side image detection system for freight train fault
货车滚动轴承早期故障轨道声学诊断系统　TADS
货车平均净载重　net average static load for wagons
货车日车公里　wagon kilometers per day, car kilometers per car per day
货车消毒线　car sterilizing siding
货车运行故障动态图像检测系统　TFDS
货车运行状态地面安全监测系统　TPDA
货单　cargo certificate, manifest, waybill, shipping list
货到付款　cash on delivery, payment on arrival, pay on delivery, spot cash
货到付款协议　take-and-pay agreement
货到交付　delivery on arrival
货交承运人（指定地点）　free carrier…（named point）（FCA）
货款结算单　statements, payment statement
货名　name of commodity, payment statement, cargo name
货盘　pallet
货棚　goods shed
货品说明综合表　summary sheets of goods
货损理算　cargo damage adjustment
货位　freight section
货位宽度　width of freight section
货位排数　row number of freight section
货位周转时间　cycling time of freight section
货物　goods, commodity, cargo, merchandise
货物保险　insurance of goods, cargo insurance
货物保险单　cargo policy, cargo insurance policy
货物标志　cargo mark, shipping mark
货物采购　procurement of goods
货物仓库　goods warehouse
货物到发波动系数　coefficient of variation for goods receiving and departure
货物发运费用　freight forward cost
货物估价单　valuation form
货物检查　cargo inspection
货物交接　delivery-receiving of goods
货物交接横列式港湾站　transverse harbor station for goods transfer
货物交接横列式工业站　transverse industrial station for goods transfer
货物进口完税单　import duty memo, customs declaration for import of goods
货物空运　airfreight
货物列车　freight train
货物列车检修作业场（列检作业场）　freight car inspection yard
货物品质证书　certificate of quality
货物清单　bill of goods, manifest, detailed list of goods
货物申报单　merchandise declaration
货物税　excise, commodity tax
货物说明书　description of goods
货物吞吐量　port's volume of freight traffic turnover
货物线　goods track
货物运价　freight rates
货物运输保险　cargo transportation insurance, cargo insurance
货物运输管理系统　freight transport management system
货物站台　freight platform
货物账款通知单　cargo accounting advice
货物装卸设备　cargo-handling equipment
货物装卸线　goods loading and unloading siding
货样　advance sample, sample goods, sample
货源选择　source selection
货运　freight, carriage, freight transport, shipment of commodities, transportation service
货运代理行　forwarder, freight agent, cargo agent
货运单　waybill, bill of freight, shipping list
货运单据　shipping documents
货运单证　cargo paper, transportation documents
货运调度电话　freight dispatching telephone
货运合同　contract of carriage, freight contract
货运距离　distance of freight carried
货运量　freight traffic volume
货运码头　freight terminal, cargo terminal, cargo berth
货运唛头　cargo mark, shipping mark
货运提单　cargo document, house bill of lading（HB/L）, bill of landing
货运条件　conditions of carriage, shipping conditions
货运业务　cargo service, freight service
货运站　freight station
货运终点站　freight terminal, cargo terminal
货运专线　freight dedicated line
货运转运商　freight forwarder
货栈　warehouse, store house, cargo terminal
货站　depot

货值提单 ad valorem bill of lading
获得 acquire, acquisition, gain, obtain, secure, procure, win, achieve
获得方 acquiring party
获利 earn, gain, make profit, earn profit, get or obtain profit, reap profits
获利能力 profitability
豁免 exempt, exemption, immunity, remit

I

IPC(期中付款证书)的签发
    issue of IPC (interim payment certificate)
IP 地址 IP address
IP 会议电视系统 IP video conference system
I 形梁 I-girder, I-beam

J

J 环障碍高差　J ring blocking step
击穿　breakdown
击穿冲击电压　breakdown impulse voltage
击穿电压　breakdown voltage
击穿放电　disruptive discharge
击实功　compactive effort
击实机　tamper
击实试验　compaction test
击实筒　compaction mould
击实土　compacted soil
击实性能　compaction performance
击实仪　compaction test apparatus
机场税　airport tax
机车不落轮车床　under-floor wheel lathe
机车车辆(动车)购置费
　　purchase expense of rolling stock (EMU)
机车乘务制　working system of locomotive crew
机车乘务组换班　locomotive crew shift change
机车出段线　track for locomotive to station
机车电台　cab radio
机车感应器　locomotive inductor
机车检修段　locomotive repair depot
机车检修率　rate of locomotives inspection and repair
机车交路　locomotive routing
机车接近通知　cab approach announcement
机车类型　type of locomotive
机车全周转时间
　　duration of locomotive complete turn-round
机车日车公里
　　average daily locomotive running kilometers
机车入段线　track for locomotive to depot
机车设备　locomotive equipment
机车台　onboard radio
机车同步操控系统　synchronized operation and
　　control system for distributed locomotives
机车信号　cab signaling
机车信号表示器　cab signal indicator
机车信号测试环线　cab signal test loop
机车信号测试区段　cab signaling testing section
机车信号发码器　cab signal code sender
机车信号钢轨最小短路电流值
　　rail minimum short circuit value for cab signal
机车信号邻线干扰
　　cab signal interference from adjacent tracks
机车信号模式　cab signaling mode (CS)
机车信号设备　cab signaling equipment
机车信号信息　cab signal message
机车信号作用点　cab signaling inductor location
机车运行安全监控装置
　　locomotive running data recorder
机车运用　locomotive operation
机车运用指标　index of locomotive operation
机车运转制　locomotive routing mode
机车折返作业　locomotive turnaround operation
机车整备　locomotive servicing
机车整车试验线　whole locomotive test track
机车综合无线通信设备　cab integrated radio com-
　　munication equipment (CIR)
机车走行公里　locomotive running kilometers
机车走行线　locomotive running track
机待线　locomotive holding track, loco waiting track
机电设备监控系统　building automation system(BAS)
机动车　vehicle, motor
机动车第三者责任险　third party motor insurance
机动车辆保险　motor insurance
机动车辆税　motor vehicle tax
机动车责任险　motor car liability insurance
机动消防泵　portable fire pump
机房平面布置图　equipment room layout plan
机构内部能力　in-house capabilities
机构自身能力
　　in-house capabilities, institutional capacity
机会　chance
机会成本　opportunity cost
机会研究　opportunity study
机架面板布置图　rack panel layout plan

机具设备　tools and equipment
机密　secret
机密文件　classified document
机器全长　overall length of TBM
机器损坏保险　machinery breakdown insurance, machinery damage insurance
机器直径　TBM diameter
机损条款　breakdown clause
机外停车　stop in advance of a signal
机务段　locomotive depot
机务段联系电路　liaison circuit among locomotive depots
机务工作量　workload of locomotive dept
机务换乘所　locomotive crew shift changing station
机务设备　locomotive facilities
机务用房　locomotive maintenance building
机务折返段　locomotive turnaround depot
机务折返所　locomotive turnaround point
机械保温车　mechanical refrigerator wagon
机械闭锁　mechanical latch, mechanical interlock
机械臂板信号机　mechanical semaphore signal
机械成孔　mechanical borehole-forming
机械除尘　mechanical dust removal
机械工　mechanic, machinist, mechanician, machine-man
机械工时定额　standard machine hour (time)
机械故障保险单　machinery breakdown policy
机械荷载　mechanical load
机械化　mechanization
机械化驼峰　mechanized hump
机械混合　mechanical mixing
机械集中联锁　mechanical interlocking
机械加工　machining
机械间接损失保险　machinery consequential loss (interruption) insurance
机械搅拌澄清池　accelerator
机械竣工　mechanical completion
机械连接　mechanical connection
机械联锁　mechanical interlocking
机械排烟　mechanical smoke exhaust
机械疲劳试验　mechanical fatigue test
机械破坏影响系数　influence coefficient of machinery damage
机械铺轨　mechanical track laying
机械强度　mechanical strength
机械倾斜仪　mechanical declinometer
机械设备安装工程　mechanical equipment installation works
机械设备价值　value of machinery
机械设备折旧　depreciation of machinery
机械设备综合单价　all-in mechanical plant rate
机械师　machinist
机械试验　mechanical test
机械寿命　mechanical life
机械送风系统　mechanical air supply system
机械锁闭　mechanical locking
机械台班　machine shift
机械台班单价　unit price of machine shift
机械台班定额　quota of machine shift
机械台班量　quantity of machine shift
机械台班消耗量定额　quota of machine shift consumption
机械台班预算价格　budget price of machine shift
机械特性　mechanical properties
机械通风　mechanical ventilation
机械通风系统　mechanical ventilation system
机械效率试验　efficiency test
机械絮凝池　mechanical flocculating tank
机械压水法　mechanical pump-in test method
机械一切险　machinery all risks insurance
机载GPS、IMU辅助摄影　air-borne GPS, IMU aided photography
迹地恢复　cut-over area recovery
积累资金　accumulated funds
积水洼地　waterlogged depression
积压　overstocking
积载空隙　broken stowage
基本比例尺　basic scale
基本比例尺地形图　basic-scale topographic map
基本变量　basic variable
基本成本估计　base cost estimate
基本承载力　basic bearing capacity
基本贷款汇率　base lending rate
基本的　basic, fundamental, substantial, essential, elementary, primary
基本电价　basic power price
基本定额　basic quota
基本费率　basis rates
基本分项工作　basic item, basic breakdown work
基本风险　prime risk, fundamental risk, basis risk
基本风压　reference wind pressure
基本工时　core working hours, basic working hours
基本工资　basic salary
基本轨　stock rail
基本耗热量　basic heat loss
基本合同责任　basic contractual responsibilities
基本价格　basic price
基本价格指数　base price index

基本建设　capital construction
基本建设费用　capital cost, capital expenditure
基本建设工程
　　capital works, capital construction projects
基本建设投资　investment in capital construction
基本建设项目　capital project
基本建设预算　capital budget
基本进路　basic route
基本竣工　substantial completion
基本库存　base stock
基本利率　basic interest rate, prime rate
基本联锁电路　fundamental interlocking circuit
基本烈度　basic intensity
基本模型　basic model
基本农田　basic farmland
基本设计　basic design
基本事实　primary fact, brass tacks, ultimate facts
基本速率接口　basic rate interface (BRI)
基本完工　substantial completion
基本文件
　　keystone document, constituent instruments
基本限界　swept envelope
基本雪压　reference snow pressure
基本养老保险费　basic pension premium
基本医疗保险费　basic medical insurance premium
基本预备费
　　basic budget reserve for unpredictable work
基本运费　base freight rate
基本站台　main platform
基本振型　basic vibration mode
基本证据　primary evidence, basic evidence
基本周期　basic cycle
基本装备　essential equipment
基本组合　basic combination
基层　base
基础　foundation
基础表达方式　primary presentation methods
基础沉陷　yielding of foundation
基础垫层　bedding layer of foundation
基础定额　fundamental quota
基础工程　foundation works, foundation engineering
基础埋置深度　burial depth of foundation
基础平面控制网(CPⅠ)
　　basic horizontal control network (CPⅠ)
基础倾覆　foundation toppling
基础上拔　foundation uplift
基础设施　infrastructure
基础设施项目　infrastructure project
基床　subgrade
基床表层　prepared subgrade
基床底层(路堤)　upper part of embankment
基床底层(路堑)　replacement layer
基床厚度　thickness of subgrade
基床加固　strengthening of subgrade
基床结构　structure of subgrade
基床软化　softening of subgrade
基床填料　fill material of subgrade
基床系数　coefficient of subgrade
基底层　basal layer
基底高程　subsoil elevation
基底构造　basal structure
基底胶结　basal cement
基底压力(接触压力)
　　base pressure (contact pressure)
基点　basis point (b. p.), starting point, centre, jig point, base station, cardinal point, Gauss point
基高比　base-height ratio
基价　base price
基建贷款　capital construction loan
基建投资　capital outlay, investment of capital construction
基建预算　construction budget
基建资金　capital fund
基金　fund
基金不足　not sufficient funds (N. S. F.)
基坑　foundation pit
基坑底隆胀　heaving of foundation pit bottom
基坑支护　retaining and protection of foundation pit
基坑总涌水量
　　total volume of water gushing into foundation pit
基面　base level, cardinal plane, datum, interarea
基期　base period
基期材料费　material expense of base period
基期单价　unit price of base period
基期电价　power price of base period
基期价格　price of base period
基期价格水平　price level of base period
基期人工费　labor cost of base period
基期设备原价
　　original price of equipment in base period
基期施工机械使用费　expenses of base period for using construction machinery
基期水价　water price of base period
基期综合工费标准
　　comprehensive labor price of base period
基群速率接口　primary rate interface (PRI)
基体　matrix
基线　baseline
基线长度中误差
　　mean square error of baseline length

基线方位角中误差
 mean square error of baseline azimuth
基线费用 base line cost
基线解算 baseline solution
基线条件 baseline condition
基线向量 baseline vector
基线预算 base line budget
基性岩浆岩 basite magmatic rock
基岩 bedrock
基岩面 bedrock surface
基岩水准点 bedrock benchmark
基于 SDH 的多业务传送平台
 SDH based multi-service transport platform
基于通信的列车控制
 communication-based train control
基于位置寻址
 location dependent addressing（LDA）
基于无线通信的列车控制
 radio communication-based train control
基于质量的选择 quality-based selection（QBS）
基于质量和价格的选择
 quality and cost based selection（QBCS）
基于资格的选择 qualifications-based selection, selection based on eligibility
基站 base transceiver station（BTS）
基站控制器 base station controller（BSC）
基站识别码 base station identification code（BSIC）
基值 base value
基桩测设 setting-out of foundation piles
基桩动测仪 foundation pile dynamic diagnosis system
基准 datum, standard, criterion, reference, basic standard
基准标高 datum grade
基准标准 benchmark standard
基准点 reference point
基准高程 levels of reference
基准计划
 baseline, reference plan, baseline program
基准建筑 reference building
基准接收机 reference receiver
基准利率 benchmark rate, base rate
基准面 datum level, base level, datum plane, reference plane, reference surface
基准年 base year, reference year, benchmark year
基准值 base value
基准配合比 mix proportion benchmark
基准频率信号 reference frequency signal
基准日期 base date
基准溶液 reference solution
基准时钟 reference clock

基准试件
 benchmark specimen, standard test specimen
基准水灰比 reference water-cement ratio
基准完成日期
 baseline finish date, base completion date
基准线 datum line, zero line, reference axis
基座阶地 bedrock seatedterrace, pedestal terrace
畸变改正 distortion correction
激磁机 exciter
激发点 shotpoint
激发极化法 induced polarization method
激光测距 laser distance measurement
激光导向机构 laser direction-guiding system
激光对射探测器 laser detector
激光投点 laser plumbing
激光准直测量 laser alignment measurement
激光准直法 laser alignment method
激励 incentive
激励性奖金 incentive bonus
激振锤 impact hammer
激振力 exciting force
激振频率 excitation frequency
及时到达 due arrival
及时交货 timely delivery, punctual delivery
及时性 timeliness, promptness
吉比特无源光网络 Gigabit passive optical network
给予协助 delivery of assistance
级别 grade, rank, level, scale, sort, rating, class
级间切换测试 level transition test
级间转换 level transition
级间转换标志牌 level transition sign board
级间转换测试 level transition test
级配 gradation
级配改良 improved gradation
级配骨料 graded aggregate
级配良好 good gradation
级配曲线 grading curve
级配砂砾石 graded sand gravel
级配碎（砾）石基床
 subgrade of graded crushed stone
级配碎石 graded crushed stone
级配碎石拌和站
 mixing station of graded broken stone
极差 range
极大风速 extreme wind speed
极点图 pole diagram, polar map
极端风向 critical wind direction
极干旱 extreme drought
极化率 polarizability
极频轨道电路 polar frequency coded track circuit

极频自动闭塞 automatic block with polar frequency impulse track circuit
极谱分析 polarographic analysis
极强烈侵蚀 extreme soil erosion
极软岩 extremely soft rock
极弱富水区 extremely weak water abundance zone
极数 number of poles
极条件 limited condition
极限 limit
极限变形 ultimate deformation
极限侧阻力 ultimate shaft resistance
极限长度 maximum allowable span length
极限承载力 ultimate bearing capacity
极限承载能力 ultimate bearing capacity
极限端阻力 ultimate tip resistance
极限开关 limit switch
极限抗拉强度 ultimate tensile strength
极限抗压强度 ultimate compressive strength
极限抗折强度 limit folding strength
极限偏差 limit deviation
极限平衡法 limit equilibrium method
极限平衡状态 limit equilibrium state
极限伸长率 ultimate elongation
极限误差 limit error
极限相对位移 ultimate relative displacement
极限应变 ultimate strain
极限应力 limiting stress
极限状态 limit state
极限状态法 limit state design method
极限状态方程 limit state equation
极限状态设计 limit state design
极限状态设计法 limit state design method
极小偏移距高频反射连续剖面法 land sonar method
极性检查电路 polarity checking circuit
极性交叉 polar transposition
极性脉冲轨道电路 polar impulse track circuit
极硬岩 extremely hard rock
极震区 meizoseismal area
即付保函 demand guarantee
即付的 prompt
即付票 sight bills
即付债务 liabilities payable on demand
即期 demand, sight
即期存款 demand deposit, deposit at call, deposit at notice, deposit at sight
即期的 sight
即期付款交单 documents against payment at sight
即期付款信用证 sight payment credit
即期汇率 spot exchange rate, sight rate
即期汇票 demand bill, demand draft, bill payable on demand, sight draft, sight bill
即期交货 prompt delivery, delivery on spot
即期票据 demand note, cote on demand, sight bill
即期外汇买卖 spot exchange transaction
即期现金报酬 immediate cash consideration
即期信用证 sight letter of credit, letter of credit at sight
即期债务 debt at call
即时的 immediate, instant, real-time, offhand
急件 urgent document, dispatch
急救 first aid, emergency treatment
急救员 first-aider
急救站 first-aid station
急流槽 steep chute
疾风 moderate gale
集成电路 integrated circuit(IC)
集成管理平台 integrated management platform
集货区 consolidated cargo (container) service area
集卡 container truck
集卡出入口通道 entrance/exit access for container truck
集控站 centralized control station
集块结构 agglomeratic texture
集块岩 volcanic agglomerate
集料冲击韧度 aggregate impact toughness
集料压碎率 aggregate crushing rate
集气罐 air collector
集群 cluster
集热器 heat collector, thermal collector
集散厅 concourse
集水 catchment, impoundment
集水井 catch pit
集水坑 catchpit
集水面积 catchment area
集水明排 open pumping
集水器 water collector
集水桶 water gathering bucket
集体抵制 group boycotts
集体行为 group action, collective behavior
集中采暖 central heating
集中道岔 centrally operated switch
集中调度 Centralized Traffic Control(CTC)
集中调度系统 centralized traffic control system
集中电源 centralized power source
集中发电站 central power station
集中分布式架构 centralized-distributed architecture
集中供电 centralized power supply
集中供暖 central heating

J

集中管理　centralized management
集中荷载（点荷载）
　　concentrated load（point load）
集中监控　centralized monitoring
集中检修　centralized repair
集中接地箱　centralized grounding box
集中控制　centralized control
集中控制道岔　centrally-controlled turnout
集中冷却系统　centralized cooling system
集中联锁　centralized interlocking
集中配置　centralized configuration
集中取土场　concentrated borrow pit
集中热水供应系统
　　central hot water supply system
集中式　centralized
集中式串联电容补偿装置
　　compensator with concentrated series capacitors
集中式空气调节系统
　　centralized air conditioning system
集中修　centralized repair
集中涌水　intensive water outflow
集装箱　container
集装箱班列　container liner train
集装箱半挂车　container semi-trailer
集装箱叉车　container forklift
集装箱拆装箱场
　　container stuffing and destuffing yard
集装箱船　container ship, container vessel, container-carrier
集装箱堆场　container yard
集装箱货场　container freight yard
集装箱货区　container freight area
集装箱货物集散站　container freight station
集装箱货运　containerized shipment
集装箱牵引车　container tractor
集装箱提单　container bill of lading
集装箱箱脚荷载　container leg load
集装箱卸箱清单　container unloading list
集装箱运输　carriage of container, container traffic, containerization
集装箱正面吊运起重机
　　container front-handling crane
集装箱装箱机　container loader
集装箱装箱清单　container loading list
集装箱装卸作业区
　　container loading and unloading operation area
集装箱作业场　container operation yard
集资　call for funds, raise funds, collect（pool）money, concentrate funds, draw money（from many sources）, pool resources, fund raising

瘠薄　barren
几何不变性　geometrical invariability
几何参数的标准值
　　standard value of geometrical parameter
几何参数的设计值
　　design value of geometrical parameter
几何尺寸　geometric dimension
几何定向　geometric orientation
几何精度　level of geometric detail
几何纠正　geometrical rectification
几何配准　geometric registration
几何相似　geometric similarity
几何信息　geometric information
挤包绝缘　extruded insulation
挤岔　trailing of a switch, splitting of point tongue
挤岔保护　trailed switch protection
挤岔报警　alarm for a trailed switch
挤出成型法　extrusion molding
挤密地基　compacted foundation
挤密喷浆法　compaction grouting method
挤密砂石桩　sand-gravel compaction pile
挤密砂桩　sand compaction pile
挤密桩　compaction pile
挤切销　dissectible pin
挤脱　trailable
挤压变形　extrusion deformation
挤压性围岩　squeezing surrounding rock
绩效报告　performance report
绩效测量基准　performance measurement baseline, performance measurement benchmark
绩效等级　performance rating
绩效管理计划　performance management plan
绩效评定　performance rating
绩效评估　performance evaluation
绩效评价
　　performance evaluation, performance appraisal
绩效月报　monthly performance report
绩效周报　weekly performance report
计费　charging
计费标准　charging standard
计费范围　charging scope
计费网关　charging gateway（CG）
计划　plan, program, scheme, project, programme, devisal, design, map out, plot
计划表　schedule
计划采购　scheduled purchasing
计划产量　scheduled output, scheduled production, planned output
计划费用　planned cost
计划风险　calculated risk

计划工程师　planner, scheduler, planning engineer
计划工期　as-planned schedule, planned project duration
计划工作预算成本　budgeted cost of work scheduled (BCWS)
计划进度　planned progress, as-planned schedule, design schedule, target advance
计划利润　target profit, planned profits
计划拟定　programming, planning
计划评审技术　program evaluation and reviews technique (PERT)
计划期限　planned period
计划日期　scheduled date
计划书　prospectus, proposal, plan
计划图　scheme drawing, planning chart
计划完工日期　scheduled completion date
计划委员会　planning commission
计划修　planned maintenance
计划修改　modification of planning
计划有效性检查　plan validity check
计划值　planned value
计价　valuation
计价过低　undervaluation
计件定价　unit pricing, piece pricing
计件工资　wages for piece work, piece wage
计件工资率　piece-work rate, piece rate
计件工作　piece work system, taskwork, jobbing, piecework, piecework job
计件折旧法　unit method of depreciation
计件制　on a piecework basis, piecework system
计量　measurement
计量单位　unit of measurement
计量方法　method of measurement
计量合同　measurement contract
计量检验　quantitative inspection
计量器具　measuring instrument
计量认证　metrology accreditation
计量型合同　metrological contract
计量原则　principle of measurement
计曲线　index contour
计权标准化声压级差　difference of sound pressure level for weighting standard
计权标准化撞击声压级　impact sound pressure level of weighting standard
计权隔声量　weighted sound reduction factor
计权规范化撞击声压级　impact sound pressure level of weighting regulation
计日工　daywork
计日工制　on a daywork basis
计日工资　daywork rate, day wage, daily wage
计日工资率　day rate
计日工作　daywork
计日工作表　daywork schedule
计日工作计划表　daywork schedule
计时工资　time wage, payment by the hour, hourly wages
计时工资率　time rate
计时观察法　timed observation method
计时卡　time card, clock card
计数检验　counting inspection
计数器计数测试　counting test of counter
计税基数　tax base
计税年度　tax year
计算长度　calculating length
计算程序　calculation program
计算高度　calculated height
计算规定　calculation rules
计算规则　calculation rules
计算机辅助设计　computer aided design
计算机辅助制图　computer aided drawing (CAD)
计算机联锁　computer based interlocking (CBI)
计算机网络　computer network
计算机制图　computer aided drawing (CAD)
计算基数　calculation base
计算价值　computed value
计算跨度　calculated span
计算拉断荷载　calculated breaking load
计算倾覆点　calculation overturning point
计算容量　calculated capacity
计算书　calculations
计算速度　computed speed
计算停车点　calculated target point
计息期　interest period
计息日　value date
计轴　axle counting
计轴轨道占用检查装置　axle counter track occupancy detection device
计轴自动站间闭塞　automatic inter-station blocking with axle counter
记存装置　register
记号　mark, sign, tick, symbolism, marking, sentinel, notation, spot mark, token
记录　record
记录错误　clerical error, misregistration
记录单元　recorder unit
记录模型　record modeling
记录图纸　record drawing
记名背书　special endorsement, endorsement in full, endorsement to order

记名提单　named bill of lading, straight bill of lading
记名债券　registered bond
记名支票　order check, signed check
记载　record
记账　keep account, book, on account (o/a)
记账单位　accounting unit, unit of account
记账货币　currency of account, money of account
记账交易　payment on open account, account dealing, open account trade
记账卡　debit card
记账员　bookkeeper, accounting clerk
技师　technician, artificer, mechanic
技术报告　technical report
技术标评审　technical bid evaluation
技术标准　technical standard, technical norms
技术参数　technical parameter
技术措施　technical measures
技术代表团　technical mission
技术方案　technical solution, technical proposal, technical scheme
技术分析　technical analysis
技术服务合同　technical services contract
技术规范　technical specifications, technical regulations
技术建议书　technical proposal
技术交底　technical instruction
技术经济指标　technical and economical indexes
技术境界标定　setting-out of technical boundary
技术诀窍　know-how
技术可行性　technical feasibility
技术秘密　know-how, technology secret
技术评价　technical evaluation, technology assessment, technical review
技术审查与批准　technical review and approval
技术审核　technical scrutiny, technology review
技术室　technical office
技术手册　technical manual
技术数据　technical data
技术水平鉴定　technical degree verification, technical level appraisal
技术特征　technical characteristics, technical feature
技术性的　technical
技术性鉴定　technical assessment, technical appraisal
技术性能　technical performance, technical characteristics, technical feature
技术引进　technology import, acquisition of technology
技术员　technician

技术援助　technical assistance
技术援助费　technical assistance fee
技术援助信贷　technical assistance credit
技术责任　technical responsibility
技术整备　technical servicing
技术整备场　technical servicing yard
技术支持　technical support
技术转让　transfer of technology, technology transfer, technical transformation, transfer of skill
技术转让费　technology transfer fee
技术咨询公司　technical consultancy firm
技术咨询顾问　technical consultant
技术资料　technical data, technical literature, technical materials
季度财务报告　quarterly financial report
季节冻结层　seasonally frozen layer
季节冻土　seasonal frozen soil
季节融化层　seasonally thawed layer
季节施工　seasonal construction
季节性冻土　seasonally frozen soil
季节性流水　seasonal running water
季节性施工　seasonal construction
既得的　vested
既得利益　vested interests
既有建筑物　existing building
既有权利　accrued rights
既有铁路　existing railway
既有线　existing line
既有线限速功能测试　speed restriction function test for existing line
既有线站场测量　survey of existing station and yard
继承的财产　inherited property
继承人　heir, inheritor, successor
继电半自动闭塞　all-relay semi-automatic block
继电保护　relay protection
继电并联传递网络　relay parallel delivery network
继电并联网络　relay parallel network
继电串联网络　relay series network
继电联锁　relay interlocking
继电器　relay
继电器间　relay room
继电器释放　relay released
继电器吸起　relay energized
继电器箱　relay cabinet
继电式电气集中联锁　all-relay electric interlocking
寄销品　consigned goods, consignment out, cosigned goods, consignment outward

加班　work overtime, extra hour work, extra hours, extra work
加班费　overtime pay
加班工时　overtime workhour, added hours
加班工资　overtime wages, premium pay, callback pay
加班工作　overtime work
加班奖金　overtime premium (bonus), attendance bonus
加班津贴　overtime allowance
加班时间　overtime, overhours
加保费　additional premium
加冰所　re-icing point
加冰线　ice supplying track
加常数　additive constant
加封　sealing
加工　process, manufacture, machining, working, handling, treating, in-process, fabrication
加工成本　processing cost, manufacturing cost, finished cost, conversion cost
加工地　place of fabrication
加工费　processing cost
加工能力　process capability, processing capacity, working ability, working capacity
加工时间　processing time
加工图　working drawings, shop drawings
加工制造的检验点　fabrication check points, manufacturing inspection point
加固　reinforce, reinforcement, consolidate, fasten, strengthening, stiffening
加固杆　reinforcing rod
加荷膨胀率　loading expansion rate
加荷平衡法　loading balance method
加荷速度　loading speed
加荷速率　rate of loading
加荷锥　conical platen
加价　price mark up
加减速顶　accelerated and decelerated retarder
加减轴作业　increase and decrease operation of traction mass
加筋　reinforcement
加筋垫层　replacement layer of tensile reinforcement
加筋土　reinforced earth
加筋土挡土墙　reinforced earth retaining wall
加筋土路基　reinforced soil embankment
加劲板　stiffened plate
加劲杆　stiffener
加劲肋　stiffener
加劲肋外伸宽度　protruding width of stiffener
加快速度　expedite, accelerate
加里东期　Caledonian age/ stage
加力牵引坡度　pusher gradient, helper gradient
加力牵引区段　section of pusher gradient, assisting section
加料器　feeder
加密基标　additional benchmark
加密控制点　densified control points
加密控制网　densified control network
加气混凝土　aeroconcrete, aerated concrete
加气剂　air entrained agent
加强层　strengthened storey
加强钢筋　additional reinforcing bar
加强线　reinforcing feeder, line feeder
加权　weighting
加权百分数　percent weighting
加权报价　weighted price
加权法　method of weighting
加权平均值　weighted average value
加权算术平均数　weighted arithmetic average, weighted arithmetic mean
加权系数　weight coefficient
加权制　weighting system
加热　heating
加热伸缩率　ratio of expansion and contraction by heating
加热损失　heating loss
加深炮孔　deepened blasting hole
加深炮孔探测　prediction by extending blast hole
加湿　humidification
加湿器　humidifier
加速偿还条款　acceleration clause
加速成本回收制度　accelerated cost recovery system
加速度　acceleration
加速度计　accelerometer
加速缓坡　gentle slope for acceleration, easy gradient for acceleration
加速竣工　accelerated completion
加速老化　accelerated aging
加速坡　accelerating grade
加速施工　acceleration, speed-up construction
加速施工指令　acceleration order
加速推送信号　humping speeding-up signal
加速折旧　accelerated depreciation
加速折旧法　accelerated method of depreciation
加算坡度　compensation gradient, conversion gradient
加压泵　pressure pump
加药间　chemical-dosing room
加腋梁　haunched beam
加载程序　loading program
加载平台　weight platform

加载设备　loading equipment
加载试机　load machine testing
加载试验　loading test
加载稳定时间　loading stabilization time
加重　aggravate, make or become heavier, increase the weight of, add to one's (tasks\worries), make or become more serious, weighting, bodiness
加州承载比　California bearing ratio (CBR)
夹层　interlayer
夹具　clamp
夹心墙　cavity wall with insulation
夹圆曲线　curve between two tangent/straight track
夹直线　tangent between curves
甲方　employer
甲供材料　employer-supplied materials, materials supplied by the employer
甲供物资　employer-supplied materials and equipment
甲蓝实验　methylene blue test
甲类其他液体储罐　type A other liquid storage tank
甲醛含量　formaldehyde content
钾钠碱度　alkalinity of potassium and sodium
钾盐　leopoldite, sylvine
价差　difference in price
价差系数　coefficient of difference in price
价差预备费　contingency for difference in price
价格　price
价格变动　price fluctuation
价格表　schedule of prices
价格波动　fluctuation of price, price fluctuation
价格波动因子　price fluctuation factor
价格补贴　price support, price subsidy, price bonification
价格不变性　invariability in price
价格差额　price margin
价格单　price list, price sheet
价格的接受者　price taker
价格的决定者　price maker
价格调整　price adjustment
价格调整合同　price adjustment contract
价格调整条款　price adjustment clause
价格调整系数　price adjustment factor
价格幅度　price range, price band
价格控制　price control
价格敏感性　price sensitivity
价格年度　price year
价格偏差　price variance
价格上涨　advancing, price escalation, rise in price
价格水平　price level
价格谈判　price bargaining
价格条件　price terms
价格贴现　discount for price
价格修正条款　price revision clause
价格指数　price index
价目表　price list, tariff, rate sheet
价值　value
价值重估　revaluation
价值分析　value analysis
价值工程　value engineering (VE)
价值工程法　value engineering method
价值管理　value management (VM)
价值规划　value planning (VP)
价值技术　value technique (VT)
价值检验证书　inspection certificate of value
价值一览表　schedule of values
架构　infrastructure
架空层　empty space
架空地线　aerial earth wire (AeW, GW)
架空电缆线路　overhead cable line
架空电力线　overhead power line
架空刚性悬挂　overhead conductor rail
架空接触轨系统　overhead conductor rail system
架空接触网　overhead contact line system
架空接触悬挂　overhead contact line(OCL)
架空线　overhead line
架立钢筋　auxiliary steel bar
架梁速度　girder erecting speed
架桥机架设法　erection by girder-erecting machine, erection by beam-erecting machine
架设　erection
架设桥梁　erection of bridge
假彩色合成　pseudo-color composite
假彩色密度编码　pseudo-color density encode
假钞　forged banknote, counterfeit money, forged note, flash money
假定　presumption, suppose, assume, presume, hypothesis, assumption, postulation
假定高程　assumed elevation
假定坐标系　assumed coordinate system
假缝　dummy joint
假冒　counterfeit, sham
假期　holiday, vacation
假日工资　premium pay, holiday pay
假设价格　notional price
假响应抑制　spurious response rejection
假账　false entry
假植　heeling-in
尖顶山　spire mountain
尖端杆　front rod of a point

尖轨　switch rail, switch blade, point blades, tongue rail
尖轨动程　throw of switch rail
尖灭　pinch out
坚持　abide, adhere, persist in, persevere in, uphold, insist on, stick to, adhere to
坚固性　soundness
坚石　hard rock
坚硬　hard
间壁　partition
间隔调速　speed control for time interval between cars
间隔铁　spacing block, separation block
间隔制动　spacing braking
间隔制动位　interval retarder location
间隔装药　discontinuous charging
间接标价法　indirect quotation
间接材料费用　indirect material cost
间接成本　indirect cost, on-costs
间接费　indirect expenses
间接费分配　overhead allocation
间接费率　rate of indirect expenses
间接费用分摊率　burden rate
间接解译标志　indirect interpretation criteria
间接开支　indirect expenses
间接贸易　indirect trade
间接排水　indirect drainage
间接平差　indirection adjustment
间接人工成本　indirect labour cost
间接融资　indirect financing
间接税　indirect tax
间接损害　indirect damage, consequential damage
间接损失　consequential damage (loss), indirect loss
间接损失保险　indirect loss insurance, consequential loss insurance
间接责任　indirect liability
间距　spacing, space between, separation distance, interval, gap
间曲线　half-interval contour
间隙　gap
间隙通过性　gap through ability
间歇采暖　intermittent heating
间歇排放　intermittent emission
间歇泉　geyser, intermittent spring
间歇作业　intermittent operation
间休室　lounge
间植灌木　alternate planting shrub
肩式交路　shoulder turnaround routing
肩回运转制　locomotive arm routing
艰难情势条款　hardship clause
监测　monitoring

监测报警值　monitoring alarm value
监测点　monitoring point
监测范围　monitoring scope
监测内容　monitoring contents
监测频次　monitoring frequency
监测频率　monitoring frequency
监测区段　monitoring sector
监测设备　monitoring equipment
监测时段　monitoring period
监测维护终端　terminal of monitoring and maintenance
监测信息 GPRS 接口服务器　monitor-GPRS interface server (M-GRIS)
监测业务终端　terminal of monitoring service
监测终端　monitoring terminal
监测重点　monitoring emphasis
监督　monitor, supervise, supervision, superintendence
监督对象　object under surveillance
监督合同能力　ability to monitor contract
监督人　superintendent, supervisor, supervisor staff
监工　ganger, superintendent, overseer, task master
监管人员　supervisory personnel, job supervisor
监护人　guardian
监控　monitor
监控单元　monitoring unit
监控工作　monitor work
监控和数据采集系统　supervisory control and data acquisition system (SCADA)
监控量测　monitoring and measurement
监控量测频率　measurement frequency
监控模块　monitoring module
监控设备　monitoring equipment
监控图像　surveillance image
监控系统　monitoring system
监控站　monitoring station
监控中心　monitoring center
监控中心服务器　monitoring center server
监控装置　monitoring device
监理　supervision
监理单位　supervision firm
监理工程师　consulting engineer, supervising engineer
监理文件　supervision document
监视　monitor, observe, oversee
监视人　overseer
兼并　merge, merger, take over, annex
兼容及扩展能力　compatibility and expansion capability
检测　testing
检测报告　inspection report
检测方法　test method

检测计划表　schedule of inspection and testing
检测连接示意图　measurement architecture
检测频次　test frequency
检测设备　inspection device
检测数据　test data
检测限差　inspection tolerance
检测与评价　testing and evaluation
检测周期　inspection period
检查报告　inspection report
检查标志　check mark
检查表　inspection list, check table
检查工作　inspection of works
检查井　manhole
检查孔　inspection hole
检查口　inspection opening
检查库　inspection workshop
检查门　access door
检查内容　inspection subject
检查桥　inspection bridge
检查日期　date of survey, date for inspection
检查员　inspector
检定　rating, verification
检定承载系数　rating load-bearing coefficient
检定洪水频率　rating flood frequency
检定流量　rated flow
检定流速　rated flow rate
检定黏结力　rated bonding force
检定容许应力　rating allowable stress
检定证书　verification certificate
检核表　checklist
检斤　weighing
检斤设备　weighing device
检举人　plaintiff, offence-reporter
检漏测试　leakage detecting test
检漏管沟　pipe ditch for leak detector
检票　check-in
检修　inspection
检修盖　access cover
检修工区　overhaul section
检修公里　running kilometers between repair intervals
检修库　maintenance workshop
检修流水线　assembly line repair
检修室　inspection and repair room
检修台位　repair position
检修停时　standing time under repair
检修线　repair track
检修修程　classification of locomotive repair
检修周期　repair cycle
检验　inspection
检验报告　survey report, test report

检验方法　inspection method
检验费　inspection fee
检验合格证书　inspection certificate
检验结果　test result
检验批　inspection lot
检验评定　inspection and evaluation
检验签证　inspection endorsement
检验日期　date for testing, date of survey
检验时间　time for tests, proving time
检验试验费　inspection and test fee
检验数量　inspection quantity
检验条款　survey clause, inspection clause
检验通知　notice of test, inspection notice
检验证书　certificate of inspection, testing certificate, test certificate, certification of proof
检验制度　inspection regime, examining system, system of inspection
剪刀撑　cross brace
剪节理　shear joint
剪跨比　shear-span to depth ratio
剪力　shear, shear force
剪力齿槽　shear alveolar, shear flute
剪力铰　shear hinge
剪力连接器　shear connector
剪力墙结构　shear wall structure
剪力滞效应　shear lag effect
剪裂缝　shear crack
剪切　shear
剪切变形　shear deformation
剪切波速　shear wave velocity
剪切波速测试　shear wave velocity measurement
（梁端轨道板）剪切连接
　（beam-end track slab）shear connection
剪切模量　shear modulus
剪切破坏　shear failure
剪切位移　shear displacement
剪切应力　shear stress
剪切应力比　shear strength stress ratio
剪应变　shearing strain
剪应力　shear stress
剪胀性　dilatancy
减加速地段
　section of acceleration and deceleration
减价　reduce the price, mark down, price cutting
减量　decrement, reduction
减免　mitigation, remission
减免税　tax relief, reduction or exemption of tax
减轻　mitigate, mitigation, alleviate, lighten, ease, alleviate, remit, relieve
减轻债务　abatement of debt

减水剂　water-reducing admixture
减水率　water-reducing rate
减税　abatement of tax, tax abatement, tax reduction
减速器　retarder
减速器长度　retarder length
减速器出口速度　exit speed of retarder
减速器单位制动能高　specific braking energy head of retarder
减速器工作状态　retarder in working state
减速器缓解时间　retarder release time
减速器缓解状态　retarder released
减速器接近限界　clearance of retarder
减速器全缓解时间　full release time of retarder
减速器全制动时间　full braking time of retarder
减速器入口速度　entrance speed at reducer
减速器制动状态　retarder in closed state
减速推送信号　humping slowing-down signal
减速信号　caution signal
减压阀　pressure relief valve
减压井　relief well
减压渣油　vacuum residuum, vacuum residue
减灾计划　disaster mitigation planning
减振　vibration reduction
减振轨道　vibration damping track
减振基础　damping foundation
减振降噪　vibration attenuation and noise reduction
减振胶垫　vibration dampening rubber pads
减振接头　vibration absorber rail joint
减振器　absorber
减振型轨道板　vibration damping track slab
减震　vibration damping
简单横向连接　simple transverse link
简单链形悬挂　simple catenary suspension
简单网络管理协议　simple network management protocol (SNMP)
简单悬挂　trolley-type suspension
简图　diagram, sketch, abbreviated drawing, diagrammatic sketch, sketch drawing, schematic diagram, block-diagram, simplified schematic
简要进度计划　summary schedule
简要说明　briefing
简易混凝土搅拌站　simple concrete mixing plant
简易水均衡法　simplified water balance method
简支梁　simply-supported girder, simply supported beam
简支梁桥　simply-supported girder bridge, simply-supported beam bridge
简支箱梁预制场　precast yard of simply-supported box girder
碱处理　alkali treatment
碱度　alkalinity
碱—骨料反应　alkali-aggregate reaction
碱硅酸反应活性矿物　alkali-silica reaction active mineral
碱含量　alkali content
碱活性　alkali activity
碱活性骨料　alkali-active aggregate
碱活性试验　alkali reactivity test
碱式氯化铝　basic aluminium chloride
碱性粗面岩　alkali trachyte
碱性花岗岩　alkali-granite
碱性流纹岩　comendite
碱性污水　alkaline sewage
碱性蓄电池　alkaline battery
碱性蓄电池间　alkaline battery storage room
碱性盐渍土　alkaline saline soil
碱性正长岩　alkali syenite
见票后定期付款汇票　bill payable at fixed date after sight
见票后（若干天）付款期票　after sight bill
见票即付　payable at sight, payable on demand, payment at sight
见票即付汇票　bill at sight, bill payable at sight
见票即付票据　demand bill note at sight
见索即付　payment on demand
见证　witness
见证检验　witnessed inspection
见证检验报告　witness inspection report
见证取样　witness sampling
见证取样检测　witnessed sampling test
建材储量　reserve of building materials
建立营地　encamp
建设—出租—移交　build-rent-transfer (BRT)
建设成本　construction cost
建设—移交—运营　build-transfer-operate (BTO)
建设—移交—租赁　build-transfer-lease (BTL)
建设—拥有—出售　build-own-sell (BOS)
建设—拥有—运营　build-own-operate (BOO)
建设—拥有—运营—补贴—移交　build-own-operate-subsidize-transfer (BOOST)
建设—拥有—运营—维护　build-own-operate-maintain (BOOM)
建设—拥有—运营—移交　build-own-operate-transfer (BOOT)
建设用地　land for construction
建设—运营—出售　build-operate-sell (BOS)
建设—运营—移交　build-operate-transfer (BOT)
建设单位管理费　administration cost of employer
建设单位管理费率　rate of administration cost of employer

J

建设单位管理其他费
  other administration costs of employer
建设单位临时设施费
  expenses for temporary facilities of employer
建设各方 parties involved in construction
建设工程档案 files of construction project
建设工程投标 bid for construction works
建设工程文件 construction project document
建设工程造价管理
  cost management of construction works
建设工程招标 bidding of construction works
建设工期 construction period
建设管理其他费
  other expenses of construction management
建设类项目 construction projects
建设期 construction period
建设期交通工具购置费 purchase expense of transportation vehicle during construction period
建设期投资贷款利息 investment loan interest during construction period
建设期债务性资金利息
  interest of debt capital during construction period
建设生产类项目
  constructive and productive engineering
建设项目管理费
  management cost of construction project
建设项目管理信息系统 construction project management information system
建设项目管理信息系统购建费 project management system cost for construction project
建设项目竣工图
  as-built drawing of construction project
建设项目竣工验收
  completion acceptance of construction project
建设项目开工报告
  construction project commencement report
建设项目可行性研究
  feasibility study for construction project
建设项目前期工作费
  preliminary work expense of construction project
建设项目设计概算
  design budgetary estimate of construction project
建设项目总投资
  total investment for construction project
建设许可证 building permit
建设周期 construction cycle
建设总工期 total construction period
建议 advising
建议书 proposal
建议书大纲 outline proposal
建议书征求函 request for proposal
建造阶段 construction stage, build stage
建造师 builder, constructor
建造周期 construction cycle, production cycle
建筑、工程、施工和设备管理
  architecture, engineering, construction and facilities management (AEC/FM)
建筑安装工程
  construction and installation works
建筑安装工程费
  cost of construction and installation works
建筑本体节能率
  building energy efficiency improment rate
建筑变形 building deformation
建筑材料 construction material
建筑产品 building products
建筑贷款 building loan, construction loan
建筑地基 building foundation
建筑费用指数 index of construction costs
建筑高度 building height
建筑接近限界 construction works
建筑工程 construction works
建筑工程保险单 construction work policy, construction insurance policy
建筑工程测量 building engineering survey
建筑工程费 cost of construction works
建筑工程公司 construction engineering corporation, building engineering company
建筑工程造价 cost of building works, construction project costs, construction engineering costs
建筑工地 construction site
建筑管理方式 construction management (CM)
建筑管理系统 building management system
建筑管制专员 commissioner of building control
建筑规范 building code
建筑合同 construction contract
建筑红线定位测量 building line survey
建筑接近限界 swept envelope
建筑节能 energy conservation in building, building energy efficiency
建筑结构 building structure
建筑结构安全等级
  safety class of building structures
建筑结构抗震设防类别
  classification for seismic fortification of buildings
建筑结构设计 building structure design
建筑界限 building boundary, construction clearance
建筑景观 architecture landscape
建筑抗震概念设计
  seismic conceptual design of building

建筑抗震设防分类　classification of seismic fortification of buildings
　　classification of seismic fortification of buildings
建筑会计　construction accounting
建筑控制线　building line
建筑垃圾清运　construction waste clearance
建筑类别　class of construction, building category
建筑密度　building density
建筑幕墙　curtain wall of building
建筑能耗综合值　building energy consumption
建筑缺陷保险　building defects insurance
建筑群　complex, building group, architectural complex
建筑设备及系统　equipment and systems of building
建筑设备设计　building services design
建筑设计　architecture, architectural design, building design
建筑师　architect
建筑施工场界　construction boundary
建筑施工场界噪声　noise at construction site boundary
建筑施工图　architectural working drawing
建筑施工噪声　construction noise
建筑条例　building code
建筑透视图　architectural perspective
建筑围护结构气密性　air tightness of building envelope
建筑维护计划　building (preventative) maintenance scheduling
建筑物沉降监测　building subsidence monitoring
建筑物耗热量指标　index of building heat loss
建筑物税　building tax
建筑物体形系数　coefficient of building shape
建筑物与构筑物　buildings and structures
建筑系统分析　building system analysis
建筑限界　structure gauge, structure clearance
建筑信息化模型　building information modeling/model (BIM)
建筑许可　construction concession, planning permission
建筑学　architecture
建筑业　construction business, construction industry, building industry
建筑账户　construction account, buildings account
建筑执照　building permit
建筑轴线测量　building axis survey
建筑装饰　building decoration
建筑资产负债表　construction balance sheet
建筑综合节能率　building energy saving rate
健康保险　health insurance
健康和安全计划　health and safety plan
健康和安全控制　health and safety control
健康及安全义务　health and safety obligation
健康证明　medical certificate, health certificate
渐进破坏　progressive failure
渐新世　Oligocene epoch
渐新统　Oligocene series
溅蚀　splash erosion
鉴别　identify, identification, distinguish, differentiate, discriminate, discern
鉴定　appraise, appraisal, identify, verification, authenticate, assay
鉴定人　appraiser, expert witness, referee, identifier, surveyor
鉴定书　testimonial, expertise report
鉴定意见　expert opinion
鉴权中心　authentication center (AuC)
箭翎线　herringbone track
姜石　loess-doll
将延误降到最低的职责　duty to minimise delay
将争议提交争议避免裁决委员会裁决　reference of a dispute to the DAAB
浆砌毛石　mortar rubble masonry
浆砌片石　mortar rubble
浆砌片石骨架　grouted rubble skeleton
浆砌石护坡　grouted pitching
浆体喷射搅拌桩　slurry injection mixing pile
浆液胶凝时间　slurry jelling time
奖惩条款　bonus-penalty clause
奖金　bonus, reward, premium money award, bounty
奖励工资　wage incentive, premium wages
奖励条款　bonus clause
降低成本　cost reduction, cut the cost, cost down, lower (reduce) production costs, reduce cost
降低额　decrease amount
降低幅度　decrease range
降低工效　decrease of work efficiency
降低质量　compromise on quality, lower the quality
降级显示　degradation indication
降价　reduce the price, price reduction, price cutting, mark down, depreciation, cut price, abate a price
降落漏斗　depression cone
降水　precipitation
降水措施　dewatering measure
降水法　dewatering method
降水井　dewatering well
降水量　amount of precipitation
降水强度　precipitation intensity
降水日　precipitation day

降水施工　dewatering
降水蓄渗工程　rainfall detention works
降温池　cooling tank
降温速率　temperature drop ratio
降温系统　cooling system
降压变电站　step-down substation
降雨历时　duration of rainfall
降雨量　rainfall
降雨强度　rainfall intensity
降噪　noise reduction
降噪系数　noise reduction coefficient (NRC)
降噪效果　noise reduction effect
降阻剂　resistance reducing agent
交变荷载　alternating load
交叉测量　cross measurement
交叉点放样　setting-out of junction
交叉渡线　scissors crossover, double crossover
交叉过失　cross-default
交叉过失条款　cross-default clause
交叉汇兑　cross exchange
交叉路　cross road, crossway
交叉式线岔
　　overhead crossing, intersecting point wiring
交叉疏解　crossing untwining
交叉索赔　cross claim
交叉责任条款　cross liability clause
交叉折扣　cross discounts
交叉支撑　X-brace
交叉中隔壁法(CRD法)　cross diaphragm method
交代结构　metasomatic texture
交单付款　cash against document
交点　intersection point
交分道岔　slip turnout
交付　deliver, delivery
交付材料　delivery of materials
交付成果　deliverables
交付行为　delivery behaviour
交互式会议业务　interactive conference service
交还　surrender, return, give back
交换　switching, exchange
交换场　exchange yard, interchange yard
交换车流　exchange traffic flow
交换性钙镁离子
　　exchangeable calcium and magnesium
交换性钾和钠含量
　　content of exchangeable potassium and sodium
交汇点　meeting point
交会法　intersection method
交货　delivery of cargo (goods)
交货承运人　delivering carrier
交货地点　delivery point, place of delivery
交货付款　cash against delivery, payment on delivery
交货港　port of delivery
交货价格　delivered price
交货期　limit of delivery
交货清单　delivery order
交货日期　date of delivery, delivery date
交货时间表　delivery schedule
交货条件　delivery terms, terms of delivery, delivered terms
交货通知　delivery advice
交货逾期赔偿　compensation for delay
交货证明　proof of delivery
交货证明书　certificate of delivery (C/D)
交际费　expenses for social intercourse, entertaining expenses
交角　intersection angle
交接　conjoin
交接场　delivery-receiving yard
交接检验　handover inspection
交接试验　acceptance test
交接线　delivery-receiving track
交接桩　stake handover
交接作业　delivery-receiving operation
交界面　interface
交流电法　A.C. electric method
交流电源　AC power supply
交流电源屏　AC power supply panel
交流二元二位轨道电路
　　AC two element two position track circuit
交流二元二位继电器
　　AC two element two position relay
交流发电机　alternator, alternating-current generator
交流供电进线　AC power supply incoming wire
交流轨道电路　AC track circuit
交流计数电码轨道电路
　　AC counting coded track circuit
交流计数电码自动闭塞　automatic block with AC counting coded track circuit
交流继电器　AC relay
交流连续式轨道电路　AC continuous track circuit
交流耐压试验　AC voltage withstand test
交流盘　AC panel
交流屏　AC panel
交流引入配电箱　AC lead-in distribution box
交流转辙机　AC point switch
交涉　negotiate, negotiation
交税　payment of tax, payment of duties
交替的
　　alternate, commutative, vicissitudinary, metagenic

交通　communication, traffic, transportation
交通安全　traffic safety
交通标志　traffic signing
交通干扰　traffic interference
交通干线　traffic artery
交通工具　transportation means
交通工具配置　configuration of transportation means
交通涵洞　traffic culvert
交通警示标记　traffic warning board, traffic warning sign
交通量　traffic volume
交通事故　traffic accident, road accident
交通信号灯　traffic lights
交通运输　transportation
交通运输能力　traffic capacity
交线条件　intersection condition
交验　handover and acceptance
交验区　delivery and inspection area
交易　deal, transaction, trade, commercial transaction
交易价格　price of transacting, transaction value
交易税　transaction tax, trade tax
交易所　exchange, bourse
交易习惯　transaction practice
交易者　negotiator, trader, negotiant, swapper, bargainer
交钥匙合同　turnkey contract
交钥匙项目　turnkey project
交织单网无线覆盖　interleaving single coverage
交织物　intertexture
交直流继电器　AC/DC relay
交直流配电箱　AC/DC distribution box
交直流系统　AC/DC power system
浇洒道路用水量　street sprinkle water consumption
浇注　pouring, casting
浇筑　cast, pour, place
浇筑预演　dry run
胶带　adhesive tape, adhesive tape, gummed tape, friction tape
胶合板　plywood, glued board, veneer board, adhesive-bonded panel, hot-press for plywood, weldwood, laminated wood, veneer, xenidium, symphylium
胶合板混凝土模板　plywood concrete forms
胶接绝缘接头　glued insulation rail joint
胶结剂　cement agent
胶结式钢轨绝缘　glued insulation rail joint
胶粒　colloidal particle
胶囊止水器　capsule sealing device

胶凝材料　cementitious material
胶凝材料抗蚀系数　cementitious material coefficient of corrosion resistance
胶塞　rubber plug
胶砂流动度　mortar fluidity
胶砂流动度测定仪　mortar fluidity tester
胶砂强度　strength of mortar
胶体质　colloidal
焦炭滤池　coke filter
角斑岩　keratophyre
角度不整合接触　angular unconformity contact
角峰　pyramidal peak
角钢　angle steel
角焊缝尺寸　size of fillet weld
角件　corner fittings, diagonal member
角砾　angular gravel
角砾混合岩　agmatite
角砾土　angular gravel soil
角砾岩　breccia
角闪石　hornblende
角闪岩　hornblendite
角岩　hornfels
角页岩　hornfels
绞车　winch, cable hoist, crab winch, hoister, wind, draw-work, windlass, cable winch, capstan, crane crab, hoist reel, hoisting winch, reel cart, rope hoist, winch capstan
绞线　stranded wire
铰接　hinge joint
铰接板梁法　hinge-jointed plate method
铰轴支座　hinge support
矫直钢轨　rail straightening
脚本　script
脚墙　toe wall
脚手板　scaffold board
脚手架　scaffold
脚手架板　scaffold board, gang board
脚手架拆搭费　charges for erection and removal of scaffold
脚手架工　scaffolding worker, scaffolder
脚注　foot-note
搅拌车　mixer truck, agitating truck
搅拌机　mixer
搅拌桩　mixed pile
缴款通知　memorandum of payment, payment notice
缴纳保金　posting bond
缴纳罚金　pay the penalty
缴清股本　paid-up capital, paid-in capital
教育费附加　education surcharge
校核基点　checking datum mark

校核容量　checked capacity
校验系数　verification coefficient
校正系数　correction coefficient
校准　calibration
校准法　calibration method
校准证书　calibration certificate
阶地　terrace
阶段发包方式　phased construction method
阶段付款　stage payment, progress billing
阶段式距离保护　section type distance protection
阶段性完工　phased completion, sectional completion
阶段招标　phased bidding. stage bidding
阶梯成本　step cost, stair-step cost
阶梯式协作货位　stepped collaborative freight section
阶梯形坡　stepped slope
阶梯状断层　step fault
阶形柱　stepped column
接车进路　receiving route
接车进路信号机　route signal for receiving
接车信号　receiving signal
接车信号机　receiving signal
接触　contact
接触变质　contact metamorphism
接触不良　poor contact, contact fault
接触导线高度　contact wire height
接触电势　touch potential
接触电位差　contact potential difference
接触电压　touch voltage
接触轨(第三轨)　conductor rail, third rail
接触滑板　contact strips
接触胶结　contact cementation
接触力　contact force
接触器　contactor
接触晒印　contact printing
接触上升泉　contact ascending spring
接触式位移量测装置
　contact type displacement measurement device
接触弹簧　contact spring
接触网　overhead contact system (OCS)
接触网高空作业车
　catenary high-altitude operation vehicle
接触网检修车　OCS inspection vehicle (car)
接触网开关集中监控系统
　centralized monitoring system of OCS disconnectors
接触网立柱　poles for overhead contact system
接触网抢修列车
　catenary emergency maintenance train
接触网维修作业车　catenary maintenance vehicle
接触网自动监测装置
　automatic monitoring device for OCS

接触线　contact wire
接触线高差　variation in contact wire height
接触线横向偏移量
　lateral deflection of contact wire
接触线坡度　gradient
接触线抬升　contact wire uplift
接触线中心锚接线夹
　mid-anchor connecting clamp for contact wire
接触线终端锚固线夹
　terminal anchor clamp for contact wire
接触线最大水平偏移量
　maximum horizontal displacement of contact wire
接触悬挂　overhead contact line/catenary
接触压力　contact pressure
接地　earthing, grounding
接地棒　earthing rod
接地保护放电装置
　discharging device for earthing protection
接地参考点　earthing reference point (ERP)
接地刀闸　earthing blade
接地电阻　earthing resistance
接地电阻测量仪　ground resistance testor
接地端子　earthing terminal
接地故障　earthing fault
接地汇集线　earthing busbar
接地极　earth electrode
接地距离保护　earthing distance protection
接地开关　earthing switch
接地面积　ground contact area
接地母排　earthing busbar
接地排　grounding bar
接地体　earth electrode
接地铜排　earthing copper bus bars
接地网　earthing mesh
接地系统　earthing system
接地线　earth wire
接地线夹　earthing clamp
接地线连接线夹
　connecting clamp of earthing conductor
接地引接线　earthing down conductor
接地装置　earth-termination system
接地阻抗　grounding impedance
接点闭合　contact closed
接点断开　contact open
接点系统　contact system
接点压力　contact pressure
接电装置　switchgear, electric hook-up
接发车进路　receiving-departure route
接缝　seam, joint
接缝填料　joint filler

接杆	extension rod
接管	take over
接管令	receiving order
接轨站	junction station
接户管	building unite pipe
接户线	service wire
接近表示	approach indication
接近发码	coding for train approaching
接近区段	approach section
接近锁闭	approach locking
接近锁闭测试	approach locking test
接近信号机	approach signal
接口	interface
接口服务器	interface server
接口设计	interface design
接力式设计—建造	novated design-build
接入层	access layer
接入节点	access node
接入设备	access device
接入网	access network (AN)
接入网关	access gateway (AG)
接闪器	lightning arrester
接收到货	take delivery, withdrawal, collection
接收电极	voltage electrode
接收光功率	receiving optical power
接收后的缺陷	defects after taking over
接收后的现场出入权	right of access after taking over
接收机天线	receiver antenna
接收井	receiving shaft
接收人	receiver, recipient
接收线圈	receiving coil
接收证书	taking-over certificate
接受报价	acceptance of offer, accept a quotation, accept an offer
接受报价者	offeree
接受报盘	entertain an offer, to accept offer
接受承兑	acceptance for honor
接受的合同款额	accepted contract amount
接受抵押人	pledgee
接受订单	accept an order
接受订货	entertain an order, accept order, execute an order
接受发盘	accept an offer
接受人	recipient, taker, accepter, receiver
接受声明	declaration of acceptance, statement of acceptance
接受索赔	accept a claim, entertain a claim
接受投标	accept the bid (tender)
接受投标书	acceptance of the bid (tender)
接受邀请	accept an invitation
接通率	call completing rate
接头	joint
接头标	joint sign
接头盒	connector box, adapter box
接头夹板	fish plate, joint bar
接头接缝拉伸强度	joint/seam tensile strength
接头拉伸试验	transverse tensile test
接头瞎缝	closed joint
接头线夹	joint clamp, splice
接头阻力	joint resistance
接线端子	connection terminal
接线箱	wiring case, junction box, connection box
接续(光缆熔接)	splicing
接续方式	connect mode
揭示牌	sign board
节点	truss joint, node, panel point
节点板	gusset plate
节段拼装法	segmental assembling method
节间	panel
节间长度	panel length
节理	joint
节理粗糙度	joint roughness
节理玫瑰图	joint rose diagram
节理密度	joint density
节理密集带	joint-intensive zone
节理面	joint plane, joint surface
节理蚀变度	joint alteration degree
节理组数	joint set number
节能	energy conservation
节能措施	energy conservation measures
节能工艺	energy conservation measures
节能技术	energy conservation process
节能减排	energy conservation and emission reduction
节能控制器	energy conservation controller
节能量	amount of energy conservation
节能率	energy conservation rate
节能目标	energy conservation target, energy efficiency targets
节能评估	energy conservation assessment
节能评价值	evaluating values of energy conservation
节能评审	energy conservation review
节能坡	energy conservation slope
节能效益	energy conservation benefit
节约能源	energy conservation
节约型社会	conservation-minded society
节约用地	optimal land utilization
节约用水	water conservation
节约资源	resources conservation
洁净气体灭火系统	clean gas fire extinguishing system

结点　nodal point
结点网　node network
结构　frame, structure, construction
结构本体混凝土　concrete of structure body
结构材料　structural material
结构侧移刚度　lateral displacement rigidity of structure
结构动力特性　structure dynamic property
结构动态特性测量　structural dynamic characteristics testing
结构分析　structural analysis
结构缝　structural joint
结构附加恒载　additional dead load on structure
结构刚度　structural stiffness
结构高度　system height
结构工程　structural works, structural engineering
结构构件垂直度　verticality of structural member
结构构件平整度　planeness of structural member
结构构件起拱　camber of structural members
结构加工　fabricate
结构胶粘剂　structural adhesive
结构结合处强度　strength of structure juncture
结构抗倾覆力矩　structural overturning moment resistance
结构抗震变形能力　anti-seismic deformation capacity of structure
结构抗震承载能力　structural bearing capacity of seismic resistance
结构抗震可靠性　structural seismic resistance reliability
结构抗震性能　structural seismic performance
结构抗震性能设计　structural seismic performance design
结构类型　structure type
结构面　structure plane
结构面闭合程度　closure degree of structural plane
结构面产状　occurrence of structural plane
结构面胶结程度　cementation degree of structural plane
结构面抗剪强度指标　shear strength index of structural plane
结构模型　structural model
结构耐久性　structure durability
结构破坏　structural failure
结构墙　structural wall
结构设计　structural design, architecture design
结构使用年限　service life of structure
结构体　structural body
结构体系　structural system

结构体系转换　structure system transformation
结构校验系数　structural verification coefficient
结构性能检验　structural performance test
结构影响系数　structural influence coefficient
结构用胶性能检验　inspection for properties of glue used in structural member
结构预制件　structural casting, structure prefabrication
结构振动控制　structural vibration control
结构整体稳固性　overall robustness of structure
结构重要性系数　importance factor of structure
结构自重　weight of structure
结构总长度　total length of structure
结构总高度　total height of structure
结构总宽度　total width of structure
结关　customs clearance, clearance, clear a port, clearance through customs
结关单　jerque note
结关手续　clearance procedure
结关文件　document on customs clearance
结合　merge, incorporate, combine, unite, link, coalition, cohesion, joint, union, join, coupling, junctura (pl. juncturae), concrescence
结合电路功能测试　combined circuit function test
结合杆　union link
结合井　combined well
结合井出水量　joint well yield
结合梁　composite girder
结合梁桥　composite girder bridge
结合水　bound water
结核状　nodular
结核状构造　concretionary structure
结汇　settlement of exchange
结晶构造　crystal structure
结晶片岩　crystalline schist
结晶质的　crystalline
结论　conclusion, ultimateness, verdict, peroration
结欠余额　balance due
结清　discharge
结清单　discharge
结实的　compact, stout, burly, well-knit, beefy, sinewy
结算单　statement of account
结算货币　currency of settlement
结算价　settlement price
结算价格　settlement price
结算期　period of settlement, accounting period
结算日　account day, settlement date
结算条款　settlement clause, settlement terms

结算协定　clearing agreement
结余　balance, surplus
结账　settle accounts, close an account
结账分录　closing entry
结账后试算表　closing trial balance
结账日期　closing date, period closing date
结转价格　transfer price
捷接线　bypass feeder
截断　cutting, cut off, block, truncature, truncation, disconnect, break, truncate
截距　intercept
截流倍数　interception ratio
截面　section
截面尺寸限值　limiting value for sectional dimension
截面刚度　rigidity of section
截面高度　height of section
截面惯性矩　moment of inertia of cross section
截面核芯面积　core area of section
截面厚度　thickness of section
截面回转半径　gyration radius of cross section
截面积　sectional area
截面剪变刚度　shearing rigidity of section
截面宽度　breadth of section
截面拉伸刚度　tensile rigidity of section
截面面积　sectional area
截面扭转刚度　torsional rigidity of section
截面翘曲刚度　warping rigidity of section
截面弯曲刚度　flexural rigidity of section
截面压缩刚度　compressive rigidity of section
截面有效高度　effective height of cross-section
截排水沟　interception and drainage ditch
截水沟　intercepting ditch
截水骨架　water-interception skeleton
截水坑　catch pit, sump
截水墙　cut-off
截水帷幕　water cutoff curtain
截止阀　globe valve, stop valve
截止日期　deadline, date of expiration (expiry), closing date, latest date, cut-off date, as-of date
截止时间　deadline, closing time
解编作业　breaking-up and marshalling operation
解除抵押　release of mortgage
解除合同　terminate a contract, rescind the contract
解除合同补偿费　compensation for cancellation of contract
解除留置权　release of liens
解除履约　release from performance
解除条款　resolutive clause
解除义务　relieve from obligations
解除责任　discharge
解读　interpretation
解雇　dismiss, fire, discharge, kickout
解雇费　termination pay, termination grant, severance pay
解理　cleavage
解理面　cleavage plane
解码器　decoder
解释　interpretation
解释权　power of interpretation
解释性备忘录　explanatory memorandum
解锁　release
解锁按钮盘　manual release button panel
解锁电路　release circuit
解锁力　releasing force
解锁条件　release requisition
解体能力　break-up capacity
解析法测图　analytical mapping
解析解　analytical solution
解析空中三角测量　analytical aerotriangulation
解译标志　interpretation mark
解约　rescission of a contract, cancel a contract, terminate a contract, break off an engagement, terminate an agreement, rescind a contract
解约权　right of rescission
介电常数　dielectric constant
介入权　step in, right of intervene
介绍简况　brief, outline
介绍信　letter of recommendation, letter of introduction
介质访问控制　media access control (MAC)
介质损耗角　dielectric loss angle
界标　landmark, monument, boundary monument, boundary sign, terminus
界面　interface
界面管理　management of interface
界限　threshold, boundary, demarcation line, dividing line, limits, bounds, boundary, range, limitation, end
界限含水率试验　water ratio limit test
界限偏心距　balanced eccentricity
界线　demarcation line, boundary line
界址点　boundary marker
界桩　boundary stake
借贷　debit and credit, borrowing
借贷成本　borrowing cost
借贷信用　creditworthiness
借方　debtor, debit
借方卡　debit card

借方栏　debit column
借方余额　debit balance
借记　debit
借据　note of hand, IOU (I Owe You), note, debit note, due bill, evidence of debt
借款保函　letter of guarantee for loan
借款单证　loan note
借款国　borrowing country
借款利率　borrowing rate, interest rate on borrowings, incremental borrowing rate
借款人　borrower
借款银行　borrowing bank, debit bank
借入　borrow
借入资本　debt capital, borrowed capital, debenture capital, loan capital
借项　debit entry, debit item, debit
借项通知单　debit memorandum (note)
借债　ask for loan, borrow money, raise (contract) a loan
金伯利岩　kimberlite
金额　amount, figure, sum, amount of money, sum of money
金刚光泽　adamantine luster
金刚石　diamond
金刚石钻进　diamond drilling
金红石　rutile
金融　finance
金融偿付能力　financial viability
金融风险　financial risk
金融工具　financial instrument
金融机构　financial institution, financier
金融家　financier
金融界　financial community, financial circle, financial interests, financial world, moneyed interest
金融票据　financial instrument, financial bill
金融期货　financial futures
金融市场　financial market, monetary markets, money market, market for funds
金融手段　financial instrument
金融性资产　financial assets
金融中介　financial intermediation
金融中心　financial center
金融咨询　financial counselling, financial consultation
金属箔防水卷材　metal foil surfaced asphalt sheet
金属导管　metal conduit
金属辐射板　metal radiant panel
金属构件　metal component
金属光泽　metallic luster
金属脚手架　iron scaffold

金属铠装开关柜　metal-clad switchgear
金属丝式应变片　metal wire strain gauge
金属线槽　metal cable tray
金属性短路　metallic short circuit
金属氧化物　metal oxide
金云母　phlogopite
津贴　allowance
筋条　fillet
仅供参考　for reference only
紧急备用动力　emergency power
紧急出口　emergency exit
紧急法令　emergency act
紧急告警　urgent alarm
紧急救济　urgent relief
紧急救援站　emergency rescue station
紧急开门按钮　emergency exit button
紧急情况　emergency, emergency circumstances, critical situation
紧急任务　urgent task
紧急疏散　emergency evacuation
紧急疏散通道　emergency evacuation channel
紧急停车测试　emergency stop test
紧急行为　emergency action
紧急制动　emergency braking
紧急制动模式曲线　emergency braking intervention profile
紧密孔隙率　compact porosity
紧密运行　tight timetable operation/tight schedule operation
紧坡地段　section of sufficient grade
紧缩银根政策　tight money policy
堇青石　cordierite
尽端式货运站　dead-end freight station
尽端式客运站　dead-end passenger station
尽端式枢纽　dead-end terminal
尽端式站台　dead-end platform
尽头信号机　signal for stub-end siding
进厂检验　factory inspection
进场道路　access route
进场费　mobilization fee
进场检验　site test, receiving inspection
进场路线　access route, approach course
进场前协议　pre-possession agreement
进场日期　date of possession
进场验收　site acceptance
进车不平衡系数　unbalanced coefficient of locomotive to shed
进程　progress, course, proceeding, process
进出口许可证　import and export license
进出站流线　(passenger) station approach flow

进出站通道　station access
进出站线路　station approach track
进出站线路疏解
　　untwining for station approach track
进度　progress, schedule
进度报告　progress report
进度表　progress chart, time schedule
进度承诺　schedule commitment
进度分析　progress analysis, schedule analysis
进度付款　progress payment
进度管理
　　progress management, schedule management
进度会　progress meeting
进度绩效指数　schedule performance index (SPI)
进度计划　progress schedule, scheduled plan
进度控制　progress control, schedule control
进度偏差　schedule variance (SV)
进度压缩　schedule compression
进度影响分析　schedule impact analysis
进度指标　progress index
进风口　air inlet
进货成本　prime cost, purchase cost, cost of goods purchased, cost of acquisition
进货代理人　buying agent
进货费用　buying expenses, purchase expense
进货运费　freight-in
进货折扣　discount on purchases
进浆速度　mortar feeding rate
进口　import, entrance
进口报关单　declaration for importation, declaration inwards, import entry
进口补报　post entry
进口材料　import material
进口代理商　import agent
进口订单　import order
进口附加税　import surtax (surcharge)
进口港　port of entry
进口关税　import tariff, import duty
进口关税险　risk of contingent import duty
进口国货币　importer's currency
进口合同　import contract
进口检疫　import quarantine
进口禁令　import ban
进口贸易　import trade
进口免税　free import
进口配额　import quota
进口批准　import license (permit)
进口设备国内运杂费　domestic freight and miscellaneous charges for imported equipment
进口设备原价　original price of imported equipment
进口申报单　import declaration
进口手续　import procedure, process of import
进口税　customs, import tax, impost, import duty
进口通知　import announcement, notice of importation
进口限额　import limit, import quota
进口限制　import restraint
进口信用证　import letter of credit
进口许可　import permit, import admission
进口许可证　import license, import permit
进口许可制　import licensing
进库材料　incoming material
进款　receipt, funds received
进料斗　feed hopper
进路　route
进路表　route table
进路表示器　route indicator
进路表示器电路　route indicator circuit
进路操纵作业　semi-automatic operation by route
进路存储器　route storage
进路电路　route selecting circuit
进路分段解锁　sectional route release
进路继电式电气集中联锁
　　route type all-relay interlocking
进路交叉　crossing of routes
进路解锁　route release
进路解锁测试　route release test
进路人工解锁　route manual release
进路适合性数据　route suitability data
进路锁闭　route locking
进路锁闭表示　route locking indication
进路信号机　route signal
进路一次解锁　once-for-all route release
进入权　access right, access, right of entry
进入现场　access to site
进入异线　enter on unexpected track
进水口　inlet, intake
进水流道　inflow runner
进弯出直　curve-in and straight-out
进线　incoming line
进线架构　incoming line framework
进行信号　proceeding signal
进展　advancement, progress, evolve, march, make progress, make headway
进展报告　progress reports
进站　entry
进站大屏　information display at departure lobby
进站检票屏　ticket checking display
进站通道屏　information display of entrance corridor
进站信号机　home signal
进账　incoming payment

进直出弯　straight-in and curve-out
近程监督分区　direct surveillance subsection
近程网路　direct surveillance network
近端串音功率和
　　power sum NEXT attenuation(loss)（PS NEXT）
近海的　maritime, coastwise
近后备保护　local backup protection
近景摄影测量　close-up photogrammetry
近零能耗建筑　nearly zero energy building
近期　short term
近期交割　near delivery
近期交货　near delivery
近似工程量清单　approximate bill of quantities
近似平差　approximate adjustment
劲性骨架混凝土　stiff-skeleton reinforced concrete
浸没　immersion
浸没比　immersion ratio
浸泡试验　immersion test
浸润线　seepage line
浸水路基　immersible subgrade
浸水膨胀装置　immersion expansion device
浸水深度　immersion depth
浸涂材料含量
　　impregnated and coated asphalt amount
浸渍材料　impregnating
禁令　ban, prohibition, injunction
禁溜线
　　prohibited rolling track, prohibited humping line
禁停标志牌　No parking sign
禁运　embargo
禁止出口　ban on export, nonexportation
禁止翻供　estoppel, estop
禁止进口　ban on import, import prohibition
禁止令
　　injunction. restraining order, writ of prohibition
禁止输入
　　import ban, inhibiting input, inhibitory input
禁止信号　prohibitive signal
经编土工格栅　warp-knitting geogrid
经常费用　constant expense, current expense, overhead expense, current expenditures, standing expenses, expense
经常开支　revenue expenditure, current expenditure, running expenses
经常收入　current income, ordinary revenue
经常项目差额
　　balance of current account, current balance
经常性修理
　　current repair, running repair, regular repair
经常修理费　regular repair cost

经度　longitude
经纪人　broker, middleman, operator, agent
经纪人佣金　brokerage, brokerage commission, brokerage fee, broker's commission
经纪行　broker, finder, commission house, brokerage house
经纪业　broking, brokerage, brokage, bkoking, commission business
经济补偿
　　financial compensation, economic compensation
经济成本　economic cost
经济传热阻　economical heat transfer resistance
经济担保　financial security, assurance of support
经济单位　economic unit
经济法　economic law
经济风险　economic risk, economic exposure
经济封锁　economic blockade
经济规律　economic law, canon of economics
经济合作　economic cooperation
经济核算　economic reckoning, economic accounting
经济滑坡　economic downturn, economic decline
经济技术对比　economic and technical comparison
经济结构　economic structure, economic pattern
经济净现值　economic net present value（ENPV）
经济内部收益率
　　economic internal return rate（EIRR）
经济批量
　　economic lot size, economic batch quantity
经济评估　economic appraisal, economic evaluation
经济评价　economic evaluation
经济权益
　　economic interest, economic rights and interests
经济师
　　economist, economic manager, economic engineer
经济实体　economic entity
经济寿命　economic life
经济寿命与残值　economic life and salvage value
经济索赔　financial claim
经济特区　special economic zone
经济危机　economic crisis
经济效益　economic benefit
经济学家　economist
经济援助　economic aid, financial aid
经济周期
　　economic cycle, trade cycle, business cycle
经纬仪　theodolite
经纬仪测绘　theodolite surveying and mapping
经纬仪测图　theodolite mapping
经纬仪三角高程测量
　　theodolite triangle elevation survey

经纬仪绳尺法　theodolite used with measuring rope
经纬仪视距法　theodolite subtense technique
经纬仪投点法　transit plotting method
经向构造　meridianal structure
经销商　dealer, distributor, agency, franchiser
经验　experience
经营　manage, run, operate
经营报表　operation statement, operating statement
经营场所　business location, establishment, purchasing place
经营费用　working expenses, operating expenses, running expenses, operating costs
经营风险　operating risk, business risks
经营利润盈余　operating surplus
经营业绩　operating performance, business performance, operation result
经营中断保险　business interruption insurance
经营周（转）期　operating cycle
晶洞　miarolitic cavity
晶体　crystal
晶系　crystal system
精度　accuracy
精度估计　precision estimation
精加工　finishing, fine machining, finish machining
精码　precise code
精密　precision
精密测距　precise distance measurement
精密定位服务　precise positioning service
精密定向　precise orientation
精密工程测量　precise engineering survey
精密工程控制网　precise engineering control network
精密量具　precision measuring instrument
精密水准测量　precise leveling
精密水准仪　precise level, precise water level
精磨　fine grinding
精确度　precision
精确度等级　accuracy class
精确时间协议　precision time protocol (PTP)
精算师　actuary
精益建造　lean construction
井点　wellpoint
井点排水　drainage by well point, wellpoint dewatering, well-point dewatering, drainage by well points
井点真空度　well point vacuum degree
井管　well casing
井间声波透视　cross-hole sonic perspective
井口装置　wellhead assembly
井群　battery of wells
井上下对照图　surface-underground contrast plan of well
井水　well water
井筒　well shaft
井筒十字中线标定　wellbore cross centerline calibration
井筒延伸测量　wellbore deepening survey
井筒中心标定　wellbore center line calibration
井下测量（又称"矿井测量"）　down hole survey (also known as "mine survey")
井下高程测量　down hole elevation measurement
井下交叉闭合导线　down hole intersecting closed traverse
井下勘探测量　down hole prospecting survey
井下空硐测量　down hole cavity survey
井液电阻率法　drilling fluid resistivity method
井字梁　grillage beam
景观　landscape
景观保护区　landscape reservation
景观照明　landscape lighting
警报　alarm
警冲标　fouling post
警冲标内方　inside of fouling post
警冲标外方　outside of fouling post
警告　warning
警告信号　warning signal
警告性标志　warning sign
警戒线　cordon
警示牌　warning sign
警惕按钮　acknowledgement button
警惕手柄　acknowledgement lever
警卫室　guardhouse
径流　runoff
径流汇集　runoff gathering
径流量　runoff
径流区　runoff area
径流系数　runoff coefficient
径流小区　runoff plot
径路标　route sign
径路探测　path detection
径向　radial direction
径向扁千斤顶法　radial flat jack technique
径向变形　radial deformation
径向试验　diametral test
径向自由膨胀率　radial free expansion rate
净保险费　net premium
净残值　net salvage value
净产值　net output

J

净成本　net cost
净吨位　net tonnage
净额　net amount
净发票价格　net invoice price
净费率　net rate
净高　clear height
净化空调系统　air conditioning purifying system
净加价百分率　net markup percentage
净价　net price
净间距　clear spacing
净浆凝结时间　setting time of cement paste
净距　clear distance
净空　clearance
净空变化　clearance change
净空高度　headroom
净空区测量　clearance limit survey
净跨　clear span
净跨度　net span
净亏损　net loss
净利润　net profit
净收入　net income, net proceeds
净收入损失　loss of net income
净收益　net earnings
净数　net
净衰耗频率特性　net attenuation frequency characteristics
净水灰比　net water-cement ratio
净损失　net loss
净投标价　net bid price
净投资收入　net return of investment
净息　net interest
净现金流量　net cash flow
净现值　net present value
净现值法　net present value
净销售额　net sales
净效益　net benefit
净营业损失　net operating loss
净运费　net freight
净值　net value
净值法　net worth method
净重　net weight
净资产　net assets
净租赁　net lease
竞争　competition, compete
竞争策略　competitive strategy, competition strategy
竞争对手　competitor
竞争能力　competitiveness
竞争性价格　competitive price
竞争性招标　competitive bidding
竞争者　competitor, rival

静变形模量　static deformation modulus
静触头　fixed contact
静弹性模量　static elasticity modulus
静定结构　statically determinate structure
静定桥梁结构　statically determinate bridge structure
静动态应变仪　static-dynamic strain gauge
静荷载　static load
静活载效应　static live load effect
静接点　break contact
静力　static force
静力触探　static sounding
静力触探试验　static cone penetration test (CPT)
静力法　static force method
静力受压弹性模量　static compressive modulus of elasticity
静力水准仪　hydrostatic level gauge
静力相似　static force similarity
静水力学天平　static water mechanics balance
静水头　hydrostatic head
静水压力　hydrostatic pressure
静水压头　hydrostatic head
静态　static state
静态标定线　static calibration track
静态标识　static sign
静态不平顺　irregularity of unloaded track
静态测试　static test
静态测试检查　static test check
静态荷载　static load
静态几何形位　static track geometry
静态接触压力　static contact force
静态立体摄影　static stereo photography
静态密封指数　static seal index
静态挠度　static deflection
静态设计　static design
静态速度曲线　static speed profile (SSP)
静态速度限制　static speed restriction
静态投资　static investment
静态投资回收期　static investment payback time
静态验收　static acceptance check
静态验收测试　static acceptance test
静态应变仪　static strain gauge
静态应力　static stress
静态作用　static action
静停时间　static standing time
静压力拔桩机　static pile extractor
静压箱　plenum chamber
静载测试仪　static loading tester
静载加载分级　static loading grading

静载锚固性能　static load anchoring performance
静载试验　static loading test
静止侧压力系数　coefficient of static lateral pressure
静止水位　static water level
静止土压力　static earth pressure
静止土压力系数　coefficient of static earth pressure
静止无功补偿装置　static VAR compensator
静置设备　still equipment
境外第三方账户　offshore escrow account
境外利率　offshore interest rate, foreign interest rate
境外银行　offshore bank
镜头　lens
镜像抑制　image rejection
纠偏转机构　rolling corrector
纠正光学条件　rectification of optical condition
纠正几何条件　rectification of geometric condition
纠正起始面　rectification of reference plane
酒店式办公楼　hotel style office building
酒精燃烧法　alcohol burning method
95%概率　95% probability
95%概率最大列车数　95% probability of maximum number of trains
旧钢轨　used rail
旧轨料　second hand rail
救援　salvage, emergency relief
救援列车　rescue train
救援列车停留线　hold track for breakdown train
救援列车演练线　rescue train rehearsal track
救援台　rescue desk
救援通道　rescue passage
救援现场　rescue scene
救援指挥　rescue command
救助费用　salvage charges
救助作业　salvage operation
就地灌筑桩　cast-in-place pile
就地控制　local control
就地培训　site training
就业保障　job security, employment protection
就业法　employment act
居住建筑　residential building
居住空间　dwelling space
居住签证　resident visa
居住许可证　residence permit
局部采暖　local heating
局部冲刷　local scour
局部冲刷坑深度　depth of local scour hole
局部电源　local power source
局部放电水平　partial discharge level
局部剪切破坏　local shear failure
局部抗压强度提高系数　increasing factor of local compressive strength
局部空气调节　local air conditioning
局部控制　local control
局部控制电路　local control circuit
局部控制盘　local control panel
局部排风罩　local exhaust hood
局部偏差　partial deviations
局部送风系统　local air supply system
局部通风　local ventilation
局部完井抽水　partially penetrating well pumping
局部应用灭火系统　local application extinguishing system
局间　inter-MSC
局间中继线　inter-office trunk line
局内　intra-MSC
局数据　office data
局域网　local area network
矩形布置　rectangular layout
矩形分幅　rectangular map subdivision
矩形框架结构　rectangle frame structure
矩形梁　rectangular beam
矩形桥墩　rectangular pier
矩阵化项目组织　matrix project organization
矩阵式机构　matrix organization
举债经营　financial leverage, leverage
举债经营比率　leverage ratio
举证责任　burden of proof
巨厚层　huge thickness layer
巨厚层滑坡　huge thickness layer landslide
巨块状　massive
巨粒土　over coarse-grained soil
巨型滑坡　huge scale landslide
巨灾损失　catastrophe loss
拒保风险　declined risk, non-insurable risk, excepted risk
拒付　dishonour, refuse, decline, protest, non-payment
拒付汇票　dishonour a bill of exchange, dishonour a bank draft
拒付声明　statement of dishonour
拒付通知　notice of dishonour
拒付通知单　notice of dishonour, protest note
拒付证书　certificate of protest, certificate of dishonour
拒付支票　declined check, dishonoured check
拒绝承兑　dishonour, non-acceptance, no acceptance (N. A.)

拒绝接受　repudiate, reject, decline
拒绝全部投标　rejection of all bids
拒绝执行　refusal of enforcement
拒赔　repudiate/reject a claim
拒收险　rejection insurance
具塞比色管　color comparison tube
具体的　specific, particular, ad hoc, given
具体留置权　particular lien
具体条件　conditions of particular application
具体条文　specific provision
具体证据　supporting details, supporting particulars
具体证明材料
　　supporting details, supporting particulars
据此　hereby
距离保护　distance protection
距离测量　distance measurement
飓风　hurricane
锯齿孔　sawtooth hole
锯齿状断口　ragged fracture
锯轨机　rail sawing machine
聚氨酯防水涂料　polyurethane waterproof coating
聚苯乙烯板块　polystyrene plate
聚苯乙烯发泡材料　expanded polystyrene
聚苯乙烯泡沫塑料
　　polystyrene foamed plastics
聚丙烯纤维水泥混凝土
　　polypropylene fiber cement concrete
聚合物材料　polymer materials
聚合物工程材料　polymer engineering materials
聚合物乳液防水涂料
　　emulsified polymer waterproof coating
聚合物砂浆　polymer mortar
聚合物水泥防水涂料
　　polymer cement waterproof coating
聚集　gather, assemble, aggregation
聚磷菌　phosphate accumulating organisms
聚氯乙烯　polyvinyl chloride(PVC)
聚氯乙烯防水卷材
　　polyvinyl chloride sheet, PVC sheet
聚氯乙烯土工膜　PVC geomembrane, polyvinyl chloride geomembrane
聚脲防水层　polyurea waterproof layer
聚羧酸系高性能减水剂　polycarboxylates high performance water-reducing admixture
聚酯毡防水卷材
　　polyester fabric reinforced waterproofing sheet
捐款　contribution, donation, subscription
捐献　contribute, donate
捐赠　contribute, donate, tip, gratuity
捐赠人　donator, contributor, donor

捐赠资本　donated capital
捐赠资产　donated assets
捐助　contribute
卷材长边　long edge of sheet
卷材短边　short edge of sheet
卷材上表面　top surface of sheet
卷尺　measuring tape, tape measure
卷扬机　winch, hoist
绢云母　sericite
决策阶段　decision stage
决策树分析　decision tree analysis
决策者　policy maker, decision maker
决定　decision, determination
决算表　final account, final statement
决算日
　　settlement day, closing day, date of final account
绝对闭合差　absolute closure difference
绝对标定法　absolute calibration method
绝对产权　absolute title
绝对承担　absolute acceptance
绝对定向　absolute orientation
绝对定向元素　absolute orientation element
绝对航高　absolute flying height
绝对免赔额　absolute deductible
绝对配额　absolute quota
绝对权益　absolute interest
绝对全损　actual total loss
绝对湿度　absolute humidity
绝对所有权　clear title
绝对条件　absolute condition
绝对误差　absolute error
绝对信号　absolute signal
绝对优势　absolute advantage
绝对优先权
　　absolute priority, liquidation preference
绝对责任　absolute liability
绝对制动距离　absolute braking distance
绝热材料　thermal insulation material
绝热温升　adiabatic temperature rise
绝缘材料　insulation material
绝缘测试　insulation test
绝缘导管　insulated conduit
绝缘等级　insulation level
绝缘电阻　insulation resistance
绝缘方式　insulation mode
绝缘轨距杆　insulated gauge rod
绝缘间隙　insulation gap
绝缘接头　insulated rail joints
绝缘节　insulated overlapped section
绝缘介质　insulating dielectric

绝缘老化　insulation aging
绝缘锚段关节　insulated overlap
绝缘母线　insulated bus
绝缘配合　insulation coordination
绝缘破损　insulation damage
绝缘强度　dielectric strength
绝缘强度试验　insulation level test
（预埋）绝缘套管　（embeded）insulation bushing
绝缘梯车　insulated ladder trolley
绝缘体　insulator
绝缘同心度　insulation concentricity
绝缘外护套　insulation outer sheath
绝缘线　insulated wire
绝缘要求　insulation requirement
绝缘转换柱　insulated transition mast
绝缘子　insulator
绝缘子串　insulator string
绝缘子漆　insulator lacquer
绝缘子清洗车　insulator cleaning vehicle
掘进过程　boring process
掘进机法　tunnel boring machine（TBM）method
掘进时间　boring time
掘进速度　boring speed
掘进行程　boring stroke
掘进循环　boring cycle
均布荷载　uniform load
均方根速度　mean square root speed
均分性能　equipartition function
均衡充电　equalizing charge
均衡生产　levelling production
均衡制动法　modulated braking method
均价　average price
均流性能　current equalization performance
均摊　share equally
均匀分布　uniform distribution
均匀温度　uniform temperature
均值　mean value
均质弹性体　homogeneous elastomer
竣工报表　statement at completion
竣工报告　completion report
竣工测量　as-built survey
竣工的工程　completed works
竣工后审查　post-completion review
竣工后验收　tests after completion
竣工记录　as-built records
竣工检验　test on completion
竣工奖金　bonus for completion
竣工期限的延长　extension of time for completion
竣工日期　date of completion, completion date
竣工时间　time for completion
竣工时间延长　extension of time for completion
竣工试验　test on completion
竣工图　as-built drawing
竣工拖延　delay in completion
竣工文件　as-built documents
竣工验收
　tests on completion, completion acceptance
竣工验收费　completion acceptance fee
竣工验收文件　completion acceptance document
竣工验收证书　final acceptance certificate
竣工证书　performance certificate, certificate of completion, completion certificate
竣工资料　as-built data

K

K_0 固结　K_0 consolidation
k 阶光通道数据单元　Optical Channel Data Unit-k (ODUk)
k 阶光通路传送单元　Optical Channel Transport Unit-k (OTUk)
卡车拖车　truck trailer
卡车装运设备　trucking equipment
卡洛变换　Karhunent-Loeve transformation
卡盘　lateral stiffener plate
卡片　card
卡套式连接　ferrule type joint
喀斯特　karst
喀斯特地貌　karst landform
喀斯特塌陷　karst collapse
开办费　initial operation cost
开办项目　preliminary items, preliminaries
开闭器　switch circuit controller
开闭所　switching post (SP), switching station
开标　opening of tender, tender opening, bid opening
开标程序　bid opening procedure
开标纪要　bid opening minutes
开标日期　date of bid opening
开采　mine, extract, exploit
开采沉陷观测　mining subsidence observation
开采沉陷图　map of mining subsidence
开采沉陷预计　prediction of mining subsidence
开槽施工　trench excavation
开敞式掘进机　open tunnel boring machine
开车　start-up
开出日期　issuing date
开发成本　development cost
开发规划　development plan
开发商　developer
开发信贷协议　development credit agreement
开发银行　development bank
开发资本　development capital
开放式办公室　open-plan office
开放信号　clearing signal
开放政策　open door policy
开放最短路径优先路由协议　open shortest path first (OSPF)
开工　commencement of work, commence
开工,延误和暂停　commencement, delays and suspension
开工会　kick-off meeting
开工令　order to commence, order of commencement
开工率　rate of operation, operating rate
开工日期　commencement date
开工通知　notice of commencement
开关操作周期　switching cycle
开关电连接跳线　electrical connection jumper from the disconnector
开关柜　switchgear
开关量　boolean quantity
开关灵敏度　switch sensitivity
开关面板　switchboard
开关设备　switchgear
开关滞后　switching hysteresis
开航日期　date of departure
开机时间　turn on time
开具发票　issue an invoice, invoice
开垦　reclamation
开口保单　open policy
开口订货单　open-end purchase order, open-end order
开口合同　cost-reimbursable contract
开口闪点　open cup flash point
开口速度　release speed
开口信用证　open letter of credit, open L/C
开裂荷载　cracking load
开路式轨道电路　normally deenergized track circuit
开盘价　opening price
开票人　drawer
开启桥　movable bridge
开启压力　opening pressure
开始采购　initiate procurement
开始记录　opening entry

开始阶段	inception stage
开式回水	open return
开式水箱	open water tank
开水器	water boiler
开通	clear
开脱性条款	exemption clause
开脱罪责的	exculpatory
开挖断面面积	excavation cross-section area
开挖面	excavation face
开挖方式	excavation method
开挖轮廓线	excavation contour
开挖直径	excavation diameter
开业会计师	practicing accountant
开证银行	issuing bank, opening bank
开支	expenses, expenditure, outlay
开支权限	spending authority
开支项目	item of expenditure, expense item
开支账	expense account
凯塞效应	Kaiser effect
凯文接法	Kelvin connection
铠装	armoured
铠装电缆	armoured cable
勘测	survey
勘测队	survey crew, investigation team, survey team
勘测设计费	expense for survey & design
勘测设计阶段测量	survey in reconnaissance and design stage
勘测图	survey maps
勘察	investigation, exploration, survey, prospect
勘察费	survey fee
勘察分级	investigation classification
勘察监理与咨询费	fees of supervision and consulting on survey works
勘察阶段	reconnaissance stage
勘察设计费	survey and design fees
勘察试验	investigation test
勘界	boundary settlement
勘探	exploration, prospecting
勘探点	exploration point
勘探开采井	exploration well
勘探孔	exploratory borehole
勘探网测量	prospecting network survey
勘探线测量	prospecting line survey
勘探线剖面图	prospecting line profile map
勘误	erratum
坎儿井	karez
看样出售	sale by sample
抗拔力	pulling resistance
抗辩	demur, contend, contradict, confute, counterplead, defence
抗剥离性	peeling resistance
抗侧力墙体结构	lateral force resisting wall
抗侧力体系	lateral resisting system
抗冲击性能	shock resistance
抗地震的	antiseismic
抗冻	freezing resistance
抗冻等级	frost resistance class
抗冻混凝土	frost-resistant concrete
抗冻融	freeze-thaw resistance
抗冻融性	freezing-thawing resistance
抗冻性	freezing resistance
抗冻性试验	frost resistibility test
抗风化能力	weather-resistant capability
抗风柱	wind-resistant column
抗浮	anti-floating
抗浮安全系数	anti-floating safety coefficient
抗干扰	anti-interference
抗干扰能力	anti-interference capability
抗旱	drought resisting
抗滑动稳定性	anti-slide stability
抗滑段	anti-slide section, anti-slip section
抗滑试验	slip resistance test
抗滑移系数	anti-sliding coefficient
抗滑支挡	anti-slide retaining
抗滑桩	anti-slide pile
抗化学腐蚀试验	chemical corrosion resistance test
抗剪断强度	shear strength
抗剪断强度试验	shear strength test by angle mould
抗剪断试验	shearing strength test
抗剪连接件	shear connector
抗剪强度	shear strength
抗剪强度指标	shear strength index
抗拉强度	tensile strength
抗老化试验	anti-aging test
抗老化性	ageing resistance
抗离析性	segregation resistance
抗力	resistance
抗裂性能	crack-resisting ability
抗硫酸盐硅酸盐水泥	"sulphate resisting Portland cement, sulphate resistance Portland cement"
抗硫酸盐结晶破坏等级	resistance class of concrete to physical sulphate attack
抗硫酸盐侵蚀	sulfate corrosion resistance
抗磨损	abrasion resistance
抗侵蚀	erosion resistance
抗侵蚀砂浆	erosion resistant mortar
抗倾覆滑移验算	overturning or slip resistance check

抗扰度　immunity to interference
抗渗　permeability resistance
抗渗等级　grade of impermeability, resistance class to hydraulic pressure
抗渗性　impermeability
抗渗压力　impermeability pressure
抗渗仪　impermeability apparatus
抗蚀系数　coefficient of corrosion resistance
抗诉　protest, counterappeal
抗弯强度　bending strength
抗微生物破坏试验　antimicrobial damage test
抗性消声器　reactive muffler
抗压极限强度　ultimate compressive strength
抗压模量　compressive modulus
抗压强度　compressive strength, compression strength
抗压强度比　ratio of compressive strength
抗液化措施　anti-liquefaction measures
抗议　protest
抗折强度　folding strength
抗震　anti-seismic
抗震措施　seismic measures
抗震等级　seismic grade
抗震防灾规划　planning for earthquake reduction and disaster prevention
抗震缝　seismic joint
抗震构造措施　seismic structural measures
抗震构造要求　earthquake-resistant detailing requirements
抗震计算方法　seismic analysis method
抗震鉴定　seismic appraisal
抗震结构　earthquake-resistant structure, antiseismic structure
抗震结构体系　seismic structural system
抗震结构整体性　seismic structural integrity
抗震墙　seismic structural wall
抗震设防标准　seismic fortification standard
抗震设防烈度　seismic precautionary intensity
抗震设防区　seismic fortification area
抗震设防区划　seismic fortification regionalization
抗震设防要求　seismic fortification requirements
抗震设计　seismic design
抗震试验　seismic test
抗震销棒　seismic nose bar
抗震支撑　earthquake-resistant support
抗震支吊架　seismic support and hanger
抗紫外线能力　ultraviolet resistance
考察　exploration, expedition, investigation, visit
考古发现　archaeological discovery
考古和地质发现　archaeological and geological findings
考勤表　time sheet
考勤卡　time card, punch card
苛性碱　caustic alkali
科里奥利效应　Coriolis effect
颗粒沉降距离　distance of particle sedimentation
颗粒分析　particle size analysis
颗粒分析试验　grain size analysis test
颗粒活性炭吸附池　granular-activated carbon adsorption tank
颗粒级配　grain gradation
颗粒级配曲线　particle grading curve
颗粒粒径　particle diameter
颗粒密度　grain density
颗粒密度校正系数　correction coefficient of particle density
壳管式冷凝器　shell and tube condenser
壳管式蒸发器　shell and tube evaporator
壳体基础　shell foundation
壳体结构　shell structure
可保财产　insurable property
可保风险　insurable risks
可保价值　insurable value
可保权益　insurable interest
可保险的　insurable
可报销的　reimbursable
可比成本　comparable cost
可比性　comparability
可避免成本　avoidable cost, escapable cost
可避免事故　avoidable accident
可变的　variable
可变荷载　variable load
可变利率　variable rate, variable interest rate, floating interest rate, adjustable interest rate
可变衰耗器　variable attenuator
可变现价值　cash value
可变现净值　net cash value
可变现资产　cashable asset
可变作用　variable action
可变作用标准值　standard value of variable action
可变作用的频遇值　frequent value of variable action
可变作用的准永久值　quasi-permanent value of variable action
可变作用的组合值　combination value of variable actions
可辨认的　discernible, decipherable
可补偿的　recoverable, reimbursable
可补偿费用　reimbursable cost

可补偿开支　reimbursable expense
可操作性　operability
可偿还的　reimbursable
可撤销的　revocable
可撤销的信用证
　　revocable letter of credit, revocable L/C
可撤销合同　voidable contract
可持续发展　sustainable development
可持续性　sustainability
可得性　availability
可动心轨辙叉
　　movable point frog, swing nose crossing
可动心轨辙叉单开道岔
　　movable point frog single turnout
可动用结余　available balance
可兑换贷款　convertible loan
可兑换的　convertible
可兑换外汇　convertible foreign exchange
可兑换证券　convertible securities
可翻转钢筋绑扎台座
　　reversible steel bar binding pedestal
可分割合同　divisible contract, severable contract
可分割信用证
　　divisible letter of credit, divisible L/C
可分摊成本　distributable cost
可管理风险　administrable risk, manageable risk
可获得的　obtainable, available
可计量性　quantification
可见光透射比　visible light transmittance
可建造性　buildability, constructability
可交付成果　deliverable
可接受的　acceptable
可接受的报价　acceptable bid
可接受的变更　acceptable variation
可接受的当地程序　acceptable local procedures
可接受的地震危害　acceptable seismic hazard
可接受的风险　eligible risk
可接受的偏离　acceptable deviation
可接受价格　acceptable price
可接受日期　acceptable date
可接受证据　admissible evidence
可靠的　reliable, authenticated, bona fide
可靠度　reliability
可靠概率　reliability probability
可靠性　reliability
可靠性管理　reliability management
可靠性设计　reliability-based design
可靠指标　reliability index
可控成本　controllable cost
可控风险　controllable risk

可控源音频大地电磁法
　　controllable-source audio magnetotelluric methods
可扩展标记语言
　　extensible markup language（XML）
可量化　quantification
可流通的　negotiable
可流通性　negotiability
可能性　possibility, probability, chance
可逆正常使用极限状态
　　reversible serviceability limit state
可曲挠橡胶接头　flexible rubber joint
可燃油品　combustible oil products
可溶铁　soluble iron
可溶物含量　dissoluble composite of membrane
可溶性硅　soluble silicon
可溶性碱含量　soluble alkali content
可溶性重金属　soluble heavy metals
可溶质　maltene, petrolene
可施工性　constructability
可施工性评审　constructability review
可收回的　recoverable
可赎回债券　redeemable bond, callable bond
可塑的　plastic
可调单价　adjustable unit price
可调底座　adjustable pedestal
可调价的固定价格合同
　　fixed price with economic price adjustment contract
　　（FP-EPA）, adjustable fixed price contract
可调节拉结件　adjustable steel tie
可调利率抵押贷款　adjustable-rate mortgage
可调托撑　adjustable fork head
可调曲柄　adjustable crank
可调总价　adjustable lump sum price
可调总价合同
　　price changeable lump sum contract
可推定的工程变更
　　constructive change, constructive variation
可推定的工程变更指令　constructive change order
可推定的加速施工　constructive acceleration
可推定的暂停施工　constructive suspension
可维护性　maintainability
可卸式止水带　detachable waterstop
可信执行保护　trusted execution protection
可行性　feasibility, practicability
可行性研究　feasibility study
可行性研究费　feasibility study fee
可行性研究阶段　feasibility study phase
可选目的地港附加费
　　optional destination additional
可选条款　optional clause

可选项　optional items
可延期债券　extendible bond, extendable bond
可研阶段　feasibility study stage
可氧化物质　oxidizable matter
可液化土层　liquefiable soil layer
可疑声源设备　suspicious sound source equipment
可议付单据　negotiable document
可银行贴现的票据　discounted bill
可用现金　available cash
可用性　availability
可用支票付款的　checkable
可预见的损失　foreseeable losses
可预料性　predictability
可原谅并应给予补偿的拖期　excusable and compensable delays
可原谅但不给予补偿的拖期　excusable but non-compensable delays
可原谅的拖期　excusable delays
可再利用材料　reusable material
可再生能源　renewable energy
可再生能源利用率　utilization ratio of renewable energy
可再循环材料　recyclable material
可转换债券　convertible bond
可转让定期存单　negotiable certificate of deposit
可转让汇票　negotiable draft
可转让票据　negotiable paper, negotiable instrument, negotiable bill
可转让期票　negotiable promissory note/time note/time bill/period bill
可转让提单　negotiable bill of lading
可转让信用证　transferable letter of credit, negotiable L/C
可转让性　negotiability
可转让证券　transferable/negotiable security
可转让支票　negotiable check (cheque)
可转移风险　transferable risks
可资本化成本　capitalizable cost
可自由兑换的货币　convertible currency
可自由兑换的纸币　convertible paper money
可自由支配的基金　discretionary funds
可钻性　drillability
可作证据的文件　admissible document
克拉索夫斯基椭球　Krasovsky ellipsoid
刻度放大镜　scale magnifying glass
刻度显微镜　scale microscope
刻图　engraving
刻图膜　scribing coating
客车车底取送线　passenger train-set taking-out and placing-in track
客车车底停留线　passenger train-set stabling siding
客车车辆段　passenger car depot
客车车辆设备　passenger car facilities
客车技术整备所(库列检)　passenger car technical servicing depot
客车技术整备线　passenger train technical servicing siding
客车配属辆数　number of allocated passenger cars
客车运行安全监控系统　train coach running safety diagnosis system, monitoring system for safe operation of passenger train, TCDS
客车整备所横列布置　transverse arrangement of passenger car servicing post
客车整备所纵列布置　longitudinal arrangement of passenger car servicing post
客车整备线　passenger car servicing siding
客观概率　objective probability
客观理由　objective reason
客观事实　objective fact
客观性　objectivity
客观证据　objective evidence
客户　customer, client
客户端　client
客户服务中心　passenger service center
客户关系管理　customer relationship management
客户账　customer's account
客货共线　mixed passenger and freight railway
客货运量　passenger and freight volume
客货运业务　passenger and freight service
客货纵列式区段站　longitudinal district station for passenger and freight service
客票系统　ticketing system
客土　borrowed soil
客土喷播植草　spraying grass seeds on borrow soil
客土植草　grass planting with borrowed soil
客土植生　planting on borrow soil
客运广播　public address system
客运机务段　locomotive depot for passenger service
客运量　passenger capacity, passenger traffic volume
客运列车断电过分相系统　passenger train neutral-section passing system with no power consumption
客运业务　passenger service
客运用房　building for passenger service
客运站　passenger railway station, passenger station
客运整备场　passenger car servicing depot
客运专线　passenger dedicated line
客运作业管理　passenger transport operation system

课税	taxation, levy a tax, imposition of tax

课税　taxation, levy a tax, imposition of tax
课税对象　object of taxation
课税豁免　tax exemption
课税基础　tax base
坑凹回填　pit refilling
坑道平面图　underground tunnel plan
坑硐展示图　developing chart of exploratory drift
坑探　test pitting
坑探工程测量　pitting engineering survey
空白背书　endorsement in blank, blank endorsement, open endorsement
空白背书汇票　bill endorsed in blank
空白票据　blank bill
空白试验　blank test
空白提单　blank bill of lading
空白信用证　blank letter of credit
空白支票　blank check, bounced check
空舱费　dead freight
空档　stop short
空吊　air hoist
空斗墙　rowlock wall
空腹拱　spandrel-unfilled arch
空腹拱桥　spandrel-unfilled arch bridge
空腹屋架　vierendeel truss
空间　space
空间包含　spatial containment
空间变换　spatial transformation
空间定位　spatial localization
空间分解　spatial decomposition
空间工作性能　spatial behaviour
空间管节点　multiplanar tubular joint
空间管理和追踪　space management and tracking
空间后方交会　spatial resection
空间间隔制　space-interval system
空间结构　spatial structure
空间结构单元　spatial structure element
空间框架　space frame
空间前方交会　spatial intersection
空间网架　space lattice
空间效果　spatial effect
空间信息　spatial information
空间组成　spatial composition
空气穿透试验　air penetration test
空气弹簧隔振器　air-cushion vibration absorber
空气调节　air conditioning
空气调节机房　air conditioner room
空气调节设备　air conditioning equipment
空气调节系统　air conditioning system
空气动力　aerodynamic force
空气动力性噪声　aerodynamic noise
空气动力学　aerodynamics
空气动力学效应　aerodynamic effect
空气放电　air discharge
空气分布器　air distributor
空气分布特性指标　air diffusion performance index(ADPI)
空气过滤器　aerofilter
空气含量　air content
空气加热器　air heater
空气夹层　air blanket
空气间隙　air gap
空气洁净度　air cleanliness
空气洁净度等级　air cleanliness class
空气绝缘　air insulation
空气绝缘间隙　electrical clearance
空气绝缘开关柜　air insulated switchgear (AIS)
空气绝缘组合电器　air insulated switchgear (AIS)
空气开关　air switch, air-break switch, airbreak switch
空气幕　air curtain
空气幕沉井法　open caisson method with injected air curtain
空气热源　air-source heat
空气声　air borne sound
空气湿度　air humidity
空气温度　air temperature
空气污染物　air pollutant
空气压力　air pressure
空气压缩机　air compressor
空气压缩机室　air compressor cabin
空气预热器　air preheater
空气源热泵　air source heat pump
空气质量　air quality
空态　empty state
空调　air conditioning
空调度日数　cooling degree days
空调工程　air conditioning engineering
空调系统　air conditioning system
空头　bear, short-seller, shorting, short-selling
空头支票　bad/bounced/dishonoured/dud/ rubber check
空隙率　porosity
空线　empty track
空箱　empty container
空箱堆垛机　empty container stacker
空心板　hollow core slab
空心板桥　voided slab bridge, hollow slab bridge
空心桥墩　hollow pier
空心线圈　hollow coil

K

空心砖	hollow brick
空心钻	core drill
空穴	cavity
空压机	air compressor
空运	airlift, transport by air
空运保险	air cargo insurance
空运承运人	air carrier
空运单条款	air waybill conditions of contract, air waybill terms
空运发货单	air consignment note (ACN)
空运货物	air cargo, air freight
空运货物保险	air cargo insurance
空运收据	air freight receipt
空运提单	air waybill (AWB)
空运险	air transportation risks
空运一切险	air transportation all risks
空运直达提单	through air waybill
空载	no-load
空载调试	non-load test
空载试机	no-load machine testing
空载损耗	no-load loss
空载运行	idle running
空中三角测量	aerial triangulation
空中索道	aerial cableway, overhead cableway
孔板送风	air supply from perforated ceiling
孔道压浆	duct grouting
孔洞	void
孔径	opening size
孔口	borehole collar
孔口距	punch to punch distance
孔内回填	borehole backfilling
孔内摄像	down-hole imaging
孔雀石	malachite
孔位间距	hole spacing
孔隙	pore, void
孔隙比	void ratio
孔隙胶结	pore cementation
孔隙率	porosity
孔隙气压力	pore air pressure
孔隙水	pore water
孔隙水压力	pore water pressure
孔隙水压力监测	monitoring of pore water pressure
孔隙水压力系数	pore water pressure coefficient
孔隙压力	pore pressure
孔隙压力比	pore pressure ratio
孔隙应力	pore stress
孔压静力触探试验	cone penetration test
控告方	plaintiff, accuser
控告人	accuser, accusant, plaintiff
控股公司	holding company
控股股东	majority shareholder, majority stockholder
控股人	majority shareholder, majority stockholder
控股有限公司	holding company limited
控诉	accuse, denounce
控制爆破	controlled blasting
控制标准	control standard
控制测量	control survey
控制点	control point
控制电缆	control cable
控制对象	controlled object
控制工程	critical works
控制荷载	controlled loading
控制回路	control circuit
控制母线	control busbar
控制盘	control panel
控制屏	control panel
控制权	control right, controlling interest
控制室	control room
控制输出时延	control output delay
控制台	control console
控制台单元	control desk element
控制台室	console room
控制条件	control requisition
控制图	control chart
控制网选点	point selection for control network
控制网优化设计	optimal design of control network
控制信号	control signal
控制站(主站)	control station (master station)
控制账户	control (controlling) account
控制指标	control index
控制周期	control cycle
口岸	port
口头报价	verbal quotation
口头变更指令	oral instruction of variation
口头陈述	oral statement
口头承诺	verbal commitment, verbal promise
口头答辩	oral pleading
口头的	verbal, oral, word of mouth
口头合同	oral contract, verbal contract
口头命令	verbal order
口头申请	verbal request
口头声明	oral statement
口头听证会	oral hearing
口头通知	oral notice
口头协议	oral agreement, parol agreement, verbal agreement
口头形式	oral form
口头约定	verbal agreement
口头证据	oral evidence
口头指令确认书	confirmation of oral instruction

口头指示	oral instruction
扣板式扣件	clamp fastening
扣车	detaining cars
扣车条件	specified conditions for detaining cars
扣除额	deduction
扣发部分 IPC 期中支付的款项	withholding (amounts in) an IPC
扣发工资	payroll deduction
扣发支付款	payment withheld
扣减	deduct
扣减保留金	reduce retention
扣件	fastening, fastener, clip
扣缴	withholding
扣款	deduct/withhold a payment
扣压力	clamping force
扣押令	garnishee order, distress warrant, writ of attachment
扣押权	lien, right of distraint
枯井	dry well
枯水季节	dry season
枯水期	rainless period
枯水位	mean water level during dry seasons
苦橄玢岩	picrite-porphyrite
苦橄岩	picrite
苦咸水	brackish water
库存	stock, inventory, reserve
库存储备量	inventory
库存短缺	lack of stock, shortage of stock
库存盘点	stock taking, inventory checking
库存清单	inventory list
库存现金	cash on hand
库仑—纳维强度理论	Coulomb-Navier strength theory
库仑土压力理论	Coulomb's earth pressure theory
库仑理论	Coulomb theory
库仑土压力	Coulomb earth pressure
库容测量	reservoir storage survey
库水位	reservoir level
跨步电势	step potential
跨步电位差	step potential difference
跨步电压	step voltage
跨度	span
跨高比	span-depth ratio
跨国公司	multinational company, transnational company, transnational corporation
跨国企业	multinational enterprises (MNE), transnational enterprise (TNE)
跨河桥	river-crossing bridge
跨河水准测量	river-crossing leveling
跨径	span
跨距	span length
跨孔 CT	cross-hole CT
跨孔超声波测试仪	cross-hole ultrasonic tester
跨区间无缝线路	trans-section continuously welded rail track
跨双线腕臂结构	cantilever structure across two tracks
跨条	cross bar
跨线列车	cross-line train, over-line train
跨线漏斗仓	overline hopper bunker
跨线桥	overpass bridge
跨线运行	movement across lines
跨越轨道馈线	across-track feeder
跨中荷载	midspan load
跨专业	multidiscipline
会计	accounting
会计报表	accounting report, accounting statement
会计变更	accounting changes
会计程序	accounting procedure
会计单位	accounting unit, accounting entity
会计等式	accounting equation
会计法	accounting law
会计方法	accounting method
会计分录	accounting entry, journal entry
会计分期	accounting period
会计工作	accounting, accountancy
会计惯例	accounting convention, accounting practice
会计恒等式	accounting equation
会计计价	accounting valuation
会计记录	accounting records
会计监督	accounting supervision
会计科目	account title, account heading
会计科目表	account chart
会计科目一览表	chart of accounts, list of account titles
会计控制	accounting control
会计年度	accounting year, financial year, fiscal year
会计凭证	accounting document, accounting voucher
会计期间	accounting period
会计人员	accounting personnel
会计师	accountant
会计师事务所	accounting firm
会计原理	accounting principles
会计账簿	book of accounts
会计主管	accounting manager, accounting supervisor, accountant in charge
会计主体	accounting entity
块石	rubble
块石路面	stone-block pavement

块石土	subangular boulder
块体	block
块体饱和密度	bulk saturation density
块体孔洞率	hollow ratio of masonry unit
块体理论	block theory
块体密度	bulk density
块体性能检验	performance test of masonry units
块状	massive
块状构造	massive structure
快动继电器	quick-acting relay
快冻法	rapid freezing and thawing method
快剪	quick shear
快剪试验	quick shear test
快速定性滤纸	rapid qualitative filter paper
快速固结试验	quick consolidation test
快速剪切试验	quick shear test
快速静态测量	fast static surveying
快速路径法	fast track method
快速砂浆棒法	accelerating mortar-bar method
快速砂浆棒膨胀率	expansion rate of accelerating mortar bar
快速铁路	fast-speed railway
快速响应洒水喷头	quick response sprinkler
快速响应早期灭火喷头	quick response early fire extinguishing sprinkler
快速压缩试验	quick compression test
快速以太网	Fast Ethernet(FE)
快速运动图像处理	fast moving image processing
快速转辙机	quick-acting switch machine
快吸继电器	quick pick-up relay
快装锅炉	compact boiler
宽动态功能	wide dynamic range
宽轨距铁路	broad-gauge railway
宽轨枕	broad sleeper
宽跨比	width to span ratio
宽容条款	tolerance clause
宽限期	grace period
宽限日期	days of grace
宽张节理	wide tension joint
款到即付	pay when paid
款项余额	balance of payment

狂风	whole gale
矿产资源	mineral resources
矿区规划	mining area planning
矿山法	mining method
矿石	ore
矿物掺合料	mineral admixtures
矿物成分	mineral composition
矿物粒料	mineral aggregate
矿物粒料黏附性	adhesion of mineral aggregate
矿物乳化沥青	mineral powder asphalt emulsion
矿渣	slag
矿渣骨料混凝土	slag concrete aggregate
矿渣硅酸盐水泥	Portland-slag cement
矿渣混凝土	slag concrete
矿渣水泥	slag cement
框标	fiducial mark
框标距	distance of fiducial marks
框架—剪力墙结构	frame-shear wall structure
框架结构	frame structure
框架梁护坡	frame beam slope protection
框架平面控制网	framework of plane control network
框架填充墙	infilled wall in frame structure
框架—筒体结构	frame-tube structure
亏舱	broken stowage
亏空	deficit, in debt
亏损	loss, deficit, negative capital
亏损账户	deficit account
馈线	feeder
馈线保护测控单元	measure and control unit of feeder protection
捆	bale
困难地段	section with difficult conditions
扩大基础	spread foundation
扩大基础加固法	strengthening method by spread foundation
扩大指标估算法	index expansion estimation method
扩展度	spread
扩展基础	spread foundation
扩展时间	flow time
扩展时间 T500	slump flow time T500

L

LED 色灯信号机机构　LED color light signal mechanism
LEED 评估　sustainability LEED (leadership in energy and environmental design) evaluation
L 形站台　L-shaped platform
L 型仪充填比　L box filling ratio
垃圾堆场　landfill, rubbish dump, garbage dump, dumping ground
垃圾分类　refuse classification
垃圾清运　garbage clearance
垃圾转运设施　refuse transfer facilities
垃圾转运站　refuse transfer station
拉拔摩擦试验　drawing friction test
拉斑玄武岩　tholeiite
拉板连接　tie-plate connection
拉长石　labradorite
拉出值　stagger
拉断荷载　breaking load
拉断张力　failing tensile stress
拉杆拱　tie-arch
拉杆式水泵　drawbar pump
拉钩检查距离　car spacing for uncoupled inspection
拉辉煌斑岩　odinite
拉结钢筋　tie bar
拉力试验机　tensile testing machine
拉钮　pull-out button
拉伸模量　tensile modulus
拉伸黏结强度　tensile adhesive strength
拉伸破裂　extension fracture
拉伸蠕变　tensile creep
拉伸试验　tensile test
拉伸速率　tensile rate
拉伸性能　tensile property
拉通测试　trial run test
拉线　backstay, guy
拉线底座　base plate of backstay
拉线回头　returning tail
拉线盘　anchor plate
蜡封　wax-sealed
蜡封法　wax coating method
蜡含量　wax content
蜡组分　wax composition
来样加工　processing with client supplied designs, processing with foreign designs
来源　source
兰金土压力理论　Rankine's earth pressure theory
拦挡　tailing hold
拦挡措施　tailing hold measures
拦沙凼　wash trap
拦湾砂坝　bay sandbank
拦渣坝　slag trapping dam
拦渣工程　slag trapping works
拦渣率　percentage of dammed slag or ashes
栏杆　rail, railing
蓝晶石　kyanite, cyanite
蓝晒图　blueprint drawing
蓝图　blueprint
缆道　cableway
缆索　cable
缆索吊装法　erection by cableway hoisting method
缆索起重机　cable crane
滥用　abuse
滥用法律　abuse of law
滥用权力　abuse of power
滥用信用　abuse of credit
滥用职权　abuse of authority
廊道　corridor
浪涌　surge
浪涌保护　surge protection
浪涌保护器　surge protective devices (SPD)
劳动安全卫生　labor safety and hygiene, labor safety and health
劳动安全卫生设施　labor safety and hygiene facilities
劳动保护　labor protection

劳动保护费　labor protection fee
劳动保险费　labor insurance premium
劳动保险制度　employment insurance system, social security system
劳动报酬　labour remuneration, remuneration
劳动定额　work quota, production rate
劳动法　labour laws
劳动纪律　employee discipline, labour discipline
劳动力　labor force
劳动力充裕　labour abundant
劳动力过剩　labour surplus
劳动力损失　loss of labour productivity
劳动密集　labour intensive
劳动生产率　labour productivity, workforce productivity
劳动生产能力　labour capacity
劳动条件　working conditions
劳动卫生　labor hygiene
劳动效率　labour efficiency
劳工保险　worker's compensation insurance
劳工法　labour law, employment law
劳工工资　wage, workman's compensation insurance
劳工监督　labour monitoring
劳工遣返　repatriation of worker
劳合社保险单　Lloyd's insurance policy
劳力不足　labour shortage
劳务成本计算　calculation of labour cost
劳务费　labour service charge
劳务费率　labour service rate
劳务分包　labour only subcontracting
劳务分包商　labour only subcontractor
劳务合同　labour supply contract, contract for the supply of labour
劳务计划　labour supply planning
劳务收入　labour service income
劳务统计报表　statement of labour services
劳务协议　labour supply agreement
劳资法庭　industrial court
劳资关系　labour relations, industrial relations
劳资合同　labour-management contract
劳资集体谈判协议　collective agreement, collective labour agreement, collective bargaining agreement
劳资纠纷　labour dispute, conflict between capital and labour, industrial dispute
劳资纠纷调解　conciliation of labour disputes
劳资纠纷仲裁　labour arbitration, industrial arbitration
劳资双方　labour and management
劳资协议　labour agreement, labour-management contract
劳资争议　labour dispute, labour unrest, industrial dispute
老化　aging
老化系数　aging coefficient
老黄土　old loess
老年人住宅　house for the aged
勒夫波　Love wave
雷暴日　thunderstorm day
雷达测试台　radar test board
雷达测速器　radar speedometer
雷达穿透　radar penetrating
雷达法　radar method
雷达有效作用距离　effective action distance of radar
雷达自检　radar self test
雷电　lightning and thunder
雷电冲击耐受电压　lightning impulse withstand voltage
雷电防护区　lightning protection zone(LPZ)
雷电防护系统　lightning protection system (LPS)
雷电干扰　lightning interference
雷电感应　lightning induction
雷电过电压　lightning overvoltage
雷电(大气)过电压保护　lightning (atmospheric) overvoltage protection
雷电浪涌侵入　thunder surge invasion
雷电耐压　lightning impulse withstand voltage
雷电闪络　lightning flash-over
雷击　lightning strike
雷击过电压　lightning overvoltage
雷氏沸煮箱　redwood boiling box
肋拱桥　multi-rib arch bridge
肋腋板　haunch board
类比法　analogism
类比预测法　analogy predicted method
累积百分声级　accumulated percentile sound level
累积百分Z振级　accumulated percentile Z vibration level
累积损伤　cumulative damage
累积温度　accumulated temperature
累积折旧　accumulated depreciation
累计成本　accumulated cost
累计金额　accumulated amount, cumulative amount
累计利润　accumulated profit
累计利息　accrued interest
累计偏差　accumulated deviations
累计筛余　cumulative sieve residue
累计筛余百分率　percentage of cumulative sieve residue
累计损失　accumulated loss

累计盈余　accumulated surplus
累计责任　aggregate liability
累计责任赔偿总限额　aggregate limit of liability
累计折耗　accumulated depletion
累计折旧　accumulated depreciation
累计总额　accumulated amount, cumulative total, grand total
累进偿付　graduated payment
累进的　progressive
累进税　progressive tax
棱角状　angular shape
棱镜反光镜　prism reflector
冷藏车　refrigerator car, reefer
冷风机组　cooling unit
冷风渗透耗热量　infiltration heat loss
冷负荷　cooling load
冷滑
　　cold running, non-energized inspection running
冷胶粘剂　cold adhesive
冷接触　cold contact
冷凝器　condenser
冷凝温度　condensing temperature
冷凝压力　condensing pressure
冷气机　air cooler
冷却　cooling
冷却方式　cooling-down mode
冷却水　cooling water
冷却水费　cooling water expense
冷却水箱　cooling water box
冷却塔　cooling tower
冷却系统　cooling system
冷热源　cooling and heating sources
冷生构造　cryostructure
冷水　cold water
冷水机　water chiller
冷水机组　water chilling unit
冷弯薄壁型钢结构
　　cold bending thin-walled steel structure
冷弯检验　cold bending test
冷弯试验　cold bend test
冷源系统能效系数
　　energy efficiency coefficient of cold source system
离岸成本加保险费(价)　cost and insurance (C&I)
离岸成本加运费(价)　cost and freight (CFR)
离岸堤　offshore embankment
离岸港　departing port
离岸合同　offshore contract
离岸价　free on board (FOB)
离岸价并理舱　free on board stowed (FOBS)
离岸价并平舱　free on board trimmed (FOBT)
离去表示　departure indication
离去区段　departure section
离散点　discrete points
离散元法　discrete element method
离石黄土　Lishi loess
离退休职工　retired staff
离网型光伏发电系统　off-grid PV system
离析　segregation
离析率　segregation rate
离线　contact loss
离线率　percentage of contact loss
离线售票　off-line ticketing
离线诊断　off-line diagnosis
离心泵　centrifugal pump
离心玻璃棉　centrifugal glass-wool
离心含水当量法
　　centrifuge moisture equivalent method
离心机　centrifuge
离心力　centrifugal force
离心力率　centrifugal force ratio
离心式鼓风机　centrifugal blower
离心式通风机　centrifugal ventilator
离心式压缩机　centrifugal compressor
离心水泵　centrifugal pump
离职补偿金　separation pay, severance pay
离子交换法　ion exchange method (IX)
离子交换树脂　ion exchange resin
离子交换吸附量　ion exchange adsorption capacity
离子选择电极法　ion-selective electrode method
李氏量瓶法　Lee's volumetric flask method
里表温差
　　temperature difference between inside and outside
里程　kilometrage, mileage
里程碑进度计划　milestone schedule
里程碑日期　milestone date
里程丈量　kilometer measure
里程桩　kilometer stone
理财　manage money, manage wealth
理论分析值　theoretical analysis value
理论价格　theoretical price
理论配合比　theoretical mix proportion
理赔　settle a claim, claim settlement
理赔代理人　claim settling agent, claim agent
理赔费用　claim expense
理赔检验代理人　settling and survey agent
理赔理算人　claim adjuster
理事会　governing board
理算　adjust, adjustment
锂辉石　spodumene
锂铍石　liberite

力工　manual labour
力矩　force moment
力学点压测试　mechanical point pressure test
力学性能　mechanical properties
力学性指标　mechanical indicators
历史成本　historical cost
历史洪水位　historic flood level
立法　make/enact laws, legislate
立法变动调整　adjustments for changes in law
立法机构　legislature
立方体标准试件　standard specimen of cube
立方体试件　cube specimen
立杆　vertical rod
立管　riser
立即付款　immediate payment, prompt cash
立即交货　immediate delivery
立即赔偿　immediate compensation
立即折返制　quick turnaround system
立即折返作业　quick turnaround operation
立即装运　immediate shipment
立交桥　interchange, flyover, overpassing
立接台　automatic answering desk
立井定向测量　shaft orientation survey
立面图　elevation, elevation drawing
立剖面　sectional elevation
立体复层绿化带　multilayered three-dimensional green belt
立体交叉　grade separation, flyover crossing
立体模型测量　stereoscopic model surveying
立体摄影机　stereometric camera
立体疏解　vertical untwining
立体像对　stereo pair
立体植被护坡网　3D vegetation net for slope protection
立约能力　capacity to contract
立约人　promisor
立轴式钻机　spindle type drilling machine
立柱　post
励磁电路　excitation circuit
励磁特性　excitation characteristic
励磁条件　excitation requisition
利率　interest rate
利率调整　interest rate adjustment
利率上下限　interest rate collar
利率上限　interest rate cap
利率套购　interest rate arbitrage
利率下限　interest rate floor
利润　profit
利润表　income statement
利润分配　profit distribution
利润估算　profit estimation
利润汇总　profit pooling
利润加成　profit markup
利润率　profit ratio, profit margin
利润税　profit tax
利润损失　loss of profit
利润损失保险　loss of profit insurance
利润预测　profit forecast
利息　interest
利息差额　net interest margin
利益　benefit, interest, gain
利益相关者　stakeholder
利用方　volume of utilization
利用量　recycled quantity
利用料　recycled material
利用率　recycled ratio
利用系数　recycled coefficient
沥青　asphalt
沥青层　bituminous layer
沥青防水层　bituminous water-proof coating
沥青灌浆　bituminous grouting
沥青混合料　bituminous mixture
沥青混凝土　asphalt concrete
沥青混凝土拌和站　mixing station of bituminous concrete
沥青混凝土路面　asphalt concrete pavement
沥青混凝土铺面　asphalt concrete pavement
沥青搅拌设备　asphalt mixing equipment, premix asphalt plant
沥青砂浆　asphalt mortar
沥青水泥砂浆　asphalt-cement mortar
例会　regular meeting
例外补救　exceptional remedy
例外的　exceptional, particular
例外事件　exceptional event
例外管理　management by exception
例外事项报告　exception report
例外条款　exception clause
例行程序　routine procedure
例行检查　routine inspection
例行评审会议　regular review meetings
砾类土　gravelly soil
砾砂　gravel sand
砾石土　gravelly soil
砾土　gravel soil
砾岩　conglomerate
砾状　psephitic
粒度　particle size
粒度韵律　granularity rhythm
粒径　grain size

粒径分布曲线　grain size distribution curve
粒状　granular
粒子计数器　particle counter
粒组　grain grade, particle fraction
连带保证人　joint sureties
连带责任　joint and several liability
连岛砂坝　island-connecting sandbar
连拱作用　effect of continuous arch
连挂区　coupling area
连挂速度　coupling speed
连环式构造　serial type structure
连接板　junction plate
连接棒　connecting rod
连接点　tie point
连接丢失概率　connection loss rate (CLR)
连接杆　connection rod
连接件　connecting piece
连接器　connector
连接销　connecting pin
连接允许控制　connection admission control (CAC)
连梁　coupling beam
连墙杆　wall-linking rod
连墙件　wall-linking element
连锁反应　chain reaction
连锁风险　chain risks
连通试验　connection test
连续/间断式测力轮对　continuous/intermittent inspection wheel set
连续拌和机　continuous mixer
连续采暖　continuous heating
连续倒塌　progressive collapse
连续电流额定值　continuous current rating
连续刚构　continuous rigid frame
连续拱桥　continuous arch bridge
连续灌注混凝土　continuous concreting
连续合同　continuing contract
连续降雨量　consecutive rainfall
连续粒级　continuous size fraction
连续梁　continuous girder, continuous beam
连续梁桥　continuous girder bridge, continuous beam bridge
连续片状多年冻土　continuous permafrost zone
连续日　consecutive days, running days
连续生产方式　sequential construction approach
连续式调速　continuous speed control
连续式轨道电路　continuous track circuit
连续式机车信号　continuous cab signaling
连续数据传输　continuous data transmission
连续压实检测　continuous compaction test
连续压实控制　continuous compaction control (CCC)

连续作业　continuous operation
连肢墙　coupled-wall
莲花状构造　lotus-form structure
联动响应　coordinating and response
联合保险　joint underwriting
联合保险单　joint insurance policy
联合报价　combined offer
联合测定法　combined measurement method
联合筹资　joint fundraising
联合除尘　combined dust removal
联合贷款　syndicated loan
联合担保　joint guarantee
联合抵押　joint mortgage
联合基础　combined foundation
联合凭证　combined certificate
联合融资　co-financing
联合试运转及工程动态监测费　joint trial operation and engineering dynamic supervision fees
联合体　consortium
联合体成员　consortium members
联合体承诺书　JV undertaking
联合投标　joint tendering, joint bid
联合洗井法　combined flushing
联合运货　multimodal transport, combined transport
联合运输单据　combined transport document (CTD)
联合运输人　multimodal transport operator (MTO)
联合账户　joint account
联合招标　joint invitations to bid/tender
联机状态　on-line state
联机作业　on-line operation
联络　liaise, liaison
联络办事处　liaison office
联络官　liaison officer
联络通道　connection passage
联络线　connecting line
联盟　federation, confederation, alignment
联盟承包商　alliance contractor
联盟合同　alliance contract
联名　joint names
联名保证　joint guarantee
联锁　interlocking
联锁表　interlocking table
联锁道岔　interlocking switch
联锁计算机　interlocking computer
联锁块铺面　interlocking block pavement
联锁区　interlocking zone
联锁设备　interlocking equipment
联锁试验　interlocking test
联锁图表　interlocking chart
联锁脱轨器　interlocked derailer

L

联锁箱　point detector
联锁箱联锁　interlocking by point detector
联调联试　integrated commissioning
联调联试及运行试验
　　joint commissioning and running test
联网退票　online ticket refund
联系测量　connection survey
联系电路　liaison circuit
联系廊　connection corridor
联系三角形法　connection triangle method
联系数　correlate
联系四边形法　connection quadrangle method
联营　joint operation
联营体负责人　JV's lead partner
联营体伙伴　joint venture partner
联营银行　affiliated bank
联运费率　combined transport freight rate
联运集装箱　intermodal container
联运提单　combined transport bill of lading（C. T. B/L），through bill of lading
联运运费　through freight
链斗式挖泥机　bucket ladder dredger
链接距离　linking distance
链接信息　linking information
链路带宽峰值　link peak bandwidth
链路发现协议　link discovery protocol
链形网　chain network
良好级配土　well-graded soil
梁　beam，girder
梁板结构　beam and slab structures
梁端防水装置　beam-end waterproof device
梁端缓冲梁　buffer beam at girder end
梁端竖向转角
　　vertical angle of rotation of beam-end
梁端有效支承长度
　　beam-end effective supporting length
梁端转角　rotation angle at girder end
梁高　girder depth，beam depth
梁轨相互作用
　　girder-rail interaction，beam and track interaction
梁式桥　girder-type bridge，beam-type bridges
梁腋　haunching of beam，haunching of girder
梁柱式支架　beam-column type falsework，beam and post falsework
两班制　two-shifts
两倍照准差　doubled collimation error discrepancy
两边支承板　two-side supported plate
两步贷款　two-step loan
两点检查　released by checking two sections
两端固定梁　beam with both ends built-in

两端张拉　tensioning at both ends
两段零序电流保护
　　two section of zero-sequence current protection
两化改正　two-ization amendment
两铰拱桥　two hinged arch bridge
两阶段招标　two-stage tendering
两讫　delivery versus payment（DVP），a done deal
两台夹两线布置
　　two platforms mingling with two tracks layout
两台夹一线布置
　　two platforms mingling with one track layout
两通阀　two-way valve
亮度　brightness
谅解备忘录　memorandum of understanding（MOU）
量本利分析　cost-volume-profit（CVP）analysis
量测范围　measuring range
量测摄影机　metric camera
量测仪器　measuring instrument
量程　measuring range
量度　measure
量规　gauge
量积法　volume measurement method
量取　measuring
量筒法　graduated cylinder method
量值溯源　traceability of magnitude
料石　dressed stone
瞭望视距　visible range for watching
列表　list
列车编组计划组号
　　car group numbers of train marshalling plan
列车侧向通过速度　lateral passing speed of train，diverging speed of train
列车超速防护　automatic train protection（ATP）
列车超速防护系统
　　automatic train protection system（ATP）
列车冲击力　impact force of train
列车出轨　train derailment
列车带电概率　energized probability of train
列车带电平均电流
　　average current of charging train
列车待避　train refuge
列车到发信息
　　information of train arrival and departure
列车电流有效值　effective current value of trains，r.m.s current of trains
列车调度电话　train dispatching telephone
列车调度指挥系统
　　train dispatching and commanding system（TDCS）
列车动荷载　train dynamic load
列车对数　train pairs

列车风压力　train wind pressure
列车服务号　train service number
列车荷载　train load
列车横向摇摆力　lateral sway force of train
列车活载　train live load
列车间隔　train interval, train headway
列车交会　train passing, train crossing, train meeting
列车交路　train routing
列车接近报警器　train approaching warning device
列车接近一次通知　train approach notice
列车接口单元　train interface unit (TIU)
列车进路　train route
列车控制系统　train control system
列车离心力　centrifugal force of train
列车冒进防护　train trip
列车密集到发　intensive train receiving and departure
列车平均电流　average current of train
列车牵引力　tractive force of train
列车竖向动力　vertical dynamic force of train
列车竖向活载动力系数　dynamic coefficient of vertical live load of train
列车竖向静活载　vertical static live load of train
列车竖向振动加速度　vertical vibration acceleration of train
列车数据　train data
列车速度检查仪　train speed monitoring device
列车通过　train passing
列车脱轨载荷　derailment load of train
列车脱线　train derailment
列车完整性　train integrity
列车位置表示　train position indication
列车无线调度通信　train radio dispatching communication
列车信号机　train signal
列车摇摆力　sway force of train
列车有效电流　effective current of train
列车越行　train overtaking
列车运行调整计划　train operation regulation plan
列车运行后方　in rear of
列车运行监控记录装置　train operation monitoring and recording device (LKJ)
列车运行监控装置　train operation monitoring and record device
列车运行控制车载设备　onboard equipment of train control system
列车运行控制方式　train operation control mode
列车运行控制类电路交换数据业务服务质量　QoS of train control CSD
列车运行控制系统　train control system
列车运行控制中心　train control center (TCC)
列车运行控制(列控)中心　train operation control center
列车运行前方　in advance of
列车直向通过速度　train straight through speed
列车制动力　braking force of train
列车种类别疏解　untwining for train types
列车自动调速　automatic train speed regulation
列车自动防护系统　automatic train protection system
列车自动防护　automatic train protection (ATP)
列车自动驾驶系统　automatic train operation (ATO) system
列车自动监控　automatic train supervision (ATS)
列车自动监控系统　automatic train supervision (ATS) system
列车自动控制　automatic train control (ATC)
列车自动限速　automatic train speed restriction
列车自动运行系统　automatic train operation (ATO) system
列车最小、最大安全后端位置　train minimum / maximum safe rear end position
列出的　listed
列检动态检车室　dynamic car inspection room
列检作业区　train inspection area
列控中心　Train Control Center (TCC)
列入短名单的公司　short-listed firms, short-listed company
列位　EMU maintenance bay
列植　linear planting
劣等的　inferior
劣化　degradation
劣质混凝土　poor quality concrete, faulty concrete, inferior concrete
烈度　intensity
烈度分布　intensity distribution
烈度异常　abnormal intensity
烈度异常区　abnormal intensity area
烈风　strong gale
裂缝　crack
裂缝测量　gap survey
裂缝观测　crack observation
裂缝监测　crack monitoring
裂缝宽度　crack width
裂谷　rift valley
裂膜纱织土工布　slit and split film yarn woven geotextiles
裂膜丝机织土工布　slit and split film silk woven geotextiles
裂纹　crack
裂纹扩展　crack growth

裂隙构造　fissure structure
裂隙含水层　fracture aquifer
裂隙水　crack water
裂隙黏土　fissured clay
邻带方里网　grid of neighboring zone
邻近地域　adjacent regions
邻近建筑物　adjacent building
邻区段干扰　adjacent section interference
邻线干扰　interference from adjacent line
林草覆盖率
　　percentage of the forestry and grass coverage
林地　forest land
林区　forest region
临管线　temporary management line
临管线火车
　　train for temporarily management line
临管线火车运价　train freight rate of temporarily management line
临界点　critical point
临界高度　critical height
临界含水率　critical water content
临界孔隙比　critical void ratio
临界跨距　critical span length
临界深度　critical depth
临界水力梯度　critical hydraulic gradient
临界速度　critical speed
临进设施费　expense of temporary facilities
临时便线　temporary railway
临时裁决　interim award
临时成本　contingent cost
临时出口　temporary export
临时贷款　temporary loan, bridging loan
临时电力线　temporary power lines
临时电力线路　temporary power line
临时渡口　temporary ferry crossing
临时发票　provisional invoice, proforma invoice
临时费
　　incidental/contingent/nonrecurring expenses
临时分录账　blotter
临时付款　provisional payment
临时高压消防系统
　　temporary high-pressure fire system
临时给水　temporary water supply
临时给水干管
　　temporary water supply trunk pipeline
临时工　casual worker/labourer, jobber, temp
临时工程　temporary works
临时工程施工器材年使用率
　　annual usage rate of contractor's construction materials for temporary works

临时工程用地　land for temporary works
临时工作　casual work, odd job
临时供电　temporary power supply
临时供水　temporary water supply
临时估价　provisional estimation
临时雇工　casual employment
临时荷载　temporary load
临时集中发电　temporary centralized power generation
临时建筑物　temporary buildings
临时建筑物、构筑物
　　temporary buildings and structures
临时解雇　temporary layoff
临时进口　temporary import
临时开支　interim/temporary charge
临时码头　temporary wharf
临时内燃集中发电站
　　temporary internal combustion power station
临时排水　temporary drainage
临时设施　temporary facilities
临时收据　temporary receipt
临时通信　temporary communication
临时通信线路　temporary communication line
临时限速　temporary speed restriction (TSR)
临时限速服务器
　　Temporary Speed Restriction Server(TSRS)
临时协议　provisional agreement
临时信号　temporary signal
临时性收支　non-recurring incomes and expenses
临时性账户　temporary account
临时延期决定　interim determination of extension
临时验收　provisional acceptance
临时移动用户识别码
　　temporary mobile subscriber identity (TMSI)
临时用地　temporary land
临时预付款　temporary advance
临时再保险　facultative reinsurance
临时站场建筑设备　temporary construction and equipment of station and yard
临时争议评判委员会
　　ad-hoc dispute adjudication board(ad-hoc DAB)
临时证书　provisional certificate
临时支撑　temporary shoring, temporary support, temporary strutting
临时仲裁　ad hoc arbitration
临时柱　temporary column
临塑荷载　critical plastic load
临险抢护　emergency repair
临修　casual repair
临修库　casual repair workshop
临修线　casual repair track

淋浴器　shower device
磷光　phosphorescence
磷化物　phosphide
磷灰石　apatite
磷灰岩　phosphorite
磷酸盐　phosphate
檩条　purlin
灵敏度　sensitivity
灵敏度余量　surplus sensitivity
灵敏系数　sensitivity coefficient
菱镁矿　magnesite
菱铁矿　siderite
零层端子　terminals of layer 0 of relay racks
零担货场　less-than-carload freight yard, part-load freight yard
零担货物　less-than-carload goods, less-than-truck-load goods
零地电位差　zero ground potential difference
零点漂移　zero drift
零点校核　check of zero
零点校正　zero correction
零断面路基　subgrade without cutting and filling
零活　casual work, odd job
零件　parts, elements
零立体效应　impossible stereoscopic effect
零能耗建筑　zero energy building
零漂　null shift
零色散波长范围　zero dispersion wavelength range
零事故　zero-accident
零售价　retail price
零售商　tradesman, retailer, retail dealer
零星工程　sporadic works
零星用料　miscellaneous material
零序电流保护　zero sequence current protection
零序增量　zero sequence current increment
龄期　age
领班　ganger, foreman
领工区　work sub-section
领货单　stock requisition form
领料单　material requisition form, stock requisition form
领料汇总单　material requisition summary
领事发票　consular invoice
领事馆　consulate
溜车不利条件　unfavorable condition for car rolling
溜放部分　rolling section of hump
溜放进路　rolling route
溜放进路自动控制　automatic control of humping route

溜放速度　rolling speed
溜放线　rolling track
溜坍　topsoil slip
溜逸　roll away
留边　selvedge
留成利润　retained profit
留存收益　retained earnings/income/surplus
留存收益表　statement of retained earnings/income/surplus
留样　reserved sample
留置　detention
留置权　lien
留置权书　letter of setoff, lien letter
流冰　drift ice
流程图　flow chart, flow diagram
流出　outflow
流动比率　current ratio, liquidity ratio
流动财产　floating property
流动度　fluidity
流动度比　ratio of fluidity
流动负债　liquid/circulating/current liabilities
流动机械年运行次数　yearly operation times of mobile machinery
流动接收机　roving receiver
流动沙丘　moving dune
流动性　fluidity
流动债务　current debt
流动装卸机械　mobile loading and unloading machinery
流动资本　floating/current/fluid/liquid/circulating capital
流动资产　liquid/current/floating/circulating assets, current asset
流动资产净额　net current asset
流动资金总额　gross working capital
流量　flow, discharge
流量表　flowmeter
流量发生器　traffic generator
流量计　flowmeter
流量箱　scaled water tank
流面构造　planar flow structure
流劈理　flow cleavage
流平性　levelling property
流沙　quicksand
流数据　streamed data
流水地貌　fluvial geomorphology/landform
流水生产法　assembly line method
流水压力　pressure of flowing water
流水账　blotter
流速　flow speed

L

流速指数	index of flow velocity
流塑	fluid-plastic
流塑状态	flow-plastic state
流通	circulate
流通存单	negotiable certificate of deposit
流通汇票	negotiable draft
流通加工区	circulation and processing area
流通票据	negotiable instrumen/paper/bill/note
流通期票	negotiable promissory note/time note/term bill/period bill
流通税	turnover tax
流通提单	negotiable bill of lading
流通信用证	negotiable letter of credit, negotiable L/C
流通支票	negotiable check (cheque)
流土	soil flow
流网	flow net
流纹构造	fluidal structure
流纹岩	rhyolite
流线	flow line
流向	flow direction
流行	prevail
流行性疾病	epidemic
流域	watershed / catchment basin
琉璃瓦	enameled tile
硫含量	sulphur content
硫化物	sulfide
硫黄锚固	sulphur anchorage
硫酸盐	sulfate
硫酸盐侵蚀	sulphate corrosion
硫酸盐渍土	sulfate saline soil
六方晶系	hexagonal system
六类线	category 6 cable
隆起	uplift
垄断	monopolize, corner
垄断价格	monopoly/administered/cartel price
楼板	floor slab
楼层侧移刚度	lateral displacement rigidity of floor
楼面反应谱	floor response spectrum
楼梯	stairs
楼梯间	staircase
镂空砖	hollow brick, air brick
漏报率	missing rate
漏电	electric leakage
漏电流	leakage current
漏斗	depression cone
漏斗仓	hopper bunker
漏斗法	funnel method
漏风量	air leakage
漏风率	air system leakage ratio
漏感	leakage inductance
漏光检测	air leak check with lighting
漏解锁	missing release
漏抗	leakage reactance
漏气	gas leakage
漏声	sound leakage, acoustic leakage
漏水	water leakage
漏税	tax dodging, evade taxes, tax evasion
漏锁闭	missing locking
漏项	missing item
漏泄同轴电缆	leakage coaxial cable (LCX)
漏油	oil leakage
炉渣	boiler slag
卤代烷灭火器	halogenated agent extinguisher
卤代烷灭火系统	halogenated agent extinguishing system
卤化物	haloids
陆地声呐法	land sonar method
陆路共通地点	overland common point
陆上运输保险	overland transportation insurance
陆相	continental facies
陆运	land transportation
陆运承运人	land carrier
陆运可达地点	overland common point
陆运提单	inland bill of lading
录像存储回放	video storage and playback
录音记录仪	audio recorder
路拌	road mixing
路标	fingerpost, signpost, guide/finger post
路厂(矿)联设工业站	combined industrial station
路堤	embankment
路堤基床	subgrade of embankment
路堤路堑过渡段	cut-fill transition section
路堤式路堑	embankment type cutting
路堤式卸车线	embankment unloading track
路堤填料	embankment fill material
路堤填土速率	filling rate of embankment
路堤中心	embankment center
路堤锥体	cone of embankment
路段	railway section
路段设计速度	design speed of railway section
路幅	breadth of road
路港联设港湾站	combined harbor station
路拱	camber
路货	afloat goods, afloat cargo
路基	earthworks
路基保温层	thermal insulation layer of earthworks
路基本体	subgrade noumenon
路基边坡绿化	subgrade slope greening

路基病害	earthworks defect
路基病害整治	treatment of earthworks defect
路基沉降	earthworks settlement
路基地段	at-grade section
路基动应力	dynamic stress of earthworks
路基冻害	frost damage of earthworks
路基段声屏障	sound barrier on subgrade
路基高程	subgrade elevation
路基工程	earthworks
路基工后沉降	post-construction settlement of subgrade
路基涵洞过渡段	earthworks-culvert transition section
路基横断面	cross section of earthworks
路基面	track formation
路基面沉降加宽	track formation widening for settlement
路基面加宽值	widening value of track formation
路基面宽度	width of track formation
路基面形状	track formation shape
路基面中心	track formation center
路基桥梁过渡段	subgrade-bridge transition section
路基融沉	thawing settlement of earthworks
路基设计高程	design elevation of earthworks
路基声屏障	sound barriers on subgrade
路基隧道过渡段	earthworks-tunnel transition section
路基坍塌	earthworks collapse
路基稳定	subgrade stability
路基纵断面	longitudinal section of earthworks
路肩	shoulder
路肩高程	shoulder elevation
路肩宽度	shoulder width
路肩抬高	shoulder heightening
路面	pavement
路面沉陷	road settlement
路面鼓胀	pavement expansion
路面结构	pavement structure
路面宽度	pavement width
路面破碎机	pavement breaker
路面形状	pavement shape
路牌	tablet
路牌携带器	tablet pouch
路牌自动授收机	automatic tablet exchanger
路企直通运输	direct transport between CR network and enterprise
路签	train staff
路签携带器	staff pouch
路签自动授收机	automatic staff exchanger
路堑	cutting
路堑边坡	cutting slope
路堑基床	subgrade of cutting
路堑声屏障	sound barrier on cutting
路桥过渡段声屏障	sound barrier on subgrade-bridge transition section
路数	number of channels
路网性编组站	railway network marshalling station
路线	route
路线测量	route survey
路线图	route map
路由	routing
路由反射器	route reflector (RR)
路由器	router
路缘石	curbstone
露点	dew point
露点温度	dew-point temperature
露天爆破	surface blasting
露天存货	open storage
露天堆场	open-stacking area
露天作业	site operations, field operation
露头	outcrop
卵石	cobble
卵石土	cobble soil
伦敦银行同业拆借利率	London interbank offered rate (LIBOR)
轮班	shift work
轮班工作制	shift system
轮乘制	rotating system
轮渡栈桥	ferry trestle bridge
轮对踏面诊断线	wheelset tread diagnosis track
轮轨动力学	wheel-rail dynamics
轮轨关系	wheel-rail interaction
轮轨间拉弧	wheel-rail arc discharge
轮轨接触	wheel-rail contact
轮轨接触踏面	wheel-track contact tread
轮轨润滑	wheel-rail lubrication
轮轨式提梁机	track-wheel girder lifter
轮轨游间	clearance between wheel flange and gauge line
轮轨噪声	wheel-rail noise
轮轨作用力	wheel-rail interaction forces
轮廓线	outline, form line, contour
(图样中的)轮廓线	contour line
轮胎起重机	tire-mounted crane
轮胎式搬梁机	rubber-wheel girder moving machine
轮胎式起重机	rubber tired crane, wheel crane
轮胎式挖掘机	wheel excavator
轮胎式装载机	wheel loader
轮信号	wheel signal

轮修　alternative maintenance
轮椅坡道　wheelchair ramp
轮缘　flange
轮载　wheel load
轮重　wheel load
轮重减载率　reduction rate of wheel load
罗盘　compass
罗盘仪测量　compass survey
逻辑地线　logic earth wire
螺钉　screw
螺杆式空气压缩机　screw compressor
螺杆式压缩机　screw compressor
螺孔裂纹　bolt hole crack
螺孔密封圈　bolt hole sealing washer
螺母　nut
螺栓　bolt
螺栓扳手　bolt wrench
螺栓端杆　shank
螺栓连接钢结构　bolted steel structure
螺栓拧紧度　bolt tightening degree
螺栓销　bolt pin
螺纹道钉　screw spike
螺纹钢筋　twisted steel
螺纹环规　thread ring gage
螺纹筋　deformed steel bar
螺纹连接　threaded connection
螺纹塞规　screw plug gauge
螺纹塞通规　screw plug go-gauge
螺纹中径　pitch diameter of thread
螺旋板载荷试验　chasing load test
螺旋箍筋　spiral stirrup
螺旋喷射桩　auger-cast pile
螺旋式风速风向传感器　screw-type wind speed and direction sensor
螺旋卸煤机　spiral coal unloader
裸露斑　naked spots
裸露面　exposed surface
裸露型岩溶区　exposed karst area
裸装货　nude cargo
洛杉矶磨耗　Los Angeles abrasion
洛杉矶磨耗机　Los Angeles rattler
洛杉矶磨耗率　Los Angeles abrasion rate
洛阳铲　Luoyang shovel
洛泽式桥(又称"直悬杆式刚性拱刚性梁桥")　Lohse bridge(also known as "rigid arch bridge with rigid tie and vertical suspenders")
落道　track lowering
落道量　track lowering
落梁施工　construction for lowering the girder (beam) into place
落石　rockfall
落石冲击力　impact force of falling stone
落水洞　sinkhole, ponor
落物监测　falling objects monitoring
落下门限　fall threshold
吕梁期　Lüliangian age/stage
吕荣单位　Lugeon unit
旅客乘降所　passenger stopping point
旅客乘坐舒适度指标　ride comfort index of passenger
旅客服务信息系统　passenger service information system
旅客基本站台　main passenger platform
旅客列车地面卸污设施　ground sewage discharge facility for passenger trains
旅客列车给水栓　water supply spigot for passenger train
旅客列车给水栓室　water supply spigot manholes for passenger train
旅客列车给水站　water supply station for passenger train
旅客列车广播设备　passenger train broadcasting equipment
旅客列车检修所(客列检)　passenger car inspection depot
旅客列车上水设备　water supply spigot for passenger train
旅客列车上水设备井室　water supply spigot well chamber for passenger train
旅客列车卸污站(点)　waste discharge station (spot) for passenger train
旅客列车卸污装置　sewage discharge equipment for passenger train
旅客天桥　passenger overpass, passenger footbridge
旅客携带物品安全检查设施　passenger-carrying luggage security inspection facilities
旅客信息系统　passenger information system
旅客站房　passenger station building
旅客站台　passenger platform
旅客中间站台　intermediate passenger platform
旅客最高聚集人数　maximum passenger number gathered
旅行时间目标值　target value of travel time
旅行信用证　circular letter of credit, traveler's letter of credit
旅行支票　traveller's check
铝包钢绞线　Al-clad steel stranded wire
铝包钢芯铝绞线　Aluminium Conductors, Aluminium Clad Steel Reinforced (ACSR/AS or ACSR/AW)

铝合金　aluminum alloy
铝护套　aluminium sheathed
铝热焊　thermit welding
履带式吊车　crawler crane
履带式起重机　crawler crane, caterpillar crane
履带式推土机　crawler dozer
履带式拖拉机　track-type tractor, crawler tractor
履带式挖掘机　crawler excavator, track excavator
履带式桩架　crawler pile frame
履带式装载机　tracked loader, crawler loader
履历表　curriculum vitae (CV), resume
履行合同　carry out /implement /execute/fulfil a contract, contract performance
履行义务　fulfill an obligation
履行职责　perform/discharge/fulfil a duty
履约　honour an agreement, fulfill a contract
履约保函　performance security
履约保函的返还　return of the performance security
履约保函的索赔　claim under the performance security
履约保证书　performance guarantee
履约不能　impossibility of performance
履约信用证　performance letter of credit
履约证明　proof of performance
履约证书　performance certificate
律师服务费　counsel/ attorney/legal fee, legal service charge
律师事务所　law firm, law office
律师委员会　bar council
律师协会　bar association
率定系数　calibration coefficient
绿地　green area
绿地率　greening rate
绿化　virescence, greening, planting
绿化分隔带　median strip, central reservation, green median strip
绿化工程　greening engineering
绿化用水量　green belt sprinkling water consumption
绿篱　hedge
绿帘石　pistacite
绿泥石　chlorite
绿色防护　greening protection
绿色防护设计　greening design
绿色铁路客站　green railway station
绿色照明　green lighting
绿脱石　nontronite
绿柱石　beryl
氯化铵—乙醇法　ammonium chloride-ethanol method
氯化物　chloride
氯化物含量　chloride content
氯离子含量　chlorion content
氯离子扩散系数　chlorion diffusion coefficient
氯离子浓度　chloride concentration
氯盐环境　chloride environment
氯盐渍土　chloride saline soil
滤波　filtering
滤池　filtration tank
滤毒室　gas-filtering room
滤毒通风　gas filtration ventilation
滤料　filtering media
滤膜　filter membrane
滤清器　filter
滤速　filtration rate
滤网　strainer
滤油　oil filtering
滤纸　filter paper
略图　sketch

M

m 值法　m method
马刀树　diverted tree, bent tree, tilted tree
马兰黄土　Malan loess
马赛克效应　mosaic effect
马蹄形隧道　horseshoe-shaped tunnel
马歇尔试验　Marshall stability test
码变换和速率适配单元
　　transcoding and rate adaption unit (TRAU)
码头　wharf, dock
码头泊位　berth, mooring
码头到仓库　pier-to-house (P/H)
码头到码头　pier-to-pier
码头到内地仓库　pier-to-inland depot
码头费　quayage, wharfage, dockage
码头交货价
　　free on quay (FOQ), free on wharf (FOW)
码头至码头运输　quay-to-quay transportation
埋地卧式油罐　buried horizontal tank
埋钉法　nail burying method
埋管机　pipe layer
埋入式连续桩板结构
　　embedded continuous pile-slab structure
埋设位置　laying place
埋深　burial depth
埋石　monumentation
埋置深度　cover, overburden
埋置式桥台　buried abutment
买方递盘　purchase offer, buying offer
买方负责　caveat emptor
买方市场　buyer's market
买方信贷　buyer's credit
买卖合同　sales contract, purchase contract, contract of sale
买入的汇票
　　draft purchased, bill of exchange purchased
买入价值　entry value
买主垄断价格　oligopsony price
麦克风　microphone
麦美奇岩　meimechite
卖方负责　caveat venditor
卖方工厂交货价格　ex-factory price
卖方利益险　contingency insurance covering sellers' interest only
卖方市场　seller's market
卖方信贷　seller's/supplier's credit
卖据　bill of sale
卖主垄断价格　oligopoly price
(电杆)迈步　offset
脉冰　vein ice
脉冲编码调制　pulse code modulation (PCM)
脉冲澄清池　pulsator
脉冲峰头电压　impulse peak head voltage
脉冲峰尾电压　impulse peak tail voltage
脉冲轨道电路　impulse track circuit
脉冲荷载　pulse load
脉冲继电器　pulse relay
脉冲式轨道电路　pulse track circuit
脉冲自动闭塞
　　automatic block with impulse track circuit
脉动法　pulsation method
满水试验　full water test
满堂式支架　full-type falsework
满堂支架法　full falsework method
满线　full track
慢剪　slow shear
慢剪试验　slow shear test
慢速定量滤纸　slow quantitative filter paper
芒硝　mirabilite
忙时话务量　traffic volume in busy hours
盲沟　filter ditch
盲谷　blind valley
盲管　filter pipe
毛刺　burr
毛费率　gross rate
毛价　gross price
毛利　gross profit

毛利率　gross profit ratio/margin, gross profit margin ratio
毛利润　gross profit
毛石　rubble
毛石砌体　rubble masonry
毛体积密度　bulk density
毛细带　capillary zone
毛细管　capillary
毛细管饱和法　capillary saturation method
毛细管水　capillary water
毛细管水上升高度　capillary water rising height
毛细泌水率　bleeding rate of capillary
毛细水　capillary water
毛细水隔断层　insulating layer of capillary water
毛细水上升　capillary rise
毛细水上升高度　height of capillary rise
毛值　gross value
毛重　gross weight
锚板　anchor plate
锚垫板　anchor backing plate
锚定板挡土墙　anchor plate retaining wall
锚定板抗拔力　uplift resistance of anchor plate
锚定板式桥台　anchor plate abutment
锚碇　anchor, anchorage
锚段　tensioning section
锚段长度　tension length
锚段关节　overlap
锚杆　rock bolt, anchor bolt
锚杆挡土墙　anchor bolt retaining wall
锚杆拉拔仪　anchor rod pull-out device
锚杆无损检测　bolt nondestructive detection
锚杆轴力　axial force of the anchor rod
锚固　anchorage
锚固板　anchor plate
锚固段　anchorage section
锚固力　anchorage force
锚固密实度　anchoring density
锚固性　anchorage property
锚筋　anchor reinforcement
锚具　anchorage device
锚孔　anchor span
锚跨　anchor span
锚栓　anchor bolt
锚索　anchor cable
锚支定位卡子　clamp holder for out-of-running CW
锚座　anchor socket
卯酉圈曲率半径　radius of curvature in prime vertical
铆钉　rivet
铆接　riveting
铆接钢结构　riveted steel structure
铆接钢梁　riveted steel girder
铆接钢桥　riveted steel bridge
冒顶　roof fall
冒进防护　overrunning protection
冒进信号　overrun a signal
冒牌商标　trademark counterfeiting/infringement, counterfeit trade-mark
贸易壁垒　trade barrier
贸易代表团　trade mission
贸易代理合同　commercial agency contract
贸易关系　trade relation
贸易惯例　trade custom, trade usage, trade practice
贸易逆差　trade deficit
贸易平衡　balance of trade
贸易入超　trade deficit
贸易术语　trade terms
贸易顺差　trade surplus
贸易谈判　trade negotiation
贸易条款　trade terms
贸易条约　commercial treaty
贸易限制　trade restriction
贸易协定　trade agreement, trade pact
贸易协会　chamber of trade
贸易折扣　trade discount
帽梁　cap beam
帽石　capping stone
媒体网关　media gateway (MGW)
煤　coal
煤层　coal seam
煤层采空区　coal goaf
煤沥青　coal pitch
煤系地层　coal measure strata
煤巷　coal road
每米制动能高　energy head of braking per meter
每秒百万包　million packet per second
每秒试呼次数　call attempt per second (CAPS)
每人平均值　per capita
每日保险费　daily premium
每日单价　daily price
每日津贴　daily allowance, per diem allowance
每日施工作业　daily construction activities
每月付款　monthly payment
每月期中付款证书　monthly interim payment certificate
每月详细进度表　monthly detailed schedule
每周劳务报告　weekly labour report
每昼夜取送车次数　number of times of taking-out and placing-in every 24 hours
每昼夜行车次数　running times of trains per day and night

每昼夜行车对数　pairs of trains operating per day and night
美元信贷　dollar credit
镁盐侵蚀　magnesium salt erosion
门磁　door contact
门禁　entrance guard, access control
门禁卡　access control card
门禁系统　access control system
门区　gate area
门区自动系统　automatic system at gate area
门式螺旋卸车机　portal-type screw unloader
门式铺轨排机　gantry-type track panel laying machine
门式起重机　gantry crane, portal crane
门式起重机走行轨　running rail of portal crane
门限值　threshold value
门形架构　portal structure
蒙绘　mask artwork
蒙特卡罗分析　Monte Carlo analysis
蒙特卡罗模拟　Monte Carlo simulation
蒙脱石　montmorillonite
蒙脱石含量　montmorillonite content
弥散系数　dispersion coefficient
迷流保护　stray current protection
糜棱结构　mylonitic texture
糜棱岩　mylonite
泌水　bleeding
泌水率　bleeding rate
密闭阀门　airtight valve
密闭节理　closed joint
密闭门　air-tight door
密闭通道　airtight passage
密闭罩　airtight cover
密度计　density gauge
密度计法　hydrometer method
密封的投标指令　sealed bid instruction
密封垫　gasket
密封垫沟槽　gasket groove
密封法　sealing method
密封盖　seal cover
密封圈　seal ring
密封试验　tightness test
密封投标　sealed bid/tender
密封性　leakproofness
密集波分复用　dense wavelength division multiplexing (DWDM)
密码键盘　password keyboard
密实　compactness
密实度　degree of compaction
密贴　closure
密贴调整杆　adjustable switch operating rod
密贴检查器　switch closure detector
密钥测试　key test
密植　compact planting
免除合同义务　release/exempt from contract obligation, discharge of contractual obligations
免除双重税收　double taxation relief
免除责任　exempt from liability, immune from liability
免除债务　release from debt/liability, remit a debt, debt discharge/relief/cancellation
免费　free of charge
免费送货　free delivery
免费提供的材料　free issue materials
免费医疗　free health care, free medical care
免关税　free of duty
免检　exempt from inspection
免赔额　deductible, excess
免赔期限　waiting period
免赔条款　deductible clause, franchise clause
免收运费　freight-free
免税单　bill of sufferance, exemption certificate
免税港　tax haven
免税货进口报关单　customs declaration form for importing duty-free goods
免税货物　duty-free goods, non-dutiable goods
免税进口　duty-free importation
免税利润　tax-free profit
免税期　tax holiday
免税区　free trade zone, duty-free zone
免税条款　exemption clause
免税证明　tax exemption certification
免责　exempt from liability, immune from liability
免责条款　exculpatory clause, exclusion of liability clause, exemption clause, escape clause
免责条款(不担责)　disclaimer
面板　panel
面波　surface wave
面积矩　area moment
面密度　areal density
面漆　finish coating
面水准测量　ground leveling survey
面砟　top ballast
面砟带　surface ballast belt
面值　face amount (value), nominal value
面状符号　area symbol
瞄直法　sighting line method
秒表　second chronograph
秒脉冲　1 Pulse Per Second (1PPS)
灭弧机构　arc-distinguishing mechanism
灭弧室　arc-distinguishing chamber, arc chute

灭火花电路	spark extinguishing circuit
灭火剂	fire extinguishing agent
灭火器	fire extinguisher
民法	civil law
民法典	civil code
民间融资建议	private finance initiatives (PFI)
民间骚乱	civil commotion
民事权利	civil right
民事诉讼	civil action/lawsuit/suit
民事损害赔偿	civil damage compensation
民事责任	civil liability
民事责任险	civil liability insurance
民用建筑	civil building
敏感点	sensitive point
敏感性分析	sensitivity analysis
名义成本	nominal cost
名义尺寸	nominal dimension
名义代理人	ostensible/nominal agent
名义合伙人	nominal partner, ostensible partner
名义汇率	nominal exchange rate
名义价值	nominal value
名义金额	nominal amount
名义利率	nominal interest rate
名义数量	nominal quantity
名义账户	nominal account
名义值	nominal value
名义资本	nominal capital
明德林解答	Mindlin's solution
明洞	open cut tunnel
明沟排水	open drainage
明桥面	open deck
明渠	open channel
明设	exposed installation
明示承诺	express undertaking
明示放弃	express waiver
明示规定	express provision
明示弃权书	express waiver
明示条款	express term
明示同意	express consent
明示协议	express agreement
明示转让	express assignment
明挖法	open cut method, cut and cover method
明挖基础	open cut foundation
明细分类账	detailed ledger, subsidiary ledger
明细记录	itemized statement
明细账	detailed account
明细账目	detailed ledger, subsidiary ledger
明显缺陷	obvious defect
明线	open wire
明线线路	open line
冥古宇	Hadean eonothem
铭牌	nameplate
命令存储测试	command storage test
模板	formwork
模板拆除	formwork removal, form removal
模板工	formwork fixer, formworker
模板工程	formwork engineering
模板台车	formwork jumbo
模板体系	formwork system
模板支撑	formwork support
模板支架	formwork support
模具	mould
模量	modulus
模拟地震震动试验	earthquake simulation test
模拟复合视频信号	analog composite video signal
模拟空中三角测量	analog aerial triangulation
模拟雷击试验	simulation lightning test
模拟量	analog quantity
模拟专线电路	analog private line
模拟子钟	analog slave clock
模腔温度	moulding chamber temperature
模式	mode, schema
模态分析	modal analysis
模型比例尺	model scale
模型变形	model deformation
模型材料	model material
模型单元	model unit
模型基点	anchor point of model
模型基线	model baseline
模型精度	level of details, level of model definition
模型连接	model connectivity
模型设计	model design
模型试验	model test
模型视图定义	model view definition (MVD)
模型要素	model elements
模型要素组合	model elements combination
模型置平	model leveling
模型资源	model resource
模型坐标	model coordinates
模筑混凝土	in-situ-cast concrete
膜分离	membrane separation
膜过滤	membrane filtration
膜密度	film density
膜生物反应器	membrane bio-reactor (MBR)
摩擦板	friction plate
摩擦电流	frictional working current
摩擦角	friction angle
摩擦结合式高强度螺栓	high-strength friction grip bolt
摩擦连接器	friction clutch

摩擦特性　frictional characteristic
摩擦系数　friction coefficient
摩擦型锚杆　friction rockbolt
摩擦桩　friction pile
摩尔—库仑定律　Mohr-Coulomb Law
摩尔—库仑理论　Mohr-Coulomb theory
摩尔浓度　Molar concentration
摩尔应力圆　Mohr's stress circle
摩尔质量　Molar mass
摩阻比　friction-resistance ratio
摩阻力　frictional resistance
磨轨车　rail grinding car
磨轨机　rail grinding machine
磨耗　wear
磨耗仪　abrasion tester
磨片　abrasive disc
磨石机　stone mill
磨蚀环境　abrasion environment
磨损　abrasion, wear, wear and tear
磨损量　wearing capacity
磨细矿渣粉　grounded furnace slag
抹灰工　plasterer, plaster worker
抹面　finishing
抹面机　finishing machine
抹子　trowel, plasterer's float
墨卡托投影　Mercator projection
默认值　default value
默示　imply
默示保证　implied warranty
默示工作　implied work
默示合同　implied contract
默示权力　implied power
默示条款　implied terms
默示异议　implied objection
没收条款　forfeiture clause
没有争议避免裁决委员会　no DAAB in place
某些权利(如矿权、地权、特许权等)使用费　royalty
母公司　parent company, mother company
母公司担保　parent company guarantee
母联　bus coupling
母排　bus bar
母体试验室　parent laboratory
母线　bus conductor, bus bar
母线电流　busbar current
母线电压　busbar voltage
母线桥　busbar bridge
母岩抗压强度　compressive strength of source rocks
母岩强度　strength of source rocks
母钟　master clock
木板桩　plank pile
木材　timber
木工　carpenter
木结构　timber structure, wood structure
木料　lumber, timber
木模板　timber/plywood formwork
木枕　wooden sleeper
木枕削平机　wooden sleeper adzing machine
木枕钻孔机　wooden sleeper drilling machine
木桩　timber pile
目标成本　target cost
目标成本管理　target cost management
目标成本合同　target cost contract
目标点　target point
目标管理　management by objectives(MBO), target management, objective management
目标合同　target contract
目标价格　target price
目标进度计划　target schedule
目标距离　target distance
目标—距离控制曲线　target-distance control curve
目标可靠度指标　target reliability index
目标可靠指标　target reliability index
目标控制　target control
目标利润　target profit
目标日期　target date
目标市场　target market
目标速度　target speed
目标速度监视区　target speed surveillance area
目测法　visual method
目的　goal, object, purpose, objective
目的地付款　payable at destination
目的地国家　country of destination
目的地交货(价)　delivered at place (DAP)
目的地交货类　free on board destination
目的地码头交货(价)　delivered at terminal (DAT), delivered ex quay (DEQ)
目的调速　target speed control
目的港　destination port, port of destination, port of arrival
目的港船上交货(价)　delivered ex ship
目的信令点编码　destination point code (DPC)
目的制动　target braking
目的制动位　target braking location
目镜　eyepiece
目视比浊法　visible turbidimetric method
目视法　visual method
目视检验　visual test
目视行车模式　on sight mode (OS)
钼蓝光度法　molybdenum blues photometric method
墓穴　tomb, grave

N

N 年重现期　return period of N years
N 线　neutral wire
纳氏比色管　Nessler tube
纳税发票　tax invoice
纳税后净收益　net income/earnings after tax
纳税能力　ability to pay tax, taxability, taxable capacity
纳税人　taxpayer, tax bearer
纳税日　tax day
纳税申报表　income tax return (form), tax file number declaration form
纳税义务　tax obligation
钠长岩　albitite
耐崩解试验　slaking test
耐崩解指数　slaking index
耐冲击电压额定值　rated value of impulse withstand voltage
耐冲击性　resistance to impact
耐臭氧老化　resistance to ozone ageing
耐冻系数　frost resistance coefficient
耐冻性　frost resistance
耐腐蚀轨　corrosion resistant rail
耐化学侵蚀　resistance to chemical erosion
耐环境应力开裂　resistance to environment stress cracking
耐火材料　refractory material, refractory, fireproof material
耐火等级　fire resistance rating
耐火混凝土　refractory/fireproof/fire-resistant concrete
耐火极限　fire resistance limit
耐火水泥　refractory cement
耐火砖　refractory brick, fire brick
耐碱性　alkali resistance
耐静水压　resistance to static hydraulic pressure
耐久性　durability
耐久性混凝土　durable concrete
耐久性能试验　durability test
耐久性指标　durability index
耐磨轨　wear resistant rail
耐磨性　abrasion resistance
耐气候老化　resistance to weathering
耐热性　resistance to heat
耐热氧化　resistance to thermal oxidation
耐酸材料　acid-resistant material, acid proof material
耐酸混凝土　acid-resistant concrete
耐压试验　voltage withstand test
耐用年限　service life, durable life, useful life
耐用总台班　total available service-life machine shift
耐张杆　strain pole, tension pole
耐张绝缘子　tension insulator, strain insulator
耐张线夹　strain clamp, tension clamp
耐张转角杆　angle strain pole
南向接口　southbound interface
南亚热带　south subtropics
难燃烧体　hard-combustible substance
难溶盐含量　content of non-soluble salt
难行车　hard rolling car
难行线　hard rolling track
难以理解　clouded
挠度　deflection
挠度观测　deflection observation
挠度校验系数　verification coefficient of deflection
挠度仪　flexometer
挠曲二阶效应　second order effect due to displacement
挠曲力　bending force in CWR on bridge
挠性　deflection
内部保护　internal protection
内部边界网关协议　internal border gateway protocol (IBGP)
内部端口　internal port
内部防雷　internal lightning protection
内部静荷载　internal static load
内部会计　internal accounting

内部控制　internal control
内部缺陷　internal defect
内部审计　internal auditing
内部收益率　internal rate of return（IRR）
内部网关协议　internal gateway protocol（IGP）
内部效益　internal benefit
内部协同　inner cooperation
内部装修　interior decoration
内插法　interpolation
内插高程点　interpolated elevation point
内插曲面　interpolated curved surface
内插误差方程式　interpolated error equation
内插圆半径　radius of interpolation circle
内衬不锈钢管　lined stainless steel pipe
内撑式停车防溜器
　　inner-support parking anti-rolling device
内存　memory
内存利用率　memory useage
内叠阶地　in-laid terrace
内定向　interior orientation
内定向元素　element of interior orientation
内分点法　method of interior points
内河运输保险　inland marine insurance
内径　inner diameter
内涝防治系统
　　local flooding prevention and control system
内力　internal force
内力调整系数　internal force adjustment factor
内力重分布　internal force redistribution
内陆海关关税　inland customs duty
内陆运输　inland transportation
内陆运输保险单　inland transit insurance policy
内摩擦角　internal friction angle
内排水系统　internal drainage system
内墙　partition wall
内燃叉车　diesel forklift
内燃道岔磨轨机
　　diesel turnout rail grinding machine
内燃钢轨钻孔机　diesel rail drilling machine
内燃轨型磨轨机　diesel rail grinding machine
内燃锯轨机　diesel rail sawing machine
内燃螺栓扳手　diesel bolt wrench
内燃牵引　diesel traction
内燃液压起拨道机
　　diesel hydraulic track lifting and lining machine
内容分发网络　content delivery network（CDN）
内锁闭装置　internal locking device
内销　domestic sales
内债　internal debt
内账　private ledger

内支撑　internal support
内装修工　interior finish worker
能高　energy head
能耗　energy consumption
能耗汇总　total energy consumption
能耗系统　energy consumption system
能耗指标　energy consumption index
能见度　visibility
能力设计　capacity design
能量分析　energy analysis
能量平衡表　energy balance sheet
能流图　energy flow diagram
能评阶段　energy conservation assessment stage
能效标准　energy efficiency standard
能效水平　energy efficiency level
能效限定值
　　minimum allowable value of the energy efficiency
能效指标　energy efficiency index
能源储存　energy storage
能源分配　energy distribution
能源供应　energy supply
能源购入　energy acquisition
能源加工转换　energy processing and conversion
能源利用效率　power utilization efficiency
能源输送　energy transportation
能源消费影响　energy consumption influence
能源消费账单　bill of power consumption
能源优化　energy optimization
尼尔森式洛泽梁桥（又称"斜悬杆式刚性拱刚性梁桥"）　Nielsen type Lohse bridge（also known as "rigid arch bridge with rigid tie and inclined suspenders"）
泥板岩　argillite
泥灰岩　marlite, marlstone
泥浆　slurry
泥浆泵　slurry pump
泥浆池　slurry tank
泥浆套沉井法
　　open caisson method with slurry coating
泥裂构造　mud crack structure
泥龄　sludge age（SRT）
泥流陡坎　mudflow scarp
泥漠　argillaceous desert
泥盆纪　Devonian period
泥盆系　Devonian system
泥石流　debris flow
泥石流堵塞系数
　　obstructive coefficient of debris flow
泥石流流域　catchment of debris flow
泥石流扇　debris flow fan

泥水平衡盾构　slurry shield
泥炭　peat
泥炭质土　peat soil
泥土筛分　dirt screen, soil screen
泥瓦工　mason
泥岩　mudstone
泥质　argillaceous
泥质胶结　argillaceous cementation
泥质岩　pelitic rock
霓霞正长岩　aegirine nepheline syenite
拟完工程计划投资
　　investment of work proposed to be finished
拟稳平差　quasi-stable adjustment
拟用于本工程的设备和材料
　　plant and materials intended for the works
逆变器　inverter
逆差　trade deficit
逆磁性矿物　diamagnetism mineral
逆断层　reverse fault
逆反摄影测量　reverse photogrammetry
逆行检测　retrograde detection
逆掩断层　overthrust
逆转点法　reversal points method
溺谷相　liman facies
年(365天)　year
年报酬　annual remuneration/recompense/pay
年成交额　annual turnover
年地表径流深度　annual surface runoff depth
年地表滞水深度
　　annual surface water stagnation depth
年地下径流深度
　　annual underground runoff depth
年度报告　annual report
年度报税表　annual return form, tax return form
年度财务报表　annual financial statement
年度结算　year-end settlement of account
年度决算　annual final accounts
年度决算书　annual statement of final accounts
年度审计报告　annual audit report
年度维修　annual maintenance, yearly maintenance
年度休假　annual leave
年度预算　annual budget, yearly budget
年度支出　annual expenditure
年度支付额　annual disbursements
年度支付最高限额　annual disbursement ceiling
年回报率　annual rate of return
年检费　annual inspection fee
年鉴　year book
年降水量　annual precipitation
年金　annuity
年金保险　annuity insurance
年金金额　amount of an annuity
年净利润　annual net profit
年利率　annual interest rate
年平均地温　annual average ground temperature
年平均降水量　annual average precipitation
年平均气温　annual average temperature
年曝光量　yearly light exposure
年生产能力　annual production capacity (APC)
年使用费率　annual use fee rate
年收入　annual income/earnings/revenue
年输送能力　annual traffic capacity
年通货膨胀率　annual inflation rate
年息　interest per annum
年销售额　annual sales
年销售量　annual sales volume
年用电量　yearly power consumption
年蒸发蒸散量
　　annual evaporation & evapotranspiration capacity
年终调整　year-end adjustment
年终奖　year-end bonus
年终审计　year-end audit
年综合能源消费量
　　annual comprehensive energy consumption
年租　annual rental
黏度　viscosity
黏度分级　viscosity classification
黏附率　adhesion rate
黏附性　adhesion
黏结　cohere, cement, bind
黏结点　bonding node
黏结力　cohesive force
黏结强度　bonding strength
黏聚力　cohesion
黏聚性　viscidity
黏粒　clay particle
黏粒含量　clay particles content
黏土　clay
黏土灌浆　clay grouting
黏土矿物含量　clay minerals content
黏土沙障　clay sand barrier
黏土围堰止水　clay cofferdam sealing
黏性土　cohesive soil
黏性土滑坡　clay landslide
黏质黄土　clayey loess, viscous loess
黏滞系数　coefficient of viscosity
碾压法　rolling compaction method
碾压机　road roller, soil compactor
碾压机械　rolling compaction machinery
碾压设备　compaction equipment

N

碾压时间　duration of rolling compaction
碾压式土坝　rolled earthfill dam, rolled earth dam
碾压试验　rolling compaction test
鸟瞰图　bird's-eye view
镍含量　nickel content
拧紧扭矩　tightening torque
凝固强度　setting strength
凝固时间　setting time
凝灰结构　tuffaceous texture
凝灰岩　tuff
凝胶时间　gelation time
凝结时间　setting time
凝结水背压力　back pressure of steam trap
凝结水泵　condensate pump
凝结水管　condensation pipe
凝结水盘　condensating drain pan
凝结水箱　condensation water tank
牛顿流体　Newtonian fluid
牛轭湖　oxbow lake
牛轭湖相　banco facies
牛腿　bracket
扭断层　torsion fault
扭剪式高强度螺栓　torshear type high strength bolt
扭剪试验　torsional shear test
扭矩　torque
扭矩扳手　torque wrench
扭力　torque force
扭曲　twist
农田灌溉　agricultural irrigation
浓度　concentration
浓缩　concentration
女儿墙　parapet
暖棚法　greenhouse method
暖气片　heating radiator
暖温带　warm temperate zone

N

O

欧拉临界力　Euler's critical load
欧拉临界应力　Euler's critical stress
欧元　euro
欧洲货币　eurocurrency
欧洲货币单位　european currency unit(ECU)
欧洲美元　eurodollar
欧洲商业票据　eurocommercial paper
欧洲市场　euromarket
欧洲银团贷款　eurosyndicated loans
欧洲银行　Eurobank
偶发事故条款　contingency clause
偶发噪声　sporadic noise
偶然荷载　accidental load
偶然设计状况　occasional design state
偶然事件　accident, contingency
偶然误差　random error
偶然作用　accidental action
耦合　coupling
耦合损耗　coupling loss
耦合振动体系　coupled vibration system

P

pH 值　pH value, hydrogen ion concentration
PP 管材　PP pipe
PVC 管材　PVC pipe
P 波　P-wave
爬电距离　creepage distance
爬模　climbing formwork
爬升模板　climbing form
爬行　creeping
拍卖　auction, public sale
拍卖底价　upset price, auction reserve price
排出管　outlet pipe
排放标准(气)　emission standard
排放标准(水)　discharge standard
排放口　discharge outlet
排放浓度(气)　emission concentration
排放浓度(水)　effluent concentration
排放物　emission
排风风道　exhaust air duct
排风机　exhaust fan
排风温度　exhaust air temperature
排洪　flood discharge
排架　bent frame
排架式桥墩　bent-type pier
排列进路　route setting
排泥阀　mud valve
排气阀　exhaust valve
排气管　exhaust pipe
排气管道　exhaust duct
排气孔　exhaust vent
排气通风　exhaust ventilation
排气温度　exhaust temperature
排气系统　exhaust ventilation system
排气压力　exhaust pressure
排水　drainage
排水泵　discharge pump
排水泵站　drainage pumping station
排水槽　drainage channel
排水带通水量　the discharge capacity of prefabricated band-shaped drains
排水定额　quota of water discharge
排水法　drainage method
排水反复直接剪切试验　drainage repeated direct shear strength test
排水干沟　main drainage ditch
排水干管　trunk drain
排水工程　sewage (waste water) engineering
排水沟　drainage ditch
排水固结　drainage consolidation
排水管　drainage pipe
排水管道　discharge pipe
排水涵洞　drainage culvert, discharge culvert
排水横坡　drainage cross slope
排水量　water discharge, displacement
排水盲沟　drainage blind ditch, pipeline, trench
排水明沟　drainage open ditch
排水区　discharge area
排水渠　drainage channel, discharge canal, offtake
排水砂井　drainage sand well
排水设施　wastewater facilities
排水系统　sewerage system, drainage system
排水制度　sewer system
排水总管　main drain
排土场　refuse dump
排土场平面图　waste dump plan
排污阀　drain valve
排污管　sanitary sewer, foul sewer
排污降温池　sewage discharge cooling tank
排污权交易　emission trading
排泄　discharge
排泄系数　discharge coefficient
排序　ranking
排烟　smoke exhaust
排烟设施　fume extractor
排烟竖井　smoke shaft
排烟系统　smoke exhaust system

排烟罩	fume hood
排桩	campshed
牌价	list price, initial price
牌照	licence, licence plate
牌照费	licence fee, permit fee
牌照税	permit fee, license tax, plate tax
派发红股	bonus issue, scrip issue, bonus share
Π形梁	Π-shaped girder, Π-shaped beam
攀藤植物	vine
盘存	take inventory/stock
盘存单	inventory sheet
盘存截止日	inventory cut-off date
盘存折旧法	inventory method of depreciation
盘管	coil
盘右	face right
盘左	face left
判读	interpretation
判决	verdict, judge, judgment, sentence
判例	precedent, authority
判例法	case law, common law
旁路母线	interbus, bypass busbar
旁通管	bypass pipe
旁弯	sweep
旁向倾角	lateral dip
旁向重叠	lateral overlap
旁压试验	pressure-meter test (PMT)
旁压仪模量	modulus of pressure meter
旁站	on-site supervision
旁折光	lateral refraction
旁证	collateral evidence
旁注	marginal note, sidenote
抛撑	throwing support
抛锚险	breakdown cover
抛石	riprap
抛石防护	riprapping protection
刨床	planer, planing machine
跑车方式	vehicle moved procedure
炮检距	source-receiver offset
炮眼	blasthole
炮眼痕迹保存率	preservation rate of blasthole trace
泡沫沥青	foamed asphalt
泡沫灭火剂	foam fire extinguishing agent
泡沫灭火器	foam fire extinguisher
泡沫灭火系统	foam extinguishing system
陪审团	jury
培训	training
培训班	training course
培训计划	training program
培训评估	training evaluation
培养皿	culture dish
赔偿	indemnify, indemnification, compensate, compensation, reimburse, reimbursement, restitution
赔偿保证书	letter of indemnity
赔偿理算	adjustment of claim
赔偿契约	deed of indemnity
赔偿协议	indemnity agreement
赔偿责任	indemnity liability
赔偿总额	aggregate limit of indemnity
赔付率	claim ratio, loss ratio
赔款	indemnity, damages, compensation
赔款准备金	claim reserve
配电	power distribution
配电盘	switchboard
配电盘	electric switchboard
配电屏	power distribution panel
配电所	distribution substation
配电网	power distribution network
配电箱	distribution box
配额	quota, ration
配箍率	stirrup reinforcement ratio
配轨	rail positioning
配合比	mix proportion
配合比设计	mix proportion design
配合比选定试验	mix proportion selection test
配合辅助工程费	cost of coordination and supporting works
配件	accessories, fittings, parts, mountings
配件检修中心	repair center for spare parts
配件配送中心	distribution for spare parts
配筋	reinforcement
配筋不足	under-reinforced
配筋率	reinforcement ratio
配筋砌体	reinforced masonry
配筋砌体构件	reinforced masonry structure
配料	batching
配料仓	batching bin
配模	allotype
配盘	drum allocation
配属机车	allocated locomotives
配水点	water distribution point
配水管道	water distribution pipeline
配水管网	distribution system, pipe system
配套工程	supporting works, auxiliary project
配线	wiring
配线表	wiring schedule
配线箱	wiring closet, distribution box
配砟整形车	ballast distributing and profiling car

配制	preparation
配制强度	preparation strength
配置数据	configuration data
配重块	balancing weight
喷播植草	grass sowing by spraying
喷出岩	extrusive rock
喷大板切割法	large slab spraying and cutting method
喷混植生	spray sowing
喷浆	guniting
喷浆机	shotcrete machine
喷口送风	air supply from nozzle outlet
喷锚衬砌	shotcrete and bolt lining
喷锚支护	shotcrete and rockbolt support
喷抛丸设备	shot peening equipment
喷漆机	painting machine
喷漆库	painting workshop
喷漆库线	painting track
喷气孔水	fumarole water
喷枪	spray gun
喷砂除锈	derusting by sandblast
喷射混凝土	shotcrete
喷射混凝土机械手	shotcreting manipulator, shotcreting robot
喷射混凝土修理	repair by shotcreting
喷水	water spray
喷水消防系统	sprinkler system
喷涂聚脲防水涂料	spray polyurea waterproofing coating
喷雾防尘装置	moist dust control system
喷嘴	nozzle
盆地	basin
盆式橡胶支座	pot rubber bearing
棚洞	shed tunnel
硼砂	borax
膨胀管	expansion pipe
膨胀剂	swelling agent
膨胀接头	expansion joint
膨胀力	swelling force
膨胀量	swelling capacity
膨胀率	swelling ratio
膨胀锚杆	expandable bolt
膨胀潜势	swelling potential
膨胀试验	expansion test
膨胀水泥	expansive cement
膨胀水箱	expansion tank
膨胀土	swelling soil
膨胀土改良	improvement of swelling soil
膨胀土滑坡	expansive soil landslide
膨胀土路基	swelling soil subgrade
膨胀压力	swelling pressure
膨胀岩	swelling rock
碰壳保护	shell leakage protection
碰损破碎险	risk of clash and breakage
碰撞	collide, collision
碰撞检查	collision detection, clash detection
碰撞险	collision insurance
批次	lot, batch
批单	endorsement, indorsement
批发	wholesale
批发价	wholesale price, trade price
批发商	distributor, wholesaler, wholesale dealer
批发业务	wholesale business
批复概算	approved budgetary estimate
批量生产	batch production, mass production
批注	indorse, endorse
批准	approval
批准程序	procedure of approval
批准的	approved
批准的变更	approved variation
批准的供货商名单	approved suppliers list
批准的进度计划	accepted programme, approved programme
批准的控制估算	initial approved cost (IAC)
批准的投标人名单	approved bidders list, approved tenderers list, prequalified bidders/tenderers
批准的延期	authorized extension
批准合同	contract endorsement
批准用于施工图纸	drawings issued "approved for construction" (AFC)
批准用于详细工程设计图纸	drawing issued "approved for design" (AFD)
劈理	cleavage
劈裂法	splitting method
劈裂抗拉强度	splitting tensile strength
劈裂试验(巴西试验)	split test (Brazilian test)
皮带输送机	belt conveyor
皮重	tare, tare weight (gross)
临近物业	adjacent property
疲劳	fatigue
疲劳列车	fatigue train
疲劳裂缝	fatigue crack
疲劳强度	fatigue strength
疲劳曲线斜率	slope of fatigue curve
疲劳容许应力幅度	allowable stress amplitude of fatigue
疲劳失效	fatigue failure
疲劳试验	fatigue test
疲劳性能	fatigue behaviour
疲劳验算	fatigue check
疲劳应力幅	fatigue stress amplitude

疲劳阻力	fatigue resistance
匹配	matching
偏差	deviation
偏差分析	deviation analysis
偏光显微镜	polarized microscope
偏极继电器	polar biased relay
偏角	deflection angle
偏角法	declination method
偏离折价	priced deviation
偏心荷载	eccentric load
偏心矩	eccentric moment
偏心距增大系数	eccentricity amplification coefficient
偏心块起振试验	eccentric block vibration test
偏心率	eccentricity ratio
偏心受拉	eccentrically tensioned
偏心受压	eccentric compression
偏心受压构件	eccentric compressive member
偏心压力法	eccentric compressive method
偏心影响系数	eccentric influence coefficient
偏压衬砌	asymmetrically-loaded lining
偏压力	asymmetrical pressure
偏压隧道	asymmetrically-loaded tunnel
偏移	deviation, offset
偏移距	offset distance
偏移模量	offset modulus
偏载系数	unbalance loading factor
偏振模色散	polarization mode dispersion
片理	schistosity
片麻岩	gneiss
片麻状构造	gneissic
片石	rubble
片石混凝土	rubble concrete
片石气冷路基	air-cooled rubble embankment
片蚀	sheet erosion
片毡	flake surfaced asphalt felt
片状	schistose
片状层	sheet layer
片状颗粒	flaky particle
片状指数	flake index, schistose index, flakiness index
漂浮物	drifts
漂浮油	floating oil
漂石	boulder
漂石土	bouldery soil
漂移测试	drift test
票额屏	information display of tickets
票汇	remittance by banker's draft
票据	document, bill, paper, note, instrument
票据迟到拒绝承兑	dishonour by non-acceptance
票据迟到拒绝付款	dishonour by non-payment
票据打印机	voucher printer
票据拒付证明	protest of bill
票据期限	tenor
票据贴现率	bill rate, acceptance rate
票面价值	par, par value, nominal value
票面金额	face amount (value), nominal value
票务	ticketing
票证	coupon
拼接板	splice plate
拼装式桥墩	prefabricated bridge pier
贫水区	water-poor zone
频差	frequency difference
频发噪声	frequent noise
频率	frequency
频率曲线	frequency curve
频率式轨道电路	frequency track circuit
频率特性	frequency characteristic
频率同步	frequency synchronization
频率响应	frequency response
频率准确度	frequency accuracy
频谱	frequency spectrum
频谱分析	frequency spectrum analysis
频谱修正量	frequency spectrum correction
频闪效应	stroboscopic effect
频闪装置	flickering device
频域	frequency domain
频域分辨率	frequency domain resolution
频遇组合	frequent combination
品牌	brand
品行证明书	character reference
品质	quality
品质检验证书	inspection certificate of quality
品质证明	certificate of quality, hallmark
聘请	engage, retain
聘请费	retainer fee
聘用	engage, retain
平安险	free from particular average (FPA)
平板车	flat truck (lorry), platform truck
平板荷载试验	slab loading test
平板式混凝土振捣器	plate concrete vibrator
平板拖车	trailer flat
平板型网架	plate-type space grid
平板仪	plane-table
平板仪测量	plane table survey
平板仪测图	plane table mapping
平板载荷试验	plate loading test
平板支座	plate bearing
平差值	adjusted value
平导	parallel heading

平等互利　equality and mutual benefit
平等交换　give-and-take
平等原则　principle of equality
平底船　barge
平地机　grader
平顶冰川　flat-top glacier
平顶山　mesa
平动—扭转耦联　translation-torsion coupling
平过道　cross-track passage
平衡表　balance sheet
平衡传输线　balanced transmission line
平衡负载　balanced load
平衡账户　balancing account
平价　par
平价汇率　par exchange rate
平交道口　level crossing, grade crossing
平截面假定　plane cross-section assumption
平距　horizontal distance
平均保险费　level premium
平均单位成本　average unit cost
平均端到端延迟(传输时间)　mean end-to-end transfer delay
平均风速　average wind velocity
平均工时数　average hours of work
平均功率因数　mean power factor
平均固结度　average degree of consolidation
平均海(水)面　mean sea level
平均厚度法　average thickness method
平均还款期　average repayment maturity
平均恢复前时间　mean time to restoration
平均积雪深度　average snow depth
平均价格　average price
平均年降雨量　mean annual rainfall/precipitation
平均年限折旧法　straight line method of depreciation
平均皮重　average tare
平均曲率半径　mean radius of curvature
平均时用水量　average hourly water consumption
平均使用年限　average life
平均停工时间　mean down time
平均无功功率　average reactive power
平均无故障时间　mean time between failures
平均误差　average error
平均线性超挖量　average linear overexcavation
平均有功功率　average active power
平均有效电压　root mean square voltage, r.m.s voltage
平均照度　average illumination
平均折旧法　average depreciation method, linear depreciation method
平均直径　average diameter
平均值　average value
平流沉淀池　horizontal flow sedimentation tank
平流沉砂池　horizontal flow grit chamber
平路机　road grader
平面标准箱位　container slot
平面布置　plane layout
平面布置图　layout plan
平面尺寸　plan view size
平面调车区集中联锁　centralized interlocking for flat shunting area
平面管节点　uniplanar tubular joint
平面监测网　horizontal monitoring control network
平面交叉　level crossing
平面结构　plane structure
平面控制测量　horizontal control survey
平面控制点　horizontal control point
平面控制网　horizontal control network
平面溜放测试　plane rolling test
平面翘曲　plane warping
平面曲线　horizontal curve
平面曲线测设　plane curve location
平面设计　layout design
平面渗透系数　coefficient of planar permeability
平面示意图　schematic plan
平面疏解　plane untwining
平面图　plan
平面位置　plane position
平面应变试验　plane strain test
平面坐标　plane coordinates
平刨　plane
平坡　flat slope
平时通风　peacetime ventilation
平水期　normal flow period
平顺性(接触线)　straightness
平台　platform
平台宽度　width of berm
平头式牵引车　flat-head tractor
平推法　flat stacking
平腕臂　top cantilever tube
平稳运行　smooth running
平巷　heading
平行不整合接触　parallel unconformity contact
平行贷款　parallel loans
平行导坑　parallel adit, parallel heading
平行导坑法　prediction by parallel heading
平行工序　parallel process
平行检验　parallel inspection
平行检验报告　parallel testing report
平行进路　parallel route

平行市场	parallel market
平行试验	parallel test
平行作业	parallel operation
平旋桥	swing bridge
平移断层	parallel displacement fault
平原	plain
平整度	flatness, smoothness
平整土地测量	survey for land smoothing
平直度	straightness
评标	evaluation of bids, bid evaluation, tender evaluation
评标报告	report on bid evaluation
评标价	evaluated bid price
评标委员会	bid evaluation committee
评定	evaluation
评定标准	evaluation standard
评定方法	evaluation method
评定价值	appraised value
评定结论	evaluation result
评定指标	evaluation index
评分比较法	scoring model method
评估	evaluation, appraisal, assessment
评估过程	evaluation process
评估使用年限	estimated service life
评估因素	evaluation factor
评价标准	evaluation criteria
评价程序	evaluation procedure
评价意见	comment, observation
评审期	review period
评审委员会	board of review
凭单	indenture, document
凭单付款	remittance against documents
凭单证付款	payable against documents
凭单支票	voucher check
凭发票付款	payment on invoice
凭规格、等级或标准买卖	sale by specification, grade or standard
凭事先通知终止合同	termination by notice
凭样品成交	sale by sample
凭账单付款	payment on statement
凭证	document, voucher, scrip
屏蔽地线	shielded ground wire
屏蔽接地	shield earthing
屏蔽线	shielded wire
坡道	slope, ramp, grade
坡道阻力	gradient resistance
坡顶	slope top
坡度	gradient
坡度标	gradient post
坡度测设	grade location
坡度差	difference in gradient
坡度尺	slope scale
坡度减缓	gradient elimination
坡度牵出线	draw-out track at grade
坡度折减	gradient compensation, gradient reduction
坡段	grade section
坡段长度	length of grade section
坡积裙	talus apron
坡积土	slope wash
坡积物	slope wash
坡积相	slope wash facies
坡脚	slope toe
坡立谷	polje
坡面	slope face
坡桥	bridge on slope
坡腰	mid-slope
破冰体	pier nose (to break up or deflect floating ice or drifts)
破产	bankruptcy, bankrupt, insolvency, insolvent
破产案产业管理人	receiver
破产产业管理人	administrator in a bankrupt estate
破产倒闭	bankruptcy
破产法	act of insolvency, act of bankruptcy, insolvent law
破产法案	bankruptcy act
破产管理人	bankruptcy administrator
破产清算人	insolvency assignee, liquidator
破产清算书	statement of liquidation
破产人的债权人	creditor of bankruptcy
破产债务人	insolvent debtor
破产者	bankrupt, insolvent
破产资产管理人	assignee in bankruptcy
破封	break a seal
破坏比	failure ratio
破坏荷载	failure load
破坏阶段设计法	plastic stage design method
破坏机理	failure mechanism
破坏模式	failure mode
破坏强度	breaking strength
破坏试验	break-down test
破坏、损失及花费	damages, losses and expenses
破坏行为	sabotage
破坏性试验	destructive test
破劈理	fracture cleavage
破碎机	cracker
破碎岩滑坡	fractured rock landslide
破损风险	risk of breakage
破损检验	destructive test
破损阶段设计法	plastic stage design method
剖面	section

剖面图 sectional drawing, sectional drawing, profile	普速铁路 conventional speed railway

剖面图　sectional drawing, sectional drawing, profile
剖面线　section line
铺草皮　turfing
铺底流动资金　initial operation fund
铺地砖　tile
铺管　piping
铺管机　pipe layer
铺轨　rail laying
铺轨长度　track laying length
铺轨机　track-laying machine
铺轨列车　track-laying train
铺架工程　track laying and girder erecting works
铺架基地　track laying and girder erecting base
铺路机　paving machine, paver
铺面　paving
铺面垫层　pavement bedding course
铺面基层　pavement base course
铺面面层　pavement surface course
铺面设计荷载　design load of pavement
铺面砖　tiling
铺砌　paving
铺设　pave, placing
铺设机　laydown machine
铺网法　fabric sheet reinforced earth
铺筑　lay
普惠制　generalized system of preferences (GSP)
普惠制单据　generalized system of preferences documents
普速车场　conventional train yard
普速铁路　conventional speed railway
普通测量学　elementary geodesy
普通承兑　general acceptance
普通单网无线覆盖　single coverage
普通地图　general map
普通法　common law
普通法系　common law system
普通钢筋　common steel bar
普通钢筋强度等级　strength class of steel bar
普通工人　general labour, unskilled labour
普通股　equity share
普通硅酸盐水泥　ordinary Portland cement
普通合伙　general partnership
普通汇票　clean draft
普通混凝土　common concrete
普通货物站台　common freight platform
普通快滤池　common rapid filter
普通路由封装　generic routing encapsulation (GRE)
普通年金　ordinary annuity
普通日记簿　general journal
普通事故保险　ordinary accident insurance
普通载货汽车　ordinary freight truck
普通凿井法施工测量　construction survey of conventional shaft sinking method
普通站台　common platform
普通支票　open cheque
曝气沉砂池　aeration grit chamber
曝气生物滤池　biological aerated filter (BAF)

Q

七氟丙烷灭火系统	seven fluorin propane fire extinguishing system
栖息地	habitat
期初差额	opening balance
期初余额	initial balance, beginning balance, opening balance
期汇	forward exchange
期货	forward, futures
期货差价	forward margin
期货抵补	forward cover
期货订单	order for future delivery
期货汇率	forward exchange rate
期货价格	forward price, futures price
期货交易	futures, forward dealings, futures dealings
期货贸易	futures trading
期货市场	futures market
期间成本	interim cost
期间费用	interim expenses
期满	expire, expiration, expiry
期满日	date of expiration (expiry)
期末存货	ending inventory, closing stock
期末余额	ending balance, closing balance
期票	promissory note, term bill
期权	option
期权购买价	option purchase price
期权交易定金	option money
期权买方	option buyer
期权卖方	option seller
期限	period, term, duration
期中财务报表	interim financial statement
期中付款	interim payment
期中付款证书	interim payment certificate
期中审计	interim audit
期中索赔	interim claim
期中验收证书	interim acceptance certificate
期中业绩	interim performance
期中支付证书	interim payment certificate (IPC)
期中资产负债表	interim balance sheet
欺诈行为	barratry, fraudulent act, fraudulent practice
7d 饱和无侧限抗压强度	7d saturated unconfined compressive strength
其他材料	other materials
其他材料费	other material expenses
其他费	other charges
其他机械	other machines
其他有关费用	other related expenses
其他站线	other station tracks
歧视	discrimination, prejudice
棋盘格式构造	chess board structure
起爆	detonation
起爆器	blaster
起保日	attachment date
起草	draft, draw
起草合同	draft a contract, draw up a contract
起草纪要	draft of minutes
起测基点	starting datum mark
起长货物	lengthy cargo
起程运输险	over carriage risk
起出	exceed, excess
起道	track lifting
起道钉机	spike puller
起道机	track lifting tool, track jack
起吊套管	hoist sleeving
起动缓坡	gentle slope for starting
起额保险	over insurance
起额条款	excess clause
起拱点	springline
起拱线	springing line
起居室	living room
起落架	chassis
起模点	start location in the TSM
起讫里程	beginning and ending mileage
起砂	chalking
起升高度	elevating height
起始点(日)	starting-point
起始数据	initial data, known data

起始数据误差　initial data error
起诉　sue, charge, accuse, take legal action, prosecution
起诉人　suitor, complainant, plaintiff
起诉书　bill of complaint
起算点（日）　starting-point
起息日　date of value, value date
起运国　country of departure
起重船　pontoon crane, floating crane
起重横梁　transverse floorbeam used for hoisting operation
起重葫芦　hoist crane
起重机　crane
起重机船　crane barge
起重机荷载　crane load
起重机梁　crane girder
起重绞车　crane winch
企业　enterprise
企业财产保险　enterprise property insurance
企业贷款　business loan
企业定额测定费　enterprise quota measurement fee
企业法　law of enterprises
企业附属石油库　oil depot attached to enterprise
企业管理　business management
企业管理费　enterprise management fee
企业国有化　nationalization of enterprise
企业合并　amalgamation of enterprises, merge
企业环境风险指数　business environmental risk index
企业级项目管理　enterprise project management
企业集团　group of enterprise
企业家　enterpriser, entrepreneur
企业社会责任　corporate social responsibility
企业业主　corporate owner
启动　mobilization, initiation, startup
启动电池　activated battery
启动费　mobilization fee
启动器　initiator
启动时间　starting time
启封　unpack
启运港　port of departure
气场式风速风向传感器　gas field wind speed and direction sensor
气锤　air hammer
气动力　aerodynamic force
气动阻力系数　aerodynamic drag factor
气浮池　floatation tank
气浮溶气罐　dissloved air vessel

气焊　acetylene welding, gas welding
气焊工　gas welder
气候　climate
气候补偿器　climate compensator
气候特征　climate characteristics
气候条件　climatic conditions
气候异常情况　climate extremes
气孔构造　vesicular structure
气力输送　pneumatic conveying
气量法　gasometric method
气流组织　airflow organization
气密层　air tightness layer
气密性材料　air tightness material
气密性混凝土　airtight concrete
气密性试验　air tightness test
气囊法　rubber balloon method
气囊式容积测定仪　rubber balloon volume meter
气泡　bubble
气泡间距　air bubble spacing
气泡间距系数　bubble spacing coefficient
气溶胶灭火剂　aerosol fire extinguishing agent
气溶胶灭火系统　gas aerosol fire extinguishing system
气态水　vaporous water
气体传递法　gas transfer method
气体绝缘组合电器　gas insulated switchgear (GIS)
气体灭火剂　gas fire extinguishing agent
气体体积滴定法　volumetric method of gas volume
气温　air temperature
气温年较差　annual temperature range
气温日较差　diurnal temperature range
气温最大月平均日较差　maximum monthly average diurnal temperature range
气相　gaseous phase
气相色谱仪　gas chromatograph
气象　meteorology
气象监测　meteorological monitoring
气象台　weather station
气象条件　meteorological condition
气象修正　meteorological correction
气象预报　weather forecast
气象资料　meteorological data
气压表　gas-pressure meter
气压给水　pneumatic water supply
气压供水设备　air pressure water supply equipment
气压灌浆泵　air pressure grouting pump
气压焊　gas pressure welding, oxy-acetylene welding
气压焊轨车　gas pressure rail welding machine
气压监测设备　air pressure monitoring device
气压密封指数　pressurized seal index

气压水罐　air-pressure water tank
气源热泵　gas source thermal pump
弃方量　discarded earthwork volume
弃权条款　waiver clause
弃土　spoil
弃土场　spoil area
弃土场协议　spoil ground agreement
弃土挡土墙　retaining wall
弃土堆　spoil bank
弃土坑　dump pit
弃土石方　waste soil and rock volume
弃渣　cuttings, muck
弃渣场　spoil area, spoil disposal area, muck disposal area
弃渣防护　muck protection
汽车起重机　truck crane, lorry crane
汽车运价　truck freight price
汽车运价率　truck freight price rate
汽车运输　delivering by truck
汽车运输便道　temporary truck road
汽车运输便道运距　delivery distance by temporary truck road
汽锤　steam hammer
汽笛　siren, whistle
汽—水换热器　steam-water heat exchanger
汽油捣固镐　gasoline tamping pick
汽油捣固机　gasoline tamping machine
契约　covenant, deed, indenture, contract
契约废除证明　certificate of rescission
契约式合营　contractual joint venture
契约式联营合同　contractual joint-venture contract
砌块　building block
砌块砌体结构　block masonry structure
砌块强度等级　strength class of masonry block
砌石工程　stonework
砌体　masonry
砌体材料最低强度等级　lowest strength class of masonry material
砌体结构局部尺寸限值　local dimension limits of masonry structure
砌体结构总高度限值　limiting value for total height of masonry structure
砌体强度　masonry strength
砌体强度标准值　standard value of masonry strength
砌体强度等级　strength grade of masonry
砌体砂浆　masonry mortar
砌体式声屏障　masonry sound barrier
砌体质量检验　quality inspection of masonry
砌筑墙体　masonry wall
砌筑体　masonry

器材　equipment, material
千分表　dial indicator
千斤顶　jack
千枚岩　phyllite
千枚状构造　phyllitic structure
千糜岩　phyllonite
千兆以太网　Gigabit Ethernet(GE)
迁移　remove, removal, relocation
迁移费　compensation for removal
牵出线　shunting neck, switching lead, lead track, draw-out track
牵头承包商　lead contractor
牵头方　lead partner
牵引变电所　traction substation (TS, TSS)
牵引变压器　traction transformer
牵引变压器接线形式　winding connection of traction transformer
牵引车　tractor
牵引电流　traction current
牵引定数　tonnage rating
牵引供电系统　traction power supply system
牵引供电系统仿真　traction power supply system simulation
牵引供电远动系统　remote control system of traction power supply, supervisory control and data acquisition system (SCADA)
牵引回流　traction return current
牵引回流横向连接　traction return current transverse link
牵引交路　traction routing
牵引力　tractive force, tractive effort
牵引能耗　traction energy consumption
牵引入　pull-in
牵引时分　traction time
牵引式滑坡　traction-type landslide
牵引网　contact line system, traction network
牵引网等效阻抗　equivalent impedance of traction network, equivalent impedance of contact line system
牵引网电压损失　voltage loss of traction network, voltage loss of contact line system
牵引网干扰电流　interference current of traction network, interference current of contact line system
牵引网阻抗　impedance of traction network, impedance of contact line system
牵引小车　pushing carriage
牵引褶曲　drag fold
牵引褶皱　drag fold
牵引质量　tractive tonnage, tractive mass

牵引种类 type of traction
牵纵拐肘 escapement
铅垂向 Z 振级 vertical Z vibration degree
铅矾 anglesite
铅含量 lead content
铅护套 lead sheath
铅酸免维护蓄电池 lead-acid maintenance-free battery
签单即付运费 bill-of-lading freight
签订 enter into, conclude
签订协议 conclude an agreement
签订协议各方 parties to an agreement
签发 issue
签发日期 date of issue
签发证书 grant a certificate, issue a certificate
签发最终付款证书 issue of FPC (final payment certificate)
签名 signature
签收 sign for, receipt
签署 sign, affix
签署合同 execute a contract, sign a contract
签署同意 sign-off
签署者 signatory
签署证书 sign a certificate
签约前谈判 pre-acceptance negotiation
签约日期 date of contract
签证 visa
签证费 certificate fee
签注 endorse, endorsement, indorse, indorsement
签字 signature, sign
签字权 power to sign
签字受雇 sign on
签字样本 specimen signature
签字移交 sign over
前端采集设备 front-end acquisition device
前端分析 front-end analysis
前端附属设备 front-end auxiliary device
前端工程设计 front end engineering design (FEED)
前端设备 front-end equipment
前方交会 forward intersection
前附函 covering letter
前接点 front contact
前期工程 advance works
前期规划 advanced planning
前墙 front wall
前圈 front coil
前述条款 preceding clause
前提 precondition, prerequisite
前向纠错 forward error correction (FEC)
前移式叉车 forward forklift

前支承 front support
前重后轻的报价 front loaded tender/bid
钳工 benchworker
钳形电流表 clamp-on ammeter
潜孔钻 down-the-hole drill
潜孔钻机 down-the-hole drill
潜流水 subsurface flow
潜热 latent heat
潜蚀 suffosion
潜水泵 submersible pump
潜水面 phreatic surface
潜水钻机 submersible drill
潜在风险 potential risk
潜在客户 prospective client
潜在缺陷 latent defect
潜在缺陷保险 latent defects insurance
潜在市场 potential market
潜在投标人 potential tenderer
浅部缺陷 shallow defect
浅层滑坡 shallow landslide
浅层土加固 consolidation of shallow soil
浅成岩 hypabyssal rock
浅海相 neritic facies
浅基 shallow foundation
浅路堑 shallow cutting
浅埋车站 shallow-buried station
浅埋隧道 shallow tunnel
浅滩磨蚀角 shoal erosion angle
浅源地震 shallow focus earthquake
遣返 repatriation
遣返费 repatriation fee
遣散 demobilize, demobilization
遣散费 release pay, cost of repatriation, compensation for removal, separation pay
欠超高 cant deficiency, deficient superelevation
欠超高时变率 time-varying rate of cant deficiency
欠超高允许值 allowable cant deficiency
欠付费用 back charge
欠固结 underconsolidation
欠固结土 underconsolidated soil
欠据 debit instrument
欠款 debt, arrears, outstanding amount
欠条 credit note, IOU (I Owe You)
欠挖 under-excavation
欠薪 back pay
欠压告警 undervoltage alarm
欠债 debt, owe
堑顶包角 wrapping of slope top of cutting
嵌缝材料 caulking material
嵌入阶地 intrenched terrace

嵌岩灌注桩	rock-socketed bored cast-in-situ pile
嵌岩桩	rock-socketed pile
强冻胀	intensively frost heave
强冻胀土	strong frost heaving soil
强度	strength
强度包线	strength envelope
强度标准值	standard value of strength
强度等级	strength grade
强度设计值	design value of strength
强度试验	strength test
强度试验仪	strength tester
强度损失	strength loss
强度验算	strength checking computation
强度值	strength value
强风	strong breeze
强风化	heavy weathering, heavily weathered
强腐蚀	strong corrosion
强富水区	strong water abundance zone
强夯	dynamic compaction
强夯法	tamping method
强夯置换	dynamic compaction replacement
强加	impose, imposition
强剪弱弯	strong shear capacity and weak bending capacity
强节点弱构件	strong node weak component
强结合水	strongly bound water
强力保持率	strength retention rate
强烈侵蚀	extensive soil erosion
强迫振动法	forced vibration method
强迫振动频率	forced frequency
强迫振动试验	forced vibration test
强热带风暴	severe tropical storm
强酸酸度	acidity of strong acid
强透水性	strong permeability
强震动记录器	strong-motion recorder
强支撑框架	frame braced with strong bracing system
强制的	mandatory, compulsory
强制对中	forced centering
强制对中标	forced centering sign
强制令	injunction
强制滤速	compulsory filtration rate
强制破产	involuntary bankruptcy
强制清算	forced liquidation
强制式混凝土搅拌机	forced concrete mixer
强制式搅拌机	forced mixer
强制司法解决	obligatory judicial settlement
强制条款	compulsory clause
强制停业处理	compulsory liquidation
强制性保险	mandatory insurance
强制要求	mandatory requirement
强制执行	enforce, enforcement
强制仲裁	obligatory arbitration, compulsory arbitration, mandatory arbitration
强制注销	forced deregistration
强轴	major axis
强柱弱梁	strong column and weak beam
墙板结构	wall-slab structure
墙壁辐射采暖	radiant wall heating
墙梁	wall beam
墙面垂直度	degree of gravity vertical for wall surface
墙面平整度	wall planeness
墙面贴砖	wall tile
墙腰	wall waist
墙肢	wall-column
抢修	emergency repair
抢修基地	emergency maintenance base
乔木	arbor
桥	bridge
桥渡设计	design of bridge crossing
桥墩	pier
桥墩局部冲刷	local scour around pier
桥墩阻水面积	water blocking area of pier
桥涵	bridge and culvert
桥涵附属工程	ancillary engineering of bridge and culvert
桥涵计算跨径	calculated span of bridge and culvert
桥涵净跨径	clear span of bridge and culvert
桥涵扩孔	opening enlargement of bridge and culvert
桥涵水文	hydrology of bridge and culvert
桥跨结构	bridge superstructure
桥跨结构(上部结构)	bridge superstructure (superstructure)
桥栏杆	bridge rail
桥梁CAD	bridge CAD
桥梁标	bridge post
桥梁标准活载	standard live load of bridge
桥梁标准设计	standard design of bridge
桥梁测量	bridge survey
桥梁承载能力	load-bearing capacity of bridge
桥梁大修	bridge overhaul
桥梁道砟槽	ballast trough of bridge
桥梁的检测与评价	testing and evaluation of bridge
桥梁顶升	jacking up of bridge
桥梁动载试验	bridge dynamic load test
桥梁段声屏障	sound barrier on bridge
桥梁墩台定位	location of bridge pier and abutment
桥梁墩台防撞	collision prevention of pier/abutment
桥梁改造	bridge renovation
桥梁高度	bridge height

桥梁工程　bridge engineering, bridge works
桥梁合龙　bridge closure
桥梁荷载谱　bridge load spectrum
桥梁荷载试验　bridge load test
桥梁横向刚度　lateral rigidity of bridge
桥梁护轨　bridge guard rail
桥梁护木　guard timber of bridge
桥梁极限状态设计　limit state design of bridge
桥梁技术档案　bridge technical archives
桥梁加固　strengthening of bridge
桥梁检查车　bridge inspection car
桥梁检定　bridge rating
桥梁检定试验　bridge rating test
桥梁建筑界限　vehicular clearance limit above bridge floor
桥梁结构激振方法　excitation methods of bridge structure
桥梁经常保养　regular maintenance of bridge
桥梁控制测量　bridge construction control survey
桥梁跨度　bridge span
桥梁挠度　bridge deflection
桥梁疲劳剩余寿命　residual fatigue life of bridge
桥梁评价　bridge assessment
桥梁浅基　shallow foundation of bridge
桥梁浅基防护　protection of shallow foundation of bridge
桥梁全长　total length of bridge
桥梁上部结构　bridge superstructure
桥梁声屏障　sound barriers on bridges
桥梁水毁　bridge damage caused by scour and hydraulic loads
桥梁下部结构　bridge substructure
桥梁养护　bridge maintenance
桥梁支座砂浆　bridge bearing mortar
桥梁轴线测设　bridge axis location
桥梁专用检测车　inspection-vehicle used only for bridge
桥梁自振频率　natural frequency of bridge
桥梁综合维修　comprehensive repair of bridge
桥门架　portal frame, portal bracing
桥门楣梁　architrave
桥面　bridge deck, bridge floor
桥面板　bridge deck
桥面板单元　bridge deck plate unit, bridge deck slab unit
桥面板块　bridge deck plate, bridge deck slab
桥面保护层　wearing surface of bridge floor, protective layer of bridge floor
桥面防水层　waterproof layer of bridge floor
桥面横坡　cross slope of the deck surface
桥面净空　clearance above bridge deck
桥面伸缩装置　bridge deck expansion device
桥面系　bridge deck system
桥面纵坡　longitudinal slope of the deck surface
桥前壅水　backwater on the upstream side of bridge
桥前壅水高度　backwater height on the upstream side of bridge
桥前最大壅水高度　maximum backwater height in front of bridge
桥上人行道　pedestrian walkway on bridge
桥式起重机　bridge crane, overhead crane
桥隧守护电话　bridge and tunnel guard telephone
桥塔　bridge tower
桥台　abutment
桥台侧墙　side-wall of abutment
桥台新建辅助挡土墙加固法　abutment strengthening method by constructing new auxiliary retaining wall
桥头搭板　transition slab at bridge end
桥头引道　bridge approach
桥头引线　bridge approach
桥位　bridge site
桥位地形图　topographic map of bridge site
桥位地质剖面图　geological profile of bridge site
桥位选择　bridge site selection
桥下净空　clearance under bridge superstructure
桥下净空高度　under-clearance height of bridge
桥下一般冲刷　general scour under bridge
桥形接线　bridge connection
桥枕　bridge sleeper
桥址水文观测　hydrologic observation at bridge site
翘曲　warp, warping
撬棍　crow bar, track shifting bars
切层滑坡　insequent landslide
切沟　dissected valley
切换号码　handover number (HON)
切石机　stone cutting machine
切土刀　soil knife
切土器　soil miller
切线　tangent
切线支距法　method of tangent offsets
切向冻胀力　tangential frost-heave force
切向分力　tangential force components
切削加工　machining
侵犯商标权　trade mark infringement
侵犯专利权　infringement of patent, patent infringement
侵权行为　infringement, tort

侵权行为人　tortfeasor, infringer
侵权性质　nature of tort
侵入冰　intrusive ice
侵入限界绝缘　insulated joints located within clearance
侵入岩　intrusive rock
侵蚀　erosion
侵蚀程度　degree of erosion
侵蚀基准面　erosion basis
侵蚀阶地　erosion terrace
侵蚀类型　erosion type
侵蚀平原　erosion plain
侵蚀坡　erosion slope
侵蚀泉　erosional spring
侵蚀性二氧化碳　corrosive carbon dioxide
侵蚀性介质　aggressive media
侵吞公款　defalcation
侵限绝缘测试　intrusion insulation test
亲笔签名　autograph, sign manual
亲水矿物　hydrophilic mineral
亲水性　hydrophilicity
青苗补偿费　existing plant compensation cost
轻便铁道　portable railway
轻度侵蚀　mild soil erosion
轻负荷臂　light load arm
轻骨料混凝土　lightweight aggregate concrete
轻瓦斯保护　light gas protection
轻物质　lightweight matter
轻物质含量　light matter content, content of material lighter than 2000kg/m³
轻型动力触探试验　light dynamic penetration test
轻型动力触探仪　light duty dynamic cone penetrometer
轻型轨道　light track
轻型轨道车　light rail car
轻型击实　light compaction
轻型击实试验　light compaction test
轻质混凝土　lightweight concrete
轻质墙　light-weight wall
轻作业　light work
氢氰酸　hydrocyanic acid
氢氧化物　hydroxide
倾倒变形　toppling deformation
倾覆　overturning
倾覆稳定系数　anti-overturning stability coefficient
倾角　dip angle
倾角仪　inclinometer
倾向　dip
倾向断层　dip fault
倾向节理　dip joint
倾斜　tilt, inclination
倾斜测量　oblique survey, tilt survey
倾斜产状　tilt occurrence
倾斜度　inclination
倾斜改正　oblique correction
倾斜观测　tilt observation
倾斜计算装置　tilt calculator
倾斜摄影　oblique photography
倾斜误差　tilt error
倾斜褶皱　skewed fold, inclined fold
清偿　liquidate
清偿不足额判决　deficiency judgement
清偿能力　liquidity
清偿责任　liability for satisfaction
清偿债务　discharge of debt, satisfy liabilities, liquidation of debt
清方　clearing
清分系统　clearing house system
清关　customs clearance, clearance
清关代理人　customs clearance agent
清关费　charges for customs clearance
清关证明　clear certificate
清关证书　customs clearance certificate
清绘　fair drawing
清基　stripping
清洁生产　clean production
清洁提单　clean bill of lading
清洁通风　cleaning ventilation
清孔　borehole cleaning
清理等级　cleaning class
清理费用　disposal cost
清理现场　site clearance
清扫　cleaning
清扫间　broom closet
清扫孔　cleaning hole
清扫口　cleanout
清筛道床　ballast cleaning
清水池　clear water reservoir
清税　tax clearance
清算　liquidation, clear an account, audit
清算代理人　clearing (clearance) agent
清算管理人　equity receiver
清算价值　liquidation value
清算银行　clearing bank
清洗箱　cleaning box
氰化物　cyanide
请求权　right of claim
请求人　claimant, claimer
穹窿　vault, dome

丘陵	hill
求积仪法	planimeter method
求助按钮	call button
求助系统	call system
求助主机	host for call system
球头挂板	ball-clevis
球头挂钩	ball-hook
球头挂环	ball-eye
球形垫块	spherical cushion block
球形钢支座	spherical steel bearing
球形摄像机	dome camera
球形支座	spherical bearing
球状构造	orbicular structure
球状体	spheroid
裘布依理论式	Dupuit theoretical formula
区地质图	regional geological map
区段	district
区段调度	section dispatching
区段列车	district train
区段试运行证书	section commissioning certificate
区段锁闭	section locking
区段占用表示	section occupation indication
区段站	district station
区间	section
区间闭塞	section blocked
区间渡线	section crossover
区间封锁	section closed up
区间空闲	section cleared
区间联系电路	liaison circuit with block signaling
区间适配设备	section adapter
区间通过能力	section carrying capacity
区间通信	section communication
区间无缝线路	section continuously welded rail track
区间信号	section signal
区间引入线缆	section lead-in cable
区间占用	section occupied
区间自动拨叫试验	section automatic dialing test
区域	zone, region, area
区域导航定位系统	local navigation positioning system
区域地质	regional geology
区域地质测量	regional geological survey
区域供热	district heating
区域规划	zoning
区域划分图	zoning plan
区域基准时钟	local primary reference clock
区域基准钟	local primary reference source (LPRS)
区域级集成管理平台	regional integrated management platform
区域价格	zone price
区域监控中心	regional monitoring center
区域节点	zone node
区域水系图	regional hydrographic network map
区域网	block
区域网络	regional network
区域网平差	block adjustment
区域性编组站	regional marshalling station
曲梁	curved beam
曲率	curvature
曲率差	curvature difference
曲率系数	curvature coefficient
曲墙式衬砌	lining with curved walls
曲线半径	radius of curve
曲线标	curve post
曲线测设	setting-out of curve
曲线超高	curve superelevation, curve cant
曲线超高递减率	decline rate of curve superelevation
曲线超高递减顺坡率	superelevation runoff rate on curve, superelevation rate on curve
曲线法(又称"赢值法")	curve method (also known as "earned value management")
曲线附加阻力	additional curve resistance
曲线回归法	curvilinear regression method, curve estimation
曲线加宽	curve widening
曲线尖轨	curved switch rail
曲线控制点	curve control point
曲线偏角	curve deflection angle
曲线桥	curved bridge
曲线设计超高	designed superelevation of curve
曲线隧道	curved tunnel
曲线外侧加宽值	widening value at the outer side of the curved embankment
曲线要素	elements of curve
曲线圆顺度	curve smoothness
曲线正矢	curve versine
曲线阻力	curve resistance
曲中点	curve middle point
驱逐出境	deportation
屈服	yield
屈服点	yield point
屈服负荷	yield load
屈服力	yield point
屈服强度	yield strength
屈服强度(屈服点)	yield strength (yield point)
屈服强度下限	lower limit of yield strength
屈服准则	yield criterion

屈曲　buckling
趋肤深度　skin depth
(断层)趋势　strike
渠道　channel
渠道测量　canal survey
取得争议避免裁决委员会的决定
　　obtaining of DAAB decision
取费　charging
取费标准　charging standard
取款凭单　bill of credit
取料场　borrow area
取暖　heating
取票　collect ticket
取水口　water intake
取水头部　intake head
取送车　placing-in and taking-out of train
取送车费(调车费)
　　vehicle delivery expenses (shunting charge)
取土　soil borrowing
取土场　borrow area
取土场协议　borrow area agreement
取土坑　borrow pit
取土器　soil sampler
取消闭塞　cancel a block
取消付款　forfeiture of payment
取消合同　contract cancellation
取消进路　route cancellation
取消赎回权　foreclosure
取消资格　disqualification
取样　sampling
取样频率　sampling frequency
去耦网络　decoupling network
去斜处理　deskew processing
圈梁　ring beam
权　weight
权衡　trade off
权矩阵　weight matrix
权力　power
权力委托　delegation of authority
权利人　obligee
权利失效　lapse
权利要求书　claim
权利转让　assignment
权逆阵　inverse of weight matrix
权系数　weight coefficient
权限　line of authority
权限的解释　interpretation of authority
权益　equity, benefited interest, interest
权益比率　equity ratio
权益转让　assignment of interests

权益资本　equity capital
权责发生制　accrual basis
权责发生制会计　accrual basis accounting
权重　weighting
权重值　weighted value
全并联供电　entirely parallel feeding
全补偿链形悬挂
　　completely compensated overhead contact line, automatically tensioned overhead contact line
全补偿直链形悬挂
　　automatically tensioned polygonal contact line
全部重置成本　full reinstatement cost
全部付讫　payment in full
全部检验　one-hundred-percent inspection
全部接收　blanket acceptance
全部同意　blanket approval
全部预期费用　all expected costs
全部预期效益　all expected benefits
全长黏结锚杆　full-length bonded bolt
全程全网　the whole process the whole network
全程统一运费率　freight all kind rate, FAK rate
全程运价　whole course transport price
全断面道床夯实机
　　full section ballast consolidating machine
全断面道砟清筛机
　　full section ballast cleaning machine
全断面法　full-face method
全断面换砟机
　　full section ballast replacement machine
全断面隧道硬岩掘进机
　　full-face tunnel boring machine for hard rock
全断面预注浆　full-face pre-grouting
全额　in full
全额保险　full insurance, full value insurance
全额承保　full coverage
全额支付　payment in full
全额追索　full recourse
全封闭　fully enclosed
全封闭声屏障　enclosed sound barrier
全功能光通路
　　Optical Channel with full functionality (Och)
全过程风险　throughout risk
全焊钢桥　all-welded steel bridge
全缓解时间　full release time
全晶质结构　holocrystalline texture
全局码　global title (GT)
全空气系统　all air system
全孔一次性注浆　full hole one-time grouting
全立交　total interchange
全面采暖　overall heating

全面检修　overhaul
全面均衡分析　general equilibrium analysis
全面排风　overall air exhaust
全面通风　overall ventilation
全面质量管理　total quality control（TQC），total quality management
全能法测图　universal method of photogrammetric mapping
全球导航卫星定位系统　global navigation satellite system(GNSS)
全球定位系统　global positioning system（GPS）
全球卫星定位系统　global positioning system（GPS）
全球小区识别码　cell global identifier(CGI)
全权　full authority
全权处理　sole discretion
全权代表　plenipotentiary
全权委托客户　discretionary client
全权信托　discretionary trust
全热　total heat
全热换热器　full heat exchanger
全热交换效率　total heat exchange efficiency
全日负荷曲线　full-time load curve
全日平均电流　full-time average current
全生命期　life cycle
全生命周期成本　life-cycle costs
全生命周期评估　life cycle assessment
全式提单　long-form bill of lading
全寿命　life-cycle
全寿命周期　whole life cycle
全寿命周期费用　life-cycle cost（LCC）
全损　total loss
全套清洁已装船提单　full set of clean on board bills of lading
全套提单　full set of bills of lading, complete set of bills of lading
全套文件　full set of documents
全体人员　personnel
全网基准钟　principal reference clock(PRC)
全险　all risks（a/r, A. R.）
全新世　Holocene epoch
全新统　Holocene series
全压　total pressure
全淹没灭火系统　total flooding extinguishing system
全圆方向观测法　method of direction observation in rounds
全站仪　total station instruments
全站仪数字化测图　digital mapping with total station instruments
全制动时间　full braking time
全自动水准仪　auto level
泉点　spring point
泉群　spring groups
泉水　spring water
泉水温度计　spring thermometer
拳头钩　fist hook
缺乏证据　absence of proof, lack of evidence
缺货成本　stockout cost
缺水地区　water-deficient area
缺陷　defect
缺陷反射波　flaw echo
缺陷和拒收　defects and rejection
缺陷界面　defect interface
缺陷清单　defects list, flaw list, deficiency list
缺陷通知期　defects notification period（DNP）
缺陷通知期限的延长　extension of defects notification period
缺陷修补　defects remediation, remedying of defects
缺陷修补费用　cost of remedying defects
缺项材料　missing item of material
缺项设备　missing item of equipment
缺氧/好氧脱氮工艺　anoxic/oxic process
缺氧区　anoxic zone
确定赔偿额　assess the damages
确定授标　confirmation of award
确定性负债　determinable liability
确定性估算　definitive estimate
确切证据　conclusive evidence
确认保证　affirmative warranty
确认车　confirmation car
确认函　letter of acknowledgement
确认书　confirmation, letter of confirmation
确认样品　confirmation sample
确认银行　confirming bank
确认中心　acknowledgement center（AC）
裙房　podium
群体行为　mass behavior, group behavior
群体意识　collective consciousness
群桩　group of piles

R

燃点	ignition point, fire point
燃弧时间	arc time, arcing time
燃料动力费	fuel and power cost
燃料费	fuel cost
燃煤锅炉	coal-fired boiler
燃气锅炉	gas-fired boiler
燃气热水机组	gas-fired hot water unit
燃烧试验箱	combustion test chamber
燃烧体	combustible substance
燃烧性能	combustion performance
燃油热水机组	fuel oil hot water unit
燃油箱	fuel tank
让步措施	concession method
让价	price concession
让与	cede to, transfer
让与人	assignor
让与条件	conditions of grant
扰动地表	disturbed land surface
扰动地表面积	area of disturbed land surface
扰动土	disturbed soil
扰动土地整治率	treatment percentage of disturbed land
扰动土样	disturbed soil sample
扰动样	disturbed sample
扰流板	spoiler
绕渗	by-pass seepage
绕行地段	detouring section
绕组温升	temperature rise of winding
热棒路基	thermal pipe subgrade
热备份	hot standby
热备盘	hot spare drives
热备用	hot standby
热崩溃	thermal runaway
热泵	heat pump
热泵式空气调节器	heat-pump air conditioner
热插拔	hot plugging
热储	geothermal reservoir
热储盖层	geothermal reservoir caprock
热储构造	geothermal reservoir structure

热处理	heat treatment
热带风暴	tropical storm
热带气旋	tropical cyclone
热带气压	tropical atmospheric pressure
热岛效应	heat island effect
热电厂	thermal power plant
热电偶	thermoelectric couple
热分析	thermal analysis
热风采暖	hot air heating
热风幕	warm air curtain
热风速仪	thermal anemometer
热负荷	thermal load
热感应法	thermoinduction method
热管	heat pipe
热红外扫描	thermal-infrared scanning
热滑	hot running, energized inspection running
热计量表	heat meter
热接触	thermocontact
热浸镀锌	hot-dip galvanization
热浸镀锌钢	hot-dipped galvanized steel
热空气老化	hot air aging
热扩散系数	thermal diffusivity
热老化试验	heat aging test
热力继电器	thermal relay
热力膨胀阀	thermal expansion valve
热力入口	heat inlet
热力岩溶	thermal karst
热量装置	heat metering device
热流计	heat flow meter
热媒	heating medium
热媒参数	heating medium parameter
热敏电阻温度计	thermistor thermometer
热膨胀系数	coefficient of thermal expansion
热平衡	heat balance
热谱分析	thermal spectrum analysis
热熔防水卷材	torch-applied asphalt sheet
热熔胶粘剂	heat-melting adhesives
热熔连接	hot-melt conjunction

热融湖塘	thermokarst lake
热融滑塌	thaw slumping
热融滑坍	thawing landslide
热湿比	heat-humidity ratio
热湿交换	heat and moisture transfer
热水采暖	hot water heating
热水供应系统	hot water supply system
热水管	hot water pipe
热水锅炉	hot-water boiler
热水循环流量	hot water circulating flow
热塑性弹性体	thermoplastic elastomer
热塑性垫圈	thermoplastic gasket
热塑性聚烯烃（TPO）防水卷材 thermoplastic polyolefin (TPO) waterproof sheet
热塑性橡胶	thermoplastic rubber
热网	heating network
热稳定电流	thermal stability current, rated short-time withstand current
热稳定性	thermal stability
热压	hot pressing
热应力	thermal stress
热源	heat source
热轧	hot-rolling
热轧钢轨	hot-rolled rail
热轧钢筋	hot-rolled bar
热重分析	thermogravimetric analysis
热阻	thermal resistance
人防有效面积	effective area of civil air defence
人工边坡	artificial slope
人工标志	artificial mark
人工单价（又称"工资单价"） unit price of labor (also known as "unit salary")
人工捣实混凝土	hand-compacted concrete
人工地震试验	artificial earthquake test
人工防渗	artificial seepage prevention
人工费	labor cost
人工费价差	labor cost difference
人工费用	labour cost
人工分路	manual shunting
人工工时定额	standard labour hour (time)
人工护道	artificial berm
人工恢复	manual recovery
人工接地体	artificial earth electrode
人工节理	artificial joint
人工解锁	manual release
人工铺轨	manual track laying
人工风化	artificial weathering
人工砂	manufactured sand
人工湿地	artificial wetland, constructed wetland
人工填土	artificial fill
人工消耗量	labor consumption
人工消耗量定额	quota of labor consumption
人工源电磁频率测深法 artificial source electromagnetic frequency sounding method
人工杂填土	artificial miscellaneous fill
人工周转率	labour turnover rate
人工综合单价	all-in labour rate
人工座席	customer service representative (CSR)
人机界面	man-machine interface (MMI), driver-machine interface (DMI)
人激振动试验	artificial vibration test
人均小时产量	output per man-hour
人孔	manhole
人孔井盖	manhole cover
人力	manpower
人力搬运	hand haulage
人力曲线	manpower curves
人力施工	manual construction
人力资源	human resources, labour resources
人力资源管理	management of human resources
人民防空地下室	civil air defence basement
人民防空工程	civil air defence works
人群密度	crowd density
人群密度估计	crowd density estimation
人群异常行为检测 crowd abnormal behavior detection
人身保险	personal insurance, insurance for life
人身伤害	bodily injury, personal injury
人身伤害和财产损失 injury to persons and damage to property
人身事故	accident to workmen
人身意外保险	personal accident insurance
人身意外伤害险	life accident insurance
人身意外伤亡	accidental bodily injury
人身意外事故	personal accident
人身与财产损害	damage to persons and property
人事变动	changes in personnel
人事部门	personnel department
人事经理	staff manager, personnel manager
人体散热量	heat dissipation from occupants
人体散湿量	moisture release from occupants
人头税	head tax
人为风险	intentional risk
人为故障	human failure
人为坑洞	man-made cavities
人为拖延手段	intentional obstruction
人为误差	personal error
人为障碍	intentional obstruction
人文环境	humanistic environment
人行道	sidewalk

人行道荷载　pedestrian walkway load
人行过道　pedestrian cross-walk, foot crossing
人行横道　pedestrian crossing
人行桥　pedestrian bridge
人行天桥　pedestrian overpass
人员的健康和安全　health and safety of personnel
人员的招募　recruitment of persons
人员角色　people roles
人员配备　staffing
人员配备计划　manning schedule
人员招募　staff acquisition
人造大理石　artificial marble
人造立体效应　artificial stereoscopic effect
人字排水坡　herringbone drainage slope
人字坡道　double spur ramp, herring-bone ramp
刃脊　serrate ridge
刃脚　cutting edge
任命机构　appointing authority
任命证书　deed of appointment
任期　terms of office
任务　task
任务单　work order
任务进度表　objective schedule
任选目的港　optional port of destination
任选卸货港　optional port of discharge
任意带　arbitrary zone
任意投影　arbitrary projection
任意投影带　arbitrary projection zone
任意中央子午线　arbitrary central meridian
任意轴子午线　arbitrary axis meridian
韧度　toughness
韧性　ductility
日班　day shift
日报表　daily statement
日变　diurnal variation
日变化系数　daily variation coefficient
日常维修　routine maintenance, operational maintenance
日程表　schedule, agenda, itinerary
日工资　day rate, daily pay (wage)
日记账　journal
日技术服务费　daily technical service fee
日降雨量　daily rainfall
日接送量　daily reception amount
日解体能力　daily breaking-up capacity
日均到达箱　daily average quantity of container received
日均发货量　daily average volume of freight dispatched
日均发送箱　daily average quantity of container dispatched
日均中转箱　daily average quantity of container for transshipment
日均作业箱数　daily average handling quantity of container
日历　calendar
日历年　calendar year
日历日　calendar day
日历月　calendar month
日时间　time of day (ToD)
日息　daily interest, interest per diem
日用资金　day-to-day money
日照标准　sunlight standard
日志　diurnal journal, log book
冗余　redundancy
冗余结构测试　redundant structure test
冗余配置　redundancy configuration
荣誉证书　honorary certificate
容积　cubic measure, volume
容积率　plot ratio
容积热容量　volumetric heat capacity
容积式换热器　volumetric heat exchanger
容量　capacity
容量法　volumetric method
容砂瓶　sand containing bottle
容箱数　number of contained containers
容许变形值　allowable deformation value
容许沉降　allowable settlement
容许承载力　allowable bearing capacity
容许冲刷　allowable scour
容许高厚比　allowable ratio of height to sectional thickness
容许轨道温降　allowable rail temperature drop
容许轨道温升　allowable rail temperature rise
容许荷载　allowable load
容许抗拉强度　allowable tensile strength
容许弯曲拉伸应力　allowable bending tensile stress
容许强度检定　allowable strength rating
容许偏差　allowable deviation
容许设备温度　allowable equipment temperature
容许速度　allowable speed, permissible speed
容许土压力　allowable soil pressure
容许温差　allowable temperature difference
容许误差　allowable error, tolerance
容许信号　permissive signal
容许应力　allowable stress
容许应力法　allowable stress method
容许应力设计法　allowable stress design method
溶槽　karst groove
溶点　melting point
溶洞　karst cave

溶洞顶板　karst cave roof
溶洞距路基安全距离
　　safe distance between karst cave and subgrade
溶斗　doline funnel
溶痕　karst trace
溶剂　solvent
溶剂混溶法　solvent mixing method
溶解度　dissolubility
溶解性固体　dissolved solids
溶解性侵蚀　dissolved erosion
溶解氧　dissolved oxygen
溶孔　dissolution pore
溶滤变形系数
　　coefficient of leaching deformation
溶盘　solution pan
溶蚀　dissolution, solution
溶蚀裂隙　corrosion fissure
溶蚀准平原　karst peneplain
溶隙　solution crack, dissolved fissure
溶液除湿机　solution dehumidifier
溶液体积　solution volume
溶胀　swelling
熔断器　fuse
熔断器断丝报警　fuse burnout alarm
熔覆合金　cladding alloy
熔融分解　decomposition by fusion
熔丝　fuse
熔岩被　lava sheet
熔岩流　lava flow
熔岩流地形　lava flow landform
融沉　thaw collapse
融沉系数　thaw-settlement coefficient
融冻变形　thawing deformation
融冻泥流　solifluction
融化沉降量　thawing settlement
融化下沉系数　thaw subsidence coefficient
融化压缩系数　thaw-compressibility coefficient
融化指数　thawing index
融区　talik
融通　accommodation
融通背书　accommodation endorsement
融通背书人　accommodation endorser
融通票据　accommodation paper, accommodation bill, accommodation note
融通支票　accommodation check
融陷　thaw collapse
融陷性　thaw collapsibility
融资　finance, financing
融资费　financing charges
融资计划　financing plan

融资结构　financing structure
融资利率　financing interest rates
融资条件　financing terms
融资租赁　finance lease
柔性　flexibility
柔性墩　flexible pier
柔性防护网　flexible protective net
柔性防水套管　flexible waterproof casing
柔性接触网　flexible OCS
柔性接口铸铁管　flexible joint cast-iron pipe
柔性连接　flexible connection
柔性路面　flexible pavement
柔性桥墩　flexible pier
柔性系杆　flexible tie bar
柔性桩　flexible pile
揉皱　crumple
蠕变　creepage
蠕变变形　creep deformation
蠕变试验　creep test
蠕动　creep
蠕滑　creep
蠕移搬运　creep transport
乳化剂　emulsifier
入港费用　inward charges
入港申报　entry declaration
入港税
　　harbor dues, keelage, port charge, harbor duty
入户管　service pipe
入境　entrance
入境报关单　declaration inwards
入境签证　entrance visa, entry visa
入境签证处　immigration office
入境文件　entry documents
入境证书　entry certificate
入口电流　entrance current
入口平台　entrance platform
入库单　godown entry
入库许可证　permit for warehousing
入侵报警系统　intrusion alarm system
入侵防范　intrusion detection
入侵监测　intrusion detection
入侵检测　intrusion detection
入侵检测系统　intrusion detection system(IDS)
入侵预防系统　intrusion prevention system(IPS)
入渗系数　infiltration coefficient
入所轮修　alternative maintenance at inspection and service point
入土角　starting angle
入选的投标人　selected bidder (tenderer)
入选名单　short list

入账	enter up an account	软式透水管	flexible permeable hose
入账价格	entry price	软塑	soft-plastic
入字形构造	lambda type structure, λ-type structure	软通货	soft currency
褥垫层	cushion layer	软铜编织	flexible braided copper wire
软贷款	soft loan	软土	soft soil
软定位器	steady arm for curve line	软土基础	soft soil foundation
软管	hose	软土区路基	subgrade in mollisol region
软横跨	head-span	软土特性	characteristics of mollisol
软化水	softened water	软岩	soft rock
软化系数	softening coefficient	软硬岩接触带	soft and hard rock contact zone
软件	software	软质岩	soft rock
软件安全完整性等级	software safety integrity level	瑞典圆弧法	Swedish circle method
软件版本	software version	瑞雷波法	Rayleigh wave method
软件副本	soft copy	瑞雷面波	Rayleigh wave
软交换机	soft switch(SS)	瑞利波	Rayleigh wave
软块石	soft blocky stone	润滑油	lubricant
软母线	flexible busbar	润滑油液位	lubricating oil level
软黏土	soft clay	润湿剂	wetting agent
软弱夹层	weak intercalated layer	弱冻胀	weakly frost heave
软弱结构	weak structure	弱冻胀土	weak frost heaving soil
软弱结构面	weak structural plane	弱风化	slight weathering
软弱面	weak plane	弱腐蚀	weak corrosion
软弱土	soft soil	弱富水区	weak water abundance zone
软弱土层	weak soil layer	弱结合水	loosely bound water
软弱土地	weak soil	弱透水性	weak permeability
软弱围岩	weak surrounding rock	弱支撑框架	frame braced with weak bracing system
软石	soft stone	弱轴	minor axis

R

S

SAN 交换机　SAN switch
SF$_6$ 断路器　sulphur hexafluoride circuit-breaker, SF$_6$ circuit-breaker
SF$_6$ 封闭式组合电器　SF$_6$ enclosed switchgear
S 形构造　S-shaped structure
洒水车　motor flusher, spraying car, water truck
洒水喷头　sprinkler head
塞钉式钢轨接续线　plug bond
三班工作制　three-shift work
三边测量　trilateration
三边网　trilateration network
三叉式应变计　tri-directional strain gauge
三点法　three-point method
三点检查　route release by checking three sections
三点支承　three-point supporting
三叠纪　Triassic period
三叠系　Triassic system
三方晶系　trigonal system
三级排放标准　third class discharge standard
三级评定　third class assessment
三角测量　triangulation
三角点　triangulation point
三角高程测量　trigonometric leveling
三角高程导线测量　trigonometric level traverse-leveling
三角坑　twist, warp
三角控制网　triangulation control network
三角锁　triangulation chain
三角网　triangulation network
三角线　wye track
三角形法　triangle method
三角形角度闭合差　triangular closure error
三角形连接　delta connection
三角形枢纽　triangle junction terminal
三角形网　triangulation network
三角形网测量　triangular network survey
三角形屋架　triangular roof truss
三角堰　triangular weir
三角洲相　delta facies
三角锥体网架　triangular pyramid space grids
三铰拱　three-hinged arch
三铰拱桥　three hinged arch bridge
三脚架　tripod
三开对称道岔　three-way symmetrical turnout
三联井　trigeminy well
三七灰土　3∶7 lime/soil
三通阀　three-way valve
三通管　pipe tee
三维导线测量　three-dimensional traverse survey
三维立体景观　three-dimensional stereoscopic scenes
三维网　three-dimensional network
三显示自动闭塞　three-aspect automatic blocking
三相 V,v 结线　three-phase Vv connection
三相 V,v 结线牵引变压器　three-phase Vv connection traction transformer
三相 V,x 结线　three-phase Vx winding connection
三相 YN,d11 结线　three-phase（YN, d11）winding connection
三相一二相平衡结线　three-phase/two-phase balanced connection
三相一二相平衡牵引变压器　three-phase/two-phase balanced traction transformer
三相多段式电流保护　three-phase multi-stage section current protection
三相牵引变压器　three-phase traction transformer
三相四线制　three-phase four-wire system
三相同期性　three-phase synchronism
三相图　three phase diagram
三斜晶系　triclinic system
三轴不固结不排水剪试验　triaxial unconsolidated and undrained shear test
三轴不排水剪切试验　triaxial undrained shear test
三轴侧向应力　triaxial lateral stress
三轴剪切试验　triaxial shear test
三轴抗压强度　triaxial compressive strength
三轴伸长试验　triaxial extension test

三轴压缩　triaxial compression
三轴压缩试验　triaxial compression test
三轴仪　triaxial apparatus
三轴轴向应力　triaxial axial stress
3D 控制和规划　3D control and planning
3D 协调　3D coordination
3 人组成的争议避免裁决委员会
　　three-member DAAB
Ⅲ型轨道板预制场
　　precast yard for Ⅲ type track slab
伞括保险　umbrella cover
伞式责任保险　umbrella liability insurance
散堆装货区　bulk goods loading area
散堆装货物货场　bulk goods loading yard
散工　day work
散流器　air diffuser
散流器送风　diffuser air supply
散落堆积　scattered accumulation
散热量　heat dissipating capacity
散热器　radiator
散热器采暖　radiator heating
散热器调节阀　radiator valve
散热强度　heat dissipation intensity
散湿量　moisture release
散体材料桩　pile of granular material
散体力学　mechanics of granular media
散装材料　bulk material
散装的　bulk laden in bulk
散装货船　bulk cargo carrier
散装货物　bulk
散装水泥　bulk cement, loose cement
扫地杆　bottom horizontal tube, floor bracing
扫描　scanning
扫描分辨率　scanning resolution
扫描数字化　scan-digitizing
扫描样点数　number of scanning sampling point
扫描仪　scanner
扫尾工作清单　punch list
色灯电锁器联锁　interlocking by electric locks with color light-signals
色灯信号机　color-light signal
色度　chromaticity
色度色散系数　chromatic dispersion coefficient
色卢铁解答　Cerruti's solution
色品　chromaticity
色品图　chromaticity diagram
色品坐标　chromaticity coordinates
色谱标准溶液　chromatography standard solution
色谱间　chromatography room
色容差　color difference

色散特性　dispersion characteristics
色散系数　dispersion coefficient
色温　color temperature
森林公园　forest park
森林植被分布　distribution of forest vegetation
森林植被恢复费　forest vegetation recovery expense
杀毒软件　antivirus software
杀价　cut down
沙暴　sandstorm
沙地　sandy land
沙堆　dune
沙害　sand hazard
沙漠　desert
沙漠化土地　desertified land
沙漠相　desert facies
沙丘　sand dune
沙丘链　dune range
沙土液化　sandy soil liquefaction
沙障　sand barrier
沙州　shoal
砂　sand
砂坝　sandbank
砂坝相　sand bar facies
砂(污泥)斗　sand(sludge) hopper
砂浆　mortar
砂浆棒膨胀率　mortar bar expansion rate
砂浆饱满度　fullness of mortar
砂浆保水性　water retentivity of mortar
砂浆剥离　mortar peeling off
砂浆稠度　mortar consistency
砂浆稠度仪　mortar consistometer
砂浆分层度仪　mortar layering degree apparatus
砂浆含气量测定仪　mortar air content tester
砂浆搅拌机　grout mixer
砂浆抗压强度　compressive strength of mortar
砂浆抗压强度换算值　equivalent value for compressive strength of mortar
砂浆抗压试件　mortar compressive specimen
砂浆锚杆　mortar bolt
砂浆配合比　mortar mix ratio
砂浆配合比设计　mix proportion design of mortar
砂浆强度等级　strength class of mortar
砂浆剩余系数法　residual coefficient of mortar
砂浆弹性模量测定仪
　　mortar elasticity modulus tester
砂浆性能检验　performance test of mortar
砂类土　sandy soil
砂砾石　sandy gravel, sand and gravel
砂砾石、碎砖三合土
　　tabia with sandy gravel and broken brick

S

砂粒　sand grain
砂滤池　grit filter
砂面防水卷材　sand surfaced asphalt sheet
砂石桩复合地基　composite foundation with sandgravel piles
砂土　sandy soil
砂土液化　sandy soil liquefaction
砂楔　sand wedge
砂芯玻璃坩埚　sand core glass crucible
砂岩　sandstone
砂与骨料比　sand and aggregate ratio
砂质黄土　sandy loess
砂质黏土　sand clay
砂(碎石)桩　sand (gravel) pile
砂状　psammitic
砂嘴　spit
砂嘴相　sand spit phase
筛板塔　sieve-plate tower
筛分　sieving
筛分骨料　screening aggregate
筛分机　screening machine
筛孔　sieve pore
筛孔边长尺寸　side length size of sieve pore
筛孔尺寸　screen size
筛上剩余颗粒　remaining particles on sieve
筛上试样质量　mass of oversize sample on sieve
筛析法　sieve analysis method
筛析机　sifter
筛下试样质量　mass of undersized sample
筛选制　screen system
晒蓝　blue printing process
晒图机　blueprinter
山　mountain
山顶　mountaintop
山脊　mountain ridge
山间盆地　intermountane basin
山麓　piedmont
山麓冰川　piedmont glacier
山麓冲积平原　piedmont alluvial plain
山脉　mountain range
山坡　mountain slope, hillside
山丘　hill
山体　massif
山体滑坡　landslide
山字形构造　epsilon-type structure
删除的工作　omitted work
删减　omissions
闪避　dodge, evade, avoid
闪长玢岩　diorite-porphyrite
闪长岩　diorite
闪点　flash point
闪光电源　flashing power source
闪光对焊　flash butt welding
闪光(接触)焊　flash butt welding
闪光信号　flashing signal
闪红光带　red light strip flash
闪辉正煌岩　vogesite
闪络　flashover
闪络保护　flashover protection
闪络保护地线　ground electrode of flashover protection
闪斜煌斑岩　spessartite
闪锌矿　sphalerite
苫盖　cover
扇形张裂缝　fan-shaped tension crack
善意被背书人　bona-fide endorsee
善意持有人　bona-fide holder
善意过失　error in good faith
善意投标人　bona fide bidder
膳食供应　accommodation
伤害保险　injury insurance
伤亡人员　casualty
商标　trade mark, merchandise mark
商标所有权　ownership of trade marks
商定金额　agreed sum
商定条件　agreed terms
商法　law of merchant, commercial law, business law
商行　business, firm
商号　firm, house
商号票据　house bill
商会　chamber of commerce, chamber
商检人　surveyor
商贸行名录　trade directories
商品　commodity, goods, merchandise
商品混凝土　commercial concrete, ready-mixed concrete
商品混凝土车　ready-mixed concrete truck
商品价格　commodity price
商品检验　commodity inspection
商品交易会　trade fair
商品名称　name of commodity
商品目录　catalogue
商品盘存　merchandise inventory
商事法庭　commercial court
商谈　negotiate
商务　commerce, commercial affairs, trade
商务备选方案　alternative of financial nature
商务标　financial proposal, commercial proposal
商务标评审　commercial bid evaluation
商务参赞　commercial counselor

商务代表 commercial representative, trade representative
商务索赔 commercial claim
商务条款 commerce clause, commercial terms
商务写字楼 commercial office building
商务选择性报价 commercial alternative quotation
商业保险 commercial insurance
商业承兑汇票 commercial acceptance bill
商业代理行 commercial agency
商业贷款 commercial loan
商业单据 commercial paper
商业发票 commercial invoice
商业法规 commercial code
商业风险 commercial risk
商业公司 commercial company
商业广告 commercial
商业合同 commercial contract
商业汇票 commercial bill, commercial draft, trade bill
商业机构 business organization
商业交易 business transaction
商业可行性 business feasibility
商业秘密 business secret
商业票据 commercial paper
商业信贷 commercial credit
商业信函 commercial correspondence
商业信用证 commercial letter of credit
商业银行 commercial bank, merchant bank
商业折扣 commercial discount, trade discount
商业周期 business cycle
商住楼 commercial and residential building
上奥陶统 upper Ordovician series
上白垩统 upper Cretaceous series
上部尺寸 upper size
上部道床 upper ballast bed
上部道床碎石 gravel for upper ballast bed
上部定位索 upper cross-span wire
上部结构 superstructure
上部清液 supernatant
上层滞水 perched groundwater
上承式桥 deck bridge
上道试验 track test
上电锁闭测试 power-on locking test
上叠阶地 on-laid terrace
上二叠统 upper Permian series
上覆荷载 overlying load
上刚下柔多层房屋 upper rigid and lower flexible complex multistorey building
上更新统 upper Pleistocene series
上古生界 upper Palaeozoic erathem/group
上寒武统 upper Cambrian series
上跨 overpass
上联设备 uplink equipment
上泥盆统 upper Devonian series
上盘 top wall
上(晚)青白口世 upper (late) qingbaikouan epoch
上(晚)青白口统 upper (late) qingbaikouan series
上柔下刚多层房屋 upper flexible and lower rigid complex multistorey building
上三叠统 upper Triassic series
上升泉 ascending spring
上石炭统 upper Carboniferous series
上市公司 listed company
上市证券 listed securities
上税单 duty memo
上诉 appeal
上诉保证书 appeal bond
上诉程序 procedure for appeal
上诉法院 court of appeal
上诉委员会 appeal board, board of review
上碗扣 upper bowl down
上下视差 vertical parallax
上下行并联供电 parallel feeding for up and down tracks
上下行分开供电 separate feeding for up and down tracks
上限截止频率 upper cut-off frequency
上新世 Pliocene epoch
上新统 Pliocene series
上行波 upward traveling wave
上行区间接口 up direction section interface
上行下给式 downfeed system
上行线 up track
上仰角 elevation angle
上元古界 upper Proterozoic group
上涨费用 escalation
上震旦统 upper Sinian series
上志留统 upper Silurian series
上侏罗统 upper Jurassic series
烧杯 beaker
烧结多孔砖 sintered porous brick
烧结普通砖 sintered common brick
烧失量 loss on ignition
稍密 slightly dense
稍湿 slightly humid
少报 understatement
少冰冻土 ice-poor permafrost
少付 underpayment
少支架法 falsework method with only a small quantity of support points

赊购　account purchase, credit purchase, tick, on the nod
赊销　charge sales, credit sale, sale on account
赊账　on account (o/a), on trust, open account, payment on open account
赊账支付　payment on account
蛇纹石　serpentine
蛇纹岩　serpentinite
蛇形丘　esker, oskar
设备　facility, equipment, plant, apparatus, fixtures, instrument
设备材料和工艺　plant, material and workmanship
设备安装　erection of plant, erection of equipment, mounting of equipment
设备安装工　fitter
设备保险　equipment insurance
设备保养　equipment maintenance, maintenance of plant
设备采购　equipment procurement
设备残值　equipment residual values, remanent value of equipment
设备层　equipment floor
设备场　equipment works, equipment yard
设备成本计算　costing of plant
设备单价　equipment unit price
设备单价汇总表　summary sheet of equipment unit prices
设备的拆除　dismantling of plant
设备的记录　plant records
设备的维护　maintenance of plant
设备费　equipment cost
设备费价差　difference in price of equipment
设备干预　equipment intervention
设备告警　equipment alarm
设备、工器具购置费　purchase expense for equipment, tools and apparatus
设备供货贷款　equipment supply loan
设备供应合同　supply of equipment contract
设备供应和安装合同　supply of equipment with erection contract
设备购置费　equipment procurement cost
设备故障　equipment fault
设备规格　equipment specification
设备基础　equipment foundation
设备集中站　equipment centralized station
设备技术资料　equipment technical document
设备空间　device space
设备库区　plant depot
设备利用率　capacity operating rate
设备能力　machine capability
设备平面布置图　equipment layout plan
设备启动测试　device starting test
设备清单　equipment list
设备区　equipment area
设备散热量　heat dissipation from equipment
设备散湿量　moisture release from equipment
设备时间核对　equipment time checking
设备识别寄存器　equipment identity register (EIR)
设备使用年限　duration of service
设备台账　equipment account
设备停用　equipment out-of use
设备外壳　equipment enclosure
设备维护　equipment maintenance
设备维修　equipment maintenance
设备闲置时间　machine idle time
设备详细估算　detailed equipment estimation
设备型号　equipment model
设备性能　equipment performance
设备选型　equipment selection
设备原价　original price of equipment
设备运行状态　operating status of equipment
设备运杂费　equipment freight and miscellaneous charges
设备运杂费费率　equipment freight and miscellaneous rates
设备再出口保函　guarantee for re-export of equipment
设备折旧　equipment depreciation, depreciation of equipment
设备支架　equipment support
设备制动优先　ATP with high priority
设备种类　equipment category
设备租赁　equipment leasing
设备租赁商　equipment lessor
设备租用费　equipment rental
设定价值　declared value
设防　setting of protected area
设计　design, engineer, layout
设计备选方案　design alternatives
设计变更　design alteration
设计变更建议书　engineering change proposal (ECP)
设计标准　design standard
设计参数　design parameter
设计单位　design unit, designer
设计单元　design unit
设计地震　design earthquake
设计地震动参数　design parameter of ground motion
设计方案　design approach, design proposal

设计方案论证	design reviews
设计分包者	design subcontractor
设计负荷	design load
设计概算	budget at design stage
设计高程	design elevation, design level
设计工程师	design engineer
设计工况	design conditions
设计工期	design construction period
设计工作	design work
设计—管理	design-management
设计规范	design code, design specification
设计合同	design contract
设计和规划	design and planning
设计和建造	design and build
设计荷载	design load
设计荷载标准	design load standard
设计洪水过程线	design flood hydrograph
设计洪水频率	design flood frequency
设计洪水频率水位	design flood frequency water level
设计活载	design live-load
设计基本地震加速度	design basic seismic acceleration
设计基准	design baseline
设计基准期	design reference period
设计建模	design modeling
设计—建设—运营	design-build-operate (DBO)
设计—建设—运营移交	design-build-operate-transfer (DBOT)
设计—建造	design-build (DB)
设计—建造合同	design-build contract
设计—建造竣工检验	test on completion of design-build
设计—建造竣工时间	time for completion of design-build
设计建造开工	commencement of design-build
设计—建造最终支付证书	final payment certificate of design-build project
设计阶段	design stage
设计接头等级	design joint grade
设计经理	engineering manager
设计开挖线(又称"计价线")	design excavation line (pay line)
设计枯水位	design low water level
设计烈度	design intensity
设计临界高度	design critical height
设计流量	design discharge
设计流速	design flow velocity
设计路段	railway section under design
设计路肩高程	design shoulder elevation
设计目标	design objective
设计能力	design capacity
设计年度	design year
设计评估	design evaluation
设计前估算	pre-design estimate
设计强度	design strength
设计深化	design development
设计审查	design audit, design review
设计师	designer
设计使用年限	design service life
设计使用期限	design service life
设计数据	design data
设计数据包	design data package
设计水位	design water level
设计说明	design specification
设计速度	design speed
设计锁定轨温	design fastening-down rail temperature, design stress-free rail temperature, neutral rail temperature
设计特征周期	design characteristic period
设计图样	design draft
设计图纸	design drawing
设计围岩分级	design surrounding rock classification
设计文件	design documentation
设计细则	design details
设计限值	design limit
设计小时供热量	designed hourly heat supply
设计小时耗热量	design hourly heat consumption
设计行包库存件数	design capacity of luggage office
设计行为	design behavior
设计压力	design pressure
设计要求	design requirement
设计用水量	design water consumption
设计原则	design principle
设计—招标—建造	engineer procurement construction (EPC)
设计职业责任险	professional indemnities
设计状况	design situation
设计准则	design criteria
设计资料	design data
设计资源	design resources
设计组	design team
设计最大日用水量	design maximum daily water consumption
设施	facilities
设施供应	facility provision
设施管理	facility management
设施使用权	right of facility

设施提供者　facility provider
社会保险　social insurance
社会保障　social security
社会保障费　social security cost
社会风险　social risks
社会福利　social welfare, public welfare
社会福利条款　social welfare clause
社会环境调查　social-environmental investigation
社会经济环境影响评价
　　social-economic environment impact assessment
社会经济目标　socio-economic objective
社会影响评价　social impact assessment
社会折现率　social rate of discount
射流　jet
射流反循环钻进　jet reverse circulation drilling
射流风机　jet fan
射流区　jet zone
涉外民事法律关系　civil legal relations with foreign element, foreign-related civil legal relations
涉外项目　foreign-related project
涉外争议　foreign-related disputes
涉外仲裁　foreign-related arbitration
摄影比例尺　photographic scale
摄影测量　photogrammetry
摄影测量内插　photogrammetric interpolation
摄影测量坐标系
　　photogrammetric coordinate system
摄影方向　photographic direction
摄影航高　photographic flying height
摄影航线　flight line of aerial photography
摄影机主机　camera mainframe
摄影基线　photographic baseline
摄影站　exposure station
摄影主光轴　optical axis of camera
摄影纵距　longitudinal distance of photography
申报　declare
申报保险单　declaration policy
申报表　declaration form
申报出口　entry of goods outward
申报货物　declare goods
申报价值　declared value
申报进口　entry of goods inward
申报实情责任　duty of disclosure
申请方法　method of application
申请费　application fee
申请人　applicant, declarant, claimant (claimer)
申请书　letter of application
申请特别承诺
　　application for special commitment
申诉　appeal
申诉人　complainant, declarant
伸长率　elongation rate
伸顶通气管　extension vent pipe
伸缩缝　expansion joint
伸缩接头　expansion joint
伸缩力　longitudinal expansion-contraction force in CWR on bridge
伸缩区　breathing zone
伸缩弯　flexible bend
身份认证　identity authentication
身份识别　universal serial bus key (USBKey)
身份证件识读设备　identity card reader
身体伤害　bodily injury
砷含量　arsenic content
深槽　trench
深层搅拌法　deep mixing method
深层土加固　consolidation of deep soil
深度处理　advanced treatment
深度基准面　depth datum
深海盆地　deep-sea basin
深海相　abyssal facies
深井泵　deep well pump
深井法　deep well method
深井水泵　deep well pump
深孔爆破　deep hole blasting
深孔水平钻探
　　prediction by drilling long horizontal hole
深孔温度计　deep hole thermometer
深路堑　deep cutting
深埋水准点　deep-buried benchmark
深埋隧道　deep tunnel
深受弯构件　deep flexural member
深水温度计　deep water thermometer
深源地震
　　deep-focus earthquake, palintectic earthquake
审查　review
审查期　review period
审定　authorize, examine and approve
审核结果　audit findings
审核期　review period
审核人　auditor
审计　audit
审计机构　auditing body
审计师　auditor, controller
审计条款　auditing clauses
审计团　audit mission
审计线索　audit trail
审计员　auditor
审理　try, trial, hear, hearing
审理辩护费用　costs

审判记录　minutes of trial
审判庭　adjudication division
审判员　judge
审批过程　approval process
审议　review
审议过程　review process
肾状　reniform
甚低频发　very low frequency（VLF）
渗沟　sewer
渗管　perforated drainage pipe
渗井　seepage well
渗径　seepage paths
渗流　seepage
渗流力　seepage force
渗流水力坡降　seepage hydraulic gradient
渗漏　leakage
渗漏水　leakage
渗漏险　risk of leakage
渗渠出水量　infiltration channel discharge
渗水　water seepage
渗水池　seepage pond
渗水量　seepage volume
渗水深度　water seepage depth
渗水隧洞　drainage tunnel
渗水土　permeable soil
渗水土路基　permeable soil subgrade
渗透　permeation, infiltration
渗透变形　seepage deformation
渗透流速　seepage velocity
渗透率　permeability
渗透破坏　seepage failure
渗透潜蚀　osmotic erosion
渗透试验　permeability test
渗透水力梯度　hydraulic gradient of permeability
渗透水量　amount of seepage
渗透系数　permeability coefficient
渗透性　permeability
渗透压法　osmotic pressure method
渗透仪　permeameter
渗油性　oil permeability
升板结构　lift-slab structure
升降机　lift（elevator）
升降桥　vertical-lift bridge
升水　premium
升压变电站　step-up substation
生产报表　manufacturing statement
生产成本　cost of production, production cost
生产定额　job rate, output quota, production quota
生产附属房屋　auxiliary building

生产工人辅助工资　supplementary wages of workers
生产工人劳动保护费　labor protection fees for workers
生产管理　production control
生产管理制度　management operating system（MOS）
生产计划　production plan
生产奖金　production bonus
生产经理　line manager, production manager
生产矿井测量　operating mine survey
生产力损失　loss of productivity
生产量　volume of production
生产流程　line of production
生产率　productivity, production rate
生产能力　productivity, output capacity, production capacity
生产能力利用率　production capacity ration
生产能力指数法　method of capacity index
生产期　production term
生产设备和材料的所有权　ownership of plant and materials
生产数据　production data
生产损失　loss of production
生产通知单　factory order
生产污水　production sewage
生产线　assembly line, production line
生产线性能考核　production line performance test
生产性建设项目　productive construction project
生产许可证　production license
生产用水量　production process water consumption
生产职工培训费　training expense of production staff
生产指标　production quota, production target
生产准备费　production preparation fee
生产准备费用　setup cost
生产资料　means of production, capital goods
生活补贴　subsistence allowance
生活房屋　domestic building
生活费　cost of living
生活供水点　household water supply point
生活供水站　household water supply station, domestic water supply station
生活垃圾　domestic garbage
生活区　accommodation camp, living quarters, colony
生活设施　living facilities
生活污水　domestic sewage（wastewater）
生活饮用水　drinking water
生活用水量　domestic and public water consumption
生石灰　quicklime

生死两全保险　endowment assurance
生态　ecology
生态功能保护区　ecological function protection area
生态环境　ecological environment
生态环境建设总体规划　general plan of ecological environment construction
生态环境特征　characteristics of ecological environment
生态环境质量　ecological environment quality
生态建设　ecological construction
生态敏感与脆弱区　ecological sensitive and vulnerable area
生态平衡　ecological balance
生态效益　ecological benefit
生物除臭　biological deodorization
生物除磷　biological phosphorus removal
生物处理　biological treatment
生物堆积　biogenic accumulation
生物法　biological method
生物反硝化　bio-denitrification
生物反应池　biological reaction tank
生物风化　biologic weathering
生物接触氧化　bio-contact oxidation
生物结构　biogenetic texture
生物量　biomass
生物膜法　biomembrane process
生物破坏影响系数　influence coefficient of biological damage
生物稳定性　biological stability
生物硝化　bio-nitrification
生物预处理　biological pre-treatment
生物转盘　rotating biological contactor（RBC）
生效　come into force, enter into effect, go into force, validation
生效日期　effective date
生效条件　entry into force conditions
生育保险费　birth insurance premium
声波　sound wave
声波测井　acoustic logging
声波法　acoustic wave method
声波反射法　acoustic wave reflection method
声波感应法　sound wave induction method
声波激振器　sound wave vibration generator
声波探测　acoustic exploration
声波透射法　cross-hole sonic logging
声波透视交会法　acoustic perspective intersection method
声测管　sounding pipe
声幅测井　acoustic amplitude logging
声光报警　audible and visual alarm
声光报警器　audio and visual alarm
声级　sound level
声级计　sound level meter
声校准器　acoustic calibrator
声明　declare, declaration, state, statement
声屏障　sound barrier
声屏障安全门　emergency exit of sound barrier
声屏障插入损失　insertion loss of sound barrier
声屏障单元板　acoustic panel of sound barrier
声屏障隔声性能　sound insulation property of sound barrier
声屏障共振响应　resonance response of sound barrier
声屏障构件　sound barrier members
声屏障固有频率　natural frequency of sound barrier
声屏障荷载组合　loads combination on sound barrier
声屏障横断面图　cross-sectional drawing of sound barrier
声屏障基础　foundation of sound barrier
声屏障接口设计　interface design of sound barrier
声屏障结构设计　structural design of sound barrier
声屏障立面　profile of sound barrier
声屏障疲劳强度　fatigue strength of sound barrier
声屏障平面　plane of sound barrier
声屏障声学设计　acoustic design of sound barrier
声屏障元件　sound barrier element
声强　sound intensity
声时　sound duration
声速　acoustic velocity
声速测井　acoustic velocity logging
声学　acoustics
声学参数　acoustic parameter
声学探测　acoustic sounding
声学性能　acoustic performance
声压　sound pressure
声压级　sound pressure level
声源　sound source
声源频谱特性　sound source spectrum characteristics
牲畜给水栓　livestock spigot
牲畜装卸线　livestock loading and unloading track
绳索取芯钻进　wireline core drilling
胜诉的一方　winning party
剩余工期　remaining duration
剩余使用寿命　residual life
剩余收益　residual income
剩余污泥　excess activated sludge
剩余物　remainder
剩余资产　residual assets

失去联锁　interlocking loss
失去时效的　expiry
失去时效的债权　barred claim
失去占用表示　occupation loss indication
失稳　loss of stability
失效　failure
失效保险单　lapsed policy
失效荷载　failure
失效法律　expiring laws
失效概率　probability of failure
失效机理　failure mechanism
失效模式　failure mode
失效原因　failure cause
失效支票　out-of-date check
失序　disorderly
失压保护　loss-of-voltage protection
失业　unemployment
失业保险　unemployment insurance
失业保险费　unemployment insurance expense
失业救济金　unemployment benefit
失业率　unemployment rate
失职　breach of duty, omission, official misconduct, neglect of duty
施工　construct, construction, execution
施工安全　construction safety
施工报告　construction report
施工变更指示　variation order
施工便道　temporary road for construction
施工便桥　temporary bridge for construction
施工标准　standard of construction, construction standard
施工布置图　construction layout
施工参数　construction parameter
施工测量　construction survey
施工场地图　site plan, layout
施工成本　construction cost
施工成本概算　construction cost estimating
施工成本控制　construction cost control
施工程序　construction procedure
施工措施费　expense of construction measures
施工单位　construction organization
施工单位营业执照　builder's licence
施工导流　construction diversion
施工队　construction team, gang
施工方案　construction scheme, construction method statement
施工方法　construction method, construction means, method of construction
施工方格网　construction square control network
施工放样　construction layout, construction staking-out
施工分包合同　construction subcontract
施工缝　construction joint
施工服务　construction service
施工复测　construction resurvey
施工干扰　construction disturbance
施工工棚　construction camp
施工工期　construction period
施工管理承包　construction management contracting
施工管理费　construction management fee
施工管理合同　construction management contract
施工管理员　construction superintendent
施工规范　construction specification/code
施工规划　construction planning
施工过程　construction process
施工过渡措施　construction transition measures
施工合同　construction contract
施工合同管理　construction contract management
施工合同授标书　construction contract award
施工和检修集中荷载　construction and inspection concentrated load
施工荷载　construction load
施工划拨用地　area allotted for the construction
施工机械　constructional mechanism, construction plant, constructional plant
施工机械费预算　equipment cost estimating
施工机械使用费　charge for using construction machinery
施工机械台时费　equipment charge out rates
施工计划　construction program, construction plan
施工计划进度　construction schedule
施工记录　construction record
施工技术　construction technique
施工技术规范　construction specifications
施工加密控制网　densified control network of construction
施工监察员　construction inspector
施工监测人员　construction inspector
施工监督　construction supervision
施工监理费　construction supervision fee
施工监理费率　construction supervision charge rate
施工监理与咨询费　construction supervision and consulting fee
施工检查　construction inspection
施工检测　construction inspection
施工检测人员　construction inspector
施工阶段　construction phase
施工阶段验算　check in construction stage
施工进场道路　construction access road
施工进度　construction progress
施工进度表　work-schedule

施工进度纲要　outline programme for construction
施工进度核查单　construction schedule check list
施工进度汇总表　construction summary schedule
施工进度计划　construction schedule
施工进度计划横道图
　　Gantt chart of construction schedule
施工进度控制　construction progress control
施工经理　construction manager
施工经验　construction experience
施工控制网　construction control network
施工临时行车限界　clearance for temporary train operation during construction
施工流程图　construction flow chart
施工能力　construction ability
施工排水　drainage during construction
施工平面布置图　construction plan
施工平面图　construction plan
施工期　construction period
施工期废水　construction wastewater
施工期限
　　construction period, period of construction
施工前阶段　pre-construction stage
施工抢险　emergency rescue in construction
施工区段　construction section
施工日报表　daily construction report
施工日历　construction calendar
施工日志
　　daily record of construction, construction diary
施工设备　construction plant, construction equipment, construction machinery
施工设备情况报告
　　construction equipment status report
施工设计　construction design
施工设施费　expense of construction facilities
施工升降机　construction elevator
施工剩余物资　construction surplus materials
施工手段　construction way, construction method, construction means
施工水位　construction water level
施工顺序　construction sequence
施工速度　construction speed
施工损耗　construction loss
施工索赔　construction claims
施工索赔管理　construction claim management
施工锁定轨温
　　fastening-down rail temperature in construction
施工条件　construction condition
施工通道　construction access
施工图　construction drawing, shop drawing, working drawing
施工图阶段　construction document design phase
施工图设计　construction drawing design
施工图设计概要　detailed design brief
施工图设计阶段
　　design stage of construction drawing
施工图审查费　review fee for construction drawings
施工图预算　budget for construction drawings
施工围岩分级
　　construction surrounding rock classification
施工文件　construction document
施工系统设计　construction system design
施工现场（工地）　construction site, site
施工现场津贴　construction site allowance
施工详图　construction details
施工详细情况　particulars of construction
施工项目　construction project
施工协调　construction coordination
施工协调员　construction coordinator
施工协议书　construction agreement
施工许可　construction permit
施工许可证　construction license
施工营地　construction camp
施工预拱度　construction pre-camber
施工预算　construction estimate
施工灾害　construction disaster
施工质量　construction quality
施工质量控制等级
　　grade of construction quality control
施工中间进度表　construction intermediate schedule
施工注意事项　construction precautions
施工装备　construction equipment
施工准备　construction preparation
施工咨询费　construction consulting fee
施工总工期　total construction period
施工总平面布置示意图　general schematic layout diagram of construction
施工总平面图　general/master construction plan
施工组织调查
　　investigation for construction organization
施工组织方案　construction organization plan
施工组织方案意见　construction organization plan guidance, construction scheme
施工组织管理
　　organization and management of construction
施工组织计划　construction organization plan
施工组织设计　project excution plan, construction method statement
施工组织设计意见
　　construction organization design guidance, preliminary construction plan

施工作业	construction operation
施工作业区	working area
施工作业指导书	construction operation guide
施救费用	rescue cost
湿地公园	wetland park
湿度	humidity
湿度测量	humidity measurement
湿法除尘	wet dust removal
湿负荷	moisture load
湿工况	wet condition
湿化	humidifying
湿化试验	slaking test
湿化速度	rate of slaking
湿化仪	slaking device
湿空气	damp air
湿密度	wet density
湿喷法	wet-mix shotcreting method
湿喷混凝土机	wet shotcreting machine
湿喷机	wet shotcreting machine
湿喷机械手	wet shotcreting manipulator
湿球黑球温度指数	wet bubble globe temperature (WBGT) index
湿球温度	wet-bulb temperature
湿润	humid
湿筛法	wet sieving method
湿式除尘器	wet-type dust collector
湿式凝结水管	wet condensation pipe
湿式喷水灭火系统	wet sprinkling system
湿式吸收氧化法	wet oxidation absorption
湿式消火栓	wet hydrant
湿土法	wet soil method
湿陷量计算值	calculated value of wetting-collapse settlement
湿陷起始压力	initial collapse pressure
湿陷系数	collapsibility coefficient
湿陷性黄土	collapsible loess
湿陷性黄土路基	collapsible loess subgrade
湿陷性土	collapsible soil
湿研磨分散法	wet lapping dispersion method
十年责任险	decennial liability insurance
十字板剪切试验	vane shear test
十字板剪切仪	cross plate shear strength apparatus
十字板头	cross plate head
十字撑	cross brace
十字石	staurolite
十字形接头	cross-type joint
十字形枢纽	cross-type junction terminal
石	stone
石材	stone
石场	stone field, felsenmeer
石方工程	stoneworks
石粉含量	fine content, crusher dust content
石膏	gypsum
石膏岩	gyprock
石拱桥	stone arch bridge
石锅	stone pot
石花	cave flower
石环	stone ring
石灰	lime
石灰改良土	lime-stabilized soil, lime-stabilized soil
石灰砂浆	lime mortar
石灰土	limestone soil
石灰土挤压桩	limestone soil squeezing pile
石灰岩	limestone
石灰桩法	lime pile method
石帘	stone curtain
石林	stone forest
石榴子石	granat
石幔	stone curtain, stone sheet
石棉	asbestos
石漠	hammada, rock desert
石墨	graphite
石瀑布	stone waterfall
石砌体结构	stone masonry structure
石圈	stone circle
石笋	stalagmite
石炭纪	Carboniferous period
石炭系	Carboniferous system
石条	stone stripes
石窝	stone nest
石芽	clint
石盐	halite
石英	quartz
石英粗面岩	quartz-trachyte
石英角斑岩	quartz-keratophyre
石英砂	quartz sand
石英砂岩	quartz sandstone
石英岩	quartzite
石质路基	rock subgrade
石质路堑	rock cutting
时标网络图	time-scaled network diagram
时差	time difference
时程分析法	time history analysis method
时分复用	time division multiplex (TDM)
时价	current price, prevailing price, running price
时价表	price current
时间成本	time cost
时间基准信号	time reference signal
时间期限	time limits

时间曲线	time-dependent curve
时间相似	time similarity
时间延误	time delay
时间因数	time factor
时距曲线	hodograph
时限	time limit
时效期限	limitation period
时延	delay, latency
时域信号	time-domain signal
时钟同步	clock synchronization
时钟系统	clock system
识别评估	recognition and assessment
实测值	measured value
实尺模型	full-size model
实地测试法	field testing method
实地调查	site visit, field investigation
实腹拱	spandrel-filled arch
实腹拱桥	spandrel-filled arch bridge
实腹式钢柱	solid-web steel column
实干时间	hard drying time
实际成本	actual cost (AC), real cost
实际成本法	actual cost method
实际附加成本	actual additional cost
实际工期	as-built schedule
实际购货订单价格	actual purchase order price
实际汇率	real exchange rate
实际价格	actual price
实际价值	actual value
实际建成的	as constructed
实际交货	actual delivery
实际进度	actual progress
实际竣工日期	physical completion date
实际竣工时间	actual completion time
实际开支成本	out-of-pocket cost
实际利率	actual interest rate
实际利润	actual profit
实际量	physical volume
实际皮重	actual tare, real tare
实际全损	actual total loss
实际容积	physical volume
实际损失	actual loss
实际损失率	actual loss ratio
实际完工	practical completion
实际违约	actual breach
实际现金价值	actual cash value
实际债务	actual debt
实际折旧	actual depreciation
实际直接成本	applied direct cost
实际重量	actual weight (A/W)
实价	net price

实缴股本	contributed capital
实例模型	instance model
实名验证系统	real-name authentication system
实名制	real-name validation
实名制售票	real-name ticketing
实盘	firm offer
实施	execute, execution, implement, enforce, enforcement
实施方法	manner of execution, means of execution
实施方式	manner of execution
实施性施工组织设计	operative construction organization design, executive construction plan
实时差分改正	real-time differences correction
实时传送	real-time transmission
实时动态定位	real-time dynamic positioning
实时监控	real-time monitoring
实体	entity
实体法	substantive law
实体桥墩	solid pie
实体组成	entity composition
实物担保	real security
实物法	real object method
实物计价法	real object valuation method
实物检测	prototype inspect
实物量法	real object measuring method
实物盘存法	physical inventory method
实物证据	physical evidence
实物支付	in-kind payment, payment in kind, pay in kind
实物资本	physical capital
实物资产	tangible assets
实物资源	physical resources, material resources
实心板	solid slab
实业界	business circle
实账户	real account
实质竣工证书	certificate of practical completion, certificate of substantial completion
实质性更改	substantial change
实质性规定	substantial provision
实质性竣工	substantial completion
实质性条款	substantial clauses
实质性修改	substantial modification
实质性证据	substantial evidence
拾振器	vibration pickup
食品供应	supply of foodstuffs
矢高	rise
矢跨比	rise to span ratio
使用费	charge for use
使用率	occupancy rate

使用面积	usable floor area
使用年限	tenure of use, life expectancy, durable year
使用期	term of service
使用期限	service life
使用寿命	service life
使用税	use tax
使用条件	operating condition, terms of service
使用需求	utilization requirements
使用与否均须付款合同	tolling agreement, through-put contract
始触区	fitting-free area
始发地	place of departure
始发站	originating station, departure station
始新世	Eocene epoch
始新统	Eocene series
示波器	oscilloscope
示范协议	model agreement
示坡线	slope indicating line
示意图	schematic drawing
示踪法	tracer method
示踪剂	tracer
示踪试验	tracer test
世界货币	universal currency (money)
世界市场价格	world price
市场波动	market fluctuation
市场定位	market orientation
市场分配	market allocation
市场分析	market analysis
市场份额	market share
市场划分	market allocation
市场汇率	market exchange rate
市场价值	market value
市场利率	market rate
市场趋势	market tendency
市场信息	market intelligence
市场需求	market demand
市场占有率	market share
市价	market price
市政工程测量	public works survey
事故	accident
事故保险	accident insurance
事故报告	accident report
事故报警信号	failure alarming signal
事故调查	accident investigation
事故描述	accident narrative
事故排烟	smoke exhaust in accident
事故通风	emergency ventilation
事故油池	emergency oil disposal tank
事故预防	accident prevention
事故照明	emergency lighting

事先审查	prior review
事先协商	prior consultation
饰面工程	face work
饰面石	facing stone
试车	commissioning, test run, initial operation
试车组	commissioning team
试剂	reagent
试件	specimen
试件承压面积	pressure bearing area of specimen
试件破坏荷载	destructive load of specimen
试坑	test pit
试块	test blocks
试模	mold testing
试配	trial mixture
试配强度	trial mixture strength
试体	specimen
试体成型	specimen molding
试验	test
试验报告	test report
试验步骤	testing procedure
试验参数	testing parameter
试验段	test section
试验墩	test pier
试验方法	test method
试验费	test expense
试验分室	branch laboratory
试验荷载	test load
试验荷载等级	testing load grade
试验荷载工况	working condition of testing load
试验荷载效率	test load efficiency
试验记录	test record
试验间	test room
试验检测	test detection
试验检测机构	test detection institution
试验检测机构资质	qualification of test detection institution
试验检查	test inspection
试验结果	test result
试验孔	test hole
试验路堤	embankment under test
试验日期	date for testing
试验手册	test manual
试验塔	test tower
试验委托书	letter of authority for test
试验误差	test error
试验现场	testing ground
试验项目	test items
试验消火栓	test fire hydrants
试验性施工	trial construction
试验压力	test pressure

试验样品　test specimen
试验组　testing group
试样　test sample
试样分解　sample decomposition
试样水浸出液　lixiviant of water sample
试样制备　specimen preparation
试用　trial, probation
试用期　probationary period, period of probation
试运行　trial run, trial operation
试运行费用　commissioning costs
试运行规范　commissioning codes
试运行期　commissioning period
试运行证书　commissioning certificate
试运转　test run
试桩　test pile
视察　inspect, inspection
视察员　inspector
视差法测距　distance measuring by parallax method
视电阻率　apparent resistivity
视电阻率法　apparent resistivity method
视距法　stadia method
视觉信号　visual signal
视觉作业　visual task
视频编码器　video encoder
视频采集点　video collection point
视频测试卡　video test card
视频传输码流　video transmission code stream
视频光端机　video optical transceiver
视频柜　video cabinet
视频核心节点　video core node
视频盒　video box
视频汇集点　video convergence site
视频监控　video monitoring
视频监控系统　video surveillance system
视频接入节点　video access node
视频解码器　video decoder
视频控制箱　video control box
视频联动功能　video linkage function
视频流　video streaming
视频流路数　number of video streaming
视频内容分析　video content analysis
视频区域节点　video regional node
视频源切换　video source switching
视频转发　video forwarding
视倾角　apparent dip
视线高程　elevation of sight
视在功率　apparent power
视准线长度　length of collimation line
视准线法　collimation line method
适当降价　modest price reduction

适当涨价　modest price increase
适度价格　moderate price
适度设防　moderate fortification
适航性　seaworthiness
适航证明书　certificate of seaworthiness
适生植物　adaptable plants
适宜工作日　weather working days
适应性规划　adaptive planning
适应性试验　compatibility test
适用法律　governing law, applicable law
适用汇率　applicable exchange rate (AER)
适用条款　applicable provision
适用性　applicability
室内净高　interior clear height
室内消火栓　indoor fire hydrant
室外配电装置　outdoor power distribution equipment
室外消火栓　outdoor fire hydrant
室形指数　room index
释放时间　drop away time
释放值　release value
收到日期　date of receipt
收发器　transceiver
收发设备　receiver and transmitter
收费　charge
收费道路　toll road
收费过高　overcharge
收工　cease work
收购　purchase, buy
收回　recover, recall, regain
收回保证金　withdraw deposit
收回报价　withdraw an offer
收回贷款　call in a loan
收货　take over, take delivery
收货单　mate's receipt
收货回单　acknowledgement
收货人　consignee
收货通知　receiving note
收集资料　collect data
收件人　addressee
收据　receipt
收款便条　receipt slip
收款人　remittee, payee
收敛计　convergence indicator
收料员　receiving clerk
收盘汇率　closing rate
收盘价　closing price
收讫通知书　acknowledgement
收取　collect
收容盘　container
收入　income, revenue, proceeds

收入保险　income insurance
收入成本　revenue cost
收入项目　revenue items
收市　closing
收税　collection of tax
收税员　tax collector
收缩　shrinkage
收缩缝　shrinking joint, contraction joint
收缩率　shrinkage rate
收缩率比　ratio of shrinkage
收缩皿法　shrinkage method
收缩容许量　shrinkage allowance
收缩试验　shrinkage test
收缩系数　shrinkage coefficient
收缩仪　contractometer
收缩应力　shrinkage stress
收条　receipt
收尾　closeout
收益　income, gain, earnings, revenue
收益表　income sheet, earning statement
收益分割　income splitting
收益分配　income distribution
收益汇总账户　income summary account
收益扣除额　income deduction
收益率　earning rate, yield rate, rate of return
收益率评估法　rate of return method
收益账户　income account
收砟机　ballast collector
收账　collections
收账代理人　collecting agent
收支　incomes and outgoings
收支表　account of receipts and payments
收支差额　balance of payment
收支赤字　deficit balance
收支两讫　account balanced
收支逆差　balance of payments deficit
收支平衡　balance, on the balance
收支顺差　balance of payments surplus
手柄　handle, knob
手册　handbook
手车式开关柜
　　handcart switchgear, withdrawable switchgear
手车位置指示器　handcart work position indicator
手持金属探测仪　handheld metal detector
手持式应变仪　hand-held strain gauge
手持式凿岩机　handheld rock drill
手持台　handheld
手锤　hammer
手动/电动操作机构箱
　　manual/motorized operating mechanism box
手动调压　manual voltage regulation
手动隔离开关　manual disconnector
手动控制　manual control
手动栏木　manual operated barrier
手动释放　manual release
手机端售票　smartphone ticket sales
手孔　hand hole
手提电动捣固机
　　portable electric tamper, electric pick
手提风动捣固机　portable pneumatic tamper
手提内燃捣固机　portable diesel tamper
手提式灭火器　portable fire extinguisher
手头现金　petty cash
手推车　trolley
手信号　hand signal
手续费　commission charge
手摇泵　hand pump
守车　caboose, guard's van
首波　head wave
首次核定估算　first check estimate (FCE)
首次要求即付　payable upon first demand
首次要求即付保函　guarantee on the first demand
首件定标　standardization of sample works
首期保费　initial premium
首期付款　initial payment
首期建筑　priority construction
首曲线　intermediate contour
首席财务官　chief finance officer
首席承保人　leading underwriter
首席代表　chief delegate
首席会计师　chief accountant
首席律师　leading counsel
首席执行官　chief executive officer (CEO)
首席仲裁员　presiding arbitrator
寿命　service life
受潮受热险
　　damage caused by sweating & heating
受电侧　receiving end
受电端　receiving end
受电弓　pantograph
受电弓摆动范围　sway of pantograph
受电弓横向偏移　lateral movement of pantograph
受电弓滑板　contact strip
受电弓滑板支架　contact strip support of pantograph
受电弓晃动　sway and skew of the pantograph
受电弓始触区　registration-fitting-free area
受雇者　employee
受合同约束　bound by contract
受话灵敏度　voice receiving sensitivity
受贿　acceptance of bribes, corruption

受惠国　beneficiary country
受惠人　beneficiary
受货人　vendee
受控公司　controlled company
受款人　payee
受拉区　tensile region
受拉区混凝土塑性影响系数
　　plasticity coefficient of concrete in tensile region
受理申诉　hear a claim
受流质量　quality of current collection
受盘人　offeree
受票人　drawee
受权人　attorney
受让人　assignee, endorsee, indorsee, assigns
受弯钢筋　bar subjected to bending moment
受弯构件　bending member
受委付人　abandonee
受委托人　trustee
受限射流　confined Jet
受信放大器　receiving amplifier
受训人　trainee
受压构件承载能力影响系数　influence coefficient of bearing capacity of compression member
受压区　compression zone
受压区高度　depth of compression zone
受押人　mortgagee
受益方　benefited party
受益权　beneficial interest
受益人　beneficiary
受益业主　beneficial owner
受援国　recipient country, assisted country
受约人　offeree, promisee
授标　tender award
授标函　letter of award
授标后会议　post-award meeting
授标后压价　post-bid shopping
授标决定　award decision
授标前会议　pre-award meeting
授标通知　award notification, notification of award
授标准则　award criteria
授权　authorize, authorization, delegate, delegation
授权代表　authorised representative
授权的权力　authority to delegate
授权范围　terms of reference (TOR), limits of authority
授权付款　authorized payment
授权人签名　authorized signature
授权书　power of attorney, letter of attorney, written authorization, commission of authority
授权文件　vesting instrument

授权银行　authorized bank
授予　award, grant, vest, confer
授予合同　award of contract
售后服务　after-sales service
售后回租　leaseback
售价　selling price
售票　ticket sales
售票处　ticket office
售票窗口屏　ticket counter display
售票交易　ticket transaction
售票量　volume of ticket sales
书面　written/in writing
书面报表　written statement
书面变更命令　written variation order
书面裁决　written decision
书面合同　literal contract
书面结清单　written discharge
书面警告　written warning
书面决定　written decision, decision in writing
书面批准　written approval
书面请求　written request
书面确认　confirmation in writing
书面申请　written application
书面声明　written statement
书面通知　written notice, notice in writing
书面文件　written document
书面协议　written agreement, agreement in writing
书面形式　in writing
书面应允　written consent
书面证据　documentary evidence, written evidence
书写　writing
书写错误　clerical error
枢纽前方站　station in advance of terminal
枢纽遥控　remote control of junction terminal
枢纽指挥　hub command
梳齿刮刀　comb scraper
舒适性空气调节　comfort air conditioning
疏导　dredging
疏忽　negligence, laches
疏解线路　untwining line
疏浚　dredging
疏浚工程　dredging works
疏散标志　emergency exit sign
疏散出口　evacuation exit
疏散走道　evacuation walk
疏水器　steam trap
疏松砂　loose sand
疏淤系数　dredging coefficient
输出　output
输出电压　output voltage

输出功率　output power
输出阻抗　output impedance
输电　electrical distribution
输电线路　transmission line
输入　input
输入灵敏度　input sensitivity
输入阻抗　input impedance
输沙量　sediment runoff
输水道　conduit
输水管　delivery pipe
输水管道　water delivery pipeline
输送带　conveyer belt
输送机　conveyer
输油管道测量　oil pipeline survey
赎单　retiring a bill
赎回　redeem
赎回价格　call price, redemption price
赎票　retiring a bill
熟练　proficiency
熟练工人　skilled worker, skilled labour, journeyman, old hand
熟石灰　white lime, slaked lime, drowned lime
熟土　mellow soil
属地化管理　localized management
属性　attribute, property
属性集　property set
术语　terminology
树根桩　root pile
树龄　tree age
树枝状　dendritic
树脂　resin
树脂光泽　resinous luster
树脂锚杆　resin rockbolt
树种　species of trees
竖杆　vertical member
竖基尺视差法　subtense method with vertical staff
竖截面　vertical section
竖井　shaft
竖井联系测量　shaft connection survey
竖流沉淀池　vertical flow settling tank
竖盘指标差　index error of vertical circle
竖曲线　vertical curve
竖曲线半径　radius of vertical curve
竖曲线测设　vertical curve location
竖式　vertical type
竖向布置图　vertical layout, profile
竖向残余徐变变形　vertical residual creep deformation
竖向测量　vertical survey
竖向分区　vertical division block
竖向刚度　vertical stiffness
竖向挠度　vertical deflection
竖向施工缝　vertical construction joint
竖向支撑　vertical bracing
竖向主框架　main vertical framework
竖旋桥　bascule bridge
数额　amount
数据　data
数据备份　data backup
数据编辑　data editing
数据编码　data encoding
数据采集　data collection
数据采集仪器　data acquisition instrument
数据处理　data processing
数据处理设备　data processing device
数据点　data point
数据调整表　table of adjustment data
数据分析　data analysis
数据获取　data acquisition
数据库　database
数据库服务器　database server
数据库管理系统　database management system (DMS)
数据库维护　database maintenance
数据链路　data link
数据通道　data channel
数据通信　data communication
数据通信网　data communication network
数据网　data network
数据网络综合分析仪　data network comprehensive analyzer
数控绘图　digital control drawing
数量　quantity
数量检验证书　inspection certificate of quantity
数量折扣　quantity discount
数量指标　quantity index
数码航摄仪　digital aerial camera
数目错误　numerical error
数学模型法　mathematical model method
数值　numerical value
数值解　numerical solution
数字　numbers
数字表面模型　digital surface model (DSM)
数字错误　numerical error
数字地籍　digital cadastre
数字地面模型　digital terrain model
数字地图　digital map
数字地形图　digital topographic map
数字高程模型　digital elevation model (DEM)
数字化测图　digital mapping

数字化横断面　digital cross section
数字化加工　digital fabrication
数字化铁路　digitalized railway
数字接口　digital interface
数字客运广播机
　　digital passenger service broadcast machine
数字配线架　digital distribution frame（DDF）
数字式子钟　digital slave clock
数字视频信号　digital video signal
数字数据性能分析仪
　　digital data performance analyzer
数字通道　digital channel
数字线划图　digital line graphic（DLG）
数字栅格地图　digital raster graphic
数字正射影像　digital orthophoto map（DOM）
数字正射影像图　digital orthophoto map
数字专线电路　digital private line
衰耗器　attenuator
衰耗系数　attenuation coefficient
衰减串音比　attenuation to crosstalk ratio（ACR）
衰减时　decay time
衰减系数　attenuation coefficient
衰退　decline, decay, slump
甩挂作业　coupling and uncoupling operation
栓接板面　faying surface
栓接钢桥　bolted steel bridge
双壁钢围堰　double-wall steel cofferdam
双边供电　double-end feeding
双边合同　bilateral contract
双边文件　bilateral document
双边文书　bilateral document
双边协议　bilateral agreement
双侧壁导坑法　double side heading method
双侧壁法　double side heading method
双层百叶型风口
　　double-layer shutter-type air outlet
双层存梁　girder storage in double layers
双层集装箱　double-deck container
双层集装箱班列　double-deck container liner train
双层结构　bi-layer structure
双层桥　double-deck bridge
双层信封投标方式　two-envelope bid system
双掺　double-doped
双承力索吊弦线夹
　　dropper clip for twin messenger wires
双代号网络
　　activity-on-arrow（AOA）, arrow diagram
双代号网络图　arrow network
双电网传感器/监测电网
　　double grid transducer
双电网传感器　dual power network sensor, double grid transducer
双动双管取芯钻进
　　double-swivel double-tube core drilling
双端接地　double-end grounding
双断　double break
双耳连接器　clevis end fitting
双耳楔形线夹　clevis end wedge-type clamp
双发　dual-transmitter
双方　both parties
双方车站分设横列式港湾站
　　transverse type harbour station built separately in both terminals
双方车站分设横列式工业站
　　transverse type industrial station built separately in both terminals
双方车站联设横列式港湾站
　　transverse type harbour station built jointly in both terminals
双方车站联设横列式工业站
　　transverse type industrial station built jointly in both terminals
双方车站联设双向混合式港湾站
　　bidirectional combined-type harbour station built jointly in both terminals
双方车站联设双向混合式工业站
　　bidirectional combined-type industrial station built jointly in both terminals
双方车站联设纵列式港湾站
　　longitudinal type harbour station built jointly in both terminals
双方车站联设纵列式工业站
　　longitudinal type industrial station built jointly in both terminals
双方同意　mutual consent
双方应允　mutual consent
双封套投标方法　two-envelop bid system
双管采暖系统　double-pipe heating system
双轨条轨道电路　double rail track circuit
双轨楔体焊接　double track wedge welding
双护盾掘进机　double-shield TBM
双环杆　double eye-end rod
双机热备　dual machine hot standby
双机主备　dual machine backup
双铰拱　two-hinged arch
双介质摄影测量　two-medium photogrammetry
双金属温度计　bimetallic thermometer
双进路　two-way route
双控制器磁盘阵列　dual-controller disk array
双口双阀消火栓　duplex double valve fire hydrant

双块式轨枕　bi-block sleeper
双块式轨枕预制场
　　double-block type track sleeper precast yard
双块式无砟轨道　bi-block ballastless track
双联板　double strap
双联井　duplex well
双梁式架桥机
　　double-armed girder-erecting machine
双列布置　double row layout
双溜放　double humping
双溜放作业　double-rolling operation
双流功能　dual stream function
双（单）轮车　two-wheeled（single-wheeled）car
双面调车信号机
　　signal for shunting forward and backward
双面索斜拉桥　double-plane cable-stayed bridge
双面斜道　two-sided ramp
双母线结线　double bus connection
双排桩　double campshed
双频　double frequency
双频感应器　double frequency inductor
双曲拱　double-curvature arch
双曲拱桥　double-curvature arch bridge
双曲线法　hyperbolic curve method
双刃滚刀　double-edge disc cutter
双头螺栓扳手　double-end bolt wrench
双推单溜　double humping and single rolling
双推双溜　double humping and double rolling
双驼峰　double-hump
双腕臂底座　twin cantilever bracket
双腕臂上底座　upper bracket for twin cantilevers
双腕臂下底座　lower bracket for twin cantilevers
双系或双机同步及切换测试
　　dual-system／dual-locomotive synchronization and switching test
双线　double-track
双线臂板信号机
　　double-wire operated semaphore signal
双线法　double-line method
双线路堤　double-track embankment
双线路堑　double-track cutting
双线桥　double-track bridge
双线隧道　double-track tunnel
双线铁路　double-track railway
双线循环式　double-line reciprocating type
双向板　two-way slab
双向编组站　bidirectional marshalling station
双向混合式编组站
　　bidirectional combined-type marshalling station
双向配筋　two-way reinforcement
双向铺轨　track laying using two sets of track laying machinery
双向土工格栅　bidirectional geogrid
双向音视频功能试验
　　bi-direction audio and video function test
双向运行自动闭塞
　　bi-directional automatic blocking
双向自动闭塞
　　double-direction running automatic block
双向纵列式编组站
　　bidirectional longitudinal type marshalling station
双信号选择性　dual signal selectivity
双悬臂式架桥机
　　double cantilever girder-erecting machine
双液浆　double-fluid grout
双引下接地
　　earthing of double down-conductors
双赢方案　win-win solution
双赢解决办法　win-win solution
双支撑　double-support
双支撑移动机构
　　double-support moving mechanism
双肢柱　double-limb column
双重保险　double insurance
双重关税　dual tariff
双重货币记录　dual currency record
双重货币债券　dual currency bond
双重绝缘　double insulation
双重控制　dual control
双重税收　double taxation
水泵接合器　pump adapter
水泵站　pump station
水表　water meter
水成岩　aqueous rock
水处理　water treatment
水处理厂　water treatment plant
水处理构筑物　water treatment structure
水锤压力　surge pressure
水袋　water bag
水道标　sign for water pipe
水道整治工程　channel regulation works
水底隧道　subaqueous tunnel, underwater tunnel
水电效应法　hydroelectricity method
水电站　hydropower station
水封　water seal
水浮力　water buoyancy
水工建筑　hydraulic structure
水工结构　hydraulic structure
水功能　water function
水沟　drainage ditch

水管　water pipe
水管内径　inside diameter of water pipe
水害断道　railway line break down due to flood
水害复旧　restoration after flood damage
水害抢修　rush repair of railway damage caused by flood
水鹤表示器　water crane indicator
水环热泵空气调节系统　water loop heat pump air conditioning system
水灰比　cement-water ratio, cementitious material water ratio, water cement ratio
水浇地　irrigable land
水胶比　water to cementitious material ratio
水解酸化　hydrolytic acidification
水浸　water immersion
水浸探测器　water immersion detector
水库　reservoir
水库地段路基　subgrade in reservoir section
水库水位　reservoir water level
水库坍岸　reservoir bank collapse
水库淤积　reservoir siltation
水冷　water cooling
水冷式冷凝器　water-cooled condenser
水力半径　hydraulic radius
水力冲填　hydraulic fill
水力除尘　wet-type dust removal
水力发电站　hydro-power station
水力混合　hydraulic mixing
水力计算　hydraulic calculation
水力警铃　hydraulic alarm
水力劈裂法　hydraulic fracturing technique
水力坡度　hydraulic slope, hydraulic gradient
水力失调　hydraulic disorder
水力梯度　hydraulic gradient
水力学性能　hydraulics property
水力循环澄清池　circulator
水利　water conservancy
水利工程　hydraulic engineering, hydraulic works
水利资源　water resources
水量评价　water quantity evaluation
水流断面　active cross-section
水流扩散角　angle of stream spreading
水流量　water flow capacity
水流偏转角　angle of turning flow
水流指示器　water flow indicator
水陆联运提单　overland bill of lading
水路　water way
水轮机　turbine, hydrographic turbine
水面坡度　slope of water surface
水幕　water curtain
水幕喷头　sprinkler for water curtain
水幕系统　drencher systems
水泥比表面积测定仪　tester for specific surface area of cement
水泥标准稠度仪　cement standard consistency meter
水泥仓　cement bunker, cement silo
水泥槽　cement trough
水泥粉煤灰碎石桩　cement-fly ash-gravel pile(CFG)
水泥粉煤灰碎石桩复合地基　composite foundation with cement-fly ash-gravel piles
水泥粉煤灰土　cement fly ash soil
水泥负压筛　negative pressure sieving of cement
水泥改良土　cement-improved soil
水泥裹砂喷射混凝土　cement sand shotcrete
水泥含量　cement content
水泥恒温恒湿养护箱　constant temperature and humidity cement curing box
水泥混凝土铺面　cement concrete pavement
水泥加固　cement stabilization
水泥浆　cement paste, cement grout, grouts
水泥浆试件　cement paste specimen
水泥浆体材料　cement paste material
水泥胶砂　cement mortar
水泥胶砂振实台　swing table for cement mortar
水泥深层搅拌桩复合地基　composite foundation with cement deep mixed piles
水泥净浆　cement paste
水泥净浆搅拌机　cement paste mixer
水泥净浆流动度　fluidity of cement paste
水泥颗粒　cement particle
水泥抹面　cement plastering
水泥牌号　cement brand
水泥灌浆　cement injection
水泥强度等级　strength grade of cement
水泥乳化沥青砂浆　cement-emulsified asphalt mortar(CAM/CEAM)
水泥砂浆　cement mortar
水泥砂浆基板　basal plate for cement mortar
水泥输送泵　cement pump
水泥水化热　hydration heat of cement
水泥土　cement soil
水泥土挤密桩　cement-soil compaction pile
水泥土挤压桩　cement soil squeezing pile
水泥土搅拌桩　cement-soil mixing pile
水喷雾灭火系统　water spray extinguishing system
水平　cross level
水平层理　horizontal bedding
水平产状　horizontal attitude

水平尺 levelling instrument
水平地震系数 horizontal seismic coefficient
水平冻胀力 horizontal frost-heave force
水平杆 horizontal bar
水平固结系数 horizontal consolidation coefficient
水平角 horizontal angle
水平角方向观测 direction observation for horizontal angle
水平角较差限差 tolerance of horizontal angles discrepancy
水平接地极 horizontal earth electrode
水平接地体 horizontal earth electrode
水平径流带 horizontal runoff zone
水平面 water level, level
水平偏移 horizontal deflection
水平渗透试验 horizontal permeability test
水平声波剖面法 horizontal acoustic profile method
水平施工缝 horizontal construction joint
水平天窗 horizontal window time
水平同步法 horizontal synchronization method
水平位移 horizontal displacement
水平旋喷桩 horizontal jet grouting pile
水平旋转角度 horizontal rotating angle
水平仪 water level
水平匀布压力 horizontal uniformly-distributed pressure
水平折光差 horizontal refraction error
水平支撑 horizontal bracing
水平支承 horizontal supporting
水平主应力 horizontal principal stress
水平钻井 horizontal drilling
水热蚀变 hydrothermal alteration
水溶性 water solubility
水溶盐 water-soluble salt
水溶液 water solution
水上起重机 pontoon crane
水上钻孔 offshore boring
水深测量 sounding
水生植物 hygrophyte
水蚀 water erosion
水—水换热器 water-water heat exchanger
水塔 water tower
水塔架 water tower rack
水头 water head
水头差 water head difference
水头损失 head loss
水土保持 soil and water conservation
水土保持措施典型设计图 typical design drawing for soil and water conservation measures
水土保持措施总体布局图 general layout diagram for soil and water conservation measures
水土保持方案 soil and water conservation scheme
水土保持方案报告编制与评估费 report compilation and assessment fees for water and soil conservation plan
水土保持方案报告书 soil and water conservation scheme report
水土流失防治区划分图 zoning map for soil and water conservation
水土保持监测 soil and water conservation monitoring
水土保持监测点位布局图 monitoring point layout diagram for soil and water conservation
水土保持监理 supervision of soil and water conservation
水土保持监理费 supervision fee of soil and water conservation
水土保持的措施 aspect of water-and-soil conservation measures
水土保持林 soil and water conservation forest
水土保持设施 soil and water conservation facilities
水土保持投资估算 investment estimation for soil and water conservation facilities
水土保持总体规划 general plan of soil and water conservation facilities
水土分算 separate calculation of water and soil pressure
水土合算 combined calculation of water and soil pressure
水土流失 soil erosion and water loss
水土流失防治分区 prevention and control zoning of soil erosion and water loss
水土流失防治分区图 prevention and control zoning chart of soil erosion and water loss
水土流失防治责任范围 the range of responsibility for soil erosion control
水土流失防治责任范围图 the range of responsibility map for soil erosion control
水土流失控制量 controlled quantity of soil erosion area
水土流失类型 type of soil erosion and water loss
水土流失面积 area of soil erosion and water loss
水土流失强度 intensity of soil erosion and water loss
水土流失危害 damage of soil erosion and water loss
水土流失现状图 status quo map for water and soil erosion
水土流失形式 form of soil erosion and water loss

水土流失因子　factor of soil erosion and water loss
水土流失预测　forecast of soil erosion and water loss
水土流失重点监督区　key supervision region of soil erosion and water loss
水土流失重点预防保护区　key protection region of soil erosion and water loss
水土流失重点治理区　key rehabilitation region of soil erosion and water loss
水土流失总量　amount of soil erosion
水土流失总治理度　soil erosion and water loss control ratio
水土流失综合治理　comprehensive control of soil erosion and water loss
水位　water level
水位传递法　water level transfer method
水位计　water stage gauge
水位降低　drawdown
水位线　waterline
水温　water temperature
水文测绘　hydrographic surveying and charting
水文测井　hydrogeological logging
水文测量　hydrographic survey
水文的　hydrological
水文地质　hydrogeology
水文地质调绘　hydrogeological investigation
水文地质断面图　hydrogeological section map
水文地质分区　hydrogeological zoning
水文地质勘察　hydrogeological investigation
水文地质条件　hydrogeological condition
水文地质资料　hydrological and geological data
水文地质钻探　hydrogeological drilling
水文调查　hydrographic survey
水文断面　hydrological cross-section
水文计算　hydrological computation
水文气候条件　hydrologic and climatic condition
水文数据　hydrological data
水文条件　hydrological conditions
水文站　hydrological station
水文资料　hydrologic data
水稳性　water stability
水污染　water pollution
水雾喷头　sprinkler for water mist
水洗湿筛分析法　wet sieve analysis method
水系分布　water system distribution
水系灭火剂　water fire extinguishing agent
水系统　water system
水系统竖向分区　vertical zoning of water system
水系图　hydrographical chart
水下岸坡　submarine bank slope
水下爆破　underwater blasting
水下地形　underwater topography
水下地形测量　underwater topographic survey
水下防护工程　underwater protection works
水下横断面测量　underwater cross-section survey
水下浇筑混凝土　underwater concreting
水下砂堤　underwater sand embankment
水下隧道　underwater tunnel
水下纵断面测量　underwater profile survey
水下作业　underwater operation
水险　marine insurance
水压　hydraulic pressure
水压爆破　water pressure blasting
水压试验　hydrostatic test
水压致裂法　hydrofracturing method
水堰　dam, weir
水养护　water cure
水样　water sample
水源　water source
水源保护区　water source protection zone
水源地　water source location
水源涵养林　water conservation forest
水源涵养能力　water conservation capacity
水源涵养区　water conservation area
水源热泵　water-source heat pump
水源卫生防护　hygiene protection for water source
水跃　hydraulic jump
水云母　hydromica
水运　water way
水运货区　freight area for water transport
水灾　flood
水灾险　flood insurance
水闸　sluice
水蒸气渗透系数　water vapor permeation coefficient
水蒸气压力　pressure of water vapour
水质　water quality
水质恶劣地区　poor water quality area
水质分析　water quality analysis
水质分析试验　water quality analysis test
水质简分析　brief water quality analysis
水质评价　water quality evaluation
水质全分析　overall water quality analysis
水中称量法　underwater weighing method
水中养护　curing in water
水柱压力　water column pressure
水柱压水法　water column pump-in test method
水准测段　leveling section
水准测量　leveling

水准尺	leveling rod
水准点	benchmark
水准管	level tube
水准基点	base benchmark
水准投标	level tendering
水准网	leveling network
水准仪	level
水准仪绳尺法	level rope tape method
水准原点	leveling origin
水资源论证	water resource assessment
水渍险	with particular average (WPA), with average (W. A.)
水阻试验	water resistance test
税	tax
税额	tax amount
税法	tax law, law of tax
税法漏洞	tax loophole
税后价格	price after tax
税后利润	after-tax profit, profit after tax
税后收益	earnings after tax (EAT)
税金	taxes
税款	imposition, dues
税款减免	tax credit
税款专用	earmarking of taxes
税率	tax rate
税目	tax items
税前利润	profit before tax, before tax profit
税前收益	before tax income
税收	revenue, tax
税收负担	tax burden
税务法院	tax court
税务检查员	surveyor of taxes
税务局	taxation office
税务员	tax collector
税制	taxation
顺坝	longitudinal dike
顺层滑坡	consequent landslide
顺层劈理	bedding cleavage
顺差	active balance, surplus
顺磁性矿物	paramagnetic mineral
顺列式枢纽	longitudinal arrangement type junction terminal
顺坡	run off
顺驼峰方向	along humping direction
顺向单开道岔	trailing single turnout
顺向连接	same direction connection
顺向重叠进路	route with overlapped section in the same direction
瞬变电磁法	transient electromagnetic method
瞬变压力	transient pressure
瞬时沉降	immediate settlement
瞬时分路	instantaneous shunting
瞬时分路不良	instantaneous loss of shunting
瞬时风速	instantaneous wind speed
瞬时荷载	transient load
瞬时间隙	instantaneous gap
瞬时制	short time
瞬态激振法	transient exciting method
瞬态面波法	transient surface wave method
瞬态振动	transient vibration
说明	describe, description
说明书	instructions
司法惯例	juridical practice
司法记录单元	juridical recorder unit (JRU)
司法记录器	juridical recorder unit
司法权	jurisdiction
司法委员会	bar council
司法协助	judicial assistance
司机—车载设备接口	driver machine interface
司机号	driver's identification
司机制动优先	driver with high priority
司库	treasurer
丝绢光泽	silky luster
丝扣	threaded coupler
私法	private law
私人财产	personal property, personal estate
私人的	personal, private
私人支票	individual check
私人主动融资	private finance initiatives (PFI)
私人助理	personal assistant
私下和解	private settlement
私营部门参与	private sector participation (PSP)
私营工程合同	contract of privately performed work
私营公司	private company
私营企业	private enterprise
私有化	privatization
私有设施实体或单位	private utility entities
斯柯特结线	Scott connection
死滑坡	dead landslide
死区段	dead section
死亡抚恤金	death benefit (gratuity)
死亡和伤残补助金	death and disability award
死亡事故	fatal accident
四边支承板	four-side supported plate
四点检查	released by checking four sections
四分法	quartering method
四角锥体网架	square pyramid space grids
四显示自动闭塞	four-aspect automatic blocking
四线接口	four-wire interface
四线接收电平	four-wire reception level

四组分法　four components method
4D 建模　4D modeling
4 毫米锁闭　4 mm locking
似 t_0 时间剖面图　pseudo-t_0 time profile
似大地水准面　quasi-geoid
似内摩擦角　equivalent internal friction angle
似碳质　carboids
松弛时间　relaxation time
松动爆破　loosening blasting
松动岩石　loose rock
松软土　mollisol
松软土路基　mollisol subgrade
松散　loose
松散结构　loose structure
松散土层　loose soil layer
松散型联营体　separated joint venture
松散压力　loosening pressure
松散岩质路堑　loose rock cutting
松土机　ripper
送电端　feeding end
送风　air supply
送风方式　air supply mode
送货单　delivery note
送货费用　delivery expense
送货回单　delivery receipt
送货令　delivery order, bill of lading(B/L)
送检　submission for inspection
送受分开电路　circuit with sending and receiving separated
送受话声音调整　transmitting and receiving voice regulation
送样　sample presentation
送桩　pile follower
苏长岩　norite
诉讼　proceedings, litigation, suit, legal action lawsuit
诉讼标的　object of action
诉讼财产管理人　receiver
诉讼程序　litigation procedure
诉讼当事人　litigant
诉讼法　procedural law, adjective law
诉讼费　legal costs, costs
诉讼费加损害赔偿费　costs and damages
诉讼理由　count of lawsuit
诉讼权　right of action
诉讼人席位　floor of the court
诉讼时效　limitation of action, prescription
诉讼时效法规　statute of limitation (prescription)
诉讼项目　action item
诉讼中止令　prohibition
诉因　cause
诉诸法律　litigate
诉诸仲裁　initiating arbitration
诉状　petition, pleadings
素混凝土　plain concrete
素混凝土结构　plain concrete structure
素混凝土面层　unreinforced surface
素混凝土桩　plain concrete pile
素土　plain soil
速差式自动闭塞　speed-different mode automatic blocking
速差制信号　speed signaling
速度　velocity, speed, rate
速度场　velocity field
速度传感器　speed sensor
速度目标值　speed target value
速度系数　speed factor
速断　instantaneous tripping
速断保护　instantaneous trip protection
速率　rate
速凝混凝土　fast-setting concrete
速凝剂　accelerating agent
速凝水泥　fast-setting cement, quick cement, rapid hardening cement, ferro-crete
速遣费　dispatch money, despatch money
宿舍区　dormitory area
塑料薄膜　plastic film
塑料防水卷材　plastic waterproof sheet
塑料管　plastic pipe
塑料排水　plastic drain
塑料排水板　plastic drain sheet
塑料排水带　plastic drainage belt
塑料填料　plastic media
塑料土工格栅　plastic geogrid
塑料制品　plastics
塑流　plastic flow
塑限　plastic limit
塑性　plasticity
塑性变形　plastic deformation
塑性混凝土　quaking concrete
塑性铰　plastic hinge
塑性平衡状态　state of plastic equilibrium
塑性破坏　plastic failure
塑性区　plastic zone
塑性图　plasticity chart
塑性土　plastic soil
塑性位移　plastic displacement
塑性应变　plastic strain
塑性指数　plasticity index
溯源　tracing, trace to the source

溯源侵蚀　headward erosion
酸不溶物含量　content of acid non-soluble substance
酸处理　acid treatment
酸度　acidity
酸度计　acidity meter
酸化处理　acidizing
酸溶法　acid pasting
酸性高锰酸钾法　acidic potassium permanganate method
酸性侵蚀　acid erosion
酸性污水　acid sewage
酸性中和池　neutralization tank
酸雨　acid rain
酸雨控制区　acid rain control zone
酸值　acid value
随乘制　caboose working system
随机抽样　random sampling
随机检验　random testing
随机样品　random sample
随意　at discretion
碎斑结构　porphyroclastic texture
碎部测量　detail survey
碎部点　detail point
碎块石　broken block stone
碎块石气冷路基　air-cooled broken block stone embankment
碎块石通风路堤　broken stone-ventilated embankment
碎块状　fragmental
碎砾石　crushed gravel
碎裂岩　cataclasite
碎落台　stage for heaping soil and broken rock
碎石　crushed stone
碎石道床　ballast bed
碎石垫层　broken stone cushion
碎石机　crusher
碎石撒铺机　broken stone spreader
碎石土　gravelly soil
碎石岩堆　crushed scree, crushed talus
碎石桩　gravel pile
碎屑结构　clastic texture
碎屑岩堆　clastic scree, clastic talus
隧道　tunnel
隧道爆破效应　blasting effect of tunnel
隧道标　tunnel post
隧道测量　tunnel survey
隧道施工超前地质预报　advance geological prediction for tunnel construction
隧道衬砌　tunnel lining
隧道衬砌断面　cross-section of lined tunnel
隧道电缆槽　cable trough of tunnel
隧道断面　cross-section of tunnel
隧道防火措施　tunnel fire prevention measure
隧道防排水　waterproofing and drainage of tunnel
隧道防水　waterproofing of tunnel
隧道附属构筑物　auxiliary structure of tunnel
隧道工程　tunnelling
隧道拱圈(又称"拱圈")　arch ring of tunnel
隧道建筑限界　structure gauge of tunnel
隧道净空断面　clear cross-section of tunnel
隧道净空　tunnel clearance
隧道净空变化　tunnel convergence
隧道掘进　tunnelling advancement
隧道掘进机　tunnel boring machine (TBM)
隧道掘进设备　tunnelling plant
隧道开挖　tunnel excavation
隧道开挖断面　cross-section of excavated tunnel
隧道漏水　water leakage of tunnel
隧道路基　tunnel subgrade
隧道门　tunnel portal
隧道模　tunnel form
隧道内测量　survey inside the tunnel
隧道排水　drainage of tunnel
隧道群　tunnel group
隧道施工通风　ventilation during tunnel construction
隧道通风　tunnel ventilation
隧道外测量　survey outside the tunnel
隧道涌水量　water inflow into tunnel
隧道运营通风　ventilation during tunnel operation
隧道凿岩机　tunnel drill, jumbo drill
隧道照明　tunnel lighting
隧道支撑　tunnel support
隧道作业　tunnelling operation
隧底隆起　tunnel floor upheaval
隧洞挖掘机　tunnel boring machine
燧石　flint, chert
损害　damage, prejudice, nuisance
损害保险　insurance of damage
损害程度　extent of damage
损害估算人　damage surveyor
损害赔偿　compensation for damage
损害赔偿费限额　limit of liquidated damages
损害赔偿金　damages
损害索赔　damage claim
损害责任　liability for damage
损耗　depletion, waste, loss, wear and tear
损耗部件　wearing parts

损耗费	cost of wear and tear
损耗量	amount of waste
损耗率	rate of waste
损耗容许量	shrinkage allowance
损坏	deterioration, breakdown
损坏风险	risk of damage
损坏计量师	damage surveyor
损坏赔偿	indemnity for damage
损坏赔偿条款	ad damnum clause
损坏水土保持设施面积	area of damaged soil and water conservation facilities
损坏植被面积	area of damaged vegetation
损失	loss
损失舱位	broken stowage
损失告知	loss advice
损失估计	loss assessment
损失机会	chance of loss
损失减轻	loss relief
损失减少	loss abatement
损失控制	loss control
损失理算师	loss adjuster
损失率	loss ratio
损失频率	loss frequency
损失评定人	loss assessor
损失条款	loss clause
损失通知	notice of loss
损失通知书	loss advice
损失预防	loss prevention
损失证明	proof of loss
损蚀	deterioration
损益	gain and loss, loss and gain, profit and loss, break-even
损益报表	operation statement
损益表	income sheet (statement), profit and loss statement, statement of profit and loss
损益分配	division of gain or loss
损益平衡分析	break-even analysis
损益平衡图	break-even chart
损益账	profit and loss account
梭式矿车	shuttle mine car
梭头	nose of guard rail, shuttle end
缩短轨	shortened rail, curtailed rail
缩减投资	disinvestment
缩颈	necking down
缩径	diameter reducing
缩限	shrinkage limit
缩性指数	shrinkage index
所得	income
所得附加税	income tax surcharge
所得税	income tax, tax on income
所得税扣款	income tax deduction
所得税申报表	income tax return
所得税预扣法	pay-as-you-earn (PAYE)
所欠余额	balance due
所用变压器	auxiliary transformer
所用电	auxiliary power supply
所用电源	auxiliary power supply
所有权	proprietary, proprietary right, pro-prietorship, ownership, title, right of ownership, possession
所有权凭证	document of title
所有权证据	evidence of title
所有权转移	ownership transfer, passage of title
所有人	proprietary, owner
所有制	ownership
所在地	locality
索鞍	cable saddle
索铲挖土机	dragline excavator
索夹	cable clip
索价	asked (asking) price
索具	rigging
索力测试	cable force test
索力控制	cable force control
索赔	claim
索赔报告	statement of claim
索赔程序	procedure for claims
索赔的认可或决定	agreement or determination of the claim
索赔的支付	payment for claims
索赔额	amount of claim, claim money
索赔理算	adjustment of claim
索赔率	claim ratio
索赔清单	statement of claim, claim statement
索赔权	right of claim, right to claim
索赔人	claimant, claimer
索赔时限	time of validity of a claim
索赔事件	claim event
索赔书	affidavit of claim
索赔通知书	notice of claim
索赔文件	document for claim, claim document
索赔悬案	outstanding claim
索赔意识	claim consciousness, sense of claims
索赔预防管理	preventive claims management
索赔证明	substantiation of claim, proof of claim
索平面	cable plane
索取	claim
索取额	amount of claim, claim money
索塔	cable support tower
索要补偿	claim for compensation

索要损害赔偿　claim for damages
索引　index
锁闭　locking
锁闭电路　locking circuit
锁闭杆　locking rod
锁闭机构　locking mechanism
锁闭力　locking force

锁闭条件　locking requisition
锁闭系统　locking system
锁臂　hammerlock
锁定荷载　lock-in load
锁口　collar
锁销　lockpin

T

TADS 铁路车辆滚动轴承故障轨旁声学诊断系统　train acoustic detection system
TFDS 货车故障轨旁图像检测系统　train of freight failures detection system
TPDS 铁路车辆运行品质轨旁动态监测系统　train performance detection system
T 形刚构桥　T-shaped rigid frame bridge
T 形接头　T-shaped joint
T 形截面　T-shaped cross-section
T 形梁　T-girder, T-beam
T 形梁桥　T-girder bridge, T-beam bridge
T 形梁制存梁场　T-girder fabrication and storage yard
T 形螺栓　T-shape bolt
T 形线夹　T-connector
弹劾　impeach
弹簧补偿器　tensioning spring
弹簧补偿装置　tensioning spring
弹簧操作机构　spring operating mechanism
弹簧道钉　elastic spike
弹簧防爬器　spring rail anchor
弹簧隔振器　spring vibration absorber
弹力继电器　spring-type relay
弹塑性分析　elastic-plastic analysis
弹条　clip
弹条式扣件　elastic clip fastening
弹性　elasticity
弹性变形　elastic deformation
弹性波　elastic wave
弹性波 CT 法　elastic wave CT method
弹性波法　elastic wave method
弹性波反射法　elastic wave reflection method
弹性波勘探　elastic wave exploration
弹性不均匀度　variation in elasticity, non-uniformity
弹性地基板　elastic foundation plate
弹性地基梁　beam on elastic foundation
弹性垫板　resilient pad
弹性垫层　elastic cushion
弹性吊索　stitch wire
弹性吊索线夹　stitch wire clamp
弹性吊索支座　stitch wire support
弹性反力　elastic reaction
弹性方案　elastic analysis scheme
弹性工时　flexible working hours（FWH）, flexitime
弹性轨枕　elastic sleeper
弹性汇率　flexible exchange rate
弹性挤开　gauge elastically widened（elastic squeeze out）
弹性简单悬挂　trolley-type suspension with bridle wire
弹性抗力　elastic resistance
弹性抗力系数　elastic resistance coefficient
弹性抗震设计　elasticity seismic design
弹性扣件　elastic clip, elastic fastening
弹性理论　theory of elasticity
弹性链形悬挂　stitched catenary suspension, catenary suspension with stitch wire
弹性模量　elasticity modulus
弹性位移　elastic displacement
弹性限位板　elastic position-limiting plate
弹性压力　elastic pressure
弹性应变　elastic strain
弹性预算　flexible budget
弹性支撑　elastic support
弹性支承块　elastic bearing block
弹性支承块式轨道　low vibration track（LVT）
弹性支承块式无砟轨道　low vibration track（LVT）, ballastless track with elastic bearing block
弹性支座连续梁　elastically supported continuous girder
探地雷达　ground penetrating radar（GPR）
调幅抑制　amplitude-modulation suppression
调高垫板　heightening pad
调高价格　escalation price
调高条文　escalation clause

调高总价合同	escalation lump sum contract
调价	revision of price, price adjustment, escalation
调价公式	price adjustment formula
调价价格	escalation price
调价条款	escalation clause
调焦误差	focusing error
调节	regulate, regulation
调节沉淀隔油	regulation, sedimentation, oil separation
调节阀	regulating valve
调节架	adjusting bracket
调解	conciliate, conciliation, mediate, mediation
调解程序	conciliation procedure
调解及仲裁规则	rules of conciliation and arbitration
调解人	conciliator, mediator, intermediary
调解委员会	conciliation committee, commission of conciliation
调梁线	car sill straightening siding
调试	commissioning
调试库	test and commissioning workshop
调速顶	speed control retarder
调速阀	speed valve
调速系统	speed control system
调停	mediate, mediation
调停费	intermediation rate
调停员	mediator
调谐匹配单元	tuning and matching unit
调谐区标志牌	sign board for tuning zone
调休制	lodging system
调压器	voltage regulator
调压装置	voltage regulating device
调音台	audio console
调整	adjustment
调整参考表	reference list of adjustment
调整电压	adjusting voltage
调整后的价格	adjusted price
调整进度表	revise a schedule
调整数据表	table of adjustment data
调整系数	adjustment multiplier
调整余量	margin for adjustment
调整状态	adjustment state
调直	straightening
调直机	straightener
调值总价合同	escalation lump sum contract
调制解调器	modem
调治构造物	river training structure
塌岸	bank collapse
塌方	cave-in, collapse
塌落拱	collapse arch
塌落扩展度	slump spread
塌陷	collapse
塌陷区	subsidence area
塔式起重机	tower crane
塔式生物滤池	biotower
踏勘	reconnaissance
踏面	tread
胎基材料	base material
台班	machine shift
台班产量	output by one machine shift
台班费	fee of one machine shift
台班小时	hours in one machine shift
台背斜	anticlise
台秤	platform scale
台风	typhoon
台后基坑	foundation pit behind abutment
台后填方	filling behind abutment
台阶	step
台阶(隧道开挖)	bench
台阶法	bench-cut method
台阶开挖	bench excavation
台口式路基	benched subgrade
台帽	abutment cap
台身	abutment stem
台时	machine hour
台位利用系数	utility factor of the position
台向斜	syneclise
台账	standing book
抬道	track lifting
抬道量	track lifting amount
抬起高度	uplifting height
抬升	uplift
抬升量	uplift
太古代	Archaeozoic era
太古界	Archaeozoic erathem
太古宇	Archean eonothem
太古宙	Archean eon
太平门	emergency door
太沙基固结理论	Terzaghi's consolidation theory
太阳方位角	solar azimuth
太阳辐射	solar radiation
太阳辐射热	solar radiation heat
太阳辐照量	solar irradiation
太阳高度角	solar altitude
太阳能	solar energy
太阳能集热器	solar collector
太阳能热水器	solar energy heater
太阳能热水系统	solar water-heating system
泰山期	Taishanian age/stage
坍岸线	bank slumping line
坍方	rock slide

坍滑　collapse and slide
坍落度　slump
坍落度保留值　slump retain value
坍落度试验　slump test
坍塌　collapse
贪污　corruption, embezzlement, peculation
贪污行为　corrupt practice
摊铺机　paver
摊铺平整　spreading evenness
摊销　amortization
摊销量　amortization amount
摊销率　amortization rate
谈判　negotiate, negotiation
谈判策略　negotiating strategies
谈判程序　negotiating procedure
谈判范围　scope for negotiation
谈判失败　fail in negotiation
谈判实力　bargaining power
谈判者　negotiator
炭黑含量　content of carbon black
炭质页岩　carbonaceous shale
探槽　exploratory trench
探测　detect
探测器　detector
探测深度　investigation depth
探测站　detection station
探杆　feeler lever
探井　exploratory well
探井器　well detector
探亲假　home leave
探伤　flaw detection
探伤检查　flaw detection
探伤仪　fault detector, flaw detector
探照灯　search light
探照式色灯信号机　colour searchlight signal
碳当量　carbon equivalent
碳滑板　carbon contact strip
碳化　carbonization
碳化钙　calcium carbide
碳化钙减量法　calcium carbide decrement method
碳化环境　carbonization environment
碳化深度　carbonation depth
碳素轨　carbon rail
碳素结构钢　carbon structural steel
碳酸根含量　carbonate content
碳酸钠　sodium carbonate
碳酸铅　lead carbonate
碳酸盐　carbonate
碳酸盐岩　carbonatite

碳纤维加固　strengthening method by bonding carbon fiber
掏槽眼　cut hole
掏金洞　gold digging cave
掏煤洞　coal digging cave
掏砂洞　sand digging cave
逃避　dodge, evade, avoid
逃税　evade taxes, tax evasion, tax dodging
逃税人　tax evader
逃税手段　tax shelter
陶粒混凝土　ceramsite concrete
讨价还价　price bargaining, price haggling
套管　casing pipe
套管单耳　eye clamp
套管式冷凝器　tube-in-tube condenser
套管双耳　clevis end holder
套管钻机　casing drilling rig
套汇　cross exchange, arbitrage
套利　arbitrage, covered-interest
套利率　interest rate of arbitrage
套期保值　hedging
套算汇率　cross rate
套筒　sleeve
套筒补偿器　sleeve compensator
套芯解除法　overcoring relief method
套型　dwelling type
特别成本　abnormal cost
特别的　extraordinary, special
特别恶劣的天气　exceptionally inclement weather
特别费用　extraordinary cost
特别附加税　special surtax
特别规定　special provisions
特别检查　special inspection
特别利润　abnormal profit
特别提款权　special drawing rights (SDRs)
特别折旧　abnormal depreciation, special discount
特长　specialty
特长隧道　extra-long tunnel
特大桥　very long bridge (with length more than 500 m)
特大型车站　super large station
特大型建设项目　mega construction project
特大型旅客车站　super-large passenger train station
特点　characteristics
特定的　specific, particular, ad hoc, given
特定留置权　particular lien
特惠　special preference
特惠关税　preferential duties
特惠税率　preferential tariff
特级道砟　special grade ballast
特权　privilege

特设仲裁　ad hoc arbitration
特深埋隧道　extra-deep tunnel
特殊保护区　special protection area
特殊补救办法　exceptional remedy
特殊产品　specialty
特殊的　exceptional, particular
特殊风险
　　special risks, abnormal risk, exceptional risk
特殊附加险　special additional risk
特殊合同条件　particular conditions
特殊荷载　special load
特殊混凝土　special concrete
特殊紧急事件　exceptional urgency
特殊力　special force
特殊路基　special subgrade
特殊缺水地区　severely water-deficient area
特殊砂浆　special mortar
特殊设防　special fortification
特殊施工条件下的附加费用　additional cost under special construction condition
特殊事件　exceptional event
特殊试验　special test
特殊条件路基　subgrade in special conditions
特殊条款　special provisions
特殊条文　special provisions
特殊土　special soil
特殊土路基　subgrade of special soil
特殊显色指数　special colour rendering index
特殊性岩土　special rock and soil
特殊岩土　special rock and soil
特殊应用条件　conditions of particular application
特型定位器　T-type steady arm
特型软定位器
　　T-type steady arm for curve line with bridle wire
特型旋转腕臂底座　T-type hinged cantilever bracket
特性　quality
特许　concession, franchise, charter
特许贷款　concessionary loan
特许的　concessionary, concessional, patent
特许公司　concessionary, concession company
特许会计师　chartered accountant (CA)
特许经营税　franchise taxes
特许期　concessionary period
特许权　franchise, concession
特许权出让人　franchiser
特许权受让人　franchisee, concessionaire
特许使用费　override
特许协议　franchise agreement, concession agreement
特有条款　specific provision

特征裂缝宽度　characteristic crack width
特征值　characteristic value
特征周期　characteristic period
特种车辆活载　live load of special vehicle
特种工程结构　special engineering structure
特种混凝土　special concrete
特种水泥　special cement
特种土工材料　special geotextile material
特种作业　special operation
剔除法　exclusion method
梯度比　gradient ratio
梯架　ladder rack
梯形法　trapezoidal method
梯形撕裂强度　trapezoidal tearing strength
梯形屋架　trapezoidal roof truss
梯形堰　trapezoidal weir
梯子　ladder
提倡　advocate
提倡者　advocate
提成费　royalty
提出索赔　file a claim
提存费用　deposit expense
提存账户　drawing account
提存支票　drawing cheque
提单　bill of lading (B/L)
提单副本　bill of lading copy (B/L copy)
提单日期　date of bill of lading
提单运费　bill-of-lading freight
提单正本　bill of lading original (B/L original)
提纲　outline plan
提供方便　accommodation
提供劳务合同　contract for the supply of labour
提供援助　delivery of assistance
提供资金　fund
提钩地段　release-coupler section
提货　take delivery, withdrawal, collection
提货单　delivery order, bill of lading (B/L)
提货即付款协议　take-and-pay agreement
提货通知　cargo delivery notice
提货与否均需付款协议
　　take-or-pay agreement
提及　refer to, mention
提价　price mark up
提交　submit, submission, produce, presentation
提交争议后双方的义务
　　the parties' obligations after the reference
提款　draw, drawing, withdraw, withdraw deposit, withdrawal
提款申请　withdrawal application
提款账　drawing account

提款账户　drawing account
提款支票　drawing cheque
提拉压缩式止水器
　　lifting compression type sealing device
提捞法　bailing method
提梁上桥区　area for lifting girder up to bridge
提名　nomination, nominate
提起诉讼　lawsuit
提前偿付条款　acceleration clause
提前承兑　rebated acceptance
提前竣工　earlier completion
提前竣工奖金　bonus for early completion
提前取款罚金　early withdrawal penalty
提前提款罚金　early withdrawal penalty
提前完成计划　ahead of schedule
提前完工　accelerated completion
提前完工奖励　incentives for early completion, early completion bonus
提取　withdraw, collect
提取现金　cash drawing
提升　promote, promotion
提示　presentment
提示人　presenter
提示信息　reminder
提水试验　water lifting test
提水筒　bailing barrel
提桶洗井法　pail flushing
提要　brief, outline
提议　proposal
体波　body wave
体格检查　medical examination
体积　cubic measure, volume
体积法　volumetric method
体积含冰量　volumetric ice content
体积力　body force
体积模量　bulk modulus
体积浓度　volume concentration
体积配筋率　reinforcement ratio per unit volume
体积压缩系数
　　coefficient of volume compressibility
体检证明　medical certificate
体力劳动者　manual labour
体内预应力　internal prestress
体缩率　volumetric shrinking ratio
体外预应力　external prestress
体外预应力加固法
　　strengthening method by external prestressing
体系　system
体系结构　architecture
体系文件　system document

体应变　volumetric strain
替代　substitute, substitution, supersede
替代办法　alternative, alternative solution
替代材料与设备　alternative material and equipment
替代方案　alternative, alternative solution
替代进口　import substitution
替代契约　deed of substitution
替代人　substitute
替代条款　alternative provisions, alternative clause
替代条文　alternative provisions, alternative clause
替换　substitution
（日历）天　（calendar）day
天窗　maintenance window
天窗架　skylight frame
天顶距　zenith distance
天沟　overhead ditch
天平　balance
天桥　over-bridge, overpass, overpassing
天然材料　natural materials
天然场大地电磁法
　　natural field magnetotelluric method
天然地基　natural ground
天然地震试验　natural earthquake test
天然干密度　natural dry density
天然含水量　natural water content
天然含水率　natural moisture content
天然护道　natural berm
天然级配　prototype gradation, naturally graded
天然建筑材料　natural construction materials
天然孔隙比　natural void ratio
天然沥青　rock asphalt
天然密度　natural density
天然密实度　natural compactness
天然桥　natural bridge
天然砂　natural sand
天然休止角　natural repose angle
天然植被　natural vegetation
天然资源　natural resources
天文台　observatory
天线　antenna
天灾　act of God
添加　add
添加剂　annexing agent
填迟日期　postdate
填充层　fill layer
填充剂　filler
填方　fill
填方材料　fill materials
填料　fill material
填料费　charge for filling material

填料集中拌和站　centralized mixing station of filler
填料类别　category of fill material
填料粒径　grain size of fill material
填料试验　test of fill material
填料塔　packed tower
填石　rockfill
填土　earth fill, embankment
填土场　landfill site
填土厚度　depth of filling
填土速率　filling rate
填项　entry
填早日期　backdate, foredate, antedate
填筑　reclamation, placement
填筑层　fill layer
填筑路堤　earth-filled embankment
填筑土　compacted filling soils
条带拉伸试验　strip-tensile test
条带状构造　banded structure, streaked structure
条带状混合岩　banded migmatite, striped migmatite
条分法　slices method
条缝型风口　slot type air outlet
条痕　streak
条件　condition, terms
条件电源　conditional power source
条件方程　condition equation
条件方程式　conditional equation
条件方程式常数项　constant term of conditional equation
条件苛刻的贷款　hard loan
条件平差　condition adjustment
条款　article, clause, terms
条款草案　draft provision
条款与条件　terms and conditions
条例　regulation, rule, ordinance, act
条目　entry
条目说明　description of items
条文初稿　draft provision
条形荷载　strip load
条形基础　strip foundation
条形混凝土铺面　stripe-shape concrete pavement
条约　pact, treaty
调整钢轨间隙　adjustment of rail gaps
挑梁　cantilever beam
跳仓施工法　alternative bay construction method
跳停　tripping
跳线　jumper
跳线肩架　jumper cross arm
跳线线夹　jumper clamp
跳运　saltation transport
跳闸　trip, tripping
贴附射流　attached jet
贴面砖　tiling
贴水　at a discount, premium, agio
贴现　discount
贴现的现金流量　discounted cash flow (DCF)
贴现回收期　discounted payback period
贴现经纪人　discount broker
贴现率　discount rate, rate of discount
贴现票据　note on discount
贴现期　discount period
贴现系数　discount factor
贴现银行　discount bank
贴现值　discounted value
铁磁性矿物　ferromagnetic mineral
铁道电气化　railway electrification
铁垫板　iron pad
铁禁　CR Prohibition
铁路边界　railway boundary
铁路边界噪声　railway noise on the boundary alongside railway line
铁路边界噪声限值　railway noise limit on the boundary alongside railway line
铁路便桥　railway temporary bridge
铁路到货通知　railway advice
铁路等级　railway classification
铁路工程　railway engineering
铁路工程测量　railway engineering survey
铁路工程绿色通道　Green Corridor for Railways
铁路工程信息模型　railway engineering information modeling/model
铁路工程要素模型　railway engineering feature model
铁路工业站　railway industrial station
铁路供配电系统　power supply and distribution system of railway
铁路航空摄影测量(铁路航测)　railway aerial photogrammetry
铁路回用水　railway reuse water
铁路货区　railway freight area
铁路给水厂(所)　water supply plant(station) of railway
铁路建设基金　railway construction fund
铁路建设基金费率　railway construction fund rate
铁路建筑限界　railway structure gauge
铁路交货　on rail
铁路交货价　free on rail (FOR)
铁路紧急呼叫　railway emergency call (REC)
铁路精密工程测量控制网　surveying control network of railway precision engineering

铁路景观用水　railway landscape water
铁路局界站　boundary station of railway administration
铁路局中心系统　centeral system of railway administration
铁路客运服务信息系统　railway passenger transport service information system
铁路客站建筑环境负荷减少　building environment load reduction of railway station
铁路客站建筑环境质量　building environment quality of railway station
铁路路基设计　railway embankment design
铁路路网规划　railway network planning
铁路旅客车站　railway passenger station
铁路轮渡　railway train ferry
铁路桥　railway bridge
铁路生产污水　sewage produced during railway operation
铁路生活杂用水　railway non-drinking water
铁路声屏障　sound barrier along railway
铁路枢纽　railway terminal, railway junction
铁路数字移动通信系统　Global System for Mobile Communications-Railway(GSM-R)
铁路隧道　railway tunnel
铁路提货单　railway bill of lading
铁路通信　railway communication
铁路托运单　railway consignment note
铁路网　railway network
铁路限界　railway clearance
铁路线路　railway line
铁路信号　railway signaling
铁路信号安全通信协议　railway signal safety communication protocol
铁路选线　railway location
铁路油品装卸线　loading and unloading line for railway oil products
铁路运费　railway freight
铁路运输　carriage by rail
铁路运输及海运　rail and ocean
铁路运输及空运　rail and air
铁路运输及水运　rail and water
铁路运营养护　railway operation and maintenance
铁路噪声　railway noise
铁路主要技术标准　main technical standards for railway
铁路专用材料　dedicated materials for railway project
铁路专用线　industrial siding, special spur track, private siding
铁路专用移动通信系统　railway dedicated mobile communication system
铁路自然灾害及异物侵限监测系统　natural disaster and foreign object intrusion monitoring system for railway
铁路综合接地　railway integrated grounding
铁路综合视频监控系统　railway integrated video surveillance system
铁塔基础　tower foundation
铁鞋　brake shoe
铁鞋制动　skate brake
铁质胶结　ferruginous cement
听觉信号　audible signal
听证会　hearing
庭审　tribunal hearing
停泊地　anchorage
停泊费　groundage, harbor dues, port dues, berthage
停泊时间　lay days
停泊税　anchorage
停车标　stop sign
停车场　parking lot, stabling yard
停车空间　parking space
停车器　stopping device
停车位置测试　parking location test
停车信号　stop signal
停电　power outage
停电作业　working with power cut-off
停港费　keelage
停工　suspension of works
停工令　suspension order
停工时间　downtime, idle time
停机时间　downtime, idle time
停靠港　port of call
停业　closing, winding up
停站时间　dwell time
停止　cease, cessation, stop, stoppage
停止运货　stoppage in transit
停止支付　non-payment
停止支付通知　caveat
通常值　ordinary value
通道　access road
通电检查　power-on check
通风　ventilation
通风道　ventilating duct
通风工程　ventilation engineering
通风管　draft tube, pipe vents
通风管道　ventilating duct
通风管路堤　duct-ventilated embankment
通风管路基　duct-ventilated subgrade
通风耗热量　ventilation heat loss
通风机　ventilation fan
通风井　ventilating shaft

通风口　vent, air-vent
通风量　ventilation rate
通风屋顶　ventilated roof
通风系统　ventilating system
通风装置　ventilating unit, ventilation device, aerator
通缝　straight joint
通缝破坏　straight-line joint failure
通告　advertisement, announcement
通过　pass, pass through
通过按钮电路　through button circuit
通过车场　transit yard
约定最终报表　agreed final statement
通过进路　through route
通过立井导入高程测量
　　height measurement by vertical shaft
通过率　passing rate
通过能力　carrying capacity
通过式货运站　through-type freight station
通过式客运站　through -type passenger station
通过信号　through signal
通过信号机　block signal
通航净空　navigational clearance
通航水位　navigable water level
通话柱　communication post
通货紧缩　deflation
通货膨胀　inflation, currency inflation
通货膨胀调整　inflation adjustment
通气管　ventilation pipe
通气帽　ventilation cap
通球试验　pigging test
通融索赔　ex gratia claim
通商口岸　treaty port
通水量试验　discharge capacity test
通所道路　access road
通透螺栓　through bolt
通信　communication
通信电缆　communication cable
通信电源及机房环境监控系统
　　communication power and equipment room environment monitoring system
通信会话管理测试
　　communication session management test
通信机房　communication equipment room
通信控制服务器
　　communication and control server(CCS)
通信楼机房
　　equipment room in communication building
地址簿　address book
通信前置处理机　communication front-end processor
通信室　communication room

通信枢纽　communication center
通信系统　communication system
通信线路　communication line
通信业务　communication service
通信站　communication station
通信综合网络管理(综合网管)
　　integrated communication network management
通行　prevail, transit
通行地沟　accessible trench
通行费　toll
通行汇率　prevailing rate
通行列车的站线　station track of trains passing
通行权　wayleaves, passage
通行税　transit tax, transit duty (dues), toll, passenger duty, pike
通讯屏　communication panel
通讯社　news agency
通用财务报表　all-purpose financial statement
通用分组无线业务
　　general packet radio service (GPRS)
通用高厚比　normal height-thickness ratio
通用固定带式输送机
　　universal fixed belt conveyor
通用硅酸盐水泥　common portland cement
通用式机车信号　universal cab signal
通用手持台
　　general purpose handset/handheld (GPH)
通用要求条款　common requirement clause
通用中间格式
　　common intermediate format (CIF)
通知　notification, notice
通知偿还　call/notice of payment
通知存款　call deposit
通知贷款　call loan
通知单　advice note, notification
通知函　circular letter
通知及其他沟通形式
　　notice and other communications
通知交货　delivery on call
通知期限　notice period
通知设备　annunciating device
通知手续费　advising charges
通知书　letter of advice, letter of notice, notification, note
通知行　advising bank, notifying bank
同步传递模式　synchronous transfer mode(STM)
同步传送模块 n 级
　　synchronous transport module level n(STM-N)
同步供给单元　synchronous supply unit(SSU)
同步光纤网络　synchronous optical network

同步接口　synchronous interface
同步控制器　synchronous controller
同步数字体系
　　synchronous digital hierarchy(SDH)
同步状态信息　synchronization status message(SSM)
同程式系统　reversed return system
同等机会　equal opportunity
同等机会条款　equal opportunity clause
同工同酬　equal pay for equal work
同级扩展　interpolation of the same accuracy
同盟　confederation
同盟费率　conference rate
同名像点　homologous point
同期记录　contemporary records
同时发生　concur
同时观测有效卫星数　number of effectively observed satellites at the same time
同事　associate
同条件养护试件
　　specimen under the same curing condition
同位素示踪测井　isotope tracer logging
同席人员　table
同相单边供电
　　single-end feeding with phase of same sequence
同相供电　cophase traction power supply
同相轴　event
同向曲线　curves in the same direction
同心圆　concentric circles
同心状　concentric
同行评议　peer review
同业　profession
同业工会　craft union, trade association
同意按钮盘　agreement button panel
同站址双网覆盖　co-located double coverage
同轴电缆　coaxial cable
同轴电力电缆供电方式
　　coaxial power cable feeding system
同轴度公差　axiality tolerance
铜棒　copper bar
铜管椭圆度　copper pipe ovality
铜含量　copper content
铜合金绞线承力索
　　copper alloy stranded messenger wire
铜合金接触导线　copper alloy contact wire
铜铝过渡设备线夹　Al-Cu transition connector
铜排　copper bar
统筹法　program evaluation and reviews technique (PERT)
统计　statistics
统计表　returns/statistical chart
统计参数　statistic parameter
统计检验法　statistical testing method
统计数字　statistics
统计推断方法　statistical inference method
统计周期　statistic cycle
统计资料　statistics
统一发票　uniform invoice
统一费率　flat rate
统一惯例　uniform customs
统一税率　flat rate
统一眩光值　unified glare rating
统驭账户　control (controlling) account
筒仓　silo
筒式柴油打桩锤　tubular diesel pile hammer
筒式搅拌机　drum mixer
筒体结构　tube structure
筒中筒结构　tube in tube structure
头等风险　primary risk
头脑风暴法　brainstorming
头衔　title
投保　effect insurance, insure against
投保单　application for insurance, proposal form
投保方　insuring party
投保金额
　　insurance amount, sum insured, insured amount
投保人　assured, applicant for insurance, policy holder, insurant, insured, person insuring
投保书　proposal, proposal of insurance
投保项目　insured item
投标　bid, bidding, submission of bid (tender), tender, tendering
投标包干价格分解
　　breakdown of lump sum bid price
投标保函　bid bond, bid guarantee, letter of guarantee for bid, tender guarantee
投标保证　bid security
投标保证声明　bid-securing declaration
投标保证书　bid guarantee, tender guarantee
投标报价　bid price
投标报价汇总表　summary of tender
投标表册　bid tabulations
投标步骤　bid process
投标程序　bid procedure
投标澄清会议　bid clarification meeting
投标担保　bid bond, tender bond
投标单价　bid unit price
投标递交函　bid submission sheet
投标方　tendering party
投标费　bid fee
投标费用　cost of tendering, bid cost

投标格式　bid form
投标估算　tender estimate
投标函　letter of tender
投标核查　bid examination
投标候选人　candidate for tendering
投标汇总　bid summary
投标货币　bid currencies
投标价　bid price, tender price, price tendered
投标价目表　bid schedule of prices
投标阶段　bid phase
投标截止期　deadline for receipt of tenders
投标金额　tender sum
投标期　bid period
投标前现场调查　pre-bid site visit
投标人　bidder, tenderer
投标人的义务　bidder's obligation
投标人会议　tenderer's conference, bidder's conference
投标人名单　tender list, bid list
投标人退还文件　bidder's return of documents
投标人须知　instructions to bidders
投标人质疑　tenderer's query
投标人资格　bidder's qualification
投标人资格预审　bidder's prequalification
投标日期　bid due date, bid date
投标审核　examination of bid
投标时间　bidding time
投标实质内容　bid substance
投标手续　tender procedures
投标书　tender, letter of tender
投标书附录　appendix to bid
投标书格式　form of tender, tender form
投标书签收　bid receipt
投标通知　bidding advice
投标文件　tender
投标文件包　bid package
投标文件内容　bid package contents
投标文件有效期　bid validity period, validity of bid (tender)
投标压价　bid shopping
投标邀请函　bid invitation letter, invitation for bid (IFB), invitation to tender
投标要求　bid requirement
投标意向书　intention for bid (IFB)
投标语言　bid language
投标预备会　pre-bid meeting
投标者　bidder, tenderer
投标准备　bid preparation, preparation of bid

投产　put into production
投机　venture, speculation
投机风险　speculative risk
投机商　speculator, profiteer
投机资本　venture capital
投加单元　dosing unit
投料试车　start-up
投料试生产　commissioning test run
投料顺序　mixing procedure
投票　vote
投入　input, invest
投入运营　go into operation
投入资本　vested capital
投诉　complain
投药　chemical dosing
投药中和　medication neutralization
投影差　relief displacement
投影长度变形值　deformation value of projection length
投影断链　projection of broken chain
投影面高程　elevation of projective plane
投影器主距　principal distance of projector
投影晒印　projection printing
投资　invest, investment
投资补贴额　investment allowance
投资构成　investment composition
投资规模　investment scale
投资回报　returns on the investment, investment return
投资回报率　rate of return on investment, rate of investment return
投资回收期　investment recovery period, payback period
投资阶段　investment phase
投资评价　investment appraisal
投资前研究　pre-investment studies
投资入股型联营体　equity joint venture
投资收益率　return on investment
投资信托　investment trust
投资银行　investment bank
投资预估算　investment pre-estimate
投资预算　investment budget
投资者　investor
投资证券　investment securities
投资周转　investment turnover
投资总额　total investment amount
透辉石　diopside
透镜径向畸变　lens radial distortion
透镜切向畸变　lens tangential distortion
透镜式色灯信号机　multi-lens color light signal

透镜体　lenticle
透明度　diaphaneity, transparency
透明隔声材料　transparent sound insulation material
透明幕墙　transparent curtain wall
透气量　air permeability
透气系数　permeability coefficient
透气系数测定仪　tester for permeability coefficient
透气性　permeability
透闪石　tremolite
透视图　perspective
透水层　permeable bed
透水层交界面　permeable layer interface
透水路堤　pervious embankment
透水性　permeability
透支　overdraft, overdraw
透支保函　overdraft guarantee
透支限额　limit of overdrawn account
透支账户　overdraft account
凸窗　bay window
凸坡　convex slope
凸形挡台　bollard
突发噪声　burst noise
突加荷载法　suddenly applied load method
突然降价法　sudden markdown method
突水　water inrush
图标　title block
图表　graph, chart, diagram
图层　layer
图根点　mapping base point
图根控制　mapping control
图号区　drawing number box
图解　graph, diagram
图解图根点　graphical mapping control point
图框　border
图框外边线　outer border line
图框线　border line
图廓　map border
图廓整饰　map margin decoration
图例　legend
图名　drawing title
图像　image
图像变换　image transformation
图像采集设备　image acquisition equipment
图像处理　image processing
图像分辨率　image resolution
图像服务器　image server
图像显示设备　image display equipment
图像帧率　frame rate
图像综合测试仪　comprehensive image tester
图形　figure

图形编辑　graphic editing
图形处理　graphic processing
图形条件　graphic condition
图形显示　graphical display
图形用户接口　graphical user interface（GUI）
图样　drawing
图章　seal
图纸　drawings
图纸登记册　drawing register
图纸目录　drawing list
图纸说明　drawing notes
途停　stopping halfway
涂层　coating
涂层厚度测定仪　coating thickness tester
涂盖材料　coating
涂料　coating
涂面工作　face work
涂膜制备　coating preparation
涂装　coating
土坝　earth dam
（盾构）土仓　excavation chamber
土层尖灭　pinch-out of soil layer
土层突变　abrupt change of soil layer
土的本构关系(本构模型)
　　constitutive relation（constitutive model）of soil
土的现场鉴别　field identification of soil
土堤　embankment, earth embankment
土地　land
土地补偿费　land compensation fee
土地处理　land treatment
土地复耕　land rehabilitation
土地复垦　land reclamation
土地改良　land improvement
土地规划测量　land planning survey
土地类型　land type
土地利用现状图　present land use map
土地扰动　land disturbance
土地使用费　land use fee
土地使用费(税)　royalties
土地使用权出让金
　　charge for the right of land use
土地使用税　land use tax
土地税　land tax
土地所有权　property in land
土地通行权　easement
土地信息系统　land information system
土地预审　pre-examination for building land
土地征用　expropriation of land
土地征用补偿费
　　compensation fees for land expropriation

土地征用管理费　management fees for land expropriation
土地征用及拆迁补偿费　compensation fees for land expropriation and demolition
土地征用权　domain
土地整理　land consolidation
土地整治　land reclamation
土地整治工程　land reclamation works
土地证　land certificate
土地转让证　land patent
土地租约　ground lease
土钉　soil nail
土钉墙　soil-nailed wall
土动态特性试验　soil dynamic characteristics test
土方工程　ground works, earthwork
土方工程进度表　schedule of earthwork
土方工程量　volume of earthwork
土方修整　grading
土工布　geotextile fabric
土工复合材料　geocomposite
土工格室　geocell
土工格栅　geogrid
土工工程措施　soil engineering measure
土工合成材料　geosynthetics
土工离心模试验　geotechnical centrifugal model test
土工离心模型试验　geotechnical centrifugal model test
土工模袋　geotextile bag
土工膜　geomembrane
土工膨润土垫　geosynthetic clay liner
土工试验　geotechnical test
土工特种材料　special geotextile material
土工网垫　geomat
土工织物　geotextile
土工织物沉枕　geotextile sinking pillow
土工织物的厚度　geotextile thickness
土骨架　soil skeleton
土滑堆积　soil slip accumulation
土建　civil work
土建工程合同　civil contract
土建公司　civil engineering firm
土建交接检验　civil engineering handover inspection
土建投资　civil engineering investments
土结构相互作用　soil-structure interaction
土类分级　soil classification
土粒比重　specific weight of soil particle
土粒粒径　particle size of soil
土木工程　civil work, civil engineering
土木工程师　civil engineer
土木工程程序　civil engineering procedure
土木工程造价　cost of civil engineering works
土木建筑　civil construction
土球　ball clay
土壤承载力　bearing capacity of soil
土壤电阻率(大地电导率)　soil resistivity (earth conductivity)
土壤含水量　soil moisture content, soil moisture
土壤类型　soil type
土壤流失控制比　controlled ratio of soil erosion
土壤流失量　amount of soil erosion
土壤流失容许量　soil loss tolerance
土壤侵蚀　soil erosion
土壤侵蚀分类分级　classification of soil erosion
土壤侵蚀模数　soil erosion modulus
土壤侵蚀强度分布图　distribution diagram of soil erosion intensity
土壤侵蚀强度因子　soil erosion intensity factor
土壤全氮含量　total nitrogen content in soil
土壤水　soil water
土壤条件　soil conditions
土壤污染　soil pollution
土壤盐渍化　salinization of soil
土塞效应　plugging effect
土石坝　earth and rock fill dam
土石方　earthwork and stonework
土石方调配　cut-fill balance
土石方工程　earthworks and stoneworks
土石方流向框图　earthwork flow diagram
土石方平衡表　earthwork balance sheet
土石方运距　haul distance of earthwork and stonework
土石分类　classification of soil and rock
土体　soil mass
土体增密法　soil densification method
土体重度　unit weight of soil mass
土楔　soil wedge
土压力　earth pressure
土压平衡盾构　earth pressure balanced shield (EPB shield)
土样　soil sample
土质边坡　soil slope
土质调查　soil investigation
土质改良　soil improvement
土质滑坡　soil landslide
土质路基　soil subgrade

土质路堑　soil cutting
土柱高度　height of soil column
土状　earthy
土状断口　earthy fracture
湍流　turbulent flow
湍流度　turbulivity
团队精神　team spirit
团体　public body
推测　presumption
推车式灭火器　transportable fire extinguisher
推迟　defer, postpone, postponement
推定价值　constructed value
推定全损　constructive total loss, technical total loss
推定条款　constructive clause
推定占有　constructive possession
推峰速度　humping speed
推峰速度自动控制　automatic control of humping speed
推覆体　nappe
推荐　recommend, recommendation, nomination, nominate
推荐信　letter of recommendation
推进机构　thrust system
推送　push
推送部分　pushing section, humping section
推送进路　pushing route
推送坡　pushing slope
推送速度　humping speed
推送线　pushing track
推送信号　pushing signal
推算坐标　derived coordinates
推土机　bulldozer
推销商　promoter
推销商品的信件　call letter
推移式滑坡　thrust-type landslide
退保　surrender
退还保险费　premium returns
退还担保　back bond
退还预付款　restitution of advance payment
退货　sales returns
退货凭单　merchandise credit slip
退货运费　back freight
退款　draw-back, refund
退料单　materials return report
退票　refund
退票通知单　protest jacket
退税　tax refund, refund of duty, tax rebate
退休　retirement
退休金　pension
退约条款　denunciation clause

托付　consignment
托管　entrust
托管人　trustee
托换技术　underpinning technique
托架　bracket
托盘　tray
托盘止水器　tray sealing device
托收　collect, collection
托收单　order for collection
托收汇票　bill for collection, collect a bill, collection bill
托收票据　bills for collection (BC)
托收人　billing agent
托收委托书　collection order
托收银行　collecting bank, remitting bank
托运　consignment
托运单　consignment bill, forwarding order
托运人　consignor consigner
托座　bracket
拖布池　mop pool
拖长的暂停　prolonged suspension
拖车　tow truck, trailer
拖挂式运输车辆　articulated transport vehicle
拖挂式载重车　coupled truck
拖拉法　dragging method
拖拉机　tractor
拖拉架设法　erection by traction method
拖期　behind schedule, schedule slippage, slippage
拖期付款　delayed payment
拖期竣工　delayed completion
拖欠风险　default risk
拖欠款　back money
拖延　delay, prolong
拖延策略　delaying tactics
拖运　haul, haulage
脱氟率　rate of defluorinate
脱轨　derail
脱轨表示器　derailment indicator
脱轨器　derailer
脱轨系数　derailment factor, derailment coefficient
脱焊　sealing-off
脱机状态　off-line state
脱机作业　off-line operation
脱模　demoulding
脱模剂　release agent
脱色　decoloration
脱线修　off line maintenance
脱鞋器　skate throw-off device
脱盐率　rate of desalination
陀螺定向测量　gyrostatic orientation survey

陀螺定向光电测距导线
　　gyrophic orientation geodimeter traverse
陀螺定向误差　　gyro orientation error
陀螺方位角　　gyro azimuth
陀螺仪子午线　　gyro meridian
驼峰　　hump
驼峰编组场　　hump marshaling yard
驼峰编组场头部
　　head end of hump yard, grouping of a hump yard
驼峰车辆溜放速度减速器　　humping retarder
驼峰电气集中　　electric interlocking for hump yard
驼峰调车进路控制
　　shunting route control for hump yard
驼峰调车人员　　hump shunter
驼峰调速设备　　hump speed regulator
驼峰调速系统　　hump speed control system
驼峰动力机械室　　hump control equipment room
驼峰峰顶　　hump crest
驼峰峰顶平台　　platform of hump crest
驼峰复式信号机　　humping signal repeater
驼峰钩车溜放进路控制
　　route control for cut rolling
驼峰机车遥控　　remote control of hump engines
驼峰机械修理室　　hump mechanics repair room
驼峰集中联锁
　　centralized interlocking for hump yard
驼峰计算点　　calculation point of hump
驼峰解体能力　　humping capacity
驼峰解体作业量
　　workload of break-up operation at hump yard
驼峰跨线桥　　hump flyover
驼峰立交桥　　hump overpass
驼峰推峰机车信号　　cab signaling for humping
驼峰推峰机车遥控
　　cab remote control for humping
驼峰推送进路控制
　　pushing route control for hump yard
驼峰推送线　　pushing track of hump
驼峰线路平面　　hump track plan
驼峰信号　　hump signaling
驼峰信号机　　hump signal
驼峰信号楼　　hump signal cabin
驼峰转线　　hump shunting
妥协　　compromise
椭球扁率　　flattening of ellipsoid
椭球长半轴　　semi-major axis of ellipsoid
椭球短半轴　　semi-minor axis of ellipsoid
椭球偏心率　　eccentricity of ellipsoid
椭圆度　　ovality
椭圆极化　　elliptic polarization
拓扑结构　　topological structure

T

U

U 形桥台　U-shaped abutment

U 形型钢　U-shaped section steel

V

V 形滤池　V filter
V 形桥墩　V-type pier

V 形天窗　"V" maintenance window
未到货通知　notice of non-delivery

W

WGS-84 年世界大地坐标系
　　World Geodetic System 1984
挖方　　excavation, cut
挖沟　　trench
挖沟机　　trenching machine, trench digger, trencher, ditcher, channeller
挖井基础　　excavated shaft foundation
挖掘　　excavation, cutting, digging
挖掘机　　excavator
挖掘机械　　excavating machinery
挖掘起重两用机　　shovel crane
挖孔桩　　excavated and cast-in-place pile
挖泥船　　dredger
挖探　　pit exploration
挖土机　　excavator
挖装机　　crawling loader
洼地　　swale, depression
蛙式打夯机　　frog rammer, jumping rammer
瓦　　tile
瓦工　　bricklayer
瓦斯　　gas
瓦斯保护　　gas protection
瓦斯含量　　content of gas
瓦斯监测　　gas monitoring
瓦斯浓度　　gas density
瓦斯压力　　gas pressure force
瓦斯压力法　　gas pressure method
外包　　outsourcing
外包式正线　　straddle-type main track
外币　　foreign currency
外币需求　　foreign currency requirements
外币折算风险　　translation risk
外币支付　　payment in foreign currencies
外部保护　　external protection
外部采购　　outsourcing
外部尺寸　　external dimension
外部电源　　power source from the public grid
外部端口　　external port
外部防雷　　external lightning protection
外部回路　　external circuit
外部条件　　physical condition
外部吸气罩　　capturing hood
外部协同　　outer cooperation
外部障碍　　physical obstruction
外埠付款汇票　　domiciled bill (draft)
外插角　　outward inclination angle
外定向元素　　extra orientation element
外观检查　　visual inspection
外观质量　　quality of appearance
外轨超高　　superelevation of outer rail
外国代理机构　　foreign agency
外国公司　　foreign corporation
外国技工　　expatriate craftsmen
外国投资　　foreign investment
外国银行　　foreign bank
外汇　　foreign exchange
外汇波动　　foreign exchange fluctuation
外汇储备　　exchange reserve
外汇短缺　　short of exchange
外汇额度　　exchange quota
外汇风险　　foreign exchange risk, foreign exchange exposure, exchange risk
外汇管理规定　　exchange control regulations
外汇管制　　exchange control, foreign exchange control
外汇换算损益　　translation gain or loss
外汇汇率　　currency rate
外汇交易　　foreign exchange transaction, exchange dealings
外汇牌价　　foreign exchange quotation
外汇牌价表　　list of exchange rate quotation
外汇升水　　exchange premium
外汇税　　exchange tax
外汇贴水　　exchange discount
外汇限制　　exchange restriction
外汇赢利　　foreign exchange earning

外籍劳工　expatriate labour
外加变形　imposed deformation
外加费用　extra cost, extras
外加剂　additive
外界条件　environmental conditions
外径　outer diameter
外壳防护等级（IP 代码）
　　enclosure protection class（IP code）
外壳接地　earthing of casing, earthing of enclosure
外壳膨胀　enclosure expansion
外控点　photogrammetry control point
外来风险　extraneous risks
外力　external force
外贸手续费　commission charge for foreign trade
外排水系统　external drainage system
外派雇员　expatriate
外派津贴　assignment allowance
外墙　external wall
外墙平均传热系数　average heat transfer coefficient of building external wall
外锁闭装置　external locking device
外贴止水带　externally bonded water stop tie
外围护　enclosure
外线电阻检测
　　resistance detecting for outside line
外线端阻抗　impedance at outside line
外业图标　fieldwork title block
外移桩　offset stake
外运提单　outward bill of lading
外在缺陷　patent defects
外债　foreign debt, external debt
外资　foreign capital
弯板机　plate bender
弯钢筋机　steel bender
弯钩　hook
弯管补偿器　expansion loop
弯管机　pipe bender, pipe bending machine
弯筋机　bender
弯进直出　curve-in and straight-out
弯矩　bending moment
弯矩调幅系数
　　moment amplitude modulation coefficient
弯起钢筋　bent-up bar
弯桥　curved bridge
弯曲　bend
弯曲度　curvature
弯曲破坏　bending failure
弯曲蠕变　bending creep
弯曲蠕变劲度　stiffness of bending creep
弯曲蠕变柔量　compliance of bending creep
弯头　elbow
弯液面校正值　meniscus adjusted value
弯折变形　buckling deformation
弯折性能　buckling properties
完成进度　achievement of progress
完成进度计划　fulfilment of schedule
完工报告　closed-out report
完工成本　finished cost
完工担保　completion guarantee
完工估算　estimate at completion（EAC）
完工阶段　stage of completion
完工日期　date of completion, time for completion
完工预算　budget at completion（BAC）
完井抽水　full penetration well pumping
完全成本　full cost, absorption cost
完全承保　full coverage
完全横向连接　integrated transverse link
完全监控模式　full supervision mode（FS）
完全锁闭　complete locking
完全信托　complete trust
完全责任　full liability
完全追索　full recourse
完税后交货　delivery duty paid（DDP）
完税货价　price duty paid
完税价值
　　duty-paying value, dutiable value, tariff value
完整井　completely penetrating well
完整岩石　intact rock
玩忽　neglect, negligence
玩忽职守
　　dereliction, neglect of duty, misconduct in office
挽回　retrieve
晚奥陶世　late Ordovician epoch
晚白垩世　late Cretaceous epoch
晚第三纪　neogene period
晚二叠世　late Permian epoch
晚更新世　late Pleistocene epoch, epi pleistocene
晚古生代　late Paleozoic era
晚寒武世　late Cambrian epoch
晚泥盆世　late Devonian epoch
晚三叠世　late Triassic epoch
晚石炭世　late Carboniferous epoch
晚震旦世　late Sinian epoch
晚志留世　late Silurian epoch
晚侏罗世　late Jurassic epoch
碗扣节点　upside down bowl-type node
碗扣式脚手架　cuplock scaffolding
万能材料试验机
　　universal material testing machine
万能道尺　universal rail gauge

万能杆件　fabricated universal steel member
万用表　multimeter
腕臂　cantilever
腕臂偏移　cantilever displacement
腕臂上底座　uppercantilever bracket
腕臂下底座　lower cantilever bracket
网点板法　grid-point method
网格尺寸　grid size
网格间距　grid spacing
网关　gateway（GW）
网关 GPRS 支持节点
　　gateway GPRS support node（GGSN）
网关移动交换中心
　　gateway mobile switching center（GMSC）
网框地漏　net frame floor drain
网络　network
网络安全　network security
网络测试仪　network tester
网络带宽　network bandwidth
网络等级　network level
网络电缆测试仪　network cable tester
网络分析　network analysis
网络附属存储　network attached storage（NAS）
网络故障　network fault
网络管理（网管）　network management
网络管理（网管）服务器
　　network management server
网络管理（网管）设备
　　network management equipment
网络管理（网管）系统
　　network management system（NMS）
网络管理（网管）中心
　　network management center
网络管理（网管）终端
　　network management terminal
网络计划　network program
网络计划形式　network form
网络交换机　switch
网络节点　network node
网络结构　network structure
网络进度计划法　network scheduling technique
网络设备　network equipment
网络时间处理服务器
　　network time processing server
网络时间协议　network time protocol（NTP）
网络时延　network delay
网络数据　network data
网络跳线　patch cable
网络通信　network communication
网络图　network chart（diagram）

网络性能分析仪　network performance analyzer
网络性能指标　network performance index
网络优化调整　network optimization and adjustment
网络运行状态监测
　　network operation status monitoring
网络资源　network resource
网络综合分析仪　comprehensive network analyzer
网桥　network bridge
网守　Gatekeeper（GK）
网元　network element
网元管理系统　element management system
网元级管理系统　element management system（EMS）
网栅　grid，mesh
网栅间隔　mesh spacing
网站　website
网状钢筋　mesh reinforcement
网状构造　reticular structure
网状系统　network
往测与返测　direct and reversed measurements
往返测　round-trip survey
往返票　round trip ticket，return ticket
往返运费　freight out and home
往复式空气压缩机　reciprocating compressor
往复式水泵　reciprocating pump
往来函件　transmittal，correspondence
往来银行　correspondent bank
往来账户　current account，reciprocal account
往来账结余　balance of current account
旺季　peak season
危害程度　hazard extent
危机管理　crisis management，disaster management
危桥　unsafe bridge
危险　danger，hazard，risk，peril
危险侧输出　wrong side output
危险地段　hazardous section
危险点　danger point
危险工作津贴　danger money
危险化学品　hazardous chemicals
危险化学品工业站
　　industrial station for hazardous chemicals
危险化学品货场　yard for hazardous chemicals
危险货物仓库　dangerous goods warehouse
危险货物货场　dangerous goods yard
危险建筑物　dangerous building
危险品　dangerous goods（articles）
危险品仓库　hazardous cargo warehouse
危险区　danger area
危险物品　dangerous goods
危险信号　danger signal
微波测距　microwave distance measurement

微波式雨量传感器　microwave rainfall sensor
微穿孔板消声器　micropunch plate muffler
微电极测井法　microelectrode logging method
微调垫板　fine adjusting pad
微分纠正　differential rectification
微分相位　differential phase (DP)
微分增益　differential gain (DG)
微风　gentle breeze
微腐蚀　slight corrosion
微观环境　micro environment
微晶石英　microcrystalline quartz
微孔过滤　microfiltration
微裂纹　microcrack
微气泡　microbubble
微三角形法　exiguous triangle method
微生物降解　micro-biological degradation
微形桩　mini pile, micropile
微型计算机(微机)服务器　microcomputer server
微压计　micromanometer
微张节理　slightly opened joint
违背　break, breach, default
违法　breach of law, illegality
违法乱纪　malfeasance
违法行为　illegal act, tort
违法行为者　tortfeasor
违反　contravene, breach, violate, offend
违反法律　violate a law
违反合同　break a contract, breach of contract, violation of contract
违反义务行为　act against duty
违反责任行为　act against duty
违反专业职责的责任　liability for breach of professional duty
违犯　violate, infringe
违规报告　non-conformance report
违禁品　contraband, prohibited articles (goods)
违约　fail, default, in default, breach of contract, non-performance
违约当事人　delinquent party
违约罚款　contractual fines, penalty of breach of contract, penal sum
违约方　default party, party in breach
违约风险　default risk
违约金　breach of contract damages
违约赔偿金　damages for default
违约事件　event of default
违约通知　notice of default
违约行为　noncompliance
违章操作　unprofessional operation, operation against rule

围标　bid-rigging
围护结构　retaining structure
围护结构(房建)　building envelope
围护结构传热系数　heat transfer coefficient of building envelope
围护结构热工性能权衡判断　balance of thermal performance of building envelope
围护墙　enclosure wall
围垦工程　reclamation works
围栏　fence
围檩(腰梁)　waling
围墙　enclosure
围岩　surrounding rock
围岩变形　surrounding rock deformation
围岩分级　surrounding rock classification
围岩级别　grade of surrounding rock
围岩加固　surrounding rock consolidation
围岩内部位移　internal displacement of surrounding rock
围岩压力　surrounding rock pressure
围岩注浆　grouting for surrounding rock
围岩自承能力　self-support capacity of surrounding rock
围岩自稳时间　self-support time of surrounding rock
围岩自稳性　self-support capability of surrounding rock
围堰　cofferdam
围障　enclosure
唯一标识符　unique identifier
唯一代理　exclusive agency
唯一代理人　sole agent
帷幕灌浆　curtain grouting
帷幕注浆　curtain grouting
维勃稠度　Vebe consistence
维护　maintain, maintenance
维护操作通道　maintenance and operation channel
维护费　maintenance fee
维护费用　cost of upkeep, costs of maintenance
维护管理终端　maintenance and management terminal
维护基标　fiducial mark maintenance
维护系数　maintenance factor
维修　repair
维修保函　maintenance guarantee
维修保留金　maintenance retention fund
维修保留金保函　maintenance retention guarantee
维修备用金　reserve for repair
维修车间　repair workshop, maintenance workshop
维修担保　maintenance bond

维修费	repair fee
维修费准备	reserve for repair
维修工程津贴	allowance for maintenance of works
维修工区	repair section
维修工区线	repair section track
维修管理	maintenance management
维修基地	maintenance base
维修期	maintenance period, warranty period
维修手册	maintenance manual
维修条件	terms of service
维修项目	maintenance projects
维修证书	maintenance certificate
卫生	hygiene
卫生间	toilet
卫生器具	sanitary ware
卫生器具当量	sanitary ware equivalent
卫生设备	sanitary facilities
卫星	satellite
卫星定位	satellite positioning
卫星定位测量	satellite positioning survey
卫星定位测量控制网	satellite positioning control network
卫星定位静态测量	satellite static positioning survey
卫星接收机	satellite receiver
卫星截止高度角	satellite cut-off elevating angle
卫星链路	satellite link
卫星图像	satellite image
卫星遥感照片	satellite remote sensing photo
卫星终端设备	satellite terminal device
卫星钟	satellite clock
未被平衡加速度	unbalanced acceleration
未标价的工程量表	unpriced bill of quantities
未标价工程量清单	unpriced bill of quantities
未偿本金	outstanding principal
未偿清货款	outstandings
未偿损失	outstanding losses
未偿外债	outstanding external debt
未偿债务	debt outstanding, unpaid liabilities
未捣混凝土	unrammed concrete
未捣实混凝土	unrammed concrete
未到期的	undue
未到期汇票	bill undue
未到期票据	undue note
未到期债务	undue debt
未抵押资产	unpledged assets
未冻含水率	unfrozen water content
未兑现支票	outstanding check, uncashed check
未发货订单	unfilled order
未分配利润	undistributed profit, undivided profit
未风化	unweathered
未付的	unpaid, outstanding
未付的应付款	outstanding dues
未付款	unpaid moneys
未付利息	unpaid interest
未付赔款	outstanding losses
未付薪金	unpaid wages and salaries
未付债务	outstanding liabilities
未固结不排水三轴试验	unconsolidated-undrained triaxial test
未耗成本	unexpired cost
未划线支票	uncrossed check, open cheque
未交订货	outstanding order, non-delivery
未交付订单	back order
未结清的余额	balance outstanding
未结清账户	open account, unsettled account
未尽义务	unfulfilled obligation
未经检验的	off-test
未经授权的	unauthorized
未决赔款	outstanding claim
未决事件	pending issue
未决问题	pending question
未来价值	future value
未了索要	outstanding claim
未了责任	outstanding liabilities
未履行	fail, default, in default, breach of contract, non-performance
未履行合同	failure of performance
未能交货	failure to deliver
未能收回的金额	amount not recovered
未能通过竣工试验	failure to pass tests on completion
未能修补缺陷	failure to remedy defects
未能预见的地质条件	unforeseen grounds conditions
未能预见的现场条件	unforeseen site conditions
未能指定争议避免裁决委员会成员	failure to appoint DAAB member
未能遵守争议避免裁决委员会的决定	failure to comply with DAAB's decision
未签字的	unsigned
未清算账目	outstandings, unliquidated account
未清余额	outstanding balance
未清债务	open debt, outstanding debt
未清账款	outstanding account
未入账收入	unrecorded revenue
未收回金额	amount outstanding
未索赔奖励	no-claim bonus
未索赔退款	no-claim return

未索赔折扣　no-claim discount
未摊销成本　unamortized cost
未通过的检验　failed test
未完成的工作
　　outstanding work, unfinished work
未完工程　construction in progress
未完工作　outstanding work
未完税后交货(价)　delivered duty unpaid (DDU)
未预见的条件　unexpected condition
未预见用水量　unforeseen demand
未中标者　unsuccessful bidder (tenderer)
伟晶岩　pegmatite
伪动力试验　pseudo-dynamic test
伪静力试验　pseudo-static test
伪距　pseudo-range
伪造　fabricate, forge, counterfeit
伪造记录　false entry
伪造签字　forged signature
伪造文件　forged document
位错　dislocation
位移　displacement
位移传感器　displacement sensor
位移放大系数　displacement dynamic magnification factor (DDMF)
位移观测　displacement observation
位移计　displacement meter
位移延性系数　displacement ductility factor
位于　locate
位置　location, locality
尾部反坡　counter grade at yard end
尾端休眠测试　tail sleeping test
尾矿坝　tailings dam
尾矿库　tailing pond
尾沙库　tail sand store
尾水管　draft tube
尾纤　cable pigtail
尾纤活动连接器　pigtail connector
纬度　latitude
纬向构造　latitudinal structure
委付通知　notice of abandonment
委派　delegate, delegation, appoint
委派管理　administration of assignment
委弃通知　notice of abandonment
委任　appoint
委任书　letter of attorney
委任条款　terms of appointment
委任者　mandatory, appointer
委托　entrust, authorize
委托代理人　entrusted agent
委托加工　manufacturing consignment

委托贸易　commission trade
委托人　client, principal, entruster, consignor, consigner
委托试验　commissioned test
委托书　certificate of entrustment, power of attorney, commission, letter of delegation, letter of proxy, trust deed
委托书格式　form of proxy
委托通知　vesting notice
委员会　council, committee, board, commission
温差　temperature difference
温差弯矩　temperature moment
温度　temperature
温度变化　temperature variation
温度变化的影响　temperature variation influence
温度测点　temperature measuring point
温度场　temperature field
温度荷载　temperature load
温度计　thermometer
温度跨度
　　bridge span length influenced by temperature
温度力　rail temperature force/load
温度裂缝　temperature cracking
温度升高　temperature rise
温度梯度　temperature gradient
温度应力　temperature stress
温度影响修正　temperature effect modification
温度作用　temperature action
温感　temperature detector
温暖地区　warm region
温漂　temperature excursion
温升峰值　peak value of temperature rise
温室气体　greenhouse gas
文本　version, text
文档分解结构　documentation breakdown structure
文件　file, document, present
文件查阅　inspection of documents
文件传送　document transmittal
文件的歧义　ambiguity in document
文件审查　inspection of documents
文件优先顺序　priority of document
文件证明书　affidavit of document
文教区　district of culture and education
文克勒假定　Winkler's assumption
文明施工措施费
　　fee of civilized construction measures
文书工作　paper work
文物　culture relics
文物保护　cultural relics protection
文物保护费　expense for preservation of cultural relics

文物保护区　historic reservation
文物保护影响评估报告
　　heritage conservation impact assessment report
纹沟　ripple
紊流　turbulent flow
稳定岸坡角　stable bank slope angle
稳定边坡　stabilized slope
稳定分析　stability analysis
（社会）稳定风险　social stability risk
稳定光源　stabilized light source
稳定计算　stability calculation
稳定剂　stabilizer
稳定力系　stabilized force system
稳定裂纹扩展　stable crack growth
稳定流　steady flow
稳定流抽水试验　steady flow pumping test
稳定渗流　steady seepage
稳定数　stability number
稳定塘　stabilization pond
稳定系数　stability factor
稳定性　stability
稳定运行　stable operation
稳固　stability
稳态比较法　stable state comparison method
稳态传热　steady-state heat transfer
稳态动测法　steady dynamic measurement
稳态强迫振动法　steady forced vibration method
稳态噪声　steady noise
稳态振动　steady vibration
稳压泵　stabilized pressure pump
稳压层　plenum space
稳压器　voltage stabilizer
问询　inquire
问责矩阵　accountability matrix
涡流激振　vortex-induced oscillation
涡轮发电机　turbo-generator
涡轮机　turbine
涡轮流量计　turbine flowmeter
涡轮式通风机　turbo-fan
涡轮状构造　turbine-like structure
窝工　run idle
窝工费用　idle cost
窝工时间　downtime, idle time, standing time
卧室　bedroom
握持拉伸　holding tension
握持力　grasping force
握持强度　grasping strength
圬工　masonry
圬工工程　masonry work
圬工梁裂损　fracture of masonry beam

圬工墙　masonry wall
圬工桥　masonry bridge
污废合流　confluence of sewage and wastewater
污泥　sludge
污泥产率　sludge yield
污泥处理　sludge treatment
污泥堆场　sludge yard
污泥焚烧　sludge incineration
污泥负荷　sludge loading
污泥干化　sludge drying
污泥干化场　sludge drying yard
污泥固体负荷　sludge solid loading
污泥含水量　sludge water content
污泥回流比　return sludge ratio
污泥龄　sludge retention time (SRT)
污泥农用　sludge farm application
污泥浓度　sludge concentration
污泥浓缩　sludge thickening
污泥浓缩池　sewage thicker
污泥热干化　sludge heat drying
污泥土地利用　sludge land application
污泥脱水　sludge dewatering
污泥脱水机　sludge dewatering machine
污泥消化　sludge digestion
污泥综合利用　sludge integrated application
污染　contaminate, contamination, pollute, pollution
污染土　contaminated soil
污染物　contamination, pollutant
污染物排放标准　pollution discharge standard
污染物总量控制
　　pollutant discharge gross controlling
污染系数　contamination coefficient
污染险　risk of contamination
污染因子　contamination factor / pollution factor
污染源　source of pollution
污水　sewage
污水泵站　sewage pumping station
污水池　sewage pool
污水处理　sewage treatment
污水处理厂（站）
　　sewage treatment plant (station) (WWTP)
污水二级排放标准
　　second class discharge standard
污水工程　sewerage
污水管　pipe sewer, sewer, sanitary sewer
污水和废气治理
　　waste water and exhaust gas treatment
污水水质　sewage water quality
污水再生利用　wastewater reuse
污水资源化　reclamation of sewage

污水自然处理	natural treatment of sewage
污物箱	dirt box
诬告	accuse falsely, malicious prosecution
屋顶	roof
屋顶通风机	roof ventilator
屋盖	roof
屋盖支撑系统	roof-bracing system
屋架	roof truss
屋面板	roof board
屋面梁	roof beam
无泵反循环钻进	reverse circulation pumpless drilling
无补偿悬挂	uncompensated suspension
无残值	zero salvage value
无侧限抗压强度	unconfined compressive strength
无侧限抗压强度试验	unconfined compressive strength test
无侧移框架	frame without sideway
无岔区段	switchless section
无差别待遇	non-discriminatory treatment
无偿的	free, gratuitous
无偿援助	non-reimbursable assistance
无磁屏蔽	non-magnetic shield
无担保贷款	unsecured loan, straight loan, open credit
无担保合同	naked contract
无担保投标	unsecured bid
无担保投标文件	unsecured bid
无担保债权人	unsecured creditor
无担保债券	debenture
无担保债务	unsecured debt
无电概率	non-energized probability
无电区	neutral zone
无钉铺设	non-nail laying
无阀滤池	valveless filter
无法兑付的支票	uncollectible check
无纺土工织物	non-woven geotextile
无风险	devoid of risk
无缝道岔	CWR turnout
无缝钢管	weldless steel tube
无缝管	seamless pipe
无缝线路	continuously welded rail track (CWR track)
无缝线路稳定性	CWR track stability
无跟单信用证	clean letter of credit
无功补偿	reactive power compensation
无功电流	reactive current, idle current
无功电压降	reactive voltage drop
无功反转正计	var-hour meters for reactive energy
无功伏安	volt-ampere reactive (var)
无功功率	reactive power
无功功率因数	reactive power factor
无管网灭火装置	fire extinguishing equipment without network
无龟裂	crack-free
无规振动	random vibration
无轨运输	trackless transportation
无荷载膨胀率试验	no-load expansion rate test
无机纤维胎基	mineral fibric base
无极继电器	neutral relay
无价值担保	dead security
无交叉线岔	tangential overhead crossing
无铰拱	fixed arch
无铰拱桥	fixed arch bridge
无绝缘轨道电路	jointless track circuit
无力偿付债务	insolvency
无力支付	non-payment
无利息	ex-interest
无梁楼盖	flat slab
无码区	codeless zone
无黏结预应力混凝土结构	unbonded pre-stressed concrete structure
无黏性粗粒土	cohesionless coarse grained soil
无黏性土	cohesionless soil
无赔款奖金	no-claim bonus
无赔款退费	no-claim return
无赔款折扣	no-claim discount
无缺陷管理	zero defects management
无缺陷开车计划	flawless start-up initiative
无人继承的财产	bona vacantia
无人增音站	unattended repeater station
无砂透水混凝土	no-sand pervious concrete
无损检测	non-destructive test (NDT)
无条件保函	guarantee on the first demand, unconditional guarantee
无条件背书	absolute endorsement
无条件承兑	unconditional acceptance
无条件接受	absolute acceptance
无条件紧急停车消息	unconditional emergency stop message
无条件信用证	unconditional letter of credit
无条件银行保函	unconditional bank guarantee
无条件银行保证书	unconditional bank guarantee
无污染	free from contamination
无息贷款	free loan, interest-free credit, passive loan, interest-free loan
无息信贷	interest-free credit
无息债券	passive bond
无限竞争性公开招标	unlimited competitive open bidding
无限竞争性招标	unlimited competitive bidding

无限期合同　open-end contract
无限责任　unlimited liability
无线闭塞中心　radio block center（RBC）
无线电波透视　radio wave penetration
无线调车机车信号和监控　Shunting Train Protection（STP）
无线话筒　wireless microphone
无线盲区　radio blind zone
无线通信　wireless communication，radio communication
无线终端　mobile station
无线子系统　radio subsystem，base station subsystem（BSS）
无效合同　contract void，void contract
无效性　invalidity
无薪休假　leave without pay
无信用　bad faith
无形财产　intangible property
无形的　intangible
无形动产　intangible movables
无形固定资产　fixed intangible assets，intangible fixed assets
无形价值　intangible value
无形贸易　invisible trade
无形商品　intangible goods
无形资本　immaterial capital
无形资产　intangible assets，intangible property，intangibles，non-visible property，invisible asset
无形资产摊销费　amortization charge of intangible assets
无序行为　disorderly conduct
无压管道　non-pressure pipeline
无压力涵洞　culvert in the case of both inlet and outlet unsubmerged
无烟煤　anthracite
无异议　no-objection
无源光网络　passive optical network（PON）
无源应答器　fixed balise
无约束力的合同　unbinding contract
无约束力的决定　non-binding decision
无约束力的仲裁　non-binding arbitration
无载调压变压器　transformer with no-load tap changer
无责任　non-responsibility
无砟道岔　ballastless turnout
无砟道床　ballastless trackbed
无砟轨道　ballastless track
无砟轨道桥梁　ballastless track bridge
无砟无枕梁　girder without ballast and sleeper
无障碍设施　accessible facilities
无障碍通路　accessible passage
无障碍住房　accessible housing
无争议条款　non-contest clause
无支撑纯框架　unbraced frame
无支付能力　failure
无主物　bona vacantia
无追索　non-recourse
无追索权　non-recourse，without recourse
无资格　disqualification，incapability
无组织进风　unorganized air supply
无组织排风　unorganized air exhaust
五金　hardware
五类线　category 5 cable
五牌一图　five boards and one layout plan
五日生化需氧量容积负荷　volumetric loading of biochemical oxygen demand for 5 days（BOD5）
五台期　Wutain age／stage
五氧化二磷含量　Content of phosphorus pentoxide
5T　TFDS，THDS，TADS，TPDS，TCDS
5″、2″、6″级仪器　level 5″,2″,6″instrument
午城黄土　Wucheng loess
舞弊　fraud，collusion
物方空间坐标系　object space coordinate system
物化法　physicochemical process
物价　commodity price
物价暴涨　inflation
物价变化系数　price fluctuation factor
物价变动余裕　dearness allowance
物价波动调价条款　escalation clause
物价飞涨　soaring prices
物价加权指数　price-weighted index
物价津贴　dearness allowance
物价上涨　price escalation
物价上涨指数　escalation index
物价稳定　price stability
物价指数　commodity price index，index of prices
物镜前（后）节点　lens front（back）node
物理端口　physical port
物理风化　physical weathering
物理改良　physical improvement
物理改良土　physically improved soil
物理勘探　geophysical prospecting
物理力学性状　physical and mechanical characteristics
物理力学指标　physical and mechanical index
物理洗井　physical flushing
物理性质　physical property
物理性指标　physical index
物理硬化　physical hardening
物力　resources
物力资源　physical resources，material resources

物料运输车　material transportation car
物流　logistics
物流保障　logistics support
物品　goods, article
物权　property
物探　geophysical prospecting
物探法　physical exploration method
物探反演　geophysical inversion
物探勘测　geophysical prospecting
物探异常带　geophysical prospecting abnormal zone
物探正演　geophysical forward modeling
物物交换　barter, trade off
物业管理　facility management
物证　exhibit, material evidence, proof
物质的　material
物质损失　material damage
物种数量　species quantity
物资　goods
物资部　purchasing department
物资储运费　charge for storage & freight of goods
物资清关　clearance of goods
物资所有权　ownership of goods and materials
误报率　rate of false report in earthquake prediction
误差　error
误差传播　error propagation
误差范围　error range
误差放大因子　error enlarging factor
误差检验　error test
误差椭圆　error ellipse
误动作　malfunction
误解　misunderstanding, mistake
误码性能　bit error rate (BER) performance
误期罚款　penalty for delay
误期费用　cost of delay
误期赔偿金　delay damages
误期损害赔偿费　liquidated damages for delay, delay damages
误期责任　liability for delay
误用失效　misuse failure

X

X 射线　X-ray
X 射线衍射分析　X ray diffraction analysis
X 数字用户线　X digital subscriber line（XDSL）
X 形支撑　X-shaped support
吸附剂　adsorbent
吸附水含量　absorption water content
吸隔声复合板　sound absorptive and insulation composite panel
吸隔声复合结构　sound absorptive and insulation compound structure
吸光度　absorbancy
吸流变压器　booster transformer
吸流变压器供电方式（BT 供电方式）　booster transformer feeding system, BT feeding system
吸起门限　pick-up threshold
吸起时间　pick-up time
吸起值　pick-up value
吸取　absorption
吸上电流　boosting current
吸上线　boosting wire
吸声　sound absorption
吸声板　acoustical board
吸声材料　sound absorption material
吸声系数　sound absorption coefficient
吸声性能　sound absorption property
吸收能力　absorptive capacity
吸收器　absorber
吸收式制冷机　absorption refrigerating machine
吸收式制冷循环　absorption refrigeration cycle
吸水管　suction pipe
吸水量　water absorbing capacity
吸水率　water absorption rate
吸水性　water absorption
吸水性试验　water absorption capacity test
吸污车　suction-type sewer scavenger
吸音板　abatvoix
吸着含水率　sorbed water content
吸着水　hydroscopic moisture

矽卡岩　skarn
息差　margin
息票　coupon
稀释液　diluent
溪水　stream water
习惯　custom, usage
习惯法　customary law, common law
习惯皮重　customary tare
洗车机　train washing plant
洗涤污水　washing wastewater, laundry sewage
洗罐线　tank washing siding
洗罐站　tank washing point
洗井　well flushing
洗脸盆　washbasin
洗筛　screen washing
洗刷污水　sewage from vehicle washing
洗刷消毒所　washing and disinfecting point
洗消间　decontamination room
铣磨车　milling train
喜马拉雅期　Himalayan age, Himalayan
系杆　tie bar, tie member
系杆拱　tied arch
系梁　collar beam
系数　factor, coefficient
系统　system
系统标定法　system calibration method
系统布线　system wiring
系统测试　system testing
系统风险　systematic risks
系统工程　system engineering
系统功能　system function
系统管理　system management
系统监控　system monitoring
系统联调　system commissioning
系统锚杆　systematic rock bolt
系统软件　system software
系统试验　system test
系统数据　system data

系统误差　systematic error
系统验收　system acceptance
系统优化　system optimization
细部　detail
细长颗粒　elongated particle
细度　fineness
细度模量　fineness modulus
细沟　groove
细骨料　fine aggregate
细骨料混凝土　fine concrete
细集料　fine aggregate
细角砾土　fine angular gravel soil
细节　detail, detailed particulars
细节充分的索赔　fully detailed claim
细晶岩　aplite
细砾　fine gravel
细粒土　fine-grained soil
细粒土塑性图　plasticity chart of fine-grained soil
细料石　fine dressed stone
细目　particular
细砂　fine sand
细筛　fine sieve
细筛分析　undersize sieve analysis
细水雾　water mist
细圆砾土　fine round gravel soil
细则　abstract of particulars, by-law, details
隙动差　lost motion
瞎炮　misfire
峡谷　canyon
峡湾　fiord
狭缝法试验　slit method test
狭窄空间　confined space
霞石　nepheline
霞石正长岩　nepheline syenite
下奥陶统　lower Ordovician series
下白垩统　lower Cretaceous series
下班　off-duty
下班时间　closing time
下部结构　substructure
下部填土　lower filling
下沉度　sinkage
下沉量　sinkage
下撑式组合梁　down-supported composite beam
下承锚底座　lower anchor bracket
下承式桥　through bridge
下定位索　lower cross-span wire
下二叠统　lower Permian series
下峰信号　hump trimming signal
下更新统　lower Pleistocene series
下古生界　lower Paleozoic erathem
下寒武统　lower Cambrian series
下降泉　descending spring
下拉荷载　downdrag
下锚段衬砌　lining of anchor section
下锚基础　anchor foundation
下锚拉线　anchor backstay
下锚拉线底座　bracket for backstay
下锚支　outgoing contact line
下锚柱　anchor pole
下泥盆统　lower Devonian series
下盘　footwall
下坡道防护电路　protection circuit for heavy down grade approaching
下三叠统　lower Triassic series
下石炭统　lower Carboniferous series
下水道　sewer
下水道工程　sewerage
下碗扣　under bowl up
下卧层　underlying stratum
下行波　downward traveling wave
下行方向　down direction
下行区间接口　down direction section interface
下行上给式　upfeed system
下行线　down track
下元古界　lower Proterozoic group
下震旦统　lower Sinian series
下志留统　lower Silurian series
下侏罗统　lower Jurassic series
下走线　downward routing
夏季空气调节室外计算干球温度　design outdoor dry-bulb temperature for air conditioning in summer
夏季空气调节室外计算日平均温度　design outdoor daily mean temperature for air conditioning in summer
夏季空气调节室外计算湿球温度　design outdoor wet-bulb temperature for air conditioning in summer
夏季通风室外计算温度　design outdoor temperature for ventilation in summer
夏季通风室外计算相对湿度　design outdoor relative humidity for air conditioning in summer
先导段　precursor section
先决条件　condition precedent, prerequisite, precondition, conditions precedent
先例　precedent
先期固结压力　preconsolidation pressure
先期交款　advance contribution
先期开工段　construction section in early stage
先期违约　anticipatory breach

先验权　prior weight
先验权中误差　mean square error of prior weight
先张法　pretensioning
先张法预应力　pre-tensioned prestressing, pretension
先张法预应力混凝土结构　pre-tensioned prestressed concrete structure
先张法预应力梁　pretensioned concrete girder
纤维板　fiber board
纤维背衬　fibrous backing
纤维复合材料　fibrous composite material
纤维土　fiber reinforced soil
纤维杂质含量　fiber impurities content
纤维增强砂浆　fiber reinforced mortar
纤维状　fibrous
纤维状断口　fibrous fracture
氙灯　xenon lamp
氙灯老化　xenon lamp aging
氙弧灯老化试验箱　xenon lamp aging test chamber
闲人莫入　off limits, no attendance
闲置率　vacancy rate
闲置设备　idle equipment, standby equipment, standing plant
闲置生产能力　idle capacity
闲置资金　dead money, idle money
弦杆　chord member
弦线偏距　chord deflection distance
弦线支距法　chord offset method
涎流冰　salivary flow ice
衔接线路　connecting track
衔接站　junction station
显晶质结构　phanerocrystalline texture
显热　sensible heat
显热交换效率　sensible heat exchange efficiency
显色剂　color developing agent
显色溶液　chromogenic solutions
显色性　color rendering
显色指数　color rendering index
显生宙　Phanerozoic eon
显示　indication
显示方式　mode of indication
显示距离　sighting distance
显示设备　display equipment
现场　field, site
现场安全费用　cost of site security
现场安全计划　project safety program
现场安装　erection on site, field erection
现场搬运　handling in field
现场办事处　field office
现场保安　security of the site, site security
现场保安费用　cost of site security

现场保安计划　project safety program
现场布置图　site layout
现场采购主管　field procurement supervisor
现场采集设备　field data acquisition equipment
现场测量　site survey
现场测试　spot test
现场查勘　site investigation
现场抽查　spot check, snap check
现场代表　field representative
现场的占有　possession of site
现场调查　field survey, site investigation
现场动员　field mobilization
现场费用　field cost
现场服务　field service
现场工程师　site engineer, field engineer
现场工作　field work
现场工作人员　field staff
现场观测　field observation
现场管理　site management
现场管理费　site overhead cost, job site overhead
现场管理人员　site management
现场焊　site welding
现场会议纪要　site meeting minutes
现场计量　field measurement
现场监督　on-site supervision
现场检查　spot inspection, on-site inspection
现场检查人员　field inspection staff
现场检验　on-site inspection
现场交货　delivery on field
现场搅拌混凝土　job mixed concrete
现场进入权　right of access to the site
现场经理　site manager
现场勘探　site exploration
现场考察　job site visit, site visit, field trip, field investigation, site inspection
现场控制器　field controller
现场量测　field measurement
现场培训　on-site training
现场平面图　site plan
现场清理　site clearance
现场设施　site facilities
现场审计　on-the-spot audit
现场生活设施　site accommodation
现场施工经理　field construction manager
现场施工组织　site organization
现场实测　field measurement
现场使用权　right to the use of a site
现场试验　field test
现场视察　inspection of site
现场首席工程师　chief resident engineer

现场首席建筑师　chief resident architect
现场数据和基准　site data and items of reference
现场条件变化　differing site conditions（D.S.C）
现场通信平台　onsite communication platform
现场外装配　offsite fabrication
现场项目人员　field project staff
现场销售　field sales
现场修理　spot repair
现场原位测试　in-situ test
现场杂费　oncost
现场指导　site instruction
现场指挥　site direction
现场指令　field order
现场治安　site security
现场资料　site data
现场作业　site operations, field operation
现车修　repair of wagon on hand, wagon on hand
现代化　modernization
现地工作站　field work station
现付　spot payment
现购　cash purchase
现汇　spot exchange
现汇汇率　spot rate
现汇交易　spot exchange transaction
现货　goods in stock, spot, actual goods, goods on the spot
现货价格　spot price
现货交易　spot transaction
现货市场　physical market
现货业务　spot transaction
现浇板柱结构　cast-in-situ slab-column structure
现浇钢筋混凝土结构　cast-in-place reinforced concrete structure
现浇混凝土　cast-in-place concrete
现浇混凝土结构　cast-in-place concrete structure
现浇混凝土桩　in-situ concrete pile
现金　cash, ready cash, money in hand
现金簿　cash book
现金出纳机　cash register
现金储备　cash reserve
现金存款　cash deposit, primary deposit
现金贷方　cash credit
现金担保　cash guarantee
现金购买　cash purchase
现金股息　cash dividend
现金管理账户　cash management account（CMA）
现金红利　cash bonus
现金汇入　inward cash remittance
现金基金　cash fund
现金奖金　cash bonus
现金奖励　cash bonus
现金交易　money transaction, on cash
现金交易市场　cash market
现金结算　cash settlement
现金借方　cash debit
现金流表　cash flow statement, statement of cash flow
现金流出量　cash outflows
现金流风险　cash flow risk
现金流估计　cash flow estimate
现金流管理　cash flow management
现金流净值　cash flow net
现金流量　cash flow
现金流量图　cash flow diagram
现金流入量　cash inflows
现金流图　cash flow diagram
现金赔款　cash losses
现金日报表　daily cash report
现金收入凭证　cash receipt voucher
现金收入日记账　cash receipt journal
现金收支表　statement of receipt and disbursement
现金损失　cash losses
现金销售　cash sales
现金溢缺　cash over and short
现金余额　cash balance
现金账　cash account, cash book
现金账户　cash account
现金折扣　cash discount
现金支出　cash credit, cash outlay
现金支出日记账　cash disbursement journal
现金支付　cash payment, payment in cash
现金支付费用　out-of-pocket expenses
现金资产　cash assets
现款　spot cash
现款交易　no credit
现时工资　current labour rates
现行成本　current cost
现行重置成本　current replacement cost
现行的进度计划　current programme
现行法令　current decrees
现行费率　prevailing rate
现行价格　current price, prevailing price
现行价格指数　current price index
现行市价　current market value
现有存货　stock in hand
现值　present value
现状建模　existing conditions modeling
限定　definition, restriction
限定价格　price fixing
限度　limitation
限额　limit, quota

限额保函　limited amount guarantee
限额保证书　limited amount guarantee
限高　height permitted
限界　clearance, gauge
限界改善　clearance improvement
限界检查　clearance checking
限界门　height limiting portal
限流　current-limiting
限时人工解锁　manual time release
限速拆分功能
　　speed limiting and splitting function
限速地段
　　speed restriction section, speed limit section
限位凹槽　position-limiting trough
限位器　position-limiting device
限位销　stop pin
限压型 SPD　voltage limiting type SPD
限值　limit value
限制电压　threshold voltage
限制粒径　constrained particle size
限制膨胀率　expansion rate in restrict condition
限制坡度　ruling gradient
限制区间　carrying capacity limiting section
限制速度　limited speed
限制条件　reservation, side conditions, qualification
限制性贷款　tied loan
限制性契约　negative covenant
限制性条件　proviso
限制性条款　proviso clause, qualifying clause, restrictive clause
限制性行车许可　limit of movement authority
限制性援助　tied aid
线岔　overhead crossing
线电压　line voltage
(布)线管　conduit
线焊机　seam welder
线荷载　linear load
线间沟　ditch between tracks
线间距
　　distance between centers of tracks, track spacing
线间距加宽
　　widened distance between centers of tracks
线宽　line width
线宽组　line group
线缆屏蔽　cable shielding
线缆综合测试仪　cable comprehensive tester
线路　line, route, track
线路变压器组接线
　　line-transformer bank connection
线路标志　track sign, route sign
线路标桩　track stake
线路参数测试　track parameter test
线路测量　route survey
线路长度　railway line length
线路大修　track overhaul
线路点　field location
线路高程控制测量　route vertical control survey
线路号适配测试　line number matching test
线路环阻　wire loop resistance
线路基桩　track survey reference stake
线路建筑长度　length of track construction
线路接线　line connection
线路竣工测量　as-built route survey
线路开放　route scheme available
线路类别　track category
线路年输送能力　annual railway traffic capacity
线路平面　track plan
线路平面控制测量
　　route planimetric control survey
线路平面控制网(CPⅡ)
　　route horizontal control network (CPⅡ)
线路平面图　route plan
线路区段　track section
线路疏解　untwining for leading line
线路水准基点　route benchmark
线路衰耗　line attenuation
线路速度限制　track speed restriction
线路所　block house, block post
线路所通过信号机　block signal at block post
线路图　layout chart, circuit diagram
线路维修　track maintenance
线路维修规则　rules of track maintenance
线路有关工程　track-related works
线路有效长度　effective length of track
线路运营长度
　　length of railway in operation, operating distance
线路展线系数
　　coefficient of line extension for the route
线路占用表示　track occupancy indication
线路遮断表示器　track obstruction indicator
线路中线　route centerline
线路中心线　track centerline, centre of alignment
线路中修　intermediate repair of track
线路纵断面　profile
线路纵断面图　railway route profile
线路走向　track alignment
线膨胀系数　coefficient of linear expansion
线平式站房　track level station building
线圈　coil
线群出站信号机　group departure signal

线上(站后工程)　E&M works
线上式站房　station building above the track level
线蚀　liner erosion
线束减速器　group retarder
线束性布置　track group layout
线速转发　wire-speed forwarding
线缩率　linear shrinkage ratio
线条　bar
线条图　bar chart, Gantt chart
线下(站前工程)　civil works, under-track works
线下工程竣工测量
　　as-built survey of civil works
线下式站房　station building below the track level
线形三角锁　linear triangulation chain
线形三角网　linear triangulation network
线形锁　linear triangulation chain
线形网　linear triangulation network
线性比例极限　linear scale limit
线性度　linearity
线性荷载　linear load
线性黏弹性　linear viscoelasticity
线应变　linear strain
线胀系数　coefficient of linear expansion
线状符号　line symbol
宪法　constitution
陷阱　pitfall
陷落洞　subsidence hole
陷塘　subsidence pool
乡土树种　indigenous species of trees
乡土植物　indigenous plant
详勘　detailed investigation
详式提单　long-form bill of lading
详图(大样图)　detail drawing
详细报表　detailed account
详细的支撑材料　detailed supporting particulars
详细费用　detailed cost
详细估算　detailed take-off, detailed estimate
详细计划　detailed program
详细计划表　detailed schedule
详细技术要求　detail requirements
详细设计　detailed design, detailed engineering
详细依据　detailed supporting particulars
详细摘量　detailed take-off, detailed estimate
详细装箱单　detailed packing list
相变特性　phase transition properties
相错式接头　staggered joint
相等物　equivalent
相电压　phase voltage
相对闭合差　relative misclosure
相对变形　relative deformation
相对标定法　relative calibration method
相对残余挠度　relative residual deflection
相对残余应变　relative residual strain
相对沉降量　relative settlement
相对定向　relative orientation
相对定向元素　relative orientation element
相对动弹模量　relative dynamic elastic modulus
相对高差　relative altitude difference
相对航高　relative flying height
相对价格　relative price
相对介电常数
　　relative dielectric constant, relative permittivity
相对密度　relative density
相对耐久性　relative durability
相对湿度　relative humidity
相对式接头　opposite joint, square joint
相对误差　relative error
相对误差椭圆　relative error ellipse
相对中误差　relative mean square error
相关成本　relevant cost
相关服务　incidental service
相关平差　correlative adjustment
相关色温　related color temperature
相关系数　correlation coefficient
相关校验　correlation test
相互保障　mutual indemnification
相互补偿　mutual indemnification
相互参照条款　cross-reference clause
相互理解　mutual understanding
相互矛盾　contradict, contradiction
相互认可　cross-acceptance
相互赊欠　swap credits
相间短路　interphase short-circuit
相间故障　phase fault, phase to phase fault
相邻凹槽中心间距
　　center to center spacing of adjacent grooves
相邻道岔　adjacent turnout
相邻点间距离　distance between adjacent points
相邻点间相对中误差
　　relative mean error between adjacent points
相邻股道　adjacent track
相邻荷载　neighboring loads
相邻坡段坡度差　gradient difference between adjacent grade sections
相敏轨道电路　phase sensitive track circuit
相容性　compatibility
相似级配法　similar gradation method
相位差　phase difference
相位法测距　distance measurement by phase
相位角　phase angle

相位特征　phase characteristics
相序表　phase-sequence meter
相序轮换　phase sequence exchange
相应距离　appropriate distance
相应速度范围　appropriate speed range
香港银行同业拆放利率
　　Hongkong interbank offered rate（HIBOR）
香花石　hsianghualite
箱　case
箱涵　box culvert
箱区横向通道　lateral aisle in container area
箱式变电所　container substation
箱式变电站
　　box-type substation, container substation, compact substation, prefabricated substation
箱式高温炉　box-type high temperature furnace
箱位边缘　edge of container slot
箱位数　number of container slot
箱形大梁　box girder
箱形拱桥　box arch bridge
箱形基础　box foundation
箱形梁　box girder, box beam
箱形梁桥　box girder bridge
箱形褶皱　box fold
箱梁　box girder, box beam
镶嵌图　mosaic map
响墩信号　detonating signal, torpedo
响岩　phonolite
响应时间　response time
响应性投标　responsive bid
响应招标文件要求
　　responsive to bidding documents
向斜　syncline
向斜谷　synclinal valley
项目　project, item
项目报告　project report
项目备选方案　project alternative
项目参与者　project participant
项目程序手册　project procedure manual
项目持续时间　project duration
项目持续性评价　project sustainability assessing
项目筹备　project preparations
项目筹融资费　project financing cost
项目代表　project representative
项目代码　project code
项目调试工程师　project commissioning engineer
项目发起人/投资人　project sponsor
项目范围　project scope
项目方案识别/鉴定　project identification
项目费用　project cost

项目分析　project analysis
项目负责机构　project entity
项目负责人　project superintendent
项目概要　project brief
项目各方　parties to a project
项目工程师　project engineer
项目工期　project duration
项目管理　project management
项目管理承包　project management contracting（PMC）
项目管理承包商
　　project management contractor
项目管理团队
　　project management team（PMT）
项目规程　project specification
项目规范　project specification
项目规模　project size
项目合同　contract for project
项目后评价　project post-evaluation
项目后评审　post project critique
项目机构　project organization
项目机会　project opportunities
项目基准日期　project base date
项目绩效　project performance
项目计划的更新　project plan update
项目计划实施　project plan execution
项目监督员　project supervisor, project superintendent, project monitor
项目监控　project monitoring
项目建议书　project proposal
项目阶段　project phase
项目结构　project structure
项目进度计划　project schedule
项目进展情况报告　project status report
项目经理　project manager
项目经理助理　assistant project manager
项目竣工报告　project completion report
项目开办　set-up of a project
项目开工
　　start-up of a project, commencement of a project
项目控制　project control
项目扩建　project extension
项目流程　project procedures
项目描述　project description
项目目标　project objective, project goal
项目内容确定　project definition
项目评估　project appraisal, project evaluation
项目评估文件　project appraisal document（PAD）
项目期末评估　end-of-project evaluation
项目启动　project startup
项目启用日期　commercial operation date（COD）

项目起始　project inception
项目日志　project diary
项目融资　project financing
项目筛选　screening of projects
项目审计　project audit
项目审批过程　project approval process
项目生命周期　project life cycle
项目实施计划　plan of operations
项目实体　project entity
项目手册　project manual
项目说明　project description
项目所在地　project location
项目谈判　project negotiation
项目通讯录　project directory
项目投资决策　project investment decision-making
项目文件　project documentation
项目误工时间　lost project time
项目协调　project coordination
项目协调员　project coordinator
项目协议　project agreement
项目型组织　projectized organization
项目选定　project selection
项目要求　project demands
项目业务　activities of project
项目影响评估　project impact assessment
项目预测　project forecast
项目预评估　project pre-appraisal
项目预算　project budget
项目约束因素　project constraints
项目运营　project operation
项目暂停　project suspension
项目执行　project execution
项目执行概况　project executive summary
项目执行计划　project implementation schedule, project execution plan
项目执行评估报告　project performance assessment report (PPAR)
项目执行审计报告　project performance audit report (PPAR)
项目执行与监督　project execution and supervision
项目职员　project staff
项目质量检测　project quality test
项目周期　project cycle
项目主管　project executive, project superintendent, project director
项目准备　project preparation
项目资金　project funding
项目组　project team
项目作业　project activities
巷道坡度线标定　setting-out of roadway slope
巷道碎部测量　detail survey of roadway
巷道验收丈量　acceptance measurement of roadway
巷道中线标定　center line of roadway setting out
象限角　bearing angle
像场角　objective angle of image field
像点位移　shift of image point
像点坐标　image coordinate
像空间坐标系　image space coordinate system
像片变形改正　correction of photograph distortion
像片地质判读(又称"像片地质解译")　geological interpretation of photograph
像片平高控制点　horizontal and vertical photo control point, full control point
像元　picture element, pixel
像主点　principal point of photograph
像主点落水　principal point of photograph on water
相底点　photo nadir point
相片调绘　photo annotation
相片归心　photo centering
相片基线　photo base
相片纠正　photo rectification
相片控制点　photo control point
相片平面图　photo-plane
相片索引图　photograph index
相片旋角　swing angle of photo
橡胶　rubber
橡胶垫板　rubber pad
橡胶防水卷材　rubber waterproof sheet
橡胶隔振器　rubber vibration absorber
橡胶支座　rubber bearing
橡胶止水带　rubber water stop tie
橡皮土　rubbery soil
消波设施　attenuating shock wave equipment
消除　eliminate
消毒　disinfection
消毒检验证书　disinfection inspection certificate
消防备用照明　reserve lighting for fire risk
消防泵　fire pump
消防泵站　fire pump station
消防队　fire brigade
消防控制室　elimination control room
消防炮　fire monitor
消防器材　fire-fighting equipment
消防设备　fire fighting equipment
消防设施　fire-fighting facilities
消防疏散标志灯　marking lamp for fire evacuation
消防疏散照明　lighting for fire evacuation
消防疏散照明灯　light for fire evacuation
消防水池　fire reservoir
消防水带　fire hose

消防水带和水枪　fire hose and nozzle
消防水枪　fire fighting squirt
消防水源　fire water source
消防吸水管　suction pipe for firefighting
消防用水量　fire water consumption
消费　consume, consumption, expenditure
消费贷款　consumer loan
消费品　consumer goods
消费品价格指数　consumer price index
消费品进口报关单　entry for consumption
消费税　excise, consumption tax, excise tax
消费信贷　consumer credit
消耗　consume, use up, expend
消耗品　consumables
消化池　digester
消化时间　digest time
消化污泥　digested sludge
消火栓　fire hydrant
(石灰)消解　slake
消力池　stilling basin, plunge pool
消能减震　energy dissipation and vibration damping
消声材料　sound-deadening material
消声器　silencer, muffler
消声弯头　bend muffler
消息传递部分　message transfer part
消烟除尘　abatement of smoke and dust
萧条　depression
硝酸　nitric acid
硝酸亚铁　ferrous nitrate
硝酸盐氮　nitrate nitrogen
硝酸银滴定法　silver nitrate volumetric method
销货成本　cost of goods sold
销货毛利　gross profit on sales
销路　marketing outlet
销售代理商　selling agent
销售点终端　point of sales (PoS)
销售额　sales turnover
销售发票　sales invoice
销售费用　marketing expenses, selling cost
销售合同　contract of sales, sales contract
销售回扣　sales rebate
销售价　selling price
销售经理　sales manager
销售毛利　sales margin
销售渠道　distribution outlet, market channel
销售权　power of sale
销售确认书　sales confirmation
销售税　sales tax
销售条件　conditions of sale, terms of sale
销售协定　selling agreement

销售佣金　sales commission
销售账　sales account
销售折扣　discount on sales
销售组合　marketing mix
销账　charge off
小半径曲线梁　girder for small-radius curve
小半径曲线黏降
　reduction of adhesion at small radius curve
小比例尺地形图　small-scale topographical map
小避车洞　small refuge niche
小便槽　urinal
小便器　urine device
小费　tip, gratuity
小轨道电路　small track circuit
小角度法　minor angle method
小角法　minor angle method
小里程端　small mileage end
小梁　joist
小流域治理　minor drainage basin management
小能力驼峰　small capacity hump
小偏心受压构件
　compression member with small eccentricity
小汽车班列　car liner trains
小汽车存放区　car storage area
小汽车交验区　car delivery and inspection area
小汽车零配件库　warehouse of car spare parts
小汽车装车区　car loading area
小汽车作业场　car operation yard
小签　initial, initialization
小桥　short bridge (with length not more than 20 m)
小区广播　zone public address system
小区广播中心　cell broadcast center (CBC)
小三角测量　minor triangulation
小时变化系数　hourly variation coefficient
小时工资　hourly wage rate, wage per hour
小写金额　amount in figures
小心轻放　handle with care
小型编组站　small sized marshaling station
小型车站　small scale station
小型低门架叉车
　small scale low portal-frame forklift
小型滑坡　small scale landslip
小型机服务器　minicomputer server
小型机具使用费　charge for using small scale machines and tools
小型交易会　minifair
小型临时设施　small scale temporary facilities
小型临时设施费
　expense of small scale temporary facilities
小型旅客车站　small passenger station

小型审判 mini-trial
小型线路机械 light track maintenance machinery
小型液压捣固机 light hydraulic tamper
小型枕底清筛机 light duty ballast undercutting cleaner
小型自卸车 small dumper
小修 small-scale maintenance, minor repair
小样本方法 small sample method
小直径连续装药 continuous charging of small-diameter cartridges
小阻力扣件 small resistance fastening
小组 gang, team, crew
肖氏硬度 Shore hardness
效果 effect
效力 force, effect
效率 efficiency
效率降低 loss of efficiency
效益 benefit, profitability
效益成本比 benefit-cost ratio (BCR)
协调 coordinate, coordination, trade-off
协调会 coordination meeting
协调人 coordinator
协调中心 coordination center
协定 agreement, convention
协定费率 agreed rate
协定价格 conventional price
协定运费率 agreed rate
协会 association, institute, institution
协会罢工、暴动及民变险条款 institute strikes, riots, and civil commotions clauses
协会货物条款 institute cargo clauses (ICC)
协会货物条款(A) institute cargo clauses (A)
协会货物条款(B) institute cargo clauses (B)
协会货物条款(C) institute cargo clauses (C)
协会战争险条款 institute war clauses
协商合同 negotiation contract
协商解决 settlement by agreement, negotiated settlement
协商债务偿还方案(避免法院清盘令) compounding a debt
协同设计 design cooperation
协议 protocol, agreement, arrangement, treaty
协议额 agreement amount
协议范围 extent of agreement, scope of agreement
协议分析仪 protocol analyzer
协议利益 benefit of agreement
协议书 form of agreement, agreement form, contract agreement
协议书规定的货币 currency of agreement
协议书语言 language of agreement
协议条文 articles of agreement
协议终止合同 termination by agreement
协议转换器 protocol converter
协助 assistance
协作 cooperation, collaboration, team work, collaborate
协作合同 contract of association
协作型联营体 cooperative joint venture
协作责任 duty of cooperation
胁迫行为 coercive practice
斜层理 diagonal bedding
斜长花岗岩 plagioclase granite
斜长石 plagioclase
斜长岩 plagioclasite
斜道 chute
斜断层 diagonal fault, oblique fault
斜方晶系 orthorhombic system
斜构件 diagonal member
斜谷 diagonal valley
斜管沉淀池 tube settler
斜管(板)沉淀池 inclined tube (plate) sedimentation tank
斜交断层 inclined fault
斜交角 skew angle, oblique angle
斜交节理 oblique joint
斜交桥 skew bridge
斜角式存放 angled storage
斜截面 oblique section
斜筋 diagonal bar
斜井 inclined shaft
斜距 slope distance
斜拉桥 cable-stayed bridge
斜拉条 diagonal brace
斜拉线(电力) backstay wire
斜缆 inclined cable
斜链形悬挂 inclined catenary suspension
斜坡 slope
斜坡防洪工程 flood prevention works with sloping faces
斜坡防护 sloping protection
斜坡式低货位 slope-type low freight section
斜坡走道 inclined walks
斜切式洞门 bamboo-truncated portal, truncated portal
斜索 inclined cable, stay cable
斜推法 incline pushing method
斜腿刚构 slant-legged rigid frame
斜腿刚构桥 slant-legged rigid frame bridge
斜腕臂 slanted cantilever tube

斜向箍筋　inclined stirrup
斜桩　batter pile, battered pile
谐波电流　harmonic current
谐波放大　harmonic amplification
谐波干扰　harmonic interference
谐波含有率　harmonic ratio
谐波校验　harmonic check
谐波失真　harmonic distortion
谐波振荡　harmonic resonance
谐振峰　harmonic peak
谐振频率　harmonic frequency
携带带式输送机　portable belt conveyor
泄力杆　tension releasing pole
泄流轮对　leakage flow wheel set
泄漏　leakage
泄漏电流　leakage current
泄漏阻抗　leakage impedance
泄露　leakage
泄水道　sluice
泄水洞　water discharging tunnel
泄水管　drain pipe
泄水涵洞　emptying culvert
泄水孔　drainage opening, weep hole
泄水引流　sluicing drainage
泄压装置　pressure relief device
潟湖　lagoon
潟湖相　lagoon facies
卸岸日期　date of landing
卸车线　unloading track
卸荷板　relieving slab
卸荷带　unloading zone
卸荷节理　unloading joint
卸货　discharge, discharge of cargo (goods), clear a ship, unload
卸货地点　landing place
卸货费　landing charges, discharging expenses
卸货港　discharging port, port of discharge, unloading port, port of delivery
卸货记录　landing account
卸货价格　landed price
卸货量　outturn
卸货码头　discharging quay
卸货日期　date of discharge
卸货通知单　landing order
卸货证书　landing certification
卸货重量　landed weight
卸料场　dumping place
卸料点　unloading site
卸料斗　discharge hopper
卸污单元　waste discharge unit
卸污线　sewage disposal track
卸油线　oil unloading track
卸载　unloading
懈怠行为　act of omission
蟹爪式装岩机　crab rock loader
心轨　frog rail
心形环　thimble
芯线感应电位　inductive potential of core wire
芯线色别　core wire color
芯柱　core column
辛迪加贷款　syndicated loan
锌含量　zinc content
新奥法　new austrian tunnelling method (NATM)
新材料　new material
新风机组　fresh air unit
新风冷负荷　cooling load from outdoor air
新风量　fresh air volume
新风系统　fresh air system
新构造运动　neotectonic movement
新黄土　new loess
新建车站　new station
新建路基　new subgrade
新建铁路　new railway
新建铁路线　new railway line
新结构　new structure
新能源　new energy
新生代　Cainozoic era
新生界　Cainozoic erathem/group
新太古代　Neoarchean era
新太古界　Neoarchean erathem
新鲜岩石　fresh rock
新元古代　Neoproterozoic era
新月形沙丘　crescent dune
新增成本　additional cost
新增工作　additional work
薪金　salary
信贷　credit
信贷保函　credit guarantee
信贷保证类保险　credit and surety insurance
信贷额度　lines of credit
信贷风险　credit risk
信贷公司　finance company
信贷市场　credit market
信贷条件　credit terms
信贷协议　credit agreement
信贷银行　credit bank
信贷政策　credit policy
信函　letter, communication
信号标志　signal sign
信号标志牌　signal sign board

信号表示	signal indication
信号传输线	signal transmission line
信号灯泡	signal bulb
信号点	signal location
信号电缆	signal cable
信号叠加次数	signal superimposing times
信号阀	signal valve
信号放大器	signal amplifier
信号复示器	signal repeater
信号关闭	signal at stop
信号关闭表示	stop signal indication
信号机	signal
信号机点灯	signal lighting
信号机点灯电路	signal lighting circuit
信号机后方	in rear of a signal
信号机前方	in advance of a signal
信号集中监测	Centralized Signaling Monitoring (CSM)
信号接口单元	signal interface unit
信号开放	signal at clear
信号开放表示	clear signal indication
信号控制电路	signal control circuit
信号楼	signal tower
信号桥	signal bridge
信号失真度	signal distortion
信号握柄	signal lever
信号无效标	sign for signal out of service
信号显示	signal indication
信号显示关系	signal indication relation
信号线	signal line
信号选别器	signal slot
信号允许	signal authorization (SA)
信汇	mail transfer (M/T)
信汇通知书	mail transfer advice
信令点	signaling point (SP)
信令分析仪等	signaling analyzer
信令网关	Signaling Gateway (SG)
信令转接点	signaling transfer point (STP)
信任	confidence, trust
信使	messenger
信守合同	honour the contract
信托	entrust, trust
信托财产	trust property
信托服务	fiduciary service
信托公司	trust company
信托基金	trust fund
信托契约	deed of trust
信托人	trustor
信托收据	trust receipt
信托受益人	cestui que trust
信托书	declaration of trust, letter of trust
信托银行	trust bank
信托账户	account in trust
信息	information, message
信息安全	information security
信息包	information packet
信息查询系统	enquiry system
信息查询终端	enquiry terminal
信息处理平台	information processing platform
信息交付手册	information delivery manual (IDM)
信息管理平台	information management platform
信息管理系统	information management system (IMS)
信息化	informatization
信息化管理	information technology-based management
信息化应用系统	information application system
信息技术	Information Technology (IT)
信息价	information-guided price
信息粒度	information granularity
信息模型	information model
信息设施系统	information facility system
信息深度	level of information detail
信息数据库	information data bank
信息显示时延	information display delay
信息直采系统	direct information collection system
信用	credit, honour
信用保险	credit insurance
信用保险单	credit policy
信用贷款	fiduciary loan
信用分析	credit analysis
信用卡	credit card
信用赊账	on credit
信用债券	debenture
信用证	letter of credit (L/C)
信用证金额	amount of the credit
信用证申请书	application for letter of credit
信用证失效日期	letter of credit expiration date
信用证条件	terms of credit
信用证修改书	amendment of letter of credit
信用证样本	specimen of letter of credit
信用证正本	original letter of credit
信誉	reputation
信元差错率	cell error rate (CER)
信元传送时延	cell transfer delay (CTD)
信元丢失率	cell lose rate (CLR)
信元时延变化	cell delay variation (CDV)
信源	input source

信噪比　signal to noise ratio
星形连接　star connection
刑法　criminal law
刑事责任　criminal liability, criminal responsibility
行包安全检查设施
　　security inspection facility of luggage and parcel
行包服务信息系统
　　luggage and parcel service information system
行包管理信息系统
　　luggage and parcel management information system
行包广播系统
　　public address system of luggage and parcel
行包视频监视
　　video surveillance system of luggage and parcel
行包显示系统
　　information display system of luggage and parcel
行包信息系统
　　luggage and parcel information system
行车安全　running safety
行车安全限值　limit value for traffic safety
行车道　road way
行车方向别疏解　untwining for train direction
行车干扰　train operation disturbance
行车干扰范围　range of train operation disturbance
行车干扰施工增加费　additional fee of construction by train operation disturbance
行车干扰项目　items of train operation disturbance
行车记录设备　train movement recording equipment
行车速度　running speed
行车信号　running signal
行车信号机　train signal
行车许可　movement authority
行车许可测试　movement authority test
行车许可的取消　revocation of movement authority
行车许可终点　end of movement authority
行车指挥方式　train operation command mode
行车组织　train operation organization
行程　itinerary
行道树　street tree
行动纲领　action programme
行贿　bribery
行人横通道　pedestrian cross passage
行驶日志　logbook
行为　action
行为标准　code of conduct
行为人　actor
行为守则　conduct code, code of conduct
行为准则　standard of conduct
行邮行包作业场　post and parcel operation yard
行政部门　administrative department, administration
行政措施　administration measure
行政当局　administering authority
行政法　administration law
行政法庭　administrative tribunal
行政费　overhead
行政管理　administration, administrative management
行政管理费　expenditure on administration, administrative overhead
行政管理人员　administrative personnel, administrative staff, administrator
行政惯例　administration practice
行政命令　administration order
形式发票　proforma invoice
型钢　shaped steel
型号　model
型式检验　type test
型式检验报告　type inspection report
型式检验试件　type inspection specimen
型式试验　type test
杏仁状　amygdaloidal
杏仁状构造　amygdaloidal structure
性能　performance
性能保证　performance assurance, guarantee of performance, performance guarantee
性能标准　performance criteria
性能标准说明书　performance specification
性能分级　performance grading
性能化设计　performance oriented design
性能检验　performance test
性能考核　performance test
性能指标　performance matrix, performance index
性质　nature, property, character
胸径　diameter at breast height
雄黄　realgar
休会　adjourn
休假　leave, off-duty
休眠模式　sleeping mode
休息日　off-day, rest day
休止　cease, cessation
休止角　angle of repose
修补　repair, rectify, remedy, patch
修补工作　remedial work
修补缺陷　remedying defects
修补缺陷后的进一步试验
　　further tests after remedying defects
修补施工现场外的缺陷工作
　　remedying of defective work off site
修车台位　position for repairing cars
修车台位长度　position length for repairing car

修车线　repair siding
修订　amend, amendment, revise
修订计划　revised programme
修复　make good, restore, restoration, rehabilitation
修复—运营—移交　rehabilitate-operate-transfer（ROT）
修改　amend, amendment, revise, revision, modify, modification, make over
修改合同　revise a contract
修改书　addendum
修改通知单　amendment advice
修理　fix, repair, mend
修理费　repair charge
修理工　mechanic, technician
修理工具　repair kit
修理性打磨　corrective grinding
修配间　repair shop
修缮和扩建　betterment and extension
修缮经费　betterments
修整　refitting, refurbishment, retrofit
修正　correct, modify, remedy
修正的格里菲斯准则　modified Griffith criterion
修正的计划　revised programme
修正合同　amendment of contract
修正系数　correction coefficient
锈蚀　rustiness
溴化锂吸收式制冷机　lithium-bromide absorption refrigerating machine
虚报　false declaration
虚报账目　cook the accounts, cook the books
虚报支出　padding, mispresent expenditure
虚假的　artificial, false
虚假利润　false profit
虚拟化　virtualization
虚拟局域网　virtual local area network（VLAN）
虚拟链路　virtual link
虚拟专用网　Virtual Private Network（VPN）
虚拟自动闭塞　automatic virtual block
虚拟组织　virtual organization
虚盈实亏　false profit
虚账户　nominal account
需求　demand
需求预测　demand forecast
需要　require, requirement
需要复原的表面　surfaces requiring reinstatement
需用功率　power demand
许可　approve, permit, consent
许可人　licensor
许可证　permit, licence, license, letters

许可证颁发人　licenser, licensor
许可证法　licensing law
许可证交易　tradable permits, tradable emissions permit
许可证接受人　licencee, licensee
许可证协议　licensing agreement
许诺　promise, undertaking
序贯平差　sequential adjustment
序列号　serial number
序批式活性污泥法　sequencing batch reactor（SBR）
序时账簿　chronological books
续保　renewal of insurance
续订合同　renew a contract
续流　follow current
絮粒　floc particles
絮粒体　floc
絮凝　flocculation
絮状构造　flocculent structure
蓄电池　storage battery
蓄电池组　storage battery
蓄热　heat accumulation
蓄热法　method of heat accumulation
蓄热水箱　thermal storage water tank
蓄热系数　coefficient of thermal storage
蓄水池　reservoir
蓄水塘　water storage pond
宣告破产　declare bankruptcy
宣判　adjudicate
宣誓　vow
宣誓书　affidavit
玄武玻璃细碧岩　basaltic glass spilite
玄武岩　basalt
悬臂　cantilever
悬臂板　cantilever slab
悬臂杆　cantilever pole
悬臂架设法　cantilever erection method
悬臂浇筑法　cast-in-place cantilever method
悬臂结构　cantilever structure
悬臂梁　cantilever beam
悬臂梁桥　cantilever bridge
悬臂螺旋卸车机　cantilever screw unloading machine
悬臂拼接法　precast segmental construction by cantilever method
悬臂拼装法　precast segmental construction by cantilever method
悬臂桥　cantilever bridge
悬臂式挡土墙　cantilever retaining wall
悬臂式铺轨机　cantilever rail laying machine

X

悬臂式铺轨排机　track panel laying machine with cantilever
悬臂式起重机　cantilever crane
悬臂支架　cantilever bracket, cantilever brace
悬冰川　hanging glacier
悬垂线夹　suspension clamp
悬吊管　suspension pipe
悬吊滑轮　suspension pulley
悬浮物　suspended matter
悬沟　hanging gully
悬挂带零位观测　tape zero observation
悬挂结构　suspended structure
悬挂泉　suspended spring
悬浇连续梁　cast-in-situ continuous girder without support
悬式绝缘子　suspension insulator
悬索　suspension cable
悬索桥　suspension bridge
悬液　suspension
悬移质　suspended load
旋流沉砂池　vortex-type grit chamber
旋流风口　swirl air outlet
旋喷桩　jet grouting pile
旋喷桩复合地基　composite foundation of piles
旋挖钻机　rotary drilling rig
旋转薄膜烘箱试验　rolling thin film oven test
旋转布水器　rotary distributor
旋转单耳　swivel with eye
旋转式钻机　rotary drill
旋转送风口　rotary air supply outlet
旋转腕臂　hinged cantilever, swivel cantilever
旋转蒸发仪　rotary evaporimetry
选厂测量　surveying for site selection
选定的分包商　selected subcontractor
选路　route selection
选路电路　route selecting circuit
选路制信号　route signaling
选频电平表　selective level meter
选频放大器　frequency-selective amplifier
选线　location, route selection
选线设计　route design
选项　option
选择标准　selection criteria
选择税　alternative duty
选择投标人　bidder selection
选择投标人准则　bidder selection criteria
选择性招标　selected bidding (tendering), selective bidding (tendering)
选址　siting, site selection
选址查勘　site selection investigation
眩光　glare
眩光值　glare rating
雪崩　avalanche
雪崩槽　avalanche slot
雪害地区路基　subgrade in snow disaster region
雪荷载　snow load
雪深计　snow depth meter
雪深监测报警　snow depth monitoring alarm
雪蚀洼地　nivation swale
雪线　snowline
削价　price cutting
削减　cutback
巡检　patrol inspection
巡视小道　patrol path
询价　enquire, enquiry, inquire, inquiry, solicitation
询价采购　purchase inquiry
询价函件　letter of inquiry
询价文件　enquiry documents
询盘　enquiry, inquiry
询问　query
询问者　inquirer
循环泵　circulating pump
循环附加流量　circulating additional flow
循环管　circulating pipe
循环加载试验　cyclic loading test
循环检查制　cyclic scanning system
循环信用证　revolving letter of credit
循环资金　revolving fund
循回式运转制　locomotive loop routing
训练　train

Y

压差指数　differential pressure index
压电激振器　piezoelectric exciter
压电式测试系统　piezoelectric test system
压电式加速度传感器　piezoelectric acceleration sensor
压覆矿藏评估费　assessment fee for mineral resources unavailabled because of the construction
压覆矿产资源评估　assessment of overlaid mineral resources
压沟坡　pressure channel ditch
压钩坡　coupler compressing grade
压浆浆体　grouting slurry
压接标志　crimping mark
压力表　pressure gauge
压力传感器　pressure sensor
压力阀　pressure valve
压力拱　pressure arch
压力管道　pressure pipeline
压力灌浆　pressure grouting
压力灌浆止水　pressure grouting sealing
压力涵洞　pressure culvert
压力盒　pressure cell
压力计算高度　pressure calculation height
压力泌水率　bleeding rate at pressure
压力泌水仪　pressure bleeding meter
压力泡　pressure bulb
压力喷浆　pneumatic mortar, gunite
压力式涵洞　culvert in the case of both inlet and outlet submerged
压力式温度计　pressure type thermometer
压力试验机　compression testing machine
压力释放装置　pressure relief device
压力隧道　pressure tunnel
压力主管　pressuring main
压力注浆　pressure grouting
压路机　roller
压敏电阻　varistor, piezoresistor
压模　compression moulding
压扭性断层　compressional torsion fault
压屈强度　compressive strength
压实　compaction
压实标准　compaction requirements
压实程度　compaction degree
压实地基　compacted ground
压实度　compactness
压实方法　compaction method
压实工具　compactor
压实填土　compacted fill
压实系数　compacting coefficient
压实性　compactability
压水设备　pump-in test device
压水试验　water pump-in test
压碎　crush
压碎结构　pressure texture, crush texture
压碎岩　cataclastic rock
压碎指标　crush index
压缩　compression
压缩变形　compression deformation
压缩机　compressor
压缩空气　compressed air
压缩空气管道　compressed air duct
压缩模量　compression modulus
压缩式制冷循环　compression refrigeration cycle
压缩系数　compression coefficient
压缩性　compressibility
压缩应变　compressive strain
压缩指数　compression index
压土机　compactor
压型钢板　profiled steel sheet
压性断层　compressional fault
压性断裂　compresional fault
压样器　pressure sampling machine
压应力　compressive stress
压重　pressure weights
押汇银行　negotiating bank
押金　deposit, cash deposit as collateral, antecedent moneyguarantee deposit

雅丹地貌　Yardang landform
亚干旱　sub drought
亚甲基蓝分光光度法
　　methylene blue spectrophotometric method
亚硫酸盐渍土　sulfurous acid saline soil
亚氯酸钠　sodium chlorite
亚氯盐渍土　subchloride saline soil
亚黏土　sandy clay
亚湿润　sub-humid
亚硝酸盐氮　nitrite nitrogen
垭口　col
咽喉区　throat area
咽喉信号机　signal in throat section
烟　smoke
烟囱架　chimney rack
烟囱效应　chimney effect
烟道　flue
烟感　smoke detector
烟雾灭火系统　smoke extinguishing system
延长工期索赔　claim for extension of time
延长有效期　extend validity
延迟　defer, delay, postpone
延迟交货　late delivery
延迟接受　late acceptance
延迟时间　delay time
延迟装运　late shipment
延度　ductility
延缓偿付期　moratorium
延交定货　back order
延米　linear metre
延期　extension, postponement, deferral
延期偿付权　moratorium
延期费用　extension fee, deferment charge
延期付款　defer payment, deferred payment, payment deferred
延期付款保函　deferred payment guarantee
延期付款销售
　　deferred payment sale, installment sale
延期付款信用证　deferred payment credit
延期交货　deferred delivery
延期利息　deferred interest
延期年金　deferred annuity
延期支付　postponed payment
延伸率　elongation
延时　time delay
延时效应　time-delay effect
延误　delay
延误的检验　delayed test
延误的试验　delayed tests
延误的图纸　delayed drawings
延误及/或成本　delay and/or cost
延性　ductility, stretchability
延性抗震设计　ductility seismic design
延性框架　ductile frame
延性破坏　ductile failure
延性设计　ductility design
延续进路　successive route
延展性　malleability, ductility
严格标准　strict standard
严格责任　strict liability
严寒地区　severe cold region
严密平差　rigorous adjustment
严密性试验　tightness test
严重渎职　serious misconduct/malfeasance
严重风化　serious weathering
严重过失　serious misconduct
严重缺陷　serious defect
严重违约　material breach of contract, serious breach of contract
严重雪害　serious snow damage
严重遗漏　material omission
岩爆　rock burst
岩崩　rockfall
岩层　rock stratum
岩层产状　occurences of rock formation
岩层滑坡　rock landslide
岩层节理统计分析　statistic analysis of rock joints
岩层倾角　dip angle of rock formation
岩层倾向　dip direction of rock formation
岩层软硬不均
　　hard-soft heterogeneity of rock formation
岩层走向　strike of rock formation
岩床　sill
岩堆　scree, talus
岩堆床　talus bed, scree bed
岩堆地段路基　subgrade in talus section
岩堆休止角
　　repose angle of scree, repose angle of talus
岩基　batholith
岩浆岩(火成岩)　magmatic rock (igneous rock)
岩浆作用　magmatism
岩块　rock block
岩块的横波速度　transverse wave velocity of rock
岩块的纵波速度
　　longitudinal wave velocity of rock
岩矿样品　samples of rock minerals
岩沥青　rock asphalt
岩盘　laccolith
岩墙　dike
岩溶　karst

岩溶地段路基　subgrade in karst section
岩溶发育程度　extent of karst development
岩溶基准　karst base level
岩溶裂隙充填系数　fissure filling coefficient of karst
岩溶裂隙率　karst fissure ratio
岩溶流　lava flow
岩溶路基　karst subgrade
岩溶盆地　karst basin, polje
岩溶泉　karst spring
岩溶水　karst water
岩溶洼地　karst depression
岩石　rock
岩石饱和吸水率　water saturated absorptivity of rock
岩石饱水系数　water-saturation coefficient of rock
岩石薄片鉴定　rock slice identification
岩石弹性泊松比　elastic poisson's ratio of rock
岩石的物理性质　physical properties of rock
岩石点荷载强度试验　point loading strength test of rock
岩石冻融系数　freezing and thawing coefficient of rock
岩石冻融质量损失率　freezing and thawing mass loss rate of rock
岩石分级　rock classification
岩石分类　rock classification
岩石风化程度　weathering degree of rock
岩石工程　rock engineering
岩石坚硬程度　hardness of rock
岩石抗剪断强度试验　rock shear strength test
岩石抗剪强度试验　rock shear strength (direct shear) test
岩石抗拉强度　rock tensile strength
岩石抗拉强度试验　rock tensile strength test
岩石可钻性　rock drillability
岩石块体密度　density of rock block
岩石块体自由浸水饱和密度　free soaking saturation density of rock block
岩石扩容　dilatancy of rock
岩石力学　rock mechanics
岩石力学性质　rock mechanical property
岩石密度　rock density
岩石耐崩解指数　slaking index of rock
岩石膨胀性试验　swelling test of rock
岩石膨胀压力　swelling pressure of rock
岩石三轴压缩强度试验　triaxial compression strength test of rock
岩石声波测试　rock sonic measurement
岩石声发射　acoustic emission of rock
岩石试验　rock test
岩石吸水率　water absorption of rock
岩石研磨性　rock abrasiveness
岩石原位直接剪切试验　in-situ direct shear test of rock
岩石质量指标　rock quality designation (RQD)
岩石柱法　rock column method
岩石柱膨胀率　expansion rate of rock column
岩体　rock mass
岩体变形　rock mass deformation
岩体变形试验　rock mass deformation test
岩体构造　structure of rock mass
岩体基本质量　basic quality of rock mass (BQ)
岩体结构类型　structural type of rock mass
岩体结构面　structural plane of rock mass
岩体结构面直剪试验　direct shear strength test for discontinuities
岩体孔隙压力　rock mass pore pressure
岩体类型　type of rock mass
岩体内摩擦角　internal friction angle of rock mass
岩体破坏荷载　rock mass fracture load
岩体破裂压力　rock mass fracture pressure
岩体强度试验　rock mass strength test
岩体顺层　bedding of rock mass
岩体完整性系数　rock mass integrity coefficient
岩体完整性指数(岩体速度指数)　intactness index of rock mass (velocity index of rock mass)
岩体应力　rock mass stress
岩体直剪试验　rock mass direct shear strength test
岩体质量指标　rock mass quality designation
岩体重张压力　rock mass reopening pressure
岩体主要结构面　main structural plane of rock mass
岩土参数空间变异性　spatial variability of geotechnical parameter
岩土参数统计分析　statistic analysis of geotechnical parameter
岩土工程　geotechnical engineering
岩土工程分级　geotechnical engineering classification
岩土工程勘察　geotechnical engineering investigation
岩土工程勘察水平　geotechnical engineering investigation level
岩土构筑物　geostructure
岩土界面　rock-soil interface
岩土矿物　rock-soil mineral
岩土膨胀压力　swelling pressure of rock and soil
岩土试样　rock-soil sample
岩土体　rock and soil mass
岩土性质　geotechnical property

岩相	lithofacies, petrofacies
岩相法	lithofacies method
岩屑	detritus, debris
岩屑砂岩	lithic sandstone
岩芯	rock core
岩芯管	core barrel
岩芯回收率	core recovery
岩芯样品	rock core sample
岩芯钻	core drill
岩性	lithology
岩盐	halite
岩样	rock sample
岩株	stock
沿岸堤	longshore embankment
研究开发费	research and development cost
研究试验费	research and test cost
研究所	institute
盐海	salt sea
盐湖	salt lake
盐碱地	saline-alkali land
盐类结晶破坏环境	salt physical attacking environment
盐类结晶型侵蚀	salt crystallization erosion
盐水(人工冻结)	brine
盐酸容量法	hydrochloric acid volumetric method
盐田	salt pan
盐岩	halite
盐沼	saltmarsh
盐渍度	salinity
盐渍化	salinization
盐渍化冻土	saline permafrost
盐渍土	saline soil
盐渍土地区	saline soil region
盐渍土路基	saline soil subgrade
盐渍岩	saline rock
颜色平滑度	color smoothness
衍生属性	derived attribute
掩蔽面积	sheltering area
掩埋阶地	buried terrace
眼球状混合岩	augen migmatite
演示	presentment
演示人	presenter
厌氧/好氧除磷工艺	anaerobic/oxic process
厌氧/缺氧/好氧脱氮除磷工艺 anaerobic/anoxic/oxic process(AAO)
厌氧(好氧)处理	anaerobic (aerobic) treatment
厌氧区	anaerobic zone
厌氧稳定塘	anaerobic pond
厌氧消化	anaerobic digestion
验槽	trenching for inspection
验工计价	measurement and valuation
验关	customs examination, customs inspection
验明	identify
验收	acceptance
验收报告	acceptance report
验收标准	standard for acceptance
验收规范	acceptance specification
验收记录	acceptance record
验收结论	acceptance result
验收日期	date of acceptance
验收试验	acceptance test
验收证书 acceptance certificate, taking-over certificate
验收准则	acceptance criteria
验算点法	checking point method
验证	verification
验证方法	means of verification
堰	barrage
堰板	weir plate
堰测法	weir method
堰顶	weir crest
堰槛	weir sill
堰塞湖	dammed lake
燕山期	Yanshan age, Yanshan
扬程	head of delivery
扬声器	loudspeaker
扬水站	lift station
羊背石	roche moutonnee, sheepback rock
羊足碾	goat-foot roller, sheep-foot roller
羊足压路机	sheep-foot roller
阳离子	cation
阳离子交换量	cation exchange capacity
阳离子乳化剂	cationic emulsifier
阳离子乳化沥青	cationic emulsified asphalt
阳台	balcony
阳像	positive image
洋脊	ocean ridge
洋盆	ocean basin
洋中脊	mid-ocean ridge
仰拱	invert
仰拱曲模	curved formwork for invert construction
仰拱填充	invert filling
仰拱栈桥	invert trestle
仰斜排水孔	backward-slanting drain hole
仰斜式钻孔	upward inclined borehole
养护	maintenance
养护费	maintenance expense
养护覆盖物	curing mat
养护龄期	curing age
养护维修	maintenance and repair

养老基金　pension fund
养老金　pension
养路费　road maintenance costs
养路费及车船使用税　road maintenance expense and vehicle and vessel use tax
养路机械作业平台　work platform of maintenance machinery
氧化沟　oxidation ditch
氧化沥青　oxidized asphalt
氧化镁含量　magnesium oxide content
氧化锰含量　manganese oxide content
氧化锌避雷器　zinc-oxide arrester
氧化亚铁含量　ferrous oxide content
氧气切割器　oxygen lance
样板房　model house
样板工程　sample works, pilot works
样本　specimen
样品　sample
样品室　sample room
腰梁　waist beam
邀请函　letter of invitation (LOI)
邀请招标　selective tendering, selected bidding
邀请招标(又称"有限竞争性招标")　selected bidding (also known as "limited competitive bidding")
邀约报价　offer
摇摆力　nosing force
摇摆柱　leaning column
摇轴支座　rocker bearing
遥测　telemetering
遥调　teleregulation
遥感　remote sensing
遥感勘测　remote sensing prospecting
遥感平台　remote sensing platform
遥感数据　remote sensing data
遥感图像　remote sensing image
遥感图像判释　remote sensing image interpretation
遥感制图　remote sensing mapping
遥控　remote control
遥信　teleindication
药剂固定储备量　standby reserve of chemical
要求　claim, request, requirement
要素　element
要约人　offerer, offeror
要约邀请　invitation for offer
钥匙路签　staff with a key
野生动物栖息地　wildlife habitat
野外地质图　field geological map
野外作业　field work

业绩　performance
业绩评价　performance evaluation
业务范围　business line
业务管理点　service management point (SMP)
业务管理接入点　service management access point (SMAP)
业务交换点　service switching point (SSP)
业务节点　service node
业务节点接口　service node interface (SNI)
业务开发　business development
业务开支　operating expenses
业务控制点　service control point (SCP)
业务支撑系统　Business Support System (BSS)
业主　owner, client, employer, proprietor, building owner
业主财产保险　insurance of client's property
业主产权　proprietary equity
业主代表　employer's representative
业主的保障　indemnities by employer
业主的财务安排　employer's financial arrangements
业主供货范围　scope of supply by owner (employer)
业主顾问　client adviser
业主机具　employer's equipment
业主权益　proprietary interest, proprietary equity
业主人员　owner's (employer's) personnel
业主认可　acceptance by owner (employer)
业主索赔　claim by owner (employer)
业主违约　default of owner (employer)
业主要求的变更　variation by request for proposal
业主主导的设计团队　employer-led design teams
业主自便终止　termination at (for) employer's convenience
叶状剥落　exfoliation
页岩　shale
页岩沥青　shale tar
夜班　night shift, graveyard shift
夜班津贴　night duty allowance
夜间施工　construction at night
夜间施工增加费　additional fee for construction at night
夜间施工增加费率　additional rate for construction at night
夜间信号　night signal
夜视功能　night vision
夜视图像　night vision image
液动冲击钻进　hydraulic percussion drilling
液灌汽车　tank truck
液化　liquefaction
液化安全系数　safety factor of liquefaction

液化等级	liquefaction grade
液化地基	liquefied ground
液化点	liquefaction point, liquidizing point
液化气体	liquefied gas
液化强度	liquefaction strength
液化势	liquefaction potential
液化土层	liquefied soil layer
液化应力	liquefaction stress
液化应力比	liquefaction stress ratio
液化指数	liquefaction index
液晶显示屏	liquid crystal display (LCD)
液氯	liquid chlorine
液氯消毒法	chlorine disinfection
液态二氧化碳	liquid carbon dioxide
液体称量法	liquid weighing method
液体货物	liquid goods
液体货物货场	liquid goods yard
液体静力水准测量	hydrostatic leveling
液位计	liquid level meter
液限	liquid limit
液相	liquid phase
液性指数	liquidity index
液压拨道器	hydraulic track lining tool
液压操作机构	hydraulic operating mechanism
液压打桩机	hydraulic pile driver
液压捣固车	hydraulic tamper, hydraulic tamping car
液压捣固机	hydraulic tamper, hydraulic tamping car
液压激振试验	hydraulic vibration test
液压计	hydraulic pressure gauge
液压精密螺栓扳手	hydraulic precise bolt wrench
液压汽车起重机	hydraulic truck crane
液压起道器	hydraulic track lifting tool, hydraulic rail jack
液压千斤顶	hydraulic jack
液压式沉降仪	hydraulic settlement device
液压式挖土机	hydraulic excavator
液压匀轨机	hydraulic rail gap adjusting device
液压凿岩台车	hydraulic rock-drilling jumbo
液压直轨器	hydraulic rail straightener
一班(制)	single shift
一般材料	general materials
一般冲刷	general scour
一般代理	general agency
一般抵押	general mortgage
一般地段	section with common conditions
一般地区	ordinary region
一般堆积土	general deposited soil
一般规定	general provisions
一般合同条件	general conditions
一般留置权	general lien
一般路基	ordinary subgrade
一般侵权行为	general tort
一般权利	general right
一般缺陷	common defect
一般条件	general conditions
一般物价水准	general price level
一般显色指数	general colour rendering index
一般项目	general item
一般要求	general requirement
一般义务	general obligation, general responsibilities
一般责任	general responsibilities
普通照明	general lighting
一布一膜复合土工膜	one fabric and one membrane composite geomembrane
一侧式正线	one-sided main line
一次参数	primary parameter
一次侧	high voltage side, primary side
一次电池供电	primary cell power supply
一次调整	adjustment at once
一次二阶矩法	first-order second-moment method
一次回风	primary return air
一次回路	primary circuit
一次群速率	primary rate
一次性成本	one-off cost
一次性付清债务	one-off debt pay off
一次性支出	one-time expenses
一次支付(整付)	lump-sum payment
一次自动重合闸	single-shot automatic reclosing
一岛一道	one island and one track
一段零序电流保护	one section of zero-sequence current protection
一级处理	primary treatment
一级道砟	first grade ballast
一级分区	first-level subregion
一级负荷贯通线	run-through power line of load level I
一级检修	first-level inspection
一级能效	first-level energy efficiency
一级排放标准	first class discharge standard
一级评价	first class assessment
一级水源保护区	first class district of source water protection zone
一阶弹性分析	first order elastic analysis
一阶非线性分析	first order nonlinear analysis
一览表	schedule, list
一揽子	package
一揽子采购	procurement packages
一揽子采购合同	blanket purchase contract

一揽子成本	lump sum cost
一揽子抵押	package mortgage
一揽子合同	blanket contract, package contract
一揽子交易	package deal, one block deal
一揽子索赔	package of claims, global package
一揽子投标	package bid
一揽子项目	package project
一揽子协议	umbrella agreement
一批	batch
一切险	all risks (a/r, A. R.)
一切险保险	all risks insurance
一切险保险单	all-risk policy
一切险合同	all risks contract
一送多受	single transmitting and multiple receiving track circuit
一送一受	single feeding and single receiving
一线一台布置	one track and one platform layout
一站式采购	one-stop shopping
一站枢纽	terminal with one station
一站直达	nonstop arrival
1 人组成的争议避免裁决委员会	sole-member DAAB
1 号数字用户信令系统	digital subscriber signaling system No. 1 (DSS1)
Ⅰ(Ⅱ,Ⅲ,Ⅳ)类桩	Ⅰ(Ⅱ,Ⅲ,Ⅳ) type pile
Ⅰ类变更	class Ⅰ alteration
Ⅰ类接入节点	Class Ⅰ access node
伊利石	illite
伊利石含量	illite content
医疗	medical treatment
医疗保险	health insurance
医疗费	medical fee
医疗费用保险	medical expense insurance
医疗证明	medical certificate
依合同	by contract
依法解除履约责任	release from performances under the law
依法占有	possession by law
依据合同	under contract
仪表管理	instrument management
仪表间	instrument room
仪器	apparatus, instrument
(水质分析)仪器设备	instruments and apparatus
夷平面	planation surface
移动备用	movable standby
移动闭塞	moving block
移动带式输送机	mobile belt conveyor
移动点对点短消息发送成功率	success ratio of point-to-point (PP) short message service (SMS)
移动交换中心	mobile switching center (MSC)
移动交换中心服务器	MSC Server
移动角	displacement angle
移动模架	movable scaffolding system (MSS, used for span-by-span casting construction)
移动模架法	movable formwork method
移动盆地	moving basin
移动式搅拌机	portable agitator
移动式卷扬机	traveling hoist
移动式龙门起重机	traveling gantry crane
移动式闪光焊轨车	movable flash welding machine
移动式卸污	movable facility for sewage discharge
移动通信系统	mobile communication system
移动信号	movable signal
移动业务交换中心	mobile service switching center (MSC)
移动用户 ISDN 号码	mobile subscriber ISDN number (MSISDN)
移动用户漫游号码	mobile subscriber roaming number (MSRN)
移动支架	movable support system (used for span-by-span precast segmental construction)
移动终端(台)	mobile station (MS)
移动终端呼叫移动终端	fixed to mobile call, mobile to mobile call
移动终端呼叫有线固定终端	mobile to fixed call
移动终端售票	mobile terminal ticket sales
移交检核表	handover checklist
移交前的使用	use before taking over
移交证书	taking-over certificate, handing-over certificate
移居国外者	expatriate
移民安置	resettlement
移民工程	resettlement
移民规模	resettlement scale
移民局	immigration office
移频轨道电路	frequency shift track circuit
移频自动闭塞	frequency shift modulated automatic block
移挖作填	cutting and filling
移位作业	position-shift operation
移液管	transfer pipette
移液管法	pipette method
移走	removal
移走有缺陷的工程	removal of defective work
遗留物检测	remnant detection
遗漏	omit, omission
遗漏错误	error of omission
乙醇	alcohol
乙炔焊接	acetylene welding

Y

乙烯—醋酸乙烯聚合物防水卷材
  ethylene vinyl acetate copolymer（EVA）sheet
乙烯—乙酸乙烯共聚物土工膜
  ethylene vinyl acetate copolymer geomembrane
乙种密度计　Grade B density gauge
已背书债券　endorsed bond
已承兑汇票　accepted bill
已承兑信用证　accepted letter of credit
已兑现支票　cashed check
已分摊成本　allocated cost, absorbed cost
已付贷款　loan serviced/paid
已付合同保证金　contract deposit paid
已付金额　disbursements to date（DTD）
已付款　account paid
已耗成本　expired cost
已还清的贷款　paid-up loan
已获利润　profit earned
已获收益　earned income
已获营业收入　earned revenue
已缴许可证费　paid-up licence fee
已缴资本　paid-up capital, paid-in capital
已结清账户　closed account
已提货提单　accomplished bill of lading
已贴现票据　bill discounted, discounted notes
已完成工时　earned man-hours
已知损失　known loss
已知危险　known hazards
已装船　on board
已装船货物　afloat cargo, afloat goods
已装船提单
  shipped bill of lading, on board bill of lading
已装船清洁提单　clean shipped bill of lading,
  clean-on-board bill of lading
以 IP 承载语音传输
  voice over internet protocol（VoIP）
以桥代路　subgrade replacement with bridge
以太网　ethernet
以太网无源光网络
  Ethernet Passive Optical Network（EPON）
义务　duty, obligation, liability
义务人　obligor
议标　negotiated bidding
议标合同　negotiation contract
议定　negotiate
议定价格　agreed price
议定书　protocol
议付　negotiation
议付结算　settlement by negotiation
议付手续费　negotiation commission
议付银行　negotiating bank
议价　bargain, negotiated price
议价能力　bargaining position
议价条件　negotiating condition
议事记录　minutes of proceedings
议事日程　agenda
议院　chamber
异步控制器　asynchronous controller
异步转移模式　asynchronous transfer mode（ATM）
异常　abnormality
异常场　anomalous field
异常的
  abnormal, exceptional, extraordinary, special
异常恶劣的气候条件
  exceptionally adverse climatic conditions
异常费用　extraordinary cost
异常事件　exceptional event
异常事件的后果　consequences of an exceptional event
异常事件的通知　notice of an exceptional event
异常意外　exceptional urgency
异程式系统　direct return system
异地数据备份　remote data backup
异物监测　foreign object monitoring
异物侵限　foreign object intrusion
异霞正长岩　lujavrite
异型钢轨　compromise rail
异型接头夹板　compromise joint bar
异议　disagreement
异议程序　objection procedure
抑制性关税　prohibitive duty
易地安家补助费　resettlement subsidy
易货　barter, swap
易货贸易　barter trade
易燃材料　inflammable material
易燃品　inflammable, flammable material
易燃油品　inflammable oil products
易溶盐　soluble salt
易溶盐含量　diffluent salt content
易行车　easy rolling car
易行线　easy rolling track
意见　opinion, suggestion
意见一致　consensus, agree
意外的　contingent, unexpected, accidental
意外开支　contingent expenses, contingency, unforeseen expenses, unexpected expenses
意外利益　windfall, unexpected benefits
意外事故　accident
意外事故保险
  contingency insurance, accident insurance
意外事故赔偿　accident compensation
意外事件预防员　accident prevention officer

意外事项准备金　contingent reserve
意外损害　accidental damage
意外损失　accidental loss
意外损失基金　contingency reserve
意外闲置　unexpected idling
意向　intent, intention
意向书　letter of intent
意向协定　intention agreement, agreement of intent
意愿租赁　tenancy at will
意旨　intendment
溢出带　overflow belt
溢出泉　overflow spring
溢短装限度　tolerance
溢洪道　spillway, overflow
溢价　at a premium, above par, premium
溢流　overflow
溢流阀　overflow valve
翼轨　wing rail
翼墙　wing wall
翼缘　flange
翼缘板　flange slab; flange plate
翼缘板外伸宽度　protruding width of flange
因合同落空而终止　termination by frustration
因素　element, factor
阴离子乳化剂　anionic emulsifier
阴离子乳化沥青　anionic emulsified asphalt
阴离子洗涤剂　anionic detergent
阴谋破坏　sabotage
阴像　negative image
阴影法　shadow method
音频电路　audio circuit
音频二线端　audio two-wire port
音频回线　audio loop cable
音频四线端　audio four-wire port
音频线路　audio line
音频选号接口　audio selective call interface
音视频编码标准
　Audio Video coding Standard (AVS)
音视频信息　audio and video information
音视频终端　audio and video terminal
音响按钮　button for audible device
铟钢尺　invar rods
铟瓦尺　invar level rod
铟瓦基线尺　invar baseline tape
银货两讫　cash on delivery (COD)
银行保函　bank guarantee
银行保证金　bank deposit
银行保证书　bank guarantee
银行本票　banks promissory note
银行承兑票据　bank acceptance note

银行承兑信用证　banker's acceptance credit
银行存款　bank deposit, deposit at bank
银行存款余额　bank balance
银行存折　bank book, pass book
银行贷款　bank financing, bank loan
银行贷款项目　bank-financed project
银行电汇　bank cable transfer
银行发票　banker's invoice
银行汇款　bank transfer
银行汇款手续费　bank remittance fee
银行汇票
　bank's (banker's) draft, bank's (banker's) bill
银行活期存款　bank current deposits
银行即期汇票　bank sight draft
银行间贷款　inter-bank loan
银行间的转账　bank transfer
银行控股公司　bank holding company
银行利差　banker's markup
银行利率　bank rate
银行留置权　banker's lien
银行买价　bank's (banker's) buying rate
银行卖价　bank's (banker's) selling rate
银行票据　bank bill
银行手续费　bank charge, agio
银行贴现　bank discount
银行贴现率　bank discount rate
银行同业拆息率　interbank offered rate
银行透支　bank overdraft
银行信贷　bank credit
银行信用证　banker's letter of credit
银行优惠利率　bank prime rate
银行愿担保的项目　bankable project
银行账户　bank account
银行支票　bank (banker's) check
银行资金融通　bank accommodation
银行资助　bank financing
银行资助的咨询服务
　bank financed consulting services
银团贷款　syndicated loan
引爆　detonation
引出线　lead wire
引导接车模式　mode of receiving trains by the pilot or the call-on signal
引导进路及信号测试　calling-on route and signal test
引导模式　calling-on mode (CO)
引导信号　calling-on signal
引导信息　guidance
引进技术和进口设备其他费用
　other expense for introduction of foreign technology and imported equipment

引气剂　air entraining admixture, air entraining agent
引前相　leading phase, wild phase
引桥　approach bridge
引入管　inlet pipe
引入线　lead-in line
引入线路　approach track
引上电缆　upward leading cable
引伸仪　extensometer
引水　diversion
引水隧洞　diversion tunnel
引下电缆　down lead cable
引下线　down-conductor
引用半径　reference radius
引诱　inducement
引张线法　method of tension wire alignment
饮用水　tap water, potable water
饮用水水源保护区　drinking water source protection zone
隐蔽工程　concealed works
隐蔽损失　hidden loss
隐伏断层　blind fault
隐伏裂纹、间隙　hidden cracks/gap
隐伏岩溶　hidden karst
隐伏岩溶图　hidden karst map
隐含回购　implied repo
隐患　risk
隐晶质结构　cryptocrystalline texture
隐瞒情况不报　non-disclosure
印花　stamp
印花税　stamp tax
印花税票　revenue stamp
印记　imprint, seal
印章　stamp, seal
印支期　Indo-Chinese epoch
应变　strain
应变测点　strain measuring point
应变法　strain method
应变花　strain rosette
应变计　strain gauge
应变空间　strain space
应变控制试验　strain-controlled test
应变量测　strain measurement
应变软化　strain softening
应变时效　strain ageing
应变式测力传感器　strain gauge force sensor
应变仪　strain gauge
应变硬化　strain hardening
应偿债务　debt repayable
应答器　balise
应答器报文　balise telegram
应答器传输模块　balise transmission module
应答器地面电子单元　lineside electronic unit（LEU）
应答器读写工具　balise programming tool
应答器链接　balise linking
应答器信息接收单元　balise transmission module（BTM）
应答器信息接收天线　transponder information receiving antenna
应答器组　balise group
应答器坐标系　balise coordinate system
应得的权利　entitlement
应得权益　due
应付承兑票据　acceptance payable
应付贷款　loan payable
应付工资　accrued payroll, wages payable
应付股利　dividend payable
应付关税　liable to customs duty
应付款　payment due, dues
应付款凭单　payable voucher, notes payable
应付利息　accrual of interest, interest payable
应付票据　bill payable, note payable
应付期　payable period
应付税　tax due
应付所得税　income tax payable
应付债券　bond payable
应付账款　account payable
应付账款登记簿　account payable register
应付账款明细账　account payable ledger
应急操作台　emergency operation console
应急储备金　contingency reserve provision for contingency
应急处理方案　scheme for emergency treatment
应急措施　emergency measure
应急费　contingency fee
应急费暂定金　provisional sums for contingency
应急工作模式　emergency operating mode, emergency mode of operations
应急广播　emergency broadcasting
应急基金　contingency fund
应急计划　contingency plan
应急救援指挥中心　emergency rescue command center
应急年金　contingent annuity
应急设施　emergency facilities
应急通信　emergency communication
应急通信接入　emergency communication access
应急响应系统　emergency response system
应急用款　contingency allowance
应急预案　emergency counterplan
应急照明　emergency lighting

应急值班台　emergency on-duty console
应急指挥台　emergency command console
应计费用　accrued charge
应计负债　accrued liabilities
应计和递延账户　accrued and deferred accounts
应计利息　accrued interest
应计收益　accrued income
应计税金　tax accrued
应计账户　accrued account
应计折旧　accrued depreciation
应计折旧资产　depreciable assets
应力　stress
应力比修正系数　modification factor of stress ratio
应力波　stress wave
应力铲　stress spade
应力法　stress method
应力分布　stress distribution
应力幅　stress range, stress amplitude
应力幅容许值　allowable stress amplitude
应力恢复法　stress recovery method
应力迹线　stress trajectory
应力集中　stress concentration
应力降低带　stress reduction zone
应力解除法　stress relief method
应力空间　stress space
应力控制试验　stress-controlled test
应力历史　stress history
应力路径　stress path
应力水平　stress level
应力松弛　stress relaxation
应力应变关系　stress-strain relationship
应力圆　stress circle
应纳税工资　taxable salary
应纳税货物　taxable goods
应纳税利润　taxable profit
应纳税人　taxable person
应纳税收入　taxable income
应收　due from, accrue
应收承兑汇票　acceptance receivable
应收贷款　loan receivable
应收分期账款　installment accounts receivable
应收合同款　contract price receivable
应收票据　bill receivable, note receivable
应收应付日期　accrual date
应收账款　account receivable, debt receivable
应收账款回收期　accounts receivable collection period
应收账款明细账　account receivable ledger
应收账款融资　account receivable financing
应收账款账户　customer's account
应收账款周转率　accounts receivable turnover
应收账款周转天数　accounts receivable collection period
应用等级　application level
应用服务器　application server
应用软件　application software
应征税款　tax accrued
英安岩　dacite
英美法系　common law system, Anglo-American law system
英闪岩　tonalite
膺架式架设法　erection by falsework method
迎风坡　windward slope
荧光　fluorescence
盈亏　gain or loss
盈亏平衡表　break-even chart
盈亏平衡点　break-even point
盈亏平衡费　break-even cost
盈亏平衡分析　break-even analysis
盈亏平衡图　break-even chart
盈利　earnings
盈利能力　profitability
盈余　gain, margin, surplus
萤石　fluorite
营地　camp
营房建筑测量　barrack's survey
营房设备　camp equipment
营救　rescue
营利性项目　profit-oriented project
营销　marketing
营销辅助决策　marketing decision support
营业报表　business report, statement of operation
营业地点　business place
营业额　turnover, volume of business
营业负债　working liabilities
营业利润　operating profit, operation profit, business profits
营业利润分摊　allocation of business profits
营业毛利　gross operating spread
营业申请　application for business
营业时间　business hours
营业收入　operation revenue, operating revenue
营业收入总额　total revenue
营业税　business tax
营业损失　operating loss
营业线　lines in service
营业线火车　trains running on lines in service
营业线火车运价　train freight on lines in service
营业线施工配合费　coordination fee for construction concerning lines in service

Y

营业线施工配合费率　coordination fee rate for construction concerning lines in service
营业盈余　earned surplus, earning surplus
营业账户　operating account
营业支出　revenue expenditure
营业执照　business license
营业周期　operating cycle
营业主任　sales manager
营业资本　operating capital
营业租赁　operating lease
营运资本收益　working capital gains/income
赢得合同　win a contract
赢得值　earned value
赢得值原理　earned value concept
影响半径　influence radius
影响力　impact, influence
影响评价报告　impact evaluation report
影响图　influence diagram
影响线　influence line
影像地质图　photogeological map
影像分辨率　image resolution
影音采集设备　video/audio acquisition device
影子价格　shadow price
硬币清分机　coin sorter
硬导体　rigid conductor
硬点　hard spot, hard point
硬度　hardness
硬度变化　variation in hardness
硬度计　durometer
硬副本　hard-copy
硬横跨　portal structure
硬横梁　cross beam
硬化点　hardening point
硬化混凝土　hardened concrete
硬化剂　hardening agent
硬架支模　rigid-frame formwork
硬件　hardware
硬件配置　hardware configuration
硬壳　duricrust
硬锚　fixed termination
硬盘存储器　hard disk memory unit
硬盘空间利用率　hard disk utilization ratio
硬盘录像机　digital video recorder (DVR)
硬盘资源　hard disk resource
硬塑　stiff-plastic
硬通货　hard currency, strong currency
硬通货贷款　hard loan
硬土　hard soil
硬弯　hard bending, kink
硬岩　hard rock

硬质合金钻进　tungsten-carbide drilling
硬质岩　hard rock
佣金　commission, commission charges
佣金经纪人　comission broker
拥护　advocate
壅水　backwater
壅水高　backwater height
壅水曲线　backwater profile
壅水曲线全长　total length of back water curve
永磁操作机构　permanent magnet operating mechanism
永冻层　permafrost
永冻层上水　suprapermafrost water
永冻层上限　permafrost table
永冻层透水　permafrost permeable
永久变形缝　permanent deformation joint
永久冻土带　permafrost zone
永久冻土下位水　subpermafrost water
永久工程　permanent works
永久荷载　permanent load
永久荷载分项系数　partial factor of permanent load
永久界桩　permanent boundary marker
永久链路　permanent link
永久性桥　permanent bridge
永久性投资　permanent investment
永久硬度　permanent hardness
永久债券　perpetual bond
永久柱　permanent column
永久资产　permanent assets
永久租赁　perpetual lease
永久作用　permanent action
永久作用标准值　standard value of permanent action
涌泥　mud gushing
涌水　water gushing
涌水量　water outflow
涌水试验　water flow test
涌水压力　water inflow pressure
用地　land
用地复垦　land reclamation
用地红线　boundary line of land
用地界　land boundary
用地界桩　land boundary marker
用地勘界费　land boundary settlement cost
用地图　land map
用电安全　electrical safety
用电量　power consumption
用电率　power consumption rate
用电许可　electrical permit

用户	user
用户话机	user telephone
用户监控终端	user monitoring terminal
用户接口	user interface
用户数据	user data
用户水表	domestic water meter, residential water meter
用户网络接口	user network interface (UNI)
用户终端	user terminal
用具	implement, appliance, tool
用料清单	bill of materials
用料审批表	material request form
用能设备	energy consumption equipment
用水定额	quota of water consumption
用水量	water consumption
用途	function, use, usage, purpose
优点	merit, advantage
优惠	preference, favour
优惠贷款	concessional loan, soft loan
优惠贷款利率	prime interest rate
优惠贷款限额	concessional line of credit
优惠待遇	favourable status
优惠额	margin of preference
优惠关税	concessional tariff
优惠价	favourable price
优惠利率	favourable interest rate, concessional rate, preferential rate of interest
优惠贸易协定	preferential trade agreement
优惠期	days of grace
优惠税目	tax preference items (TPIS)
优惠税则	preferential tariff
优惠条件	easy terms, favourable condition, favourable terms
优惠支付	exgratia payment
优级纯	guaranteed reagent (GR)
优良工程	high quality project
优良品质	fine quality
优势	advantage
优先	supersede, precede, preference
优先次序	order of precedence, priority
优先抵押权	underlying mortgage
优先购买权	preemption, preemptive right, right of preemption
优先购置权	preemptive right
优先股	preferred stock
优先权	preference, priority, option, right of priority, precedence
优先权利要求	first right
优先顺序	priority
优先索赔	prior claims
优先投资	investment priority
优先于	prevail, override, precede, over-ride
优先债权人	senior creditor
优质	quality
优质标记	hallmark
优质工程	high-quality project
优质竣工证书	excellent execution certificate
幽谷	glen
由买方选择	at buyer's option
由卖方选择	at seller's option
邮戳日期	date of postmark
油处理间	oil treatment room
油断路器	oil circuit-breaker
油罐车	oil (tank) truck
油罐区	oil tank area
油罐容量	oil tank capacity
油罐组	oil tank set
油浸变压器	oil-immersed transformer
油浸式变压器	oil-immersed transformer
油浸式电压互感器	oil-immersed voltage transformer
油库	oil storage
油冷却器	oil cooler
油毛毡	asphalt felt, malthoid, hair felt
油漆	paint
油漆工	paint worker, painter
油漆沥青	bitumen for paint
油漆台位	painting position
油气压力	oil gas pressure
油燃料价格	fuel price
油溶性	oil solubility
油色谱在线监测	oil chromatographic online monitor
油位计	oil level indicator
油压表	oil pressure gauge
油压千斤顶	oil jack
油页岩	oil shale
油毡	asphalt felt
油毡原纸	paper felt base
油枕	oil conservator
油脂光泽	greasy luster
游标卡尺	vernier caliper
游离CaO含量	free CaO content
游离二氧化碳	free carbon dioxide
游离性余氯	free residual chlorine
游资	hot money, speculative capital/money, floating capital
友好	goodwill
友好合作	friendly cooperation
友好解决	amicable settlement
友好解决协议	amicable composition

友好协商	friendly consultation
友善条款	goodwill clause
有保留接受	qualified acceptance
有侧移框架	frame with sidesway
有偿贷款	onerous loan
有持续影响的索赔	claims of continuing effect
有重分布的一阶或二阶线弹性分析	elastic analysis of first order or second order curve with repetition distribution
有担保贷款	secured loan
有担保债券	backed bond
有抵押品的贷款	collateralized loan
有毒的	toxic
有毒有害物质	poisonous and hazardous substances
有法定资格的	competent
有法律效力的协议	legally-binding agreement
有分歧	at odds
有风险	at risk
有缝线路	jointed track
有功电流	active current
有功功率	active power
有功损耗	active power loss
有轨运输	track-mounted transportation
有害冻胀	harmful frost heaving
有害冻胀深度	harmful frost heaving depth
有害工业废水	hazardous industrial wastewater
有害空间	gap in the frog, gap at the common crossing, unguided part in frog, the gap between the wing rail and the point
有害裂缝	hazardous crack
有害气体	hazardous gas
有害物控制检测	pest control inspection
有荷载膨胀率试验	loaded expansion rate test
有机过氧化物	organic peroxide
有机结合料	organic binder
有机磷	organophosphorus
有机磷含量	organophosphorus content
有机物含量	organic content
有机盐	organic salt
有机质	organic matter
有机质含量	organic matter content
有机质土	organic soil
有极继电器	polarized relay
有竞争力的价格	keen price
有竞争力的投标书	competitive tender
有库存	in stock
有利地段	favorable section
有缺陷的材料	defective material
有缺陷的材料及工艺	faulty material and workmanship
有缺陷的工作	defective work, faulty work
有缺陷的设计	faulty design
有熔断指示器的熔断器	indicating fuse
有时效限制的债务	time-limited debt (obligation), barred debt (obligation)
有胎沥青防水卷材	reinforced asphalt sheet
有特殊作业要求的集装箱	container with special operation requirement
有息贷款	lend at interest
有息债务	active debt
有限元法	finite element method
有限公司	limited company
有限合伙公司	limited partnership
有限竞争性选择招标	limited competitive selected bidding
有限责任	limited liability, incorporated liability
有限责任保单	limited policy
有限责任公司	limited liability company
有限责任合伙人	limited partner
有限追索	limited recourse
有线电视	cable TV
有线调度通信系统	wired dispatching communication system
有线固定终端呼叫	fixed to mobile call
有效	in force, validity
有效保证	effective guarantee
有效波	useful wave
有效程度	effectiveness
有效单价	effective rate
有效法向应力	effective normal stress
有效合同	valid contract
有效合同价	effective contract price
有效厚度	effective thickness
有效钾含量	available potassium content
有效静荷载	effective static load
有效抗剪强度	effective shear strength
有效抗剪强度指标	effective shear strength index
有效孔隙率	effective porosity
有效控制距离	effective control distance
有效宽度	effective width
有效宽度系数	effective width coefficient
有效粒径	effective particle size
有效磷含量	available phosphorus content
有效期	valid period, period of validity, term of validity
有效日期	date of validity
有效条款	effective terms
有效性	effectiveness, availability, validity
有效悬臂长度	effective length of cantilever
有效氧化钙	effective calcium oxide

有效异常	effective anomaly
有效应力	effective stress
有效应力法	effective stress method
有效应力分析	effective stress analysis
有效应力原理	principle of effective stress
有效预应力值	effective prestress value
有效直径	effective diameter
有效主应力比	effective principal stress ratio
有形财产	visible means
有形固定资产	fixed tangible assets
有形贸易	visible trade
有形资产	material assets, tangible assets
有压管道	pressure pipeline
有义务的	bound, liable
有源光网络	active optical network (AON)
有源应答器	switchable balise, controllable balise
有约束力的	binding
有约束力的合同	binding contract
有约束力的决定	binding decision
有约束力的签字	binding signature
有载调压变压器	transformer with on-load tap changer (OLTC)
有载自振频率	load-carrying natural frequency
有砟道床	ballasted trackbed
有砟轨道	ballast track
有砟轨道道岔	ballasted turnout
有黏结预应力混凝土结构	bonded prestressed concrete structure
有组织进风	organized air supply
有组织排风	organized air exhaust
右开道岔	right hand turnout
诱导器	induction unit
诱导式空气调节系统	induction air conditioning system
诱导通风	inductive ventilation
诱发地质灾害	induced geological hazards
迂回保护电路	alternative protection circuit
迂回电路	alternative circuit
迂回进路	bypass route
迂回线	detour line
淤堵试验	colmation test
淤积	siltation
淤泥	silt
淤泥质土	mucky soil
淤砂	siltation sand
余额	balance
余额递减折旧法	declining balance method of depreciation, reducing balance depreciation method
余款	money remaining
余热	waste heat
余湿	moisture excess
余压	residual pressure
余压回水	back pressure return
余氧	residual oxygen
余值	remaining value
鱼腹式梁	lenticular beam
鱼类产卵场	fish spawning ground
鱼鳞坑	fish-scale pit
鱼尾板扳手	fishplate wrench
逾期交付	overdue delivery
逾期利息	overdue interest
逾期票据	overdue bill
逾期未交货物	overdue delivery
逾越	overstep
羽毛状节理	feather joint
雨季	rainy season
雨季施工	construction in rainy season
雨季滞水	stagnant water in rainy season
雨量传感器	rainfall sensor
雨量计	rain gauge
雨量监测	rainfall monitoring
雨量监测报警	rainfall monitoring alarm
雨量器	precipitation gauge
雨淋灭火系统	spray extinguishing system
雨落水管	downspout
雨棚	canopy, platform awning
雨水	rainwater
雨水泵站	storm water pumping station
雨水槽	gutter
雨水斗	roof drain
雨水管	storm sewer
雨水管渠设计	rainwater pipe channel design
雨水井	rainwater catch-basin
雨水口	gutter, rain inlet
雨水排水系统	rainwater drainage system
语音	voice
语音广播	voice broadcast service (VBS)
语音呼叫	voice call
语音呼叫中心	voice call center
语音配线架	voice distribution frame (VDF)
语音业务和非列车运行控制类电路交换数据业务服务质量	QoS of voice and non train control Circuit Switched Data (CSD)
语音组呼	voice group call service (VGCS)
峪	vale
预办闭塞	preworking a block
预拌	premixing
预拌混凝土	ready-mix concrete

预拌混凝土车　ready-mix truck
预报　forecast
预备　prepare, get ready for
预备的　standby, preliminary
预备费　budget reserve for unpredictable work
预备工程　preliminary works
预备进口报关单　preliminary entry
预备诉讼行为　preliminary act
预拨经费　advance appropriation
预测　forecast, projection, prediction
预沉　pre-sedimentation
预处理　pre-treatment
预打磨　pre-grinding
预垫款　advance call
预调试　precommissioning
预叠加电码化　pre-overlapped coding
预订　book, reserve
预定日期　target date
预定损失率　assumed loss ratio
预定违约金　liquidated damages
预防　prevent, prevention
预防措施　preventive measure
预防性维修　preventive maintenance
预付　pay in advance, advancement, cash in advance, imprest
预付保险费　deposit premium
预付费用　prepaid expenses
预付分包商款　advances to subcontractor
预付汇款　advance remittance
预付款　advance payment, advance deposit
预付款保函　advanced payment guarantee
预付款保证　advance payment security
预付款担保　advance payment bond
预付款的偿还　repayment of advance
预付款的支付　payment of advance
预付款条款　prepayment clause
预付款证明　advanced payment certificate
预付现金　advance in cash, cash advance
预付运费　advance freight, prepaid freight
预告标　warning signs for approaching a station
预告信号　distant signal
预告信号机　distant signal
预拱度　pre-camber
预估工程量　estimated quantities
预计不满意者的百分数　predicted percentage of disaffected (PPD)
预计财务报表　projected financial statement
预计成本　predicated cost, projected cost
预计到达时间　estimated time of arrival (ETA)
预计费用　estimated cost

预计风险　calculated risk
预计离港时间　estimated time of departure (ETD)
预计平均热感觉指数　predicted mean heat sensation value (PMV)
预计使用年限　expected life, estimated physical life
预计收入　anticipated revenue
预计卸货完成时间　estimated time of finishing discharging (ETFD)
预计最终成本　forecast final cost
预见　foresee
预见性　foreseeability
预绞式护线条　preformed armor rod
预缴保费　advance premium
预警系统　early warning system
预开发票　proforma invoice
预可行性研究　pre-feasibility study
预可研　preliminary feasibility study
预扣税款　withholding tax
预扣税款凭证　tax withholding certificate
预拉荷载　pre-tensioning load
预料　anticipate, predict
预裂爆破　pre-split blasting
预裂缝　pre-cut notch
预留变形　deformation allowance
预留变形量　deformation allowance
预留弛度　pre-sag
预留电化股道　electrified track in plan
预留二线　second line reserved
预留轨缝　reserved rail joint gap
预留孔　preformed hole
预留款　holdback
预留利润　allowance for profit
预留线　reserved track
预留线(路)　reserved line
预埋管　embedded pipe
预埋件　embedded part
预埋套管　embedded sleeve, plastic dowel
预埋注浆管　embedded scouting pipe
预排进路　route presetting
预评估　preappraisal
预期　anticipate, anticipation, prospect
预期成本　anticipated cost
预期价格　anticipated price
预期利润　anticipated profit
预期利润损失保险　loss of advanced profits insurance
预期利息　anticipated interest
预期收益　anticipated gain, prospective yield
预期收益率　required rate of return

预期投标者　prospective bidder (tenderer)
预期运费　anticipated freight
预试运行　pre-commissioning
预收合同款　contract price received in advance
预收款项　advance collections
预算　budget, estimate
预算拨款　budget allocation
预算成本　estimated cost, budgeted cost, budget cost
预算单价法　budgetary unit price method
预算导则　estimate guideline
预算定额　budgetary quota
预算费　budget
预算工时　budgeted man-hour
预算汇总　budget summary
预算价格　budgetary price
预算控制　budget control
预算书　budget document
预算造价　budgetary construction cost
预算总额　budget amount
预提税　withholding tax
预填骨料　prepacked aggregate
预投资研究　pre-investment studies
预先　in advance
预先报关单　pre-entry
预先承兑　anticipated acceptance
预先警告　advance warning
预先申报　pre-entry
预先锁闭　advance locking
预压地基　preloading foundation
预压法　preloading method
预氧化　pre-oxidization
预应力　prestress
预应力传递长度　transfer length of prestress
预应力度　degree of prestressing
预应力钢材　prestressed steel
预应力钢绞线　prestressing strand
预应力钢结构　prestressed steel structure
预应力钢筋　prestressing bar
预应力钢筋混凝土　prestressed reinforced concrete
预应力钢筋混凝土杆　prestressed reinforced concrete pole
预应力钢筋混凝土桥　prestressed concrete bridge
预应力钢丝束　prestressing tendon
预应力混凝土杆　prestressed concrete pole
预应力混凝土结构　prestressed concrete structure
预应力混凝土梁　prestressed concrete beam (girder)
预应力混凝土桥　prestressed concrete bridge
预应力混凝土柱　prestressed concrete pole
预应力混凝土桩　prestressed concrete pile
预应力筋　prestressing bar
预应力筋强度等级　strength class of prestressed tendon
预应力锚杆　prestressed anchor rod
预应力锚索　prestressed anchor cable
预应力损失　loss of prestress
预约保单　open policy
预约保险　open cover
预约金　subscription
预支付　pay in advance, make advance
预制　prefabricate
预制板　prefabricated slab
预制厂　factory for prefabrication
预制场　prefabrication yard
预制钢壳钻孔基础　drilled shaft foundation with prefabricated steel shells
预制构件　prefabricated member/element/component
预制轨道板　precast track slab
预制混凝土　precast concrete
预制混凝土构件　precast concrete member
预制混凝土空心块　precast hollow concrete block
预制混凝土楼板　precast concrete slab
预制混凝土土桩　precast concrete pile
预制模板　prefab-form, shuttering
预制水泥块　cement block
预制桩　precast pile
预制装配管道　precast fabricated pipe
预制装配式房屋　prefabricated house, prefab
预注浆　pre-grouting
预钻式旁压试验　pre-drilling lateral pressure test
预作用灭火系统　preaction system
域间接口　inter-domain interface (IrDI)
域名服务器　domain name server (DNS)
域名系统　domain name system
阈值报警　threshold alarm
遇忙回呼　completion of calls to busy subscriber (CCBS)
遇水膨胀式止水带　water swelling water stop tie
遇水膨胀止水条　water swelling strip
遇险　emergency
遇险信号　distress call
元古代　Proterozoic era, Agnotozoic era
元古界　Proterozoic erathem, Algonkian system
元古宇　Proterozoic eonothem
元古宙　Proterozoic eon
元素　element
园地　garden plot
园林建筑　garden architecture
园林小品　small garden ornament
员工和劳务　staff and labour

员工和劳务的雇佣　engagement of staff and labour
员工设施　facilities for staff and labour
原案　original bill
原保险　original insurance
原边侧　high voltage side, primary side
原材料　raw materials
原产地　origin, country of origin
原产地标志　origin marking
原产地证明书　certificate of origin（C/O）, evidence of origin
原地貌土壤侵蚀模数　background soil erosion modulus
原稿　manuscript
原告　claimant（claimer）, complainant, plaintiff
原构件　existing structural member
原合同　original contract
原价　original price
原件　original
原理　principle
原料　feedstock
原生节理　primary joint
原生矿物　original mineral, primary mineral
原生林　original forest
原生植被　native vegetation
原始保险费　original premium
原始成本　original cost
原始成本加成　original mark-up
原始单据　original document
原始发票　original invoice
原始费用　baseline cost
原始记录　original record
原始价值　original value
原始凭单　original voucher
原始凭证　source document, underlying document
原始森林地区　virgin forest area
原始森林地区额外建设成本　additional cost of construction in virgin forest area
原始数据　first-hand data, initial data, raw data, primary data
原始文件　original document, source document
原始账　blotter
原始证据　primary evidence
原始资本　seed capital
原始资料　primary data, original data
原水　raw water
原位测试　in-situ testing
原位检测　in situ test
原位试验　in-situ test
原污泥　raw sludge
原型　original, prototype
原型试验　prototype testing
原样品　original sample
原因　cause
原则　principle
原值　original value
原状取土器　undisturbed soil sampler
原状土样　undisturbed soil sample
原状样　undisturbed sample
原状样品　undisturbed sample
原子吸收光谱法　atomic absorption spectrometry
原子荧光光谱仪　atomic fluorescence spectrometer
原子钟　atomic clock
圆顶山　round top mountain
圆端形桥墩　round-ended pier
圆管涵　pipe culvert
圆棱状　subrounded
圆砾　pebble
圆频率　circular frequency
圆球顶破强度　ball-burst strength
圆曲线　circular curve
圆曲线半径　radius of circular curve
圆曲线测设　circular curve locating
圆形桥墩　circular pier
圆形隧道　circular tunnel
圆周角条件　condition of circumference angle
圆柱筛筒　drum sieve
圆柱头焊钉　cheese head stud
援助　assistance
援助国　donor country
远程试验　remote test
远程网路　relayed surveillance network
远程维护　remote maintenance
远动　remote control
远动系统　remote control system
远动终端　remote terminal unit（RTU）
远动终端设备　remote terminal unit（RTU）
远端闭音　remote microphone off
远端拨入用户验证服务　remote authentication dial in user service（RADIUS）
远红外　far infrared
远后备保护　remote backup protection
远期　long term
远期差价　forward margin
远期的　forward
远期付款交单　forward payment bill
远期工程　long term works
远期合同　forward contract
远期汇率　forward rate, forward exchange rate
远期交货　forward delivery
远期交易　forward

Y

远期外汇　forward exchange
远期信用证　usance letter of credit
远洋班轮　ocean liner
远洋船舶　ocean vessel
远洋货轮　oceangoing freighter
远洋运输　ocean carriage
远运土　long distance transported soil
约定　appointment, engagement, commitment
约定补偿　agreed compensation
约定价格合同　stipulated price contract
约定金额　stipulated sum
约定金额合同　stipulated sum contract
约定目的港　agreed port of destination
约定皮重　computed tare
约定时间　commitment time
约束　restrain
约束变形　restrained deformation
约束点　constraint point
约束混凝土　confined concrete
约束力　binding
约束平差　constraint adjustment
约束砌体　confined masonry
约束条件　restrictions
约束条款　binding clause
约束性规定　restrictive regulation
约束性合同　binding contract
约因　consideration
月报表　monthly statement, monthly return
月报告　monthly report
月度对账单　monthly statement of account
月度状态报告　monthly status review
月工资　monthly wages
月汇总表　monthly summary
月检修　monthly inspection
月结算报告　monthly settlement report
月结算表　monthly balance sheet
月结算单　monthly statement
月津贴　monthly allowance
月进度报告　monthly progress report
月进度审查会议　monthly progress review meeting
月息　monthly interest
月薪　salary, monthly pay
跃层住宅　duplex apartment
越冬场　overwintering ground
越岭隧道　mountain-crossing tunnel
越区供电　over-section feeding
越区切换中断时间　handover interruption time
越权行为　act in excess of authority, ultra vires act
越行　overtaking
越行站　overtaking station
越野车　off-road vehicle
云煌岩　minette
云镜控制　pan tilt and zoom (PTZ) control
云母　mica
云母长英角岩　mica felsic hornfels
云母含量　mica content
云母角岩　mica hornfels
云母片岩　mica schist
云台　pan-tilt head
云斜煌岩　kersantite, kersanton
云英岩　greisen
匀质性　homogeneity
允留天窗打靶　target shooting with allowable possessive interval
允许　allow, allowance, permit, permission
允许成本　allowable cost
允许开采量　safe yield
允许推送信号　start humping signal
允许信号　proceeding signal
允许振速　allowable vibration velocity
运动黏度　kinematic viscosity
运动图像专家组　moving picture experts group (MPEG)
运费　freight charge
运费保险　freight insurance
运费保险单　freight policy
运费、保险费付至　carriage and insurance paid to (CIP)
运费待付　carriage forward
运费单　freight note, freight bill
运费到付　freight to collect, freight to be paid, express collect
运费吨　freight ton
运费付至　carriage paid to (CPT)
运费基价　basic freight rate
运费率　freight rate, rate of freight
运费免付　carriage free
运费审查　freight audit
运费条款　freight clause
运费一览表　schedule of freight rates
运费已付　freight paid, carriage paid
运费已预付　freight prepaid
运费由收货人付　carriage forward, freight to collect, freight forward
运货代理商　shipping agent
运货费　cartage
运价　freight price
运价表　freight list (F/L)
运价规则　freight price provisions
运价号　freight price number
运价里程　freight price mileage

运价率　freight price rate number
运距　haul distance
运输　carriage, transport, traffic
运输保险　insurance in transit, transportation insurance, marine insurance
运输便道　temporary road
运输车　carrier vehicle
运输车辆保险　vehicle insurance
运输成本　transportation cost
运输承运人的索赔　transportation carrier's claim
运输代理行　freight forwarder
运输单据　documentary of carriage
运输吨数　tonnage
运输方法　delivery methods
运输方法比重　proportion of delivery methods
运输方式　delivery means
运输费　delivery charge
运输服务　traffic services
运输工　haulier
运输工具　carrier, conveyance, transportation carrier
运输工具保险　conveyance insurance
运输管理　traffic management
运输合同　contract of carriage, contract of affreightment
运输机械重复作用荷载　repeating load of transportation machinery
运输计划　transportation planning, traffic plan
运输距离　delivery distance
运输量　traffic volume
运输能力　transportation capability
运输设备　hauling equipment, transportation equipment
运输损耗费　cost of wear and tear during delivery
运输损耗费费率　rate of wear and tear during delivery
运输损失　loss of traffic
运输通道　delivery passageway
运水车　water truck
运送　deliver, transport
运送材料　delivery of materials
运送的货物　delivered goods, freight
运送费用　delivery cost
运行方向　running direction
运行监控记录装置　operation monitoring and recording device
运行检验　performance test, operational test
运行阶段　operation phase
运行时分　running time
运行试验　trial run test
运行图　train diagram
运行图描绘仪　train diagram plotter
运行正常　proper operation
运营　operation
运营成本　operation cost, operating cost, running cost
运营初期　initial period of operation
运营调度管理系统　operation and dispatching management system
运营动力系数　operating dynamic force coefficient
运营服务　operation service
运营服务期　operation service period
运营服务最终支付证书　final payment certificate operation service
运营干扰　operation interference
运营管理体系　operation management system
运营管理要求　operation management requirement
运营和养护手册　operation and maintainance manuals
运营荷载　operating load
运营活载　live operating load
运营及维护承包商　operation and maintenance contractor
运营及维护计划　operation and maintenance plan
运营及维护手册　operation and maintenance manual
运营阶段　operation phase
运营速度　running speed, operation speed
运营条件　operation condition
运营铁路　operating railway
运营通风道　operation ventilating duct
运营维修合同　operation and maintenance contract
运营性能　operation performance
运营性能检验　inspection of operation performance
运营性能检验判别值　critera for judging the traffic serviceability
运营许可证　operating license
运营养护设备　operation maintenance equipment
运营支撑系统　operation support system(OSS)
运用　apply, use, utilize, exercise, operate
运用机车　locomotive in operation
运用检修　operation maintenance
运杂费　freight and miscellaneous charges
运杂费单价分析　unit price analysis of freight and miscellaneous charges
运载　carry
运载工具　vehicle
运转　operation
运转时间　duration of runs
运转室　train operation office

Z

ZC 活载　ZC live load
ZK 活载　ZK live load
ZPW-2000(UM)系列轨道电路　ZPW-2000 (UM) series track circuit
Z 计权振动加速度级　Z-weighted vibration acceleration level
杂费　incidental, sundry
杂散电流保护　stray current protection
杂砂岩　greywacke
杂税　irregular tax
杂填土　miscellaneous fill
杂物　sundry
杂项　incidental, sundry
杂项开支　miscellaneous expenses, sundry expenses
杂项收入　sundry revenue
杂音　noise
杂音电压　noise voltage
杂音防卫度　signal to noise ratio
杂音计　noise meter, psophometer
杂质含量　impurity content
灾备中心　disaster recovery center
灾害　disaster, catastrophe
灾害监测系统　disaster monitoring system (DMS)
灾难　disaster, catastrophe
栽植法建植草坪　plangting grass root or culm
载荷　load
载荷板试验　plate load test
载荷试验　load test
载流量　current carrying capacity
载流能力　current-carrying capability
载重　burden, loading, loading capacity
再保险　reinsurance
再保险合同　reinsurance contract
再出口　re-export
再出口证书　certificate of re-export
再次保证　reassure
再次分包　sub-subcontracting
再抵押　submortgage
再归属　revest
再进口　re-import
再开始　resumption
再生产成本　reproduction cost
再生段　regenerator section
再生水　reclaimed water
再生水厂　reclaimed water plant
再用轨　second-hand rail, relay rail
再用轨料　second hand track material
再用轨料整修管理费　renovation management expense of used rails
再招标　retender(rebid)
在船上　on board
在建工程　construction in progress, work in progress
在票据上背书　back a bill
在途货物　goods in transit
在途账　account in transit
在线式 UPS　online UPS
在线诊断　off-line diagnosis
在修机车　locomotive under repair
在役钢轨　in-service rail
在站停留时间　station standing time
在职培训　or-the-job training (OJT)
暂保单　binder, cover note (C/N), risk note, insurance note
暂保收据　binding receipt
暂定价格　provisional price
暂定价格指数　provisional index
暂定金　reserve
暂定金额　provisional sum
暂定项目　optional items
暂付款项　temporary payment
暂缓　abeyance
暂记账户　clearing account. suspense account
暂时停工　suspension of work
暂时停工费用　cost of suspension
暂时停工命令　order to suspend
暂时硬度　temporary hardness

暂收款账户	advance received account
暂停拨款	suspension of disbursements
暂停付款	suspension of payment
暂行办法	provisional procedures
暂行标准	tentative standard
暂行条例	interim regulation, provisional regulation
暂行规定	interim provision
赞助	sponsor, support
遭受延误	suffer delay
凿方切割法	chisel cutting method
凿石机	rock cutter
凿岩工	driller
凿岩机	rock drill
凿岩台车	rock drilling jumbo
早奥陶世	early Ordovician epoch
早白垩世	early Cretaceous epoch
早拆模板体系	early removal formwork system
早第三纪	Paleogene period
早二叠世	early Permian epoch
早更新世	early Pleistocene epoch
早古生代	Eopaleozoic, early Paleozoic era
早寒武世	early Cambrian epoch
早泥盆世	early Devonian epoch
早期警告	early warning
早期强度	early strength
早强混凝土	early strength concrete
早强水泥	high-early-strength cement
早三叠世	early Triassic epoch
早石炭世	early Carboniferous epoch
早震旦世	early Sinian epoch
早志留世	early Silurian epoch
早侏罗世	early Jurassic epoch
造桥机	bridge fabrication machine
造岩矿物	rock-forming mineral
噪声	noise
噪声测量值修正	correction of noise measurement value
噪声防治	noise prevention
噪声级	noise level
噪声控制	noise control
噪声控制标准	noise control standard
噪声敏感建筑	noise-sensitive building
噪声频谱特性	spectral characteristics of noise
噪声评价	noise assessment
噪声评价数	noise rating number
噪声探测器	noise detector
噪声限值	noise limit value
噪声源强	noise source intensity
噪限灵敏度	noise-limited sensitivity
责任	liability, responsibility
责任保险	insurance for liability, liability insurance
责任的限定	limitation of liability
责任范围	extent of liability, scope of cover, scope of liability, limitation of liability
责任方	party liable
责任分担	apportionment of liabiliy, allocation of responsibility
责任分担条款	contribution clause
责任分界线	interface of responsibilities
责任风险	liability risk
责任期限	duration of liability
责任人	responsible person
责任条款	liability clause
责任限度	limitation of liability
责任证明	accountability verification
增补基桩加固法	strengthening method by supplementary foundation piles
增长	increase, grow, growth, accrue
增长率	growth rate
增大截面加固法	strengthening method by increasing cross section
增大系数	amplifying coefficient
增额	increment, addition
增股筹资	equity financing
增加	increase, addition
增加额	additional amount
增加费	additional expenses
增加费率	additional rate
增加费用	additional expense
增加幅度	increase range
增加人工投入	additional input of labour
增建第二线	construction of second track
增建二线	construction of the second line
增黏剂	tackifier
增强材料	reinforcement material
增强型位置寻址	enhanced location dependent addressing (eLDA)
增压泵	booster pump
增益	gain
增长率	growth rate
增值	added value, increment, appreciation. value added
增值保险	increased value insurance
增值税	value added tax (VAT), added-value tax
增值条款	value-added terms/clause
增值资产	accrued asset
赠款	endowment, grant
赠品	gift, present
赠券	coupon
赠送人	presenter

赠予　present, gift
轧制型钢梁　rolled steel beam
闸楼　operating control-point
砟肩　shoulder of ballast bed
砟肩堆高　shoulder hump, hump of ballast shoulder
诈骗　deceit, defraud
栅栏　fence
栅条絮凝池　grid flocculating tank
炸药　explosive, dynamite, percussion powder, blasting powder
摘车临修　casual repair of vehicles detached from train
摘挂列车　pick-up and drop-off train
摘要　brief, abstract
窄轨距铁路　narrow-gauge railway
债本比　debt to equity ratio
债款　debt, liability
债权　financial claim, obligatory right
债权人　creditor, claimant (claimer) obligee, debtee
债权受益人　creditor beneficiary
债券　bond, security
债券利率　bonding rale
债券市场　bond market
债务　liability, debt, debt service, financial obligation, engagements
债务变更契约　deed of novation
债务和解　composition
债务解除证书　certificate of release
债务清偿收据　acquittance
债务确认书　cognovit
债务人　debtor, obligor, loanee
债务危机　debt crisis
债务证明书　debt certificate
债务转让　assignment of debt
债务资金　debt capital
债息　debt service
债主　obligee
粘贴钢板加固法　strengthening method by bonding steel plate
展期　continuation, renewal
展期条款　continuation clause
展示件　exhibit
展线　line extension
展线系数　coefficient of line extension
展性　malleability
占线表示　occupancy indication
占用费　occupancy expenses
占用率　occupancy rate
占用权　occupancy right

占用许可证　occupancy permit
占用资金　occupation of fund
占有　occupation, possession
占有留置权　possessory lien
占有权　right of possession
占有人　occupant occupier
占有诉讼　action for possession
占有证明书　certificate of occupancy
栈单　warehouse certificate, landing a count
栈桥　trestle
栈桥式卸车线　trestle-type unloading line
战略　strategy
战胜　defeat
战时通风　wartime ventilation
战争保险　war risk, insurance, insurance against war risk
站场　station and yard
站场电话　station and yard telephone
站场基线　station site baseline
站场极坐标测量　polar-coordinate measurement at station site
站场路基　subgrade in station and yard
站场绿化　greening for station area
站场通信　station and yard communication
站场线路　station and yard line
站房对侧右端　right side opposite to station building
站房平台　station building terrace
站房中心位置　station center
站后工程　E&M works
站机　station equipment
站间距离　distance between stations
站间联系电路　liaison circuit among stations
站间行车电话　inter-station train operation telephone
站内道口联系电路　liaison circuit with highway crossings within the station
站内联络线　in-station connecting line
站坪　station site
站坪长度　length of station site
站坪坡度　grade of station site
站前工程　civil works, under-track works
站台安全标线　safety marking of platform
站台边缘　platform edge
站台到发信息屏　platform display
站台端部　end of platform
站台高度　platform height
站台斜坡　platform slope
站台雨棚　platform shelter
站线　station track, siding
站线道床　ballast bed of station track

Z

站型　station type
站修所　freight car repair point at station
站修线　station repair track
站修作业场　freight car repair yard at station
张断层　tension fault
张节理　tension joint
张拉试验　tensile test
张拉锁件　tensioning lockpiece
张力补偿　tensioning
张力补偿装置　tensioning device
张力差　variation of tension
张力增量　tension increment
张裂缝　tension crack
张裂隙　tension fissure
张扭性断层　tension-shear fault
张线式位移量测装置
　　wire supported displacement measuring apparatus
涨价　escalation, appreciation
涨落　fluctuation
涨缩潜势　swelling and shrinkage potential
章程　charter, constitution, articles, statute
掌子面　tunnel face
账　account
账簿　account book
账单　account bill
账号　account number
账户　account
账户成交量　account turnover
账户代号　account code
账户分类　account classification
账户结平　account balanced
账户名称　account title, title of account
账户式资产负债表
　　account form of balance sheet
账户一览表　chart of accounts
账户营业额　account turnover
账户余额　account balance
账户转账　account conversion, account transfer
账款回收期　collection period
账面　book
账面成本　book cost
账面价值　carrying value, book value
账面金额　carrying amount
账面利润　book profit, paper profit
账面盘存　book inventory
账面收益　accounting income
账面损失　book loss, paper loss
账面盈余　book surplus, paper profit
账面余额　balance of account, book balance
账目　account

账目编号　code of accounts
账目摘要　abstract of account
胀轨跑道　buckling of track
胀破强度　burst tearing strength
胀破试验　burst tearing test
障碍和污染物质
　　physical obstructions and pollutions
障碍物　obstruction, obstacle, bar
嶂谷　narrow gorge
招标　bid (tender) invitation, call for bids (tender), invitation to bid (tender), request for bid (tender)
招标澄清会议　tender clarification meeting
招标服务费　bidding service fee
招标公告　tendering publicity
招标控制价　bidding control price
招标时间表　tender timetable
招标条件　tendering conditions
招标通告　advertisement for bid (tender)
招标通知　bid invitation, request for proposal, tendering notice
招标图纸　tender drawing
招标委员会　tender committee
招标文件　bidding documents
招标文件补遗　bid addenda
招标文件的澄清
　　clarification of bidding (tender) documents
招标文件的修改
　　amendment of bidding (tender) documents
招待费　entertainment expense, hospitality expense
招工　job opening
招募劳工　labour recruitment
招聘　recruit, recruitment
招投标咨询服务费　bidding consulting service fee
招致增加费用　incure cost
沼气　sludge gas, marsh gas
沼泽　marsh, swamp
沼泽沉积　swamp deposit
沼泽地区　marshy area
沼泽水　marsh water
沼泽相　swamp facies
兆欧表　tramegger
照查锁闭　crosscheck locking
照查条件　check requisition
照度　illumination
照度标准值　standard brightness level
照度均匀度　uniformity of illumination
照管　custody
照管工程的责任　liability for care of the works
照管工程的职责　responsibility for care of the works

照管责任　duty of care
照看和保管文件　care and supply of document
照明　lighting
照明方式　lighting system
照明功率密度　lighting power density
照明散热量　heat dissipation from lighting
照明系统总功率降低率　reduction rate of the total installed capacity of lighting system
照准点　sighting point
照准点归心　reduction to target centre
照准误差　error of sighting
遮板　parapet
遮断信号　obstruction signal
遮断信号机　obstruction signal
遮断预告信号机　approach obstruction signal
遮栏　barrier
遮阳棚路基　sunshade embankment
遮阳系数　shading coefficient
折板絮凝池　folded-plate flocculating tank
折叠　fold
折返环线　turnaround loop
折返线　turnaround track
折耗备抵　depletion allowance
折耗性资产　depletive assets
折换　translate, convert
折减系数　reduction coefficient
折角车流　reflected traffic flow
折旧　depreciate, depreciation
折旧备抵　allowance for depreciation
折旧不足　underdepreciation
折旧成本　depreciation cost
折旧方法　depreciation method
折旧费　depreciation cost
折旧费率　depreciation rate
折旧后净收益　net income after depreciation
折旧基金　depreciation fund
折旧基数　depreciation base
折旧率　depreciation rate
折旧年限　period of depreciation
折旧期　period of depreciation
折旧准备　depreciation reserve, reserve for depreciation
折扣　discount, rebate
折扣率　discount rate
折扣期限　discount period
折扣系数　discount factor
折射波法　refraction method
折算长度　effective length
折算系数　conversion coefficient
折损　depletion

折现　discount
折现回收期　discounted payback period
折现率　discount rate, rate of discount
折现现金流量　discounted cash flow (DCF)
折余成本　depreciated cost
折余价值　depreciated value
折衷方法　compromise
辙叉　frog, common crossing
辙叉角　crossing angle, frog angle
辙叉心轨尖端　actual point of frog
辙叉心轨理论尖端　theoretical point of frog
褶曲　fold
褶皱　fold
阵型分解法　the formation of decomposition method
针刺土工织物　needle-punched geotextile
针片状颗粒含量　content of elongated and flaky particles
针入度　penetration
针入度分级　penetration grading
针入度指数　penetration index
针式绝缘子　pin insulator
针状　acicular
针状颗粒　acicular particle
针状指数　elongation index
诊断　diagnosis
枕间夯实机　crib consolidator
枕木　sleeper
枕状构造　pillow structure
珍稀濒危物种　rare and endangered species
珍稀动植物栖息地　habitat of rare plants and animals
珍稀野生动物　rare wildlife
珍珠光泽　pearly luster
真空泵　vacuum pump
真空抽气饱和　vacuum saturation
真空抽气法　vacuum pumping method
真空断路器　vacuum circuit breaker
真空断路器操作小车　vacuum circuit breaker handcart
真空阀　vacuum valve
真空干燥法　vacuum drying method
真空干燥器　vacuum drying apparatus
真空干燥箱　vacuum drying box
真空盒试验　vacuum box test
真空接触器　vacuum contactor
真空毛细管法黏度　vacuum capillary viscometer
真空排水　vacuum drainage
真空排水系统　vacuum drainage system
真空破坏器　vacuum breaker

真空水泵　vacuum pump
真空预压　vacuum preloading
真空预压法　vacuum preloading method
真空站（真空中心）　vacuum station (center)
真倾角　true dip
真三轴试验　true triaxial test
真实记录　factual record
真实理由　bona fide reason
真实性　authenticity
真误差　true error
真相　naked truth
真子午线　true meridian
振冲法　vibroflotation method
振荡器　oscillator
振捣　vibrating
振捣器　vibrator
振动　vibration
振动棒　vibrator tamper
振动沉拔桩机　vibratory pile driver-extractor
振动传感器　vibration sensor
振动锤击法　vibration hammering method
振动打桩机　vibrating pile driver
振动夯　vibration rammer
振动级　vibration level
振动加速度　vibration acceleration
振动敏感建筑　vibration-sensitive buildings
振动碾实　vibrating rolling
振动频率　vibration frequency
振动嵌入法　vibration embedded
振动筛　vibrating sieve
振动速度　vibration speed
振动台试验　shaking table test
振动压路机　vibratory roller
振动压实值　vibration compaction value
振动源强　vibration source intensity
振动碾压机　vibration compactor, vibratory roller
振动桩锤　vibratory pile hammer
振幅　amplitude
振稳密度　soil density after vibration liquefaction
振弦式土压力盒　vibrating-wire earth pressure cell
振型　vibration mode
振型参与系数　mode participation coefficient
振型分解法　modal analysis method
震旦纪　Sinian period
震旦系　Sinian system
震动衰减　vibration attenuation
震动钻进　vibration drilling
震害　seismic hazard, earthquake damage
震害调查　earthquake damage investigation

震级　earthquake magnitude
震陷　earthquake subsidence
震源　earthquake focus
震源深度　focal depth
震中　epicenter
震中距　epicentral distance
震中烈度　epicentral intensity
震中区　epicentral region
争辩者　contestant
争端及仲裁　disputes and arbitration
争端　dispute
争议　dispute
争议避免裁决委员会
　　DAAB/Dispute Avoidance/Adjudication Board
争议避免裁决委员会程序规则
　　DAAB procedural rules
争议避免裁决委员会的规则　DAAB's rules
争议避免裁决委员会的活动　DAAB's activities
争议避免裁决委员会的决定
　　the DAAB's decision
争议避免裁决委员会的期限　term of the DAAB
争议避免裁决委员会的权限　powers of the DAAB
争议避免裁决委员会的组成
　　constitution of the DAAB
争议避免裁决协议书　DAAB agreement
争议避免裁决协议引起的争议
　　dispute under the DAAB agreement
争议的解决　settlement of disputes
争议解决替代方式
　　alternative dispute resolution (ADR)
争议评判员　dispute adjudicator
争议审议委员会　disputes review board (DRB)
争议审议专家　disputes review expert
争议事宜　matters in dispute
争执　dispute
争执点　point in dispute
争执方　contestant
征收　impose, demand
征收附加税　imposition of surcharge
征收税款　levy
征税　collect duties, levy duties on, taxation, tax, levy
征税依据　tax base
征用　requisition, expropriation, take over for use
征用土地　requisitioning of land
征用土地安置补偿费
　　resettlement subsidies for land expropriation
征占地面积　land acquisition area
挣值分解结构　earned value breakdown structure
挣值管理　earned value management
蒸发冷凝　evaporative condensation

蒸发冷却　evaporative cooling
蒸发量　evaporation capacity
蒸发器　evaporator
蒸发式冷凝器　evaporative condenser
蒸发式冷气机　evaporative air cooler
蒸发温度　evaporating temperature
蒸发压力　evaporating pressure
蒸干法　steam seasoning
蒸馏水　distilled water
蒸馏装置　distillation apparatus
蒸汽采暖　steam heating
蒸汽打桩机　steam pile driver
蒸汽管　steam pipe
蒸汽锅炉　steam boiler
蒸汽加湿器　steam humidifier
蒸汽喷射器　steam ejector
蒸汽喷射式制冷循环　steam-jet refrigeration cycle
蒸汽喷射系统　steam injection system
蒸汽养护　steam curing
蒸压粉煤灰普通砖　autoclaved flyash-lime brick
蒸压灰沙普通砖　autoclaved sand-lime brick
蒸压灰砂普通砖　autoclaved lime-sand brick
整备待班线　servicing temporary rest track
整备能力　servicing capacity
整备台位　servicing position
整备线配置系数　allocation factor of service track
整笔支付　single payment
整车　block train
整车货场　car-load freight yard
整船包价　lump-sum freight
整定　setting
整定值　setting value
整合接触　conformable contact
整理资料　process data
整列装卸　loading and unloading of the whole train
整流继电器　rectifier relay
整流模块　rectifier module
整流器　rectifier
整批采购　bulk procurement
整套承包制合同　all-in contract
整套服务　integrated service
整套购买　basket purchase
整体道床轨道　monolithic ballastless track
整体的　integrated
整体吊弦　integrated dropper
整体剪切破坏　overall shear failure
整体浇筑混凝土　monolithic concrete
整体抗倾覆稳定　overall overturning stability
整体式衬砌　monolithic lining
整体式空气调节器　integrated air conditioner
整体式声屏障　integrated sound barrier
整体式制冷设备　packaged refrigeration device
整体稳定　overall stability
整体性　integrity
整体状构造　integral cryostructure
整箱货　full container load (FCL)
整修管理费　renovation cost
整修管理费率　renovation management rate
整正曲线　curve alignment adjusting
整正水平　adjusting of cross level
整直机　straightening machine
整治措施　renovation measures
整铸辙叉　one-piece cast frog, cast manganese frog, cast monobloc crossing
整装设备　packaged equipment
正本　original, text
正变质岩　orthometamorphite
正长斑岩　orthophyre
正长石　orthoclase
正长岩　syenite
正常报价　arm's length quotation
正常场(背景值)　normal field (background value)
正常的　natural, normal
正常的服务　normal services
正常的收缩　normal shrinkage
正常动作继电器　normal acting relay
正常费用　normal cost
正常工作模式　normal operating mode, normal mode of operations
正常工作时间　straight time
正常固结土　normally consolidated soil
正常结余　ordinary balance
正常情况　normal condition
正常使用极限状态　serviceability limit state
正常使用条件　average service conditions
正常税　regular tax
正常损耗　normal loss
正常条件　normal condition
正常涌水量　normal water inflow
正常折旧　normal depreciation, ordinary depreciation
正垂线法　direct plummeting method
正锤线观测(又称"正锤法")　direct plummet observation (also known as "direct plummet method")
正当成本　legitimate cost
正当持票人　holder in due course
正当的　justifiable
正当解雇　fair dismissal
正地形　positive relief
正定位　pull-off

正洞导坑法　prediction by pilot heading of main tunnel
正断层　normal fault
正断面图　normal section
正方晶系　tetragonal system
正方向　forward direction
正方形布置　square layout
正方形分幅　square map subdivision
正滚刀　face disc cutter
正火　normalizing
正交桥　right bridge
正交异型板　orthotropic plate
正截面　normal section
正镜　direct telescope
正馈线　negative feeder (AF)
正立体法　ortho-stereoscopy
正面冲突　head-on collision
正面条款　face clause
正片　positive
正三角形布置　regular triangle layout
正射投影　orthographic projection
正射影像地图　orthophoto map
正射影像图　orthophotoquad
正式承兑　formal acceptance
正式代表　official representative
正式的　formal, official
正式发票　formal invoice, official invoice
正式工　permanent labourer
正式合同　contract under seal, formal contract, sealed contract, official contract
正式价格　official price
正式确认　formal confirmation
正式收据　official receipt
正式条款　formal clause
正式通知　formal notice
正式文本　official text
正式协定　formal agreement
正式验收　formal acceptance
正式邀请　formal invitation
正式要求　formal request, demand
正式译本　official translation
正式语言　official language
正式注册　official register
正水头　positive hydraulic head
正态分布　normal distribution
正现金流量　positive cash flow
正线　main line
正线发车模式　main track departure mode
正线数目　number of main line
正线通过模式　main track passage mode
正线通过一级二场横列式　transverse layout of a through industrial (or harbour) station with two yards in one stage on main line
正向铲挖土机　face shovel
正像　positive image
正循环旋转钻机　direct circulation drilling rig
正压区　positive pressure area
正应力　normal stress
正褶皱　normal fold
正直摄影　normal case photography
正轴投影　normal projection
正装　right-handed machine
证词　attestation, evidence, proof
证件　credentials
证据　evidence, attestation, proof, substantiation
证明报告　certified report
证明函　supporting letter
证明拒付　protest
证明书　testimonial
证明文件　supporting document
证明有罪　convict
证券　security, stock, paper
证券持有人　security holder
证券交易所指数　stock exchange index
证券市场　security market
证人　witness, evidence, substantiator
证实　verify, verification, substantiate, justification
证书　certificate, letters
证言　witness, testimony
政策　policy
政党　political party
政府　government, state
政府拨款　government grant
政府部门　government department
政府采购　government procurement
政府采购政策　government procurement policy
政府担保　government guarantee
政府当局　public authorities
政府的承诺　government commitment
政府干预　government intervention
政府官员　public official
政府机构　public body
政府税收　government revenue
政府特派员　commissioner
政府投资　government investment, state investment
政府信贷　government credit
政府业主　government owner
政府预算　government budget
政府债券　government bond

政府质量稽查人员　country and city inspectors
政令　government decree, decree
政治风险　political risk
帧频　frame frequency
之字力　zigzag force, lateral force
支撑　support
支撑板　poling board
支撑管式止水器　the support tube sealing device
支撑架　support frame
支撑力　braced force
支撑靴　gripper
支撑靴座　gripper pedestal
支承板　baseplate
支承长度限值　limiting value for supporting length
支承机构　support mechanism
支承加劲肋　bearing stiffener
支承桩　bearing pile
支持　favour, support
支持函　supporting letter
支持结构　support structures
支持绝缘子　support insulator
支持器　holder
支持物　holder
支持装置　supporting assembly
支出　expenditure, outgo
支出费用　disbursement
支出项目　items of expenditure
支出预算　budget of expenditure
支出证明书　certificate of expenditure
支挡结构　retaining structure
支挡式结构　buttressed structure
支导线　open traverse
支道　branch passage
支洞　adit
支墩　rest pier
(支架的)支墩　pile
支付百分比　disbursement percentage
支付保险费　premium payment
支付表单　schedule of payments
支付次数　frequency of payment
支付担保　payment bond
支付的款项　payment
支付方式　method of payment, mode of payment, way of payment
支付合同　contract of payment
支付货币　currencies of payment
支付计划　payment schedule
支付进度表　payment schedule
支付宽限　grace of payment
支付里程碑　payment milestone
支付能力　ability to pay, solvency
支付逆差　adverse balance of payment
支付凭单　disbursement voucher, payment voucher, pay order
支付期票　honour a bill
支付日期　due date, date of payment
支付申请　application for payment
支付时间　time for payment
支付手段　means of payment
支付条件　payment terms, terms of payment
支付条款　settlement terms, payment provisions, terms of payment
支付协议　payment agreement
支付证书　certificate of payment
支管　branch pipe
支护结构　supporting structure
支架　support, bracket
支架法　falsework method
支架现浇施工　cast-in-place construction on falsework
支架现浇箱梁　cast-in-situ box girder with scaffolding support
支架预压　falsework preloading
支流　tributary
支票　check, cheque
支票簿存根　check book stubs
支票簿　check book
支票存根　check stub
支票登记簿　check register
支票兑现　cash a cheque
支票账户　checking account
支水准路线　spur leveling line
支线　branch line
支柱　pole, mast
支柱侧面限界　horizontal distance between the midpoint of the connection line of the TORs and the track-side face of the pole (TP)
支柱基础　mast foundation, pole foundation
支座　bearing, bearing seat
枝状管网　branch system
知识产权　intellectual property rights
知识产权和工业产权　intellectual and industrial property rights
知识分子　intellectual
织造土工织物　woven geotextile
执行　implement, carry out, execute, perform
执行董事　executive director, managing director
执行董事会　board of executive directors
执行范围　scope of execution

执行高层　top executive
执行合同　contract performance
执行机构　executing agency, performing organization
执行进度　implementation schedule
执行器　actuator
执行人　executor
执行委员会　executive committee, executing agency
执行中的项目　operational project
执业工程师　professional engineer
执业工程师证书　professional engineer license
执业管理会计师　certified management accountant (CMA)
执业会计师　public accountant
执照　licence, license, permit, diploma
执照费　fee for permit
执照税　excise, licence duty
执照有效期　duration of licence
直壁式低货位　straight wall type low freight section
直尺　rail straightness gauge
直达波法　direct wave method
直达港　direct port
直达货运　through freight
直达列车　through train
直达提单　direct bill of lading
直达运输　direct shipment
直方图　histogram
直观法　direct observation method
直轨器　rail straightening machine
直击雷　direct lightning stroke
直剪　direct shear
直剪快剪试验　quick direct shear test
直剪慢剪试验　slow direct shear test
直剪摩擦试验　direct shear friction test
直剪试验　direct shear test
直角拐肘　right angle crank
直角坐标网　rectangular coordinate network
直接报价　direct quotation
直接材料　direct material
直接裁决　direct verdict
直接采购　direct purchase, direct shopping
直接成本　direct cost, prime cost
直接成本计算法　direct costing
直接冻融法　direct freezing-thawing method
直接费　direct cost
直接费用　direct cost
直接付款　direct payment, direct debit
直接工程费　direct engineering cost
直接供电方式　direct feeding system
直接观测法　direct observation method
直接观察法　method of direct observation
直接管理费　direct overhead
直接管理费账户　direct overhead account
直接剪切试验　direct shear strength test
直接解译标志　direct interpretation mark
直接借记　direct debit
直接雷击　direct lightning stroke
直接贸易　direct trade
直接目的地　immediate destination
直接平差　direct adjustment
直接人工费　direct labour cost
直接融资　direct financing
直接受益人　immediate beneficiary
直接税　direct tax
直接损害　direct damage
直接损失　direct loss, direct damage
直接提单　straight bill of lading
直接现汇　direct cash remittance
直接线性变换　direct linear transformation
直接销售　direct sale
直接销账　direct write-off
直接协议　direct agreement
直接眩光　direct glare
直接影响区　probable impact area
直接原因　immediate cause
直接支付　direct payment
直接属性　direct attribute
直接装运　direct shipment
直进弯出　straight-in and curve-out
直径　inside diameter
直立产状　upright attitude
直立褶皱　upright fold
直连式存储　Direct-Attached Storage (DAS)
直链形悬挂　polygonal catenary
直流电　direct current
直流电法　direct current electric method
直流电平携带码　DC Level Shift (DCLS)
直流电压互感器　DC voltage transformer
直流电阻　direct-current resistance
直流隔断器　DC block
直流供电制　DC power supply system
直流继电器　DC relay
直流盘　DC panel
直流配电设备　DC power distribution device
直流屏　DC panel
直流输出　DC output
直流源屏　DC power supply panel
直埋电缆　directly buried cable (DBC)
直射眩光　direct glare
直伸三角形（又称"延伸三角形"）　straight triangle (also known as "extended triangle")

直通列车　transit train
直通模式　direct mode
直线　straight line, tangent
直线杆　suspension pole
直线折旧法　average method of depreciation, straight line method of depreciation
直向进路　straight route
直行坡　straight slope
直译　literal translation
直饮水系统　fine drinking water system
值班　on duty
值班采暖　standby heating
值班工程师　shift engineer
值班工区　on-duty section
值班台　on-duty console
值守房屋　guard room
职称　job title
职工保险　worker's insurance
职工福利费　welfare expense of employee
职工教育经费　employee education fund
职工死亡丧葬补助费、抚恤费　funeral grant and pension cost for death of employees
职工养老金　employee's pension fund
职工忠诚保险　fidelity bond (insurance)
职能　function
职能部门主管人员　staff executive
职能经理　functional manager
职能组织　functional organization
职权　authority
职权范围　reference
职位　position, capacity, post
职位空额　job vacancy
职务津贴　duty allowance
职业　occupation, profession, calling
职业安全　occupational safety
职业保障保险　professional indemnity insurance
职业病　occupational disease
职业道德　professional ethics
职业道德准则　code of ethics
职业的　professional
职业疏忽　professional negligence
职业行为准则　professional code of conduct
职业责任　professional responsibility, professional duty, professional liability
职业责任保险　professional liability insurance
职员　clerk, employee, staff, personnel
职员的变更　changes in personnel
职员的供应　supply of personnel
职责　duty, obligation, responsibility, role
职责范围　responsibility range, sphere of responsibility
职责委托　delegation of duties
植被　vegetation
植被调查　vegetation survey
植被覆盖率　vegetation coverage rate
植被恢复　revegetation
植被恢复率　revegetation percentage
植被恢复系数　revegetation coefficient
植被建设工程　vegetation construction works
植被类型　vegetation type
植草　grass planting
植草边坡　seeded slope
植筋　post-installed reinforcing bar, post-installed rebar
植生带　Lawn nursery strip
植生袋　Seed-nutriment-soil sack
植树绿化　greening with trees
植物保护带　vegetation screen
植物防护　Protection by plants
植物混播混种　mixed sowing and planting
植物群落　phytocoenosium, plant community
止付　withhold payment
止浆墙　grout-stopping wall
止水　water seal
止水带　waterstop
止水片　water stop
止水条　water stop strip
止水岩盘　waterstop laccolite
只保全损险　insurance against total loss only (TLO)
只读记录　un-editable record
只供材料　supply only materials
纸币　paper
纸币清分机　banknote sorter
纸黄金　paper gold
纸上定线　route mapping
指标　index
指标优化　index optimization
指导　guide, direct, direction, instruct, instruction
指导性施工组织设计　instructive construction organization design, guiding construction plan
指定　designate, nominate, nomination
指定代表　designated representative
指定的承包商　nominated contractor
指定的暂定金额　specified provisional sums
指定分包商　nominated subcontractor
指定交货地点　named place of delivery
指定目的地　named place of destination
指定启运地　named departure point

指定人提单　order bill of lading
指定人支票　order check
指定日期
　　specified date, named date, appointed day
指定收货人　named consignee
指定银行　authorized bank
指定装船港　named port of shipment
指挥　command, superintendence
指挥链　chain of command
指挥者　superintendent
指控　charge, accuse
指令　instruction, command
指令变更　variation by instruction
指南　guideline, manual
指派　designate
指示　indicate, indication, instruct, instruction
指示剂　indicator
指示剂法　indicator method
指示提单　order bill of lading
指示物　indicator
指示性标志　indicative mark
指数　index
志留纪　Silurian period
志留系　Silurian system
制裁　sanction
制单　vouching
制定　work out, formulate, institution, lay down
制动撑架　braking-force bracing
制动墩　braking-force pier
制动方式　brake mode
制动功　braking work
制动构件　brake member
制动接口单元　brake interface unit
制动力　braking force
制动能高　energy head of braking
制动曲线　braking curve
制动时间　braking time
制动位　retarder location
制度　system
制冷　refrigeration
制冷机房　refrigerating machine room
制冷剂　refrigerant
制冷量　refrigerating capacity
制冷系统　refrigerating system
制冷性能系数
　　coefficient of refrigerating performance
制冷循环　refrigeration cycle
制梁区　girder fabrication area
制梁台座　girder fabrication pedestal
制票机　ticket printer

制图专家系统　cartographic expert system
制图综合　cartographic generalization
制印　map process and printing
制约因素　restrictive element
制造　produce, manufacture
制造成本
　　factory cost, manufacturing cost, fabrication cost
制造费用　overhead charges (cost), manufacturing
　　expenses, factory expenses
制造商　manufacturer
制造图　manufacturing drawing
制造证明书　certificate of manufacture
制作　produce, production, fabricate, fabrication
制作场　fabricating yard
质保大纲　quality assurance programme
质量保证　quality assurance
质量保证计划　quality assurance plan
质量保证期　warranty
质量保证书　quality guarantee
质量保证体系　quality assurance system
质量标准　quality standards
质量成本　cost concerning quality
质量担保　warranty bond
质量分数　mass fraction
质量管理体系　quality management system
质量记录　quality record
质量监督　quality surveillance
质量检验　quality inspection
质量鉴定　appraisal of quality
质量控制　quality control
质量浓度　mass concentration
质量评估方法　quality evaluation methods
质量评价　quality evaluation
质量审查　quality review
质量审核　quality audit
质量体系　quality system
质量维修保函
　　letter of guarantee for maintenance
质量验收　quality acceptance
质量以买方样品为准
　　quality as per buyer's sample
质量以卖方样品为准
　　quality as per seller's sample
质量证明　quality certificate
质询　challenge
质询程序　challenge procedure
质疑　query
质追踪系统　quality tracking system
治安　security
致密性　compactness

秩亏网平差　rank defect network adjustment
蛭石　vermiculite
智能化电源设备　intelligent power supply equipment
智能化集成系统　intelligent integration system
智能建筑　intelligent building
智能平台管理接口　intelligent platform management interface（IPMI）
智能全站仪　robotic total station
智能外设　intelligent peripheral（IP）
智能网　intelligent network（IN）
滞付金　retention money
滞洪工程　flood-retarding project
滞后　lag
滞后工期　lag duration
滞后相　lagging phase
滞回曲线　hysteretic curve
滞留　demurrage
滞纳金　fine for delayed payment
滞纳税款　delinquent tax
滞期费　demurrage, demurrage cost
滞销货　dead stock
置存成本　carrying cost
置存价值　carrying value
置换、掺料与化学处理法　replacement, admixture and chemical processing method
置换通风　displacement ventilation
中奥陶世　middle Ordovician epoch
中奥陶统　middle Ordovician series
中班　swing shift
中班工人　swing shiftman
中部平原　central plain
中层滑坡　middle layer landslide
中长距离预报　medium and long distance forecast
中长隧道　medium-long tunnel
中承式　half-through type
中承式桥　half-through bridge
中粗砂　medium-coarse sand
中等富水区　medium water abundance zone
中等价格　moderate price
中等品质　fair average quality（FAQ）
中度侵蚀　moderate erosion
中断　interruption, discontinue
中风化　moderate weathering
中腐蚀　medium corrosion
中隔壁法（CD法）　central diaphragm method（CD method）
中更新世　middle Pleistocene epoch
中更新统　middle Pleistocene series
中国列车运行控制系统0级　Chinese train control system level 0（CTCS-0）
中国列车运行控制系统1级　Chinese train control system level 1（CTCS-1）
中国列车运行控制系统2级　Chinese train control system level 2（CTCS-2）
中国列车运行控制系统3级　Chinese train control system level 3（CTCS-3）
中国列车运行控制系统4级　Chinese train control system level 4（CTCS-4）
中国列车运行控制系统　CTCS Chinese Train Control System
中国列车运行控制系统CTCS　Chinese train control system（CTCS）
中国铁路列控系统　China train control system（CTCS）
中寒武世　middle Cambrian epoch
中寒武统　middle Cambrian series
中和法　neutralization method
中和轨温　neutral rail temperature
中和面　neutral plane
中和轴高度　height of neutral axis
中厚层　medium thickness layer
中—活载　standard live load of Chinese railway
中继点　relay node
中继段　repeater section
中继方式图　trunking diagram
中继链路带宽峰值　trunk peak bandwidth
中继网关　trunk gateway（TG）
中间层　intermediate floor
中间电缆盒　intermediate cable terminal box
中间调解　mediation
中间加劲肋　intermediate stiffener
中间架构　intermediate framework
中间坡　intermediate slope
中间漆　intermediate coating
中间人　intermediary, intermediate, middleman
中间商　middleman, broker
中间试验费　intermediate test cost
中间系统到中间系统协议　intermediate system-to-intermediate system（IS-IS）
中间站　intermediate station
中间站台　intermediate platform
中间柱　intermediate pole（mast）, single cantilever pole（mast）
中介　intermediation
中介人　finder, broker, intermediate
中介人佣金　finder's fee
中介物　intermediary
中介业务　intermediary business

中空注浆锚杆　hollow grouted rockbolt
中立的　neutral
中立国　neutral state
中埋式止水带　buried water stop tie
中密　medium density
中能力驼峰　middle capacity hump
中泥盆世　middle Devonian epoch
中泥盆统　middle Devonian series
中频　intermediate frequency
中平　centerline stake leveling
中平测量　profile leveling
中期　medium term, intermediate term
中期付款申请　application for interim payment
中期评估　mid-term evaluation
中桥　medium bridge (with length from 21 m to 100 m)
中热带　medium tropic
中溶盐含量　content of moderately soluble salt
中软土　medium-soft soil
中三叠世　middle Triassic epoch
中三叠统　middle Triassic series
中砂　medium sand
中山　medium mountain
中生代　Mesozoic era
中生界　Mesozoic erathem/ group
中石炭世　middle Carboniferous epoch
中石炭统　middle Carboniferous series
中水　reclaimed water
中水系统　reclaimed water system
中速定量滤纸　quantitative filter paper of moderately speed
中途停运权　stoppage in transit
中途折返　midway return operation
中途折回　turnback halfway
中外合资企业　sino-foreign joint venture
中温带　middle temperate zone
中温消化　mesophilic digestion
中误差　mean squares error
中线　midline
中线测量　centerline survey
中线高程　midline elevation
中线控制桩　midline control stake
中线位置　midline position
中心服务器　center server
中心滚刀　center disc cutter
中心荷载(轴心荷载)　centric load (centric axial load)
中心级集成管理平台　central integrated management platform
中心矩法　central moment method
中心控制　centralized control
中心里程　center mileage
中心锚结　mid-point anchor
中心锚结线夹　mid-point anchor clamp
中心排水沟　central drainage ditch
中心频率　center frequency
中心试验室　central laboratory
中心位置　central position
中心线　center line
中心站　central station
中心柱　center mast of overlap
中心桩　central stake
中新世　Miocene epoch
中新统　Miocene series
中行车　medium rolling car
中型编组站　middle sized marshaling station
中型车站　medium scale station
中型滑坡　medium scale landslide
中型旅客车站　medium passenger station
中型清筛机　medium ballast cleaning machine
中性保护导体　neutral protection conductor
中性点　neutral point
中性点接地　neutral point earthing
中性段　neutral section
中性面　neutral plane
中性区段　neutral section
中性提单　neutral party bill of lading
中性液体　neutral liquid
中修　medium-scale maintenance, medium repair
中压缩性　medium compressibility
中亚热带　mid-subtropics
中央处理器　Central Processing Unit(CPU)
中央银行　central bank
中央子午线　centerline meridian
中硬土　medium-hard soil
中元古代　Mesoproterozoic
中源地震　intermediate-focus earthquake
中震旦世　middle Sinian epoch
中震旦统　middle Sinian series
中止　suspend, suspension, stoppage
中止合同　suspension of contract
中止谈判　suspend talks
中止条款　cesser clause
中志留世　middle Silurian epoch
中志留统　middle Silurian series
中侏罗世　middle Jurassic epoch
中侏罗统　middle Jurassic series
中转　transit
中转车流　transfer traffic flow
中转改编车流　transfer remarshaling traffic flow
中转港　port of transshipment

中转集装箱　transfer container
中转作业　transfer operation
中桩　center stake
中桩高程测量(又称"纵断面水准测量")
　　center stake leveling (also known as "profile leveling")
中桩高程测量(中平)　center stake leveling (CSL)
中桩(中线桩)　center line stake
终裁　final award
终点　end point
终端电缆盒　cable terminal box
终端杆　terminal pole, dead-end pole
终端杆塔　terminal support, dead-end support
终端工作站　terminal work station
终端架构　terminal framework
终结　terminate, termination
终结账户　terminal accounts
终凝　final setting
终碛　terminal moraine
终碛堤　terminal moraine levee
终碛垄　terminal moraine ridge
终身保险　insurance for life
终值　final value, maturity value, terminal value
终止　terminate, termination, cease, cessation, expire, expiration
终止合同　terminate a contract
终止合同的条款　stop clause
终止后承包商的义务
　　contractor's obligation after termination
终止后的付款　payment after termination
终止日期　date of termination
终止时的付款　payment on termination
终止诉讼　closure of the proceedings, termination of the proceedings
终止通知　termination notice
终止责任　cessation of liability
钟差　clock error
钟乳石　stalactite
钟乳状　stalactitic
种植土　planting soil
种植穴槽　Planting pit (trough)
种子发芽率　rate of emergence
种子含水率　seed moisture content
中标　award of contract, win a contract
中标函　letter of acceptance, award letter
中标合同　contract awarded
中标合同价　accepted contract amount
中标人　winning bidder
中标书　letter of acceptance
中标通知　notice of award, letter of acceptance

中标意向书　intent to award, letter of intent
中标者　successful bidder (tenderer)
仲裁　arbitrate, arbitration
仲裁裁决　arbitral decision, arbitration award
仲裁程序　arbitral procedure, arbitration procedure, procedure of arbitration
仲裁代理人　arbitration agent
仲裁地点　place of arbitration
仲裁法　arbitration law
仲裁费　arbitration fee
仲裁规则　arbitration rules
仲裁解决　settlement by arbitration
仲裁申请　application for arbitration
仲裁条款　arbitration clause, reference clause
仲裁庭　arbitral tribunal, arbitration tribunal, tribunal, forum for arbitration
仲裁委员会　arbitration board
仲裁小组　arbitration panel
仲裁协议　arbitration agreement
仲裁语言　language of arbitration
仲裁员　arbitrator, arbiter, referee
重锤夯实法　heavy tamping method
重大偏离　material/major/substantial deviation
重大事件　milestone, major event
重大修改
　　material alteration/modification/amendment
重点工程　priority project
重点设防　intensive fortification
重点隧道工程弃渣防护图
　　design drawing for excavation waste dump protection of key tunnel engineering
重度　specific weight
重度值　unit weight value
重负荷臂　heavy load arm
重过失行为　reckless misconduct
重晶石　barite
重力坝　gravity dam
重力场　gravity field
重力分布　gravity distribution
重力荷载代表值　representative value of gravity load
重力基准网　gravity datum network
重力继电器　gravitation type relay
重力加速度　gravity acceleration
重力勘探　gravity prospecting
重力流管道　gravity flow pipe
重力侵蚀　gravity erosion
重力式挡土墙　gravity retaining wall
重力式浸水挡土墙　immersible gravity retaining wall
重力式桥墩　gravity pier
重力式桥台　gravity abutment

重力数据库　gravimetric data base
重力水　gravity water
重力仪　gravimeter
重联　coupled
重联机车　double heading locomotives
重量法　gravimetric method
重黏土　heavy clay
重视　value
重塑强度　remoulded strength
重碳酸盐　hydrocarbonate
重瓦斯保护　heavy gas protection
重型动力触探　heavy dynamic penetration test
重型动力触探仪　heavy duty dynamic cone penetrometer
重型轨道　heavy track
重型轨道车　heavy rail car
重型击实　heavy-duty compaction
重型击实试验　heavy compaction test
重型卡车　heavy-duty truck
重型起重机　heavy lift
重型线路机械　heavy track maintenance machinery
重要用户　very important person(VIP)
重载铁路　heavy-haul railway
重作业　heavy work
舟桥　bateau bridge, pontoon bridge
周报表　weekly returns
周边眼　contour hole
周边眼装药结构　charging structure of contour hole
周工资　weekly wages
周计划　weekly scheduling
周界安全防范　perimeter security protection
周末班　weekend shift period/cycle
周期　period
周期荷载　periodic load
周期信用证　periodic credit
周期性负载　periodic load
周围　surroundings
周围情况　environmental conditions turnover
周转材料　revolving materials
周转次数　turnover frequency
周转额　turnover
周转轨　inventory rails
周转金　working fund
周转率　turnover rate
周转设备　general plant
周转资产　working assets
周转资金　working capital
轴测投影图　isometric drawing
轴力　axial force
轴力标准值　standard value of axial force
轴流风机　axial fan
轴流式通风机　axial ventilator
轴流水泵　axial pump
轴面劈理　axial plane cleavage
轴线　axis
轴线控制网　axial control network
轴线投测　axis projection surveying
轴向变形　axial deformation
轴向荷载　axial load
轴向拉力　axial tensile force
轴向压力　axial pressure
轴向应变　axial strain
轴向应力　axial stress
轴向自由膨胀率　axial free swelling ratio
轴心抗拉极限强度　ultimate axial tensile strength
轴心抗压极限强度　ultimate axial compressive strength
轴心抗压强度　axial compressive strength
轴心受压构件稳定系数　stability coefficient of axial compression member
轴压比　axial compression ratio
轴重　axle load
帚状构造　brush structure
昼间信号　day signal
昼夜施工　around-the-clock job
昼夜通用信号　signal for both day and night
侏罗纪　Jurassic period
侏罗系　Jurassic system
株距　intra-line spacing
逐跨施工法　span-by-span construction method
逐条记载　itemize
主办人　sponsor
主包工程　main works
主保护　primary protection, main protection
主变保护测控单元　measure and control unit of traction transformer protection
主承包商　principal contractor
主持会议　officiate, chair the meeting
主持人　host
主导风向　prevailing wind direction
主导可变作用　dominant variable action
主导因子　dominant factor
主导语言　ruling language
主灯丝　main filament
主灯丝断丝报警　main filament burnout alarm
主动控制　active control
主动土压力　active earth pressure
主动质量阻尼器控制系统　active mass damper control system
主干道　trunk road

主干对绞电缆	trunk twisted pair cable
主干汇流排	main bus-bar
主干线路	main circuit
主固结	primary consolidation
主管部门	department in charge
主管当局	competent authorities
主管法庭	competent court
主管工程师	engineer in charge
主管人	controller, person in charge, superintendent
主光轴偏角	averted angle of principal optic axis
主轨道电路	main track circuit
主合点	principal vanishing point
主合同	main contract, prime contract
主合同条款	main contract clauses
主合同文件	main contract documents
主河槽	main river channel
主桁架	primary truss
主滑段	main slide section
主接线	single line diagram
主节点	major node
主筋	main reinforcement
主进度计划	master schedule
主控项目	critical item
主控站	master control station
主控制室	main control room
主类	primary type
主梁	main girder
主梁中心距	center distance between main girders
主频率	main frequency
主桥	main bridge
主权贷款	sovereign loan
主权利	principal rights
主人	host
主任	director
主时钟	master clock
主隧道(又称"正洞")	main tunnel
主塔	king-tower
主题	subject
主体	entity
主体工程	main works
主体结构	main structure
主体信号机	main signal
主通气立管	main ventilation riser
主席	chairman
主箱场	main container yard
主信用证	overriding credit
主要备选方案	major alternative
主要材料	primary material
主要材料预算价格表	budgetary price sheet of primary materials
主要成本	prime cost, first cost
主要成本加定比酬金	prime cost plus percentage fee
主要成本加固定酬金	prime cost plus fixed fee
主要承重构件	main load-carrying member
主要工程数量	main quantities
主要合伙人	senior partner
主要荷载	main load
主要角焊缝	main fillet welds
主要缺陷	major defect
主要人员	key personnel
主要施工设备	major items of construction plant
主要市场	primary market
主要事实	primary fact
主要污染源	major pollution source
主要巷道平面图	main workings plan
主要营业地	principal place of business
主要预算	main budget
主要责任	ultimate liability
主要债务	primary liability
主要债务人	principal debtor
主要证据	evidence in chief
主应变	principal strain
主应力差	principal stress difference
主振频率	master oscillator frequency
主振型	principal vibration mode
主轴线测设	setting-out of main axis
煮沸法	boiling method
助理	assistant
助理工程师	assistant engineer
助凝剂	coagulant aid
助手	assistant
住房	housing, lodging quarters
住房公积金	housing fund
住宅	house
住宅单元	dwelling unit
住宅建设	housing development
住宅建设基金	housing fund
住宅建筑	residential building
住宅区	residential quarters
贮备溶液	stock solution
贮料堆	stock pile
贮、配水构筑物	structure for water storage and distribution
贮药间	chemical storage tank
贮液器	liquid receiver
贮油池	oil basin (oil leakage pool)
注册	register, registration
注册产权	registered title
注册成本工程师	certified cost engineer

Z

注册承包商　licensed contractor
注册地　country of incorporation
注册工程师　chartered engineer
注册工料测量师　chartered quantity surveyor
注册公司　registered company
注册建筑师　licensed architect
注册建筑师考试
　　architect registration exam（ARE），architect certification examination
注册会计师　chartered accountant（CA），certified accountant
注册商标　registered trade mark
注册设计　registered design
注册证书　certificate of registry，certification
注册资本　registered capital
注浆　grouting
注浆泵　grouting pump
注浆泵压力　pressure of grouting pump
注浆充填率　grouting filling ratio
注浆防水　waterproofing by grouting
注浆加固　grouting reinforcement
注浆量　grouting volume
注浆流量　grouting flow rate
注浆深度　grouting depth
注浆压力　grouting pressure
注模成型法　injection molding
注释　comment
注水试验　water injecting test
注销　deregistration
注意　attention, notice
注意信号　caution signal
驻班制　crew shift changing at turnaround depot system, shifting system
驻地工程师　resident engineer
驻地首席工程师　chief resident engineer
驻地项目代表　resident project representative
驻国外代表　representative abroad
驻站联络员　station liaison officer
柱板式声屏障　post panel sound barrier
柱锤冲扩桩
　　piles thrusted-expanded with column-hammer
柱锤重扩柱　hammer enlargement pile
柱腹板节点域　panel zone of column web
柱式桥墩　column-type pier
柱状　columnar
铸铁管　cast iron pipe
铸铁散热器　cast-iron radiator
筑岛围堰　artificial island cofferdam
筑堤　dyke
筑路　road building, pave

抓铲挖掘机　clamshell bucket
抓斗式门式起重机　grab type portal crane
抓斗式起重机　clamshell crane, grab crane
抓斗式挖泥船　clamshell dredge, grab dredger
抓斗式挖土机
　　clamshell excavator, clamshell shovel, grab
抓土斗　clamshell
专家　expert, specialist
专家库　pool of experts
专家评审　professional review
专家委员会　expert committee（council），peer review, expert panel
专家意见　professional comment
专利　patent
专利保护　patent protection
专利产品　proprietary product
专利持有人　patent holder
专利代理人　patent agent
专利法　patent law
专利费　patent fee, licence fee
专利局　patent office
专利批准者　patentor
专利品　proprietary articles
专利权　patent, patent right
专利权人　proprietor
专利权使用费　patent royalty
专利权所有人　patentee
专利许可证　patent license
专利证书　letter of patent, certificate of patent
专卖　monopoly
专卖价格　monopoly price
专卖品　proprietary articles
专卖权　monopoly right
专门技术　know-how
专门律师　barrister
专门人员　specialist
专题地图　thematic map
专线电路　private-line circuit
专线会议电视系统
　　private-line video conference system
专业　profession, discipline
专业承包商　special contractor, specialist contractor, professional constructor, trade contractor
专业分包商
　　specialist subcontractor, trade sub-contractor
专业服务　specialist services, professional service
专业服务费　professional fee
专业工种承包商　trade contractor
专业化　specialization
专业化修制　specialized repair system

专业技能　expertise
专业技术　professional skill, professional craftsmanship, professional technique
专业领域　disciplines
专业模型几何表达等级　geometric expression level of professional model
专业人员　professional
专业设计师　design professional
专业性货场　specialized goods yard
专业证人　professional witness
专营合同　exclusive contract
专营权　franchise
专用　earmark
专用合同条件　special (particular) conditions of contract
专用税　objective tax
专用条件　conditions of particular application
专用通气立管　dedicated ventilation riser
专用通信　private communication
专有的　proprietary
专有技术　proprietary technology
专有技术合同　know-how contract
专有技术许可证　know-how license
专有名词　technical terms
专员　commissioner
专制行为　autocratic acts brick
砖　brick
砖工　brick worker
砖过梁　brick lintel
砖混结构　brick-concrete structure
砖木结构　masonry-timber structure
砖坯　raw brick
砖砌体结构　brick masonry structure
砖砌体墙　brick masonry wall
砖砌体柱　brick masonry column
砖石结构　brick masonry structure
砖筒拱　cylindrical brick arch
转包　sublet, subcontract
转车盘　turning jack
转船　tranship
转船附加费　transhipment surcharge
转船提单　transhipment bill of lading
转刺　point transfer
转贷　on lending
转道空闲　detour cleared
转道占用　detour occupied
转抵押　repledge
转动次数　rotation times
转换　conversion
转换层　transfer storey
转换轨　transfer track
转换结构构件　transfer member
转换跨距　transition span length
转换时间　switching time
转换锁闭器　switch-and-lock mechanism
转换(支)柱　transition mast of overlap
转极时间　pole-changing time
转极值　pole-changing value
转记　carry down carried forward, carried down
转嫁风险　transfer risks
转交　forward, transfer
转角杆　angle pole
转角架构　angle framework
转角量测　intersection angle measurement
转借　underlease
转借人　sub-borrower
转开信用证　back-to-back letter of credit
转口贸易　transit trade
转口税　transit duty (dues)
转口信用证　transit letter of credit
转轮除湿机　rotary dehumidifier
转轮式换热器　rotary heat exchanger
转盘式钻机　rotary drilling machine
转让　transfer, transference, assign, assignment, demise
转让费　royalty, assignment fee (charge)
转让契据　deed of transfer
转让人　assigner, assignor, indorser, endorser
转让手续费　negotiation commission
转让书　letter of assignment
转让证书　deed of conveyance, assignment
转手贸易　switch trade
转输流量　flow feeding the reservoir in network
转体法　rotation method
转体施工　erection by rotation method
转筒式混凝土搅拌机　rotary drum concrete mixer
转线列车　shunting trains
转向杆　steering rod
转向架检修库　bogie inspection and repair workshop
转向架租用费　bogie lease charge
转向角　steering angle
转向设备　turning equipment
转押　submortgage
转移风险　transfer of risks
转移价格　transfer price
转移责任　hold harmless
转运　tranship, transhipment, transship, transshipment
转运港　port of transshipment
转运公司　forwarder

转运提单　transhipment bill of lading
转账凭证　transfer voucher, journal voucher
转账通知单　account transfer memo
转账支付　payment by transfer
转辙机　switch machine
转辙机安装装置　switch machine installation
转辙机表示缺口　switch machine indicating gap, switch gap
转辙器　switch
转辙锁闭器　plunger lock
转辙装置　switching device
转子流量计　rotameter
转租　assignment of lease, sublease, relet
转租人　subtenant
桩　pile
桩板结构　pile-slab structure
桩板式挡土墙　pile-slab retaining wall
桩侧阻力　lateral pile resistance
桩长　pile length
桩垂直度　pile verticality
桩锤　rammer
桩底持力层　the bearing stratum of pile bottom
桩端阻力　tip resistance, end resistance
桩筏结构　pile raft structure
桩工机械　piling machinery
桩基　pile foundation
桩基础　pile foundation
桩基等效沉降系数　equivalent settlement coefficient of pile foundation
桩基计算 m 值法　m-method of pile foundation calculation
桩架　pile frame
桩径　pile diameter
桩距　spacing of pile
桩帽　pile cap, head of pile
桩群　pile cluster
桩身　pile shaft
桩身截面　cross section of pile shaft
桩身内力测试　internal force test of pile shaft
桩身缺陷　pile defects
桩身完整性　pile integrity
桩身应变　strain of pile shaft
桩头　head of pile
桩头处理　pile top preparation
桩网结构　pile-net structure
桩位　pile position
装备　equipment, furnishings
装车道　loading track
装车台　loading platform
装车线　loading track
装船　loading on board
装船付现　cash on shipment (COS)
装船期　period for shipment
装船日期　date of shipment
装船通知　shipment advice, notice of shipment, shipping note
装船许可证　lading permit
装船指示　shipping instructions
装货　loading, on load cargo
装货单　shipping order
装货地　place of loading
装货港　loading port, lading port
装货国　country of embarkation
装货日期　date of loading
装货重量　shipping weight
装配　assemble, assembly, fabricate, fit
装配场　fabricating yard, place of assembly
装配车间　fitting shop, assembly shop
装配成本　fabrication cost, erection cost, mounting cost
装配方式　assembly mode
装配件　fittings
装配式衬砌　assembled lining, prefabricated lining
装配式混凝土结构　precast concrete structure
装配式结构　prefabricated structure
装配图　erection diagram, assembly drawing, mounting drawing
装配线　assembly line
装配整体式混凝土结构　precast integral concrete structure
装砂机　sand loader
装饰　upholster, decoration
装填　load
装箱单　packing list, packing slip (sheet)
装卸　loading and unloading
装卸场　loading and unloading yard
装卸次数　loading and unloading times
装卸单价　unit price of loading and unloading
装卸费　charges of loading and unloading
装卸机械停放间　handling machinery storage shed
装卸检修作业场　in-service freight car inspection yard
装卸期限　lay days
装卸设备　handling facility
装卸时间　lay time
装卸线　loading and unloading siding
装卸有效长度　effective loading and unloading length
装卸作业区　loading and unloading operation area

装修　decoration
装修工程　finishing work
装岩机　rock loader, muck loader
装运　shipment
装运单据　shipping documents
装运付款　cash on shipment（COS）
装运港　port of shipment
装运港交货类　port delivery
装运期　time of shipment
装运申请　application for shipment
装运时间　time of shipment
装运条件　terms of shipment
装运误期费　demurrage
装载　load, loading, lading
装载过多　overcharge
装载机　loader
装载机(履带式)　loading shovel(crawler)
装载机(轮式)　loading shovel(wheeled)
装置　device, apparatus, mounting, fitting, fixture
状态修　condition-based repair, health repair
撞击力　collision force
撞击声　crashing sound
追偿权　right of reimbursement
追钩　catch up
追加保险　additional cover
追加保证金的通知　margin call（notice）
追加拨款　additional appropriation
追加的　additional, cumulative
追加订单　additional order
追加订货　additional order
追加利息　add-on interest
追加预算　supplementary budget
追加账单　supplemental bill
追索权　recourse
追尾　rear-end collision
追踪间隔　headway, headway of trains
锥坡　truncated conical slope
锥体护坡　truncated conical revetment
锥形反转出料混凝土搅拌机　conical reversing concrete mixer
锥形瓶　conical flask
锥形倾翻出料混凝土搅拌机　tapered tilting concrete mixer, conical tilting concrete mixer
坠陀　weight
坠陀串　weight sets
坠陀杆　support bar for weight
坠陀限制架　weight guide tube
坠砣抱箍　weight guide strap
缀板　batten plate
缀材(缀件)　lacing and batten elements
缀条　lacing bar
准备工作及审查　preparation and review
准备金　reserve funds, provision
准会员　associate member
准据法　proper law
准平原　peneplain
准确称取　accurately weighing
准确度　accuracy rating
准司法的　quasi-judicial
准同步数字系列　plesiochronous digital hierarchy（PDH）
准线　alignment
准许　permit, permission, empower
准移动闭塞　quasi-moving block
准永久组合　quasi-permanent combination
准予　grand, permit, approve
准则　code, criteria, principle
准仲裁员　quasi-arbitrator
卓越周期　predominant period
灼烧失量法　method of ignition loss
灼烧失量含量　content of ignition loss
浊度　turbidness, turbidity
酌处权　discretion
着色法　staining method
咨询　consultation
咨询费　consulting fee
咨询分包　sub-consultancy
咨询分包人　sub-consultant
咨询服务　consulting service, consultancy service, adviser service
咨询服务采购　procurement of consulting services
咨询服务合同　contract for consulting services
咨询服务用户手册　handbook of users of consulting services
咨询工程师　consulting engineer
咨询公司　consulting firm, consultant company（corporation）
咨询人员　consultant, advocate
咨询委员会　consultative committee, board of reference, advisory committee
咨询协议　consulting agreement
咨询专家　expert consultant, consultant
咨询专家的责任　liability of the consultant
资本　capital, principal
资本成本　cost of capital
资本负债　capital liability
资本公积　capital reserves
资本红利　capital bonus
资本基金　capital fund

资本结构	capital composition structure
资本金	capital fund, net capital (N/C)
资本净收益	net capital gains
资本亏损	capital deficit
资本市场	capital market
资本收益率	capital return
资本损益	capital gain or loss
资本投资	capital investment
资本形成	capital formation
资本性账户	capital account
资本性资产	capital assets
资本盈利	capital surplus
资本预算	capital budget
资本增值	capital appreciation
资本折旧	depreciation of capital
资本支出	capital expenditure capital charges, capital outlay
资本周转率	capital turnover rate
资本转移税	capital transfer tax
资本准备金	capital reserve
资本租赁	capital lease
资产	asset
资产报废	asset retirement
资产重置计划	assets replacement schedule
资产重置资金	assets replacement fund
资产担保	assets cover
资产抵偿	assets cover
资产负债表	balance sheet, statement of asset and liabilities
资产负债表日期	date of balance sheet
资产负债管理	asset and liability management (ALM)
资产负债数据	balance sheet data
资产估价	assets valuation
资产管理	asset management
资产净额	net assets
资产净值	net asset value
资产留置权	encumbrance, charge on assets
资产评估	property valuation
资产清算人	liquidator
资产收益	return on assets
资产与负债	assets and liabilities
资产账户	assets account
资产折旧	assets depreciation
资产折旧幅度	assets depreciation range
资产周转率	assets turnover
资产总额	total asses
资方	capital
资格	eligibility, capacity, qualification
资格后审	post qualification
资格鉴定	competency certification
资格文件	qualification documents
资格预审	prequalification
资格预审不合格	failure of prequalification
资格预审申请	prequalification application
资格预审文件	prequalification documents
资格预审邀请书	invitation for prequalification
资格证书	qualification certificate
资金	finance, financial resources, capital, fund
资金安排	financial arrangement
资金不足	capital scarcity
资金成本	cost of funds
资金充足	abundance of capital
资金筹集费	capital expenses
资金分配	allocation of funds
资金结算网	fund settlement network
资金来源	source of funds
资金流动	cash flow
资金流动折现评估法	discounted cash flow method
资金流分析	cash flow analysis
资金流入	inflow of fund
资金流转	capital circulation
资金密集项目	capital intensive project
资金渠道	financial channel
资金缺额担保	deficiency guarantee
资金时间价值	time value of capital
资金投入	funding
资本外逃	capital flight
资金限制	limitation of funds
资金运用	use of funds
资金支出	expenditure of fund
资料解释	data interpretation
资审合格的承包商	prequalified contractor
资审合格的投标人	prequalified tenderer
资信证明	certificate of credit standing
资信状况	credit standing (status)
资讯	information
资用压力	available pressure
资源	resources
资源分解结构	resource breakdown structure (RBS)
资源负荷曲线	resource loading curve, bell curve
资源计划	resource planning
资源量	resource quantity
资源配置方案	resource allocation plan
资源选线	resources-based railway location
资源依赖	resource dependent
资质说明	statement of qualification
资助	fund, subsidize
资助费用	back-stopping cost
资助计划	financing plan

子类	subtype
子条款	sub-clause
子网连接保护	Subnetwork Connection Protection (SNCP)
子午圈曲率半径	curvature radius of meridian
子午线	meridian
子午线收敛角	meridian convergence angle
子项目	sub-project
子钟	slave clock
紫外线	ultraviolet (UV)
紫外线剂量	ultraviolet dose
紫外线消毒法	ultraviolet disinfection
仔细检查	scrutinize, scrutiny
自保持	self-holding
自保电路	stick circuit
自闭电路	stick circuit
自闭条件	stick requisition
自闭性	self-closing
自筹资金	self-finance
自定成本	discretionary cost
自动闭塞	automatic block
自动闭塞电力线路	run-through power line for automatic block system (ABS line)
自动闭塞供电线路	automatic block power line
自动闭塞联系电路	liaison circuit with automatic blocks
自动闭塞信号线路	automatic block signal line
自动操纵作业	automatic operation
自动抄车号	automatic car identification
自动倒机	automatic switchover
自动点灯	automatic lighting
自动调节	automatic regulation
自动调压	automatic voltage regulation
自动断面仪	automatic profiler
自动放弃	waiver
自动分保	obligatory reinsurance
自动扶梯	escalator
自动过分相	neutral section auto-passing
自动化驼峰	automatic hump
自动化制图	automatic cartography
自动缓解	automatic release
自动绘图	automatic plotting
自动检票机	automatic ticket gate
自动进路触发	automatic route trigger
自动开闭器	switch circuit controller
自动控温控湿设备	automatic temperature and humidity controlling device
自动栏木	automatic barrier
自动排气活门	automatic exhaust valve
自动喷水灭火系统	automatic sprinkling system
自动平路机	self-propelled blader
自动铺路机	motorpaver
自动启闭喷头	automatic open-close sprinkler
自动取款机	cash dispenser
自动取票机	automatic ticket collection machine
自动申请破产	voluntary bankruptcy
自动升降机	auto-lift
自动售票机	ticket vending machine, automatic ticket machine
自动停车	automatic train stop
自动停车装置	automatic train stop device
自动通过按钮电路	automatic passing button circuit
自动通过进路	automatic passing route
自动投切	auto-switching
自动稳压	automatic voltage regulation
自动限时解锁	automatic time release
自动巡检	automatic inspection
自动增益控制	automatic gain control
自动站间闭塞	interstation auto-block
自动整平捣固车	automatic lifting-lining-tamping train
自动终端信息业务	automatic terminal information service (ATIS)
自动终止条款	automatic termination clause
自动重合闸	auto-reclosing
自动转账服务	automatic transfer service
自负额	deductible
自负额条款	excess clause
自负风险	own risk
自负损害	own damage
自负责任	own risk
自复式按钮	nonstick button
自灌充水	self-priming
自恢复	self recovery
自检	self test
自检校法	self calibration method
自进式锚杆	self-advancing rockbolt
自来水厂	water works
自来水价格	tap water price
自冷	self cooling
自留式压水法	retention pump-in test method
自流平砂浆	self-leveling mortar
自流泉	artesian spring
自流水	artesian water
自流水盆地泉	artesian basin spring
自流装车	loading by gravity
自律机	autonomous computer
自密实混凝土	self-compacting concrete
自耦变压器	auto-transformer

自耦变压器所　auto-transformer post（ATP）
自耦变压器中线　neutral wire of auto-transformer
自然保护区　natural reserve
自然边界测量　natural boundary survey
自然材料　natural materials
自然采光　daylighting
自然沉淀　plain sedimentation
自然底数　natural base, base of natural logarithm
自然地理　physical geography
自然电场法　natural electric field method
自然电位法　spontaneous potential method, self-potential method
自然防渗　natural anti-seepage
自然风险　natural risk, physical risk
自然风险因素　physical hazard
自然拱　natural arch
自然滑坡　natural landslide
自然恢复期　spontaneous recovery period
自然接地体　natural earth electrode
自然扩散法　natural diffusion method
自然排风　natural exhaust
自然排烟　natural smoke exhaust
自然人　natural person
自然损耗　natural wastage, fair wear and tear
自然条件　natural conditions, physical condition
自然通风　natural ventilation
自然物质条件　natural physical conditions
自然养护　natural curing
自然灾害　natural disaster
自然灾害及异物侵限监测系统
　　natural disaster and foreign object intrusion monitoring system
自然灾害损失　loss from natural disaster
自然增长　accrue
自然增值　accretion, unearned increment
自然障碍　physical obstruction
自然资源　natural resources
自稳　self-support
自我保险　self-insurance
自校　self-correcting
自卸卡车　dumper, dump truck, tip lorry
自卸汽车　dump truck
自行设计　design in-house
自营（自建）工程　force account, direct labour
自由裁量权　discretion
自由测站边角交会法
　　free station linear intersection method
自由度　degree of freedom
自由段　free section
自由兑换货币　free convertible currency
自由兑换外汇　free foreign exchange
自由港　free port, open port, free-trade port
自由货币　free currency
自由浸水法　free water immersion method
自由竞争　free competition
自由落锤　drop hammer
自由贸易区　free trade area
自由膨胀率　free swelling ratio
自由射流　free jet
自由水　free water
自由网　free network
自由网平差　adjustment of free network
自由振动　free vibration
自由振动法　free vibration method
自由振动试验　free vibration test
自有资金　own fund
自愈环电路　self-healing ring circuit
自愿保险　voluntary insurance
自愿免赔额　voluntary deductibles
自愿清偿　voluntary liquidation
自粘防水卷材
　　self-adhesive waterproofing membrane
自诊断　self diagnosis
自诊断法　self-diagnosis method
自振频率　natural vibration frequency
自振周期　natural vibration period
自重　dead weight
自重湿陷系数　coefficient of self-weight collapsibility
自重压力　gravity pressure
自重应力　self-weight stress
自主选择终止　optional termination
自阻抗　self-impedance
自钻式锚杆　self-drilling rockbolt
自钻式旁压仪　self-boring pressure meter
字面解释　literal interpretation
恣意行为　reckless misconduct
纵波　longitudinal wave
纵波波速　longitudinal wave velocity
纵断层　longitudinal fault
纵断面　profile
纵断面设计　profile design
纵断面图　profile diagram
纵谷　longitudinal valley
纵梁　stringer, longitudinal beam
纵列配置　longitudinal arrangement
纵列式　longitudinal layout
纵列式编组站　longitudinal type marshalling yard, longitudinal type classification yard
纵列式区段站　longitudinal type district station
纵向缝　longitudinal seam

纵向钢筋	longitudinal reinforcing bar, longitudinal reinforcement bar, longitudinal bar
纵向谷	longitudinal valley
纵向加劲肋	longitudinal stiffener
纵向接缝	longitudinal joint
纵向力	longitudinal force
纵向梁	longitudinal beam
纵向盲管	longitudinal filter pipe
纵向排水设备	longitudinal drainage device
纵向偏差	longitudinal deviation
纵向沙丘	longitudinal dune
纵向受拉钢筋应变不均匀系数	nonuniformity coefficient of tensile steel strain
纵向水平支撑	longitudinal horizontal bracing
纵向撕裂力	vertical tear force
纵向拖拉法	erection by longitudinal traction method
纵向位移	longitudinal displacement
纵轴	vertical axis
总包合同	main contract
总包价格	lump sum price
总保险单	master policy
总变化系数	peak variation factor
总布置图	general arrangements
总部	headquarters, head office, principal office
总部费用	head office cost
总部管理费	general overhead, head office overhead
总裁	president
总采购通告	general procurement notice
总成本	complete cost, total cost
总承包合同	general contract, main contract
总代理	general agency
总代理人	general agent
总贷款	overall loan
总氮	total nitrogen (TN)
总抵押	general mortgage
总额	total amount
总发电量	gross generation
总费用	total cost
总分类账	key ledger
总分类账户	general ledger account
总概算	total budgetary estimate
总概(预)算	total budgetary estimate (budget)
总工程师	chief engineer, engineer in chief
总公司	head office parent company, main office
总功率	total power
总估算	total estimate
总估算表	sheet of total estimate
总估算汇总表	summary sheet of total estimate
总顾问	principal consultant
总管	main
总和	sum
总会计师	accountant general, controller
总价	total price, allin price
总价成本	lump sum cost
总价付款	lump sum payment
总价合同	lump sum contract
总监理工程师	chief supervisor, general foreman
总碱度	general alkalinity
总碱量	total alkali content
总建筑面积	gross floor area, overall floorage
总建筑师	chief architect
总进度计划	master programme, master schedule
总经理	general manager, managing director, president
总经销	exclusive distribution
总控制账户	master control account
总矿化度	total mineralization
总括保险单	blanket policy
总括保证	blanket bond
总括条款	umbrella article
总括性利率	all-in rate
总磷	total phosphorus (TP)
总领班	chief foreman
总贸易体系	general trade system
总配线架	main distribution frame (MDF)
总平面	general layout
总平面布置围	general layout
总平面设计	site planning
总平面图	master plan
总铅量	total lead
总清单	master list
总设计师	chief designer
总伸长率	percentage of total elongation
总时差	total float time, total float
总收入	gross income, total income
总收益	gross earnings
总数	amount, sum
总酸度	total acidity
总体布置图	general plan, general arrangement drawings
总体规定	general specification
总体规划	general plan
总体计划	umbrella programme
总体设计	general design, overall design
总体说明书	general description
总体要求	general requirements
总体预测	macro-forecast
总投资	gross investment
总推力	total thrust
总协议	umbrella agreement

总谐波电流　total harmonic current（THC）
总谐波电压　total harmonic voltage（THV）
总谐波畸变率　total harmonic distortion（THD）
总行　main office
总应力　total stress
总应力法　total stress method
总应力分析　total stress analysis
总硬度　general hardness
总预估算　total pre-estimate
总预估算表　sheet of total pre-estimate
总预估算汇总表
　　summary sheet of total pre-estimate
总预算　total budget
总载重吨位　deadweight tonnage（DWT）
总则　general provisions, general articles
总账　general account, ledger gross weight
总支撑力　total supporting force
总装模型　assembly model
总咨询师　principal consultant
综合保单　comprehensive policy
综合变更控制　integrated change control
综合布线　premises distribution system
综合部分负荷性能系数
　　integrated part load value（IPLV）
综合超前地质预报
　　comprehensive advance geological prediction
综合措施　comprehensive measures
综合单价　comprehensive unit price
综合单价法　comprehensive unit price method
综合法测图　photo planimetric method of photogrammetric mapping
综合防雷　integrated lightning protection
综合费用　general expense
综合分析　comprehensive analysis
综合负荷贯通线
　　run-through power line of comprehensive loads
综合概（预）算
　　comprehensive budgetary estimate（budget）
综合工程地质图
　　comprehensive engineering geological map
综合工费　comprehensive expense of labors
综合工费标准
　　standard of comprehensive expense of labors
综合工费类别
　　category of comprehensive expense of labors
综合估算　comprehensive estimate
综合估算表　sheet of comprehensive estimate
综合估算汇总表
　　summary sheet of comprehensive estimate
综合观测点　comprehensive observation point

综合管线图　synthesis plan of pipelines
综合计算法　comprehensive calculation method
综合价格　composite price
综合架　composite rack
综合监控室　control room
综合检测　comprehensive inspection
综合检测车　comprehensive inspection car
综合检测车库　comprehensive inspection car shed
综合检测列车　comprehensive inspection train
综合交通枢纽　integrated transport terminal
综合接地　integrated earthing
综合接地系统　integrated earthing system
综合接入设备　Integrated Access Device（IAD）
综合解决办法　compound settlement
综合开发　comprehensive development
综合勘察　integrated investigation
综合客运交通枢纽
　　comprehensive passenger traffic terminal/hub
综合利用项目　multipurpose project
综合楼　comprehensive building
综合能耗　comprehensive energy consumption
综合企业　complex
综合汽车保单
　　comprehensive automobile liability policy
综合生活污水　comprehensive sewage（wastewater）
综合视频监控　integrated video surveillance
综合收益表　consolidated income statement
综合水文地质图
　　integrated hydrogeological map
综合税率　composite rate of tax
综合索赔　compound claim
综合维修　comprehensive maintenance
综合维修车间
　　comprehensive maintenance workshop
综合维修工区
　　comprehensive maintenance workshop/work area
综合物价指数　overall price index
综合物探　integrated geophysical prospecting
综合显示屏　information display
综合显示系统　passenger information display system
综合险　all risks（A.R.）, wrap-up
综合性货场　comprehensive goods yard
综合性计划　umbrella programme
综合选线　comprehensive railway location, integrated route selection
综合压水试验　comprehensive water pump-in test
综合业务数字网
　　integrated service digital network（ISDN）
综合一览表　comprehensive list
综合引入柜　comprehensive lead-in cabinet

综合预估算　comprehensive pre-estimate
综合预估算表　sheet of comprehensive pre-estimate
综合预估算汇总表　summary sheet of comprehensive pre-estimate
综合预算　comprehensive budget
综合运输　multimodal transport
综合责任保单　comprehensive general liability policy
综合招标文件　comprehensive tender documents
综合指标法　comprehensive index method
综合指数　composite index
综合质量评定　overall quality assessment
综合治理　comprehensive treatment
综合自动化　integrated automation
综合自动化系统　integrated automation system
综述　overview
走滑　strike-slip
走廊　passage
走廊回风　air return through corridor
走私　smuggle
走私货　contraband
走线架　cable tray
走向　trend, strike
走向断层　strike fault
走向节理　strike joint
走行距离　running distance
走行时分　running time
走行线　running track
足尺模型　full-size model
租船　charter
租船方　charter party
租船合同　charter contract, charter party
租船人　charterer
租船运费　chartered freight
租船运输　shipping by chartering
租购　hire purchase, installment buying
租借　hire, lease, rent
租借权　lease, leasehold, tenancy
租借物　leasehold
租金　rent, rental
租金收入　rental
租赁　lease, hire, rent
租赁保函　leasing guarantee
租赁公司　leasing company
租赁购买　lease purchase
租赁合同　contract of lease, contract of hire
租赁权　leasehold
租赁人　tenant
租赁融资　lease financing
租期　chartered period, tenancy, term of lease, lease, leasehold

租让协议　concession agreement
租用　hire, rent
租用费　lease charges
租用条件　conditions of hire
租用土地　leased land
租用协议书　agreement for hire, agreement of lease
租约　lease, lease agreement, agreement for hire
族库　family library
阻火圈　firestop collar
阻抗　impedance
阻抗电压　impedance voltage
阻抗复合消声器　impedance muffler
阻抗元件　impedance component
阻力功　resistance work
阻力系数　resistance coefficient
阻尼比　damping ratio
阻尼因数　damping factor
阻尼振动　damped vibration
阻燃　flame retardant
阻燃材料　flame retardant material
阻燃防水卷材　fire-retardant asphalt sheet
阻燃剂　flame retardant
阻燃沥青　fire-retardant asphalt
阻塞比　blockage ratio
阻性消声器　dissipative muffler
阻锈剂　rust inhibitor
组合　combination
组合道岔　combined turnouts
组合电器　switchgear
组合调车进路测试　integrated shunting route test
组合端子　terminals of a unit block
组合钢模板　combined steel formwork
组合构件　combined member
组合柜　unit block rack
组合继电器　combination relay
组合架　unit block assembly rack
组合梁　built-up girder, composite girder
组合梁桥　composite girder bridge
组合楼盖　composite floor
组合式电气集中联锁　unit-block type relay interlocking
组合式桥台　composite abutment
组合式枢纽　combined-type junction terminal
组合式信号机构　modular type signal mechanism
组合式辙叉　assembled frog, built-up common crossing
组合屋架　composite roof truss
组合系数　coefficient of combination
组呼号码　group call number (GCN)
组呼寄存器　group call register (GCR)

Z

组拼式架桥机　assembly type girder-erecting machine
组匣　modular block
组匣端子　terminals of a modular block
组匣柜　modular block rack
组织分解结构　organizational breakdown structure
组织角色　organizational roles
组装　assembly
组装式制冷设备　assembling refrigeration device
钻爆法　drill and blast method
钻弓　collapse of pantograph
钻机　drilling rig
钻架　drilling rig
钻井　drilled well, well drilling
钻探工程测量　drilling engineering survey
钻具组　drilling set
钻孔　borehole
钻孔变形计法试验　test of borehole deformation
钻孔机　driller
钻孔排水　drainage by borehole drilling
钻孔偏斜率　borehole deflection rate
钻孔取芯　core drilling
钻孔取芯法　core-drilling method
钻孔取芯机　core-drilling machine
钻孔瓦斯涌出初速度法　drilling gas gushing initial velocity method
钻孔位置测量　hole position survey
钻孔直径　hole size
钻孔桩　bored pile, drilled pile
钻井平台　drilling platform
钻石机　stone driller
钻探　drilling
钻探日志　boring log
钻探设备　boring rig
钻头　drill bit
钻屑指标法　drilling chip index method
钻芯法　core drilling method
最不利计算荷载　most unfavorable calculated load
最大常用制动　maximum service brake
最大超高允许值　maximum allowable superelevation
最大持续工作电流　maximum continuous working current
最大持续运行电压　maximum continuous operating voltage
最大冲击负荷　maximum impact load
最大点超挖量　maximum point overexcavation
最大分子吸水率　maximum molecular water-absorption rate
最大风速　maximum wind speed
最大负荷电流　maximum load current
最大附加应力限值　limiting value of maximum subsidiary stress
最大干密度　maximum dry density
最大公称粒径　nominal maximum aggregate size
最大轨温变化幅度　maximum variation of rail temperature
最大金额　maximum amount
最大孔隙比　maximum void ratio
最大粒径　maximum size
最大量　maximum amount
最大挠度　maximum deflection
最大赔偿额　maximum liability, maximum compensation
最大偏差　maximum deviation
最大平面主应力　maximum plane principal stress
最大坡度　maximum gradient
最大起重量　maximum hoisting capacity
最大曲线半径　maximum radius of curve
最大熵法　maximum entropy method
最大声级　maximum sound level
最大时用水量　maximum hourly water consumption
最大输出功率　maximum output power
最大竖曲线半径　maximum radius of vertical curve
最大瞬时风速　maximum instantaneous wind speed
最大限制信号　most restrictive signal
最大应力幅　maximum stress range
最大涌水量　maximum water inflow
最大允许入口速度　maximum allowable entry speed
最大允许信号　most permission signal
最大值　maximum value
最低保险费　minimum premium
最低保证金　minimum deposit
最低报价　lowest offer, floor bid
最低标　lowest bid (tender)
最低额　minimum amount
最低罚款　minimum fine
最低轨温　minimum rail temperature
最低合闸电压　minimum closing voltage
最低价格　floor price, bottom price, minimum price
最低价投标人　lowest bidder (tenderer)
最低气温　minimum temperature
最低水位　lowest water level
最低限价　price floor
最低限速　minimum speed limit
最低预付保险费　minimum deposit
最低支付限额　minimum amount of payment
最低值　threshold, minimum,
最多风向　dominant wind direction
最高保额条款　peak value clause
最高保证价格　maximum guaranteed price

最高标价	highest bid, bid ceiling
最高成本	cost ceiling
最高成本限价合同	guaranteed maximum cost contracts
最高法院	supreme court
最高轨温	maximum rail temperature
最高级别会谈	summit talk
最高价格	price ceiling
最高气温	maximum temperature
最高气压标准	highest air pressure standard
最高日供水量	maximum daily water supply
最高容许浓度	maximum permissible concentration
最高水位	highest water level
最高限额	ceiling amount, maximum limit
最高限价	ceiling price
最高行车速度	highest running speed
最后成本	final cost
最后的支付	final payment, complete payment
最后检查	final inspection
最后进价法	last invoice price method
最后决策人	final decision maker
最后通牒	ultimatum
最惠国待遇	most-favoured-nation treatment
最惠国关税率	most-favoured-nation tariff rates
最惠国条款	most-favoured-nation clause
最佳掺合料	best mineral admixture
最佳掺量	optimum dosage
最佳配比	optimum mix proportion
最近相关应答器组	last relevant balise group
最冷月平均气温	average temperature of the coldest month
最热月平均气温	average temperature of the hottest month
最热月平均温度	mean temperature in the hottest month
最弱边	weakest side
最弱点	weakest point
最晚开工日期	late start date
最晚日期	latest date
最限制模式曲线	most restrictive mode curve
最限制速度曲线	most restrictive speed profile (MRSP)
最小二乘法	least square method
最小二乘平差	least squares adjustment
最小服务水头	minimum service head
最小干密度	minimum dry density
最小净高	minimum clear height
最小净距	minimum clearance
最小可用接收电平	minimum available receiving level
最小孔隙比	minimum pore ratio
最小拉断荷载	the minimum breaking load
最小模型单元	minimal model unit
最小平面主应力	minimum plane principal stress
最小坡段长度	minimum length of grade section
最小曲线半径	minimum radius of curve
最小竖曲线半径	minimum radius of vertical curve
最小行车间隔	minimum headway
最小值	minimum value
最小转弯半径	minimum turning radius
最易行车	easiest rolling car
最优含水量	optimum moisture content
最优含水率	optimum water content
最优惠利率	prime rate
最优批量	economic lot size, optimum lot size
最早开工日期	early start date
最终报表	final statement
最终报表草案	draft final statement
最终报表草稿	draft final statement
最终裁决	final verdict
最终产品	end-product
最终沉降	final settlement
最终发票	final invoice
最终付款	final payment
最终估算	final estimate
最终价格	final price
最终结账单	statement of final account
最终进度	definitive schedule
最终竣工	final completion
最终竣工证书	final completion certificate
最终目的港	final destination
最终设计	final design
最终受益人	ultimate beneficiary
最终损失	ultimate loss
最终验收	final acceptance
最终验收证书	final acceptance certificate
最终用户	end user
最终账目	final account
最终证书	final certificate
最终支付证书	final payment certificate (FPC), certificate of final payment
最终仲裁	terminal arbitration
醉汉林	drunken forest
遵守法律	compliance with laws
遵守国际惯例	follow the international practice
遵守合同	compliance with the contract, abide by the counteract, keep a contract
遵守协议	abide by the agreement
遵循判例原则	principle of stare decisis
左开道岔	left hand turnout
左右视差	horizontal parallax

佐藤邦明非稳定流式　Misaki Sato Kuniki unsteady-state flow formula
作废　cancel, cancellation, become null and void, stand void
作业层　operating team
作业干扰　operation disturbance
作业工程量表　operational bill of quantities
作业过程回放　operation process playback
作业计划　plan of operations
作业交底　operation instruction
作业进度安排　scheduling of activities
作业进度表　schedule of activities
作业描述　job description
作业区　operation area
作业日志　job log
作业手持台　operational purpose handset (OPH)
作业台架　operation platform
作业循环　job cycle
作用　action
作用半径　action radius
作用代表值　representative value of an action
作用的标准值　standard value of actions
作用的代表值　representative value of actions
作用的设计值　design value of actions
作用的组合　action combination
作用（荷载）　action (load)
作用距离　contact length
作用设计值　design value of an action
作用效应　action effect
作用效应分项系数　partial factor of action effect
作用效应基本组合　fundamental combination for action effects
作用效应偶然组合　accidental combination of action effects
作用效应系数　coefficient of action effect
作用效应组合　combination of action effects
作用组合　combination of actions
坐标　coordinates
坐标方位角　coordinate azimuth
坐标格网　coordinate grid
坐标系　coordinate system
坐标系统　coordinate system
坐标增量　coordinate increment
坐标增量闭合差　closing error in coordinate increment
坐标中误差　mean square error of coordinates
坐标转换　coordinate transformation
座式继电器　shelf-type relay, desk type relay
做功行程　power stroke

Z

PART II

英汉部分

A

a done deal 两讫
A. C. electric method 交流电法
Advanced Audio Coding-Low Delay（AAC-LD）
　高级音频编码技术—低延迟规格
abandon 撤销
abandoned assets 废弃资产
abandoned property 废弃财产
abandoned works 废弃工程
abandonee 财产受领人,受委付人
abandonment of appeal 放弃上诉
abandonment of claim 放弃索赔权
abandonment of contract 放弃合同
abandonment of right 放弃权利
abate a price 还价,降价,减价
abatement 冲销
abatement of action 撤销诉讼
abatement of debt 减轻债务
abatement of smoke and dust 消烟除尘
abatement of tax 减税
abatvoix 吸音板
abbreviated drawing 简图
abeyance 产权待定,暂缓
abide 坚持
abide by the agreement 遵守协议
abide by the counteract 遵守合同
ability to monitor contract 监督合同能力
ability to pay 偿付能力,支付能力,购买力
ability to pay tax 纳税能力
ability to work 工作能力
abnormal 异常的
abnormal cost
　非正常成本,反常费用,特别成本
abnormal depreciation
　特别折旧,反常贬值
abnormal gains 非正常收益
abnormal intensity 烈度异常
abnormal intensity area 烈度异常区
abnormal loss 非正常损失

abnormal profit
　非正常利润,反常利润,特别利润
abnormal risk 特殊风险
abnormality 异常
above par 溢价
abrasion 磨损
abrasion environment 磨蚀环境
abrasion geomorphy 海蚀地貌
abrasion resistance 抗磨损性,耐磨性
abrasion tester 磨耗仪
abrasive disc 磨片
abrasive machining of rail support stand
　承轨台磨削加工
abroad 海外
abrogate the original contract 废除原合同
abrupt change of soil layer 土层突变
abscissa 横坐标
abscissa axis 横轴
absence of proof 缺乏证据
absolute acceptance 绝对承担,无条件接受
absolute advantage 绝对优势
absolute braking distance 绝对制动距离
absolute calibration method 绝对标定法
absolute closure difference 绝对闭合差
absolute condition 绝对条件
absolute deductible 绝对免赔额
absolute endorsement 单纯背书,无条件背书
absolute error 绝对误差
absolute flying height 绝对航高
absolute humidity 绝对湿度
absolute interest 绝对权益
absolute liability 绝对责任
absolute orientation 绝对定向
absolute orientation element 绝对定向元素
absolute priority 绝对优先权
absolute quota 绝对配额
absolute signal 绝对信号
absolute title 绝对产权

absolute (clean)-acceptance 单纯承兑
absorb the price difference 分担差价
absorbancy 吸光度
absorbed cost 已分摊成本
absorber 减振器,吸收器
absorption 吸取
absorption cost 完全成本
absorption refrigerating machine
　吸收式制冷机
absorption refrigeration cycle
　吸收式制冷循环
absorption water content 吸附水含量
absorptive capacity 吸收能力
abstract 提要,介绍简况,摘要
abstract of account 账目摘要
abstract of particulars 细则
abstract of title 产权归属说明书
abstract quotation 报价摘要
abundance of capital 资金充足
abuse 滥用
abuse of authority 滥用职权
abuse of credit 滥用信用
abuse of law 滥用法律
abuse of power 滥用权力
abutment 桥台
abutment cap 台帽
abutment stem 台身
abutment strengthening method by constructing
　new auxiliary retaining wall
　桥台新建辅助挡土墙加固法
abutment with cantilevered retaining wall
　耳墙式桥台
abutting joint 对接接头
abyssal facies 深海相
AC continuous track circuit
　交流连续式轨道电路
AC counting coded track circuit
　交流计数电码轨道电路
AC lead-in distribution box 交流引入配电箱
AC panel 交流盘,交流屏
AC point switch 交流转辙机
AC power supply 交流电源
AC power supply incoming wire 交流供电进线
AC power supply panel 交流电源屏
AC relay 交流继电器
AC track circuit 交流轨道电路
AC two element two position relay
　交流二元二位继电器
AC two element two position track circuit
　交流二元二位轨道电路

AC voltage withstand test 交流耐压试验
AC/DC distribution box 交直流配电箱
AC/DC power system 交直流系统
AC/DC relay 交直流继电器
accessible housing 无障碍住房
accessible passage 无障碍通路
accelerate 加快速度
accelerated aging 加速老化
accelerated and decelerated retarder
　加减速顶
accelerated completion
　加速竣工,提前完工
accelerated cost recovery system
　加速成本回收制度
accelerated curing of concrete
　混凝土快速养护
accelerated depreciation 加速折旧
accelerated method of depreciation
　加速折旧法
accelerating admixture 促凝外加剂
accelerating agent 速凝剂
accelerating grade 加速坡
accelerating mortar-bar method
　快速砂浆棒法
acceleration 加速度,加速施工
acceleration clause
　加速偿还条款,提前偿付条款
acceleration order 加速施工指令
accelerator 促凝剂,机械搅拌澄清池
accelerometer 加速度计
accept 承兑,承诺
accept a claim 接受索赔
accept a quotation 接受报价
accept an invitation 接受邀请
accept an offer 接受发盘
accept an order 接受订单
accept insurance 承保
accept order 接受订货
accept the bid (tender) 接受投标
acceptable 合格的,可接受的
acceptable bid 可接受报价
acceptable date 可接受日期
acceptable deviation 可接受的偏离
acceptable local procedures 可接受的当地程序
acceptable materials 合格材料
acceptable price 可接受价格
acceptable product 合格产品
acceptable quality 合格质量
acceptable seismic hazard
　可接受的地震危害

acceptable variation　可接受的变更
acceptance　承保,承兑,承诺,验收
acceptance amount　承兑金额
acceptance bank　承兑银行
acceptance bill　承兑汇票,承兑票据
acceptance by owner (employer)
　业主认可
acceptance certificate of the contract goods
　合同货物验收证书
acceptance certificate　验收证书
acceptance commission　承兑汇票手续费
acceptance contract　承兑合同
acceptance credit
　承兑汇票,承兑信贷,承兑信用证
acceptance criteria　验收准则
acceptance for carriage　承运
acceptance for honor　接受承兑
acceptance letter of credit　承兑信用证
acceptance measurement of roadway
　巷道验收丈量
acceptance of a project　工程验收
acceptance of bribes　受贿
acceptance of offer　接受报价
acceptance of risks　承担风险
acceptance of the bid (tender)　接受投标书
acceptance of works　工程验收
acceptance payable　应付承兑票据
acceptance rate　票据贴现率
acceptance receivable　应收承兑汇票
acceptance record　验收记录
acceptance register　承兑票据登记簿
acceptance report　验收报告
acceptance result　验收结论
acceptance specification　验收规范
acceptance test　交接试验,验收试验
accepted bill　已承兑汇票
accepted contract amount
　接受的合同款额,中标合同价
accepted letter of credit　已承兑信用证
accepted programme　批准的进度计划
accepter　承诺人,接受人
accepting bank　承兑银行
accepting house　承兑商行
acceptor　承兑人,承付人,承诺人
access　进入权
access control　门禁
access control card　门禁卡
access control system　门禁系统
access cover　检修盖
access device　接入设备
access door　检查门
access gateway (AG)　接入网关
access layer　接入层
access network (AN)　接入网
access node　接入节点
access right　进入权
access road　通道,通所道路
access route　进场路线
access to entrance and exit　出入口通道
access to site　进入现场
accessible facilities　无障碍设施
accessible trench　通行地沟
accession tax　财产增益税
accessories　配件
accessory contract　附加合同,附约
accessory debtor　从属债务人
accident　偶然事件,事故,意外事故
accident compensation　意外事故赔偿
accident insurance　事故保险,意外事故保险
accident investigation　事故调查
accident narrative　事故描述
accident prevention officer　意外事件预防员
accident prevention　安全措施,事故预防
accident report　事故报告
accident to workmen　人身事故
accident work injury　工伤事故
accidental　意外的
accidental action　偶然作用
accidental bodily injury　人身意外伤亡
accidental combination of action effects
　作用效应偶然组合
accidental damage　意外损害
accidental load　偶然荷载
accidental loss　意外损失
accommodation　膳食供应,提供方便,融通
accommodation bill　融通票据
accommodation camp　生活区
accommodation check　融通支票
accommodation endorsement　融通背书
accommodation endorser　融通背书人
accommodation note　融通票据
accommodation paper　融通票据
accomplished bill of lading　已提货提单
accord and satisfaction　合意解决
according to　按照
account as recorded in a ledger
　分类账科目
account　账,账户,账目
account balance　账户余额
account balanced　收支两讫,账户结平

A

account bill	账单
account book	账簿
account chart	会计科目表
account classification	账户分类
account code	账户代号
account conversion	账户转换
account day	过户结账日,结算日
account dealing	记账交易
account form of balance sheet	账户式资产负债表
account heading	会计科目
account in transit	在途账
account in trust	信托账户
account number	账号
account of receipts and payments	收支表
account paid	已付款
account payable	应付账款
account payable ledger	应付账款明细账
account payable register	应付账款登记簿
account purchase	赊购
account receivable	应收账款
account receivable financing	应收账款融资
account receivable ledger	应收账款明细账
account title	会计科目
account transfer	账户转账
account transfer memo	转账通知单
account turnover	账户成交量,账户营业额
accountability matrix	问责矩阵
accountability system for construction safety	安全生产责任制
accountability verification	责任证明
accountancy	会计工作
accountant	会计师
accountant general	总会计师
accountant in charge	会计主管
accounting	核算,会计,会计工作
accounting changes	会计变更
accounting clerk	记账员
accounting control	会计控制
accounting convention	会计惯例
accounting document	会计凭证
accounting entity	会计单位,会计主体,会计分录
accounting equation	会计等式,会计恒等式
accounting firm	会计师事务所
accounting income	账面收益
accounting law	会计法
accounting manager	会计主管
accounting method	会计方法
accounting period	会计分期,会计期间,结算期
accounting personnel	会计人员
accounting practice	会计惯例
accounting principles	会计原理
accounting procedure	会计程序
accounting records	会计记录
accounting released	公布账目
accounting report	会计报表
accounting statement	会计报表
accounting supervision	会计监督
accounting supervisor	会计主管
accounting unit	会计单位,记账单位
accounting valuation	会计计价
accounting voucher	会计凭证
accounting year	会计年度
accounts receivable collection period	应收账款回收期,应收账款周转天数
accounts receivable turnover	应收账款周转率
accredited	被委任的
accredited party	被授权方
accretion	自然增值
accrue	增长,应收,自然增长
accrual basis	权责发生制
accrual basis accounting	权责发生制会计
accrual date	应收应付日期
accrual of interest	应付利息
accrued account	应计账户
accrued and deferred accounts	应计和递延账户
accrued asset	增值资产
accrued charge	应计费用
accrued depreciation	应计折旧
accrued income	应计收益
accrued interest	累计利息,应计利息
accrued liabilities	应计负债
accrued payroll	应付工资
accrued rights	既有权利
accumulate	堆积
accumulated amount	累计金额
accumulated cost	累计成本
accumulated depletion	累计折耗
accumulated depreciation	累积折旧,累计折旧
accumulated deviations	累计偏差
accumulated funds	积累资金,公积金
accumulated loss	累计损失
accumulated percentile sound level	累积百分声级
accumulated percentile Z vibration level	累积百分Z振级
accumulated profit	累计利润
accumulated surplus	累计盈余

accumulated temperature 累积温度	acoustic leakage 漏声
accumulation landform 堆积地貌	acoustic logging 声波测井
accumulation landslide 堆积层滑坡	acoustic panel of sound barrier 声屏障单元板
accumulation of risk 风险累积	acoustic parameter 声学参数
accumulation plain 堆积平原	acoustic performance 声学性能
accumulation terrace 堆积阶地	acoustic perspective intersection method
accuracy 精度	声波透视交会法
accuracy class 精确度等级	acoustic sounding 声学探测
accuracy rating 准确度	acoustic velocity 声速
accurately weighing 准确称取	acoustic velocity logging 声速测井
accuse 控诉,起诉,指控	acoustic wave method 声波法
accuse falsely 诬告	acoustic wave reflection method 声波反射法
accused person 被告	acoustical board 隔音板,吸声板
accuser 控告人,控告方	acoustics 声学
access control 访问控制	acquire 获得
access route 进场道路	acquiring enterprise 购方企业
acetylene welding 乙炔焊接,气焊	acquiring party 购买方,获得方
achieve 达到,获得	acquisition 获得
achievement of progress 完成进度	acquisition control 采购控制
acicular 针状	acquisition cost 购置成本
acicular particle 针状颗粒	acquisition evaluation 采购评估
acid erosion 酸性侵蚀	acquisition of property 购置财产
acid pasting 酸溶法	acquisition of technology 技术引进
acid rain 酸雨	acquisition unit 采集单元
acid rain control zone 酸雨控制区	acquittance 债务清偿收据
acid sewage 酸性污水	across-track feeder 跨越轨道馈线
acid storage room 储酸室	act 代理,法案,法令,条例
acid treatment 酸处理	act against duty
acid value 酸值	违反义务行为,违反责任行为
acidic potassium permanganate method	act in excess of authority 越权行为
酸性高锰酸钾法	act of bankruptcy 破产法
acidity 酸度	act of God 天灾
acidity meter 酸度计	act of insolvency 破产法
acidity of strong acid 强酸酸度	act of omission
acidizing 酸化处理	懈怠行为,(法定义务的)不作为
acid-resistant concrete 耐酸混凝土	acting manager 代理经理
acid-resistant material 耐酸材料	action 行为,作用
acid proof material 耐酸材料	action (load) 作用(荷载)
acknowledgement 收货回单,收讫通知书,承认	action combination 作用的组合
acknowledgement button 警惕按钮	action effect 作用效应
acknowledgement center (AC) 确认中心	action for negligence 过失侵权诉讼
acknowledgement lever 警惕手柄	action for possession 占有诉讼
acknowledgment of receipt 回执	action item 诉讼项目
acoustic amplitude logging 声幅测井	action programme 行动纲领
acoustic calibrator 声校准器	action radius 作用半径
acoustic design of sound barrier	activated battery 启动电池
声屏障声学设计	activated carbon adsorption tank 活性炭吸附池
acoustic emission of rock 岩石声发射	activated sludge 活性污泥
acoustic enclosure (shield) 隔声罩	activated sludge process 活性污泥法
acoustic exploration 声波探测	active account 活跃账户

active balance 顺差
active carbon 活性炭
active carbon adsorption 活性炭吸附
active control 主动控制
active cross-section 水流断面
active current 有功电流
active debt 有息债务
active earth pressure 主动土压力
active fault 活动断层,活断层
active fault zone 活动断裂带
active landslide 活动滑坡
active layer 活动层
active layer water 活动层水
active mass damper control system
  主动质量阻尼器控制系统
active mineral 活性矿物
active optical network(AON) 有源光网络
active power 有功功率
active power loss 有功损耗
active region 活动区
activities of project 项目业务
activity 单项活动,活度
activity bill of quantities 单项工程量清单
activity index 活动性指数,活性指数
activity-on-arrow(AOA) 双代号网络
activity-on-node(AON) 单代号网络
actor 行为人
actual additional cost 实际附加成本
actual breach 实际违约
actual cash value 实际现金价值
actual completion time 实际竣工时间
actual cost(AC) 实际成本
actual cost method 实际成本法
actual debt 实际债务
actual delivery 实际交货
actual depreciation 实际折旧
actual goods 存货,现货
actual interest rate 实际利率
actual length of turnout 道岔实际长度
actual loss 实际损失
actual loss ratio 实际损失率
actual point of frog 辙叉心轨尖端
actual price 实际价格
actual profit 实际利润
actual progress 实际进度
actual purchase order price
  实际购货订单价格
actual tare 实际皮重
actual total loss 绝对全损,实际全损
actual value 实际价值

actual weight(A/W) 实际重量
actuary 固定资产统计师,精算师
actuator 执行器
ad damnum clause 损坏赔偿条款
ad hoc arbitration 临时仲裁,特设仲裁
ad valorem bill of lading
  从价提单,货值提单
ad valorem duties 从价税
ad valorem freight 从价运费
ad valorem import duty 从价进口税
ad valorem rate of duty 从价税率
ad valorem tariff 从价关税率
ad valorem tax 从价税
adamantine luster 金刚光泽
adaptable plants 适生植物
adapter box 接头盒
adaptive planning 适应性规划
add 添加
add to one's(tasks/worries) 加重
added-value tax 增值税
added hours 加班工时
added value 增值
addendum 附加物,修改书,补遗
addition 增额,增加
additional 额外的,追加的
additional amount 增加额
additional appropriation 追加拨款
additional assured 附加受保人
additional benchmark 加密基标
additional charge 附加费用
additional charge of electrification
  电气化附加费
additional clause 附加条款
additional conductor 附加导线(电力)
additional contract clauses 附则,合同补充条款
additional cost 新增成本,额外成本,附加费
additional cost of construction in virgin forest area
  原始森林地区额外建设成本
additional cost of construction 额外建设成本
additional cost under special construction condition 特殊施工条件下的附加费用
additional cover 追加保险
additional curve resistance 曲线附加阻力
additional dead load on structure 结构附加恒载
additional expenses 增加费,增加费用
additional fee for construction at night
  夜间施工增加费
additional fee of construction by train operation disturbance 行车干扰施工增加费
additional force 附加力

additional freight	附加运费
additional heat loss	附加耗热量
additional input of labour	增加人工投入
additional load	附加荷载
additional location survey	补充定线测量
additional measure point	补充测点
additional order	追加订单,追加订货
additional payment	额外付款
additional premium	附加保险费,加保费
additional provision	附加条款
additional rate	附加费率,增加费率
additional rate for construction at night	
夜间施工增加费率	
additional rate of electrification	
电气化附加费费率	
additional reinforcing bar	加强钢筋
additional resistance of turnouts	道岔附加阻力
additional risk	附加险
additional safety factor	附加安全系数
additional service	附加服务
additional stress	附加应力
additional survey	补充勘测
additional tensile strength	附加抗拉强度
additional track circuit	附加轨道电路
additional work	额外工作,新增工作,附加工作
additional working condition	附加工况
additive	外加剂
additive constant	加常数
address book	地址簿
address correction	地址更正
address modification	地址变更
address resolution protocol（ARP）	
地址解析协议	
addressee	收件人
addresser	发件人,发信人
add-drop multiplexer（ADM）	分插复用器
add-on	附加
add-on interest	追加利息
adequacy of insurance	保险的完备性
adhere	坚持
adhesion	附着度,黏附性
adhesion contract	附意合同
adhesion of mineral aggregate	
矿物粒料黏附性	
adhesion rate	黏附率
adhesive strength of moist surface	
潮湿基面黏结强度	
adhesive tape	胶带
adhesive-bonded panel	胶合板
adiabatic temperature rise	绝热温升
adit	支洞
adit excavation	洞探
adjacent building	邻近建筑物
adjacent property	邻近物业
adjacent regions	邻近地域
adjacent section interference	邻区段干扰
adjacent track	相邻股道
adjacent turnout	相邻道岔
adjective law	诉讼法,程序法
adjourn	休会
adjudicate	宣判
adjudication	裁决
adjudication division	审判庭
adjudication fee	法庭费用
adjudication order	裁决令
adjudication rule	裁决规则
adjudicator	裁决人
adjust	理算
adjustable crank	可调曲柄
adjustable fixed price contract	
可调价的固定价格合同	
adjustable fork head	可调托撑
adjustable interest rate	可变利率
adjustable lump sum price	可调总价
adjustable pedestal	可调底座
adjustable steel tie	可调节拉结件
adjustable switch operating rod	密贴调整杆
adjustable unit price	可调单价
adjustable-rate mortgage	可调利率抵押贷款
adjusted price	调整后的价格
adjusted value	平差值
adjuster	海损理算人
adjusting bracket	调节架
adjusting of cross level	整正水平
adjusting voltage	调整电压
adjustment	调整,理算
adjustment at once	一次调整
adjustment letter	海损精算书
adjustment multiplier	调整系数
adjustment of average	海损理算
adjustment of claim for general average	
共同海损赔偿理算	
adjustment of claim	赔偿理算,索赔理算
adjustment of free network	自由网平差
adjustment of general average	共同海损理算
adjustment of rail gaps	调整铁轨间隙
adjustment state	调整状态
adjustments for changes in cost	
成本变动调整	
adjustments for changes in law	立法变动调整

admeasurement 测量
admeasurement type of contract 合同计量类型
administering authority 行政当局
administration 行政部门,行政管理
administration cost 管理成本
administration cost of employer
    建设单位管理费
administration law 行政法
administration measure 行政措施
administration of assignment 委派管理
administration order 行政命令
administration practice 管理规定,行政惯例
administration rules 管理规定
administrative department 行政部门
admistrative management 行政管理
administrative overhead 行政管理费
administrative personnel 行政管理人员
administrative staff 行政管理人员
administrative tribunal 行政法庭
administrator 行政管理人员
administrator in a bankrupt estate
    破产产业管理人
administrable risk 可管理风险
admissible document 可作证据的文件
admissible evidence 可接受证据
admission 承认
admix 混合
admixture 掺合料
admixture and chemical processing method
    置换、掺料与化学处理法
adsorbent 吸附剂
adulterate 掺假
advance anchor bolt 超前锚杆
advance appropriation 预拨经费
advance call 预垫款
advance collections 预收款项
advance contribution 先期交款
advance deposit 预付款
advance detection 超前探测
advance drilling forecast method
    超前钻探预报法
advance exploration drilling 超前钻探
advance freight 预付运费
advance geological prediction for tunnel construction 隧道施工超前地质预报
advance grouting 超前预注浆
advance heading 超前导坑
advance heading forecast method
    超前导坑预报法
advance in cash 预付现金

advance locking 预先锁闭
advance payment 预付款
advance payment bond 预付款担保
advance payment for contract 合同预付款
advance payment security 预付款保证
advance premium 预缴保费
advance received account 暂收款账户
advance remittance 预付汇款
advance sample 货样
advance small duct 超前小导管
advance support 超前支护
advance warning 预先警告
advance works 前期工程,前期工作
advanced certified final drawings(ACF)
    供货厂商先期确认图
advanced certified vendors'drawings
    供货厂商先期确认图
advanced payment certificate 预付款证明
advanced payment guarantee 预付款保函
advanced planning 前期规划
advanced repair 高级检修
advanced treatment 深度处理
advancement 进展,预付
advances to subcontractor 预付分包商款
advancing 价格上涨
advantage 优点,优势
adverse balance of international trade
    国际贸易逆差
adverse balance of payment 支付逆差
adverse physical conditions 不利自然条件
adverse weather 恶劣天气
adverse weather conditions 不利的天气条件
advertisement for bid(tender) 招标通告
advertisement 通告
advice for collection of documentary bill
    跟单汇票托收委托书
advice note 通知单
advice of arrival 到货通知,抵埠通知
advice of payment 付款通知
adviser 顾问
adviser service 咨询服务
advising 建议
advising bank 通知行
advising charges 通知手续费
advisor 顾问
advisory committee 顾问委员会,咨询委员会
advocate 辩护人,提倡,提倡者,拥护,咨询人员
ad-hoc dispute adjudication board(ad-hoc DAB)
    临时争议评判委员会
aegirine nepheline syenite 霓霞正长岩

aeolian 风成的
aeolian deposit 风积层
aeolian landform 风积地貌
aeolian loess 风成黄土
aeolian mushroom 风蚀蘑菇
aeolian sands 风积沙
aerated concrete 加气混凝土
aeration grit chamber 曝气沉砂池
aeration zone 包气带
aerator 通风装置
aerial cableway 空中索道
aerial earth wire (AeW,GW) 架空地线
aerial photo 航空照片
aerial photogrammetry 航空摄影测量
aerial photographic gap 航空摄影漏洞
aerial photographic absolute gap
 航空摄影绝对漏洞
aerial photographic relative gap
 航空摄影相对漏洞
aerial photographic scale 航空摄影比例尺
aerial photography 航空摄影
aerial photogrammetry 航空摄影测量学
aerial remote sensing 航空遥感
aerial triangulation 空中三角测量
aerobic 好氧
aerobic digestion 好氧消化
aerobic pond 好氧稳定塘
aerobic treatment 好氧处理
aerobic zone 好氧区
aeroconcrete 加气混凝土
aerodynamic drag factor 气动阻力系数
aerodynamic effect 空气动力学效应
aerodynamic force 空气动力,气动力
aerodynamic noise 空气动力性噪声
aerodynamics 空气动力学
aerofilter 空气过滤器
aerosol fire extinguishing agent 气溶胶灭火剂
affidavit 宣誓书
affidavit of claim 索赔书
affidavit of document 文件证明书
affiliate 分公司
affiliate bank 分行
affiliated bank 联营银行
affiliation 附属
affine plotting 变换光束测图
affirmative warranty 确认保证
affix 签署
affordability 承担能力
afloat cargo 已装船货物,路货
afloat goods 已装船货物,路货

after action report (AAR) 后审查
after sight bill 见票后(若干天)付款期票
aftercare engineer 后照管工程师
afterwards backup 后期支护
after-sales service 售后服务
after-tax profit 税后利润
age 龄期
age limit for subsequent safety assessment
 后续安全评估的年限
age of vessel 船龄
ageing resistance 抗老化性
agreement of intent 意向协定
agency 代理,代理机构,代理权,经销商
agency agreement 代理协议
agency commission 代理手续费
agency contract 代理合同
agency fee 代理费
agenda 日程表,议事日程
agent 代理人,代理商,经纪人
agent bank 代理银行
agent firm 代理公司
agent's tort 代理人侵权行为
agglomeratic texture 集块结构
aggravate 加重
aggregate 骨料
aggregate bin 骨料仓
aggregate crushing rate 骨料压碎率
aggregate gradation 骨料级配
aggregate impact toughness 骨料冲击韧度
aggregate liability 累计责任
aggregate limit of indemnity 赔偿总额
aggregate processing plant 骨料加工厂
aggregate segregation 骨料分离
aggregate-cement ratio 骨料水泥比
aggregate limit of liability 累计责任赔偿总限额
aggregation 聚集,汇总
aggressive media 侵蚀性介质
aging 老化
aging coefficient 老化系数
agio 银行手续费,贴水
agitating truck 搅拌车
agmatite 角砾混合岩
Agnotozoic era 元古代
agree 意见一致,达成协议
agreed compensation 约定补偿
agreed final statement 约定最终报表
agreed port of destination 约定目的港
agreed price 议定价格
agreed rate 协定运费率,协定费率
agreed sum 商定金额

agreed terms 商定条件
agreement 协议,协定
agreement amount 协议额
agreement button panel 同意按钮盘
agreement for hire 租赁协议,租用协议书
agreement form 协议书
agreement in writing 书面协议
agreement of dispute resolution 和解协议
agreement of lease 租用协议书
agreement of reimbursement 偿付协议
agreement of understanding 非正式协议
agreement or determination of the claim
 索赔的认可或决定
agricultural irrigation 农田灌溉
ahead of schedule 提前完成计划
aide-memoire 备忘录
air blanket 空气夹层
air blower 鼓风机
air borne sound 空气声
air brick 镂空砖
air bubble spacing 气泡间距
air bubble spacing factor of concrete
 混凝土气泡间距系数
air cargo 空运货物
air cargo insurance 空运保险,空运货物保险
air carrier 空运承运人
air cleanliness 空气洁净度
air cleanliness class 空气洁净度等级
air collector 集气罐
air compressor 空气压缩机,空压机
air compressor cabin 空气压缩机室
air conditioner room 空气调节机房
air conditioning 空调,空气调节
air conditioning engineering 空调工程
air conditioning equipment 空气调节设备
air conditioning purifying system
 净化空调系统
air conditioning system
 空调系统,空气调节系统
air consignment note(ACN)
 空运发货单,航空托运单
air content 空气含量
air cooler 冷气机
air cooling 风冷
air curtain 空气幕
air diffuser 散流器
air diffusion performance index(ADPI)
 空气分布特性指标
air discharge 空气放电
air distributor 空气分布器
air duct 风道
air duct hanger 风管吊架
air duct support 风管支架
air duct system 风管系统
air entrained agent 加气剂
air entraining admixture 引气剂
air entraining agent 引气剂
air freight 航空货运,航空货费,空运货物
air freight receipt 空运收据
air gap 空气间隙
air hammer 气锤
air heater 空气加热器
air hoist 空吊
air humidity 空气湿度
air inlet 进风口
air insulated switchgear(AIS)
 空气绝缘开关柜,空气绝缘组合电器
air insulation 空气绝缘
air leak check with lighting 漏光检测
air leakage 漏风量
air line 航线
air penetration test 空气穿透试验
air permeability 透气量
air pick 风镐
air pipeline pressure governor
 风管路调压设备
air pollutant 空气污染物
air pollution 大气污染
air preheater 空气预热器
air pressure 空气压力
air pressure drilling 风压钻进
air pressure grouting pump 气压灌浆泵
air pressure monitoring device 气压监测设备
air pressure water supply equipment
 气压供水设备
air quality 空气质量
air reservoir 储风罐
air return mode 回风方式
air return through corridor 走廊回风
air route 航线
air source heat pump 空气源热泵
air speed (通风)风速
air supply 送风
air supply from nozzle outlet 喷口送风
air supply from perforated ceiling 孔板送风
air supply mode 送风方式
air switch 空气开关
air system leakage ratio 漏风率
air temperature 气温,空气温度
air tightness layer 气密层

air tightness material　气密性材料
air tightness of building envelope
　建筑围护结构气密性
air tightness test　气密性试验
air transportation all risks　空运一切险
air transportation cargo insurance
　航空运输货物保险
air transportation risks　空运险
airway　航线
air waybill（AWB）　空运提单
air waybill conditions of contract　空运单条款
air waybill terms　空运单条款
airbreak switch　空气开关
airflow organization　气流组织
airfreight　货物空运
airlift　空运
airport tax　机场税
airtight concrete　气密性混凝土
airtight cover　密闭罩
airtight door　密闭门
airtight passage　密闭通道
airtight valve　密闭阀门
air-borne GPS，IMU aided photography
　机载 GPS、IMU 辅助摄影
air-break switch　空气开关
air-circulating oven　鼓风烘箱
air-cooled broken block stone embankment
　碎块石气冷路基
air-cooled condenser　风冷式冷凝器
air-cooled rubble embankment　片石气冷路基
air-cooled unit　风冷机组
air-cushion vibration absorber　空气弹簧隔振器
air-dried soil　风干土
air-pressure water tank　气压水罐
air-raid shelter　防空洞
air-source heat　空气热源
air-vent　通风口
air-way bill　航空货运单
aisle　过道
alarm　报警,告警,警报
alarm at level crossing　道口报警
alarm facilities　报警设施
alarm for a trailed switch　挤岔报警
alarm host　报警主机
alarm resetting　报警复位
alarm terminal　报警终端
alarm valve　报警阀
albitite　钠长岩
alcohol burning method　酒精燃烧法
alcohol　乙醇

aleuritic　粉砂状
Algonkian system　元古界
alienate　产权转移
alignment of track　轨向
alignment　定线；准线,联盟
alkali activity　碱活性
alkali content　碱含量(含碱量)
alkali reactivity of aggregate　骨料的碱活性
alkali reactivity test　碱活性试验
alkali reactivity test of aggregate
　骨料碱活性试验
alkali resistance　耐碱性
alkali syenite　碱性正长岩
alkali trachyte　碱性粗面岩
alkali treatment　碱处理
alkaline battery　碱性蓄电池
alkaline battery storage room　碱性蓄电池间
alkaline saline soil　碱性盐渍土
alkaline sewage　碱性污水
alkalinity　碱度
alkalinity of potassium and sodium
　钾钠碱度
alkali-active aggregate　碱活性骨料
alkali-aggregate reaction　碱—骨料反应
alkali-granite　碱性花岗岩
alkali-silica reaction active mineral
　碱硅酸反应活性矿物
all air system　全空气系统
all expected benefits　全部预期效益
all expected costs　全部预期费用
all risks（a/r,A.R.）　全险,一切险,综合险
all risks contract　一切险合同
all risks insurance　一切险保险
all risks marine insurance　海上综合保险
alliance contract　联盟合同
alliance contractor　联盟承包商
allocate　拨(款)
allocate cost　分摊成本
allocated cost　已分摊成本
allocated locomotives　配属机车
allocation　拨款
allocation factor of service track
　整备线配置系数
allocation of business profits　营业利润分摊
allocation of funds　资金分配
allocation of risks　风险分担
allotment　拨款
allotment advice　拨款通知
allotype　配模
allow　允许

allowable bearing capacity　容许承载力
allowable bending tensile stress
　容许弯曲拉伸应力
allowable cant deficiency　欠超高允许值
allowable cost　允许成本
allowable deformation value　容许变形值
allowable deviation　容许偏差
allowable equipment temperature　容许设备温度
allowable error　容许误差
allowable load　容许荷载
allowable rail temperature drop　容许轨道温降
allowable rail temperature rise　容许轨道温升
allowable ratio of height to sectional thickness
　容许高厚比
allowable scour　容许冲刷
allowable settlement　容许沉降
allowable slenderness ratio of steel member
　钢构件容许长细比
allowable soil pressure　容许土压力
allowable speed　容许速度
allowable strength rating　容许强度检定
allowable stress　容许应力
allowable stress amplitude of fatigue
　疲劳容许应力幅度
allowable stress amplitude　应力幅容许值
allowable stress design method
　容许应力设计法
allowable stress method　容许应力法
allowable temperature difference　容许温差
allowable tensile strain of reinforcement
　钢筋容许拉伸应变
allowable tensile strength　容许抗拉强度
allowable value of deflection of structural members　构件挠度容许值
allowable value of deformation of steel member
　钢构件变形容许值
allowable value of deformation of structural members　构件变形容许值
allowable vibration velocity　允许振速
allowance　补贴,允许
allowance clause　短溢装条款
allowance for bad debts　备抵坏账
allowance for depreciation　折旧备抵,备抵折旧
allowance for maintenance of works
　维修工程津贴
allowance for profit　预留利润
allowance for sales discount　备抵销货折扣
allowance provision　津贴,补助费
alloy rail　合金轨
alluvial deposit　冲积堆

alluvial fan　冲积扇
alluvial flat　河漫滩
alluvial flat facies　河漫滩相
alluvial plain　冲积平原
alluvial soil　冲积土
alluvial-proluvial plain　冲洪积平原
alluviation　冲积
alluvium　冲积土
all-in　混合料
all-in contract　整套承包制合同
all-in labour rate　人工综合单价
all-in material rate　材料综合单价
all-in mechanical plant rate　机械设备综合单价
all-in price　总价
all-in rate　总括性利率
all-purpose financial statement　通用财务报表
all-relay electric interlocking
　继电式电气集中联锁
all-relay interlocking for shunting area
　调车区电气集中联锁
all-relay semi-automatic block　继电半自动闭塞
all-risk policy　一切险保险单
all-weld tensile test　焊缝金属拉伸试验
all-welded steel bridge　全焊钢桥
allocation of responsibility　责任分担
along humping direction　顺驼峰方向
alongside bill of lading　船边交货提单
along-track feeder　合架供电线
flexible arch bridge with rigid tie
　刚性系杆柔性拱桥
alteration　改动,更改
alteration of contract　合同变更
alteration of works　工程变更
altered stress　变异应力
alternate　代理人,交替的
alternate planting shrub　间植灌木
alternating load　交变荷载
alternating-current generator　交流发电机
alternative　备选的
alternative bay construction method　跳仓施工法
alternative bid　备选投标书
alternative circuit　迂回电路
alternative clause　替代条款,替代条文
alternative dispute resolution（ADR）
　争议解决替代方式
alternative duty　选择税
alternative item　备选项目
alternative maintenance　轮修
alternative maintenance at inspection and service point　入所轮修

alternative material and equipment
　替代材料与设备
alternative of financial nature　商务备选方案
alternative offer　备选报价
alternative plan　备选方案
alternative protection circuit　迂回保护电路
alternative provisions　替代条款,替代条文
alternative route　变更进路
alternative solution　替代方案,替代办法
alter　改动,更改
alternator　交流发电机
altitude projection surface　标高投影面
Aluminium Clad Steel Reinforced（ACSR/AS or ACSR/AW）铝包钢芯铝绞线
Aluminium Conductors　铝包钢芯铝绞线
aluminium sheathed　铝护套
aluminium-steel composite conductor rail
　钢铝复合接触轨
aluminum alloy　铝合金
aluminum conductor steel reinforced（ACSR）
　钢芯铝绞线
Al-clad steel stranded wire　铝包钢绞线
Al-Cu transition connector　铜铝过渡设备线夹
amalgamation　合并,混合
amalgamated balance sheet　合并资产负债表
amalgamation of enterprises　企业合并
ambient noise　背景噪声
ambient noise at boundary　厂界环境噪声
ambient temperature　环境温度
ambiguity in document　文件的歧义
ameliorative measures　改良措施
amend　修改,修订,更正,补遗
amendment　修改,修订,更正
amendment advice　修改通知单
amendment of bidding（tender）documents
　招标文件的修改
amendment of contract　修正合同
amendment of letter of credit　信用证修改书
amicable composition　友好解决协议
amicable settlement　友好解决
ammonium chloride-ethanol method
　氯化铵—乙醇法
ammonium persulfate spectrophotometry
　过硫酸铵分光光度法
amorphous body　非晶质体
amorphous texture　非晶质结构
amortization　摊销,分期偿还
amortization amount　摊销量
amortization charge of intangible assets
　无形资产摊销费
amortization loan　分期偿还贷款
amortization of fixed asset　固定资产摊销
amortization rate　摊销率,分期偿还率
amortization schedule　分期偿付计划
amortized mortgage loan　分期偿还抵押贷款
amortizing loan　分期偿还贷款
amount　金额,数额,总数
amount allocated　拨款额;分配额
amount in figures　小写金额
amount in words　大写金额
amount insured　保险金额
amount not recovered　未能收回的金额
amount of a draft　汇票金额
amount of an annuity　年金金额
amount of claim　索赔额,索取额
amount of energy conservation　节能量
amount of insurance　保险金额
amount of money　金额
amount of passenger train sets　车底数
amount of precipitation　降水量
amount of seepage　渗透水量
amount of soil erosion
　水土流失总量,土壤流失量
amount of the credit　信用证金额
amount of waste　损耗量
amount outstanding　未收回金额
amount secured　担保金额
amplifier　功率放大器
amplifying coefficient　增大系数
amplitude　波幅;幅值;振幅
amplitude of snake-like movement
　车辆蛇形摆幅
amplitude vs frequency characteristic
　幅频特性
amplitude-frequency curve　幅频曲线
amplitude-modulation suppression　调幅抑制
amygdaloidal　杏仁状
amygdaloidal structure　杏仁状构造
anaerobic（aerobic）treatment
　厌氧(好氧)处理
anaerobic digestion　厌氧消化
anaerobic pond　厌氧稳定塘
anaerobic zone　厌氧区
anaerobic/anoxic/oxic process（AAO）
　厌氧/缺氧/好氧脱氮除磷工艺
anaerobic/oxic process
　厌氧/好氧除磷工艺
analog aerial triangulation　模拟空中三角测量
analog composite video signal
　模拟复合视频信号

analog private line 模拟专线电路
analog quantity 模拟量
analog slave clock 模拟子钟
analogism 类比法
analogy predicted method 类比预测法
analysis index 分析指标
analysis of cost variance 成本差异分析
analysis price 分析价
analysis sieve 分析筛
analytical aerotriangulation
　解析空中三角测量
analytical balance 分析天平
analytical mapping 解析法测图
analytical reagent(AR) 分析纯
analytical solution 解析解
anchor 锚碇
anchor backing plate 锚垫板
anchor backstay 下锚拉线
anchor bolt 锚栓;地脚螺栓,锚杆
anchor bolt retaining wall 锚杆挡土墙
anchor cable 锚索
anchor foundation 下锚基础
anchor plate 锚板,拉线盘,锚固板
anchor plate abutment 锚定板式桥台
anchor plate retaining wall 锚定板挡土墙
anchor point of model 模型基点
anchor pole 下锚柱
anchor reinforcement 锚筋
anchor rod pull-out device 锚杆拉拔仪
anchor socket 锚座
anchor span 锚孔
anchorage 锚固,停泊地,停泊税,锚碇
anchorage device 锚具
anchorage force 锚固力
anchorage length of steel bar 钢筋锚固长度
anchorage property 锚固性
anchorage sealing 封锚
anchorage section 锚固段
anchoring density 锚固密实度
anchoring shotcrete with wire mesh on slope
　边坡挂网锚喷防护
ancient and rare trees 古树名木
ancient channel/riverway 古河道
ancillary benefits 辅助收益
ancillary engineering of bridge and culvert
　桥涵附属工程
ancillary restrictions 附加限制
andesite 安山岩
anemometrograph 风速风向计
angle framework 转角架构

angle of repose 休止角
angle of stream spreading 水流扩散角
angle of turning flow 水流偏转角
angle pole 转角杆
angle steel 角钢
angle strain pole 耐张转角杆
angled storage 斜角式存放
anglesite 铅矾
Anglo-American law system 英美法系
angular gravel 角砾
angular gravel soil 角砾土
angular shape 棱角状
angular unconformity contact 角度不整合接触
anionic detergent 阴离子洗涤剂
anionic emulsified asphalt 阴离子乳化沥青
anionic emulsifier 阴离子乳化剂
anisotropic consolidation 不等向固结
anisotropy 各向异性
anisotropy index 各向异性指数
annex 附件,兼并
annexed leveling line 附加水准路线
annexed traverse 附加导线(航测)
annexing agent 添加剂
annotated photograph 调绘相片
annotation 调绘
announce 公布
announced bid price 唱标价
announcement 公告,通告
annual audit report 年度审计报告
annual average ground temperature
　年平均地温
annual average precipitation 年平均降水量
annual average temperature 年平均气温
annual budget 年度预算
annual comprehensive energy consumption
　年综合能源消费量
annual cooling demand 供冷年耗冷量
annual disbursement ceiling
　年度支付最高限额
annual disbursements 年度支付额
annual evaporation & evapotranspiration capacity
　年蒸发蒸散量
annual expenditure 年度支出
annual final accounts 年度决算
annual financial statement 年度财务报表
annual funding amount 分年度资金供应量
annual heating demand 供暖年耗热量
annual income/earnings/revenue 年收入
annual inflation rate 年通货膨胀率
annual inspection fee 年检费

annual interest rate 年利率
annual investment amount 分年度投资额
annual investment schedule 分年度投资表
annual leave 年度休假
annual maintenance 年度维修
annual net profit 年净利润
annual precipitation 年降水量
annual production capacity（APC）
年生产能力
annual railway traffic capacity
线路年输送能力
annual rate of return 年回报率
annual remuneration/recompense/pay
年报酬
annual rental 年租
annual report 年度报告
annual return form 年度报税表
annual sales 年销售额
annual sales volume 年销售量
annual statement of final accounts 年度决算书
annual surface runoff depth
年地表径流深度
annual surface water stagnation depth
年地表滞水深度
annual temperature range 气温年较差
annual traffic capacity 年输送能力
annual turnover 年成交额
annual underground runoff depth
年地下径流深度
annual usage rate of contractor's construction
临时工程施工器材年使用率
annual use fee rate 年使用费率
annualization 按年计算
annuity 年金
annuity insurance 年金保险
annul 废除
annular vent pipe 环形通气管
annulment of award 撤销授标
annulment of contract 撤销合同
annunciating device 通知设备
anomalous field 异常场
anoxic zone 缺氧区
antecedent moneyguarantee deposit 押金
antedate 倒填日期,填早日期
antedated check 倒填日期支票
antenna 天线
anthracite 无烟煤
anticipated acceptance 预先承兑
anticipated cost 预期成本
anticipated freight 预期运费

anticipated gain 预期收益
anticipated interest 预期利息
anticipated price 预期价格
anticipated profit 预期利润
anticipated revenue 预计收入
anticipate 预料,预期
anticipation 预期
anticipatory breach 先期违约
anticlinal valley 背斜谷
anticline 背斜
anticlise 台背斜
anticorrosion measures 防腐蚀措施
anticorrosive 防腐
anticorrosive paint 防锈漆
antimicrobial damage test
抗微生物破坏试验
antique 古物
antiquities 古董
antirust 防锈的
antiseismic 抗地震的
antiseismic structure 抗震结构
anti-aging test 抗老化试验
anti-avoidance measures 反避税措施
anti-breakage midpoint anchor 防断中心锚结
anti-creep strut 防爬支撑
anti-creeper 防爬器
anti-creeping device 防窜中心锚结
anti-dry floor drain 防涸地漏
anti-dumping duty 反倾销税
anti-evasion measures 反逃税措施
anti-explosion blanket 防爆毯
anti-explosion floor drain 防爆地漏
anti-explosion tank 防爆罐
anti-explosion wave digestion tank
防爆波化粪池
anti-explosion wave electric cable well
防爆波电缆井
anti-falling safety device 防坠安全器
anti-floating 抗浮
anti-floating safety coefficient 抗浮安全系数
anti-freezing 防冻
anti-interference 抗干扰
anti-interference capability 抗干扰能力
anti-liquefaction measures 抗液化措施
anti-overturning stability coefficient
倾覆稳定系数
anti-seismic deformation capacity of structure
结构抗震变形能力
anti-slide pile 抗滑桩
anti-slide retaining 抗滑支挡

anti-slide section 抗滑段
anti-slide stability 抗滑动稳定性
anti-sliding coefficient 抗滑移系数
anti-sliding stability coefficient 滑动稳定系数
anti-slip floor 防滑地面
anti-slip section 抗滑段
anti-static floor 防静电地板
anti-trust law 反托拉斯法
anti-virus 病毒防范
anti-virus software 杀毒软件
apartment-office building 公寓式办公楼
apatite 磷灰石
aplite 细晶岩
apportionment of liabiliy 责任分担
apparatus 设备,仪器,装置
apparent density 堆积密度,表观密度
apparent dip 视倾角
apparent power 视在功率
apparent resistivity method 视电阻率法
apparent resistivity 视电阻率
apparent viscosity 表观黏度
appeal 上诉,申诉
appeal board 上诉委员会
appeal bond 上诉保证书
appear in court 出庭
appearance quality 观感质量
appendix 附件
appendix to bid 投标书附录
appendix to contract 合同附件
appliance 用具
applicability 适用性
applicable exchange rate (AER) 适用汇率
applicable law 适用法律
applicable law of contract 合同准据法
applicable provision 适用条款
applicant 申请人
applicant for insurance 投保人
application fee 申请费
application for arbitration 仲裁申请
application for business 营业申请
application for export licence
出口许可证申请书
application for insurance 投保单
application for interim payment
中期付款申请
application for letter of credit 信用证申请书
application for payment 付款申请
application for shipment 装运申请
application for special commitment
申请特别承诺

application level 应用等级
application server 应用服务器
application software 应用软件
applied direct cost 实际直接成本
apply 运用
apply for reimbursement 报销
apply to the customs 报关
appoint 委派,委任
appointed day 规定日期,指定日期
appointee 被委任者
appointer 委任者
appointing authority 任命机构
appointment 约定
apportionment 分摊数额
appraisal 评定,评估,鉴定
appraisal of quality 质量鉴定
appraise 鉴定
appraised value 评定价值
appraiser 估价人,鉴定人
appreciation 增值,涨价
appreciation of a currency 货币升值
approach 方法
approach bridge 引桥
approach course 进场路线
approach indication 接近表示
approach locking 接近锁闭
approach locking test 接近锁闭测试
approach obstruction signal
遮断预告信号机
approach section 接近区段
approach section of highway level crossing
道口接近区段
approach signal 接近信号机
approach track 引入线路
appropriate 拨(款)
appropriate distance 相应距离
appropriate speed range 相应速度范围
appropriation 拨款
approval 批准
approval notice of the contract 合同批准通知
approval of preliminary design 初步设计批复
approval process 审批过程
approval test 合格性检验
approve 许可,准予
approved 批准的
approved bidders list 批准的投标人名单
approved budgetary estimate 批复概算
approved capital 核准资本
approved programme 批准的进度计划
approved suppliers list 批准的供货商名单

approved tenderers list 批准的投标人名单
approved variation 批准的变更
approximate adjustment 近似平差
approximate bill of quantities 近似工程量清单
approximate estimate 估算
aqueduct 渡槽
aqueous rock 水成岩
aquifer 储水层,含水层
aquifer outcrop areas 含水层露头地区
aquifuge 隔水层
arbiter 仲裁员;公断人
arbitrage 套汇,套利
arbitral award 裁决书
arbitral decision 仲裁裁决
arbitral procedure 仲裁程序
arbitral tribunal 仲裁庭
arbitrary axis meridian 任意轴子午线
arbitrary central meridian 任意中央子午线
arbitrary projection 任意投影
arbitrary projection zone 任意投影带
arbitrary zone 任意带
arbitrate 仲裁
arbitration 仲裁,裁决
arbitration agent 仲裁代理人
arbitration agreement 仲裁协议
arbitration award 仲裁裁决,公断书
arbitration board 仲裁委员会
arbitration clause 仲裁条款
arbitration fee 仲裁费
arbitration law 仲裁法
arbitration panel 仲裁小组
arbitration procedure 仲裁程序
arbitration rules 仲裁规则
arbitration tribunal 仲裁庭
arbitrator 仲裁员,公断人,裁决人
arbor 乔木
arc chute 灭弧室
arc strike 电弧擦伤
arc time 燃弧时间
arc welding joint 电弧焊接头
arc welding of rebar 钢筋电弧焊
arch 拱;拱部
arch bridge 拱桥;拱式桥
arch crown 拱顶
arch culvert 拱涵
arch dam 拱坝
arch impost 拱座
arch rib 拱肋
arch ring of tunnel 隧道拱圈(简称拱圈)
arch ring 拱圈
arch rise 拱矢
arch soffit 拱腹
arch springing 拱脚
arch stone 拱石
arch structure 拱结构
arch thrust 拱推力
archaeological and geological findings 考古和地质发现
archaeological discovery 考古发现
archaeozoic era 太古代
archaeozoic erathem 太古界
archean eon 太古宙
archean eonothem 太古宇
arched girder 拱梁
arched roof truss 拱形屋架
arched slab 拱板
architect 建筑师
architect certification examination 建筑师认证考试
architect registration exam (ARE) 注册建筑师考试
architectural complex 建筑群
architectural design 建筑设计
architectural perspective 建筑透视图
architectural working drawing 建筑施工图
architecture 建筑、工程、施工和设备管理,建筑设计,体系结构,建筑学
architecture design 结构设计
architecture, engineering, construction and facilities management(AEC/FM) 建筑、工程、施工和设备管理
architecture landscape 建筑景观
architrave 桥门楣梁
archiving 归档
arcing time 燃弧时间
arc-chord length 弧弦长
arc-distinguishing chamber 灭弧室
arc-distinguishing mechanism 灭弧机构
area 地区,区域
area allotted for the construction 施工划拨用地
area for lifting girder up to bridge 提梁上桥区
area moment 面积矩
area of conversion cross section 换算截面面积
area of damaged soil and water conservation facilities 损坏水土保持设施面积
area of damaged vegetation 损坏植被面积
area of disturbed land surface 扰动地表面积

area of soil erosion and water loss 水土流失面积
area ratio of window to wall 窗墙面积比
area symbol 面状符号
areal density 面密度
argillaceous 泥质
argillaceous cementation 泥质胶结
argillaceous desert 泥漠
argillite 泥板岩
arid region 干旱地区
arkose 长石砂岩
arkose quartzite 长英岩
armoured 铠装
armoured cable 铠装电缆
arm's length quotation 正常报价
arm's length transaction 公平交易
aromatics of asphalt 芳香酚
around-the-clock job 昼夜施工
arrange insurance 办理保险
arrangement 协议
arrangement of reinforcement 钢筋布置
arrears 欠款
arrestment 财产扣押
arrival 到达
arrival contract 到货合同
arrival notice 到货通知,抵埠通知
arrival quality 到货质量
arrival terms 到货条件
arrive 到达
arriving angle 出土角
arrow diagram 双代号网络
arrow network 双代号网络图
arsenic content 砷含量
artesian basin spring 自流水盆地泉
artesian spring 自流泉
artesian water 自流水
article 条款,物品
articles 章程
articles of agreement 协议条文
articulated transport vehicle 拖挂式运输车辆
artificer 技师
artificial 虚假的
artificial berm 人工护道
artificial earth electrode 人工接地体
artificial earthquake test 人工地震试验
artificial fill 人工填土
artificial island cofferdam 筑岛围堰
artificial joint 人工节理
artificial marble 人造大理石
artificial mark 人工标志
artificial miscellaneous fill 人工杂填土

artificial permafrost table 多年冻土人为上限
artificial person 法人
artificial seepage prevention 人工防渗
artificial slope 人工边坡
artificial source electromagnetic frequency sounding method 人工源电磁频率测深法
artificial stereoscopic effect 人造立体效应
artificial vibration test 人激振动试验
artificial weathering 人工风化
artificial wetland 人工湿地
as constructed 实际建成的
asbestos 石棉
ascending spring 上升泉
ash content 灰分
ask for loan 借债
ask for payment 催付,催缴
asked (asking) price 索价
aspect of water-and-soil conservation measures 水土保持的措施
asphalt 沥青
asphalt concrete 沥青混凝土
asphalt concrete pavement 沥青混凝土路面,沥青混凝土铺面
asphalt felt 油毛毡,油毡
asphalt mixing equipment 沥青搅拌设备
asphalt mortar 沥青砂浆
asphalt-cement mortar 沥青水泥砂浆
assay 化验,鉴定
assembled frog 组合式辙叉
assembled lining 装配式衬砌
assemble 汇编,聚集,装配
assembler 汇编
assembling refrigeration device 组装式制冷设备
assembling reinforcement 绑扎钢筋
assembly 汇编,装配,组装
assembly drawing 安装图,装配图
assembly line 生产线,装配线
assembly line method 流水生产法
assembly line repair 检修流水线
assembly mode 装配方式
assembly model 总装模型
assembly of track section 轨排拼装
assembly shop 装配车间
assembly type girder-erecting machine 组拼式架桥机
assertion 断言
assess 估价,估算
assess the damages 确定赔偿额
assessed value 估定价值
assessment 评定,评估,估价

assessment fee for geological hazard risk 地质灾害危险性评估费
assessment fee for mineral resources unavailabled because of the construction 压覆矿藏评估费
assessment fee for seismic safety 地震安全性评估费
assessment of overlaid mineral resources 压覆矿产资源评估
assessor 估价财产人
asset 资产
asset and liability management(ALM) 资产负债管理
asset management 资产管理
asset retirement 资产报废
assets 财产
assets account 资产账户
assets and liabilities 资产与负债
assets cover 资产担保,资产抵偿
assets depreciation 资产折旧
assets depreciation range 资产折旧幅度
assets replacement fund 资产重置资金
assets replacement schedule 资产重置计划
assets turnover 资产周转率
assets valuation 资产估价
assignee 受让人
assignee in bankruptcy 破产资产管理人
assigner 转让人
assignment 权利转让,转让证书
assignment allowance 外派津贴
assignment fee(charge) 转让费
assignment of contract 合同转让
assignment of contract rights 合同权益转让
assignment of debt 债务转让
assignment of interests 权益转让
assignment of lease 转租
assignment of policy 保险单转让
assignor 让与人,转让人
assigns 受让人
assistance 协助,援助
assistant 助理,助手
assistant engineer 助理工程师
assistant heat source 辅助热源
assistant locomotive 补机
assistant project manager 项目经理助理
assistant superintendent 副院长,车间副主任
assisted country 受援国
assisting section 加力牵引区段
associate 合伙人,同事,合伙人
associate member 准会员
association 协会
assume 假定
assumed coordinate system 假定坐标系
assumed elevation 假定高程
assumed loss ratio 预定损失率
assumption 假定
assurance of support 经济担保
assured 保险受益人,被保险人,投保人
assure 保证
assurer 保险人,承保人
accusant 控告人
asymmetrical pressure 偏压力
asymmetrical erosion and siltation 不对称侵蚀淤积
asymmetrical impulse track circuit 不对称脉冲轨道电路
asymmetrically-loaded lining 偏压衬砌
asymmetrically-loaded tunnel 偏压隧道
asynchronous controller 异步控制器
asynchronous transfer mode(ATM) 异步转移模式
as-built data 竣工资料
as-built documents 竣工文件
as-built drawing 竣工图
as-built drawing of construction project 建设项目竣工图
as-built drawing of project 工程竣工图
as-built records 竣工记录
as-built route survey 线路竣工测量
as-built schedule 实际工期
as-built survey 竣工测量
as-built survey of civil works 线下工程竣工测量
as-of date 截止日期
as-planned schedule 计划工期,计划进度
at a discount 贴水
at a premium 溢价
at buyer's option 由买方选择
at current cost 按现时成本
at discretion 随意
AT feeding system AT 供电方式
at maturity 到期
at odds 有分歧
at par 按面值
at risk 有风险
AT section AT 段
at seller's option 由卖方选择
atlas 地图集
atmosphere 大气
atmospheric pollution 大气污染

atmospheric pressure 大气压力
atmospheric refraction 大气折光
atomic absorption spectrometry
  原子吸收光谱法
atomic clock 原子钟
atomic fluorescence spectrometer
  原子荧光光谱仪
ATP with high priority 设备制动优先
attached account 被查封账户
attached clause 附加条款
attached concrete vibrator
  附着式混凝土振捣器
attached jet 贴附射流
attached public houses 附建公共用房
attachment date 起保日
attachment device 附着装置
attachment of risk 风险责任的起期
attendance 出席
attendance bonus 加班奖金
attention 注意
attenuating shock wave equipment 消波设施
attenuation coefficient 衰耗系数,衰减系数
attenuation ratio of dynamic stress
  动应力衰减比
attenuation to crosstalk ratio (ACR)
  衰减串音比
attenuator 衰耗器
attestation 证词,证据
attitude 产状
attorney 初级律师,代办人,受权人
attribute 属性
at-grade section 路基地段
at-risk CM 风险型工程管理模式
AU pointer adjustment AU 指针调整
auction 拍卖
auction reserve price 拍卖底价
audible and visual alarm 声光报警
audible signal 听觉信号
audio and video information 音视频信息
audio and video terminal 音视频终端
audio and visual alarm 声光报警器
audio cable 广播电缆
audio circuit 音频电路
audio console 调音台
audio four-wire port 音频四线端
audio line 音频线路
audio loop cable 音频回线
audio recorder 录音记录仪
audio selective call interface
  音频选号接口

audio two-wire port 音频二线端
audio video coding standard(AVS)
  音视频编码标准
audit 查账,清算,审计
audit findings 审核结果
audit mission 审计团
audit trail 查账追踪,审计线索
audited financial statement 财务审计报表
auditing body 审计机构
auditing clauses 查账条款,审计条款
auditor 查账人,审核人,审计员,审计师
augen migmatite 眼球状混合岩
auger-cast pile 螺旋喷射桩
austenitic stainless steel 奥氏体不锈钢
authenticate 鉴定
authenticated 可靠的
authentication center (AuC) 鉴权中心
authenticity 真实性
authorised representative 授权代表
authority 判例,职权
authority to delegate 授权的权力
authorization 核准,授权
authorize 委托,托管,核准,审定,授权
authorized bank 授权银行,指定银行
authorized capital 核准资本
authorized capital stock
  法定股本,核定股本
authorized extension 批准的延期
authorized party 被授权方
authorized payment 授权付款
authorized person 被授权方
authorized signature 授权人签名
auto level 全自动水准仪
autoclaved flyash-lime brick
  蒸压粉煤灰普通砖
autoclaved lime-sand brick 蒸压灰砂普通砖
autoclaved sand-lime brick 蒸压灰沙普通砖
autocratic acts brick 专制行为
autograph 亲笔签名
automatic answering desk 立接台
automatic barrier 自动栏木
automatic block 自动闭塞
automatic block power line
  自动闭塞供电线路
automatic block signal line
  自动闭塞信号线路
automatic block with AC counting coded track circuit 交流计数电码自动闭塞
automatic block with coded track circuit
  电码自动闭塞

automatic block with impulse track circuit
脉冲自动闭塞
automatic block with polar frequency impulse track circuit 极频自动闭塞
automatic car identification 自动抄车号
automatic cartography 自动化制图
automatic control of humping route
溜放进路自动控制
automatic control of humping speed
推峰速度自动控制
automatic exhaust valve 自动排气活门
automatic gain control 自动增益控制
automatic hump 自动化驼峰
automatic inspection 自动巡检
automatic inter-station blocking with axle counter
计轴自动站间闭塞
automatic level crossing announcement
道口自动通知
automatic level crossing barrier
道口自动栏杆
automatic level crossing signal 道口自动信号
automatic lifting-lining-tamping train
自动整平捣固车
automatic lighting 自动点灯
automatic monitoring device for OCS
接触网自动监测装置
automatic open-close sprinkler
自动启闭喷头
automatic operation 自动操纵作业
automatic passing button circuit
自动通过按钮电路
automatic passing route 自动通过进路
automatic plotting 自动绘图
automatic profiler 自动断面仪
automatic regulation 自动调节
automatic release 自动缓解
automatic route trigger 自动进路触发
automatic sprinkling system
自动喷水灭火系统
automatic staff exchanger 路签自动授收机
automatic switchover 自动倒机
automatic system at gate area 门区自动系统
automatic tablet exchanger
路牌自动授收机
automatic temperature and humidity controlling device 自动控温控湿设备
automatic terminal information service (ATIS)
自动终端信息业务
automatic termination clause
自动终止条款
automatic ticket collection machine
自动取票机
automatic ticket gate 自动检票机
automatic ticket machine 自动售票机
automatic time release 自动限时解锁
automatic train control（ATC）
列车自动控制
automatic train door control 车门自动控制
automatic train identification system
车号自动识别系统
automatic train operation（ATO）**system**
列车自动运行系统,列车自动驾驶系统
automatic train protection system
列车超速防护系统,列车自动防护系统
automatic train protection（ATP）
列车超速防护,列车自动防护
automatic train speed regulation
列车自动调速
automatic train speed restriction
列车自动限速
automatic train stop 自动停车
automatic train stop device 自动停车装置
automatic train supervision（ATS）
列车自动监控
automatic train supervision（ATS）**system**
列车自动监控（ATS）系统
automatic transfer service 自动转账服务
automatic virtual block 虚拟自动闭塞
automatic voltage regulation
自动调压,自动稳压
automatic voltage regulator
电压自动调整器
automatically tensioned overhead contact line
全补偿链形悬挂
automatically tensioned polygonal contact line
全补偿直链形悬挂
autonomous computer 自律机
auto-lift 自动升降机
auto-reclosing 自动重合闸
auto-switching 自动投切
auto-transformer feeding system
AT 供电方式
auto-transformer post（ATP） 自耦变压器所
auto-transformer 自耦变压器
auxiliary book 辅助账簿
auxiliary building 生产附属房屋
auxiliary bus bar 辅助母线
auxiliary circuit 辅助回路
auxiliary container yard 辅助箱场
auxiliary deflection angle 分转向角

auxiliary enterprise 附属企业
auxiliary equipment 附属设备,辅助设备
auxiliary facility 辅助设施
auxiliary intersection point 副交点
auxiliary marshalling yard 辅助调车场
auxiliary materials 辅助材料
auxiliary messenger wire 辅助承力索
auxiliary operation facilities 辅助生产设施
auxiliary pier 辅助墩
auxiliary power supply 所用电,所用电源
auxiliary project 配套工程
auxiliary prompt test 辅助提示测试
auxiliary protection 辅助保护
auxiliary rail 辅助轨
auxiliary repair 辅修
auxiliary station track 次要站线
auxiliary steel bar 架立钢筋
auxiliary structure of tunnel
　隧道附属构筑物
auxiliary structures 附属建筑物
auxiliary switch 辅助开关
auxiliary transformer 所用变压器
auxiliary ventilation riser 副通气立管
available balance 可动用结余
available cash 可用现金
available phosphorus content 有效磷含量
available potassium content 有效钾含量
available pressure 资用压力
availability 可得性,可用性,有效性
avalanche 雪崩
avalanche slot 雪崩槽
average 海损
average active power 平均有功功率
average agent 海损代理人
average agreement 海损协议
average bond 共同海损保证书
average contribution 海损分摊
average current of charging train
　列车带电平均电流
average current of feeding section
　供电臂平均电流
average current of train 列车平均电流
average daily locomotive running kilometers
　机车日车公里
average daily operation time of forklift
　叉车日均作业时间
average degree of consolidation 平均固结度
average depreciation method 平均折旧法
average diameter 平均直径
average error 平均误差
average heat transfer coefficient of building external wall 外墙平均传热系数
average hourly water consumption
　平均时用水量
average hours of work 平均工时数
average illumination 平均照度
average life 平均使用年限
average linear overexcavation
　平均线性超挖量
average method of depreciation
　直线折旧法
average policy 海损保险单
average price 均价,平均价格
average reactive power 平均无功功率
average repayment maturity 平均还款期
average service conditions 正常使用条件
average snow depth 平均积雪深度
average taker 海损理算人
average tare 平均皮重
average temperature of the coldest month
　最冷月平均气温
average temperature of the hottest month
　最热月平均气温
average temperature outside during heating period
　采暖期室外平均温度
average thickness method 平均厚度法
average unit cost 平均单位成本
average value 平均值
average wind velocity 平均风速
averaged length of car 车辆平均长度
averted angle of principal optic axis
　主光轴偏角
avoid 躲避,闪避,规避,逃避
avoidable accident 可避免事故
avoidable cost 可避免成本
avoidance 避免
avoidance of disputes 避免争议
avoidance of double taxation 避免双重征税
avoidance of interference
　避开干扰,避免干扰
avoidance of tax 避税
award 裁定,裁决书,授予
award criteria 授标准则
award decision 授标决定
award letter 中标函,中标书
award notification 授标通知
award of contract 授予合同,中标
axial compression ratio 轴压比
axial compressive strength 轴心抗压强度
axial control network 轴线控制网

axial deformation　轴向变形
axial fan　轴流风机
axial force　轴力
axial force of the anchor rod　锚杆轴力
axial free swelling ratio　轴向自由膨胀率
axial load　轴向荷载
axial plane cleavage　轴面劈理
axial pressure　轴向压力
axial pump　轴流水泵
axial strain　轴向应变
axial stress　轴向应力
axial tensile force　轴向拉力
axial ventilator　轴流式通风机
axiality tolerance　同轴度公差
axis　轴线
axis projection surveying　轴线投测
axle counter track occupancy detection device　计轴轨道占用检查装置
axle counting　计轴
axle load　轴重
azimuth　方位角,航线
azimuth closing error of traverse　导线方位角闭合差
azimuth condition　方位角条件

B

back 背面,背书
back a bill 在票据上背书
back a check 背书支票
back bond 退还担保,保管证书,反担保
back charge 欠付费用
back coil 后圈
back contact 后接点
back door 非法途径
back flashover 反击
back freight 回程运费,退货运费
back money 过期未付款,拖欠款
back order 延交订货,未交付订单
back pay 欠薪
back pressure 反压力
back pressure of steam trap 凝结水背压力
back pressure return 余压回水
back scheduling 倒排工期
back to back 背对背
backbone layer 骨干层
backbone network 骨干网络
backbone synchronization network 骨干同步网
backbone transmission network 骨干传输网
backdate 倒填日期,填早日期
backed bond 有担保债券
backfill 回填,回填料
backfill material 回填料
backfilling 回填料
backfilling grouting 回填注浆
backfilling soil 回填土
backflow pollution 回流污染
backflow preventer
  倒流防止器,防回流装置
background 背景
background material 背景材料
background noise 背景噪声
background soil erosion modulus
  原地貌土壤侵蚀模数
backhoe 反铲挖土机
backing weld 垫板焊
backlight effect 背光效果
backlog 订单积压
backstay 拉索
backstay wire 斜拉线(电力)
backup 待用品
backup data 备查资料
backup plan 后备计划
backup protection 后备保护
backup system 后配套
backward-slanting drain hole 仰斜排水孔
backwater 壅水
backwater height 壅水高
backwater height on the upstream side of bridge
  桥前壅水高度
backwater on the upstream side of bridge
  桥前壅水
backwater profile 壅水曲线
back-end analysis 后端分析
back-passing arrangement of turnouts
  道岔顺向布置
back-pressure back flow 背压回流
back-pressure platform 反压平台
back-stopping cost 资助费用
back-to-back (letter of) credit
  背对背信用证
back-to-back account 对开账户
back-to-back letter of credit 转开信用证
back-up equipment 后配套设备
bad account 呆账,坏账
bad debt 呆账,坏账
bad faith 无信用
bad loans 呆账,坏账
bad packing 包装不良
bad/bounced/dishonoured/dud/rubber check
  空头支票
bad-debt provision 坏账准备
baffle block 挡块

baffling 不能理解的
bagged cement 袋装水泥
bail 保释金,保释
bail bond 保释金保函
bailee 被保释人
bailer 保释人
bailing barrel 提水筒
bailing method 提捞法
bailment 保释
bailor 保释人
bainite rail 贝氏体钢轨
balance 天平,余额,结余,收支平衡
balance amount 差额
balance due 结欠余额,所欠余额
balance of account 账面余额
balance of current account
 经常项目差额,往来账结余
balance of international indebtedness
 国际借贷差额
balance of payment 款项余额,收支差额
balance of payments deficit 收支逆差
balance of payments surplus 收支顺差
balance of revenue and expenditure
 财政收支平衡
balance of thermal performance of building envelope 围护结构热工性能权衡判断
balance of trade 贸易平衡
balance outstanding 未结清的余额
balance sheet 资产负债表,平衡表
balance sheet data 资产负债数据
balance weight 砝码
balance weight retaining wall 衡重式挡土墙
balanced eccentricity 界限偏心距
balanced load 平衡负载
balanced transmission line 平衡传输线
balancing account 平衡账户
balancing weight 配重块
balcony 阳台
bale 捆
bale capacity 包装容积
balise 应答器
balise coordinate system 应答器坐标系
balise group 应答器组
balise linking 应答器链接
balise programming tool 应答器读写工具
balise telegram 应答器报文
balise transmission module（BTM）
 应答器传输模块,应答器信息接收单元
ball clay 土球
ball socket end clamp 杵座鞍子

ball socket with clevis 杵座双耳
ball with eye rod 杵环杆
ballast 道砟
ballast bed 碎石道床
ballast bed depression 道床沉陷
ballast bed of station track 站线道床
ballast bed resistance 道床电阻
ballast cleaning 道砟清筛,清筛道床
ballast cleaning machine 道床清扫机,道砟清筛机
ballast cleaning machine with removed track
 panels 大揭盖清筛机
ballast coefficient 道床系数
ballast collector 收砟机
ballast compaction 夯实道床
ballast compactor 道床夯拍机
ballast consolidating 夯实道床
ballast contamination 道床脏污
ballast cover 道床覆盖
ballast density 道床密度
ballast depression trough 道砟陷槽
ballast distributing and profiling car
 道床配砟整形车,配砟整形车
ballast fouling 道床脏污
ballast grading 道砟级配
ballast maintenance 道床作业
ballast plough 道砟犁
ballast raker 扒砟机
ballast regulation 道床整形
ballast replacement 道砟更换
ballast replacement machine 道砟更换机
ballast resistance 道砟电阻
ballast resistivity 道砟电阻率
ballast shoulder 道床砟肩
ballast shoulder consolidating machine
 道床边坡夯实机
ballast slope 道床边坡
ballast storage yard 存砟场
ballast tamping 捣固道床
ballast track 有砟轨道
ballast trimming 道床整形
ballast trough 道砟槽
ballast trough of bridge 桥梁道砟槽
ballasted deck 道砟桥面
ballasted track 有砟轨道
ballasted trackbed 有砟道床
ballasted turnout 有砟轨道道岔
ballastless track 无砟轨道
ballastless track bridge 无砟轨道桥梁
ballastless track with elastic bearing block
 弹性支承块式无砟轨道

ballastless trackbed 无砟道床
ballastless turnout 无砟道岔
ball-burst strength 圆球顶破强度
ball-clevis 球头挂板
ball-eye 球头挂环
ball-hook 球头挂钩
bamboo-truncated portal 斜切式洞门
ban 禁令
ban on export 禁止出口
ban on import 禁止进口
banco facies 牛轭湖相
banded clay 带状黏土
banded migmatite 条带状混合岩
banded structure 带状构造,条带状构造
bank (banker's) check 银行支票
bank acceptance note 银行承兑票据
bank accommodation 银行资金融通
bank account 银行账户
bank balance 银行存款余额
bank bill 银行票据
bank book 银行存折
bank cable transfer 银行电汇
bank charge 银行手续费
bank collapse 塌岸
bank credit 银行信贷
bank current deposits 银行活期存款
bank deposit 银行保证金,银行存款
bank discount 银行贴现
bank discount rate 银行贴现率
bank financed consulting services
 银行资助的咨询服务
bank financing 银行贷款,银行资助
bank guarantee 银行保函,银行保证书
bank holding company 银行控股公司
bank loan 银行贷款
bank of deposit 存款银行
bank overdraft 银行透支
bank prime rate 银行优惠利率
bank protection work 护岸工程
bank rate 银行利率
bank remittance fee 银行汇款手续费
bank sight draft 银行即期汇票
bank slope 岸坡
bank slumping line 坍岸线
bank statement 对账单
bank transfer 银行汇款,银行间的转账
bankable project 银行愿担保的项目
banker's acceptance credit 银行承兑信用证
banker's invoice 银行发票
banker's letter of credit 银行信用证
banker's lien 银行留置权
banker's markup 银行利差
banking locomotive 补机
banking protection works 护岸工程
banknote sorter 纸币清分机
bankrupt 破产,破产者
bankruptcy 破产倒闭,破产
bankruptcy act 破产法案
bankruptcy administrator 破产管理人
banks promissory note 银行本票
bank's (banker's) bill 银行汇票
bank's (banker's) buying rate 银行买价
bank's (banker's) draft 银行汇票
bank's (banker's) selling rate 银行卖价
bank-financed project 银行贷款项目
bar 线条,障碍物
bar association 律师协会
bar chart 甘特图,横道图
bar council 律师委员会,司法委员会
bar cutter 钢筋截断机
bar screen 格栅
bar shearing machine 钢筋切断机,钢筋弯曲机
bar splice 钢筋接头
bar splicing 钢筋搭接
bar structure 杆系结构
bar subjected to bending moment 受弯钢筋
bar thermometer 棒状温度计
bareboat charter 光船租赁
bargain 议价
bargainer 交易者
bargaining position 议价能力
bargaining power 谈判实力
barge 驳船,平底船
barite 重晶石
barrack's survey 营房建筑测量
barrage 坝,挡水建筑物,堰
barratry 不法行为,违法行为,欺诈行为
barred claim 失去时效的债权
barred debt (obligation)
 有时效限制的债务
barren 瘠薄
barrier 遮栏
barrister 大律师,专门律师
barter 物物交换,易货贸易,易货
barter trade 易货贸易
basal cement 基底胶结
basal conglomerate 底砾岩
basal layer 基底层
basal plate for cement mortar
 水泥砂浆基板

basal structure	基底构造
basalt	玄武岩
basaltic glass spilite	玄武玻璃细碧岩
bascule bridge	竖旋桥
base	底座,基层
base benchmark	水准基点
base completion date	基准完成日期
base cost estimate	基本成本估计
base date	基准日期
base freight rate	基本运费
base lending rate	基本贷款汇率
base level	基面,基准面
base line	底线
base line budget	基线预算
base line cost	基线费用
base line of section	断面基线
base material	胎基材料
base metal of steel-bar	钢筋母材
base of natural logarithm	自然底数
base period	基期
base plate	底板,底盘
base plate of backstay	拉线底座
base plate of steel pole	钢柱底座
base pressure (contact pressure)	基底压力(接触压力)
base price	标底,底价,基价
base price index	基本价格指数
base price of materials	材料基价
base rate	基准利率
base slab	底板
base station	基点
base station controller(BSC)	基站控制器
base station identification code (BSIC)	基站识别码
base station subsystem (BSS)	无线子系统
base stock	基本库存
base transceiver station (BTS)	基站
base value	基值,基准值
base year	基准年
based on	按照
baseline condition	基线条件
baseline cost	原始费用
baseline finish date	基准完成日期
baseline program	基准计划
baseline solution	基线解算
baseline vector	基线向量
baseline	基准计划,基线
basement	地下室
baseplate	支承板
base-height ratio	基高比
basic	基本的
basic aluminium chloride	碱式氯化铝
basic bearing capacity	基本承载力
basic breakdown work	基本分项工作
basic budget reserve for unpredictable work	基本预备费
basic combination	基本组合
basic contractual responsibilities	基本合同责任
basic cycle	基本周期
basic design	基本设计
basic evidence	基本证据
basic farmland	基本农田
basic freight rate	运费基价
basic heat loss	基本耗热量
basic horizontal control network (CPⅠ)	基础平面控制网(CPⅠ)
basic information system of land	国土基础信息系统
basic intensity	基本烈度
basic interest rate	基本利率
basic item	基本分项工作
basic medical insurance premium	基本医疗保险费
basic model	基本模型
basic pension premium	基本养老保险费
basic power price	基本电价
basic price	基本价格
basic quality of rock mass (BQ)	岩体基本质量
basic quota	基本定额
basic rate interface (BRI)	基本速率接口
basic route	基本进路
basic salary	基本工资
basic scale	基本比例尺
basic standard	基准
basic variable	基本变量
basic vibration mode	基本振型
basic working hours	基本工时
basically stable low-temperature permafrost	低温基本稳定冻土区
basic-scale topographic map	基本比例尺地形图
basin	盆地
basis point (b.p.)	基点
basis rates	基本费率
basis risk	基本风险
basite magmatic rock	基性岩浆岩
basket purchase	整套购买
basket unit	复合货币单位

blasting powder 炸药
batch 批次,一批
batch budgeting 分批预算
batch costing 分批成本预算法
batch production 批量生产
batching 配料
batching bin 配料仓
batching plant
混凝土拌和厂,混凝土搅拌站,混凝土拌和楼,混凝土搅拌楼
bateau bridge 舟桥
batholith 岩基
bathyal facies 次深海相
batten plate 缀板
batter pile 斜桩
battered pile 斜桩
battery bank 电池组
battery cell 单体蓄电池
battery jar 电池槽
battery locomotive 电瓶车
battery of wells 井群
bay sandbank 拦湾砂坝
bay window 凸窗
beach 海滩
beaker 烧杯
beam 梁
beam and post falsework 梁柱式支架
beam and slab structures 梁板结构
beam and track interaction 梁轨相互作用
beam depth 梁高
beam on elastic foundation 弹性地基梁
beam with both ends built-in 两端固定梁
beam-column type falsework 梁柱式支架
beam-end effective supporting length
梁端有效支承长度
beam-end waterproof device 梁端防水装置
beam-type bridges 梁式桥
bear 承担,空头
bear a loss 负担损失
bear expenses 承担费用
bear legal liability 承担法律责任
bearer bill of lading 不记名提单
bearer bond 不记名债券
bearer channel connection (BCC)
承载通路连接
bearer cheque 不记名支票
bearer network 承载网
bearer platform 承载平台
bearing 支座
bearing angle 象限角

bearing capacity 承载力,承载能力
bearing capacity of soil 土壤承载力
bearing pile 承重桩,支承桩
bearing plate 承压板
bearing ratio 承载比
bearing seat 支座
bearing stiffener 支承加劲肋
bearing stratum 持力层
bearing stress 承压应力
bearing structure 承重结构
bearing wall 承重墙
beat down 跌价
become null and void 作废
bedding 层理
bedding cleavage 顺层劈理
bedding course 垫层
bedding layer of foundation 基础垫层
bedding of rock mass 岩体顺层
bedding structure 层理构造
bedrock 基岩
bedrock benchmark 基岩水准点
bedrock seatedterrace 基座阶地
bedrock surface 基岩面
bedroom 卧室
beefy 结实的
before tax income 税前收益
before tax profit 税前利润
beginning and ending mileage 起讫里程
beginning balance 期初余额
behind schedule 拖期
beidellite 贝得石
bell curve 资源负荷曲线
belt conveyor
传送带,皮带输送机,带式输送机
belt loader 带式装料机
bench 台阶(隧道开挖)
bench excavation 台阶开挖
benched subgrade 台口式路基
benchmark 标杆管理,水准点
benchmark rate 基准利率
benchmark specimen 基准试件
benchmark standard 基准标准
benchmark year 基准年
benchmarking 标杆管理
benchworker 钳工
bench-cut method 台阶法
bend 弯曲
bend muffler 消声弯头
bender 弯筋机
bending creep 弯曲蠕变

bending failure 弯曲破坏
bending force in CWR on bridge 挠曲力
bending member 受弯构件
bending moment 弯矩
bending strength 抗弯强度
beneficial interest 受益权
beneficial owner 受益业主
beneficiary 受惠人,受益人
beneficiary country 受惠国
benefit 补助金,利益,效益
benefit of agreement 协议利益
benefit of insurance 保险利益
benefited interest 股权,权益
benefited party 受益方
benefit-cost ratio(BCR) 效益成本比
bent cap 盖梁
bent frame 排架
bent tree 马刀树
bent-type pier 排架式桥墩
bent-up bar 弯起钢筋
berm 护道
berth 码头泊位,泊位,船位
berth charter 班轮条件租赁,舱位包租
berth clause 泊位包租条款
berthage 泊位,停泊费
beryl 绿柱石
best mineral admixture 最佳掺合料
best observation period for EDM 电磁波测距最佳观测时间段
betterment 不动产增值
betterment and extension 修缮和扩建
betterments 修缮经费
bevel angle 半坡角度
bid 报价,投标
bid(tender)**invitation** 招标
bid addenda 招标文件补遗
bid bond 投标担保,投标保函
bid ceiling 最高标价
bid clarification meeting 投标澄清会议
bid cost 投标费用
bid currencies 投标货币
bid date 投标日期
bid division 分标
bid due date 投标日期
bid evaluation 评标
bid evaluation committee 评标委员会
bid examination 投标核查
bid fee 投标费
bid for construction works 建设工程投标
bid for engineering project 工程项目投标
bid form 投标格式
bid guarantee 投标保证书,投标保函
bid invitation 招标通知
bid invitation letter 投标邀请函
bid language 投标语言
bid list 投标人名单
bid lot 标段
bid opening 开标
bid opening minutes 开标纪要
bid opening procedure 开标程序
bid package 投标文件包
bid package contents 投标文件内容
bid period 投标期
bid phase 投标阶段
bid preparation 投标准备,编制投标文件,编标
bid price 投标价,标价,投标报价
bid procedure 投标程序
bid process 投标步骤
bid receipt 投标书签收
bid requirement 投标要求
bid schedule of prices 投标价目表
bid security 投标保证
bid shopping 投标压价
bid submission sheet 投标递交函
bid substance 投标实质内容
bid summary 投标汇总
bid tabulations 投标表册
bid unit price 投标单价
bid validity period 投标文件有效期
bid withdrawal 撤回投标书
bidder 投标人,投标者
bidder selection 选择投标人
bidder selection criteria 选择投标人准则
bidder's conference 投标人会议
bidder's obligation 投标人的义务
bidder's prequalification 投标人资格预审
bidder's qualification 投标人资格
bidder's return of documents 投标人退还文件
bidding 投标
bidding advice 投标通知
bidding consulting service fee 招投标咨询服务费
bidding control price 招标控制价
bidding documents 招标文件
bidding of construction works 建设工程招标
bidding of engineering project 工程项目招投标
bidding service fee 招标服务费
bidding sheet 标价单

bidding time 投标时间
bidirectional combined-type harbour station built jointly in both terminals
 双方车站联设双向混合式港湾站
bidirectional combined-type industrial station built jointly in both terminals
 双方车站联设双向混合式工业站
bidirectional combined-type marshalling station
 双向混合式编组站
bidirectional geogrid 双向土工格栅
bidirectional longitudinal type marshalling station
 双向纵列式编组站
bidirectional marshalling station
 双向编组站
bid-rigging 围标
bid-securing declaration 投标保证声明
big refuge niche 大避车洞
bilateral agreement 双边协议
bilateral contract 双边合同
bilateral document 双边文件,双边文书
bill 单据,票据,法案
bill at sight 见票即付汇票
bill discounted 已贴现票据
bill endorsed in blank 空白背书汇票
bill for collection 托收汇票
bill for remittance 汇票
bill of approximate quantity contract
 估计工程量单价合同
bill of complaint 起诉书
bill of credit 取款凭单,付款通知
bill of draft 汇票
bill of entry 报关单
bill of estimate 估价单
bill of exchange（B/E） 汇票
bill of exchange purchased 买入的汇票
bill of freight 货运单
bill of goods 货物清单
bill of lading（B/L） 提单,提货单,送货令
bill of lading copy（B/L copy）
 提单副本
bill of lading original（B/L original）
 提单正本
bill of landing 货运提单
bill of materials（BOM）
 材料表,用料清单
bill of maturity 到期票据
bill of parcel 包裹单
bill of payment 付款清单
bill of power consumption 能源消费账单
bill of quantities contract 合同清单

bill of quantities 工程量表,工程量清单
bill of sale 发货单,卖据
bill of sufferance 待检查物品单,免税单
bill of variations 工程变更单
bill of works 工程报表
bill payable 应付票据
bill payable at fixed date after sight
 见票后定期付款汇票
bill payable at sight 见票即付汇票
bill payable by installments 分期汇票
bill payable on demand 即期汇票
bill rate 票据贴现率
bill receivable 应收票据
bill undue 未到期汇票
billing agent 托收人
bills for collection（BC） 托收票据
bill-of-lading freight
 提单运费,签单即付运费
BIM application model deliverables
 BIM 应用模型
BIM design deliverables BIM 设计交付物
BIM execution plan BIM 执行计划书
BIM modeling software BIM 建模软件
BIM views deliverables BIM 视图成果
bimetallic thermometer 双金属温度计
bind 黏结
binder 承保协议,暂保单
binding 有约束力的,约束力
binding clause 约束条款
binding contract
 有约束力的合同,约束性合同
binding decision 有约束力的决定
binding receipt 暂保收据
binding signature 有约束力的签字
biogenetic texture 生物结构
biogenic accumulation 生物堆积
biologic weathering 生物风化
biological aerated filter（BAF）
 曝气生物滤池
biological deodorization 生物除臭
biological method 生物法
biological phosphorus removal 生物除磷
biological pre-treatment 生物预处理
biological reaction tank 生物反应池
biological stability 生物稳定性
biological treatment 生物处理
biomass 生物量
biomembrane process 生物膜法
biotite 黑云母
biotower 塔式生物滤池

Biot's consolidation theory 比奥固结理论
bio-contact oxidation 生物接触氧化
bio-denitrification 生物反硝化
bio-nitrification 生物硝化
birdcaging 灯笼(导线缺陷)
bird's-eye view 鸟瞰图
birth insurance premium 生育保险费
Bishop's simplified method of slice
　毕肖普简化条分法
bit error rate 比特误码率
bit error rate (BER) performance 误码性能
bitumen for paint 油漆沥青
bituminous grouting 沥青灌浆
bituminous layer 沥青层
bituminous water-proof coating 沥青防水层
bituminous mixture 沥青混合料
bi-block ballastless track 双块式无砟轨道
bi-block sleeper 双块式轨枕
bi-direction audio and video function test
　双向音视频功能试验
bi-directional automatic blocking
　双向运行自动闭塞
bi-layer structure 双层结构
bkoking 经纪业
black globe temperature 黑球温度
Blaine method 勃氏法
blank bill 空白票据
blank bill of lading 空白提单
blank check 空白支票
blank endorsement 不记名背书,空白背书
blank letter of credit 空白信用证
blank test 空白试验
blanket acceptance 全部接收
blanket approval 全部同意
blanket bond 总括保证
blanket contract 一揽子合同
blanket policy 总括保险单
blanket purchase contract 一揽子采购合同
blast 爆破
blaster 起爆器
blasthole 炮眼
blasting compaction method 爆炸挤密法
blasting effect of tunnel 隧道爆破效应
blasting noise 爆破噪声
blasting seismic effect 爆破地震效应
blasting vibration 爆破振动
blastproof partition wall 防爆墙
bleed valve 放气阀
bleeding 泌水
bleeding rate 泌水率
bleeding rate at normal pressure 常压泌水率
bleeding rate at pressure 压力泌水率
bleeding rate of capillary 毛细泌水率
blend 混合
blend sand 混合砂
blending ratio 混合比
blending 混合
blind ditch 暗沟
blind fault 隐伏断层
blind valley 盲谷
block 块体,区域网,截断
block adjustment using bundle method
　光线束法区域网平差
block adjustment using independent-model method
　独立模型法区域网平差
block adjustment 区域网平差
block door 堵门
block house 线路所
block instrument 闭塞机
block line 闭塞线
block masonry structure 砌块砌体结构
block post 线路所
block resistance property 防堵性
block section 闭塞分区
block signal 通过信号机
block signal at block post
　线路所通过信号机
block theory 块体理论
block train 整车
block type 闭塞类型
blockage ratio 阻塞比
blocked account 冻结账户
blocked currency 冻结货币
blocked deposit 冻结存款
blocked fund 冻结资金
blocking 闭塞
blocking concrete 封端混凝土
block-diagram 简图
blotter 临时分录账,流水账,原始账
blower 吹风机,鼓风机
blowing rate 风量
blowout basin 风蚀盆地
blue printing process 晒蓝
blue vitriol 胆矾
blueprint 蓝图
blueprint drawing 蓝晒图
blueprint of the project 工程蓝图
blueprinter 晒图机
board 董事会,委员会
board chairman 董事主席

board meeting　董事会会议
board of directors　董事会
board of executive directors　执行董事会
board of reference　咨询委员会
board of review　评审委员会,上诉委员会
boat　船
bodily injury　人身伤害,身体伤害
bodiness　加重
body corporate　法人团体
body force　体积力
body of rod　杆体
body wave　体波
bogie inspection and repair workshop　转向架检修库
bogie lease charge　转向架租用费
boiler　锅炉
boiler room　锅炉房
boiler slag　炉渣
boiling method　沸煮法,煮沸法
boiling spill oil　沸溢性油品
bollard　凸形挡台
bolt　螺栓
bolt hole crack　螺孔裂纹
bolt hole sealing washer　螺孔密封圈
bolt nondestructive detection　锚杆无损检测
bolt pin　螺栓销
bolt tightening degree　螺栓拧紧度
bolt wrench　螺栓扳手
bolted steel bridge　栓接钢桥
bolted steel structure　螺栓连接钢结构
bona fide　可靠的
bona fide bidder　善意投标人
bona fide reason　真实理由
bona vacantia　无人继承的财产,无主物
bona-fide endorsee　善意被背书人
bona-fide holder　合法持票人,善意持有人
bond　担保,公债,政府债券,债券
bond market　债券市场
bond payable　应付债券
bonded area　保税区
bonded goods　保税货物
bonded port　保税港
bonded prestressed concrete structure　有黏结预应力混凝土结构
bonded stores　保税仓库
bonded warehouse　保税仓库
bonding agent　担保代理人
bonding capacity　担保额度,担保能力
bonding company　担保公司

bonding node　黏结点
bonding rate　担保费率,债券利率
bonding strength　黏结强度
bonus　额外津贴,奖金,红利
bonus clause　奖励条款
bonus for completion　竣工奖金
bonus for early completion　提前竣工奖金
bonus issue　派发红股
bonus share (stock)　红利股
bonus share　派发红股
bonus-penalty clause　奖惩条款
book　记账,预订,账面
book balance　账面余额
book cost　账面成本
book inventory　账面盘存
book loss　账面损失
book of accounts　会计账簿
book profit　账面利润
book surplus　账面盈余
book value　账面价值
booking office machine　窗口售票机
booking order　订单
bookkeeper　簿记员,记账员
bookkeeping　簿记
boolean quantity　开关量
boom　繁荣
boom hoist　臂式起重机
booster pump　增压泵
booster transformer　吸流变压器
booster transformer feeding system　吸流变压器供电方式(BT供电方式)
boosting current　吸上电流
boosting wire　吸上线
borax　硼砂
border　图框
border gateway (BG)　边界网关
border gateway protocol (BGP)　边界网关协议
border line　图框线
bored pile　钻孔桩
borehole　钻孔
borehole backfilling　孔内回填
borehole cleaning　清孔
borehole collar　孔口
borehole deflection rate　钻孔偏斜率
borehole-forming　成孔
boring cycle　掘进循环
boring log　钻探日志
boring process　掘进过程

boring rig　钻探设备
boring speed　掘进速度
boring stroke　掘进行程
boring time　掘进时间
borrow　借入
borrow area　取料场,取土场
borrow area agreement　取土场协议
borrow money　借债
borrow pit　取土坑
borrowed capital　借入资本,债务资金
borrowed soil　客土
borrower　借款人
borrowing　借贷
borrowing bank　借款银行
borrowing cost　借贷成本
borrowing country　借款国
borrowing rate　借款利率
both parties　双方
bottom horizontal tube　扫地杆
bottom price　底价,最低价格
bottom shearing force method/quasi-static method　底部剪力法/拟静力法
boulder　漂石
bouldery soil　漂石土
bounced check　空白支票
bound　有义务的
bound by contract　受合同约束
bound water　结合水
boundary line　界线
boundary line of land　用地红线
boundary lines of roads　道路红线
boundary map for construction land　工程用地红线图
boundary marker　界址点
boundary monument　界标
boundary settlement　勘界
boundary sign　界标
boundary stake　界桩
boundary station of railway administration　铁路局界站
boundary　边界,厂界,地界,分界线,界限
bounds　界限
bounty　奖金
bourse　交易所
Boussinesq theory　布辛涅斯克理论
box arch bridge　箱形拱桥
box beam　箱形梁,箱梁
box culvert　箱涵
box fold　箱形褶皱
box foundation　箱形基础

box girder　箱形梁,箱形大梁
box girder bridge　箱形梁桥
box-type high temperature furnace　箱式高温炉
box-type substation　箱式变电站
boycott　抵制
brace　撑杆
braced force　支撑力
bracket　牛腿,托架,托座,支架
bracket for backstay　下锚拉线底座
brackish water　苦咸水
brainstorming　头脑风暴法
brake interface unit　制动接口单元
brake member　制动构件
brake mode　制动方式
brake shoe　铁鞋
braking curve　制动曲线
braking force　制动力
braking force of train　列车制动力
braking release mode curve　缓解制动模式曲线
braking time　制动时间
braking work　制动功
braking-force bracing　制动撑架
braking-force pier　制动墩
branch　分公司
branch affiliate　分支机构
branch center　分中心
branch connection　分支接线,分支结线
branch laboratory　试验分室
branch line　岔线,支线
branch office　分公司
branch passage　支道
branch pipe　叉管,支管
branch switch　分路道岔
branch system　枝状管网
branching parallel jumper　分支并联跳线
brand　品牌
brand name　标牌
brass tacks　基本事实
breach　不履行,违背,违反
breach of contract　不履行合同,毁约,违反合同,违约,不作为,未履行
breach of contract damages　违约金
breach of contractor　承包商违约
breach of duty　失职
breach of law　违法
breach of promise　毁约
breadth of road　路幅
breadth of section　截面宽度

breadth of wall between windows 窗间墙宽度
break 暴跌,毁坏,截断,违背
break a contract 违反合同
break a seal 破封
break contact 静接点
break off an engagement 解约
break through survey 贯通测量
breakage 断线
breakdown 击穿,损坏
breakdown clause 机损条款
breakdown cover 抛锚险
breakdown impulse voltage 击穿冲击电压
breakdown of lump sum bid price
  投标包干价格分解
breakdown of price 单价分析
breakdown price 分项价格
breakdown reappearance 故障再现
breakdown voltage 击穿电压
breaking coil 分闸线圈
breaking load 断裂荷载,拉断荷载
breaking strength 破坏强度
breaking time 分闸时间
breaking up ice run to avoid collision
  防撞破凌
breaking-up and marshalling operation
  解编作业
breakout boot 分支手套
breakthrough （隧道）贯通
breakwater 防波堤
break-down test 破坏试验
break-even 损益
break-even analysis
  保本分析,损益平衡分析,盈亏平衡分析
break-even chart
  保本图,损益平衡图,盈亏平衡图
break-even cost 盈亏平衡费
break-even point 保本点,盈亏平衡点
break-over voltage 导通电压
break-up capacity 解体能力
breathing zone 伸缩区
breccia 角砾岩
bribe 贿赂,贿赂物
bribery 行贿
bribery crime 贿赂罪
bribes 贿赂费
brick 砖
brick lintel 砖过梁
brick masonry column 砖砌体柱
brick masonry structure
  砖砌体结构,砖石结构

brick masonry wall 砖砌体墙
brick worker 砖工
bricklayer 瓦工
brick-concrete structure 砖混结构
bridge 桥
bridge and culvert 桥涵
bridge and tunnel guard telephone
  桥隧守护电话
bridge approach 桥头引道,桥头引线
bridge assessment 桥梁评价
bridge axis location 桥梁轴线测设
bridge bearing mortar 桥梁支座砂浆
bridge CAD 桥梁 CAD
bridge closure 桥梁合龙
bridge connection 桥形接线
bridge construction control survey
  桥梁控制测量
bridge crane 桥式起重机
bridge damage caused by scour and hydraulic loads
  桥梁水毁
bridge deck 桥面板,桥面
bridge deck expansion device 桥面伸缩装置
bridge deck plate 桥面板块
bridge deck plate unit 桥面板单元
bridge deck slab 桥面板块
bridge deck slab unit 桥面板单元
bridge deck system 桥面系
bridge deflection 桥梁挠度
bridge dynamic load test 桥梁动载试验
bridge engineering 桥梁工程
bridge erection by floating crane method
  浮运架桥法
bridge fabrication machine 造桥机
bridge financing 过渡性融资
bridge floor 桥面
bridge guard rail 桥梁护轨
bridge height 桥梁高度
bridge inspection car 桥梁检查车
bridge lighting 灯桥
bridge load spectrum 桥梁荷载谱
bridge load test 桥梁荷载试验
bridge loan 过渡贷款
bridge maintenance 桥梁养护
bridge on slope 坡桥
bridge overhaul 桥梁大修
bridge post 桥梁标
bridge rail 桥栏杆
bridge rating 桥梁检定
bridge rating test 桥梁检定试验
bridge renovation 桥梁改造

bridge site　桥位
bridge site selection　桥位选择
bridge sleeper　桥枕
bridge span　桥梁跨度
bridge span length influenced by temperature
　温度跨度
bridge substructure　桥梁下部结构
bridge superstructure（superstructure）
　桥跨结构（上部结构）
bridge survey　桥梁测量
bridge technical archives　桥梁技术档案
bridge tower　桥塔
bridge works　桥梁工程
bridge/culver by jack-in construction method
　顶进桥涵
bridging agreement　关联协议
bridging loan　临时贷款
bridle wire guiding bracket　吊索导向托座
bridle wire-and-pulley suspension　吊索滑轮装置
bridle wire　吊索
brief　提要,介绍简况,摘要
brief water quality analysis　水质简分析
briefing　简要说明
brightness　亮度
brine　盐水（人工冻结）
brittle failure　脆断,脆性破坏
brittle fracture of rail　钢轨折断
brittle fracture　脆性断裂
brittle transition temperature　脆性转变温度
brittleness　脆性
broad sleeper　宽轨枕
broadcast communication　广播通信
broadcast ephemeris　广播星历
broad-gauge railway　宽轨距铁路
brokage　经纪业
broken block stone　碎块石
broken chain　断链
broken height　断高
broken pile　断桩
broken rail dead zone　断轨盲区
broken rail detection sensitivity
　断轨检点灵敏度
broken rail detection　断轨检查
broken rail gap　断缝
broken rail protection　断轨保障
broken space　舱位损失
broken stone cushion　碎石垫层
broken stone spreader　碎石撒铺机
broken stone-ventilated embankment
　碎块石通风路堤

broken stowage
　积载空隙,亏舱,损失舱位
broker　经纪人,经纪行,中间商,中介人
brokerage　回扣,经纪人佣金,经纪业
brokerage commission　经纪人佣金
brokerage fee　经纪人佣金
brokerage house　经纪行
broker's commission　经纪人佣金
broking　经纪业
broom closet　清扫间
brush structure　帚状构造
BT feeding system
　吸流变压器供电方式（BT 供电方式）
bubble　气泡
bubble spacing coefficient　气泡间距系数
buchite　玻化岩
bucket　铲斗,吊罐
bucket combined coal unloader
　斗式联合卸煤机
bucket elevator　斗式升降机,斗式提升机
bucket excavator　斗式挖土机
bucket ladder dredger　链斗式挖泥机
bucket loader　斗式装载机
buckling　屈曲
buckling deformation　弯折变形
buckling of track　胀轨跑道
buckling properties　弯折性能
budget　预算费,预算
budget allocation　预算拨款
budget amount　预算总额
budget at completion（BAC）　完工预算
budget at design stage　设计概算
budget control　预算控制
budget cost　估算成本,预计费用,预算成本
budget document　预算书
budget for construction drawings
　施工图预算
budget of expenditure　支出预算
budget price of machine shift
　机械台班预算价格
budget reserve for unpredictable work　预备费
budget summary　预算汇总
budget year　财政年度
budgetary construction cost　预算造价
budgetary estimate
　概算,概算价值,概算造价
budgetary estimate（budget）of single construction
　单项概（预）算
budgetary estimate making hierarchies
　编制层次

budgetary estimate making regulation
编制办法
budgetary estimate making unit 编制单元
budgetary estimate quota 概算定额
budgetary price 预算价格
budgetary price of materials 材料预算价格
budgetary price sheet of primary materials
主要材料预算价格表
budgetary quota 预算定额
budgetary reserve for rise of construction price
工程造价增长预备/留费
budgetary unit price method 预算单价法
budgeted cost 估算成本,预计费用,预算成本
budgeted cost of work scheduled(BCWS)
计划工作预算成本
budgeted man-hour 预算工时
buffer beam at girder end 梁端缓冲梁
buffer bumper 缓冲装置
buffer fund 缓冲基金
buffer inventory 保险储备存量,缓冲库存
buffer stock 保险储备存量,缓冲库存
buffer structure 缓冲结构
buffer zone 缓冲区
buffeting 抖振
build stage 建造阶段
buildability 可建造性
builder 建造师
builder's licence 施工单位营业执照
Building Automation System(BAS)
机电设备监控系统
building(preventative)**maintenance scheduling**
建筑维护计划
building and removing cost 搭拆费
building axis survey 建筑轴线测量
building block 砌块
building boundary 建筑界限
building category 建筑类别
building code 建筑规范,建筑条例
building construction engineering
房屋建筑工程
building decoration 建筑装饰
building defects insurance 建筑缺陷保险
building deformation 建筑变形
building density 建筑密度
building design 建筑设计
building energy consumption
建筑能耗综合值
building energy efficiency 建筑节能
building energy efficiency improment rate
建筑本体节能率
building energy saving rate
建筑综合节能率
building engineering company
建筑工程公司
building engineering survey 建筑工程测量
building envelope 围护结构(房建)
building environment load reduction of railway station 铁路客站建筑环境负荷减少
building environment quality of railway station
铁路客站建筑环境质量
building for passenger service 客运用房
building foundation 建筑地基
building group 建筑群
building height 建筑高度
building industry 建筑业
building information modeling/model(BIM)
建筑信息化模型
building inspector 房屋检测人员
Building Integrated Timing Supply(BITS)
大楼综合定时供给设备
building line 建筑控制线,房屋界线
building line survey 建筑红线定位测量
building loan 建筑贷款
building management system
建筑管理系统
building owner 业主
building permit 建设许可证,建筑执照
building products 建筑产品
building services design 建筑设备设计
building structure 建筑结构
building structure design 建筑结构设计
building subsidence monitoring
建筑物沉降监测
building system analysis 建筑系统分析
building tax 房产税,建筑物税
building unite pipe 接户管
buildings account 建筑账户
buildings and structures 建筑物与构筑物
build-operate-sell(BOS) 建设—运营—出售
build-operate-transfer(BOT)
建设—运营—移交
build-own-operate(BOO) 建设—拥有—运营
build-own-operate-maintain(BOOM)
建设—拥有—运营—维护
build-own-operate-subsidize-transfer(BOOST)
建设—拥有—运营—补贴—移交
build-own-operate-transfer(BOOT)
建设—拥有—运营—移交
build-own-sell(BOS) 建设—拥有—出售
build-rent-transfer(BRT) 建设—出租—移交

build-to-suit 定制建造
build-transfer-lease (BTL) 建设—移交—租赁
build-transfer-operate (BTO) 建设—移交—运营
built-up common crossing 组合式辙叉
built-up girder 组合梁
bulged fishplate 鼓包夹板
bulk 散装货物
bulk cargo carrier 散装货船
bulk cement 散装水泥
bulk density 块体密度,毛体积密度
bulk goods loading area 散堆装货区
bulk goods loading yard 散堆装货物货场
bulk laden in bulk 散装的
bulk material 大宗材料,散装材料
bulk modulus 体积模量
bulk procurement 整批采购
bulk saturation density 块体饱和密度
bulldozer 推土机
bundled tube structure 成束筒结构
bunker train 槽式列车
buoy water level gauge 浮标水位计
buoyancy 浮力
buoyant unit weight 浮重度
burden 载重
burden of proof 举证责任
burden rate 间接费用分摊率
bureau of shipping 船级社
burette 滴定管
burial depth 埋深
burial depth of foundation 基础埋置深度
burial depth of pipe top 管顶埋深
burial depth of the pipe 管道埋深
buried abutment 埋置式桥台
buried concrete 地下混凝土
buried horizontal tank 埋地卧式油罐
buried pipe 暗管
buried terrace 掩埋阶地
buried water stop tie 中埋式止水带
buried wiring 暗线
burly 结实的
burr 毛刺
burst noise 突发噪声
burst of rail base 轨底崩裂
burst of rail end 轨端崩裂
burst tearing strength 胀破强度
burst tearing test 胀破试验
bus bar 汇流条,母排,母线
bus conductor 汇集线,母线
bus coupling 母联

busbar bridge 母线桥
busbar current 母线电流
busbar voltage 母线电压
business 工商企业,商行
business circle 实业界
business condition 行情
business cycle 经济周期,商业周期
business development 业务开发
business environmental risk index
 企业环境风险指数
business feasibility 商业可行性
business hours 营业时间
business interruption insurance
 经营中断保险
business law 商法
business license 营业执照
business line 业务范围
business loan 企业贷款
business location 经营场所
business management 企业管理
business organization 商业机构
business performance 经营业绩
business place 营业地点
business profits 营业利润
business report 营业报表
business risks 经营风险
business secret 商业秘密
business support system (BSS)
 业务支撑系统
business tax 营业税
business transaction 商业交易
butt joint 对接
button 按钮
button for audible device 音响按钮
button indication 按钮表示
button indicator 按钮表示器
buttressed structure 支挡式结构
buy 收购
buy back deal 回购交易
buyer's credit 买方信贷
buyer's market 买方市场
buying agent 进货代理人
buying expenses 进货费用
buying offer 购货发盘,购买要约,买方递盘
buying order 购货单
buy-back 返销,回销
buy-back agreement 返销协议
buy-back of product 产品回购,回购产品
buzzer 蜂鸣器
by contract 依合同

by share　按份额
bypass busbar　旁路母线
bypass feeder　捷接线
bypass pipe　旁通管
bypass route　迂回进路
by-law　地方法规,细则
by-pass seepage　绕渗

C

cab approach announcement　机车接近通知
cab integrated radio communication equipment（CIR）　机车综合无线通信设备
cab radio　机车电台
cab remote control for humping　驼峰推峰机车遥控
cab signal code sender　机车信号发码器
cab signal indicator　机车信号表示器
cab signal interference from adjacent tracks　机车信号邻线干扰
cab signal message　机车信号信息
cab signal test loop　机车信号测试环线
cab signaling　机车信号
cab signaling equipment　机车信号设备
cab signaling for humping　驼峰推峰机车信号
cab signaling inductor location　机车信号作用点
cab signaling mode（CS）　机车信号模式
cab signaling testing section　机车信号测试区段
cable　电缆, 缆索
cable box　电缆盒
cable bracket　电缆架
cable branch box　电缆分支箱
cable branching terminal box　分向电缆盒
cable chamber　电缆腔
cable clamp　电缆线卡
cable clip　索夹
cable comprehensive tester　线缆综合测试仪
cable control length　电缆控制长度
cable cover　电缆盖板
cable crane　缆索起重机
cable drum　电缆盘
cable duct　电缆沟（线路两侧预留的）
cable fault detector　电缆故障探测仪
cable fault tester　电缆故障测试仪
cable force control　索力控制
cable force test　索力测试
cable hoist　绞车
cable inflation　电缆充气
cable interlayer　电缆夹层
cable joint　电缆接头
cable ladder　电缆支架
cable ladder（tray）　电缆桥架
cable layout　电缆配线图
cable manhole　电缆检修孔
cable mark　电缆标志
cable pigtail　尾纤
cable plane　索平面
cable rack　电缆支架
cable rate　电汇费率
cable reel　电缆盘
cable riser　电缆支架
cable route　电缆线路
cable saddle　索鞍
cable shaft　电缆井, 电缆竖井
cable shielding　线缆屏蔽
cable sleeve　电缆套管
cable stocking　钢丝网套
cable support　电缆支架
cable support tower　索塔
cable tee connector　电缆分线夹
cable terminal　电缆终端头
cable terminal box　终端电缆盒
cable terminal box on a post　杆上电缆盒
cable terminal pole　电缆终端杆
cable transfer　电汇
cable tray　走电缆槽, 电缆沟
cable trench　电缆沟（需要回填土的）, 电缆沟
cable trench cover　电缆沟盖板
cable trough　电缆沟, 电缆槽
cable trough of tunnel　隧道电缆槽
cable TV　有线电视
cable winch　绞车

cableway 缆道
cable-stayed bridge 斜拉桥
cabling 布线
caboose 守车
caboose working system 随乘制
cadastral information system
　地籍信息系统
cadastral map 地籍图
cadastre 不动产清册
cadmiferous sewage 含镉污水
cadmium content 镉含量
Cainozoic era 新生代
Cainozoic erathem/group 新生界
caisson 沉箱
caisson foundation 沉箱基础
caisson pile 沉箱桩,管柱桩
calcantite 胆矾
calcareous cementation 钙质胶结
calcareous shale 钙质页岩
calcite 方解石
calcium carbide 碳化钙
calcium carbide decrement method
　碳化钙减量法
calcium magnesium silicate hornfels
　钙镁硅酸盐角岩
calculated breaking load 计算拉断荷载
calculated capacity 计算容量
calculated height 计算高度
calculated length of railway vehicles
　车辆计算长度
calculated risk 计划风险,预计风险
calculated span 计算跨度
calculated span of bridge and culvert
　桥涵计算跨径
calculated target point 计算停车点
calculated value of wetting-collapse settlement
　湿陷量计算值
calculating length 计算长度
calculation base 计算基数
calculation of labour cost 劳务成本计算
calculation overturning point 计算倾覆点
calculation parameter of standard load
　标准荷载计算参数
calculation point of hump 驼峰计算点
calculation program 计算程序
calculation rules 计算规定,计算规则
calculations 计算书
Caledonian age/stage 加里东期
calendar 日历
calendar day 日历日

calendar month 日历月
calendar year 日历年
calibration 标定,校准
calibration certificate 校准证书
calibration coefficient 率定系数
calibration method 校准法
California bearing ratio (CBR)
　加州承载比
call 催缴
call attempt per second (CAPS)
　每秒试呼次数
call barring service 呼叫限制
call button 求助按钮
call completing rate 接通率
call deposit 通知存款
call for bids (tender) 招标
call for funds 集资
call in a loan 收回贷款
call letter 催款信,推销商品的信件
call loan 短期同行拆借,活期贷款,通知贷款
call loss probability 呼损率
call money 活期贷款
call price 赎回价格
call queuing 呼叫列队
call signal 呼叫信号
call system 求助系统
call waiting 呼叫等待
call/notice of payment 通知偿还
callable bond 可赎回债券
callback pay 加班工资
calling 职业
calling-on mode (CO) 引导模式
calling-on route and signal test
　引导进路及信号测试
calling-on signal 引导信号
camber 拱度,路拱
camber of structural members
　结构构件起拱
cambist 汇兑商
Cambrian period 寒武纪
Cambrian system 寒武系
camera mainframe 摄影机主机
camp 营地
camp equipment 营房设备
campshed 排桩
canal survey 渠道测量
cancel 撤销,作废
cancel a block 取消闭塞
cancel a contract 撤销合同,解约
cancel after verification 核销

canceled check 付讫支票
cancellation 作废
cancellation of a contract 撤销合同
cancellation of licence 吊销执照
cancellation of protected area 撤防
candidate for tendering 投标候选人
cannibal repair 互换修
canon of economics 经济规律
canopy 雨棚
cant 超高,行话
cant deficiency 欠超高
cant excess 过超高
cant surplus 过超高
cantilever 腕臂,悬臂
cantilever beam 挑梁,悬臂梁
cantilever brace 悬臂支架
cantilever bracket 悬臂支架
cantilever bridge 悬臂梁桥,悬臂桥
cantilever crane 悬臂式起重机
cantilever displacement 腕臂偏移
cantilever erection method 悬臂架设法
cantilever pole 悬臂杆
cantilever rail laying machine
　悬臂式铺轨机
cantilever retaining wall 悬臂式挡土墙
cantilever screw unloading machine
　悬臂螺旋卸车机
cantilever slab 悬臂板
cantilever structure 悬臂结构
cantilever structure across two tracks
　跨双线腕臂结构
canyon 峡谷
cap beam 帽梁
capacitance and dielectric loss
　电容和介质损耗
capacitance compensation 电容补偿
capacitor bank 电容器组
capacitor charge 电容器充电
capacitor discharge 电容器放电
capacitor reactance 电容器电抗
capacitor room 电容器室
capacitor voltage transformer
　电容式电压互感器
capacitor 电容器
capacity 容量,职位,资格
capacity design 能力设计
capacity operating rate 设备利用率
capacity to contract 缔约能力,立约能力
capillary 毛细管
capillary rise 毛细水上升

capillary saturation method 毛细管饱和法
capillary water 毛细管水,毛细水
capillary water rising height
　毛细管水上升高度
capillary zone 毛细带
capital 资本,资方,资金
capital account
　固定资产账户,资本性账户
capital and interest 本利
capital appreciation 资本增值
capital assets 固定资产,资本性资产
capital authorized 法定资本
capital bonus 股票股利,资本红利
capital budget 基本建设预算,资本预算
capital circulation 资金流转
capital composition structure 资本结构
capital construction 基本建设
capital construction loan 基建贷款
capital construction projects 基本建设工程
capital cost 基本建设费用
capital deficit 资本亏损
capital equipment 固定设备
capital charges 资本支出
capital expenditure 基本建设费用
capital expenses 资金筹集费,经费支出
capital flight 资本外逃
capital formation 资本形成
capital fund 基建资金,资本基金,资本金
capital gain or loss 资本损益
capital goods 生产资料
capital intensive project 资金密集项目
capital investment 资本投资
capital lease 资本租赁
capital liability 资本负债
capital market 资本市场
capital outlay 基建投资,资本支出
capital project 基本建设项目
capital repair fund 大修基金
capital reserve 资本准备金
capital reserves 资本公积
capital return 资本收益率
capital scarcity 资金不足
capital stock 股本
capital surplus 资本盈利
capital transfer tax 资本转移税
capital turnover rate 资本周转率
capital works 基本建设工程
capitalizable cost 可资本化成本
capitation 按人计算
capping stone 帽石

capstan 绞车
capsule sealing device 胶囊止水器
capturing hood 外部吸气罩
car accelerator 车辆加速器
car delivery and inspection area
　小汽车交验区
car depot 车辆段
car energy head 车辆能高
car group numbers of train marshalling plan
　列车编组计划组号
car inspection and repair facilities
　车辆检修设备
car kilometers per car per day
　货车日车公里
car liner trains 小汽车班列
car loading area 小汽车装车区
car operation yard 小汽车作业场
car retarder 车辆减速器
car rolling down resistance 车辆溜放阻力
car sill straightening siding 调梁线
car spacing for uncoupled inspection
　拉钩检查距离
car sterilizing siding 货车消毒线
car storage area 小汽车存放区
car technical servicing yard
　车辆技术整备场
car wheelset repair shop 车轮厂
carboids 似碳质
carbon contact strip 碳滑板
carbon dioxide fire extinguishing agent
　二氧化碳灭火剂
carbon dioxide fire extinguishing system
　二氧化碳灭火系统
carbon equivalent 碳当量
carbon rail 碳素轨
carbon structural steel 碳素结构钢
carbonaceous shale 炭质页岩
carbonate 碳酸盐
carbonate content 碳酸根含量
carbonation depth 碳化深度
carbonation of concrete 混凝土碳化
carbonatite 碳酸盐岩
Carboniferous period 石炭纪
Carboniferous system 石炭系
carbonization 碳化
carbonization environment 碳化环境
card 卡片
card of construction site 工点卡片
card reader 读卡器
cardinal changes 根本性变更
cardinal plane 基面
cardinal point 基点
care and supply of document
　照看和保管文件
care of works and indemnities
　工程照管和免责
cargo 船货,货物
cargo accounting advice 货物账款通知单
cargo agent 货运代理行
cargo berth 货运码头
cargo certificate 货单
cargo damage adjustment 货损理算
cargo delivery notice 提货通知,到货通知
cargo document 货运提单
cargo inspection 货物检查
cargo insurance 货物运输保险,货物保险
cargo insurance policy 货物保险单
cargo marine insurance 海洋货运保险
cargo mark 货物标志,货运唛头
cargo name 货名
cargo paper 货运单证
cargo policy 货物保险单
cargo service 货运业务
cargo terminal 货运码头,货运终点站,货栈
cargo transportation insurance
　货物运输保险
cargo-handling equipment 货物装卸设备
carpenter 木工
carriage 货运,运输
carriage and insurance paid to (CIP)
　运费、保险费付至
carriage by rail 铁路运输
carriage by road 公路运输
carriage forward 运费由收货人付,运费待付
carriage free 运费免付
carriage of container 集装箱运输
carriage paid 运费已付
carriage paid to (CPT) 运费付至
carried down 转记
carrier 承运人,运输工具
carrier and interference ratio 干扰保护比
carrier vehicle 运输车
carrier's liability insurance
　承运人责任保险
carrier's lien 承运人留置权
carry 运载
carry down carried forward 转记
carry out 执行
carry out/implement/execute/fulfil a contract
　履行合同

carrying amount 账面金额
carrying capacity 通过能力
carrying capacity limiting section
  限制区间
carrying capacity of receiving-departure track
  到发线通过能力
carrying cost 置存成本
carrying test 搭载测试
carrying value 账面价值,置存价值
cars per cut 钩车
cartage 运货费
cartographic expert system 制图专家系统
cartographic generalization 制图综合
cartography 地图制图学
car-load freight yard 整车货场
case 案例,箱
case law 判例法
cash 兑现,现金
cash a cheque 支票兑现
cash account 现金账,现金账户
cash advance 预付现金
cash against delivery 交货付款
cash against document 交单付款
cash and delivery 付款交货
cash assets 现金资产
cash balance 现金余额
cash before delivery (CBD) 付款后交货
cash bonus 现金红利,现金奖金,现金奖励
cash book 现金簿,现金账
cash credit 现金贷方,现金支出
cash debit 现金借方
cash deposit 现金存款
cash deposit as collateral 押金
cash disbursement journal 现金支出日记账
cash discount 现金折扣
cash dispenser 自动取款机
cash dividend 现金股息
cash drawing 提取现金
cash flow 现金流量,资金流动
cash flow analysis 资金流分析
cash flow diagram 现金流量图,现金流图
cash flow estimate 现金流估计
cash flow management 现金流管理
cash flow net 现金流净值
cash flow risk 现金流风险
cash flow statement 现金流表
cash fund 现金基金
cash guarantee 现金担保
cash in advance 预付
cash inflows 现金流入量

cash losses 现金赔款,现金损失
cash management account (CMA)
  现金管理账户
cash market 现金交易市场
cash on delivery (COD) 银货两讫,货到付款
cash on hand 库存现金
cash on shipment (COS)
  装船付现,装运付款
cash outflows 现金流出量
cash outlay 现金支出
cash over and short 现金溢缺
cash payment 现金支付
cash purchase 现购,现金购买
cash receipt journal 现金收入日记账
cash receipt voucher 现金收入凭证
cash register 现金出纳机
cash remittance note 汇款单
cash reserve 现金储备
cash sales 现金销售
cash settlement 现金结算
cash value 可变现价值
cash with order 订货付现
cashable asset 可变现资产
cashed check 已兑现支票
cashier 出纳员
cashier's cheque 本票
casing drilling rig 套管钻机
casing pipe 护管壁,套管
cast 浇筑
cast iron pipe 铸铁管
cast manganese frog 整铸辙叉
cast monobloc crossing 整铸辙叉
casting 浇注,灌注
cast-in-place cantilever method
  悬臂浇筑法
cast-in-place concrete 现浇混凝土
cast-in-place concrete structure
  现浇混凝土结构
cast-in-place construction on falsework
  支架现浇施工
cast-in-place pile 就地灌筑桩
cast-in-place reinforced concrete structure
  现浇钢筋混凝土结构
cast-in-situ box girder with scaffolding support
  支架现浇箱梁
cast-in-situ continuous girder without support
  悬浇连续梁
cast-in-situ slab-column structure 现浇板柱结构
cast-iron radiator 铸铁散热器
casual employment 临时雇工

casual repair 临修
casual repair of vehicles detached from train 摘车临修
casual repair track 临修线
casual repair workshop 临修库
casual work 临时工作,零活
casual worker/labourer 临时工
casualty 伤亡人员
cataclasite 碎裂岩
cataclastic rock 压碎岩
catalogue 商品目录
catastrophe 灾害,灾难
catastrophe loss 巨灾损失
catch pit 集水井,截水坑
catch siding 安全线
catch up 追钩
catchment area 汇流面积,汇水面积,集水面积
catchment area survey 汇水面积测量
catchment 集水
catchment of debris flow 泥石流流域
catchpit 集水坑
category 5 cable 五类线
category 6 cable 六类线
category of comprehensive expense of labors 综合工费类别
category of fill material 填料类别
catenary emergency maintenance train 接触网抢修列车
catenary high-altitude operation vehicle 接触网高空作业车
catenary maintenance vehicle 接触网维修作业车
catenary suspension with stitch wire 弹性链形悬挂
cation 阳离子
cation exchange capacity 阳离子交换量
cationic emulsified asphalt 阳离子乳化沥青
cationic emulsifier 阳离子乳化剂
caulking material 嵌缝材料
cause 诉因,原因
caustic alkali 苛性碱
caution signal 减速信号,注意信号
cave axis 洞轴
cave body 洞体
cave deposit 洞穴堆积
cave flower 石花
caveat 停止支付通知
caveat emptor 买方负责
caveat venditor 包退包换

caveat venditor 卖方负责
cavern 洞穴
cave-in 塌方
cavity 空穴
cavity wall with insulation 夹心墙
CBR burst strength CBR 顶破强度
cease 停止,休止
cease work 收工
cede to 让与
ceiling 顶棚
ceiling amount 最高限额
ceiling board 顶棚
ceiling fan 吊扇
ceiling hanger 顶棚吊顶
ceiling price 最高限价
ceiling radiant heating 顶棚辐射采暖
ceiling screen 挡烟垂壁
ceiling speed surveillance area 顶棚速度监视区
cell broadcast center(CBC) 小区广播中心
cell concrete 多孔混凝土
cell delay variation(CDV) 信元时延变化
cell error rate(CER) 信元差错率
cell global identifier(CGI) 全球小区识别码
cell lose rate(CLR) 信元丢失率
cell transfer delay(CTD) 信元传送时延
cement 黏结
cement agent 胶结剂
cement block 预制水泥块
cement brand 水泥牌号
cement bunker 水泥仓
cement concrete pavement 水泥混凝土铺面
cement content 水泥含量
cement fly ash soil 水泥粉煤灰土
cement grout 水泥浆
cement injection 水泥灌浆
cement mortar 水泥胶砂,水泥砂浆
cement particle 水泥颗粒
cement paste 水泥浆,水泥净浆
cement paste material 水泥浆体材料
cement paste mixer 水泥净浆搅拌机
cement paste specimen 水泥浆试件
cement plastering 水泥抹面
cement pump 水泥输送泵
cement sand shotcrete 水泥裹砂喷射混凝土
cement silo 水泥仓
cement soil 水泥土
cement soil squeezing pile 水泥土挤压桩

cement stabilization 水泥加固
cement standard consistency meter 水泥标准稠度仪
cement trough 水泥槽
cementation degree of structural plane 结构面胶结程度
cementitious material coefficient of corrosion resistance 胶凝材料抗蚀系数
cementitious material 胶凝材料
cementitious material water ratio 水灰比
cement-emulsified asphalt mortar（CAM/CEAM）水泥乳化沥青砂浆
cement-flyash-gravelpile（CFG）水泥粉煤灰碎石桩
cement-improved soil 水泥改良土
cement-soil compaction pile 水泥土挤密桩
cement-soil mixing pile 水泥土搅拌桩
cement-water ratio 水灰比
center disc cutter 中心滚刀
center distance between main girders 主梁中心距
center frequency 中心频率
center line 中心线
center line of roadway setting out 巷道中线标定
center line stake 中桩（中线桩）
center mast of overlap 中心柱
center mileage 中心里程
center server 中心服务器
center stake 中桩
center stake leveling（also known as "profile leveling"）中桩高程测量（又称"纵断面水准测量"）
center stake leveling（CSL）中桩高程测量（中平）
center to center distance between tower feet 根开（铁塔）
center to center spacing of adjacent grooves 相邻凹槽中心间距
central system of railway administration 铁路局中心系统
centering element 归心元素
centering under point 点下对中
centerline meridian 中央子午线
centerline position of track slab 轨道板中线位置
centerline stake leveling 中平
centerline survey 中线测量
central bank 中央银行
central diaphragm method（CD method）中隔壁法（CD 法）
central drainage ditch 中心排水沟
central heating 集中采暖,集中供暖
central hot water supply system 集中热水供应系统
central integrated management platform 中心级集成管理平台
central laboratory 中心实验室
central moment method 中心矩法
central plain 中部平原
central position 中心位置
central power station 集中发电站
central processing unit（CPU）中央处理器
central reservation 绿化分隔带
central stake 中心桩
central station 中心站
centralized 集中式
centralized air conditioning system 集中式空气调节系统
centralized concrete mixing plant 混凝土集中拌和站
centralized configuration 集中配置
centralized control 集中控制,中心控制
centralized control station 集控站
centralized cooling system 集中冷却系统
centralized grounding box 集中接地箱
centralized interlocking 集中联锁
centralized interlocking for flat shunting area 平面调车区集中联锁
centralized interlocking for hump yard 驼峰集中联锁
centralized management 集中管理
centralized mixing station of filler 填料集中拌和站
centralized monitoring 集中监控
centralized monitoring system of OCS disconnectors 接触网开关集中监控系统
centralized power source 集中电源
centralized power supply 集中供电
centralized repair 集中检修,集中修
centralized signaling monitoring（CSM）信号集中监测
centralized traffic control（CTC）集中调度
centralized traffic control（CTC）**system** 集中调度系统
centralized-distributed architecture 集中分布式架构
centrally operated switch 集中道岔
centrally-controlled turnout 集中控制道岔
centre 基点

centre of alignment 线路中心线
centric load (centric axial load) 中心荷载(轴心荷载)
centrifugal blower 离心式鼓风机
centrifugal compressor 离心式压缩机
centrifugal force 离心力
centrifugal force of train 列车离心力
centrifugal force ratio 离心力率
centrifugal glass-wool 离心玻璃棉
centrifugal pump 离心泵,离心水泵
centrifugal ventilator 离心式通风机
centrifuge 离心机
centrifuge moisture equivalent method 离心含水当量法
ceramic ferrule 磁环
ceramic sheath 瓷护套
ceramic tile 瓷砖
ceramsite concrete 陶粒混凝土
Cerruti's solution 色卢铁解答
certificate 单证,证书
certificate fee 签证费
certificate for export 出口检验证
certificate for payment 付款证明
certificate of completion 竣工证书
certificate of credit standing 资信证明
certificate of delivery (C/D) 交货证明书
certificate of deposit 存款单
certificate of dishonour 拒付证书
certificate of entrustment 委托书
certificate of expenditure 支出证明书
certificate of final payment 最终支付证书
certificate of incorporation 公司注册证书
certificate of inspection 检验证书
certificate of insurance 保险凭证,保险证书,保单,保险单
certificate of manufacture 制造证明书
certificate of materials 材料证明
certificate of occupancy 占有证明书
certificate of origin (C/O) 原产地证明书,产地证书
certificate of patent 专利证书
certificate of payment 支付证明
certificate of practical completion 实质竣工证书
certificate of protest 拒付证书
certificate of quality 货物品质证书,品质证明
certificate of registry 注册证书
certificate of release 债务解除证书
certificate of rescission 契约废除证明
certificate of re-export 再出口证书
certificate of seaworthiness 适航证明书

certificate of shipment 出口许可证
certificate of substantial completion 实质竣工证书
certification 注册证书,合格证
certification of proof 检验证书
certified accountant 注册会计师,特许会计师
certified check (cheque) 保付支票
certified cost engineer 注册成本工程师
certified final drawings (CF) 供货厂商最终确认图
certified management accountant (CMA) 执业管理会计师
certified report 证明报告
certified vendor drawings (CD) 供货厂商最终确认图
certifier 工程签证人
cessation 停止,休止
cessation of employer's liability 雇主责任的终止
cessation of liability 终止责任
cesser clause 中止条款
cestui que trust 信托受益人
chain network 链形网
chain of command 指挥链
chain reaction 连锁反应
chain risks 连锁风险
chair the meeting 主持会议
chairman 董事长,主席
chairman of the board 董事长,主席
chalcopyrite 黄铜矿
chalking 起砂
challenge 质询
challenge procedure 质询程序
chamber 商会,议院
chamber blasting 峒室爆破
chamber of commerce 商会
chamber of trade 贸易协会
chance 可能性,机会
chance of loss 损失机会
change 变更,改动
change clause 变更条款
change control 变更控制
change in cost 费用变更
change instruction (CI) 变更指令
change log 变更日志
change of ownership 变更所有权
change order 变更命令,变更指令
change order log 变更命令记录簿
change proposal 变更建议书

change request 变更请求
changeover section
　地面转换自动过分相区段
changes in personnel
　人事变动,职员的变更
channel 管渠,渠道
channel dredging 河渠疏浚
channel regulation works 水道整治工程
channel roughness coefficient 河槽糙率系数
channel steel 槽钢
channel surveying reference level 航道绘图水位
channel survey 航道测量
channel width 河槽宽度
channeller 挖沟机
character 性质
character reference 品行证明书
characteristic combination 标准组合
characteristic crack width 特征裂缝宽度
characteristic period 特征周期
characteristic period of response spectrum
　反应谱特征周期
characteristic period of the acceleration response
　spectrum 地震动加速度反应谱特征周期
characteristic value 特征值
characteristic value of material properties
　材料性能的标准值
characteristic value of subsoil bearing capacity
　地基承载力特征值
characteristic value of the vertical bearing capaci-
　ty of a single pile 单桩竖向承载力特征值
characteristics 特点
characteristics of ecological environment
　生态环境特征
characteristics of mollisol 软土特性
charge 费用,起诉,收费,指控
charge for filling material 填料费
charge for overweight 超重费
charge for storage & freight of goods
　物资储运费
charge for the right of land use
　土地使用权出让金
charge for trouble 酬劳费
charge for use 使用费
charge for using construction machinery
　施工机械使用费
charge for using small scale machines and tools
　小型机具使用费
charge for using tools and appliances
　工具用具使用费
charge off 冲销,核销,销账

charge on assets 资产留置权
charge sales 赊销
charges for customs clearance 清关费
charges for erection and removal of scaffold
　脚手架拆搭费
charges for installation and removal and off-site
　delivery 安拆费及场外运费
charges for procurement 采购费
charges of loading and unloading 装卸费
charge-amplifier 电荷放大器
charging 充电,计费,取费
charging along detonating fuse 导爆索装药
charging gateway (CG) 计费网关
charging impact wrench 充电式冲击扳手
charging line 供料线,供水管
charging module 充电模块
charging pressure 充装压力
charging scope 计费范围
charging source chamber 充电电源间
charging standard 计费标准,取费标准
charging structure of contour hole
　周边眼装药结构
chart 海图,图表
chart of accounts
　会计科目一览表,账户一览表
charter 公司执照,特许,章程,租船
charter by voyage 航次租船
charter contract 租船合同
charter of company 公司章程
charter party 租船方,租船合同
chartered accountant (CA)
　注册会计师,特许会计师
chartered engineer 注册工程师
chartered freight 租船运费
chartered period 租期
chartered quantity surveyor
　注册工料测量师
charterer 租船人
chasing load test 螺旋板载荷试验
chassis 起落架
chattel 动产
chattel mortgage 动产抵押
chattering 颤振
cheap credit 低息贷款
cheap money 低息贷款
check 核实,支票
check and approve 核准
check book 支票簿
check book stubs 支票簿存根
check gauge 查照间隙

check in construction stage 施工阶段验算
check mark 核对符号,检查标志
check of zero 零点校核
check rail of turnout 道岔护轨
check register 支票登记簿
check requisition 照查条件
check sheet 对账单
check stub 支票存根
check table 检查表
check up account 核对账目
checkable 可用支票付款的
checked capacity 校核容量
checking account 活期账户,支票账户
checking datum mark 校核基点
checking point method 验算点法
checklist 核对清单,检核表
check-in 检票
cheese head stud 圆柱头焊钉
chemical accumulation 化学堆积
chemical amendments 化学改良法
chemical analysis 化学分析
chemical constitution 化学结构
chemical corrosion 化学侵蚀
chemical corrosion resistance test
  抗化学腐蚀试验
chemical dosing 投药
chemical erosion environment
  化学侵蚀环境
chemical flushing 化学洗井
chemical grouting 化学灌浆
chemical improved soil 化学改良土
chemical methods 化学法
chemical oxygen demand (COD)
  化学需氧量
chemical sedimentation 化学沉淀法
chemical stability 化学稳定性
chemical storage tank 贮药间
chemical weathering 化学风化
chemical-dosing room 加药间
cheque 支票
chert 燧石
chess board structure 棋盘格式构造
chief accountant 首席会计师
chief architect 总建筑师
chief delegate 首席代表
chief designer 总设计师
chief engineer 总工程师
chief executive officer (CEO)
  首席执行官
chief finance officer 首席财务官
chief foreman 总领班
chief of customs 海关关长
chief resident architect 现场首席建筑师
chief resident engineer
  现场首席工程师,驻地首席工程师
chief supervisor 总监理工程师
chimney effect 烟囱效应
chimney rack 烟囱架
China train control system (CTCS)
  中国铁路列控系统,中国列车运行控制系统
Chinese train control system level 0 (CTCS-0)
  中国列车运行控制系统 0 级
chipping machine 混凝土打毛机
chisel cutting method 凿方切割法
chloride 氯化物
chloride concentration 氯离子浓度
chloride content 氯化物含量
chloride environment 氯盐环境
chloride saline soil 氯盐渍土
chlorine dioxide disinfection
  二氧化氯消毒法
chlorine disinfection 液氯消毒法
chlorineion content 氯离子含量
chlorion diffusion coefficient
  氯离子扩散系数
chlorite 绿泥石
choke transformer 扼流变压器
choking coil 扼流线圈
chord deflection distance 弦线偏距
chord member 弦杆
chord offset method 弦线支距法
chromatic dispersion coefficient
  色度色散系数
chromaticity 色度,色品
chromaticity coordinates 色品坐标
chromaticity diagram 色品图
chromatography room 色谱间
chromatography standard solution
  色谱标准溶液
chromium compounds 铬化物
chromium gel reprint 铬胶翻版
chromogenic solutions 显色溶液
chronological books 序时账簿
chute 斜道
cinnabar 辰砂
circuit breaker (CB) 断路开关,断路器
circuit diagram 电路图,线路图
circuit failure 电路故障
circuit switching 电路交换
circuit switchover 电路倒换

circuit table 电路台账
circuit with multiple transit sections
　多转接段电路
circuit with sending and receiving separated
　送受分开电路
circular curve 圆曲线
circular curve locating 圆曲线测设
circular frequency 圆频率
circular junction terminal 环形枢纽
circular letter 通知函
circular letter of credit 旅行信用证
circular pier 圆形桥墩
circular pole of equal diameter 等径圆杆
circular structure 环状构造
circular tunnel 圆形隧道
circulate 流通
circulating additional flow 循环附加流量
circulating factor of depot repairing
　段修循环系数
circulating pipe 循环管
circulating pump 循环泵
circulation and processing area 流通加工区
circulator 水力循环澄清池
circumferential 环向
circumferential filter pipe 环向盲管
circumferential joint 环向缝
cirque 冰斗
civil action/lawsuit/suit 民事诉讼
civil air defence basement 人民防空地下室
civil air defence works 人民防空工程
civil building 民用建筑
civil code 民法典
civil commotion 民间骚乱
civil construction 土木建筑
civil contract 土建工程合同
civil damage compensation 民事损害赔偿
civil engineer 土木工程师
civil engineering 土木工程
civil engineering firm 土建公司
civil engineering handover inspection
　土建交接检验
civil engineering investments 土建投资
civil engineering procedure 土木工程程序
civil law 大陆法，民法
civil law system 大陆法系
civil legal relations with foreign element
　涉外民事法律关系
civil liability 民事责任
civil liability insurance 民事责任险
civil right 民事权利

civil work 土木工程，土建
civil works 线下（站前工程），站前工程
cladding alloy 熔覆合金
claim 权利要求书，索赔索取，要求
claim adjuster 理赔理算人
claim agent 理赔代理人
claim assessor 估损人
claim by owner (employer) 业主索赔
claim consciousness 索赔意识
claim document 索赔文件
claim event 索赔事件
claim expense 理赔费用
claim for compensation
　索赔补偿费，索要补偿
claim for damages
　索赔损害赔偿费，索要损害赔偿
claim for extension of time 延长工期索赔
claim for extra cost 额外费用索赔
claim money 索赔额，索取额
claim ratio 赔付率，索赔率
claim reserve 赔款准备金
claim settlement 理赔
claim settling agent 理赔代理人
claim statement 索赔报告，索赔清单
claim under the performance security
　履约保函的索赔
claimant (claimer) 索赔人,请求人
claimant (claimer) 申请人
claimant (claimer) obligee 债权人
claimee 被索赔人
claimer 请求人,索赔人
claims for payment and /or EOT
　费用和工期延长（EOT）的索赔
claims of continuing effect
　有持续影响的索赔
clamp 夹具
clamp fastening 扣板式扣件
clamp for midpoint anchor rope of messenger wire
　承力索中心锚结绳线夹
clamp holder for out-of-running CW
　锚支定位卡子
clamping force 扣压力
clamp-on ammeter 钳形电流表
clamshell 抓土斗
clamshell bucket
　蛤壳式抓斗/抓铲挖掘机
clamshell crane 抓斗式起重机
clamshell dredge 抓斗式挖泥船
clamshell excavator 抓斗式挖土机
clamshell shovel 抓斗式挖土机

clarification 澄清
clarification of bidding (tender) documents 招标文件的澄清
clash detection 碰撞检查
class 级别
class of construction 建筑类别
class rate 分级费率
Class Ⅰ access node Ⅰ类接入节点
Class Ⅱ access node Ⅱ类接入节点
classification 等级
classification for seismic fortification of buildings 建筑结构抗震设防类别
classification of frost heaving 冻胀分级
classification of geological complexity 地质复杂程度分级
classification of locomotive repair 检修修程
classification of seismic fortification of buildings 建筑抗震设防分类
classification of soil and rock 土石分类
classification of soil erosion 土壤侵蚀分类分级
classified depreciation 分类折旧
classified document 机密文件
classified inspection 分级检验
classⅠalteration Ⅰ类变更
clastic scree 碎屑岩堆
clastic talus 碎屑岩堆
clastic texture 碎屑结构
clause 条款
claw bolt 钩螺栓
clay 黏土
clay cofferdam sealing 黏土围堰止水
clay grouting 黏土灌浆
clay landslide 黏性土滑坡
clay minerals content 黏土矿物含量
clay particle 黏粒
clay particles content 黏粒含量
clay sand barrier 黏土沙障
clayey loess 黏质黄土
clean (bill for) collection 光票托收
clean (letter of) credit 光票信用证
clean bill 光票
clean bill of lading 清洁提单
clean draft 普通汇票,光票
clean gas fire extinguishing system 洁净气体灭火系统
clean letter of credit 无跟单信用证
clean production 清洁生产
clean shipped bill of lading 已装船清洁提单
cleaning 清扫
cleaning box 清洗箱
cleaning class 清理等级
cleaning hole 清扫孔
cleaning ventilation 清洁通风
cleanliness of ballast surface 道砟表面清洁度
cleanout 清扫口
clean-on-board bill of lading 已装船清洁提单
clear 开通
clear a bill 付清
clear a port 出港,结关
clear a ship 卸货
clear an account 清算
clear certificate 清关证明
clear cross-section of tunnel 隧道净空断面
clear distance 净距
clear height 净高
clear signal indication 信号开放表示
clear spacing 净间距
clear span 净跨
clear span of bridge and culvert 桥涵净跨径
clear title 绝对所有权
clear water reservoir 清水池
clearance 海关放行证,清关,结关,净空,限界
clearance above bridge deck 桥面净空
clearance between wheel flange and gauge line 轮轨游间
clearance change 净空变化
clearance checking 限界检查
clearance for temporary train operation during construction 施工临时行车限界
clearance improvement 限界改善
clearance limit survey 净空区测量
clearance of goods 物资清关
clearance of retarder 减速器接近限界
clearance permit 出港许可证
clearance procedure 结关手续
clearance through customs 结关
clearance under bridge superstructure 桥下净空
clearing 清方
clearing (clearance) agent 报关代理人,清算代理人
clearing account 待清理账户,暂记账户
clearing agreement 结算协定
clearing bank 清算银行
clearing house system 清分系统
clearing signal 开放信号

cleavage 解理,劈理
cleavage plane 解理面
clerical error 笔误,书写错误,记录错误
clerk 办事员,职员
clerk of the works 工程管理员
clevis end fitting 双耳连接器
clevis end holder 套管双耳
clevis end wedge-type clamp
双耳楔形线夹
client 当事人,顾客,客户,客户端,委托人,业主
client adviser 业主顾问
client concerned 当事人
cliff 陡崖
climate 气候
climate characteristics 气候特征
climate compensator 气候补偿器
climate extremes 气候异常情况
climatic conditions 气候条件
climbing formwork 爬模
climbing form 爬升模板
clint 石芽
clip 弹条,扣件
clock card 计时卡,工时记录卡,考勤卡
clock error 钟差
clock synchronization 时钟同步
clock system 时钟系统
close an account 结账
close up 封锁
closed account 已结清账户
closed entry control curve 闭口控制曲线
closed full flow return 闭式满管回水
closed joint 接头瞎缝,密闭节理
closed leveling line (route) 闭合水准路线
closed market 封闭式市场
closed mean square error 闭合中误差
closed return 闭式回水
closed water tank 闭式水箱
closed-end investment fund 定额投资基金
closed-loop coding 闭环电码化
closed-out report 完工报告
closeout 收尾
closet 壁柜
close-up photogrammetry 近景摄影测量
closing 收市,停业
closing balance 期末余额
closing circuit 合闸回路
closing coil 合闸线圈
closing date 结账日期,截止日期
closing day 决算日
closing entry 结账分录

closing error in coordinate increment
坐标增量闭合差
closing power source bus 合闸母线
closing price 收盘价
closing rate 收盘汇率
closing signal 关闭信号
closing stock 期末存货
closing time 合闸时间,截止时间,下班时间
closing trial balance 结账后试算表
closure 合龙,密贴
closure degree of structural plane
结构面闭合程度
closure error of azimuth 方位角闭合差
closure error of traverse 闭合导线误差
closure joint 合拢
closure of the proceedings 终止诉讼
closure rail 导轨
closure survey traverse 闭合测量导线
cloudburst 暴雨
clouded 待定
cluster 集群
coagulant aid 助凝剂
coagulant 混凝剂
coal 煤
coal consumption 耗煤
coal digging cave 掏煤洞
coal goaf 煤层采空区
coal measure strata 煤系地层
coal pitch 煤沥青
coal road 煤巷
coal seam 煤层
coalition 结合
coal-fired boiler 燃煤锅炉
coarse aggregate 粗骨料
coarse angular gravel soil 粗角砾土
coarse dressed stone 粗料石
coarse grained soil 粗颗粒土
coarse particles 粗颗粒
coarse round gravel soil 粗圆砾土
coarse sand 粗砂
coarse sieve 粗筛
coarse-grained soil 粗粒土
coassignee 合伙受让人
coast 海岸
coastal plain 滨海平原
coastal subgrade 滨海路基
coasting 惰行
coastwise 近海的
coating 涂层,涂盖材料,涂料,涂装
coating preparation 涂膜制备

coating thickness tester 涂层厚度测定仪
coaxial cable 同轴电缆
coaxial power cable feeding system
　　同轴电力电缆供电方式
cobble 鹅卵石,卵石
cobbly soil 粗砾土,卵石土
code 代码,法典,法规,规范,准则
code missing 掉码
code of accounts 账目编号
code of conduct 行为标准,行为守则
code of ethics 职业道德准则
code of survey area 测区代号
code relay 电码继电器
code requirement 法规要求
code transmitter 发码器
code verification 规范验证
coded track circuit
　　电码轨道电路,电码化轨道电路
codeless zone 无码区
coder-decoder 编解码器
coding 编码,电码化
coding for station receiving-departure route
　　车站接发车进路电码化
coding for tracks in station 车站股道电码化
coding for train approaching 接近发码
coding overlapped on track circuit
　　轨道电路电码化
coefficient 系数
coefficient of action effect 作用效应系数
coefficient of building shape 建筑物体形系数
coefficient of cars not in service 非运用车系数
coefficient of combination 组合系数
coefficient of corrosion resistance
　　抗蚀系数
coefficient of difference in price of materials
　　材料价差系数
coefficient of difference in price 价差系数
coefficient of dynamic force 动力系数
coefficient of kinetic viscosity
　　动力黏滞系数
coefficient of leaching deformation
　　溶滤变形系数
coefficient of line extension 展线系数
coefficient of line extension for the route
　　线路展线系数
coefficient of linear expansion
　　线膨胀系数,线胀系数
coefficient of non-uniformity 不均匀系数
coefficient of permeability normal to the plane
　　垂直渗透系数
coefficient of planar permeability
　　平面渗透系数
coefficient of refrigerating performance
　　制冷性能系数
coefficient of resistance 电阻系数
coefficient of secondary consolidation
　　次固结系数
coefficient of secondary stress 次应力系数
coefficient of self-weight collapsibility
　　自重湿陷系数
coefficient of static earth pressure
　　静止土压力系数
coefficient of static lateral pressure
　　静止侧压力系数
coefficient of subgrade
　　地基系数,基床系数
coefficient of subsoil K30 地基系数 K30
coefficient of thermal expansion
　　热膨胀系数
coefficient of thermal storage 蓄热系数
coefficient of train derailment
　　车辆脱轨系数
coefficient of transmissibility 导水系数
coefficient of variation 变异系数
coefficient of variation for goods receiving and departure 货物到发波动系数
coefficient of viscosity 黏滞系数
coefficient of volume compressibility
　　体积压缩系数
coefficient of working condition
　　工作条件系数
coercive practice 胁迫行为
cofferdam 围堰
cofinancing 共同资助
cognovit 被告承认书,债务确认书
cohere 黏结
cohesion 黏聚力,结合
cohesionless coarse grained soil
　　无黏性粗粒土
cohesionless soil 无黏性土
cohesive force 黏结力
cohesive soil 黏性土
coil 盘管,线圈
coin sorter 硬币清分机
coke filter 焦炭滤池
col 垭口
cold adhesive 冷胶粘剂
cold area 高寒区
cold bend test 冷弯试验
cold bending test 冷弯检验

cold bending thin-walled steel structure
冷弯薄壁型钢结构
cold contact　冷接触
cold desert zone　寒漠带
cold region　寒冷地区
cold running　冷滑
cold temperate zone　寒温带
cold water　冷水
colinearity condition equation　共线条件方程
collaborate　协作
collaboration　协作
collaboration contract　合作合同
collapse　坍塌,塌陷,毁坏,塌方
collapse accumulation　崩塌堆积
collapse and slide　坍滑
collapse arch　塌落拱
collapse joint　崩塌节理
collapse of pantograph　刮弓,打弓,钻弓
collapse-proof shed　防倒塌棚架
collapsibility coefficient　湿陷系数
collapsible form　活动模板
collapsible loess subgrade
湿陷性黄土路基
collapsible loess　湿陷性黄土
collapsible soil　湿陷性土
collar　锁口
collar beam　系梁
collateral　从属抵押品,附属担保品
collateral acceptance　担保承兑
collateral bond　担保债券
collateral contract　附属合同
collateral damages　附带损害
collateral evidence　旁证
collateral loan　抵押贷款
collateral mortgage　担保品抵押
collateral rights　从权利
collateral warranty　附带担保,副担保书
collateral warranty agreement
附属担保协议
collateralized loan　有抵押品的贷款
collect　收取,提取,托收
collect (pool) **money**　集资
collect a bill　托收汇票
collect and edit　汇编
collect data　收集资料
collect duties　征税
collect ticket　取票
collecting agent　代收人,收账代理人
collecting bank　代收银行,托收银行
collection　汇编,汇总,提货,接收到货,托收

collection bill　托收汇票
collection of customs duty　关税征收
collection of tax　收税
collection on clean bill　光票托收
collection on documents　跟单托收
collection order　托收委托书
collection period　账款回收期
collections　收账
collective agreement　劳资集体谈判协议
collective bargaining agreement
劳资集体谈判协议
collective behavior　集体行为
collective consciousness　群体意识
collective labour agreement
劳资集体谈判协议
collide　碰撞
collimation line method　视准线法
collision　碰撞
collision detection　碰撞检测
collision force　撞击力
collision insurance　碰撞险
collision prevention for pier and abutment
墩台防撞
collision prevention of pier/abutment
桥梁墩台防撞
colloidal　胶体质
colloidal particle　胶粒
collude　串通
collusion　串通,舞弊
collusive bid (tender)　串通投标
collusive practice　串通行为
colluvial　崩积的
colluvial loess　崩积黄土
colmation test　淤堵试验
colony　生活区
color comparison tube　比色管,具塞比色管
color composite　彩色合成
color developing agent　显色剂
color difference　色容差
color engineering drawing　工程彩色制图
color film　彩色片
color infrared film　彩色红外片
color infrared photography　彩色红外摄影
color rendering index　显色指数
color rendering　显色性
color smoothness　颜色平滑度
color temperature　色温
color-light signal　色灯信号机
colour searchlight signal
探照式色灯信号机

columnar 柱状
column-type pier 柱式桥墩
comb scraper 梳齿刮刀
combination 合并,组合
combination of action effects 作用效应组合
combination of actions 作用组合
combination of load effect 荷载效应组合
combination of long-term action effects
　长期效应组合
combination of short-term action effects
　短期效应组合
combination of TSP and SP 分区兼开闭所
combination relay 组合继电器
combination value of live load
　活荷载组合值
combination value of variable actions
　可变作用的组合值
combine 结合
combined calculation of water and soil pressure
　水土合算
combined certificate 联合凭证
combined circuit function test
　结合电路功能测试
combined dust removal 联合除尘
combined financial statement 合并财务报表
combined flushing 联合洗井法
combined foundation 联合基础
combined harbor station 路港联设港湾站
combined industrial station
　路厂(矿)联设工业站
combined measurement method
　联合测定法
combined member 组合构件
combined offer 合并发盘,联合报价
combined quotation 合并报价
combined sewage pumping station
　合流污水泵站
combined steel formwork 组合钢模板
combined system 合流制
combined transport freight rate 联运费率
combined transport bill of lading (C. T. B/L)
　联运提单
combined transport 联合运货
combined transport document (CTD)
　联合运输单据
combined turnouts 组合道岔
combined well 结合井
combined-type junction terminal
　组合式枢纽
combustible oil products 可燃油品

combustible substance 燃烧体
combustion performance 燃烧性能
combustion test chamber 燃烧试验箱
come into force 生效
comendite 碱性流纹岩
comfort air conditioning 舒适性空气调节
comission broker 佣金经纪人
command 说明书,指令,指挥
command storage test 命令存储测试
commence 开工
commencement date 开工日期
commencement of a project 项目开工
commencement of design-build
　设计建造开工
commencement of work 开工
comment 评价意见,注释
commerce 商务
commerce clause 商务条款
commercial 商业广告
commercial acceptance bill 商业承兑汇票
commercial affairs 商务
commercial agency 商业代理行
commercial agency contract 贸易代理合同
commercial alternative quotation
　商务选择性报价
commercial and residential building 商住楼
commercial bank 商业银行
commercial bid evaluation 商务标评审
commercial bill 商业汇票
commercial claim 商务索赔
commercial code 商业法规
commercial company 商业公司
commercial concrete 商品混凝土
commercial contract 商业合同
commercial correspondence 商业信函
commercial counselor 商务参赞
commercial court 商事法庭
commercial credit 商业信贷
commercial discount 商业折扣
commercial draft 商业汇票
commercial insurance 商业保险
commercial invoice 商业发票
commercial law 商法
commercial letter of credit 商业信用证
commercial loan 商业贷款
commercial office building 商务写字楼
commercial operation date (COD)
　项目启用日期
commercial paper 商业单据,商业票据
commercial proposal 商务标

commercial representative 商务代表
commercial risk 商业风险
commercial set 成套商业单据
commercial terms 商务条款
commercial transaction 交易
commercial treaty 贸易条约
commission 代理佣金,委托书,委员会,佣金
commission business 经纪业
commission charge 手续费
commission charge for foreign trade 外贸手续费
commission charges 佣金
commission house 经纪行
commission of authority 授权书
commission of conciliation 调解委员会
commission trade 委托贸易,经济贸易
commissioned test 委托试验
commissioner 地方长官,政府特派员,专员
commissioner of building control 建筑管制专员
commissioning 调试,试车
commissioning certificate 试运行证书
commissioning codes 试运行规范
commissioning costs 试运行费用
commissioning period 试运行期
commissioning team 试车组
commissioning test run 投料试生产
commit 承诺
commit a crime 犯罪
commitment 承诺,承诺付款额,约定
commitment and award 承诺与授予
commitment authority 承诺权
commitment authorization 承诺授权书
commitment charge (fee) 承诺费
commitment document 承诺文件
commitment letter 承诺信
commitment time 承诺时限,约定时间
commitment value 承诺价值
committee 委员会
commixture 混合
commodity 货物,商品
commodity inspection 商品检验
commodity price index 物价指数
commodity price 物价,商品价格
commodity tax 货物税
common battery telephone 共电电话
common box 公用箱
common channel signaling 公共信道信令
common concrete 普通混凝土
common crossing 辙叉

common defect 一般缺陷
common earthing 共用接地
common facilities 公共设施
common freight platform 普通货物站台
common intermediate format (CIF) 通用中间格式,标准化图像格式
common law 惯例法,习惯法,判例法,普通法
common law system 普通法系,英美法系
common market 共同市场
common mistake 共同错误
common mode test 共模试验
common platform 普通站台
common portland cement 通用硅酸盐水泥
common rapid filter 普通快滤池
common requirement clause 通用要求条款
common seal 公章
common steel bar 普通钢筋
communication 交通,通信,信函
communication and control server (CCS) 通信控制服务器
communication and signal inspection car 电务检测车
communication cable 通信电缆
communication center 通信枢纽
communication duty room of chemical defense 防化通信值班室
communication equipment room 通信机房
communication front-end processor 通信前置处理机
communication line 通信线路
communication panel 通讯屏
communication post 通话柱
communication power and equipment room environment monitoring system 通信电源及机房环境监控系统
communication room 通信室
communication service 通信业务
communication session management test 通信会话管理测试
communication station 通信站
communication system 通信系统
communications and signalling 供电工程
communication-based train control 基于通信的列车控制
commutative 交替的
commutator 换向器
compact 结实的
compact boiler 快装锅炉
compact planting 密植
compact porosity 紧密孔隙率

compact substation 箱式变电站
compactability 压实性
compacted fill 压实填土
compacted filling soils 填筑土
compacted foundation 挤密地基
compacted ground 压实地基
compacted soil 击实土
compacting coefficient 压实系数
compaction 夯实,压实
compaction degree 压实程度
compaction equipment 碾压设备
compaction grouting method 挤密喷浆法,压密注浆法
compaction method 压实方法
compaction mould 击实筒
compaction performance 击实性能
compaction pile 挤密桩
compaction requirements 压实标准
compaction test 击实试验
compaction test apparatus 击实仪
compactive effort 击实功
compactness 密实,压实度,致密性
compactor 夯具,压实工具,压土机
company 公司
company act 公司条例,公司法
company law 公司法
company limited by shares 股份有限公司
company property 公司财产
comparability 可比性
comparable cost 可比成本
comparative balance sheet 比较资产负债表
comparative financial statement 比较财务报表
comparator 比长仪
compass 罗盘
compass survey 罗盘仪测量
compatibility 相容性
compatibility and expansion capability 兼容及扩展能力
compatibility test 适应性试验
compensate 补偿,抵偿
compensation 补偿,赔偿,赔款
compensation capacitor 补偿电容
compensation events 补偿事件
compensation fees for land expropriation 土地征用补偿费
compensation fees for land expropriation and demolition 土地征用及拆迁补偿费
compensation for cancellation of contract 解除合同补偿费
compensation for damage 损害赔偿
compensation for delay 交货逾期赔偿
compensation for injury 工伤补偿
compensation for removal 迁移费,遣散费
compensation gradient 加算坡度
compensation insurance 补偿保险
compensation level surface 抵偿高程面
compensation of additional cost 附加费用的补偿
compensation terms 补偿条款
compensation trade 补偿贸易
compensator 补偿器
compensator with concentrated series capacitors 集中式串联电容补偿装置
compensator with decentralised series capacitors 分散式串联电容补偿装置
compete 竞争
competency 缔约能力
competency certification 资格鉴定
competent 有法定资格的
competent authorities 主管当局
competent court 主管法庭
competition 竞争
competition strategy 竞争策略
competitive bidding 公开招标,竞争性招标
competitive price 竞争性价格
competitive strategy 竞争策略
competitive tender 有竞争力的投标书
competitiveness 竞争能力
competitor 竞争对手,竞争者
compilation 汇编
compilation and assessment fees of environmental impact report 环境影响报告编制与评估费
compilation content 编制内容
compilation fee of flood influence assessment report 洪水影响评价报告编制费
compilation of budget 编制预算
compile 汇编
compiled original 编绘原图
complain 投诉
complainant 起诉人,申诉人,索赔人
complement 补充,补码
complementary 补充的
complete cost 总成本
complete locking 完全锁闭
complete payment 最后的支付
complete plant 成套设备
complete set of bills of lading 全套提单
complete set of drawings 成套图纸
complete set of equipment 成套设备

complete trust 完全信托
completed works 竣工的工程
completely compensated overhead contact line 全补偿链形悬挂
completely penetrating well 完整井
completion acceptance 竣工验收
completion acceptance document 竣工验收文件
completion acceptance fee 竣工验收费
completion acceptance of construction project 建设项目竣工验收
completion certificate 竣工证书
completion date 竣工日期
completion guarantee 完工担保
completion of calls to busy subscriber (CCBS) 遇忙回呼
completion of works 工程竣工
completion report 竣工报告
completion settlement of project 工程竣工结算
complete set of equipment 成套设备
complex 建筑群,综合企业
complex tariff 复式税则
compliance of bending creep 弯曲蠕变柔量
compliance verification documentation 合规性验证文件
compliance verification system 合规性验证体系
compliance with a schedule 符合进度表
compliance with laws 遵守法律
compliance with the contract 遵守合同
comply with 按照
component 部件
component library 构件库
components of rail joint fastening 钢轨接头配件
composite abutment 组合式桥台
composite belt 复合带
composite electrode 复合电极
composite floor 组合楼盖
composite foundation of piles 旋喷桩复合地基
composite foundation with cement deep mixed piles 水泥深层搅拌桩复合地基
composite foundation with cement-fly ash-gravel piles 水泥粉煤灰碎石桩复合地基
composite foundation with rammed soil-cement piles 夯实水泥土桩复合地基
composite foundation with sandgravel piles 砂石桩复合地基
composite geomembrane insulating course 复合土工膜隔断层
composite geomembrane 复合土工膜
composite geotextile 复合土工布,复合土工织物
composite girder 结合梁,组合梁
composite girder bridge 结合梁桥,组合梁桥
composite ground 复合地基
composite index 综合指数
composite insulator 复合绝缘子
composite lining 复合衬砌,复合式衬砌
composite malthoid 复合油毡
composite material duct 复合材料风管
composite member 叠合构件
composite mineral admixture 复合掺合料
composite mortar 混合砂浆
composite pile foundation 复合基桩
composite price 综合价格
composite rack 综合架
composite rate of tax 综合税率
composite roof truss 组合屋架
composite shear strength modulus 复合剪切模量
composite sleeper 合成轨枕
composite slip surface 复合滑动面
composite soil nailing wall 复合土钉墙
composite steel and concrete beam 钢与混凝土组合梁
composite structure 混合结构
composite tube 复合管
composite wall 复合墙
composition 和解协议,债务和解
compound 混合,混合料
compound amount 复利
compound claim 综合索赔
compound curve 复曲线
compound dunes 复合型沙丘
compound duties 复合关税,混合关税
compound duty 混合税
compound earthing mesh 复合接地网
compound interest 复利
compound rate 复利率
compound settlement 综合解决办法
compound stirrup 复合箍筋
compound suspension catenary 复链形接触悬挂
compound tariff 复合关税,混合关税,混合税率
compounding 复利计算,混合
compounding a debt 协商债务偿还方案(避免法院清盘令)

comprehensive image tester
　图像综合测试仪
comprehensive advance geological prediction
　综合超前地质预报
comprehensive analysis　综合分析
comprehensive automobile liability policy
　综合汽车保单
comprehensive budget　综合预算
comprehensive budgetary estimate (budget)
　综合概(预)算
comprehensive building　综合楼
comprehensive calculation method
　综合计算法
comprehensive control of soil erosion and water loss　水土流失综合治理
comprehensive development　综合开发
comprehensive energy consumption　综合能耗
comprehensive engineering geological map
　综合工程地质图
comprehensive estimate　综合估算
comprehensive expense of labors　综合工费
comprehensive freight rat
　公路综合运价率
comprehensive general liability policy
　综合责任保单
comprehensive goods yard　综合性货场
comprehensive index method　综合指标法
comprehensive inspection car　综合检测车
comprehensive inspection car shed
　综合检测车库
comprehensive inspection　综合检测
comprehensive inspection train
　综合检测列车
comprehensive labor price of base period
　基期综合工费标准
comprehensive lead-in cabinet　综合引入柜
comprehensive list　综合一览表
comprehensive maintenance workshop
　综合维修车间
comprehensive maintenance workshop/work area
　综合维修工区
comprehensive maintenance　综合维修
comprehensive measures　综合措施
comprehensive network analyzer
　网络综合分析仪
comprehensive observation point
　综合观测点
comprehensive passenger traffic terminal/hub
　综合客运交通枢纽
comprehensive policy　综合保单
comprehensive pre-estimate　综合预估算
comprehensive railway location　综合选线
comprehensive repair of bridge
　桥梁综合维修
comprehensive sewage (wastewater)
　综合生活污水
comprehensive tender documents
　综合招标文件
comprehensive treatment　综合治理
comprehensive unit price　综合单价
comprehensive unit price for power supply for construction　工程用电综合单价
comprehensive unit price for water supply for construction　工程用水综合单价
comprehensive unit price method
　综合单价法
comprehensive water pump-in test
　综合压水试验
compresional fault　压性断裂
compressed air　压缩空气
compressed air duct　压缩空气管道
compressed air supply　(施工)供风
compressibility　压缩性
compression　压缩
compression coefficient　压缩系数
compression deformation　压缩变形
compression index　压缩指数
compression member with large eccentricity
　大偏心受压构件
compression member with small eccentricity
　小偏心受压构件
compression modulus　压缩模量
compression moulding　压模
compression refrigeration cycle
　压缩式制冷循环
compression strength　抗压强度
compression testing machine　压力试验机
compression zone　受压区
compressional fault　压性断层
compressional torsion fault　压扭性断层
compressive elastic modulus of concrete
　混凝土受压弹性模量
compressive modulus　抗压模量,压缩模量
compressive rigidity of members
　构件抗压刚度
compressive rigidity of section
　截面压缩刚度
compressive strain　压缩应变
compressive strength of mortar
　砂浆抗压强度

compressive strength of source rocks
　母岩抗压强度
compressive strength　抗压强度,压屈强度
compressive stress　压应力
compressor　压缩机
comprise　包括
compromise　和解,妥协,折衷方法
compromise joint bar　异型接头夹板
compromise on quality　降低质量
compromise rail　异型钢轨
compulsory　强制的
compulsory arbitration　强制仲裁
compulsory clause　强制条款
compulsory filtration rate　强制滤速
compulsory liquidation　强制停业处理
compulsory third party insurance
　第三方责任强制保险
computation　核算
computed speed　计算速度
computed tare　约定皮重
computed value　计算价值
computer aided design　计算机辅助设计
computer aided drawing（CAD）
　计算机制图,计算机辅助制图
computer based interlocking（CBI）
　计算机联锁
computer network　计算机网络
computerized tomography　层析成像
concave platform　凹形站台
concave slope　凹坡
concave washer　凹形垫块
concealed installation　暗设
concealed works　隐蔽工程
concentrate funds　集资
concentrated borrow pit　集中取土场
concentrated load（point load）
　集中荷载(点荷载)
concentration　浓度,浓缩
concentration of calcium and magnesium ions
　钙镁离子浓度
concentric　同心状
concentric circles　同心圆
conceptual design　概念设计,方案设计
concession　给予特许,专营权,特许
concession agreement　特许协议,租让协议
concession company　特许公司
concession method　让步措施
concession of custom duty　关税减让
concession of tariff　关税减让
concessionaire　特许权受让人

concessional　特许的
concessional line of credit　优惠贷款限额
concessional loan　优惠贷款
concessional rate　优惠利率
concessional tariff　优惠关税
concessionary　特许公司,特许的
concessionary loan　特许贷款
concessionary period　特许期
conchoidal fracture　贝状断口
conciliate　调解,和解
conciliation　调解,和解
conciliation committee　调解委员会
conciliation of labour disputes
　劳资纠纷调解
conciliation procedure　调解程序
conciliator　调解人
conclude　缔结,签订,达成
conclude a contract　缔结和约,订立合同
conclude a transaction　成交
conclude a treaty　缔约
conclude an agreement　签订协议
conclusion　缔结,签订,结论
conclusion of contract　合同缔结
conclusive evidence　确切证据
concourse　集散厅
concrescence　结合
concrete　混凝土
concrete additive　混凝土外加剂
concrete aggregate　混凝土骨料
concrete air content　混凝土含气量
concrete air content measuring instrument
　混凝土含气量测定仪
concrete anti permeability apparatus
　混凝土抗渗仪
concrete base　混凝土底座
concrete block　混凝土块,混凝土砌块
concrete brick　混凝土块,混凝土砌块
concrete bridge　混凝土桥
concrete broad sleeper　混凝土宽枕
concrete cable-stayed bridge　混凝土斜拉桥
concrete casting temperature　混凝土入模温度
concrete column　混凝土柱
concrete column cap　混凝土柱帽
concrete compressive strength
　混凝土抗压强度
concrete consistency　混凝土稠度
concrete core wall　混凝土心墙
concrete corrosion resistance　混凝土抗腐蚀性
concrete cover　钢筋保护层,混凝土保护层
concrete cover tester　混凝土保护层测定仪

concrete cover to reinforcement
　钢筋混凝土保护层
concrete crack　混凝土裂缝,混凝土裂纹
concrete creepage　混凝土徐变
concrete curing　混凝土养护
concrete delivery pump　混凝土输送泵
concrete equipment　混凝土设备
concrete formwork　混凝土模板
concrete foundation　混凝土基础
concrete freezing and thawing cycle test
　混凝土冻融循环试验
concrete freezing resistance　混凝土抗冻性
concrete lining　混凝土衬砌
concrete mast　混凝土支柱
concrete mixer　混凝土搅拌机
concrete mixing plant
　混凝土拌和厂,混凝土搅拌站,混凝土拌和楼,混凝土搅拌楼
concrete mixing ratio　混凝土配合比
concrete of structure body
　结构本体混凝土
concrete pavement　混凝土块路面
concrete paver　混凝土摊铺机
concrete placement　混凝土浇筑
concrete pole　混凝土支柱
concrete pump　混凝土泵
concrete pump truck　混凝土泵车
concrete reinforcement　混凝土配筋
concrete retarder　混凝土缓凝剂
concrete shrinkage　混凝土收缩
concrete skip　混凝土吊斗
concrete slab　混凝土板
concrete sleeper　混凝土枕
concrete sleeper bolt drilling and pulling machine
　混凝土枕螺栓钻取机
concrete sleeper turnout　混凝土枕道岔
concrete slump　混凝土坍落度
concrete specimen　混凝土试件
concrete strength　混凝土强度
concrete structural column　混凝土构造柱
concrete structure　混凝土结构
concrete supporting layer
　混凝土支撑层,混凝土支承层
concrete track slab　混凝土道床板
concrete truck　混凝土搅拌车
concrete turnout slab　混凝土道岔板
concrete vibrating stand　混凝土振动台
concrete worker　混凝土工
concrete-filled steel tube arch bridge
　钢管混凝土拱桥
concrete-filled steel tube bridge
　钢管混凝土桥
concrete-filled steel tube　钢管混凝土构件
concreting　混凝土浇筑
concretionary structure　结核状构造
concur　同时发生
concurrent delay　共同延误
condemned work　不合格的工作
condensate pump　凝结水泵
condensating drain pan　凝结水盘
condensation pipe　凝结水管
condensation water tank　凝结水箱
condenser　冷凝器
condenser charge　电容器充电
condensing pressure　冷凝压力
condensing temperature　冷凝温度
condition　条件
condition adjustment　条件平差
condition adjustment with parameters
　附参数条件平差
condition equation　条件方程
condition of circumference angle　圆周角条件
condition precedent　先决条件
condition subsequent　后继条件
conditional equation　条件方程式
conditional power source　条件电源
conditions for employment　雇用条件
conditions of carriage　货运条件
conditions of contract/these conditions
　合同条件/本条件
conditions of engagement　雇用条件
conditions of grant　让与条件
conditions of hire　租用条件
conditions of particular application
　特殊应用条件,具体条件,专用条件
conditions of sale　销售条件
conditions precedent　先决条件
condition-based repair　状态修
conduct code　行为守则
conductive grease　电力复合脂
conductivity　导电率,电导率
conductivity cell constant　电导池常数
conductivity method　电导法
conductor bar　滑触线
conductor rail　接触轨(第三轨)
conduit　导管,输水道,(布)线管,管道
conduit cover slab　槽道盖板
cone of embankment　路堤锥体
cone penetration test　孔压静力触探试验
confederation　联盟,同盟

conference 会谈，会议
conference dispatching room 会议调度车间
conference extension 会议分机
conference rate
  班轮公会运价，海运公会运价，同盟费率
conference switchboard 会议总机
conference system 会议系统
confer 授予
confidence 信任
confidential 保密的
confidential clause 保密条款
confidential details 保密事项
confidentiality 保密
configuration data 配置数据
configuration of transportation means
  交通工具配置
confined aquifer 承压含水层
confined area 承压区
confined concrete 约束混凝土
confined jet 受限射流
confined masonry 约束砌体
confined space 狭窄空间
confined water 承压水
confined water head 承压水头
confirmation 确认书，保兑
confirmation car 确认车
confirmation in writing 书面确认
confirmation of award 确定授标
confirmation of oral instruction
  口头指令确认书
confirmation sample 确认样品
confirmed letter of credit 保兑信用证
confirming bank 保兑银行，确认银行
conflagration 大火灾，火灾
conflict 冲突
conflict between capital and labour
  劳资纠纷
conflict of laws 法律冲突
conflict rules 冲突法规
conflicting route 敌对进路
conflicting signal 敌对信号
confluence amount 汇流量
confluence of sewage and wastewater 污废合流
conformable contact 整合接触
conformal projection 等角投影/正形投影
conformity test 合格性检验
confute 驳斥，抗辩
conglomerate 砾岩
Congo red test paper 刚果红试纸
conical flask 锥形瓶

conical platen 加荷锥
conical reversing concrete mixer
  锥形反转出料混凝土搅拌机
conical tilting concrete mixer
  锥形倾翻出料混凝土搅拌机
conjoin 交接
conjuncture 行情
commencement 开工，延误和暂停
commencement of works 工程开工
connect mode 接续方式
connecting clamp of earthing conductor
  接地线连接线夹
connecting leveling line 附合水准路线
connecting line 联络线
connecting piece 连接件
connecting pin 连接销
connecting rod of turnout 道岔连接杆
connecting rod 连接棒
connecting track 衔接线路
connecting traverse 附合导线
connection admission control (CAC)
  连接允许控制
connection box 接线箱
connection corridor 联系廊
connection establishment delay (CED)
  呼叫(连接)建立时间
connection establishment error ratio (CER)
  呼叫(连接)建立失败概率
connection loss rate (CLR) 连接丢失概率
connection of steel bars 钢筋连接
connection passage 联络通道，横通道
connection quadrangle method
  联系四边形法
connection rod 连接杆
connection survey 联系测量
connection terminal 接线端子
connection test 连通试验
connection triangle method 联系三角形法
connection tunnel 横通道
connector 连接器
connector box 接头盒
consecutive days 连续日
consecutive rainfall 连续降雨量
consensus 意见一致
consent 许可
consent award 合意裁决
consequences of an exceptional event
  异常事件的后果
consequences of employer's suspension
  雇主暂停后果

consequent landslide 顺层滑坡
consequential damage (loss)
　从属损失,间接损失
consequential damage 间接损害
consequential loss insurance 间接损失保险
conservation-minded society 节约型社会
consideration 对价,约因
consideration money 酬金
consigned goods 寄销品
consignee 收货人
consigner 发货人,委托人
consignment 托运,托付
consignment bill 托运单
consignment out 寄销品
consignment outward 寄销品
consignor 发货人,委托人
consignor consigner 托运人
consistency 稠度
consistency limit 稠度界限
console room 控制台室
consolidate 加固
consolidated balance sheet
　合并资产负债表
consolidated cargo (container) service area
　集货区
consolidated drained shear test
　固结排水剪试验
consolidated financial statement
　合并财务报表
consolidated income statement 综合收益表
consolidated quick shear 固结快剪
consolidated quick shear test
　固结快剪试验
consolidated undrained shear test
　固结不排水剪试验
consolidated-drained triaxial test
　固结排水三轴试验
consolidated-undrained triaxial test
　固结不排水三轴试验
consolidation 固结
consolidation apparatus 固结仪
consolidation coefficient 固结系数
consolidation curve 固结曲线
consolidation grouting 固结灌浆
consolidation of deep soil 深层土加固
consolidation of shallow soil 浅层土加固
consolidation settlement 固结沉降
consolidation stress 固结应力
consolidation stress ratio 固结应力比
consolidation test 固结试验

consolidometer 固结仪
consortium 国际财团,联合体,合资企业
consortium agreement 合资企业协议
consortium bank 合资银行
consortium company 合资公司
consortium members 联合体成员
consortium of contractors 承包商联合体
constant 恒量
constant annuity 定额年金
constant cost 不变成本,固定成本
constant cross-section column 等截面柱
constant error 常差
constant expense 经常费用
constant head method 常水头法
constant speed 定速
constant stress press machine 恒应力压力机
constant temperature and humidity cement curing
　box 水泥恒温恒湿养护箱
constant temperature curing box
　恒温养护箱
constant temperature oven 恒温烘箱
constant tension wire barrow 恒张力放线车
constant term of conditional equation
　条件方程式常数项
constant-volume air conditioning system
　定风量空气调节系统
constituent instruments 基本文件
constituted authority 合法当局
constitution 宪法,章程
constitution of the DAAB
　争议避免裁决委员会的组成
constitution of track circuit 轨道电路构成
constitutive relation 本构关系
constitutive relation (constitutive model) of soil
　土的本构关系(本构模型)
constrained particle size 限制粒径
constraint adjustment 约束平差
constraint point 约束点
construct 施工
constructability 可建造性,可施工性
constructability review 可施工性评审
constructed value 估定价值,推定价值
constructed wetland 人工湿地
construction 结构,施工
construction ability 施工能力
construction access 施工通道
construction access road 施工进场道路
construction account 建筑账户
construction accounting 建筑会计
construction adit 辅助坑道

construction agreement 施工协议书
construction and facilities management（AEC/FM）
建筑、工程、施工和设备管理
construction and inspection concentrated load
施工和检修集中荷载
construction and installation works
建筑安装工程
construction at night 夜间施工
construction balance sheet 建筑资产负债表
construction boundary 建筑施工场界
construction budget 基建预算
construction business 建筑业
construction calendar 施工日历
construction camp 施工工棚,施工营地
construction claim management
施工索赔管理
construction claims 施工索赔
construction clearance 建筑界限
construction concession 建筑许可,施工许可
construction condition 施工条件
construction consulting fee 施工咨询费
construction contract 建筑合同,施工合同
construction contract award
施工合同授标书
construction contract management
施工合同管理
construction contracting
承包工程,工程承包
construction control network 施工控制网
construction coordination 施工协调
construction coordinator 施工协调员
construction cost
工程造价,建设成本,施工成本
construction cost control 施工成本控制
construction cost estimating 施工成本概算
construction cost index 工程造价指数
construction cost information 工程造价信息
construction cycle 建造周期
construction delay 工期拖延
construction design 施工设计
construction details 施工详图
construction diary 施工日志
construction disaster 施工灾害
construction disturbance 施工干扰
construction diversion 施工导流
construction document 施工文件
construction document design phase
施工图阶段
construction drawing 施工图
construction drawing design 施工图设计

construction elevator 施工升降机
construction engineering corporation
建筑工程公司
construction engineering costs
建筑工程造价
construction equipment 施工设备,施工装备
construction equipment status report
施工设备情况报告
construction estimate 施工预算
construction experience 施工经验
construction flow chart 施工流程图
construction for lowering the girder（beam）**into place** 落梁施工
construction in progress 未完工程,在建工程
construction in rainy season 雨季施工
construction industry 建筑业
construction inspection 施工检查,施工监测
construction inspector
施工监察员,施工监测人员,施工检测人员
construction insurance policy
建筑工程保险单
construction intermediate schedule
施工中间进度表
construction joint 施工缝
construction layout 施工布置图,施工放样
construction license 施工许可证
construction load 施工荷载
construction loan 建筑贷款
construction loss 施工损耗
construction machinery 施工设备
construction management（CM）
建筑管理方式
construction management contract
施工管理合同
construction management contracting
施工管理承包
construction management fee 施工管理费
construction manager 施工经理
construction material 建筑材料
construction means 施工方法,施工手段
construction method 工法,施工方法,施工手段
construction method statement
施工方案,施工组织设计
construction noise 建筑施工噪声
construction of buildings 房屋建筑
construction of policy 保险单的解释
construction of second track/line 增建第二线
construction operation 施工作业
construction operation guide
施工作业指导书

construction organization 施工单位
construction organization design guidance
　施工组织设计意见
construction organization plan
　施工组织方案,施工组织计划
construction organization plan guidance
　施工组织方案意见
construction parameter 施工参数
construction period
　工期,建设工期,施工期限,施工工期
construction period quota 定额工期
construction permit 施工许可
construction phase 施工阶段
construction plan
　施工平面布置图,施工平面图,施工计划
construction planning 施工规划
construction plant
　施工设备,施工场地,施工机械
construction precautions 施工注意事项
construction preparation 施工准备
construction pre-camber 施工预拱度
construction procedure 施工程序
construction process 施工过程
construction program 施工计划
construction progress 施工进度
construction progress control
　施工进度控制
construction project 施工项目
construction project commencement report
　建设项目开工报告
construction project costs 建筑工程造价
construction project document
　建设工程文件
construction project management information system 建设项目管理信息系统
construction projects 建设类项目
construction quality 施工质量
construction record 施工记录
construction report 施工报告
construction resurvey 施工复测
construction safety 施工安全
construction schedule
　施工计划进度,施工进度计划
construction schedule check list
　施工进度核查单
construction scheme 施工组织方案意见,施工方案
construction section 施工区段
construction section in early stage
　先期开工段
construction sequence 施工顺序

construction service 施工服务
construction site 施工现场(工地),工地
construction site allowance 施工现场津贴
construction specification/code 施工规范
construction specifications 施工技术规范
construction speed 施工速度
construction stage 建造阶段
construction staking-out 施工放样
construction standard 施工标准
construction subcontract 施工分包合同
construction summary schedule
　施工进度汇总表
construction superintendent 施工管理员
construction supervision 施工监督
construction supervision and consulting fee
　施工监理与咨询费
construction supervision charge rate
　施工监理费率
construction supervision fee 施工监理费
construction surplus materials 施工剩余物资
construction surrounding rock classification
　施工围岩分级
construction survey 施工测量
construction survey by caissons
　沉井法施工测量
construction survey of conventional shaft sinking method 普通凿井法施工测量
construction survey of track works
　轨道施工测量
construction system design 施工系统设计
construction team 施工队
construction technique 施工技术
construction transition measures
　施工过渡措施
construction waste clearance 建筑垃圾清运
construction wastewater 施工期废水
construction water level 施工水位
construction way 施工手段
construction work policy 建筑工程保险单
construction works 建筑工程
constructional column 构造柱
constructional mechanism 施工机械
constructional plant 施工机械,施工设备
constructional reinforcement 构造配筋
constructive acceleration 可推定的加速施工
constructive and productive engineering
　建设生产类项目
constructive change 可推定的工程变更
constructive change order
　可推定的工程变更指令

constructive clause 推定条款
constructive possession 推定占有
constructive suspension
　可推定的暂停施工
constructive total loss 推定全损
constructive variation 可推定的工程变更
constructor 建造师
construction square control network
　施工方格网
consular invoice 领事发票
consulate 领事馆
consult 磋商
consultancy service 咨询服务
consultant 顾问,咨询人员,咨询专家
consultant company (corporation) 咨询公司
consultation 磋商,咨询
consultative committee 咨询委员会
consulting agreement 咨询协议
consulting engineer 监理工程师,咨询工程师
consulting fee 咨询费
consulting firm 咨询公司
consulting service 咨询服务
consumables 消耗品
consume 消费,消耗
consumer credit 消费信贷
consumer goods 消费品
consumer loan 消费贷款
consumer price index 消费品价格指数
consumption 消费
consumption of material 材料消耗
consumption tax 消费税
contact 接触,(开关)触头
contact ascending spring 接触上升泉
contact cementation 接触胶结
contact closed 接点闭合
contact fault 接触不良
contact force 接触力
contact length 作用距离
contact line system 牵引网
contact loss 离线
contact metamorphism 接触变质
contact open 接点断开
contact potential difference 接触电位差
contact pressure 接触压力,接点压力
contact printing 接触晒印
contact spring 接触弹簧
contact strip support of pantograph
　受电弓滑板支架
contact strip 受电弓滑板
contact strips 接触滑板

contact system 接点系统
contact type displacement measurement device
　接触式位移量测装置
contact wire 接触线
contact wire height 接触导线高度,导高
contact wire uplift 接触线抬升
contactless card 非接触式卡
contactor 接触器
contacts operated by semaphore
　臂板接触器
contain 包含
contained in spatial structure 被空间包含
container 集装箱,收容盘
container bill of lading 集装箱提单
container forklift 集装箱叉车
container freight area 集装箱货区
container freight station
　集装箱货物集散站
container freight yard 集装箱货场
container front-handling crane
　集装箱正面吊运起重机
container leg load 集装箱箱脚荷载
container liner train 集装箱班列
container loader 集装箱装箱机
container loading and unloading operation area
　集装箱装卸作业区
container loading list 集装箱装箱清单
container operation yard 集装箱作业场
container semitrailer for road transport
　公路运输用集装箱半挂车
container semi-trailer 集装箱半挂车
container ship 集装箱船
container slot 平面标准箱位
container stuffing and destuffing yard
　集装箱拆装箱场
container substation 箱式变电所,箱式变电站
container tractor 集装箱牵引车
container tractor for road transport
　公路运输用集装箱牵引车
container traffic 集装箱运输
container truck 集卡
container unloading list 集装箱卸箱清单
container vessel 集装箱船
container with special operation requirement
　有特殊作业要求的集装箱
container yard 集装箱堆场
containerization 集装箱运输
containerized shipment 集装箱货运
container-carrier 集装箱船
containment 包容

contaminate 污染
contaminated soil 污染土
contamination 污染物,污染
contamination coefficient 污染系数
contamination factor/pollution factor 污染因子
contemporary records 同期记录
contend 抗辩
content 含量
content delivery network (CDN)
　内容分发网络
content of acid non-soluble substance
　酸不溶物含量
content of calcium ion 钙离子含量
content of carbon black 炭黑含量
content of carbon dioxide 二氧化碳含量
content of dioxide 二氧化物含量
content of elongated and flaky particles
　针片状颗粒含量
content of exchangeable potassium and sodium
　交换性钾和钠含量
content of fluorine 氟含量
content of gas 瓦斯含量
content of ignition loss 灼烧失量含量
content of material lighter than 2000kg/m³
　轻物质含量
content of moderately soluble salt
　中溶盐含量
content of non-soluble salt 难溶盐含量
content of phosphorus pentoxide
　五氧化二磷含量
content of titanium dioxide 二氧化钛含量
contestant 争辩者,争执方
continental facies 陆相
continental law 大陆法
continental law system 大陆法系
continental rise 大陆隆
continental shelf 大陆架
continental slope 大陆坡
contingency 不可预见费,偶然事件,意外开支
contingency allowance 应急用款
contingency clause 偶发事故条款
contingency cost 不可预见费
contingency evaluation 不可预见性评估
contingency fee 应急费
contingency for difference in price 价差预备费
contingency fund 应急基金
contingency insurance 意外事故保险
contingency insurance covering sellers' interest only
　卖方利益险
contingency plan 应急计划

contingency reserve 意外损失基金
contingency reserve provision for contingency
　应急储备金
contingency sum 不可预见费
contingent 意外的
contingent annuity 应急年金
contingent cost 临时成本
contingent expenses 或有费用,意外开支
contingent interest 或有权益
contingent liabilities 或有负债
contingent profit 或有利润
contingent reserve 意外事项准备金
continuation 展期
continuation clause 展期条款
continue 持续
continuing contract 连续合同
continuous arch bridge 连续拱桥
continuous beam bridge 连续梁桥
continuous beam 连续梁
continuous bucket ditcher 多斗挖沟机
continuous cab signaling 连续式机车信号
continuous charging of small-diameter cartridges
　小直径连续装药
continuous compaction control (CCC)
　连续压实控制
continuous compaction test 连续压实检测
continuous concreting 连续灌注混凝土
continuous current rating 连续电流额定值
continuous data transmission 连续数据传输
continuous girder 连续梁
continuous girder bridge 连续梁桥
continuous heating 连续采暖
continuous mixer 连续拌和机
continuous operation 连续作业
continuous permafrost zone 连续片状多年冻土
continuous rigid frame 连续刚构
continuous size fraction 连续粒级
continuous speed control 连续式调速
continuous track circuit 连续式轨道电路
continuous/intermittent inspection wheel set
　连续/间断式测力轮对
continuously welded rail track (CWR track)
　无缝线路
contour 轮廓线
contour hole 周边眼
contour interval 等高距
contour line 等高线,(图样中的)轮廓线
contour map 等高线图
contour map of groundwater level
　地下水等水位线图

contra account　抵消账户
contra proferentum　反义居先原则
contraband　违禁品,走私货
contract　承包,合同,契约
contract administration　合同管理
contract agreement　合同协议书,协议书
contract amount　合同额,合同价格
contract arbitration fees　合同仲裁费
contract authorization　合同授权
contract awarded　中标合同
contract balance　合同节余额
contract based on unit price　单价合同
contract bond　合同担保
contract cancellation　取消合同
contract change　合同变更
contract clause　合同条款
contract close-out　合同收尾
contract completion certificate　合同完成证书
contract completion date　合同完成日期
contract consciousness　合同意识
contract constraint　合同约束
contract currency　合同规定的货币
contract data　合同数据,合同数据表格资料
contract debt　合同债务
contract deposit paid　已付合同保证金
contract dispute　合同争议
contract documents　合同文件
contract document analysis　合同文件分析
contract document review　合同文件审核
contract draft　合同草稿
contract duty　合同义务
contract endorsement　批准合同
contract engineer　合同工程师
contract execution　合同实施
contract expiry　合同期满
contract file　合同档案,合同文件
contract files　合同卷宗
contract for consulting services
　咨询服务合同
contract for goods　订货合同
contract for labour　包工合同
contract for labour and materials
　包工包料合同
contract for project　项目合同
contract for purchase　购货合同
contract for service　服务合同
contract for the supply of labour
　提供劳务合同,劳务合同
contract for work and materials
　包工包料合同

contract form　合同格式
contract formation　合同构成
contract implementation　合同实施
contract interface　合同接口
contract language　合同语言
contract law　合同法
contract ledger　合同分类账
contract management　合同管理
contract manager　合同经理
contract negotiation　合同谈判
contract notarial fees　合同公证费
contract object　合同标的
contract obligation　合同义务
contract of adhesion　附加合同,附约
contract of affreightment　运输合同
contract of association　协作合同
contract of carriage　运输合同,货运合同
contract of compensation　补偿合约
contract of copartnery　合伙契约
contract of employment　雇佣合同
contract of hire　租赁合同
contract of hire of labour　雇工合同
contract of insurance　保险合同
contract of lease　租赁合同
contract of marine insurance
　海上保险契约
contract of novation　更替型合同
contract of ocean carriage　海运合同
contract of payment　支付合同
contract of privately performed work
　私营工程合同
contract of property insurance
　财产保险合约
contract of sale　买卖合同
contract of sales　销售合同
contract overexpenditure　合同超支额
contract overrun　合同超支额
contract package　合同包
contract package scope　合同范围
contract payment bond　合同支付担保
contract payment guarantee
　合同支付担保
contract performance　履行合同,执行合同
contract period　合同有效期,合同期
contract price
　承包合同价,合同价格,合同约定价格
contract price and payment　合同价格和付款
contract price receivable　应收合同款
contract price received in advance
　预收合同款

contract project 合同项目
contract provisions 合同规定
contract records 合同记录
contract renewal 合同续订
contract review 合同审核
contract risk 合同风险
contract scope changes 合同范围变更
contract serial number 合同序号
contract signature date 合同签署日期
contract size 合同规模
contract stipulations 合同规定
contract sum 合同价格
contract suspension 合同暂停
contract termination 合同终止
contract terms 合同条款
contract type 合同类型
contract under seal 盖章合同,正式合同
contract underrun 合同节余额
contract value 合同价值
contract variation 合同变更
contract verification 合同审核
contract version 合同版本
contract void 无效合同
contracted repair 包修制
contracting 承包
contracting firm 承包企业
contracting party 订约人
contracting strategy 发包策略
contraction joint 收缩缝
contractometer 收缩仪
contractor 承包单位,承包商,订约人
contractor furnished equipment
  承包商供应设备
contractor invoice 承包商发票
contractor payment request
  承包商付款请求
contractor payment system
  承包商付款系统
contractor short-list 承包商短名单
contractor supervisor 工地监工员
contractor's affidavit 承包商宣誓书
contractor's all risks insurance (C.A.R)
  承包工程一切险,承包商全险保险,工程施工一切险
contractor's claims release 承包商放弃索赔
contractor's claim 承包商的索赔
contractor's default 承包商违约
contractor's documents 承包商文件
contractor's equipment floater
  承包商设备保险单,承包商设备运输险

contractor's equipment
  承包商机具,承包商设备
contractor's facilities 承包商设施
contractor's fee 承包商的酬金
contractor's financing 承包商融资
contractor's general obligations
  承包商的一般义务
contractor's joint venture 承包商联营体
contractor's liability insurance
  承包商责任保险
contractor's obligation after termination
  终止后承包商的义务
contractor's operations on site
  承包商的现场作业
contractor's personnel 承包商人员
contractor's profit 承包商利润
contractor's proposals 承包商建议书
contractor's records 承包商的记录
contractor's representative 承包商代表
contractor's risk and cost
  承包商的风险和成本
contractor's staff 承包商的职员
contractor's superintendence 承包商的监督
contractor's traffic 承包商的交通运输
contractor-financed contract
  承包商带资承包合同
contractor-led design teams
  承包商主导的设计团队
contractual arrangement 合同安排
contractual capacity 缔约能力
contractual commitments 合同承诺
contractual fines 违约罚款
contractual input 合同项下的投入
contractual joint venture 契约式合营
contractual joint-venture contract
  契约式联营合同
contractual liabilities 合同责任
contractual obligation 合同义务
contractual practice 合同惯例
contractual relationship 合同关系
contractual release 合同解除
contractual restrictions 合同约束
contractual right 合同权利
contractual specification 合同规定
contractual usage 合同惯例
contradict 相互矛盾,反驳,抗辩
contradiction 相互矛盾
contrast 对比
contravene 违反,反驳
contribute 捐献,捐赠,捐助

contributed capital 实缴股本
contributing insurance 分摊保险
contribution 捐款,分担
contribution clause 责任分担条款
contribution value 分摊价值
contributory negligence 共同过错
contributor 捐赠人
control (controlling) account 控制账户,统驭账户
control busbar 控制母线
control cable 控制电缆
control chart 控制图
control circuit 二次回路,控制回路
control console 控制台
control cycle 控制周期
control desk element 控制台单元
control index 控制指标
control output delay 控制输出时延
control panel 控制盘,控制屏
control point 控制点
control requisition 控制条件
control right 控制权
control room 综合监控室,控制室
control signal 控制信号
control standard 控制标准
control station (master station) 控制站(主站)
control survey 控制测量
controllable balise 有源应答器
controllable cost 可控成本
controllable risk 可控风险
controllable-source audio magnetotelluric methods 可控源音频大地电磁法
controlled blasting 控制爆破
controlled company 受控公司
controlled loading 控制荷载
controlled object 控制对象
controlled price 管制价格
controlled quantity of soil erosion area 水土流失控制量
controlled ratio of soil erosion 土壤流失控制比
controlled station (slave station) 被控站(子站)
controlled-release chemical disinfection 缓释药剂消毒
controller 审计师,主管人,总会计师
controller of customs 海关署长
controller of public address system 广播控制器

controlling interest 控制权
controlling survey inside tunnel 洞内控制测量
controlling survey outside tunnel 洞外控制测量
convenience of the public 公众的便利
convention 常规,公约,惯例,会议,协定
convention on the recognition and enforcement of foreign arbitral awards 承认和执行外国仲裁裁决公约
conventional price 协定价格
conventional speed railway 普速铁路
conventional train yard 普速车场
convergence indicator 收敛计
convergence layer 汇聚层
convergence node 汇聚节点
conversion 兑换,转换
conversion coefficient 换算系数,折算系数
conversion cost 加工成本
conversion gradient 加算坡度
conversion of currency 货币兑换
conversion price 兑换价格
conversion rate 兑换率,汇价
convert 兑换
converted length 换算长度
converted soil column 换算土柱
converted traffic volume of level crossing 道口折算交通量
converted train pairs 换算列车对数
convertibility 货币兑换性
convertible 可兑换的
convertible bond 可转换债券
convertible currency 可自由兑换的货币
convertible foreign exchange 可兑换外汇
convertible loan 可兑换贷款
convertible paper money 可自由兑换的纸币
convertible securities 可兑换证券
convex slope 凸坡
convey 传送
conveyance 运输工具
conveyance insurance 运输工具保险
conveyance of estate 财产转让
conveyer 输送机,传送机,传送设备
conveyer belt 输送带,传送带
conveying system 传送系统
conveyor 传送设备
convict 证明有罪,犯罪
cook the accounts 虚报账目
cook the books 虚报账目
cooling 冷却

cooling and heating sources 冷热源
cooling degree days 空调度日数
cooling load 冷负荷
cooling load from outdoor air 新风冷负荷
cooling system 降温系统,冷却系统
cooling tank 降温池
cooling tower 冷却塔
cooling unit 冷风机组
cooling water 冷却水
cooling water box 冷却水箱
cooling water expense 冷却水费
cooling-down mode 冷却方式
cooperation 协作
cooperation contract 合作合同
cooperative joint venture 协作型联营体
coordinate 协调
coordinate azimuth 坐标方位角
coordinate grid 坐标格网
coordinate increment 坐标增量
coordinate system 坐标系,坐标系统
coordinate transformation 坐标转换
coordinates 坐标
coordinating and response 联动响应
coordination 协调
coordination center 协调中心
coordination fee for construction concerning lines in service 营业线施工配合费
coordination fee rate for construction concerning lines in service 营业线施工配合费率
coordination meeting 协调会
coordination of work 工作协调
coordinator 协调人
copartnery 合伙关系
cophase traction power supply 同相供电
copper alloy contact wire 铜合金接触导线
copper alloy stranded messenger wire 铜合金绞线承力索
copper bar 铜棒,铜排
copper content 铜含量
copper pipe ovality 铜管椭圆度
copy 抄件,副本,复印件
copyright 版权
cordierite 堇青石
cordon 警戒线
core area of section 截面核芯面积
core barrel 岩芯管
core column 芯柱
core competence 核心竞争力
core competitiveness 核心竞争力
core drill 空心钻,岩芯钻

core drilling 钻孔取芯
core drilling method 钻芯法
core network 核心网
core node 核心节点
core recovery 岩芯回收率
core temperature of concrete 混凝土芯部温度
core wire color 芯线色别
core working hours 基本工时
core-drilling machine 钻孔取芯机
core-drilling method 钻孔取芯法
Coriolis effect 科里奥利效应
corner 垄断
corner fittings 角件
corner stone 奠基石
corporate acquisition 公司收购
corporate assets 公司资产
corporate bond 公司债券
corporate charter 公司执照
corporate income tax 公司所得税
corporate merger 公司合并
corporate owner 法人业主,企业业主
corporate profit tax 公司利润税
corporate restructuring 公司重组
corporate social responsibility 企业社会责任
corporate tax 公司税
corporation act (law) 公司法
corporation by laws 公司章程
corporation regulation 公司条例
corporation seal 公司印章
corporation tax (CT) 公司税
corporation tax act (CTA) 公司税法
corporation 股份有限公司
corpus 本金,汇编
correct 修正
corrected bid price 改正后的投标价
correction coefficient 校正系数,修正系数
correction coefficient of particle density 颗粒密度校正系数
correction factor for orientation 朝向修正率
correction for tape length 尺长改正
correction of noise measurement value 噪声测量值修正
correction of photograph distortion 像片变形改正
corrective grinding 修理性打磨
corrective maintenance 故障检修
correlate 联系数
correlation coefficient 相关系数

correlation test 相关校验
correlative adjustment 相关平差
correspondence 往来函件
correspondent bank 代理银行,往来银行
corridor 廊道
corrosion 腐蚀
corrosion environment 腐蚀环境
corrosion fissure 溶蚀裂隙
corrosion inhibitor for steel 钢筋阻锈剂
corrosion of steel bar 钢筋锈蚀
corrosion preventive 防腐剂,防锈剂
corrosion resistant rail 耐腐蚀轨
corrosion-induced crack of steel girder
  钢梁腐蚀裂纹
corrosion-proof 防腐蚀的
corrosive carbon dioxide 侵蚀性二氧化碳
corrosiveness 腐蚀性
corrosiveness of groundwater
  地下水侵蚀性
corrugated compensator 波纹补偿器
corrupt 贿赂
corrupt practice 贿赂行为,贪污行为
corruption 受贿,贪污
corundum 刚玉
coset 层系组
cost 成本
cost account 成本账户,成本核算
cost accounting 成本会计
cost allocation 成本分摊
cost analysis 成本分析
cost and commitment 成本与承诺费
cost and freight (CFR)
  成本加运费(价),离岸成本加运费(价)
cost and insurance (C&I)
  离岸成本加保险费(价)
cost benefit 成本收益
cost breakdown 成本分解
cost breakdown detail 成本分类细则
cost breakdown structure 成本分解结构
cost ceiling 最高成本
cost clerk 成本管理员
cost code 成本编码
cost code system 成本编码系统
cost concerning construction period
  工期成本
cost concerning quality 质量成本
cost consultant 成本咨询顾问
cost contribution 成本分摊
cost control 成本管理,成本控制
cost curve 成本曲线
cost cutting 成本削减
cost down 降低成本
cost engineer 成本工程师
cost estimate 成本估算,费用估算
cost estimation 成本预算
cost factor 成本因素
cost forecasting 成本预测
cost impact analysis 成本影响分析
cost index 费用指数
cost input 成本投入
cost items 成本项目
cost making method 编制方法
cost making period price 编制期价格
cost making period 编制期
cost making year 编制年度
cost management of construction works
  建设工程造价管理
cost monitoring 费用监测
cost of acquisition 进货成本
cost of bond 担保成本
cost of building works 建筑工程造价
cost of capital 资本成本
cost of civil engineering works
  土木工程造价
cost of construction and installation works
  建筑安装工程费
cost of construction works 建筑工程费
cost of coordination and supporting works
  配合辅助工程费
cost of delay 误期费用
cost of fire protection 防火费用
cost of funds 资金成本
cost of goods purchased 购货成本,进货成本
cost of goods sold 销货成本
cost of living 生活费
cost of overhaul 大修费用
cost of production 生产成本
cost of remedying defects 缺陷修补费用
cost of repatriation 遣散费
cost of safety program 安全计划费用
cost of site security
  现场安全费用,现场保安费用
cost of subcontracted works 分包工程费
cost of suspension 暂时停工费用
cost of tendering 投标费用
cost of transitional works 过渡工程费
cost of upkeep 维护费用
cost of wear and tear 损耗费
cost of wear and tear during delivery
  运输损耗费

cost overrun 成本超支,费用超支
cost planning 费用计划
cost plus profit 成本加利润
cost recovery 成本回收
cost reduction 降低成本
cost reimbursable 成本补偿
cost reimbursement 费用补偿
cost reimbursement contract 成本补偿合同
cost schedule 成本明细表
cost sheet 成本单
cost target contract 成本目标合同
cost variance 成本差异,成本偏差
cost, insurance and freight (CIF) 到岸价格
cost, insurance, freight and commission (CIF and C.) 成本、保险费、运费加佣金(价),到岸价格加佣金
cost, insurance, freight and war-risks (CIF. and W.) 成本、保险费、运费加战争险价
cost, insurance, freight, ex-ships hold (CIF ex-ships hold) 成本、保险费、运费加船舱底交货(价),到岸轮船舱底交货
cost, insurance, freight, landed terms (CIF landed terms) 成本、保险费、运费加卸货费(价),到岸价格加卸货费
cost, insurance, freight, liner terms (CIF liner terms) 成本、保险费、运费加班轮费用(价),到岸价格加班轮条件
cost, insurance, freight under ship's tackle 成本、保险费、运费加吊钩下交货价
costing 成本计算
costing of plant 设备成本计算
costs 审理辩护费用,诉讼费
costs and damages 诉讼费加损害赔偿费
costs of maintenance 维护费用
cost-and-fee contract 成本加酬金合同
cost-benefit analysis (CBA) 成本效益分析
cost-benefit evaluation 成本效益评价
cost-benefit ratio 成本效益比
cost-effective analysis 成本效益分析
cost-plus contract 成本加成合同
cost-plus pricing 成本加成计价法
cost-plus-award-fee contract 成本加激励酬金合同,成本加奖金合同
cost-plus-fee contract 成本加酬金合同
cost-plus-fixed-fee contract 成本加固定酬金合同
cost-plus-fluctuating-fee contract 成本加浮动酬金合同
cost-plus-incentive-fee contract 成本加激励酬金合同,成本加奖金合同
cost-plus-percentage-fee contract 成本加定比酬金合同
cost-plus-upset-maximum contract 成本加固定最大酬金合同
cost-reimbursable contract 开口合同
cost-volume-profit (CVP) analysis 本量利分析
cost-volume-profit analysis 本量利分析,成本、数量、利润分析
cote on demand 即期票据
Coulomb earth pressure 库仑土压力
Coulomb theory 库仑理论
Coulomb's earth pressure theory 库仑土压力理论
Coulomb-Navier strength theory 库仑-纳维强度理论
council 委员会
counsel 辩护律师,法律顾问
counsel/attorney/legal fee 律师服务费
counselor 辩护律师,顾问
count of lawsuit 诉讼理由
counter grade at yard end 尾部反坡
counter guarantee 反担保函
counter intercom 窗口对讲器
counter offer 还价,还盘
counterappeal 抗诉
counterchange 互换
countercharge 反控诉
counterclaim 反诉,反索赔
counterclaim for contractor's defaults 对承包商违约的反索赔
counterfeit 假冒,伪造
counterfeit money 假钞
counterfeit trademark 冒牌商标
counterfort retaining wall 扶壁式挡土墙
countermeasure 对策
counterplead 抗辩
counterpurchase 反购,互购
countersignature block 会签栏
countersign 副签,会签
countertrade 对等贸易,反向贸易
countervailing credit 背对背信用证
countervailing duty 抵消税,反补贴税,反倾销税
counter-notice 回函
counter-bid 还价
counter-force device 反力装置
counting inspection 计数检验
counting test of counter 计数器计数测试
country 国家
country and city inspectors 政府质量稽查人员

country of departure　起运国
country of destination　目的地国家
country of dispatch　发货国
country of embarkation　装货国
country of incorporation　注册地
country of origin　原产地
country of payment　付款国
country quota　国别配额
country risk　国别风险
couper's cabin at hump crest
　峰顶联结员室
coupled　重联
coupled truck　拖挂式载重车
coupled vibration system　耦合振动体系
coupled-wall　连肢墙
coupler buffer device　车钩缓冲装置
coupler compressing grade　压钩坡
coupling　结合,耦合
coupling and uncoupling operation
　甩挂作业
coupling area　连挂区
coupling beam　连梁
coupling loss　耦合损耗
coupling speed　连挂速度
coupon　票证,息票,赠券
course　进程
course line　航线
court　法庭,法院
court fee　法庭费用
court of appeal　上诉法院
covenant　契约
cover
　包括,抵偿,覆盖,苫盖,埋置深度
cover and cut-bottom up　盖挖顺筑法
cover note (C/N)　暂保单,承保单
cover plate　盖板
coverage　承保险别
coverage of survey area　测区范围
covered karst area　覆盖型岩溶区
covered-interest　套利
covering letter　前附函
covering soil　表层覆土
cover-excavation method　盖挖法
co-acceptor　共同承兑人
co-assurer　共同承保人
co-beneficiary　共同受益人
co-borrower　共同借款人
co-debtor　共同债务人
co-financing　联合融资
co-guarantor　共同担保人

co-insurance　共同保险
co-located double coverage
　同站址双网覆盖
co-manager　共同管理人
co-operation　合作
co-partnership company　合资公司
co-production　合作生产
CR Prohibition　铁禁
crab rock loader　蟹爪式装岩机
crab winch　绞车
crack　裂缝,裂纹
crack growth　裂纹扩展
crack monitoring　裂缝监测
crack observation　裂缝观测
crack water　裂隙水
crack width　裂缝宽度
cracker　破碎机
cracking load　开裂荷载
crack-free　无龟裂
crack-resisting ability　抗裂性能
craft　船
craft union　同业工会
craftsman　工匠
crane　起重机
crane barge　起重机船
crane crab　绞车
crane girder　机重机梁
crane load　机重机荷载
crane winch　起重绞车
crank　拐肘
crash　暴跌
crash costs　赶工成本
crash duration　赶工工期
crashing sound　撞击声
crawler crane/caterpillar crane　履带式起重机
crawler dozer　履带式推土机
crawler excavator　履带式挖掘机
crawler loader　履带式装载机
crawler pile frame　履带式桩架
crawler tractor　履带式拖拉机
crawling loader　挖装机
credentials　证件
credit　贷记,贷项,信贷,贷款,信用
credit agreement　信贷协议
credit analysis　信用分析
credit and surety insurance　信贷保证类保险
credit balance　贷方余额
credit bank　信贷银行
credit card　信用卡
credit column　贷方栏

credit guarantee 信贷保函
credit insurance 信用保险
credit line 贷款额度
credit market 信贷市场
credit memorandum (memo) 贷项通知单
credit note 贷项通知单,欠条
credit policy 信贷政策,信用保险单
credit purchase 赊购
credit risk 信贷风险
credit sale 赊销
credit side 贷方
credit standing (status) 资信状况
credit terms 信贷条件
creditor 贷方,债权人
creditor beneficiary 债权受益人
creditor of bankruptcy 破产人的债权人
creditworthiness 借贷信用
creek ditch 浜沟
creep 蠕动,蠕滑
creep deformation 蠕变变形
creep of concrete 混凝土蠕变
creep test 蠕变试验
creep transport 蠕移搬运
creepage 蠕变
creepage distance 爬电距离
creeping 爬行
creolization 混合
crescent dune 新月形沙丘
crest 坝顶
crest value 峰值
Cretaceous period 白垩纪
Cretaceous system 白垩系
crew 小组
crew shift changing at turnaround depot system 驻班制
crib consolidator 枕间夯实机
crime 犯罪
criminal law 刑法
criminal liability 刑事责任
criminal responsibility 刑事责任
crimping mark 压接标志
crisis management 危机管理
criteria 标准,尺度,准则
critera for judging the traffic serviceability 运营性能检验判别值
criterion 基准
critical activity 关键活动
critical date schedule 关键日期计划表
critical depth 临界深度
critical event 关键事件

critical height 临界高度
critical hydraulic gradient 临界水力梯度
critical item 主控项目
critical items list 关键项目清单
critical path 关键路径,关键线路
critical path method (CPM) 关键路径方法,关键路径网络图
critical path schedule 关键路线进度表
critical plastic load 临塑荷载
critical point 关键点,临界点
critical process 关键工序
critical situation 紧急情况
critical span length 临界跨距
critical speed 临界速度
critical void ratio 临界孔隙比
critical water content 临界含水率
critical wind direction 极端风向
critical works 控制工程
cross (crossed) check (cheque) 横线支票,划线支票
cross bar 跨条
cross beam 横梁,硬横梁
cross brace 剪刀撑,十字撑
cross claim 交叉索赔
cross diaphragm method (CRD method) 交叉中隔壁法(CRD 法)
cross discounts 交叉折扣
cross exchange 交叉汇兑,套汇
cross fault 横断层
cross level 水平
cross liability clause 交叉责任条款
cross license 互换许可证
cross link (eye/eye) 单耳连接器
cross measurement 交叉测量
cross passage 横通道
cross plate head 十字板头
cross plate shear strength apparatus 十字板剪切仪
cross rate 套算汇率
cross road 交叉路
cross section 断面,横断面,横截面
cross section drawing 横断面图
cross section of earthworks 路基横断面
cross section of pile shaft 桩身截面
cross slope of the deck surface 桥面横坡
cross tunnel 横通道
crosscheck locking 照查锁闭
crossing angle 辙叉角
crossing barrier 道口栏木
crossing nose 叉心

crossing of routes 进路交叉
crossing station 会让站
crossing untwining 交叉疏解
crossover 渡线
crosstalk attenuation tester 串音衰耗测试器
crosstalk interference 串音干扰
crossway 交叉路
cross-acceptance 相互认可
cross-bar 横杆
cross-default clause 交叉过失条款
cross-default 交叉过失
cross-hole CT 跨孔 CT
cross-hole sonic logging 声波透射法
cross-hole sonic perspective 井间声波透视
cross-hole ultrasonic tester
 跨孔超声波测试仪
cross-line train 跨线列车
cross-reference clause 相互参照条款
cross-section of excavated tunnel
 隧道开挖断面
cross-section of lined tunnel 隧道衬砌断面
cross-section of tunnel 隧道断面
cross-section survey
 断面测量,横断面测量
cross-sectional drawing of sound barrier
 声屏障横断面图
cross-span structure 横跨结构
cross-span wire clamp 定位索线夹
cross-span wire 定位索
cross-track passage 平过道
cross-turnout pavement at hump crest
 峰顶跨道岔铺面
cross-type joint 十字形接头
cross-type junction terminal 十字形枢纽
cross-wall 冰坎
crow bar 撬棍
crowd abnormal behavior detection
 人群异常行为检测
crowd density 人群密度
crowd density estimation 人群密度估计
crown beam 冠梁
crown diameter 冠幅
crown settlement 拱顶下沉
CRTS-Ⅰ slab ballastless track
 CRTS-Ⅰ型板式无砟轨道
CRTS-Ⅰ bi-block CRTS-Ⅰ型双块式
CRTS-Ⅰ slab CRTS-Ⅰ型板式
CRTS-Ⅱ bi-block CRTS-Ⅱ型双块式
CRTS-Ⅱ slab ballastless track
 CRTS-Ⅱ型板式无砟轨道

CRTS-Ⅱ slab CRTS-Ⅱ型板式
CRTS-Ⅲ slab ballastless track
 CRTS-Ⅲ型板式无砟轨道
CRTS-Ⅲ slab CRTS-Ⅲ型板式
crucible 坩埚
crumple 揉皱
crush 压碎
crush index 压碎指标
crush texture 压碎结构
crushed gravel 碎砾石
crushed scree 碎石岩堆
crushed stone 碎石
crushed talus 碎石岩堆
crusher 碎石机
crusher dust content 石粉含量
crushing of rail head 轨头压溃
crust 地壳
crustal stress 地壳应力
cryostructure 冷生构造
cryptocrystalline texture 隐晶质结构
crystal 晶体
crystal structure 结晶构造
crystal system 晶系
crystalline 结晶质的
crystalline schist 结晶片岩
crystalloblastic texture 变晶结构
cubage load of volatile solids
 挥发性固体容积负荷
cube specimen 立方体试件
cubic measure 体积,容积
cubic system 等轴晶系
cuesta 单面山
cultivated land 耕地
cultural relics protection 文物保护
culture dish 培养皿
culture relics 文物
culvert 电缆管道,涵洞
culvert in the case of both inlet and outlet submerged 压力式涵洞
culvert in the case of both inlet and outlet unsubmerged 无压力涵洞
culvert in the case of only one of the inlet/outlet submerged 半压力式涵洞
culvert span 涵洞孔径
culvert survey 涵洞测量
culvert water inlet 涵洞进水口
culvert water outlet 涵洞出水口
cumulative 追加的
cumulative amount 累计金额
cumulative damage 累积损伤

cumulative sieve residue 累计筛余
cumulative total 累计总额
cuplock scaffolding 碗扣式脚手架
cup-type foundation 杯形基础
cup-type wind speed and direction sensor 风杯式风速风向传感器
curb 抵制
curbstone 路缘石
curing age 养护龄期
curing at moisture-retention and heat-insulation 保温保湿养护
curing in water 水中养护
curing mat 养护覆盖物
currencies of payment 支付货币
currency 货币
currency adjustment factor 币值调整因数
currency appreciation 货币升值
currency conversion 货币兑换
currency convertibility 货币可兑换性,货币自由兑换性
currency depreciation 货币贬值
currency devaluation 货币贬值
currency exchange 货币兑换
currency exchange adjustment 汇率调整
currency futures contract 货币期货合同
currency hedge 货币套期保值
currency inflation 通货膨胀
currency market 货币市场
currency of account 记账货币
currency of agreement 协议书规定的货币
currency of contract 合同规定的货币
currency of settlement 结算货币
currency option 货币期权
currency proportion 货币比例
currency rate 外汇汇率
currency reserve 货币储备
currency restriction 货币限制
currency revaluation 货币升值
currency risk 货币风险
currency swap 货币掉期,货币互换
current account 活期账户,往来账户
current appropriation 本年度拨款
current asset 流动资产
current balance 经常项目差额
current basis 按现值
current bedding 波状层理
current carrying capacity 载流量
current cost 现行成本
current debt 短期债务,流动债务
current decrees 现行法令
current deposit 活期存款
current electrode 发射电极,供电电极
current electrode spacing 供电电极距
current element 电流元件
current equalization performance 均流性能
current expenditures 经常费用
current expenditure 经常性开支
current expense 本期费用,经常费用
current income 本期收益,经常收入
current increment protection 电流增量保护
current investment 短期投资
current labour rates 现时工资
current liabilities 短期债务
current loan 短期银行贷款
current market value 现行市价
current period 本期
current price 时价,现行价格
current price index 现行价格指数
current programme 现行的进度计划,当前实施计划
current protection 电流保护
current ratio 流动比率
current repair 经常性修理
current replacement cost 现行重置成本
current return via protective wire 保护线 PW 线回流
current return via return conductor 回流线回流
current revenue 当期营业收入
current transformer 电流互感器
current wage bulletin 当前工资简报
current waveform 电流波形
current-carrying capability 载流能力
current-limiting 限流
current-voltage protection 电流电压保护
curriculum vitae(CV) 履历表
curtailed rail 缩短轨
curtain grouting 帷幕灌浆,帷幕注浆
curtain wall of building 建筑幕墙
curvature 曲率,弯曲度
curvature coefficient 曲率系数
curvature difference 曲率差
curvature radius of meridian 子午圈曲率半径
curvature radius of normal section arc 法截弧曲率半径
curve alignment adjusting 整正曲线
curve between two tangent/straight track 夹圆曲线
curve calibration 测量曲线

curve cant 曲线超高
curve control point 曲线控制点
curve deflection angle 曲线偏角
curve estimation 曲线回归法
curve method (also known as "earned value management") 曲线法(又称"赢值法")
curve middle point 曲中点
curve post 曲线标
curve resistance 曲线阻力
curve smoothness 曲线圆顺度
curve superelevation 曲线超高
curve versine 曲线正矢
curve widening 曲线加宽
curved beam 曲梁
curved bearing 弧形支座
curved bridge 曲线桥,弯桥
curved cantilever 弓形腕臂
curved formwork for invert construction 仰拱曲模
curved holder for earth wire 地线弯卡
curved stock rail 导轨
curved switch rail 曲线尖轨
curved tunnel 曲线隧道
curves in the same direction 同向曲线
curve-in and straight-out 进弯出直,弯进直出
curvilinear regression method 曲线回归法
cushion course 垫层
cushion layer 褥垫层
custody 保管,照管
custom 常规,风俗习惯,惯例,习惯
custom of port 港口惯例
custom union 关税同盟
customary law 惯例法,习惯法
customary tare 习惯皮重
customer relationship management 客户关系管理
customer service representive (CSR) 人工座席
customer's credits 顾客信贷
customer's account 客户账,应收账款账户
customer 顾客,客户
customs 海关,进口税
customs agency 报关代理行
customs agent 报关代理人
customs appraised value 海关估价
customs barrier 关税壁垒
customs bond 海关保税保证书
customs brokerage 海关佣金
customs broker 报关行,报关经纪人
customs clearance 海关放行证,清关,结关
customs clearance agent 清关代理人
customs clearance certificate 清关证书
customs clearing charges (fee) 报关费
customs consignee 海关委托人
customs declaration 报关
customs declaration form 海关申报单
customs declaration form for importing duty-free goods 免税货进口报关单
customs declaration for import of goods 货物进口完税单
customs dues 关税
customs duties 保护性关税
customs duty 关税
customs entry 报关单,海关登记,海关进口手续
customs examination 海关检验,验关
customs examination list 海关验货单
customs formalities 海关手续
customs house 海关
customs house officer 海关官员
customs import tariff 海关进口税则
customs inspection 验关
customs invoice 海关发票
customs law 海关法
customs pass 海关通行证
customs permit 海关许可证
customs procedures 海关手续
customs receipt 海关收据
customs regulations 海关条例
customs tariff 海关税则
customs territory 关境,海关境域
customs valuation 海关估价
cut 挖方
cut and cover method 明挖法
cut down 杀价
cut hole 掏槽眼
cut off 截断
cut price 降价,减价
cut section 分割区段
cut the cost 降低成本
cutback 削减
cutoff angle of a luminaire 灯具遮光角
cutter head 刀盘
cutter head bearing 刀盘轴承
cutter head micromotion mechanism 刀盘微动机构
cutter head power 刀盘功率
cutter head rotation speed 刀盘转速
cutter head sealing 刀盘密封
cutter head thrust 刀盘推力
cutter head torque 刀盘扭矩

cutter housing 刀座
cutter hub 刀体
cutter ring 刀圈
cutter ring diameter 刀圈直径
cutter ring life 刀圈寿命
cutter shaft 刀轴
cutter spacing 刀间距
cutting 截断,路堑,挖掘
cutting and filling 移挖作填
cutting edge 刃脚
cutting edge of open caisson 沉井刃脚
cutting ring 环刀
cutting slope 路堑边坡
cuttings 弃渣
cutting-ring method 环刀法
cut-and-cover works 单建掘开式工程
cut-and-fill 半堤半堑,半填半挖
cut-fill balance 土石方调配
cut-fill transition section 路堤路堑过渡段
cut-fill volume evaluated based on average cross section 断面方
cut-off 防渗墙,截水墙
cut-off date 截止日期
cut-off period 不得超过的期限
cut-over area recovery 迹地恢复
cuvette 比色皿
CWR track stability 无缝线路稳定性
CWR turnout 无缝道岔
cyanide 氰化物
cyanite 蓝晶石
cycle advance of blasting 爆破循环进尺
cycle length 盾环进尺
cyclic loading test 循环加载试验
cyclic scanning system 循环检查制
cycling time of freight section 货位周转时间
cylindrical brick arch 砖筒拱

D

D/A draft 承兑汇票
DAAB agreement 争议避免裁决协议书
DAAB procedural rules
　争议避免裁决委员会程序规则
DAAB/Dispute Avoidance/Adjudication Board
　争议避免裁决委员会
DAAB's activities
　争议避免裁决委员会的活动
DAAB's rules 争议避免裁决委员会的规则
dacite 英安岩
daily allowance 每日津贴
daily average handling quantity of container
　日均作业箱数
daily average quantity of container dispatched
　日均发送箱
daily average quantity of container for transshipment 日均中转箱
daily average quantity of container received
　日均到达箱
daily average volume of freight dispatched
　日均发货量
daily breaking-up capacity 日解体能力
daily cash report 现金日报表
daily construction activities 每日施工作业
daily construction report 施工日报表
daily interest 日息
daily pay (wage) 日工资
daily premium 每日保险费
daily price 每日单价
daily rainfall 日降雨量
daily reception amount 日接送量
daily record of construction 施工日志
daily statement 日报表
daily stock of freight cars 货车保有量
daily technical service fee 日技术服务费
daily variation coefficient 日变化系数
daily wage 计日工资
dam 坝,水堰
dam construction survey 堤坝施工测量
damage 毁坏,损害
damage caused by sweating & heating
　受潮受热险
damage claim 损害索赔
damage of soil erosion and water loss
　水土流失危害
damage surveyor
　损坏计量师,损害估算人
damage to persons and property
　人身与财产损害
damage to works 对工程的损害
damages 赔款,破坏、损失及花费,损害赔偿金
damages for default 违约赔偿金
dammed lake 堰塞湖
damp 潮湿
damp air 湿空气
damped vibration 阻尼振动
dampening rubber 减振胶垫
damper 防振锤
damping factor 阻尼因数
damping foundation 减振基础
damping ratio 阻尼比
damp-proof coating 防潮层
danger 危险
danger area 危险区
danger money 危险工作津贴
danger point 危险点
danger signal 危险信号
dangerous building 危险建筑物
dangerous goods (articles)
　危险品,危险物品
dangerous goods warehouse 危险货物仓库
dangerous goods yard 危险货物货场
Danxia landform 丹霞地貌
Darcy law 达西定律
data 数据
data acquisition 数据获取

data acquisition instrument 数据采集仪器
data analysis 数据分析
data backup 数据备份
data channel 数据通道
data collection 数据采集
data communication 数据通信
data communication network 数据通信网
data editing 数据编辑
data encoding 数据编码
data interpretation 资料解释
data link 数据链路
data network 数据网
data network comprehensive analyzer 数据网络综合分析仪
data point 数据点
data processing 数据处理
data processing device 数据处理设备
database 数据库
database maintenance 数据库维护
database management system（DMS） 数据库管理系统
database server 数据库服务器
date draft 定期汇票
date due 到期日
date for inspection 检查日期
date for testing 检验日期,试验日期
date of acceptance 验收日期
date of arrival 到达日
date of balance sheet 资产负债表日期
date of bid opening 开标日期
date of bill of lading 提单日期
date of completion 竣工日期,完工日期
date of contract 签约日期
date of delivery 交货日期
date of departure 开航日期
date of discharge 卸货日期
date of draft 汇票支付日期
date of expiration（expiry） 截止日期,期满日
date of final account 决算日
date of issue 签发日期
date of landing 卸岸日期
date of letter 发函日期
date of loading 装货日期
date of payment 付款日,支付日期
date of possession 进场日期
date of postmark 邮戳日期
date of receipt 收到日期
date of shipment 装船日期
date of survey 测量日期,检查日期,检验日期
date of termination 终止日期
date of validity 有效日期
date of value 起息日
datum 基面,基准
datum grade 基准标高
datum level 基准面
datum line 基准线
datum plane 基准面
（calendar）day （日历）天
day bill 定期票据
day loan 按日计息贷款
day rate 计日工资率,日工资
day shift 白班,日班
day signal 昼间信号
day wage 计日工资
day work 散工
daylight factor 采光系数
daylighting 采光,自然采光
days of grace 宽限日期,优惠期
days of heating period 采暖期天数
daywork 计日工,计日工作
daywork rate 计日工资
daywork schedule 计日工作表,计日工作计划表
day-time 白天
day-to-day money 日用资金
DC block 直流隔断器
DC level shift（DCLS） 直流电平携带码
DC output 直流输出
DC panel 直流盘,直流屏
DC power distribution device 直流配电设备
DC power supply panel 直流源屏
DC power supply system 直流供电制
DC relay 直流继电器
DC voltage transformer 直流电压互感器
dead account 呆账,坏账
dead asset 报废资产
dead capital 呆滞资本
dead freight 空舱费
dead landslide 死滑坡
dead load 恒荷载,恒载,呆滞贷款
dead loss 纯损失
dead money 闲置资金
dead season 淡季
dead section 死区段
dead section of track circuit 轨道电路死区段
dead security 无价值担保
dead stock 呆滞存货,滞销货
dead weight 自重
dead zone 分相区

deadline 截止日期,截止时间
deadline for receipt of tenders 投标截止期
deadweight tonnage(DWT) 总载重吨位
dead-end freight station 尽端式货运站
dead-end passenger station 尽端式客运站
dead-end platform 尽端式站台
dead-end pole 终端杆
dead-end support 终端杆塔
dead-end terminal 尽端式枢纽
deaerator 除氧装置
deal 交易
dealer 经销商
dear money 高息贷款
dearness allowance 物价津贴,物价变动余裕
death and disability award 死亡和伤残补助金
death benefit(gratuity) 死亡抚恤金
debenture 公司债券,海关退税单,无担保债券,信用债券
debenture capital 借入资本,债务资金
debit 负债人,借方,借记,借项
debit and credit 借贷
debit balance 借方余额
debit bank 借款银行
debit card 记账卡,借方卡
debit column 借方栏
debit entry 借项
debit instrument 欠据
debit item 借项
debit memorandum(note) 借项通知单
debit note 借据
debris 废弃物,岩屑
debris flow 泥石流
debris flow fan 泥石流扇
debt 欠款,欠债,债款,债务
debt at call 即期债务
debt capital 借入资本,债务资金
debt certificate 债务证明书
debt crisis 债务危机
debt discharge/relief/cancellation 免除债务
debt due 到期债务
debt outstanding 未偿债务
debt receivable 应收账款
debt repayable 应偿债务
debt rescheduling 重订还债期限
debt retirement 还债
debt service analysis 偿债能力分析
debt service 还本付息,债务,债息
debt to equity ratio 负债资产比,债本比
debtee 债权人

debtor 负债人,借方,债务人
debt-equity ratio 贵务-产权比率
decant pond 沉淀井
decay 毁坏,衰退
decay time 衰减时
deceit 诈骗
decennial liability insurance 十年责任险
decentralized and autonomous constraints 分散自律约束条件
decentralized and autonomous control 分散自律控制
decentralized and autonomous CTC system 分散自律调度集中系统
decentralized structure 分散构造
decibel 分贝
decipherable 可辨认的
decision 决定
decision in writing 书面决定
decision maker 决策者
decision stage 决策阶段
decision tree analysis 决策树分析
deck bridge 上承式桥
declarant 报关人,申请人,申诉人
declaration 声明
declaration for exportation 出口报关
declaration for importation 进口报关单
declaration form 申报表
declaration inwards 进口报关单,入境报关单
declaration of acceptance 接受声明
declaration of trust 信托书
declaration outward 出口报关
declaration policy 申报保险单
declare 申报,声明
declare at the customs 报关
declare bankruptcy 宣告破产
declare goods 申报货物
declare off 毁约
declared value 设定价值,申报价值
declination method 偏角法
decline 拒付,衰退
decline an offer 不接受报价
decline rate of curve superelevation 曲线超高递减率
declined risk 拒保风险
declining balance method of depreciation 余额递减折旧法
declining rate of gauge widening 轨距加宽递减率
decoder 解码器
decoiling device 放线装置

decoloration 脱色
decomposition by fusion 熔融分解
decomposition temperature 分解温度
decontamination room 洗消间
decoration 装饰,装修
decoupling network 去耦网络
decrease 递减
decrease amount 降低额
decrease of work efficiency 降低工效
decrease range 降低幅度
decree 法令,政令
decrement 贬值,减量
dedicated materials for railway project 铁路专用材料
dedicated ventilation riser 专用通气立管
deduct 扣减
deduct/withhold a payment 扣款
deductible clause 免赔条款
deductible 免赔额,自负额
deduction 扣除额
deed 契约
deed of appointment 任命证书
deed of assignment 财产转让契约
deed of conveyance 转让证书
deed of guarantee 担保契约
deed of indemnity 赔偿契约
deed of mortgage 抵押契约
deed of novation 债务变更契约
deed of partnership 合伙契约
deed of substitution 替代契约
deed of transfer 转让契据
deed of trust 信托契约
deed of undertaking 保证契约
deep cutting 深路堑
deep flexural member 深受弯构件
deep gutterway 高式水沟
deep hole blasting 深孔爆破
deep hole thermometer 深孔温度计
deep mixing method 深层搅拌法
deep tunnel 深埋隧道
deep water thermometer 深水温度计
deep well 管井
deep well method 深井法
deep well pump 深井泵,深井水泵
deepened blasting hole 加深炮孔
deeply inclined strata 陡倾岩层
deep-buried benchmark 深埋水准点
deep-focus earthquake 深源地震
deep-sea basin 深海盆地
deface 毁坏

defalcation 侵吞公款
default 不出庭,不履行义务,违背,违约,不作为,未履行
default by contractor 承包商违约
default of owner (employer) 业主违约
default of payment 不履行付款义务
default of subcontractor 分包商的违约
default party 违约方
default risk 拖欠风险,违约风险
default value 默认值
defeasance clause 废除条款
defeated party 败诉方
defeated suit 败诉
defect 缺陷,战胜
defect interface 缺陷界面
defect types 病害类型
defective goods 次品
defective material 有缺陷的材料
defective pile 不合格桩
defective shunting 分路不良
defective work 有缺陷的工作
defects after taking over 接收后的缺陷
defects and rejection 缺陷和拒收
defects list 缺陷清单
defects notification period (DNP) 缺陷通知期
defects remediation 缺陷修补
defence counsel 辩护律师
defence 辩护,抗辩
defend 保卫,辩护
defendant 被告
defense 辩护
defense/prevention against claim 防范索赔
defer payment 延期付款
deferment charge 延期费用
deferment of a project 工程延期
defer 推迟,延迟
deferral 延期
deferred annuity 延期年金
deferred assets 递延资产
deferred charges (expenses) 递延费用
deferred cost 递延成本
deferred credits 递延贷项
deferred debits 递延借项
deferred delivery 延期交货
deferred equity 递延股权
deferred interest 延期利息
deferred liabilities 递延负债
deferred payment 延期付款
deferred payment credit 延期付款信用证
deferred payment guarantee 延期付款保函

deferred payment sale 延期付款销售
deferred premium 递延保险金
deferred revenue (income) 递延收入
deficiency 不足额
deficiency guarantee 资金缺额担保
deficiency judgement 清偿不足额判决
deficiency list 缺陷清单
deficient 不足
deficient superelevation 欠超高
deficit 赤字,亏空,亏损
deficit account 亏损账户
deficit balance 收支赤字
deficit budget 赤字预算
deficit financing 赤字财政
deficit spending 赤字开支
definite appropriation 定额拨款
definite price 固定价格
definition 定义,限定
definition phase 定义阶段
definitive estimate 确定性估算
definitive schedule 最终进度
deflation 吹蚀,通货紧缩
deflation hollow 风蚀洼地
deflation unaka 风蚀残丘
deflection 挠度,挠性
deflection angle 偏角
deflection observation 挠度观测
deflection of measure point 测点变位
deflector 导流板
deformation 变形
deformation allowance 预留变形,预留变形量
deformation analysis 变形分析
deformation check 变形验算
deformation control network 变形控制网
deformation factor 变形因子
deformation joint 变形缝
deformation modulus 变形模量
deformation monitoring 变形监测
deformation monitoring measurement 变形监控量测
deformation observation control network 变形观测控制网
deformation of river bed 河床变迁
deformation parameter 变形参数
deformation pressure 形变压力
deformation second-order effect 变形二阶效应
deformation survey 变形测量
deformation value of projection length 投影长度变形值
deformed steel bar 螺纹筋

defraud 诈骗
degassing method 抽气法
degradation 劣化
degradation indication 降级显示
degree of approximation 逼近度
degree of compaction 密实度
degree of consolidation 固结度
degree of erosion 侵蚀程度
degree of freedom 自由度
degree of gravity vertical for wall surface 墙面垂直度
degree of prestressing 预应力度
degree of risk 风险度
degree of safety 安全度
degree of separation 分离度
degressive depreciation 递减折旧
dehumidification 除湿
dehydrator 除水器
delay 时延,推迟,延迟,拖延,延误
delay and/or cost 误期及/或成本
delay damages 误期赔偿金,误期损害赔偿费
delay in completion 竣工拖延
delay time 延迟时间
delayed completion 拖期竣工
delayed drawings 延误的图纸
delayed payment 拖期付款,付款延误
delayed test 延误的检验,延误的试验
delaying tactics 拖延策略
delays and suspension 开工、延误和暂停
delays by subcontractor 分包商的误期
delays caused by authorities 当局造成的延误
delays in engineering 工程延误
delegate 授权,委派
delegation 代表团,授权,委派
delegation by the engineer 工程师的委托
delegation of authority 权力委托
delegation of duties 职责委托
delict 不法行为,违法行为
decline 拒绝接受
declined check 拒付支票
delinquent party 违约当事人
delinquent tax 滞纳税款
deliver 传送,递交,交付,运送
deliverable 可交付成果
deliverables 交付成果
delivered at frontier 边境交货
delivered at place (DAP) 目的地交货(价)
delivered at terminal (DAT) 目的地码头交货(价)

delivered ex quay (DEQ) 目的地码头交货(价)
delivered duty unpaid (DDU)
　未完税后交货(价)
delivered ex ship (DES)
　船上交货,目的港船上交货(价)
delivered goods 运送的货物
delivered price 交货价格
delivered terms 交货条件
delivering by train 火车运输
delivering by truck 汽车运输
delivering carrier 交货承运人
delivery 交付
delivery advice 交货通知
delivery against acceptance 承兑交货
delivery against payment 付款交货
delivery and inspection area 交验区
delivery behaviour 交付行为
delivery charge 运输费
delivery cost 运送费用
delivery date 交货日期
delivery distance 运输距离
delivery distance by temporary truck road
　汽车运输便道运距
delivery duty paid (DDP)
　完税后交货
delivery expense 送货费用
delivery ex-warehouse 仓库交货
delivery in instalment 分批交货
delivery means 运输方式
delivery methods 运输方法
delivery note 送货单
delivery of assistance 提供援助,给予协助
delivery of cargo (goods) 交货
delivery of materials 交付材料,运送材料
delivery on arrival 货到交付
delivery on call 通知交货,按通知交货
delivery on field 现场交货
delivery on payment 付款交货
delivery on spot 即期交货
delivery order 交货清单,提货单,送货令
delivery passageway 运输通道
delivery pipe 输水管
delivery point 交货地点
delivery receipt 送货回单
delivery schedule 交货时间表
delivery terms 交货条件
delivery test 出厂试验
delivery versus payment (DVP) 两讫
delivery-receiving of goods 货物交接
delivery-receiving of wagon 车辆交接
delivery-receiving operation 交接作业
delivery-receiving track 交接线
delivery-receiving yard 交接场
delta connection 三角形连接
delta facies 三角洲相
deluge sprinkler 大水滴喷头
demand 即期,需求,征收,正式要求
demand and supply 供求
demand bill 即期汇票
demand bill note at sight 见票即付票据
demand deposit 活期存款,即期存款
demand draft 即期汇票
demand forecast 需求预测
demand guarantee 即付保函
demand loan 活期贷款
demand note 即期票据
demarcation 分界,划分
demarcation line
　(各类地质结构构造的)分界线,界限,界线
Demilitarized Zone (DMZ) 隔离区
demobilization 遣散,撤场
demobilize 遣散,撤场
demolish 拆除
demolition 拆迁
demolition and relocation cost
　拆迁成本,拆迁费
demolition and resettlement 拆迁安置
demolition compensation 拆迁补偿
demolition cost 拆除费
demolition permit 拆迁许可
demolition range 拆迁范围
demolition works 拆除工程
demolitioner 拆迁人
demoulding 脱模
demountable truss 拆装式桁架
demurrage 滞留,装运误期费,滞期费
demurrage cost 滞期费
demur 抗辩
dendritic 树枝状
denounce 控诉
dense wavelength division multiplexing (DWDM)
　密集波分复用
densified control network of construction
　施工加密控制网
densified control network 加密控制网
densified control points 加密控制点
density gauge 密度计
density of air 大气密度
density of rock block 岩石块体密度
denudated mountain 剥蚀残山

denudation 剥蚀
denudation plain 剥蚀平原
denudation slope 剥蚀坡
denunciation clause 退约条款
depart 出发
departing port 离岸港
department 部门
department in charge 主管部门
department manager 部门经理
departure 出发
departure indication 离去表示
departure indicator 发车表示器
departure indicator circuit 发车表示器电路
departure route 发车进路
departure section 离去区段
departure signal
　出站信号机,发车信号,发车信号机
departure station 始发站
departure track 出发线
departure yard 出发场
dependent signal 从属信号机
deplete 耗尽
depletion 损耗,折损
depletion allowance 折耗备抵
depletion reserve 耗减准备
depletive assets 折耗性资产
deportation 驱逐出境
deposit 保证金,存款,押金
deposit accounts 储蓄存款
deposit at bank 银行存款
deposit at call 即期存款
deposit at notice 即期存款
deposit at sight 即期存款
deposit expense 提存费用
deposit premium 预付保险费
deposit rate 存款利率
deposit receipt 存款收据
deposit slip 存款单
depositional plain 沉积平原
depositor 储户
depot 仓库,货站
depot repair 段修
depot track 段管线
depreciable assets 应计折旧资产
depreciate 折旧
depreciated cost 折余成本
depreciated value 折余价值
depreciation 贬值,降价,减价,折旧
depreciation base 折旧基数
depreciation cost 折旧成本,折旧费

depreciation fund 折旧基金
depreciation method 折旧方法
depreciation of capital 资本折旧
depreciation of equipment 设备折旧
depreciation of fixed assets 固定资产折旧
depreciation of machinery 机械设备折旧
depreciation of value 贬值
depreciation rate 折旧费率,折旧率
depreciation reserve 折旧准备
depression 洼地,萧条
depression cone 降落漏斗,漏斗
deprive 剥夺
depth datum 深度基准面
depth of atmosphere/atmospheric effect
　大气影响深度
depth of ballast bed 道床厚度
depth of compression zone 受压区高度
depth of filling 填土厚度
depth of frost 冻结深度
depth of local scour hole 局部冲刷坑深度
depth of sharp atmospheric effect
　大气影响急剧层深度
depth ratio 充满度
depth to span ratio 高跨比
derail 脱轨
derailer 脱轨器
derailment coefficient 脱轨系数
derailment factor 脱轨系数
derailment indicator 脱轨表示器
derailment load of train 列车脱轨载荷
deregistration 注销
dereliction 玩忽职守
dereliction of duty 渎职
derived attribute 衍生属性
derived coordinates 推算坐标
derogation 部分废除
derrick 抱杆
derusting by sandblast 喷砂除锈
descaling by brush 钢丝刷除锈
descaling by flame 火焰除锈
descending spring 下降泉
describe 说明
description 说明
description of goods 货物说明书
description of items 分项说明,条目说明
description of materials 材料说明
description of project 工程说明书
description of station 点之记
description of works and fees
　工程及费用名称

description of works 工程描述
desert 沙漠
desert facies 沙漠相
desertified land 沙漠化土地
desiccation fissure 干缩裂缝
design 计划,设计
design alteration 设计变更
design alternatives 设计备选方案
design and build 设计和建造
design and planning 设计和规划
design approach 设计方案
design audit 设计审查
design baseline 设计基准
design basic seismic acceleration
　设计基本地震加速度
design behavior 设计行为
design budgetary estimate of construction project
　建设项目设计概算
design capacity 设计能力
design capacity of luggage office
　设计行包库存件数
design characteristic period 设计特征周期
design code 设计规范
design conditions 设计工况
design construction period 设计工期
design contract 设计合同
design cooperation 协同设计
design criteria 设计准则
design critical height 设计临界高度
design data 设计数据,设计资料
design data package 设计数据包
design details 设计细则
design development 设计深化
design discharge 设计流量
design documentation 设计文件
design draft 设计图样
design drawing for excavation waste dump protection of key tunnel engineering
　重点隧道工程弃渣防护图
design drawing 设计图纸
design earthquake 设计地震
design elevation 设计高程
design elevation of earthworks
　路基设计高程
design engineer 设计工程师
design evaluation 设计评估
design excavation line (pay line)
　设计开挖线(或称计价线)
design fastening-down rail temperature
　设计锁定轨温

design flood frequency 设计洪水频率
design flood frequency water level
　设计洪水频率水位
design flood hydrograph 设计洪水过程线
design flow velocity 设计流速
design hourly heat consumption
　设计小时耗热量
design intensity 设计烈度
design in-house 自行设计
design joint grade 设计接头等级
design level 设计高程
design limit 设计限值
design live-load 设计活载
design load 设计负荷,设计荷载
design load of pavement 铺面设计荷载
design load standard 设计荷载标准
design low water level 设计枯水位
design maximum daily water consumption
　设计最大日用水量
design modeling 设计建模
design objective 设计目标
design of bridge crossing 桥渡设计
design of typical construction site
　典型工点设计
design outdoor daily mean temperature for air conditioning in summer
　夏季空气调节室外计算日平均温度
design outdoor dry-bulb temperature for air conditioning in summer
　夏季空气调节室外计算干球温度
design outdoor relative humidity for air conditioning in summer 夏季通风室外计算相对湿度
design outdoor relative humidity for air conditioning in winter 冬季空气调节室外计算相对湿度
design outdoor temperature for air conditioning in winter 冬季空气调节室外计算温度
design outdoor temperature for heating
　采暖室外计算温度
design outdoor temperature for ventilation in summer 夏季通风室外计算温度
design outdoor temperature for ventilation in winter 冬季通风室外计算温度
design outdoor wet-bulb temperature for air conditioning in summer
　夏季空气调节室外计算湿球温度
design parameter 设计参数
design parameter of ground motion
　设计地震动参数
design pressure 设计压力
design principle 设计原则

design professional 专业设计师
design proposal 设计方案
design reference period 设计基准期
design requirement 设计要求
design resources 设计资源
design review 设计审查
design reviews 设计方案论证
design schedule 计划进度
design service life
　设计使用年限,设计使用期限
design shoulder elevation 设计路肩高程
design situation 设计状况
design specification 设计规范,设计说明
design speed 构造速度,设计速度
design speed of railway section 路段设计速度
design stage 设计阶段
design stage of construction drawing
　施工图设计阶段
design standard 设计标准
design strength 设计强度
design stress-free rail temperature
　设计锁定轨温
design subcontractor 设计分包者
design surrounding rock classification
　设计围岩分级
design team 设计组
design unit 设计单位,设计单元
design value of a load 荷载设计值
design value of actions 作用的设计值
design value of an action 作用设计值
design value of axial tensile strength of concrete
　混凝土轴心抗拉强度设计值
design value of bearing capacity of members
　构件承载能力设计值
design value of bending compressive strength of
　concrete 混凝土弯曲抗压强度设计值
design value of compressive strength of steel bar
　钢筋抗压强度设计值
design value of concrete strength
　混凝土强度设计值
design value of earthquake-resistant strength of
　materials 材料抗震强度设计值
design value of geometrical parameter
　几何参数设计值
design value of load 荷载作用设计值
design value of material property
　材料性能设计值
design value of material strength
　材料强度设计值
design value of strength 强度设计值

design value of tensile strength of steel bar
　钢筋抗拉强度设计值
design water consumption 设计用水量
design water level 设计水位
design work 设计工作
design year 设计年度
designate 指定,指派
designated representative 指定代表
designed hourly heat supply
　设计小时供热量
designed superelevation of curve
　曲线设计超高
designer 设计单位,设计师
design-build(DB) 设计—建造
design-build contract 设计—建造合同
design-build-operate(DBO)
　设计—建设—运营
design-build-operate-transfer(DBOT)
　设计—建设—运营移交
design-management 设计—管理
desilting basin 沉砂池
desk type relay 座式继电器
deskew processing 去斜处理
despatch 调度
despatch money 速遣费
destination point code(DPC)
　目的信令点编码
destination port 目的港
destroy 毁坏,毁灭
destruction 毁灭
destructive load of specimen 试件破坏荷载
destructive test 破坏性试验,破损检验
detachable waterstop 可卸式止水带
detail 细部,细节
detail drawing 详图(大样图)
detail fracture of rail head 轨头微细波纹
detail point 碎部点
detail requirements 详细技术要求
detail survey 碎部测量
detail survey of roadway 巷道碎部测量
detailed account 详细报表,明细账
detailed cost 详细费用
detailed design 详细设计
detailed design brief 施工图设计概要
detailed engineering 详细设计
detailed equipment estimation
　设备详细估算
detailed estimate 详细估算,详细摘量
detailed investigation 详勘
detailed ledger 明细分类账,明细账目

detailed list of goods 货物清单
detailed packing list 详细装箱单
detailed particulars 细节
detailed program 详细计划
detailed project report 工程详细报告
detailed schedule 详细计划表
detailed supporting particulars
　详细的支撑材料,详细依据
detailed take-off 详细估算,详细摘要
details 细则
detained goods 被扣货物
detaining cars 扣车
detect 探测
detection station 探测站
detector 探测器
detention 留置
deteriorate 恶化
deterioration 变质,损蚀,恶化,损坏
determinable liability 确定性负债
determination 裁定,决定
determination of impact coefficient
　冲击系数测定
deterministic design method 定值设计法
detonate 爆破
detonating signal 响墩信号
detonation 起爆,引爆
detour cleared 转道空闲
detour line （铁路）便线,迂回线
detour occupied 转道占用
detouring section 绕行地段
detritus 岩屑
devaluation 贬值
devaluation adjustment 货币贬值调整
devaluation of the currency 货币贬值
devastate 毁坏
develop 发展
developer 开发商
developing chart of exploratory drift
　坑硐展示图
development 发展
development bank 发展银行,开发银行
development capital 开发资本
development cost 开发成本
development credit agreement
　开发信贷协议
development forum 发展论坛
development fund 发展基金
development plan 开发规划
deviation 偏差,偏移
deviation analysis 偏差分析

deviation of plumb line 垂线偏差
device 装置
device space 设备空间
device starting test 设备启动测试
devisal 计划
devoid of risk 无风险
Devonian period 泥盆纪
Devonian system 泥盆系
dew point 露点
dewatering measure 降水措施
dewatering method 降水法
dewatering 降水施工
dewatering well 降水井
dew-point temperature 露点温度
diabase 辉绿岩
diagnosis 诊断
diagonal bar 斜筋
diagonal bedding 斜层理
diagonal brace 斜拉条
diagonal deviation 对角线差
diagonal fault 斜断层
diagonal member 斜构件,角件
diagonal valley 斜谷
diagram 简图,图表,图解
diagrammatic sketch 简图
dial 度盘
dial indicator 百分表,千分表
diamagnetism mineral 逆磁性矿物
diameter at breast height 胸径
diameter reducing 缩径
diametral test 径向试验
diamond 金刚石
diamond drilling 金刚石钻进
diaphaneity 透明度
diaphragm 防渗墙,横隔板
diapir 底辟
diastimeter 测距仪
diatomaceous earth 硅藻土
dickite 迪凯石
dielectric constant 介电常数
dielectric loss angle 介质损耗角
dielectric strength 绝缘强度
diesel bolt wrench 内燃螺栓扳手
diesel engine 柴油机
diesel engine forklift
　柴油发动机叉车
diesel forklift 内燃叉车
diesel hydraulic track lifting and lining machine
　内燃液压起拨道机
diesel pile driver 柴油打桩机

diesel rail drilling machine　内燃钢轨钻孔机
diesel rail grinding machine
　内燃轨型磨轨机
diesel rail sawing machine　内燃锯轨机
diesel tamping machine　柴油捣固机
diesel traction　内燃牵引
diesel turnout rail grinding machine
　内燃道岔磨轨机
difference　差额
difference in gradient　坡度差
difference in price　价差
difference in price of equipment　设备费价差
difference in price of materials　材料价差
difference of GPS　差分 GPS
difference of sound pressure level for weighting standard　计权标准化声压级差
different speed restriction　不同速度限制
differential correction　差分改正
differential current element　差流元件
differential gain（DG）　微分增益
differential mode test　差模试验
differential phase（DP）　微分相位
differential pressure flowmeter　差压流量计
differential pressure index　压差指数
differential protection　差动保护
differential rectification　微分纠正
differential settlement　差异沉降,沉降差
differential thermal analysis　差热分析
differentiate　鉴别
differentiated services（DiffServ）　差分服务
differentiation　差异性
differing site conditions（D.S.C）
　现场条件变化
diffluent salt content　易溶盐含量
diffuser air supply　散流器送风
diffusion coefficient of chloride ion of concrete
　混凝土氯离子扩散系数
digest time　消化时间
digested sludge　消化污泥
digester　消化池
digging　挖掘
digital aerial camera　数码航摄仪
digital cadastre　数字地籍
digital channel　数字通道
digital control drawing　数控绘图
digital cross section　数字化横断面
digital data performance analyzer
　数字数据性能分析仪
digital distribution frame（DDF）
　数字配线架
digital elevation model（DEM）
　数字高程模型
digital fabrication　数字化加工
digital interface　数字接口
digital line graphic（DLG）　数字线划图
digital map　数字地图
digital mapping　数字化测图
digital mapping with total station instruments
　全站仪数字化测图
digital orthophoto map（DOM）
　数字正射影像图
digital passenger service broadcast machine
　数字客运广播机
digital payment　电子支付
digital private line　数字专线电路
digital raster graphic　数字栅格地图
digital slave clock　数字式子钟
digital subscriber signaling system No.1（DSS1）
　1号数字用户信令系统
digital surface model（DSM）　数字表面模型
digital terrain model　数字地面模型
digital topographic map　数字地形图
digital video recorder（DVR）　硬盘录像机
digital video signal　数字视频信号
digitalized railway　数字化铁路
dike　护堤,岩墙
dilatancy　剪胀性
dilatancy of rock　岩石扩容
diluent　稀释液
diluvial soil　洪积土
dimension　尺寸
dimensional deviation　尺寸偏差
diminishing assets　递耗资产
diopside　透辉石
diorite　闪长岩
diorite-porphyrite　闪长玢岩
dip　倾向
dip angle　倾角
dip angle for lateral slope of ground
　地面横坡倾角
dip angle of rock formation　岩层倾角
dip direction of rock formation　岩层倾向
dip fault　倾向断层
dip joint　倾向节理
diploma　执照
dipped rail joint　钢轨低接头
direct　指导
direct adjustment　直接平差
direct agreement　直接协议
direct and reversed measurements　往测与返测

direct attribute	直接属性
direct bill of lading	直达提单
direct cash remittance	直接现汇
direct circulation drilling rig	正循环旋转钻机
direct cost	直接成本,直接费用
direct costing	直接成本计算法
direct current	直流电
direct current electric method	直流电法
direct damage	直接损害,直接损失
direct debit	直接付款,直接支付,直接借记
direct engineering cost	直接工程费
direct fastening	不分开式扣件
direct feeding system	直接供电方式
direct feeding system with return conductor	带回流线的直接供电方式
direct financing	直接融资
direct freezing-thawing method	直接冻融法
direct glare	直接眩光,直射眩光
direct information collection system	信息直采系统
direct interpretation mark	直接解译标志
direct labour	自营(自建)工程
direct labour cost	直接人工费
direct lightning stroke	直击雷,直接雷击
direct linear transformation	直接线性变换
direct loss	直接损失
direct material	直接材料
direct method of allocation of cost	成本直接分摊法
direct mode	直通模式
direct observation method	直观法,直接观测法
direct overhead	直接管理费
direct overhead account	直接管理费账户
direct payment	直接付款,直接支付
direct plummet observation (also known as "direct plummet method")	正锤线观测(又称"正锤法")
direct plummeting method	正垂线法
direct port	直达港
direct purchase	直接采购
direct quotation	直接报价
direct return system	异程式系统
direct sale	直接销售
direct shear	直剪
direct shear friction test	直剪摩擦试验
direct shear strength test	直接剪切试验
direct shear strength test for discontinuities	岩体结构面直剪试验
direct shear test	直剪试验
direct shipment	直达运输,直接装运
direct shopping	直接采购
direct surveillance network	近程网路
direct surveillance subsection	近程监督分区
direct tax	直接税
direct telescope	正镜
direct trade	直接贸易
direct transport between CR network and enterprise	路企直通运输
direct verdict	直接裁决
direct wave method	直达波法
direct write-off	直接销账
direction	方位,所在地,指导
direction angle	方向角
direction observation for horizontal angle	水平角方向观测
directional antenna	定向天线
directional drilling method	定向钻法
directional switch	方向转接器
directional traffic power source	方向电源
direction-annexed traverse	方向附合导线
directly buried cable (DBC)	直埋电缆
director	董事,主任
directors and officers liability insurance	董事及高级职员责任险
directory	地址录,汇编
Direct-Attached Storage (DAS)	直连式存储
direct-current resistance	直流电阻
dirt box	污物箱
dirt screen	泥土筛分
dirty bill of lading	不洁提单
disablement pension	残疾抚恤金
disagreement	异议
disassembly	拆迁,拆卸
disaster	灾害,灾难
disaster management	危机管理
disaster mitigation planning	减灾计划
disaster monitoring system (DMS)	灾害监测系统
disaster prevention system	防灾系统
disaster prevention ventilation	防灾通风
disaster recovery center	灾备中心
disbursement	偿付款,支出费用,放款
disbursement clause	船舶费用条款
disbursement insurance	船舶费用保险
disbursement percentage	支付百分比
disbursement procedure	付款程序
disbursement voucher	支付凭单
disbursements to date (DTD)	已付金额
disc cutter	滚刀

discarded earthwork volume 弃方量
discernible 可辨认的
discern 鉴别
discharge
放电,解除责任,排泄,结清,结清单,解雇,流量,卸货
discharge area 排水区
discharge canal 排水槽,排水渠
discharge capacity 放电容量
discharge capacity test 通水量试验
discharge coefficient 排泄系数
discharge cross-section 过水断面
discharge culvert 排水涵洞
discharge current 放电电流
discharge gap 放电间隙
discharge hopper 卸料斗
discharge of cargo (goods) 卸货
discharge of contractual obligations
免除合同义务
discharge of contract 合同解除
discharge of debt 清偿债务
discharge outlet 排放口
discharge pipe 排水管道
discharge pump 排水泵
discharge standard 排放标准(水)
discharge time 放电时间
discharge tube 放电管
discharger 放电器
discharging coil 放电线圈
discharging device for earthing protection
接地保护放电装置
discharging expenses 卸货费
discharging port 卸货港
discharging quay 卸货码头
discipline 专业
disciplines 各专业,专业领域
disclaim 放弃
disclaimer 不承认,放弃者,免责条款(不担责)
disclaimer of responsibility 放弃责任
discomfort glare 不舒适眩光
disconnect 截断
disconnecting switch pole 隔离开关杆
disconnector 隔离开关
discontinue 中断
discontinuous charging 间隔装药
discordant contact 不整合接触
discount 贴现,折现,折扣
discount bank 贴现银行
discount broker 贴现经纪人
discount factor 贴现系数,折扣系数

discount for price 价格贴现
discount of draft 汇票贴现
discount on purchases 进货折扣
discount on sales 销售折扣
discount period 贴现期,折扣期限
discount rate 贴现率,折扣率,折现率
discounted bill 可银行贴现的票据
discounted cash flow (DCF)
贴现的现金流量,折现现金流量
discounted cash flow method
资金流动折现评估法
discounted notes 已贴现票据
discounted payback period
贴现回收期,折现回收期
discounted value 贴现值
discrepancy 不符合,不一致
discrete element method 离散元法
discrete points 离散点
discretion 酌处权,自由裁量权
discretionary client 全权委托客户
discretionary cost 自定成本
discretionary funds 可自由支配的基金
discretionary trust 全权信托
discriminate 辨别
discrimination 辨别,歧视
dishing liquid limit method 碟式仪法
dishonour 拒付,拒绝承兑
dishonour a bill 不承兑期票,不支付期票
dishonour by non-acceptance
票据迟到拒绝承兑
dishonour by non-payment
票据迟到拒绝付款
dishonour a bank draft 拒付汇票
dishonour a bill of exchange 拒付汇票
dishonoured check 拒付支票
disinfection 消毒
disinfection inspection certificate
消毒检验证书
disintegration 崩解
disintegration quantity 崩解量
disinvestment 撤资,缩减投资
disk space 磁盘空间
disk-type apparatus 碟式仪
disk-type liquid-plastic limit apparatus
蝶式液塑限仪
dislation 错落体
dislocation 错落,位错
dismantlement 拆除
dismantle 拆除
dismantling of plant 设备的拆除

dismiss 驳回,解雇
disorderly 失序
disorderly conduct 无序行为
dispatch 调度,发送,急件
dispatch area 出货区
dispatch list 发货单
dispatch money 速遣费
dispatching console 调度台
dispatching control 调度控制
dispatching extension 调度电话分机
dispatching post 调度所
dispatching supervision 调度监督
dispatching supervision system 调度监督系统
dispatching switch 调度交换机
dispatching switchboard 调度总机
dispatching user zone ID 调度用户区域标识
dispersion characteristics 色散特性
dispersion coefficient 弥散系数,色散系数
dispersive clay 分散性黏土
displacement 排水量,位移
displacement angle 移动角
displacement ductility factor 位移延性系数
displacement dynamic magnification factor (DDMF) 位移放大系数
displacement meter 位移计
displacement observation 位移观测
displacement sensor 位移传感器
displacement ventilation 置换通风
display equipment 显示设备
disposal 出售,处理
disposal cost 清理费用
disposal of fixed assets 固定资产的处置
disposal price 出售价格
dispose 出售,处理
disposition 出售
disproof 驳斥,反驳
dispute 争端,争议,争执
dispute adjudicator 争议评判员
dispute under the DAAB agreement 争议避免裁决协议引起的争议
disputes and arbitration 争端及仲裁
disputes review board (DRB) 争议审议委员会
disputes review expert 争议审议专家
disqualification 不合格,取消资格,无资格
disqualified goods 不合格货物
disruptive discharge 击穿放电
dissected valley 切沟
dissectible pin 挤切销
dissipative muffler 阻性消声器
dissloved air vessel 气浮溶气罐
dissolubility 溶解度
dissoluble composite of membrane 可溶物含量
dissolution 溶蚀
dissolution of contract 合同解除
dissolution pore 溶孔
dissolved erosion 溶解性侵蚀
dissolved fissure 溶隙
dissolved oxygen 溶解氧
dissolved solids 溶解性固体
distance between adjacent points 相邻点间距离
distance between centers of tracks 线间距
distance between stations 站间距离
distance measurement 距离测量
distance measurement by phase 相位法测距
distance measuring by parallax method 视差法测距
distance measuring instrument 测距仪
distance of fiducial marks 框标距
distance of freight carried 货运距离
distance of particle sedimentation 颗粒沉降距离
distance protection 距离保护
distance-to-coupling measurement 测长
distant signal 预告信号,预告信号机
distillation apparatus 蒸馏装置
distilled water 蒸馏水
distinguish 鉴别
distortion correction 畸变改正
distress call 遇险信号
distress warrant 扣押令
distributable cost 可分摊成本
distributed 分布式
distributed capacitance 分布电容
Distributed deny-of-service (DDoS) 分布式拒绝服务
distributed load 分布荷载
distributed power generation 分散发电
distributing terminal board 分线盘
distribution 分发,分销
distribution bar 分布钢筋
distribution box 分线箱,配电箱,配线箱
distribution diagram of soil erosion intensity 土壤侵蚀强度分布图

distribution for spare parts	配件配送中心
distribution network	分销网
distribution of forest vegetation	森林植被分布
distribution of risks	风险分散
distribution outlet	销售渠道
distribution reinforcement	分布钢筋
distribution substation	配电所
distribution system	配水管网
distributor	经销商,批发商
distributor method	分料器法
district	区段
district attorney	地区检察官
district auditor	地区审计员
district court	地区法庭
district heating	区域供热
district of culture and education	文教区
district station	区段站
district train	区段列车
district tribunal	地区法庭
disturbance	干扰
disturbed land surface	扰动地表
disturbed sample	扰动样
disturbed soil	扰动土
disturbed soil sample	扰动土样
ditch	管渠
ditch between tracks	线间沟
ditcher	挖沟机
diurnal journal	日志
diurnal temperature range	气温日较差
diurnal variation	日变
dive culvert	倒涵管
diverging route	侧向进路
diverging speed of train	列车侧向通过速度
diverging track of turnout	道岔侧股
diversification of risk	风险分散
diversion	导流,引水
diversion channel	导流渠
diversion structures	导流建筑物
diversion trench	导流槽
diversion tunnel	导流洞,引水隧洞
diverted tree	马刀树
divestiture	剥夺
divide	划分
dividend	股息,红利
dividend earned	股利收入
dividend payable	应付股利
dividend payout ratio	股利支付率
dividing	划分
dividing line	界限
divisible contract	可分割合同
divisible L/C	可分割信用证
divisible letter of credit	可分割信用证
division	部门,分公司
division controller	部门主会计师
division of gain or loss	损益分配
division value	分度值
divisional works	分部工程
dock	船坞,码头
dockage	船坞费,码头费
document	单据,票据,单证,凭单,凭证,文件
document against payment (D/P)	付款交单
document for claim	索赔文件
document of project preparation stage	工程准备阶段文件
document of title	所有权凭证
document on customs clearance	结关文件
document transmittal	文件传送
documentary bill (draft)	跟单汇票
documentary collection	跟单托收
documentary evidence	书面证据
documentary letter of credit	跟单信用证
documentary of carriage	运输单据
documents against acceptance (D/A)	承兑交单
documents against payment at sight	即期付款交单
documentation breakdown structure	文档分解结构
dodge	躲避,闪避,规避,逃避
doline	斗淋
doline funnel	溶斗
dollar credit	美元信贷
dolomite	白云石,白云岩
dolomitic limestone	白云石质灰岩
domain	产业所有权,土地征用权
domain name server (DNS)	域名服务器
domain name system	域名系统
dome	穹窿
dome camera	球形摄像机
domestic agent	国内代理人
domestic and public water consumption	生活用水量
domestic arbitral award	国内仲裁裁决
domestic building	生活房屋
domestic cargo transportation insurance	国内货运保险
domestic contract	国内合同
domestic contractor	当地承包商
domestic cost	国内费用

domestic exchange 国内汇兑
domestic finance 国内财政
domestic freight and miscellaneous charges for imported equipment 进口设备国内运杂费
domestic garbage 生活垃圾
domestic inflation rate 国内通货膨胀率
domestic manufacture 本国制成品
domestic market price 国内市场价格
domestic partner 国内合伙人
domestic preference 国内优惠
domestic priority 国内优先
domestic project 国内工程项目
domestic remittance 国内汇兑
domestic resources cost 国内资源成本
domestic sales 内销
domestic sewage(wastewater) 生活污水
domestic tax 国内税
domestic trade 国内贸易
domestic turnover 国内销售额
domestic water meter 用户水表
domestic water supply station 生活供水站
domestic 本国的,国产的
domiciled bill(draft) 外埠付款汇票
dominant factor 主导因子
dominant variable action 主导可变作用
dominant wind direction 最多风向
donate 捐献,捐赠,捐助
donated assets 捐赠资产
donated capital 捐赠资本
donation 捐款
donator 捐赠人
donor 捐赠人
donor country 援助国
door contact 门磁
dormitory area 宿舍区
dormitory van 工程宿营车
dosing unit 投加单元
double 2-vote-2 redundant structure 2×2取2冗余结构
double break 双断
double bus connection 双母线结线
double campshed 双排桩
double cantilever girder-erecting machine 双悬臂式架桥机
double crossover 交叉渡线
double eye-end rod 双环杆
double frequency 双频
double frequency inductor 双频感应器
double grid transducer 双电网传感器/监测电网
double handling 二次搬运,二次装卸
double heading locomotives 重联机车
double humping 双溜放
double humping and double rolling 双推双溜
double humping and single rolling 双推单溜
double insulation 双重绝缘
double insurance 双重保险
double rail track circuit 双轨条轨道电路
double replacement 互换
double row layout 双列布置
double side heading method 双侧壁导坑法,双侧壁法
double signal location 并置信号点
double spur ramp 人字坡道
double strap 双联板
double taxation 双重税收
double taxation relief 免除双重税收
double track wedge welding 双轨楔休焊接
doubled collimation error discrepancy 两倍照准差
double-account system 复式账户制
double-armed girder-erecting machine 双梁式架桥机
double-block type track sleeper precast yard 双块式轨枕预制场
double-curvature arch 双曲拱
double-curvature arch bridge 双曲拱桥
double-deck bridge 双层桥
double-deck container 双层集装箱
double-deck container liner train 双层集装箱班列
double-direction running automatic block 双向自动闭塞
double-doped 双掺
double-edge disc cutter 双刃滚刀
double-end bolt wrench 双头螺栓扳手
double-end feeding 双边供电
double-end grounding 双端接地
double-fluid grout 双液浆
double-hump 双驼峰
double-layer shutter-type air outlet 双层百叶型风口
double-limb column 双肢柱
double-line method 双线法
double-line reciprocating type 双线循环式
double-pipe heating system 双管采暖系统
double-plane cable-stayed bridge 双面索斜拉桥

double-rolling operation 双溜放作业
double-shield TBM 双护盾掘进机
double-support 双支撑
double-support moving mechanism
　双支撑移动机构
double-swivel double-tube core drilling
　双动双管取芯钻进
double-track 双线
double-track bridge 双线桥
double-track cutting 双线路堑
double-track railway 双线铁路
double-track tunnel 双线隧道
double-track embankment 双线路堤
double-wall steel cofferdam 双壁钢围堰
double-wire operated semaphore signal
　双线臂板信号机
dowel steel 传力杆
down direction 下行方向
down direction section interface 下行区间接口
down hole cavity survey 井下空硐测量
down hole elevation measurement
　井下高程测量
down hole intersecting closed traverse
　井下交叉闭合导线
down hole prospecting survey
　井下勘探测量
down hole survey (also known as "mine survey")
　井下测量(又称"矿井测量")
down lead cable 引下电缆
down payment 初次付款,定金
down payment guarantee 定金保函
down tools 罢工
down track 下行线
downdrag 下拉荷载
downfeed system 上行下给式
downspout 雨落水管
downtime 窝工时间,停机时间,停工时间
downward routing 下走线
downward traveling wave 下行波
down-conductor 引下线
down-hole imaging 孔内摄像
down-supported composite beam
　下撑式组合梁
down-the-hole drill 潜孔钻,潜孔钻机
draft 草案,草稿,草图,草拟,起草,汇票
draft a contract 起草合同
draft final statement
　最终报表草案,最终报表草稿
draft of minutes 起草纪要
draft provision 条款草案,条文初稿

draft purchased 买入的汇票
draft tube 通风管,尾水管
drag coefficient of wind load
　风荷载体形系数,风荷载阻力系数
drag factor of wind load
　风荷载体形系数,风荷载阻力系数
drag fold 牵引褶皱,牵引褶曲
dragging method 拖拉法
dragline excavator
　索铲挖土机/拉铲挖掘机
drain pipe 泄水管
drain valve 排污阀
drainage 排水
drainage blind ditch 排水盲沟,管道,沟槽
drainage by borehole drilling 钻孔排水
drainage by well point 井点排水
drainage by well points 井点排水
drainage channel 排水槽,排水渠
drainage cross slope 排水横坡
drainage culvert 排水涵洞
drainage ditch 排水沟,水沟
drainage material of composite geomembrane
　复合土工排水材料
drainage method 排水法
drainage open ditch 排水明沟
drainage opening 泄水孔
drainage pipe 排水管
drainage pumping station 排水泵站
drainage sand well 排水砂井
drainage system 排水系统
drainage tunnel 排水洞
drainage consolidated shear 固结排水剪
drainage consolidation 排水固结
drainage repeated direct shear strength test
　排水反复直接剪切试验
drainage during construction 施工排水
drainage of tunnel 隧道排水
draw 草拟,起草,提款
draw money (from many sources) 集资
draw up a contract 起草合同
drawbar pump 拉杆式水泵
drawdown 水位降低
drawee 付款人,受票人
drawer 出票人,开票人
drawing 草拟,起草,绘图,提款,图样
drawing account 提存账户,提款账户
drawing cheque 提存支票,提款支票
drawing friction test 拉拔摩擦试验
drawing issued "approved for design" (AFD)
　批准用于详细工程设计图纸

drawing list　图纸目录
drawing notes　图纸说明
drawing number box　图号区
drawing polyester film　绘图聚酯薄膜
drawing register　图纸登记册
drawing title　图名
drawings issued "approved for construction"（AFC）
　批准用于施工图纸
drawings　图纸
draw-back　退款
draw-out track　牵出线
draw-out track at grade　坡度牵出线
draw-work　绞车
dredger　挖泥船
dredger fill　冲填土
dredging　疏导,疏浚
dredging coefficient　疏淤系数
dredging works　疏浚工程
dregs　沉渣
drencher systems　水幕系统
dressed stone　料石
drier　干料
drift angle　风流偏角,航偏角
drift ice　流冰
drift test　漂移测试
drifts　漂浮物
drill and blast method　钻爆法
drill bit　钻头
drillability　可钻性
drilled pile　钻孔桩
drilled shaft foundation with prefabricated steel shells　预制钢壳钻孔基础
drilled well　管井,钻井
driller　凿岩工,钻孔机
drilling　钻探
drilling chip index method　钻屑指标法
drilling engineering survey
　钻探工程测量
drilling exploration of foundations of piers and abutments for inspection purpose
　墩台基础钻探测量
drilling fluid resistivity method
　井液电阻率法
drilling gas dynamic phenomenon
　打钻瓦斯动力现象
drilling gas gushing initial velocity method
　钻孔瓦斯涌出初速度法
drilling platform　钻井平台
drilling rig　钻机,钻架
drilling set　钻具组

drinking water　生活饮用水
drinking water source protection zone
　饮用水水源保护区
drive test　动态测试
driver machine interface
　司机—车载设备接口
driver with high priority　司机制动优先
driver's identification　司机号
driver-machine interface（DMI）　人机界面
driving hole　辅助眼
driving inspection　传动检查
driving system　传动系统
drop away time　释放时间
drop chute　跌水槽
drop hammer　自由落锤
drop test of rail　钢轨落锤试验
drop tube　吊柱
dropper　吊弦
dropper clip　吊弦线夹
dropper clip for messenger wire
　承力索吊弦线夹
dropper clip for twin messenger wires
　双承力索吊弦线夹
dropper clip of single messenger wire
　单承力索吊弦线夹
dropper spacing　吊弦间距
dropwise add　滴入（加）
drop-out fuse　跌落式熔断器
drought　干旱
drought resisting　抗旱
drowned lime　熟石灰
drowned valley　沉溺谷
drug　毒品
drum allocation　配盘
drum mixer　滚筒式拌和机,筒式搅拌机
drum sieve　圆柱筛筒
drum tension crack　鼓式张裂缝
drumlin　鼓丘
drunken forest　醉汉林
dry air　干空气
dry and wet alternating environment
　干湿交替环境
dry bridge　旱桥
dry concrete　干硬性混凝土
dry condensation pipe　干式凝结水管
dry condition　干工况
dry density　干密度,干重度
dry drilling technology　干法成孔工艺
dry evaporator　干式蒸发器
dry farm　旱地

dry filtering 干过滤
dry hydrant 干式消火栓
dry materials 干料
dry masonry 干砌片石
dry pitching 干砌石护坡
dry powder fire extinguisher 干粉灭火器
dry rubble 干砌片石
dry run 浇筑预演
dry season 枯水季节
dry shotcreting machine 干喷混凝土机
dry shrinkage 干缩
dry sieving method 干筛法,干筛分析法
dry soil 干土
dry soil method 干土法
dry sprinkling system 干式喷水灭火系统
dry tamped cement mortar 干捣水泥砂浆
dry type air-core reactor 干式空芯电抗器
dry valley 干谷
dry well 枯井
dryer 干燥器
drying and watering cycle 干湿循环
drying oven 干燥箱
dry-bulb temperature 干球温度
dry-mix shotcreting method 干喷法
dry-stone masonry 干砌石圬工
dry-type transformer 干式变压器
dual control 双重控制
dual currency bond 双重货币债券
dual currency record 双重货币记录
dual machine backup 双机主备
dual machine hot standby 双机热备
dual monitors at ticket counter 窗口双屏
dual power network sensor 双电网传感器
dual signal selectivity 双信号选择性
dual stream function 双流功能
dual tariff 双重关税
dual-controller disk array
  双控制器磁盘阵列
dual-system/dual-locomotive synchronization and
  switching test 双系或双机同步及切换测试
dual-transmitter 双发
duct grouting 孔道压浆
ductile failure 延性破坏
ductile frame 延性框架
ductility 韧性,延度,延性,延展性
ductility design 延性设计
ductility seismic design 延性抗震设计
duct-ventilated embankment 通风管路堤
duct-ventilated subgrade 通风管路基
due 到期应付,应得权益

due arrival 及时到达
due bill 借据
due date (pay day) 付款日,支付日期
due date checklist 到期清单
due from 应收
dues 税款,应付款
dug well 大口井
dummy joint 假缝
dump pit 弃土坑
dump truck 自卸卡车,自卸汽车
dumper 翻斗车,自卸卡车
dumping ground 垃圾堆场
dumping place 卸料场
dun 催债
dune 沙堆
dune range 沙丘链
duplex apartment 跃层住宅
duplex double valve fire hydrant
  双口双阀消火栓
duplex well 双联井
duplicate 抄件,副本,复制,复制品
duplicate invoice 发票副本
Dupuit theoretical formula 裘布依理论式
durability 耐久性
durability index 耐久性指标
durability of concrete 混凝土耐久性
durability test 耐久性能试验
durable concrete 耐久性混凝土
durable life 耐用年限
durable year 使用年限
duration 存续期,期限
duration calculation 工期计算
duration compression 工期压缩
duration of contract 合同期,合同有效期
duration of liability 责任期限
duration of licence 执照有效期
duration of locomotive complete turn-round
  机车全周转时间
duration of rainfall 降雨历时
duration of rolling compaction 碾压时间
duration of runs 运转时间
duration of service 设备使用年限
duration of short-circuit current
  短路电流(持续)时间
duricrust 硬壳
durometer 硬度计
dust 粉尘
dust board 挡尘板
dust bowl 风沙区
dust content 粉尘含量

dust concentration 粉尘浓度,含尘浓度
dust removal 除尘
dust removal efficiency 除尘效率
dust remover 除尘器
dust sampler 粉尘采样仪
dust screen inspection and cleaning
防尘网检查清洗
dust-proof 防尘
dutiable value 完税价值
duty 关税,义务,职责
duty allowance 职务津贴
duty memo 上税单
duty of care 照管责任
duty of cooperation 协作责任
duty of disclosure 申报实情责任
duty paid 关税已付
duty to minimise delay
将延误降到最低的职责
duty unpaid 关税未付
duty-free goods 免税货物
duty-free importation 免税进口
duty-free zone 免税区
duty-paying value 完税价值
dwarf signal 矮型信号机
dwell time 停站时间
dwelling space 居住空间
dwelling type 套型
dwelling unit 住宅单元
dyke 筑堤
dynamic acceptance test 动态验收测试
dynamic action 动态作用
dynamic behavior 动态性能
dynamic car inspection room
列检动态检车室
dynamic characteristic 动态性能
dynamic coefficient of vertical live load of train
列车竖向活载动力系数
dynamic compaction 强夯
dynamic compaction replacement 强夯置换
dynamic deflection 动态挠度
dynamic deformation 动态变形
dynamic deformation modulus 动态变形模量
dynamic design 动态设计
dynamic elasticity modulus 动弹性模量
dynamic elastic modulus tester
动弹模量测定仪
dynamic host configuration protocol（DHCP）
动态主机配置协议
dynamic investment 动态投资
dynamic investment pay-back period
动态投资回收期
dynamic load 动荷载,动态荷载
dynamic load performance 动载性能
dynamic loading test 动载试验
dynamic management 动态管理
dynamic mass 动态质量
dynamic parameter identification
动态参数识别
dynamic penetration test 动力触探试验
dynamic perforation 动态穿孔
dynamic performance 动态性能
dynamic reactive power compensator
动态无功补偿装置
dynamic resistance strain gauge
动态电阻应变仪
dynamic risk 动态风险
dynamic seal index 动态密封指数
dynamic shear strength modulus
动剪切模量
dynamic sign 动态标识
dynamic similarity 动力相似
dynamic single shear test 动单剪试验
dynamic stability current 动稳定电流
dynamic state 动态
dynamic stereo photography 动态立体摄影
dynamic strength 动强度
dynamic strength test 动强度试验
dynamic stress 动态应力,动应力
dynamic stress of earthworks 路基动应力
dynamic test 动态试验
dynamic torsional shear test 动扭剪试验
dynamic track geometry 动态几何形位
dynamic track stabilizer
动力稳定机,轨道动力稳定车
dynamic train speed profile 动态速度曲线
dynamic triaxial test
动三轴试验,动力三轴试验
dynamic uplift 动态抬升
dynamic viscosity 动力黏度
dynamic water level 动力水位
dynamic wind pressure 动态风压
dynamical magnification 动态放大倍数
dynamite 炸药
dynamometer 测力计
dynamometric device 测力装置
dynamotor 电动发电机

E

E&M works	线上(站后工程)
earlier completion	提前竣工
early Cambrian epoch	早寒武世
early Carboniferous epoch	早石炭世
early completion bonus	提前完工奖励
early Cretaceous epoch	早白垩世
early Devonian epoch	早泥盆世
early Jurassic epoch	早侏罗世
early Ordovician epoch	早奥陶世
early Paleozoic era	早古生代
early Permian epoch	早二叠世
early Pleistocene epoch	早更新世
early removal formwork system	早拆模板体系
early Silurian epoch	早志留世
early Sinian epoch	早震旦世
early start date	最早开工日期
early strength	早期强度
early strength concrete	早强混凝土
early Triassic epoch	早三叠世
early warning	早期警告
early warning system	预警系统
early withdrawal penalty	提前取款罚金,提前提款罚金
earmark	专用
earmarking of taxes	税款专用
earn	获利
earn profit	获利
earned income	已获收益
earned man-hours	已完成工时
earned revenue	已获营业收入
earned surplus	营业盈余
earned value	赢得值
earned value breakdown structure	挣值分解结构
earned value concept	赢得值原理
earned value management	挣值管理
earnest money	保证金,定金
earning rate	收益率
earning statement	收益表
earning surplus	营业盈余
earnings	收益,盈利
earnings after tax (EAT)	税后收益
earth and rock fill dam	土石坝
earth conductivity	大地导电率
earth covering	覆土
earth current	地中电流
Earth curvature	地球曲率
earth dam	土坝
earth electrode	接地体,接地极
earth ellipsoid	地球椭球
earth embankment	土堤
earth fill	填土
earth pressure	土压力
earth pressure balanced shield (EPB shield)	土压平衡盾构
earth resistivity	大地电阻率
earth return current	地回流
earth wire	地线,接地线
earth wire clamp	地线线夹
earth wire clamp for overhead conductor rail	汇流排地线线夹
earthing	接地
earthing blade	接地刀闸
earthing busbar	接地汇集线,接地母排
earthing clamp	接地线夹
earthing connection inspection	地线连接检查
earthing copper bus bars	接地铜排
earthing distance protection	接地距离保护
earthing down conductor	接地引接线
earthing fault	接地故障
earthing mesh	接地网
earthing network	地网
earthing of casing	外壳接地
earthing of enclosure	外壳接地
earthing of double down-conductors	双引下接地

earthing reference point (ERP)　接地参考点
earthing resistance　接地电阻
earthing rod　接地棒
earthing switch　接地开关
earthing system　接地系统
earthing terminal　接地端子
earthquake　地震
earthquake acceleration meter
　地震加速度计
earthquake damage　震害
earthquake damage grade of engineering structure
　工程结构地震破坏等级
earthquake damage investigation　震害调查
earthquake design state　地震设计状况
earthquake disaster　地震灾害
earthquake dynamic water pressure method
　地震动水压力法
earthquake focus　震源
earthquake grouping　地震群集
earthquake intensity　地震强度
earthquake magnitude　地震震级,震级
earthquake monitoring　地震监测
earthquake monitoring alarm and early warning
　地震监测报警预警
earthquake monitoring sensor
　地震监测传感器
earthquake monitoring station　地震监测台站
earthquake peak acceleration
　地震峰值加速度
earthquake simulation test
　模拟地震震动试验
earthquake subsidence　震陷
earthquake wave　地震波
earthquake zone　地震带
earthquake-resistant detailing requirements
　抗震构造要求
earthquake-resistant structure　抗震结构
earthquake-resistant support　抗震支撑
earthwork　土方工程
earthwork and stonework　土石方
earthwork balance sheet　土石方平衡表
earthwork flow diagram　土石方流向框图
earthworks　路基,路基工程
earthworks and stoneworks　土石方工程
earthworks collapse　路基坍塌
earthworks defect　路基病害
earthworks settlement　路基沉降
earthworks-culvert transition section
　路基涵洞过渡段
earthworks-tunnel transition section
　路基隧道过渡段
earthworm-like freight section
　地龙式协作货位
earthy　土状
earthy fracture　土状断口
earth's core　地核
earth-filled embankment　填筑路堤
earth-rammer　夯土机
earth-retaining component　挡土构件
earth-securing mesh cushion
　固体网垫
earth-termination system　接地装置
ease　减轻
easement　地役权,土地通行权,附属建筑物
easiest rolling car　最易行车
easy gradient for acceleration　加速缓坡
easy money　低息贷款
easy rolling car　易行车
easy rolling track　易行线
easy terms　优惠条件
eccentric block vibration test
　偏心块起振试验
eccentric compression　偏心受压
eccentric compressive member
　偏心受压构件
eccentric compressive method
　偏心压力法
eccentric influence coefficient
　偏心影响系数
eccentric load　偏心荷载
eccentric moment　偏心矩
eccentrically tensioned　偏心受拉
eccentricity amplification coefficient
　偏心距增大系数
eccentricity of ellipsoid　椭球偏心率
eccentricity ratio　偏心率
ecological balance　生态平衡
ecological benefit　生态效益
ecological construction　生态建设
ecological environment　生态环境
ecological environment quality
　生态环境质量
ecological function protection area
　生态功能保护区
ecological sensitive and vulnerable area
　生态敏感与脆弱区
ecology　生态
economic accounting　经济核算
economic aid　经济援助

economic and technical comparison
　经济技术对比
economic appraisal　经济评估
economic batch quantity　经济批量
economic benefit　经济效益
economic blockade　经济封锁
economic compensation　经济补偿
economic cooperation　经济合作
economic cost　经济成本
economic crisis　经济危机
economic cycle　经济周期
economic decline　经济滑坡
economic downturn　经济滑坡
economic engineer　经济师
economic entity　经济实体
economic evaluation　经济评估,经济评价
economic exposure　经济风险
economic interest　经济权益
economic internal return rate（EIRR）
　经济内部收益率
economic law　经济法,经济规律
economic life　经济寿命
economic life and salvage value
　经济寿命与残值
economic lot size　经济批量,最优批量
economic manager　经济师
economic net present value（ENPV）
　经济净现值
economic pattern　经济结构
economic reckoning　经济核算
economic rights and interests　经济权益
economic risk　经济风险
economic structure　经济结构
economic unit　经济单位
economical heat transfer resistance
　经济传热阻
economist　经济师,经济学家
edge of container slot　箱位边缘
edge processing　边缘处理
education surcharge　教育费附加
effect　效果,效力
effect insurance　投保
effect of continuous arch　连拱作用
effective action distance of radar
　雷达有效作用距离
effective anomaly　有效异常
effective area of civil air defence
　人防有效面积
effective calcium oxide　有效氧化钙
effective contract price　有效合同价

effective control distance　有效控制距离
effective current coefficient of feeding section
　供电臂有效电流系数
effective current of feeding section
　供电臂有效电流
effective current of train　列车有效电流
effective current value of trains
　列车电流有效值
effective date　生效日期
effective date of contract　合同生效日期
effective diameter　有效直径
effective guarantee　有效保证
effective height of cross-section
　截面有效高度
effective length　折算长度
effective length of cantilever
　有效悬臂长度
effective length of receiving-departure track
　到发线有效长度
effective length of track　线路有效长度
effective loading and unloading length
　装卸有效长度
effective normal stress　有效法向应力
effective particle size　有效粒径
effective pore size　等效孔径
effective porosity　有效孔隙率
effective prestress value　有效预应力值
effective principal stress ratio
　有效主应力比
effective rate　有效单价
effective shear strength　有效抗剪强度
effective shear strength index
　有效抗剪强度指标
effective static load　有效静荷载
effective stress　有效应力
effective stress analysis　有效应力分析
effective stress method　有效应力法
effective terms　有效条款
effective thickness　有效厚度
effective width　有效宽度
effective width coefficient　有效宽度系数
effectiveness of contract　合同生效,合同效力
effectiveness　有效程度,有效性
efficiency　效率
efficiency test　机械效率试验
effluent concentration　排放浓度(水)
elastic analysis of first order or second order curve
　with repetition distribution
　有重分布的一阶或二阶线弹性分析
elastic analysis scheme　弹性方案

elastic bearing block 弹性支承块
elastic clip 弹性扣件
elastic clip fastening 弹条式扣件
elastic cushion 弹性垫层
elastic deformation 弹性变形
elastic displacement 弹性位移
elastic fastening 弹性扣件
elastic foundation plate 弹性地基板
elastic modulus of concrete
　混凝土弹性模量
elastic modulus of rail support
　钢轨支点弹性模量
elastic poisson's ratio of rock
　岩石弹性泊松比
elastic position-limiting plate 弹性限位板
elastic pressure 弹性压力
elastic reaction 弹性反力
elastic resistance 弹性抗力
elastic resistance coefficient 弹性抗力系数
elastic sleeper 弹性轨枕
elastic spike 弹簧道钉
elastic strain 弹性应变
elastic support 弹性支撑
elastic wave 弹性波
elastic wave CT method 弹性波CT法
elastic wave exploration 弹性波勘探
elastic wave method 弹性波法
elastic wave reflection method
　弹性波反射法
elastically supported continuous girder
　弹性支座连续梁
elasticity modulus 弹性模量
elasticity modulus of materials
　材料弹性模量
elasticity 弹性
elasticity seismic design 弹性抗震设计
elastic-plastic analysis 弹塑性分析
elbow 弯头
electric arc welder 电弧焊机
electric arc welding 电弧焊
electric bending resistance machine 电动抗折机
electric boiler 电锅炉
electric cab signaling 电式机车信号
electric center line of wheel sensor
　车轮传感器的电气中心线
electric compressor 电动压缩机
electric concentration 电气集中
electric conveyer 电动传送设备
electric energy metering device
　电能计量装置

electric field strength 电场强度
electric field treatment 电场法
electric flux 电通量
electric forklift 电力叉车
electric generator 发电机
electric heat oven 电热鼓风烘箱
electric heat tracing 电伴热
electric heater 电加热器
electric hoist (also known as "electric block")
　电动起重机(又称"电动葫芦"),电动卷扬机
electric hook-up 接电装置
electric hot plate 电热板
electric interlocking 电气集中联锁
electric interlocking for hump yard
　驼峰电气集中
electric isolation 电气隔离
electric leakage 漏电
electric lock 电锁器
electric locking 电气锁闭
electric locomotive 电力机车
electric logging 电测井
electric motor 电动机
electric multiple units (EMU)
　动车组,电动车组
electric pick 手提电动捣固机,电镐
electric power 电力工程
electric power dispatching telephone
　电力调度电话
electric profiling 电测剖面法
electric profiling method 电剖面法
electric rail drilling machine
　电动钢轨钻孔机
electric semaphore signal 电动臂板信号机
electric siren 电笛
electric staff block system 电气路签闭塞
electric staff instrument 电气路签机
electric switch machine 电动转辙机
electric switchboard 配电盘
electric tablet block system 电气路牌闭塞
electric tablet instrument 电气路牌机
electric traction 电力牵引
electric traction interference 电力牵引干扰
electric vibrator 电动振捣器
electric water heater 电热水器
electric water level gauge 电测水位计
electric welding 电焊
electric whistle 电笛
electric winch 电动卷扬机
electrical bridge 电桥
electrical clearance 空气绝缘间隙

electrical connection at overlap
　关节电连接
electrical connection between MW and CW
　横向电连接
electrical connection between tracks
　股道间电连接
electrical connection clamp　电连接线夹
electrical connection clamp for messenger wire
　承力索电连接线夹
electrical connection clamp for overhead conductor rail　汇流排电连接线夹
electrical connection jumper from the disconnector
　开关电连接跳线
electrical distribution　输电
electrical endurance　电寿命
electrical energy loss　电能损失
electrical energy quality analysis
　电能质量分析
electrical energy quality monitoring
　电能质量监测
electrical engineer　电气工程师
electrical heating method　电加热法
electrical installation　电气安装
electrical insulated joint　电气绝缘节
electrical interlocking　电气联锁
electrical level　电平
electrical lighting　电气照明
electrical logging apparatus　电测仪器
electrical logging measuring device
　电测式量测装置
electrical method　电法
electrical permit　用电许可
electrical prospecting　电法勘探
electrical prospecting instrument
　电法勘探仪
electrical protection　电气防护
electrical repair shop　电修间
electrical safety　用电安全
electrical sectioning　电分段
electrical sectioning device
　分段装置(电分段装置)
electrical sounding method　电测深法
electrical supervisory channel（ESC）
　电监控通路
electrical test　电气试验
electrical testing vehicle　电气试验车
electrically heated drying oven　电热干燥箱
electricity price　电价
electrification　电气化
electrification interference　电气化干扰
electrification mileage　电气化里程
electrification section　电气化区段
electrification transformation　电气化改造
electrified railway
　电气化铁道,电气化铁路
electrified track　电化股道,电化线路
electrified track in plan　预留电化股道
electrochemical probe method
　电化学探头法
electrochemical process　电化法
electrochemical stabilization　电化学加固
electrode spacing　电极距
electrodialysis process（ED）　电渗析法
electrolyte　电解液
electromagnetic compatibility（EMC）
　电磁兼容
electromagnetic distance meter instrument(EDMI)
　电磁波测距仪
electromagnetic distance metering（EDM）
　电磁波测距
electromagnetic environment　电磁环境
electromagnetic induction　电磁感应
electromagnetic induction method
　电磁感应法
electromagnetic interference（EMI）　电磁干扰
electromagnetic logging　电磁测井
electromagnetic pollution　电磁污染
electromagnetic pulse　电磁脉冲
electromagnetic radiation　电磁辐射
electromagnetic radiation protection
　电磁污染防护
electromagnetic reflection method
　电磁波反射法
electromagnetic relay　电磁继电器
electromagnetic shielding　电磁屏蔽
electromagnetic spectrum device
　电磁频谱仪
electromagnetic test system
　电磁式测试系统
electromagnetic track relay
　电磁式轨道继电器
electromagnetic valve　电磁阀
electromagnetic wave CT　电磁波CT
electromagnetic wave method　电磁波法
electromagnetic wave transmission
　电磁波透射法
electromagnetism　电磁
electronic balance　电子天平
electronic bid opening procedures
　电子方式开标程序

electronic bid submission procedures
电子方式投标程序
electronic document management system
电子文档管理系统
electronic execution unit 电子执行单元
electronic inclinometer 电子倾斜仪
electronic information system
电子信息系统
electronic scale 电子秤
electronic strike 电子锁
electronic tachometer 电子速测仪
electronic tachometer measurement
电子速测仪测量
electronic truck scale 电子汽车衡
electroplating 电镀
electro-hydraulic switch machine
电液转辙机
electro-magnetic current transformer
电磁式电流互感器
electro-mechanical interlocking
电机集中联锁
electro-optical distance measurement
光电测距
electro-optical distance measurement instrument
光电测距仪
electro-osmotic drainage 电渗法
electro-pneumatic conveyer 电空传送设备
electro-pneumatic switch machine
电空转辙机
electro-pneumatic valve 电空阀
element 单元,构件,元素,要素,因素
element management system (EMS)
网元级管理系统
element of interior orientation 内定向元素
elemental bill of quantities 单元工程清单
elementary 基本的
elementary geodesy 普通测量学
elements 零件
elements of curve 曲线要素
elevated fire tank 高位消防水箱
elevated line 高架线
elevated tank 高位水池
elevated waiting room 高架候车室
elevating height 起升高度
elevation angle 上仰角
elevation annotation point 高程注记点
elevation control network 高程控制网
elevation control point 高程控制点
elevation control survey 高程控制测量
elevation difference 高差

elevation drawing 立面图
elevation mean square error 高程中误差
elevation of ground leveling 场坪标高
elevation of projective plane 投影面高程
elevation of sight 视线高程
elevation of top surface 顶面高程
elevation point 高程点
elevation point by independent intersection
独立交会高程点
elevation survey 高程测量
elevation synchronization method 高差同步法
elevation system 高程系统
elevation 标高,高程,立面图
elevator 电梯
elevator liability insurance 电梯责任保险
elide 忽略
eligibility 合格性,资格
eligibility limit 合格性限制
eligible 合格的
eligible bidder 合格投标者
eligible bill 合格票据
eligible contractor 合格承包商
eligible paper 合格票据
eligible product 合格产品
eligible risk 可接受的风险
eligible source country 合格来源国
eligible tenderer 合格投标者
eliminate 消除
elimination 冲销
elimination control room 消防控制室
elliptic polarization 椭圆极化
elongated particle 细长颗粒
elongation 延伸率
elongation at break 断裂伸长率
elongation index 针状指数
elongation rate 伸长率
eluvial facies 残积相
embankment 堤,路堤,填土,土堤
embankment center 路堤中心
embankment fill material 路堤填料
embankment of the benchland 河滩路堤
embankment type cutting 路堤式路堑
embankment under test 试验路堤
embankment unloading track
路堤式卸车线
embankment with riverbank scouring
河岸冲刷路堤
embargo 禁运
embedded continuous pile-slab structure
埋入式连续桩板结构

embedded part 预埋件
embedded pipe 预埋管
embedded scouting pipe 预埋注浆管
embedded sleeve 预埋套管
embezzlement 贪污
emergency 紧急情况,遇险
emergency act 紧急法令
emergency action 紧急行为
emergency braking 紧急制动
emergency braking intervention profile
　紧急制动模式曲线
emergency broadcasting 应急广播
emergency circumstances 紧急情况
emergency command console 应急指挥台
emergency communication 应急通信
emergency communication access
　应急通信接入
emergency counterplan 应急预案
emergency door 太平门,安全门
emergency evacuation 紧急疏散
emergency evacuation channel
　紧急疏散通道
emergency exit 安全出口,紧急出口
emergency exit button 紧急开门按钮
emergency exit of sound barrier
　声屏障安全门
emergency exit sign 疏散标志
emergency facilities 应急设施
emergency joint bar 钢轨急救器
emergency lighting 事故照明,应急照明
emergency maintenance base 抢修基地
emergency measure 应急措施
emergency mode of operations
　应急工作模式
emergency oil disposal tank 事故油池
emergency on-duty console 应急值班台
emergency operating mode 应急工作模式
emergency operation console 应急操作台
emergency power 紧急备用动力
emergency pump 备用泵
emergency relief 救援
emergency repair 临险抢护,抢修
emergency rescue command center
　应急救援指挥中心
emergency rescue in construction 施工抢险
emergency rescue station 紧急救援站
emergency response system 应急响应系统
emergency shaft 备用井
emergency station control 非常站控
emergency stop test 紧急停车测试

emergency treatment 急救
emergency treatment after failure 故障办理
emergency ventilation 事故通风
emission 排放物
emission concentration 排放浓度(气)
emission standard 排放标准(气)
emission trading 排污权交易
employee 雇员,受雇者,职员
employee discipline 劳动纪律
employee education fund 职工教育经费
employee experience profile 雇员履历表
employee's pension fund 职工养老金
employer 雇主,甲方,业主
employer's default 雇主违约
employer's equipment 业主机具
employer's financial arrangements
　业主的财务安排
employer's liability 雇主的责任
employer's liability insurance
　雇主的责任保险
employer's obligation 雇主的义务
employer's representative 业主代表
employer's risks 雇主的风险
employer's suspension 雇主暂停
employer's taking over 雇主的接收
employer-led design teams
　业主主导的设计团队
employer-supplied materials and equipment
　甲供物资
employer-supplied materials
　甲供材料、雇主供材料
employment 雇佣
employment act 就业法
employment contract 雇佣合同
employment insurance system 劳动保险制度
employment law 劳动法,劳工法
employment permit 工作许可,雇工许可证
employment protection 就业保障
empower 准许
empty container 空箱
empty container stacker 空箱堆垛机
empty space 架空层
empty state 空态
empty track 空线
emptying culvert 泄水涵洞
EMU depot (section) 动车段(所)
EMU depot access track
　动车组进出段(所)线
EMU facilities 动车组设备
EMU maintenance bay 列位

EMU management information system　动车组管理信息系统
EMU operation shed　动车运用所
EMU running shed　动车所
EMU running test track　动车组试验线
EMU stabling siding　动车组存放线
EMU stabling yard　动车组存车场
EMU transfer track　动车组出入段(所)
emulsified polymer waterproof coating
　聚合物乳液防水涂料
emulsifier　乳化剂
enameled tile　琉璃瓦
encamp　建立营地
enclosed construction　封闭施工
enclosed sound barrier/enclosed noise barrier
　封闭式声屏障,全封闭声屏障
enclosure　围墙,围障,外围护
enclosure expansion　外壳膨胀
enclosure protection class(IP code)
　外壳防护等级(IP 代码)
enclosure wall　围护墙
encumbrance　不动产债权,资产留置权
end　界限
end of movement authority　行车许可终点
end of platform　站台端部
end point　终点
end resistance　桩端阻力
end spine　端刺
end to end call connection establishment delay
　端到端呼叫(连接)建立时间
end transverse floorbeam　端横梁
end user　最终用户
end wall　端墙
end wall axis of warehouse　仓库端墙轴线
endangered wildlife　濒危野生动物
ending balance　期末余额
ending inventory　期末存货
endorse　背书,批注,签注
endorsed bond　已背书债券
endorsee　被背书人,受让人
endorsement　背书,批单,签注
endorsement in blank　不记名背书,空白背书
endorsement in full　记名背书
endorsement to order　记名背书
endorser　背书人,转让人
endowment　赠款
endowment assurance　生死两全保险
end-of-project evaluation　项目期末评估
end-product　最终产品
end-to-end delay　端到端时延
energized bay　带电间隔
energized compartment　带电间隔
energized inspection running　热滑
energized probability　带电概率
energized probability of train　列车带电概率
energized structure　带电结构
energy acquisition　能源购入
energy analysis　能量分析
energy balance sheet　能量平衡表
energy conservation　节能,节约能源
energy conservation and emission reduction
　节能减排
energy conservation assessment　节能评估
energy conservation assessment stage
　能评阶段
energy conservation benefit　节能效益
energy conservation controller　节能控制器
energy conservation in building　建筑节能
energy conservation measures
　节能措施,节能工艺
energy conservation process　节能技术
energy conservation rate　节能率
energy conservation review　节能评审
energy conservation slope　节能坡
energy conservation target　节能目标
energy consumption　能耗
energy consumption equipment　用能设备
energy consumption index　能耗指标
energy consumption influence
　能源消费影响
energy consumption shear strength modulus
　耗能剪切模量
energy consumption system　能耗系统
energy dissipation and vibration damping
　消能减震
energy distribution　能源分配
energy efficiency coefficient of cold source system
　冷源系统能效系数
energy efficiency index　能效指标
energy efficiency level　能效水平
energy efficiency standard　能效标准
energy efficiency targets　节能目标
energy flow diagram　能流图
energy head　能高
energy head of braking　制动能高
energy head of braking per meter
　每米制动能高
energy optimization　能源优化
energy performance equivalent building of railway station　等效客站能耗计算模型

energy processing and conversion
　能源加工转换
energy storage　能源储存
energy supply　能源供应
energy transportation　能源输送
energy-efficient　高效节能
enforce　强制执行,实施
enforcement　强制执行,实施
engage　聘请,聘用
engagement　雇佣,约定
engagement clause　保证条款
engagement of staff and labour
　员工和劳务的雇佣
engagements　债务
engineer　工程师,设计
engineer in charge　主管工程师
engineer in chief　总工程师
engineer procurement construction（EPC）
　设计—招标—建造
engineering analogy method　工程类比法
engineering analysis　工程分析
engineering breakdown struture（EBS）
　工程分解结构
engineering change proposal（ECP）
　设计变更建议书
engineering construction quota
　工程建设定额
engineering consultancy firm
　工程咨询公司
engineering consulting contract
　工程咨询合同
engineering contract fee　工程承包费
engineering control network　工程控制网
engineering cost　工程成本
engineering design phase/stage
　工程设计阶段
engineering earthquake resistance　工程抗震
engineering entity quality　工程实体质量
engineering geological column
　工程地质柱状图
engineering geological condition
　工程地质条件
engineering geological drilling exploration
　工程地质钻探
engineering geological evaluation
　工程地质评价
engineering geological investigation and mapping
　工程地质测绘
engineering geological investigation report
　工程地质勘察报告

engineering geological map　工程地质图
engineering geological mapping
　工程地质调绘
engineering geological profile
　工程地质剖面图
engineering geological prospecting
　工程地质勘探
engineering geological route selection
　工程地质选线
engineering geology　工程地质
engineering geology manual
　工程地质手册
engineering interface　工程接口
engineering investigation　工程勘察
engineering laboratory　工程试验室
engineering landslide　工程滑坡
engineering manager　设计经理,工程部经理
engineering measure　工程措施
engineering monitoring　工程监测
engineering photogrammetry
　工程摄影测量
engineering physical exploration
　工程物理勘探
engineering quality and safety supervision fee
　工程质量安全监督费
engineering quality inspection fee
　工程质量检测费
engineering quantity　工程数量
engineering remote sensing　工程遥感
engineering report　工程报告
engineering scope database
　工程范围数据库
engineering service loan　工程服务贷款
engineering settlement（final accounting）**period**
　工程结(决)算期
engineering structure　工程结构
engineering structure design　工程结构设计
engineering supervision and consulting service fees
　工程监理与咨询服务费
engineering supervision fee　工程监理费
engineering survey　工程测量
engineering train　工程列车
engineering vessel　工程船舶
engineering water　工程用水
engineer's consent　工程师的同意
engineer's determination　工程师的确定
engineer's duties and authority
　工程师的职责和权限
engineer's initial response
　工程师的初始响应

engineer's inspection and investigation
　工程师的检查和调查
engineer's interim certificate
　工程师的期中支付证书
engineer's representative　工程师代表
Engler viscosity　恩式黏度
engraving　刻图
enhanced location dependent addressing（eLDA）
　增强型位置寻址
enhanced multi-level precedence and pre-emption
　service（eMLPP）　多优先级功能
enhanced pool with chemical flocculation
　化学絮凝强化池
enquire　询价
enquiry　询价,询盘
enquiry documents　询价文件
enquiry system　信息查询系统
enquiry terminal　信息查询终端
ensure　保证
enter　登记
enter into　缔结,签订
enter into a contract　订合同
enter into a contract with
　缔结和约,订立合同
enter into effect　生效
enter on unexpected track　进入异线
enter up an account　入账
enterprise　企业
enterprise management fee　企业管理费
enterprise owned by sole investor
　独资企业
enterprise project management
　企业级项目管理
enterprise property insurance　企业财产保险
enterprise quota measurement fee
　企业定额测定费
enterpriser　企业家
entertain a claim　接受索赔
entertain an offer　接受报盘
entertain an order　接受订货
entertaining expenses　交际费
entertainment expense　招待费
enthalpy　焓值
enthalpy-humidity diagram　焓湿图
entirely parallel feeding　全并联供电
entitative quality of concrete
　混凝土实体质量
entitle　给予权利
entitlement　应得的权利
entity　个体,实体,主体

entity composition　实体组成
entrance　进口,入境
entrance and exit line for depot　出入段线
entrance current　入口电流
entrance guard　门禁
entrance platform　入口平台
entrance speed at reducer　减速器入口速度
entrance visa　入境签证
entrance/exit　出入口
entrance/exit access for container truck
　集卡出入口通道
entrance/exit inspection　出入库检测
entrepreneur　企业家
entrust　委托,托管,信托
entrusted agent　委托代理人
entruster　委托人
entry　进站,填项,条目
entry and exit procedural　出入境手续
entry certificate　入境证书
entry declaration　入港申报
entry documents　入境文件
entry for consumption　消费品进口报关单
entry for home use
　国内消费品进口报关单
entry into force conditions　生效条件
entry of contract into force　合同生效
entry of goods inward　申报进口
entry of goods outward　申报出口
entry outward　出口报关单
entry price　入账价格
entry value　买入价值
entry visa　入境签证
envelope curve　包络线
environment　环境
environment and power monitoring system
　环境及电源监控系统
environment contamination　环境污染
environment engineering　环境工程
environment resource　环境资源
environmental action grade　环境作用等级
environmental analysis　环境分析
environmental benefit　环境效益
environmental carrying capacity　环境承载力
environmental characteristics　环境特征
environmental condition
　环境条件,外界条件
environmental conditions turnover　周围情况
environmental disaster　环境灾害
environmental friendly route selection
　环境保护选线

environmental geological conditions
　环境地质条件
environmental geology　环境地质
environmental hydrogeology
　环境水文地质
environmental impact　环境影响
environmental impact assessment (EIA)
　环境影响评价
environmental impcat statement (EIS)
　环境影响报告
environmental management system
　环境管理体系
environmental micro-vibration　环境微振动
environmental monitoring　环境监控
environmental monitoring system
　环境监测系统
environmental noise　环境噪声
environmental noise measuring method
　环境噪声测量方法
environmental noise monitoring points
　环境噪声监测点位
environmental noise pollution　环境噪声污染
environmental pollution　环境污染
environmental protection　环境保护
environmental protection expenditure
　环境保护费
environmental protection policy
　环境保护政策
environmental quality standard for surface water
　地表水环境质量标准
environmental risk insurance
　环境风险保险
environmental stress cracking time
　环境应力开裂时间
environmental supervision　环境监理
environmental survey　环境调查
environmental vibration test　环境振动试验
environmentally sensitive area　环境敏感区
Eocene epoch　始新世
Eocene series　始新统
eolian soil　风积土
Eopaleozoic　早古生代
epicenter　震中
epicentral distance　震中距
epicentral intensity　震中烈度
epicentral region　震中区
epidemic　流行性疾病
epi pleistocene　晚更新世
epoxy coating　环氧涂层
epoxy concrete　环氧混凝土

epoxy resin coated steel bar
　环氧树脂涂层钢筋
epsilon-type structure　山字形构造
equal level far end crosstalk attenuation (loss)
　(ELFEXT)　等电平远端串音衰减
equal opportunity　同等机会
equal opportunity clause　同等机会条款
equal pay for equal work　同工同酬
equal viscosity temperature　等黏温度
equality and mutual benefit　平等互利
equalizing charge　均衡充电
equally tilted photograph　等倾摄影
equatorial plane　赤平面
equatorial tropics　赤道热带
equidistant projection　等距投影
equilateral turnout　对称道岔
equipartition function　均分性能
equipment　器材,设备
equipment account　设备台账
equipment alarm　设备告警
equipment and systems of building
　建筑设备及系统
equipment area　设备区
equipment category　设备种类
equipment centralized station　设备集中站
equipment charge out rates
　施工机械台时费
equipment cost　设备费
equipment cost estimating
　施工机械费预算
equipment depreciation　设备折旧
equipment enclosure　设备外壳
equipment fault　设备故障
equipment floor　设备层
equipment foundation　设备基础
equipment freight and miscellaneous charges
　设备运杂费
equipment freight and miscellaneous rates
　设备运杂费费率
equipment identity register (EIR)
　设备识别寄存器
equipment insurance　设备保险
equipment intervention　设备干预
equipment layout plan　设备平面布置图
equipment leasing　设备租赁
equipment lessor　设备租赁商
equipment list　设备清单
equipment maintenance
　设备保养,设备维护,设备维修
equipment model　设备型号

equipment out-of use 设备停用
equipment performance 设备性能
equipment procurement 设备采购
equipment procurement cost 设备购置费
equipment rental 设备租用费
equipment residual values 设备残值
equipment room in communication building
　通信楼机房
equipment room layout plan
　机房平面布置图
equipment selection 设备选型
equipment specification 设备规格
equipment supply loan 设备供货贷款
equipment support 设备支架
equipment technical document
　设备技术资料
equipment time checking 设备时间核对
equipment unit price 设备单价
equipment works 设备场
equipment yard 设备场
equipotential 等电位
equipotential connection 等电位连接
equipotential line 等势线
equitable mortgage 衡平法按揭
equity 产权,股票,股权,权益
equity capital 产权资本,权益资本
equity financing 增股筹资
equity fund 股票基金
equity holder 股本持有者
equity joint venture
　产权式合营,投资入股型联营体
equity joint-venture contract
　股权式联营合同
equity market 股票市场
equity ownership 产权所有权
equity ratio 权益比率
equity receiver 清算管理人
equity share 普通股
equivalent 相等物
equivalent A-weighted sound level
　等效 A 声级
equivalent base shear method 底部剪力法
equivalent continuous A-weighted sound pressure level 等效连续 A 声级
equivalent impedance of contact line system
　牵引网等效阻抗
equivalent impedance 当量阻抗
equivalent impedance of traction network
　牵引网等效阻抗
equivalent internal friction angle 似内摩擦角

equivalent length 当量长度
equivalent moment coefficient
　等效弯矩系数
Equivalent n-th harmonic 等效 n 次谐波
equivalent projection 等积投影
equivalent replacement method 等量代替法
equivalent settlement coefficient of pile foundation
　桩基等效沉降系数
equivalent shear wave velocity
　等效剪切波速
equivalent slenderness ratio 换算长细比
equivalent sound level 等效声级
equivalent uniform live load
　等效均布活荷载,换算均布活载
equivalent uniform load 等效均布荷载
equivalent value for compressive strength of mortar 砂浆抗压强度换算值
erbium-doped fiber (EDF) 掺铒光纤
erection 架设,安装
erection all risks (EAR) 安装工程一切险
erection by beam-erecting machine
　架桥机架设法
erection by cableway hoisting method
　缆索吊装法
erection by falsework method
　膺架式架设法
erection by girder-erecting machine
　架桥机架设法
erection by incremental launching method
　顶推式架设法
erection by longitudinal traction method
　纵向拖拉法
erection by rotation method 转体施工
erection by traction method 拖拉架设法
erection cost 安装费,装配成本
erection diagram 装配图
erection information 安装资料
erection of bridge 架设桥梁
erection of equipment 设备安装
erection of plant 设备安装
erection on site 现场安装
erode 毁坏
erosion 侵蚀
erosion basis 侵蚀基准面
erosion plain 侵蚀平原
erosion resistance 抗侵蚀
erosion resistant mortar 抗侵蚀砂浆
erosion slope 侵蚀坡
erosion terrace 侵蚀阶地
erosion type 侵蚀类型

erosional spring　侵蚀泉
erratum　勘误
error　错误，误差
error ellipse　误差椭圆
error enlarging factor　误差放大因子
error in good faith　善意过失
error of omission　过失罪，遗漏错误
error of sighting　照准误差
error propagation　误差传播
error range　误差范围
error test　误差检验
error-free period　传输无差错时间
escalation　调价，上涨费用，涨价
escalation clause
　调高条文，调价条款，物价波动调价条款
escalation index　物价上涨指数
escalation lump sum contract
　调值总价合同，调高总价合同
escalation of fault　故障升级
escalation price　调价价格，调高价格
escalator　自动扶梯
escapable cost　可避免成本
escape clause　免责条款
escapement　牵纵拐肘
escrow account　第三方托管账户
escrow deposit　代理存款
esker　蛇形丘
essence　本质
essence of insurance　保险要素
essential　基本的
essential equipment　基本装备
established international practice
　公认的国际惯例
establishment　经营场所
estate　财产，地产
estimate　估价，估算，预算
estimate at completion (EAC)　完工估算
estimate documentation　估价文件
estimate guideline　预算导则
estimate of cost　成本估算
estimate sheet　估价单
estimate summary　汇总估价表
estimated cost
　估算成本，预计费用，预算成本
estimated liabilities　估计负债
estimated physical life　预计使用年限
estimated price　估计价格
estimated quantities
　估算工程量，预估工程量
estimated residual value　估计残值
estimated salvage value　估计残值
estimated service life　评估使用年限
estimated time of arrival (ETA)
　预计到达时间
estimated time of departure (ETD)
　预计离港时间
estimated time of finishing discharging (ETFD)
　预计卸货完成时间
estimater　估价人
estimator　估算师
estop　禁止翻供
estoppel　禁止翻供
estuarine delta　河口三角洲
ethernet　以太网
ethernet passive optical network (EPON)
　以太网无源光网络
ethical standard　道德标准
ethics　道德准则
ethylene vinyl acetate copolymer (EVA) sheet
　乙烯—醋酸乙烯聚合物防水卷材
ethylene vinyl acetate copolymer geomembrane
　乙烯—乙酸乙烯共聚物土工膜
Euler's critical load　欧拉临界力
Euler's critical stress　欧拉临界应力
euro　欧元
Eurobank　欧洲银行
eurocommercial paper　欧洲商业票据
eurocurrency　欧洲货币
eurodollar　欧洲美元
euromarket　欧洲市场
european currency unit (ECU)
　欧洲货币单位
eurosyndicated loans　欧洲银团贷款
evacuation exit　疏散出口
evacuation walk　疏散走道
evade　躲避，闪避，规避，逃避
evade taxes　逃税，漏税
evaluated bid price　评标价
evaluating values of energy conservation
　节能评价值
evaluation　评定，评估
evaluation by track inspection car
　轨检车评分
evaluation criteria　评价标准
evaluation factor　评估因素
evaluation index　评定指标
evaluation method　评定方法
evaluation of bids　评标
evaluation of settlement　沉降评估
evaluation procedure　评价程序

evaluation process 评估过程
evaluation result 评定结论
evaluation standard 评定标准
evaporating pressure 蒸发压力
evaporating temperature 蒸发温度
evaporation capacity 蒸发量
evaporative air cooler 蒸发式冷气机
evaporative condensation 蒸发冷凝
evaporative condenser 蒸发式冷凝器
evaporative cooling 蒸发冷却
evaporator 蒸发器
event 同相轴
event of default 违约事件
evergreen credit 常用贷款
evidence 证词,证件,证据,证人
evidence in chief 主要证据
evidence of debt 借据
evidence of origin 原产地证明书
evidence of payment 付款证明
evidence of title 所有权证据
evolve 进展
ex gratia claim 道义索赔,通融索赔
ex parte 单方面
ex store 仓库交货,仓库交货价
ex works（EXW） 工厂交货
exacerbate 恶化
examination 测验
examination of bid 投标审核
examine 核查
examine and approve 核准,审定
examining system 检验制度
example 范例
excavated and cast-in-place pile 挖孔灌注桩
excavated shaft foundation 挖井基础
excavating machinery 挖掘机械
excavation 挖方,挖掘
excavation chamber （盾构）土仓
excavation contour 开挖轮廓线
excavation cross-section area 开挖断面面积
excavation diameter 开挖直径
excavation face 开挖面
excavation method 开挖方式
excavation of foundations of piers and abutments for inspection purpose 墩台基础挖验
excavator 挖掘机,挖土机
exceed 超过
exceed the budget 超出预算
excellent execution certificate 优质竣工证书
except 不包括
excepted risk 除外风险,拒保风险

exception clause 除外条款,例外条款
exception report 例外事项报告
exceptional 特殊的,例外的,异常的
exceptional event 例外事件,特殊事件,异常事件
exceptional remedy 特殊补救办法,例外补救
exceptional risk 特殊风险
exceptional service 额外服务
exceptional urgency 特殊紧急事件,异常意外
exceptionally adverse climatic conditions 异常恶劣的气候条件
exceptionally inclement weather 特别恶劣的天气
excess 超出额,免赔额,起出
excess activated sludge 剩余污泥
excess clause 起额条款,自负额条款
excess hydrostatic pressure 超静水压力
excess pore pressure ratio 超孔压比
excessive joint gap 大轨缝
excessive residual voltage for branching 分路残压超标
excessive resistance for branching 分路电阻超标
eurrency exchange adjustment 汇率调整
exchange 兑换,互换,换汇,汇兑,交换,交易所
exchange bank 汇兑银行
exchange control regulations 外汇管理规定
exchange control 外汇管制
exchange cost 换汇成本
exchange dealings 外汇交易
exchange discount 外汇贴水
exchange premium 外汇升水
exchange proviso clause 汇率保值条款
exchange quota 外汇额度
exchange rate 兑换率,汇率
exchange rate adjustment 汇率调整
exchange rate hedging clause 汇率保值条款
exchange reserve 外汇储备
exchange restriction 外汇限制
exchange risk 汇兑风险,外汇风险
exchange tax 外汇税
exchange traffic flow 交换车流
exchange yard 交换场
exchangeable calcium and magnesium 交换性钙镁离子
excise 货物税,消费税,执照税
excise tax 消费税

excitation characteristic 励磁特性
excitation circuit 励磁电路
excitation frequency 激振频率
excitation methods of bridge structure
 桥梁结构激振方法
excitation requisition 励磁条件
excite （声波）发射
exciter 激磁机
exciting force 激振力
exclude 不包括
excluded liability 除外责任
exclusion 不保事项,除外责任条款
exclusion clause 除外条款
exclusion method 剔除法
exclusion of liability clause 免责条款
exclusive agency 独家代理,唯一代理
exclusive agent 独家代理人
exclusive contract 专营合同
exclusive dealer 独家经销商
exclusive distribution 独家经销,总经销
exclusive market 独销市场
exclusive patent right 独家专利权
exclusive selling agent 独家销售代理商
exclusive use for the works 工程专用
exculpatory 开脱罪责的
exculpatory clause 免责条款
excusable and compensable delays
 可原谅并应给予补偿的拖期
excusable but non-compensable delays
 可原谅但不给予补偿的拖期
excusable delays 可原谅的拖期
execute 实施,执行
execute a contract 签署合同
execute an order 接受订货
executing agency 执行机构,执行委员会
execution 施工,实施
execution of contract 合同生效
execution of the works 工程实施
executive 高级管理人员
executive board 常务董事会
executive committee 执行委员会
executive construction plan
 实施性施工组织设计
executive director 执行董事
executory consideration 待结付的补偿
executory contract 待履行的合同
executor 执行人
exempt 豁免
exempt from inspection 免检
exempt from liability 免责

exemption 豁免
exemption certificate 免税单
exemption clause
 开脱性条款,免税条款,免责条款
exercise 运用
exfoliation 叶状剥落
exhaust 耗尽
exhaust air duct 排风风道
exhaust air temperature 排风温度
exhaust duct 排气管道
exhaust fan 排风机
exhaust pipe 排气管
exhaust pressure 排气压力
exhaust temperature 排气温度
exhaust valve 排气阀
exhaust vent 排气孔
exhaust ventilation system 排气系统
exhaust ventilation 排气通风
exhibit 物证,展示件
exiguous triangle method 微三角形法
existing building 既有建筑物
existing conditions modeling 现状建模
existing line 既有线
existing line reconstruction 改建既有线
existing plant compensation cost 青苗补偿费
existing railway 既有铁路
existing structural member 原构件
exit 出口,出站
exit button 出门按钮
exit documents 出境文件
exit speed of retarder 减速器出口速度
expand 发展
expandable bolt 膨胀锚杆
expanded polystyrene 聚苯乙烯发泡材料
expansion joint
 膨胀接头,伸缩缝,伸缩接头
expansion loop 弯管补偿器
expansion pipe 膨胀管
expansion rate in restrict condition
 限制膨胀率
expansion rate of accelerating mortar bar
 快速砂浆棒膨胀率
expansion rate of rock column
 岩石柱膨胀率
expansion tank 膨胀水箱
expansion test 膨胀试验
expansive cement 膨胀水泥
expansive soil landslide 膨胀土滑坡
expatriate 外派雇员,移居国外者
expatriate craftsmen 外国技工

expatriate labour 外籍劳工
expected life 预计使用年限
expedite 加快速度
expedite deliveries 催促交货
expediting 催交
expedition 考察
expend 消耗
expendable fund 备用资金
expenditure 开支,消费,支出
expenditure of fund 资金支出
expenditure on administration 行政管理费
expense 费用,经常费用
expense account 开支账
expense allocation 费用分摊
expense for preservation of cultural relics 文物保护费
expense for survey & design 勘测设计费
expense item 开支项目
expense of construction facilities 施工设施费
expense of construction measures 施工措施费
expense of site clearing 场地清理费
expense of small scale temporary facilities 小型临时设施费
expense of temporary facilities 临进设施费
expense ratio 费用率
expenses 开支
expenses for administration 办公费
expenses for social intercourse 交际费
expenses for temporary facilities of employer 建设单位临时设施费
expenses for using fixed assets 固定资产使用费
expenses of base period for using construction machinery 基期施工机械使用费
expenses of large scale temporary facilities and transitional works 大型临时设施和过渡工程费
experience 经验
expert 专家
expert committee (council) 专家委员会
expert consultant 咨询专家
expert opinion 鉴定意见
expert panel 专家委员会
expert witness 鉴定人
expertise 专业技能
expertise report 鉴定书,证明书
expiration 耗尽,期满
expiration date 到期日
expiration of contract 合同到期,合同期满
expire 期满
expired cost 已耗成本
expiring laws 失效法律
expiry 期满,失去时效的
explanatory memorandum 解释性备忘录
explode 爆破
exploit 开采
exploration 勘察,勘探,考察
exploration point 勘探点
exploration well 勘探井
exploratory borehole 勘探孔
exploratory trench 探槽
exploratory well 探井
explosion action 爆炸作用
explosion proof 防爆
explosion-proof area 防爆区
explosion-proof electric apparatus 防爆电气设备
explosive 爆破材料,炸药
explosive detector 爆炸物测探仪器
export 出口
export bank guarantee 出口银行保函
export credit 出口信贷
export credit guarantee 出口信贷担保
export credit insurance 出口信用保险
export documents 出口担保,出口单证
export duty 出口税
export entry 出口报关单
export incense (permit) 出口许可证
export invoice 出口发票
export letter of credit 出口信用证
export price 出口价
export restriction 出口限制
export shipping instructions 出口装船须知
export subsidy 出口补贴
export tariff 出口关税
export tax 出口税
exposed installation 明设
exposed karst area 裸露型岩溶区
exposed surface 裸露面
exposure 暴露
exposure diversification 风险分散
exposure station 摄影站
express agreement 明示协议
express assignment 明示转让
express collect 运费到付
express consent 明示同意
express provision 明示规定
express term 明示条款

express undertaking	明示承诺
express waiver	明示放弃,明示弃权书
expression	措辞
expression of partial factor	分项系数表达式
expressway	高速公路
Express-G	EXPRESS 语言的图形子集
expropriation	剥夺所有权,征用
expropriation of land	土地征用
extend	给予
extend validity	延长有效期
extendable bond	可延期债券
extended clamp for suspension	长吊环
extended drop bracket	长定位单环
extended steady ring	长定位环
extended twin drop bracket	长定位双环
extendible bond	可延期债券
extensible markup language (XML) 可扩展标记语言	
extension	延期
extension fee	延期费用
extension fracture	拉伸破裂
extension of contract period	合同期的延长
extension of defects notification period 缺陷通知期限的延长	
extension of time (EOT)	工期延长
extension of time for completion 竣工期限的延长,竣工时间延长	
extension of works	工程扩建
extension rod	接杆
extension vent pipe	伸顶通气管
extensive soil erosion	强烈侵蚀
extensometer	引伸仪
extent of agreement	协议范围
extent of damage	损害程度
extent of karst development	岩溶发育程度
extent of liability	责任范围
exterminate	毁灭
external affairs	对外事务
external circuit	外部回路
external concrete vibrator 附着式混凝土振捣器	
external debt	外债
external dimension	外部尺寸
external drainage system	外排水系统
external force	外力
external lightning protection	外部防雷
external locking device	外锁闭装置
external port	外部端口
external prestress	体外预应力
external protection	外部保护
external trade	对外贸易
external wall	外墙
external works	附属工程
externally bonded water stop tie	外贴止水带
extinguish	偿清
extra	额外的
extra allowance	额外津贴
extra charges (expenses)	额外开支
extra coefficient	富余系数
extra cost	额外成本,额外费用,外加费用
extra hour work	加班
extra hours	加班
extra orientation element	外定向元素
extra premium	附加保险费
extra profit	额外利润
extra time	额外时间
extra wage	附加工资
extra work	额外工作,加班
extract	开采
extrados	拱背线
extraneous risks	外来风险
extraordinary cost	特别费用,异常费用
extraordinary item	非经常性项目
extraordinary	特别的,异常的
extras	额外成本,额外费用,外加费用
extra-deep tunnel	特深埋隧道
extra-long tunnel	特长隧道
extreme drought	极干旱
extreme soil erosion	极强烈侵蚀
extreme wind speed	极大风速
extremely hard rock	极硬岩
extremely soft rock	极软岩
extremely weak water abundance zone 极弱富水区	
extruded insulation	挤包绝缘
extrusion deformation	挤压变形
extrusion molding	挤出成型法
extrusive rock	喷出岩
ex-contractual claims	合同外索赔
ex-factory	工厂交货
ex-factory price	出厂价,卖方工厂交货价格
ex-gratia payment	道义支付,优惠支付
ex-interest	无利息
ex-warehouse	仓库交货价
ex-works price	工厂交货价
eye clamp	定位环,吊环,套管单耳
eye end rod	耳环杆
eyepiece	目镜
e-payment	电子支付
E-ticket	电子票

F

fabric reinforcement 钢筋网
fabric sheet reinforced earth 铺网法
fabric switch 光纤存储交换机
fabricate 结构加工,伪造,制作,装配
fabricated universal steel member
　万能杆件
fabricating yard 制作场,装配场
fabrication 加工,制作
fabrication check points
　加工制造的检验点
fabrication cost 制造成本,装配成本
face amount (value) 面值,票面金额
face clause 正面条款
face disc cutter 正滚刀
face left 盘左
face right 盘右
face shovel 正向铲挖土机
face to face negotiation 当面谈判
face work 涂面工作,饰面工程
face-passing arrangement of turnouts
　道岔对向布置
facilities for staff and labour 员工设施
facility 设备,工具
facility management 设施管理,物业管理
facility provider 设施提供者
facility provision 设施供应
facing single turnout 对向单开道岔
facing stone 饰面石
facsimile (fax) 传真
facsimile telegraph 传真电报
facsimile transmission 传真发送
factor 系数,因素
factor of soil erosion and water loss
　水土流失因子
factorage 代理商佣金,代理业
factoring charges 代理融通费
factoring company 代理融通公司
factory cost 制造成本

factory expenses 制造费用
factory for prefabrication 预制厂
factory inspection 进厂检验
factory order 生产通知单
factory painting 工厂漆
factory price 出厂价
factory tax 出厂税
factual record 真实记录
facultative reinsurance 临时再保险
fail 违约,不作为,未履行
fail in negotiation 谈判失败
failed test 未通过的检验
failing tensile stress 拉断张力
failure 不履行,失效,无支付能力
failure alarming signal 事故报警信号
failure cause 失效原因
failure load 破坏荷载,失效荷载
failure mechanism 失效机理,破坏机理
failure mode 失效模式,破坏模式
failure of performance 未履行合同
failure of prequalification 资格预审不合格
failure ratio 破坏比
failure to appoint DAAB member
　未能指定争议避免裁决委员会成员
failure to comply with DAAB's decision
　未能遵守争议避免裁决委员会的决定
failure to deliver 未能交货
failure to pass tests on completion
　未能通过竣工试验
failure to perform 不能履行
failure to predict an earthquake 地震漏报
failure to remedy defects 未能修补缺陷
fail-safe 故障—安全
fair average quality (FAQ) 中等品质
fair competition 公平竞争
fair dealing 公平交易
fair dismissal 合理驳回,正当解雇
fair drawing 清绘

fair market price 公平市价
fair price 公平价格
fair trading act 公平交易法
fair wear and tear 自然损耗
fairness 公平性
FAK rate 全程统一运费率
fall due 到期
fall threshold 落下门限
falling objects monitoring 落物监测
false 虚假的
false declaration 虚报
false entry 假账,伪造记录
false indication of a switch 道岔错误表示
false profit 虚假利润,虚盈实亏
falsework method with only a small quantity of support points 少支架法
falsework method 支架法
falsework preloading 支架预压
family library 族库
fan 风扇
fan blower 鼓风机
fan filter unit (FFU,FMU) 风机过滤器单元
fan-coil unit 风机盘管机组
fan-shaped tension crack 扇形张裂缝
far infrared 远红外
Faraday cage 法拉第笼
farmland occupation tax 耕地占用税
Fast Ethernet (FE) 快速以太网
fast moving image processing 快速运动图像处理
fast static surveying 快速静态测量
fast track method 快速路径法
fasten 加固
fastener 扣件
fastening-down rail temperature in construction 施工锁定轨温
fastening 扣件
fast-setting cement 速凝水泥
fast-setting concrete 速凝混凝土
fast-speed railway 快速铁路
fat concrete 富混凝土
fatal accident 死亡事故
fatigue 疲劳
fatigue behaviour 疲劳性能
fatigue check 疲劳验算
fatigue crack 疲劳裂缝
fatigue damage of steel girder 钢梁疲劳损伤
fatigue failure 疲劳失效
fatigue of contact wire 导线疲劳
fatigue resistance 疲劳阻力
fatigue strength 疲劳强度
fatigue strength of sound barrier 声屏障疲劳强度
fatigue stress amplitude 疲劳应力幅
fatigue test 疲劳试验
fatigue train 疲劳列车
fault accumulation 故障积累
fault block landform 断块地貌
fault board 故障板件
fault breccia 断层角砾岩
fault detector 探伤仪
fault diagnosis 故障诊断
fault displacement 断距
fault fractured zone 断层破裂带
fault gouge 断层泥
fault identification device 故障判别装置
fault line 断层线
fault locating 故障测距,故障定位
fault management 故障管理
fault plane 断层面
fault restoration 故障复原
fault scarp 断层崖
fault spring 断层泉
fault surface 断层面
fault test 故障测试
fault treatment 故障办理
fault valley 断层谷
fault wall 断盘
fault zone 断层带
faulty concrete 劣质混凝土
faulty design 有缺陷的设计
faulty excessive out-of-tolerance 过失性大超差
faulty material and workmanship 有缺陷的材料及工艺
faulty trackside acoustic detection system of train rolling bearing 车辆滚动轴承故障轨边声学诊断系统
fault 断层,故障
faulty work 工作缺陷,有缺陷的工作
favorable section 有利地段
favour 优惠,支持
favourable condition 优惠条件
favourable interest rate 优惠利率
favourable price 优惠价
favourable status 优惠待遇
favourable terms 优惠条件
fax machine 传真机
faying surface 栓接板面
FC switch 光纤交换机

feasibility 可行性
feasibility study 可行性研究
feasibility study fee 可行性研究费
feasibility study for construction project 建设项目可行性研究
feasibility study phase 可行性研究阶段
feasibility study stage 可研阶段
feather joint 羽毛状节理
fecal sewage 粪便污水
federation 联盟
fee 报酬,费用
fee for permit 执照费
fee of civilized construction measures 文明施工措施费
fee of one machine shift 台班费
feed hopper 进料斗,供料斗
feed pipe 供水管
feedback 反馈
feeder 供电电缆,加料器,馈线
feeder cable 供电电缆
feeder road 公路支线
feeding end 送电端
feeding point 供电上网(点)
feeding section 供电臂
feedstock 原料
feeler lever 探杆
fees and expenses 费用和开支
fees of supervision and consulting on survey works 勘察监理与咨询费
feldspar 长石
felsenmeer 石场
fence 围栏,栅栏
ferriage 渡船费
ferromagnetic mineral 铁磁性矿物
ferrous nitrate 硝酸亚铁
ferrous oxide content 氧化亚铁含量
ferro-crete 速凝水泥
ferruginous cement 铁质胶结
ferrule type joint 卡套式连接
ferry trestle bridge 轮渡栈桥
ferryboat 渡轮
fiber board 纤维板
fiber channel(FC) 光纤通道
fiber end face 光纤端面
fiber impurities content 纤维杂质含量
fiber optical transceiver 光纤收发器
fiber reinforced mortar 纤维增强砂浆
fiber reinforced soil 纤维土
fiber to the building/curb(FTTB/C) 光纤到楼宇/分线盒

fiber to the home(FTTH) 光纤到户
fibrous 纤维状
fibrous backing 纤维背衬
fibrous composite material 纤维复合材料
fibrous fracture 纤维状断口
fidelity bond(insurance) 职工忠诚保险
FIDIC 国际咨询工程师联合会
fiducial mark maintenance 维护基标
fiducial mark 框标
fiduciary loan 信用贷款
fiduciary service 信托服务
field 场地,工地
field book 工地记录本
field connection 工地装配
field construction manager 现场施工经理
field controller 本地控制器,现场控制器
field cost 现场费用
field data acquisition equipment 现场采集设备
field engineer 现场工程师
field erection 现场安装
field geological map 野外地质图
field identification of soil 土的现场鉴别
field inspection 工地视察
field inspection staff 现场检查人员
field investigation 实地调查,现场考察
field laboratory 工地试验室
field location 线路点
field measurement 现场计量,现场量测,现场实测
field mobilization 现场动员
field observation 现场观测
field office 现场办事处
field operation 现场作业,露天作业
field order 现场指令
field painting 工地漆
field procurement supervisor 现场采购主管
field project staff 现场项目人员
field representative 现场代表
field sales 现场销售
field service 现场服务
field staff 现场工作人员
field strength coverage 场强覆盖
field survey 现场调查
field test 现场试验
field testing method 实地测试法
field trip 现场考察
field work 现场工作,野外作业
field work station 现地工作站

fieldwork title block 外业图标
figure 金额,图形,插图
figure of the earth 地球形状
filament burnout 灯丝断丝
filament burnout alarm 灯丝断丝报警
filament knitted geotextile 长丝针织土工布
filament transfer device 灯丝转换装置
filament woven geotextile 长丝机织土工布
file 备案,档案
file a claim 提出索赔,呈交要求
file a record 备案
file data 档案资料
files of construction project 建设工程档案
fill 填方
fill layer 填充层,填筑层
fill material 填料
fill material of group A A组填料
fill material of subgrade 基床填料
fill materials 填方材料
fill ratio 充水比
fill replacement 换填
filler 填充剂
fillet 筋条
filling ability 充填性
filling behind abutment 台后填方
filling degree 充盈度
filling layer 充填层
filling pad 充填式垫板
filling pile 灌注桩
filling rate 填土速率
filling rate of embankment 路堤填土速率
fill-mass landslide 充填体滑坡
film density 膜密度
film water 薄膜水
filter 过滤器,滤清器
filter course 过滤层
filter ditch 盲沟
filter membrane 滤膜
filter paper 滤纸
filter pipe 盲管
filtering 滤波
filtering media 滤料
filtration 过滤
filtration efficiency 过滤效率
filtration rate 滤速
filtration tank 滤池
final acceptance 最终验收
final acceptance certificate
　竣工验收证书,最终验收证书
final account 决算表,最终账目

final award 终裁
final certificate 最终证书
final completion 最终竣工
final completion certificate 最终竣工证书
final contract review 合同最终评审
final cost 最后成本
final decision maker 最后决策人
final design 最终设计
final destination 最终目的港
final estimate 最终估算
final inspection 最后检查
final invoice 最终发票
final payment 最后的支付,最终付款
final payment certificate（FPC） 最终支付证书
final payment certificate of design-build project
　设计—建造最终支付证书
final payment certificate operation service
　运营服务最终支付证书
final price 最终价格
final resistance of filter 过滤器终阻力
final setting 终凝
final settlement 最终沉降,决算表,最终账目
final statement 最终报表
final value 终值
final verdict 最终裁决
finance 金融,融资,资金
finance company 信贷公司
finance lease 融资租赁
financial 财政的
financial ability 财力
financial accounting 财务会计
financial accounting standards
　财务会计标准
financial accounts 财务账目
financial aid 财务援助,财政资助,经济援助
financial analysis 财务分析
financial appraisal 财务评估
financial arrangement 资金安排
financial assets 财务资产,金融性资产
financial audit 财务审计
financial bill 金融票据
financial budget 财务预算
financial capacity 财务能力
financial center 金融中心
financial channel 资金渠道
financial circle 金融界
financial claim 经济索赔,债权
financial closing 财务清账
financial commissioner 财务专员
financial community 金融界

financial compensation 经济补偿
financial condition 财务状况
financial consultation 财务咨询,金融咨询
financial cost 财务成本,财务费用
financial counselling 财务咨询,金融咨询
financial counsellor (consultant) 财务顾问
financial data 财务数据
financial default 不履行债务
financial document 财务文件
financial embarrassment 财政拮据
financial evaluation 财务评价
financial expenses 财务成本,财务费用
financial futures 金融期货
financial guarantee 财务担保
financial institution 金融机构
financial instrument
　　金融工具,金融手段,金融票据
financial interests 金融界
financial intermediation 金融中介
financial lease 财务租赁
financial leverage 财务杠杆,举债经营
financial management 财务管理
financial market 金融市场
financial means 财务收入
financial memorandum 财务备忘录
financial obligation 债务
financial penalty 罚款
financial position 财务状况
financial projection 财务预测
financial proposal 财务建议书,商务标
financial rate of return 财务收益率
financial ratio 财务比率
financial report 财务报表,财务报告
financial resources 财政资源,资金
financial risk 金融风险
financial security 经济担保
financial settlement 财务结算
financial stakeholder 财务干系人
financial statement 财务报告
financial status 财务状况
financial viability 金融偿付能力
financial world 金融界
financial year 财政年度,会计年度
financier 金融机构,金融家
financing 筹资,融资
financing charges 融资费
financing cost 筹资成本
financing interest rates 融资利率
financing plan 融资计划,资助计划
financing structure 融资结构
financing terms 融资条件
finder 经纪行,中介人
finder's fee 中介人佣金
findings 调查结果
fine 罚金
fine adjusting pad 微调垫板
fine adjustment of track slab 轨道板精调
fine aggregate 细骨料,细集料
fine angular gravel soil 细角砾土
fine concrete 细骨料混凝土
fine content 石粉含量
fine dressed stone 细料石
fine drinking water system 直饮水系统
fine for delayed payment 滞纳金
fine gravel 细砾
fine grinding 精磨
fine machining 精加工
fine quality 优良品质
fine round gravel soil 细圆砾土
fine sand 细砂
fine sieve 细筛
fineness 细度
fineness modulus 细度模量
fine-grained soil 细粒土
fingerpost 路标
finish coating 面漆
finish machining 精加工
finished cost 加工成本,完工成本
finished product 成品
finished product factory 成品厂
finishing 精加工,抹面
finishing machine 抹面机
finishing work 装修工程
finite element method 有限元法
fiord 峡湾
fiorite 硅华
fire 火灾,解雇
fire alarm 火灾报警
fire alarm system (FAS) 火灾报警系统
fire and extended cover insurance
　　火灾和拓展范围险
fire brick 耐火砖
fire brigade 消防队
fire extinguisher 灭火器
fire extinguishing agent 灭火剂
fire extinguishing equipment without network
　　无管网灭火装置
fire fighting equipment 消防设备
fire fighting squirt 消防水枪
fire hose 消防水带

fire hose and nozzle 消防水带和水枪
fire hydrant 消火栓
fire insurance 火灾保险
fire monitor 消防炮
fire on the sea 海上火灾
fire perils 火灾风险事故
fire plume 火羽流
fire point 燃点
fire protecting performance/fire resistance 防火性能
fire pump 消防泵
fire pump station 消防泵站
fire radiation 火源辐射
fire reservoir 消防水池
fire resistance limit 耐火极限
fire resistance rating 耐火等级
fire risk 火灾风险
fire risk accident 火灾风险事故
fire risk level 火灾危险等级
fire separation clearance 防火净距
fire stopping 防火封堵
fire suppression and barrier wall 挡油墙
fire water consumption 消防用水量
fire water source 消防水源
fireproof 防火
fireproof air duct 防火风管
fireproof casing 防火套管
fireproof distance 防火间距
fireproof door 防火门
fireproof material 耐火材料
fireproof partition 防火隔墙
fireproof valve 防火阀
firestop collar 阻火圈
firewall 防火墙
fire-fighting equipment 消防器材
fire-fighting facilities 消防设施
fire-fighting water curtain belt 防火水幕带
fire-protection evacuation walk 避难走道
fire-retardant asphalt sheet 阻燃防水卷材
fire-retardant asphalt 阻燃沥青
firm 商号,商行
firm commitment 不变承诺
firm contract 不可撤销的合同
firm fixed price contract (FFP) 固定价格合同
firm lump sum contract 固定总价合同
firm offer 实盘
first aid 急救
first approach section 第一接近区段
first arrival 初至
first check estimate (FCE) 首次核定估算
first class assessment 一级评价
first class discharge standard 一级排放标准
first class district of source water protection zone 一级水源保护区
first cost 主要成本
first departure section 第一离去区段
first grade ballast 一级道砟
first loss insurance 第一损失保险
first mortgage 第一抵押权
first order elastic analysis 一阶弹性分析
first order nonlinear analysis 一阶非线性分析
first priority 第一优先权
first right 优先权利要求
first-aid station 急救站
first-aider 急救员
first-hand data 原始数据
first-hand information 第一手资料
first-level energy efficiency 一级能效
first-level inspection 一级检修
first-level subregion 一级分区
first-order second-moment method 一次二阶矩法
fiscal 财政的
fiscal agent 财务代理人
fiscal crisis 财政危机
fiscal measures 财政措施
fiscal policy 财政政策
fiscal revenue 财政收入
fiscal year 财政年度,会计年度
fish plate 接头夹板
fish spawning ground 鱼类产卵场
fishplate wrench 鱼尾板扳手
fish-scale pit 鱼鳞坑
fissure filling coefficient of karst 岩溶裂隙充填系数
fissure structure 裂隙构造
fissured clay 裂隙黏土
fist hook 拳头钩
fit 装配
fitter 设备安装工
fitting 装置
fitting shop 装配车间
fittings 配件,装配件
fitting-free area 始触区
five boards and one layout plan 五牌一图
fix 修理
fixed arch 无铰拱
fixed arch bridge 无铰拱桥

fixed assets 固定资产
fixed assets net value 固定资产净值
fixed assets salvage value 固定资产残值
fixed assets tax 固定资产税
fixed balise 无源应答器
fixed bearing 固定支座
fixed blocking 固定闭塞
fixed capital 固定资本
fixed charges 固定费用
fixed contact 静触头
fixed cost 固定成本,固定费用
fixed credit line 固定信贷额
fixed cross section 固定断面
fixed deposit 定期存款
fixed distributor 固定布水器
fixed dune 固定沙丘
fixed equipment 固定设备
fixed error 固定误差
fixed expenses 固定费用,固定开支
fixed facility for sewage discharge by vacuum 固定式真空卸污
fixed fee 固定酬金
fixed focus camera 定焦摄像机
fixed head water injection 固定水头注水
fixed intangible assets 无形固定资产
fixed labour rates 固定劳工工资等级
fixed overhead 固定管理费
fixed point detection 定点检测
fixed point error 定点误差
fixed position type 固定台位式
fixed price 固定价格
fixed price contract 固定价格合同
fixed price contract with incentives 带奖励的固定价格合同
fixed price plus incentive fee contract 固定价格加激励酬金合同
fixed price with economic price adjustment contract (FP-EPA) 可调价的固定价格合同
fixed property 不动产,固定资产
fixed rate item 固定费率项目
fixed rate loan 固定利率贷款
fixed royalty 固定提成
fixed signal 固定信号
fixed speed limit 固定限速
fixed spot alarm 定点报警
fixed support 固定支架
fixed tangible assets 有形固定资产
fixed termination 硬锚
fixed to mobile call 移动终端呼叫移动终端,有线固定终端呼叫

fixed type gravity sewage discharge 固定式重力卸污
fixed unit price contract 固定单价合同
fixed volume method 固定体积法
fixed wages 固定工资
fixed water level 固定水位
fixed-asset investment 固定资产投资
fixed-boom crane 固定臂起重机
fixed-fee contract 固定酬金合同
fixed-percentage-of-cost method (of depreciation) 成本定率(折旧)法
fixed-percentage-on-declining-balance method 定率递减折旧法
fixed-term contract 定期合同
fixed-type switchgear 固定式开关柜
fixing device 固定装置
fixture 附属装置,装置
fixtures 设备
flake failure 白点
flake index 片状指数
flake surfaced asphalt felt 片毡
flakiness index 片状指数
flaky particle 片状颗粒
flame photometry 火焰光度法
flame retardant 阻燃,阻燃剂
flame retardant material 阻燃材料
flameproof electrical equipment 隔爆电气设备
flammable material 易燃品
flange 法兰,轮缘,翼缘
flange connection 法兰连接
flange plate 翼缘板
flange slab 翼缘板
flangeway of level crossing 道口轮缘槽
flash butt welding 闪光对焊,闪光(接触)焊
flash money 假钞
flash point 闪点
flashing power source 闪光电源
flashing signal 闪光信号
flashover 闪络
flashover protection 闪络保护
flash-butt welding of rebar 钢筋闪光对焊
flat dilatometer 侧胀板头
flat dilatometer test 扁铲侧胀试验
flat jack technique 扁千斤顶法
flat rate 比例税率,统一费率,统一税率
flat ratio 扁平率
flat slab 无梁楼盖
flat slope 平坡

flat stacking　平推法
flat truck（lorry）　平板车
flatness　平整度
flattening of ellipsoid　椭球扁率
flat-head tractor　平头式牵引车
flat-top glacier　平顶冰川
flaw detection　探伤检查
flaw detector　探伤仪
flaw echo　缺陷反射波
flaw list　缺陷清单
flawless start-up initiative
　无缺陷开车计划
fleet policy　车（船）队保险单
flexibility　柔性
flexible bend　伸缩弯
flexible braided copper wire　软铜编织
flexible budget　变动预算,弹性预算
flexible busbar　软母线
flexible connection　柔性连接
flexible exchange rate　弹性汇率
flexible joint cast-iron pipe
　柔性接口铸铁管
flexible OCS　柔性接触网
flexible pavement　柔性路面
flexible permeable hose　软式透水管
flexible pier　柔性墩,柔性桥墩
flexible pile　柔性桩
flexible protective net　柔性防护网
flexible rubber joint　可曲挠橡胶接头
flexible tie bar　柔性系杆
flexible waterproof casing　柔性防水套管
flexible working hours（FWH）　弹性工时
flexitime　弹性工时
flexometer　挠度仪
flexural rigidity of members　构件抗弯刚度
flexural rigidity of section　截面弯曲刚度
flickering device　频闪装置
flight　班机
flight block　航摄分区,航空摄影分区
flight level difference　航高差
flight line of aerial photography　摄影航线
flight strip design　航带设计
flight trajectory　航迹线
flint　燧石
float bridge　浮桥
float time　浮动时间,浮时
floatation tank　气浮池
floating bridge　浮桥
floating caisson foundation　浮式沉井基础
floating capital　短期流动资金,游资

floating charge　浮充,浮充充电
floating charge current　浮充电流
floating charge power supply　浮充供电
floating charge voltage　浮充电压
floating crane　起重船,浮式起重机
floating debt　短期债务
floating exchange rate　浮动汇率
floating interest rate　浮动利率,可变利率
floating oil　漂浮油
floating property　流动财产
floating rate note（FRN）　浮动利率票据
floating seal　浮动密封
floating weighing method　浮称法
floating/current/fluid/liquid/circulating capital
　流动资本
floc　絮粒体
floc particles　絮粒
flocculation　絮凝
flocculent structure　絮状构造
flood　洪水,水灾
flood control and draining project
　防洪排导工程
flood control function　防洪功能
flood control level　防洪水位
flood control reach　防洪河段
flood discharge　洪水流量,排洪
flood frequency　洪水频率
flood insurance　水灾险
flood inundation of railway　洪水淹没
flood level　洪水位
flood level in return period of 100 years
　百年洪水位
flood mark　洪水标记
flood peak　洪峰
flood plain　河漫滩
flood plain facies　河漫滩相
flood prevention works with sloping faces
　斜坡防洪工程
flood survey　洪水调查
floodplain　河滩
flood-retarding project　滞洪工程
floor　地面
floor bid　最低报价
floor bracing　扫地杆
floor broker　场内经纪商
floor drain　地漏
floor height　层高
floor of the court　诉讼人席位
floor price　底价,最低价格
floor response spectrum　楼面反应谱

floor slab 楼板
flow 流量
flow chart 程序图,流程图
flow cleavage 流劈理
flow diagram 流程图
flow direction 流向
flow feeding the reservoir in network 转输流量
flow line 流线
flow net 流网
flow of rail head 轨头肥边
flow speed 流速
flow time 扩展时间
flowmeter 流量表,流量计
flow-plastic state 流塑状态
fluctuate 波动
fluctuating price contract 浮动价格合同
fluctuation 波动,涨落
fluctuation of price 价格波动
flue 烟道
fluidal structure 流纹构造
fluidity 流动度,流动性
fluidity of cement paste 水泥净浆流动度
fluid-plastic 流塑
fluorescence 荧光
fluoride 氟化物
fluorite 萤石
flushing cycle 冲洗周期
flushing fluid 冲洗液
fluvial facies 河成相
fluvial geomorphology/landform 流水地貌
fluvial sand 河砂
fluvioglacial terrace 冰水阶地
fly 航行
fly ash 粉煤灰
flying form 飞模
flyover 立交桥
flyover crossing 立体交叉
foam extinguishing system 泡沫灭火系统
foam fire extinguisher 泡沫灭火器
foam fire extinguishing agent 泡沫灭火剂
foamed asphalt 泡沫沥青
focal depth 震源深度
focusing error 调焦误差
foil strain gauge 箔式应变片
fold 折叠,褶曲,褶皱
folded-plate concrete structure 混凝土折板结构
folded-plate flocculating tank 折板絮凝池
folding strength 抗折强度

follow current 续流
follow the international practice 遵守国际惯例
follow-up investment 后续投资
foot crossing 人行过道
foot plank 步行板
footwall 下盘
foot-note 脚注
for reference only 仅供参考
force 效力
force account 自营(自建)工程
force majeure 不可抗力
force majeure clause 不可抗力条款
force moment 力矩
force of law 法律效力
forced centering 强制对中
forced centering sign 强制对中标
forced concrete mixer 强制式混凝土搅拌机
forced deregistration 强制注销
forced frequency 强迫振动频率
forced liquidation 强制清算
forced mixer 强制式搅拌机
forced vibration method 强迫振动法
forced vibration test 强迫振动试验
forecast 预报,预测
forecast final cost 预计最终成本
forecast of soil erosion and water loss 水土流失预测
foreclosure 取消赎回权
foredate 倒填日期,填早日期
foreign agency 外国代理机构
foreign bank 外国银行
foreign borrowing 对外借贷
foreign branch 国外分支机构
foreign capital 外资
foreign corporation 外国公司
foreign currency 外币
foreign currency requirements 外币需求
foreign debt 外债
foreign draft 国外汇票
foreign exchange 外汇
foreign exchange control 外汇管制
foreign exchange earning 外汇赢利
foreign exchange exposure 外汇风险
foreign exchange fluctuation 外汇波动
foreign exchange gains and losses 汇兑损益
foreign exchange quotation 外汇牌价
foreign exchange risk 外汇风险
foreign exchange transaction 外汇交易
foreign interest rate 境外利率

foreign investment 国外投资,外国投资
foreign market 国外市场
foreign object intrusion 异物侵限
foreign object monitoring 异物监测
foreign subsidiary 国外子公司
foreign trade 对外贸易
foreign-related arbitration 涉外仲裁
foreign-related civil legal relations 涉外民事法律关系
foreign-related disputes 涉外争议
foreign-related project 涉外项目
foreman 工长,领班
forepoling 超前小导管
foresee 预见
foreseeability 预见性
foreseeable losses 可预见的损失
forest against flood 防水林
forest land 林地
forest park 森林公园
forest region 林区
forest vegetation recovery expense 森林植被恢复费
forfeit 罚金
Forfeiting 福费廷交易
forfeiture 罚金
forfeiture clause 没收条款
forfeiture of payment 取消付款
forge 锻造,伪造
forged banknote 假钞
forged document 伪造文件
forged note 假钞
forged signature 伪造签字
forklift 叉车
form 表格
form line 轮廓线
form of agreement 协议书
form of letter of guarantee 保函样本
form of proxy 委托书格式
form of report 报告书格式
form of soil erosion and water loss 水土流失形式
form of tender 投标书格式
form removal 模板拆除
formal 正式的
formal acceptance 正式承兑,正式验收
formal agreement 正式协定
formal clause 正式条款
formal confirmation 正式确认
formal contract 盖章合同,正式合同
formal invitation 正式邀请

formal invoice 正式发票
formal law 成文法
formal notice 正式通知
formal request 正式要求
formaldehyde content 甲醛含量
formality of contract 合同格式
formation lithology 地层岩性
formtraveler (used for cast-in-place cantilever construction) 挂篮
formula price adjustment 公式调价法
formulate 编制,制订
formwork 模板
formwork engineering 模板工程
formwork fixer 模板工
formwork jumbo 模板台车
formwork removal 模板拆除
formwork support 模板支撑,模板支架
formwork system 模板体系
formworker 模板工
forum for arbitration 仲裁庭
forward 递交,发送,远期的,远期交易,转交
forward contract 远期合同
forward cover 期货抵补
forward dealings 期货交易
forward delivery 远期交货
forward direction 正方向
forward error correction (FEC) 前向纠错
forward exchange 期汇,远期外汇
forward exchange rate 期货汇率,远期汇率
forward forklift 前移式叉车
forward intersection 前方交会
forward margin 期货差价,远期差价
forward payment bill 远期付款交单
forward price 期货价格
forward rate 远期汇率
forwarder 代运人,转运公司,货运代理行
forwarding agency 承运商
forwarding order 托运单
fossil 化石
foul bill of lading 不洁提单
foul sewer 排污管
fouling post 警冲标
foundation 基础
foundation engineering 基础工程
foundation of sound barrier 声屏障基础
foundation pile dynamic diagnosis system 基桩动测仪
foundation pit 基坑
foundation pit behind abutment 台后基坑
foundation soil 地基

foundation toppling 基础倾覆
foundation uplift 基础上拔
foundation works 基础工程
four components method 四组分法
Fourier transform 傅里叶变换
four-aspect automatic blocking
　四显示自动闭塞
four-side supported plate 四边支承板
four-wire interface 四线接口
four-wire reception level 四线接收电平
Fraass breaking point 弗拉斯脆点
Fraass bursting point 弗拉斯脆点
fractile 分位值
fracture 断口,断裂
fracture aquifer 裂隙含水层
fracture cleavage 破劈理
fracture elongation 断裂延伸率
fracture load 断裂负荷
fracture of masonry beam 圬工梁裂损
fracture toughness 断裂韧度
fracture zone 断裂破碎带
fractured rock landslide 破碎岩滑坡
fragmental 碎块状
frame 结构
frame beam slope protection 框架梁护坡
frame braced with strong bracing system
　强支撑框架
frame braced with weak bracing system
　弱支撑框架
frame frequency 帧频
frame rate 图像帧率
frame structure 框架结构
frame with sidesway 有侧移框架
frame without sidesway 无侧移框架
framework 骨架
framework of plane control network
　框架平面控制网(CPO)
frame-shear wall structure 框架—剪力墙结构
frame-tube structure 框架—筒体结构
franchise 给予特许,专营权,特许
franchise agreement 特许协议
franchise clause 免赔条款
franchise taxes 特许经营税
franchisee 特许权受让人
franchiser 经销商,特许权让与人
fraud 舞弊
fraudulent act 欺诈行为
fraudulent practice 欺诈行为
free 无偿的
free alongside ship (F.A.S) 船边交货价

free CaO content 游离 CaO 含量
free carbon dioxide 游离二氧化碳
free carrier... (named point)(FCA)
　货交承运人(指定地点)
free competition 自由竞争
free convertible currency 自由兑换货币
free currency 自由货币
free delivery 免费送货
free export 出口免税
free foreign exchange 自由兑换外汇
free from contamination 无污染
free from particular average (FPA)
　单独海损不赔偿,平安险
free health care 免费医疗
free import 进口免税
free issue materials 免费提供的材料
free jet 自由射流
free loan 无息贷款
free medical care 免费医疗
free network 自由网
free of charge 免费
free of duty 免关税
free on board (FOB) 离岸价
free on board destination 目的地交货类
free on board stowed (FOBS) 离岸价并理舱
free on board trimmed (FOBT) 离岸价并平舱
free on quay (FOQ) 码头交货价
free on rail (FOR) 铁路交货价
free on wharf (FOW) 码头交货价
free port 自由港
free residual chlorine 游离性余氯
free section 自由段
free soaking saturation density of rock block
　岩石块体自由浸水饱和密度
free station linear intersection method
　自由测站边角交会法
free swelling ratio 自由膨胀率
free trade area 自由贸易区
free trade zone 保税区,免税区
free vibration 自由振动
free vibration method 自由振动法
free vibration test 自由振动试验
free water 自由水
free water immersion method 自由浸水法
freeze 冻结
freeze-thaw creeping flow 冻融蠕流
freeze-thaw erosion 冻融侵蚀
freeze-thaw erosion area 冻融侵蚀区
freeze-thaw resistance 抗冻融
freeze-thaw sorting 冻融分选

freezing and thawing coefficient of rock 岩石冻融系数
freezing and thawing mass loss rate of rock 岩石冻融质量损失率
freezing breaking point 冻裂点
freezing index 冻结指数
freezing layer 冻结层
freezing method 冻结法
freezing resistance 抗冻,抗冻性
freezing temperature 冻结温度
freezing-thawing cycle 冻融循环
freezing-thawing damage 冻融破坏
freezing-thawing loss rate 冻融损失率
freezing-thawing loss ratio L or Q 冻融损失率 L 或 Q
freezing-thawing 冻融
freezing-thawing resistance 抗冻融性
free-trade port 自由港
freight agent 货运代理行
freight all kind rate 全程统一运费率
freight and miscellaneous charges 运杂费
freight area for water transport 水运货区
freight audit 运费审查
freight bill 运费单
freight car 货车
freight car depot 货车车辆段
freight car facilities 货车车辆设备
freight car inspection yard 货物列车检修作业场(列检作业场)
freight car repair point at station 站修所
freight car repair yard at station 站修作业场
freight car technical handing-over yard 车辆技术交接作业场
freight charge 运费
freight clause 运费条款
freight conference 海运公会,航运公会
freight contract 货运合同
freight dedicated line 货运专线
freight dispatching telephone 货运调度电话
freight forward 运费由收货人付
freight forward cost 货物发运费用
freight forwarder 货运转运商,运输代理行
freight insurance 运费保险
freight list (F/L) 运价表
freight note 运费单
freight out and home 往返运费
freight paid 运费已付
freight platform 货物站台
freight policy 运费保险单
freight prepaid 运费已预付
freight price 运价
freight price mileage 运价里程
freight price number 运价号
freight price provisions 运价规则
freight price rate number 运价率
freight rate 运费率
freight rates 货物运价
freight section 货位
freight service 货运业务
freight station 货运站
freight storage yard 堆货场
freight terminal 货运码头,货运终点站
freight to be paid 运费到付
freight to collect 运费到付,运费由收货人付
freight ton 运费吨
freight traffic volume 货运量
freight train 货物列车
freight transport 货运
freight transport management system 货物运输管理系统
freight yard 货场
freight-free 免收运费
freight-in 进货运费
frequency 频率
frequency accuracy 频率准确度
frequency characteristic 频率特性
frequency curve 频率曲线
frequency difference 频差
frequency domain 频域
frequency domain resolution 频域分辨率
frequency of payment 支付次数
frequency of wind direction 风向频率
frequency response 频率响应
frequency shift modulated automatic block 移频自动闭塞
frequency shift track circuit 移频轨道电路
frequency spectrum 频谱
frequency spectrum analysis 频谱分析
frequency spectrum correction 频谱修正量
frequency synchronization 频率同步
frequency track circuit 频率式轨道电路
frequency-selective amplifier 选频放大器
frequent combination 频遇组合
frequent noise 频发噪声
frequent value of a load 荷载频遇值
frequent value of variable action 可变作用的频遇值
frequently occurred earthquake 多遇地震

fresh air system 新风系统
fresh air unit 新风机组
fresh air volume 新风量
fresh concrete 混凝土拌和物
fresh concrete temperature 混凝土拌合物温度
fresh gale 大风
fresh rock 新鲜岩石
fresh water 淡水
freshwater lake facies 淡水湖泊相
Fresnel zone 菲涅尔区
friction angle 摩擦角
friction clutch 摩擦连接器
friction coefficient 摩擦系数
friction pile 摩擦桩
friction plate 摩擦板
friction rockbolt 摩擦型锚杆
friction tape 胶带
frictional characteristic 摩擦特性
frictional resistance 摩阻力
frictional working current 摩擦电流
friction-resistance ratio 摩阻比
friendly consultation 友好协商
friendly cooperation 友好合作
fringe benefits 附加福利
fringe cost 附加费
frog 辙叉
frog angle 辙叉角
frog heel 道岔辙叉跟
frog point rail 叉心
frog rail 心轨
frog rammer 蛙式打夯机
front coil 前圈
front contact 前接点
front end engineering design (FEED) 前端工程设计
front end of turnout 道岔始端
front length of turnout 道岔前长
front loaded 不平衡(报价)
front loaded tender/bid 前重后轻的报价
front rod of a point 尖端杆
front support 前支承
front view of slope protection 边坡防护正面图
front wall 前墙
frontier 国境
front-end acquisition device 前端采集设备
front-end analysis 前端分析
front-end auxiliary device 前端附属设备
front-end equipment 前端设备
frost damage of earthworks 路基冻害
frost depth 冻深

frost heave 冻胀
frost heave grade 冻胀等级
frost heaving force 冻胀力
frost heaving mound 冻胀丘
frost heaving ratio 冻胀率
frost line 冰冻线
frost resistance 耐冻性
frost resistance class 抗冻等级
frost resistance class of concrete 混凝土抗冻等级
frost resistance coefficient 耐冻系数
frost resistance of concrete 混凝土抗冻性能
frost resistibility test 抗冻性试验
frost-heave capacity 冻胀量
frost-resistant concrete 抗冻混凝土
frozen account 冻结账户
frozen assets 冻结资产
frozen pulling stone 冻拔石
frozen rail joint 冻结接头
frozen soil 冻土
frozen soil thermal conductivity 冻土导热系数
frozen strength 冻结强度
frozen structure soil 冻结结构土
frustrated contract 不能履行的合同
frustration of contract 合同落空
fuel and power cost 燃料动力费
fuel cost 燃料费
fuel electric plant 火力发电厂
fuel oil hot water unit 燃油热水机组
fuel price 油燃料价格
fuel tank 燃油箱
fuel-burning power plant 火力发电厂
fulfill a contract 履约
fulfill an obligation 履行义务
fulfilment of contract 合同履行
fulfilment of schedule 完成进度计划
full authority 全权
full braking time 全制动时间
full braking time of retarder 减速器全制动时间
full container load (FCL) 整箱货
full control point 相片平高控制点
full cost 完全成本
full coverage 完全承保,全额承保
full falsework method 满堂支架法
full heat exchanger 全热换热器
full hole one-time grouting 全孔一次性注浆
full insurance 全额保险

full liability 完全责任
full penetration well pumping 完井抽水
full recourse 完全追索,全额追索
full reinstatement cost 全部重置成本
full release time 全缓解时间
full release time of retarder
减速器全缓解时间
full section ballast cleaning machine
全断面道砟清筛机
full section ballast consolidating machine
全断面道床夯实机
full section ballast replacement machine
全断面换砟机
full set of bills of lading 全套提单
full set of clean on board bills of lading
全套清洁已装船提单
full set of documents 全套文件
full supervision mode (FS) 完全监控模式
full track 满线
full value insurance 全额保险
full water columns 充实水柱
full water test 满水试验
fullness of mortar 砂浆饱满度
fully detailed claim 细节充分的索赔
fully enclosed 全封闭
full-face method 全断面法
full-face pre-grouting 全断面预注浆
full-face tunnel boring machine for hard rock
全断面隧道硬岩掘进机
full-length bonded bolt 全长黏结锚杆
full-size model 实尺模型,足尺模型
full-term DAB 常任争议评判委员会
full-time average current 全日平均电流
full-time load curve 全日负荷曲线
full-type falsework 满堂式支架
fumarole water 喷气孔水
fume extractor 排烟设施
fume hood 排烟罩

function 用途,职能
function area 功能区
function number (FN) 功能号
functional addressing (FA) 功能寻址
functional earthing 工作接地
functional manager 职能经理
functional organization 职能组织
functional replacement 功能置换
functional test 功能检验,功能试验
fund 基金,提供资金,资金,资助
fund raising 筹资,集资
fund settlement network 资金结算网
fundamental 基本的
fundamental breach 根本性违约
fundamental combination for action effects
作用效应基本组合
fundamental interlocking circuit 基本联锁电路
fundamental quota 基础定额
fundamental risk 基本风险
fundamental wire pair of cable 电缆基本线对
funded debt 长期债务
funding 资金投入
funds received 进款
funeral grant and pension cost for death of employees 职工死亡丧葬补助费、抚恤费
funnel method 漏斗法
furnish 供应
furnishings 供应,装备
further tests after remedying defects
修补缺陷后的进一步试验
fuse 熔断器,熔丝
fuse burnout alarm 熔断器断丝报警
future value 未来价值
futures 期货
futures dealings 期货交易
futures market 期货市场
futures price 期货价格
futures trading 期货贸易

G

gabbro 辉长岩
gain 获得,获利,利益,收益,盈余,增益
gain and loss 损益
gain or loss 盈亏
galena 方铅矿
gallop 驰振
galloping inflation 恶性通货膨胀
galloping 驰振
galvanized iron 白铁皮,镀锌铁皮
galvanized iron wire 镀锌铁丝
galvanizing 镀锌
gang 施工队,小组
gang board 脚手(架)板
gang cost 班组费用
ganger 监工,领班
gantry crane 门式起重机
gantry-type track panel laying machine 门式铺轨排机
Gantt chart 甘特图,横道图
Gantt chart of construction schedule 施工进度计划横道图
gap 间隙
gap at the common crossing 有害空间
gap in the frog 有害空间
gap sealing formwork 封边模板
gap survey 裂缝测量
gap through ability 间隙通过性
gap-graded soil 不连续级配土
garbage 废弃物
garbage clearance 垃圾清运
garbage dump 垃圾堆场
garden architecture 园林建筑
garden plot 园地
garnishee order 扣押令
gas 瓦斯
gas aerosol fire extinguishing system 气溶胶灭火系统
gas chromatograph 气相色谱仪
gas density 瓦斯浓度
gas field wind speed and direction sensor 气场式风速风向传感器
gas filtration ventilation 滤毒通风
gas fire extinguishing agent 气体灭火剂
gas insulated switchgear (GIS) 气体绝缘开关柜,气体绝缘组合电器
gas leakage 漏气
gas monitoring 瓦斯监测
gas particulate filter 过滤吸收器
gas pressure force 瓦斯压力
gas pressure method 瓦斯压力法
gas pressure rail welding machine 气压焊轨车
gas pressure welding 气压焊
gas protection 瓦斯保护
gas protection passage 防毒通道
gas source thermal pump 气源热泵
gas supply pressure 供气压力
gas transfer method 气体传递法
gas welder 气焊工
gas welding 气焊
gaseous phase 气相
gasket 垫片
gasket groove 密封垫沟槽
gasoline tamping machine 汽油捣固机
gasoline tamping pick 汽油捣固镐
gasometric method 气量法
gas-filtering room 滤毒室
gas-fired boiler 燃气锅炉
gas-fired hot water unit 燃气热水机组
gas-pressure meter 气压表
gate area 门区
Gatekeeper (GK) 网守
gateway (GW) 网关
gateway GPRS support node (GGSN) 网关GPRS支持节点
gateway mobile switching center (GMSC) 网关移动交换中心

gather 汇总,聚集
gauge 标准尺,量规,轨距,范围,限界
gauge apron 轨距挡板
gauge disc cutter 边滚刀
gauge elastically widened (elastic squeeze out)
  弹性挤开
gauge length 轨距,轨距长度
gauge rod 轨距杆
gauge side of rail 钢轨工作边
gauge widening 轨距加宽
gauss method of reduction 高斯约化法
Gauss point 基点
Gaussian planimetric rectangular coordinate system
  高斯平面直角坐标系
gaussian projection plane 高斯投影面
gauss-Kruger projection 高斯—克吕格投影
gelation time 凝胶时间
gelenite 方铅矿
general acceptance 普通承兑
general account 总账
general agency 一般代理,总代理
general agent 总代理人
general alkalinity 总碱度
general arrangement drawings 总体布置图
general arrangements 总布置图
general articles 一般规定,总则
general average (G. A.) 共同海损
general average act 共同海损行为
general average adjustment 共同海损理算
general average clause 共同海损条款
general average contribution
  共同海损分摊
general average deposit 共同海损保证金
general average disbursement insurance
  共同海损费用保险
general average fund 共同海损基金
general average guarantee
  共同海损保函,共同海损担保书
general average loss 共同海损损失
general average security 共同海损担保
general average statement 共同海损理算书
general colour rendering index 一般显色指数
general conditions 一般合同条件,一般条件
general conditions of dispute avoidance/adjudication agreement 避免/裁决争议协议的一般条件
general contract 总承包合同
general contracting for engineering project
  工程项目总承包
general contractual liabilities
  合同一般责任

general deposited soil 一般堆积土
general description 总体说明书
general design 总体设计
general equilibrium analysis 全面均衡分析
general expense 综合费用
general foreman 总监理工程师
general hardness 总硬度
general item 一般项目
general journal 普通日记簿
general labour 普通工人
general layout 总平面,总平面布置围
general layout diagram for soil and water conservation measures 水土保持措施总体布局图
general ledger account 总分类账户
general lien 一般留置权
general lighting 普通照明
general manager 总经理
general map 普通地图
general materials 一般材料
general mortgage 一般抵押,总抵押
general obligation 一般义务
general obligations of the parties
  当事双方的一般义务
general overhead 总部管理费
general packet radio service (GPRS)
  通用分组无线业务
general partnership 普通合伙
general plan 总体布置图,总体规划
general plan of ecological environment construction 生态环境建设总体规划
general plan of soil and water conservation facilities 水土保持总体规划
general plant 周转设备
general practice 惯例
general price level 一般物价水准
general procurement notice 总采购通告
general provisions 一般规定,总则
general purpose handset/handheld (GPH)
  通用手持台
general requirement 一般要求,总体要求
general responsibilities 一般义务,一般责任
general right 一般权利
general schematic layout diagram of construction
  施工总平面布置示意图
general scour 一般冲刷
general scour under bridge 桥下一般冲刷
general specification 总体规定
general tort 一般侵权行为
general trade system 总贸易体系
general/master construction plan 施工总平面图

generalized system of preferences（GSP） 普惠制
generalized system of preferences documents 普惠制单据
generally accepted accounting principles（GAAP） 公认会计原则
generating capacity 发电能力
generating station 发电站
generator 发电机，发生器
generator set 发电机组
generic routing encapsulation（GRE） 普通路由封装
gentle breeze 微风
gentle slope 缓坡
gentle slope for acceleration 加速缓坡
gentle slope for starting 起动缓坡
geocell 土工格室
geocentric coordinate system 地心坐标系
geochron 地质年代
geocomposite 土工复合材料
geodetic control data base 大地控制数据库
geodetic coordinate 大地坐标
geodetic coordinate system 大地坐标系
geodetic datum 测量基准
geodetic height 大地高
geodetic leveling difference 大地水准面差距
geodetic origin 大地原点
geodetic surveying 大地测量
geodetic surveying system 大地测量系统
geographic coordinate graticule 地理坐标网
geographic information 地理信息
geographic information system 地理信息系统
geographic（al）position 地理位置
geographical coordinate reference system 地理坐标参考系
geographic-name data base 地名数据库
geogrid 土工格栅
geoid 大地水准面
geologic survey 地质测量
geological abbreviated drawing 地质缩图
geological analysis method 地质分析法
geological boundary 地质界线
geological condition 地质条件
geological cross section 地质横剖面图
geological environment 地质环境
geological environmental factor 地质环境要素
geological hazard 地质灾害
geological hazard assessment 地质灾害危险性评估
geological interpretation 地质判释
geological interpretation of photograph 相片地质判读（又称"相片地质解译"）
geological investigation 地质勘探
geological investigation and mapping 地质调绘
geological location 地质选点
geological longitudinal profile 地质纵剖面图
geological longitudinal section drawing 地质纵断面图
geological mapping 地质素描，地质填图
geological mapping method 地质作图法
geological plane map 地质平面图
geological prediction 地质超前预报
geological profile 地质剖面图
geological profile of bridge site 桥位地质剖面图
geological radar 地质雷达
geological sketch 地质素描
geological structure 地质构造
geological survey method 地质调查法
geological test 地质测试
geology forecast 超前地质预报
geomagnetic field 地磁场
geomat 土工网垫
geomechanical model test 地质力学模型试验
geomembrane 土工膜
geometric dimension 几何尺寸
geometric expression level of component model 构件模型几何表达等级
geometric expression level of professional model 专业模型几何表达等级
geometric information 几何信息
geometric orientation 几何定向
geometric registration 几何配准
geometric similarity 几何相似
geometrical invariability 几何不变性
geometrical rectification 几何纠正
geomorphic unit 地貌单元
geomorphological map 地貌图
geomorphy 地貌
geophysical forward modeling 物探正演
geophysical inversion 物探反演
geophysical prospecting 地球物理勘探，物理勘探，物探勘测
geophysical prospecting abnormal zone 物探异常带
geostructure 岩土构筑物

geosyncline 地槽
geosynthetic clay liner 土工膨润土垫
geosynthetics 土工合成材料
geotechnical centrifugal model test
　土工离心模型试验
geotechnical engineering 岩土工程
geotechnical engineering classification
　岩土工程分级
geotechnical engineering investigation
　岩土工程勘察
geotechnical engineering investigation level
　岩土工程勘察水平
geotechnical property 岩土性质
geotechnical test 土工试验
geotextile 土工织物
geotextile bag 土工模袋
geotextile fabric 土工布
geotextile sinking pillow 土工织物沉枕
geotextile thickness 土工织物的厚度
geotherm 地热
geothermal gradient 地温梯度
geothermal heat pump 地源热泵
geothermal reservoir caprock 热储盖层
geothermal reservoir structure 热储构造
geothermal reservoir 热储
geo-robot 测量机器人
get or obtain profit 获利
get ready for 预备
geyser 间歇泉
gift 赠品,赠予
Gigabit Ethernet (GE) 千兆以太网
Gigabit passive optical network
　吉比特无源光网络
girder 大梁,梁
girder depth 梁高
girder erecting speed 架梁速度
girder fabrication area 制梁区
girder fabrication pedestal 制梁台座
girder for small-radius curve
　小半径曲线梁
girder storage area 存梁区
girder storage in double layers 双层存梁
girder storage in single layer 单层存梁
girder storage pedestal 存梁台座
girder storage period 存梁周期
girder without ballast and sleeper
　无砟无枕梁
girder-rail interaction 梁轨相互作用
girder-type bridge 梁式桥
give back 交还

give-and-take 平等交换
glacial deposition plain 冰积平原
glacial deposit 冰川沉积
glacial drift 冰碛
glacial erosion scarp 冰蚀崖
glacial facies 冰川相
glacial landform 冰川地貌
glacial marginal fan 冰前扇地
glacier 冰川
glacier bed 冰床
glacier trough 冰川槽谷
glaciofluvial fans 冰水扇
glare 眩光
glare by reflection 反射眩光,反射炫光
glare rating 眩光值
glass electrode 玻璃电极
glass fiber felt 玻纤毡
glass fiber felt base 玻璃纤维薄毡
glass fiber grid 玻纤网
glass fiber mat waterproof sheet
　玻璃纤维毡防水卷材
glass fiber reinforced polyester felt
　玻纤增强聚酯毡
glassfiber reinforced plastic
　玻璃纤维增强塑料
glassfiber reinforced plastic cantilever
　玻璃钢腕臂
glassy 玻璃质的
glassy lustre 玻璃光泽
glauconite 海绿石
glazier 玻璃工
glen 幽谷
gliding mark 浮游测标
global navigation satellite system (GNSS)
　全球导航卫星定位系统
global package 一揽子索赔
global positioning system (GPS)
　全球卫星定位系统,全球定位系统
global system for mobile communications-railway
　(GSM-R) 铁路数字移动通信系统
global title (GT) 全局码
globe valve 截止阀
glued board 胶合板
glued insulation rail joint
　胶接绝缘接头,胶结式钢轨绝缘
gneiss 片麻岩
gneissic 片麻状构造
go into force 生效
go into operation 投入运营
goal 目的

goat-foot roller 羊足碾
godown entry 入库单
goggle 护目镜
gold digging cave 掏金洞
good faith 诚信
good gradation 级配良好
Goodman empirical formula 古德曼经验公式
goods 货物,商品,物品,物资
goods in stock 存货,现货
goods in transit 在途货物
goods loading and unloading siding 货物装卸线
goods on the spot 存货,现货
goods shed 货棚
goods track 货物线
goods warehouse 货物仓库
goodwill 友好
goodwill clause 友善条款
governing board 理事会
governing law 管辖法律,适用法律
government 政府
government bond 公债,政府债券
government budget 政府预算
government commitment 政府承诺
government credit 政府信贷
government decree 政令
government department 政府部门
government grant 政府拨款
government guarantee 政府担保
government intervention 政府干预
government investment 政府投资
government owner 政府业主
government procurement 政府采购
government procurement policy 政府采购政策
government revenue 政府税收
GPRS home subscriber server (GROS) GPRS 归属服务器
GPRS interface server (GRIS) GPRS 接口服务器
GPRS service switching point (GPRSSSP) GPRS 业务交换点
grab 抓斗式挖土机
grab crane 抓斗式起重机
grab dredger 抓斗式挖泥船
grab type portal crane 抓斗式门式起重机
graben 地堑
graben valley 地堑谷
grace of payment 支付宽限
grace period 宽限期

gradation 级配
grade 等级,级别,坡道
grade B density gauge 乙种密度计
grade crossing 道口,平交道口
grade location 坡度测设
grade of construction quality control 施工质量控制等级
grade of impermeability 抗渗等级
grade of station site 站坪坡度
grade of surrounding rock 围岩级别
grade or standard 凭规格、等级或标准买卖
grade section 坡段
grade separation 立体交叉
grade shift 等级转换
graded aggregate 级配骨料
graded crushed stone 级配碎石
graded gravel layer 承托层
graded measuring 分级计量
graded sand gravel 级配砂砾石
graded stockpiling 分级堆放
grader 分选机,平地机
gradient 接触线坡度,坡度
gradient compensation 坡度折减
gradient difference between adjacent grade sections 相邻坡段坡度差
gradient elimination 坡度减缓
gradient post 坡度标
gradient ratio 梯度比
gradient reduction 坡度折减
gradient resistance 坡道阻力
gradient within the turnout area 道岔区坡
grading 土方修整
grading curve 级配曲线
grading proportion of coarse aggregate 粗骨料分级比例
graduated cylinder method 量筒法
graduated payment 累进偿付
grain density 颗粒密度
grain gradation 颗粒级配
grain grade 粒组
grain size 粒径
grain size analysis test 颗粒分析试验
grain size distribution curve 粒径分布曲线
grain size of fill material 填料粒径
granat 石榴子石
grand 准予
grand total 累计总额
grandfather clause 不追溯条款
granite 花岗岩
granite porphyry 花岗斑岩

granite-pegmatite　花岗伟晶岩
granodiorite-porphyry　花岗闪长斑岩
granodiorite　花岗闪长岩
grant　补贴,授予,赠款
grant a certificate　签发证书
grant of representation　代表权的授予
granular　粒状
granularity rhythm　粒度韵律
granular-activated carbon adsorption tank
　颗粒活性炭吸附池
graph　图表,图解
graphic condition　图形条件
graphic editing　图形编辑
graphic processing　图形处理
graphical display　图形显示
graphical mapping control point　图解图根点
graphical user interface（GUI）　图形用户接口
graphite　石墨
grasping force　握持力
grasping strength　握持强度
grass planting　植草
grass planting with borrowed soil　客土植草
grass seed　草种
grass sowing by spraying　喷播植草
grassland　草原
graticule　格子线
grating sensor　光栅传感器
gratuitous　无偿的
gratuity　小费,捐赠,福利
grave　墓穴
gravel for upper ballast bed　上部道床碎石
gravel pile　碎石桩
gravel sand　砾砂
gravel soil　砾土
gravelly soil　砾类土,砾石土,碎石土
graveyard shift　夜班
gravimeter　重力仪
gravimetric data base　重力数据库
gravimetric method　重量法
gravimetric method of animal glue
　动物胶凝聚重量法
gravimetric method of perchloric acid dehydration
　高氯酸脱水质量法
gravitation type relay　重力继电器
gravity abutment　重力式桥台
gravity acceleration　重力加速度
gravity dam　重力坝
gravity datum network　重力基准网
gravity distribution　重力分布
gravity erosion　重力侵蚀

gravity field　重力场
gravity fire reservoir　高位消防水池
gravity flow pipe　重力流管道
gravity foundation　承重基础
gravity loading storage　滑坡仓
gravity pier　重力式桥墩
gravity pressure　自重压力
gravity prospecting　重力勘探
gravity retaining wall　重力式挡土墙
gravity water　重力水
gray level　灰阶
grease tank　隔油池,隔油井
greasy luster　油脂光泽
green area　绿地
green belt sprinkling water consumption
　绿化用水量
green corridor for railways　铁路工程绿色通道
green lighting　绿色照明
green median strip　绿化分隔带
green railway station　绿色铁路客站
greenhouse gas　温室气体
greenhouse method　暖棚法
greening　绿化
greening design　绿色防护设计
greening design drawing of typical sections
　典型地段绿化图
greening engineering　绿化工程
greening for station area　站场绿化
greening protection　绿色防护
greening rate　绿地率
greening with trees　植树绿化
greisen　云英岩
greyscale　灰度级
greywacke　杂砂岩
grid　网栅
grid flocculating tank　栅条絮凝池
grid interval　格网间隔
grid of neighboring zone　邻带方里网
grid plate　格网板
grid size　网格尺寸
grid spacing　网格间距
grid-point method　网点板法
Griffith criterion　格里菲斯准则
grillage beam　井字梁
grinding and assembling area　打磨装配区
gripper（TBM）　撑靴,支撑靴
gripper pedestal　支撑靴座
grit chamber　沉砂池
grit filter　砂滤池
gritstone　粗砂岩

gross domestic product（GDP）
国内生产总值,国内总产值
gross earnings 总收益
gross error 粗差
gross error checking 粗差检验
gross fixed investment 固定投资总额
gross floor area 总建筑面积
gross generation 总发电量
gross income 总收入
gross investment 总投资
gross national income（GNI） 国民收入总值
gross national product（GNP） 国民生产总值
gross operating spread 营业毛利
gross premium 保险费总额
gross price 毛价
gross profit 毛利,毛利润
gross profit margin ratio 毛利率
gross profit on sales 销货毛利
gross profit ratio/margin 毛利率
gross rate 毛费率
gross value 毛值
gross weight 毛重
gross working capital 流动资金总额
ground 场地
ground anchor 地锚
ground application node 地面应用节点
ground beam 底梁
ground cable 地下电缆
ground contact area 接地面积
ground control segment 地面控制部分
ground depression measurement 地表下沉量测
ground electrical power source for EMUs
动车组地面电源
ground electrode of flashover protection
闪络保护地线
ground elevation 地面高程
ground feature 地物
ground feature point 地物点
ground fissure 地裂缝
ground fracture 地裂
ground heave 地鼓
ground lease 土地租约,场地租约
ground leveling survey 面水准测量
ground microtremor testing 地基微动测定
ground micro-tremor 地脉动
ground moraine 底碛
ground nadir point 地底点
ground penetrating radar（GPR）
地质雷达,探地雷达
ground penetrating radar method 地质雷达法

ground resistance testor 接地电阻测量仪
ground roughness 地面粗糙度
ground settlement 地面沉降
ground sewage discharge facility for passenger trains 旅客列车地面卸污设施
ground stabilization 地基加固
ground stress field 地应力场
ground surface 地面
ground surface settlement 地表下沉
ground surface subsidence or upheaval
地表沉降或隆起
ground temperature annual change in depth
地温年变化深度
ground temperature zoning 地温分区
ground track 地面线
ground treatment 地基处理,地基加固
ground water 地下水
ground water abundant area 地下水富集区
ground works 土方工程
groundage 港口费用,停泊费
grounded furnace slag 磨细矿渣粉
grounding 接地
grounding bar 接地排
grounding impedance 接地阻抗
groundwater control 地下水控制
groundwater dynamics 地下水动力学
groundwater dynamics method
地下水动力学法
groundwater level 地下水位
groundwater monitoring 地下水监测
groundwater pollution 地下水污染
groundwater recharge 地下水补给量
groundwater regime 地下水动态
groundwater runoff 地下径流
groundwater storage
地下水存储量,地下水储存量
ground-train information transmission
地对车信息传输
group action 集体行为
group behavior 群体行为
group boycotts 集体抵制
group call number（GCN） 组呼号码
group call register（GCR） 组呼寄存器
group departure signal 线群出站信号机
group method of depreciation 分类折旧法
group of enterprise 企业集团
group of piles 群桩
group retarder 线束减速器
grouped observation 分组观测
grouping of a hump yard 驼峰编组场头部

grout mixer 砂浆搅拌机
grout pump 灌浆泵
grouted pitching 浆砌石护坡
grouted rubble skeleton 浆砌片石骨架
grouting 灌浆,注浆
grouting depth 注浆深度
grouting filling ratio 注浆充填率
grouting flow rate 注浆流量
grouting for surrounding rock 围岩注浆
grouting for the backside void of segment lining 壁后注浆
grouting machine 灌浆机
grouting pressure 灌浆压力,注浆压力
grouting pump 注浆泵
grouting reinforcement 注浆加固
grouting slurry 压浆浆体
grouting test 灌浆试验
grouting volume 注浆量
grouts 水泥浆
grout-stopping wall 止浆墙
growth 增长
growth rate 增长率
growth rate of construction cost 工程造价增长率
grow 发展,增长
GRP cantilever 玻璃钢腕臂
GSM service switching point (GSMSSP) GSM业务交换点
guarantee 保函,保证书,保证
guarantee deposit 保证金
guarantee for re-export of equipment 设备再出口保函
guarantee insurance 保证保险
guarantee of insurance 保险担保书
guarantee of performance 性能保证
guarantee on the first demand 首次要求即付保函,无条件保函
guarantee period 保证期
guarantee rate 保证率
guarantee security 担保
guaranteed maximum cost contracts 最高成本限价合同
guaranteed maximum price 保证最大价格
guaranteed reagent (GR) 优级纯
guarantor 保证人,担保人

guaranty period 保证期
guard 保卫
guard rail 护轮轨
guard rail of turnout 道岔护轨
guard railing 防护栏杆
guard room 值守房屋
guard stake 护桩
guard timber of bridge 桥梁护木
guardhouse 警卫室
guardian 监护人
guard's van 守车
guesstimate 粗估
guidance 引导信息
guidance sign 导向标志
guide 指导
guide line 标线
guide plate 轨距挡板
guide strap 抱箍(坠陀限制架)
guide wheel 导轮
guide/finger post 路标
guideline 指南
guidelines for procurement 采购指南
guiding construction plan 指导性施工组织设计
guiding track bracket 导轨架
guild regulations 行规
gulf 海湾
gulley 隘谷,沟谷
gully 冲沟
gummed tape 胶带
gunite 压力喷浆
guniting 喷浆
gusset plate 节点板
gutter 边沟,雨水槽,雨水口
guy 拉线
gyprock 石膏岩
gypsum 石膏
gyration radius of cross section 截面回转半径
gyro azimuth 陀螺方位角
gyro meridian 陀螺仪子午线
gyro orientation error 陀螺定向误差
gyrophic orientation geodimeter traverse 陀螺定向光电测距导线
gyrostatic orientation survey 陀螺定向测量
G-M method G-M法

H

H pipe　H形管
habitat of rare plants and animals
　珍稀动植物栖息地
habitat　栖息地
Hadean eonothem　冥古宇
hail　冰雹
hair felt　油毛毡，油毡
half circular routing system of locomotive
　半循环运转制
half kilometer post　半公里标
half-interval contour　间曲线
half-power bandwidth method
　半功率带宽法
half-power point bandwidth　半功率点带宽
half-through bridge　中承式桥
half-through type　中承式
halite　盐岩，石盐，岩盐
hallmark　货物品质证书，品质证明，优质标记
halloysite　埃洛石
halogenated agent extinguisher
　卤代烷灭火器
halogenated agent extinguishing system
　卤代烷灭火系统
haloids　卤化物
hammada　石漠
hammer　手锤
hammer enlargement pile　柱锤重扩桩
hammering check　锤击检查
hammering method　锤击法
hammerlock　锁臂
hand barrow　担架
hand haulage　人力搬运
hand hole　手孔
hand pump　手摇泵
hand rail　扶手
hand signal　手信号
handbook　手册
handcart switchgear　手车式开关柜
handcart work position indicator
　手车位置指示器
handheld　手持台
handheld metal detector　手持金属探测仪
handheld rock drill　手持式凿岩机
handing-over certificate
　接收证书，移交证书
handle　处理，手柄
handle with care　小心轻放
handling　处理，加工
handling charges　搬运费
handling expenses　搬运费
handling facility　装卸设备
handling fee　案件处理费
handling in field　现场搬运
handling machinery storage shed
　装卸机械停放间
handover and acceptance　交验
handover checklist　移交检核表
handover inspection　交接检验
handover interruption time
　越区切换中断时间
handover number（HON）　切换号码
hand-compacted concrete　人工捣实混凝土
hand-held strain gauge　手持式应变仪
hanger　吊架
hanging bar　吊筋
hanging basket　吊篮
hanging glacier　悬冰川
hanging gully　悬沟
happen　发生
harbor dues　港务费，入港税，停泊费
harbor duty　港口税，入港税
harbor project　港湾项目
harbor regulations　港口条例
harbor works　港湾工程
harbour breakwater　港湾防波堤
harbour station　港湾站

hard 坚硬	haunched beam 加腋梁
hard bending 硬弯	haunching of beam 梁腋
hard costs 工程直接费	haunching of girder 梁腋
hard currency 硬通货	hazard 公害,危险
hard disk memory unit 硬盘存储器	hazard extent 危害程度
hard disk resource 硬盘资源	hazardous cargo warehouse 危险品仓库
hard disk utilization ratio 硬盘空间利用率	hazardous chemicals
hard drying time 实干时间	化学危险品,危险化学品
hard loan 条件苛刻的贷款,硬通货贷款	hazardous crack 有害裂缝
hard point 硬点	hazardous gas 有害气体
hard rock 硬质岩,坚石,硬岩	hazardous industrial wastewater
hard rolling car 难行车	有害工业废水
hard rolling track 难行线	hazardous section 危险地段
hard soil 硬土	head end of hump yard 驼峰编组场头部
hard spot 硬点	head hardened rail 淬火轨
hardened concrete 硬化混凝土	head loss 水头损失
hardening agent 硬化剂	head of delivery 扬程
hardening point 硬化点	head of pile 桩帽,桩头
hardhat 安全帽	head office 总部
hardness 硬度	head office cost 总部费用
hardness of rock 岩石坚硬程度	head office overhead 总部管理费
hardship clause 艰难情势条款	head office parent company 总公司
hardware 五金,硬件	head tax 人头税
hardware configuration 硬件配置	head wave 首波
hard-combustible substance 难燃烧体	heading 平巷
hard-copy 硬副本	headquarters 总部
hard-soft heterogeneity of rock formation	headroom 净空高度
岩层软硬不均	headward erosion 溯源侵蚀
harmful frost heaving 有害冻胀	headway 追踪间隔
harmful frost heaving depth 有害冻胀深度	headway of trains 追踪间隔
harmonic amplification 谐波放大	head-on collision 正面冲突
harmonic check 谐波校验	head-span 软横跨
harmonic current 谐波电流	head-span wire 横承力索
harmonic distortion 谐波失真	head-span wire clamp 横承力索线夹
harmonic frequency 谐振频率	health and safety control 健康和安全控制
harmonic interference 谐波干扰	health and safety obligation
harmonic peak 谐振峰	健康及安全义务
harmonic ratio 谐波含有率	health and safety of personnel
harmonic resonance 谐波振荡	人员的健康和安全
haul 拖运	health and safety plan 健康和安全计划
haul distance 运距	health certificate 健康证明
haul distance of earthwork and stonework	health insurance 健康保险,医疗保险
土石方运距	health repair 状态修
haul distance of highway transportation	heap collapse 堆塌
公路运距	hear a claim 受理申诉
haulage 拖运	heares legitimus 合法继承人
haulier 承运人,运输工	hearing 听证会
hauling equipment 运输设备	heat accumulation 蓄热
haunch 拱腰	heat aging test 热老化试验
haunch board 承托,肋腋板	heat and moisture transfer 热湿交换

heat balance 热平衡
heat collector 集热器
heat dissipating capacity 散热量
heat dissipation from equipment 设备散热量
heat dissipation from lighting 照明散热量
heat dissipation from occupants 人体散热量
heat dissipation intensity 散热强度
heat efficiency of boiler 锅炉热效率
heat exchanger 换热器
heat flow meter 热流计
heat inlet 热力入口
heat insulation 隔热
heat island effect 热岛效应
heat loss 耗热量
heat meter 热计量表
heat metering device 热量装置
heat pipe 热管
heat pump 热泵
heat screen 隔热屏
heat source 热源
heat transfer 传热
heat transfer coefficient 传热系数
heat transfer coefficient of building envelope 围护结构传热系数
heat transfer efficiency 换热效率
heat treatment 热处理
heat/smoke detector 感温/感烟探测器
heating 采暖,加热,取暖
heating cable 发热电缆
heating degree days 采暖度日数
heating loss 加热损失
heating medium 热媒
heating medium parameter 热媒参数
heating network 热网
heating pipe 采暖管道
heating radiator 暖气片
heating system 供暖系统
heat-humidity ratio 热湿比
heat-insulating material 隔热材料
heat-melting adhesives 热熔胶粘剂
heat-pump air conditioner 热泵式空气调节器
heavily weathered 强风化
heaving of foundation pit bottom 基坑底隆胀
heavy and bulky goods area 长大笨重货区
heavy clay 重黏土
heavy compaction test 重型击实试验
heavy construction 大型工程
heavy duty dynamic cone penetrometer 重型动力触探仪
heavy duty full section ballast cleaning machine 大型全断面清筛机
heavy duty switch machine 大功率转辙机
heavy dynamic penetration test 重型动力触探
heavy gas protection 重瓦斯保护
heavy lift 重型起重机
heavy load arm 重负荷臂
heavy maintenance 大修
heavy metals contained sewage 含重金属污水
heavy rail car 重型轨道车
heavy tamping method 重锤夯实法
heavy track 重型轨道
heavy track maintenance machinery 重型线路机械
heavy weathering 强风化
heavy work 重作业
heavy-duty compaction 重型击实
heavy-duty truck 重型卡车
heavy-haul railway 重载铁路
hedge 绿篱
hedging 套期保值
heel contact 动接点
heeling-in 假植
height above sea level 海拔
height anomaly 高程异常
height difference 高低差
height limiting portal 限界门
height measurement by vertical shaft 通过立井导入高程测量
height of capillary rise 毛细水上升高度
height of converted soil 换算土柱高度
height of layered filling 分层填筑高度
height of neutral axis 中和轴高度
height of section 截面高度
height of soil column 土柱高度
height permitted 限高
height traverse 高程导线
height variation coefficient of wind pressure 风压高度变化系数
heightening pad 调高垫板
height-diameter ratio 高径比
heir 继承人
helper gradient 加力牵引坡度
helper locomotive 补机
helper locomotive section 补机地段
helper locomotive station 补机始终点站
hematite 赤铁矿
herbs 草本植物

Hercynian age/stage 海西期
hereby 据此
heritage conservation impact assessment report
 文物保护影响评估报告
herringbone drainage slope 人字排水坡
herringbone track 箭翎线
herring-bone ramp 人字坡道
hexagonal system 六方晶系
hidden cracks/gap 隐伏裂纹、间隙
hidden karst 隐伏岩溶
hidden karst map 隐伏岩溶图
hidden loss 隐蔽损失
high compressibility 高压缩性
high density profiling method 高密度剖面法
high elasticity synthetic rubber membrane
 高弹性人造橡胶薄膜
high embankment 高路堤
high fill and deep cut 高填深挖
high flood plain terraces 高漫滩阶地
high frequency switch 高频开关
high frequency switching power supply
 高频开关电源
high ground temperature 高地温
high impedance protection 高阻保护
high mode 高阶振型
high mountain 高山
high performance concrete 高性能混凝土
high pile cap 高桩承台
high platform 高站台
high polymer waterproof sheet
 高分子防水卷材
high pressure jet grouting pile 高压旋喷桩
high pressure pump 高压泵
high pressure system 高压系统
high price 高价
high priced bid 高标价投标
high quality project 优良工程
high resistance wheel set 高阻轮对
high risk works 高风险工程
high signal 高柱信号机
high slope 高边坡
high strength bolt 高强度螺栓
high stress repeated tensile and compression test
 高应力反复拉压试验
high temperature muffle furnace
 高温茂福炉
high terrace 高阶地
high tide level 高潮位
high type pavement 高级路面
high voltage circuit breaker 高压断路器
high voltage gas insulated switchgear
 高压全封闭式组合电器
high voltage power distribution room
 高压配电室
high voltage side 高压侧,一次侧,原边侧
high voltage test 高压试验
highest air pressure standard
 最高气压标准
highest bid 最高标价
highest bidder 报价最高的投标人
highest running speed 最高行车速度
highest water level 最高水位
highland 高地
highway 公路
highway crossing outdoor audible device
 道口室外音响器
highway crossing signal 道口信号机
highway engineering 公路工程
highway level crossing announcing device
 道口通知设备
highway level crossing flashing signal
 道口闪光信号
high (low)-rate biofilter
 高(低)负荷生物滤池
high-definition camera 高清摄像机
high-density electrical method
 高密度电法
high-early strength cement 早强水泥
high-flying highway 高架公路
high-level data link control (HDLC)
 高级数据链路控制协议
high-level talks 高层谈判
high-pass filter 高通滤波器
high-pressure fire system
 高压消防系统
high-quality cement 高强度等级水泥
high-quality project 优质工程
high-rise building 高层建筑
high-rise structure 高耸结构
high-speed photography 高速摄影
high-speed railway network 高速铁路网
high-speed railway (HSR) 高速铁路
high-speed track inspection car
 高速轨检车
high-speed yard 高速车场
high-strain dynamic testing 高应变法
high-strength cement 高强水泥
high-strength concrete 高强混凝土
high-strength friction grip bolt
 摩擦结合式高强度螺栓

high-temperature and extremely unstable area
　高温极不稳定区
high-temperature unstable area
　高温不稳定区
high-tensile steel bar　高强度钢筋
high-voltage bushing　高压套管
high-voltage insulator　高压绝缘子
high-voltage room　高压室
high-water period　丰水期
hill　丘陵，山丘
hillside　山坡
Himalayan　喜马拉雅期
Himalayan age　喜马拉雅期
hinge joint　铰接
hinge support　铰轴支座
hinged cantilever　旋转腕臂
hinge-jointed plate method　铰接板梁法
hire　雇佣，租借，租赁
hire purchase　租购
hired labour　雇工
hirer　出租人，雇主
histogram　直方图
historic flood level　历史洪水位
historic reservation　文物保护区
historical cost　历史成本
HIV/AIDS prevention　艾滋病预防
hodograph　时距曲线
hoist　卷扬机
hoist crane　起重葫芦
hoist reel　绞车
hoist sleeving　起吊套管
hoister　绞车
hoisting　吊装
hoisting winch　绞车
hold　待定
hold harmless　转移责任
hold track for breakdown train
　救援列车停留线
hold track for reserved locomotive
　备用机车停留线
holdback　预留款
holder　支持器，支持物
holder in due course　正当持票人
holding company　控股公司
holding company limited　控股有限公司
holding tension　握持拉伸
hold-in　保持入
hole man　爆破工
hole position survey　钻孔位置测量
hole size　钻孔直径

hole spacing　孔位间距
holiday　假期
holiday pay　假日工资
holiday with pay　带薪休假期
hollow brick　空心砖，镂空砖
hollow coil　空心线圈
hollow core slab　空心板
hollow grouted rockbolt　中空注浆锚杆
hollow pier　空心桥墩
hollow ratio of masonry unit　块体孔洞率
hollow slab bridge　空心板桥
Holocene epoch　全新世
Holocene series　全新统
holocrystalline texture　全晶质结构
home consumption　国内消费
home country　本国
home leave　探亲假
home leave allowance　回国探亲津贴
home location register（HLR）
　归属位置寄存器
home made　国内制造
home office　公司本部
home office cost　公司本部费用
home signal　进站信号机
home-freight　国内运费，回程运费
homogeneity　匀质性
homogeneous elastomer　均质弹性体
homologous point　同名像点
honeycomb　蜂窝
honeycomb structure　蜂窝结构
Hongkong interbank offered rate（HIBOR）
　香港银行同业拆放利率
honorarium　补偿金
honorary certificate　荣誉证书
honour　承兑，信用
honour a bill　承兑票据，支付期票
honour a cheque　兑付支票
honour an agreement　履约
honour one's liability　承担赔偿责任
honour the contract　信守合同
hook　挂钩，弯钩
hook clip　定位钩
hook end clamp　钩头鞍子
hooked bolt　钩螺栓
hookswitch　叉簧
hoop　管箍，抱箍（支柱上）
hoop reinforcement　环筋，环向筋
hopper bunker　漏斗仓
horizontal acoustic profile method
　水平声波剖面法

horizontal agreement　横向协议
horizontal and vertical photo control point
　相片平高控制点
horizontal angle　水平角
horizontal attitude　水平产状
horizontal axis　横轴
horizontal bar　水平杆
horizontal bearing capacity of single pile
　单桩水平承载力
horizontal bedding　水平层理
horizontal bracing　水平支撑
horizontal consolidation coefficient
　水平固结系数
horizontal construction joint　水平施工缝
horizontal control network　平面控制网
horizontal control point　平面控制点
horizontal control survey　平面控制测量
horizontal curve　平面曲线
horizontal deflection　水平偏移
horizontal displacement　水平位移
horizontal distance between the midpoint of the connection line of the TORs and the track-side face of the pole（TP）支柱侧面限界
horizontal distance　平距
horizontal drilling　水平钻井
horizontal earth electrode
　水平接地极,水平接地体
horizontal flow grit chamber　平流沉砂池
horizontal flow sedimentation tank
　平流沉淀池
horizontal frost-heave force　水平冻胀力
horizontal jet grouting pile　水平旋喷桩
horizontal monitoring control network
　平面监测网
horizontal parallax　左右视差
horizontal permeability test　水平渗透试验
horizontal pipe　横管
horizontal principal stress　水平主应力
horizontal refraction error　水平折光差
horizontal rotating angle　水平旋转角度
horizontal runoff zone　水平径流带
horizontal seismic coefficient　水平地震系数
horizontal supporting　水平支承
horizontal synchronization method
　水平同步法
horizontal type　横式
horizontal uniformly-distributed pressure
　水平匀布压力
horizontal wheel　导线平轮
horizontal wheel assembly　导线平轮组

horizontal window time　水平天窗
hornblende　角闪石
hornblendite　角闪岩
hornfels　角页岩,角岩
horseshoe-shaped tunnel　马蹄形隧道
horst　地垒
hose　软管
hospitality expense　招待费
host　主持人,主人
host country　东道国
host for call system　求助主机
host government　东道国政府
hostilities　敌对行为
hot air aging　热空气老化
hot air heating　热风采暖
hot money　短期流动资金,游资
hot plugging　热插拔
hot pressing　热压
hot running　热滑
hot spare drives　热备盘
hot standby　热备用,热备份
hot water circulating flow　热水循环流量
hot water heating　热水采暖
hot water pipe　热水管
hot water supply system　热水供应系统
hotel style office building　酒店式办公楼
hot-dip galvanization　热浸镀锌
hot-dipped galvanized steel　热浸镀锌钢
hot-melt conjunction　热熔连接
hot-press for plywood　胶合板
hot-rolled bar　热轧钢筋
hot-rolled rail　热轧钢轨
hot-rolling　热轧
hot-water boiler　热水锅炉
hourly variation coefficient　小时变化系数
hourly wage rate　小时工资
hourly wages　计时工资
hours in one machine shift　台班小时
house　商号,住宅
house bill　公司汇票,商号票据
house bill of lading（HB/L）货运提单
house for the aged　老年人住宅
household heat metering　分户热计量
household water supply point　生活供水点
household water supply station　生活供水站
housing　住房
housing construction safety assessment
　房屋建筑安全评估
housing development　住宅建设
housing fund　住房公积金,住宅建设基金

hsianghualite	香花石
hub command	枢纽指挥
huge scale landslide	巨型滑坡
huge thickness layer	巨厚层
huge thickness layer landslide	巨厚层滑坡
hull insurance	船舶保险,船舶险
hull policy	船体保险单
human failure	人为故障
human resources	人力资源
humanistic environment	人文环境
humidification	加湿
humidifier	加湿器
humidifying	湿化
humidity	湿度,潮湿程度
humidity measurement	湿度测量
humid	湿润,潮湿
hump	驼峰
hump control equipment room	驼峰动力机械室
hump crest	峰顶,驼峰峰顶
hump crest height	峰高
hump crest platform	峰顶平台
hump flyover	驼峰跨线桥
hump marshaling yard	驼峰编组场
hump mechanics repair room	驼峰机械修理室
hump of ballast shoulder	砟肩堆高
hump overpass	驼峰立交桥
hump shunter	驼峰调车人员
hump shunting	驼峰转线
hump signal	驼峰信号机
hump signal cabin	驼峰信号楼
hump signaling	驼峰信号
hump speed control system	驼峰调速系统
hump speed regulator	驼峰调速设备
hump track plan	驼峰线路平面
hump trimming signal	下峰信号
humping back signal	后退信号
humping capacity	驼峰解体能力
humping retarder	驼峰车辆溜放速度减速器
humping section	推送部分
humping signal repeater	驼峰复式信号机
humping slowing-down signal	减速推送信号
humping speed	推峰速度,推送速度
humping speeding-up signal	加速推送信号
humus soil	腐殖土
hurricane	飓风
hush money	贿赂费
hyalopsite	黑曜岩
hybrid	混合
hybrid control	混合控制
hydration heat of cement	水泥水化热
hydraulic alarm	水力警铃
hydraulic calculation	水力计算
hydraulic disorder	水力失调
hydraulic engineering	水利工程
hydraulic excavator	液压式挖土机
hydraulic fill	水力冲填
hydraulic fracturing technique	水力劈裂法
hydraulic gradient	水力坡度,水力梯度
hydraulic gradient of permeability	渗透水力梯度
hydraulic jack	液压千斤顶
hydraulic jump	水跃
hydraulic loading rate	表面负荷
hydraulic mixing	水力混合
hydraulic operating mechanism	液压操作机构
hydraulic percussion drilling	液动冲击钻进
hydraulic pile driver	液压打桩机
hydraulic precise bolt wrench	液压精密螺栓扳手
hydraulic pressure	水压
hydraulic pressure gauge	液压计
hydraulic radius	水力半径
hydraulic rail gap adjusting device	液压匀轨机
hydraulic rail jack	液压起道器
hydraulic rail straightener	液压直轨器
hydraulic rock-drilling jumbo	液压凿岩台车
hydraulic settlement device	液压式沉降仪
hydraulic slope	水力坡度
hydraulic structure	水工建筑,水工结构
hydraulic tamper	液压捣固机,液压捣固车
hydraulic tamping car	液压捣固机,液压捣固车
hydraulic track lifting tool	液压起道器
hydraulic track lining tool	液压拨道器
hydraulic truck crane	液压汽车起重机
hydraulic vibration test	液压激振试验
hydraulic works	水利工程
hydraulics property	水力学性能
hydrocarbonate	重碳酸盐
hydrocyanic acid	氢氰酸
hydrochloric acid volumetric method	盐酸容量法
hydroelectricity method	水电效应法
hydrofracturing method	水压致裂法

hydrogen ion concentration PH 值
hydrogen peroxide 过氧化氢
hydrogeochemical map of groundwater
　地下水水化学图
hydrogeological condition 水文地质条件
hydrogeological drilling 水文地质钻探
hydrogeological investigation
　水文地质勘察,水文地质调绘
hydrogeological logging 水文测井
hydrogeological section map
　水文地质断面图
hydrogeological zoning 水文地质分区
hydrogeology 水文地质
hydrographic survey 水文测量,水文调查
hydrographic surveying and charting
　水文测绘
hydrographic turbine 水轮机
hydrographical chart 水系图
hydrologic and climatic condition 水文气候条件
hydrologic data 水文资料
hydrologic observation at bridge site
　桥址水文观测
hydrological 水文的
hydrological and geological data
　水文地质资料
hydrological computation 水文计算
hydrological conditions 水文条件
hydrological cross-section 水文断面
hydrological data 水文数据
hydrological station 水文站
hydrology of bridge and culvert 桥涵水文
hydrolytic acidification 水解酸化
hydrometer method 密度计法
hydromica 水云母
hydrophilic mineral 亲水矿物
hydrophilicity 亲水性
hydropower station 水电站
hydroscopic moisture 吸着水
hydrostatic head 静水压头,静水头
hydrostatic level gauge 静力水准仪
hydrostatic leveling 液体静力水准测量
hydrostatic pressure 静水压力
hydrostatic test 水压试验
hydrothermal alteration 水热蚀变
hydroxide 氢氧化物
hygiene protection for water source
　水源卫生防护
hygiene 卫生
hygrophyte 水生植物
hypabyssal rock 浅成岩
hyperbolic curve method 双曲线法
hypocrystalline texture 半晶质结构
hypothecate 抵押
hypothecated assets
　被抵押资产,抵押资产
hypothecation 财产抵押行为
hypothesis 假定
hysteretic curve 滞回曲线
H-shaped section steel H 形型钢
H-shaped steel pole H 形钢柱

I

ice bed 冰床
ice coating 覆冰
ice cover 冰盖
ice fall 冰瀑布
ice interlayer 冰夹层
ice lake 冰湖
ice load 冰荷载,覆冰荷载
ice mound 冰丘
ice pressure 冰压力
ice sheet 冰盾
ice supplying track 加冰线
ice tongue 冰舌
ice wedge 冰楔
ice-moderate permafrost 多冰冻土
ice-poor permafrost 少冰冻土
ice-rich permafrost 富冰冻土
ice-saturated permafrost 饱冰冻土
IDA credit 国际开发协会信贷
identification 鉴别
identification of risks 风险辨识
identifier 鉴定人
identify 鉴别,鉴定,验明
identity authentication 身份认证
identity card reader 身份证件识读设备
idle 怠工
idle capacity 闲置生产能力
idle cost 窝工费用
idle current 无功电流
idle equipment 闲置设备
idle money 闲置资金
idle running 空载运行
idle time 窝工时间,停机时间,停工时间
idocrase 符山石
igneous rock 火成岩
ignition point 燃点
ignore 驳回,忽略
illegal 非法的
illegal act 不法行为,违法行为
illegal contract 非法合同
illegal payment 非法支付
illegal profit 非法利润
illegality 非法行为,违法
illicit payment 非法支付
illiquid fund 非流动资金
illite 伊利石
illite content 伊利石含量
illumination 照度
image 图像
image acquisition equipment 图像采集设备
image coordinate 像点坐标
image display equipment 图像显示设备
image processing 图像处理
image rejection 镜像抑制
image resolution 图像分辨率,影像分辨率
image server 图像服务器
image space coordinate system 像空间坐标系
image transformation 图像变换
imbricate fault 叠瓦式断层
immaterial capital 非物质资本,无形资本
immediate 即时的
immediate beneficiary 直接受益人
immediate cash consideration 即期现金报酬
immediate cause 直接原因
immediate compensation 立即赔偿
immediate delivery 立即交货
immediate destination 直接目的地
immediate payment 立即付款
immediate settlement 瞬时沉降
immediate shipment 立即装运
immersed pipeline method 沉管法
immersed tube 沉管,沉管隧道
immersible concrete vibrator 插入式混凝土振捣器

immersible gravity retaining wall
重力式浸水挡土墙
immersible subgrade 浸水路基
immersion 浸没
immersion depth 浸水深度
immersion expansion device
浸水膨胀装置
immersion ratio 浸没比
immersion test 浸泡试验
immigration office 入境签证处,移民局
immovables 不动产
immune from liability 免除责任,免责
immunities of the carrier 承运人责任豁免
immunity 豁免
immunity to interference 抗扰度
impact 影响力
impact ductility 冲击韧性
impact earthquake 冲击地震
impact evaluation report 影响评价报告
impact factor 冲击系数,冲击因数
impact force 冲击力
impact force of falling stone 落石冲击力
impact force of train 列车冲击力
impact hammer 激振锤
impact load 冲击负载,冲击荷载
impact method 冲击法
impact rolling 冲击碾压
impact sound pressure level of weighting regulation 计权规范化撞击声压级
impact sound pressure level of weighting standard 计权标准化撞击声压级
impact tester 冲击仪
impact vibration 冲击振动
impact vibration exciter 冲击激振器
impact wave 冲击波
impartiality 公正性
impeach 弹劾
impedance 阻抗
impedance at outside line 外线端阻抗
impedance component 阻抗元件
impedance muffler 阻抗复合消声器
impedance of contact line system 牵引网阻抗
impedance of feeder cable 供电线阻抗
impedance of traction network 牵引网阻抗
impedance voltage 阻抗电压
impede 妨碍
impurity content 杂质含量
impermeability 抗渗性
impermeability apparatus 抗渗仪
impermeability pressure 抗渗压力
impermeable layer(aquiclude)
不透水层(隔水层)
impermeable soil subgrade 非渗水土路基
impersonal entity 法人单位
impervious blanket 防渗铺盖
impervious soil 非渗水土
implement 实施,用具,执行
implementation of contract 合同履行
implementation schedule 执行进度
implication 暗示
implied contract 默示合同
implied objection 默示异议
implied power 默示权力
implied repo 隐含回购
implied terms 默示条款
implied warranty 默示保证
implied work 默示工作
imply 暗示,默示
import 进口
import admission 进口许可
import agent 进口代理商
import and export license 进出口许可证
import announcement 进口通知
import ban 进口禁令,禁止输入
import contract 进口合同
import declaration 进口申报单
import duty 进口关税,进口税
import duty memo 货物进口完税单
import entry 进口报关单
import letter of credit 进口信用证
import license 进口许可证
import licensing 进口许可制
import limit 进口限额
import material 进口材料
import order 进口订单
import permit 进口许可,进口许可证
import procedure 进口手续
import prohibition 禁止进口
import quarantine 进口检疫
import quota 进口配额,进口限额
import restraint 进口限制
import substitution 替代进口
import surtax(surcharge) 进口附加税
import tariff 进口关税
import tax 进口税
import trade 进口贸易
importance factor of structure
结构重要性系数
importer's currency 进口国货币
impose 强加,征收

imposed deformation　外加变形
imposition　强加,税款
imposition of surcharge　征收附加税
imposition of tax　课税
impossibility of performance　不能履约
impossible stereoscopic effect　零立体效应
impost　进口税
impoundment　集水
imprecise terms　不明确的条文
impregnated and coated asphalt amount　浸涂材料含量
impregnating　浸渍材料
imprest　预付
imprest cash　定额备用现金
imprest fund　定额备用金
imprest system　定额备用制
imprint　印记
improper　不合格的
improved gradation　级配改良
improved soil　改良土
improvement cost　改建费用,改进成本
improvement of swelling soil　膨胀土改良
impulse current　冲击电流
impulse discharge voltage　冲击放电电压
impulse grounding resistance　冲击接地电阻
impulse load　冲击负载
impulse peak head voltage　脉冲峰头电压
impulse peak tail voltage　脉冲峰尾电压
impulse track circuit　脉冲轨道电路
in accordance with　根据
in accordance with contract　按照合同
in advance　预先
in advance of　列车运行前方
in advance of a signal　信号机前方
in bad faith　恶意
in compliance with　按照
in current price　按现价
in debt　赤字,亏空
in default　违约,不作为,未履行
in force　有效
in full　全额
in rear of　列车运行后方
in rear of a signal　信号机后方
in short supply　供不应求
in stock　有库存
in writing　书面形式
inability to perform　不能履行
inactive money　呆滞资金
inactive stock　呆滞存货
inactive trust　不主动信托

inadequate　不充分的,不足
inalienable　不可分割的
inappropriate　不当的
incapability　无资格
incentive　激励
incentive bonus　激励性奖金
incentives for early completion　提前完工奖励
inception report　初始报告
inception stage　开始阶段
incidental　附带事件,杂费,杂项
incidental expenses　附带费用
incidental revenue　附带收入
incidental service　附带服务,相关服务
incidental/contingent/nonrecurring expenses　临时费
inclement weather　恶劣天气
inclination　倾斜,倾斜度
incline pushing method　斜推法
inclined cable　斜缆,斜索
inclined catenary suspension　斜链形悬挂
inclined fault　斜交断层
inclined fold　倾斜褶皱
inclined shaft　斜井
inclined stirrup　斜向箍筋
inclined tube (plate) sedimentation tank　斜管(板)沉淀池
inclined walks　斜坡走道
inclinometer　倾角仪
inclinometer tube　测斜管
include　包含
inclusive　包括的
income　收入,收益,所得
income account　收益账户
income deduction　收益扣除额
income distribution　收益分配
income insurance　收入保险
income sheet (statement)　损益表,收益表
income splitting　收益分割
income statement　利润表
income summary account　收益汇总账户
income tax　所得税
income tax deduction　所得税扣款
income tax payable　应付所得税
income tax return　所得税申报表
income tax return form　纳税申报表
income tax surcharge　所得附加税
incomes and outgoings　收支
incoming line　进线
incoming line framework　进线架构

incoming material　进库材料
incoming payment　进账
inconvenience　不方便
inconvertibility　不可兑换
inconvertible currency
　不能自由兑换的货币
incorporate　结合
incorporated company　股份公司
incorporated liability　有限责任
incorporation　归并
incorporation procedure　公司注册手续
incorporator　公司创办人
increase　增长
increase and decrease operation of traction mass
　加减轴作业
increase range　增加幅度
increase the weight of　加重
increased value insurance　增值保险
increasing cost　递增成本
increasing factor of local compressive strength
　局部抗压强度提高系数
increment　增额,增值
incremental borrowing rate　借款利率
incremental launching method　顶推法
incumbrance　财产抵押行为
incur cost　招致增加费用
indemnification　保障,赔偿
indemnify　保障,补偿,赔偿
indemnifying party　保障方
indemnities by contractor　承包商的保障
indemnities by employer
　业主的保障,雇主提供的保障
indemnity　补偿,赔款
indemnity agreement　保障协议,赔偿协议
indemnity clause　保护条款,保障条款
indemnity for damage　损坏赔偿
indemnity for risk　风险赔偿
indemnity liability　赔偿责任
indemnity of insurance　保险赔偿
indent　订货,订货单
indenture　凭单,契约
independence and impartiality　独立和公正
independent accountant　独立会计师
independent agent　独立代理人
independent audit　独立审计
independent claim settling clerk
　独立理赔人
independent compliance audit
　独立符合性审计
independent contractor　独立承包商,独立订约人

independent coordinate system　独立坐标系
independent engineer　独立工程师
independent engineering coordinate system
　工程独立坐标系
independent feeder　独立供电线
independent foundation　独立基础
independent insurer　独立保险人
independent party　独立一方
independent power source　独立电源
index　指标,索引,指数
index calculation method of budgetary estimate
　indexes　概算指标计价法
index contour　计曲线
index error of vertical circle　竖盘指标差
index expansion estimation method
　扩大指标估算法
index method of budgetary estimate
　概算指标估算法
index of building heat loss
　建筑物耗热量指标
index of construction costs　建筑费用指数
index of estimate　估算指标
index of flow velocity　流速指数
index of locomotive operation
　机车运用指标
index of prices　物价指数
index of wage　工资指数
index optimization　指标优化
indicate　表明,指示
indicating fuse　有熔断指示器的熔断器
indication　表明,表示,显示,指示
indication circuit　表示电路
indication cycle　表示周期
indication lamp　表示灯
indication panel　表示盘
indication requisition　表示条件
indication rod　表示杆
indication system for traction power supply system
　供电复示系统
indicative mark　指示性标志
indicator　表示器,指示剂,指示物
indicator method　指示剂法
indices for contract price adjustment formula
　合同价格调整公式指数
indigenous contractor　本土承包商
indigenous plant　乡土植物
indigenous species of trees　乡土树种
indirect cost　间接成本
indirect damage　间接损害
indirect drainage　间接排水

indirect expenses 间接费,间接开支
indirect fastening 分开式扣件
indirect financing 间接融资
indirect interpretation criteria 间接解译标志
indirect labour cost 间接人工成本
indirect liability 间接责任
indirect loss 间接损失
indirect loss insurance 间接损失保险
indirect material cost 间接材料费用
indirect quotation 间接标价法
indirect tax 间接税
indirect trade 间接贸易
indirection adjustment 间接平差
individual 个人的,个体
individual check 私人支票
individual consultant 个人咨询专家
individual depreciation 单独折旧
individual design 个别设计
individual enterprise 个体企业
individual estimate 单项估算
individual estimate sheet 单项估算表
individual income 个人所得
individual income tax 个人所得税
individual job procedure 单项工作程序
individual owner 个体业主
individual pre-estimate sheet 单项预估算表
individual pre-estimate 单项预估算
individual proprietorship 独资
individual test 单体试验
indivisible 不可分割的
indivisible obligation 不可分债务
indoor fire hydrant 室内消火栓
indorse 背书,批注,签注
indorsee 被背书人,受让人
indorsement 背书,批单,签注
indorser 背书人,转让人
indo-Chinese epoch 印支期
induced current 感应电流
induced geological hazards 诱发地质灾害
induced polarization method 激发极化法
induced voltage 感应电压
inducement 引诱
induction 感应
induction air conditioning system 诱导式空气调节系统
induction height survey 导入高程测量
induction unit 诱导器
inductive potential of core wire 芯线感应电位
inductive thunder 感应雷
inductive ventilation 诱导通风
inductively coupled plasma atomic emission spectrometry 电感耦合等离子体原子发射光谱法
industrial and commercial income tax 工商所得税
industrial arbitration 劳资纠纷仲裁
industrial building 工业建筑
industrial court 劳资法庭
industrial dispute 劳资纠纷,劳资争议
industrial frequency grounding resistance 工频接地电阻
industrial frequency single-phase AC traction system 单相工频交流制
industrial injury 工伤
industrial injury insurance premium 工伤保险费
industrial personal computer 工控机
industrial property right 工业产权
industrial property rights 工业产权
industrial relations 劳资关系
industrial rules 行规
industrial siding 铁路专用线
industrial station 工业站
industrial station for hazardous chemicals 危险化学品工业站
industrial ventilation 工业通风
industrial wastewater 工业废水
industrialization 工厂化
industry foundation classes (IFC) 工业基础类
industry practice 行业惯例
industry routine 行业惯例
industry tax 产业税
inefficiency 低效率
inequality 不平等
inertia moment of conversion section 换算截面惯性矩
inertial surveying system 惯性测量系统
inevitable 不可避免的
inexcusable delays 不可原谅的拖期
inferior 劣等的
inferior concrete 劣质混凝土
infilled wall in frame structure 框架填充墙
infiltration 渗透
infiltration channel discharge 渗渠出水量
infiltration coefficient 入渗系数
infiltration ditch of side slope 边坡渗沟
infiltration heat loss 冷风渗透耗热量
inflammable 易燃品
inflammable material 易燃材料

inflammable oil products 易燃油品
inflation 通货膨胀,物价暴涨
inflation adjustment 通货膨胀调整
inflation pressure 充气压力
inflator 充气机
inflexibility 横向刚度
inflow of fund 资金流入
inflow runner 进水流道
influence 影响力
influence coefficient of bearing capacity of compression member 受压构件承载能力影响系数
influence coefficient of biological damage 生物破坏影响系数
influence coefficient of creep of material 材料蠕变影响系数
influence coefficient of damage due to chemicals 化学剂破坏影响系数
influence coefficient of machinery damage 机械破坏影响系数
influence diagram 影响图
influence line 影响线
influence radius 影响半径
informal agreement 非正式协定
informal assistance 非正式协助
informal contract 非正式合同
informal record 非正式记录
information application system 信息化应用系统
information data bank 信息数据库
information delivery manual(IDM) 信息交付手册
information 信息,资讯
information display 综合显示屏
information display at arrival lobby 出站大屏
information display at departure lobby 进站大屏
information display delay 信息显示时延
information display in waiting hall 候车引导屏
information display of entrance corridor 进站通道屏
information display of exit corridor 出站通道屏
information display of tickets 票额屏
information display system of luggage and parcel 行包显示系统
information facility system 信息设施系统
information granularity 信息粒度
information management platform 信息管理平台
information management system(IMS) 信息管理系统
information model of urban rail transit engineering 城市轨道交通工程信息模型
information model 信息模型
information of train arrival and departure 列车到发信息
information packet 信息包
information processing platform 信息处理平台
information security 信息安全
information technology-based management 信息化管理
information-guided price 信息价
informatization 信息化
infrared 红外
infrared detection 红外勘探,红外探测
infrared distance measurement 红外测距
infrared journal temperature detection system 红外线轴温探测系统
infrared opposite emission detector 红外对射探测器
infrared photography 红外摄影
infrared radiator 红外线辐射器
infrared thermometer 红外线测温仪
infrastructure 基础设施,架构,公共基础设施
infrastructure project 基础设施项目
infringement 侵权行为
infringement of patent 侵犯专利权
infringe 违犯
infringer 侵权行为人
inherited property 继承的财产
inheritor 继承人
inhibiting input 禁止输入
initial 草签,小签
initial a contract 草签合同
initial approved cost(IAC) 批准的控制估算
initial balance 期初余额
initial budget 初始预算
initial collapse pressure 湿陷起始压力
initial control estimate(ICE) 初期控制估算
initial data 起始数据,原始数据
initial data error 起始数据误差
initial displacement test 初位移试验
initial exemption 初期豁免
initial expenses 创办费
initial filtrated water 初滤水
initial ground stress 初始地应力
initial ground stress field 初始地应力场

initial modulus of elasticity	初始模量
initial operation	试车
initial operation cost	开办费
initial operation fund	铺底流动资金
initial payment	首期付款
initial period of operation	运营初期
initial premium	首期保费
initial price	初期价格,牌价
initial programme	初始计划
initial resistance of filter	过滤器初阻力
initial risk	初始风险
initial setting	初凝
initial setting time	初凝时间
initial settlement	初始沉降
initial shear stress ratio	初始剪应力比
initial speed test	初速度试验
initial stage	初期
initial strength	初始强度
initial stress	初始应力
initial water level	初始水位
initialization	小签
initialling	草签
initiate procurement	开始采购
initiating arbitration	诉诸仲裁
initiation	启动
initiator	启动器
injection molding	注模成型法
injunction	禁令,禁止令,强制令
injury insurance	伤害保险
injury on job	工伤
injury to employees	雇员伤害
injury to persons and damage to property	人身伤害和财产损失
injustice	不公平
inland bill of lading	国内提单,陆运提单
inland bill of lading clause	国内提单条款
inland customs duty	内陆海关关税
inland marine insurance	内河运输保险
inland transit insurance policy	内陆运输保险单
inland transportation	内陆运输
inlet	进水口
inlet pipe	引入管
inlet time	地面集水时间
inner bottom of pipe	管道内底
inner contour of lining	衬砌内轮廓
inner cooperation	内部协同
inner diameter	内径
inner-support parking anti-rolling device	内撑式停车防溜器
input	输入,投入
input impedance	输入阻抗
input sensitivity	输入灵敏度
input source	信源
inquire	问询,询价
inquirer	调查人,询问者
inquiry	询价,询盘
inquiry in public participation	公共参与调查
inquiry response time	查询响应时间
insect and pest nuisance	虫害
insequent landslide	切层滑坡
insertion loss (IL)	插入损耗,插入损失
insertion loss of sound barrier	声屏障插入损失
inside diameter	内径
inside diameter of water pipe	水管内径
inside of fouling post	警冲标内方
insist on	坚持
insolvency	破产,无力偿付债务
insolvency assignee	破产清算人
insolvent	破产,破产者
insolvent debtor	破产债务人
insolvent law	破产法
inspection	核查,检验,检修,视察
inspection and evaluation of concrete strength	混凝土强度检验评定
inspection and evaluation	检验评定
inspection and repair room	检修室
inspection and test fee	检验试验费
inspection bridge	检查桥
inspection certificate of origin	产地检验证书
inspection certificate of quality	品质检验证书
inspection certificate of quantity	数量检验证书,工程量检查证
inspection certificate	检验合格证书
inspection certificate of value	价值检验证书
inspection clause	检验条款
inspection device	检测设备
inspection endorsement	检验签证
inspection fee	检验费
inspection for properties of glue used in structural member	结构用胶性能检验
inspection hole	检查孔
inspection list	检查表
inspection lot	检验批
inspection method	检验方法

inspection notice 检验通知
inspection of accounts 查账
inspection of documents
　文件查阅,文件审查
inspection of operation performance
　运营性能检验
inspection of site 现场视察
inspection of works 检查工作
inspection opening 检查口
inspection period 检测周期
inspection quantity 检验数量
inspection regime 检验制度
inspection report 检测报告,检查报告
inspection subject 检查内容
inspection tolerance 检测限差
inspection workshop 检查库
inspection-vehicle used only for bridge
　桥梁专用检测车
inspect 视察
inspector 检查员,视察员,检测员
installation and commissioning 安装调试
installation and removal expenses
　安装拆卸费
installation cost 安装工程费
installation curve 安装曲线
installation diagram 安装图
installation fee 安装费
installation quantity curve
　安装工作量曲线
installation test 安装测试
installation tools 安装工具
installation works 安装工程
installed capacity 安装容量
installment 分期付款,分期支付
installment accounts receivable
　应收分期账款
installment buying/hire/purchase 分期购买
installment contract 分期合同
installment sale 分期销售,延期付款销售
installment shipment 分批装运
instance model 实例模型
instantaneous gap 瞬时间隙
instantaneous loss of shunting
　瞬时分路不良
instantaneous shunting 瞬时分路
instantaneous trip current protection
　电流速断保护
instantaneous trip protection 速断保护
instantaneous tripping 速断
instantaneous wind speed 瞬时风速

instant 即时的
institute 协会,研究所
institute cargo clauses (ICC)
　协会货物条款
institute cargo clauses 协会货物条款
institute war clauses 协会战争险条款
institute strikes, riots, and civil commotions clauses
　协会罢工,暴动及民变险条款
institution 协会,制订
institutional capacity
　机构内部能力,机构自身能力
instruct 指导,指示
instruction 说明书,指令,指导,指示
instruction for variation 变更命令
instruction to contractor 给承包商的指示
instructions to bidders 投标人须知
instructive construction organization design
　指导性施工组织设计
instrument 单据,票据,工具,设备,仪器
instrument management 仪表管理
instrument of surveying and mapping
　测绘仪器
instrument room 仪表间
instrument transformer 互感器
instruments and apparatus
　(水质分析)仪器设备
insular shelf 岛架
insular slope 岛坡
insulated bus 绝缘母线
insulated conduit 绝缘导管
insulated gauge rod 绝缘轨距杆
insulated joints located within clearance
　侵入限界绝缘
insulated joints within a turnout 岔中绝缘
insulated ladder trolley 绝缘梯车
insulated overlap 绝缘锚段关节
insulated overlapped section 绝缘节
insulated rail joints 绝缘接头
insulated transition mast 绝缘转换柱
insulated wire 绝缘线
insulating course 隔断层
insulating dielectric 绝缘介质
insulating layer of capillary water
　毛细水隔断层
insulation aging 绝缘老化
(embedded) insulation bushing
　(预埋)绝缘套管
insulation concentricity 绝缘同心度
insulation coordination 绝缘配合
insulation damage 绝缘破损

insulation gap 绝缘间隙
insulation level 绝缘等级
insulation level test 绝缘强度试验
insulation material 绝缘材料
insulation mode 绝缘方式
insulation outer sheath 绝缘外护套
insulation requirement 绝缘要求
insulation resistance 绝缘电阻
insulation test 绝缘测试
insulator 绝缘子,绝缘体
insulator cleaning vehicle 绝缘子清洗车
insulator lacquer 绝缘子漆
insulator string 绝缘子串
insurable 可保险的
insurable interest 可保权益
insurable property 可保财产
insurable risks 可保风险
insurable value 可保价值
insurance 保险
insurance against accident to workmen
　工伤事故保险
insurance against loss in weight
　承保短量险
insurance against total loss only（TLO）
　只保全损险
insurance against war risk 战争保险
insurance agent 保险代理人
insurance amount 保险额,投保金额
insurance applicant 保险申请人
insurance assessment 保险估价
insurance assessor 保险公估人
insurance broker 保险经纪人
insurance certificate
　保单,保险单,保险凭证,保险证书
insurance claim 保险索赔
insurance clauses 保险条款
insurance company 保险公司
insurance compensation 保险赔偿
insurance contract 保险合同
insurance cover（coverage） 保险范围,保险总额
insurance documents 保险单据
insurance for liability 责任保险
insurance for life 人身保险,终身保险
insurance fund 保险基金
insurance group 保险集团
insurance in transit 运输保险
insurance incident 保险事件
insurance indemnity 保险赔偿
insurance interest 保险利益
insurance law 保险法
insurance liability 保险责任
insurance note 暂保单
insurance of client's property
　业主财产保险
insurance of damage 损害保险
insurance of goods 货物保险
insurance of works 工程保险
insurance period 保险期限
insurance policy 保单,保险单
insurance practice 保险惯例
insurance premium 保险费,保险金
insurance rate 保险费率
insurance risk 保险风险
insurance slip 承保条
insurance subject 保险标的
insurance surveyor 保险鉴定人
insurance to be provided by the contractor
　承包商提供的保险
insurant 投保人,被保险人
insure 办理保险,承保
insure against 投保
insured
　保险客户,保险受益人,被保险人,投保人
insured amount 保险额,投保金额,保险总额
insured item 投保项目
insured letter 保价信
insured liability 保险责任
insured loss 被保损失
insured object 保险对象
insured perils 被保风险
insured property 被保险财产
insured value 保险价值
insurer 保险人,保险人,承保人
insuring party 投保方
insurrection 暴动
intact rock 完整岩石
intactness index of rock mass（velocity index of rock mass） 岩体完整性指数(岩体速度指数)
intake 进水口
intake head 取水头部
intangible 无形的
intangible assets 无形资产
intangible fixed assets 无形固定资产
intangible goods 无形商品
intangible movables 无形动产
intangible property 无形财产,无形资产
intangible value 无形价值
intangibles 无形资产
integral cryostructure 整体状构造
integrated 整体的

integrated access device(IAD) 综合接入设备
  综合接入设备
integrated air conditioner
  整体式空气调节器
integrated automation 综合自动化
integrated automation system
  综合自动化系统
integrated change control 综合变更控制
integrated circuit(IC) 集成电路
integrated commissioning 联调联试
integrated communication network management
  通信综合网络管理(综合网管)
integrated dropper 整体吊弦
integrated earthing 综合接地
integrated earthing system 综合接地系统
integrated geophysical prospecting 综合物探
integrated hydrogeological map
  综合水文地质图
integrated investigation 综合勘察
integrated lightning protection 综合防雷
integrated management platform
  集成管理平台
integrated part load value(IPLV)
  综合部分负荷性能系数
integrated route selection 综合选线
integrated service 整套服务
integrated service digital network(ISDN)
  综合业务数字网
integrated shunting route test
  组合调车进路测试
integrated sound barrier
  整体式声屏障
integrated transport terminal
  综合交通枢纽
integrated transverse link
  完全横向连接
integrated video surveillance
  综合视频监控
integrity 诚信,整体性
intellectual 知识分子
intellectual property rights 知识产权
intelligent building 智能建筑
intelligent integration system
  智能化集成系统
intelligent network(IN) 智能网
intelligent peripheral(IP) 智能外设
intelligent platform management interface(IPMI)
  智能平台管理接口
intelligent power supply equipment
  智能化电源设备

intendment 意旨
intensified anti-corrosion measures
  防腐蚀强化措施
intensity 烈度
intensity distribution 烈度分布
intensity of radioactivity 放射强度
intensity of soil erosion and water loss
  水土流失强度
intensive fortification 重点设防
intensive train receiving and departure
  列车密集到发
intensive water outflow 集中涌水
intensively frost heave 强冻胀
intent 意向
intent to award 中标意向书
intention 动机,意向
intention for bid(IFB) 投标意向书
intention agreement 意向协定
intentional act 故意行为
intentional obstruction
  人为拖延手段,人为障碍
intentional risk 人为风险
intentional tort 故意侵权行为
inter working function(IWF)
  互联功能单元
inter-domain interface(IRDI)
  域间接口
interaction behavior between pantograph and OCS
  弓网关系
interactive conference service
  交互式会议业务
interactive marine and terrestrial deposit
  海陆交互沉积
interarea 基面
interbank offered rate 银行同业拆息率
interbedded water 层间水
interbus 旁路母线
intercept 截距
intercepting ditch 截水沟
interception and drainage ditch 截排水沟
interception ratio 截流倍数
interchange 互换,立交桥
interchange yard 交换场
intercity railway 城际铁路
interconversion 互换
interest 股权,权益,利息,利益
interest compound 复利
interest due 到期利息
interest of debt capital during construction period
  建设期债务性资金利息

interest on late payments 迟付款项利息
interest payable 应付利息
interest payment date 付息日
interest per annum 年息
interest per diem 日息
interest period 计息期
interest rate 利率
interest rate adjustment 利率调整
interest rate arbitrage 利率套购
interest rate cap 利率上限
interest rate collar 利率上下限
interest rate floor 利率下限
interest rate of arbitrage 套利率
interest rate on borrowings 借款利率
interest-bearing note 带息票据
interest-free credit 无息贷款,无息信贷
interest-free loan 无息贷款
interface 界面,交界面,接口
interface design 接口设计
interface design of sound barrier
　声屏障接口设计
interface of responsibilities 责任分界线
interface server 接口服务器
interfere 妨碍
interference 妨碍,干扰
interference anomaly 干扰异常
interference current of contact line system
　牵引网干扰电流
interference current of traction network
　牵引网干扰电流
interference from adjacent line 邻线干扰
interfering wave 干扰波
interfluve 河间地块
interfluve depression 河间洼地
interfusion 混合
interim acceptance certificate 期中验收证书
interim audit 期中审计
interim award 临时裁决
interim balance sheet 期中资产负债表
interim claim 期中索赔
interim cost 期间成本
interim determination of extension
　临时延期决定
interim expenses 期间费用
interim financial statement 期中财务报表
interim payment 期中付款
interim payment certificate（IPC）
　期中付款证书,期中支付证书
interim performance 期中业绩
interim provision 暂行规定
interim regulation 暂行条例
interim/temporary charge 临时开支
interior clear height 室内净高
interior decoration 内部装修
interior finish worker 内装修工
interior orientation 内定向
interlaminar cleavage 层间劈理
interlayer 夹层
interleaving paper 隔离纸
interleaving single coverage
　交织单网无线覆盖
interlock 闭锁
interlocked derailer 联锁脱轨器
interlocking 联锁
interlocking block pavement 联锁块铺面
interlocking by electric locks 电锁器联锁
interlocking by electric locks with color light-signals　色灯电锁器联锁
interlocking by electric locks with electric semaphore　电动臂板电锁器联锁
interlocking by electric locks with semaphore
　臂板电锁器联锁
interlocking by point detector 联锁箱联锁
interlocking chart 联锁图表
interlocking computer 联锁计算机
interlocking device 闭锁装置
interlocking equipment 联锁设备
interlocking loss 失去联锁
interlocking switch 联锁道岔
interlocking system of semaphore signal
　臂板电锁器联锁
interlocking table 联锁表
interlocking test 联锁试验
interlocking zone 联锁区
intermediary 调解人,中间人,中介物
intermediary business 中介业务
intermediate 中间人,中介人
intermediate cable terminal box
　中间电缆盒
intermediate coating 中间漆
intermediate contour 首曲线
intermediate floor 中间层
intermediate framework 中间架构
intermediate frequency 中频
intermediate passenger platform
　旅客中间站台
intermediate platform 中间站台
intermediate pole（mast） 中间柱
intermediate repair of track 线路中修
intermediate slope 中间坡

intermediate station　中间站
intermediate stiffener　中间加劲肋
intermediate system to intermediate system（IS-IS）
　中间系统到中间系统协议
intermediate term　中期
intermediate test cost　中间试验费
intermediate-focus earthquake　中源地震
intermediation　中介
intermediation rate　调停费
intermittent device　点式设备
intermittent emission　间歇排放
intermittent heating　间歇采暖
intermittent mode　点式
intermittent operation　间歇作业
intermittent speed control　点式调速
intermittent spring　间歇泉
intermittent transmission　点式传输
intermittent-continuous mode　点连式
intermittent-continuous speed control
　点连式调速
intermix　混合
intermodal container　联运集装箱
intermountane basin　山间盆地
internal accounting　内部会计
internal auditing　内部审计
internal benefit　内部效益
internal border gateway protocol（IBGP）
　内部边界网关协议
internal concrete vibrator
　插入式混凝土振捣器
internal control　内部控制
internal debt　内债
internal defect　内部缺陷
internal displacement of surrounding rock
　围岩内部位移
internal drainage system　内排水系统
internal filling of concrete
　混凝土内部充填物
internal force　内力
internal force adjustment factor
　内力调整系数
internal force redistribution　内力重分布
internal force test of pile shaft　桩身内力测试
internal friction angle　内摩擦角
internal friction angle of rock mass
　岩体内摩擦角
internal friction angle under consolidated-undrained shear　固结不排水剪切内摩擦角
internal friction angle under undrained shearing
　不排水剪切内摩擦角

internal gateway protocol（IGP）
　内部网关协议
internal lightning protection　内部防雷
internal locking device　内锁闭装置
internal port　内部端口
internal prestress　体内预应力
internal protection　内部保护
internal rate of return（IRR）　内部收益率
internal static load　内部静荷载
internal support　内支撑
internal tax　国内税
international arbitral award　国际仲裁裁决书
international arbitral tribunal　国际仲裁法庭
international cargo transportation insurance
　国际货物运输保险
international commercial terms
　国际贸易术语
international competitive bidding（ICB）
　国际竞争性招标
international construction project　国际工程
international convention　国际公约,国际惯例
international corporation　国际公司
international currency　国际通行货币
international customs　国际惯例
international double tax imposition
　国际双重征税
international double taxation　国际双重征税
international fair　国际博览会
international finance　国际金融
international framework for dictionaries（IFD）
　国际字典框架
international freight charge　国际运费
international law　国际法
international mobile subscriber identity（IMSI）
　国际移动用户识别码
international practice　国际惯例
international price　国际价格
international project　国际工程
international rules for the interpretation of trade terms（INCOTERMS）
　国际贸易术语解释通则
international sanctions　国际制裁
international shopping　国际询价采购
international syndicated loan
　国际银团贷款
international tax avoidance　国际避税
international taxation agreement　国际税收协定
International Telecommunication Union telecommunication sector（ITU-T）
　国际电信联盟远程通信标准化组

international trade 国际贸易
international trade currency 国际贸易货币
international trade law 国际贸易法
international validity 国际效力
internationally supervised containers
　　国际监管箱
internet data center（IDC）
　　互联网数据中心
internet protocol（IP） 互联网协议
Internet protocol version 4（IPv4）
　　互联网协议第 4 版
internet protocol version 6（IPv6）
　　互联网协议第 6 版
interoperability 互联互通
interphase short-circuit 相间短路
interpolated curved surface 内插曲面
interpolated elevation point 内插高程点
interpolated error equation
　　内插误差方程式
interpretation 判读；解读，解释
interpolation of the same accuracy 同级扩展
interpolation 内插法
interpretation mark 解译标志
interpretation of authority 权限的解释
interpretation of contract 合同解释
interpretation of law 法律的解释
interrogation 查问
interruption 中断
intersection 道路交叉口
intersecting point wiring 交叉式线岔
intersection angle measurement 转角量测
intersection angle 交角
intersection condition 交线条件
intersection method 交会法
intersection point 交点
intersection point of turnout 道岔中心
interstation auto-block 自动站间闭塞
interstation train operation telephone
　　站间行车电话
intertexture 交织物
intertidal zone 潮间带
interval 间距
interval between sounding points
　　测深点间距
interval of isoline 等值距
interval of topographical point 地形点间距
interval retarder location 间隔制动位
（brake）intervention curve
　　（制动）干预曲线
inter-bank loan 银行间贷款

inter-line spacing 行距
inter-MSC 局间
inter-office trunk line 局间中继线
intrados 拱腹线
intra-line spacing 株距
intra-MSC 局内
intrenched terrace 嵌入阶地
introduction of construction site 工点说明
intrusion alarm system 入侵报警系统
intrusion detection
　　入侵检测，入侵监测，入侵防范
intrusion detection system（IDS）
　　入侵检测系统
intrusion insulation test 侵限绝缘测试
intrusion prevention system（IPS）
　　入侵预防系统
intrusive ice 侵入冰
intrusive rock 侵入岩
invalid code 非法码字
invalidate the contract 废约
invalidity 无效性
invar baseline tape 钢瓦基线尺
invar level rod 钢瓦尺
invar rods 钢钢尺
invariability in price 价格不变性
inventory 存货，现货，库存，库存储备量
inventory allowance 存货允许限度
inventory checking 库存盘点
inventory control 存货管理
inventory cut-off date 盘存截止日
inventory data 存货数据
inventory list 库存清单
inventory method of depreciation
　　盘存折旧法
inventory rails 周转轨
inventory sheet 存货盘点表，盘存单
inventory turnover 存货周转
inventory valuation 存货估价
inverse analysis 反演分析
inverse attribute 反向属性
inverse of weight matrix 权逆阵
inverse plummet observation（also known as "inverse plummeting"）
　　倒锤线观测（又称"倒锤法"）
inversion anticline 倒转背斜
invert 仰拱
invert filling 仰拱填充
invert trestle 仰拱栈桥
inverted attitude 倒转产状
inverted filter 反滤层

inverted filter layer of groundwater intake structure 地下水取水构筑物反滤层
inverted siphon 倒虹吸管
inverted siphon culvert 倒虹吸涵
inverted strata 倒转岩层
inverter 逆变器
invest 投入,投资
investigation 调查,勘察,考察
investigation classification 勘察分级
investigation depth 探测深度
investigation for construction organization 施工组织调查
investigation team 勘测队
investigation test 勘察试验
investment 投资
investment allowance 投资补贴额
investment appraisal 投资评价
investment bank 投资银行
investment budget 投资预算
investment composition 投资构成
investment estimation for soil and water conservation facilities 水土保持投资估算
investment in capital construction 基本建设投资
investment loan interest during construction period 建设期投资贷款利息
investment of capital construction 基建投资
investment of the said year 当年投资
investment of work proposed to be finished 拟完工程计划投资
investment phase 投资阶段
investment pre-estimate 投资预估算
investment priority 优先投资
investment recovery period 投资回收期
investment return 投资回报
investment scale 投资规模
investment securities 投资证券
investment trust 投资信托
investment turnover 投资周转
investor 投资者
invisible asset 无形资产
invisible trade 无形贸易
invitation for bid (IFB) 投标邀请函
invitation for offer 要约邀请
invitation for prequalification 资格预审邀请书
invitation to bid (tender) 招标
invitation to tender 投标邀请函
invoice 发货清单,发票,开具发票
invoice value 发票价值
invoice with document attached 附有单证的发票

involuntary bankruptcy 强制破产
inward cash remittance 现金汇入
inward charges 入港费用
in-house capabilities 机构内部能力,机构自身能力
in-house capacity 厂内生产能力
in-kind payment 实物支付
in-laid terrace 内叠阶地
in-process 加工
in-running contact line 工作支
in-service freight car inspection yard 装卸检修作业场
in-service rail 在役钢轨
in-site parking lot 场内停车场
in-site road 场内道路
in-situ concrete pile 现浇混凝土桩
in-situ direct shear test of rock 岩石原位直接剪切试验
in-situ test 现场原位测试,原位试验
in-situ testing 原位测试
in-situ-cast concrete 模筑混凝土
in-station connecting line 站内联络线
in-train repair 不摘车修理
iodide 碘化物
iodine spectrophotometric method 碘量分光光度法
iodometry 碘量法
ion exchange adsorption capacity 离子交换吸附量
ion exchange method 离子交换法
ion exchange resin 离子交换树脂
ionospheric delay 电离层延迟
ion-selective electrode method 离子选择电极法
IOU (I owe you) 欠条
IP address IP 地址
IP video conference system IP 会议电视系统
iron pad 铁垫板
iron scaffold 金属脚手架
irradiance 辐射照度
irreconcilable 不可调解的
irredeemable currency 不能自由兑换的货币
irrefutable 驳不倒的
irregular lump test 不规则块体试验
irregular tax 杂税
irregular triangulateration network 不规则三角网
irregularity of track under train load 动态不平顺

I

irregularity of unloaded track 静态不平顺
irreversible serviceability limit state
不可逆正常使用极限状态
irrevocable 不可撤销的
irrevocable credit 不可撤销的信用证
irrevocable documentary（letter of）**credit**
不可撤销的跟单信用证
irrevocable letter of credit
不可撤销的信用证
irrevocable letter of guarantee
不可撤销的保函
irrigable land 水浇地
irrigation 灌溉
irrigation canal 灌渠
irrigation channel 灌溉渠
island 岛屿
island arc 岛弧
island platform 岛式站台
island shelf 岛架
island slope 岛坡
island talik 岛状融区
island-connecting sandbar 连岛砂坝
island-like permafrost region 岛状冻土区
isobaric waterline method 等压水位线法
isobath 等深线
isobath interval 等深距
isolating transformer 隔离变压器
isolation layer 隔离层
isolation mode 隔离模式
isolation of risk 风险的分离
isolation ventilation 隔绝通风
isoline 等值线
isoline method 等值线法

isometric drawing 轴测投影图
isoseismal 等震线
isoseismal map 等震线图
isothermal jet 等温射流
isotope tracer logging 同位素示踪测井
isotropic consolidation 等向固结
issuance 颁布
issue 颁布，颁发，签发，发行
issue a certificate 签发证书
issue an invoice 开具发票
issue bidding documents 颁发招标文件
issue of FPC（final payment certificate）
签发最终付款证书
issue of IPC（interim payment certificate）
IPC（期中付款证书）的签发
issue of material 材料发放
issuing bank 开证银行
issuing date 开出日期
Information Technology（IT） 信息技术
item 项目
item depreciation 单项折旧
item of expenditure 开支项目
item of works 分项工程
itemize 逐条记载
itemized price 分项价格
itemized statement 明细记录
items of expenditure 支出项目
items of train operation disturbance
行车干扰项目
itinerary 航线，日程表，行程
I-beam 工形梁，工字梁，I形梁
I-girder 工形梁，工字梁，I形梁
I-shaped section steel 工字钢

J

J ring blocking step　J 环障碍高差
jack　千斤顶
jacking block　顶铁
jacking mechanism　顶升机构
jacking up of bridge　桥梁顶升
jack-hammer　冲击钻孔机
jack-in construction method　顶进法
jargon　行话
jenny scaffold　活动脚手架
jerque note　海关检查证,结关单
jerquer　船货检查员
jet　射流
jet fan　射流风机
jet grouting method　高压喷射注浆法
jet grouting pile　旋喷桩
jet grouting pile constructed from ground surface
　地表旋喷桩
jet reverse circulation drilling
　射流反循环钻进
jet zone　射流区
jig point　基点
jitter　抖动
job changes　工程变更
job completion　工程竣工,工作完成
job cost journal　工程成本日记账
job cost ledger　工程成本分类账
job cost record　工程成本记录
job cost sheet　分批成本单
job cycle　工作周期,作业循环
job description　作业描述
job log　作业日志
job lot method　分批法
job mixed concrete　现场搅拌混凝土
job opening　招工
job organization　工程组织机构
job overhead cost　工程费
job performance　工作业绩
job rate　生产定额
job record　工作记录
job security　就业保障
job site　工地
job site cleanup　工地清理
job site facilities　工地设施
job site overhead　现场管理费
job site survey　工地勘察
job site visit　现场考察
job specification　操作规程,工作规范
job supervisor　监管人员
job title　职称
job vacancy　职位空额
jobber　临时工
jobbing　计件工作
join　结合
joinder　共同诉讼
joint　接缝,节理,接头,结合
joint account　联合账户
joint act　共同行为
joint alteration degree　节理蚀变度
joint and several liability
　共同和各自的责任,连带责任,各自负有连带和单
　独责任,连带责任
joint bar　接头夹板
joint bid　联合投标
joint clamp　接头线夹
joint commissioning and running test
　联调联试及运行试验
joint creditor　共同债权人
joint density　节理密度
joint filler　接缝填料
joint fundraising　联合筹资
joint guarantee　联合担保,联名保证
joint insurance policy　联合保险单
joint insured cross liability clause
　共保交叉责任条款
joint invitations to bid/tender　联合招标
joint liability　共同义务

joint mortgage　联合抵押
joint names　联名
joint operation　联营
joint ownership　共同所有权
joint plane　节理面
joint production　合作生产
joint resistance　接头阻力
joint rose diagram　节理玫瑰图
joint roughness　节理粗糙度
joint set number　节理组数
joint sign　接头标
joint state and private enterprise　公私合营企业
joint sureties　连带保证人
joint surface　节理面
joint tenant　共同租赁人
joint tendering　联合投标
joint trial operation and engineering dynamic supervision fees　联合试运转及工程动态监测费
joint underwriting　联合保险
joint venture　合资企业
joint venture agreement　合资企业协议
joint venture bank　合资银行
joint venture company　合资公司
joint venture partner　联营体伙伴
joint venture railway　合资铁路
joint well yield　结合井出水量
joint/seam tensile strength　接头接缝拉伸强度
jointed track　有缝线路
jointless track circuit　无绝缘轨道电路
joint-intensive zone　节理密集带

joist　小梁
journal　分录簿, 日记账
journal entry　分录, 会计分录
journal voucher　分录凭单, 转账凭证
journeyman　熟练工人
judge　法官, 审判员, 判决
judgment　判决
judicial assistance　司法协助
judicial person　法人
jumbo drill　钻孔台车
jumper　跳线
jumper clamp　跳线线夹
jumper cross arm　跳线肩架
jumping rammer　蛙式打夯机
junction box　接线箱
junction plate　连接板
junction station　接轨站, 衔接站
junctura（pl. juncturae）　结合
junior accountant　初级会计师
Jurassic period　侏罗纪
Jurassic system　侏罗系
juridical practice　司法惯例
juridical recorder unit（JRU）　司法记录单元
juridical recorder unit　司法记录器
jurisdiction　管辖权, 司法权, 法律管辖区
jury　陪审团
justifiable　正当的
justification　证实
JV undertaking　联合体承诺书
JV's lead partner　联营体负责人

K

K_0 consolidation　K_0固结
Kaiser effect　凯塞效应
kame　冰砾阜
kaolin　高岭土
kaolinite　高岭石
kar　冰斗
karez　坎儿井
Karhunent-Loeve transformation　卡洛变换
karst　岩溶,喀斯特
karst base level　岩溶基准
karst basin　岩溶盆地
karst cave　溶洞
karst cave roof　溶洞顶板
karst collapse　喀斯特塌陷
karst depression　岩溶洼地
karst fissure ratio　岩溶裂隙率
karst groove　溶槽
karst landform　喀斯特地貌
karst peneplain　溶蚀准平原
karst spring　岩溶泉
karst subgrade　岩溶路基
karst trace　溶痕
karst water　岩溶水
keelage　入港税,停港费
keen price　有竞争力的价格
keep　保持
keep a contract　遵守合同
keep account　记账
keeper　保管人
Kelvin connection　凯文接法
keratophyre　角斑岩
kersantite　云斜煌岩
key component　关键部件,关键组成部分
key event schedule　关键事件进度表
key ledger　总分类账
key milestone　关键里程碑
key performance index　关键绩效指标
key personnel　关键人员,主要人员
key protection region of soil erosion and water loss　水土流失重点预防保护区
key rehabilitation region of soil erosion and water loss　水土流失重点治理区
key supervision region of soil erosion and water loss　水土流失重点监督区
key test　密钥测试
Keyboard Video Mouse (KVM)　多计算机切换器
keystone document　基本文件
kickback　回扣
kickout　解雇
kick-off meeting　开工会
kidnap ransom insurance　绑架赎金险
kilometer measure　里程丈量
kilometer post　公里标
kilometer stake　公里桩
kilometer stone　里程桩
kilometrage　里程
kilowatt-hour meter　电表
kimberlite　金伯利岩
kinematic envelope　车辆动态包络线
kinematic load gauge　车辆的动态限界
kinematic viscosity　运动黏度
king-tower　主塔
kink　硬弯
kitchen　厨房
knob　手柄
known data　起始数据
known hazards　已知危险
known loss　已知损失
know-how　技术诀窍,专门技术,技术秘密
know-how contract　专有技术合同
know-how license　专有技术许可证
Krasovsky ellipsoid　克拉索夫斯基椭球
kyanite　蓝晶石

L

L box filling ratio　L 型仪充填比
label　标记,标签,标识
labor consumption　人工消耗量
labor cost　人工费
labor cost difference　人工费价差
labor cost of base period　基期人工费
labor force　劳动力
labor hygiene　劳动卫生
labor insurance premium　劳动保险费
labor protection　劳动保护
labor protection fee　劳动保护费
labor protection fees for workers　
　生产工人劳动保护费
labor safety and health　劳动安全卫生
labor safety and hygiene　劳动安全卫生
labor safety and hygiene facilities　
　劳动安全卫生设施
laboratory　化验间
labour　工人
labour abundant　劳动力充裕
labour agreement　劳资协议
labour and management　劳资双方
labour arbitration　劳资纠纷仲裁
labour capacity　劳动生产能力
labour cost　人工费用
labour discipline　劳动纪律
labour dispute　劳资纠纷,劳资争议
labour disturbance　工潮
labour efficiency　工作效率,劳动效率
labour hour rate　工时率
labour intensive　劳动密集
labour law　劳动法,劳工法
labour monitoring　劳工监督
labour only subcontracting　劳务分包
labour only subcontractor　劳务分包商
labour practice　雇工惯例
labour productivity　劳动生产率
labour recruitment　招募劳工
labour relations　劳资关系
labour remuneration　劳动报酬
labour resources　人力资源
labour service charge　劳务费
labour service income　劳务收入
labour service rate　劳务费率
labour shortage　劳力不足
labour supply agreement　劳务协议
labour supply contract　劳务合同
labour supply planning　劳务计划
labour surplus　劳动力过剩
labour turnover rate　人工周转率
labour union　工会
labour unrest　劳资争议
labour-management contract　劳资合同,劳资协议
labradorite　拉长石
laccolith　岩盘
laches　迟误,疏忽
lacing and batten elements　缀材(缀件)
lacing bar　缀条
lack of evidence　缺乏证据
lack of materials　材料短缺
lack of stock　库存短缺
lacustrine deposit　湖积
lacustrine plain　湖积平原
ladder　梯子
ladder rack　梯架
ladder track with multiple frog angles　
　复式梯线
lading　船货,装载
lading permit　装船许可证
lading port　装货港
lag　滞后
lag duration　滞后工期
lagging jack　拱架
lagging phase　滞后相
lagoon　潟湖
lagoon facies　潟湖相

lake 湖泊
lake water 湖水
lambda type structure 人字形构造
lamellar tearing 层状裂纹
laminar flow 层流
laminated layer 薄细层
laminated reinforced concrete flexural member
  叠合式混凝土受弯构件
laminated rubber bearing 板式橡胶支座
laminated wood 胶合板
lamprophyre 煌斑岩
land acquisition area 征占地面积
land boundary 用地界
land boundary marker 用地界桩
land boundary settlement cost 用地勘界费
land boundary survey 地界测量
land carrier 陆运承运人
land certificate 地契,土地证
land compensation fee 土地补偿费
land consolidation 土地整理
land disturbance 土地扰动
land for construction 建设用地
land for temporary works 临时工程用地
land improvement 土地改良
land information system 土地信息系统
land map 用地图
land patent 土地转让证
land planning survey 土地规划测量
land price 地价
land reclamation
  土地复垦,用地复垦,土地整治
land reclamation works 土地整治工程
land rehabilitation 复耕,土地复耕
land sonar method
  陆地声呐法,极小偏移距高频反射连续剖面法
land subsidence 地面沉降,地面沉陷
land tax 土地税
land transportation 陆运
land treatment 土地处理
land trust certificate 地产信托证
land type 土地类型
land use fee 土地使用费
land use tax 土地使用税
landed cost 到岸成本
landed price 抵岸价,卸货价格
landed property 地产
landed quality 到岸品质
landed weight 卸货重量
landfill 垃圾堆场
landfill site 填土场

landform 地貌
landform line 地形线
landform observation point 地貌观测点
landform unit 地貌单元
landing a count 栈单
landing account 卸货记录
landing certification 卸货证书
landing charges 卸货费
landing order 卸货通知单
landing place 卸货地点
landing stage 趸船,浮码头
landmark 界标
landscape 景观
landscape lighting 景观照明
landscape reservation 景观保护区
landslide 滑坡,山体滑坡,滑坡塌方
landslide bed 滑坡床
landslide deposit 滑坡堆积
landslide depression 滑坡洼地
landslide joint 滑坡节理
landslide mass 滑坡体
landslide monitoring 滑坡监测
landslide platform 滑坡台地
landslide size 滑坡规模
landslide terrace 滑坡台坎
land 用地,土地
Langer bridge
  朗格尔式桥(又称"刚性系杆柔性拱桥")
language of agreement 协议书语言
language of arbitration 仲裁语言
language of contract 合同语言
lapped length of steel bar 钢筋搭接长度
lapse 权利失效
lapsed policy 失效保险单
larceny 盗窃
large capacity hump 大能力驼峰
large mileage end 大里程端
large panel concrete structure
  混凝土大板结构
large passenger station 大型旅客车站
large scale landslip 大型滑坡
large scale marshalling station 大型编组站
large scale material storehouse 材料厂
large scale mine car 大型矿车
large scale temporary facilities
  大型临时设施
large slab spraying and cutting method
  喷大板切割法
large station 大型车站
large station building 大型站房

large track maintenance machinery depot 大型养路机械段
large track maintenance machinery repair workshop 大机检修库
large-diameter well yield 大口井出水量
large-scale aerial photogrammetry 大比例尺航空摄影测量
large-scale enterprise 大型企业
large-scale topographical map 大比例尺地形图
large-scale topographic mapping 大比例尺地形测图
large-size turnout 大号码道岔
laser alignment measurement 激光准直测量
laser alignment method 激光准直法
laser detector 激光对射探测器
laser direction-guiding system 激光导向机构
laser distance measurement 激光测距
laser plumbing 激光投点
last 持续
last invoice price method 最后进价法
last relevant balise group 最近相关应答器组
late acceptance 延迟接受
late bid 迟到的投标书
late Cambrian epoch 晚寒武世
late Carboniferous epoch 晚石炭世
late Cretaceous epoch 晚白垩世
late delivery 延迟交货
late Devonian epoch 晚泥盆世
late Jurassic epoch 晚侏罗世
late Ordovician epoch 晚奥陶世
late Paleozoic era 晚古生代
late payment 迟到的付款
late Permian epoch 晚二叠世
late Pleistocene epoch 晚更新世
late shipment 延迟装运
late Silurian epoch 晚志留世
late Sinian epoch 晚震旦世
late start date 最晚开工日期
late Triassic epoch 晚三叠世
latency 时延
latent defects insurance 潜在缺陷保险
latent defect 潜在缺陷
latent heat 潜热
lateral aisle in container area 箱区横向通道
lateral arrangement 横列配置
lateral axle 横轴
lateral bending 侧向弯曲
lateral bracing system 侧向水平联结系
lateral collision protection 侧撞防护
lateral confinement 侧限
lateral deviation 横向偏差
lateral deflection of contact wire 接触线横向偏移量
lateral dip 旁向倾角
lateral displacement 侧向位移
lateral displacement rigidity of floor 楼层侧移刚度
lateral displacement rigidity of structure 结构侧移刚度
lateral drainage facility 横向排水设备
lateral effective stress 侧向有效应力
lateral enlargement factor 横向增大系数
lateral error of traverse 导线横向误差
lateral force 之字力
lateral force factor 横向水平力系数
lateral force resisting wall 抗侧力墙体结构
lateral intersection 侧方交会
lateral launching of beam 横移梁
lateral launching of girder 横移梁
lateral logging 横向测井
lateral moraine 侧碛
lateral moraine ridge 侧碛垅
lateral movement of pantograph 受电弓横向偏移
lateral overlap 旁向重叠
lateral passing speed of train 列车侧向通过速度
lateral pile resistance 桩侧阻力
lateral pressure 侧向压力
lateral pressure coefficient 侧压力系数
lateral refraction 旁折光
lateral reinforcement 横向钢筋
lateral resistance of track bed 道床横向阻力
lateral resisting system 抗侧力体系
lateral rigidity of bridge 桥梁横向刚度
lateral slope of ground 地面横坡
lateral stiffener 横卧板,横向加劲肋
lateral stiffener plate 卡盘
lateral stiffness 横向刚度
lateral stop block 侧向挡块
lateral structure 横向结构物
lateral sway force of train 列车横向摇摆力

lateral tear force 横向撕裂力
lateral train reception and departure 侧向接发列车
lateral vibration acceleration 横向振动加速度
lateral vibration amplitude 横向振幅
laterite 红土
latest date 最晚日期,截止日期
latitude 纬度
latitudinal structure 纬向构造
latticed steel column 格构式钢柱
launching 步进
launching shaft 工作井
laundry sewage 洗涤污水
lava flow 岩溶流,熔岩流
lava flow landform 熔岩流地形
lava sheet 熔岩被
law circle 法律界
law court 法院
law firm 律师事务所
law governing the contract 合同管辖法
law of company 公司法
law of contract 合同法
law of contract jurisdiction 合同管辖法
law of enterprises 企业法
law of insurance 保险法
law of merchant 商法
law of nations 国际法
law office 律师事务所
lawful 法定的,合法的
lawful bearer 合法持票人
lawful earned income 合法收入
lawful money 法定货币
lawful right 合法权利
lawful successor 合法继承人
lawn 草坪
lawn nursery strip 植生带
laws 法律
lawsuit 提起诉讼
lay 放置,铺筑
lay days 停泊时间,装卸期限
lay down 制订
lay duty on imports 对进口货课税
lay time 装卸时间
laydown machine 铺设机
layer 图层
layered bedding 分层铺垫
layered filling 分层填筑
layering degree 分层度
layer-wise rolling and compaction 分层碾压
layer-wise summation method 分层总和法
laying place 埋设位置
laying through track 过轨敷设
layout 布局,草稿,草图,设计,施工场地图
layout chart 线路图
layout design 平面设计
layout plan 平面布置图,布置图
layout survey 定线测量
lay-down yard 材料设备存放场
licence 许可证
total lead 总铅量
lead carbonate 碳酸铅
lead content 铅含量
lead contractor 牵头承包商
lead partner 牵头方
lead rail 导轨
lead sheath 铅护套
lead time 备购时间,订货周期
lead track 牵出线
lead wire 引出线
leading counsel 首席律师
leading hand 工头
leading locomotive 本务机车
leading phase 引前相,超前相
leading underwriter 首席承保人
leading unit 本务端设备
leady sewage 含铅污水
lead-acid maintenance-free battery 铅酸免维护蓄电池
lead-in line 引入线
leakage 渗漏水,泄漏,泄露,渗漏
leakage coaxial cable (LCX) 漏泄同轴电缆
leakage current 泄漏电流,漏电流
leakage detecting test 检漏测试
leakage detector 查漏仪
leakage flow wheel set 泄流轮对
leakage impedance 泄漏阻抗
leakage inductance 漏感
leakage reactance 漏抗
leakproofness 密封性
lean construction 精益建造
leaning column 摇摆柱
lease 租借权,出租,租借,租赁,租期,租约
lease agreement 租约
lease charges 租用费
lease financing 租赁融资
lease purchase 租赁购买
leaseback 回租,售后回租
leased land 租用土地

leasehold 租借权，租借物，租赁权，租期
leaseholder 承租人
leasing company 租赁公司
leasing guarantee 租赁保函
least square method 最小二乘法
least squares adjustment 最小二乘平差
leave 休假
leave with pay 带薪休假
leave without pay 无薪休假
LED color light signal mechanism
  LED 色灯信号机机构
ledger 分户账，分类账
ledger form 分类账表格
ledger gross weight 总账
ledger journal 分类日记账
leeward slope 背风坡
Lee's volumetric flask method 李氏量瓶法
left hand turnout 左开道岔
left-handed machine 反装
leg length 焊脚尺寸
legal 法定的，法律的，合法的
legal action lawsuit 诉讼
legal act 法律行为
legal adviser 法律顾问
legal agent 法定代理人
legal assets 法定资产
legal authority 合法当局
legal authorization 合法授权
legal basis 法律依据
legal capacity 法定身份
legal capital (value) 法定资本
legal compensation 法定赔偿
legal construction 法律释义
legal consultation 法律咨询
legal costs 诉讼费
legal document 法律文件
legal entity 法定单位，法人实体，法人单位
legal fact 法律事实
legal holiday 法定假日
legal insurance 法定保险
legal liability 法定负债，法律责任
legal liquidation 法定清算
legal mortgage 法定权益按揭，合法抵押
legal person 法人
legal personality 法人资格
legal proceedings 法律诉讼程序
legal provisions 法律规定
legal representative 法定代表，法定代理人
legal requests 合法请求，合理索赔
legal right 法定权利

legal rules 法律规定
legal sanction 法律制裁
legal service charge 律师服务费
legal standing 法律身份
legal system 法系
legal tender 法定货币
legal title 法定所有权，法定资格
legal weight 法定重量
legality 合法，合法性
legally-binding agreement
  有法律效力的协议
legend 图例
legislate 立法
legislation 法规
legislature 立法机构
legitimacy 合法
legitimate 合法的
legitimate claim 合法请求，合理索赔
legitimate cost 正当成本
legitimate heir 合法继承人
legitimate income 合法收入
legitimate right 合法权利
lend at interest 有息贷款
lender 出借人，贷款方
lending limit 贷款限额
lending rate 贷款利率
lending term 贷款期限，贷款条件
length of collimation line 视准线长度
length of grade section 坡段长度
length of railway in operation
  线路运营长度
length of station site 站坪长度
length of track construction 线路建筑长度
length variation in Gaussian projection
  高斯投影长度变形
lengthened chain 长链
lengthy cargo 起长货物
length-fixed rail 定尺钢轨
lens 镜头
lens front (back) node 物镜前(后)节点
lens radial distortion 透镜径向畸变
lens tangential distortion 透镜切向畸变
lenticle 透镜体
lenticular beam 鱼腹式梁
leopoldite 钾盐
lessee 承租人
lessor 出租人
less-than-carload freight yard 零担货场
less-than-carload goods 零担货物
less-than-truckload goods 零担货物

let 出租
letter 信函
letter of acceptance 中标函,中标书,中标通知
letter of acknowledgement 回函,确认函
letter of advice 通知书
letter of application 申请书
letter of assignment 转让书
letter of assurance 保函,保证书
letter of attorney 授权书,委任书
letter of authority for test 试验委托书
letter of award 授标函
letter of confirmation 确认书
letter of credit (L/C) 信用证
letter of credit at sight 即期信用证
letter of credit expiration date
　信用证失效日期
letter of delegation 委托书
letter of deposit 抵押证书
letter of guarantee for bid 投标保函
letter of guarantee for loan 借款保函
letter of guarantee for maintenance
　质量维修保函
letter of guarantee (L/G) 保函,保证书
letter of hypothecation 抵押证书
letter of indemnity 赔偿保证书
letter of inquiry 询价函件
letter of intent 意向书,中标意向书
letter of introduction 介绍信,推荐信
letter of invitation (LOI) 邀请函
letter of notice 通知书
letter of offer 报价函
letter of patent 专利证书
letter of proxy 委托书
letter of recommendation 介绍信,推荐信
letter of setoff 留置权书
letter of subrogation 代位授权书
letter of tender 投标函,投标书
letter of trust 信托书
letters 许可证,证书
leucite 白榴石
leucite phonolite 白榴石响岩
level 级别,水平面,水准仪,高程
level 5″,2″,6″ instrument
　5″、2″、6″级仪器
level crossing 道口,平交道口,平面交叉
level crossing cabin 道口房
level crossing obstruction signal
　道口遮断信号
level crossing pavement 道口铺面
level crossing safety 道口安全

level crossing signal 道口信号
level grade between opposite gradients 分坡平段
level meter 电平表
level of details 模型精度
level of geometric detail 几何精度
level of information detail 信息深度
level of model definition 模型精度
level oscillator 电平振荡器
level premium 平均保险费
level rope tape method 水准仪绳尺法
level stretch of grade crossing 道口平台
level tendering 水准投标
level transition 级间转换
level transition sign board
　级间转换标志牌
level transition test
　级间转换测试,级间切换测试
level tube 水准管
leveling 水准测量
leveling network 水准网
leveling origin 水准原点
leveling rod 水准尺
leveling section 水准测段
levelling 抄平
levelling instrument 水平尺
levelling production 均衡生产
levelling property 流平性
levels of protection 防护等级
levels of reference 基准高程
lever arm oedometer 杠杆固结仪
lever rule method 杠杆原理法
leverage 财务杠杆,举债经营,杠杆作用
leverage ratio 杠杆比率,举债经营比率
leveraged lease 衡平租赁
lever-type pressure apparatus
　杠杆压力仪装置
levy 征收税款,征税
levy a fine 罚款
levy a tax 课税
levy duties on 征税
lex non scripta 不成文法
lex scripta 成文法
liabilities 负债
liabilities account 负债账户
liabilities payable on demand 即付债务
liability 义务,责任,债款,债务
liability clause 责任条款
liability for acceptance 承兑责任
liability for breach of professional duty
　违反专业职责的责任

L

liability for care of the works
　照管工程的责任
liability for damage　损害责任
liability for delay　误期责任
liability for fault　过失责任
liability for satisfaction　清偿责任
liability insurance　责任保险
liability of the consultant　咨询专家的责任
liability reserves　负债准备金
liability risk　责任风险
liable　有义务的
liable to customs duty　应付关税
liaise　联络
liaison　联络
liaison circuit　联系电路
liaison circuit among locomotive depots
　机务段联系电路
liaison circuit among stations
　站间联系电路
liaison circuit between yards
　场间联系电路
liaison circuit with automatic blocks
　自动闭塞联系电路
liaison circuit with block signaling
　区间联系电路
liaison circuit with highway crossings within the station　站内道口联系电路
liaison office　联络办事处
liaison officer　联络官
liberite　锂铍石
licence　牌照,执照
licence duty　执照税
licence fee　牌照费,专利费
licence plate　牌照
licencee　许可证接受人
license　许可证,执照
license tax　牌照税
licensed architect　注册建筑师
licensed contractor　注册承包商
licensee　许可证接受人
licenser　出证方,许可证颁发人
licensing agreement　许可证协议
licensing law　许可证法
licensor　出证方,许可证颁发人,许可人
licit　合法的
lien　抵押权,扣押权,留置权
lien letter　留置权书
life accident insurance　人身意外伤害险
life cycle　全生命期
life cycle assessment　全生命周期评估

life expectancy　使用年限
life of contract　合同有效期
life of product　产品寿命
life-cycle　全寿命
life-cycle cost（LCC）
　全寿命周期费用,全生命周期成本
lift　电梯
lift（elevator）　升降机
lift bucket　吊斗
lift shaft　电梯井
lift station　扬水站
lifting compression type sealing device
　提拉压缩式止水器
lifting height　拔起高度
lifting rope　吊绳
lift-slab structure　升板结构
light compaction　轻型击实
light compaction test　轻型击实试验
light distribution　光强分布
light duty ballast undercutting cleaner
　小型枕底清筛机
light duty dynamic cone penetrometer
　轻型动力触探仪
light dynamic penetration test
　轻型动力触探试验
light emitting diode（LED）　发光二极管
light flux　光通量
light for fire evacuation　消防疏散照明灯
light gas protection　轻瓦斯保护
light hydraulic tamper　小型液压捣固机
light load arm　轻负荷臂
light matter content　轻物质含量
light rail car　轻型轨道车
light source　光源
light strip　光带
light track　轻型轨道
light track maintenance machinery
　小型线路机械
light water level gauge　灯光水位计
light work　轻作业
lighten　减轻
lighting　照明
lighting for fire evacuation　消防疏散照明
lighting of the site　工地照明
lighting power density　照明功率密度
lighting system　照明方式
lightning（atmospheric）overvoltage protection
　雷电(大气)过电压保护
lightning and thunder　雷电
lightning arrester　接闪器

lightning arrestor 防雷保安器
lightning flash-over 雷电闪络
lightning impulse withstand voltage
　雷电冲击耐受电压
lightning induction 雷电感应
lightning interference 雷电干扰
lightning net 避雷网
lightning overvoltage
　雷电过电压,雷击过电压
lightning protection 防雷
lightning protection box 防雷箱
lightning protection cable cabinet
　防雷分线柜
lightning protection component tester
　防雷元件测试仪
lightning protection components 防雷元件
lightning protection earth wire 防雷地线
lightning protection equipment 防雷设备
lightning protection system（LPS）
　雷电防护系统
lightning protection zone（LPZ）
　雷电防护区
lightning rod 避雷针
lightning strike 雷击
lightning strip 避雷带
lightning-proof transformer 防雷变压器
lightweight aggregate concrete
　轻骨料混凝土
lightweight concrete 轻质混凝土
lightweight matter 轻物质
light-spot indication 光点式表示
light-strip indication 光带式表示
light-weight wall 轻质墙
lignite 褐煤
liman facies 溺谷相
limburgite 玻基辉岩
lime 石灰
lime mortar 石灰砂浆
lime pile method 石灰桩法
lime soil 灰土
lime soil squeezing pile 灰土挤压桩
limestone 石灰岩
limestone soil 石灰土
limestone soil squeezing pile
　石灰土挤压桩
lime-soil（cement-soil）compaction pile
　灰土（水泥土）挤密桩
lime-soil compaction pile 灰土挤密桩
lime-soil pile 灰土桩
lime-stabilized soil 石灰改良土

limit deviation 极限偏差
limit equilibrium method 极限平衡法
limit equilibrium state 极限平衡状态
limit error 极限误差
limit folding strength 极限抗折强度
limit of delivery 交货期
limit of liquidated damages
　损害赔偿费限额
limit of movement authority
　限制性行车许可
limit of overdrawn account 透支限额
limit state 极限状态
limit state design method
　极限状态设计法,极限状态法
limit state design of bridge
　桥梁极限状态设计
limit state design 极限状态设计
limit state equation 极限状态方程
limit switch 极限开关
limit value 限值
limit value for traffic safety 行车安全限值
limitation 界限,限度
limitation of action 诉讼时效
limitation of funds 资金限制
limitation of liability
　责任的限定,责任限度,责任范围
limitation of retention money 保留金限额
limitation period 时效期限
limited amount guarantee
　限额保函,限额保证书
limited company 有限公司
limited competitive selected bidding
　有限竞争性选择招标
limited condition 极条件
limited duration guarantee 定期保函
limited liability 有限责任
limited liability company
　股份有限公司,有限责任公司
limited partnership 有限合伙公司
limited partner 有限责任合伙人
limited policy 有限责任保单
limited recourse 有限追索
limited speed 限制速度
limiting stress 极限应力
limiting value for sectional dimension
　截面尺寸限值
limiting value for supporting length
　支承长度限值
limiting value for total height of masonry structure
　砌体结构总高度限值

limiting value of maximum subsidiary stress
最大附加应力限值
limits 界限,范围,极限,限额
limits of authority 授权范围,工作大纲
limonite 褐铁矿
line 管线,航线,线路
line attenuation 线路衰耗
line connection 线路接线
line extension 展线
line feeder 加强线
line group 线宽组
line manager 生产经理
line number matching test
线路号适配测试
line of authority 权限
line of production 生产流程
line symbol 线状符号
line voltage 线电压
line width 线宽
linear depreciation method 平均折旧法
linear intersection 测边交会法
linear load 线荷载,线性荷载
linear metre 延米
linear planting 列植
linear scale limit 线性比例极限
linear shrinkage ratio 线缩率
linear strain 线应变
linear triangulation chain
线形三角锁,线形锁
linear triangulation network
线形三角网,线形网
linear viscoelasticity 线性黏弹性
linearity 线性度
linear-angular combined intersection
边角联合交会
linear-angular intersection
边角交会,边角交会法
lined stainless steel pipe 内衬不锈钢管
liner 衬垫(物),班轮
liner erosion 线蚀
liner transport 班轮运输
lines in service 营业线
lines of credit 信贷额度
lineside electronic unit（LEU）
应答器地面电子单元
line-transformer bank connection
线路变压器组接线
lining 衬砌
lining corrosion 衬砌腐蚀
lining crack 衬砌裂损

lining deformation 衬砌变形
lining of anchor section 下锚段衬砌
lining seepage 衬砌渗水情况
lining thickness 衬砌厚度
lining with curved walls 曲墙式衬砌
link 结合
link discovery protocol 链路发现协议
link peak bandwidth 链路带宽峰值
linking distance 链接距离
linking information 链接信息
lintel 过梁
lip of rail head 轨头肥边
lip synchronization 唇音同步
liquefaction 液化
liquefaction grade 液化等级
liquefaction index 液化指数
liquefaction point 液化点
liquefaction potential 液化势
liquefaction strength 液化强度
liquefaction stress 液化应力
liquefaction stress ratio 液化应力比
liquefiable soil layer 可液化土层
liquefied gas 液化气体
liquefied ground 液化地基
liquefied soil layer 液化土层
liquid carbon dioxide 液态二氧化碳
liquid chlorine 液氯
liquid crystal display（LCD） 液晶显示屏
liquid goods 液体货物
liquid goods yard 液体货物货场
liquid level meter 液位计
liquid limit 液限
liquid phase 液相
liquid receiver 储液器
liquid weighing method 液体称量法
liquid/circulating/current liabilities
流动负债
liquid/current/floating/circulating assets
流动资产
liquidate 清偿
liquidated damages 预定违约金
liquidated damages for delay
误期损害赔偿费
liquidation 变现,偿还债务,清算
liquidation of debt 清偿债务
liquidation preference 绝对优先权
liquidation value 清算价值
liquidator 破产清算人,资产清算人
liquidity 清偿能力
liquidity index 液性指数

liquidity ratio 偿依能力比率,流动比率
liquidizing point 液化点
Lishi loess 离石黄土
list 列表,一览表
list of account titles
　会计科目一览表,账户一览表
list of construction sites 工点表
list of exchange rate quotation
　外汇牌价表
list price 牌价
listed 列出的
listed company 上市公司
listed securities 上市证券
literal contract 成文合同,书面合同
literal interpretation 字面解释
literal translation 直译
lithic sandstone 岩屑砂岩
lithium-bromide absorption refrigerating machine
　溴化锂吸收式制冷机
lithofacies 岩相
lithofacies method 岩相法
lithology 岩性
litigant 诉讼当事人
litigate 诉诸法律
litigation 诉讼
litigation procedure 诉讼程序
littoral facies 滨海相
live load 活载
live load coefficient 活载系数
live load of road 公路活载
live load of special vehicle 特种车辆活载
live operating load 运营活载
live part 带电体
live working 带电作业
livestock loading and unloading track
　牲畜装卸线
livestock spigot 牲畜给水栓
living facilities 生活设施
living quarters 生活区
living room 起居室
lixiviant of water sample 试样水浸出液
Lloyd's insurance policy 劳合社保险单
load 负荷,载荷,装填,装载
load arrangement 荷载布置
load balancer 负载均衡器
load capacity 负荷容量
load case 荷载工况
load combination 荷载组合
load conversion coefficient 荷载换算系数
load effect 荷载效应
load efficiency 荷载效率
load equipartition system 负荷均分系统
load factor rating 承载系数检定
load holding duration 持荷时间
load machine testing 加载试机
load rate 荷载率,负荷率,荷重率
load standard value 荷载标准值
load strength 荷载强度
load switch 负荷开关
load test 荷载试验,荷载检验,载荷试验
load test for composite ground
　复合地基载荷试验
load test of composite ground with single pile
　单桩复合地基载荷试验
load test track 负荷试验线
loaded expansion rate test
　有荷载膨胀率试验
loader 搬运工,装载机
loading 荷载,载重,装货,装载
loading and unloading 装卸
loading and unloading line for railway oil products
　铁路油品装卸线
loading and unloading of the whole train
　整列装卸
loading and unloading operation area
　装卸作业区
loading and unloading siding 装卸线
loading and unloading times 装卸次数
loading and unloading yard 装卸场
loading arm 鹤管
loading balance method 加荷平衡法
loading berm 反压护道
loading by gravity 自流装车
loading capacity 载重
loading equipment 加载设备
loading expansion rate 加荷膨胀率
loading on board 装船
loading platform 装车台
loading port 装货港
loading program 加载程序
loading shovel (crawler) 装载机(履带式)
loading shovel (wheeled) 装载机(轮式)
loading speed 加荷速度
loading stabilization time 加载稳定时间
loading test 加载试验
loading track 装车道,装车线
loads combination on sound barrier
　声屏障荷载组合
load-breaking capacity 带载分闸能力
load-bearing capacity factor 承载力因数

load-bearing capacity of bridge
桥梁承载能力
load-bearing capacity of disc cutter
滚刀承载能力
load-bearing capacity of member
构件承载能力
load-carrying natural frequency
有载自振频率
load-making capacity 带载合闸能力
loan 贷款
loan agreement 贷款协议
loan amount with interest 还息贷款额
loan capital 借入资本,债务资金
loan ceiling 贷款限额
loan committee 贷款委员会
loan consortium 贷款财团
loan currency 贷款货币
loan document 贷款文件
loan interest 贷款利息
loan interest rate 贷款利率
loan note 借款单证
loan on actual estate 不动产抵押贷款
loan payable 应付贷款
loan receivable 应收贷款
loan repayment period 贷款偿还期
loan repayment 偿还贷款
loan serviced/paid 已付贷款
loanee 债务人
local 本地人
local agent 当地代理人
local air conditioning 局部空气调节
local air supply system 局部送风系统
local application extinguishing system
局部应用灭火系统
local area network 局域网
local authority 地方当局
local backup protection 近后备保护
local competitive bidding (LCB)
国内竞争性招标
local contractor 本土承包商,当地承包商
local control
就地控制,本地控制,局部控制
local control circuit 局部控制电路
local control panel 局部控制盘
local court 地方法院
local craft terminal (LCT) 本地维护终端
local currency 本币,当地货币
local dimension limits of masonry structure
砌体结构局部尺寸限值
local exhaust hood 局部排风罩

local expenditures 当地开支
local experience 地区经验
local flooding prevention and control system
内涝防治系统
local government 当地政府
local heating 局部采暖
local interest rate 当地利率
local labour 当地工人
local marshalling station
地方性编组站
local material 地材,当地材料
local navigation positioning system
区域导航定位系统
local personnel 当地人员
local power source 局部电源,地方电源
local power supply authority
地方供电部门
local price 当地价格
local primary reference clock
区域基准时钟
local primary reference source (LPR)
区域基准钟
local railway 地方铁路
local resident 当地居民
local scour 局部冲刷
local scour around pier 桥墩局部冲刷
local shear failure 局部剪切破坏
local shopping 当地购买
local statute 当地法规
local supplier 当地供应商
local tax 地方税
local telephone network 本地电话网
local ventilation 局部通风
local worker 当地工人
locality 地区,方位,所在地,位置
localization information 定位信息
localized management 属地化管理
locally operated switch 非集中道岔
locate 位于
location 场所,位置,选线
location dependent addressing (LDA)
基于位置寻址
location mark 定位标志
location of bridge pier and abutment
桥梁墩台定位
location of sounding point 测深定位
location reference 定位基准点
location repair 定位修
location survey 工程定位复测
locking 锁闭

locking circuit	锁闭电路
locking force	锁闭力
locking mechanism	锁闭机构
locking requisition	锁闭条件
locking rod	锁闭杆
locking system	锁闭系统
lockpin	锁销
lock-in load	锁定荷载
loco invoice	产地交货单
loco price	产地交货价格
loco waiting track	机待线
locomotive arm routing	肩回运转制
locomotive crew shift change	机车乘务组换班
locomotive crew shift changing station	机务换乘所
locomotive depot	机务段
locomotive depot for passenger service	客运机务段
locomotive equipment	机车设备
locomotive facilities	机务设备
locomotive holding track	机待线
locomotive in operation	运用机车
locomotive inductor	机车感应器
locomotive long runs	长交路
locomotive loop routing	循回式运转制
locomotive maintenance building	机务用房
locomotive operation	机车运用
locomotive repair depot	机车检修段
locomotive routing	机车交路
locomotive routing mode	机车运转制
locomotive running data recorder	机车运行安全监控装置
locomotive running kilometers	机车走行公里
locomotive running track	机车走行线
locomotive servicing	机车整备
locomotive turnaround depot	机务折返段
locomotive turnaround operation	机车折返作业
locomotive turnaround point	机务折返所
locomotive under repair	在修机车
lodging quarters	住房
lodging system	调休制
loess	黄土
loess bridge	黄土桥
loess collapsibility test	黄土湿陷性试验
loess hill	黄土峁,黄土丘陵
loess hillock	黄土峁,黄土丘陵
loess landslide	黄土滑坡
loess pile	黄土桩
loess plain	黄土平原
loess plateau	黄土高原
loess plate	黄土碟
loess ridge	黄土梁
loess sink hole	黄土陷穴
loess subgrade	黄土路基
loess tableland	黄土塬
loess well	黄土井
loess-doll	姜石
loess-like soil	黄土状土
log book	日志
logbook	航海日志,航空日志,行驶日志
logic earth wire	逻辑地线
logic state of block section	闭塞分区逻辑状态
logistics	后勤,物流
logistics support	后勤保障,物流保障
Lohse bridge (also known as "rigid arch bridge with rigid tie and vertical suspenders")	洛泽式桥(又称"直悬杆式刚性拱刚性梁桥")
loitering detection	逗留检测
London interbank offered rate (LIBOR)	伦敦银行同业拆借利率
long bridge (with length from 101m to 500m)	大桥(长度为101~500m)
long distance forecast	长距离预报
long distance manual exchange system	长途人工交换系统
long distance transported soil	远运土
long edge of sheet	卷材长边
long length charges	超长附加费
long list	长名单
long loop impedance	长回路阻抗
long price	高价
long rail continuous method	单枕长轨连续铺设法
long rail storage area	长钢轨存放区
long rail string	长轨条
long rod insulator with eye end cap	带耳环的长棒式绝缘子
long route	长交路
long sleeper embedded track	长枕埋入式轨道
long steep grade	长大坡道
long term	远期
long term rigidity of members	构件长期刚度
long term works	远期工程
long tunnel	长隧道
long wave irregularity	长波不平顺

longitude 经度
longitudinal arrangement of passenger car servicing post 客车整备所纵列布置
longitudinal arrangement type junction terminal 顺列式枢纽
longitudinal arrangement 纵列配置
longitudinal bar 纵向钢筋
longitudinal beam 纵梁,纵向梁
longitudinal bending coefficient of components 构件纵向弯曲系数
longitudinal connection of track slabs 轨道板纵向连接
longitudinal deviation 纵向偏差
longitudinal dike 顺坝
longitudinal displacement 纵向位移
longitudinal distance of photography 摄影纵距
longitudinal district station for passenger and freight service 客货纵列式区段站
longitudinal drainage device 纵向排水设备
longitudinal dune 纵向沙丘
longitudinal error of traverse 导线纵向误差
longitudinal expansion-contraction force in CWR on bridge 伸缩力
longitudinal fault 纵断层
longitudinal filter pipe 纵向盲管
longitudinal force 纵向力
longitudinal horizontal bracing 纵向水平支撑
longitudinal horizontal force of long steel rails 长钢轨纵向水平力
longitudinal joint 纵向接缝
longitudinal layout 纵列式
longitudinal level 高低
longitudinal reinforcement bar 纵向钢筋
longitudinal reinforcing bar 纵向钢筋
longitudinal resistance of track bed 道床纵向阻力
longitudinal seam 纵向缝
longitudinal section of earthworks 路基纵断面
longitudinal section of retaining wall 挡土墙纵断面
longitudinal slope of the deck surface 桥面纵坡
longitudinal stiffener 纵向加劲肋
longitudinal tilt 航向倾角
longitudinal type classification yard 纵列式编组站
longitudinal type district station 纵列式区段站
longitudinal type harbour station built jointly in both terminals 双方车站联设纵列式港湾站
longitudinal type industrial station built jointly in both terminals 双方车站联设纵列式工业站
longitudinal type marshalling yard 纵列式编组站
longitudinal valley 纵向谷,纵谷
longitudinal wave 纵波
longitudinal wave velocity 纵波波速
longitudinal wave velocity of rock 岩块的纵波速度
longshore embankment 沿岸堤
longitudinal overlap 航向重叠
long-distance circuit 长途电路
long-distance communication system 长途通信系统
long-distance line 长途线路
long-distance telephone network 长途电话网
long-form bill of lading 详式提单,全式提单
long-lead items 长周期采购项目
long-lived assets 长期资产
long-run agreement 长期协议
long-span structure 大跨度结构
long-term claim 长期债权
long-term debt 长期债务
long-term forecast 长期预测
long-term investment 长期投资
long-term lease 长期租赁
long-term liabilities 长期负债
long-term loan 长期贷款
long-term modulus 长期模量
long-term planning 长期规划
long-term policy 长期保单
long-term rental 长期租用
long-term stability 长期稳定性
loop 环线,回线环路
loop account 回线台账
loop pipe network 环状管网
loop resistance 环路电阻
looped power supply 环状供电
loose 松散
loose cement 散装水泥
loose rock cutting 松散岩质路堑
loose rock 松动岩石

loose sand	疏松砂
loose soil layer	松散土层
loose structure	松散结构
loosely bound water	弱结合水
loosening blasting	松动爆破
loosening pressure	松散压力
Los Angeles abrasion rate	洛杉矶磨耗率
Los Angeles abrasion	洛杉矶磨耗
Los Angeles rattler	洛杉矶磨耗机
lose sight of	忽略
losing a suit	败诉
losing party	败诉方
loss	亏损，损耗，损失
loss abatement	损失减少
loss adjuster	损失理算师
loss advice	出险通知，损失通知书，损失告知
loss and gain	损益
loss assessment	损失估计
loss assessor	损失评定人
loss clause	损失条款
loss control	损失控制
loss frequency	损失频率
loss from natural disaster	自然灾害损失
loss of advanced profits insurance	预期利润损失保险
loss of efficiency	效率降低
loss of indication of a switch	道岔失去表示
loss of labour productivity	劳动力损失
loss of net income	净收入损失
loss of prestress	预应力损失
loss of production	生产损失
loss of productivity	生产力损失
loss of profit	利润损失
loss of profit insurance	利润损失保险
loss of stability	失稳
loss of traffic	运输损失
loss of voltage	电压损失
loss on devaluation	货币贬值损失
loss on ignition	烧失量
loss prevention	损失预防
loss ratio	赔付率，索赔率，损失率
loss relief	损失减轻
losses and expenses	破坏、损失及花费
loss-of-voltage protection	失压保护
lost motion	隙动差
lost project time	项目误工时间
lot	批次
lotus-form structure	莲花状构造
loudspeaker	扬声器
lounge	间休室
louver	百叶窗
Love wave	勒夫波
low compressibility	低压缩性
low dipping stratum	缓倾岩层
low embankment	低路堤
low emissivity coated glass	低发射率膜玻璃
low fill and shallow cut	低填浅挖
low frequency alternate action	低周反复作用
low mountain	低山
low performance damages	功能欠佳赔偿费
low pile cap	低桩承台
low pressure fire water supply system	低压消防给水系统
low pressure membrane filter device	低压膜过滤装置
low pressure system	低压系统
low signal	矮型信号机
low strain reflected wave method	低应变反射波法
low temperature air supply air conditioning system	低温送风空气调节系统
low temperature drying method	低温烘干法
low temperature properties	低温性能
low temperature refrigerator	低温冰柜
low temperature test	低温试验
low vibration track (LVT)	弹性支承块式无砟轨道
low voltage side	低压侧，二次侧，次边侧
lower (reduce) production costs	降低成本
lower anchor bracket	下承锚底座
lower bracket for twin cantilevers	双腕臂下底座
lower Cambrian series	下寒武统
lower cantilever bracket	腕臂下底座
lower Carboniferous series	下石炭统
lower Cretaceous series	下白垩统
lower cross-span wire	下定位索
lower Devonian series	下泥盆统
lower explosion limit	爆炸极限
lower filling	下部填土
lower Jurassic series	下侏罗统
lower limit of yield strength	屈服强度下限
lower Ordovician series	下奥陶统
lower Paleozoic erathem	下古生界
lower Permian series	下二叠统
lower Pleistocene series	下更新统
lower Proterozoic group	下元古界

lower Silurian series 下志留统
lower Sinian series 下震旦统
lower the quality 降低质量
lower Triassic series 下三叠统
lowest bid (tender) 最低标
lowest bidder (tenderer) 最低价投标人
lowest offer 最低报价
lowest strength class of masonry material
　砌体材料最低强度等级
lowest water level 最低水位
low-heat cement 低热水泥
low-lying land 低洼地
low-power sewage treatment facilities
　低动力污水处理设施
low-rate trickling filters 低负荷生物滤池
low-strain integrity testing 低应变法
low-temperature and basically stable area
　低温基本稳定区
low-temperature stable area 低温稳定区
low-voltage circuit breaker 低压断路器
low-voltage power distribution 低压配电
lubricant 润滑油
lubricating oil level 润滑油液位
Lugeon unit 吕荣单位
luggage and parcel information system
　行包信息系统
luggage and parcel management information system
　行包管理信息系统
luggage and parcel service information system
　行包服务信息系统
lujauvrite 异霞正长岩岩
lumber 木料
luminaire efficacy 灯具效能
luminaire efficiency 灯具效率
luminescence 发光性
luminous efficacy 发光效能
luminous flux maintenance factor
　光通量维持率
luminous intensity 发光强度
lump sum contract 总价合同
lump sum cost 一揽子成本,总价成本
lump sum items 包干项
lump sum on firm bill of quantities
　固定工程量总价合同
lump sum payment 总价付款
lump sum price 总包价格
lump sum remuneration 包干酬金
lump-sum freight 整船包价
lump-sum payment 一次支付(整付)
lump-sum price with bill of quantities
　附工程量表的总价
lump-sum price with schedule of rates
　附费率表的总价
Luoyang shovel 洛阳铲
luster 光泽
Lüliangian age/stage 吕梁期
L-shaped platform L形站台

M

m method　m 值法
machine capability　设备能力
machine hour　台时
machine idle time　设备闲置时间
machine shift price of cost making period
　编制期机械台班单价
machine shift　台班,机械台班
machineman　机械工
machinery all risks insurance　机械一切险
machinery breakdown insurance
　机器损坏保险
machinery breakdown policy
　机械故障保险单
machinery consequential loss（interruption）insurance　机械间接损失保险
machinery damage insurance
　机器损坏保险
machining　机械加工,切削加工,加工
machinist　机械工,机械师
macrostructure　宏观结构
macro-forecast　宏观预测,总体预测
magmatic rock（igneous rock）
　岩浆岩(火成岩)
magmatism　岩浆作用
magnesite　菱镁矿
magnesium oxide content　氧化镁含量
magnesium salt erosion　镁盐侵蚀
magnetic anomaly　磁异常
magnetic azimuth　磁方位角
magnetic circuit system　磁路系统
magnetic declination　磁偏角
magnetic field intensity　磁场强度
magnetic inclination　磁倾角
magnetic medium thermal paper ticket
　磁介质纸质热敏票
magnetic meridian　磁子午线
magnetic method　磁法
magnetic prospecting　磁法勘探

magnetic shielding　磁屏蔽
magnetic stirrer　磁力搅拌机
magnetic susceptibility　磁化率
magnetite　磁铁矿
magneto telephone　磁石电话
magnetotelluric sounding and profiling method
　大地电磁测深及剖面法
mail transfer（M/T）　信汇
mail transfer advice　信汇通知书
main　总管
main bridge　主桥
main budget　主要预算
main bus-bar　主干汇流排
main circuit　主干线路
main container yard　主箱场
main contract　主合同,总包合同,总承包合同
main contract clauses　主合同条款
main contract documents　主合同文件
main control room　主控制室
main distribution frame（MDF）　总配线架
main drain　排水总管
main drainage ditch　排水干沟
main filament　主灯丝
main filament burnout alarm
　主灯丝断丝报警
main fillet welds　主要角焊缝
main frequency　主频率
main girder　主梁
main line　正线
main line of turnout　道岔主线
main load　主要荷载
main load-carrying member　主要承重构件
main office　总公司,总行
main passenger platform　旅客基本站台
main pipe　干管
main platform　基本站台
main protection　主保护
main quantities　主要工程数量

main reinforcement 主筋
main river channel 主河槽
main signal 主体信号机
main slide section 主滑段
main structural plane of rock mass
　岩体主要结构面
main structure 主体结构
main supply 供电干线
main technical standards for railway
　铁路主要技术标准
main track circuit 主轨道电路
main track departure mode 正线发车模式
main track passage mode 正线通过模式
main tunnel 主隧道(也称正洞)
main ventilation riser 主通气立管
main vertical framework 竖向主框架
main workings plan 主要巷道平面图
main works 主体工程,主包工程
mainstream 干流
maintain 保持,维护
maintainability 可维护性
maintenance 保持,保养,维护,养护
maintenance and management terminal
　维护管理终端
maintenance and operation channel
　维护操作通道
maintenance and repair 养护维修
maintenance base 维修基地
maintenance bond 维修担保
maintenance center for hotbox detection system
　红外线轴温探测设备检测所(红外所)
maintenance certificate 维修证书
maintenance charge 保养费
maintenance expense 养护费
maintenance factor 维护系数
maintenance fee 维护费
maintenance guarantee 维修保函
maintenance management 维修管理
maintenance manual 维修手册
maintenance of plant 设备保养,设备的维护
maintenance of value 保持价值
maintenance of works 工程维修
maintenance period 维修期
maintenance projects 维修项目
maintenance retention fund 维修保留金
maintenance retention guarantee
　维修保留金保函
maintenance window 天窗
maintenance workshop 检修库,维修车间
major alternative 主要备选方案

major axis 强轴
major defect 主要缺陷
major event 重大事件
major items of construction plant
　主要施工设备
major node 主节点
major pollution source 主要污染源
major repair cost 大修修理费
majority rule 多数裁定原则
majority shareholder 控股股东,控股人
majority stockholder 控股股东,控股人
make advance 垫付,预支付
make an offer 发盘
make good 修复
make good on general average
　共同海损补偿
make headway 进展
make or become heavier 加重
make or become more serious 加重
make over 修改;修订;更正
make profit 获利
make progress 进展
make remittance 汇寄,汇款
make/enact laws 立法
make-up pump 补给水泵
making and breaking current 分合闸电流
making coil 合闸线圈
making time 合闸时间
malachite 孔雀石
Malan loess 马兰黄土
malfeasance 渎职,违法乱纪
malfunction 误动作
malicious damage 恶意破坏
malicious prosecution 诬告
malleability 延展性,展性
maltene 可溶质
malthoid 油毛毡,油毡
man day 工日
man hour 工时
manage 经营
manage money 理财
manage wealth 理财
manageable risk 可管理风险
management accounting 管理会计
management agreement 管理协定
management by exception 例外管理
management by objectives (MBO)
　目标管理
management consultant 管理顾问
management contract 管理合同

management contracting 管理承包
management contractor 管理承包商
management control system 管理控制系统
management cost 管理费
management cost of construction project
　建设项目管理费
management fee lump sum contract
　管理费总价合同
management fees for land expropriation
　土地征用管理费
management function 管理职能
management information 管理信息
management information system（MIS）
　管理信息系统
management measure 管理措施
management of construction cost
　工程造价管理
management of human resources
　人力资源管理
management of interface 界面管理
management operating system（MOS）
　生产管理制度
management plan 管理计划
management strategy 管理策略
managerial accountant 管理会计师
managerial accounting 管理会计
managing director 执行董事,总经理
mandatory 强制的,委任者
mandatory arbitration 强制仲裁
mandatory insurance 强制性保险
mandatory requirement 强制要求
manganese oxide content 氧化锰含量
manhole 检查井,人孔
manhole cover 人孔井盖
manifestation 表现
manifest 仓单,船货清单,货单,货物清单
manner of execution 实施方法,实施方式
manners and customs 风俗习惯
manning schedule 人员配备计划
manpower 人力
manpower curves 人力曲线
mantle 地幔
manual 指南
manual construction 人力施工
manual control 手动控制
manual disconnector 手动隔离开关
manual labour 体力劳动者,力工
manual non-time release 不限时人工解锁
manual operated barrier 手动栏木
manual rates 标准保险费率

manual recovery 人工恢复
manual release 人工解锁,手动释放
manual release button panel 解锁按钮盘
manual shunting 人工分路
manual time release 限时人工解锁
manual track laying 人工铺轨
manual voltage regulation 手动调压
manual/motorized operating mechanism box
　手动/电动操作机构箱
manufacture 加工,制造
manufactured sand 人工砂
manufacturer 厂家,制造商
manufacturer's certificate 厂商证明书
manufacturer's agent 厂商代理人
manufacturer's invoice 厂商发票
manufacturing consignment 委托加工
manufacturing cost 加工成本,制造成本
manufacturing drawing 制造图
manufacturing expenses 制造费用
manufacturing inspection point
　加工制造的检验点
manufacturing statement 生产报表
manuscript 原稿
man-day quota 工天定额
man-machine interface（MMI） 人机界面
man-made cavities 人为坑洞
map 地图
map annotation 地图注记
map border 图廓
map compilation 地图编制
map database 地图数据库
map database management system
　地图数据库管理系统
map decoration 地图整饰
map margin decoration 图廓整饰
map of mining subsidence 开采沉陷图
map out 计划
map plate-making 地图制版
map printing 地图印刷
map process and printing 制印
map projection 地图投影
map specifications 地图规范
mapping base point 图根点
mapping by picket-point method
　测记法成图
mapping control 图根控制
marble 大理岩(石)
marcasite 白铁矿
march 进展
margin 保护余量,边际,息差,盈余

margin call (notice)　追加保证金的通知
margin for adjustment　调整余量
margin of preference　优惠额
marginal cost　边际成本
marginal costing　边际成本
marginal income　边际收益
marginal note　旁注
marginal profit　边际利润
marginal revenue　边际收入
marginal tropics　边缘热带
marine arch　海蚀拱桥
marine bill of lading　海运提单
marine chart　海图
marine deposit　海相沉积
marine deposition plain　海积平原
marine erosion cliff　海蚀崖
marine facies　海相
marine geomorphy　海洋地貌
marine insurance　海运保险,水险,运输保险
marine insurance policy　海运保险单
marine law　海商法
marine origin　海成
marine platform　海蚀平台
marine pollution　海洋污染
marine premium　海运保险费
marine soil　海积土
marine stack　海蚀岩柱
marine structure　海上建筑物
marine window　海蚀窗
maritime　海运的,近海的
maritime arbitration commission　海事仲裁委员会
maritime claim　海事索赔
maritime court　海事法庭
maritime customs　海关
maritime law　海商法
maritime loss　海损
maritime perils　海上风险
maritime port　海港
maritime transportation insurance　海洋运输保险
maritime works　海工建筑
mark　标记,标志,记号
mark down　降价,减价
mark stamping of rails　钢轨打标记
marker bed　标志层
market allocation　市场分配,市场划分
market analysis　市场分析
market channel　销售渠道
market demand　市场需求

market exchange rate　市场汇率
market fluctuation　市场波动
market for funds　金融市场
market information　行情
market intelligence　市场信息
market orientation　市场定位
market price　市价
market quotations　行情
market rate　市场利率
market share　市场份额,市场占有率
market tendency　市场趋势
market value　市场价值
marketing　营销
marketing decision support　营销辅助决策
marketing expenses　销售费用
marketing mix　销售组合
marketing outlet　销路
marking　标识,记号
marking lamp for fire evacuation　消防疏散标志灯
markstone　标石
mark-up　标高金,成本加成
marlite　泥灰岩
marlstone　泥灰岩
marsh　沼泽
marsh gas　沼气
marsh water　沼泽水
marshaling workload　改编作业量
Marshall stability test　马歇尔试验
marshalling line　编组线
marshalling station　编组站
marshalling track　编组线
marshalling yard　编组站
marshalling-departure track　编发线
marshy area　沼泽地区
mask artwork　蒙绘
mason　泥瓦工
masonry　圬工,砌体,砌筑体
masonry bridge　圬工桥
masonry mortar　砌体砂浆
masonry sound barrier　砌体式声屏障
masonry strength　砌体强度
masonry wall　砌筑墙体,圬工墙
masonry work　圬工工程
masonry-timber structure　砖木结构
mass behavior　群体行为
mass concentration　质量浓度
mass concentration of phenol　酚的质量浓度
mass concrete　大体积混凝土

mass fraction 质量分数
mass of oversize sample on sieve
  筛上试样质量
mass of undersized sample 筛下试样质量
mass per unit area 单位面积质量
mass production 批量生产
massif 山体
massive 巨块状,块状
massive structure 块状构造
mast 支柱
mast foundation 支柱基础
master clock 主时钟,母钟
master control account 总控制账户
master control station 主控站
master list 总清单
master oscillator frequency 主振频率
master plan 总平面图
master policy 总保险单
master programme 总进度计划
master schedule 主进度计划,总进度计划
matching 匹配
material 材料,器材
material alteration/modification/amendment
  重大修改
material and workmanship
  设备,材料和工艺
material assets 有形资产
material breach of contract 严重违约
material certification 材料合格证
material consumption amount 材料消耗量
material consumption norm 材料消耗定额
material cost 材料费,材料成本
material damage 物质损失
material delivered from temporary large size storage site 厂发料
material delivery note 材料出库单
material departure point 发料点
material evidence 物证
material exception report (MER)
  材料异常报告
material expense of base period
  基期材料费
material handling 材料转运
material omission 严重遗漏
material purchase and storage expenses
  材料采购及保管费
material receipt 材料收据
material receiving report 材料签收报告
material request form 用料审批表
material requisition form 领料单

material requisition summary 领料汇总单
material resources 物力资源,实物资源
material specification 材料明细表
material store 材料库
material supply 材料供应
material supply plan
  材料供应方案/计划
material take-off (MTO) 材料统计
material testing machine 材料试验机
material transport plan 材料运输方案
material transportation car 物料运输车
material types 材料种类
material/major/substantial deviation
  重大偏离
materials for temporary works
  临时工程施工器材年使用率
materials planning 材料计划
materials purchasing 材料购买
materials return report 退料单
materials supplied by the employer
  甲供材料,雇主供材料
mate's receipt 收货单
mathematical model method 数学模型法
matrix 基体
matrix organization 矩阵式机构
matrix project organization
  矩阵化项目组织
matters in dispute 争议事宜
matured liability 到期负债
maturity date 偿还日
maturity of a draft 汇票支付日期
maturity value 到期值,终值
maximum allowable entry speed
  最大允许入口速度
maximum allowable span length
  极限长度
maximum allowable superelevation
  最大超高允许值
maximum amount 最大金额,最大量
maximum backwater height in front of bridge
  桥前最大壅水高度
maximum compensation 最大赔偿额
maximum continuous operating voltage
  最大持续运行电压
maximum continuous working current
  最大持续工作电流
maximum current of feeding section
  供电臂最大电流
maximum daily water supply
  最高日供水量

maximum deflection 最大挠度
maximum deviation 最大偏差
maximum dry density 最大干密度
maximum effective current of feeding section 供电臂最大有效电流
maximum entropy method 最大熵法
maximum gradient 最大坡度
maximum guaranteed price 最高保证价格
maximum hoisting capacity 最大起重量
maximum horizontal displacement of contact wire 接触线最大水平偏移量
maximum hourly water consumption 最大时用水量
maximum impact load 最大冲击负荷
maximum instantaneous wind speed 最大瞬时风速
maximum liability 最大赔偿额
maximum limit 最高限额
maximum load current 最大负荷电流
maximum molecular water-absorption rate 最大分子吸水率
maximum monthly average diurnal temperature range 气温最大月平均日较差
maximum output power 最大输出功率
maximum passenger number gathered 旅客最高聚集人数
maximum permissible concentration 最高容许浓度
maximum plane principal stress 最大平面主应力
maximum point overexcavation 最大点超挖量
maximum radius of curve 最大曲线半径
maximum radius of vertical curve 最大竖曲线半径
maximum rail temperature 最高轨温
maximum range of EDM 电磁波测距最大测程
maximum service brake 最大常用制动
maximum size 最大粒径
maximum sound level 最大声级
maximum stress range 最大应力幅
maximum temperature 最高气温
maximum value 最大值
maximum variation of rail temperature 最大轨温变化幅度
maximum void ratio 最大孔隙比
maximum water inflow 最大涌水量
maximum wind speed 最大风速
meadow 草地
mean down time 平均停工时间

mean end-to-end transfer delay 平均端到端延迟(传输时间)
mean height surface of survey area 测区平均高程面
mean power factor 平均功率因数
mean radius of curvature 平均曲率半径
mean rolling speed of car 车辆平均溜放速度
mean sea level 平均海(水)面
mean square error of angle measurement 测角中误差
mean square error of azimuth 方位角中误差
mean square error of baseline azimuth 基线方位角中误差
mean square error of baseline length 基线长度中误差
mean square error of coordinates 坐标中误差
mean square error of distance measurement 测距中误差
mean square error of positions 点位中误差
mean square error of prior weight 先验权中误差
mean square error of side length 边长中误差
mean square error of unit weight 单位权中误差
mean square root speed 均方根速度
mean squares error 中误差
mean temperature in the hottest month 最热月平均温度
mean time between failures 平均无故障时间
mean time to restoration 平均恢复前时间
mean value 均值
mean water level during dry seasons 枯水位
mean annual rainfall/precipitation 平均年降雨量
meandering coefficient of traverse 导线曲折系数
means 方法
means of execution 实施方法
means of payment 支付手段
means of production 生产资料
means of verification 验证方法
measure 测量,措施,量度
measure and control unit of feeder protection 馈线保护测控单元
measure and control unit of traction transformer protection 主变保护测控单元

measure of security　安全措施
measure value modification　测值修正
measured value　实测值
measuring installation　测量安置
measurement　测量,计量,衡量
measurement and cost reimbursement contract
　测量与成本补偿合同
measurement and inspection　测量检查
measurement and valuation　验工计价
measurement architecture
　检测连接示意图
measurement contract　计量合同
measurement frequency　监控量测频率
measurement items　措施项目
measuring　测量,量取
measuring electrode　测量电极
measuring electrode spacing　测量电极距
measuring gauge length　测量标距
measuring instrument　计量器具,量测仪器
measuring line　测线
measuring peg　测桩
measuring point　测点
measuring range　量测范围,量程
measuring tape　卷尺
measuring time-window　测量时窗
mechanic　机械工,技师,修理工
mechanical air supply system
　机械送风系统
mechanical borehole-forming　机械成孔
mechanical completion　机械竣工
mechanical connection　机械连接
mechanical declinometer　机械倾斜仪
mechanical dust removal　机械除尘
mechanical equipment installation works
　机械设备安装工程
mechanical fatigue test　机械疲劳试验
mechanical flocculating tank
　机械絮凝池
mechanical indicators　力学性指标
mechanical interlock　机械闭锁
mechanical interlocking
　机械集中联锁,机械联锁
mechanical latch　机械闭锁
mechanical life　机械寿命
mechanical load　机械荷载
mechanical locking　机械锁闭
mechanical mixing　机械混合
mechanical point pressure test
　力学点压测试
mechanical properties　机械特性,力学性能
mechanical properties of materials
　材料力学性能
mechanical pump-in test method
　机械压水法
mechanical refrigerator wagon　机械保温车
mechanical semaphore signal
　机械臂板信号机
mechanical smoke exhaust　机械排烟
mechanical strength　机械强度
mechanical test　机械试验
mechanical track laying　机械铺轨
mechanical ventilation　机械通风
mechanical ventilation system　机械通风系统
mechanician　机械工
mechanics of fracture　断裂力学
mechanics of granular media　散体力学
mechanization　机械化
mechanized hump　机械化驼峰
mediate　调解,调停
media access control（MAC）
　介质访问控制
media gateway（MGW）　媒体网关
median strip　绿化分隔带
mediation　调停,调解,中间调解
mediator　调解人,调停员
medical certificate
　健康证明,体检证明,医疗证明
medical examination　体格检查
medical expense insurance　医疗费用保险
medical fee　医疗费
medical treatment　医疗
medication neutralization　投药中和
medium and long distance forecast
　中长距离预报
medium ballast cleaning machine
　中型清筛机
medium bridge（with length from 21m to 100m）
　中桥（长度为 21~100m）
medium compressibility　中压缩性
medium corrosion　中腐蚀
medium density　中密
medium mountain　中山
medium passenger station　中型旅客车站
medium repair　中修
medium rolling car　中行车
medium sand　中砂
medium scale landslide　中型滑坡
medium scale station　中型车站
medium term　中期
medium thickness layer　中厚层

medium tropic 中热带
medium water abundance zone 中等富水区
medium-coarse sand 中粗砂
medium-hard soil 中硬土
medium-long tunnel 中长隧道
medium-scale maintenance 中修
medium-soft soil 中软土
meeting 会议
meeting attendance form 会议签到单格式
meeting notes 会议纪要
meeting place 会场
meeting point 交汇点
mega construction project 特大型建设项目
mega project 大型工程
meimechite 麦美奇岩,玻基橄榄岩
meizoseismal area 极震区
mellow soil 熟土
melting point 溶点
member 杆件
member fabrication in plant 工厂化
membership 成员资格
membrane 薄膜,防渗护面
membrane bio-reactor（MBR） 膜生物反应器
membrane filtration 膜过滤
membrane separation 膜分离
memorandum 备忘录,非正式记录
memorandum of association 公司章程
memorandum of deposit 抵押证书
memorandum of payment 缴款通知
memorandum of understanding（MOU） 谅解备忘录
memory 内存
memory card 存储卡
memory device 存储设备
memory useage 内存利用率
memo 备忘录
mend 修理
meniscus adjusted value 弯液面校正值
mention 提及
Mercator projection 墨卡托投影
merchandise 货物,商品
merchandise credit slip 退货凭单
merchandise declaration 货物申报单
merchandise inventory 商品盘存
merchandise mark 商标
merchant bank 商业银行
mercury content 汞含量
mercury vapor meter 汞蒸气测定仪
merge 合并,兼并,结合,企业合并
merge offer 合并报价,合并发盘
merger 兼并
meridian 子午线
meridian convergence angle 子午线收敛角
meridianal structure 经向构造
merit 优点
merits 法律依据
mesa 平顶山
mesh 网栅
mesh reinforcement 网状钢筋,钢筋网
mesh spacing 网栅间隔
mesophilic digestion 中温消化
Mesoproterozoic 中元古代
Mesozoic era 中生代
Mesozoic erathem/group 中生界
message 信息
message transfer part 消息传递部分
messenger 信使
messenger wire 承力索,吊线
messenger wire clamp 承力索线夹
messenger wire sag 承力索弛度
messenger wire splice 承力索接头线夹
metagenic 交替的
metal cable tray 金属线槽
metal component 金属构件
metal conduit 金属导管
metal detector door 安全门
metal foil surfaced asphalt sheet 金属箔防水卷材
metal oxide 金属氧化物
metal radiant panel 金属辐射板
metal wire strain gauge 金属丝式应变片
metallic luster 金属光泽
metallic short circuit 金属性短路
metal-clad switchgear 金属铠装开关柜
metamorphic conglomerate 变质砾岩
metamorphic rock 变质岩
metamorphic structure 变成构造
metamorphism 变质作用
metasandstone 变质砂岩
metasomatic texture 交代结构
meteorological condition 气象条件
meteorological correction 气象修正
meteorological data 气象资料
meteorological monitoring 气象监测
meteorology 气象
method 方法
method of application 申请方法
method of capacity index 生产能力指数法

method of construction 施工方法
method of direct observation 直接观察法
method of direction observation in rounds
全圆方向观测法
method of direction observation
方向观测法
method of equal-weight substitution
等权代替法
method of fixed percentage on cost
成本固定百分比(折旧)法
method of heat accumulation 蓄热法
method of ignition loss 灼烧失量法
method of interior points 内分点法
method of measurement 计量方法
method of payment 支付方式
method of redress 补救办法
method of sampling 抽样方法
method of tangent offsets 切线支距法
method of tension wire alignment
引张线法
method of traverse line intersecting
方向线交会法
method of unit estimation 单位估价法
method of weighting 加权法
methylene blue spectrophotometric method
亚甲基蓝分光光度法
methylene blue test 甲蓝实验
metric camera 量测摄影机
metric conversion 公制换算
metric measure 公制计量
metric system 公制
metrological contract 计量型合同
metrology accreditation 计量认证
miarolitic cavity 晶洞
mica 云母
mica content 云母含量
mica felsic hornfels 云母长英角岩
mica hornfels 云母角岩
mica schist 云母片岩
micro environment 微观环境
microbubble 微气泡
microcomputer server
微型计算机(微机)服务器
microcrack 微裂纹
microcrystalline quartz 微晶石英
microelectrode logging method
微电极测井法
microfiltration 微孔过滤
micromanometer 微压计
microphone 话筒,麦克风
micropile 微形桩
micropunch plate muffler 微穿孔板消声器
microwave distance measurement
微波测距
microwave rainfall sensor
微波式雨量传感器
micro-biological degradation 微生物降解
middle Cambrian epoch 中寒武世
middle Cambrian series 中寒武统
middle capacity hump 中能力驼峰
middle Carboniferous epoch 中石炭世
middle Carboniferous series 中石炭统
middle Devonian epoch 中泥盆世
middle Devonian series 中泥盆统
middle Jurassic epoch 中侏罗世
middle Jurassic series 中侏罗统
middle layer landslide 中层滑坡
middle Ordovician epoch 中奥陶世
middle Ordovician series 中奥陶统
middle part of shunting yard 调车场中部
middle Pleistocene epoch 中更新世
middle Pleistocene series 中更新统
middle Silurian epoch 中志留世
middle Silurian series 中志留统
middle Sinian epoch 中震旦世
middle Sinian series 中震旦统
middle sized marshaling station
中型编组站
middle temperate zone 中温带
middle Triassic epoch 中三叠世
middle Triassic series 中三叠统
middleman 经纪人,中间人,中间商
midline 中线
midline control stake 中线控制桩
midline elevation 中线高程
midline position 中线位置
midpoint anchor clamp for messenger wire
承力索中心锚结线夹
midspan load 跨中荷载
midway return operation 中途折返
mid-anchor connecting clamp for contact wire
接触线中心锚接线夹
mid-ocean ridge 洋中脊
mid-point anchor 中心锚结
mid-point anchor clamp 中心锚结线夹
mid-section impedance 段中阻抗
mid-slope 坡腰
mid-subtropics 中亚热带
mid-term evaluation 中期评估
mid-track 道心

mild soil erosion 轻度侵蚀
mileage 里程
milestone 重大事件
milestone date 里程碑日期
milestone payment 按里程碑付款
milestone schedule 里程碑进度计划
milling train 铣磨车
million packet per second 每秒百万包
Mindlin's solution 明德林解答
mined-out area 采空区
mineral admixtures 矿物掺合料
mineral aggregate 矿物粒料
mineral composition 矿物成分
mineral fibric base 无机纤维胎基
mineral powder asphalt emulsion
　矿物乳化沥青
mineral resources 矿产资源
minette 云煌岩
mine 开采
mingle 混合
mini pile 微形桩
minicomputer server 小型机服务器
minifair 小型交易会
minimal model unit 最小模型单元
minimum 最低值
minimum allowable value of the energy efficiency
　能效限定值
minimum amount 最低额
minimum amount of payment 最低支付限额
minimum available receiving level
　最小可用接收电平
minimum clear height 最小净高
minimum clearance 最小净距
minimum closing voltage 最低合闸电压
minimum deposit
　最低保证金,最低预付保险费
minimum dry density 最小干密度
minimum fine 最低罚款
minimum headway 最小行车间隔
minimum length of grade section
　最小坡段长度
minimum plane principal stress
　最小平面主应力
minimum pore ratio 最小孔隙比
minimum premium 最低保险费
minimum price 最低价格
minimum radius of curve 最小曲线半径
minimum radius of vertical curve
　最小竖曲线半径
minimum rail temperature 最低轨温

minimum service head 最小服务水头
minimum speed limit 最低限速
minimum temperature 最低气温
minimum thickness of concrete cover
　混凝土保护层最小厚度
minimum thickness of reinforced concrete cover
　钢筋混凝土保护层最小厚度
minimum turning radius 最小转弯半径
minimum value 最小值
mining area planning 矿区规划
mining method 矿山法
mining subsidence observation
　开采沉陷观测
minister 部长
ministry 部
mini-trial 小型审判
minor angle method 小角法,小角度法
minor axis 弱轴
minor defect 次要缺陷
minor drainage basin management
　小流域治理
minor repair 小修
minor triangulation 小三角测量
minusing 差减法
minute book 会议记录本
minutes 会议纪要
minutes of proceedings 议事记录
minutes of the meeting 会议纪要
minutes of trial 审判记录
Miocene epoch 中新世
Miocene series 中新统
mirabilite 芒硝
Misaki Sato Kuniki unsteady-state flow formula
　佐藤邦明非稳定流式
miscellaneous expenses 杂项开支
miscellaneous fill 杂填土
miscellaneous local taxes 地方杂税
miscellaneous material 零星用料
misclosure 闭合差
misclosure of round 归零差
misconduct in office 玩忽职守
misconduct offense 渎职罪
mise-a-la-masse method 充电法
misfire 瞎炮
mispresent expenditure 虚报支出
misregistration 记录错误
misrepresentation 不实陈述,讹传
missing item 漏项
missing item of equipment 缺项设备
missing item of material 缺项材料

missing locking 漏锁闭
missing rate 漏报率
missing release 漏解锁
mission 代表团
mission allowance 出差津贴
mistake 错误,误差,误解
misunderstanding 误解
misuse failure 误用失效
mitigate 减轻
mitigation 减免,减轻
mitigating action 缓解措施
mix 混合,混合料
mix proportion 拌和比,混合比,配合比
mix proportion benchmark 基准配合比
mix proportion design of mortar
  砂浆配合比设计
mix proportion design 配合比设计
mix proportion selection test
  配合比选定试验
mix ratio 拌和比
mixed cementation 混合胶结
mixed chromogenic reagent 混合显色剂
mixed cost 混合成本
mixed direct and indirect fastening
  半分开式扣件
mixed duties 混合关税,混合税
mixed liquid recycle 混合液回流
mixed passenger and freight railway
  客货共线
mixed pile 搅拌桩
mixed pumping test 混合抽水试验
mixed sand 混合砂
mixed single and double pipe heating system
  单双管混合式采暖系统
mixed soil 混合土
mixed solution 混合溶液
mixed sowing and planting 植物混播混种
mixed tariff 混合关税,混合税率
mixed-in-place 工地搅拌
mixer 搅拌机,拌和机
mixer truck 搅拌运料车
mixing 混合
mixing area 拌和区
mixing of concrete 混凝土拌和
mixing plant 拌和站
mixing procedure 投料顺序
mixing station of bituminous concrete
  沥青混凝土拌和站
mixing station of graded broken stone
  级配碎石拌和站

mixing station of improved soil
  改良土拌和站
mixing water 拌和水
mixture 混合,混合料
mixture properties 拌和物性能
mixture ratio 混合比
mix-up 混合
mm locking 毫米锁闭
mobile belt conveyor 移动带式输送机
mobile communication system
  移动通信系统
mobile loading and unloading machinery
  流动装卸机械
mobile service switching center(MSC)
  移动业务交换中心
mobile staging 活动脚手架
mobile station(MS) 移动终端(台),无线终端
mobile subscriber ISDN number(MSISDN)
  移动用户ISDN号码
mobile subscriber roaming number(MSRN)
  移动用户漫游号码
mobile switching center(MSC)
  移动交换中心
mobile terminal ticket sales 移动终端售票
mobile to fixed call
  移动终端呼叫有线固定终端
mobile to mobile call
  移动终端呼叫移动终端
mobilization 动员,启动
mobilization advance 动员预付款
mobilization charges 动员费
mobilization fee 启动费,动员费
mobilize 动员,调遣
modal analysis 模态分析
modal analysis method 振型分解法
mode 模式
mode of indication 显示方式
mode of payment 支付方式
mode of receiving trains by the pilot or the call-on signal 引导接车模式
mode participation coefficient
  振型参与系数
model 型号
model agreement 合同范本,示范协议
model baseline 模型基线
model connectivity 模型连接
model contract 标准合同,合同范本
model coordinates 模型坐标
model deformation 模型变形
model design 模型设计

model elements　模型要素
model elements combination
　模型要素组合
model house　样板房
model leveling　模型置平
model material　模型材料
model resource　模型资源
model scale　模型比例尺
model test　模型试验
model unit　模型单元
model view definition（MVD）
　模型视图定义
modem　调制解调器
moderate erosion　中度侵蚀
moderate fortification　适度设防
moderate gale　疾风
moderate price　中等价格,适度价格
moderate weathering　中风化
modernization　现代化
modest price increase　适当涨价
modest price reduction　适当降价
modification　更改,修改,修订,更正
modification factor of stress ratio
　应力比修正系数
modification of contract　合同变更
modification of planning　计划修改
Modified Griffith criterion
　修正的格里菲斯准则
modify　修改,修订,更正,更改,修正
modifying agent　改性剂
modular block　组匣
modular block rack　组匣柜
modular type signal mechanism
　组合式信号机构
modulated braking method　均衡制动法
modulus　模量
modulus of pressure meter　旁压仪模量
modulus of resilience　回弹模量
Mohr's stress circle　摩尔应力圆
Mohr-Coulomb Law　摩尔—库仑定律
Mohr-Coulomb theory　摩尔—库仑理论
moist　潮湿
moist dust control system　喷雾防尘装置
moisture　潮湿
moisture content　含湿量
moisture excess　余湿
moisture load　湿负荷
moisture proof　防潮
moisture release from equipment　设备散湿量
moisture release from occupants　人体散湿量

moisture release　散湿量
Molar concentration　摩尔浓度
Molar mass　摩尔质量
mold testing　试模
molding　（试件）成型
molding temperature　成型温度
molecular association　分子缔合
molecular water absorption ratio　分子吸水率
mollisol　松软土
mollisol subgrade　松软土路基
molybdenum blues photometric method
　钼蓝光度法
moment amplitude modulation coefficient
　弯矩调幅系数
moment of inertia of cross section
　截面惯性矩
momentum gradient　动能坡度
monadnock　残丘
monetary　财政的,货币的
monetary assets　货币性资产
monetary authorities　财政当局
monetary capital　货币性资金
monetary exchange rate
　货币汇率,货币汇率
monetary gain or loss　货币损益
monetary liabilities　货币债务
monetary market　货币市场
monetary markets　金融市场
monetary policy　货币政策
monetary restraint　货币限制
monetary stability　币值稳定
monetary unit　货币单位
monetary value　币值
money　货币
money assets or liabilities
　货币性资产或负债
money at call　短期放款,短期同行拆借
money equivalent　等值货币
money in hand　现金
money market　货币市场,金融市场
money of account　记账货币
money order　汇款单
money remaining　余款
money returned　还债
money transaction　现金交易
money turnover　货币周转
moneyed interest　金融界
money's worth　等值货币价值
monitor　监督,监控,监视
monitor work　监控工作

monitoring 监测
monitoring alarm value 监测报警值
monitoring and measurement 监控量测
monitoring center 监控中心
monitoring center server 监控中心服务器
monitoring contents 监测内容
monitoring device 监控装置
monitoring emphasis 监测重点
monitoring equipment 监控设备,监测设备
monitoring frequency 监测频率,监测频次
monitoring module 监控模块
monitoring of deformation of surrounding rock 洞室围岩变形监测
monitoring of pore water pressure 孔隙水压力监测
monitoring period 监测时段
monitoring point 监测点
monitoring point layout diagram for soil and water conservation 水土保持监测点位布局图
monitoring scope 监测范围
monitoring sector 监测区段
monitoring station 监控站
monitoring station for train operation safety 车辆运行安全监测站
monitoring system 监控系统
monitoring system for safe operation of passenger train 客车运行安全监控系统
monitoring terminal 监测终端
monitoring unit 监控单元
monitor-GPRS interface server（M-GRIS） 监测信息 GPRS 接口服务器
monkey engine 锤式打桩机
monobucket excavator 单斗挖土机
monoclinal valley 单斜谷
monocline 单斜
monoclinic system 单斜晶系
monolithic ballastless track 整体道床轨道
monolithic concrete 整体浇筑混凝土
monolithic lining 整体式衬砌
monomineral 单矿物
monopolize 垄断
monopoly 专卖
monopoly contract 独家承包合同
monopoly price 专卖价格
monopoly right 专卖权
monopoly/administered/cartel price 垄断价格
monorail trolley 单轨小车
Monte Carlo analysis 蒙特卡罗分析
Monte Carlo simulation 蒙特卡罗模拟
monthly 按月计
monthly allowance 月津贴
monthly balance sheet 月结算表
monthly detailed schedule 每月详细进度表
monthly inspection 月检修
monthly interest 月息
monthly interim payment certificate 每月期中付款证书
monthly pay 月薪
monthly payment 按月支付,每月付款
monthly performance report 绩效月报
monthly progress report 月进度报告
monthly progress review meeting 月进度审查会议
monthly report 月报告
monthly return 月报表
monthly statement 月结算单,月报表
monthly settlement report 月结算报告
monthly statement of account 月度对账单
monthly status review 月度状态报告
monthly summary 月汇总表
monthly wages 月工资
montmorillonite 蒙脱石
montmorillonite content 蒙脱石含量
monumentation 埋石
monument 界标
monzonite 二长岩
mooring 码头泊位
mop pool 拖布池
morainal topography 冰碛地形
moraine hill 冰碛丘陵
moraine kame 冰碛阜
morainic clay 冰碛黏土
moral risk 道德风险
moral standard 道德准则
moratorium 延缓偿付期,延期偿付权
more or less clause（M/L clause） 短溢装条款
mortar 砂浆
mortar air content tester 砂浆含气量测定仪
mortar bar expansion rate 砂浆棒膨胀率
mortar bolt 砂浆锚杆
mortar compressive specimen 砂浆抗压试件
mortar consistency 砂浆稠度
mortar consistometer 砂浆稠度仪
mortar elasticity modulus tester 砂浆弹性模量测定仪
mortar feeding rate 进浆速度

mortar fluidity　胶砂流动度
mortar fluidity tester　胶砂流动度测定仪
mortar for concrete small hollow block
　混凝土砌块专用砂浆
mortar layering degree apparatus
　砂浆分层度仪
mortar mix ratio　砂浆配合比
mortar peeling off　砂浆剥离
mortar rubble　浆砌片石
mortar rubble masonry　浆砌毛石
mortarless wall　干砌墙
mortgage　按揭,抵押,抵押单,抵押款,抵押权
mortgage bond　抵押债券
mortgage clause　抵押条款
mortgage loan　抵押贷款
mortgagee
　承按人,承押人,抵押贷款人,受押人
mortgagor　按揭人,出押人,抵押借款人,抵押人
mosaic effect　马赛克效应
mosaic map　镶嵌图
most permission signal　最大允许信号
most restrictive mode curve
　最限制模式曲线
most restrictive signal　最大限制信号
most restrictive speed profile（MRSP）
　最限制速度曲线
most unfavorable calculated load
　最不利计算荷载
most unfavorable combination of load effect
　荷载效应最不利组合
most-favoured-nation clause　最惠国条款
most-favoured-nation tariff rates
　最惠国关税率
most-favoured-nation treatment　最惠国待遇
mother company　母公司
motive　动机
motor　机动车
motor car liability insurance　机动车责任险
motor flusher　洒水车
motor insurance　机动车辆保险
motor vehicle tax　机动车辆税
motorized disconnector with short-circuit indicator
　带短路指示器电动隔离开关
motorized disconnector　电动隔离开关
motorized operating mechanism
　电动操作机构
motormixer　混凝土搅拌车
motorpaver　自动铺路机
motor-type code sender　电动机式发码器
mould　模具

moulding chamber temperature　模腔温度
mountain　山
mountain glacier　高山冰川
mountain range　山脉
mountain ridge　山脊
mountain slope　山坡
mountainside tunnel　傍山隧道
mountaintop　山顶
mountain-crossing tunnel　越岭隧道
mounting　配件
mounting cost　装配成本
mounting drawing　装配图
mounting height　安装高度
mounting of equipment　设备安装
mounting rack　安装架,工作台
movable bearing　活动支座
movable bridge　活动桥,开启桥
movable facility for sewage discharge
　移动式卸污
movable flash welding machine
　移动式闪光焊轨车
movable formwork method　移动模架法
movable point frog　可动心轨辙叉
movable point frog single turnout
　可动心轨辙叉单开道岔
movable property　动产
movable scaffolding system（MSS,used for span-by-span casting construction）　移动模架
movable signal　移动信号
movable standby　移动备用
movable support system（used for span-by-span precast segmental construction）　移动支架
movable support　活动支架
movement across lines　跨线运行
movement authority　行车许可
movement authority test　行车许可测试
moving basin　移动盆地
moving block　移动闭塞
moving dune　流动沙丘
moving image　活动图像
moving picture experts group（MPEG）
　运动图像专家组
MSC Server　移动交换中心服务器
muck　弃渣
muck disposal area　弃渣场
muck loader　装岩机
muck protection　弃渣防护
mucking　出渣
mucky soil　淤泥质土
mud crack structure　泥裂构造

mud gushing 涌泥
mud valve 排泥阀
mudflow scarp 泥流陡坎
mudstone 泥岩
mud-pumping 翻浆冒泥
muffler 消声器
multiaspect seismic fortification
多道抗震设防
multiband image 多波段图像
multidiscipline 跨专业
multilateral agreement 多边协定
multilateral aid 多边援助
multilateral clearing 多边清算
multilateral contract 多边合同
multilateral cooperation 多边合作
multilateral settlement 多边结算
multilateral tariff treaty 多边税收协定
multilateral trade 多边贸易
multilayer rectangular arrangement
多层矩形布置
multilayered three-dimensional green belt
立体复层绿化带
multimedia 多媒体
multimeter 万用表
multimodal transport operator（MTO）
联合运输人
multimodal transport
多式联运,多种方式联运,综合运输
multimodal transport 联合运货
multimode optical fiber 多模光纤
multinational company 跨国公司
multinational enterprises（MNE） 跨国企业
multipath effect 多路径效应
multiplanar tubular joint 空间管节点
multiple bidding 多合同招标
multiple contracting 多合同发包
multiple coverage（overlay） 多次覆盖(叠加)
multiple line insurance
多险种保险,复合保险
multiple payments（equal cash flow）
多次支付(等额现金流)
multiple perils insurance 多种风险保险
multiple pushing and double rolling
多推双溜
multiple tariff system 多重关税制,复式税则
multiple taxation 复税制
multiplex equipment 复用设备
multiplexer 复用器
multiplexing section 复用段
multiple-shot reclosing 多次重合闸

multiple-step income statement 分步收益表
multiple-track tunnel 多线隧道
multiple-well pumping test 多井抽水试验
multipoint control unit（MCU）
多点控制单元(设备)
multipoint displacement meter 多点位移计
multipoint excitation 多点激振
multiprocessor 多处理器
multipurpose project 综合利用项目
multispectral image 多光谱图像
multistage anaerobic treatment 多段厌氧处理
multistage measuring instrument of energy consumption 多级用能计量措施
multitemporal image 多时像图像
multi-bucket excavator 多斗挖土机
multi-driver communication 多驾驶员通信
multi-feature pulse 多特征脉冲
multi-frequency signal display
多频信号显示器
multi-lens color light signal
透镜式色灯信号机
multi-level architecture 多级架构
multi-party arbitration 多方仲裁
multi-plan bidding 多方案报价法
multi-protocol BGP（MP-BGP） 多协议 BGP
multi-protocol label switching（MPLS）
多协议标签交换,多协议标记交换
multi-rib arch bridge 肋拱桥
Multi-Service Transport Platform（MSTP）
多业务传送平台
multi-storey stereoscopic waiting room
多层立体式候车室
multi-tower structure 多塔楼结构
multi-track bridge 多线桥
muscovite 白云母
mutual benefit 互惠,互利
mutual consent 双方同意,双方应允
mutual deviation 互差
mutual exchange 互换
mutual funds 共同基金,互惠基金
mutual impedance 互阻抗
mutual indemnification
相互补偿,相互保障
mutual insurance company 互助保险公司
mutual understanding 互相谅解,相互理解,互谅
mutually preferential tariff 互惠关税
mylonite 糜棱岩
mylonitic texture 糜棱结构
m-method of pile foundation calculation
桩基计算 m 值法

N

nail burying method 埋钉法
naked contract 无担保合同
naked spots 裸露斑
naked truth 真相
name of commodity 货名,商品名称
named bill of lading 记名提单
named consignee 指定收货人
named date 规定日期,指定日期
named departure point 指定启运地
named place of delivery 指定交货地点
named place of destination 指定目的地
named port of shipment 指定装船港
nameplate 铭牌
nappe 推覆体
narrow gorge 嶂谷
narrow margin 薄利
narrow-gauge railway 窄轨距铁路
nation 国家
national bond 国家公债
national competitive bidding
　国内竞争性招标
national coordinate system 国家坐标系
national customs territory 国家海关辖区
national debt 国债
national dividend 国民所得
national economic evaluation 国民经济评价
national finance 国家财政
national insurance 国家保险
national key cultural relics protection units
　国家重点文物保护单位
national market 国内市场
national product 国民总收入
national railway 国家铁路
national revenue 国家税收
national sovereignty 国家主权
national standard 国家标准
national statute 国家法令
national tax 国税

national treatment 国民待遇
nationality 国籍
nationalization of enterprise 企业国有化
nationals 国民
native 本国的,国产的,本国人,本地人
native vegetation 原生植被
natural anti-seepage 自然防渗
natural arch 自然拱
natural base 自然底数
natural berm 天然护道
natural boundary survey 自然边界测量
natural bridge 天然桥
natural compactness 天然密实度
natural conditions 自然条件
natural construction materials 天然建筑材料
natural curing 自然养护
natural density 天然密度
natural diffusion method 自然扩散法
natural disaster and foreign object intrusion monitoring system for railway
　铁路自然灾害及异物侵限监测系统
natural disaster and foreign object intrusion monitoring system
　自然灾害及异物侵限监测系统
natural disaster 自然灾害
natural dry density 天然干密度
natural earth electrode 自然接地体
natural earthquake test 天然地震试验
natural electric field method 自然电场法
natural exhaust 自然排风
natural field magnetotelluric method
　天然场大地电磁法
natural frequency 固有频率
natural frequency of bridge 桥梁自振频率
natural frequency of sound barrier
　声屏障固有频率
natural ground 天然地基
natural landslide 自然滑坡

natural materials 天然材料,自然材料
natural moisture content 天然含水率
natural permafrost table 冻土天然上限
natural person 自然人
natural physical conditions 自然物质条件
natural repose angle 天然休止角
natural reserve 自然保护区
natural resources 天然资源,自然资源
natural risk 自然风险
natural sand 天然砂
natural scour of river channel 河槽天然冲刷
natural smoke exhaust 自然排烟
natural treatment of sewage 污水自然处理
natural vegetation 天然植被
natural ventilation 自然通风
natural vibration frequency 自振频率
natural vibration period 自振周期
natural void ratio 天然孔隙比
natural wastage 自然损耗
natural water content 天然含水量
naturally graded 天然级配
nature 性质
nature of tort 侵权性质
nature of works 工程性质
nautical mile 海里
navigable water level 通航水位
navigate 航行
navigation satellite global positioning system 导航卫星全球定位系统
navigational clearance 通航净空
navvy 工人
near delivery 近期交割,近期交货
nearly zero energy building 近零能耗建筑
neat plaster 纯灰浆
necking down 缩颈
needle-punched geotextile 针刺土工织物
negative apparent velocity method 负视速度法
negative assets account 负债账户,负资产账户
negative capital 亏损
negative cash flow 负现金流量
negative covenant 限制性契约
negative delay 负延时
negative feeder (AF) 正馈线
negative film 负片
negative growth 负增长
negative hardness 负硬度
negative hydraulic head 负水头
negative image 阴像

negative pressure area 负压区
negative pressure sieving of cement 水泥负压筛
negative pressure suction erosion 负压吸蚀作用
negative relief 负地形
negative sequence 负序
negative sequence compensation degree 负序补偿度
negative sequence component 负序分量
negative sequence current increment 负序增量
negative sequence current 负序电流
negative skin friction 负摩阻力
neglect 忽略
neglect of duty 失职,玩忽职守
neglection 忽略
negligence 玩忽,过失,疏忽
negligent act 过失行为
negligent crime 过失罪
negotiability 可流通性,可转让性
negotiable bill of lading 可转让提单,流通提单
negotiable bill 可转让票据
negotiable certificate of deposit 可转让定期存单,流通存单
negotiable check (cheque) 可转让支票,流通支票
negotiable document 可议付单据
negotiable draft 可转让汇票,流通汇票
negotiable instrumen/paper/bill/note 流通票据,可转让票据
negotiable L/C 可转让信用证,流通信用证
negotiable letter of credit 流通信用证
negotiable paper 可转让票据
negotiable promissory note/time note/term bill/period bill 流通期票
negotiable promissory note/time note/time bill/period bill 可转让期票
negotiable 可流通的
negotiant 交易者
negotiate 交涉,商谈,议定,谈判
negotiated bidding 议标
negotiated price 议价
negotiated settlement 协商解决
negotiating bank 议付银行/押汇银行
negotiating condition 议价条件
negotiating procedure 谈判程序
negotiating strategies 谈判策略
negotiation 交涉,谈判,议付

negotiation commission　议付手续费,转让手续费
negotiation contract　协商合同,议标合同
negotiator　交易者,谈判者
neighboring loads　相邻荷载
Neoarchean era　新太古代
Neoarchean erathem　新太古界
neogene period　晚第三纪
Neoproterozoic era　新元古代
neotectonic movement　新构造运动
nepheline　霞石
nepheline syenite　霞石正长岩
neritic facies　浅海相
Nessler tube　纳氏比色管
net　净数
net amount　净额
net account due　到期付款净额
net asset value　资产净值
net assets　净资产,资产净额
net attenuation frequency characteristics　净衰耗频率特性
net average static load for wagons　货车平均净载重
net benefit　净效益
net bid price　净投标价
net capital (N/C)　纯资本,资本金
net capital gains　资本净收益
net cash flow　净现金流量
net cash value　可变现净值
net cost　净成本
net current asset　流动资产净额
net earnings　净收益
net expenditure　纯支出
net frame floor drain　网框地漏
net freight　净运费
net income　净收入
net income after depreciation　折旧后净收益
net income/earnings after tax　纳税后净收益
net interest　净息
net interest margin　利息差额
net invoice price　净发票价格
net lease　净租赁
net liabilities　负债净额
net loss　净亏损,净损失
net markup percentage　净加价百分率
net national product (NNP)　国民生产净值
net operating loss　净营业损失
net output　净产值
net platform at hump crest　峰顶净平台
net premium　净保险费
net present value　净现值,净现值法
net price　净价,实价
net proceeds　净收入
net profit　纯利,净利润
net rate　纯费率,净费率
net return of investment　净投资收入
net sales　净销售额
net salvage value　净残值
net span　净跨度
net tonnage　净吨位
net value　净值
net value of fixed assets　固定资产净值
net water-cement ratio　净水灰比
net weight　净重
net worth method　净值法
network　管网,网络,网状系统
network analysis　网络分析
Network Attached Storage (NAS)　网络附属存储
network bandwidth　网络带宽
network bridge　网桥
network cable tester　网络电缆测试仪
network chart (diagram)　网络图
network communication　网络通信
network data　网络数据
network delay　网络时延
network element　网元
network equipment　网络设备
network fault　网络故障
network form　网络计划形式
network level　网络等级
network management center　网络管理(网管)中心
network management equipment　网络管理(网管)设备
network management server　网络管理(网管)服务器
network management system (NMS)　网络管理(网管)系统
network management terminal　网络管理(网管)终端
network management　网络管理(网管)
network node　网络节点
network of flight strip　航线网
network operation status monitoring　网络运行状态监测
network optimization and adjustment　网络优化调整

network performance analyzer
网络性能分析仪
network performance index 网络性能指标
network program 网络计划
network resource 网络资源
network scheduling technique 网络进度计划法
network security 网络安全
network structure 网络结构
network tester 网络测试仪
network time processing server
网络时间处理服务器
network time protocol(NTP)
网络时间协议
neutral liquid 中性液体
neutral party bill of lading 中性提单
neutral plane 中和面,中性面
neutral point 中性点
neutral point earthing 中性点接地
neutral protection conductor 中性保护导体
neutral rail temperature
设计锁定轨温,中和轨温
neutral relay 无极继电器
neutral section 中性区段,中性段
neutral section auto-passing 自动过分相
neutral state 中立国
neutral wire of auto-transformer
自耦变压器中线
neutral wire N 线
neutral zone 分相区,无电区
neutralization method 中和法
neutralization tank 酸性中和池
New Austrian Tunnelling Method(NATM)
新奥法
new energy 新能源
new loess 新黄土
new material 新材料
new railway 新建铁路
new railway line 新建铁路线
new station 新建车站
new structure 新结构
new subgrade 新建路基
news agency 通讯社
Newtonian fluid 牛顿流体
niche 壁龛
nickel content 镍含量
Nielsen type Lohse bridge (also known as "rigid arch bridge with rigid tie and inclined suspenders")
尼尔森洛泽梁桥,又称"斜悬杆式刚性拱刚性梁桥"
night duty allowance 夜班津贴

night shift 夜班
night signal 夜间信号
night vision 夜视功能
night vision image 夜视图像
nitrate nitrogen 硝酸盐氮
nitric acid 硝酸
nitrite nitrogen 亚硝酸盐氮
nivation swale 雪蚀洼地
no acceptance (N. A.) 拒绝承兑
no attendance 闲人莫入
no credit 现款交易
no DAAB in place
没有争议避免裁决委员会
No parking sign 禁停标志牌
no trespassing 不准进入
nodal point 节点
node 节点
node network 节点网
nodular 结核状
noise 杂音,噪声
noise assessment 噪声评价
noise at boundary 厂界噪声
noise at construction site boundary
建筑施工场界噪声
noise control 噪声控制
noise control standard 噪声控制标准
noise detector 噪声探测器
noise level 噪声级
noise limit value 噪声限值
noise meter 杂音计
noise prevention 噪声防治
noise rating number 噪声评价数
noise reduction 降噪
noise reduction coefficient (NRC) 降噪系数
noise reduction effect 降噪效果
noise source intensity 噪声源强
noise voltage 杂音电压
noise-limited sensitivity 噪限灵敏度
noise-sensitive building 噪声敏感建筑
nominal 额定的
nominal account 名义账户,虚账户
nominal accuracy 标称精度
nominal accuracy of EDM
电磁波测距标称精度
nominal amount 名义金额
nominal capacity 标称容量
nominal capital 名义资本
nominal cost 名义成本
nominal current 标称电流
nominal diameter 公称直径

nominal dimension 标称尺寸,名义尺寸
nominal exchange rate 名义汇率
nominal force 公称力
nominal frequency 标称频率
nominal impedance 标称阻抗
nominal interest rate 额定利率,名义利率
nominal length 公称长度
nominal load 额定荷载
nominal maximum aggregate size
最大公称粒径
nominal particle size 公称粒径
nominal partner 名义合伙人
nominal quantity 名义数量
nominal sound pressure level 标称声压级
nominal value
名义值,名义价值,票面价值,面值,票面金额
nominal voltage 标称电压
nominate 提名,推荐,指定
nominated contractor 指定的承包商
nominated subcontractor 指定分包商
nomination 提名,推荐,指定
nominee 被任命人,被提名人
non equipment centralized station
非设备集中站
non-transferable credit 不可转让信用证
nonbearing wall 非承重墙
noncompliance 不遵守,违约行为,不符合
noncompliance with contractual conditions
不符合合同条件
noncompliance with specifications
不符合技术规范
nonexportation 禁止出口
non-leakage flow wheel set 非泄流轮对
nonmetallic air duct 非金属材料风管
nonpolarizable electrode 不极化电极
nonprofit-oriented project 非营利性项目
nonstick button 自复式按钮
nonstop arrival 一站直达
nonstructural joint 非结构节理
non-traditional water source 非传统水源
nontransferable letter of credit
不可转让信用证
nontronite 绿脱石
nonuniformity coefficient of tensile steel strain
纵向受拉钢筋应变不均匀系数
non-visible property 无形资产
non-acceptance 不接受,拒绝承兑
non-alkali-active aggregate 非碱活性骨料
non-assignable 不可转让的
non-bearing boiler 非承压锅炉

non-binding arbitration 无约束力的仲裁
non-binding decision 无约束力的决定
non-breathing zone 固定区
non-centralized interlocking 非集中联锁
non-combustible substance 不燃烧体
non-competitive bid 非竞争性报价
non-condensable gas separator
不凝性气体分离器
non-conformance report
违规报告,不合要求报告
non-conforming product 不合格产品
non-contact IC card 非接触式IC卡
non-contact measurement
非接触测量,非接触量测
non-contest clause 无争议条款
non-crystalline 非晶质体
non-delivery 未交定货
non-destructive test (NDT) 无损检测
non-disclosure 保密,隐瞒情况不报
non-discountable bill 非贴现票据
non-discriminatory treatment 无差别待遇
non-dutiable goods 免税货物
non-elastic deformation 非弹性变形
non-electrified line 非电化线路
non-electrified track 非电化股道
non-eligible 不合格的
non-eligible country 不合格来源国
non-energized inspection running 冷滑
non-energized probability 无电概率
non-energized section
(列控系统)分相区
non-excusable delays 不可原谅的拖期
non-execution 不执行
non-forfeiture condition 不作废条款
non-geometric information 非几何信息
non-implementation of contract
合同不履行
non-insulated overlap 非绝缘锚段关节
non-insulated transition mast
非绝缘转换(支)柱
non-insurable risk 拒保风险
non-interlocked zone 非联锁区
non-interlocking switch 非联锁道岔
non-isothermal jet 非等温射流
non-linear distortion 非线性失真
non-linear error 非线性误差
non-load test 空载调试
non-magnetic shield 无磁屏蔽
non-mechanized hump 非机械化驼峰
non-metallic short circuit 非金属性短路

non-metric camera 非量测摄影机
non-monetary assets 非货币性资产
non-monetary liabilities 非货币性负债
non-nail laying 无钉铺设
non-negotiable 不可转让的
non-negotiable bill of lading 不可转让提单
non-negotiable document 不可转让单据
non-operating expenses 非营业费用
non-operating income 非营业收入
non-operating outlay 非营业性支出
non-operating revenue 非营业收入
non-payment 拒付,停止支付,无力支付
non-performance 违约,不作为,未履行
non-performance of contract 合同不履行
non-pressure pipeline 无压管道
non-price criteria 非价格准则
non-productive construction project
非生产性建设项目
non-prosecution 不起诉
non-recourse 无追索,无追索权
non-recurring incomes and expenses
临时性收支
non-reimbursable assistance 无偿援助
non-responsibility 无责任
non-responsive bid 不符合要求的投标
non-route shunting circuit 非进路调车电路
non-self-weight collapsible loess
非自重湿陷性黄土
non-separation agreement 不可分割协议书
non-stable permafrost region at high temperature
高温不稳定冻土区
non-standard circular cone specimen
非标准圆锥台体试件
non-steady noise 非稳态噪声
non-tilting mixer 鼓筒式混凝土搅拌机
non-topographic photogrammetry
非地形摄影测量
non-trade receipt 非贸易收入
non-trading asset 固定资产
non-uniformity 弹性不均匀度
non-uniformity coefficient
不均匀程度系数
non-vital circuit 非安全电路
non-waiver 不弃权
non-woven geotextile 无纺土工织物
norite 苏长岩
norm 标准
normal acting relay 正常动作继电器
normal and reverse locking 定反位锁闭
normal case photography 正直摄影

normal condition 正常情况,正常条件
normal consistency 标准稠度
normal contact 定位接点
normal cost 正常费用
normal depreciation 正常折旧
normal distribution 正态分布
normal equation 标准方程
normal fault 正断层
normal field (background value)
正常场(背景值)
normal flow period 平水期
normal fold 正褶皱
normal frost-heave force 法向冻胀力
normal height-thickness ratio 通用高厚比
normal hour 标准工时
normal locking 定位锁闭
normal loss 正常损耗
normal mode of operations 正常工作模式
normal operating mode 正常工作模式
normal position indication 定位显示
normal projection 正轴投影
normal section 正截面,正断面图
normal services 正常的服务
normal shrinkage 正常的收缩
normal stress 法向应力,正应力
normal tension 法向拉力
normal water inflow 正常涌水量
normal water level 常水位
normalizing 正火
normally closed contacts 常闭节点
normally closed disconnector
常闭隔离开关
normally consolidated soil 正常固结土
normally deenergized track circuit
开路式轨道电路
normally energized track circuit
闭路式轨道电路
normally open contacts 常开节点
normally open disconnector 常开隔离开关
northbound interface 北向接口
northern subtropics 北亚热带
nose of guard rail 梭头
nose-like hump 鼻状凸丘
nosing force 摇摆力
not sufficient funds (N.S.F.)
存款不足,基金不足
notarial acts 公证手续
notarial certificate 公证证书
notarial document 公证文件
notarization 公证

notarize 公证
notary 公证人
notary public 公证人
notation 记号
note 单据,票据,便条,借据,通知书
note of hand 借据
note on discount 贴现票据
note receivable 应收票据
notes payable 应付款凭单,应付票据
notice 布告,通知,注意
notice and other communications 通知及其他沟通形式
notice by fax 传真通知
notice in writing 书面通知
notice of abandonment 委付通知,委弃通知
notice of an exceptional event 异常事件的通知
notice of arrival 到货通知,抵埠通知
notice of award 中标通知
notice of change 变更通知
notice of claim 索赔通知书
notice of commencement 开工通知
notice of default 违约通知
notice of dishonour 拒付通知,拒付通知单
notice of dissatisfaction (NOD) 不满意通知
notice of importation 进口通知
notice of loss 损失通知
notice of non-delivery 提货不着通知单,未到货通知
notice of shipment 装船通知
notice of test 检验通知
notice period 通知期限
notice to correct 改正通知
notification 布告,通知,通知单,通知书
notification of award 授标通知
notifying bank 通知行
notional price 假设价格
novated design-build 接力式设计—建造
novation contract 更替型合同
nozzle 喷嘴
no-claim bonus 无赔款奖金,未索赔奖励
no-claim discount 无赔款折扣,未索赔折扣
no-claim return 无赔款退费,未索赔退款

no-interest-bearing note 不带息票据
no-load 空载
no-load expansion rate test 无荷载膨胀率试验
no-load loss 空载损耗
no-load machine testing 空载试机
no-load test for transformer 变压器空载试验
no-objection 无异议
no-sand pervious concrete 无砂透水混凝土
nuclear assembly 核装置
nuclear device 核装置
nuclear magnetic resonance method 核磁共振探视法
nuclear ray method 核子射线法
nuclear risk 核风险
nucleon density and humidity tester 核子密度湿度测试仪
nude cargo 裸装货
nuisance 妨害,损害
null shift 零漂
number of allocated passenger cars 客车配属辆数
number of channels 路数
number of closed loops 闭合环边数
number of contained containers 容箱数
number of container slot 箱位数
number of disc cutters 滚刀数
number of effectively observed satellites at the same time 同时观测有效卫星数
number of freight cars on hand 货车保有量
number of main line 正线数目
number of poles 极数
number of scanning sampling point 扫描样点数
number of times of taking-out and placing-in every 24 hours 每昼夜取送车次数
number of video streaming 视频流路数
numbering error 编号错误
numbers 数字
numerical error 数字错误,数目错误
numerical solution 数值解
numerical value 数值
nummary 货币的
nut 螺母

O

object 标的(物),对象,目的
object matter of insurance 保险标的
object of action 诉讼标的
object of insurance 保险标的
object of taxation 课税对象
object space coordinate system
　物方空间坐标系
object under surveillance 监督对象
objection 妨碍
objection procedure 异议程序
objective 目的
objective angle of image field 像场角
objective evidence 客观证据
objective fact 客观事实
objective management 目标管理
objective probability 客观概率
objective reason 客观理由
objective schedule 任务进度表
objective tax 对物税,专用税
objectivity 客观性
obligation 义务,职责
obligatory arbitration 强制仲裁
obligatory judicial settlement 强制司法解决
obligatory reinsurance 固定分保,自动分保
obligatory right 债权
obligee 权利人,债主
obligor 义务人,债务人
oblique angle 斜交角
oblique correction 倾斜改正
oblique fault 斜断层
oblique joint 斜交节理
oblique photography 倾斜摄影
oblique section 斜截面
oblique survey 倾斜测量
observation 评价意见,注释
observation data 观测数据
observation equation (also known as "error equation")
　观测方程(又称"误差方程")
observation error 观测误差
observation hole 灌注孔、观察孔
observation instrument 观测仪器
observation monument 观测墩
observation of slope stability
　边坡稳定性观测
observation of subsidence deformation
　沉降变形观测
observation period 观测周期
observation pillar 观测桩
observation point 观测点
observation session 观测时段
observation set 测回
observation station 观测站
observation station of surface movement
　地表移动观测站
observation target 觇标,测量觇标
observation well 观测孔
observatory 天文台
observe 监视
observed profile for settlement
　沉降观测断面
obsidian 黑曜岩
obstacle 障碍物
obstacle board (补偿坠陀)挡板
obstruct 妨碍
obstruction 障碍物
obstruction signal
　遮断信号,遮断信号机
obstructive coefficient of debris flow
　泥石流堵塞系数
obstructive failure 妨害失效
obtain 达到,获得
obtaining of DAAB decision
　取得争议避免裁决委员会的决定
obvious defect 明显缺陷
occasional combination of loads
　荷载偶然组合

occasional design state 偶然设计状况
occupancy expenses 占用费
occupancy indication 占线表示
occupancy permit 占用许可证
occupancy rate 使用率,占用率
occupancy right 占用权
occupant occupier 占有人
occupation 占有,职业
occupation loss indication 失去占用表示
occupation of fund 占用资金
occupational disease 职业病
occupational safety 职业安全
occur 发生
occurrence 产状,发生
occurences of rock formation 岩层产状
occurrence of structural plane 结构面产状
ocean and rail (O. & R.) 海陆联运
ocean basin 洋盆
ocean bill of lading 海运提单
ocean carriage 海运,远洋运输
ocean carrier 海运承运人
ocean freight 海运费
ocean liner 远洋班轮
ocean marine cargo (transportation) insurance 海洋运输货物保险
ocean ridge 海岭,洋脊
ocean vessel 远洋船舶
ocean waybill 海运提单
oceangoing freighter 远洋货轮
oceanic basin 大洋盆地
OCS inspection vehicle (car) 接触网检修车
octave-band sound-pressure level 倍频带声压级
odd job 临时工作,零活
odinite 拉辉煌斑岩
off limits 闲人莫入
off line maintenance 脱线修
off season 淡季
off set 冲账
offal 次品
offence 犯法
offence of bribery 贿赂罪
offence of dereliction of duty 渎职罪
offence-reporter 检举人
offend 违反
offer 报价,发盘,邀约报价
offer period 报价有效期
offered price 出售价格
offered rate 贷款利率
offeree 接受报价者,受盘人,受约人

offerer 报价人,发盘人,要约人
offeror 报价人,发盘人,要约人
offhand 即时的
office automation system 办公信息系统
office building 办公建筑
office data 局数据
office expenses 办公费
office hours 办公时间
office network 办公网
office overhead costs 办公室管理费
office premises 办公用房
officer 办事员,公务员
official 正式的
official contract 盖章合同,正式合同
official devaluation 法定贬值
official exchange rate 法定汇率,官方汇率
official gazette 官方公报
official holiday 法定假日
official language 正式语言
official letter 公函
official misconduct 失职
official price 法定价格,官方价值,正式价值
official rate 法定利率,官方兑换率,法定汇率
official receipt 正式收据
official register 正式注册
official representative 正式代表
official seal 公章
official text 正式文本
official translation 正式译本
officiate 主持会议
offline UPS 后备式UPS
offset (电杆)迈步,冲销,抵消,偏移
offset account 抵消账户
offset distance 偏移距
offset modulus 偏移模量
offset of closure rail 导曲线支距
offset of lead curve 导曲线支距
offset stake 外移桩
offshore bank 境外银行
offshore boring 水上钻孔
offshore contract 离岸合同
offshore embankment 离岸堤
offshore escrow account 境外第三方账户
offshore interest rate 境外利率
offshore office 海外办事处
offsite fabrication 现场外装配
offtake 排水槽,排水渠,分输
offtake agreement 承购协议
offtake contract 承购合同
off-day 休息日

off-duty 下班,休假
off-grid PV system 离网型光伏发电系统
off-line diagnosis 在线诊断,离线诊断
off-line operation 脱机作业
off-line state 脱机状态
off-line ticketing 离线售票
off-road vehicle 越野车
off-site parking lot 场外停车场
off-test 未经检验的
official invoice 正式发票
oil basin (oil leakage pool) 贮油池
oil chromatographic online monitor
  油色谱在线监测
oil circuit-breaker 油断路器
oil conduit 导油管
oil conservator 油枕
oil converging pipe 汇油管
oil cooler 油冷却器
oil depot attached to enterprise 企业附属石油库
oil filtering 滤油
oil gas pressure 油气压力
oil jack 油压千斤顶
oil leakage 漏油
oil length 含油率
oil level indicator 油位计
oil permeability 渗油性
oil pipeline survey 输油管道测量
oil pressure gauge 油压表
oil removal facilities 除油设施
oil separation 调节沉淀隔油
oil separation and sedimentation tank
  隔油沉淀池
oil separator 隔油池
oil shale 油页岩
oil solubility 油溶性
oil storage 油库
oil storage area 储油区
oil tank area 油罐区
oil tank capacity 油罐容量
oil tank set 油罐组
oil treatment room 油处理间
oil unloading track 卸油线
oil (tank) truck 油罐车
oily production sewage 含油生产污水
oily sewage 含油污水
oil-immersed transformer
  油浸变压器,油浸式变压器
oil-immersed voltage transformer
  油浸式电压互感器
old hand 熟练工人

old loess 老黄土
Oligocene epoch 渐新世
Oligocene series 渐新统
oligopoly price 卖主垄断价格
oligopsony price 买主垄断价格
olive brilliant slate 橄辉煌板岩
olivine 橄榄石
olivine basalt 橄榄玄武岩
omissions 删减
omission 忽略,失职,遗漏
omit 忽略,遗漏
omitted work 删除的工作
on a daywork basis 计日工制
on a monthly basis 按月计
on a piecework basis 计件制
on a turnkey basis 采取交钥匙的形式
on account (O/A) 记账,赊账
on board 已装船,在船上
on board bill of lading 已装船提单
on cash 现金交易
on credit 信用赊账
on deck bill of lading 舱面交货提单
on deck risk 舱面货物险
on duty 当班,值班
on job lab 工地试验室
on lending 转贷
on load cargo 装货
on rail 铁路交货
on schedule 按预定计划
on sight mode (OS) 目视行车模式
on the balance 收支平衡
on the ground 当场
on the nod 赊购
on trust 赊账
onboard communication unit 车载通信单元
onboard equipment 车载设备
onboard equipment of train control system
  列车运行控制车载设备
onboard radio 机车台
onboard vital computer 车载安全计算机
once-for-all route release 进路一次解锁
oncost 现场杂费
one block deal 一揽子交易
one fabric and one membrane composite geomembrane 一布一膜复合土工膜
one island and one track 一岛一道
one section of zero-sequence current protection
  一段零序电流保护
one track and one platform layout 一线一台布置
onerous loan 有偿贷款

one-hundred-percent inspection 全部检验
one-off cost 一次性成本
one-off debt pay off 一次性付清债务
one-piece cast frog 整铸辙叉
one-pipe series-loop heating system 单管顺序式采暖系统
one-sided main line 一侧式正线
one-stop shopping 一站式采购
one-time expenses 一次性支出
one-way concrete slab 混凝土单向板
one-way slab 单向板
one-way slope 单面坡道
one-way slope tunnel 单面坡隧道
online monitoring of transformer 变压器在线监测
online ticket refund 联网退票
online ticket sales 互联网售票
online UPS 在线式UPS
onshore contract 岸上合同
onsite communication platform 现场通信平台
on-board juridical recorder unit（JRU）车载司法记录单元
on-board rail lubricator 车载钢轨涂油器
on-board satellite terminal 车载卫星终端
on-costs 间接成本
on-duty console 值班台
on-duty section 值班工区
on-laid terrace 上叠阶地
on-line operation 联机作业
on-line state 联机状态
on-load loss 负载损耗
on-site custody fee 工地保管费
on-site inspection 现场检查，现场检验
on-site supervision 旁站，现场监督
on-site training 现场培训
on-the-job training 岗上培训
on-the-spot audit 现场审计
oolitic 鲕状，粒岩的
oolitic structure 鲕状构造
opal 蛋白石
open account 赊账，未结清账户
open account trade 记账交易
open bid（tender）公开投标
open bidding（tendering）公开招标
open bill of lading 不记名提单
open caisson 沉井
open caisson foundation 沉井基础
open caisson method with injected air curtain 空气幕沉井法
open caisson method with slurry coating 泥浆套沉井法
open channel 明渠
open cheque 普通支票，未划线支票
open competition 公开竞争
open cover 承保单，预约保险
open credit 无担保贷款
open cup flash point 开口闪点
open cut foundation 明挖基础
open cut method 明挖法
open cut tunnel 明洞
open debt 未清债务
open deck 明桥面
open door policy 开放政策
open drainage 明沟排水
open endorsement 空白背书
open L/C 开口信用证
open letter of credit 开口信用证
open line 明线线路
open policy 预约保单，开口保单
open port 自由港
open pumping 集水明排
open return 开式回水
open rib 板肋
open shortest path first（OSPF）开放最短路径优先路由协议
open storage 露天存货
open traverse 支导线
open tunnel boring machine 开敞式掘进机
open water tank 开式水箱
open well 大口井
open wire 明线
opening balance 期初差额，期初余额
opening bank 开证银行
opening circuit 分闸回路
opening coil 分闸线圈
opening enlargement of bridge and culvert 桥涵扩孔
opening entry 开始记录
opening of tender 开标
opening pressure 开启压力
opening price 开盘价
opening size 孔径
opening time 分闸时间
open-end contract 无限期合同
open-end order 开口订货单
open-end purchase order 开口订货单
open-plan office 开放式办公室
open-stacking area 露天堆场
operability 可操作性

operate 经营,运用
operating account 营业账户
operating capital 营业资本
operating condition 使用条件
operating console 操纵台
operating control-point 闸楼
operating cost 运营成本
operating costs 经营费用
operating cycle 经营周(转)期,营业周期
operating distance 线路运营长度
operating dynamic force coefficient
　运营动力系数
operating expenses 业务开支,经营费用
operating lease 营业租赁
operating license 运营许可证
operating load 运营荷载
operating loss 营业损失
operating mechanism for motorized disconnector
　电动开关操作机构
operating mine survey 生产矿井测量
operating performance 经营业绩
operating pipe 工作管
operating profit 营业利润
operating railway 运营铁路
operating rate 开工率
operating revenue 营业收入
operating risk 经营风险
operating rod for driving a switch 动作连接杆
operating statement 经营报表
operating status of equipment 设备运行状态
operating stroke 工作行程
operating surplus 经营利润盈余
operating system 操作系统
operating team 作业层
operation 操作,运营,运转
operation against rule 违章操作
operation and dispatching management system
　运营调度管理系统
operation and display interface
　操作及显示界面
operation and maintainance manuals
　运营和养护手册
operation and maintenance center (OMC)
　操作与维护中心
operation and maintenance contract
　运营维修合同
operation and maintenance contractor
　运营及维护承包商
operation and maintenance cost
　操作和维修费用
operation and maintenance manual
　操作和维修手册,运营及维护手册
operation and maintenance plan
　运营及维护计划
operation area 作业区
operation base point 工作基点
operation condition 运营条件
operation cost 运营成本
operation counter 动作计数器
operation disturbance 作业干扰
operation duty test 动作负载试验
operation inspection 操作检查
operation instruction 作业交底
operation interference 运营干扰
operation maintenance 运用检修
operation maintenance equipment
　运营养护设备
operation management requirement
　运营管理要求
operation management system
　运营管理体系
operation monitoring and recording device
　运行监控记录装置
operation performance 运营性能
operation phase 运行阶段,运营阶段
operation platform 作业台架
operation process playback 作业过程回放
operation profit 营业利润
operation result 经营业绩
operation revenue 营业收入
operation service 运营服务
operation service period 运营服务期
operation speed 运营速度
operation statement 经营报表,损益报表
operation support system (OSS) 运营支撑系统
operation terminal 操作终端
operation ventilating duct 运营通风道
operational bill of quantities 作业工程量表
operational maintenance 日常维修
operational project 执行中的项目
operational purpose handset (OPH)
　作业手持台
operational purpose handset/handheld for shunting (OPS) 调车手持台
operational specification 操作规范
operational test 运行检验
operative construction organization design
　实施性施工组织设计
operative test 工艺性试验
operator 操作工,经纪人

opinion 意见
opportunity cost 机会成本
opportunity study 机会研究
opposite arrangement of turnouts
道岔对向布置
opposite connection 对向连接
opposite joint 相对式接头
opposite planting 对植
optic fibre 光纤
optical alignment 光学准直
optical attenuator 光衰耗器
optical axis of camera 摄影主光轴
optical cable 光缆
optical cable monitoring system
光缆监测系统
optical centering device 光学对中器
optical channel 光通道,光纤通道
Optical Channel Data Unit (ODU)
光通道数据单元
Optical Channel Data Unit-k (ODUk)
k 阶光通道数据单元
optical channel payload unit
光通路净荷单元
Optical Channel Transport Unit-k (OTUk)
k 阶光通路传送单元
optical channel transport unit
光通路传送单元
Optical Channel with full functionality (Och)
全功能光通路
optical connection 光纤连接
optical distribution frame (ODF)
光纤配线架,光缆配线架 ODF
optical distribution network (ODN)
光分配网络
optical eletrical cable lead-in cabinet
光电缆引入柜
optical eletrical cable lead-in 光电缆引入
optical fiber fusion splicer 光纤熔接机
optical fiber line auto switch protection equipment
(OLP) 光纤线路自动切换保护装置
optical fiber monitoring system
光纤监测系统
optical image processing 光学图像处理
optical line terminal (OLT) 光线路终端
optical mosaic 光学镶嵌
optical multiplex section 光复用段
optical multiplex section protection (OMSP)
光复用段保护
optical network unit (ONU) 光网络单元
optical power 光功率

optical power meter 光功率计
optical ranging condition 光距条件
optical repeater 光中继器
optical signal to noise ratio (OSNR) 光信噪比
optical stereoscopic model 光学立体模型
optical supervisory channel (OSC)
光监控通路
optical time-domain reflectometer (OTDR)
光时域反射仪
optical transmission section (OTS) 光传送段
optical transponder unit (OTU)
光转换器单元
optical transport network (OTN) 光传送网
optical-mechanical rectification
光学机械纠正
optimal design of control network
控制网优化设计
optimal land utilization 节约用地
optimum dosage 最佳掺量
optimum lot size 最优批量
optimum mix proportion 最佳配比
optimum moisture content 最优含水量
optimum water content 最优含水率
option 期权,选项,优先权
option buyer 期权买方
option money 期权交易定金
option purchase price 期权购买价
option seller 期权卖方
optional clause 可选条款
optional destination additional
可选目的地港附加费
optional equipment 备用设备
optional items 可选项,可选条款,暂定项目
optional port of destination 任选目的港
optional port of discharge 任选卸货港
optional termination 自主选择终止
options analysis 备选方案分析
optoelectronic isolator 光电隔离器
oral 口头的
oral agreement 口头协议
oral contract 口头合同
oral evidence 口头证据
oral form 口头形式
oral hearing 口头听证会
oral instruction 口头指示
oral instruction of variation 口头变更指令
oral notice 口头通知
oral pleading 口头答辩
oral statement 口头陈述,口头声明
orbicular structure 球状构造

order 次序,订货,订货单
order bill of lading 指定人提单,指示提单
order check 记名支票,指定人支票
order file 订货档案,订货卷宗
order for collection 托收单
order for future delivery 期货订单
order for variation 变更指令
order form 订货单格式
order of commencement 开工令
order of precedence 优先次序
order quantity 订货量
order sheet 订货单
order to commence 开工令
order to suspend 暂时停工命令
orderer 订货人
ordering contract 订货合同
ordering cost 订货费用
ordinance 法令,条例
ordinary accident insurance 普通事故保险
ordinary annuity 普通年金
ordinary balance 正常结余
ordinary depreciation 正常折旧
ordinary freight truck 普通载货汽车
ordinary Portland cement 普通硅酸盐水泥
ordinary region 一般地区
ordinary revenue 经常收入
ordinary subgrade 一般路基
ordinary value 通常值
Ordovician period 奥陶纪
Ordovician system 奥陶系
ore 矿石
organic binder 有机结合料
organic content 有机物含量
organic matter content 有机质含量
organic matter 有机质
organic peroxide 有机过氧化物
organic salt 有机盐
organic soil 有机质土
organization and management of construction 施工组织管理
organizational breakdown structure 组织分解结构
organizational roles 组织角色
organized air exhaust 有组织排风
organized air supply 有组织进风
organophosphorus 有机磷
organophosphorus content 有机磷含量
orientation connection survey (also known as "connection survey") 定向连接测量(简称"连接测量")

orientation element 方位元素
orientation point 定向点
orienting line 方位线
origin 原产地
origin marking 原产地标志
original 原件,原型,正本
original bill 汇票正本,原案
original contract 原合同
original cost 原始成本
original data 原始资料
original document 原始单据,原始文件
original forest 原生林
original insurance 原保险
original invoice 原始发票
original letter of credit 信用证正本
original mark-up 原始成本加成
original mineral 原生矿物
original of the contract 合约正本
original policy 保险单正本
original premium 原始保险费
original price 原价
original price of equipment 设备原价
original price of equipment in base period 基期设备原价
original price of imported equipment 进口设备原价
original price of material 材料原价
original printing 出版原图
original record 原始记录
original sample 原样品
original value 原值,原始价值
original voucher 原始凭单
originating station 始发站
original 正本
orthoclase 正长石
orthographic projection 正射投影
orthometamorphite 正变质岩
orthophoto map 正射影像地图
orthophotoquad 正射影像图
orthophyre 正长斑岩
orthorhombic system 斜方晶系
orthotropic plate 正交异型板
ortho-stereoscopy 正立体法
or-the-job training (OJT) 在职培训
oscillator 振荡器
oscilloscope 示波器
oskar 蛇形丘
osmotic erosion 渗透潜蚀
osmotic pressure method 渗透压法
ostensible/nominal agent 名义代理人

ostensible partner 名义合伙人
other administration costs of employer
　建设单位管理其他费
other charges 其他费
other expense for introduction of foreign technology and imported equipment
　引进技术和进口设备其他费用
other expenses of construction management
　建设管理其他费
other insurance required by laws and local practice 法律和当地惯例要求的其他保险
other machines 其他机械
other material expenses 其他材料费
other materials 其他材料
other related expenses 其他有关费用
other station tracks 其他站线
out ward clearance certificate
　出口结关证书
outboard delivery 船边交货
outcrop 露头
outdoor fire hydrant 室外消火栓
outdoor power distribution equipment
　室外配电装置
outer border line 图框外边线
outer cooperation 外部协同
outer diameter 外径
outflow 流出
outgo 超过,支出
outgoing contact line 非工作支,下锚支
outgoing feeder 出线
outlay 开支
outlet air velocity 出口风速
outlet pipe 排出管
outline 草案,轮廓线,提要,介绍简况,摘要
outline construction scheme
　概略施工组织方案意见
outline design 纲要设计
outline of engineering geological investigation
　工程地质勘查大纲
outline plan 提纲,概要计划,初步计划
outline programme for construction
　施工进度纲要
outline programme 工程计划概要
outline proposal 建议书大纲
output 输出
output by one machine shift 台班产量
output capacity 生产能力
output impedance 输出阻抗
output of supplying water 供水量
output per man-hour 人均小时产量

output power 输出功率
output quota 产量定额,生产定额
output voltage 输出电压
outside of fouling post 警冲标外方
outside turnout locking device
　道岔外锁闭装置
outsourcing 外包,外部采购
outspend 超支
outstanding 未付的
outstanding account 未清账款
outstanding amount 欠款
outstanding balance 未清余额
outstanding check 未兑现支票
outstanding claim
　索赔悬案,未了索要,未决赔款
outstanding debt 未清债务
outstanding dues 未付的应付款
outstanding external debt 未偿外债
outstanding liabilities 未付债务,未了责任
outstanding loss reserve 待定赔款准备金
outstanding losses 未偿损失,未付赔款
outstanding order 未交订货
outstanding principal 未偿本金
outstanding work 未完成的工作
outstandings 未偿清货款,未清算账目
outturn 卸货量
outward bill of lading 外运提单
outward inclination angle 外插角
outward port charges 出港手续费
outwash 冰水沉积
out-of-date check 过期支票,失效支票
out-of-date equipment 过时设备
out-of-pocket cost
　付现成本,实际开支成本
out-of-pocket expenses
　付现费用,现金支付费用
ovality 椭圆度
oven 烘箱
oven drying method 烘干法
over carriage risk 起程运输险
over coarse-grained soil 巨粒土
over consolidation ratio (OCR) 超固结
over insurance 起额保险
over interest 过期利息
overall air exhaust 全面排风
overall design 总体设计
overall floorage 总建筑面积
overall heating 全面采暖
overall length of TBM 机器全长
overall loan 总贷款

overall overturning stability 整体抗倾覆稳定
overall price index 综合物价指数
overall quality assessment 综合质量评定
overall robustness of structure
　结构整体稳固性
overall shear failure 整体剪切破坏
overall stability 整体稳定
overall stability coefficient of steel beam
　钢梁整体稳定系数
overall ventilation 全面通风
overall water quality analysis 水质全分析
overbreak 超挖
overburden 埋置深度,覆盖层
overburden pressure 覆盖压力
overburden thickness 覆盖层厚度,覆盖厚度
overcharge 收费过高,装载过多
overconsolidated 超固结
overconsolidated soil 超固结土
overcoring relief method 套芯解除法
overcorrection 过度改正
overcurrent 过电流
overcurrent protection 过电流保护
overdraft 透支
overdraft account 透支账户
overdraft guarantee 透支保函
overdraw 透支
overdue bill 逾期票据
overdue check 过期支票
overdue delivery
　逾期交付,逾期未交货物
overdue interest 逾期利息
overdue payment
　过期未付款,拖欠款,到期未付款
overdue risk 船期延误保险条款
overestimate 高估
overexcavation 超挖
overexpenditure 超支
overfill 超填
overflow 溢洪道,溢流
overflow belt 溢出带
overflow spring 溢出泉
overflow valve 溢流阀
overhaul 全面检修
overhaul section 检修工区
overhead 行政费
overhead account 管理费账户
overhead allocation
　管理费分配,间接费分配
overhead cable line 架空电缆线路
overhead cableway 空中索道

overhead charges (cost) 制造费用
overhead conductor rail clamp
　汇流排定位线夹
overhead conductor rail
　汇流排,架空刚性悬挂
overhead conductor rail system
　架空接触轨系统
overhead contact line system with compound suspension 复链形接触网
overhead contact line system 架空接触网
overhead contact line (OCL)/catenary
　架空接触悬挂,接触悬挂
overhead contact system (OCS) 接触网
overhead crane 桥式起重机
overhead crossing 交叉式线岔,线岔
overhead ditch 天沟
overhead expense 经常费用
overhead line 架空线
overhead power line 架空电力线
overhours 加班时间
overland bill of lading 水陆联运提单
overland common point
　陆路共通地点,陆运可达地点
overland transportation insurance
　陆上运输保险
overlap 重叠,锚段关节,过走防护区
overlap joint 搭接节点
overlap length 搭接长度
overlap section 重叠区段
overlap track circuit 叠加轨道电路
overlapped coding 叠加电码化
overlapping delays 共同延误
overlapping insurance 重复保险
overlength charges 超长附加费
overline hopper bunker 跨线漏斗仓
overload 超载,过负荷
overload capability 过负荷能力
overload curve 过负荷曲线
overload protection 过负荷保护
overlook 忽略
overlying load 上覆荷载
overlying soil thickness on pipe
　管道覆土厚度
overpass 上跨,天桥
overpass bridge 跨线桥
overpassing 立交桥,高架桥,天桥
overpressure ventilation 超压排风
override 代理佣金,特许使用费,优先于
overriding credit 主信用证
overrun 超过

overrun a signal 冒进信号
overrunning protection 冒进防护
overseas 海外
overseas agents 海外代理商
overseas allowance 海外津贴
overseas branch 国外分部
overseas investment 海外投资
overseas market 海外市场
overseas project 国外项目,海外工程
overseas training 国外培训
overseas works 国外工程
oversee 监视
overseer 监工,监视人
oversize 超大体积
overspeed protection 超速防护
overspeeding in coupling 超速连挂
overstate 高估
overstep 逾越
overstocking 积压
overtaking 越行
overtaking station 越行站
overthrust 逆掩断层
overtime 加班时间
overtime allowance 加班津贴
overtime pay 加班费
overtime premium (bonus) 加班奖金
overtime wages 加班工资
overtime work hour 加班工时
overtime work 加班工作
overturned anticline 倒转背斜
overturning 倾覆
overturning or slip resistance check 抗倾覆滑移验算
overview 概况,综述
overvoltage 过电压

overvoltage protection 过电压保护
overvoltage protection device 过电压保护装置
overweight 超重
overwintering ground 越冬场
over-bridge 天桥
over-discharge 过放电
over-line train 跨线列车
over-ride 优先于
over-section feeding 越区供电
owe 欠债
own damage 自负损害
own fund 自有资金
own risk 自负风险,自负责任
owner 所有人,业主
owner of title 产权所有人
ownership 所有权,专有技术权,所有制
ownership of goods and materials 物资所有权
ownership of plant and materials 生产设备和材料的所有权
ownership of trade marks 商标所有权
ownership transfer 所有权转移
owner's (employer's) personnel 业主人员
oxbow lake 牛轭湖
oxic 好氧
oxic sludge age 好氧泥龄
oxic zone 好氧区
oxidation ditch 氧化沟,活性氧化沟
oxidizable matter 可氧化物质
oxidized asphalt 氧化沥青
oxygen lance 氧气切割器
oxy-acetylene welding 气压焊
ozone 臭氧
ozone disinfection 臭氧消毒
ozone oxidation method 臭氧氧化法

P

pack 包装,打包
package 包裹,包装,一揽子
package bid 一揽子投标
package contract 一揽子合同
package deal 一揽子交易
package model 封装模型
package mortgage 一揽子抵押
package of claims 一揽子索赔
package project 一揽子项目
package technology 成套技术
packaged equipment 整装设备
packaged refrigeration device
　整体式制冷设备
packaging 包装
packed goods area 成件包装货区
packed tower 填料塔
packet control 分组控制
packet loss rate 丢包率
packet switched domain 分组域
packet switching 分组交换
Packet Transport Network (PTN) 分组传送网
packing and marking 包装与标记
packing cost 包装成本
packing expense 包装费
packing instructions 包装须知
packing list 装箱单
packing slip (sheet) 包装单,装箱单
pact 公约,条约
pad 垫板
pads 减振胶垫
padding 虚报支出
paid check 付讫支票
paid holiday 带薪休假期
paid off 付讫,付清的
paid-in capital 已缴资本,缴清股本
paid-up capital 已缴资本,缴清股本
paid-up licence fee 已缴许可证费
paid-up loan 已还清的贷款

pail flushing 提桶洗井法
paint 油漆
paint worker 油漆工
painter 油漆工
painting machine 喷漆机
painting position 油漆台位
painting track 喷漆库线
painting workshop 喷漆库
pairs of trains operating per day and night
　每昼夜行车对数
Paleoarchean era 古太古代
Paleoarchean erathem 古太古界
Paleocene epoch 古新世
Paleocene series 古新统
Paleogene period 早第三纪
Paleoproterozoic 古元古代
paleosoil 古土壤
Paleozoic erathem/group 古生界
Paleozoic era 古生代
palimpsest structure 变余构造
palimpsest texture 变余结构
palintectic earthquake 深源地震
pallet 锤垫,货盘
pan tilt and zoom (PTZ) control 云镜控制
pandect 汇编
panel 节间,面板,单元板
panel length 节间长度
panel point 节点
panel zone of column web 柱腹板节点域
pantograph bow 弓头
pantograph head 弓头
pantograph 受电弓
pan-tilt head 云台
pan-tilt-zoom camera 带云台的摄像机
paper 单据,票据,证券,纸币
paper felt base 油毡原纸
paper gold 纸黄金
paper loss 账面损失

paper profit 账面利润,账面盈余
paper work 文书工作
par 等价,平价,票面价值
par exchange rate 平价汇率
par value 票面价值
parallel adit 平行导坑
parallel arrangement type terminal 并列式枢纽
parallel branching railway connector
  并联分支钢轨连接线
parallel capacitor 并联电容器
parallel capacitor compensation 并联电容器补偿
parallel condition 并联条件
parallel displacement fault 平移断层
parallel double-track 并行双线
parallel feeding for up and down tracks
  上下行并联供电
parallel heading 平导,平行导坑
parallel inspection 平行检验
parallel load equipartition performance
  并联负载均分性能
parallel loans 平行贷款
parallel market 平行市场
parallel operation 平行作业
parallel process 平行工序
parallel route 平行进路
parallel running 并列运行
parallel test 平行试验
parallel testing report 平行检验报告
parallel track circuit 并联式轨道电路
parallel unconformity contact 平行不整合接触
parallel UPS 并联冗余
parallel water supply 并联供水
parallel-averted photography 等偏摄影
paramagnetic mineral 顺磁性矿物
parameter 参数
parameter adjustment with conditions (also known as "condition adjustment with indirection")
  附条件参数平差(又称"附条件的间接平差")
parapet 遮板,女儿墙
parapet wall 护墙
para-metamorphite 副变质岩
parcel 包裹
parent company 母公司
parent company guarantee 母公司担保
parent laboratory 母体试验室
parking location test 停车位置测试
parking lot 停车场
parking space 停车空间
parking track for large track maintenance machinery 大型养路机械停放线

parol agreement 口头协议
part of works 分部工程
partial compensation 部分补偿
partial coverage 部分保险,部分赔付
partial delivery 部分交货
partial deviations 局部偏差
partial discharge level 局部放电水平
partial factor 分项系数
partial factor design method
  分项系数设计方法
partial factor for load 荷载分项系数
partial factor of action effect
  作用效应分项系数
partial factor of load 荷载作用分项系数
partial factor of material property
  材料性能分项系数
partial factor of permanent load
  永久荷载分项系数
partial load 不满载
partial loss 部分损失
partial payment 部分支付
partial possession 部分占有
partial shipment 分批装运
partial supervision mode (PS)
  部分监控模式
partially penetrating well 非完整井
partially penetrating well pumping
  局部完井抽水
partially prestressed concrete beam
  部分预应力混凝土梁
partially prestressed concrete bridge
  部分预应力混凝土桥
participating loan 共同贷款
particle counter 粒子计数器
particle diameter 颗粒粒径
particle fraction 粒组
particle grading curve 颗粒级配曲线
particle size 粒度
particle size analysis 颗粒分析
particle size of soil 土粒粒径
particular 特殊的,例外的,细目
particular average 单独海损
particular conditions 特殊合同条件
particular lien
  个别留置权,特定留置权,具体留置权
particulars 单独事项
particulars of construction 施工详细情况
parties involved in construction 建设各方
parties to a project 项目各方
parties to an agreement 签订协议各方

parties to contract 合同各方
partition 分区,间壁,划分
partition wall 隔墙,内墙
partitioning waterproofing 分区防水
partly-exposed basement 半地下室
partner 合股人,合伙人
partnering 伙伴关系
partnership 合伙,合伙关系,合伙企业,伙伴关系
partnership agreement 合伙契约
partnership assignee 合伙受让人
partnership business establishment 合伙企业
partnership contract 合伙契约
partnership enterprise 合伙企业
partnership trustee 合伙受托人
parts 零件,配件
party in breach 违约方
party liable 责任方
party/parties 合同一方/当事人
part-cut and part-fill 半堤半堑,半填半挖
part-load freight yard 零担货场
pass 通过
pass book 银行存折
pass through 通过
passage 通行权,走廊
passage of title 所有权转移
passenger and freight service 客货运业务
passenger and freight volume 客货运量
passenger capacity 客运量
passenger car depot 客车车辆段
passenger car facilities 客车车辆设备
passenger car inspection depot
　旅客列车检修所(客列检)
passenger car servicing depot 客运整备场
passenger car servicing siding 客车整备线
passenger car technical servicing depot
　客车技术整备所(库列检)
passenger dedicated line 客运专线
passenger footbridge 旅客天桥
passenger information display system
　综合显示系统
passenger information system 旅客信息系统
passenger overpass 旅客天桥
passenger platform 旅客站台
passenger railway station 客运站
passenger service 客运业务
passenger service information system
　旅客服务信息系统
passenger station 客运站
passenger station building 旅客站房
passenger stopping point 旅客乘降所

passenger traffic volume 客运量
passenger train broadcasting equipment
　旅客列车广播设备
passenger train neutral-section passing system with no power consumption
　客运列车断电过分相系统
passenger train technical servicing siding
　客车技术整备线
passenger train-set stabling siding
　客车车底停留线
passenger train-set taking-out and placing-in track
　客车车底取送线
passenger transport operation system
　客运作业管理
passenger-carrying luggage security inspection facilities 旅客携带物品安全检查设施
passing error 贯通误差
passing of the risk 风险转移
passing protected section 过走防护区段
passing rate 通过率
passing station 会让站
passive bond 无息债券
passive control 被动控制
passive earth pressure 被动土压力
passive infrared detector
　被动红外探测器
passive loan 无息贷款
passive optical network(PON)
　无源光网络
passenger service center 客户服务中心
password keyboard 密码键盘
past-due 过期
past-due bill(note) 过期票据
patch 修补
patch cable 网络跳线
patchy permafrost 岛状多年冻土
patent 特许的,专利,专利权
patent agent 专利代理人
patent defects 外在缺陷
patent fee 专利费
patent holder 专利持有人
patent infringement 侵犯专利权
patent law 专利法
patent license 专利许可证
patent office 专利局
patent protection 专利保护
patent right 专利权
patent royalty 专利权使用费
patentee 专利权所有人
patentor 专利批准者

path detection 径路探测
pathway 航线
patrol inspection 巡检
patrol path 巡视小道
pave 铺设,筑路
pavement 路面
pavement base course 铺面基层
pavement bedding course 铺面垫层
pavement breaker 路面破碎机
pavement expansion 路面鼓胀
pavement of concrete block 混凝土块路面
pavement shape 路面形状
pavement structure 路面结构
pavement surface course 铺面面层
pavement width 路面宽度
paver 铺路机,摊铺机
paving 铺面,铺砌
paving machine 铺路机
pawn ticket 抵押凭证
pay 报酬,工资
pay a debt 还债
pay at fixed price 按固定价格付款
pay back 偿付,偿还,付还
pay back debts 偿还债务
pay by installments 分期付款
pay cash 付现
pay cheque 工资支票
pay date 发薪日
pay day 过户结账日
pay excess fare 补票
pay in advance 预付,预支付
pay in full 付清
pay in kind 实物支付
pay off 偿清,付清
pay off the principal and interest 付清本息
pay on delivery 货到付款
pay order 支付凭单
pay the penalty 缴纳罚金
pay to 汇付
pay when paid 款到即付
payable against documents 凭单证付款
payable at destination 目的地付款
payable at sight 见票即付
payable on demand 见票即付
payable period 应付期
payable upon first demand 首次要求即付
payable voucher 应付款凭单
payback method 回收期评估法
payback period 投资回收期,回收期
payday 发薪日

payee 收款人,受款人
payer 付款人
paying agent 付款代理人
paying bank 付款银行
paying list 付款清单
paying out 放线
payment 付款,支付的款项
payment abroad 国外付款
payment after termination 终止后的付款
payment after termination by contractor 承包商终止后的支付
payment after termination for contractor's default 承包商过错终止后的支付
payment after Termination for Employer's Convenience 雇主决定终止后的付款
payment agreement 支付协议
payment at maturity 到期付款
payment at sight 见票即付
payment bond 支付担保
payment by draft 汇票支付
payment by the hour 计时工资
payment by transfer 拨付,转账支付
payment certificate 付款证书
payment credit 付款信用证
payment deferred 延期付款
payment due 应付款
payment for acceleration 赶工费用
payment for claims 索赔的支付
payment guarantee 付款保函
payment in cash 现金支付
payment in due course 到期支付
payment in foreign currencies 外币支付
payment in full 全部付讫,全额支付
payment in kind 实物支付
payment milestone 支付里程碑
payment notice 缴款通知
payment of advance 预付款的支付
payment of duties 交税
payment of tax 交税
payment on account 分期支付,赊账支付
payment on arrival 货到付款
payment on delivery 交货付款
payment on demand 见索即付
payment on fixed price basis 按固定价格付款
payment on invoice 凭发票付款
payment on open account 记账交易,赊账
payment on statement 凭账单付款
payment on termination 终止时的付款
payment on terms 按条件付款,定期付款

payment order 付款通知
payment provisions 支付条款
payment schedule 支付计划,支付进度表
payment statement 货款结算单,货名
payment terms 支付条件
payment voucher 支付凭单
payment withheld 扣发支付款
payment-by-results 按成果付酬工资制
payroll 工资表
payroll check 工资支票
payroll deduction 扣发工资
payroll form 工资表格
payroll records 工资记录
payroll tax 工薪税
pay-as-you-earn (PAYE) 所得税预扣法
peacetime ventilation 平时通风
peak discharge 洪峰流量
peak flow 洪峰流量
peak forest terrain 峰林地形
peak hill 峰丘
peak hour volume 高峰小时发送量
peak season 旺季
peak strength 峰值强度
peak time 高峰
peak to peak value 峰峰值
peak traffic flow 高峰交通量
peak traffic hour power demand
  高峰小时功率需求
peak value 峰值
peak value clause 最高保额条款
peak value of temperature rise 温升峰值
peak variation factor 总变化系数
pearly luster 珍珠光泽
peat 泥炭
peat soil 泥炭质土
peatificated permafrost 冻结泥炭化土
pebble 圆砾
peculation 贪污
pecuniary allowances for job 岗位津贴
pecuniary penalty 罚金
pedestal of steel pole 钢柱底座
pedestal terrace 基座阶地
pedestrian bridge 人行桥
pedestrian cross passage 行人横通道
pedestrian crossing 人行横道
pedestrian cross-walk 人行过道
pedestrian island 安全岛
pedestrian overpass 人行天桥
pedestrian walkway load 人行道荷载
pedestrian walkway on bridge 桥上人行道

peel strength 剥离强度
peeling resistance 抗剥离性
peer review 同行评议,专家委员会
pegmatite 伟晶岩
pelitic rock 泥质岩
penal sum 罚金,违约罚款
penalty 处罚,罚款
penalty clause 惩罚条款,罚金条款
penalty for delay 误期罚款
penalty of breach of contract 违约罚款
pending issue 未决事件
pending question 未决问题
pendulum type coder 摆式发码器
peneplain 准平原
penetrating crack 贯穿性裂缝
penetrating vibrator 插入式混凝土振捣器
penetration 贯入度,针入度
penetration grading 针入度分级
penetration index 针入度指数
penetration inspection 贯入法检测
penetration rate 贯入量
penetration resistance apparatus 贯入阻力仪
penetration resistance 贯入阻力
penetration test apparatus 长杆贯入仪
penetrometer 贯入仪
pension 抚恤金,退休金,养老金
pension fund 养老基金
people roles 人员角色
per annum 按年计
per capita 每人平均值
per diem allowance 每日津贴
per diem 按日计
percent 百分比
percent weighting 加权百分数
percentage 百分率
percentage of contact loss 离线率
percentage of coverage 覆盖率
percentage of cumulative sieve residue
  累计筛余百分率
percentage of dammed slag or ashes 拦渣率
percentage of return air 回风百分比
percentage of the forestry and grass coverage
  林草覆盖率
percentage of total elongation 总伸长率
perched groundwater 上层滞水
percussion drill 冲击式钻机
percussion powder 炸药
percussive drilling 冲击钻进
perforated asphalt felt 带孔油毡
perforated drainage pipe 渗管

perform 执行
perform/discharge/fulfil a duty 履行职责
performance 性能,业绩,表现
performance appraisal 绩效评价
performance assurance 性能保证
performance certificate 竣工证书,履约证书
performance criteria 性能标准
performance evaluation
　绩效评估,业绩评价,绩效评价
performance function 功能函数
performance grading 性能分级
performance guarantee 履约保证书
performance index 性能指标
performance letter of credit 履约信用证
performance management plan
　绩效管理计划
performance matrix 性能指标
performance measurement baseline
　绩效测量基准
performance measurement benchmark
　绩效测量基准
performance of contract 合同履行,合同实施
performance oriented design 性能化设计
performance rating 绩效评定,绩效等级
performance report 绩效报告
performance security 履约保函
performance specification
　性能标准说明书
performance test 性能检验,性能考核,运行检验
performance test of masonry units
　块体性能检验
performance test of mortar 砂浆性能检验
performance test of steel bar
　钢筋性能检验
performance test of structural member
　构件性能检验
performing organization 执行机构
peridotite 橄榄岩
periglacial landform 冰缘地貌
periglacial process 冰缘作用
periglacial region 冰缘区
peril 风险事故,危险
perils of the sea 海上风险,海难
perimeter security 边界保护
perimeter security protection
　周界安全防范
period 期限,周期
period bill 定期汇票
period closing date 结账日期
period for shipment 装船期

period of construction
　工期,建设工期,施工期限,施工工期,工程期限
period of contract 合同期
period of depreciation 折旧年限,折旧期
period of insurance 保险期限
period of probation 试用期
period of settlement 结算期
period of validity 有效期
period of warranty 保修期
periodic bill 定期汇票
periodic credit 周期信用证
periodic inspection 定期检查
periodic inventory 定期盘存
periodic load 周期荷载,周期性负载
periodic measurement 定期测量
periodic meeting 定期会议
periodic payment 定期付款
periodic report 定期报告
periodical deposit 定期存款
periodical repair 定期修
periodical statement 定期报表
performance guarantee 性能保证
permafrost 永冻层
permafrost base 冻土下限
permafrost landform 冻土地貌
permafrost permeable 永冻层透水
permafrost subgrade 冻土路基
permafrost swamp 冻土沼泽
permafrost table 冻土上限,永冻层上限
permafrost thawing circle 冻土融化圈
permafrost zone 永久冻土带
permanent 长时制
permanent action 永久作用
permanent assets 固定资产,永久资产
permanent boundary marker 永久界桩
permanent bridge 永久性桥
permanent column 永久柱
permanent deformation joint 永久变形缝
permanent hardness 永久硬度
permanent investment 永久性投资
permanent labourer 正式工
permanent link 永久链路
permanent load 永久荷载
permanent magnet operating mechanism
　永磁操作机构
permanent standby 固定备用
permeability
　透水性,渗透性,渗透率,透气性
permeability coefficient of concrete
　混凝土透气系数

permeability coefficient 渗透系数,透气系数	personnel manager 人事经理
permeability resistance 抗渗	perspective 透视图
permeability test 渗透试验	pervious embankment 透水路堤
permeability tester 电通量测定仪	pest control inspection 有害物控制检测
permeable bed 透水层	petition 诉状
permeable layer interface 透水层交界面	petrification 化石
permeable soil 渗水土	petrofacies 岩相
permeable soil subgrade 渗水土路基	petrolene 可溶质
permeameter 渗透仪	petty cash 备用现金,手头现金
permeation 渗透	pH value pH 值
permanent works 永久工程	pH value of groundwater 地下水 pH 值
Permian period 二叠纪	phanerocrystalline texture 显晶质结构
Permian system 二叠系	Phanerozoic eon 显生宙
permissible speed 允许速度	phase angle 相位角
permission 允许,准许	phase break 电分相
permissive signal 容许信号	phase break device 分相绝缘器
permissive signal for reverse direction 反向容许信号	phase break with overlaps 关节式电分相
	phase characteristics 相位特征
permit 许可,许可证,允许,执照,准许,准予	phase difference 相位差
permit fee 牌照费,牌照税	phase fault 相间故障
permit for warehousing 入库许可证	phase sensitive track circuit 相敏轨道电路
permit for withdrawing 出库许可证	phase sequence exchange 相序轮换
permutation 互换	phase to phase fault 相间故障
peroration 结论	phase transition properties 相变特性
perpetual bond 永久债券	phase voltage 相电压
perpetual lease 永久租赁	phased bidding 阶段招标
persevere in 坚持	stage bidding 阶段招标
persist in 坚持	phased completion 阶段性完工
persistent design state 持久设计状况	phased construction method 阶段发包方式
person in charge 主管人	phase-sequence meter 相序表
person insuring 投保人	phenolic mastic 酚醛胶泥
personal 个人的,私人的	phenolphthalein indicator 酚酞指示剂
personal accident 人身意外事故	phenols 酚类
personal accident insurance 人身意外保险	phlogopite 金云母
personal assets 个人资产	phonolite 响岩
personal assistant 私人助理	phosphate 磷酸盐
personal effects 个人财产	phosphate accumulating organisms 聚磷菌
personal error 人为误差	phosphide 磷化物
personal estate 私人财产	phosphorescence 磷光
personal income tax 个人所得税	phosphorite 磷灰岩
personal injury 人身伤害,身体伤害	phosphorus removal 除磷
personal insurance 人身保险	photo annotation 相片调绘
personal liability 个人责任	photo base 相片基线
personal property 动产,个人财产,私人财产	photo centering 相片归心
personal protective equipment 个人劳保用品	photo control point 相片控制点
	photo nadir point 相底点
personal tort 个人侵权行为	photo planimetric method of photogrammetric mapping 综合法测图
personnel 全体人员,职员	photo rectification 相片纠正
personnel department 人事部门	photoelectric converter 光电转换器

photoelectric deflectometer 光电式挠度仪
photoelectric distance measuring traverse 光电测距导线
photoelectric parameter 光电参数
photoelectric type flexural meter 光电式挠度仪
photoelectric type liquid-plastic limit combined tester 光电式液塑限联合测定仪
photogeological map 影像地质图
photogrammetric coordinate system 摄影测量坐标系
photogrammetric interpolation 摄影测量内插
photogrammetry 摄影测量
photogrammetry control point 外控点
photograph index 相片索引图
photographic baseline 摄影基线
photographic direction 摄影方向
photographic flying height 摄影航高
photographic scale 摄影比例尺
photosensitive material 感光材料
photo-plane 相片平面图
phreatic surface 潜水面
phyllite 千枚岩
phyllitic structure 千枚状构造
phyllonite 千糜岩
physical and mechanical characteristics 物理力学性状
physical and mechanical index 物理力学指标
physical capital 实物资本
physical completion date 实际竣工日期
physical condition 外部条件,自然条件
physical evidence 实物证据
physical exploration method 物探法
physical flushing 物理洗井
physical geography 自然地理
physical hardening 物理硬化
physical hazard 自然风险因素
physical improvement 物理改良
physical index 物理性指标
physical inventory method 实物盘存法
physical market 现货市场
physical obstruction 外部障碍,自然障碍
physical obstructions and pollutions 障碍和污染物质
physical port 物理端口
physical properties of rock 岩石的物理性质
physical property 物理性质
physical resources 物力资源,实物资源
physical risk 自然风险
physical volume 实际量,实际容积
physical weathering 物理风化
physically improved soil 物理改良土
physicochemical process 物化法
phytocoenosium 植物群落
pick-up threshold 吸起门限
pick-up and drop-off train 摘挂列车
pick-up time 吸起时间
pick-up value 吸起值
picrite 苦橄岩
picrite-porphyrite 苦橄玢岩
picture element 像元
piece pricing 计件定价
piece rate 计件工资率
piece wage 计件工资
piece work system 计件工作
piecework 计件工作
piecework job 计件工作
piecework system 计件制
piece-work rate 计件工资率
piedmont 山麓
piedmont alluvial plain 山麓冲积平原
piedmont glacier 山麓冰川
pier 墩,桥墩
pier cap 墩帽
pier nose (to break up or deflect floating ice or drifts) 破冰体
pier shaft 墩身
piercer 冲孔器
piercing strength 刺破强度
pier-to-house (P/H) 码头到仓库
pier-to-inland depot 码头到内地仓库
pier-to-pier 码头到码头
piezoelectric acceleration sensor 压电式加速度传感器
piezoelectric exciter 压电激振器
piezoelectric test system 压电式测试系统
piezometric head 测压管水头
piezoresistor 压敏电阻
pigging test 通球试验
pigtail connector 尾纤活动连接器
pike 关卡
pile 桩,(支架的)支墩
pile cap 承台,桩帽
pile cap effect coefficient 承台效应系数
pile casing 护筒
pile cluster 桩群
pile defects 桩身缺陷

pile diameter 桩径
pile driver 打桩机
pile extractor 拔桩机
pile follower 送桩
pile foundation 桩基础,桩基
pile frame 桩架
pile integrity 桩身完整性
pile length 桩长
pile of granular material 散体材料桩
pile position 桩位
pile raft structure 桩筏结构
pile shaft 桩身
pile top preparation 桩头处理
pile verticality 桩垂直度
piles thrusted-expanded with column-hammer 柱锤冲扩桩
pile-net structure 桩网结构
pile-plank structure 板桩结构
pile-slab retaining wall 桩板式挡土墙
pile-slab structure 桩板结构
piling machinery 桩工机械
pillar 墩
pillow structure 枕状构造
pilot tunnel 导洞
pilot works 样板工程
pin for steady arm 定位器销钉
pin insulator 针式绝缘子
pinch out 尖灭
pinch-out of soil layer 土层尖灭
pipage 管道运输
pipe 管道
pipe anticorrosion 管道防腐
pipe bender 弯管机
pipe bending machine 弯管机
pipe clamp 管卡
pipe compensator 导管调整器
pipe culvert 管涵,圆管涵
pipe ditch for leak detector 检漏管沟
pipe fittings 管道配件
pipe installation 导管装置
pipe jacking method 顶管法
pipe jacking through track 顶管过轨
pipe layer 埋管机,铺管机
pipe pile 管桩
pipe pile foundation 管桩基础
pipe radiator 光面管散热器
pipe roof 超前管棚
pipe run 管道,管线
pipe sewer 污水管
pipe shaft 管道井

pipe system 配水管网
pipe tee 三通管
pipe trench 管沟
pipe vents 通风管
pipe wall thickness 管道壁厚
pipe work 管道工程
pipeline 管道,管线,排水盲沟,管道,沟槽
pipeline project 管线工程项目
pipeline surveying 管道测量
pipeline thermal 管道保温
pipette method 移液管法
pipe-roof grouting 管棚注浆
piping 管涌,铺管
piping and instrument diagram (PID/P&ID) 管道仪表流程图
piping erection 管道安装
piping layout drawing 管道平面布置图
piping planning 管道平面设计图
pisolitic texture 豆状结构
pistacite 绿帘石
piston 活塞
piston compressor 活塞式压缩机
piston flushing 活塞洗井法
piston subassembly 活塞组合件
pit exploration 挖探
pit refilling 坑凹回填
pitch diameter of thread 螺纹中径
pitfall 陷阱
pitot tube 毕托管
pitting engineering survey 坑探工程测量
pixel 像元
place 场所,浇筑
place an order 订购,订货
place of arbitration 仲裁地点
place of assembly 装配场
place of delivery 交货地点
place of departure 始发地
place of fabrication 加工地
place of incorporation 公司注册地
place of loading 装货地
place of payment 付款地点
placement 填筑
placing 铺设
placing plant 混凝土浇筑设备
placing-in and taking-out of train 取送车
plagioclase 斜长石
plagioclase granite 斜长花岗岩
plagioclasite 斜长岩
plain 平原

plain concrete 素混凝土
plain concrete pile 素混凝土桩
plain concrete structure 素混凝土结构
plain sedimentation 自然沉淀
plain soil 素土
plaintiff 检举人,控告方,控告人,起诉人,原告
plan of observation points 观测点位置图
plan of operations
  项目实施计划,作业计划
plan validity check 计划有效性检查
plan view size 平面尺寸
planar flow structure 流面构造
planation surface 夷平面
plane 平刨
plane coordinates 平面坐标
plane cross-section assumption 平截面假定
plane curve location 平面曲线测设
plane layout 平面布置
plane of sound barrier 声屏障平面
plane position 平面位置
plane rolling test 平面溜放测试
plane strain test 平面应变试验
plane structure 平面结构
plane table mapping 平板仪测图
plane table survey 平板仪测量
plane untwining 平面疏解
plane warping 平面翘曲
planeness of structural member
  结构构件平整度
planer 刨床
plane-table 平板仪
planting grass root or culm
  栽植法建植草坪
planimeter method 求积仪法
planing machine 刨床
plank 板
plank pile 木板桩
planned cost 计划费用
planned maintenance 计划修
planned output 计划产量
planned period 计划期限
planned profits 计划利润,目标利润
planned progress 计划进度
planned project duration 计划工期
planned value 计划值
planner 计划工程师
planning 规划,编制计划,计划拟定
planning authority 规划当局
planning budget 编制预算
planning chart 计划图

planning commission 计划委员会
planning consent 规划同意书
planning engineer 计划工程师
planning for earthquake reduction and disaster prevention 抗震防灾规划
planning permission 规划许可,建筑许可
planning survey 规划测量
planning-based railway location 规划选线
plant 工厂,设备,设备,材料和工艺,方案,计划,计划书,平面图
plant and materials intended for the works
  拟用于本工程的设备和材料
plant assets 固定资产
plant capacity 工厂生产能力
plant community 植物群落
plant depot 设备库区
plant records 设备的记录
planting 绿化
planting grass in skeleton 骨架内植草
planting on borrow soil 客土植生
Planting pit(trough) 种植穴槽
planting soil 种植土
plasma 等离子体
plaster 灰浆
plaster worker 抹灰工
plasterer 抹灰工
plasterer's float 抹子
plastic 可塑的
plastic deformation 塑性变形
plastic design of steel structure
  钢结构塑性设计
plastic displacement 塑性位移
plastic dowel 预埋套管
plastic drain 塑料排水
plastic drain sheet 塑料排水板
plastic drainage belt 塑料排水带
plastic failure 塑性破坏
plastic film 塑料薄膜
plastic flow 塑流
plastic geogrid 塑料土工格栅
plastic hinge 塑性铰
plastic limit 塑限
plastic media 塑料填料
plastic pipe 塑料管
plastic soil 塑性土
plastic stage design method
  破损阶段设计法,破坏阶段设计法
plastic strain 塑性应变
plastic waterproof sheet 塑料防水卷材
plastic zone 塑性区

plasticity 塑性
plasticity chart 塑性图
plasticity chart of fine-grained soil 细粒土塑性图
plasticity coefficient of concrete in tensile region 受拉区混凝土塑性影响系数
plasticity index 塑性指数
plastics 塑料制品
plate 板,板块
plate bearing 平板支座
plate bender 弯板机
plate concrete vibrator 平板式混凝土振捣器
plate girder 板梁
plate heat exchanger 板式换热器
plate load test 载荷板试验
plate loading test 平板载荷试验
plate tax 牌照税
plate weir 薄壁堰
plateau 高原
plateau frigid zone 高原寒带
plateau subfrigid zone 高原亚寒带
plateau subtropics 高原亚热带
plateau temperate zone 高原温带
plated structure 板系结构
plate-type smoke outlet 板式排烟口
plate-type space grid 平板型网架
platform 地台,平台
platform awning 雨棚
platform display 站台到发信息屏
platform edge 站台边缘
platform height 站台高度
platform of hump crest 驼峰峰顶平台
platform scale 台秤
platform shelter 站台雨棚
platform slope 站台斜坡
platform truck 平板车
platinum dish 铂器皿
pleadings 诉状
pledge 保证,抵押物,抵押
pledge against a loan 抵押借款
pledgee 接受抵押人
pledger 抵押人
Pleistocene epoch 更新世
Pleistocene series 更新统
plenipotentiary 全权代表
plenum chamber 静压箱
plenum space 稳压层
plesiochronous digital hierarchy(PDH) 准同步数字系列

Pliocene epoch 上新世
Pliocene series 上新统
plot 计划
plot ratio 容积率
plotting magnification factor 测图放大系数
plug bond 塞钉式钢轨接续线
plugging effect 土塞效应
plug-in relay 插入式继电器
plumber 管道工
plumbing 管道工程
plumbing survey 垂直度测量
plumpness of mortar grouting 灌注砂浆饱满度
plunge pool 消力池
plunger lock 转辙锁闭器
pluvial 洪积的
pluvial facies 洪积相
plywood 胶合板
plywood concrete forms 胶合板混凝土模板
pneumatic clamp retarder 风压钳夹式减速器
pneumatic conveying 气力输送
pneumatic drill 风钻
pneumatic gravity-like reducer 风压重力式减速器
pneumatic mortar 压力喷浆
pneumatic pick 风镐
pneumatic rock drill 风动凿岩机
pneumatic water supply 气压给水
podium 裙房
point bearing pile 端承桩
point blades 尖轨
point detector 联锁箱
point in dispute 争执点
point load test 点荷载试验
point loading strength index 点荷载强度指数
point loading strength test of rock 岩石点荷载强度试验
point of change from spiral to circular curve(SC) 缓圆点
point of change from spiral to tangent(ST) 缓直点
point of contract 合同要点
point of gradient change 变坡点
point of sales(PoS) 销售点终端
point selection for control network 控制网选点
point symbol 点状符号

point transfer 转刺
points and crossings 道岔
point-continued type speed control system
　点连式调速系统
point-to-point protocol 点对点协议
point-to-point speech service
　点对点普通语音通信业务
poisonous and hazardous substances
　有毒有害物质
Poisson ratio 泊松比
polar biased relay 偏极继电器
polar coordinate method with EDMI
　电磁波测距仪极坐标法
polar frequency coded track circuit
　极频轨道电路
polar impulse track circuit
　极性脉冲轨道电路
polar map 极点图
polar transposition 极性交叉
polarity checking circuit 极性检查电路
polarizability 极化率
polarization mode dispersion 偏振模色散
polarized microscope 偏光显微镜
polarized relay 有极继电器
polarographic analysis 极谱分析
polar-coordinate measurement at station site
　站场极坐标测量
pole 电杆,支柱
pole diagram 极点图
pole foundation 支柱基础
poles for overhead contact system
　接触网立柱
pole-changing time 转极时间
pole-changing value 转极值
police management information system
　公安管理信息系统
policy 保单,保险单,政策
policy holder 保单持有人,保险客户,投保人
policy maker 决策者
poling board 支撑板
political party 政党
political risk 政治风险
polje 坡立谷,岩溶盆地
pollutant 污染物
pollutant discharge gross controlling
　污染物总量控制
pollute 污染
pollution 污染
pollution discharge standard
　污染物排放标准

polycarboxylates high performance water-reducing admixture 聚羧酸系高性能减水剂
polyconic projection 多圆锥投影
polyester fabric reinforced waterproofing sheet
　聚酯毡防水卷材
polygon adjustment 多边形平差
polygon three-dimensional slope protection network 多边形立体护坡网
polygonal catenary 直链形悬挂
polygonal top-chord roof truss 多边形屋架
polymer cement waterproof coating
　聚合物水泥防水涂料
polymer engineering materials
　聚合物工程材料
polymer materials 聚合物材料
polymer mortar 聚合物砂浆
polypropylene fiber cement concrete
　聚丙烯纤维水泥混凝土
polystyrene foamed plastics
　聚苯乙烯泡沫塑料
polystyrene plate 聚苯乙烯板块
polyurea waterproof layer 聚脲防水层
polyurethane waterproof coating
　聚氨酯防水涂料
polyvinyl chloride（PVC） 聚氯乙烯
polyvinyl chloride geomembrane
　聚氯乙烯土工膜
polyvinyl chloride sheet
　聚氯乙烯防水卷材
pond 池塘
ponor 落水洞
pontoon 趸船
pontoon bridge 浮桥,舟桥
pontoon crane 水上起重机,起重船
pool of experts 专家库
pool resources 集资
poor contact 接触不良
poor quality concrete 劣质混凝土
poor water quality area
　水质恶劣地区
poorly-graded soil 不良级配土
porcelain post insulator
　瓷支持绝缘子,瓷支柱绝缘子
pore 孔隙
pore air pressure 孔隙气压力
pore cementation 孔隙胶结
pore pressure 孔隙压力
pore pressure ratio 孔隙压力比
pore stress 孔隙应力
pore water 孔隙水

pore water pressure 孔隙水压力
pore water pressure coefficient
孔隙水压力系数
porosity 孔隙率,空隙率
porous brick 多孔砖
porphyritic structure 斑状构造
porphyroclastic texture 碎斑结构
port 港口,口岸
port authority 港务局
port charge 港口费用,入港税
port clearance 出港结关
port congestion surcharge 港口拥挤附加费
port delivery 装运港交货类
port distribution diagram (table)
端口运用图(表)
port distribution table 端口运用台账
port dues 港口费用,港口税,停泊费
port handling capacity 港口吞吐量
port of arrival 目的港
port of call 停靠港
port of delivery 交货港,卸货港
port of departure 出发港,启运港
port of destination 目的港
port of discharge 发货港,卸货港
port of embarkation 出发港
port of entry 进口港
port of exit 出口港
port of shipment 装运港
port of transshipment 中转港,转运港
port rate 端口速率
port surcharge 港口附加费
port works 港口工程
portable agitator 移动式搅拌机
portable belt conveyor 携带带式输送机
portable diesel tamper 手提内燃捣固机
portable electric tamper
手提电动捣固机,电镐
portable fire extinguisher 手提式灭火器
portable fire pump 机动消防泵
portable pneumatic tamper
手提风动捣固机
portable radio 便携电台
portable railway 轻便铁道
portable terminal 便携终端
portal 洞口,洞门
portal bracing 桥门架
portal buffer structure 洞口缓冲结构
portal crane 门式起重机
portal frame 桥门架
portal structure 门形架构,硬横跨

portal wall 洞门墙
portal-type screw unloader
门式螺旋卸车机
porter 搬运工,装载机
portion 部分
Portland cement 硅酸盐水泥
Portland slag cement 硅酸盐矿渣水泥
Portland-composite cement 复合硅酸盐水泥
Portland-fly ash cement
粉煤灰硅酸盐水泥
Portland-pozzolana cement
火山灰质硅酸盐水泥
Portland-slag cement 矿渣硅酸盐水泥
port's volume of freight traffic turnover
货物吞吐量
position 职位
position error 点位误差
position for repairing cars 修车台位
position length for repairing car
修车台位长度
position of steel bars 钢筋位置
positioning block 定位块
position-limiting device 限位器
position-limiting trough 限位凹槽
position-shift operation 移位作业
positive 正片
positive cash flow 正现金流量
positive hydraulic head 正水头
positive image 阳像,正像
positive pressure area 正压区
positive relief 正地形
possession 所有权,专有技术权,占有
possession by law 依法占有
possession of site 现场的占有
possessive interval for process 过程天窗
possessory lien 占有留置权
possibility 可能性
post 过账,立柱,职位
post and parcel operation yard
行邮行包作业场
post entry 进口补报
post evaluation 后评价
post grouting for cast-in-situ pile
灌注桩后注浆
post panel sound barrier 柱板式声屏障
post project critique 项目后评审
post qualification 资格后审
post review 后审查
post tensioning cable 后张钢丝索
postdate 填迟日期

posting 过账
posting bond 缴纳保金
posting reference 过账依据
postpone 推迟,延迟
postpone payment 迟付
postponed payment 延期支付
postponement 推迟,延迟,延期
postulation 假定
postweld heat treatment 焊后热处理
post-poured strip 后浇带
post-award meeting 授标后会议
post-bid shopping 授标后压价
post-buckling strength of web plate 腹板屈曲后强度
post-completion review 竣工后审查
post-construction settlement 工后沉降
post-construction settlement of subgrade 路基工后沉降
post-grant review 后审查
post-installed rebar 植筋
post-installed reinforcing bar 植筋
post-processed differential correction 后处理差分改正
post-tensioned concrete girder 后张法预应力梁
post-tensioned prestressed concrete structure 后张法预应力混凝土结构
post-tensioned prestressing 后张法预加应力
post-tensioning bonded and prestressed concrete structure 后张法有黏结预应力混凝土结构
post-tensioning 后张法
pot hole 锅穴
pot rubber bearing 盆式橡胶支座
potable water 饮用水
potential market 潜在市场
potential risk 潜在风险
potential tenderer 潜在投标人
potentiometric tester 电位测量仪
potentiometric titration 电位滴定法
potentiometry 电位法
pour 浇筑
pouring 浇注,灌注
pouring hole 灌注孔,观察孔,灌注孔
powder extinguishing system 干粉灭火系统
powder injection mixing pile 粉体喷射搅拌桩
powder jet mixing pile 粉喷桩

powder surfaced asphalt felt 粉毡
powdered activated carbon adsorption 粉末活性炭吸附
power 电力,权力
power cable 电力电缆,动力电缆
power cable material 电力线材
power capacity 电源容量
power consumption 耗电,用电量
power consumption rate 用电率
power cut 动力切断
power demand 需用功率
power density 功率密度
power dispatching center 电力调度中心
power distribution 配电
power distribution network 配电网
power distribution panel 配电屏
power energy loss 电能损失
power factor 功率因数
power factor compensation 功率因数补偿
power frequency electric field 工频电场
power frequency flashover voltage 工频闪络电压
power frequency magnetic field 工频磁场
power frequency withstand voltage 工频耐压
power frequency withstand voltage r.m.s 工频耐压有效值
power generating rail car 发电轨道车
power generation 发电
power grid 电网
power grid sensor 电网传感器
power harmonic analyzer 电力谐波分析仪
power head drilling rig 动力头式钻机
power house (plant) 发电厂
power lightning protection box 电源防雷箱
power line 电源线
power loss 功率损耗
power of attorney 授权书,委托书
power of interpretation 解释权
power of representation 代理权
power of sale 销售权
power outage 停电
power plant 电厂,电站
power price of base period 基期电价
power project 电力工程
power purchase agreement 购电协议
power remote control system 电力远动系统
power resources 电力资源

power room 动力车间
power source for indication lamp 表示灯电源
power source for switch operation 道岔动作电源
power source from the public grid 外部电源
power splitter 功分器
power station 电厂，发电站
power strip test board 电源板测试台
power stroke 做功行程
power sum ELFEXT attenuation（loss）（PS ELF-EXT）等电平远端串音功率和
power sum NEXT attenuation（loss）（PS NEXT）近端串音功率和
power supply 电源
power supply and distribution system of railway 铁路供配电系统
power supply equipment maintenance management department 供电段
power supply for operation 操作电源
power supply line 供电线路
power supply maintenance 供电维修
power supply mode 供电方式
power supply plan 供电方案
power supply room 电源室
power supply terminal 电源端子
power supply voltage 电源电压
power switching over panel 电源转换屏
power switching station 电力开闭所
power to sign 签字权
Power Usage Effectiveness（PUE）电能利用效率
power utilization efficiency 能源利用效率
powerhouse of car retarder 车辆减速器动力室
powers of the DAAB 争议避免裁决委员会的权限
power-on check 通电检查
power-on locking test 上电锁闭测试
PP pipe PP管材
practicability 可行性
practical completion 实际完工
practice 惯例
practicing accountant 开业会计师
prairie 草原
pre（-）stressed reinforced concrete 预应力钢筋混凝土
preaction system 预作用灭火系统
preappraisal 预评估

precast concrete 预制混凝土
precast concrete member 预制混凝土构件
precast concrete pile 预制混凝土土桩
precast concrete slab 预制混凝土楼板
precast concrete structure 装配式混凝土结构
precast fabricated pipe 预制装配管道
precast hollow concrete block 预制混凝土空心块
precast integral concrete structure 装配整体式混凝土结构
precast pile 预制桩
precast segmental construction by cantilever method 悬臂拼装法，悬臂拼接法
precast track slab 预制轨道板
precast yard for rail sleeper 轨枕预制场
precast yard for track slab 轨道板预制场
precast yard for Ⅱ type track slab Ⅱ型轨道板预制场
precast yard for Ⅲ type track slab Ⅲ型轨道板预制场
precast yard of simply-supported box girder 简支箱梁预制场
precede 优先，优先于
precedence 优先权
precedence diagram 单代号网络
precedence network 单代号网络图
precedent 判例，先例
preceding clause 前述条款
precipitation 降水
precipitation day 降水日
precipitation gauge 雨量器
precipitation intensity 降水强度
precise code 精码
precise distance measurement 精密测距
precise engineering control network 精密工程控制网
precise engineering survey 精密工程测量
precise engineering survey of high speed railway 高速铁路精密工程测量
precise level 精密水准仪
precise leveling 精密水准测量
precise orientation 精密定向
precise positioning service 精密定位服务
precise water level 精密水准仪
precision 精密，精确度
precision estimation 精度估计
precision measuring instrument 精密量具
Precision Time Protocol（PTP）精确时间协议

precommissioning 预调试
precondition 前提,先决条件
preconsolidation pressure 先期固结压力
precursor section 先导段
predicated cost 预计成本
predict 预料
predictability 可预料性
predicted mean heat sensation value（PMV）
  预计平均热感觉指数
predicted percentage of disaffected（PPD）
  预计不满意者的百分数
prediction 预测
prediction by advance heading
  超前导坑预测法
prediction by drilling long horizontal hole
  深孔水平钻探
prediction by extending blast hole
  加深炮孔探测
prediction by parallel heading 平行导坑法
prediction by pilot heading of main tunnel
  正洞导坑法
prediction of mining subsidence
  开采沉陷预计
predominant period 卓越周期
preemption 优先购买权
preemptive call 话路强插
preemptive right 优先购买权,优先购置权
pre-entry 预先报关单,预先申报
prefab 预制装配式房屋
prefabricate 预制
prefabricated bridge pier 拼装式桥墩
prefabricated concrete blocks 混凝土预制块
prefabricated house 预制装配式房屋
prefabricated lining 装配式衬砌
prefabricated member/element/component
  预制构件
prefabricated slab 预制板
prefabricated structure 装配式结构
prefabricated substation 箱式变电站
prefabrication yard 预制场
prefab-form 预制模板
preference 优惠,优先,优先权
preference for domestic contractors
  对国内承包商的优惠
preference for domestic manufacturers
  对国内制造商的优惠
preferential duties 特惠关税
preferential rate of interest 优惠利率
preferential tariff 特惠税率,优惠税则
preferential trade agreement 优惠贸易协定

preferred stock 优先股
preformed armor rod 预绞式护线条
preformed hole 预留孔
pre-investment studies
  投资前研究,预投资研究
prejudice 歧视,损害
preliminaries 开办项目
preliminary 预备的
preliminary acceptance certificate
  初步验收证书
preliminary act 预备诉讼行为
preliminary budget 初步预算
preliminary computation 初步计算
preliminary construction plan
  施工组织设计意见
preliminary design 初步设计
preliminary design stage 初步设计阶段
preliminary drawings 初步设计图纸
preliminary entry 预备进口报关单
preliminary estimate 初步估算
preliminary evaluation 初步评价
preliminary feasibility study 预可研
preliminary items 开办项目
preliminary proposal 初步建议书
preliminary survey 初测
preliminary traverse 初测导线
preliminary vendor drawings（PD）
  供货厂商先期确认图
preliminary works 预备工程
preliminary work expense of construction project
  建设项目前期工作费
preloading foundation 预压地基
preloading method 预压法
preloading with surcharge fill 堆载预压
premises distribution system 综合布线
premium 保险费,保险金,升水,贴水,溢价
premium money award 奖金
premium pay 加班工资,假日工资
premium payment 支付保险费
premium rate 保险费率
premium returns 额外利润,退还保险费
premium wages 奖励工资
premix asphalt plant 沥青搅拌设备
premixing 预拌
prepacked aggregate 预填骨料
prepaid expenses 预付费用
prepaid freight 预付运费
preparation 配制
preparation and review 准备工作及审查
preparation expenses 筹备费

preparation of bid 投标准备,编制投标文件
preparation of contract documents 合同文件的编制
preparation strength 配制强度
prepare 编制,预备
prepared subgrade 基床表层
prepayment clause 预付款条款
prequalification 资格预审
prequalification application 资格预审申请
prequalification documents 资格预审文件
prequalified bidders 批准的投标人名单
prequalified contractor 资格审查合格的承包商
prequalified tenderer 资格审查合格的投标人
prerequisite 必要的,必要条件,前提,先决条件
prescription 诉讼时效
presence 出庭,出席
present 出示,出席,文件,赠品,赠予
present land use map 土地利用现状图
present value 现值
present value of cost 成本现值
presentation 提交
presentation of evidence 出示证据
presenter 提示人,演示人,赠送人
presentment 提示,演示
presentment for acceptance 承兑提示
presentment for payment 付款提示
preservation rate of blasthole trace 炮眼痕迹保存率
preservative substance 防腐剂
preserve 保持
presetting period 初凝时期
president 行长,总裁,总经理
presiding arbitrator 首席仲裁员
pressure arch 压力拱
pressure bearing area of specimen 试件承压面积
pressure bleeding meter 压力泌水仪
pressure bulb 压力泡
pressure calculation height 压力计算高度
pressure cell 压力盒
pressure channel ditch 压沟坡
pressure culvert 压力涵洞
pressure gauge 压力表
pressure grouting 压力注浆,压力灌浆
pressure grouting sealing 压力灌浆止水
pressure of backfilled soil 回填土压力
pressure of flowing water 流水压力
pressure of grouting pump 注浆泵压力
pressure of water flow in aqueduct 渡槽流水压力
pressure of water vapour 水蒸气压力
pressure pipe 承压管
pressure pipeline 压力管道,有压管道
pressure pump 加压泵
pressure relief device 泄压装置,压力释放装置
pressure relief valve 减压阀
pressure sampling machine 压样器
pressure sensor 压力传感器
pressure texture 压碎结构
pressure tunnel 压力隧道
pressure type thermometer 压力式温度计
pressure valve 压力阀
pressure weights 压重
pressure(-)meter test(PMT) 旁压试验(PMT)
pressure-superposed water supply 叠压供水
pressuring main 压力主管
pressurized seal index 气压密封指数
prestress 预应力
prestressed anchor cable 预应力锚索
prestressed concrete beam(girder) 预应力混凝土梁
prestressed concrete bridge 预应力混凝土桥
prestressed concrete pile 预应力混凝土桩
prestressed concrete pole 预应力混凝土柱,预应力混凝土杆
prestressed concrete structure 预应力混凝土结构
prestressed reinforced concrete pole 预应力钢筋混凝土杆
prestressed steel 预应力钢材
prestressed steel structure 预应力钢结构
prestressing bar 预应力(钢)筋
prestressing strand 预应力钢绞线
prestressing tendon 预应力钢丝束
presume 假定
presumption 假定,推测
presumption of law 法律上的推定
pretension 先张法预应力
pretensioned concrete girder 先张法预应力梁
pretensioning 先张法
prevail 流行,通行,优先于
prevailing price 时价,现行价格

prevailing rate 通行汇率,现行费率
prevailing wind direction 主导风向
prevention 预防
prevention and control zoning chart of soil erosion and water loss 水土流失防治分区图
prevention and control zoning of soil erosion and water loss 水土流失防治分区
prevent 预防
preventive claims management 索赔预防管理
preventive maintenance 预防性维修
preventive measure 预防措施
preworking a block 预办闭塞
pre-acceptance negotiation 签约前谈判
pre-award meeting 授标前会议
pre-bid meeting 标前会议,投标预备会
pre-bid site visit 投标前现场调查
pre-camber 预拱度
pre-commissioning 预试运行
pre-construction stage 施工前阶段
pre-contract procedures 合同前的程序
pre-cut notch 预裂缝
pre-design estimate 设计前估算
pre-drilling lateral pressure test 预钻式旁压试验
pre-examination for building land 土地预审
pre-feasibility study 预可行性研究
pre-grinding 预打磨
pre-grouting 预注浆
pre-grouting performed from ground surface 地面预注浆
pre-hump crest receiving yard 峰前到达场
pre-overlapped coding 预叠加电码化
pre-oxidization 预氧化
pre-possession agreement 进场前协议
pre-sag 预留弛度
pre-sedimentation 预沉
pre-setting 初凝
pre-split blasting 预裂爆破
pre-stressed anchor rod 预应力锚杆
pre-tensioned prestressed concrete structure 先张法预应力混凝土结构
pre-tensioned prestressing 先张法预应力
pre-tensioning load 预拉荷载
pre-treatment 预处理
price 定价,价格,行情
price adjustment 调价,价格调整
price adjustment clause 价格调整条款
price adjustment contract 价格调整合同
price adjustment factor 价格调整系数
price adjustment formula 调价公式
price after tax 税后价格
price at factory 厂价
price band 价格幅度
price bargaining 价格谈判,讨价还价
price bonification 价格补贴
price by investigation 调查价
price ceiling 最高价格
price changeable lump sum contract 可调总价合同
price concession 让价
price control 价格控制
price current 时价表
price cutting 降价,减价,削价
price difference 差价
price duty paid 完税货价
price escalation 价格上涨,物价上涨
price fixing 限定价格
price floor 最低限价
price fluctuation 价格变动,价格波动
price fluctuation factor 价格波动因子,物价变化系数
price haggling 讨价还价
price index 价格指数
price indication 参考价格
price level 价格水平
price level of base period 基期价格水平
price level of cost making period 编制期价格水平
price list 价目表,价格单
price loco 当地价格,购买地价格
price maker 价格的决定者
price margin 价格差额
price mark up 加价,提价,加价
price of base period 基期价格
price of ex-factory 工厂交货价
price of transacting 交易价格
price range 价格幅度
price reduction 降价,减价
price revision clause 价格修正条款
price sensitivity 价格敏感性
price sheet 价格单
price stability 物价稳定
price subsidy 价格补贴
price support 价格补贴
price taker 价格的接受者
price tendered 投标价
price terms 价格条件
price variance 价格偏差
price year 价格年度

priced bill of quantities 标价的工程量表
priced contract with activity schedule 带有分项工程表的标价合同
priced contract with bill of quantities 带有工程量表的标价合同
priced deviation 偏离折价
price-level-adjusted statement 按物价水平调整的报表
price-weighted index 物价加权指数
pricing 定价,标价
prima facie 表面的
prima facie evidence 初步证据
primary 基本的
primary cell power supply 一次电池供电
primary circuit 一次回路
primary circulating system 第一循环管
primary consolidation 主固结
primary data 原始数据,原始资料
primary deposit 现金存款
primary earthquake disaster 地震原生灾害
primary evidence 基本证据,原始证据
primary fact 基本事实,主要事实
primary highway 公路干线
primary joint 原生节理
primary liability 主要债务
primary market 初级市场,主要市场
primary material 主要材料
primary mineral 原生矿物
primary parameter 一次参数
primary presentation methods 基础表达方式
primary protection 主保护
primary rate 一次群速率
primary rate interface (PRI) 基群速率接口
primary return air 一次回风
primary risk 头等风险
primary settling tank 初次沉淀池
primary shotcreting 初喷
primary side 高压侧,一次侧,原边侧
primary sludge 初沉污泥
primary support 初期支护
primary treatment 一级处理
primary truss 主桁架
primary type 主类
prime coating 底漆
prime contract 主合同
prime cost plus fixed fee 主要成本加固定酬金
prime cost plus percentage fee 主要成本加定比酬金
prime cost 直接成本,直接费用,进货成本,主要成本
prime interest rate 优惠贷款利率
prime rate 基本利率,最优惠利率
prime risk 基本风险
principal 本金,当事人,委托人,资本
principal amount 贷款本金
principal and interest 本利,本息
principal consultant 总顾问,总咨询师
principal contractor 主承包商
principal debtor 主要债务人
principal distance of projector 投影器主距
principal office 总部
principal payment 本金支付
principal payment date 本金偿还日
principal place of business 主要营业地
principal point of photograph 像主点
principal point of photograph on water 像主点落水
Principal Reference Clock (PRC) 全网基准钟
principal rights 主权利
principal strain 主应变
principal stress difference 主应力差
principal sum 本金,本钱
principal vanishing point 主合点
principal vibration mode 主振型
principle 原理,原则,准则
principle of compensation 补偿原则
principle of effective stress 有效应力原理
principle of equality 平等原则
principle of good faith 诚信原则
principle of measurement 计量原则
principle of stare decisis 遵循判例原则
printer 打印机
prior claims 优先索赔
prior consultation 事先协商
prior review 事先审查
prior weight 先验权
priority 优先次序,优先权,优先顺序
priority construction 首期建筑
priority of contract documents 合同文件的优先次序
priority of document 文件优先顺序
priority project 重点工程
prism reflector 棱镜反光镜
private 个人的
private bidding (tendering) 不公开投标
private communication 专用通信
private company 私营公司
private enterprise 私营企业

private finance initiatives（PFI）
　私人主动融资,民间融资计划
private international law　国际私法
private law　私法
private ledger　内账
private sector participation（PSP）
　私营部门参与
private settlement　私下和解
private siding　铁路专用线
private utility entities
　私有设施实体或单位
private-line circuit　专线电路
private-line video conference system
　专线会议电视系统
privatization　私有化
privilege　特权
privity of contract
　合同关系不涉及第三者原则
pro rata　按比例
pro rata distribution　按比例分摊
pro rata liability system　比例责任制
probabilistic design method　概率设计法
probabilistic limit state design method
　概率极限状态设计法
probability　可能性
probability analysis　概率分析
probability distribution　概率分布
probability estimate　概率估算
probability of failure　失效概率
probable impact area　直接影响区
probation　试用
probationary period　试用期
procedural law　诉讼法,程序法
procedure　程序
procedure for appeal　上诉程序
procedure for claims　索赔程序
procedure for concluding a contract
　合同签订程序
procedure of approval　批准程序
procedure of arbitration　仲裁程序
procedure of customs　报关程序
proceeding　进程,程序
proceeding signal　允许信号,进行信号
proceedings　汇编,诉讼
proceeds　收入
process　工艺,加工,进程
process analysis　工序分析
process capability　加工能力
process chart　工艺流程图
process control diagram（PCD）　工艺控制图

process control　过程控制;工序控制
process costing　分步成本计算法
process data　整理资料
process design　工艺设计
process diagram　工艺流程图
process engineer　工艺工程师
process flow chart　工艺流程图
process flow diagram（PFD）　工艺流程图
process of export　出口手续
process of import　进口手续
process package　工艺包
process plant　工艺设备
process release　工艺发表
process unit　工艺装置
processing capability　处理能力
processing capacity　加工能力
processing cost　加工成本,加工费
processing efficiency　处理效率
processing time　加工时间
processing unit　处理单元
processing with client supplied designs
　来样加工
processing with foreign designs　来样加工
proclamation　公告
procure　采购,获得
procurement　采购
procurement administration　采购管理
procurement audit　采购审计
procurement clerk　采购员
procurement methods　采购办法
procurement of consulting services
　咨询服务采购
procurement of goods　货物采购
procurement of materials　材料采购
procurement of works　工程采购
procurement packages　采购包,一揽子采购
procurement planning　采购计划编制
procurement program　采购计划
procurement restraints　采购限制
procurement schedule　采购工作计划
procurement status report　采购进度报告
procure-upgrade-operate（PUO）
　购买—更新—运营
produce　出示,提交,制造,制作
product appraisal certificate　产品鉴定证书
product liability insurance　产品责任保险
product life cycle　产品生命周期
product quality guarantee　产品质量保证
product tax　产品税
production　出示,制作

production area of track section
轨排生产区
production bonus 生产奖金
production capacity ration
生产能力利用率
production capacity 生产能力
production check estimate（PCE）
二次核定估算
production control 生产管理
production cost 产品成本,生产成本
production cycle 建造周期
production data 生产数据
production license 生产许可证
production line 生产线
production line of track section
轨排生产作业线
production line performance test
生产线性能考核
production manager 生产经理
production method of depreciation
产量折旧法
production plan 生产计划
production preparation fee 生产准备费
production process water consumption
生产用水量
production quantity guarantee 产量保证
production quota 生产定额,生产指标
production rate 劳动定额,生产率
production sewage 生产污水
production target 生产指标
production term 生产期
production test 产品试板
productive construction project
生产性建设项目
productivity 生产率,生产能力
profession 同业,职业,职业,专业
professional 职业的,专业人员
professional code of conduct 职业行为准则
professional comment 专家意见
professional constructor 专业承包商
professional craftsmanship 专业技术
professional duty 职业责任
professional engineer license
执业工程师证书
professional engineer 执业工程师
professional ethics 职业道德
professional etiquette 行规
professional fee 专业服务费
professional indemnity insurance
职业保障保险

professional indemnity 职业责任险
professional liability 职业责任
professional liability insurance 职业责任保险
professional negligence 职业疏忽
professional responsibility 职业责任
professional review 专家评审
professional service 专业服务
professional skill 专业技术
professional technique 专业技术
professional witness 专业证人
proficiency 熟练
profile
（线路）纵断面,概况,高低,剖面图,竖向布置图
profile design 纵断面设计
profile diagram 纵断面图
profile leveling 中平测量
profile of sound barrier 声屏障立面
profile scanning 断面扫描
profile settlement tube 沉降剖面管
profiled steel sheet 压型钢板
profit 利润
profit after tax 税后利润
profit and loss 损益
profit and loss account 损益账
profit and loss statement 损益表
profit before tax 税前利润
profit distribution 利润分配
profit earned 已获利润
profit estimation 利润估算
profit for the term 本期利润,当期利润
profit forecast 利润预测
profit margin 利润率
profit markup 利润加成
profit pooling 利润汇总
profit ratio 利润率
profit tax 利润税
profitability 获利能力,效益,盈利能力
profitability analysis 财务盈利能力分析
profiteer 投机商
profit-oriented project 营利性项目
proforma invoice 形式发票,预开发票,临时发票
program 程序,方案,计划
program backup 后备计划
program evaluation and reviews technique（PERT）
统筹法,计划评审技术
program flow chart 程序流程图
programme 程序,计划
programming 程序设计,计划拟定
progress 进程,进度,进展
progress analysis 进度分析

progress billing 阶段付款
progress chart 进度表
progress control 进度控制
progress index 进度指标
progress management 进度管理
progress meeting 进度会
progress payment 进度付款
progress report 进度报告
progress schedule 进度计划
progressive 累进的
progressive collapse 连续倒塌
progressive failure 渐进破坏
progressive tax 累进税
prohibited articles（goods） 违禁品
prohibited humping line 禁溜线
prohibited rolling track 禁溜线
prohibition 禁令,诉讼中止令
prohibitive duty 高额关税,抑制性关税
prohibitive signal 禁止信号
project 计划,项目
project activities 项目作业
project agreement 项目协议
project alternative 项目备选方案
project analysis 项目分析
project appraisal 项目评估
project appraisal document（PAD）
　项目评估文件
project approval process 项目审批过程
project audit 项目审计
project base date 项目基准日期
project brief 项目概要
project budget 项目预算
project charter 核准书
project code 项目代码
project commissioning engineer
　项目调试工程师
project completion report 项目竣工报告
project constraints 项目约束因素
project contract 工程合同
project contracting 承包工程,工程承包
project control 项目控制
project coordination 项目协调
project coordinator 项目协调员
project cost 项目费用
project cycle 项目周期
project definition 项目内容确定
project demands 项目要求
project description 项目描述,项目说明
project design 工程设计
project design plan 工程设计方案

project diary 项目日志
project directory 项目通讯录
project director 项目主管
project documentation 项目文件
project duration 项目持续时间,项目工期
project engineer 项目工程师
project entity 项目负责机构,项目实体
project evaluation 项目评估
project execution 项目执行
project excution plan 施工组织设计
project execution and supervision
　项目执行与监督
project execution plan 项目执行计划
project executive 项目主管
project executive summary 项目执行概况
project extension 项目扩建
project financing 项目融资
project financing cost 项目筹融资费
project forecast 项目预测
project funding 项目资金
project goal 项目目标
project identification
　项目(方案)识别,项目(方案)鉴定
project impact assessment 项目影响评估
project implementation schedule
　项目执行计划
project inception 项目起始
project inspection reports 工程检查报告
project insurance 工程保险
project insurance expenses 工程保险费
project investment 工程投资
project investment decision-making
　项目投资决策
project life cycle 项目生命周期
project location 工程地点,项目所在地
project management 项目管理
project management contracting（PMC）
　项目管理承包
project management contractor
　项目管理承包商
project management system cost for construction
　project 建设项目管理信息系统购建费
project management team（PMT）
　项目管理团队
project manager 项目经理
project manual 项目手册
project monitor 项目监督员
project monitoring 项目监控
project negotiation 项目谈判
project objective 项目目标

project operation	项目运营
project opportunities	项目机会
project organization	项目机构
project participant	项目参与者
project performance	项目绩效
project performance assessment report (PPAR)	项目执行评估报告
project performance audit report (PPAR)	项目执行审计报告
project phase	项目阶段
project plan execution	项目计划实施
project plan update	项目计划的更新
project pollution discharge fees	工程排污费
project post-evaluation	项目后评价
project preparation(s)	项目准备,项目筹备
project pre-appraisal	项目预评估
project procedure manual	项目程序手册
project procedures	项目流程
project profile	工程概况
project program	工程计划
project property insurance	工程财产保险
project proposal	项目建议书
project proposal for approval	核准书
project quality test	项目质量检测
project quota measurement fee	工程定额测定费
project report	项目报告
project representative	项目代表
project risk	工程风险
project safety program	现场安全计划,现场保安计划
project schedule	项目进度计划
project scope	项目范围
project selection	项目选定
project size	项目规模
project specification	项目规程,项目规范
project sponsor	项目发起人,项目投资人
project staff	项目职员
project startup	项目启动
project status report	项目进展情况报告
project structure	项目结构
project superintendent	项目负责人,项目监督员,项目主管
project supervisor	项目监督员
project suspension	项目暂停
project sustainability assessing	项目可持续性评价
project team	项目组
project warranty	工程保修
projected cost	预计成本
projected financial statement	预计财务报表
projection	预测
projection by suspended plumb	吊锤投影
projection of broken chain	投影断链
projection printing	投影晒印
projectized organization	项目型组织
prolong	拖延
prolonged delay	持续的误期
prolonged suspension	停工延期,持续的暂时停工
proluvial fan	洪积扇
promise	许诺
promisee	受约人
promisor	订约人,立约人
promissory note	本票,期票
promote	提升,促进
promoter	推销商
promotion	提升,促进,促销
prompt	催促,催款单,付款期限,即付的
prompt cash	立即付款
prompt delivery	即期交货
promptness	及时性
proof	物证,证词,证据
proof of claim	索赔证明
proof of delivery	交货证明
proof of loss	损失证明
proof of performance	履约证明
proof to the contrary	反面证据
proper law	准据法
proper law of the contract	合同管辖法,合同准据法
proper operation	运行正常
property	财产,财产权,物权,性质,属性
property assets	房地产
property claim	产权要求
property company	房地产公司
property damage	财产损失
property dispute	产权纠纷
property in land	土地所有权
property insurance	财产保险
property insurance premium	财产保险费
property right	产权
property set	属性集
property valuation	资产评估
proportion	比例,比率,部分
proportion of delivery methods	运输方法比重
proportioning by weight	按重量比配合
proposal	方案,计划书,提议,建议书,投保书
proposal form	投保单

proposal of insurance　投保书
proprietary　所有权,专有技术权,所有人,专有的
proprietary articles　专利品,专卖品
proprietary equity
　股东权益,业主产权,业主权益
proprietary interest　业主权益
proprietary product　专利产品
proprietary right　所有权,专有技术权
proprietary technology　专有技术
proprietor　业主,专利权人
prosecution　起诉
prospect　勘察,预期
prospecting　勘探
prospecting line profile map　勘探线剖面图
prospecting line survey　勘探线测量
prospecting network survey　勘探网测量
prospective bidder（tenderer）　预期投标者
prospective borrower　贷款对象
prospective client　潜在客户
prospective yield　预期收益
prospectus　计划书
protect　保护
protected section　防护区段
protection　保护
protection and indemnity clause
　保赔保险条款
protection area　保护面积
protection at level crossing　道口防护
protection by plants　植物防护
protection circuit for heavy down grade approaching
　下坡道防护电路
protection circuit for switching midway in receiving-departure track　到发线出岔电路
protection cover　护罩
protection culvert　防护涵洞
protection door　防护门
protection fence　防护栅栏
protection malfunction　保护误动作
protection of shallow foundation of bridge
　桥梁浅基防护
protection panel　保护屏
protection section　保护区段
protection setting value　保护整定值
protection tube　防护套管
protection wall　防护墙
protection works　防护工程
protection zone　保护区
protectionism　保护主义
protective belt　防护带
protective coating of steel bridge　钢梁油漆

protective conductor　保护导体
protective cover　防护罩
protective device　保护器
protective earthing　保护接地
protective layer　保护层
protective layer of bridge floor　桥面保护层
protective measure(s)
　保护措施,防护措施,安全措施
protective mode　保护模式
protective radius　保护半径
protective range　保护范围
protective steel pipe　防护钢管
protective switch　防护道岔
protective transformer　防护变压器
protective turnout test　防护道岔测试
protective unit　防护单元
protective wire（PW）　保护线（PW线）
protector　保安器
Proterozoic eon　元古宙
Proterozoic eonothem　元古宇
Proterozoic erathem　元古界
Proterozoic era　元古代
protest　拒付,抗诉,抗议,(证明)拒付
protest jacket　退票通知单
protest note　拒付通知单
protest of bill　票据拒付证明
protocol　草案,协议,议定书
protocol analyzer　协议分析仪
protocol converter　协议转换器
prototype　原型
prototype gradation　天然级配
prototype inspect　实物检测
prototype testing　原型试验
protruding joint bar　鼓包夹板
protruding width of flange　翼缘板外伸宽度
protruding width of stiffener
　加劲肋外伸宽度
prove　核实
providing a guarantee　出具保函
providing a receipt　出具收据
proving time　检验时间
provision　供应,准备金
provision for bad debts　备抵坏账
provision for depreciation　备抵折旧
provisional acceptance　临时验收
provisional agreement　临时协议
provisional certificate　临时证书
provisional estimation　临时估价
provisional index　暂定(价格)指数
provisional invoice　临时发票

provisional payment 临时付款
provisional price 暂定价格
provisional procedures 暂行办法
provisional regulation 暂行条例
provisional sum 暂定金额
provisional sums for contingency
  应急费暂定金
provisions of contract 合同规定,合同条款
proviso 保留条件,限制性条件
proviso clause 但书,保留条款,限制性条款
proxy 代理权
pro-prietorship 所有权,专有技术权
psammitic 砂状
psephitic 砾状
pseudo-color composite 假彩色合成
pseudo-color density encode
  假彩色密度编码
pseudo-dynamic test 伪动力试验
pseudo-range 伪距
pseudo-static test 伪静力试验
pseudo-stereoscope 反立体镜
pseudo-t_0 time profile 似t_0时间剖面图
psophometer 杂音计
psychrometer 干湿球温度表
public accountant 执业会计师
public address system of luggage and parcel
  行包广播系统
public address system
  (客运)广播,广播系统
public assets 公共资产
public authorities 政府当局,公共机构
public bidding 公开招标
public body 团体,政府机构
public building 公共建筑
public emergency call 公众紧急呼叫
public facilities 公共设施
public green area 公共绿地
public grid 公共电网
public holiday 公共假日
public law 公法
public liability 公共责任
public liability insurance 公众责任险
public money 公款
public notary 公证人
public offer 公开报价
public official 政府官员
public policy 公共政策
public private partnership(PPP)
  公私伙伴关系
public relation 公共关系
public sale 拍卖
public security system 公共安全系统
public services 公用事业
public switched telephone network(PSTN)
  公共交换电话网
public utility 公用设施,公用事业
public welfare 公共福利,社会福利
public works 公共工程,市政工程,公用工程
public works survey 市政工程测量
publish 颁布,发行,公布
pull down 拆除
pulley 滑轮
pulley assembly tensioning device
  滑轮组补偿装置
pulling resistance 抗拔力
pull-in 牵引入
pull-off 正定位
pull-out button 拉钮
pulsation method 脉动法
pulsator 脉冲澄清池
pulse code modulation(PCM)
  脉冲编码调制
pulse load 脉冲荷载
pulse relay 脉冲继电器
pulse track circuit 脉冲轨道电路
pumice 浮岩
pump adapter 水泵接合器
pump station 水泵站
pumped concrete 泵送混凝土
pumping flushing 抽水洗井法
pumping station 泵站
pumping test 抽水试验
pump-in test device 压水设备
punch card 计时卡,工时记录卡,考勤卡
punch list 扫尾工作清单
punch to punch distance 孔口距
puncher 冲孔器
punching point 刺点
punching point photograph 刺点相片
punching shear failure 冲剪破坏
punching well flushing 冲孔洗井
punchlist 核对清单,检核表
punctual delivery 及时交货
punish 处罚
punitive damages 惩罚性赔偿费
purchase 采购,收购
purchase and storage expenses
  采购及保管费
purchase commitment 购货约定
purchase contract 订货合同,买卖合同

purchase cost 进货成本
purchase expense 采购费,购置费,进货费用
purchase expense for equipment
　设备、工器具购置费
purchase expense of rolling stock（EMU）
　机车车辆(动车)购置费
purchase expense of transportation vehicle during
　construction period
　建设期交通工具购置费
purchase inquiry 询价采购
purchase invoice 购货发票
purchase journal 购货日记账
purchase memorandum 采购备忘录
purchase money 定金
purchase note 购货确认书
purchase offer 买方递盘,买方出价
purchase order 订单,购货单
purchase requisition 采购申请单
purchase sample 购货样品
purchasing agency 采购代理
purchasing agent 购货代理人
purchasing clerk 采购员
purchasing commission 代购佣金
purchasing cost 购货成本
purchasing department 采购部,物资部
purchasing place 经营场所
purchasing power 购买力
purchasing strategy 采购策略
pure interest 纯利息
pure premium 纯保险费
pure risk 纯粹风险
pure shear stress 纯剪应力
pure water 纯水
purlin 檩条
purpose 目的,用途
pursuant to 根据
push 推送
push button 电钮
pusher gradient 加力牵引坡度
pushing carriage 牵引小车
pushing route 推送进路
pushing route control for hump yard
　驼峰推送进路控制
pushing section 推送部分
pushing signal 推送信号
pushing slope 推送坡
pushing track 推送线
pushing track of hump 驼峰推送线
push-off 反定位
put into production 投产
puzzling 不能理解的
PVC geomembrane 聚氯乙烯土工膜
PVC pipe 聚氯乙烯管材
PVC sheet 聚氯乙烯防水卷材
pycnometer 比重瓶
pycnometer method 比重瓶法
pyramidal peak 角峰
pyrite 黄铁矿
pyrometer 高温计
pyroxene 辉石
pyroxenite 辉岩
P-wave P波

Q

QoS of train control CSD
 列车运行控制类电路交换数据业务服务质量
QoS of voice and non train control Circuit Switched
 Data(CSD) 语音业务和非列车运行控制类电
 路交换数据业务服务质量
quaking concrete 塑性混凝土
qualification 限制条件,资格
qualification certificate 资格证书
qualification documents 资格文件
qualification of test detection institution
 试验检测机构资质
qualifications-based selection
 基于资格的选择
qualified 合格的
qualified acceptance
 附条件承兑,有保留接受
qualified contractor 合格承包商
qualified materials 合格材料
qualified piles 合格桩
qualifying clause 限制性条款
qualitative analysis 定性分析
qualitative analysis method 定性分析法
quality 特性,品质,优质
quality acceptance 质量验收
quality and cost based selection(QBCS)
 基于质量和价格的选择
quality as per buyer's sample
 质量以买方样品为准
quality as per seller's sample
 质量以卖方样品为准
quality assurance 质量保证
quality assurance plan 质量保证计划
quality assurance programme 质保大纲
quality assurance system 质量保证体系
quality audit 质量审核
quality certificate 质量证明
quality control 质量控制
quality evaluation methods 质量评估方法
quality evaluation 质量评价
quality guarantee 质量保证书
quality inspection 质量检验
quality inspection of masonry
 砌体质量检验
quality management system 质量管理体系
quality of appearance 外观质量
quality of current collection 受流质量
Quality of Service(QoS) 服务质量
quality record 质量记录
quality review 质量审查
quality standards 质量标准
quality surveillance 质量监督
quality system 质量体系
quality tracking system 质追踪系统
quality-based selection(QBS)
 基于质量的选择
quantification 可计量性,可量化
quantitative analysis method 定量分析法
quantitative filter paper of moderately speed
 中速定量滤纸
quantitative inspection 计量检验
quantity 数量,工程量
quantity discount 数量折扣,工程量折扣
quantity index 数量指标
quantity of machine shift 机械台班量
quantity of work 工作量
quantity pricing 工程量标价
quantity survey 工料测量
quantity surveying 工料测量学
quantity surveyor(QS) 工料测量师
quantity take-off 工程量计算
quarry 采掘场,采石场
quarrying 采石工程
quartering method 四分法
quarterly financial report 季度财务报告
Quarternary 第四纪
Quarternary period 第四纪

quartz 石英
quartz sand 石英砂
quartz sandstone 石英砂岩
quartzite 石英岩
quartz-keratophyre 石英角斑岩
quartz-trachyte 石英粗面岩
quasi-arbitrator 准仲裁员
quasi-geoid 似大地水准面
quasi-judicial 准司法的
quasi-moving block 准移动闭塞
quasi-official 半官方的
quasi-permanent combination of load effect 荷载效应准永久组合
quasi-permanent combination 准永久组合
quasi-permanent value of a load 荷载准永久值
quasi-permanent value of live load 活荷载准永久值
quasi-permanent value of load 荷载作用准永久值
quasi-permanent value of variable action 可变作用准永久值
quasi-stable adjustment 拟稳平差
Quaternary system 第四系
quayage 码头费
quay-to-quay transportation 码头至码头运输
quenched rail 淬火轨
quenching treatment 淬火处理
query 询问,质疑
quick cement 速凝水泥
quick compression test 快速压缩试验
quick consolidation test 快速固结试验
quick direct shear test 直剪快剪试验
quick pick-up relay 快吸继电器
quick response early fire extinguishing sprinkler 快速响应早期灭火喷头
quick response sprinkler 快速响应洒水喷头
quick shear 快剪
quick shear test 快(速)剪(切)试验
quick turnaround operation 立即折返作业
quick turnaround system 立即折返制
quicklime 生石灰
quicksand 流沙
quick-acting relay 快动继电器
quick-acting switch machine 快速转辙机
quota 定额,配额,限额
quota consumption of materials 材料定额消耗量
quota direct engineering expense 定额直接工程费
quota exchange 定额抽换
quota increase range 定额增加幅度
quota man-day 定额工天
quota measurement 定额测定
quota of labor consumption 人工消耗量定额
quota of machine shift consumption 机械台班消耗量定额
quota of machine shift 机械台班定额
quota of water consumption 用水定额
quota of water discharge 排水定额
quota price 定额价
quota system 定额体系
quota valuation 定额计价
quotation 报价单
quotation for acceleration 赶工报价
quote 报价

R

rack panel layout plan　机架面板布置图
radar method　雷达法
radar penetrating　雷达穿透
radar self test　雷达自检
radar speedometer　雷达测速器
radar test board　雷达测试台
radial deformation　径向变形
radial direction　径向
radial flat jack technique　径向扁千斤顶法
radial flow settling tank　辐流沉淀池
radial free expansion rate　径向自由膨胀率
radial gate　弧形闸门
radial structure　辐射状构造
radial well　辐射井
radiant floor heating　地板辐射采暖
radiant heating　辐射采暖
radiant wall heating　墙壁辐射采暖
radiant well yield　辐射井出水量
radiated　放射状
radiation intensity　辐射强度
radiation transformation　辐射变换
radiator　散热器
radiator heating　散热器采暖
radiator valve　散热器调节阀
radio blind zone　无线盲区
radio block center（RBC）　无线闭塞中心
radio communication　无线通信
radio communication-based train control
　基于无线通信的列车控制
radio subsystem　无线子系统
radio wave penetration　无线电波透视
radioactive contamination　放射性污染
radioactive detection method
　放射性探测法
radioactivity logging　放射性测井
radioactivity prospecting　放射性勘探
radio-noise field strength of background
　背景无线电噪声场强

radius of circular curve　圆曲线半径
radius of curvature in prime vertical
　卯酉圈曲率半径
radius of curve　曲线半径
radius of interpolation circle　内插圆半径
radius of vertical curve　竖曲线半径
raft foundation　筏形基础
ragged fracture　锯齿状断口
rail　扶手,钢轨,栏杆,护栏
rail anchor　防爬器
rail and air　铁路运输及空运
rail and ocean　铁路运输及海运
rail and water　铁路运输及水运
rail base　轨底
rail base slope　轨底坡
rail bolt hole　钢轨螺栓孔
rail bond　钢轨接续线
rail bottom inclination　轨底坡
rail brace　轨撑
rail breakage　钢轨断裂
rail breaking force in CWR on bridge　断轨力
rail cant　轨底坡
rail car　轨道车
rail car shed　轨道车库
rail corrosion　钢轨锈蚀
rail corrugation　波形磨耗
rail crack　钢轨裂纹
rail creep indication post　钢轨位移观测桩
rail creep observation pile　钢轨位移观测桩
rail creeping　钢轨爬行
rail defect　钢轨伤损
rail drilling machine　钢轨钻孔机
rail drilling tool　钢轨钻孔器
rail electrical disconnection　钢轨电气断离
rail end step in gauge line or surface
　错牙接头
rail expansion joint　钢轨伸缩调节器
rail fastening-down　钢轨锁定

rail fatigue 钢轨疲劳
rail flat car 轨道平车
rail flaw detecting 钢轨探伤
rail flaw detecting car 钢轨探伤车
rail flaw detector 钢轨探伤仪
rail fracture 钢轨断裂
rail gap adjuster 轨缝调整器
rail gap slice 轨隙片
rail grinding 钢轨打磨
rail grinding car 钢轨打磨车,磨轨车
rail grinding machine 磨轨机
rail head 轨头
rail head checks 轨头发裂
rail head reprofiling 轨头整形
rail head shelling 轨头剥离
rail head wear 轨头磨损
rail heater 钢轨加热器
rail heating 钢轨加热
rail impedance 钢轨阻抗
rail insulation 钢轨绝缘
rail joint 钢轨接头
rail joint gap 轨缝
rail laying 铺轨
rail leakage resistance 钢轨泄漏电阻
rail longitudinal connection 钢轨纵向连接
rail lubricating 钢轨涂油
rail lubricator 钢轨涂油器
rail minimum short circuit value for cab signal 机车信号钢轨最小短路电流值
rail mounted container gantry crane 轨道式集装箱门式起重机
rail mounted crane 轨行式起重机
rail pad 轨下垫板
rail plane 轨面
rail positioning 配轨
rail potential 轨道电位,钢轨电位
rail puller 钢轨拉伸器
rail repair welding 钢轨焊补,焊修钢轨
rail replacement 钢轨更换
rail replacement machine 钢轨更换机
rail return current 钢轨回流
rail sawing machine 锯轨机
rail scratch 钢轨擦伤
rail seat 承轨槽,承轨台
rail sizing 钢轨定尺
rail straightening 钢轨矫直,矫直钢轨
rail straightening machine 直轨器
rail straightness gauge 直尺
rail straightness measuring scale 钢轨直度测量尺
rail stress 钢轨应力
rail supporting modulus 钢轨基础模量
rail temperature 钢轨温度
rail temperature force/load 温度力
rail temperature monitoring 轨温监测
rail tensor 钢轨拉伸器
rail tread 钢轨踏面
rail wear 钢轨磨耗
rail wear measuring car 钢轨磨损检查车
rail wear measuring device 钢轨磨损检查仪
rail web 轨腰
rail weighing bridge 轨道衡
rail weld seam shearing machine 钢轨推凸机
rail weld trimmer 钢轨推凸机
rail welding 钢轨焊接
rail welding car 钢轨焊接车
rail welding machine 焊轨机
rail welding production line 焊轨生产线
railing 栏杆,护栏
railway advice 铁路到货通知
railway aerial photogrammetry 铁路航空摄影测量(铁路航测)
railway ballast storage yard 道砟存放场
railway bill of lading 铁路提货单
railway boundary 铁路边界
railway bridge 铁路桥
railway classification 铁路等级
railway clearance 铁路限界
railway communication 铁路通信
railway consignment note 铁路托运单
railway construction fund 铁路建设基金
railway construction fund rate 铁路建设基金费率
railway dedicated mobile communication system 铁路专用移动通信系统
railway digital mobile communication system (GSM-R) 铁路数字移动通信系统
railway electrification 铁道电气化
railway embankment design 铁路路基设计
railway emergency call (REC) 铁路紧急呼叫
railway engineering 铁路工程
railway engineering feature model 铁路工程要素模型
railway engineering information modeling/model 铁路工程信息模型
railway engineering survey 铁路工程测量
railway freight 铁路运费

railway freight area 铁路货区
railway in plateau region 高原铁路
railway industrial station 铁路工业站
railway integrated grounding 铁路综合接地
railway integrated video surveillance system 铁路综合视频监控系统
railway junction 铁路枢纽
railway landscape water 铁路景观用水
railway line 铁路线路
railway line break down due to flood 水害断道
railway line length 线路长度
railway location 铁路选线
railway location based on environmental protection factors 环保选线
railway network 铁路网
railway network marshalling station 路网性编组站
railway network planning 铁路路网规划
railway noise 铁路噪声
railway noise limit on the boundary alongside railway line 铁路边界噪声限值
railway noise on the boundary alongside railway line 铁路边界噪声
railway non-drinking water 铁路生活杂用水
railway operation and maintenance 铁路运营养护
railway passenger station 铁路旅客车站
railway passenger transport service information system 铁路客运服务信息系统
railway reuse water 铁路回用水
railway route profile 线路纵断面图
railway section 路段
railway section under design 设计路段
railway signal safety communication protocol 铁路信号安全通信协议
railway signaling 铁路信号
railway structure gauge 铁路建筑限界
railway temporary bridge 铁路便桥
railway terminal 铁路枢纽
railway train ferry 铁路轮渡
railway tunnel 铁路隧道
railway-turnout beam bridge 道岔梁桥
railway-turnout girder bridge 道岔梁桥
rail-cum-road bridge 公铁两用桥
rail-earth potential 钢轨—大地电位
rail-head edges planing machine 钢轨刨边机
rail-mounted handling and transportation machine 轨行式装运机械

rain gauge 雨量计
rain inlet 雨水口
rain proof 防雨
rainfall 降雨量
rainfall detention works 降水蓄渗工程
rainfall intensity 降雨强度
rainfall monitoring 雨量监测
rainfall monitoring alarm 雨量监测报警
rainfall sensor 雨量传感器
rainless period 枯水期
rainstorm characteristic value 暴雨特征值
rainstorm duration 暴雨历时
rainstorm intensity 暴雨强度
rainwater 雨水
rainwater catch-basin 雨水井
rainwater drainage system 雨水排水系统
rainwater pipe channel design 雨水管渠设计
rainy season 雨季
raise (contract) a loan 借债
raise funds 筹措资金,集资
rammed ground 夯实地基
rammer 夯,桩锤
ramming machine 打夯机
ramp 坡道
random error 偶然误差
random mean square error of elevation difference 高差偶然中误差
random sample 随机样品
random sampling 随机抽样
random testing 随机检验
random vibration 无规振动
range 范围,极差,界限
range of train operation disturbance 行车干扰范围
rank 级别
rank defect network adjustment 秩亏网平差
Rankine's earth pressure theory 兰金土压力理论
ranking 排序
rapakivi granite 奥长环斑花岗岩
rapid freezing and thawing method 快冻法
rapid hardening cement 速凝水泥
rapid qualitative filter paper 快速定性滤纸
rapid voltage change 电压突变
rare and endangered species 珍稀濒危物种
rare wildlife 珍稀野生动物
rate 费率,速率,比率
rate of administration cost of Employer 建设单位管理费率

rate of customs duty 海关税率
rate of defluorinate 脱氟率
rate of deformation 变形速率
rate of desalination 脱盐率
rate of discount 贴现率,折扣率,折现率
rate of emergence 种子发芽率
rate of exchange 兑换率,汇率
rate of false report in earthquake prediction
  误报率
rate of freight 运费率
rate of indirect expenses 间接费率
rate of investment return 投资回报率
rate of loading 加荷速率
rate of locomotive shed repair 段修率
rate of locomotives inspection and repair
  机车检修率
rate of operation 开工率
rate of port dues 港口税率
rate of premium 保险费率
rate of progress 工程进度
rate of purchase and storage expenses
  采购及保管费率
rate of return 收益率
rate of return method 收益率评估法
rate of return on investment 投资回报率
rate of slaking 湿化速度
rate of waste 损耗率
rate of wear and tear during delivery
  运输损耗费费率
rate sheet 价目表
rated bonding force 检定黏结力
rated breaking current 额定开断电流
rated capacity 额定容量
rated current 额定电流
rated flow 额定流量,检定流量
rated flow rate 检定流速
rated horsepower 额定马力
rated load 额定负荷
rated load of road 道路标准荷载
rated making current 额定关合电流
rated measuring range 额定量程
rated operating pressure 额定工作压力
rated peak withstand current
  动稳定电流,额定峰值耐受电流
rated power 额定功率
rated short-time withstand current
  热稳定电流
rated value 额定值
rated value of impulse withstand voltage
  耐冲击电压额定值
rated voltage 额定电压
rates of wages and conditions of labour
  工资标准和劳动条件
rating 级别,检定
rating allowable stress 检定容许应力
rating flood frequency 检定洪水频率
rating load-bearing coefficient
  检定承载系数
ratio 比率
ratio estimation method 比例估算法
ratio of compressive strength 抗压强度比
ratio of expansion and contraction by heating
  加热伸缩率
ratio of fluidity 流动度比
ratio of power consumption to heat output
  耗电输热比
ratio of shrinkage 收缩率比
ration 配额
ravage 毁坏
raw brick 砖坯
raw data 原始数据
raw materials 原材料
raw sludge 原污泥
raw water 原水
Rayleigh wave 瑞利波,瑞雷面波
Rayleigh wave method 瑞雷波法
reach an agreement 达成协议
reactance compensation 电抗补偿
reaction 反力
reaction wall 反力墙
reactive compensator with fixed parallel capacitors
  固定并联电容无功补偿装置
reactive current 无功电流
reactive muffler 抗性消声器
reactive power 无功功率
reactive power compensation 无功补偿
reactive power factor 无功功率因数
reactive voltage drop 无功电压降
reactor 电抗器
ready cash 现金
ready-mix concrete 预拌混凝土
ready-mix concrete truck
  混凝土搅拌运输车
ready-mix truck 预拌混凝土车
ready-mixed concrete 商品混凝土
ready-mixed concrete truck 商品混凝土车
read-out bid price 唱标价
reagent 试剂
real account 实账户
real cost 实际成本

real estate 不动产,房地产
real exchange rate 实际汇率
real object measuring method 实物量法
real object method 实物法
real object valuation method 实物计价法
real property 不动产,房地产
real security 实物担保
real tare 实际皮重
realgar 雄黄
realignment 改线
real-name authentication system
　实名验证系统
real-name ticketing 实名制售票
real-name validation 实名制
real-time 即时的
real-time differences correction
　实时差分改正
real-time dynamic positioning
　实时动态定位
real-time monitoring 实时监控
real-time transmission 实时传送
reap profits 获利
rear end of turnout 道岔终端
rear length of turnout 道岔后长
rear services 后勤
rear support 后支承
rear-end collision 追尾
reasonable claim 合法请求,合理索赔
reasonable price 公平价格
reassure 再次保证
rebar 钢筋
rebar layer spacing 钢筋层距
rebar mechanical splicing 钢筋机械连接
rebate 回扣,折扣
rebated acceptance 提前承兑
rebound apparatus 回弹仪
rebound ratio 回弹率
rebuilding 改建
recall 收回
recall an order 撤销订货单
receipt 签收,收条,收据,进款
receipt slip 收款便条
received for shipment bill of lading 待运提单
receiver 接收人,接受人,破产案产业管理人,诉讼财产管理人
receiver and transmitter 收发设备
receiver antenna 接收机天线
receiving amplifier 受信放大器
receiving clerk 收料员
receiving coil 接收线圈
receiving end 受电端,受电侧
receiving inspection 进场检验
receiving note 收货通知
receiving optical power 接收光功率
receiving order 接管令
receiving route 接车进路
receiving shaft 接收井
receiving signal 接车信号(机)
receiving track 到达线
receiving yard 到达场
receiving-departure route 接发车进路
receiving-departure track 到发线
receiving-departure yard 到发场
recession of contract 撤销合同
recharge area 补给区
recharge radius 补给半径
recharge rate 补给率
recipient 接收人,接受人
recipient country 受援国
reciprocal 互惠的
reciprocal account 往来账户
reciprocal agreement 互惠协定
reciprocal contract 互惠合同
reciprocal letter of credit 对开信用证
reciprocal tariff 互惠关税
reciprocal trade 互惠贸易
reciprocal treatment 互惠待遇
reciprocate 互换
reciprocating compressor
　往复式空气压缩机
reciprocating pump 往复式水泵
reciprocity clause 互惠条款
recirculation zone 回流区
reckless misconduct
　恣意行为,重过失行为
reclaimed water 中水,再生水
reclaimed water plant 再生水厂
reclaimed water system 中水系统
reclamation 回填,开垦,填筑
reclamation cost of farmland 耕地开垦费
reclamation of sewage 污水资源化
reclamation value 回收价值
reclamation works 围垦工程
recognition and assessment 识别评估
recommend 推荐
recommendation 推荐
reconciliation 和解
reconfirm 重新确认
reconnaissance 踏勘,初勘
reconnaissance stage 勘察阶段

reconstructed railway 改建铁路
reconstruction 改建,重建
record 记录,记载
record drawing 记录图纸
record modeling 记录模型
recorder unit 记录单元
recourse 追索权
recover 复原,恢复,收回
recoverable 可补偿的,可收回的
recovery 复原,恢复
recovery of property 财产收回
recovery plan (schedule) 赶工计划
recovery value 回收价值
recruit 招聘
recruitment 招聘
recruitment of persons 人员的招募
rectangle frame structure 矩形框架结构
rectangular beam 矩形梁
rectangular coordinate network 直角坐标网
rectangular layout 矩形布置
rectangular map subdivision 矩形分幅
rectangular pier 矩形桥墩
rectification of geometric condition
　纠正几何条件
rectification of optical condition
　纠正光学条件
rectification of reference plane 纠正起始面
rectifier 整流器
rectifier module 整流模块
rectifier relay 整流继电器
rectify 补救,修补
recuperate 复原,恢复
recurrence interval 重现期
recurrence interval of tide level 潮位重现期
recyclable material 可再循环材料
recycled coefficient 利用系数
recycled material 利用料
recycled quantity 利用量
recycled ratio 利用率
red balance 赤字,亏空
red bed 红层
red clay 红黏土
red clay subgrade 红黏土路基
red flag clause 关键条款
red light strip flash 闪红光带
red mud pond 赤泥库
redeem 赎回
redeemable bond 可赎回债券
redemption price 赎回价格
redeployment expense 调遣费

redress 补救
reduce cost 降低成本
reduce retention 扣减保留金
reduce the price 降价,减价
reducing balance depreciation method
　余额递减折旧法
reduction 减量
reduction coefficient 折减系数
reduction coefficient of live load
　活荷载折减系数
reduction of adhesion at small radius curve
　小半径曲线黏降
reduction or exemption of tax 减免税
reduction rate of the total installed capacity of
　lighting system 照明系统总功率降低率
reduction rate of wheel load 轮重减载率
reduction to station centre 测站归心
reduction to target centre 照准点归心
redundancy 冗余
redundancy configuration 冗余配置
redundant array of independent disks(RAID)
　独立磁盘冗余阵列
redundant array of inexpensive disk (RAID)
　磁盘阵列
redundant observation 多余观测
redundant structure test 冗余结构测试
redwood boiling box 雷氏沸煮箱
reefer 冷藏车
reel cart 绞车
refer 参考
refer to 提及
referee 仲裁员,公断人,鉴定人
reference 参考,基准,职权范围
reference axis 基准线
reference building 参照建筑,基准建筑
reference clause 仲裁条款
reference clock 基准时钟
reference earth 参考地
reference ellipsoid 参考椭球(体)
reference frequency signal 基准频率信号
reference line of turnout 道岔基线
reference list of adjustment 调整参考表
reference model 参考模型
reference of a dispute to the DAAB
　将争议提交争议避免裁决委员会裁决
reference plane 参考平面,基准面,基准计划
reference point 基准点,参照点
reference point of background noise
　背景噪声对照点
reference price 参考价格

reference radius 引用半径
reference receiver 基准接收机
reference snow pressure 基本雪压
reference solution 基准溶液
reference surface 基准面
reference water-cement ratio 基准水灰比
reference wind pressure 基本风压
reference year 基准年
refilling 回填
refinance 重新筹集资金
refitting 修整
reflectance ratio 反射比
reflected glare 反射眩光,反射炫光
reflected traffic flow 折角车流
reflected wave 反射波
reflection method 反射波法
reflector 反射镜,反射体
reflux ratio 回流比
refraction method 折射波法
refractory 耐火材料
refractory brick 耐火砖
refractory cement 耐火水泥
refractory material 耐火材料
refractory/fireproof/fire-resistant concrete 耐火混凝土
refrigerant 制冷剂
refrigerating capacity 制冷量
refrigerating machine room 制冷机房
refrigerating system 制冷系统
refrigeration 制冷
refrigeration cycle 制冷循环
refrigerator car 冷藏车
refuge 避难所
refuge niche 避车洞
refuge platform 避车台
refuge recess 避车洞
refuge room 避难屋
refuge storey 避难层
refund 偿还债务,退款,退票
refund of duty 退税
refurbishment 修整
refusal of enforcement 拒绝执行
refuse 拒付
refuse classification 垃圾分类
refuse dump 排土场
refuse transfer facilities 垃圾转运设施
refuse transfer station 垃圾转运站
refute 反驳
regain 复原,恢复,收回
regenerate 复原,恢复

regenerator section 再生段
region 地区,区域
regional cable 地区电缆
regional geological map 区地质图
regional geological survey 区域地质测量
regional geology 区域地质
regional hydrographic network map 区域水系图
regional integrated management platform 区域级集成管理平台
regional line 地区线路
regional marshalling station 区域性编组站
regional monitoring center 区域监控中心
regional network 区域网络
regional planning 地区规划
regional preference 地区性优惠
regional price differential 地区差价
regional uniform quota 地区统一定额
register 登记簿,记存装置,登记,注册
registered bond 记名债券
registered capital 注册资本
registered company 注册公司
registered design 注册设计
registered letter 挂号信
registered mail 挂号邮件
registered title 注册产权
registered trade mark 注册商标
registration 注册
registration assembly 定位装置
registration fee 案件受理费
registration mast 定位(支)柱
registration tube 定位管
registration tube brace 定位管支撑
registration tube clamp 定位管卡子
registration tube strut 定位管支撑
registration-fitting-free area 受电弓始触区
regression model 回归模型
regressive sequence 海退层序
regressive tax 递减税
regular insurance 定期保险
regular maintenance of bridge 桥梁定期保养
regular meeting 例会
regular payment 定期支付
regular repair 经常性修理
regular repair cost 定期修理费
regular review meetings 例行评审会议
regular re-measuring 定期复测
regular tax 正常税
regular triangle layout 正三角形布置

regulate 调节
regulating valve 调节阀
regulation 调节,调节沉淀隔油,条例
rehabilitate 复原,恢复
rehabilitate-operate-transfer（ROT） 改建—运营—移交,修复—运营—移交
rehabilitate-own-operate（ROO） 更新—拥有—运营
rehabilitation 修复,重建
reimbursable 可报销的,可偿还的,可补偿的
reimbursable cost 可补偿费用
reimbursable expense 可补偿开支
reimburse 补偿,偿还,赔偿
reimbursement 补偿,赔偿
reinforce 加固
reinforced asphalt sheet 有胎沥青防水卷材
reinforced concrete（RC） 钢筋混凝土
reinforced concrete bridge 钢筋混凝土桥
reinforced concrete pile 钢筋混凝土桩
reinforced concrete pole 钢筋混凝土柱
reinforced concrete pressure pipe 钢筋混凝土压力水管
reinforced concrete structure 钢筋混凝土结构
reinforced earth 加筋土
reinforced earth retaining wall 加筋土挡土墙
reinforced masonry 配筋砌体
reinforced masonry structure 配筋砌体构件
reinforced soil embankment 加筋土路基
reinforcement 加筋,配筋,加固
reinforcement bar 钢筋
reinforcement material 增强材料
reinforcement mesh/skeleton binding pedestal 钢筋网片/骨架绑扎台座
reinforcement meter 钢筋测力仪(计)
reinforcement ratio per unit volume 体积配筋率
reinforcement ratio 配筋率
reinforcement yard 钢筋加工场
reinforcing bar 钢筋
reinforcing fabric 钢筋网
reinforcing feeder 加强线
reinforcing rod 加固杆
reinstate 复原,恢复
reinstate sb. in 复原,恢复
reinstatement 恢复原状
reinstatement cost 复原费用
reinstatement value insurance 重置价值保险
reinsurance 再保险
reinsurance contract 再保险合同
reject 驳回,拒绝接受
rejection insurance 拒收险
rejection of all bids 废标,拒绝全部投标
related color temperature 相关色温
relative altitude difference 相对高差
relative calibration method 相对标定法
relative closing error of traverses 导线相对闭合差
relative deformation 相对变形
relative density 相对密度
relative dielectric constant 相对介电常数
relative durability 相对耐久性
relative dynamic elastic modulus 相对动弹模量
relative error 相对误差
relative error ellipse 相对误差椭圆
relative flying height 相对航高
relative humidity 相对湿度
relative mean error between adjacent points 相邻点间相对中误差
relative mean square error 相对中误差
relative mean square error of side length 边长相对中误差
relative misclosure 相对闭合差
relative orientation 相对定向
relative orientation element 相对定向元素
relative permittivity 相对介电常数
relative price 比价,相对价格
relative residual deflection 相对残余挠度
relative residual strain 相对残余应变
relative settlement 相对沉降量
relaxation time 松弛时间
relay 继电器
relay cabinet 继电器箱
relay energized 继电器吸起
relay interlocking 继电联锁
relay node 中继点
relay parallel delivery network 继电并联传递网络
relay parallel network 继电并联网络
relay protection 继电保护
relay released 继电器释放
relay room 继电器间
relay series network 继电串联网络
relayed surveillance network 远程网路
release 缓解,解锁
release after power-off 断电释放
release agent 脱模剂

release circuit 解锁电路
release claim 放弃索赔
release factor 返还系数
release from debt/liability 免除债务
release from performance 解除履约
release from performances under the law 依法解除履约责任
release of bank guarantee 撤销银行保函
release of liens 解除留置权
release of material 材料发放
release of mortgage 解除抵押
release of retention money 返还保留金,保留金的退还
release of security 保函退还
release of the guarantee 归还保函
release paper 隔离纸
release pay 遣散费
release requisition 解锁条件
release speed 开口速度
release value 释放值
release/exempt from contract obligation 免除合同义务
released by checking four sections 四点检查
released by checking two sections 两点检查
release-coupler section 提钩地段
releasing force 解锁力
releasing time 缓解时间
releasor 放弃权利者
relending 分贷
relet 转租
relevant cost 相关成本
reliability 可靠度,可靠性
reliability analysis of traction power supply system 供电可靠性分析
reliability index 可靠指标
reliability management 可靠性管理
reliability probability 可靠概率
reliability-based design 可靠性设计
reliable 可靠的
relief displacement 投影差
relief well 减压井
relieve 减轻
relieve from obligations 解除义务
relieving slab 卸荷板
reliquiae 化石
relocate 搬迁
relocation 搬迁,拆迁,迁移

relocation cost 搬迁费
relocation settlement costs 搬迁安置费用
remain in force 保持有效
remainder 剩余物
remaining duration 剩余工期
remaining particles on sieve 筛上剩余颗粒
remaining value 余值
remaining value salvage value 残值
remanent value of equipment 设备残值
remarshaling capacity 改编能力
remarshaling train 改编列车
remeasurement 重新计量
remeasurement contract 重新计量合同
remedial action 补救措施
remedial measure 补救措施
remedial work 修补工作,补救工作
remedy 补救,修补,修正
remedying defects 修补缺陷
remedying of defective work off site 修补施工现场外的缺陷工作
remedying of defects 缺陷修补
reminder 催单,提示信息
remission 减免
remit 汇寄,汇款,豁免,减轻
remit a debt 免除债务
remittance 汇兑,汇付,汇寄,汇款
remittance advice 汇款通知单
remittance against documents 凭单付款
remittance by banker's draft 票汇
remittance by draft 汇票汇款
remittance permit 核准书
remittance settlement 汇款结算
remittance slip 汇款通知单
remittee 收款人
remitter 汇款人
remitting bank 代收银行,托收银行,汇款银行
remnant detection 遗留物检测
remote authentication dial in user service (RADIUS) 远端拨入用户验证服务
remote backup protection 远后备保护
remote control 远动,遥控
remote control of hump engines 驼峰机车遥控
remote control of junction terminal 枢纽遥控
remote control system 远动系统
remote control system of traction power supply 牵引供电远动系统
remote data backup 异地数据备份
remote maintenance 远程维护
remote microphone off 远端闭音

remote sensing 遥感
remote sensing data 遥感数据
remote sensing image 遥感图像
remote sensing image interpretation 遥感图像判释
remote sensing mapping 遥感制图
remote sensing platform 遥感平台
remote sensing prospecting 遥感勘测
remote surveillance and telemetering for highway crossing 道口遥信遥测设备
remote terminal unit（RTU） 远动终端(设备)
remote test 远程试验
remoulded strength 重塑强度
removal 迁移,移走
removal and laying 拆铺
removal cost 拆迁成本
removal expenses 搬运费
removal of defective work 移走有缺陷的工程
removal percentage of volatile solids 挥发性固体去除率
remove 迁移
remuneration 报酬,酬金,劳动报酬
renew 复原,恢复,更新
renew a contract 续订合同
renewable energy 可再生能源
renewal 更新,展期
renewal of contract 合同续订,合同展期
renewal of insurance 续保
reniform 肾状的
renovation cost 整修管理费
renovation management expense of used rails 再用轨料整修管理费
renovation management rate 整修管理费率
renovation measures 整治措施
rent 租借,租金,租赁
rental 出租,租金,租金收入
repair 补救,维修,返修,修补,修理
repair by shotcreting 喷射混凝土修理
repair center for spare parts 配件检修中心
repair charge 修理费
repair cycle 检修周期
repair fee 维修费
repair kit 修理工具
repair of wagon on hand 现车修
repair position 检修台位
repair section 维修工区
repair section track 维修工区线
repair shop 修配间
repair siding 修车线
repair track 检修线
repair workshop 维修车间
repairs beyond the scope of repairing course 超范围维修
repartition 划分
repatriation 汇还本国,遣返
repatriation fee 遣返费
repatriation of worker 劳工遣返
repay 偿付,偿还
repay capital with interest 还本付息
repay（the）capital and interest 还本付息
repayment 偿还
repayment ability 偿还能力
repayment guarantee 偿还保函
repayment of advance payment 偿还预付款
repayment of advance 预付款的偿还
repayment of loan 偿还贷款
repayment period 偿还期
repayment schedule 还款时间表
repeated action 多次重复作用
repeated check 重复检查
repeater section 中继段
repeating indication 重复显示
repeating load of transportation machinery 运输机械重复作用荷载
repeating signal 复示信号(机)
repeating station 复示站
repeating survey 复测
repeating terminal 复示终端
rephotography 复照
replace 更换
replacement cost 更新成本,重置成本
replacement layer 基床底层(路堑)
replacement layer of compacted fill 换填垫层
replacement layer of tensile reinforcement 加筋垫层
replacement material 代用材料
replacement method by tamping lime-soil cushion 灰土换填夯实法
replacement of bearing seat 更换支座
replacement of the engineer 工程师的替换
replacement value 重置价值
repledge 转抵押
replenishment rate 补给率
reply 回复
reply（to a letter） 回函
report 报告

report compilation and assessment fees for water and soil conservation plan   水土保持方案报告编制与评估费
report form of balance sheet   报告式资产负债表
report on bid evaluation   评标报告
repose angle of scree   岩堆休止角
repose angle of talus   岩堆休止角
representative abroad   驻国外代表
representative construction site   代表性工点
representative section   代表性断面
representative trains   典型列车
representative value of actions   作用的代表值
representative value of gravity load   重力荷载代表值
representative value of load   荷载作用代表值
representative values of a load   荷载代表值
repristination   恢复原状
reproduction cost   再生产成本,重置成本
repudiate   拒绝接受
repudiate the contract   否认合同有效
repudiate/reject a claim   拒赔
repudiation of contract   放弃合同
repugnance   不一致
reputation   信誉
request   要求
request for bid (tender)   招标
request for change (RFC)   变更申请
request for information   澄清请求函
request for proposal   建议书征求函,招标通知
require   需要
required monitoring item   必测项目
required rate of return   预期收益率
requirement   需要,要求
requisite   必要的
requisite document   必备文件
requisition   征用
requisition for money (payment)   拨款要求,付款申请
requisitioning of land   征用土地
rerailing apparatus   复轨器
reschedule ticket   改签
rescind   撤销,废除
rescind a contract   解约
rescind the contract   解除合同,终止合同
rescission of a contract   解约
rescission of contract   废除合同,合同解除
rescue   营救
rescue command   救援指挥
rescue cost   施救费用
rescue desk   救援台
rescue passage   救援通道
rescue scene   救援现场
rescue train   救援列车
rescue train rehearsal track   救援列车演练线
research and development cost   研究开发费
research and test cost   研究试验费
resection   后方交会
reservation   保留,储备,限制条件
reserve   保留,储备,库存,预订,暂定金
reserve for bad debts   备抵坏账,坏账准备
reserve for depletion   耗减准备
reserve for depreciation   备抵折旧,折旧准备
reserve for repair   维修费准备,维修备用金
reserve fund   公积金
reserve funds   准备金
reserve lighting for fire risk   消防备用照明
reserve of building materials   建材储量
reserve personnel   后备人员
reserve stock   储备库存量
reserved   保留的
reserved line   预留线(路)
reserved rail joint gap   预留轨缝
reserved sample   留样
reserved track   预留线
reservoir   水库,蓄水池
reservoir (water) level   (水)库水位
reservoir bank collapse   水库坍岸
reservoir siltation   水库淤积
reservoir storage survey   库容测量
resettlement   移民工程,移民安置
resettlement scale   移民规模
resettlement subsidies for land expropriation   征用土地安置补助费
resettlement subsidy   易地安家补助费
residence permit   居住许可证
residency   常住,定居
residency system   包乘制
resident engineer   驻地工程师
resident project representative   驻地项目代表
resident representative   常驻代表
resident visa   居住签证
residential building   居住建筑,住宅建筑
residential quarters   住宅区
residential water meter   用户水表
residual assets   剩余资产
residual coefficient of mortar   砂浆剩余系数法
residual deformation   残余变形

residual deposit 残积
residual fatigue life of bridge 桥梁疲劳剩余寿命
residual income 剩余收益
residual layer 残留层
residual length of optical fiber 光纤余长
residual life 剩余使用寿命
residual oxygen 余氧
residual pressure 余压
residual risk 残留风险
residual soil 残积土
residual strength 残余强度
residual value 残值
residual vertical parallax 残余上下视差
residual voltage 残压
residual voltage peak value 残压峰值
residual/running pressure 动水压力
resignation and termination 辞职和终止
resilience index 回弹指数
resilient deformation 回弹变形
resilient pad 弹性垫板
resiliometer 回弹仪
resin 树脂
resin rockbolt 树脂锚杆
resinous luster 树脂光泽
resist 抵制
resistance 抗力
resistance class of concrete to physical sulphate attack 抗硫酸盐结晶破坏等级
resistance class to hydraulic pressure 抗渗等级
resistance coefficient 阻力系数
resistance detecting for outside line 外线电阻检测
resistance isoline 等阻线
resistance loss 电阻损失
resistance reducing agent 降阻剂
resistance strain gauge 电阻应变片,电阻应变仪
resistance strain gauge method 电阻应变片法
resistance strain sensor 电阻应变传感器
resistance strain type 电阻应变式
resistance to chemical erosion 耐化学侵蚀
resistance to environment stress cracking 耐环境应力开裂
resistance to heat 耐热性
resistance to impact 耐冲击性
resistance to ozone ageing 耐臭氧老化
resistance to static hydraulic pressure 耐静水压
resistance to thermal oxidation 耐热氧化
resistance to weathering 耐气候老化
resistance work 阻力功
resistivity 电阻率
resistivity method 电阻率法
resolution 分辨力,分辨率
resolution capacity 分辨力
resolutive clause 解除条款
resonance 共振
resonance factor 共振系数
resonance method 共振法
resonance response of sound barrier 声屏障共振响应
resonance velocity 共振速度
resonant column test 共振柱试验
resource allocation plan 资源配置方案
resource breakdown structure (RBS) 资源分解结构
resource dependent 资源依赖
resource loading curve 资源负荷曲线
resource planning 资源计划
resource quantity 资源量
resources 物力,资源,财力
resources conservation 节约资源
resources-based railway location 资源选线
respirator 呼吸器
respondent 被申请人,答辩人,被告
response 回复
response letter 回函
response spectrum 反应谱
response time 响应时间
responsibility 责任,职责
responsibility for care of the works 照管工程的职责
responsibility range 职责范围
responsible person 责任人
responsive bid 符合性投标,响应性投标
responsive to bidding documents 响应招标文件要求
rest pier 支墩
rest day 休息日
restitution 复原,恢复,赔偿,重建
restitution of advance payment 退还预付款
restitution of the guarantee 归还保函
restoration 复原,恢复,修复
restoration after flood damage 水害后复旧
restoration process 复位进程
restore 复原,恢复,修复
restoring force model 恢复力模型
restrain 约束

restrained deformation 约束变形
restraining order 禁止令,强制令
restraining rail of turnout 道岔护轨
restriction on eligibility 合格性限制
restriction(s) 约束条件,限定
restrictive clause 限制性条款
restrictive element 制约因素
restrictive endorsement 附条件背书
restrictive regulation 约束性规定
resume 复原,恢复,履历表
resumption 再开始
resumption of work 复工
resurgent 复原,恢复
resurgent valley 复活谷
resurrect 复原,恢复
retail dealer 零售商
retail price 零售价
retailer 零售商
retain 保持,保留,聘请,聘用
retained earnings/income/surplus 留存收益
retained profit 待分配利润,留成利润
retainer and success fee contract 顾问费加成功费合同
retainer fee 聘请费
retaining and protection of foundation pit 基坑支护
retaining structure 支挡结构,围护结构
retaining wall （弃土）挡土墙
retarded cement 缓凝水泥
retarder 减速器,缓凝剂
retarder in closed state 减速器制动状态
retarder in working state 减速器工作状态
retarder length 减速器长度
retarder location 制动位
retarder release time 减速器缓解时间
retarder released 减速器缓解状态
retarder within shunting track 调车线内减速器
retender(rebid) 再招标,重新招标
retention 保留
retention free amount 保留金起扣额
retention money 保留金,滞付金
retention money guarantee 保留金保函
retention option 保留权
retention percentage 保留金比例
retention period 保管期,保留期
retention pump-in test method 自留式压水法
retest 重新检验
retesting 重新试验

reticular structure 网状构造
retired staff 离退休职工
retirement 报废
retirement of fixed assets 固定资产报废
retiring a bill 赎单,赎票
retrieve 挽回
retroactive pay 补发的工资
retrofit 修整
retrograde detection 逆行检测
retroreflector 反光镜
return 返回,交还
return cable 回流电缆
return circuit (including running rail, return current rail, return conductor, earthing wire, return cable, other components conducting return currents) 回流回路,回流系统（包括走行轨、回流轨、回流线、接地线、回流电缆、导通回流组件）
return conductor 回流线,回流导体
return loss of conference room 会议室回损
return of materials 材料退回
return of the performance security 履约保函的返还
return on assets 资产收益
return on investment 投资收益率
return period of N years N年重现期
return rail 回流轨
return sludge ratio 污泥回流比
return ticket 往返票
return time 回程时间
return to 复原,恢复
return valve 回程阀
return visit 回访
return water 回水
returned sludge 回流污泥
returned value 回收价值
returning tail 拉线回头
returns of contractor's equipment 承包商设备报表
returns on the investment 投资回报
returns/statistical chart 统计表
reusable material 可再利用材料
reuse and recycling 回收利用
revaluation 重新估价,价值重估
revegetation 植被恢复
revegetation coefficient 植被恢复系数
revegetation percentage 植被恢复率
revenue 收入,收益,税收
revenue cost 收入成本
revenue expenditure 经常性开支,营业支出
revenue items 收入项目

revenue stamp 印花税票
reversal film 反转片
reversal points method 逆转点法
reverse circulation drilling rig
 反循环旋转钻机
reverse circulation pumpless drilling
 无泵反循环钻进
reverse composite irregularity of the track cross
 level and the alignment
 轨向水平逆向复合不平顺
reverse contact 反位接点
reverse curve 反向曲线
reverse departure 反发
reverse fault 逆断层
reverse filter 反滤层
reverse locking 反位锁闭
reverse osmosis process (RO) 反渗透法
reverse photogrammetry 逆反摄影测量
reverse pole-changing value 反向转极值
reverse receiving 反到
reversed return system 同程式系统
reversed S-shaped structure 反S形构造
reverse-hump direction 反驼峰方向
reversible serviceability limit state
 可逆正常使用极限状态
reversible steel bar binding pedestal
 可翻转钢筋绑扎台座
reversing drum mixer 鼓筒式混凝土搅拌机
reversing telescope 倒镜
revest 再归属
revetment 护岸,护坡
revetment and beach protection 护岸护滩
review 审查,复审,审议,核查
review fee for construction drawings
 施工图审查费
review period 评审期,审查期,审核期
review process 审议过程
revise 修改;修订;更正
revise a contract 修改合同
revise a schedule 调整进度表
revised programme 修正的计划,修订计划
revision 修改;修订;更正
revision of price 调价
revive 复原,恢复
revocable 可撤销的
revocable L/C 可撤销的信用证
revocable letter of credit 可撤销的信用证
revocation of licence 撤销执照
revocation of movement authority
 行车许可的取消

revoke 撤销
revolving fund 循环资金
revolving letter of credit 循环信用证
revolving materials 周转材料
reward 酬金,奖金
rework cost 返工成本
reworking 返工
re-bar fixer 钢筋安装工
re-bar worker 钢筋工
re-check 复核
re-evaluate 重新评估
re-export 再出口
re-icing point 加冰所
re-import 再进口
re-inspection 复检
rhyolite 流纹岩
rich concrete 富混凝土
ride comfort index of passenger
 旅客乘坐舒适度指标
ridge 海岭
riffle sampler 分样器
rift valley 裂谷
rigging 索具
right angle crank 直角拐肘
right bridge 正交桥
right hand turnout 右开道岔
right of access after taking over
 接收后的现场出入权
right of access to the site 现场进入权
right of action 诉讼权
right of claim 请求权,索赔权
right of distraint 扣押权
right of entry 进入权
right of facility 设施使用权
right of intervene 介入权
right of legal representation 法定代表权
right of ownership 所有权,专有技术权
right of possession 占有权
right of preemption 优先购买权
right of priority 优先权
right of property 财产权
right of reimbursement 追偿权
right of rescission 解约权
right of revocation 撤销权
right of way 道路通行权,过境权
right side opposite to station building
 站房对侧右端
right to access 出入权
right to claim 索赔权
right to leased property 财产租赁权

right to the use of a site 现场使用权
rightful 合法的
rights to vary 变更权
right-handed machine 正装
rigid analysis scheme 刚性方案
rigid conductor 硬导体,刚性导体
rigid connection 刚接
rigid fastening 刚性扣件
rigid foundation 刚性基础
rigid frame 刚构
rigid frame bridge 刚构桥,刚架桥
rigid pile 刚性桩
rigid tie bar 刚性系杆
rigid transverse wall 刚性横墙
rigid zone 刚域
rigidity 刚度,横向刚度
rigidity of section 截面刚度
rigidity of track panel 轨道框架刚度
rigidity of transverse wall 横墙刚度
rigidity-plasticity analysis
 刚性—塑性分析
rigidly supported continuous girder
 刚性支座连续梁
rigid-elastic analysis scheme 刚弹性方案
rigid-frame formwork 硬架支模
rigid-framed arch 刚架拱
rigid-framed structure 刚架结构
rigid-jointed plate method 刚接板梁法
rigorous adjustment 严密平差
ring and ball method 环球法
ring beam 圈梁
ring cut method 环形开挖预留核心土法
ring departure 环发
ring earthing electrode 环形接地体
ring network 环形网
ring receiving 环到
ring road 环形道路
rinse 冲洗
riot 暴乱
ripper 松土机
ripple 纹沟
ripple effect 波纹效应
ripple structure 波痕构造
riprap 抛石
riprapping protection 抛石防护
rise 矢高
rise in price 价格上涨
rise of arch 拱高
rise to span ratio 矢跨比
riser 立管

risk 风险,隐患,危险
risk acceptance criteria 风险接受准则
risk allocation 风险分担
risk allowance 风险准备金
risk analysis 风险分析
risk apportionment 风险分摊
risk assessment 风险评估
risk avoidance 风险规避
risk bearer 风险承担者
risk category 风险类别
risk contract 风险合同
risk control 风险控制
risk database 风险数据库
risk deflection 风险转移
risk estimation 风险估计
risk evaluation 风险评价
risk event 风险事件
risk factor 风险因素
risk grade 风险等级
risk identification 风险识别
risk index system 风险指标体系
risk management 风险管理
risk mitigation 风险消减
risk monitoring 风险监测
risk monitoring and control 风险监控
risk note 承保证明,暂保单
risk of breakage 破损风险
risk of clash and breakage 碰损破碎险
risk of contamination 污染险
risk of contingent import duty 进口关税险
risk of damage 损坏风险
risk of hook damage 钩损险
risk of leakage 渗漏险
risk of shortage 短量险
risk premium 风险保费
risk probability analysis 风险概率分析
risk ranking 风险分级
risk rating 风险等级划分,风险评级
risk reduction 风险分散,风险减少
risk register 风险记录单
risk registration 风险登记
risk response plan 风险应对计划
risk retention 风险自留
risk sharing 风险分担
risk speculation 风险利用
risk transfer 风险转移
risk treatment 风险处理
rival 竞争者
river bed 河床
river bed paving 河床铺砌

river bed width　河床宽度
river bottom　河底
river channel　河槽
river course　河道
river course survey　河道调查
river training structure　调治构造物
river valley　河谷
river water　河水
riverbank　河岸
riverbed gradient　河床比降
riverbed intake structure　河床式取水构筑物
riverbed scouring　河床冲刷
riverside　河岸
riverside intake structure
　岸边式取水构筑物
riverside subgrade　滨河路基
river-crossing bridge　跨河桥
river-crossing leveling　跨河水准测量
rivet　铆钉
riveted steel bridge　铆接钢桥
riveted steel girder　铆接钢梁
riveted steel structure　铆接钢结构
riveting　铆接
rizzonite　玻基辉橄岩
road　道路
road accident　交通事故
road building　筑路
road edge　道路边缘
road engineering　公路工程
road engineering survey　道路工程测量
road grader　平路机
road maintenance costs　养路费
road maintenance expense and vehicle and vessel use tax　养路费及车船使用税
road mixing　路拌
road pavement　道路铺面，道路路面
road roller　碾压机
road settlement　路面沉陷
road way　行车道
robotic total station　测量机器人，智能全站仪
roche moutonnee　羊背石
rock　岩石
rock abrasiveness　岩石研磨性
rock and soil mass　岩土体
rock asphalt　岩沥青，天然沥青
rock block　岩块
rock bolt　锚杆
rock burst　岩爆
rock classification　岩石分级，岩石分类
rock column method　岩石柱法
rock core　岩芯
rock core sample　岩芯样品
rock cutter　凿石机
rock cutting　石质路堑
rock density　岩石密度
rock desert　石漠
rock drill　凿岩机
rock drillability　岩石的可钻性
rock drilling jumbo　凿岩台车
rock engineering　岩石工程
rock landslide　岩层滑坡
rock loader　装岩机
rock mass　岩体
rock mass deformation　岩体变形
rock mass deformation test　岩体变形试验
rock mass direct shear strength test
　岩体直剪试验
rock mass engineering classification
　工程岩体分级
rock mass fracture load　岩体破坏荷载
rock mass fracture pressure　岩体破裂压力
rock mass integrity coefficient
　岩体完整性系数
rock mass pore pressure　岩体孔隙压力
rock mass quality designation
　岩体质量指标
rock mass reopening pressure
　岩体重张压力
rock mass strength test　岩体强度试验
rock mass stress　岩体应力
rock mechanical property　岩石力学性质
rock mechanics　岩石力学
rock quality designation（RQD）
　岩石质量指标
rock sample　岩样
rock shear strength（direct shear）test
　岩石抗剪（断）强度试验
rock slice identification　岩石薄片鉴定
rock slide　坍方
rock sonic measurement　岩石声波测试
rock stratum　岩层
rock subgrade　石质路基
rock tensile strength　岩石抗拉强度
rock tensile strength test　岩石抗拉强度试验
rock test　岩石试验
rocker bearing　摇轴支座
rockfall　落石，岩崩
rockfill　填石
Rockwell hardness tester for steel
　钢材洛氏硬度计

rock-fill dam 堆石坝
rock-forming mineral 造岩矿物
rock-socketed bored cast-in-situ pile
嵌岩灌注桩
rock-socketed pile 嵌岩桩
rock-soil interface 岩土界面
rock-soil mineral 岩土矿物
rock-soil sample 岩土试样
rod 标尺
role 职责
roll away 溜逸
rollability measurement 测阻
rolled earth dam 碾压式土坝
rolled earthfill dam 碾压式土坝
rolled steel beam 轧制型钢梁
roller 压路机
roller bearing 滚轴支座
rolling compaction machinery 碾压机械
rolling compaction method 碾压法
rolling compaction test 碾压试验
rolling corrector 纠偏转机构
rolling route 溜放进路
rolling section of hump 溜放部分
rolling speed 溜放速度
rolling stock auxiliary repair 车辆辅修
rolling stock depot repair 车辆段维修
rolling stock depot 车辆段
rolling stock facility 车辆设备
rolling stock operational maintenance
车辆运用维修
rolling stock purchase additional charge
车辆购置附加费
rolling thin film oven test
旋转薄膜烘箱试验
rolling track 溜放线
roll-in composite geo-membrane
辊压复合土工膜
roof 顶板,屋盖,屋顶
roof beam 屋面梁
roof board 屋面板
roof drain 雨水斗
roof fall 冒顶
roof support 顶护盾
roof truss 屋架
roof ventilator 屋顶通风机
roof-bracing system 屋盖支撑系统
room air conditioner 房间空气调节器
room index 室形指数
root development 根系发育状况
root mean square voltage 平均有效电压

root pile 树根桩
root span 根开
rope hoist 绞车
rose diagram of wind direction and wind speed
风向风频玫瑰图
rotameter 转子流量计
rotary air supply outlet 旋转送风口
rotary dehumidifier 转轮除湿机
rotary distributor 旋转布水器
rotary drill 旋转式钻机
rotary drilling 回转钻进
rotary drilling machine 转盘式钻机
rotary drilling rig 旋挖钻机
rotary drum concrete mixer
转筒式混凝土搅拌机
rotary evaporimetry 旋转蒸发仪
rotary heat exchanger 转轮式换热器
rotary sampler 回转取土器
rotating biological contactor(RBC) 生物转盘
rotating system 轮乘制
rotation angle at girder end 梁端转角
rotation method 转体法
rotation times 转动次数
rough draft 草案,草稿,草图
rough estimation 估算价
rough making 粗加工
rough orientation 粗略定向
rough plan 初步计划
rough sketch 草稿,草图
roughness 粗糙度
roughness coefficient 糙率
round top mountain 圆顶山
round trip ticket 往返票
rounded 浑圆状
round-ended pier 圆端形桥墩
round-trip survey 往返测
route 航线,进路,路线,线路
route benchmark 线路水准基点
route cancellation 取消进路
route centerline 线路中线
route control for cut rolling
驼峰钩车溜放进路控制
route design 选线设计
route horizontal control network(CPⅡ)
线路平面控制网(CPⅡ)
route indicator 进路表示器
route indicator circuit 进路表示器电路
route locating survey 定线测量
route locking 进路锁闭
route locking indication 进路锁闭表示

route manual release 进路人工解锁
route map 路线图
route mapping 纸上定线
route plan 线路平面图
route planimetric control survey
　线路平面控制测量
route presetting 预排进路
route reflector(RR) 路由反射器
route release 进路解锁
route release by checking three sections
　三点检查
route release test 进路解锁测试
route scheme available 线路开放
route selecting circuit 进路电路,选路电路
route selection 选路,选线
route setting 排列进路
route sign 径路标,线路标志
route signal 进路信号机
route signal for departure 发车进路信号机
route signal for receiving 接车进路信号机
route signaling 选路制信号
route storage 进路存储器
route suitability data 进路适合性数据
route survey 线路测量,路线测量
route table 进路表
route type all-relay interlocking
　进路继电式电气集中联锁
route vertical control survey
　线路高程控制测量
route with overlapped section in the opposite direction 对向重叠进路
route with overlapped section in the same direction 顺向重叠进路
router 路由器
routing 路由
routine inspection 定期检查,例行检查
routine maintenance 日常维修
routine procedure 例行程序
routine test 常规试验
roving receiver 流动接收机
row number of freight section 货位排数
rowlock wall 空斗墙
royalties 土地使用费(税)
royalty 产权使用费,提成费,某些权利(如矿权、地权、特许权等)使用费,转让费
rubber 橡胶
rubber balloon method 气囊法
rubber balloon volume meter
　气囊式容积测定仪
rubber bearing 橡胶支座
rubber pad 橡胶垫板
rubber plug 胶塞
rubber tired crane 轮胎式起重机
rubber vibration absorber 橡胶隔振器
rubber water stop tie 橡胶止水带
rubber waterproof sheet 橡胶防水卷材
rubbery soil 橡皮土
rubber-wheel girder moving machine
　轮胎式搬梁机
rubbish 废弃物
rubbish dump 垃圾堆场
rubble 块石,片石,毛石
rubble concrete 片石混凝土
rubble masonry 毛石砌体
ruin 毁坏,毁灭
rule 裁定,规则,条例
rules and regulations 规章制度
rules of conciliation and arbitration
　调解及仲裁规则
rules of track maintenance 线路维修规则
ruling 裁定,裁决
ruling gradient 限制坡度
ruling language 主导语言
rummage 海关检查
rum-discriminatory treatment 不歧视待遇
run 经营
run away 飞车
run error of micrometer 测微器行差
run idle 窝工
run off 顺坡
running cost 运营成本
running days 连续日
running direction 运行方向
running distance 走行距离
running expenses 经常性开支,经营费用
running kilometers between repair intervals
　检修公里
running price 时价,现行价格
running rail of portal crane
　门式起重机走行轨
running repair 经常性修理
running safety 行车安全
running signal 行车信号
running speed 行车速度,运营速度
running surface of rail 钢轨工作边
running test track 动态试验线
running time 走行时分,运行时分
running times of trains per day and night
　每昼夜行车次数
running track 走行线

running track for EMU　动车组走行线
running track for train-set placing-in and taking-out　车底取送走行线
runoff　径流(量)
runoff area　径流区
runoff coefficient　径流系数
runoff gathering　径流汇集
runoff plot　径流小区
run-through power line　电力贯通线路
run-through power line for automatic block system（ABS line）　自动闭塞电力线路
run-through power line of comprehensive loads　综合负荷贯通线
run-through power line of load level I　一级负荷贯通线
rush repair of railway damage caused by flood　水害抢修
rust inhibitor　阻锈剂
rust removal　除锈
rust-resisting material　防锈材料
rutile　金红石
rustiness　锈蚀
r.m.s current of trains　列车电流有效值
r.m.s voltage　平均有效电压

S

sabotage 破坏行为,阴谋破坏
safe box 保险箱
safe brake distance 安全制动距离
safe coupling 安全连挂
safe distance between karst cave and subgrade 溶洞距路基安全距离
safe handling 安全装卸
safe side-oriented deviation 导向安全侧偏差
safe working conditions 安全工作条件
safe yield 允许开采量
safeguard 保卫
safeguard clause 保护条款,保障条款
safety 安全,安全性
safety accessory 安全附件
safety and prevention first 安全第一,防范为主
safety brake 安全制动器,保险闸
safety class of building structures 建筑结构安全等级
safety clearance 安全净距
safety contact 安全接点
safety controls 安全装置
safety critical 安全苛求
safety distance 安全距离
safety earth wire 安全地线
safety earthing 安全接地
safety factor 安全系数
safety factor method 安全系数法
safety factor of liquefaction 液化安全系数
safety fence 安全护栏
safety helmet 安全帽
safety hook 安全钩
safety inspection 安全检查
safety installation 安全装置
safety island 安全岛
safety level 安全等级
safety marking of platform 站台安全标线
safety measure 安全措施
safety monitoring and controlling system 安全监控系统
safety monitoring 安全监控
safety precaution 安全预防措施
safety procedure 安全程序
safety production 安全生产
safety production costs 安全生产费
safety program 安全计划
safety promotion 安全宣贯
safety protection 安全防护
safety protection device 安全防护装置
safety protective distance 安全防护距离
safety railing 防护栏杆
safety regulation 安全法规
safety report 安全报告
safety representative 安全代表
safety siding 安全线
safety standard 安全标准
safety technology 安全技术
safety training 安全培训
safety valve 安全阀
safety evacuation function 安全疏散功能
sag 凹陷,弛度,弧垂
sail 航行
salary 薪金,月薪
sale 出售
sale by sample 看样出售,凭样品成交
sale by specification 凭规格、等级或标准买卖
sale on account 赊销
sales account 销售账
sales agency 代销行
sales commission 销售佣金
sales confirmation 销售确认书
sales contract 买卖合同,销售合同
sales invoice 销售发票
sales manager 销售经理,营业主任
sales margin 销售毛利
sales rebate 销售回扣

sales returns 退货
sales tax 销售税
sales turnover 销售额
saline permafrost 盐渍化冻土
saline rock 盐渍岩
saline soil 盐渍土
saline soil region 盐渍土地区
saline soil subgrade 盐渍土路基
saline-alkali land 盐碱地
salinity 盐渍度
salinization 盐渍化
salinization of soil 土壤盐渍化
salivary flow ice 涎流冰
salt crystallization erosion 盐类结晶性侵蚀
salt lake 盐湖
salt pan 盐田
salt physical attacking environment 盐类结晶破坏环境
salt sea 盐海
saltation transport 跳运
saltmarsh 盐沼
salvage （海上）救助,残料,救援
salvage charges 救助费用
salvage company 海难救援公司,打捞公司
salvage operation 救助作业
same direction connection 顺向连接
sample 标本,货样,样品
sample decomposition 试样分解
sample goods 货样
sample inspection 抽样检查
sample presentation 送样
sample room 样品室
sample splitter 分样器
sample test 抽样试验
sample works 样板工程
samples of rock minerals 岩矿样品
sampling 抽样,取样
sampling frequency 采样频率,取样频率
sampling hole 测孔
sampling inspection 抽样检查,抽样检验
sampling interval 采样间隔
sampling plan 抽样方案
sampling rate 采样率
SAN switch SAN 交换机
sanction 处罚,制裁
sand 砂
sand and aggregate ratio 砂与骨料比
sand and gravel 砂砾石

sand bar facies 砂坝相
sand barrier 沙障
sand clay 砂质黏土
sand compaction pile 挤密砂桩
sand cone method 灌砂法
sand containing bottle 容砂瓶
sand control system 防沙体系
sand core glass crucible 砂芯玻璃坩埚
sand digging cave 掏砂洞
sand dune 沙丘
sand flow 风沙流
sand grain 砂粒
sand hazard 沙害
sand loader 装砂机
sand material excavated from river course 河道取砂(砾)料
sand spit phase 砂嘴相
sand stabilization and fire prevention belt 固沙防火带
sand surfaced asphalt sheet 砂面防水卷材
sand wedge 砂楔
sand wick 袋装砂井
sand (gravel) pile 砂(碎石)桩
sand (sludge) hopper 砂(污泥)斗
sandbank 砂坝
sandstone 砂岩
sandstorm 沙暴
sandy clay 亚黏土
sandy gravel 砂砾石
sandy land 沙地
sandy loess 砂质黄土
sandy soil 砂(类)土
sandy soil liquefaction 砂土液化,沙土液化
sand-gravel compaction pile 挤密砂石桩
sanitary facilities 卫生设备
sanitary sewer 排污管,污水管
sanitary ware 卫生器具
sanitary ware equivalent 卫生器具当量
satellite 卫星
satellite clock 卫星钟
satellite cut-off elevating angle 卫星截止高度角
satellite image 卫星图像
satellite link 卫星链路
satellite positioning 卫星定位
satellite positioning control network 卫星定位测量控制网
satellite positioning survey 卫星定位测量
satellite receiver 卫星接收机
satellite remote sensing photo 卫星遥感照片

satellite static positioning survey
　卫星定位静态测量
satellite terminal device　卫星终端设备
satisfy　偿还
satisfy liabilities　清偿债务
saturated　饱和
saturated absorption rate　饱和吸水率
saturated frozen soil　饱和冻土
saturated soil　饱和土
saturated steam　饱和蒸汽
saturated unit weight　饱和重度
saturated water content　饱和含水率
saturation curve　饱和曲线
saturation degree　饱和度
saturation density　饱和密度
saturation vapor pressure　饱和蒸汽压力
saturation zone　饱水带
saturator　饱和器
saving account　储蓄账户
saving clause　但书,保留条款
saving deposit　储蓄存款
sawtooth hole　锯齿孔
saw-tooth joint failure　齿缝破坏
scaffold board　脚手(架)板
scaffolder　脚手架工
scaffolding worker　脚手架工
scaffold　脚手架
scale　尺度,等级,级别,比例尺,规模
scale effect　尺度效应
scale expansion　比例扩张
scale magnifying glass　刻度放大镜
scale mass　剥落量
scale microscope　刻度显微镜
scaled water tank　流量箱
scanner　扫描仪
scanning　扫描
scanning resolution　扫描分辨率
scan-digitizing　扫描数字化
scarp　陡坎
scattered accumulation　散落堆积
scene reorganization　场景重组
schedule　计划表,进度,日程表,一览表
schedule analysis　进度分析
schedule commitment　进度承诺
schedule compression　进度压缩
schedule control　进度控制
schedule impact analysis　进度影响分析
schedule management　进度管理
schedule of activities　作业进度表
schedule of construction　工程进度表
schedule of earthwork　土方工程进度表
schedule of erection works
　安装工程进度表
schedule of freight rates　运费一览表
schedule of guarantees　保证表
schedule of inspection and testing
　检测计划表
schedule of payment(s)
　支付表单,付款计划表
schedule of prices　价格表
schedule of rates　单价表
schedule of supplementary information
　补充资料表
schedule of values　价值一览表
schedule of works　工程进度表
schedule performance index (SPI)
　进度绩效指数
schedule slippage　拖期
schedule variance (SV)　进度偏差
scheduled completion date　计划完工日期
scheduled cost of work　工作计划成本
scheduled date　计划日期
scheduled output　计划产量
scheduled payment　定期付款
scheduled plan　进度计划
scheduled production　计划产量
scheduled purchasing　计划采购
scheduler　计划工程师
schedules　表单
scheduling of activities　作业进度安排
schema　模式
schematic design phase　方案设计阶段
schematic diagram　简图
schematic drawing　示意图
schematic plan　平面示意图
scheme　方案,计划
scheme design　方案设计
scheme drawing　方案图,计划图
scheme for emergency treatment
　应急处理方案
schistose　片状
schistose index　片状指数
schistosity　片理
scissors crossover　交叉渡线
scoop shovel　铲斗挖土机
scooptram　铲运机
scope　范围
scope change　范围变更
scope definition　范围定义
scope for negotiation　谈判范围

scope of agreement 协议范围
scope of cover 保险范围,责任范围
scope of execution 执行范围
scope of liability 责任范围
scope of services 服务范围
scope of supply 供应范围
scope of supply by contractor
　承包商供货范围
scope of supply by owner (employer)
　业主供货范围
scope of surveying and mapping 测绘范围
scope of work 工作范围
scope of work claim 工程范围变更索赔
scope statement 范围说明
scope verification 范围核实
scoring model method 评分比较法
Scott connection 斯柯特结线
scouring and depositing around pier
　墩周冲淤
scouring factor 冲刷系数
scrap rail 废轨
scraper 铲运机
scraper conveyer 刮板输送机
scratch 擦伤
scree 岩堆
scree bed 岩堆床
screen size 筛孔尺寸
screen system 筛选制
screen washing 洗筛
screening aggregate 筛分骨料
screening machine 筛分机
screening of projects 项目筛选
screw 螺钉
screw compressor 螺杆式(空气)压缩机
screw plug gauge 螺纹塞规
screw plug go-gauge 螺纹塞通规
screw spike 螺纹道钉
screw-type wind speed and direction sensor
　螺旋式风速风向传感器
scribing coating 刻图膜
scrip 凭证
scrip issue 派发红股
script 脚本
scrutinize 仔细检查
scrutiny 仔细检查
SDH based multi-service transport platform
　基于 SDH 的多业务传送平台
sea basin 海盆
sea cave 海蚀穴
sea damage 海损

sea damage terms 海损条款
sea facies 海相
sea freight 海运费
sea insurance 海运保险
sea sand 海砂
sea terrace 海积阶地
sea water 海水
seal 图章,印记,印章
seal cover 密封盖
seal ring 密封圈
sealed bid/tender 密封投标
sealed bid instruction 密封的投标指令
sealed contract 盖章合同,正式合同
sealing 加封
sealing method 密封法
sealing water proof 封闭防水
sealing-off 脱焊
seam 接缝
seam welder 滚焊机,线焊机
seamless pipe 无缝管
seamount 海山
seapeak 海峰
search light 探照灯
seashore 海滨
seasonal construction 季节(性)施工
seasonal frozen soil 季节冻土
seasonal running water 季节性流水
seasonally frozen layer 季节冻结层
seasonally frozen soil 季节性冻土
seasonally thawed layer 季节融化层
seaworthiness 适航性
secant stiffness 割线模量
second approach section 第二接近区段
second chronograph 秒表
second class discharge standard
　污水二级排放标准
second class environmental impact assessment
　二级评价
second class water conservation district
　二级水源保护区
second departure section 第二离去区段
second hand rail 旧轨料
second hand track material 再用轨料
second line reserved 预留二线
second order effect due to displacement
　挠曲二阶效应
second order elastic analysis 二阶弹性分析
second order nonlinear analysis
　二阶非线性分析
secondary beam 次梁

secondary circulating system 第二循环管
secondary consolidation 次固结
secondary consolidation settlement 次固沉降,次固结沉降
secondary deformation modulus 二次变形模量
secondary disaster of earthquake 地震次生灾害
secondary evidence 辅助证据
secondary hard rock 次坚石
secondary heavy track 次重型轨道
secondary instrument 二次仪表
secondary lining 二次衬砌
secondary meaning of words 词句引申义
secondary mineral 次生矿物
secondary parameter 二次参数
secondary pollution 二次污染
secondary presentation methods 辅助表达方式
secondary return air 二次回风
secondary salinization 次生盐渍化
secondary settling tank 二次沉淀池
secondary shotcreting 复喷
secondary side 低压侧,二次侧,次边侧
secondary side current 二次电流
secondary side equipment, equipment at secondary side 二次设备
secondary side load 二次负荷
secondary side system 二次系统
secondary sludge 二沉污泥
secondary strengthening treatment 二级强化处理
secondary stress 次(生)应力
secondary support 二次支护
secondary treatment 二级处理
secondary trunk road 次干道
secondary wiring 二次接线
seconds 次品,二流商品
second-hand equipment 二手设备
second-hand rail 再用轨
relay rail 再用轨
second-level inspection 二级检修
secrecy 保密
secret 保密的,机密
section 部分,部门,区间,截面,剖面
section adapter 区间适配设备
section automatic dialing test 区间自动拨叫试验
section blocked 区间闭塞
section carrying capacity 区间通过能力
section cleared 区间空闲
section closed up 区间封锁
section communication 区间通信
section commissioning certificate 区段试运行证书
section continuously welded rail track 区间无缝线路
section crossover 区间渡线
section dispatching 区段调度
section foreman 工段长
section form 断面形式
section insulator 分段绝缘器
section lead-in cable 区间引入线缆
section line 剖面线
section locking 区段锁闭
section manager 部门经理
section modulus of conversion section 换算截面模量
section occupation indication 区段占用表示
section occupied 区间占用
section of acceleration and deceleration 减加速地段
section of insufficient grade 非紧坡地段
section of pusher gradient 加力牵引区段
section of sufficient grade 紧坡地段
section of works 单位工程
section sign 管界标
section signal 区间信号
section size 断面尺寸
section spacing 断面间距
section type distance protection 阶段式距离保护
section with common conditions 一般地段
section with difficult conditions 困难地段
sectional area 截面(面)积
sectional calibration method 分部标定法
sectional completion 阶段性完工
sectional drawing 剖面图
sectional elevation 立剖面
sectional route release 进路分段解锁
sectional view 断(截)面图
sectional water pump-in test 分段压水试验
sectionalizing of single busbar 单母线分段
sector 部门
secure 获得
Secure Sokets Layer (SSL) 安全套接层
secured liabilities 担保负债
secured loan 抵押贷款,有担保贷款

security　安全,债券,证券,治安
security audit　安全审计
security guard　保安人员
security holder　证券持有人
security inspection facility of luggage and parcel　行包安全检查设施
security interest　担保权益,抵押权益
security market　证券市场
security measure　安全措施
security of loan　贷款担保
security of the site　现场保安
security system　保安系统
sediment　沉渣
sediment runoff　输沙量
sedimentary rock　沉积岩
sedimentation　沉淀,调节沉淀隔油
sedimentation system　沉淀系统
sedimentation tank　沉淀池
seed capital　原始资本
seed moisture content　种子含水率
seeded slope　植草边坡
seed-nutriment-soil sack　植生袋
seepage　放渗,渗流
seepage deformation　渗透变形
seepage failure　渗透破坏
seepage force　渗流力
seepage hydraulic gradient　渗流水力坡降
seepage line　浸润线
seepage paths　渗径
seepage pond　渗水池
seepage velocity　渗透流速
seepage volume　渗水量
seepage well　渗井
seepage-proof　防渗
segment　管片
segment mould　管片模具
segment of flight strip　航线段
segmental assembling method　节段拼装法
segmented advance grouting　分段前进式注浆
segmented retrograde grouting　分段后退式注浆
segregated ice　分凝冰
segregation　离析
segregation coefficient　隔离系数
segregation rate　离析率
segregation resistance　抗离析性
seismic acceleration　地震加速度
seismic accelerator　地震加速度计
seismic action　地震活动
seismic action effect　地震作用效应

seismic adjustment coefficient of subgrade bearing capacity　地基承载力抗震调整系数
seismic analysis method　抗震计算方法
seismic appraisal　抗震鉴定
seismic basic intensity　地震基本烈度
seismic belt　地震带
seismic coefficient　地震系数
seismic conceptual design of building　建筑抗震概念设计
seismic design　抗震设计
seismic design of non-structural element　非结构构件抗震设计
seismic earth pressure calculation method　地震动土压力法
seismic emergency handling　地震紧急处置
seismic exploration instrument　地震勘探仪
seismic force　地震力
seismic fortification area　抗震设防区
seismic fortification regionalization　抗震设防区划
seismic fortification requirements　抗震设防要求
seismic fortification standard　抗震设防标准
seismic grade　抗震等级
seismic ground motion parameter　地震动参数
seismic ground motion parameter zoning map　地震动参数区划图
seismic hazard　震害
seismic hazard analysis　地震危害分析
seismic influence coefficient　地震影响系数
seismic intensity　地震烈度
seismic isolation technique　隔震技术
seismic joint　防震缝,抗震缝
seismic load　地震荷载
seismic measures　抗震措施
seismic monitoring　地震监测
seismic nose bar　抗震销棒
seismic peak ground acceleration　地震动峰值加速度
seismic pit　地震坑
seismic precautionary intensity　抗震设防烈度
seismic prospecting　地震勘探
seismic resistance adjustment coefficient of components bearing capacity　构件承载力抗震调整系数
seismic resistance strength of materials　材料抗震强度

seismic safety assessment of construction site 工程场地地震安全性评价
seismic safety evaluation 地震安全性评估
seismic structural integrity 抗震结构整体性
seismic structural measures 抗震构造措施
seismic structural system 抗震结构体系
seismic structural wall 抗震墙
seismic support and hanger 抗震支吊架
seismic test 抗震试验
seismic wave 地震波
seismic wave reflection method 地震波反射法
seldomly occured earthquake 罕遇地震
selected bidder (tenderer) 入选的投标人
selected bidding (also known as "limited competitive bidding") 邀请招标（又称"有限竞争性招标"）
selected bidding (tendering) 选择性招标
selected subcontractor 选定的分包商
selection based on eligibility 基于资格的选择
selection criteria 选择标准
selective bidding (tendering) 选择性招标
selective level meter 选频电平表
selective tendering 邀请招标，选择性招标
self calibration method 自检校法
self cooling 自冷
self cooling/air cooling 自冷/风冷
self diagnosis 自诊断
self recovery 自恢复
self test 自检
self-adhesive waterproofing membrane 自黏防水卷材
self-advancing rockbolt 自进式锚杆
self-boring pressure meter 自钻式旁压仪
self-closing 自闭性
self-compacting concrete 自密实混凝土
self-correcting 自校
self-diagnosis method 自诊断法
self-drilling rockbolt 自钻式锚杆
self-finance 自筹资金
self-healing ring circuit 自愈环电路
self-holding 自保持
self-impedance 自阻抗
self-insurance 自我保险
self-leveling mortar 自流平砂浆
self-potential method 自然电位法
self-priming 自灌充水
self-propelled blader 自动平路机
self-propelled power generating car 发电走行两用车
self-support 自稳
self-support capability of surrounding rock 围岩自稳性
self-support capacity of surrounding rock 围岩自承能力
self-support time of surrounding rock 围岩自稳时间
self-weight stress 自重应力
sell 出售
seller's market 卖方市场
seller's/supplier's credit 卖方信贷
selling agent 销售代理商
selling agreement 销售协定
selling cost 销售费用
selling price 售价，销售价
selvedge 留边
semaphore contact 臂板接触器
semaphore signal 臂板信号机
semicircular terminal 半环形枢纽
semi-accessible trench 半通行地沟
semi-active control 半主动控制
semi-arid region 半干旱(地)区
semi-automatic block 半自动闭塞
semi-automatic operation by route 进路操纵作业
semi-compensated overhead contact line system 半补偿接触网
semi-dome camera 半球形摄像机
semi-enclosed sound barrier/semi-enclosed noise barrier 半封闭声屏障
semi-finished product 半成品
semi-fixed dune 半固定沙丘
semi-infinite elastic body 半无限弹性体
semi-major axis of ellipsoid 椭球长半轴
semi-metallic luster 半金属光泽
semi-minor axis of ellipsoid 椭球短半轴
semi-open office 半开放式办公室
semi-skilled labour 半熟练工
semi-trailer 半挂车
sender 发货人
sending end 供电侧
senior creditor 优先债权人
senior engineer 高级工程师
senior partner 主要合伙人
sense of claims 索赔意识
sense of contract 合同意识
sense of risks 风险意识
sensible heat exchange efficiency 显热交换效率
sensible heat 显热

sensitive point 敏感点
sensitivity 感量,灵敏度
sensitivity analysis 敏感性分析
sensitivity coefficient 灵敏系数
sensitivity of frost heaving 冻胀敏感性
sensor 传感器
sensory testing method 感官法
sentence 判决
sentinel 记号
separant 隔离剂
separate calculation of water and soil pressure
　　水土分算
separate contract(s)
　　分项发包合同,独立合同
separate contractor 独立承包商
separate feeding for up and down tracks
　　上下行分开供电
separate legal entity 独立法人
separate system 分流制
separated joint venture 松散形联营体
separated steel column 分离式钢柱
separation block 间隔铁
separation distance 间距
separation layer 隔离层
separation of track circuit 轨道电路分割
separation pay 离职补偿金,遣散费
separator 分选机
sepiolite 海泡石
septic tank 化粪池
sequencing batch reactor (SBR)
　　序批式活性污泥法
sequential adjustment 序贯平差
sequential construction approach
　　连续生产方式
sequential starting of switches 道岔顺序启动
sequential transition of switches
　　道岔顺序转换
serial number 编号,序列号
serial number of track slab 轨道板编号
serial type structure 连环式构造
sericite 绢云母
series capacitor compensation
　　串联电容器补偿
series track circuit 串联式轨道电路
series water supply 串联供水
serious breach of contract 严重违约
serious defect 严重缺陷
serious misconduct/malfeasance
　　严重渎职,严重过失
serious snow damage 严重雪害

serious weathering 严重风化
serpentine 蛇纹石
serpentinite 蛇纹岩
serrate ridge 刃脊
server 服务器
service 保养,公共设施
service agreement 服务协议书
service braking 常用制动
service braking mode curve
　　常用制动模式曲线
service charge 服务费
service contract 服务合同
service control point (SCP) 业务控制点
service gallery 辅助坑道
service life 耐用年限,寿命,使用期限,使用寿命
service life of structure 结构使用年限
service management access point (SMAP)
　　业务管理接入点
service management point (SMP)
　　业务管理点
service node 业务节点
service node interface (SNI) 业务节点接口
service passport 公务护照
service pipe 入户管
service road 便道,辅助道路
service switching point (SSP) 业务交换点
service telephone test 公务电话试验
service wire 接户线
serviceability limit state
　　正常使用极限状态
serviceability safety of building
　　房屋建筑使用安全
servicing capacity 整备能力
servicing position 整备台位
servicing temporary rest track 整备待班线
serving GPRS support node (SGSN)
　　服务 GPRS 支持节点
session initiation protocol truck (SIP Truck)
　　会话启动协议交换
set aside 驳回,撤销
set of spare parts 成套备件
set retarding-type 缓凝型
setting 整定
setting horizontal point of portal 洞口投点
setting of ground 地基下沉
setting of protected area 设防
setting out 放样
setting strength 凝固强度
setting time 凝结时间,凝固时间
setting time of cement paste 净浆凝结时间

setting value 整定值
setting-out of curve 曲线测设
setting-out of foundation piles 基桩测设
setting-out of junction 交叉点放样
setting-out of main axis 主轴线测设
setting-out of roadway slope
　巷道坡度线标定
setting-out of technical boundary
　技术边界标定
setting-out survey 放样测量
settle a claim 理赔
settle accounts 结账
settlement 沉降,沉降量
settlement agreement 和解协议
settlement by acceptance 承兑结算
settlement by agreement 协商解决
settlement by arbitration 仲裁解决
settlement by negotiation 议付结算
settlement by payment 付款结算
settlement calculation depth 沉降计算深度
settlement clause 结算条款
settlement curve 沉降曲线
settlement date 结算日
settlement day 决算日
settlement deformation monitoring
　沉降变形监测
settlement joint 沉降缝
settlement observation 沉降观测
settlement of disputes 争议的解决
settlement of exchange 结汇
settlement of project cost 工程价款结算
settlement plate 沉降板
settlement price 结算价(格)
settlement rate 沉降速率
settlement subsidies 安置补助费
settlement terms 结算条款,支付条款
settling and survey agent 理赔检验代理人
settling chamber 沉降室
settling pond 沉淀井
settling tank 澄清池
setup cost 生产准备费用
set-off 冲账,抵消
set-up of a project 项目开办
seven fluorin propane fire extinguishing system
　七氟丙烷灭火系统
severable contract 可分割合同
several liability 各自责任
severance pay 解雇费,离职补偿金
severe cold region 严寒地区
severe tropical storm 强热带风暴
severely water-deficient area
　特殊缺水地区
sewage 污水
sewage (waste water) engineering
　排水工程
sewage discharge cooling tank 排污降温池
sewage discharge equipment for passenger train
　旅客列车卸污装置
sewage disposal track 卸污线
sewage farming 灌溉田
sewage from vehicle washing 洗刷污水
sewage pool 污水池
sewage produced during railway operation
　铁路运营产生的污水
sewage pumping station 污水泵站
sewage thicker 污泥浓缩池
sewage treatment 污水处理
sewage treatment plant (station)(WWTP)
　污水处理厂(站)
sewage water quality 污水水质
sewage with pathogens 病原体污水
sewer 渗沟,下水道,污水管
sewerage 污水工程,下水道工程
sewerage system 排水系统
sewer system 排水制度
SF_6 circuit-breaker SF_6 断路器
SF_6 enclosed switchgear
　SF_6 封闭式组合电器
shading coefficient 遮阳系数
shadow method 阴影法
shadow price 影子价格
shaft 竖井
shaft connection survey 竖井联系测量
shaft friction 侧摩擦阻力
shaft orientation survey 立井定向测量
shaking table test 振动台试验
shale 页岩
shale tar 页岩沥青
shallow beam 低高度梁
shallow cutting 浅路堑
shallow defect 浅部缺陷
shallow focus earthquake 浅源地震
shallow foundation 浅基
shallow foundation of bridge 桥梁浅基
shallow landslide 浅层滑坡
shallow tunnel 浅埋隧道
shallow-buried station 浅埋车站
sham 假冒
shank 螺栓端杆
shaped steel 型钢

share clause 分摊条款
share equally 均摊
share risks 分担风险
share the price difference 分担差价
shared indemnities 共同保障
shared operation yard 共用作业场
Shared Protection Ring(SPRing)
　共享保护环
shareholder 股东
shareholder's agreement 股东协议
shareholder's equity 股东权益
shareholder's meeting 股东大会
share-holding bank 合资银行
share 分担,股票
shattered fault zone 断裂构造破碎带
shattered weathered zone 风化破碎带
shear 剪力,剪切
shear alveolar 剪力齿槽
(beam-end track slab) shear connection
　(梁端轨道板)剪切连接
shear connector 抗剪连接件,剪力连接器
shear crack 剪裂缝
shear deformation 剪切变形
shear displacement 剪切位移
shear failure 剪切破坏
shear flute 剪力齿槽
shear force 剪力
shear hinge 剪力铰
shear joint 剪节理
shear lag effect 剪力滞效应
shear modulus 剪切模量
shear strength 抗剪(断)强度
shear strength index of structural plane
　结构面抗剪强度指标
shear strength index 抗剪强度指标
shear strength stress ratio 剪切应力比
shear strength test by angle mould
　抗剪断强度试验
shear stress 剪切应力,剪应力
shear wall structure 剪力墙结构
shear wave velocity measurement
　剪切波速测试
shear wave velocity 剪切波速
shearing rigidity of members
　构件抗剪刚度
shearing rigidity of section 截面剪变刚度
shearing strain 剪应变
shearing strength test 抗剪断试验
shear-span to depth ratio 剪跨比
sheath eccentricity 护套偏心度

shed tunnel 棚洞
sheepback rock 羊背石
sheep-foot roller 羊足碾
sheep-foot roller 羊足压路机
sheet 表格
sheet erosion 片蚀
sheet layer 片状层
sheet of comprehensive estimate
　综合估算表
sheet of comprehensive pre-estimate
　综合预估算表
sheet of total estimate 总估算表
sheet of total pre-estimate 总预估算表
sheet of unit estimation 单位估计表
sheet pile 板桩
sheet-pile retaining wall 板桩式挡土墙
sheet-punching machine 冲片机
shelf-type relay 座式继电器
shell 薄壳
shell and tube condenser 壳管式冷凝器
shell and tube evaporator 壳管式蒸发器
shell foundation 壳体基础
shell leakage protection 碰壳保护
shell structure 壳体结构
sheltering area 掩蔽面积
shield 地盾,护盾
shield earthing 屏蔽接地
shield tunnel boring machine
　护盾式掘进机
shielded ground wire 屏蔽地线
shielded TBM 护盾式掘进机
shielded wire 屏蔽线
shift 轮班
shift boss 当班工长
shift engineer 值班工程师
shift of image point 像点位移
shift system 轮班工作制
shift work 轮班
shifting system 驻班制
shim 垫片
ship 船
shipment 船货,船运,装运,发货
shipment advice 装船通知
shipment of commodities 货运
shipped bill of lading 已装船提单
shipping 发货,海运
shipping agent 运货代理商
shipping bill 船货清单
shipping by chartering 租船运输
shipping company 船运公司

shipping conditions 货运条件
shipping conference 海运公会,航运公会
shipping documents 货运单据,装运单据,发货单
shipping freight 船舶运价
shipping instructions 装船指示
shipping line 航线
shipping list 发货清单,货单,货运单
shipping mark 货物标志,货运唛头
shipping note 装船通知
shipping order 装货单
shipping weight 装货重量
shoal 沙洲
shoal erosion angle 浅滩磨蚀角
shock absorber base 防震架
shock resistance 抗冲击性能
shockproof block 防震挡块
shop drawing 施工图
shop drawings 加工图
shop instruction 出厂说明书
shop testing 车间测试
shore dissolving basin 岸溶盆地
Shore hardness 肖氏硬度
shore protection 护岸
shore protection engineering 护岸工程
short 不足
short bill 短期期票
short bridge (with length not more than 20m) 小桥(长度不超过20m)
short chainage 短链
short circuit 短路
short dialing codes 短号码
short distance forecast 短距离预报
short edge of sheet 卷材短边
short lease 短期租赁
short list 短名单,入选名单
short listed firms 候选公司名单
short message service center (SMSC) 短消息服务中心
short of exchange 外汇短缺
short stiffener 短加劲肋
short subgrade 短路基
short term 近期
short term rigidity of members 构件短期刚度
short time 瞬时制
short tunnel 短隧道
short wave irregularity 短波不平顺
shortage 不足
shortage of stock 库存短缺
shortened chain 短链

shortened rail 缩短轨
shorting 空头
short-circuit capacity 短路容量
short-circuit characteristic 短路特性
short-circuit current 短路电流
short-circuit electrodynamic force 短路电动力
short-circuit fault 短路故障
short-circuit impedance 短路阻抗
short-circuit loss 短路损耗
short-listed company 列入短名单的公司
short-listed firms 列入短名单的公司
short-seller 空头
short-selling 空头
short-term contract 短期合同
short-term credit 短期信贷
short-term debt 短期债务
short-term insurance 短期保险
short-term investment 短期投资
short-term loan 短期贷款
short-term planning 短期计划
shot area 打靶区
shot peening equipment 喷抛丸设备
shotcrete 喷(射)混凝土
shotcrete and bolt lining 喷锚衬砌
shotcrete and rockbolt support 喷锚支护
shotcrete machine 喷浆机
shotcreting manipulator 喷射混凝土机械手
shotcreting robot 喷射混凝土机械手
shotpoint 激发点
shot-firer 爆破工
shoulder 路肩
shoulder ballast cleaning machine 边坡清筛机
shoulder elevation 路肩高程
shoulder heightening 路肩抬高
shoulder hump 砟肩堆高
shoulder of ballast bed 砟肩
shoulder turnaround routing 肩回式交路
shoulder width 路肩宽度
shovel 铲土机
shovel crane 挖掘起重两用机
show 表明,表现
shower device 淋浴器
show-up time 到场时间
shrinkage 收缩
shrinkage allowance 收缩容许量,损耗容许量
shrinkage coefficient 收缩系数
shrinkage index 缩性指数
shrinkage limit 缩限

shrinkage method 收缩皿法
shrinkage rate 收缩率
shrinkage stress 收缩应力
shrinkage test 收缩试验
shrinkage-compensating concrete 补偿收缩混凝土
shrinking joint 收缩缝
shrub 灌木
shunt capacitor 并联电容器
shunt capacitor bank 并联电容补偿装置
shunter's cabin 调车员室
shunting 分路
shunting area 调车作业区
shunting dead zone 分路死区
shunting effect 分路效应
shunting equipment 调车设备
shunting indicator 调车表示器
shunting indicator circuit 调车表示器电路
shunting mode (SH) 调车模式
shunting mode communication 调车作业模式通信
shunting monitoring mode 调车监控模式
shunting neck 牵出线
shunting operation without interlocking 非进路调车
shunting residual voltage 分路残压
shunting resistance 分路电阻
shunting route 调车进路
shunting route control for hump yard 驼峰调车进路控制
shunting sensitivity 分路灵敏度
shunting signal 调车信号(机)
shunting state 分路状态
shunting state of track circuit 轨道电路分路状态
shunting test 调车测试
shunting track 调车线
shunting train protection (STP) 无线调车机车信号和监控
shunting trains 转线列车
shunting transfer track 调车转线
shunting yard 调车场
shutter type air outlet 百叶形风口
shuttering 预制模板
shuttle end 梭头
shuttle mine car 梭式矿车
sick leave 病假
sick leave pay 病假工资
side and front slopes at tunnel portal 洞口边仰坡

side conditions 附带条件,限制条件
side difference tolerance 边长较差限差
side ditch 边沟,侧沟
side ditch berm 侧沟平台
side forklift 侧面式叉车
side formwork 侧模
side intermediate platform 侧式中间站台
side intersection 侧方交会
side length size of sieve pore 筛孔边长尺寸
side repair track 边修线
side stone bank 边石堤
side view 侧视图
side wall 边墙
side wear 侧面磨耗
side bearing foundation 侧向承载基础
sidenote 旁注
siderite 菱铁矿
sidewalk 人行道
side-contact conductor rail 侧接触式接触轨
side-draught hood 侧吸罩
side-on collision 侧面冲突
side-wall of abutment 桥台侧墙
siding 站线
sidings 侧线
sieve analysis method 筛析法
sieve pore 筛孔
sieve-plate tower 筛板塔
sieving 过筛,筛分
sifter 筛析机
sight 即期,即期的
sight bill (s) 即付票,即期汇票,即期票据
sight draft 即期汇票
sight letter of credit 即期信用证
sight payment credit 即期付款信用证
sight rate 即期汇率
sight test 当场检查
sightglass 观察孔
sighting distance 显示距离
sighting line method 瞄直法
sighting point 照准点
sign 标识,标志,记号,签署,签字
sign a certificate 签署证书
sign a contract 签署合同
sign at level crossing 道口标志
sign board 标志牌,揭示牌
sign board for tuning zone 调谐区标志牌
sign for 代签,签收
sign for signal out of service 信号无效标
sign for water pipe 水道标

sign manual 亲笔签名
sign on 签字受雇
sign over 签字移交
signal 信号机
signal amplifier 信号放大器
signal at clear 信号开放
signal at stop 信号关闭
signal authorization(SA) 信号允许
signal bridge 信号桥
signal bulb 信号灯泡
signal cable 信号电缆
signal control circuit 信号控制电路
signal distortion 信号失真度
signal for both day and night 昼夜通用信号
signal for shunting forward and backward 双面调车信号机
signal for stub-end siding 尽头信号机
signal in throat section 咽喉信号机
signal indication 信号显示,信号表示
signal indication relation 信号显示关系
signal interface unit 信号接口单元
signal lever 信号握柄
signal lighting 信号机点灯
signal lighting circuit 信号机点灯电路
signal line 信号线
signal location 信号点
signal repeater 信号复示器
signal sign 信号标志
signal sign board 信号标志牌
signal slot 信号选别器
signal superimposing times 信号叠加次数
signal to crosstalk ratio 串音防卫度
signal to noise ratio 杂音防卫度,信噪比
signal tower 信号楼
signal transmission line 信号传输线
signal valve 信号阀
signaling analyzer 信令分析仪等
signaling gateway(SG) 信令网关
signaling point(SP) 信令点
signaling transfer point(STP) 信令转接点
signatory 签署者
signature 签名,签字
signed check 记名支票
signing the contract 合同签署
signpost 路标
sign-off 签署同意
silencer 消声器
silica fume 硅灰
silicalite 硅质岩
silicate 硅酸盐

siliceous cementation 硅质胶结
siliceous shale 硅质页岩
silicon components 硅元件
silicon dioxide 二氧化硅
silicon molybdenum blue spectrophotometry 硅钼蓝分光光度法
silicone rubber sheath 硅橡胶护套
silky luster 丝绢光泽
sill 岩床
sillimanite 硅线石
silo 筒仓,罐
silt 淤泥
silt content 含泥量
silt grain 粉粒
siltation 淤积
siltation sand 淤砂
siltstone 粉砂岩
silty clay 粉砂质黏土
silty sand 粉砂
silty soil 粉砂质土
Silurian period 志留纪
Silurian system 志留系
silver nitrate volumetric method 硝酸银滴定法
silver-diethyldithiocarbamin acid spectrophotometry 二乙基二硫代氨基甲酸银光度法
similar gradation method 相似级配法
simple catenary suspension 简单链形悬挂
simple concrete mixing plant 简易混凝土搅拌站
simple interest 单利
simple network management protocol(SNMP) 简单网络管理协议
simple shear test 单剪试验
simple transverse link 简单横向连接
simple turnout 单开道岔
simple wall 单一墙
simplified schematic 简图
simplified water balance method 简易水均衡法
simply supported beam 简支梁
simply-supported beam bridge 简支梁桥
simply-supported girder bridge 简支梁桥
simply-supported girder 简支梁
simulation 仿真模拟
simulation lightning test 模拟雷击试验
sinewy 结实的
single-edge disc cutter 单刃滚刀
single break 单断
single bucket excavator 单斗挖土机

single cantilever pole（mast） 中间柱
single case claim 单项索赔
single construction 单项工程
single coverage 普通单网无线覆盖
single crossover 单渡线
single curve 单曲线
single drum test 单盘检测
single feeding and single receiving 一送一受
single frequency 单频
single frequency inductor 单频感应器
single groove 单面坡口
single hole method 单孔法
single humping 单溜放
single humping and single rolling 单推单溜
single layer rectangular arrangement
　单层矩形布置
single liability 单一责任
single line diagram 主接线
single line reciprocating type 单线往复式
single machine test 单机测试
single mode optical fiber 单模光纤
single payment 整笔支付
single phase load 单相负荷
single phase traction transformer
　单相牵引变压器
single pile bearing capacity 单桩承载力
single point excitation 单点激振
single point responsibility 单一负责制
single point settlement 单点沉降
single polar 单偏光镜
single rail track circuit 单轨条轨道电路
single rate 单利
single row layout 单列布置
single safety coefficient method
　单一安全系数法
single shield TBM 单护盾掘进机
single shift 一班（制）
single signal location 单置信号点
single signal selectivity 单信号选择性
single tax system 单一税制
single tender 单项招标
single test 单体试验
single track wedge-shaped welding
　单轨楔体焊接
single transmitting and multiple receiving track circuit 一送多受
single trip ticket 单程票
single turnout 单开道岔
single turnout with fixed frog
　固定辙叉单开道岔

single-armed girder-erecting machine
　单梁式架桥机
single-channel image 单路画面
single-doped 单掺
single-end earthing 单端接地
single-end feeding 单边供电
single-end feeding with phase of same sequence
　同相单边供电
single-fluid grout 单液浆
single-grained structure 单粒结构
single-hump 单驼峰
single-layer shutter-type air outlet
　单层百叶形风口
single-level architecture 单级架构
single-locomotive traction section
　单机牵引区段
single-phase ground short-circuit
　单相接地短路
single-phase three-wire system 单相三线制
single-phase winding connection 单相结线
single-plane cable-stayed bridge
　单面索斜拉桥
single-point method 单点法
single-room office 单间式办公
single-shot automatic reclosing
　一次自动重合闸
single-sided ramp 单面斜道
single-swivel double-tube core drilling
　单动双管取芯钻进
single-track 单线
single-track bridge 单线桥
single-track railway 单线铁路
single-track rock cutting 单线石质路堑
single-track section 单线地段
single-track soil cutting 单线土质路堑
single-track tunnel 单线隧道
single-tube drilling with movable casing water-blocking connector 活套闭水接头单管钻进
single-well pumping test 单井抽水试验
single-wire operated semaphore signal
　单线臂板信号机
Sinian period 震旦纪
Sinian system 震旦系
sinkage 下沉度,下沉量
sinkhole 落水洞
sinking coefficient 沉没系数
sino-foreign joint venture 中外合资企业
sintered common brick 烧结普通砖
sintered porous brick 烧结多孔砖
siphon 虹吸（管）

siphon backflow 虹吸回流
siphon culvert 虹吸涵洞
siphon cylinder method 虹吸筒法
siphon filter 虹吸滤池
siphon tube method 虹吸管法
siren 汽笛
site 场地,工地,工地,施工现场
site acceptance 进场验收
site accommodation 现场生活设施
site analysis 场地分析
site arrangement 工地布置
site assessment 场地评价
site category 场地类别
site clearance 现场清理,清理现场
site condition 场地条件
site coverage 工地范围
site data 现场资料
site data and items of reference 现场数据和基准
site diary 工地日志
site direction 现场指挥
site engineer 现场工程师
site equipment 工地设备
site exploration 现场勘探
site facilities 现场设施
site grading 场地平整,工地平整
site hut 工棚
site inspection 现场考察
site instruction 现场指导
site intensity 场地烈度
site investigation 现场查勘,现场调查
site laboratory 工地试验室
site layout 现场布置图
site leachate 场地浸淋水
site leveling 场地平整
site management 现场管理(人员)
site manager 现场经理
site meeting minutes 现场会议纪要
site operations 现场作业,露天作业
site organization 现场施工组织
site overhead cost 现场管理费
site plan 场地平面图,现场平面图,施工场地图
site planning 总平面设计
site reclamation 场地填筑
site security 现场治安,现场保安
site selection 选址
site selection investigation 选址查勘
site soil 场地土
site soil type 场地土类型
site survey 现场测量
site test 进场检验
site training 就地培训
site utilization planning 场地使用计划
site visit 实地调查,现场考察
site welding 现场焊
siting 选址
size of fillet weld 角焊缝尺寸
size of the loan 贷款额
sizer 分选机
skarn 矽卡岩,夕卡岩
skate brake 铁鞋制动
skate throw-off device 脱鞋器
skeleton 骨架
skeleton curve 骨架曲线
skeleton revetment 骨架护坡
skeleton slope protection 骨架护坡
sketch 草稿,草图,简图,略图
sketch drawing 简图
skew angle 斜交角
skew bridge 斜交桥
skewback 拱座
skewed fold 歪斜褶皱
skid resistant fastener 防滑扣件
skilled labour 熟练工人
skilled worker 熟练工人
skin depth 趋肤深度
skip car 翻斗车
skip elevator 斗式升降机,斗式提升机
skylight frame 天窗架
slab arch bridge 板拱桥
slab beam 板梁
slab culvert 盖板涵
slab loading test 平板荷载试验
slab track 板式轨道
slab-column shear wall structure 板柱—剪力墙结构
slab-type bridge 板桥
slab-type stairway 板式楼梯
slab-type turnout area 板式岔区
slack time 浮动时间
slacking at work 怠工
slag 矿渣
slag cement 矿渣水泥
slag concrete 矿渣混凝土
slag muck 废渣
slag trapping dam 拦渣坝
slag trapping works 拦渣工程
slag concrete aggregate 矿渣骨料混凝土
slake (石灰)消解
slaked lime 熟石灰

slaking device 湿化仪
slaking index 耐崩解指数
slaking index of rock 岩石耐崩解指数
slaking test 耐崩解试验,湿化试验
slang 行话
slanted cantilever tube 斜腕臂
slant-legged rigid frame 斜腿刚构
slant-legged rigid frame bridge 斜腿刚构桥
slate 板岩
slaty 板状
slaty structure 板状构造
slave clock 子钟
sleeper 轨枕,枕木
sleeper crib 轨枕盒
sleeper defect 轨枕伤损
sleeper laying 轨枕铺设
sleeper repair 轨枕修补
sleeper replacement 轨枕更换
sleeper replacement machine 轨枕更换机
sleeper-embedded ballastless track in turnout area 道岔区轨枕埋入式无砟轨道
sleeping mode 休眠模式
sleeve 衬套,套筒
sleeve compensator 套筒补偿器
slenderness ratio 长细比
slices method 条分法
sliding of slope surface layer 边坡溜坍
slide plate 滑床板
slide tongue 滑坡舌
slideway 滑道
sliding contact current method 滑动接触电流法
sliding dropper clamp of double messenger wire 滑动双承力索吊弦线夹
sliding dropper clamp 滑动吊弦线夹
sliding dropper clip for messenger wire 承力索滑动吊弦线夹
sliding layer 滑动层
sliding oil cylinder 滑动油缸
sliding price 浮动价格
sliding soil 滑动土
sliding surface 滑动面
slight corrosion 微腐蚀
slight weathering 弱风化
slightly dense 稍密
slightly humid 稍湿
slightly opened joint 微张节理
slip cleavage 滑劈理
slip cliff 滑坡壁
slip code 滑码
slip form 滑动模板
slip resistance coefficient of friction surface for high strength bolt 高强度螺栓摩擦面抗滑移系数
slip resistance test 抗滑试验
slip ring 滑环
slip turnout 交分道岔
slippage 工期落后,滑移,拖期
slip-form construction 滑模施工
slit and split film silk woven geotextiles 裂膜丝机织土工布
slit and split film yarn woven geotextiles 裂膜纱织土工布
slit method test 狭缝法试验
slope 边坡,斜坡,坡道
slope gradient 边坡坡率
slope protection with vegetation 边坡绿色防护
slope bench 边坡平台
slope collapse 边坡坍塌
slope cutting 边坡开挖
slope distance 斜距
slope face 坡面
slope indicating line 示坡线
slope of fatigue curve 疲劳曲线斜率
slope of water surface 水面坡度
slope protection 边坡防护,护坡
slope scale 坡度尺
slope spalling 边坡剥落
slope stability 边坡稳定性
slope stability factor 边坡稳定系数
slope stake 边坡桩
slope stake locating 边坡桩测设
slope toe 坡脚
slope top 坡顶
slope wash 坡积土,坡积物
slope wash facies 坡积相
slope-type low freight section 斜坡式低货位
sloping protection 斜坡防护
slot type air outlet 条缝型风口
slow assets 呆滞资产
slow direct shear test 直剪慢剪试验
slow down 放慢速度
slow pick-up time 缓吸时间
slow quantitative filter paper 慢速定量滤纸
slow release relay 缓放继电器
slow release time 缓放时间
slow setting cement 缓凝水泥
slow shear 慢剪

slow shear test 慢剪试验
slowly varying thermometer 缓变温度计
sludge 污泥
sludge age 泥龄
sludge concentration 污泥浓度
sludge dewatering 污泥脱水
sludge dewatering machine 污泥脱水机
sludge digestion 污泥消化
sludge drying 污泥干化
sludge drying yard 污泥干化场
sludge farm application 污泥农用
sludge gas 沼气
sludge heat drying 污泥热干化
sludge incineration 污泥焚烧
sludge integrated application 污泥综合利用
sludge land application 污泥土地利用
sludge loading 污泥负荷
sludge retention time (SRT) 污泥龄
sludge solid loading 污泥固体负荷
sludge thickening 污泥浓缩
sludge treatment 污泥处理
sludge water content 污泥含水量
sludge yard 污泥堆场
sludge yield 污泥产率
sluice 水闸,泄水道
sluicing drainage 泄水引流
slump 暴跌,滑塌,坍落度,衰退
slump flow time T_{500} 扩展时间 T_{500}
slump retain value 坍落度保留值
slump spread 坍落扩展度
slump test 坍落度试验
slurry 泥浆
slurry injection mixing pile 浆体喷射搅拌桩
slurry jelling time 浆液胶凝时间
slurry pump 泥浆泵
slurry shield 泥水平衡盾构
slurry tank 泥浆池
small capacity hump 小能力驼峰
small dumper 小型自卸车
small garden ornament 园林小品
small mileage end 小里程端
small passenger station 小型旅客车站
small refuge niche 小避车洞
small resistance fastening 小阻力扣件
small sample method 小样本方法
small scale landslip 小型滑坡
small scale low portal-frame forklift 小型低门架叉车
small scale station 小型车站
small scale temporary facilities 小型临时设施
small sized marshaling station 小型编组站
small track circuit 小轨道电路
small-scale maintenance 小修
small-scale topographical map 小比例尺地形图
small-sized hollow concrete block 混凝土小型空心砌块
smartphone ticket sales 手机端售票
smoke 烟
smoke bay 防烟分区
smoke detector 烟感
smoke exhaust 排烟
smoke exhaust in accident 事故排烟
smoke exhaust system 排烟系统
smoke extinguishing system 烟雾灭火系统
smoke prevention 防烟
smoke proof staircase 防烟楼梯间
smoke sensing fire detector 感烟火灾探测器
smoke shaft 排烟竖井
smooth blasting 光面爆破
smooth running 平稳运行
smooth wheel roller 光轮压路机
smoothness 平整度
smooth-wheeled roller 光轮压路机
smuggle 走私
snap check 现场抽查,现场抽查
snow depth meter 雪深计
snow depth monitoring alarm 雪深监测报警
snow load 雪荷载
snowline 雪线
snow-bearing wind 风雪流
snow-driving wind 风雪流
soaring prices 物价飞涨
social impact assessment 社会影响评价
social insurance 社会保险
social rate of discount 社会折现率
social risks 社会风险
social security 社会保障
social security cost 社会保障费
social security system 劳动保险制度
social stability risk 社会稳定风险
social welfare 社会福利
social welfare clause 社会福利条款
social-economic environment impact assessment 社会经济环境影响评价
social-environmental investigation 社会环境调查

socio-economic objective 社会经济目标
socket bonding 承插粘接
socket end wedge-type clamp
　　杵座楔形线夹
sodium carbonate 碳酸钠
sodium chlorite 亚氯酸钠
sodium hypochlorite 次氯酸钠
soft and hard rock contact zone 软硬岩接触带
soft blocky stone 软块石
soft clay 软黏土
soft copy 软件副本
soft currency 软通货
soft loan 低息贷款,软贷款,优惠贷款
soft rock 软岩,软质岩
soft soil 软弱土,软土
soft soil foundation 软土基础
soft stone 软石
Soft Switch(SS) 软交换机
softened water 软化水
softening coefficient 软化系数
softening of subgrade 基床软化
software 软件
software safety integrity level
　　软件安全完整性等级
software version 软件版本
soft-plastic 软塑
soil and water conservation 水土保持
soil and water conservation design drawing for typical borrow pit
　　典型取土场水土保持防护图
soil and water conservation design drawing for typical spoil ground
　　典型弃土场水土保持防护图
soil and water conservation facilities
　　水土保持设施
soil and water conservation forest
　　水土保持林
soil and water conservation monitoring
　　水土保持监测
soil and water conservation scheme
　　水土保持方案
soil and water conservation scheme report
　　水土保持方案报告书
soil borrowing 取土
soil classification 土类分级
soil compactor 碾压机
soil conditions 土壤条件
soil covering height 覆土高度
soil cutting 土质路堑
soil densification method 土体增密法

soil density after vibration liquefaction
　　振稳密度
soil dynamic characteristics test
　　土动态特性试验
soil engineering measure 土工工程措施
soil erosion and water loss 水土流失
soil erosion and water loss control ratio
　　水土流失总治理度
soil erosion 土壤侵蚀
soil erosion intensity factor
　　土壤侵蚀强度因子
soil erosion modulus 土壤侵蚀模数
soil flow 流土
soil improvement 土质改良
soil investigation 土质调查
soil knife 切土刀
soil landslide 土质滑坡
soil loss tolerance 土壤流失容许量
soil mass 土体
soil miller 切土器
soil moisture 土壤含水量
soil moisture content 土壤含水量
soil nail 土钉
soil pollution 土壤污染
soil resistivity (earth conductivity)
　　土壤电阻率(大地电导率)
soil sample 土样
soil sampler 取土器
soil screen 泥土筛分
soil skeleton 土骨架
soil slip accumulation 土滑堆积
soil slope 土质边坡
soil subgrade 土质路基
soil type 土壤类型
soil water 土壤水
soil wedge 土楔
soil-containing ice layer 含土冰层
soil-nailed wall 土钉墙
soil-structure interaction 土结构相互作用
solar altitude 太阳高度角
solar azimuth 太阳方位角
solar collector 太阳能集热器
solar energy 太阳能
solar energy heater 太阳能热水器
solar irradiation 太阳辐照量
solar radiation 太阳辐射
solar radiation heat 太阳辐射热
solar water-heating system
　　太阳能热水系统
soldering 焊接(用于电子设备的锡焊)

sole agency 独家代理,唯一代理
sole agent 独家代理人,唯一代理人
sole arbitrator 独任仲裁员
sole discretion 单独酌处权,全权处理
sole distributor 独家经销商
solely foreign-owned enterprise 独资企业
sole-member DAAB 1人组成的争议避免裁决委员会
solicitation 询价
solicitor 初级律师
solid content 固体含量
solid elastic index 固弹指数
solid fuel 固体燃料
solid load 固体负荷
solid phase 固相
solid pie 实体桥墩
solid reagent method 固体试剂法
solid slab 实心板
solid waste 固体废物
solid waste pollution 固体废弃物污染
solid wastes disposal 固体废物处置
solid water 固态水
solidified agent soil 固化剂土
solid-web steel column 实腹式钢柱
solifluction 融冻泥流
soluble alkali content 可溶性碱含量
soluble heavy metals 可溶性重金属
soluble iron 可溶铁
soluble salt 易溶盐
soluble silicon 可溶性硅
solution 溶蚀
solution crack 溶隙
solution dehumidifier 溶液除湿机
solution pan 溶盘
solution volume 溶液体积
solvency 偿付能力,支付能力,偿债能力
solvent 溶剂
solvent mixing method 溶剂混溶法
sorbed water content 吸着含水率
sort 级别
sorting area 分拣区
sound absorption 吸声
sound absorption coefficient 吸声系数
sound absorption material 吸声材料
sound absorption property 吸声性能
sound absorptive and insulation composite panel 吸隔声复合板
sound absorptive and insulation compound structure 吸隔声复合结构
sound arriving value 到达地完好货价

sound barrier 声屏障
sound barrier along railway 铁路声屏障
sound barrier element 声屏障元件
sound barrier members 声屏障构件
sound barrier on bridge 桥梁段声屏障
sound barrier on cutting 路堑声屏障
sound barrier on subgrade 路基段声屏障
sound barrier on subgrade-bridge transition section 路桥过渡段声屏障
sound duration 声时
sound exposure level 暴露声级
sound insulation 隔声
sound insulation property of sound barrier 声屏障隔声性能
sound insulation watching door 隔声观察窗
sound insulation window 隔声窗
sound insulator 隔声材料
sound intensity 声强
sound leakage 漏声
sound level 声级
sound level meter 声级计
sound pressure 声压
sound pressure level 声压级
sound reduction factor (index) 隔声量
sound source 声源
sound source spectrum characteristics 声源频谱特性
sound wave 声波
sound wave induction method 声波感应法
sound wave vibration generator 声波激振器
sounding 水深测量
sounding line 测深线
sounding pipe 声测管
sounding point 测深点
soundness 安定性,坚固性
soundproof door 隔声门
sound-deadening material 消声材料
source 根源,来源
source document 原始凭证,原始文件
source of funds 资金来源
source of pollution 污染源
source selection 货源选择
source-receiver offset 炮检距
south subtropics 南亚热带
southbound interface 南向接口
sovereign loan 主权贷款
space 空间
space between 间距
space frame 空间框架
space lattice 空间网架

space management and tracking
　空间管理和追踪
space remote sensing technology
　航天遥感技术
space remote sensing　航天遥感
spacer bar　定位钢筋
spacer flocculating tank　隔板絮凝池
space-interval system　空间间隔制
spacing　间距
spacing block　间隔铁
spacing braking　间隔制动
spacing of pile　桩距
spacing of reinforcement　钢筋间距
spacing of stirrup legs　箍筋肢距
spacing of transverse walls　横墙间距
spalling　掉块
span　跨度,跨径
span length　跨距
spandrel　拱肩
spandrel-filled arch　实腹拱
spandrel-filled arch bridge　实腹拱桥
spandrel-unfilled arch　空腹拱
spandrel-unfilled arch bridge　空腹拱桥
span-by-span construction method
　逐跨施工法
span-depth ratio　跨高比
spare box　备用箱
spare filament　副灯丝
spare locomotive　备用机车
spare material　备用材料
spare parts　备品,备件
spare rail（emergency rail stored along the way）
　备用轨
spare unit　备用材料,备用设备
spark extinguishing circuit　灭火花电路
spark gap　火花间隙
spatial behaviour　空间工作性能
spatial composition　空间组成
spatial containment　空间包含
spatial decomposition　空间分解
spatial effect　空间效果
spatial information　空间信息
spatial intersection　空间前方交会
spatial localization　空间定位
spatial resection　空间后方交会
spatial structure　空间结构
spatial structure element　空间结构单元
spatial transformation　空间变换
spatial variability of geotechnical parameter
　岩土参数空间变异性

special　特别的,异常的
special（particular）conditions of contract
　专用合同条件
special additional risk　特殊附加险
special cement　特种水泥
special colour rendering index
　特殊显色指数
special concrete　特殊混凝土,特种混凝土
special contractor　专业承包商
special discount　特别折扣,反常贬值
special drawing rights（SDRs）
　特别提款权
special economic zone　经济特区
special endorsement　记名背书
special engineering structure
　特种工程结构
special force　特殊力
special fortification　特殊设防
special geotextile material　特种土工材料
special grade ballast　特级道砟
special inspection　特别检查
special load　特殊荷载
special mortar　特殊砂浆
special operation　特种作业
special preference　特惠
special protection area　特殊保护区
special provisions
　特别规定,特殊条款,特殊条文
special risks　特殊风险
special rock and soil　特殊岩土
special soil　特殊土
special spur track　铁路专用线
special subgrade　特殊路基
special supervision fee for environmental protection　环境保护专项监理费
special surtax　特别附加税
special test　特殊试验
specialist　专家,专门人员
specialist contractor　专业承包商
specialist services　专业服务
specialist subcontractor　专业分包商
specialization　专业化
specialized goods yard　专业性货场
specialized repair system　专业化修制
specialty　特长,特殊产品
species of trees　树种
species quantity　物种数量
specific　特定的,具体的
specific braking energy head of retarder
　减速器单位制动能高

specific enthalpy 比焓
specific gravity 比重
specific gravity bottle 比重瓶
specific grout absorption capacity
 单位吸浆量
specific identification method 个别辨认法
specific penetration resistance（Ps）
 比贯入阻力
specific provision 特有条款,具体条文
specific surface area 比表面积
specific transmission module（STM）
 轨道信息接收单元
specific water absorption capacity
 单位吸水量
specific weight 重度
specific weight of soil particle 土粒比重
specific yield 给水度
specification 规程,规格,规范
specification compliance form 规格响应表
specifications of surveying 测量规范
specified conditions for detaining cars
 扣车条件
specified costs 规费
specified date 规定日期,指定日期
specified provisional sums
 指定的暂定金额
specified sound pressure level 规定声压级
specimen molding 试件成型
specimen of letter of credit 信用证样本
specimen planting 孤植
specimen preparation 试样制备
specimen signature 签字样本
specimen under the same curing condition
 同条件养护试件
specimen 样本,试件,试体,标本
spectral characteristics of noise
 噪声频谱特性
spectrography 光谱纯
spectrophotometer 分光光度计
spectrophotometric turbidimetry method
 分光光度比浊法
spectrum 波谱
spectrum analyzer 光谱分析仪
spectrum characteristic of ground feature
 地物波谱特性
speculation 投机
speculative capital/money
 短期流动资金,游资
speculative risk 投机风险
speculator 投机商

speed control for time interval between cars
 间隔调速
speed control retarder 调速顶
speed control system 调速系统
speed factor 速度系数
speed limit section 限速地段
speed limiting and splitting function
 限速拆分功能
speed measurement 测速
speed restriction function test for existing line
 既有线限速功能测试
speed restriction section 限速地段
speed sensor 速度传感器
speed signaling 速差制信号
speed target value 速度目标值
speed valve 调速阀
speed-different mode automatic blocking
 速差式自动闭塞
speed-up construction 加速施工
spending authority 开支权限
spessartite 闪斜煌斑岩
sphalerite 闪锌矿
sphere of responsibility 职责范围
spherical bearing 球形支座
spherical cushion block 球形垫块
spherical steel bearing 球形钢支座
spheroid 球状体
spike driver 打道钉机
spike hammer 道钉锤
spike puller 起道钉机
spillway 溢洪道
spindle type drilling machine 立轴式钻机
spiral coal unloader 螺旋卸煤机
spiral curve 缓和曲线
spiral stirrup 螺旋箍筋
spire mountain 尖顶山
spit 砂嘴
splash erosion 溅蚀
splice 叠接,接头线夹
splice plate 拼接板
splicing 接续（光缆熔接）
split air conditioner 分体式空气调节器
split of rail head 轨头劈裂
split of rail web 轨腰劈裂
split test（Brazilian test）
 劈裂试验(巴西试验)
splitting method 劈裂法
splitting of point tongue 挤岔
splitting tensile strength 劈裂抗拉强度
spodumene 锂辉石

spoil 弃土
spoil area 弃土场,弃渣场
spoil bank 弃土堆
spoil disposal area 弃渣场
spoil ground agreement 弃土场协议
spoiled product (goods) 次品
spoiler 扰流板
sponsor 出资人,主办人,赞助
spontaneous potential method 自然电位法
spontaneous recovery period 自然恢复期
sporadic noise 偶发噪声
sporadic works 零星工程
spot 场所,存货,现货
spot cash 货到付款,现款
spot check 当场检查,现场抽查
spot delivery 当场交货
spot exchange 现汇
spot exchange rate 即期汇率
spot exchange transaction
  即期外汇买卖,现汇交易
spot inspection 现场检查
spot mark 记号
spot payment 现付
spot price 现货价格
spot rate 现汇汇率
spot repair 现场修理
spot test 抽查,现场测试
spot transaction 现货交易,现货业务
spotted slate 斑点板岩
spotted structure 斑点状构造
spray extinguishing system 雨淋灭火系统
spray gun 喷枪
spray polyurea waterproofing coating
  喷涂聚脲防水涂料
spray sowing 喷混植生
spraying car 洒水车
spraying grass seeds on borrow soil
  客土喷播植草
spread 扩展度
spread foundation 扩大基础,扩展基础
spreading evenness 摊铺平整
spring groups 泉群
spring operating mechanism 弹簧操作机构
spring point 泉点
spring rail anchor 弹簧防爬器
spring thermometer 泉水温度计
spring vibration absorber 弹簧隔振器
spring water 泉水
springline 起拱点
springing line 起拱线

spring-type relay 弹力继电器
sprinkler for water curtain 水幕喷头
sprinkler for water mist 水雾喷头
sprinkler head 洒水喷头
sprinkler system 喷水消防系统
spur dike 丁坝,又称"挑水坝"
spur leveling line 支水准路线
spurious response rejection 假响应抑制
square grid 方里网
square grid point 方格网点
square joint 相对式接头
square layout 正方形布置
square map subdivision 正方形分幅
square method 方格法
square pyramid space grids 四角锥体网架
squeezing surrounding rock 挤压性围岩
stability 稳定性,稳固
stability analysis 稳定分析
stability calculation 稳定计算
stability coefficient of axial compression member
  轴心受压构件稳定系数
stability factor 稳定系数
stability number 稳定数
stability test of point location 点位稳定性检验
stabilization pond 稳定塘
stabilized force system 稳定力系
stabilized light source 稳定光源
stabilized pressure pump 稳压泵
stabilized slope 稳定边坡
stabilizer 稳定剂
stable bank slope angle 稳定岸坡角
stable crack growth 稳定裂纹扩展
stable low-temperature permafrost
  低温稳定冻土区
stable operation 稳定运行
stable state comparison method
  稳态比较法
stabling siding for spare passenger cars
  备用客车存放线
stabling siding for spare vehicles
  备用车停留线
stabling yard 场内停车场,存车场,停车场
stacking layers 堆放层数
stacking tier 堆码层数
stadia method 视距法
staff 标尺,标杆,工作人员,职员
staff acquisition 人员招募
staff and labour 员工和劳务
staff executive 职能部门主管人员
staff manager 人事经理

staff pouch　路签携带器
staff regulations　工作人员条例
staff salary　工作人员工资
staff with a key　钥匙路签
staffing　人员配备
stage for heaping soil and broken rock　碎落台
stage of completion　完工阶段
stage payment　阶段付款
stagger　拉出值
staggered joint　相错式接头
staggering　错台
stagnant water in rainy season　雨季滞水
staining method　着色法
stainless steel　不锈钢
staircase　楼梯间
stairs　楼梯
stair-step cost　阶梯成本
stake　标桩
stake handover　交接桩
stakeholder　利益相关者
stalactite　钟乳石,钟乳状
stalagmite　石笋
stale bill of lading　过期提单
stale check　过期支票
stale policy　过期保险单
stamp　印章
stamp tax　印花税
stand void　作废
standalone management　独立管理
standalone test　单体测试
standard　标准,规范,基准
standard agreement　标准协议书
standard bidding documents for works（SBDW）标准工程招标文件(SBDW)
standard brightness level　照度标准值
standard calibration site　标准检定场
standard clause　标准条款
standard collocation point　标准配置点
standard consolidation test　标准固结试验
standard contract　标准合同
standard cooling capacity　标准制冷量
standard cost　标准成本
standard cross section　标准横断面
standard curing specimen　标准养护试件
standard curing temperature　标准养护温度
standard curve　标准曲线
standard design　标准设计
standard design fee　标准设计费
standard design of bridge　桥梁标准设计

standard deviation　标准偏差
standard error　标准差
standard for acceptance　验收标准
standard form　标准格式
standard form of contract　合同范本
standard fortification　标准设防
standard frost depth　标准冻结深度
standard gauge　标准轨距
standard gauge railway　标准轨距铁路
standard grade of steel　钢材牌号
standard labour hour（time）标准人工工时,人工工时定额
standard labour rate　标准工资率
standard length rail　标准长度钢轨
standard live load　标准活载
standard live load of bridge　桥梁标准活载
standard load of road　道路标准荷载
standard machine hour（time）标准机械工时,机械工时定额
standard of comprehensive expense of labors　综合工费标准
standard of conduct　行为准则
standard of construction　施工标准
standard of fixed assets　固定资产标准
standard of surveying and mapping　测绘标准
standard operation procedures　标准操作程序
standard penetration test（SPT）标准贯入试验
standard penetrometer　标准贯入器
standard live load of Chinese railway　中—活载
standard sand　标准砂
standard shunt resistance　标准分路电阻
standard shunting sensitivity　标准分流感度,标准分路灵敏度
standard solution　标准溶液
standard specimen　标准试件
standard specimen of cube　立方体标准试件
standard sprinkler　标准喷头
standard terms　标准条款
standard test specimen　基准试件
standard thawing depth　标准融深
standard value　标准值
standard value of actions　作用的标准值
standard value of axial force　轴力标准值
standard value of axial tensile strength of concrete　混凝土轴心抗拉强度标准值
standard value of bending compressive strength of concrete　混凝土弯曲抗压强度标准值
standard value of compressive strength for concrete cube　混凝土立方体抗压强度标准值

standard value of concrete strength 混凝土强度标准值
standard value of daylight factor 采光系数标准值
standard value of earthquake action 地震作用标准值
standard value of geometrical parameter 几何参数的标准值
standard value of load 荷载作用标准值
standard value of masonry strength 砌体强度标准值
standard value of material strength 材料强度标准值
standard value of permanent action 永久作用标准值
standard value of pressure bearing strength for member end 构件端面承压强度标准值
standard value of strength 强度标准值
standard value of tensile strength of steel bar 钢筋抗拉强度标准值
standard value of variable action 可变作用标准值
standard viscometer 标准黏度计
standard working condition 标准工况
standardization 标准化
standardization management 标准化管理
standardization of sample works 首件定标
standards of industry practice 行业惯例标准
standby 备用的,预备的
standby cost 备用成本
standby equipment 备用设备,闲置设备
standby heating 值班采暖
standby letter of credit 备用信用证
standby mode 待机模式
standby power source 备用电源
standby reserve of chemical 药剂固定储备量
standby UPS 备用冗余 UPS
standing book 台账
standing director 常务董事
standing expenses 经常费用
standing order 长期订单
standing permit 长期许可证
standing plant 闲置设备
standing position 地位
standing time 窝工时间,停机时间,停工时间
standing time under repair 检修停时
star connection 星形连接

start humping signal 允许推送信号
start location in the TSM 起模点
starting angle 入土角
starting date of contract 合同生效日期
starting datum mark 起测基点
starting point 基点,起始点,起算点(日)
starting time 启动时间
startup 启动
start-up 开车,投料试车
start-up of a project 项目开工
state 声明,政府,国家
state investment 政府投资
state of block section device 闭塞分区设备状态
state of plastic equilibrium 塑性平衡状态
state of track section device 轨道区段设备状态
statement 报表,财务报表,声明
statement and supporting documents 报表和支撑文件
statement at completion 竣工报表
statement of acceptance 接受声明
statement of account 结算单
statement of asset and liabilities 资产负债表
statement of cash flow 现金流表
statement of claim 索赔报告,索赔清单
statement of defence 答辩
statement of dishonour 拒付声明
statement of expenses 费用清单
statement of final account 最终结账单
statement of financial position 财务状况表
statement of labour services 劳务统计报表
statement of liquidation 破产清算书
statement of operation 营业报表
statement of profit and loss 损益表
statement of qualification 资质说明
statement of receipt and disbursement 现金收支表
statement of retained earnings/income/surplus 留存收益表
statements 货款结算单
state-owned enterprise 国有企业
static acceptance check 静态验收
static acceptance test 静态验收测试
static action 静态作用
static calibration track 静态标定线
static compressive modulus of elasticity 静力受压弹性模量
static cone penetration test (CPT) 静力触探试验

static contact force 静态接触压力
static deflection 静态挠度
static deformation modulus 静变形模量
static design 静态设计
static earth pressure 静止土压力
static elasticity modulus 静弹性模量
static force 静力
static force method 静力法
static force similarity 静力相似
static investment 静态投资
static investment payback time
　静态投资回收期
static live load effect 静活载效应
static load 静荷载,静态荷载
static load anchoring performance
　静载锚固性能
static load gauge 车辆的静态限界
static loading grading 静载加载分级
static loading test 静载试验
static loading tester 静载测试仪
static pile extractor 静压力拔桩机
static seal index 静态密封指数
static sign 静态标识
static sounding 静力触探
static speed profile (SSP) 静态速度曲线
static speed restriction 静态速度限制
static standing time 静停时间
static state 静态
static stereo photography 静态立体摄影
static strain gauge 静态应变仪
static stress 静态应力
static test 静态测试
static test check 静态测试检查
static track geometry 静态几何形位
static VAR compensator 静止无功补偿装置
static water level 静止水位
static water mechanics balance
　静水力学天平
statically determinate bridge structure
　静定桥梁结构
statically determinate structure 静定结构
statically indeterminate bridge structure
　超静定桥梁结构
statically indeterminate structure 超静定结构
static-dynamic strain gauge 静动态应变仪
station 车站
station access 进出站通道
station and yard 站场
station and yard communication 站场通信
station and yard line 站场线路

station and yard telephone 站场电话
(passenger) station approach flow
　进出站流线
station approach track 进出站线路
station autonomous computer 车站自律机
station broadcasting 车站广播
station building above the track level
　线上式站房
station building below the track level
　线下式站房
station building terrace 站房平台
station center 站房中心位置
station communication equipment room
　车站通信机房
station control 车站控制
station dispatching switch 车站调度交换机
station distribution 车站分布
station equipment 站机
station in advance of terminal 枢纽前方站
station integrated management platform
　车站集成管理平台
station liaison officer 驻站联络员
station passenger service broadcasting equipment
　车站客运广播设备
station radio 车站电台
station repair track 站修线
station signal 车站信号
station site 站坪
station site baseline 站场基线
station standing time 在站停留时间
station throat area 车站咽喉区
station track of trains passing 通行列车的站线
station track 站线
station type 站型
stationary hydraulic lifting platform
　固定式液压升降台
stationary hydraulic yard ramp
　固定式液压登车桥
statistic analysis of geotechnical parameter
　岩土参数统计分析
statistic analysis of rock joints
　岩层节理统计分析
statistic cycle 统计周期
statistic parameter 统计参数
statistical inference method 统计推断方法
statistical testing method 统计检验法
statistics 统计,统计数字,统计资料
status of a project 工程状况
status quo map for water and soil erosion
　水土流失现状图

statute 法定,法规,法令,章程
statute law 成文法
statute of limitation（prescription）
  诉讼时效法规
statutory agent 法定代理人
statutory declaration 法定声明
statutory duty 法定义务
statutory instruments 法定文件
statutory representative 法定代表
statutory right 法定权利
statutory tax rate 法定税率
staurolite 十字石
stay cable 斜缆,斜索
steady arm 定位器
steady arm for curve line 软定位器
steady dynamic measurement 稳态动测法
steady flow 稳定流
steady flow pumping test 稳定流抽水试验
steady forced vibration method
  稳态强迫振动法
steady noise 稳态噪声
steady seepage 稳定渗流
steady vibration 稳态振动
steady-state heat transfer 稳态传热
steam boiler 蒸汽锅炉
steam curing 蒸汽养护
steam distribution header 分汽缸
steam ejector 蒸汽喷射器
steam electric plant 火力发电厂
steam hammer 汽锤
steam heating 蒸汽采暖
steam humidifier 蒸汽加湿器
steam injection system 蒸汽喷射系统
steam pile driver 蒸汽打桩机
steam pipe 蒸汽管
steam seasoning 蒸干法
steam trap 疏水器
steam-jet refrigeration cycle
  蒸汽喷射式制冷循环
steam-water heat exchanger 汽—水换热器
steel 钢材
steel anti-corrosion admixture 钢筋阻锈剂
steel arch 钢架
steel bar 钢筋
steel bar bender 钢筋弯曲机
steel bar cold-drawing machine
  钢筋冷拉机
steel bar cutter 钢筋切断机
steel bar protection property 护筋性
steel bar straightener 钢筋调直机

steel bar test 钢筋试验
steel bearing 钢支座
steel bender 弯钢筋机
steel box beam 钢箱梁
steel box girder 钢箱梁
steel bridge 钢桥
steel bridge maintenance 钢桥养护
steel cable-stayed bridge 钢斜拉桥
steel casing 钢套管
steel column base 钢柱脚
steel column component 钢柱分肢
steel erection 钢结构安装
steel fibre 钢纤维
steel fiber cement concrete
  钢纤维水泥混凝土
steel fiber reinforced concrete
  钢纤维混凝土
steel fiber reinforced shotcrete
  钢纤维喷射混凝土
steel lattice girder 钢格栅
steel mast 钢支柱(钢柱)
steel pile 钢桩
steel pipe passing through track 过轨钢管
steel pipe pile 钢管桩
steel plate 钢板
steel plate girder 钢板梁
steel pole 钢支柱(钢柱)
steel radiator 钢制散热器
steel rail polarity 钢轨极性
steel rib 钢架
steel rib installing machine 钢拱架安装器
steel sheet pile 钢板桩
steel sleeper 钢枕
steel strand 钢绞线
steel structure 钢结构
steel support 钢支架
steel tape 钢卷尺
steel tape odometer 钢尺量距
steel tapeline 钢挂尺
steel tendon 钢丝束
steel truss girder 钢桁梁
steel tubular structure 钢管结构
steel wire 钢丝
steel wire reverse bend test machine
  钢丝反复弯曲机
steep chute 急流槽
steep slope subgrade 陡坡路基
steep strata 陡立岩层
steep wall 陡壁
steering angle 转向角

steering rod 转向杆
step 措施,台阶
step cost 阶梯成本
step curve of interference current 干扰电流阶梯曲线
step fault 阶梯状断层
step in 介入权
step potential 跨步电势
step potential difference 跨步电位差
step voltage 跨步电压
steppe 草原
stepped collaborative freight section 阶梯式协作货位
stepped column 阶形柱
stepped slope 阶梯形坡
step-down substation 降压变电站
step-up substation 升压变电站
stereo pair 立体像对
stereographic projection 赤平极射投影,赤平投影
stereographic projection method 赤平投影法
stereometric camera 立体摄影机
stereoscopic model surveying 立体模型测量
stevensite 硅镁石
stick button 非自复式按钮
stick circuit 自闭电路,自保电路
stick requisition 自闭条件
stick to 坚持
sticky hook scaffold 挂扣式脚手板
stiff consistency mortar 干硬性砂浆
stiffened end of arch 护拱
stiffened plate 加劲板
stiffener 加劲杆,加劲肋
stiffening 加固
stiffness 刚度
stiffness of bending creep 弯曲蠕变劲度
stiff-plastic 硬塑
stiff-skeleton reinforced concrete 劲性骨架混凝土
still equipment 静置设备
stilling basin 消力池
stipends consideration money 补偿金
stipulated price contract 约定价格合同
stipulated sum 约定金额
stipulated sum contract 约定金额合同
stirrup 箍筋
stirrup reinforcement ratio 配箍率
stirrup spacing 箍筋间距
stitch wire 弹性吊索

stitch wire clamp 弹性吊索线夹
stitch wire support 弹性吊索支座
stitched catenary suspension 弹性链形悬挂
stock 存货,现货,储备,股票,库存,岩株,证券
stock capital 股份
stock exchange index 证券交易所指数
stock in hand 现有存货
stock ledger 存货分类账,股东分户账
stock loss fee 仓储损耗费
stock loss rate 仓储损耗费率
stock market 股票市场
stock pile 堆放,贮料堆,储存
stock pile area 堆料场
stock premium 股票溢价
stock rail 基本轨
stock requisition form 领货单,领料单
stock solution 贮备溶液
stock taking 库存盘点
stockbridge damper 防振锤
stockholder 股东
stockholder's equity 股东权益
stockout 存货短缺
stockout cost 缺货成本
stockpile 贮备,储存,堆料场
stone 石,石材
stone arch bridge 石拱桥
stone circle 石圈
stone curtain 石帘,石幔
stone cutting machine 切石机
stone driller 钻石机
stone field 石场
stone forest 石林
stone masonry structure 石砌体结构
stone mill 磨石机
stone nest 石窝
stone pot 石锅
stone ring 石环
stone sheet 石帘,石幔
stone stripes 石条
stone waterfall 石瀑布
stonework 砌石工程,石方工程
stone-block pavement 块石路面
stool device 大便器
stool groove 大便槽
stop 停止,休止
stop buffer 挡车器
stop clause 终止合同的条款
stop in advance of a signal 机外停车
stop pin 限位销
stop short 空档

stop sign 停车标
stop signal 停车信号
stop signal indication 信号关闭表示
stop valve 截止阀
stoppage 罢工,中止,罢工,停止,休止,中止
stoppage in transit 停止运货,中途停运权
stopping a train at a target point 定点停车
stopping device 停车器
stopping halfway 途停
storage 保管,照管
storage and maintenance
　采购保管和保养费
storage area 储存区
Storage Area Network(SAN)
　存储区域网络
storage area of track section 轨排存放区
storage battery 蓄电池,蓄电池组
storage battery car 电瓶车
storage bin 储料仓
storage capacity 存储能力
storage charge 保管费
storage fee 仓储费
storage model 存储模型
storage pressure 储存压力
storage quantity 存放数量
storage rate 保管费率
storage server 存储服务器
storage shear strength modulus
　储能剪切模量
storage tank 储水池
storage volume 储存量
store 储存
store house 货栈
stored value card 储值卡票
stored value ticket 储值卡票
storehouse 仓库
stores 备用品
stores on site 工地备用品
storm 暴风
storm sewer 雨水管
storm water pumping station 雨水泵站
stout 结实的
straddle forklift 插腿式叉车
straddle-type main track 外包式正线
straight bill of lading 记名提单,直接提单
straight joint 通缝
straight line 直线
straight line method of depreciation
　平均年限折旧法,直线折旧法
straight loan 无担保贷款

straight piece work system
　单纯计件工资制
straight route 直向进路
straight section length after the turnout
　岔后直线段长度
straight slope 直行坡
straight time 正常工作时间
straight track of turnout 道岔直股
straight triangle (also known as "extended triangle") 直伸三角形(又称"延伸三角形")
straight unit rate contract 纯单价合同
straight wall type low freight section
　直壁式低货位
straightener 调直机
straightening 调直
straightening machine 整直机
straightness 平顺性(接触线),平直度
straight-in and curve-out
　进直出弯,直进弯出
straight-line joint failure 通缝破坏
strain 应变
strain ageing 应变时效
strain clamp 耐张线夹
strain gauge 应变计,应变仪
strain gauge force sensor
　应变式测力传感器
strain hardening 应变硬化
strain insulator 耐张绝缘子
strain measurement 应变量测
strain measuring point 应变测点
strain method 应变法
strain of pile shaft 桩身应变
strain pole 耐张杆
strain rosette 应变花
strain softening 应变软化
strain space 应变空间
strainer 滤网
strain-controlled test 应变控制试验
strait 海峡
stranded wire 绞线
strategy 战略
stratification 层理
stratified air conditioning 分层空气调节
stratified pumping test 分层抽水试验
stratified structure 层状构造
stratigraphic age 地层时代
stratigraphic sequence 地层层序
stratigraphic structure 地层结构
stratigraphic unit 地层单元
stratum 地层

stratum boundary 地层分界线
stratum column 地层柱状图
stratum lithology 地层岩性
stratum observation point 地层观测点
stratum series 层系
straw barrier 柴草沙障
stray current protection 杂散电流保护,迷流保护
streak 条痕
streaked structure 带状构造,条带状构造
stream water 溪水
streamed data 流数据
street sprinkle water consumption 浇洒道路用水量
street tree 行道树
strength 强度
strength checking computation 强度验算
strength class of masonry block 砌块强度等级
strength class of mortar 砂浆强度等级
strength class of prestressed tendon 预应力筋强度等级
strength class of steel bar 普通钢筋强度等级
strength envelope 强度包线
strength grade 强度等级
strength grade of cement 水泥强度等级
strength grade of concrete 混凝土强度等级
strength grade of masonry 砌体强度等级
strength loss 强度损失
strength of mortar 胶砂强度
strength of source rocks 母岩强度
strength of structure juncture 结构结合处强度
strength retention rate 强力保持率
strength test 强度试验
strength tester 强度试验仪
strength value 强度值
strengthened storey 加强层
strengthening method by bonding carbon fiber 碳纤维加固
strengthening method by bonding steel plate 粘贴钢板加固法
strengthening method by changing structural system 改变结构体系加固法
strengthening method by external prestressing 体外预应力加固法
strengthening method by increasing cross section 增大截面加固法
strengthening method by pier/abutment widening 墩台拓宽加固法
strengthening method by reinforced concrete hoop or sheath 钢筋混凝土套箍或护套加固法
strengthening method by spread foundation 扩大基础加固法
strengthening method by supplementary foundation piles 增补基桩加固法
strengthening of bridge 桥梁加固
strengthening of steel girder 钢梁加固
strengthening of subgrade 基床加固
strengthening 加固
stress 应力
stress amplitude 应力幅
stress circle 应力圆
stress concentration 应力集中
stress distribution 应力分布
stress history 应力历史
stress level 应力水平
stress method 应力法
stress path 应力路径
stress range 应力幅
stress recovery method 应力恢复法
stress reduction zone 应力降低带
stress relaxation 应力松弛
stress relief method 应力解除法
stress space 应力空间
stress spade 应力铲
stress trajectory 应力迹线
stress wave 应力波
stress/corrosion-induced crack of steel girder 钢梁应力腐蚀裂纹
stress-controlled test 应力控制试验
stress-strain relationship 应力—应变关系
stretchability 延性
strict liability 严格责任
strict standard 严格标准
strike (断层)趋势,罢工,走向
strike a bargain 成交
strike an agreement 缔结协议
strike fault 走向断层
strike joint 走向节理
strike of rock formation 岩层走向
strike-slip 走滑
strikes riots and civil commotions (SRCC) 罢工险
stringer 纵梁
stringing device 放线装置
strip deformation 航线弯曲度
strip foundation 条形基础
strip load 条形荷载
strip topographic map 带状地形图

striped migmatite 条带状混合岩
stripe-shape concrete pavement 条形混凝土铺面
stripping 剥离表层土, 拆模, 清基
strip-tensile test 条带拉伸试验
stroboscopic effect 频闪效应
stroke 动程
stromatolite 叠层石
strong box 保险箱
strong breeze 强风
strong column and weak beam 强柱弱梁
strong corrosion 强腐蚀
strong currency 硬通货
strong frost heaving soil 强冻胀土
strong gale 烈风
strong node weak component 强节点弱构件
strong permeability 强透水性
strong shear capacity and weak bending capacity 强剪弱弯
strong water abundance zone 强富水区
strongly bound water 强结合水
strong-motion recorder 强震动记录器
storage server 存储服务器
structural plane of rock mass 岩体结构面
structural adhesive 结构胶粘剂
structural analysis 结构分析
structural bearing capacity of seismic resistance 结构抗震承载能力
structural body 结构体
structural casting 结构预制件
structural design 结构设计
structural design of sound barrier 声屏障结构设计
structural dynamic characteristics testing 结构动态特性测量
structural engineering 结构工程
structural failure 结构破坏
structural influence coefficient 结构影响系数
structural joint 结构缝
structural material 结构材料
structural model 结构模型
structural overturning moment resistance 结构抗倾覆力矩
structural performance test 结构性能检验
structural rail joint gap 构造轨缝
structural reinforcement 构造钢筋
structural requirements 构造要求
structural safety of building 房屋建筑结构安全
structural seismic performance 结构抗震性能
structural seismic performance design 结构抗震性能设计
structural seismic resistance reliability 结构抗震可靠性
structural slope 构造坡
structural speed 构造速度
structural steelwork 钢结构工程
structural stiffness 结构刚度
structural system 结构体系
structural type of rock mass 岩体结构类型
structural verification coefficient 结构校验系数
structural vibration control 结构振动控制
structural wall 结构墙
structural works 结构工程
structure 构造, 结构
structure above arch 拱上建筑
structure clearance 建筑限界
structure durability 结构耐久性
structure dynamic property 结构动力特性
structure for water storage and distribution 贮、配水构筑物
structure gauge 建筑限界
structure gauge of tunnel 隧道建筑限界
structure observation point 构造观测点
structure of rock mass 岩体构造
structure of subgrade 基床结构
structure plane 结构面
structure prefabrication 结构预制件
structure system transformation 结构体系转换
structure type 结构类型
strut 撑杆
stud 顶铁
stuffing and destuffing operation 拆装箱作业
stuffing and destuffing platform 拆装箱作业站台
stuffing and destuffing shed 拆装箱库
stuffing and destuffing yard 拆装箱场
styrene butadiene rubber (SBR) modified asphalt 丁苯橡胶改性沥青
sub drought 亚干旱
subangular 次棱角状
subangular boulder 块石土
subaqueous tunnel 水底隧道
sub-ballast 底砟(垫层)
sub-ballast compactor 道床底砟夯实机

sub-ballast consolidating machine 道床底砟夯实机
subchloride saline soil 亚氯盐渍土
subcontract 分包合同
subcontract package 分包合同包
subcontracting 分包
subcontractor 分包商
subdivisional works 分项工程
subgrade 基床
subgrade defect 地基缺陷
subgrade elevation 路基高程
subgrade in anti-wind corridor 防风走廊路基
subgrade in collapse and talus zone 崩塌及岩堆路基
subgrade in karst section 岩溶地段路基
subgrade in landslide section 滑坡地段路基
subgrade in mollisol region 软土区路基
subgrade in permafrost region 冻土区路基
subgrade in reservoir section 水库地段路基
subgrade in snow disaster region 雪害地区路基
subgrade in special conditions 特殊条件路基
subgrade in station and yard 站场路基
subgrade in talus section 岩堆地段路基
subgrade in wind-blown sand regions 风沙地区路基
subgrade noumenon 路基本体
subgrade of cutting 路堑基床
subgrade of embankment 路堤基床
subgrade of graded crushed stone 级配碎(砾)石基床
subgrade of special soil 特殊土路基
subgrade renovation of existing line 改建既有线路基
subgrade replacement with bridge 以桥代路
subgrade slope greening 路基边坡绿化
subgrade stability 路基稳定
subgrade widening 帮宽路基
subgrade with unfavorable geological conditions 地质不良路基
subgrade without cutting and filling 零断面路基
subgrade-bridge transition section 路基桥梁过渡段
subject 标题,主题
sublease 转租
sublet 转包
submarine bank slope 水下岸坡
submarine geomorphy 海地地貌
submersible drill 潜水钻机
submersible pump 潜水泵
submission 提交
submission for inspection 送检
submission of bid(tender) 投标
submit 提交
submortgage 分押,再抵押,转押
subnetwork connection protection(SNCP) 子网连接保护
subordinate debt 次要债务
subpermafrost water 永久冻土下位水
subquality product 不合格产品,次级品
subrogation right 代位求偿权
subrounded 圆棱状
subscription 捐款,预约金
subsequent activity 后续活动
subsequent event 后续事件
subsidence 沉降,沉陷
subsidence area 塌陷区
subsidence deformation 沉降变形
subsidence hole 陷落洞
subsidence pool 陷塘
subsidence zone 沉降带
subsidiary 附属机构
subsidiary account 辅助账户
subsidiary company 分公司
subsidiary ledger 明细分类账,明细账目
subsidiary loan agreement 附属贷款协议
subsidiary record 辅助记录
subsidiary works 附属工程
subsidize 资助
subsidy 补贴,补助金
subsistence allowance 生活补贴
subsoil 地基,地基土
subsoil bearing capacity 地基承载力
subsoil elevation 基底高程
subsoil settlement 地基沉降
substantial 基本的
substantial change 实质性更改
substantial clauses 实质性条款
substantial completion 基本竣工,基本完工,实质性竣工
substantial evidence 实质性证据
substantial modification 实质性修改
substantial provision 实质性规定
substantiate 证实
substantiation 证据
substantiation of claim 索赔证明
substantiator 证人
substantive law 实体法
substation 变电站

substitute 更换,替代,替代人
substitution 替换
substructure 地下结构,下部结构,轨下基础
subsurface erosion/piping 管涌潜蚀
subsurface flow 潜流水
subsurface runoff 地下径流
subtenant 转租人
subtense method with horizontal staff
　横基尺视差法
subtense method with vertical staff
　竖基尺视差法
subterranean stream 地下河
subtype 子类
subvolcanic rock 次火山岩
sub-borrower 转借人
sub-clause 子条款
sub-consultancy 咨询分包
sub-consultant 咨询分包人
sub-high type pavement 次高级路面
sub-humid 亚湿润
sub-project 子项目
sub-subcontracting 再次分包
sub-subtype 次子类
sub-supplier 分包供货商
sub-vail structure 轨下基础
success ratio of point-to-point (PP) short message service (SMS) 移动点对点短消息发送成功率
successful bidder (tenderer) 中标者
successive route 延续进路
successor 继承人
successor activity 后续活动
successor legitimus 合法继承人
suction pipe 吸水管
suction pipe for firefighting 消防吸水管
suction velocity at return air inlet
　回风口吸风速度
suction-type sewer scavenger 吸污车
sudden markdown method 突然降价法
suddenly applied load method 突加荷载法
sue 起诉
suffer delay 遭受延误
sufficiency of the contract amount
　合同金额的充分性
suffosion 潜蚀
suffuse degree 充盈率
suggestion 意见
suit 诉讼
suitor 起诉人
sulfate 硫酸盐
sulfate corrosion resistance 抗硫酸盐侵蚀

sulfate saline soil 硫酸盐渍土
sulfide 硫化物
sulfur determinator 定硫仪
sulfurous acid saline soil
　亚硫酸盐渍土
sulphate corrosion 硫酸盐侵蚀
sulphate resistance portland cement
　抗硫酸盐硅酸盐水泥
sulphur anchorage 硫黄锚固
sulphur content 硫含量
sulphur hexafluoride circuit-breaker
　SF_6 断路器
sum 金额,总和,总数
sum in words 大写金额
sum insured 保险额,投保金额
sum of money 金额
summarization 汇总
summary of bill of quantities
　工程量清单汇总表
summary of tender 投标报价汇总表
summary schedule 简要进度计划
summary sheet of comprehensive estimate
　综合估算汇总表
summary sheet of comprehensive pre-estimate
　综合预估算汇总表
summary sheet of equipment unit prices
　设备单价汇总表
summary sheet of total estimate
　总估算汇总表
summary sheet of total pre-estimate
　总预估算汇总表
summary sheets of goods
　货品说明综合表
summit talk 最高级别会谈
sump 截水坑
sundry 杂费,杂项,杂物
sundry expenses 杂项开支
sundry revenue 杂项收入
sunk 沉没
sunlight standard 日照标准
sunshade embankment 遮阳棚路基
super large station 特大型车站
super profit 超额利润
superelevation 超高
superelevation of outer rail 外轨超高
superelevation rate 超高顺坡率
superelevation runoff 超高顺坡
superelevation runoff rate 超高顺坡率
superelevation runoff rate on curve
　曲线超高递减顺坡率

superelevation time-varying rate 超高时变率
superheated steam 过热蒸汽
superimposed load 叠加荷载
superintendence 监督,指挥
superintendent 监督人,监工,指挥者,主管人
supernatant 上部清液
superplasticizer 高效减水剂
superposition 重叠
superposition wall 叠合墙
supersede 替代,优先
superstructure 上部结构
supervise 监督
supervising engineer 监理工程师
supervision 监督,监理
supervision document 监理文件
supervision fee of soil and water conservation
　水土保持监理费
supervision firm 监理单位
supervision of soil and water conservation
　水土保持监理
supervisor 监督人
supervisor staff 监督人
supervisory control and data acquisition system
　（SCADA）
　监控和数据采集系统,牵引供电远动系统
supervisory personnel 监管人员
super-large passenger train station
　特大型旅客车站
supplement 补充
supplemental bill 补充清单,追加账单
supplemental contract 补充合同
supplementary 补充的
supplementary agreement 补充协议
supplementary budget 追加预算
supplementary conditions 补充条件
supplementary costs 附加成本
supplementary financial statement
　补充财务报表
supplementary information 补充资料
supplementary quota 补充定额
supplementary terms of the contract
　附则,合同补充条款
supplementary wage 辅助工资
supplementary wages of workers
　生产工人辅助工资
supplier 供应商
supply 供应品,供应
supply bond 供货担保
supply channel 供应渠道
supply of equipment contract 设备供应合同
supply of equipment with erection contract
　设备供应和安装合同
supply of foodstuffs 食品供应
supply of personnel 职员的供应
supply only materials 只供材料
supply plan 供应方案
supply price 供货价格
support 支撑,赞助,支持,支架
support bar for weight 坠陀杆
support clamp for double messenger wires
　承力索双线支撑线夹
support district 保障区
support frame 支撑架
support insulator 支持绝缘子
support mechanism 支承机构
support personnel 辅助人员
support structures 支持结构
supporting assembly 支持装置
supporting details 具体证据,具体证明材料
supporting document 证明文件
supporting letter 证明函,支持函
supporting particulars 具体证明材料
supporting shell of cutter head
　刀盘支承壳体
supporting stiffness of track bed
　道床支承刚度
supporting structure 支护结构
supporting works 配套工程
suppose 假定
suprapermafrost water 永冻层上水
supreme court 最高法院
surcharge 附加费
surcharge preloading 堆载预压
surety 保证人,担保人
surety bond 保函,保证书,担保书,担保债券
surety commission 保证人佣金
surety company 担保公司
suretyship 担保人身份
surface ballast belt 面砟带
surface blasting 露天爆破
surface bubble 表面气泡
surface collapse 地面塌陷
surface crack 表面裂缝
surface drainage 表面排水
surface finish 表面装修
surface force 表面力
surface heat exchanger 表面式换热器
surface relief 地表形态
surface rolling measure 地表碾压措施
surface runoff 地表径流

surface slope 地面坡度
surface sweep washing 表面扫洗
surface treatment 表面处理
surface washing 表面冲洗
surface water 地表水
surface wave 面波
surface wave technique 表面波法
surfaces requiring reinstatement
　需要复原的表面
surface-underground contrast plan of well
　井上下对照图
surge 浪涌
surge arrester 避雷器
surge pressure 水锤压力
surge protection 浪涌保护
surge protective devices(SPD) 浪涌保护器
surplus 结余,顺差,盈余
surplus sensitivity 灵敏度余量
surplus superelevation 过超高
surrender 交还,退保
surrogate 代理
surrounding rock 围岩
surrounding rock classification 围岩分级
surrounding rock consolidation 围岩加固
surrounding rock deformation 围岩变形
surrounding rock pressure 围岩压力
surrounding rock with serious deformation risk
　大变形围岩
surroundings 周围
surtax 附加税
surveillance image 监控图像
survey adjustment 测量平差
survey and design fees 勘察设计费
survey clause 检验条款
survey control network 测量控制网
survey crew 勘测队
survey fee 勘察费
survey for land smoothing 平整土地测量
survey in reconnaissance and design stage
　勘测设计阶段测量
survey inside the tunnel 隧道内测量
survey maps 勘测图
survey marker 测量标志
survey of existing station and yard
　既有线站场测量
survey outside the tunnel 隧道外测量
survey party 测置队
survey peg 测量标桩
survey report 检验报告
survey station 测站

survey team 勘测队
surveying 测量学
surveying control network of railway precision engineering 铁路精密工程测量控制网
surveying for site selection 选址测量
surveying instrument 测量仪器
surveying picture 调绘相片
surveying stake 标杆
surveyor
　测量员,测置师,商检人,调查人,询问者,鉴定人
surveyor of customs 海关检验人员
surveyor of port 港口检验人员
surveyor of taxes 税务检查员
survey 测量,勘测,勘察
suspend 中止
suspend talks 中止谈判
suspended ceiling 吊顶
suspended ditch 吊沟
suspended load 悬移质
suspended matter 悬浮物
suspended span 吊孔(也称吊跨)
suspended spring 悬挂泉
suspended structure 悬挂结构
suspended water 包气带水
suspender 吊杆
suspense account 待清理账户,暂记账户
suspension 悬液,中止
suspension and termination by contractor
　承包商暂停和终止
suspension bridge 吊桥,悬索桥
suspension by contractor 承包商暂停
suspension cable 吊缆,悬索
suspension clamp 悬垂线夹
suspension coop 吊笼
suspension insulator 悬式绝缘子
suspension insulator with eye end cap
　耳环悬式绝缘子
suspension of contract 中止合同
suspension of disbursements 暂停拨款
suspension of payment 暂停付款
suspension of work 停工,暂时停工
suspension order 停工令
suspension pipe 悬吊管
suspension pole 直线杆
suspension pulley 悬吊滑轮
suspicious sound source equipment
　可疑声源设备
sustainability 可持续性
sustainability LEED (leadership in energy and environmental design) evaluation LEED 评估

sustainable development 可持续发展
swale 洼地
swamp 沼泽
swamp deposit 沼泽沉积
swamp facies 沼泽相
swap 互换,换汇,易货
swap credits 互惠信贷,相互赊欠
swap license 互换许可证
swapper 交易者
swash height of wave 波浪侵袭高
sway and skew of the pantograph 受电弓晃动
sway bracing 横联
sway force of train 列车摇摆力
sway of pantograph 受电弓摆动范围
Swedish circle method 瑞典圆弧法
sweep 旁弯
swelling 溶胀
swelling agent 膨胀剂
swelling and shrinkage potential 涨缩潜势
swelling capacity 膨胀量
swelling force 膨胀力
swelling potential 膨胀潜势
swelling pressure 膨胀压力
swelling pressure of rock 岩石膨胀压力
swelling pressure of rock and soil
　岩土膨胀压力
swelling ratio 膨胀率
swelling ratio under lateral restraint condition
　侧向约束膨胀率
swelling rock 膨胀岩
swelling soil 膨胀土
swelling soil subgrade 膨胀土路基
swelling test of rock 岩石膨胀性试验
swept envelope
　基本限界,建筑接近限界,建筑接近限界
swing angle of photo 相片旋角
swing bridge 平旋桥
swing nose crossing 可动心轨辙叉
swing shift 中班
swing shiftman 中班工人
swing table for cement mortar
　水泥胶砂振实台
swirl air outlet 旋流风口
switch 网络交换机,转辙器,道岔
switch and crossing 道岔
switch blade 尖轨
switch circuit controller
　开闭器,自动开闭器
switch closed up 道岔封锁
switch close-up 道岔密贴

switch closure 道岔密贴
switch closure detector 密贴检查器
switch control circuit 道岔控制电路
switch gap 转辙机表示缺口,道岔缺口
switch indication 道岔表示
switch indicator 道岔表示器
switch jumper 道岔跳线
switch lever 道岔握柄
switch lock out 道岔锁闭
switch locking 道岔锁闭
switch machine 转辙机
switch machine indicating gap
　转辙机表示缺口,道岔缺口
switch machine installation
　转辙机安装装置
switch manual release 道岔人工解锁
switch normal indication 道岔定位表示
switch rail 尖轨
switch resetting 道岔恢复
switch reverse indication 道岔反位表示
switch rod 道岔拉杆
switch sensitivity 开关灵敏度
switch starting 道岔启动
switch thrown under moving train
　道岔中途转换
switch trade 转手贸易
switch transition 道岔转换
switch with follow-up movement 带动道岔
switchable balise 有源应答器
switchboard 配电盘,开关面板
switchgear
　开关设备,组合电器,开关柜,接电装置
switching 交换
switching cycle 开关操作周期
switching device 转辙装置
switching groups feeding
　分场供电,分束供电,分场分束供电
switching hysteresis 开关滞后
switching lead 牵出线
switching overvoltage 操作过电压
switching post (SP) 开闭所
switching station 开闭所
switching time 动作时间,转换时间
switchless section 无岔区段
switchman's telephone 扳道电话
switchover measure 倒代措施
switchover time 倒换时间
switch-and-lock mechanism 转换锁闭器
switch-back curve locating 回头曲线测设
swivel cantilever 旋转腕臂

swivel with eye 旋转单耳
syenite 正长岩
sylvine 钾盐
symbolism 记号
symmetrical turnout 对称道岔
symphylium 胶合板
Synchronization Status Message(SSM)
　同步状态信息
synchronized operation and control system for distributed locomotives 机车同步操控系统
synchronous controller 同步控制器
synchronous digital hierarchy(SDH)
　同步数字体系
synchronous interface 同步接口
synchronous optical network 同步光纤网络
Synchronous Supply Unit(SSU)
　同步供给单元
Synchronous Transfer Mode(STM)
　同步传递模式
Synchronous Transport Module level n(STM-N)
　同步传送模块 n 级
synclinal valley 向斜谷
syncline 向斜
syndicated loan 联合贷款,辛迪加贷款,银团贷款
syneclise 台向斜
synthesis chart of pipelines 管道综合图
synthesis plan of pipelines 综合管线图
synthetic fibre 合成纤维
synthetic staple fiber chemical bonding nonwoven geotextile 短纤化学黏合非织造土工布
synthetic staple fiber knitted geotextile
　短纤维针织土工布
synthetic staple fiber needle-punched nonwoven geotextiles 短纤针刺非织造土工布
synthetic staple fiber nonwoven geotextile
　短纤非织造土工布
synthetic staple fiber thermal bonding nonwoven geotextile 短纤热黏非织造土工布
syphon 虹吸(管)
syphonage 虹吸(管)
system 系统,体系,制度
system acceptance 系统验收
system calibration method 系统标定法
system commissioning 系统联调
system data 系统数据
system document 体系文件
system engineering 系统工程
system function 系统功能
system height 结构高度
system management 系统管理
system monitoring 系统监控
system of inspection 检验制度
system optimization 系统优化
system software 系统软件
system testing 系统测试
system test 系统试验
system wiring 系统布线
systematic error 系统误差
systematic risks 系统风险
systematic rock bolt 系统锚杆
S-shaped structure S形构造

T

tabia with sandy gravel and broken brick 砂砾石、碎砖三合土
table 表格,同席人员
table of adjustment data 数据调整表,调整数据表
table of distribution 发文簿
tableflow 表流
tablet 路牌
tablet pouch 路牌携带器
tabular grain 扁平颗粒
tabular structure 板状构造
tache ovale 轨头核伤
tack welding 定位焊
tackifier 增黏剂
tack-free time 表干时间
TADS,TFDS,THDS,TPDS,TCDS 5T
tag 标签
tail of shunting yard 调车场尾部
tail sand store 尾沙库
tail sleeping test 尾端休眠测试
tailing hold 拦挡
tailing hold measures 拦挡措施
tailing pond 尾矿库
tailings dam 尾矿坝
tainter gate 弧形闸门
Taishanian age/stage 泰山期
take action 采取行动
take delivery 提货,接收到货
take inventory/stock 盘存
take legal action 起诉
take out insurance 办理保险
take over 接管,收货,兼并
take over for use 征用
take up 处理,付清
takeoff 估price
taker 接受人
take-and-pay agreement 提货即付款协议,货到付款协议
take-or-pay agreement 提货与否均需付款协议
take-or-pay contract 或取或付合同
taking over parts 分部工程的接收
taking over the works and sections 工程和单位工程的接收
taking-out and placing-in at designated places 定点取送
taking-over certificate 接收证书,移交证书,验收证书
talc 滑石
talik 融区
talk 会谈
taltalite 电气石
talus 岩堆
talus apron 坡积裙
talus bed 岩堆床
tamper 打夯机,击实机
tamping 捣固
tamping car 捣固车
tamping method 强夯法
tandem 汇接
tandem device 汇接设备
tandem mobile switching center(TMSC) 汇接移动交换中心
tandem shelf 汇接架
tangent 切线
tangent between curves 夹直线
tangent retarder 调车线始端减速器
tangential force components 切向分力
tangential frost-heave force 切向冻胀力
tangential overhead crossing 无交叉线岔
tangential ventilator 贯流式通风机
tangible assets 实物资产,有形资产
tank connecting device 罐体连接装置
tank delivery device 罐体输送装置
tank safety device 罐体安全装置
tank truck 液灌汽车
tank washing point 洗罐站
tank washing siding 洗罐线

tap 抽
tap changer 分接抽头
tap water 饮用水
tap water price 自来水价格
tape library 磁带库
tape measure 卷尺
tape zero observation 悬挂带零位观测
tapered tilting concrete mixer 锥形倾翻出料混凝土搅拌机
tapping 抽头
tapping voltage 分接电压
tar coated road 柏油路
tare 皮重
tare gross 除皮重量
tare weight (gross) 皮重
target advance 计划进度
target aiming control 打靶控制
target braking 目的制动
target braking location 目的制动位
target contract 目标合同
target contract with activity schedule 带有分项工程表的目标合同
target contract with bill of quantities 带有工程表的目标合同
target control 目标控制
target cost 目标成本
target cost contract 目标成本合同
target cost management 目标成本管理
target date 目标日期,预定日期
target distance 目标距离
target management 目标管理
target market 目标市场
target point 目标点
target price 目标价格
target profit 计划利润,目标利润
target reliability index 目标可靠度指标,目标可靠指标
target schedule 目标进度计划
target shooting with allowable possessive interval 允留天窗打靶
target speed 目标速度
target speed control 目的调速
target speed surveillance area 目标速度监视区
target value of travel time 旅行时间目标值
target year of design 方案设计水平年
target-distance control curve 目标—距离控制曲线
tariff 关税,关税率,海关税则,价目表
tariff agreement 关税协议

tariff barrier 关税壁垒
tariff ceiling 关税最高限额
tariff preference 关税优惠
tariff protection 关税保护
tariff quota 关税配额
tariff rate 关税率
tariff schedule 关税率表
tariff value 完税价值
task 任务
task master 工头,监工
taskwork 计件工作
total revenue 营业收入总额
tax 税,税收,征税
tax abatement 减税
tax accrued 应计税金,应征税款
tax amount 税额
tax assessor 估税人,估税员
tax avoidance 避税
tax base 计税基数,课税基础,征税依据
tax bearer 纳税人
tax burden 税收负担
tax clearance 清税
tax collector 收税员,税务员
tax court 税务法院
tax credit 抵税,税款减免
tax day 纳税日
tax dodging 逃税,漏税
tax due 应付税
tax evader 逃税人
tax evasion 逃税,漏税
tax exemption 课税豁免
tax exemption certification 免税证明
tax file number declaration form 纳税申报表
tax haven 低税地区,免税港
tax holiday 免税期
tax invoice 纳税发票
tax items 税目
tax law 税法
tax loophole 税法漏洞
tax make-up 补税
tax obligation 纳税义务
tax on income 所得税
tax on property 财产税
tax preference items (TPIS) 优惠税目
tax rate 税率
tax rebate 退税
tax reduction 减税
tax refund 退税
tax relief 减免税
tax return form 年度报税表

tax shelter　逃税手段,避税
tax surcharge　附加税
tax withholding certificate　预扣税款凭证
tax year　计税年度
taxability　纳税能力
taxable capacity　纳税能力
taxable goods　应纳税货物
taxable income　应纳税收入
taxable person　应纳税人
taxable profit　应纳税利润
taxable salary　应纳税工资
taxation　课税,税制,征税
taxation office　税务局
taxes　税金
taxitic structure　斑杂构造
taxpayer　纳税人
tax-free profit　免税利润
TBM diameter　全断面岩石掘进机直径
team　小组
team spirit　团队精神
team work　协作
technical　技术性的
technical analysis　技术分析
technical and economical indexes　技术经济指标
technical appraisal　技术性鉴定
technical assessment　技术性鉴定
technical assistance　技术援助
technical assistance credit　技术援助信贷
technical assistance fee　技术援助费
technical bid evaluation　技术标评审
technical characteristics　技术特征
technical consultancy firm　技术咨询公司
technical consultant　技术咨询顾问
technical data　技术数据,技术资料
technical degree verification　技术水平鉴定
technical evaluation　技术评价
technical feasibility　技术可行性
technical feature　技术特征,技术性能
technical instruction　技术交底
technical level appraisal　技术水平鉴定
technical literature　技术资料
technical manual　技术手册
technical materials　技术资料
technical measures　技术措施
technical mission　技术代表团
technical norms　技术标准
technical office　技术室
technical operation process at station　车站技术作业过程
technical parameter　技术参数
technical performance　技术性能
technical proposal　技术建议书
technical regulations　技术规范
technical report　技术报告
technical responsibility　技术责任
technical review　技术评价
technical review and approval　技术审查与批准
technical scheme　技术方案,技术方案
technical scrutiny　技术审核
technical services contract　技术服务合同
technical servicing　技术整备
technical servicing yard　技术整备场
technical solution　技术方案
technical specifications　技术规范
technical standard　技术标准
technical support　技术支持
technical terms　专有名词
technical total loss　推定全损
technical transformation　技术转让
technician　技师,修理工
technology　工艺
technology assessment　技术评价
technology import　技术引进
technology inspection　工艺检验
technology secret　技术秘密
technology transfer fee　技术转让费
technology transfer　技术转让
tectonic breccia　构造角砾岩
tectonic earthquake　构造地震
tectonic stress　构造应力
tectonic stress field　构造应力场
tectonic system　构造体系
tectonic zone　构造带
telegraph　电报
telegraph communication　电报通信
telegraph exchange　电报交换机
telegraph terminal　电报终端
telegraphic money order　电汇汇款单
telegraphic transfer (T/T)　电汇
teleindication　遥信
telemetering　遥测
telephone at level crossing　道口电话
telephone blocking　电话闭塞
telephone booking system　电话订票系统
telephone conference circuit　电话会议电路
telephone conference equipment　电话会议设备
telephone set　电话机
telephone switch　电话交换

telephone weighted noise voltage
　电话衡重杂音电压
teleregulation　遥调
television logging　电视测井
television signal field strength
　电视信号场强
telex　电传
tele-reply　电复
tellurian　地球仪
telluric electromagnetic sounding
　大地电磁测深
temp　临时工
temperature　温度
temperature action　温度作用
temperature coefficient of resistance
　电阻温度系数
temperature cracking　温度裂缝
temperature detector　温感
temperature difference　温差
temperature difference between inside and outside
　里表温差
temperature drop ratio　降温速率
temperature effect modification
　温度影响修正
temperature excursion　温漂
temperature field　温度场
temperature gradient　温度梯度
temperature load　温度荷载
temperature measuring point　温度测点
temperature moment　温差弯矩
temperature rise　温度升高
temperature rise of winding　绕组温升
temperature sensing fire detector
　感温火灾探测器
temperature sensitivity　感温性
temperature stress　温度应力
temperature variation　温度变化
temperature variation influence
　温度变化的影响
temporary　短时制
temporary account　临时性账户
temporary advance　临时预付款,短期垫款
temporary bridge　便桥
temporary bridge for construction　施工便桥
temporary buildings　临时建筑物
temporary buildings and structures
　临时建筑物、构筑物
temporary centralized power generation
　临时集中发电
temporary column　临时柱

temporary communication　临时通信
temporary communication line
　临时通信线路
temporary construction and equipment of station and yard　临时站场建筑设备
temporary drainage　临时排水
temporary export　临时出口
temporary facilities　临时设施
temporary ferry crossing　临时渡口
temporary hardness　暂时硬度
temporary high-pressure fire system
　临时高压消防系统
temporary import　临时进口
temporary internal combustion power station
　临时内燃集中发电站
temporary investment　短期投资
temporary land　临时用地
temporary layoff　临时解雇
temporary line　便线
temporary load　临时荷载
temporary loan　短期贷款,临时贷款
temporary management line　临管线
temporary mobile subscriber identity(TMSI)
　临时移动用户识别码
temporary payment　暂付款项
temporary power line　临时电力线路
temporary power supply　临时供电
temporary railway　临时便线
temporary receipt　临时收据
temporary rest position　待班台位
temporary road　运输便道
temporary road for construction　施工便道
temporary shoring　临时支撑
temporary signal　临时信号
temporary speed restriction(TSR)　临时限速
temporary speed restriction server(TSRS)
　临时限速服务器
temporary strutting　临时支撑
temporary support　临时支撑
temporary truck road　汽车运输便道
temporary water supply trunk pipeline
　临时给水干管
temporary water supply　临时给水,临时供水
temporary wharf　临时码头
temporary works　临时工程
tenancy　租借权,租期
tenancy at will　不定期租赁,意愿租赁
tenant　承租人,租赁人
tendency of exchange rate　汇率走势
tender　投标,投标书

tender award 授标
tender bond 投标担保
tender clarification meeting 招标澄清会议
tender committee 招标委员会
tender drawing 招标图纸
tender estimate 投标估算
tender evaluation 评标
tender evidence 出示证据
tender form 投标书格式
tender guarantee 投标保函,投标保证书
tender list 投标人名单
tender opening 开标
tender price 标底,投标价
tender procedures 投标手续
tender submission 递交投标书
tender sum 投标金额
tender timetable 招标时间表
tenderer 投标人,投标者
tenderers 批准的投标人名单
tenderer's conference 投标人会议
tenderer's query 投标人质疑
tendering conditions 招标条件
tendering notice 招标通知
tendering party 投标方
tendering publicity 招标公告
tendering 投标
tenor 票据期限
tensile adhesive strength 拉伸黏结强度
tensile creep 拉伸蠕变
tensile modulus 拉伸模量
tensile property 拉伸性能
tensile rate 拉伸速率
tensile region 受拉区
tensile retainer 定伸保持器
tensile rigidity of members 构件抗拉刚度
tensile rigidity of section 截面拉伸刚度
tensile strength 抗拉强度
tensile test 拉伸试验,张拉试验
tensile testing machine 拉力试验机
tension clamp 耐张线夹
tension crack 张裂缝
tension fault 张断层
tension fissure 张裂隙
tension increment 张力增量
tension insulator 耐张绝缘子
tension joint 张节理
tension length 锚段长度
tension pole 耐张杆
tension pulley 补偿滑轮
tension releasing pole 泄力杆

tensioning 张力补偿
tensioning at both ends 两端张拉
tensioning at one end 单端张拉
tensioning device
 补偿装置,张力补偿装置
tensioning lockpiece 张拉锁件
tensioning section 锚段
tensioning spring
 弹簧补偿器,弹簧补偿装置
tension-shear fault 张扭性断层
tentative plan 初步计划
tentative standard 暂行标准
tenure of use 使用年限
term 期限
term bill 定期汇票,期票
term credit 定期信贷,定期信用证
term deposit 定期存款
term loan 定期贷款
term loan agreement 定期贷款协议
term of contract 合同有效期
term of lease 租期
term of loan 贷款期限,贷款条件
term of service 保修期,使用期
term of the DAAB
 争议避免裁决委员会的期限
term of validity 有效期
terminal 车站,端子
terminal accounts 终结账户
terminal anchor clamp for contact wire
 接触线终端锚固线夹
terminal anchor clamp for messenger wire
 承力索终端锚固线夹
terminal arbitration 最终仲裁
terminal board 端子排
terminal box 端子箱
terminal framework 终端架构
terminal moraine 终碛
terminal moraine levee 终碛堤
terminal moraine ridge 终碛垄
terminal of monitoring and maintenance
 监测维护终端
terminal of monitoring service
 监测业务终端
terminal pole 终端杆
terminal station 端站
terminal support 终端杆塔
terminal value 终值
terminal with one station 一站枢纽
terminal work station 终端工作站
terminals of a modular block 组匣端子

terminals of a unit block　组合端子
terminals of layer 0 of relay racks　零层端子
terminate a contract　解除合同,终止合同,解约
terminate an agreement　解约
termination　终结
termination at (for) employer's convenience
　业主自便终止
termination by agreement　协议终止合同
termination by contractor　承包商终止
termination by employer　雇主终止
termination by frustration
　因合同落空而终止
termination by notice　凭事先通知终止合同
termination for contractor's default
　承包商过错终止
termination for employer's convenience
　雇主决定终止
termination grant　解雇费
termination notice　终止通知
termination of contract　合同解除
termination of the proceedings　终止诉讼
termination pay　解雇费
terminology　术语
terminus　界标
terms　条件,条款
terms and conditions　条款与条件
terms of appointment　委任条款
terms of credit　信用证条件
terms of delivery　交货条件
terms of employment　待遇,雇用条件
terms of insurance　保险条件
terms of office　任期
terms of payment　付款条件,支付条件,支付条款
terms of redemption　分期偿还条件
terms of reference (TOR)
　授权范围,工作大纲
terms of sale　销售条件
terms of service　使用条件,维修条件
terms of shipment　装运条件
terrace　阶地
terrain condition　地形条件
terrain sampling　地形采样
terrestrial photogrammetric coordinate system
　地面摄影测量坐标系
terrestrial photogrammetry　地面摄影测量
terrain　地形
territorial limitation　地区限制
territory　地域范围
Tertiary　第三纪
Tertiary period　第三纪

Tertiary system　第三系
Terzaghi's consolidation theory
　太沙基固结理论
test　测试,试验,化验
test and commissioning workshop　调试库
test blocks　试块
test case　测试案例
test certificate　检验证书
test check　抽查
test clock　测钟
test data　检测数据
test detection　试验检测
test detection institution　试验检测机构
test error　试验误差
test expense　试验费
test fire hydrants　试验消火栓
test for dynamic parameter　动力特性试验
test for suitability　合格性检验
test for switching midway in receiving-departure
　track　到发线出岔测试
test frequency　检测频次
test hole　测试孔,试验孔
test inspection　试验检查
test items　试验项目
test load　试验荷载
test load efficiency　试验荷载效率
test loop　测试环线
test manual　试验手册
test method　检测方法,试验方法
test of borehole deformation
　钻孔变形计法试验
test of california bearing ratio　承载比试验
test of departure route and section state interlocking relation
　发车进路与区间状态联锁关系测试
test of fill material　填料试验
test of switch with follow up movement
　带动道岔测试
test on completion of design-build
　设计—建造竣工检验
test on completion　竣工检验,竣工试验
test pier　试验墩
test pile　试桩
test pit　试坑
test pitting　坑探
test pressure　试验压力
test record　试验记录
test report　检验报告,试验报告
test result　检验结果,试验结果
test room　试验间

test run 试车,试运转
test sample 试样
test section 试验段
test sequence 测试序列
test specimen 试验样品
test tower 试验塔
test value 测试值
tester for permeability coefficient
　透气系数测定仪
tester for specific surface area of cement
　水泥比表面积测定仪
testimonial 鉴定书,证明书
testimony 证言
testing 检测
testing and evaluation 检测与评价
testing and evaluation of bridge
　桥梁的检测与评价
testing by the contractor 承包商试验
testing certificate 检验证书
testing ground 试验现场
testing group 试验组
testing load grade 试验荷载等级
testing parameter 试验参数
testing procedure 试验步骤
testing scaffold 测试支架
tests after completion 竣工后验收
tests on completion 竣工验收
tetragonal system 正方晶系
text 文本,正本
text to speech (TtS)
　从文本到语言(也称语音合成)
thaw collapse 融沉,融陷
thaw collapsibility 融陷性
thaw slumping 热融滑塌
thaw subsidence coefficient 融化下沉系数
thawing and compression test of frozen soil
　冻土融化压缩试验
thawing deformation 融冻变形
thawing index 融化指数
thawing landslide 热融滑坍
thawing settlement 融化沉降量
thawing settlement of earthworks 路基融沉
thaw-compressibility coefficient
　融化压缩系数
thaw-settlement coefficient 融沉系数
the amount of machine shift between major repair
　大修间隔台班
the bearing stratum of pile bottom
　桩底持力层
the contract guarantee 合同担保
the currency specified in the contract
　合同规定的货币
the DAAB's decision
　争议避免裁决委员会的决定
the discharge capacity of prefabricated band-shaped drains 排水带通水量
the formation of decomposition method
　阵型分解法
the gap between the wing rail and the point
　有害空间
the minimum breaking load 最小拉断荷载
the parties' obligations after the reference
　提交争议后双方的义务
the parties's undertaking and indemnity
　当事人的承诺和赔偿
the range of responsibility for soil erosion control
　水土流失防治责任范围
the range of responsibility map for soil erosion control 水土流失防治责任范围图
the support tube sealing device
　支撑管式止水器
the whole process the whole network 全程全网
theft insurance 盗窃保险
thematic map 专题地图
theodolite 经纬仪
theodolite mapping 经纬仪测图
theodolite subtense technique
　经纬仪视距法
theodolite surveying and mapping
　经纬仪测绘
theodolite triangle elevation survey
　经纬仪三角高程测量
theodolite used with measuring rope
　经纬仪绳尺法
theoretical analysis value 理论分析值
theoretical lead of turnout 道岔理论导程
theoretical length of turnout 道岔理论长度
theoretical mix proportion 理论配合比
theoretical price 理论价格
theory of elasticity 弹性理论
thermal analysis 热分析
thermal anemometer 热风速仪
thermal collector 集热器
thermal conductivity coefficient 导热系数
thermal diffusivity 热扩散系数
thermal expansion valve 热力膨胀阀
thermal insulation 保温
thermal insulation layer 保温层
thermal insulation layer of earthworks
　路基保温层

thermal insulation material
　保温材料,绝热材料
thermal insulation material　隔热材料
thermal insulation window　保温窗
thermal insulation works　保温工程
thermal karst　热力岩溶
thermal load　热负荷
thermal pipe subgrade　热棒路基
thermal power plant　火力发电厂,热电厂
thermal relay　热力继电器
thermal resistance　热阻
thermal runaway　热崩溃
thermal spectrum analysis　热谱分析
thermal stability　热稳定性
thermal stability current　热稳定电流
thermal storage water tank　蓄热水箱
thermal stress　热应力
thermal-infrared scanning　热红外扫描
thermistor thermometer　热敏电阻温度计
thermit welding　铝热焊
thermocontact　热接触
thermoelectric couple　热电偶
thermogravimetric analysis　热重分析
thermoinduction method　热感应法
thermokarst lake　热融湖塘
thermometer　温度计
thermophilic digestion　高温消化
thermoplastic elastomer　热塑性弹性体
thermoplastic gasket　热塑性垫圈
thermoplastic polyolefin (TPO) waterproof sheet
　热塑性聚烯烃(TPO)防水卷材
thermoplastic rubber　热塑性橡胶
thermostatic water bath　恒温水槽
theoretical point of frog　辙叉心轨理论尖端
thick layer　厚层
thick layer landslide　厚层滑坡
thick loose deposit　厚层松散堆积体
thickness gauge　厚度计
thickness of concrete cover
　钢筋保护层厚度,混凝土保护层厚度
thickness of section　截面厚度
thickness of subgrade　基床厚度
thickness of track bed　道床厚度
thick-wall open mouth soil sampler
　厚壁敞口取土器
thimble　心形环
thin film oven test　薄膜烘箱试验
thin layer　薄层
things mortgaged　抵押物
thin-wall sampler　薄壁取土器

third class assessment　三级评价
third class discharge standard
　三级排放标准
third departure section　第三离去区段
third party　第三方
third party charges　第三方收费
third party claim　第三方索赔
third party contract　第三方合同
third party insurance
　第三方保险,第三者责任险
third party liability　第三方责任
third party motor insurance
　机动车第三者责任险
third party test and inspection body
　第三方试验检测机构
third rail　接触轨(第三轨)
third window loan　第三类贷款业务
third-country currency　第三国货币
this side up　此端向上
thixotropy　触变性
tholeiite　拉斑玄武岩
thread ring gage　螺纹环规
thread twisting method　搓条法
threaded connection　螺纹连接
threaded coupler　丝扣
three hinged arch bridge　三铰拱桥
three phase diagram　三相图
three-aspect automatic blocking
　三显示自动闭塞
three-dimensional network　三维网
three-dimensional stereoscopic scenes
　三维立体景观
three-dimensional traverse survey
　三维导线测量
three-hinged arch　三铰拱
three-member DAAB
　3人组成的争议避免裁决委员会
three-phase (YN,d11) winding connection
　三相(YN,d11)结线
three-phase four-wire system　三相四线制
three-phase multi-stage section current protection
　三相多段式电流保护
three-phase synchronism　三相同期性
three-phase traction transformer
　三相牵引变压器
three-phase Vv connection　三相Vv结线
three-phase Vv connection traction transformer
　三相Vv结线牵引变压器
three-phase Vx winding connection
　三相Vx结线

three-phase/two-phase balanced connection 三相/二相平衡结线
three-phase/two-phase balanced traction transformer 三相/二相平衡牵引变压器
three-point method 三点法
three-point supporting 三点支承
three-shift work 三班工作制
three-way symmetrical turnout 三开对称道岔
three-way valve 三通阀
threshold 界限,最低值
threshold alarm 阈值报警
threshold value 门限值
threshold voltage 限制电压
thrift account 储蓄账户
throat area 咽喉区
through air waybill 空运直达提单
through bill of lading 联运提单
through bolt 通透螺栓
through bridge 下承式桥
through button circuit 通过按钮电路
through current/through fault current 穿越电流
through earthing wire 贯通地线
through freight 联运运费,直达货运
through route 通过进路
through signal 通过信号
through train 直达列车
through-type passenger station 通过式客运站
throughout risk 全过程风险
through-type freight station 通过式货运站
through-put contract 使用与否均须付款合同
throw of switch rail 尖轨动程
throw rod 动作杆
throwing support 抛撑
thrust 冲断层
thrust system 推进机构
thrust-type landslide 推移式滑坡
thunder surge invasion 雷电浪涌侵入
thunderstorm day 雷暴日
tick 记号,赊购
ticket agency 代售点
ticket checking display 进站检票屏
ticket counter display 售票窗口屏
ticket machine for excess fare 补票机
ticket office 售票处
ticket printer 制票机
ticket sales 售票
ticket transaction 售票交易
ticket vending machine 自动售票机
ticketing 票务
ticketing system 客票系统
tidal river 潮汐河流
tidal zone 潮汐区
tie bar 系杆,拉结钢筋
tie in clause 搭卖条款
tie member 系杆
tie point 连接点
tie replacing machine 轨枕抽换机
tie respacer 方枕器
tie respacing 方正轨枕
tied aid 限制性援助
tied arch 系杆拱
tied framework 绑扎骨架
tied loan 限制性贷款,附带条件贷款
tie-arch 拉杆拱
tie-plate connection 拉板连接
tight money policy 紧缩银根政策
tight timetable operation/tight schedule operation 紧密运行
tightening torque 拧紧扭矩
tightness test 密封试验,严密性试验
tile 铺地砖,瓦
tiling 贴面砖,铺面砖
till money 备用现金
tilt 倾斜
tilt calculator 倾斜计算装置
tilt error 倾斜误差
tilt observation 倾斜观测
tilt occurrence 倾斜产状
tilt survey 倾斜测量
tilted tree 马刀树
timber 木材,木料
timber pile 木桩
timber structure 木结构
timber/plywood formwork 木模板
time bill 定期汇票
time card 计时卡,工时记录卡,考勤卡
time charter 定期租船
time cost 工时成本,时间成本
time delay 时间延误,延时
time deposit 定期存款
time difference 时差
time distribution 工时分配
Time Division Multiplex(TDM) 时分复用
time draft 定期汇票
time factor 时间因数
time for completion of design-build 设计—建造竣工时间

time for completion　竣工时间,完工日期
time for payment　支付时间
time for tests　检验时间
time history analysis method　时程分析法
time keeping　工时记录
time limit　时限
time limit for acceptance　承诺期限
time loan　定期贷款
time of concentration　地面集水时间
time of day(ToD)　日时间
time of discharge　放电时间
time of duration　持续时间
time of shipment　装运期,装运时间
time of validity of a claim　索赔时限
time payment　定期付款
time rate　计时工资率
time reference signal　时间基准信号
time report　工时报告单
time schedule　进度表
time sheet　考勤表
time similarity　时间相似
time value of capital　资金时间价值
time value of money　货币时间价值
time wage　计时工资
timed observation method　计时观察法
timeliness　及时性
timely delivery　及时交货
time-delay effect　延时效应
time-dependent curve　时间曲线
time-domain signal　时域信号
time-limited debt (obligation)　有时效限制的债务
time-scaled network diagram　时标网络图
time-varying rate of cant deficiency　欠超高时变率
timing water level　测时水位
tinned plate　白铁皮
tip　小费,捐赠,福利
tip lorry　自卸卡车
tip resistance　桩端阻力
tipper　斗车
tipping bucket rainfall sensor　翻斗式雨量传感器
tippler　翻车机
tire-mounted crane　轮胎起重机
title　所有权,专有技术权,头衔
title block　图标
title deed　地契,土地证
title of account　账户名称
title of survey area　测区名称

title to property　财产所有权
title transfer　产权转移
titration　滴定,滴定法
to accept offer　接受报盘
to be repaired box　待修箱
to break the contract　毁约
toe wall　脚墙
toilet　卫生间
token　记号
tolerance　公差,溢短装限度,容许误差
tolerance clause　宽容条款
tolerance of horizontal angles discrepancy　水平角较差限差
toll　通行费
toll road　收费道路
tolling agreement　使用与否均须付款合同
tomb　墓穴
tonalite　英闪岩
tone　行情
tongue rail　尖轨
tonnage　吨位(费),运输吨数
tonnage duty(tax)　吨位税
tonnage rating　牵引定数
tonnage-time fees　吨次费
tool　工具,用具
tool rail　工具轨
tools and apparatus　设备、工器具购置费
tools and equipment　机具设备
toothed(ratchet) wheel tension assembly　补偿棘轮
top ballast　面砟
top cantilever tube　平腕臂
top cap　顶帽
top executive　执行高层
top management　高管层
top of rail (TOR)　轨顶
top plate　顶板
top soil　表层土
top surface of sheet　卷材上表面
top wall　上盘
top width of track bed　道床顶面宽度
topaz　黄玉
topographic database　地形数据库
topographic map　地形图
topographic map content elements　地形图要素
topographic map database　地形图数据库
topographic map of bridge site　桥位地形图
topographic map of construction site　工点地形图

topographic map revision 地形图修测
topographic map scale 地形图比例尺
topographic map symbols 地形图图式
topographic mapping 地形测图
topographic map-subdivision 地形图分幅
topographic original map 地形原图
topographic point 地形点
topographic survey 地形测量
topographical rectification 地形校正
topography investigation 地形地貌调查
topological structure 拓扑结构
toppling collapse 崩塌
toppling deformation 倾倒变形
topsoil 表土
topsoil slip 溜坍
torch signal 火炬信号
torch-applied asphalt sheet 热熔防水卷材
torpedo 响墩信号
torque 扭矩
torque force 扭力
torque wrench 扭矩扳手
torshear type high strength bolt 扭剪式高强度螺栓
torsion fault 扭断层
torsional rigidity of members 构件抗扭刚度
torsional rigidity of section 截面扭转刚度
torsional shear test 扭剪试验
tort 不法行为,违法行为,侵权行为
tortfeasor 侵权行为人,违法行为者
total acidity 总酸度
total alkali content 总碱量
total amount 总额
total amount of budgetary estimate 概算总额
total asses 资产总额
total available service-life machine shift 耐用总台班
total budget 总预算
total budgetary estimate（budget） 总概(预)算
total construction period 建设总工期,施工总工期
total cost 总成本,总费用
total energy consumption 能耗汇总
total estimate 总估算
total float 总时差
total float time 总时差
total flooding extinguishing system 全淹没灭火系统
total harmonic current（THC） 总谐波电流
total harmonic distortion（THD） 总谐波畸变率
total harmonic voltage（THV） 总谐波电压
total heat 全热
total heat exchange efficiency 全热交换效率
total height of structure 结构总高度
total income 总收入
total interchange 全立交
total investment amount 投资总额
total investment for construction project 建设项目总投资
total length closing error of traverse 导线全长闭合差
total length of back water curve 壅水曲线全长
total length of bridge 桥梁全长
total length of structure 结构总长度
total length of turnout 道岔全长
total liabilities 负债总额
total loss 全损
total mean square error of elevation difference 高差全中误差
total mineralization 总矿化度
total mineralization of groundwater 地下水总矿化度
total nitrogen（TN） 总氮
total nitrogen content in soil 土壤全氮含量
total phosphorus（TP） 总磷
total power 总功率
total pressure 全压
total pre-estimate 总预估算
total price 总价
total price of the package 成套设备总价
total quality control（TQC） 全面质量管理
total quality management 全面质量管理
total quantities of works 工程总量
total salary amount 工资总额
total station instruments 全站仪
total stress 总应力
total stress analysis 总应力分析
total stress method 总应力法
total supporting force 总支撑力
total thrust 总推力
total volume of water gushing into foundation pit 基坑总涌水量
total water content of frozen soil 冻土总含水率
total weight 合重
total width of structure 结构总宽度

touch potential 接触电势
touch screen dispatching console
触摸屏调度台
touch voltage 接触电压
toughness 韧度
tow truck 拖车
tower crane 塔式起重机
tower foundation 铁塔基础
toxic 有毒的
trace to the source 溯源
traceability of magnitude 量值溯源
tracer 示踪剂
tracer method 示踪法
tracer test 示踪试验
trachyte 粗面岩
tracing 溯源
track 轨道,线路
track alignment 线路走向
track auxiliary component 轨道附属设备
track bed 道床
track bed leakage resistance
轨道道床漏泄电阻
track carrying capacity 轨道承载力
track category 线路类别
track centerline 线路中心线
track circuit 轨道电路
track circuit adjustment at once
轨道电路一次调整
track circuit length 轨道电路长度
track circuit reader 轨道电路读取器
track circuit section 轨道电路区段
track condition 轨道状态
track condition test 轨道条件测试
track control network (CPⅢ)
轨道控制网(CPⅢ)
track datum mark 轨道基准点
track deformation 轨道变形
track design 轨道设计
track dynamics 轨道动力学
track engineering 轨道工程
track excavator 履带式挖掘机
track failure 轨道失效
track filter 轨道滤波器
track for locomotive to depot 机车入段线
track for locomotive to station 机车出段线
track formation 路基面
track formation center 路基面中心
track formation shape 路基面形状
track formation widening for settlement
路基面沉降加宽
track framework 轨排
track galvanic effect 轨道生电现象
track gauge 轨距
track gauge block 轨距块
track geometry spectrum 轨道谱
track geometry tolerances
轨道几何尺寸容许公差
track geometry 轨道几何形位
track group layout 线束性布置
track information receiving antenna
轨道信息接收天线
track inspection 轨道检测
track inspection car 轨道检查车,轨检车
track inspection device 轨道检测设备
track inspection trolley 轨道检查小车
track insulation 轨道绝缘
track irregularity 轨道不平顺
track jack 起道机
track laying and girder erecting base 铺架基地
track laying and girder erecting works
铺架工程
track laying length 铺轨长度
track laying using one set of track laying machinery 单向铺轨
track laying using two sets of track laying machinery 双向铺轨
track laying with replacement method
换铺法(铺轨)
track lead 钢轨引接线
track level 轨道水平尺
track level station building 线平式站房
track lifting 起道,抬道
track lifting amount 抬道量
track lifting tool 起道机
track lining 拨道
track lining machine 拨道机
track lowering 落道,落道量
track maintenance 线路维修
track maintenance and repair
轨道养护维修
track maintenance standard 轨道养护标准
track material storage area 轨料存放区
track mechanics 轨道力学
track obstruction indicator
线路遮断表示器
track occupancy indication 线路占用表示
track occupation check 轨道占用检查
track occupied 轨道占用
track overhaul 线路大修
track panel 轨排

track panel adjustment 轨排调整
track panel assembling 轨排组装
track panel assembling machine 轨排组装机
track panel base 轨排基地
track panel laying machine with cantilever 悬臂式铺轨排机
track panel transport car 轨排运送车
track parameter 轨道参数
track parameter test 线路参数测试
track plan 线路平面
track quality index (TQI) 轨道质量指数
track reactor 轨道电抗器
track residual deformation 轨道残余变形
track return system 轨回流系统
track rheostat 轨道变阻器
track section 轨道区段,线路区段
track sectioning cabin (TSC) 分区所
track sectioning post (TSP) 分区所
track shifting bars 撬棍
track side dynamic detection system for train riding quality 车辆运行品质轨边动态检测系统
track side image detection system for freight train fault 货车故障轨边图像检测系统
track sign 线路标志
track slab 轨道板
track slab deflection 轨道板偏移
track slab delivery 轨道板运输
track slab floating 轨道板上浮
track slab laying 轨道板铺设
track spacing 线间距
track speed restriction 线路速度限制
track spike 道钉
track stake 线路标桩
track storage effect 轨道电路蓄电现象
track strength 轨道强度
track structure 轨道结构
track survey reference stake 线路基桩
track system 轨道系统
track test 上道试验
track transformer box 轨道变压器箱
track treadle 轨道接触器
track unoccupied 轨道空闲
track works 轨道工程
tracked loader 履带式装载机
trackless transportation 无轨运输
trackside electronic unit 轨旁电子单元
trackside equipment for testing onboard equipment 车载地面检测设备
trackside signal 地面信号
track-bound crane 轨道起重机
track-laying machine 铺轨机
track-laying train 铺轨列车
track-mounted transportation 有轨运输
track-related works 线路有关工程
track-side rail lubricator 地面钢轨涂油器
track-type tractor 履带式拖拉机
track-wheel girder lifter 轮轨式提梁机
traction current 牵引电流
traction energy consumption 牵引能耗
traction network 牵引网
traction power supply 供电工程
traction power supply calculation 供电计算
traction power supply system 牵引供电系统
traction power supply system simulation 牵引供电系统仿真
traction return current 牵引回流
traction return current transverse link 牵引回流横向连接
traction routing 牵引交路
traction substation (TS,TSS) 牵引变电所
traction time 牵引时分
traction transformer 牵引变压器
traction-type landslide 牵引式滑坡
tractive effort 牵引力
tractive force 牵引力
tractive force of train 列车牵引力
tractive mass 牵引质量
tractive tonnage 牵引质量
tractor 牵引车,拖拉机
tradable emissions permit 许可证交易
tradable permits 许可证交易
trade 交易,商务
trade agreement 贸易协定
trade association 同业工会
trade barrier 贸易壁垒
trade bill 商业汇票
trade bill of quantities 工种工程量表
trade contractor 专业承包商,专业工种承包商
trade custom 贸易惯例
trade cycle 经济周期
trade deficit 贸易逆差,贸易入超,逆差
trade directories 商贸行名录
trade discount 贸易折扣,商业折扣
trade fair 商品交易会
trade mark 商标
trade mark infringement 侵犯商标权
trade mission 贸易代表团
trade negotiation 贸易谈判
trade off 权衡,物物交换,易货贸易

trade pact 贸易协定
trade practice 贸易惯例,行业惯例
trade price 批发价
trade relation 贸易关系
trade representative 商务代表
trade restriction 贸易限制
trade subcontractor 专业分包商
trade surplus 贸易顺差
trade tax 交易税
trade terms 贸易术语,贸易条款
trade union 工会
trade union funds 工会经费
trade usage 贸易惯例
trademark counterfeiting/infringement
　冒牌商标
trader 交易者
tradesman 零售商
trade-off 协调
traffic 交通,运输
traffic accident 交通事故
traffic artery 交通干线
traffic capacity 交通运输能力
traffic culvert 交通涵洞
traffic generator 流量发生器
traffic interference 交通干扰
traffic lights 交通信号灯
traffic management 运输管理
traffic plan 运输计划
traffic safety 交通安全
traffic services 运输服务
traffic signing 交通标志
traffic volume 话务量,交通量,运输量
traffic volume in busy hours 忙时话务量
traffic warning board 交通警示标志
traffic warning sign 交通警示标记
trailable 挤脱
trailed switch protection 挤岔保护
trailer 挂车,拖车
trailer flat 平板拖车
trailing of a switch 挤岔
trailing single turnout 顺向单开道岔
train 训练
train acoustic detection system(TADS)
　铁路车辆滚动轴承故障轨旁声学诊断系统
train approach notice 列车接近一次通知
train approaching warning device
　列车接近报警器
train coach position display 编组屏
train coach running safety diagnosis system(TCDS)
　客车运行安全监控系统

Train Control Center(TCC)
　列控中心,列车运行控制中心
train control system
　列车控制系统,列车运行控制系统
train crossing 列车交会
train data 列车数据
train derailment 列车出轨,列车脱线
train diagram 运行图
train diagram plotter 运行图描绘仪
train dispatching and commanding system(TDCS)
　列车调度指挥系统
train dispatching section 调度区段
train dispatching telephone 列车调度电话
train dynamic load 列车动荷载
train for temporarily management line
　临管线火车
train freight on lines in service
　营业线火车运价
train freight rate 火车运价
train freight rate of temporarily management line
　临管线火车运价
train headway 列车间隔
train hotbox detection system(THDS)
　车辆轴温智能探测系统
train inspection area 列检作业区
train integrity 列车完整性
train interface unit(TIU) 列车接口单元
train interval 列车间隔
train live load 列车活载
train load 列车荷载
train meeting 列车交会
train minimum/maximum safe rear end position
　列车最小/最大安全后端位置
train movement recording equipment
　行车记录设备
train number 车次
train number indication 车次表示
train of freight failures detection system(TFDS)
　货车故障轨旁图像检测系统
train operation command mode
　行车指挥方式
train operation control center
　列车运行控制(列控)中心
train operation control mode
　列车运行控制方式
train operation disturbance 行车干扰
train operation monitoring and record device
　列车运行监控装置
train operation monitoring and recording device
　(LKJ) 列车运行监控记录装置

train operation office 运转室
train operation organization 行车组织
train operation regulation plan
  列车运行调整计划
train overtaking 列车越行
train pairs 列车对数
train passing 列车通过,列车交会
train performance detection system(TPDS)
  铁路车辆运行品质轨旁动态监测系统
train position indication 列车位置表示
train radio dispatching communication
  列车无线调度通信
train refuge 列车待避
train route 列车进路
train routing 列车交路
train service number 列车服务号
train set 车组
train signal 行车信号机,列车信号机
train speed monitoring device
  列车速度检查仪
train staff 路签
train straight through speed
  列车直向通过速度
train trip 列车冒进防护
train washing plant 洗车机
train wind pressure 列车风压力
trainee 受训人
training 培训
training course 培训班
training evaluation 培训评估
training expense of production staff
  生产职工培训费
training program 培训计划
trains running on lines in service
  营业线火车
train-borne signaling 车载信号
train-set 车底
train-set parking yard 车底停留场
trajectory 航线
tramegger 兆欧表
transaction 交易
transaction practice 交易习惯
transaction tax 交易税
transaction value 成交价值,交易价格
transborder rate 过境运价
transceiver 收发器
transcoding and rate adaption unit(TRAU)
  码变换和速率适配单元
transducer 换能器
transfer 过户,汇兑,让与,转交,转让

transfer coefficient of impulse voltage
  冲击电压转移系数
transfer container 中转集装箱
transfer length of prestress
  预应力传递长度
transfer member 转换结构构件
transfer of contractual interest
  合同权益转让
transfer of funds 汇寄,汇款
transfer of lighting indication 灯光转移
transfer of risks 转移风险
transfer of skill 技术转让
transfer of technology 技术转让
transfer operation 中转作业
transfer pipette 移液管
transfer price 结转价格,转移价格
transfer remarshaling traffic flow
  中转改编车流
transfer risks 转嫁风险
transfer storey 转换层
transfer track 转换轨
transfer track for depot 出入段线
transfer traffic flow 中转车流
transfer voucher 转账凭证
transferable letter of credit 可转让信用证
transferable risks 可转移风险
transferable/negotiable security 可转让证券
transference 转让
transformer 变压器
transformer at track circuit receiving end
  轨道受电变压器
transformer reactance 变压器电抗
transformer substation 变电所
transformer with no-load tap changer
  无载调压变压器
transformer with on-load tap changer(OLTC)
  有载调压变压器
transgression sequence 海侵层序
tranship 转运
transhipment 转运
transhipment bill of lading
  转船提单,转运提单
transhipment surcharge 转船附加费
transient design state 短暂设计状况
transient electromagnetic method
  瞬变电磁法
transient exciting method 瞬态激振法
transient load 瞬时荷载
transient maximum current of feeding section
  供电臂瞬时最大电流

transient pressure 瞬变压力
transient surface wave method 瞬态面波法
transient vibration 瞬态振动
transit 通行,中转
transit country 过境国
transit duty (dues) 转口税
transit formalities 过境手续
transit letter of credit 转口信用证
transit plotting method 经纬仪投点法
transit tax 过境税,通行税
transit trade 转口贸易
transit train 直通列车
transit visa 过境签证
transit yard 通过车场
transition area 过渡区
transition curve 缓和曲线
transition curve locating 缓和曲线测设
transition facies 过渡相
transition mast of overlap 转换(支)柱
transition scheme 过渡方案
transition section 过渡段
transition section works 过渡段工程
transition slab at bridge end 桥头搭板
transition span 过渡孔
transition span length 转换跨距
transition zone 缓冲区
transitional disc cutter 过渡滚刀
transitional grade section 缓和坡段
transitional works 过渡工程
translation gain or loss 外汇换算损益
translation risk 外币折算风险
translation-torsion coupling
 平动—扭转耦联
transmission 传输
Transmission Control Protocol (TCP)
 传输控制协议
transmission interference period
 传输干扰时间
transmission level 传输电平
transmission line 传输线路,输电线路
transmission loss (TL) 传声损失
transmission network 传输网
transmission protocol 传输协议
transmission quality 传输质量
transmission system 传输系统
transmittal 往来函件
transmitting and receiving voice regulation
 送受话声音调整
transmitting level 发信电平
transmitting optical power 发送光功率

transnational company 跨国公司
transnational corporation 跨国公司
transnational enterprise (TNE) 跨国企业
transparency 透明度
transparent curtain wall 透明幕墙
transparent sound insulation material
 透明隔声材料
transponder information receiving antenna
 应答器信息接收天线
transport 运输,运送
transport and working train of welded long rails
 长钢轨运输作业列车
transport by air 空运
transport car of welded long rails
 焊接长钢轨运送车
transportable fire extinguisher
 推车式灭火器
transportation 交通,交通运输,搬运
transportation capability 运输能力
transportation carrier's claim
 运输承运人的索赔
transportation carrier 承运人,运输工具
transportation cost 运输成本
transportation documents 货运单证
transportation equipment 运输设备
transportation insurance 运输保险
transportation means 交通工具
transportation planning 运输计划
transportation service 货运
transposition 互换
transshipment 驳载,转运
transship 转运
transversal projection 横轴投影
transverse arrangement 横列配置
transverse arrangement of passenger car servicing
 post 客车整备所横列布置
transverse auxiliary arches 拱波
transverse axis 横轴
transverse circulation 横向环流
transverse diagonal brace 横向斜撑
transverse distribution 横向分布
transverse distribution bar 横向分布钢筋
transverse distribution of load
 荷载横向分布
transverse district station 横列式区段站
transverse drainage facility 横向排水设施
transverse dune 横向沙丘
transverse electrical connection 横向电连接
transverse fatigue crack in rail head
 轨头核伤

transverse fissure in rail head 轨头核伤
transverse floorbeam 横梁
transverse floorbeam used for hoisting operation 起重横梁
transverse gradient 横向坡度
transverse harbor station for goods transfer 货物交接横列式港湾站
transverse horizontal bracing 横向水平支撑
transverse industrial station for goods transfer 货物交接横列式工业站
transverse layout of a through industrial (or harbour) station with two yards in one stage on main line 正线通过一级二场横列式
transverse link 横向连接
transverse marshalling station 横列式编组站
transverse section 断面净空
transverse shaft 横轴
transverse slope 横坡
transverse tensile test 接头拉伸试验
transverse type harbour station built jointly in both terminals 双方车站联设横列式港湾站
transverse type harbour station built separately in both terminals 双方车站分设横列式港湾站
transverse type industrial station built jointly in both terminals 双方车站联设横列式工业站
transverse type industrial station built separately in both terminals 双方车站分设横列式工业站
transverse valley 横谷
transverse wave 横波
transverse wave velocity of rock 岩块的横波速度
transverse web prestressed reinforced concrete pole 横腹杆预应力钢筋混凝土支柱
trans-section continuously welded rail track 跨区间无缝线路
trap 存水弯
trapezoidal method 梯形法
trapezoidal roof truss 梯形屋架
trapezoidal tearing strength 梯形撕裂强度
trapezoidal weir 梯形堰
travel and transportation expenses 差旅交通费
travel expense 差旅费
traveler's letter of credit 旅行信用证
traveling formwork 活动模板
traveling gantry crane 移动式龙门起重机
traveling hoist 移动式卷扬机
traveller's check 旅行支票

traverse angle 导线折角
traverse control network 导线控制网
traverse network 导线网
traverse node 导线节点
traverse of location survey 定测导线
traverse point 导线点
traverse side 导线边
traversing 导线测量
tray 托盘
tray sealing device 托盘止水器
tread 踏面
tread flat 扁疤
treasurer 财务主管,司库
treasury 国库
treasury bill 国库券
treasury board 财政委员会
treating 加工
treatment 处理,待遇
treatment of earthworks defect 路基病害整治
treatment percentage of disturbed land 扰动土地整治率
treaty 条约,协议
treaty port 通商口岸
tree age 树龄
tremie concrete 导管灌注混凝土
tremolite 透闪石
trench 地沟,管道,海沟,深槽,挖沟
trench digger 挖沟机
trench excavation 开槽施工
trench exploration 槽探
trench hoe 反铲挖沟机
trench, groove, pipe and hole 沟、槽、管和洞
trencher 挖沟机
trenching for inspection 验槽
trenching machine 挖沟机
trend 走向
trestle 栈桥
trestle-type unloading line 栈桥式卸车线
trial 试用
trial construction 试验性施工
trial mixture 试配
trial mixture strength 试配强度
trial operation 试运行
trial run 试运行
trial run test 拉通测试,运行试验
triangle junction terminal 三角形枢纽
triangle method 三角形法
triangular closure error 三角形角度闭合差
triangular network survey 三角形网测量
triangular pyramid space grids 三角锥体网架

triangular roof truss 三角形屋架
triangular weir 三角堰
triangulateration 边角测量
triangulateration network 边角网
triangulation 三角测量
triangulation chain 三角锁
triangulation control network 三角控制网
triangulation network 三角网
triangulation point 三角点
Triassic period 三叠纪
Triassic system 三叠系
triaxial apparatus 三轴仪
triaxial axial stress 三轴轴向应力
triaxial compression 三轴压缩
triaxial compression strength test of rock
  岩石三轴压缩强度试验
triaxial compression test (triaxial shear test)
  三轴压缩试验(三轴剪切试验)
triaxial compressive strength
  三轴抗压强度
triaxial extension test 三轴伸长试验
triaxial lateral stress 三轴侧向应力
triaxial shear test 三轴剪切试验
triaxial unconsolidated and undrained shear test
  三轴不固结不排水剪试验
triaxial undrained shear test
  三轴不排水剪切试验
tribunal 法官席,法庭,仲裁庭
tribunal hearing 庭审
tributary 支流
tributary area 从属面积
triclinic system 三斜晶系
trigeminy well 三联井
trigonal system 三方晶系
trigonometric level traverse-leveling
  三角高程导线测量
trigonometric leveling 三角高程测量
trigonometric leveling by electromagnetic ranging
  电磁波测距三角高程测量
trilateration 三边测量
trilateration network 三边网
trip 跳闸
tripod 三脚架
tripping 况扣,侧倾,跳停
tri-directional strain gauge 三叉式应变计
troctolite 橄长岩
trolley 手推车
trolley-type suspension 简单悬挂
trolley-type suspension with bridle wire
  弹性简单悬挂

tropical atmospheric pressure 热带气压
tropical cyclone 热带气旋
tropical storm 热带风暴
troposphere delay 对流层延迟
trough iron 槽钢
trough moraine 槽碛
trough moraine ridge 槽碛垄
Trough-type beam 槽形梁
Trough-type girder 槽形梁
trowel 抹子
truck 货车
truck crane 汽车起重机
truck freight price 汽车运价
truck freight price rate 汽车运价率
truck trailer 卡车拖车
trucking equipment 卡车装运设备
true dip 真倾角
true error 真误差
true meridian 真子午线
true triaxial test 真三轴试验
truncate 截断
truncated conical revetment 锥体护坡
truncated conical slope 锥坡
truncated portal 斜切式洞门
truncation 截断
truncature 截断
trunk drain 排水干管
Trunk Gateway(TG) 中继网关
trunk line 干线
trunk long-distance communication network
  干线长途通信网
trunk peak bandwidth 中继链路带宽峰值
trunk pipeline for water supply 给水干管路
trunk road 主干道
trunk twisted pair cable 主干对绞电缆
trunking diagram 中继方式图
truss 桁架
truss arch 桁架拱
truss crossbeam 桁架横梁
truss joint 节点
trussed arch bridge 桁架拱桥
trussed bridge 桁架桥
trust 信任,信托
trust bank 信托银行
trust company 信托公司
trust deed 委托书
trust fund 信托基金
trust property 信托财产
trust receipt 信托收据
trusted execution protection 可信执行保护

trustee 受委托人,托管人
trustor 信托人
tsunami 海啸
tube boot sealing device 管靴止水器
tube cap 管帽
tube column foundation 管柱基础
tube in tube structure 筒中筒结构
tube settler 斜管沉淀池
tube structure 筒体结构
tubewell yield 管井出水量
tube-in-tube condenser 套管式冷凝器
tubular diesel pile hammer 筒式柴油打桩锤
tubular scaffold 管子脚手架
tubular steel pole 钢管柱
tuff 凝灰岩
tuffaceous texture 凝灰结构
tungsten-carbide drilling 硬质合金钻进
tuning and matching unit 调谐匹配单元
tunnel 隧道
tunnel air 地道风
tunnel boring machine(TBM) 隧道掘进机
tunnel boring machine(TBM) method 掘进机(TBM)法
tunnel clearance 隧道净空
tunnel convergence 隧道净空变化
tunnel drill 隧道凿岩机
tunnel excavation 隧道开挖
tunnel face 掌子面
tunnel fire prevention measure 隧道防火措施
tunnel floor upheaval 隧底隆起
tunnel form 隧道模
tunnel group 隧道群
tunnel in unfavorable geological conditions 不良地质隧道
tunnel in water-rich karst region 富水岩溶隧道
tunnel lighting 隧道照明
tunnel lining 隧道衬砌
tunnel portal 隧道门
tunnel post 隧道标
tunnel subgrade 隧道路基
tunnel support 隧道支护
tunnel survey 隧道测量
tunnel ventilation 隧道通风
tunnelling 隧道工程
tunnelling advancement 隧道掘进
tunnelling by shield machine 盾构法
tunnelling operation 隧道作业
tunnelling plant 隧道掘进设备
turbidity 浊度
turbidness 浊度
turbine 水轮机,涡轮机
turbine flowmeter 涡轮流量计
turbine-like structure 涡轮状构造
turbo-fan 涡轮式通风机
turbo-generator 涡轮发电机
turbulent flow 湍流,紊流
turbulivity 湍流度
turf transplanting 草块移植
turfing 铺草皮
turn on time 开机时间
turnaround track 回转线,折返线,折返环线
turnback halfway 中途折回
turning equipment 转向设备
turning jack 转车盘
turning lane for vehicles 回车道
turnkey contract 交钥匙合同
turnkey project 交钥匙项目
turnout 道岔
turnout ballast cleaning machine 道岔清筛机
turnout center 道岔中心
turnout closure detector 道岔密贴检查装置
turnout geometry inspection 道岔几何状态检测
turnout grinding car 道岔打磨车
turnout installation device 道岔安装装置
turnout laying and replacement crew 道岔铺换机组
turnout laying and replacement device 道岔铺换设备
turnout locking indication 道岔锁闭表示
turnout mast 道岔柱
turnout number 道岔号数
turnout passing speed 过岔速度
turnout setting and locking test 道岔转换及锁闭测试
turnout sleeper 岔枕
turnout sleeper components 岔枕组件
turnout stabilizer 道岔稳定车
turnout structure 道岔结构
turnout survey 道岔测量
turnout through speed 过岔速度
turnover 成交量,周转额,营业额
turnover frequency 周转次数
turnover rate 周转率
turnover tax 流通税
turn-on voltage 导通电压
twenty-foot equivalent unit(TEU) 换算箱
twin cantilever bracket 双腕臂底座
twist 扭曲,三角坑

twisted steel 螺纹钢筋
two hinged arch bridge 两铰拱桥
two platforms mingling with one track layout
　两台夹一线布置
two platforms mingling with two tracks layout
　两台夹两线布置
two section of zero-sequence current protection
　两段零序电流保护
two-aspect automatic blocking
　二显示自动闭塞
two-envelope bid system
　双层信封投标方式,双封套投标方法
two-hinged arch 双铰拱
two-ization amendment 两化改正
two-medium photogrammetry 双介质摄影测量
two-shifts 两班制
two-side supported plate 两边支承板
two-sided ramp 双面斜道
two-stage tendering 两阶段招标
two-step loan 两步贷款
two-way concrete slab 混凝土双向板
two-way reinforcement 双向配筋
two-way route 双进路
two-way slab 双向板
two-way valve 两通阀
two-wheeled (single-wheeled) car 双(单)轮车
two-wire reception level 二线接收电平
tying contract 搭卖合同
type A other liquid storage tank
　甲类其他液体储罐
type inspection report 型式检验报告
type inspection specimen 型式检验试件
type of locomotive 机车类型
type of rock mass 岩体类型
type of site environment 场地环境类型
type of soil erosion and water loss
　水土流失类型
type of track 轨道类型
type of traction 牵引种类
type of turnout 道岔类型
type test 型式检验,型式试验
typhoon 台风
typical construction site 典型工点
typical design drawing for soil and water conser-
　vation measures 水土保持措施典型设计图
typical development and construction projects
　典型开发建设项目
typified formwork 定型模板
typo 笔误,书写错误
typographical error 笔误,书写错误
T-beam T形梁
T-beam bridge T形梁桥
T-connector T形线夹
T-girder T形梁
T-girder bridge T形梁桥
T-girder fabrication and storage yard
　T形梁制存梁场
T-shape bolt T形螺栓
T-shaped cross-section T形截面
T-shaped joint T形接头
T-shaped rigid frame bridge T形刚构桥
T-type hinged cantilever bracket
　T形旋转腕臂底座
T-type steady arm T形定位器
T-type steady arm for curve line with bridle wire
　T形软定位器

U

undivided profit　未分配利润
ultimate axial compressive strength
　轴心抗压极限强度
ultimate axial tensile strength
　轴心抗拉极限强度
ultimate bearing capacity
　极限承载力,极限承载能力
ultimate beneficiary　最终受益人
ultimate compressive strain of concrete
　混凝土极限压应变
ultimate compressive strength　极限抗压强度
ultimate deformation　极限变形
ultimate elongation　极限伸长率
ultimate facts　基本事实
ultimate liability　根本责任,主要责任
ultimate limit states　承载能力极限状态
ultimate loss　最终损失
ultimate relative displacement　极限相对位移
ultimate shaft resistance　极限侧阻力
ultimate strain　极限应变
ultimate tensile strength　极限抗拉强度
ultimate tip resistance　极限端阻力
ultimate vertical bearing capacity of a single pile
　单桩竖向极限承载力
ultimateness　结论
ultimatum　最后通牒
ultra low energy building　超低能耗建筑
ultra vires act　越权行为
ultrabasic alkaline rock　超基性碱性岩
ultrabasic rock　超基性岩
ultrafiltration　超滤法
ultrafiltration membrane　超滤膜
ultrared hotbox detection system
　红外线轴温探测系统
ultrasonic blocking method　超声阻滞法
ultrasonic imaging well logging
　超声成像测井
ultrasonic method　超声波法
ultrasonic wind speed and direction sensor
　超声波式风速风向传感器
ultraviolet（UV）　紫外线
ultraviolet disinfection　紫外线消毒法
ultraviolet dose　紫外线剂量
ultraviolet resistance　抗紫外线能力
umbrella agreement　一揽子协议,总协议
umbrella article　总括条款
umbrella cover　伞括保险
umbrella liability insurance　伞式责任保险
umbrella programme　综合性计划,总体计划
umpire　仲裁员,公断人
unabsorbed cost　待摊成本
unamortized cost　未摊销成本
unattended repeater station　无人增音站
unauthorized　未经授权的
unavoidable　不可避免的
unavoidable cost　固定成本
unbalance loading factor　偏载系数
unbalanced　不平衡(报价)
unbalanced acceleration　未被平衡加速度
unbalanced bidding
　不平衡报价,不平衡投标
unbalanced bidding method　不平衡报价法
unbalanced coefficient of locomotive to shed
　进车不平衡系数
unbalanced insulation resistance
　不平衡绝缘电阻
unbalanced resistance　不平衡电阻
unbalanced traction current　不平衡牵引电流
unbalanced transmission line　非平衡传输线
unbinding contract　无约束力的合同
unblocked　不封锁
unbonded pre-stressed concrete structure
　无黏结预应力混凝土结构
unbound water　非结合水
unbraced frame　无支撑纯框架
uncashed check　未兑现支票

unclean bill of lading 不洁提单
uncollectible account 呆账，坏账
uncollectible check 无法兑付的支票
uncompensated suspension 无补偿悬挂
unconditional acceptance 无条件承兑
unconditional bank guarantee
　无条件银行保函，无条件银行保证书
unconditional emergency stop message
　无条件紧急停车消息
unconditional guarantee 无条件保函
unconditional letter of credit
　无条件信用证
unconfined compressive strength
　无侧限抗压强度
unconfined compressive strength test
　无侧限抗压强度试验
unconfirmed letter of credit 不保兑信用证
unconformable contact 不整合接触
unconsolidated and undrained shear
　不固结不排水剪
unconsolidated and undrained shear test
　不固结不排水剪试验
unconsolidated-undrained triaxial test
　未固结不排水三轴试验
uncontrollable cost 不可控制成本
uncontrollable risks 不可控风险
uncover 剥露
uncrossed check 未划线支票
under bowl up 下碗扣
under contract 依据合同
underconsolidated soil 欠固结土
underconsolidation 欠固结
underdepreciation 折旧不足
underdrain 地下排水管
underestimate 低估
underflow 底流
underground cable 地下电缆
underground cable terminal box 地中电缆盒
underground cavity 地下洞室
underground diaphragm wall 地下连续墙
underground geophysical prospecting
　地下物探
underground geophysical prospecting instrument
　地下物探仪
underground installation 地下埋设物
underground pipeline 地下管线
underground pipeline survey
　地下管线测量
underground pipelines detection 地下管线探测
underground river 暗河

underground runoff depth method
　地下径流深度法
underground runoff modulus 地下径流模数
underground station 地下车站
underground surveying 地下测量
underground track 地下线
underground tunnel plan 坑道平面图
underground water source 地下水源
underground works 地下工程
underlease 转借
underlying document 原始凭证
underlying mortgage 优先抵押权
underlying stratum 下卧层
underpass 高架桥下公路
underpass tunnel 地道
underpayment 少付
underpinning technique 托换技术
underproof 不合格的
undersize sieve analysis 细筛分析
understatement 少报
understock 存货不足
undertake 承担
undertaking 许诺
undervaluation 低估，计价过低
undervalue 低估
undervoltage alarm 欠压告警
underwater blasting 水下爆破
underwater concreting 水下浇筑混凝土
underwater cross-section survey
　水下横断面测量
underwater operation 水下作业
underwater profile survey 水下纵断面测量
underwater protection works 水下防护工程
underwater sand embankment 水下砂堤
underwater topographic survey 水下地形测量
underwater topography 水下地形
underwater tunnel 水底隧道，水下隧道
underwater weighing method 水中称量法
underwriter 保险人，保险商，担保人
underwriting 承保
under-clearance height of bridge
　桥下净空高度
under-excavation 欠挖
under-floor wheel lathe 机车不落轮车床
under-floor wheel lathe workshop 不落轮镟轮库
under-reinforced 配筋不足
under-track works
　线下（站前工程），站前工程
undistributed profit 未分配利润
undisturbed sample 原状样，原状样品

undisturbed soil sampler 原状取土器,不扰动土样,原状土样
undrained consolidated shear 固结不排水剪
undrained shear strength 不排水抗剪强度
undue 未到期的
undue debt 未到期债务
undue loss 不当损失
undue note 未到期票据
undulate diagonal bedding 波状斜层理
undulating dune zone 波状沙丘带
undulating sandy land 波状沙地
unearned increment 自然增值
unearned profit 非营业利润
unemployment 失业
unemployment benefit 失业救济金
unemployment insurance 失业保险
unemployment insurance expense 失业保险费
unemployment rate 失业率
unequal settlement 不均匀沉陷
unequal terms 不平等条款
uneven fracture 参差状断口
uneven settlement 不均匀沉降
unevenness 不均匀度
unexpected 意外的
unexpected benefits 意外利益
unexpected condition 未预见的条件
unexpected expenses 意外开支
unexpected idling 意外闲置
unexpired cost 未耗成本
unfair 不公平
unfair competition 不公平竞争,不正当竞争
unfavorable condition for car rolling 溜车不利条件
unfavorable geological phenomena 不良地质现象
unfavorable geological process 不良地质作用
unfavorable geology 不良地质
unfavorable section 不利地段
unfavourable conditions 不利条件
unfavourable geological section 地质不良地段
unfilled order 未发货订单
unfinished work 未完成的工作
unforeseeable 不可预见
unforeseeable event 不可预见的事件
unforeseeable physical conditions 不可预见的物质条件
unforeseeable physical obstructions 不可预见的外部障碍
unforeseen demand 未预见用水量
unforeseen expenses 意外开支
unforeseen grounds conditions 未能预见的地质条件
unforeseen site conditions 未能预见的现场条件
unforeseen work 不可预见的工作
unfrozen water content 未冻含水率
unfulfilled obligation 未尽义务
unguided part in frog 有害空间
uniaxial compressive strength 单轴抗压强度
uniaxial geogrid 单向土工格栅
unidirectional combined type marshalling station 单向混合式编组站
unidirectional layout 单向图形
unidirectional longitudinal type marshalling station 单向纵列式编组站
unidirectional marshalling station 单向编组站
unidirectional stretching 单向拉伸
unidirectional thrust-force pier 单向推力墩
unified glare rating 统一眩光值
uniform beam 等截面梁
uniform customs 统一惯例
uniform distribution 均匀分布
uniform invoice 统一发票
uniform load 均布荷载
uniform temperature 均匀温度
uniformity of illumination 照度均匀度
uniformization 归一化
unilateral agreement 单务协议
unilateral contract 单方合约
unilateral denunciation 单方废约,单方宣告无效
uninsurable risk 不可保风险
Uninterruptible Power Supply(UPS) 不间断电源
uninterruptible power supply 不间断供电
union 结合
union link 结合杆
uniplanar tubular joint 平面管节点
unique identifier 唯一标识符
unique method 独特方法
unit 单位,单元,部件
unit block assembly rack 组合架
unit block rack 组合柜
unit capacity estimate method 单位生产能力估算法
unit cost 单位成本
unit energy head of braking 单位制动能高
unit labour cost 单位人工成本
unit method of depreciation 计件折旧法

unit of account　记账单位
unit of measurement　计量单位
unit office　单元式办公室
unit price analysis of freight and miscellaneous charges　运杂费单价分析
unit price　单价
unit price contract　单价合同
unit price EXW　出厂单价
unit price of base period　基期单价
unit price of comprehensive expense of labors of cost making period　编制期综合工费单价
unit price of labor（also known as "unit salary"）人工单价（也称"工资单价"）
unit price of loading and unloading　装卸单价
unit price of machine shift　机械台班单价
unit price of materials　材料单价
unit price sheet of supplementary materials　补充材料单价表
unit prices of loading and unloading for train or truck　火车、汽车装卸单价
unit pricing　计件定价
unit profit　单位利润
unit project　单体工程
unit rail link　单元轨节
unit slab　轨道单元板
unit value assessment　单值评价量
unit weight　单位权,单重
unit weight of soil mass　土体重度
unit weight value　重度值
unit windage resistance　单位风阻力
unit works　单位工程
unite　结合
unit-block type relay interlocking　组合式电气集中联锁
unit-weight of material　材料单重
universal cab signal　通用式机车信号
universal currency（money）　世界货币
universal fixed belt conveyor　通用固定带式输送机
universal material testing machine　万能材料试验机
universal method of photogrammetric mapping　全能法测图
universal rail gauge　万能道尺
universal serial bus key（USBKey）　身份识别
unlawful　非法的
unlimited competitive bidding　无限竞争性招标
unlimited competitive open bidding　无限竞争性公开招标
unlimited duration guarantee　非定期保证
unlimited liability　无限责任
unliquidated account　未清算账目
unload　卸货
unloading　卸载
unloading joint　卸荷节理
unloading port　卸货港
unloading site　卸料点
unloading track　卸车线
unloading zone　卸荷带
unoccupied track length　股道空闲长度
unofficial agreement　非正式协议
unorganized air exhaust　无组织排风
unorganized air supply　无组织进风
unpack　拆包,启封
unpaid　未付的
unpaid interest　未付利息
unpaid liabilities　未偿债务
unpaid moneys　未付款
unpaid wages and salaries　未付薪金
unpassable trench　不通行地沟
unpledged assets　未抵押资产
unpredictable element　不可预见因
unpriced bill of quantities　未标价的工程量表,未标价工程量清单
unprofessional operation　违章操作
unqualified product　不合格产品
unrammed concrete　未捣实混凝土,未捣混凝土
unrecorded revenue　未入账收入
unreeling device　放线装置
unreinforced surface　素混凝土面层
unsafe bridge　危桥
unsecured bid　无担保投标,无担保投标文件
unsecured creditor　无担保债权人
unsecured debt　无担保债务
unsecured loan　无担保贷款
unsettled account　未结清账户
Unsheilded Twisted Paired（UTP）非屏蔽双绞线
unsigned　未签字的
unskilled labour　不熟练工人,普工
unstability coefficient　不平稳系数
unsteady flow pumping test　非稳定流抽水试验
unsteady flow　非稳定流
unsteady-state heat transfer　非稳态传热
unsuccessful bidder（tenderer）　未中标者
untwining for leading line　线路疏解
untwining for station approach track　进出站线路疏解

untwining for train direction 行车方向别疏解
untwining for train types 列车种类别疏解
untwining line 疏解线路
unvalued insurance 不定值保险
unwarranted 不当的
unweathered 未风化
un-editable record 不可编辑的记录
up direction section interface 上行区间接口
up to par 达到标准
up track 上行线
updated schedule 更新的进度计划
updating 更新
upfeed system 下行上给式
upgrade 更新
upgrading/renewal works 改建工程
uphold 坚持
upholster 装饰
uplift 抬升,抬升量,隆起
uplift resistance of anchor plate 锚定板抗拔力
uplifting height 抬起高度
uplink equipment 上联设备
upper (late) qingbaikouan epoch 上(晚)青白口世
upper (late) qingbaikouan series 上(晚)青白口统
upper ballast bed 上部道床
upper bowl down 上碗扣
upper bracket for twin cantilevers 双腕臂上底座
upper Cambrian series 上寒武统
upper Carboniferous series 上石炭统
upper Cretaceous series 上白垩统
upper cross-span wire 上部定位索
upper cut-off frequency 上限截止频率
upper Devonian series 上泥盆统
upper flexible and lower rigid complex multistorey building 上柔下刚多层房屋
upper Jurassic series 上侏罗统
upper Ordovician series 上奥陶统
upper Palaeozoic erathem/group 上古生界
upper part of embankment 基床底层(路堤)
upper Permian series 上二叠统
upper Pleistocene series 上更新统
upper Proterozoic group 上元古界
upper rigid and lower flexible complex multistorey building 上刚下柔多层房屋
upper Silurian series 上志留统
upper Sinian series 上震旦统
upper size 上部尺寸
upper Triassic series 上三叠统
uppercantilever bracket 腕臂上底座
upright attitude 直立产状
upright fold 直立褶皱
upset price 拍卖底价
upside down bowl-type node 碗扣节点
upward inclined borehole 仰斜式钻孔
upward leading cable 引上电缆
upward traveling wave 上行波
urban facilities 城市设施
urban maintenance and construction tax 城市维护建设税
urban sewer network 城市(镇)排水管网
urban survey 城市测量
urban wastewater 城镇污水
urban wastewater system 城镇污水系统
urge 敦促
urgent alarm 紧急告警
urgent document 急件
urgent relief 紧急救济
urgent task 紧急任务
urinal 小便槽
urine device 小便器
usable floor area 使用面积
usage 惯例,习惯,用途
usance letter of credit 远期信用证
use 用途
use before taking over 移交前的使用
use of funds 资金运用
use tax 使用税
use up 消耗
used rail 旧钢轨
useful life 耐用年限
useful wave 有效波
user 用户,运用
user data 用户数据
user handbook of consulting services 咨询服务用户手册
user interface 用户接口
user monitoring terminal 用户监控终端
user network interface(UNI) 用户网络接口
user telephone 用户话机
user terminal 用户终端
utility 公用事业
utility factor of the position 台位利用系数
utilization factor of rated load 额定荷载利用系数

utilization factor of storey height
　层高利用系数
utilization ratio of renewable energy
　可再生能源利用率
utilization requirements　使用需求
utilize　运用
U-shaped abutment　U形桥台
U-shaped section steel　U形型钢

V

V filter V形滤池
vacancy rate 闲置率
vacation 假期
vacuum box test 真空盒试验
vacuum breaker 真空破坏器
vacuum capillary viscometer
　真空毛细管法黏度
vacuum circuit breaker 真空断路器
vacuum circuit breaker handcart
　真空断路器操作小车
vacuum contactor 真空接触器
vacuum drainage 真空排水
vacuum drainage system 真空排水系统
vacuum drying apparatus 真空干燥器
vacuum drying box 真空干燥箱
vacuum drying method 真空干燥法
vacuum preloading 真空预压
vacuum preloading method 真空预压法
vacuum pump 真空泵
vacuum pumping method 真空抽气法
vacuum residue 减压渣油
vacuum residuum 减压渣油
vacuum saturation 真空抽气饱和
vacuum station（center）
　真空站（真空中心）
vacuum valve 真空阀
vacuum water saturation instrument of concrete
　混凝土真空保水机
vale 峪
valid code 合法码字
valid contract 有效合同
valid period 有效期
validate contract 合同生效
validation 生效
validity 有效,有效性
validity of an award 裁决的有效性
validity of bid（tender） 投标文件有效期
validity of contract 合同有效性
validity of offer 报价有效期
valley facies 谷地相
valley glacier 谷冰川
valley terrace 河谷阶地
valuation 估价,计价
valuation after termination for contractor's default
　承包商过错终止后的估价
valuation after termination for employer's convenience
　雇主决定终止后的估价
valuation at cost 按成本计价
valuation clause 估价条款
valuation form 货物估价单
valuation of variation 变更的估价
valuation of works 工程的估价
value 定价,估价,价值
value added 附加价值,增值
value added tax（VAT） 增值税
value analysis 价值分析
value date 计息日,起息日
value engineering（VE） 价值工程
value engineering method 价值工程法
value management（VM） 价值管理
value of insurance 保险价值
value of machinery 机械设备价值
value planning（VP） 价值规划
value technique（VT） 价值技术
value-added terms/clause 增值条款
valve type arrester 阀式避雷器
valve type track circuit 阀式轨道电路
valveless filter 无阀滤池
valve-regulated sealed lead-acid battery
　阀控式密封铅酸蓄电池
vandalism 故意破坏
vane shear test 十字板剪切试验
vanishing-point control 合点控制
vaporous water 气态水
variable 可变的
variable action 可变作用

variable attenuator 可变衰耗器
variable budget 变动预算,弹性预算
variable costing 变动成本计算
variable cost 变动成本
variable cross-section beam 变截面梁
variable frequency speed regulation constant pressure water supply system 变频调速恒压给水系统
variable head method 变水头法
variable interest rate 可变利率
variable levy 差价税
variable load 可变荷载
variable optical attenuator 光可变衰耗器
variable rate 可变利率
variable refrigerant flow multi split air conditioning system 变制冷剂流量多联分体式空气调节系统
variable stiffness leveling design 变刚度调平设计
variable-volume air conditioning system 变风量空气调节系统
variance covariance matrix (also known as "variance-covariance matrix") 方差—协方差矩阵(又称"积差阵")
variance of unit weight (also known as "variance factor") 单位权方差(又称"方差因子")
variance-covariance propagation law 方差—协方差传播律
variation 变动,变更
variation by instruction 指令变更
variation by request for proposal 业主要求的变更
variation clause 变更条款
variation control 变更控制
variation control procedure 变更控制程序
variation in contact wire height 接触线高差
variation in elasticity 弹性不均匀度
variation in hardness 硬度变化
variation of quantity 工程量变更
variation of tension 张力差
variation of work 工程变更
variation order (VO) 变更指令,施工变更指示
variation procedure 变更程序
variation proposal 变更建议书
variations and adjustments 变更和调整
varied rate 变更的单价,变更的费率
varied work 变更的工作
Variscan age/stage 华力西期
varistor 压敏电阻
vary 变更
varying head water injecting 变动水头注水
var-hour meters for reactive energy 无功反转正计
vault 穹窿
Vebe consistence 维勃稠度
vegetable field development and construction fund 菜地开发建设基金
vegetation 植被
vegetation construction works 植被建设工程
vegetation coverage rate 植被覆盖率
vegetation screen 植物保护带
vegetation survey 植被调查
vegetation type 植被类型
vehicle 车辆,机动车,运载工具
vehicle and vessel use tax 车船使用税
vehicle cleaning siding 车辆洗刷线
vehicle delivery expenses (shunting charge) 取送车费(调车费)
vehicle insurance 运输车辆保险
vehicle moved procedure 跑车方式
vehicle safety early warning system 车辆安全防范预警系统
vehicle scheduling 车辆调度
vehicle tax 车辆税
vehicle vibration period 车辆振动周期
vehicle-bridge coupling dynamic response 车桥耦合动力响应
vehicle-washing track 车辆洗刷线
vehicular clearance limit above bridge floor 桥梁建筑界限
veiling reflection 光幕反射
vein ice 脉冰
velocity 速度
velocity field 速度场
velocity of electromagnetic wave 电磁波速
venal practices 贿赂行为,贪污行为
vendee 受货人
vendor 发货人,供应商
vendor coordination meeting (VCM) 厂商协调会议
vendor list 供货商名单
veneer board 胶合板
veneer 胶合板
vent 通风口
ventilated roof 通风屋顶
ventilating duct 通风道,通风管道
ventilating shaft 通风井

ventilating system 通风系统
ventilating unit 通风装置
ventilation 通风
ventilation cap 通气帽
ventilation device 通气装置
ventilation during tunnel construction 隧道施工通风
ventilation during tunnel operation 隧道运营通风
ventilation engineering 通风工程
ventilation fan 通风机
ventilation frequency 换气次数
ventilation heat loss 通风耗热量
ventilation pipe 通气管
ventilation rate 通风量
venture 投机
venture capital 投机资本
venture investment 风险投资
verbal 口头的
verbal agreement 口头协议,口头约定
verbal commitment 口头承诺
verbal contract 口头合同
verbal order 口头命令
verbal promise 口头承诺
verbal quotation 口头报价
verbal request 口头申请
verdict 裁决,结论,判决
verification 检定,鉴定,验证,证实
verification certificate 检定证书
verification coefficient of deflection 挠度校验系数
verification coefficient 校验系数
verification of account 对账,核对账目
verify 核实,证实
verify a statement 核对清单,检核表
vermiculite 蛭石
vernier caliper 游标卡尺
version 文本
vertical angle of rotation of beam-end 梁端竖向转角
vertical axis 纵轴
vertical bracing 竖向支撑
vertical compression bearing capacity of single pile 单桩竖向抗压承载力
vertical construction joint 竖向施工缝
vertical curve 竖曲线
vertical curve location 竖曲线测设
vertical datum 高程基准
vertical deflection 竖向挠度
vertical displacement 垂直位移

vertical displacement measuring 垂直位移测量
vertical division block 竖向分区
vertical dynamic force of train 列车竖向动力
vertical earth electrode 垂直接地极,垂直接地体
vertical flow settling tank 竖流沉淀池
vertical force 垂向力
vertical joint 垂直缝
vertical layout 竖向布置图
vertical load 垂直荷载
vertical member 竖杆
vertical parallax 上下视差
vertical parallel plate 垂直并联板
vertical percolation zone 垂直渗漏带
vertical pressure 垂直压力
(track slab) vertically placed on the side (轨道板)侧置立放
vertical reaction 垂直反力
vertical residual creep deformation 竖向残余徐变变形
vertical rigidity 垂直刚度
vertical rod 立杆
vertical rotating angle 垂直旋转角度
vertical section 垂直面,竖截面
vertical single-pipe heating system 垂直单管采暖系统
vertical static live load of train 列车竖向静活载
vertical stiffness 竖向刚度
vertical storage 垂直式存放
vertical survey 高程测量,竖向测量
vertical tear force 纵向撕裂力
vertical type 竖式
vertical uniformly-distributed pressure 垂直匀布压力
vertical untwining 立体疏解
vertical uplift bearing capacity of single pile 单桩竖向抗拔承载力
vertical vibration acceleration of train 列车竖向振动加速度
vertical wheel 导线立轮
vertical window time 垂直天窗
vertical Z vibration degree 铅垂向Z振级
vertical zoning of water system 水系统竖向分区
verticality 垂直度
verticality of structural member 结构构件垂直度
vertical-displacement monitoring network 垂直位移监测网

vertical-lift bridge 升降桥
verification 证实
Very Important Person(VIP) 重要用户
very long bridge (with length more than 500 m) 特大桥
very low frequency (VLF) 甚低频发
vesicular structure 气孔构造
vest 赋予权力,给予,授予
vested 既得的
vested capital 投入资本
vested interests 既得利益
vesting 赋予权力
vesting instrument 授权文件
vesting notice 委托通知
vesting order 财产受托命令
vesuvianite 符山石
viaduct 高架桥,高架线
vibrating 振捣
vibrating pile driver 振动打桩机
vibrating rolling 振动碾实
vibrating sieve 振动筛
vibrating-wire earth pressure cell 振弦式土压力盒
vibration 减振胶垫,振动
vibration absorber rail joint 减振接头
vibration acceleration 振动加速度
vibration attenuation 震动衰减
vibration attenuation and noise reduction 减振降噪
vibration compaction value 振动压实值
vibration compactor 振动碾压机
vibration damping 减震
vibration damping track 减振轨道
vibration damping track slab 减振型轨道板
vibration drilling 震动钻进
vibration embedded 振动嵌入法
vibration frequency 振动频率
vibration hammering method 振动锤击法
vibration isolating 隔振
vibration isolation wall 隔振墙
vibration isolation and damping base 隔振减振基础
vibration isolation pipe pile 隔振管桩
vibration isolator 隔振器
vibration level 振动级
vibration measuring sensor 测振传感器
vibration mode 振型
vibration pickup 拾振器
vibration rammer 振动夯
vibration reduction 减振

vibration sensor 振动传感器
vibration source intensity 振动源强
vibration speed 振动速度
vibration-measuring amplifier 测振放大器
vibration-measuring recording device 测振记录装置
vibration-sensitive buildings 振动敏感建筑
vibrator 振捣器
vibrator poker 插入式振捣器
vibrator tamper 振动棒
vibratory pile driver-extractor 振动沉拔桩机
vibratory pile hammer 振动桩锤
vibratory roller 振动压路机,振动碾压机
vibroflotation method 振冲法
vicarious liability 代偿责任
vicarious performance 代位履行
vice versa 反之亦然
vicious circle 恶性循环
vicissitudinary 交替的
video access node 视频接入节点
video box 视频盒
video cabinet 视频柜
video collection point 视频采集点
video conference 电视电话会议,会议电视
video conference circuit 电视会议电路
video conference terminal 会议电视终端
video content analysis 视频内容分析
video control box 视频控制箱
video convergence site 视频汇集点
video core node 视频核心节点
video decoder 视频解码器
video encoder 视频编码器
video forwarding 视频转发
video linkage function 视频联动功能
video monitoring 视频监控
video optical transceiver 视频光端机
video regional node 视频区域节点
video source switching 视频源切换
video storage and playback 录像存储回放
video streaming 视频流
video surveillance system 视频监控系统
video surveillance system of luggage and parcel 行包视频监视
video test card 视频测试卡
video transmission code stream 视频传输码流
video wall 大屏幕显示设备
video/audio acquisition device 影音采集设备
vierendeel truss 空腹屋架
vine 攀藤植物

violate 违反,违犯
violate a law 违反法律
violation of contract 违反合同
virescence 绿化
virgin forest area 原始森林地区
vertical control network 高程控制网
virtual link 虚拟链路
virtual organization 虚拟组织
Virtual Private Network（VPN）
虚拟专用网
virtualization 虚拟化
virus 病毒
visa 签证
viscidity 黏聚性
viscosity 黏度
viscosity classification 黏度分级
viscous loess 黏质黄土
visibility 能见度
visible light transmittance 可见光透射比
visible means 有形财产
visible pit of track 轨道明坑
visible range for watching 瞭望视距
visible trade 有形贸易
visible turbidimetric method 目视比浊法
visit 考察
visitor location register（VLR）
拜访位置寄存器
visual inspection 观察检查,外观检查
visual method 目测法,目视法
visual signal 视觉信号
visual task 视觉作业
visual test 目视检验
vital circuit 安全电路
vital computer 安全计算机
vitreous 玻璃质的
Virtual Local Area Network（VLAN）
虚拟局域网
vogesite 闪辉正煌岩
voice 语音
voice broadcast service（VBS）
语音广播
voice call 语音呼叫
voice call center 语音呼叫中心
voice distribution frame（VDF） 语音配线架
voice group call service（VGCS） 语音组呼
voice over internet protocol（VoIP）
以IP承载语音传输
voice receiving sensitivity 受话灵敏度
void 孔洞,孔隙
void contract 无效合同
void ratio 孔隙比
voidable contract 可撤销合同
voided slab bridge 空心板桥
voids under sleeper/tie 轨道暗坑
volatile organic compound
挥发性有机化合物
volatile phenols 挥发酚
volatile solid 挥发性固体
volcanic activity 火山活动
volcanic agglomerate 集块岩
volcanic breccia 火山角砾岩
volcanic breccia structure 火山角砾构造
volcanic cone 火山锥
volcanic deposit 火山堆,火山堆积
volcanic earthquake 火山地震
volcanic landform 火山地貌
volcanism 火山活动
voltage 电压
voltage amplifier 电压放大器
voltage dip 电压下降
voltage distortion（VD） 电压畸变率
voltage drop 电压降
voltage electrode 接收电极
voltage level 电压等级
voltage limiting type(SPD) 限压型
voltage loss of contact line system
牵引网电压损失
voltage loss of traction network
牵引网电压损失
voltage protection 电压保护
voltage regulating device 调压装置
voltage regulation factor 电压调整率
voltage regulator 调压器
voltage rise 电压升
voltage stabilizer 稳压器
voltage transformer 电压互感器
voltage unbalance factor 电压不平衡度
voltage value 电压值
voltage withstand test 耐压试验
volt-ampere characteristics 伏安特性
volt-ampere reactive(var) 无功伏安
volume 体积,容积,容积
volume batching 按容积配合
volume concentration 体积浓度
volume measurement method 量积法
volume of business 营业额
volume of earthwork 土方工程量
volume of production 生产量
volume of ticket sales 售票量
volume of utilization 利用方

volumetric heat capacity　容积热容量
volumetric heat exchanger　容积式换热器
volumetric ice content　体积含冰量
volumetric loading of biochemical oxygen demand for 5 days（BOD5）　五日生化需氧量容积负荷
volumetric method　滴定法，体积法
volumetric method of gas volume　气体体积滴定法
volumetric shrinking ratio　体缩率
volumetric strain　体应变
voluntary bankruptcy　自动申请破产
voluntary deductibles　自愿免赔额
voluntary insurance　自愿保险
voluntary liquidation　自愿清偿
volcanism　火山活动
vortex-induced oscillation　涡流激振
vortex-type grit chamber　旋流沉砂池
vote　表决，投票
voting right　表决权
vouchee　被担保者
voucher　单据，票据，凭证，证件
voucher check　凭单支票
voucher printer　票据打印机
vouching　核单，制单
vow　宣誓
voyage　航次，航行
voyage charter　定程租船
V-type pier　V形桥墩

V

wage 工资,劳工工资
wage bill 工资总额单
wage ceiling 工资最高限额
wage in sliding scale 浮动工资
wage incentive 奖励工资
wage index 工资指数
wage level 工资标准,工资水平
wage per hour 小时工资
wage rate 工资标准,工资水平,工资率
wages for piece work 计件工资
wages income tax 工资所得税
wages payable 应付工资
wages sheet 工资表
wagon kilometers per day 货车日车公里
wagon loading and unloading by groups 成组装卸
wagon loading by groups 成组装车
wagon on hand 现车修
waist beam 腰梁
waiting area 候车区
waiting for the train 候车
waiting period 免赔期限
waive 不起诉,放弃
waive one's right 放弃权利
waive right of claim 放弃索赔权
waiver 自动放弃
waiver clause 放弃条款,弃权条款
waiver of claim 撤回索赔
waling 围檩(腰梁)
walk off the job 罢工
wall beam 墙梁
wall planeness 墙面平整度
wall thickness 壁厚
wall tile 墙面贴砖
wall waist 墙腰
wall with pilaster 带壁柱墙
wall-column 墙肢
wall-frame structure 壁式框架

wall-linking element 连墙件
wall-linking rod 连墙杆
wall-slab structure 墙板结构
wall-through bushing 穿墙套管
war risk 战争保险
warehouse 仓库,货栈
warehouse book 仓库账簿
warehouse certificate 仓库凭证,栈单
warehouse cost 仓储成本
warehouse of car spare parts 小汽车零配件库
warehouse receipt 仓单,仓库收据
warehouse to warehouse clause 仓至仓条款
warehouse width 仓库宽度
warehouse-keeper's order 出库通知单
warm air curtain 热风幕
warm region 温暖地区
warm temperate zone 暖温带
warning 警告
warning sign 警告性标志,警示牌
warning signal 警告信号
warning signs for approaching a station 预告标
warning speed profile 报警速度曲线
warping 翘曲
warping rigidity of section 截面翘曲刚度
warp 翘曲,三角坑
warp-knitting geogrid 经编土工格栅
warrant 担保
warrant money 保证金
warrantee 被保证人
warranty 保修,保证,担保书,质量保证期
warranty bond 质量担保
warranty expenses 保修费用
warranty period 保证期,维修期
warranty phase 保修阶段
wartime ventilation 战时通风

wash rate 冲洗强度
wash trap 拦沙函
washbasin 洗脸盆
washer 垫片,垫圈
washing and disinfecting point 洗刷消毒所
washing wastewater 冲洗废水,洗涤污水
washout 冲蚀
waste 损耗
waste discharge station (spot) for passenger train 旅客列车卸污站(点)
waste discharge unit 卸污单元
waste disposal 废料处理
waste dump plan 排土场平面图
waste gas 废气
waste heat 废热,余热
waste land 废弃地
waste soil and rock volume 弃土石方
wastewater 废水
waste water and exhaust gas treatment 污水和废气治理
wastewater facilities 排水设施
wastewater reuse 污水再生利用
wasting assets 递耗资产,耗减资产
water absorption 吸水性
water absorbing capacity 吸水量
water absorption capacity test 吸水性试验
water absorption of rock 岩石吸水率
water absorption rate 吸水率
water abundance 富水程度
water bag 水袋
water bearing sand 含水沙层
water bearing stratum 含水层
water blocking area of pier 桥墩阻水面积
water boiler 开水器
water buoyancy 水浮力
water cement ratio 水灰比
water chiller 冷水机
water chilling unit 冷水机组
water collector 集水器
water column pressure 水柱压力
water column pump-in test method 水柱压水法
water conservancy 水利
water conservation 节约用水
water conservation area 水源涵养区
water conservation capacity 水源涵养能力
water conservation forest 水源涵养林
water consumption 耗水,用水量
water content 含水率
water content ratio 含水比
water cooling 水冷
water crane indicator 水鹤表示器
water cure 水养护
water curtain 水幕
water cutoff curtain 截水帷幕
water delivery pipeline 输水管道
water discharge 排水量
water discharging tunnel 泄水洞
water distribution pipeline 配水管道
water distribution point 配水点
water divide 分水岭
water erosion 水蚀
water filling test 灌水试验
water fire extinguishing agent 水系灭火剂
water flow capacity 水流量
water flow indicator 水流指示器
water flow test 涌水试验
water function 水功能
water gathering bucket 集水桶
water gushing 涌水
water head 水头
water head difference 水头差
water immersion 水浸
water immersion detector 水浸探测器
water impermeability 不透水性
water inflow into tunnel 隧道涌水量
water inflow pressure 涌水压力
water injecting test 注水试验
water inrush 突水
water intake 取水口
water leakage 漏水
water leakage from pipeline 管网漏失水量
water leakage of tunnel 隧道漏水
water level 水平面,水平仪,水位
water level transfer method 水位传递法
water lifting test 提水试验
water loop heat pump air conditioning system 水环热泵空气调节系统
water meter 水表
water mist 细水雾
water outflow 涌水量
water pipe 水管
water pollution 水污染
water pressure blasting 水压爆破
water price of base period 基期水价
water pump-in test 压水试验
water quality 水质
water quality analysis 水质分析
water quality analysis test 水质分析试验
water quality evaluation 水质评价

water quantity evaluation 水量评价
water ratio limit test 界限含水率试验
water replacement method 灌水法
water requirement of normal consistency
　标准稠度用水量
water resistance test 水阻试验
water resource assessment 水资源论证
water resources 水利资源
water retaining capacity 持水度,持水性
water retaining works 挡水建筑物
water retention 保水性
water retentivity of mortar 砂浆保水性
water return pipe 回水管
water sample 水样
water saturated absorptivity of rock
　岩石饱和吸水率
water seal 止水,水封
water seepage 渗水
water seepage depth 渗水深度
water separator 分水器
water service 供水
water solubility 水溶性
water solution 水溶液
water source 水源
water source location 水源地
water source protection zone 水源保护区
water spray 喷水
water spray extinguishing system
　水喷雾灭火系统
water stability 水稳性
water stage gauge 水位计
water stop 止水片
water stop strip 止水条
water stop tie of steel sheet and rubber type
　钢板橡胶止水带
water stop tie of steel sheet type 钢板止水带
water storage coefficient 储水系数
water storage pond 蓄水塘
water supply 给水,供水
water supply and sewerage works
　给水排水工程
water supply capacity 给水能力
water supply fittings 给水配件
water supply machine 给水机械
water supply mode 供水方式
water supply pipe 给水管
water supply plan 供水方案
water supply plant 给水厂
water supply plant(station) of railway
　铁路给水厂(所)
water supply property 给水特点
water supply pump station 给水泵站
water supply spigot for passenger train
　旅客列车给水栓,旅客列车上水设备
water supply spigot manholes for passenger train
　旅客列车给水栓室
water supply spigot well chamber for passenger train　旅客列车上水设备井室
water supply station 给水站
water supply station for passenger train
　旅客列车给水站
water supply system 给水系统,供水系统
water swelling strip 遇水膨胀止水条
water swelling water stop tie
　遇水膨胀式止水带
water system 水系统
water system distribution 水系分布
water temperature 水温
water to cementitious material ratio 水胶比
water tower 水塔
water tower rack 水塔架
water treatment 水处理
water treatment plant 水处理厂
water treatment structure 水处理构筑物
water truck 洒水车,运水车
water vapor permeation coefficient
　水蒸气渗透系数
water way 水路,水运
water works 给水装置,自来水厂
water yield 出水量
waterline 水位线
waterlogged depression 积水洼地
waterproof 防水
waterproof apparatus 不透水仪
waterproof base course layer 防水基层
waterproof coating 防水涂料
waterproof coiled material 防水卷材
waterproof concrete 防水混凝土
waterproof layer 防水层
waterproof layer of bridge floor
　桥面防水层
waterproof seal material 防水密封材料
waterproofing and drainage of tunnel
　隧道防排水
waterproofing by grouting 注浆防水
waterproofing insulation layer 防水隔离层
waterproofing of tunnel 隧道防水
waterproofing plaster coat 防水抹面
waterproofing sheet 防水板
waterproofing worker 防水工

waterproofness 防水性
watershed 分水岭
watershed/catchment basin 流域
waterstop 止水带
waterstop laccolite 止水岩盘
watertightness 不透水性
watertightness tester 不透水仪
water-bearing ice layer 含水冰层
water-bearing zone 含水带
water-cooled condenser 水冷式冷凝器
water-deficient area 缺水地区
water-dividing dyke 分流堤
water-interception skeleton 截水骨架
water-poor zone 贫水区
water-proof and vapor-permeable material 防水透气材料
water-reducing admixture 减水剂
water-reducing rate 减水率
water-repellent admixture 防水剂
water-retaining property 保水性
water-retention consistence-increasing material 保水增稠材料
water-rich stratum 富水地层
water-saturation coefficient 饱水系数
water-saturation coefficient of rock 岩石饱水系数
water-soluble salt 水溶盐
water-source heat pump 水源热泵
water-water heat exchanger 水—水换热器
watt-hour meter 电度表
wave cut notch 海蚀壁龛
wave pressure 波浪压力
wave propagation coefficient 波动传播系数
wave propagation velocity 波传播速度
wave receiver interval 道间距
wave runup 波浪爬高
wave velocity 波速
wave velocity logging 波速测井
wave velocity well logging method 波速测井法
waveband dispersion characteristics 波段色散特性
waveform 波形
Wavelength Division Multiplexing(WDM) 波分复用
wax coating method 蜡封法
wax composition 蜡组分
wax content 蜡含量
wax-sealed 蜡封
way 道路,方法,航线

way of payment 支付方式
waybill 货单,货运单
wayleave 道路通行权,通行权
wayside inductor 地面感应器
weak corrosion 弱腐蚀
weak frost heaving soil 弱冻胀土
weak intercalated layer 软弱夹层
weak permeability 弱透水性
weak plane 软弱面
weak soil 软弱土地
weak soil layer 软弱土层
weak structural plane 软弱结构面
weak structure 软弱结构
weak surrounding rock 软弱围岩
weak water abundance zone 弱富水区
weakest point 最弱点
weakest side 最弱边
weakly frost heave 弱冻胀
wear 磨耗,磨损
wear and tear 磨损,损耗
wear resistant rail 耐磨轨
wearing capacity 磨损量
wearing parts 损耗部件
wearing surface of bridge floor 桥面保护层
weather forecast 气象预报
weather station 气象台
weather working days 适宜工作日
weathered particles 风化颗粒
weathered rock 风化岩石
weathering 风化,风化作用
weathering coefficient 风化系数
weathering crust 风化壳
weathering degree 风化程度
weathering degree of rock 岩石风化程度
weathering joint 风化节理
weathering zone 风化带
weather-resistant capability 抗风化能力
web 腹板
web member 腹杆
website 网站
wedged rail anchor 穿销防爬器
weekend shift period/cycle 周末班
weekly labour report 每周劳务报告
weekly performance report 绩效周报
weekly returns 周报表
weekly scheduling 周计划
weekly wages 周工资
weep hole 泄水孔
weigh 称量
weighing 检斤

weighing bottle 称量瓶
weighing box 称量盒
weighing device 检斤设备
weighing method 称量法,称重法
weight 砝码
weight coefficient 加权系数
weight guide strap 坠砣抱箍
weight guide tube 坠陀限制架
weight matrix 权矩阵
weight of structure 结构自重
weight platform 加载平台
weight sensing 测重
weight sets 坠陀串
weighted arithmetic average
　加权算术平均数
weighted arithmetic mean 加权算术平均数
weighted average value 加权平均值
weighted noise 衡重噪声
weighted price 加权报价
weighted sound reduction factor
　计权隔声量
weighted value 权重值
weighting system 加权制
weighting 加权,权重,加重
weir 水堰
weir crest 堰顶
weir flow 过堰流量
weir method 堰测法
weir plate 堰板
weir sill 堰槛
weld seam 焊缝
weldability of steel bar 钢筋可焊性
welded bond 焊接式钢轨接续线
welded framework 焊接骨架
welded long rail 焊接长钢轨
welded rail joint 焊接接头
welded steel beam 焊接钢梁
welded steel structure 焊接钢结构
welder 焊工
welding 焊接
welding consumable 焊接材料
welding equipment 电焊设备
welding head 焊头
welding length 焊接长度
weldless steel tube 无缝钢管
weldwood 胶合板
welfare 福利
welfare benefits 福利费
welfare expenses 福利费
welfare expense of employee 职工福利费
welfare funds 福利基金
well casing 井管
well detector 探井器
well drilling 钻井
well flushing 洗井
well logging 测井
well point vacuum degree 井点真空度
well shaft 井筒
well water 井水
wellbore center line calibration
　井筒中心标定
wellbore cross centerline calibration
　井筒十字中线标定
wellbore deepening survey 井筒延伸测量
wellhead assembly 井口装置
wellpoint 井点
wellpoint dewatering 井点排水
well-graded soil 良好级配土
well-knit 结实的
well-point dewatering 井点排水
well-sinking 沉井
wet bubble globe temperature (WBGT) index
　湿球黑球温度指数
wet condensation pipe 湿式凝结水管
wet condition 湿工况
wet density 湿密度
wet dust removal 湿法除尘
wet hydrant 湿式消火栓
wet lapping dispersion method
　湿研磨分散法
wet oxidation absorption 湿式吸收氧化法
wet shotcreting machine 混凝土湿喷机
wet shotcreting manipulator 湿喷机械手
wet sieve analysis method 水洗湿筛分析法
wet sieving method 湿筛法
wet soil method 湿土法
wet sprinkling system 湿式喷水灭火系统
wetland park 湿地公园
wetting agent 润湿剂
wet-bulb temperature 湿球温度
wet-mix shotcreting method 湿喷法
wet-type dust collector 湿式除尘器
wet-type dust removal 水力除尘
wharf 码头
wharf boat 趸船
wharfage 码头费
wheel crane 轮胎式起重机
wheel excavator 轮胎式挖掘机
wheel load 轮载
wheel loader 轮胎式装载机

wheel pair assembly shed 存轮棚
wheel signal 轮信号
wheel sliding 车轮滑行
wheel slipping 车轮空转
wheelchair ramp 轮椅坡道
wheelset storage shed 存轮棚
wheelset tread diagnosis track 轮对踏面诊断线
wheel-rail arc discharge 轮轨间拉弧
wheel-rail contact 轮轨接触
wheel-rail dynamics 轮轨动力学
wheel-rail interaction 轮轨关系
wheel-rail interaction forces 轮轨作用力
wheel-rail lubrication 轮轨润滑
wheel-rail noise 轮轨噪声
wheel-track contact tread 轮轨接触踏面
whipping effect 鞭梢效应
whistle 汽笛
white light strip 白光带
white lime 熟石灰
white-light image processing 白光图像处理
whole course transport price 全程运价
whole gale 狂风
whole life cycle 全寿命周期
whole locomotive test track 机车整车试验线
wholesale 批发
wholesale business 批发业务
wholesale dealer 批发商
wholesale price 批发价
wholesaler 批发商
wide area network 广域网
wide dynamic range 宽动态功能
wide tension joint 宽张节composed
widened distance between centers of tracks 线间距加宽
widening value 帮宽值
widening value at the outer side of the curved embankment 曲线外侧加宽值
widening value of track formation 路基面加宽值
width of ballast shoulder 道床肩宽
width of berm 平台宽度
width of freight section 货位宽度
width of track formation 路基面宽度
width to span ratio 宽跨比
wild phase 引前相，超前相
wildlife habitat 野生动物栖息地
win 获得
win a contract 赢得合同，中标
winch 绞车，卷扬机
winch capstan 绞车
wind 风，绞车
wind break and sand fixation forest 防风固沙林
wind break and sand fixation works 防风固沙工程
wind break and sand fixation 防风固沙
wind deflection 风偏
wind direction 风向
wind direction and speed meter 风速风向计
wind erosion 风蚀
wind erosion intensity 风蚀强度
wind fairing 风嘴
wind force 风力
wind force / wind power 风力等级
wind load 风荷载
wind pressure 风压
wind rose diagram 风玫瑰图
wind scale 风级，风力侵蚀
wind season 风季
wind shade 风影区
wind speed 风速
wind speed and direction sensor 风速风向传感器
wind speed monitoring alarm 风速监测报警
wind tunnel 风洞
wind valley 风蚀谷
wind velocity 风速
wind vibration 风振
wind vibration coefficient 风振系数
windfall 横财，意外利益
windfall profit 暴利
winding connection of traction transformer 牵引变压器接线形式
winding up 停业
windlass 绞车
window function 窗函数
window-type air conditioner 窗式空气调节器
windstay 防风拉线
windward slope 迎风坡
wind-erosion castle 风蚀城堡
wind-erosion landform 风蚀地貌
wind-resistant column 抗风柱
wing rail 翼轨
wing wall 翼墙，耳墙
Winkler's assumption 文克勒假定
winning bidder 中标人
winning party 胜诉的一方

winter construction 冬期施工
win-win solution 双赢方案,双赢解决办法
wire carrier 导线导轮
wire compensator 导线调整器
wire fracture 断线
wire installation 导线装置
wire loop resistance 线路环阻
wire request 电汇申请单
wire rope 钢丝绳
wire supported displacement measuring apparatus 张线式位移量测装置
wire transfer 电汇
wired dispatching communication system 有线调度通信系统
wireless communication 无线通信
wireless microphone 无线话筒
wireline core drilling 绳索取芯钻进
wiremesh 钢筋网
wire-adjusting screw 导线反正扣
wire-speed forwarding 线速转发
wire-wrapped filter tube 缠丝过滤管
wiring 布线,配线
wiring case 接线箱
wiring closet 配线箱
wiring schedule 配线表
wiring system 布线系统
with average（W.A.） 水渍险
with particular average（WPA） 单独海损赔偿,水渍险
withdraw 撤回,废除,提款,提取
withdraw an offer 收回报价
withdraw deposit 收回保证金,提款
withdrawable switchgear 手车式开关柜
withdrawal 撤回,提货,接收到货,提款
withdrawal application 提款申请
withdrawal of bid（tender） 撤销投标
withhold payment 止付
withholding 扣缴
withholding（amounts in）an IPC 扣发部分 IPC 期中支付的款项
withholding tax 预扣税款,预提税
without prejudice to 不妨害
without recourse 无追索权
witness 见证,证人,证言
witness inspection report 见证检验报告
witness sampling 见证取样
witnessed inspection 见证检验
witnessed sampling test 见证取样检测
wollastonite 硅灰石
wood structure 木结构
wooden sleeper adzing machine 木枕削平机
wooden sleeper drilling machine 木枕钻孔机
wooden sleeper 木枕
word of mouth 口头的
wording 措辞
work accident 工伤事故
work at height 高空作业
work attendance 出勤率
work breakdown structure（WBS） 工作分解结构
work capacity 工作量,工作能力
work changes 工作变动
work content 工作内容
work contracting 承包工程,工程承包
work cost budget 工程成本预算
work defect 工程缺陷
work execution flowsheet 工作执行流程表
work in progress 在建工程
work interruption 工作中断
work item 工作单项
work item or expense description 工作项目或费用名称
work order 工作通知单,任务单
work out 制订
work overtime 加班
work package 工作包
work permit 工作许可,工作许可证
work plan 工作方案,工作计划
work platform of maintenance machinery 养路机械作业平台
work procedure 工序
work program 工作方案,工作计划
work quota 劳动定额
work report 工作报告
work result 工项,工作成果
work scope description 工作范围说明
work section 工区
work sheet 工作底稿
work site 工地
work station 工作站
work sub-section 领工区
workability 和易性
workability of concrete 混凝土和易性
workday 工作日
worker's compensation insurance 劳工保险
worker's insurance 职工保险
workflow 工作流程
workforce productivity 劳动生产率
working 加工
working ability 加工能力

working accident	工伤事故
working area	施工作业区
working assets	周转资产
working at height	高处作业
working capacity	加工能力
working capital	周转资金
working capital gains/income	营运资本收益
working condition of testing load	试验荷载工况
working conditions	劳动条件,工作条件
working current	工作电流
working day	工作日
working drawing	施工图
working drawings	加工图
working duration of locomotive crew	乘务员连续工作时间
working efficiency	工作效率
working expenses	工作费用,经营费用
working face	工作面
working fund	周转金
working hours	工时,工作时间
working instruction	工作指令
working liabilities	营业负债
working mode of locomotive crew	乘务方式
working papers	工作文件,工作许可
working rules	操作规程,工作规范
working solution	工作溶液
working stroke	工作行程
working system of locomotive crew	机车乘务制
working tensile stress	工作张力
working value	工作值
working with power cut-off	停电作业
working years	工龄
workload	工作负荷,工作量
workload of break-up operation at hump yard	驼峰解体作业量
workload of locomotive dept	机务工作量
workman	工匠,工人
workmanship	工艺
workman's compensation insurance	劳工工资
workman's compensation	工人抚恤金
workpiece	工件
workplace	工作场所
workplace temperature control	防暑降温
works	工厂,工程
works statistics	工程统计
works to be measured	待验工
workshop	车间,工厂,工场
work-schedule	工作进度表,施工进度表
World Geodetic System 1984	WGS-84 年世界大地坐标系
world price	世界市场价格
woven geotextile	织造土工织物
wrapping of slope top of cutting	堑顶包角
wrap-up	综合险
writ of attachment	扣押令
writ of prohibition	禁止令,强制令
writing	书写
written agreement	书面协议
written application	书面申请
written approval	书面批准
written authorization	核准书,授权书
written consent	书面应允
written decision	书面裁决,书面决定
written discharge	书面结清单
written document	书面文件
written evidence	书面证据
written law	成文法
written notice	书面通知
written request	书面请求
written statement	书面报表,书面声明
written variation order	书面变更命令
written warning	书面警告
written/in writing	书面
wrong handling	错误办理
wrong side output	危险侧输出
wrong side-oriented deviation	导向危险侧偏差
wrongful dismissal	非法解雇
Wucheng loess	午城黄土
Wutaian age/stage	五台期
wye track	三角线

X

X digital subscriber line（XDSL） X 数字用户线
X ray diffraction analysis X 射线衍射分析
xenidium 胶合板
xenolith 捕虏体
xenon lamp 氙灯
xenon lamp aging 氙灯老化
xenon lamp aging test chamber
　氙弧灯老化试验箱
xerox copy 复印件
xylenol orange spectrophotometry
　二甲酚橙分光光度法
X-brace 交叉支撑
X-ray X 射线
X-ray inspection machine 安检仪
X-shaped support X 形支撑

Y

Yanshan 燕山期
Yanshan age 燕山期
yard 场地,工场
yard elevation 场坪高程
yard for hazardous chemicals 危险化学品货场
Yardang landform 雅丹地貌
year 年(365天)
year book 年鉴
year of loan interest payment 还息年度
yearly budget 年度预算
yearly installments 按年分期付款
yearly light exposure 年曝光量
yearly maintenance 年度维修
yearly operation times of mobile machinery 流动机械年运行次数
yearly power consumption 年用电量
year-end adjustment 年终调整
year-end audit 年终审计
year-end bonus 年终奖
year-end settlement of account 年度结算
yield 屈服,产出
yield criterion 屈服准则
yield load 屈服负荷
yield point 屈服点
yield rate 收益率
yield strength 屈服强度
yielding of foundation 基础沉陷

Z

ZC live load　ZC 活载
zenith distance　天顶距
zero correction　零点校正
zero defects management　无缺陷管理
zero dispersion wavelength range
　零色散波长范围
zero drift　零点漂移
zero energy building　零能耗建筑
zero ground potential difference　零地电位差
zero line　基准线
zero salvage value　无残值
zero sequence current increment　零序增量
zero sequence current protection
　零序电流保护
zero-accident　零事故
zeta type structure　歹字形构造
zigzag force　之字力
zinc coating　镀锌
zinc content　锌含量
zinc-oxide arrester　氧化锌避雷器
ZK live load　ZK 活载
zone　地带,区域
zone node　区域节点
zone plan　带状平面图
zone price　区域价格
zone public address system　小区广播
zone-dividing of Gaussian projection
　高斯投影分带
zoning　区域规划
zoning broadcast　分区插播
zoning map for soil and water conservation
　水土流失防治区划分图
zoning of public address system　广播分区
zoning permit　规划许可
zoning plan　区域划分图
zoning two-pipe water system
　分区两管制水系统
zoom lens camera　变焦摄像机
ZPW-2000(UM) series track circuit
　ZPW-2000(UM)系列轨道电路
Z-weighted vibration acceleration level
　Z 计权振动加速度级